Ancient Greek Philosophers

ANCIENT GREEK PHILOSOPHERS

Introduction by Ken Mondschein, PhD

Canterbury Classics

San Diego

Canterbury Classics
An imprint of Printers Row Publishing Group
9717 Pacific Heights Blvd, San Diego, CA 92121
www.canterburyclassicsbooks.com • mail@canterburyclassicsbooks.com

Introduction copyright © 2025 Printers Row Publishing Group

All rights reserved. No part of this publication may be reproduced, distributed, or transmitted in any form or by any means, including photocopying, recording, or other electronic or mechanical methods, without the prior written permission of the publisher, except in the case of brief quotations embodied in critical reviews and certain other noncommercial uses permitted by copyright law.

Printers Row Publishing Group is a division of Readerlink Distribution Services, LLC. Canterbury Classics is a registered trademark of Readerlink Distribution Services, LLC.

Correspondence concerning the content of this book should be sent to Canterbury Classics, Editorial Department, at the above address.

Publisher: Peter Norton • Associate Publisher: Ana Parker
Editorial Director: April Graham
Art Director: Charles McStravick
Editorial Team: JoAnn Padgett, Melinda Allman, Traci Douglas, Dan Mansfield
Production Team: Beno Chan, Julie Greene

Cover design: Rusty von Dyl
Endpaper image courtesy of Dreamer Company/Shutterstock.com
Original photo that inspired the cover art licensed from The British Museum

The Library of Congress has cataloged the original edition of this book as follows:
Names: Canterbury Classics (Firm), editor.
Title: Ancient Greek philosophers / Editors of Canterbury Classics.
Description: San Diego : Canterbury Classics, 2018.
Identifiers: LCCN 2018020465 (print) | LCCN 2018033613 (ebook) | ISBN 9781684125616 | ISBN 9781684125531 (leather-bound)
Subjects: LCSH: Philosophy, Ancient.
Classification: LCC B171 (ebook) | LCC B171 .A46 2018 (print) | DDC 180--dc23
LC record available at https://lccn.loc.gov/2018020465

ISBN: 978-1-6672-1164-0

Printed in Faridabad-Haryana, India
First printing, March 2025. TS/03/25
29 28 27 26 25   1 2 3 4 5

Editor's Note: The works in this book have been published in their original form to preserve the authors' intent and style.

CONTENTS

Introduction vii
The First Alcibiades (Plato) 3
Apology (Plato) 55
Crito (Plato) 87
Symposium (Plato) 103
Phaedrus (Plato) 169
Phaedo (Plato) 251
Poetics (Aristotle) 345
Rhetoric (Aristotle) 377
Memorabilia (Xenophon) 527
Hellenica (Xenophon) 679
Enchiridion (Epictetus) 937
Letter to Menoeceus (Epicurus) 955
Principal Doctrines (Epicurus) 959
Editor's Note 965

INTRODUCTION

> ...when I should remember the paragons of Hellas
> I think instead
> Of the crooks, the adventurers, the opportunists,
> The careless athletes and the fancy boys,
> The hair-splitters, the pedants, the hard-boiled sceptics
> And the Agora and the noise
> Of the demagogues and the quacks...
> ...and lastly
> I think of the slaves.
>
> Louis MacNeice (1907–1963), "The Gloomy Academic"

The Greek philosophical tradition not only laid the basis for Western thought but influenced the entire world. From its origins in the rocky islands and mountains of Greece, it was brought as far east as India by Alexander's conquests. When the Romans vanquished the successor states to Alexander's empire, they also absorbed the Greek philosophical tradition. The torch was passed in turn to both of Rome's heirs: the Byzantine Empire and the Islamic empire. Translation into Arabic of the Greek texts began in the eighth century CE during the Abbasid caliphate, especially in the famous "House of Wisdom" founded in Baghdad by the Caliph Harun al-Rashid in the late eighth century.

Beginning in the twelfth century, the works of Greek philosophy that had been lost in the West, especially those of Aristotle, were transmitted to medieval Europe by means of translations from Arabic into Latin, the common language of European scholars. Multilingual border areas, such as Sicily and Spain, were especially important in this effort. By the next century, a few brilliant scholars such as Robert Grosseteste had begun making translations into Latin directly from the Greek. Together with the Arabic translations came a rich tradition of commentaries, which medieval European writers added to as they sought to reconcile faith with reason. In an age of sectarian strife among Christians, Muslims, and Jews, Greek philosophy provided common ground on which scholars of different faiths could work together.

Though translations of Greek philosophy into European vernaculars—everyday languages such as English, Italian, and French, as opposed to scholarly Latin—probably existed from the earliest times, many important translations were produced in the late Middle Ages as powerful patrons hungered for education and practical advice for ruling. The Parisian philosopher Nicole Oresme (c. 1320–1385), for instance, produced French translations and commentaries of Aristotle's Ethics, Politics, and On the Heavens, as well as a work on economics incorrectly attributed to the philosopher, for King Charles V of France. The pace of translation increased during the Renaissance as Italian scholars sought to recover the wisdom of the ancient world and a passion for Plato swept over the peninsula. The elite of Italy, such as Cosimo de' Medici (1389–1464), would patronize scholars, such as Marsilio Ficino (1433–1499), and fund the revival of Platonic thought, which, they thought, would give them a truer understanding of God. The invention of print only increased the pace, and publishers found that editions of philosophers in Greek, Latin, and vernacular languages were a good way to turn a profit.

As part of the millennia-old tradition of translation and publication, Ancient Greek Philosophers provides—in convenient form—a précis of selected aspects of Greek philosophy. Though it contains works from several authors, it is but a toe dipped into a vast pool of thought. This introduction is not only a history and contextualization of these works, but also a brief explanation of the ideas found therein. It also takes into account some of the ways in which Greek thought not only influenced later philosophy, but also politics, literature, and art. Finally, it looks at the lives of some of the men and women who undertook the work of translating these works into English.

ORIGINS OF GREEK PHILOSOPHY

"Philosophy," from the Greek φιλοσοφία, philosophia, literally means "love of wisdom." At its core, it is nothing less than a critical, reasoned examination of the fundamental problems of existence—how we can be moral, how (and whether) we can know things for certain, and how we

Introduction

can live our best lives. However, its activities go well beyond this aim. Historically, "philosophy" meant "a body of knowledge;" thus, "natural philosophy" is an older term for what today we call "science." For the ancients, however, there was no hard-and-fast distinction between the fields of math, physiology, spiritualism, and other disciplines.

Philosophy is deeply rooted in the social conditions of ancient Athens. The Athenian democratic tradition required citizens (who were free men born in the city) to be their own lawyers, advocates, and representatives in the ecclesia, or popular assembly. To be able to speak well in public was thus an important skill for the free Athenian. Equally important was personal martial and athletic ability: To be a free citizen was to serve as a hoplite, or citizen-soldier, in the city militia. Hoplites were armed with shields and spears and fought shoulder-to-shoulder in a formation called a phalanx. Each man was protected not just by his own shield, but by the shield of the man to his right as the two sides came together in a clash called the othismos, or "push." The side that broke first would run and often be chased down and slaughtered. Battle tactics thus required virtues such as cooperation, patriotism, group cohesion, sacrificing oneself for the good of the whole, and personal toughness, while civil life required the ability to debate, manage public opinion, and maneuver in a shifting and fractious political environment. It is no coincidence that these are virtues valued by Greek philosophy.

Athens in the years after the Persian Wars (499–449 BCE) was, much like the United States after World War II, a society in its golden age. Money from the Delian League, Athens' de facto empire, poured into the city. Athens was rebuilt in grand style from the wars' devastation. It was in this environment that the sophists thrived—we could better translate the name as "wise guys" than "lovers of wisdom." These men claimed they could prove any argument or solve any problem for a fee; the term "sophist" has become considered derogatory, since writers who followed Socrates (470–399 BCE) fancied themselves in the true, elevated "philosophical" tradition and dismissed these early thinkers as amoral, hair-splitting mercenaries.

However, the lifetimes of Socrates and his student Plato (c. 420s–c. 347 BCE) saw Athenian confidence and power transition into a time of decline. Athens' growing influence brought her into conflict with Sparta, the other major power in Greece. From 431–404 BCE, the two city-states fought a destructive conflict known as the Peloponnesian War that eventually resulted in Athens' defeat. This may help to explain Plato's turn away from the world, and his critique of the democracy that had led to military and social disaster.

Socrates himself left us no writings: All we know of him we have from his students Plato and Xenophon, in whose dialogues he is a main character; from the plays of his contemporary, Aristophanes; and from a few other surviving sources. So influential was he that the thinkers before Socrates, who modern historians call the "pre-Socratics," are by and large known only from quotes and fragments in other writers' works. Some of the sources for the pre-Socratics include Plato's Parmenides and the various works of Plato's student Aristotle. The pre-Socratics included Zeno of the famous paradoxes, such as the one that states Achilles would never overtake a tortoise; Pythagoras, who saw numbers as the basis of all things; and Leucippus, who is thought to have invented atomic theory.

What did Socrates teach? Like the Sophists, Socrates believed that arête (ἀρετή), usually translated as "virtue" or "excellence," could be taught. He developed what we have come to refer to as the "Socratic method," which appears throughout the various dialogues—the method of finding truth by asking questions (ἔλεγχος, elenchus). He claimed that the wisest man is he who knows he knows nothing, and that the highest aim of human life is to seek justice, which he defined (according to Plato) as that which is pleasing to the gods. He also preached the immortality of the soul. Eventually, his critiques of how the city was being run angered the ruling Athenians enough that he was sentenced to death some eight years into the Peloponnesian War. The charge was corrupting the youth and introducing the worship of strange gods; more likely, it was that he humiliated Athenian leadership, rallied the young men around himself, and praised what was admirable about their enemies, the Spartans.

LIVES OF THE PHILOSOPHERS

Any attempt to summarize the works of the Greek philosophers must begin with Plato and Aristotle. The sixteenth-century painter Raphael's great fresco School of Athens in the Vatican rightly shows Aristotle and Plato distinguishing themselves by their gestures. The elder philosopher points up, showing his belief that truth was to be found in a higher world; Aristotle, however, gestures outwards, showing he believes truth is to be found in the present world. The following is not—can never be—comprehensive but will offer a very brief introduction to the works of Plato, Aristotle, Xenophon, Epictetus, and Epicurus.

PLATO

The philosopher and mathematician Alfred North Whitehead commented in his *Process and Reality* that "The safest general characterization of the European philosophical tradition is that it consists of a series of footnotes to Plato." Whereas Whitehead wrote half in jest, there is nonetheless a deep truth therein: Plato's significance to all subsequent philosophers cannot be understated. Philosophers from Spinoza to Hegel to Bertrand Russell either wrote in defense of, or in reaction to, Plato.

The first of Plato's works included in this volume, the Alcibiades, is often considered an excellent primer for Platonic philosophy. The titular character is a well-born young man with excellent prospects but he has a bad habit of driving off potential lovers with his cold manner. Socrates, coming to him before he is to speak in front of the ecclesia, gets him to admit he knows nothing of either virtue or politics, and that the best course is to follow the Delphic Oracle's advice, "Know Thyself" (γνῶθι σεαυτόν, gnōthi seauton) to become virtuous and thus succeed in politics and life. Though scholars since Friedrich Schleiermacher in the 1830s have cast doubts on Plato's having written it, the Alcibiades is still a good introduction to the Socratic idea of what proper education is. (The actual Alcibiades had a very checkered career in the Peloponnesian War, which gives the dialogue a certain irony.)

The next two of Plato's works that we have included, the Apology and Crito, deal directly with Socrates's trial and death. In Greek, an apology (ἀπολογία, apologia) is not something one says to mean "I'm sorry" but rather an impassioned defense. The Apology is a scathing attack on Socrates's accusers. It includes a supernatural defense: The Oracle at Delphi said Socrates is the wisest man in the land, but he does not believe himself particularly wise. The answer is that even though Socrates does not believe himself to be wise, he, unlike the others, is not operating under the delusion that he knows more than he really does. He characterizes himself as a gadfly, stinging the body politic into action.

In the Crito, meanwhile, Socrates speaks to his wealthy friend on the nature of justice and injustice, saying that even though he has been unjustly condemned, it would also be unjust to escape and that it is his duty to die.

The eighteenth-century French painter Jacques-Louis David, in his 1787 painting The Death of Socrates, signs his name beneath the figure of Crito, who is gripping Socrates's thigh, while Plato, inaccurately depicted as an old man, sits with his head bowed at the foot of the bed. The scene described in the dialogue becomes, in the painter's hands, a lesson on self-sacrifice for love of country and for truth—an appropriate sentiment on the eve on the French Revolution.

Perhaps the most perplexing of Plato's ideas found in this volume, particularly in the Phaedo, the Phaedrus, the Parmenides, and the Symposium, is his concept of the Forms. In the Phaedrus, for instance, Plato has Socrates explain that the changeable, imperfect world we perceive with our senses is not the "real" one. All of the things we give names to, including such intangible but indispensable concepts as "goodness" and "virtue," are but reflections of eternal ideas that have their own independent existence outside our mundane reality.

Plato explains this idea most famously through the metaphor of the cave in his Republic: Imagine that we are prisoners who have been chained for our entire lives in a cave. Behind us is a fire casting a light; actors come by holding shapes and use them to cast shadows on the cave wall. These shadows are all we know of the world; to us, they are "real" things—cats, tables, chairs, etc. Were we able to predict what the next shadow to be cast was, we might think we knew something about the world. Were we able to loosen our chains somewhat and turn around, then we would think we were really enlightened: reality was not the shadows, but the shadow-puppets of the cats, tables, and chairs! Then, he says, let us imagine we escaped our chains and left the cave entirely, to the world lit by the sun, and we saw the real world of which the objects in the cave were only representations. This, Plato writes, is true reality.

This idea of reality existing in a transcendental world is Plato's answer to the problem of universals. Imagine a chair. It could be a folding chair, a classroom desk-chair, a Ghyczy Garden Egg chair, or a papasan. Plato would hold that we recognize all of these things as "chairs" because they participate in a universal "chair-ness," that is, somewhere out there in the "real world" there is a Platonic Chair. The material chairs we know are but reflections—shadows on the cave wall—of this "real" ideal of a chair. Aristotle, on the other hand, says that there is no Platonic Chair, only things we call chairs. We call the Aristotelian position "nominalism" after the medieval Latin term nomina mentalia, "mental names," whereas the

Introduction

Platonic position we term Realism, after the reality of the essential forms. The message—that we must not be blinded by what we perceive with our senses, but strive to see the principles behind things and the real causes (e.g., the sun, as opposed to a mere fire)—is of no small importance to the development of Western science.

In his Symposium, Plato states that the way human beings connect to the higher realm is through the transcendental power of love. A symposium was a drinking party of the sort held by elite Athenians in a special part of the house called the andros, or "men's room." Being quite hungover from the night before, rather than participating in drunken debauchery, the guests at Plato's symposium discuss the meaning of love—specifically, eros (ἔρος), "desire" or "romantic love." Plato believed that the way human beings connect to this realm is through the transcendental power of eros, for love is nothing more than the pursuit of beauty, and, as he has Socrates say, "Is not the good also the beautiful. . . .[and] in wanting the beautiful, love wants also the good?" Or, as the poet John Keats wrote in his "Ode on a Grecian Urn" (1819):

> "Beauty is truth, truth beauty,—that is all
> Ye know on earth, and all ye need to know."

Specifically, for the ancient Greeks, this was the love of a well-born young citizen and his older male mentor. As Acusilaus, one of the guests in the Symposium, says: "I know not any greater blessing to a young man who is beginning life than a virtuous lover, or to the lover than a beloved youth." It was expected for an older man to take a well-born youth as a lover to initiate him in all the things expected of a citizen. (The Athenians were not unique in this: the Sacred Band of Thebes was an elite warrior corps of 150 pairs of male lovers.) This was not necessarily homosexual in the sense we think of it today: Plato claims that the man of true philosophical inclination, exemplified by the character of Socrates, is always seeking to achieve the higher realm but disdains the sex act itself. On the other hand, idealized contemplation of the male body—the original meaning of "Platonic love"—begets a sort of spiritual birth in the mind of the lover. Women are needed for carnal reproduction, but in Plato's world, the higher sort of parenthood belongs entirely to men. It was for the admiration of his lover that a man sought the masculine virtue essential to the well being of the city-state.

About the Translator

Benjamin Jowett (1817–1893) was a professor of Greek at Oxford and translator of Plato and Thucydides. He was also a correspondent of Florence Nightingale, who had some input into the translation. His other interests included theology (he was drawn to the Arnold school, which saw Christianity as just another mythology and caused some problems with his academic career), in "modernizing" India, and in making Plato relevant to the Victorian age. He was beloved by his students and became a much-respected figure at Oxford. As Nightingale remarked upon his death, "Mr. Jowett put as much of his genius into Plato as Plato did into Mr. Jowett."

ARISTOTLE

Unlike Socrates and Plato, who lived in the shadow of the Peloponnesian War, the career of Aristotle (384–322 BCE) coincided with the conquests of Alexander the Great (356–323 BCE) and the spread of Greek culture through the entire eastern Mediterranean and Middle East. Educated in the Academy that Plato had founded in Athens and employed as the young Alexander's tutor, Aristotle's worldview is more positive than Plato's, reflecting the times in which he lived. No less significant a philosopher than his master, he would later go on to found his own school, the Lyceum. Aristotle's surviving body of work is vast, covering fields that we would today classify as natural science (physics, biology, zoology, etc.), metaphysics, ethics, political science, logic, and language arts. If all Western philosophy is "footnotes to Plato," then all other disciplines are either grounded on the principles laid out by Aristotle, or else founded on what was written in reaction to him.

Examination of the body of Aristotle's works, known by its medieval Latin name the corpus Aristotelicum, is complicated by the fact that he did not compose his books integrally; rather, they were delivered to his audience at different times—perhaps as lectures—and edited together only after his death. Centuries later, Aristotle's influence in the Middle Ages was so great that he was simply known as "The Philosopher." While the Renaissance placed increasing emphasis on Plato (early Christian writers had been Platonists, marrying the philosophy of the elder philosopher with Christian beliefs), the Aristotelian world-system was not completely demolished until Galileo proved that Earth revolves around the sun and

Introduction

not the other way around with his observations of the lunar surface and Jupiter's moons in the sixteenth and seventeenth centuries. Newton, in the following generation, put the last nails in the coffin with his mathematical theories of how the universe functions.

Aristotle was nonetheless foundational to Western scientific thought in that it was he who expressed the idea of using logic and reason to deduce truth. It is also Aristotle who gives us the idea of using experience and sense data together with logic to discover knowable things about the world. One theory of how the Scientific Revolution emerged was that the practical skill and knowledge of craftsmen was combined with the formal Aristotelian training of educated scholars.

Aristotle's influence was no less important in the language arts. Unlike Plato's criticism of the art of rhetoric in his Gorgias (a view that he did temper in later writings), Aristotle praised the discipline of public speaking, which was needed for an active, involved life in the ancient world. His Rhetoric (from the Greek rhētorikós, ῥητορικός) contains all the elements needed to give a persuasive speech or write a scholarly work even today—citing credible sources, layers of proof, employing logic, and structuring an argument. In fact, in the Middle Ages, rhetoric, along with the Aristotelian discipline of logic and grammar (the study of Latin), formed the trivium, the basis for all education. With dialectic (establishing the truth through argument), logic and rhetoric form the basis for all Western philosophy.

Aristotle writes about the purpose of rhetoric—to persuade the listener—as well as how it can be used for good or ill. He then talks about the types of arguments and proofs—ἐνθύμημα, or enthymeme—used to persuade. Arguments can be stated, implied, or conveyed by signs. For instance, let's suppose that we're going to host a fancy British-style tea party, and I'm trying to persuade you that we should serve Earl Grey tea. I can do it by a stated argument: Earl Grey is a type of tea, and the British drink all sorts of tea, therefore the British drink Earl Grey. Alternately, I can say that they sell Earl Grey tea at Marks & Spencer—here, the idea is implicit, since you knew ahead of time Marks & Spencer is a chain of stores in Britain. Finally, I can do it by signs: I can say that Earl Grey tea is classy, and since we associate "British" things with classiness, it follows that this sort of tea would be appropriate. (Of course, as Aristotle would point out in his Logic, even if we can posit that British things are classy, not all classy things are British!) Aristotle also talks about rhetorical devices, style, metaphors, and the aims of the three types of rhetoric—deliberative (to persuade towards a course of action), forensic (discussing past actions), and epideictic (praise-and-blame, as in a funeral oration). The remainder of the work discusses the details of these sorts of rhetoric.

The Poetics, the first known work on literary theory, likewise contains ideas that would not be out of place in a guide for Hollywood screenwriters. In Greek, poietikos (ποιητικός) means simply "creativity"; accordingly, the treatise covers all forms of writing, including the three (comedy, with a happy ending; tragedy, with a sorrowful ending; and the "satyr play," or satire). Unfortunately, the second book, on comedy, has been lost, so what we have left is an explanation of tragedy. However, the concepts in the surviving portion of the Poetics been profoundly influential: The character's downfall should be as a result of their fatal flaws and hubris. The plot must unfold logically. There must be a discovery of what they had unknowingly wrought. The situation should seek to evoke catharsis, or fear and pity, in the audience. The features of tragedy are seen everywhere from Shakespeare's Macbeth to David Fincher's Se7en to Game of Thrones.

About the Translators

The *Poetics* was translated by Samuel Henry Butcher (1850–1910), an Anglo-Irish classicist who taught at Cambridge (where he had been educated), Oxford, and the University of Edinburgh. Besides Aristotle, he also translated Demosthenes's *Orations* and the *Odyssey*. The *Rhetoric* was translated by William Rhys Roberts (1858–1929), who was similarly educated at Cambridge and taught at University College, Bangor, and the University of Leeds. He published widely on ancient Greek history and on the teaching of the classics.

XENOPHON

If Plato and Aristotle were "armchair philosophers," then Xenophon epitomizes the Greek active life. A student of Socrates, he was a professional soldier whose works include treatises on horsemanship and hunting and the Anabasis, a story of the heroic retreat of 10,000 Greek mercenaries from the interior of the Persian Empire to friendly territory. The tale, a triumph of the principles of leadership taught by Socrates, may have encouraged the Macedonian king Phillip to plan his invasion of Persia. In modern times, it has been the basis for numerous works of fiction.

We have chosen to include in this volume Xenophon's Memorabilia and his Hellenica. The Memorabilia is, like Plato's Apology and Crito, a defense of Xenophon's teacher Socrates. Unlike Plato's works, it is not forensic, but rather presents many anecdotes of Socrates's life and methods of education. Xenophon's Socrates is less philosophical and more practical. Xenophon also has Socrates dealing with his accusers with a sort of suicidal arrogance, whereas Plato puts Socrates in the position of failing to defend himself in order to teach a lesson. (Xenophon also wrote an Apologia for Socrates.)

The Hellenica, a history, is in fact a continuation of Thucydides' work on the Peloponnesian War. Xenophon was in an extraordinary position to write such a work since although he was of Athenian birth, he fought for Sparta and lived there after being exiled from Athens. Xenophon was, in fact, a great admirer of the Spartans, and much of what we know of their society comes from his observations. On the other hand, he, like Plato, is somewhat cynical of democracy.

About the Translator

The translator, Henry Graham Dakyns (1838–1911) was educated at Cambridge, tutored the children of the poet Alfred, Lord Tennyson, and later became a Master at the progressive Clifton College in Bristol, England. He translated numerous works from the Greek.

EPICTETUS

While to call someone "stoic" carries the connotation of their being unfeeling or emotionless, Stoicism is, in fact, a deeply humanistic philosophy that was, and remains, hugely influential as a practical means of living a good and fulfilling life. The school was founded by Zeno of Citium (in Cyprus) in the third century CE. The name "stoic" comes from the colonnaded portico, or stoa, where Zeno and his students would meet. Like Buddhists, Stoics see suffering as inevitable. All we have control over is our own internal state—that is, how we react to adversity and how we conduct ourselves. This, and attention to our obligations to others, are the keys to living a happy life.

None of Zeno's writings survive, but we have an idea of what he taught from such sources as Epictetus (55–135 CE). Epictetus certainly had quite a bit of adversity in his own life: He was born into slavery in Greek Phrygia (modern Turkey), lived in Rome, where he gained his freedom, and died in exile in Nicopolis, Greece, after the emperor Domitian banned all philosophers around the year 93 CE. He was also disabled, having been lame since childhood (the theologian Origen even said that his master had deliberately broken his leg). Epictetus' student, the historian Arrian, wrote the Enchiridion and Discourses based on Epictetus' teaching, but the philosopher himself left no writings.

The Enchiridion is literally a "handbook" of Stoic thought, emphasizing self-control, reason, devotion to duty, and non-attachment to material things. The principles of Stoicism found their most famous expression in the Meditations of Marcus Aurelius and have discovered new relevance today; they have found application, for instance, in cognitive behavioral therapy.

About the Translator

The translator of this work, Elizabeth Carter (1717–1806), was a remarkable woman and member of the progressive Bluestocking Circle. Her philosophical translations of Epictetus brought her both fame and fortune. She was also learned in Latin, Hebrew, classical Arabic, and modern languages, and produced translations from the French.

EPICURUS

Most of Epicurus' works have been lost, though quotations in other works remain, as do various fragments (for instance, charred scrolls at the Villa of the Papyri at Herculaneum). His work is represented here with the Letter to Menoeceus and The Principal Doctrines, which were quoted by the third-century CE historian Diogenes Laërtius.

Whereas today, "Epicurean" means "one who takes joy in the finer things in life," even to the point of immoderation, the original philosophy of Epicurus (341–270 BCE) was quite different. While sometimes seen as an opposing doctrine to Stoicism, in fact, Epicureanism finds slightly different answers to the same problems. Since there is no life after death, we must find our enjoyment in this world and in living a life free from pain, fear, and suffering. Despite this, death is not to be feared—it is only non-existence, and dreading it leads to unhappiness in the here-and-now. The key to such enjoyment is moderation: Epicurus taught that an excess of anything—drinking, sex, exercise—is ultimately detrimental to the individual. One can see that this was a philosophy of those who had a degree of control over their lives and who, unlike the Stoics, were disinterested in the public good, religious piety, politics, or duty to others. Epicurus also believed in the material causes of things, which, in the form of the Roman poet Lucretius' long poem De Re Natura, would be immensely influential to Western science.

About the Translator

The works of Epicurus are translated by Robert Drew Hicks (1850—1929), a fellow of Trinity College, Cambridge. Though he went blind by 1900, he was aided by his wife, Bertha Mary Heath, who herself held an advanced degree in classics, in producing translations of Aristotle's On the Soul and of the Stoics and Epicureans, as well as a Latin dictionary in Braille.

THE ENDURING RELEVANCE OF PHILOSOPHY

Greek philosophy is as relevant today as it was in the past. As the biographies of the philosophers and translators reveal, these classics of thought belong to, and speak to, everyone, no matter where they come from or what their life circumstances might be. While the philosophers discuss how to live a happy life or rule a city-state, they also react to, as the famed classicist Mary Beard wrote, "the squalor, the slavery, the misogyny, the irrationality of antiquity."* Poverty, injustice, and prejudice are all conditions that are hardly unknown or irrelevant in our world today. The study of philosophy therefore isn't just for those with time on their hands, or who can afford to go to elite liberal-arts colleges. Just as in the ancient world, philosophy can elevate and educate people of all backgrounds. We present *Ancient Greek Philosophers* as a work from which everyone can extract meaning that can be applied to their own life. Just as Herman Melville wrote in Moby-Dick, "A whale ship was my Yale College and my Harvard," we ask that you let this book be your Yale and your Harvard.

Ken Mondschein, PhD
Northampton, Massachusetts
April 16, 2018

---

* "Do the Classics Have a Future?" Beard, Mary; the New York Review of Books, January 12, 2012, http://www.nybooks.com/articles/2012/01/12/do-classics-have-future/

PLATO

THE FIRST ALCIBIADES

BY PLATO

Translated by Benjamin Jowett

PREFACE

It seems impossible to separate by any exact line the genuine writings of Plato from the spurious. The only external evidence to them which is of much value is that of Aristotle; for the Alexandrian catalogues of a century later include manifest forgeries. Even the value of the Aristotelian authority is a good deal impaired by the uncertainty concerning the date and authorship of the writings which are ascribed to him. And several of the citations of Aristotle omit the name of Plato, and some of them omit the name of the dialogue from which they are taken. Prior, however, to the inquiry about the writings of a particular author, general considerations which equally affect all evidence to the genuineness of ancient writings are the following: Shorter works are more likely to have been forged, or to have received an erroneous designation, than longer ones; and some kinds of composition, such as epistles or panegyrical orations, are more liable to suspicion than others; those, again, which have a taste of sophistry in them, or the ring of a later age, or the slighter character of a rhetorical exercise, or in which a motive or some affinity to spurious writings can be detected, or which seem to have originated in a name or statement really occurring in some classical author, are also of doubtful credit; while there is no instance of any ancient writing proved to be a forgery, which combines excellence with length. A really great and original writer would have no object in fathering his works on Plato; and to the forger or imitator, the "literary hack" of Alexandria and Athens, the Gods did not grant originality or genius. Further, in attempting to balance the evidence for and against a Platonic dialogue, we must not forget that the form of the Platonic writing was common to several of his contemporaries. Aeschines, Euclid, Phaedo, Antisthenes, and in the next generation Aristotle, are all said to have composed dialogues; and mistakes of names are very likely to have occurred. Greek literature in the third century before Christ was almost as voluminous as our own, and without the safeguards of regular publication, or printing, or binding, or even of distinct titles. An unknown writing was naturally attributed to a known writer whose works bore the same character; and the name once appended easily obtained authority. A tendency may also be observed to blend the works and opinions of the master with those of his scholars. To a later Platonist, the difference between Plato and his imitators was not so perceptible as to ourselves. The Memorabilia of Xenophon and the Dialogues of Plato are but a part of a considerable Socratic literature which has passed away. And we must consider how we should regard the question of the genuineness of a particular writing, if this lost literature had been preserved to us.

These considerations lead us to adopt the following criteria of genuineness: (1) That is most certainly Plato's which Aristotle attributes to him by name, which (2) is of considerable length, of (3) great excellence, and also (4) in harmony with the general spirit of the Platonic writings. But the testimony of Aristotle cannot always be distinguished from that of a later age (see above); and has various degrees of importance. Those writings which he cites without mentioning Plato, under their own names, e.g. the Hippias, the Funeral Oration, the Phaedo, etc., have an inferior degree of evidence in their favor. They may have been supposed by him to be the writings of another, although in the case of really great works, e.g. the Phaedo, this is not credible; those again which are quoted but not named, are still more defective in their external credentials. There may be also a possibility that Aristotle was mistaken, or may have confused the master and his scholars in the case of a short writing; but this is inconceivable about a more important work, e.g. the Laws, especially when we remember that he was living at Athens, and a frequenter of the groves of the Academy, during the last twenty years of Plato's life. Nor must we forget that in all his numerous citations from the Platonic writings he never attributes any passage found in the extant dialogues to anyone but Plato. And lastly, we may remark that one or two great writings, such as the Parmenides and the Politicus, which are wholly devoid of Aristotelian (1) credentials may be fairly attributed to Plato, on the ground of (2) length, (3) excellence, and (4) accordance with the general spirit of his writings. Indeed the greater part of the evidence for the genuineness of ancient Greek authors may be summed up under two heads only: (1) Excellence; and (2) uniformity of tradition—a kind of evidence, which though in many cases sufficient, is of inferior value.

Proceeding upon these principles we appear to arrive at the conclusion that nineteen-twentieths of all the writings which have ever been ascribed to Plato, are undoubtedly genuine. There is another portion of them, including the Epistles, the Epinomis, the dialogues rejected by the ancients themselves, namely, the Axiochus, De justo, De virtute, Demodocus, Sisyphus, Eryxias, which on grounds, both of internal and external evidence, we are able with equal certainty to reject. But there still remains a small portion of which we are unable to affirm either that they are genuine or spurious. They may have been written in youth, or possibly like the works of some painters, may be partly or wholly the compositions of pupils; or they may have been the writings of some contemporary transferred by accident to the more celebrated name of Plato, or of some Platonist in the next generation who aspired to imitate his master. Not that on grounds either of language or philosophy we should lightly reject them. Some difference of style, or inferiority of execution, or inconsistency of thought, can hardly be considered decisive of their spurious character. For who always does justice to himself, or who writes with equal care at all times? Certainly not Plato, who exhibits the greatest differences in dramatic power, in the formation of sentences, and in the use of words, if his earlier writings are compared with his later ones, say the Protagoras or Phaedrus with the Laws. Or who can be expected to think in the same manner during a period of authorship extending over above fifty years, in an age of great intellectual activity, as well as of political and literary transition? Certainly not Plato, whose earlier writings are separated from his later ones by as wide an interval of philosophical speculation as that which separates his later writings from Aristotle.

The dialogues which have been translated in the first Appendix, and which appear to have the next claim to genuineness among the Platonic writings, are the Lesser Hippias, the Menexenus or Funeral Oration, the First Alcibiades. Of these, the Lesser Hippias and the Funeral Oration are cited by Aristotle; the first in the Metaphysics, the latter in the Rhetoric. Neither of them are expressly attributed to Plato, but in his citation of both of them he seems to be referring to passages in the extant dialogues. From the mention of "Hippias" in the singular by Aristotle, we may perhaps infer that he was unacquainted with a second dialogue bearing the same name. Moreover, the mere existence of a Greater and Lesser Hippias, and of a First and Second Alcibiades, does to a certain extent throw a doubt upon both of them. Though a very clever and ingenious work, the Lesser

Hippias does not appear to contain anything beyond the power of an imitator, who was also a careful student of the earlier Platonic writings, to invent. The motive or leading thought of the dialogue may be detected in Xen. Mem., and there is no similar instance of a "motive" which is taken from Xenophon in an undoubted dialogue of Plato. On the other hand, the upholders of the genuineness of the dialogue will find in the Hippias a true Socratic spirit; they will compare the Ion as being akin both in subject and treatment; they will urge the authority of Aristotle; and they will detect in the treatment of the Sophist, in the satirical reasoning upon Homer, in the reductio ad absurdum of the doctrine that vice is ignorance, traces of a Platonic authorship. In reference to the last point we are doubtful, as in some of the other dialogues, whether the author is asserting or overthrowing the paradox of Socrates, or merely following the argument "whither the wind blows." That no conclusion is arrived at is also in accordance with the character of the earlier dialogues. The resemblances or imitations of the Gorgias, Protagoras, and Euthydemus, which have been observed in the Hippias, cannot with certainty be adduced on either side of the argument. On the whole, more may be said in favor of the genuineness of the Hippias than against it.

The Menexenus or Funeral Oration is cited by Aristotle, and is interesting as supplying an example of the manner in which the orators praised "the Athenians among the Athenians," falsifying persons and dates, and casting a veil over the gloomier events of Athenian history. It exhibits an acquaintance with the funeral oration of Thucydides, and was, perhaps, intended to rival that great work. If genuine, the proper place of the Menexenus would be at the end of the Phaedrus. The satirical opening and the concluding words bear a great resemblance to the earlier dialogues; the oration itself is professedly a mimetic work, like the speeches in the Phaedrus, and cannot therefore be tested by a comparison of the other writings of Plato. The funeral oration of Pericles is expressly mentioned in the Phaedrus, and this may have suggested the subject, in the same manner that the Cleitophon appears to be suggested by the slight mention of Cleitophon and his attachment to Thrasymachus in the Republic; and the Theages by the mention of Theages in the Apology and Republic; or as the Second Alcibiades seems to be founded upon the text of Xenophon, Mem. A similar taste for parody appears not only in the Phaedrus, but in the Protagoras, in the Symposium, and to a certain extent in the Parmenides.

To these two doubtful writings of Plato I have added the First Alcibiades, which, of all the disputed dialogues of Plato, has the greatest merit, and is somewhat longer than any of them, though not verified by the testimony of Aristotle, and in many respects at variance with the Symposium in the description of the relations of Socrates and Alcibiades. Like the Lesser Hippias and the Menexenus, it is to be compared to the earlier writings of Plato. The motive of the piece may, perhaps, be found in that passage of the Symposium in which Alcibiades describes himself as self-convicted by the words of Socrates. For the disparaging manner in which Schleiermacher has spoken of this dialogue there seems to be no sufficient foundation. At the same time, the lesson imparted is simple, and the irony more transparent than in the undoubted dialogues of Plato. We know, too, that Alcibiades was a favorite thesis, and that at least five or six dialogues bearing this name passed current in antiquity, and are attributed to contemporaries of Socrates and Plato. (1) In the entire absence of real external evidence (for the catalogues of the Alexandrian librarians cannot be regarded as trustworthy); and (2) in the absence of the highest marks either of poetical or philosophical excellence; and (3) considering that we have express testimony to the existence of contemporary writings bearing the name of Alcibiades, we are compelled to suspend our judgment on the genuineness of the extant dialogue.

Neither at this point, nor at any other, do we propose to draw an absolute line of demarcation between genuine and spurious writings of Plato. They fade off imperceptibly from one class to another. There may have been degrees of genuineness in the dialogues themselves, as there are certainly degrees of evidence by which they are supported. The traditions of the oral discourses both of Socrates and Plato may have formed the basis of semi-Platonic writings; some of them may be of the same mixed character which is apparent in Aristotle and Hippocrates, although the form of them is different. But the writings of Plato, unlike the writings of Aristotle, seem never to have been confused with the writings of his disciples: This was probably due to their definite form, and to their inimitable excellence. The three dialogues which we have offered in the Appendix to the criticism of the reader may be partly spurious and partly genuine; they may be altogether spurious;—that is an alternative which must be frankly admitted. Nor can we maintain of some other dialogues, such as the Parmenides, and the Sophist, and Politicus, that no considerable objection can be urged against them, though greatly overbalanced by the weight (chiefly) of internal evidence in their favor. Nor, on the other hand, can we exclude a bare possibility that some dialogues which are usually rejected, such as the Greater Hippias and the Cleitophon, may be genuine. The nature and object of these semi-Platonic writings require more careful study and more comparison of them with one another, and with forged writings in general, than they have yet received, before we can finally decide on their character. We do not consider them all as genuine until they can be proved to be spurious, as is often maintained and still more often implied in this and similar discussions; but should say of some of them, that their genuineness is neither proven nor disproven until further evidence about them can be adduced. And we are as confident that the Epistles are spurious, as that the Republic, the Timaeus, and the Laws are genuine.

On the whole, not a twentieth part of the writings which pass under the name of Plato, if we exclude the works rejected by the ancients themselves and two or three other plausible inventions, can be fairly doubted by those who are willing to allow that a considerable change and growth may have taken place in his philosophy (see above). That twentieth debatable portion scarcely in any degree affects our judgment of Plato, either as a thinker or a writer, and though suggesting some interesting questions to the scholar and critic, is of little importance to the general reader.

INTRODUCTION

The First Alcibiades is a conversation between Socrates and Alcibiades. Socrates is represented in the character which he attributes to himself in the Apology of a know-nothing who detects the conceit of knowledge in others. The two have met already in the Protagoras and in the Symposium; in the latter dialogue, as in this, the relation between them is that of a lover and his beloved. But the narrative of their loves is told differently in different places; for in the Symposium Alcibiades is depicted as the impassioned but rejected lover; here, as coldly receiving the advances of Socrates, who, for the best of purposes, lies in wait for the aspiring and ambitious youth.

Alcibiades, who is described as a very young man, is about to enter on public life, having an inordinate opinion of himself, and an extravagant ambition. Socrates, "who knows what is in man," astonishes him by a revelation of his designs. But has he the knowledge which is necessary for carrying them out? He is going to persuade the Athenians—about what? Not about any particular art, but about politics—when to fight and when to make peace. Now, men should fight and make peace on just grounds, and therefore the question of justice and injustice must enter into peace and war; and he who advises the Athenians must know the difference between them. Does Alcibiades know? If he does, he must either have been taught by some master, or he must have discovered the nature of them himself. If he has had a master, Socrates would like to be informed who he is, that he may go and learn of him also. Alcibiades admits that he has never learned. Then has he inquired for himself? He may have, if he was ever aware of a time when he was ignorant. But he never was ignorant; for when he played with other boys at dice, he charged them with cheating, and this implied a knowledge of just and unjust. According to his own explanation, he had learned of the multitude. Why, he asks, should he not learn of them the nature of justice, as he has learned the Greek language of them? To this Socrates answers, that they can teach Greek, but they cannot teach justice; for they are agreed about the one, but they are not agreed about the other; and therefore Alcibiades, who has admitted that if he knows he must either have learned from a master or have discovered for himself the nature of justice, is convicted out of his own mouth.

Alcibiades rejoins, that the Athenians debate not about what is just, but about what is expedient; and he asserts that the two principles of justice and expediency are opposed. Socrates, by a series of questions, compels him to admit that the just and the expedient coincide. Alcibiades is thus reduced to the humiliating conclusion that he knows nothing of politics, even if, as he says, they are concerned with the expedient.

However, he is no worse than other Athenian statesmen; and he will not need training, for others are as ignorant as he is. He is reminded that he has to contend, not only with his own countrymen, but with their enemies—with the Spartan kings and with the great king of Persia; and he can only attain this higher aim of ambition by the assistance of Socrates. Not that Socrates himself professes to have attained the truth, but the questions which he asks bring others to a knowledge of themselves, and this is the first step in the practice of virtue.

The dialogue continues: We wish to become as good as possible. But to be good in what? Alcibiades replies, "Good in transacting business." But what business? "The business of the most intelligent men at Athens." The cobbler is intelligent in shoemaking, and is therefore good in that; he is not intelligent, and therefore not good, in weaving. Is he good in the sense which Alcibiades means, who is also bad? "I mean," replies Alcibiades, "the man who is able to command in the city." But to command what—horses or men? and if men, under what circumstances? "I mean to say, that he is able to command men living in social and political relations." And what is their aim? "The better preservation of the city." But when is a city better? "When there is unanimity, such as exists between husband and wife." Then, when husbands and wives perform their own special duties, there can be no unanimity between them; nor can a city be well ordered when each citizen does his own work only. Alcibiades, having stated first that goodness consists in the unanimity of the citizens, and then in each of them doing his own separate work, is brought to the required point of self-contradiction, leading him to confess his own ignorance.

But he is not too old to learn, and may still arrive at the truth, if he is willing to be cross-examined by Socrates. He must know himself; that is to say, not his body, or the things of the body, but his mind, or truer self. The physician knows the body, and the tradesman knows his own business, but they do not necessarily know themselves. Self-knowledge can be obtained only by looking into the mind and virtue of the soul, which is the diviner part of a man, as we see our own image in another's eye. And if we do not know ourselves, we cannot know what belongs to ourselves or belongs to others, and are unfit to take a part in political affairs. Both for the sake of the individual and of the state, we ought to aim at justice and temperance, not at wealth or power. The evil and unjust should have no power—they should be the slaves of better men than themselves. None but the virtuous are deserving of freedom.

And are you, Alcibiades, a freeman? "I feel that I am not; but I hope, Socrates, that by your aid I may become free, and from this day forward I will never leave you."

The Alcibiades has several points of resemblance to the undoubted dialogues of Plato. The process of interrogation is of the same kind with that which Socrates practices upon the youthful Cleinias in the Euthydemus; and he characteristically attributes to Alcibiades the answers which he has elicited from him. The definition of good is narrowed by successive questions, and virtue is shown to be identical with knowledge. Here, as elsewhere, Socrates awakens the consciousness not of sin but of ignorance. Self-humiliation is the first step to knowledge, even of the commonest things. No man knows how ignorant he is, and no man can arrive at virtue and wisdom who has not once in his life, at least, been convicted of error. The process by which the soul is elevated is not unlike that which religious writers describe under the name of "conversion," if we substitute the sense of ignorance for the consciousness of sin.

In some respects the dialogue differs from any other Platonic composition. The aim is more directly ethical and hortatory; the process by which the

The First Alcibiades

antagonist is undermined is simpler than in other Platonic writings, and the conclusion more decided. There is a good deal of humor in the manner in which the pride of Alcibiades, and of the Greeks generally, is supposed to be taken down by the Spartan and Persian queens; and the dialogue has considerable dialectical merit. But we have a difficulty in supposing that the same writer, who has given so profound and complex a notion of the characters both of Alcibiades and Socrates in the Symposium, should have treated them in so thin and superficial a manner in the Alcibiades, or that he would have ascribed to the ironical Socrates the rather unmeaning boast that Alcibiades could not attain the objects of his ambition without his help; or that he should have imagined that a mighty nature like his could have been reformed by a few not very conclusive words of Socrates. For the arguments by which Alcibiades is reformed are not convincing; the writer of the dialogue, whoever he was, arrives at his idealism by crooked and tortuous paths, in which many pitfalls are concealed. The anachronism of making Alcibiades about twenty years old during the life of his uncle, Pericles, may be noted; and the repetition of the favorite observation, which occurs also in the Laches and Protagoras, that great Athenian statesmen, like Pericles, failed in the education of their sons. There is none of the undoubted dialogues of Plato in which there is so little dramatic verisimilitude.

Persons of the dialogue: Alcibiades, Socrates

SOCRATES: I dare say that you may be surprised to find, O son of Cleinias, that I, who am your first lover, not having spoken to you for many years, when the rest of the world were wearying you with their attentions, am the last of your lovers who still speaks to you. The cause of my silence has been that I was hindered by a power more than human, of which I will some day explain to you the nature; this impediment has now been removed; I therefore here present myself before you, and I greatly hope that no similar hindrance will again occur. Meanwhile, I have observed that your pride has been too much for the pride of your admirers; they were numerous and high-spirited, but they have all run away, overpowered by your superior force of character; not one of them remains. And I want you to understand the reason why you have been too much for them. You think that you have no need of them or of any other man, for you have great possessions and lack nothing, beginning with the body, and ending with the soul. In the first place, you say to yourself that you are the fairest and tallest of the citizens, and this everyone who has eyes may see to be true; in the second place, that you are among the noblest of them, highly connected both on the father's and the mother's side, and sprung from one of the most distinguished families in your own state, which is the greatest in Hellas, and having many friends and kinsmen of the best sort, who can assist you when in need; and there is one potent relative, who is more to you than all the rest, Pericles the son of Xanthippus, whom your father left guardian of you, and of your brother, and who can do as he pleases not only in this city, but in all Hellas, and among many and mighty barbarous nations. Moreover, you are rich; but I must say that you value yourself least of all upon your possessions. And all these things have lifted you up; you have overcome your lovers, and they have acknowledged that you were too much for them. Have you not remarked their absence? And now I know that you wonder why I, unlike the rest of them, have not gone away, and what can be my motive in remaining.

ALCIBIADES: Perhaps, Socrates, you are not aware that I was just going to ask you the very same question: What do you want? And what is your motive in annoying me, and always, wherever I am, making a point of coming? (Compare Symp.) I do really wonder what you mean, and should greatly like to know.

SOCRATES: Then if, as you say, you desire to know, I suppose that you will be willing to hear, and I may consider myself to be speaking to an auditor who will remain, and will not run away?

ALCIBIADES: Certainly, let me hear.

SOCRATES: You had better be careful, for I may very likely be as unwilling to end as I have hitherto been to begin.

ALCIBIADES: Proceed, my good man, and I will listen.

SOCRATES: I will proceed; and, although no lover likes to speak with one who has no feeling of love in him (compare Symp.), I will make an effort, and tell you what I meant: My love, Alcibiades, which I hardly like to confess, would long ago have passed away, as I flatter myself, if I saw you loving your good things, or thinking that you ought to pass life in the enjoyment of them. But I shall reveal other thoughts of yours, which you keep to yourself; whereby you will know that I have always had my eye on you. Suppose that at this moment some God came to you and said: Alcibiades, will you live as you are, or die in an instant if you are forbidden to make any further acquisition? I verily believe that you would choose death. And I will tell you the hope in which you are at present living: Before many days have elapsed, you think that you will come before the Athenian assembly, and will prove to them that you are more worthy of honor than Pericles, or any other man that ever lived, and having proved this, you will have the greatest power in the state. When you have gained the greatest power among us, you will go on to other Hellenic states, and not only to Hellenes, but to all the barbarians who inhabit the same continent with us. And if the God were then to say to you again: Here in Europe is to be your seat of empire, and you must not cross over into Asia or meddle with Asiatic affairs, I do not believe that you would choose to live upon these terms; but the world, as I may say, must be filled with your power and name—no man less than Cyrus and Xerxes is of any account with you. Such I know to be your hopes—I am not guessing only—and very likely you, who know that I am speaking the truth, will reply, Well, Socrates, but what have my hopes to do with the explanation which you promised of your unwillingness to leave me? And that is what I am now going to tell you, sweet son of Cleinias and Dinomache. The explanation is, that all these designs of yours cannot be accomplished by you without my help; so great is the power which I believe myself to have over you and your concerns; and this I conceive to be the reason why the God has hitherto forbidden me to converse with you, and I have been long expecting his permission. For, as you hope to prove your own great value to the state, and having proved it, to attain at once to absolute power, so do I indulge a hope that I shall be the supreme power over you, if I am able to prove my own great value to you, and to show you that neither guardian, nor kinsman, nor anyone is able to deliver into your hands the power which you desire, but I only, God being my helper. When you were young (compare Symp.) and your hopes were not yet matured, I should have wasted my time, and therefore, as I conceive, the God forbade me to converse with you; but now, having his permission, I will speak, for now you will listen to me.

ALCIBIADES: Your silence, Socrates, was always a surprise to me. I never could understand why you followed me about, and now that you have begun to speak again, I am still more amazed. Whether I think all this or not, is a matter about which you seem to have already made up your mind, and therefore my denial will have no effect upon you. But granting, if I must, that you have perfectly divined my purposes, why is your assistance necessary to the attainment of them? Can you tell me why?

SOCRATES: You want to know whether I can make a long speech, such as you are in the habit of hearing; but that is not my way. I think, however, that I can prove to you the truth of what I am saying, if you will grant me one little favor.

ALCIBIADES: Yes, if the favor which you mean be not a troublesome one.
SOCRATES: Will you be troubled at having questions to answer?
ALCIBIADES: Not at all.
SOCRATES: Then please to answer.
ALCIBIADES: Ask me.
SOCRATES: Have you not the intention which I attribute to you?
ALCIBIADES: I will grant anything you like, in the hope of hearing what more you have to say.
SOCRATES: You do, then, mean, as I was saying, to come forward in a little while in the character of an adviser of the Athenians? And suppose that when you are ascending the bema, I pull you by the sleeve and say, Alcibiades, you are getting up to advise the Athenians—do you know the matter about which they are going to deliberate, better than they? How would you answer?
ALCIBIADES: I should reply, that I was going to advise them about a matter which I do know better than they.
SOCRATES: Then you are a good adviser about the things which you know?
ALCIBIADES: Certainly.
SOCRATES: And do you know anything but what you have learned of others, or found out yourself?
ALCIBIADES: That is all.
SOCRATES: And would you have ever learned or discovered anything, if you had not been willing either to learn of others or to examine yourself?
ALCIBIADES: I should not.
SOCRATES: And would you have been willing to learn or to examine what you supposed that you knew?
ALCIBIADES: Certainly not.
SOCRATES: Then there was a time when you thought that you did not know what you are now supposed to know?
ALCIBIADES: Certainly.
SOCRATES: I think that I know tolerably well the extent of your acquirements; and you must tell me if I forget any of them: according to my recollection, you learned the arts of writing, of playing on the lyre, and of wrestling; the flute you never would learn; this is the sum of your accomplishments, unless there were some which you acquired in secret; and I think that secrecy was hardly possible, as you could not have come out of your door, either by day or night, without my seeing you.
ALCIBIADES: Yes, that was the whole of my schooling.

SOCRATES: And are you going to get up in the Athenian assembly, and give them advice about writing?
ALCIBIADES: No, indeed.
SOCRATES: Or about the touch of the lyre?
ALCIBIADES: Certainly not.
SOCRATES: And they are not in the habit of deliberating about wrestling, in the assembly?
ALCIBIADES: Hardly.
SOCRATES: Then what are the deliberations in which you propose to advise them? Surely not about building?
ALCIBIADES: No.
SOCRATES: For the builder will advise better than you will about that?
ALCIBIADES: He will.
SOCRATES: Nor about divination?
ALCIBIADES: No.
SOCRATES: About that again the diviner will advise better than you will?
ALCIBIADES: True.
SOCRATES: Whether he be little or great, good or ill-looking, noble or ignoble—makes no difference.
ALCIBIADES: Certainly not.
SOCRATES: A man is a good adviser about anything, not because he has riches, but because he has knowledge?
ALCIBIADES: Assuredly.
SOCRATES: Whether their counselor is rich or poor, is not a matter which will make any difference to the Athenians when they are deliberating about the health of the citizens; they only require that he should be a physician.
ALCIBIADES: Of course.
SOCRATES: Then what will be the subject of deliberation about which you will be justified in getting up and advising them?
ALCIBIADES: About their own concerns, Socrates.
SOCRATES: You mean about shipbuilding, for example, when the question is what sort of ships they ought to build?
ALCIBIADES: No, I should not advise them about that.
SOCRATES: I suppose, because you do not understand shipbuilding—is that the reason?
ALCIBIADES: It is.
SOCRATES: Then about what concerns of theirs will you advise them?
ALCIBIADES: About war, Socrates, or about peace, or about any other concerns of the state.

SOCRATES: You mean, when they deliberate with whom they ought to make peace, and with whom they ought to go to war, and in what manner?
ALCIBIADES: Yes.
SOCRATES: And they ought to go to war with those against whom it is better to go to war?
ALCIBIADES: Yes.
SOCRATES: And when it is better?
ALCIBIADES: Certainly.
SOCRATES: And for as long a time as is better?
ALCIBIADES: Yes.
SOCRATES: But suppose the Athenians to deliberate with whom they ought to close in wrestling, and whom they should grasp by the hand, would you, or the master of gymnastics, be a better adviser of them?
ALCIBIADES: Clearly, the master of gymnastics.
SOCRATES: And can you tell me on what grounds the master of gymnastics would decide, with whom they ought or ought not to close, and when and how? To take an instance: Would he not say that they should wrestle with those against whom it is best to wrestle?
ALCIBIADES: Yes.
SOCRATES: And as much as is best?
ALCIBIADES: Certainly.
SOCRATES: And at such times as are best?
ALCIBIADES: Yes.
SOCRATES: Again; you sometimes accompany the lyre with the song and dance?
ALCIBIADES: Yes.
SOCRATES: When it is well to do so?
ALCIBIADES: Yes.
SOCRATES: And as much as is well?
ALCIBIADES: Just so.
SOCRATES: And as you speak of an excellence or art of the best in wrestling, and of an excellence in playing the lyre, I wish you would tell me what this latter is—the excellence of wrestling I call gymnastic, and I want to know what you call the other.
ALCIBIADES: I do not understand you.
SOCRATES: Then try to do as I do; for the answer which I gave is universally right, and when I say right, I mean according to rule.
ALCIBIADES: Yes.
SOCRATES: And was not the art of which I spoke gymnastic?

ALCIBIADES: Certainly.
SOCRATES: And I called the excellence in wrestling gymnastic?
ALCIBIADES: You did.
SOCRATES: And I was right?
ALCIBIADES: I think that you were.
SOCRATES: Well, now—for you should learn to argue prettily—let me ask you in return to tell me, first, what is that art of which playing and singing, and stepping properly in the dance, are parts—what is the name of the whole? I think that by this time you must be able to tell.
ALCIBIADES: Indeed I cannot.
SOCRATES: Then let me put the matter in another way: What do you call the Goddesses who are the patronesses of art?
ALCIBIADES: The Muses do you mean, Socrates?
SOCRATES: Yes, I do; and what is the name of the art which is called after them?
ALCIBIADES: I suppose that you mean music.
SOCRATES: Yes, that is my meaning; and what is the excellence of the art of music, as I told you truly that the excellence of wrestling was gymnastic—what is the excellence of music—to be what?
ALCIBIADES: To be musical, I suppose.
SOCRATES: Very good; and now please to tell me what is the excellence of war and peace; as the more musical was the more excellent, or the more gymnastical was the more excellent, tell me, what name do you give to the more excellent in war and peace?
ALCIBIADES: But I really cannot tell you.
SOCRATES: But if you were offering advice to another and said to him—This food is better than that, at this time and in this quantity, and he said to you—What do you mean, Alcibiades, by the word "better"? you would have no difficulty in replying that you meant "more wholesome," although you do not profess to be a physician, and when the subject is one of which you profess to have knowledge, and about which you are ready to get up and advise as if you knew, are you not ashamed, when you are asked, not to be able to answer the question? Is it not disgraceful?
ALCIBIADES: Very.
SOCRATES: Well, then, consider and try to explain what is the meaning of "better," in the matter of making peace and going to war with those against whom you ought to go to war? To what does the word refer?
ALCIBIADES: I am thinking, and I cannot tell.
SOCRATES: But you surely know what are the charges which we bring

against one another, when we arrive at the point of making war, and what name we give them?

ALCIBIADES: Yes, certainly; we say that deceit or violence has been employed, or that we have been defrauded.

SOCRATES: And how does this happen? Will you tell me how? For there may be a difference in the manner.

ALCIBIADES: Do you mean by "how," Socrates, whether we suffered these things justly or unjustly?

SOCRATES: Exactly.

ALCIBIADES: There can be no greater difference than between just and unjust.

SOCRATES: And would you advise the Athenians to go to war with the just or with the unjust?

ALCIBIADES: That is an awkward question; for certainly, even if a person did intend to go to war with the just, he would not admit that they were just.

SOCRATES: He would not go to war, because it would be unlawful?

ALCIBIADES: Neither lawful nor honorable.

SOCRATES: Then you, too, would address them on principles of justice?

ALCIBIADES: Certainly.

SOCRATES: What, then, is justice but that better, of which I spoke, in going to war or not going to war with those against whom we ought or ought not, and when we ought or ought not to go to war?

ALCIBIADES: Clearly.

SOCRATES: But how is this, friend Alcibiades? Have you forgotten that you do not know this, or have you been to the schoolmaster without my knowledge, and has he taught you to discern the just from the unjust? Who is he? I wish you would tell me, that I may go and learn of him—you shall introduce me.

ALCIBIADES: You are mocking, Socrates.

SOCRATES: No, indeed; I most solemnly declare to you by Zeus, who is the God of our common friendship, and whom I never will forswear, that I am not; tell me, then, who this instructor is, if he exists.

ALCIBIADES: But, perhaps, he does not exist; may I not have acquired the knowledge of just and unjust in some other way?

SOCRATES: Yes; if you have discovered them.

ALCIBIADES: But do you not think that I could discover them?

SOCRATES: I am sure that you might, if you inquired about them.

ALCIBIADES: And do you not think that I would inquire?

SOCRATES: Yes; if you thought that you did not know them.

ALCIBIADES: And was there not a time when I did so think?

SOCRATES: Very good; and can you tell me how long it is since you thought that you did not know the nature of the just and the unjust? What do you say to a year ago? Were you then in a state of conscious ignorance and inquiry? Or did you think that you knew? And please to answer truly, that our discussion may not be in vain.

ALCIBIADES: Well, I thought that I knew.

SOCRATES: And two years ago, and three years ago, and four years ago, you knew all the same?

ALCIBIADES: I did.

SOCRATES: And more than four years ago you were a child—were you not?

ALCIBIADES: Yes.

SOCRATES: And then I am quite sure that you thought you knew.

ALCIBIADES: Why are you so sure?

SOCRATES: Because I often heard you when a child, in your teacher's house, or elsewhere, playing at dice or some other game with the boys, not hesitating at all about the nature of the just and unjust; but very confident—crying and shouting that one of the boys was a rogue and a cheat, and had been cheating. Is it not true?

ALCIBIADES: But what was I to do, Socrates, when anybody cheated me?

SOCRATES: And how can you say, "What was I to do?" if at the time you did not know whether you were wronged or not?

ALCIBIADES: To be sure I knew; I was quite aware that I was being cheated.

SOCRATES: Then you suppose yourself even when a child to have known the nature of just and unjust?

ALCIBIADES: Certainly; and I did know then.

SOCRATES: And when did you discover them—not, surely, at the time when you thought that you knew them?

ALCIBIADES: Certainly not.

SOCRATES: And when did you think that you were ignorant—if you consider, you will find that there never was such a time?

ALCIBIADES: Really, Socrates, I cannot say.

SOCRATES: Then you did not learn them by discovering them?

ALCIBIADES: Clearly not.

SOCRATES: But just before you said that you did not know them by learning; now, if you have neither discovered nor learned them, how and whence do you come to know them?

ALCIBIADES: I suppose that I was mistaken in saying that I knew them through my own discovery of them; whereas, in truth, I learned them in the same way that other people learn.

SOCRATES: So you said before, and I must again ask, of whom? Do tell me.

ALCIBIADES: Of the many.

SOCRATES: Do you take refuge in them? I cannot say much for your teachers.

ALCIBIADES: Why, are they not able to teach?

SOCRATES: They could not teach you how to play at draughts, which you would acknowledge (would you not) to be a much smaller matter than justice?

ALCIBIADES: Yes.

SOCRATES: And can they teach the better who are unable to teach the worse?

ALCIBIADES: I think that they can; at any rate, they can teach many far better things than to play at draughts.

SOCRATES: What things?

ALCIBIADES: Why, for example, I learned to speak Greek of them, and I cannot say who was my teacher, or to whom I am to attribute my knowledge of Greek, if not to those good-for-nothing teachers, as you call them.

SOCRATES: Why, yes, my friend; and the many are good enough teachers of Greek, and some of their instructions in that line may be justly praised.

ALCIBIADES: Why is that?

SOCRATES: Why, because they have the qualities which good teachers ought to have.

ALCIBIADES: What qualities?

SOCRATES: Why, you know that knowledge is the first qualification of any teacher?

ALCIBIADES: Certainly.

SOCRATES: And if they know, they must agree together and not differ?

ALCIBIADES: Yes.

SOCRATES: And would you say that they knew the things about which they differ?

ALCIBIADES: No.

SOCRATES: Then how can they teach them?

ALCIBIADES: They cannot.

SOCRATES: Well, but do you imagine that the many would differ about the nature of wood and stone? are they not agreed if you ask them what

they are? and do they not run to fetch the same thing, when they want a piece of wood or a stone? And so in similar cases, which I suspect to be pretty nearly all that you mean by speaking Greek.
ALCIBIADES: True.
SOCRATES: These, as we were saying, are matters about which they are agreed with one another and with themselves; both individuals and states use the same words about them; they do not use some one word and some another.
ALCIBIADES: They do not.
SOCRATES: Then they may be expected to be good teachers of these things?
ALCIBIADES: Yes.
SOCRATES: And if we want to instruct anyone in them, we shall be right in sending him to be taught by our friends the many?
ALCIBIADES: Very true.
SOCRATES: But if we wanted further to know not only which are men and which are horses, but which men or horses have powers of running, would the many still be able to inform us?
ALCIBIADES: Certainly not.
SOCRATES: And you have a sufficient proof that they do not know these things and are not the best teachers of them, inasmuch as they are never agreed about them?
ALCIBIADES: Yes.
SOCRATES: And suppose that we wanted to know not only what men are like, but what healthy or diseased men are like—would the many be able to teach us?
ALCIBIADES: They would not.
SOCRATES: And you would have a proof that they were bad teachers of these matters, if you saw them at variance?
ALCIBIADES: I should.
SOCRATES: Well, but are the many agreed with themselves, or with one another, about the justice or injustice of men and things?
ALCIBIADES: Assuredly not, Socrates.
SOCRATES: There is no subject about which they are more at variance?
ALCIBIADES: None.
SOCRATES: I do not suppose that you ever saw or heard of men quarrelling over the principles of health and disease to such an extent as to go to war and kill one another for the sake of them?
ALCIBIADES: No indeed.

SOCRATES: But of the quarrels about justice and injustice, even if you have never seen them, you have certainly heard from many people, including Homer; for you have heard of the Iliad and Odyssey?

ALCIBIADES: To be sure, Socrates.

SOCRATES: A difference of just and unjust is the argument of those poems?

ALCIBIADES: True.

SOCRATES: Which difference caused all the wars and deaths of Trojans and Achaeans, and the deaths of the suitors of Penelope in their quarrel with Odysseus.

ALCIBIADES: Very true.

SOCRATES: And when the Athenians and Lacedaemonians and Boeotians fell at Tanagra, and afterward in the battle of Coronea, at which your father Cleinias met his end, the question was one of justice—this was the sole cause of the battles, and of their deaths.

ALCIBIADES: Very true.

SOCRATES: But can they be said to understand that about which they are quarrelling to the death?

ALCIBIADES: Clearly not.

SOCRATES: And yet those whom you thus allow to be ignorant are the teachers to whom you are appealing.

ALCIBIADES: Very true.

SOCRATES: But how are you ever likely to know the nature of justice and injustice, about which you are so perplexed, if you have neither learned them of others nor discovered them yourself?

ALCIBIADES: From what you say, I suppose not.

SOCRATES: See, again, how inaccurately you speak, Alcibiades!

ALCIBIADES: In what respect?

SOCRATES: In saying that I say so.

ALCIBIADES: Why, did you not say that I know nothing of the just and unjust?

SOCRATES: No; I did not.

ALCIBIADES: Did I, then?

SOCRATES: Yes.

ALCIBIADES: How was that?

SOCRATES: Let me explain. Suppose I were to ask you which is the greater number, two or one; you would reply "two"?

ALCIBIADES: I should.

SOCRATES: And by how much greater?

ALCIBIADES: By one.
SOCRATES: Which of us now says that two is more than one?
ALCIBIADES: I do.
SOCRATES: Did not I ask, and you answer the question?
ALCIBIADES: Yes.
SOCRATES: Then who is speaking? I who put the question, or you who answer me?
ALCIBIADES: I am.
SOCRATES: Or suppose that I ask and you tell me the letters which make up the name Socrates, which of us is the speaker?
ALCIBIADES: I am.
SOCRATES: Now let us put the case generally: Whenever there is a question and answer, who is the speaker, the questioner or the answerer?
ALCIBIADES: I should say, Socrates, that the answerer was the speaker.
SOCRATES: And have I not been the questioner all through?
ALCIBIADES: Yes.
SOCRATES: And you the answerer?
ALCIBIADES: Just so.
SOCRATES: Which of us, then, was the speaker?
ALCIBIADES: The inference is, Socrates, that I was the speaker.
SOCRATES: Did not someone say that Alcibiades, the fair son of Cleinias, not understanding about just and unjust, but thinking that he did understand, was going to the assembly to advise the Athenians about what he did not know? Was not that said?
ALCIBIADES: Very true.
SOCRATES: Then, Alcibiades, the result may be expressed in the language of Euripides. I think that you have heard all this "from yourself, and not from me"; nor did I say this, which you erroneously attribute to me, but you yourself, and what you said was very true. For indeed, my dear fellow, the design which you meditate of teaching what you do not know, and have not taken any pains to learn, is downright insanity.
ALCIBIADES: But, Socrates, I think that the Athenians and the rest of the Hellenes do not often advise as to the more just or unjust; for they see no difficulty in them, and therefore they leave them, and consider which course of action will be most expedient; for there is a difference between justice and expediency. Many persons have done great wrong and profited by their injustice; others have done rightly and come to no good.
SOCRATES: Well, but granting that the just and the expedient are ever so

much opposed, you surely do not imagine that you know what is expedient for mankind, or why a thing is expedient?

ALCIBIADES: Why not, Socrates? But I am not going to be asked again from whom I learned, or when I made the discovery.

SOCRATES: What a way you have! When you make a mistake which might be refuted by a previous argument, you insist on having a new and different refutation; the old argument is a worn-our garment which you will no longer put on, but someone must produce another which is clean and new. Now I shall disregard this move of yours, and shall ask over again: Where did you learn and how do you know the nature of the expedient, and who is your teacher? All this I comprehend in a single question, and now you will manifestly be in the old difficulty, and will not be able to show that you know the expedient, either because you learned or because you discovered it yourself. But, as I perceive that you are dainty, and dislike the taste of a stale argument, I will inquire no further into your knowledge of what is expedient or what is not expedient for the Athenian people, and simply request you to say why you do not explain whether justice and expediency are the same or different? And if you like you may examine me as I have examined you, or, if you would rather, you may carry on the discussion by yourself.

ALCIBIADES: But I am not certain, Socrates, whether I shall be able to discuss the matter with you.

SOCRATES: Then imagine, my dear fellow, that I am the demus and the ecclesia; for in the ecclesia, too, you will have to persuade men individually.

ALCIBIADES: Yes.

SOCRATES: And is not the same person able to persuade one individual singly and many individuals of the things which he knows? The grammarian, for example, can persuade one and he can persuade many about letters.

ALCIBIADES: True.

SOCRATES: And about number, will not the same person persuade one and persuade many?

ALCIBIADES: Yes.

SOCRATES: And this will be he who knows number, or the arithmetician?

ALCIBIADES: Quite true.

SOCRATES: And cannot you persuade one man about that of which you can persuade many?

ALCIBIADES: I suppose so.

SOCRATES: And that of which you can persuade either is clearly what you know?

ALCIBIADES: Yes.

SOCRATES: And the only difference between one who argues as we are doing, and the orator who is addressing an assembly, is that the one seeks to persuade a number, and the other an individual, of the same things.

ALCIBIADES: I suppose so.

SOCRATES: Well, then, since the same person who can persuade a multitude can persuade individuals, try conclusions upon me, and prove to me that the just is not always expedient.

ALCIBIADES: You take liberties, Socrates.

SOCRATES: I shall take the liberty of proving to you the opposite of that which you will not prove to me.

ALCIBIADES: Proceed.

SOCRATES: Answer my questions—that is all.

ALCIBIADES: Nay, I should like you to be the speaker.

SOCRATES: What, do you not wish to be persuaded?

ALCIBIADES: Certainly I do.

SOCRATES: And can you be persuaded better than out of your own mouth?

ALCIBIADES: I think not.

SOCRATES: Then you shall answer; and if you do not hear the words, that the just is the expedient, coming from your own lips, never believe another man again.

ALCIBIADES: I won't; but answer I will, for I do not see how I can come to any harm.

SOCRATES: A true prophecy! Let me begin then by inquiring of you whether you allow that the just is sometimes expedient and sometimes not?

ALCIBIADES: Yes.

SOCRATES: And sometimes honorable and sometimes not?

ALCIBIADES: What do you mean?

SOCRATES: I am asking if you ever knew anyone who did what was dishonorable and yet just?

ALCIBIADES: Never.

SOCRATES: All just things are honorable?

ALCIBIADES: Yes.

SOCRATES: And are honorable things sometimes good and sometimes not good, or are they always good?

ALCIBIADES: I rather think, Socrates, that some honorable things are evil.

SOCRATES: And are some dishonorable things good?

ALCIBIADES: Yes.

SOCRATES: You mean in such a case as the following: In time of war, men have been wounded or have died in rescuing a companion or kinsman, when others who have neglected the duty of rescuing them have escaped in safety?

ALCIBIADES: True.

SOCRATES: And to rescue another under such circumstances is honorable, in respect of the attempt to save those whom we ought to save; and this is courage?

ALCIBIADES: True.

SOCRATES: But evil in respect of death and wounds?

ALCIBIADES: Yes.

SOCRATES: And the courage which is shown in the rescue is one thing, and the death another?

ALCIBIADES: Certainly.

SOCRATES: Then the rescue of one's friends is honorable in one point of view, but evil in another?

ALCIBIADES: True.

SOCRATES: And if honorable, then also good: Will you consider now whether I may not be right, for you were acknowledging that the courage which is shown in the rescue is honorable? Now is this courage good or evil? Look at the matter thus: which would you rather choose, good or evil?

ALCIBIADES: Good.

SOCRATES: And the greatest goods you would be most ready to choose, and would least like to be deprived of them?

ALCIBIADES: Certainly.

SOCRATES: What would you say of courage? At what price would you be willing to be deprived of courage?

ALCIBIADES: I would rather die than be a coward.

SOCRATES: Then you think that cowardice is the worst of evils?

ALCIBIADES: I do.

SOCRATES: As bad as death, I suppose?

ALCIBIADES: Yes.

SOCRATES: And life and courage are the extreme opposites of death and cowardice?

ALCIBIADES: Yes.

SOCRATES: And they are what you would most desire to have, and their opposites you would least desire?

ALCIBIADES: Yes.

SOCRATES: Is this because you think life and courage the best, and death and cowardice the worst?
ALCIBIADES: Yes.
SOCRATES: And you would term the rescue of a friend in battle honorable, in as much as courage does a good work?
ALCIBIADES: I should.
SOCRATES: But evil because of the death which ensues?
ALCIBIADES: Yes.
SOCRATES: Might we not describe their different effects as follows: You may call either of them evil in respect of the evil which is the result, and good in respect of the good which is the result of either of them?
ALCIBIADES: Yes.
SOCRATES: And they are honorable in so far as they are good, and dishonorable in so far as they are evil?
ALCIBIADES: True.
SOCRATES: Then when you say that the rescue of a friend in battle is honorable and yet evil, that is equivalent to saying that the rescue is good and yet evil?
ALCIBIADES: I believe that you are right, Socrates.
SOCRATES: Nothing honorable, regarded as honorable, is evil; nor anything base, regarded as base, good.
ALCIBIADES: Clearly not.
SOCRATES: Look at the matter yet once more in a further light: He who acts honorably acts well?
ALCIBIADES: Yes.
SOCRATES: And he who acts well is happy?
ALCIBIADES: Of course.
SOCRATES: And the happy are those who obtain good?
ALCIBIADES: True.
SOCRATES: And they obtain good by acting well and honorably?
ALCIBIADES: Yes.
SOCRATES: Then acting well is a good?
ALCIBIADES: Certainly.
SOCRATES: And happiness is a good?
ALCIBIADES: Yes.
SOCRATES: Then the good and the honorable are again identified.
ALCIBIADES: Manifestly.
SOCRATES: Then, if the argument holds, what we find to be honorable we shall also find to be good?

ALCIBIADES: Certainly.
SOCRATES: And is the good expedient or not?
ALCIBIADES: Expedient.
SOCRATES: Do you remember our admissions about the just?
ALCIBIADES: Yes; if I am not mistaken, we said that those who acted justly must also act honorably.
SOCRATES: And the honorable is the good?
ALCIBIADES: Yes.
SOCRATES: And the good is expedient?
ALCIBIADES: Yes.
SOCRATES: Then, Alcibiades, the just is expedient?
ALCIBIADES: I should infer so.
SOCRATES: And all this I prove out of your own mouth, for I ask and you answer?
ALCIBIADES: I must acknowledge it to be true.
SOCRATES: And having acknowledged that the just is the same as the expedient, are you not (let me ask) prepared to ridicule anyone who, pretending to understand the principles of justice and injustice, gets up to advise the noble Athenians or the ignoble Peparethians, that the just may be the evil?
ALCIBIADES: I solemnly declare, Socrates, that I do not know what I am saying. Verily, I am in a strange state, for when you put questions to me I am of different minds in successive instants.
SOCRATES: And are you not aware of the nature of this perplexity, my friend?
ALCIBIADES: Indeed I am not.
SOCRATES: Do you suppose that if someone were to ask you whether you have two eyes or three, or two hands or four, or anything of that sort, you would then be of different minds in successive instants?
ALCIBIADES: I begin to distrust myself, but still I do not suppose that I should.
SOCRATES: You would feel no doubt; and for this reason—because you would know?
ALCIBIADES: I suppose so.
SOCRATES: And the reason why you involuntarily contradict yourself is clearly that you are ignorant?
ALCIBIADES: Very likely.
SOCRATES: And if you are perplexed in answering about just and unjust, honorable and dishonorable, good and evil, expedient and inexpedient, the

reason is that you are ignorant of them, and therefore in perplexity. Is not that clear?

ALCIBIADES: I agree.

SOCRATES: But is this always the case, and is a man necessarily perplexed about that of which he has no knowledge?

ALCIBIADES: Certainly he is.

SOCRATES: And do you know how to ascend into heaven?

ALCIBIADES: Certainly not.

SOCRATES: And in this case, too, is your judgment perplexed?

ALCIBIADES: No.

SOCRATES: Do you see the reason why, or shall I tell you?

ALCIBIADES: Tell me.

SOCRATES: The reason is, that you not only do not know, my friend, but you do not think that you know.

ALCIBIADES: There again; what do you mean?

SOCRATES: Ask yourself; are you in any perplexity about things of which you are ignorant? You know, for example, that you know nothing about the preparation of food.

ALCIBIADES: Very true.

SOCRATES: And do you think and perplex yourself about the preparation of food, or do you leave that to someone who understands the art?

ALCIBIADES: The latter.

SOCRATES: Or if you were on a voyage, would you bewilder yourself by considering whether the rudder is to be drawn inwards or outwards, or do you leave that to the pilot, and do nothing?

ALCIBIADES: It would be the concern of the pilot.

SOCRATES: Then you are not perplexed about what you do not know, if you know that you do not know it?

ALCIBIADES: I imagine not.

SOCRATES: Do you not see, then, that mistakes in life and practice are likewise to be attributed to the ignorance which has conceit of knowledge?

ALCIBIADES: Once more, what do you mean?

SOCRATES: I suppose that we begin to act when we think that we know what we are doing?

ALCIBIADES: Yes.

SOCRATES: But when people think that they do not know, they entrust their business to others?

ALCIBIADES: Yes.

SOCRATES: And so there is a class of ignorant persons who do not make

mistakes in life, because they trust others about things of which they are ignorant?
ALCIBIADES: True.
SOCRATES: Who, then, are the persons who make mistakes? They cannot, of course, be those who know?
ALCIBIADES: Certainly not.
SOCRATES: But if neither those who know, nor those who know that they do not know, make mistakes, there remain those only who do not know and think that they know.
ALCIBIADES: Yes, only those.
SOCRATES: Then this is ignorance of the disgraceful sort which is mischievous?
ALCIBIADES: Yes.
SOCRATES: And most mischievous and most disgraceful when having to do with the greatest matters?
ALCIBIADES: By far.
SOCRATES: And can there be any matters greater than the just, the honorable, the good, and the expedient?
ALCIBIADES: There cannot be.
SOCRATES: And these, as you were saying, are what perplex you?
ALCIBIADES: Yes.
SOCRATES: But if you are perplexed, then, as the previous argument has shown, you are not only ignorant of the greatest matters, but being ignorant you fancy that you know them?
ALCIBIADES: I fear that you are right.
SOCRATES: And now see what has happened to you, Alcibiades! I hardly like to speak of your evil case, but as we are alone I will: My good friend, you are wedded to ignorance of the most disgraceful kind, and of this you are convicted, not by me, but out of your own mouth and by your own argument; wherefore also you rush into politics before you are educated. Neither is your case to be deemed singular. For I might say the same of almost all our statesmen, with the exception, perhaps of your guardian, Pericles.
ALCIBIADES: Yes, Socrates; and Pericles is said not to have got his wisdom by the light of nature, but to have associated with several of the philosophers; with Pythocleides, for example, and with Anaxagoras, and now in advanced life with Damon, in the hope of gaining wisdom.
SOCRATES: Very good; but did you ever know a man wise in anything who was unable to impart his particular wisdom? For example, he who

taught you letters was not only wise, but he made you and any others whom he liked wise.
ALCIBIADES: Yes.
SOCRATES: And you, whom he taught, can do the same?
ALCIBIADES: True.
SOCRATES: And in like manner the harper and gymnastic master?
ALCIBIADES: Certainly.
SOCRATES: When a person is enabled to impart knowledge to another, he thereby gives an excellent proof of his own understanding of any matter.
ALCIBIADES: I agree.
SOCRATES: Well, and did Pericles make anyone wise; did he begin by making his sons wise?
ALCIBIADES: But, Socrates, if the two sons of Pericles were simpletons, what has that to do with the matter?
SOCRATES: Well, but did he make your brother, Cleinias, wise?
ALCIBIADES: Cleinias is a madman; there is no use in talking of him.
SOCRATES: But if Cleinias is a madman and the two sons of Pericles were simpletons, what reason can be given why he neglects you, and lets you be as you are?
ALCIBIADES: I believe that I am to blame for not listening to him.
SOCRATES: But did you ever hear of any other Athenian or foreigner, bond or free, who was deemed to have grown wiser in the society of Pericles,—as I might cite Pythodorus, the son of Isolochus, and Callias, the son of Calliades, who have grown wiser in the society of Zeno, for which privilege they have each of them paid him the sum of a hundred minae (about 406 pounds sterling) to the increase of their wisdom and fame.
ALCIBIADES: I certainly never did hear of anyone.
SOCRATES: Well, and in reference to your own case, do you mean to remain as you are, or will you take some pains about yourself?
ALCIBIADES: With your aid, Socrates, I will. And indeed, when I hear you speak, the truth of what you are saying strikes home to me, and I agree with you, for our statesmen, all but a few, do appear to be quite uneducated.
SOCRATES: What is the inference?
ALCIBIADES: Why, that if they were educated they would be trained athletes, and he who means to rival them ought to have knowledge and experience when he attacks them; but now, as they have become politicians without any special training, why should I have the trouble of learning and practicing? For I know well that by the light of nature I shall get the better of them.

SOCRATES: My dear friend, what a sentiment! And how unworthy of your noble form and your high estate!
ALCIBIADES: What do you mean, Socrates; why do you say so?
SOCRATES: I am grieved when I think of our mutual love.
ALCIBIADES: At what?
SOCRATES: At your fancying that the contest on which you are entering is with people here.
ALCIBIADES: Why, what others are there?
SOCRATES: Is that a question which a magnanimous soul should ask?
ALCIBIADES: Do you mean to say that the contest is not with these?
SOCRATES: And suppose that you were going to steer a ship into action, would you only aim at being the best pilot on board? Would you not, while acknowledging that you must possess this degree of excellence, rather look to your antagonists, and not, as you are now doing, to your fellow combatants? You ought to be so far above these latter, that they will not even dare to be your rivals; and, being regarded by you as inferiors, will do battle for you against the enemy; this is the kind of superiority which you must establish over them, if you mean to accomplish any noble action really worthy of yourself and of the state.
ALCIBIADES: That would certainly be my aim.
SOCRATES: Verily, then, you have good reason to be satisfied, if you are better than the soldiers; and you need not, when you are their superior and have your thoughts and actions fixed upon them, look away to the generals of the enemy.
ALCIBIADES: Of whom are you speaking, Socrates?
SOCRATES: Why, you surely know that our city goes to war now and then with the Lacedaemonians and with the great king?
ALCIBIADES: True enough.
SOCRATES: And if you meant to be the ruler of this city, would you not be right in considering that the Lacedaemonian and Persian king were your true rivals?
ALCIBIADES: I believe that you are right.
SOCRATES: Oh no, my friend, I am quite wrong, and I think that you ought rather to turn your attention to Midias the quail-breeder and others like him, who manage our politics; in whom, as the women would remark, you may still see the slaves' cut of hair, cropping out in their minds as well as on their pates; and they come with their barbarous lingo to flatter us and not to rule us. To these, I say, you should look, and then you need not trouble yourself about your own fitness to contend in such a noble arena:

There is no reason why you should either learn what has to be learned, or practice what has to be practiced, and only when thoroughly prepared enter on a political career.

ALCIBIADES: There, I think, Socrates, that you are right; I do not suppose, however, that the Spartan generals or the great king are really different from anybody else.

SOCRATES: But, my dear friend, do consider what you are saying.

ALCIBIADES: What am I to consider?

SOCRATES: In the first place, will you be more likely to take care of yourself, if you are in a wholesome fear and dread of them, or if you are not?

ALCIBIADES: Clearly, if I have such a fear of them.

SOCRATES: And do you think that you will sustain any injury if you take care of yourself?

ALCIBIADES: No, I shall be greatly benefited.

SOCRATES: And this is one very important respect in which that notion of yours is bad.

ALCIBIADES: True.

SOCRATES: In the next place, consider that what you say is probably false.

ALCIBIADES: How so?

SOCRATES: Let me ask you whether better natures are likely to be found in noble races or not in noble races?

ALCIBIADES: Clearly in noble races.

SOCRATES: Are not those who are well born and well bred most likely to be perfect in virtue?

ALCIBIADES: Certainly.

SOCRATES: Then let us compare our antecedents with those of the Lacedaemonian and Persian kings; are they inferior to us in descent? Have we not heard that the former are sprung from Heracles, and the latter from Achaemenes, and that the race of Heracles and the race of Achaemenes go back to Perseus, son of Zeus?

ALCIBIADES: Why, so does mine go back to Eurysaces, and he to Zeus!

SOCRATES: And mine, noble Alcibiades, to Daedalus, and he to Hephaestus, son of Zeus. But, for all that, we are far inferior to them. For they are descended "from Zeus," through a line of kings—either kings of Argos and Lacedaemon, or kings of Persia, a country which the descendants of Achaemenes have always possessed, besides being at various times sovereigns of Asia, as they now are; whereas, we and our fathers were but private persons. How ridiculous would you be thought if you were to make a display of your ancestors and of Salamis the island of Eurysaces, or of Aegina, the habitation of the still more ancient Aeacus, before Artaxerxes, son of Xerxes. You should consider how inferior we are to them both in the derivation of our birth and in other particulars. Did you never observe how great is the property of the Spartan kings? And their wives are under the guardianship of the Ephori, who are public officers and watch over them, in order to preserve as far as possible the purity of the Heracleid blood. Still greater is the difference among the Persians; for no one entertains a suspicion that the father of a prince of Persia can be anyone but the king. Such is the awe which invests the person of the queen, that any other guard is needless. And when the heir of the kingdom is born, all the subjects of the king feast; and the day of his birth is forever afterward kept as a holiday and time of sacrifice by all Asia; whereas, when you and I were born, Alcibiades, as the comic poet says, the neighbors hardly knew of the important event. After the birth of the royal child, he is tended, not by a good-for-nothing woman-nurse, but by the best of the royal eunuchs, who are charged with the care of him, and especially with the fashioning and right formation of his limbs, in order that he may be as shapely as possible; which being their calling, they are held in great honor. And when the young prince is seven years old he is put upon a horse and taken to the riding-masters, and begins to go out hunting. And at fourteen years of age he is handed over to the royal schoolmasters, as they are termed: these are four chosen men, reputed to be the best among the Persians of a certain age; and one of them is the wisest, another the justest, a third the most temperate, and a fourth the most valiant. The first instructs him in the magianism of Zoroaster, the son of Oromasus, which is the worship of the Gods, and teaches him also the duties of his royal office; the second, who is the justest, teaches him always to speak the truth; the third, or most temperate, forbids him to allow any pleasure to be lord over him, that he may be accustomed to be a freeman and king indeed, lord of himself first, and not a slave; the most valiant trains him to be bold and fearless, telling him that if he fears he is to deem himself a slave; whereas Pericles gave you, Alcibiades, for a tutor Zopyrus the Thracian, a slave of his who was past all other work. I might enlarge on the nurture and education of your rivals, but that would be tedious; and what I have said is a sufficient sample of what remains to be said. I have only to remark, by way of contrast, that no one cares about your birth or nurture or education, or, I may say, about that of any other Athenian, unless he has a lover who looks after him. And if you cast an eye on the wealth, the luxury, the garments with their flowing trains, the anointings with myrrh, the multitudes of attendants, and all the other bravery of the Persians, you will be ashamed when you discern your own inferiority; or if you look at the temperance and orderliness and ease and grace and magnanimity and courage and endurance and love of toil and desire of glory and ambition of the Lacedaemonians—in all these respects you will see that you are but a child in comparison of them. Even in the matter of wealth, if you value yourself upon that, I must reveal to you how you stand; for if you form an estimate of the wealth of the Lacedaemonians, you will see that our possessions fall far short of theirs. For no one here can compete with them either in the extent and fertility of their own and the Messenian territory, or in the number of their slaves, and especially of the Helots, or of their horses, or of the animals which feed on the Messenian pastures. But I have said enough of this: And as to gold and silver, there is more of them in Lacedaemon than in all the rest of Hellas, for during many generations gold has been always flowing in to them from the whole Hellenic world, and often from the barbarian also, and never going out, as in the fable of Aesop the fox said to the lion, "The prints of the feet of those going in are distinct enough"; but who ever saw the trace of money going out of Lacedaemon? And therefore you may safely infer that the inhabitants are the richest of the Hellenes in gold and silver, and that their kings are the richest of them, for they have a larger share of these things, and they have also a tribute paid to them which is very considerable. Yet the Spartan wealth, though great in comparison of the wealth of the other Hellenes, is as nothing in comparison of that of the Persians and their kings. Why, I have been informed by a credible person who went up to the king (at Susa), that he passed through a large tract of excellent land, extending for nearly a day's journey, which the people of the country called the queen's girdle, and another, which they called her veil; and several other fair and fertile districts, which were reserved for the adornment of the queen, and are named after her several habiliments. Now, I cannot help thinking to myself, What if someone were to go to Amestris, the wife of Xerxes and mother of Artaxerxes, and say to her, "There is a certain Dinomache, whose whole wardrobe is not worth fifty minae"—and that will be more than the value—"and she has a son who is possessed of a three-hundred acre patch at Erchiae, and he has a mind to go to war with your son"—would she not wonder to what this Alcibiades trusts for success in the conflict? "He must rely," she would say to herself, "upon his training and wisdom—these are the things which Hellenes value."

And if she heard that this Alcibiades who is making the attempt is not as yet twenty years old, and is wholly uneducated, and when his lover tells him that he ought to get education and training first, and then go and fight the king, he refuses, and says that he is well enough as he is, would she not be amazed, and ask "On what, then, does the youth rely?" And if we replied: He relies on his beauty, and stature, and birth, and mental endowments, she would think that we were mad, Alcibiades, when she compared the advantages which you possess with those of her own people. And I believe that even Lampido, the daughter of Leotychides, the wife of Archidamus and mother of Agis, all of whom were kings, would have the same feeling; if, in your present uneducated state, you were to turn your thoughts against her son, she too would be equally astonished. But how disgraceful, that we should not have as high a notion of what is required in us as our enemies" wives and mothers have of the qualities which are required in their assailants! O my friend, be persuaded by me, and hear the Delphian inscription, "Know thyself"—not the men whom you think, but these kings are our rivals, and we can only overcome them by pains and skill. And if you fail in the required qualities, you will fail also in becoming renowned among Hellenes and Barbarians, which you seem to desire more than any other man ever desired anything.

ALCIBIADES: I entirely believe you; but what are the sort of pains which are required, Socrates—can you tell me?

SOCRATES: Yes, I can; but we must take counsel together concerning the manner in which both of us may be most improved. For what I am telling you of the necessity of education applies to myself as well as to you; and there is only one point in which I have an advantage over you.

ALCIBIADES: What is that?

SOCRATES: I have a guardian who is better and wiser than your guardian, Pericles.

ALCIBIADES: Who is he, Socrates?

SOCRATES: God, Alcibiades, who up to this day has not allowed me to converse with you; and he inspires in me the faith that I am especially designed to bring you to honor.

ALCIBIADES: You are jesting, Socrates.

SOCRATES: Perhaps, at any rate, I am right in saying that all men greatly need pains and care, and you and I above all men.

ALCIBIADES: You are not far wrong about me.

SOCRATES: And certainly not about myself.

ALCIBIADES: But what can we do?

SOCRATES: There must be no hesitation or cowardice, my friend.
ALCIBIADES: That would not become us, Socrates.
SOCRATES: No, indeed, and we ought to take counsel together: For do we not wish to be as good as possible?
ALCIBIADES: We do.
SOCRATES: In what sort of virtue?
ALCIBIADES: Plainly, in the virtue of good men.
SOCRATES: Who are good in what?
ALCIBIADES: Those, clearly, who are good in the management of affairs.
SOCRATES: What sort of affairs? Equestrian affairs?
ALCIBIADES: Certainly not.
SOCRATES: You mean that about them we should have recourse to horsemen?
ALCIBIADES: Yes.
SOCRATES: Well, naval affairs?
ALCIBIADES: No.
SOCRATES: You mean that we should have recourse to sailors about them?
ALCIBIADES: Yes.
SOCRATES: Then what affairs? And who do them?
ALCIBIADES: The affairs which occupy Athenian gentlemen.
SOCRATES: And when you speak of gentlemen, do you mean the wise or the unwise?
ALCIBIADES: The wise.
SOCRATES: And a man is good in respect of that in which he is wise?
ALCIBIADES: Yes.
SOCRATES: And evil in respect of that in which he is unwise?
ALCIBIADES: Certainly.
SOCRATES: The shoemaker, for example, is wise in respect of the making of shoes?
ALCIBIADES: Yes.
SOCRATES: Then he is good in that?
ALCIBIADES: He is.
SOCRATES: But in respect of the making of garments he is unwise?
ALCIBIADES: Yes.
SOCRATES: Then in that he is bad?
ALCIBIADES: Yes.
SOCRATES: Then upon this view of the matter the same man is good and also bad?

ALCIBIADES: True.
SOCRATES: But would you say that the good are the same as the bad?
ALCIBIADES: Certainly not.
SOCRATES: Then whom do you call the good?
ALCIBIADES: I mean by the good those who are able to rule in the city.
SOCRATES: Not, surely, over horses?
ALCIBIADES: Certainly not.
SOCRATES: But over men?
ALCIBIADES: Yes.
SOCRATES: When they are sick?
ALCIBIADES: No.
SOCRATES: Or on a voyage?
ALCIBIADES: No.
SOCRATES: Or reaping the harvest?
ALCIBIADES: No.
SOCRATES: When they are doing something or nothing?
ALCIBIADES: When they are doing something, I should say.
SOCRATES: I wish that you would explain to me what this something is.
ALCIBIADES: When they are having dealings with one another, and using one another's services, as we citizens do in our daily life.
SOCRATES: Those of whom you speak are ruling over men who are using the services of other men?
ALCIBIADES: Yes.
SOCRATES: Are they ruling over the signal-men who give the time to the rowers?
ALCIBIADES: No; they are not.
SOCRATES: That would be the office of the pilot?
ALCIBIADES: Yes.
SOCRATES: But, perhaps you mean that they rule over flute players, who lead the singers and use the services of the dancers?
ALCIBIADES: Certainly not.
SOCRATES: That would be the business of the teacher of the chorus?
ALCIBIADES: Yes.
SOCRATES: Then what is the meaning of being able to rule over men who use other men?
ALCIBIADES: I mean that they rule over men who have common rights of citizenship, and dealings with one another.
SOCRATES: And what sort of an art is this? Suppose that I ask you again, as I did just now, "What art makes men know how to rule over their fellow

sailors"—how would you answer?
ALCIBIADES: The art of the pilot.
SOCRATES: And, if I may recur to another old instance, what art enables them to rule over their fellow singers?
ALCIBIADES: The art of the teacher of the chorus, which you were just now mentioning.
SOCRATES: And what do you call the art of fellow citizens?
ALCIBIADES: I should say "good counsel," Socrates.
SOCRATES: And is the art of the pilot evil counsel?
ALCIBIADES: No.
SOCRATES: But good counsel?
ALCIBIADES: Yes, that is what I should say—good counsel, of which the aim is the preservation of the voyagers.
SOCRATES: True. And what is the aim of that other good counsel of which you speak?
ALCIBIADES: The aim is the better order and preservation of the city.
SOCRATES: And what is that of which the absence or presence improves and preserves the order of the city? Suppose you were to ask me, what is that of which the presence or absence improves or preserves the order of the body? I should reply, the presence of health and the absence of disease. You would say the same?
ALCIBIADES: Yes.
SOCRATES: And if you were to ask me the same question about the eyes, I should reply in the same way, "the presence of sight and the absence of blindness"; or about the ears, I should reply, that they were improved and were in better case, when deafness was absent, and hearing was present in them.
ALCIBIADES: True.
SOCRATES: And what would you say of a state? What is that by the presence or absence of which the state is improved and better managed and ordered?
ALCIBIADES: I should say, Socrates: the presence of friendship and the absence of hatred and division.
SOCRATES: And do you mean by friendship agreement or disagreement?
ALCIBIADES: Agreement.
SOCRATES: What art makes cities agree about numbers?
ALCIBIADES: Arithmetic.
SOCRATES: And private individuals?
ALCIBIADES: The same.

SOCRATES: And what art makes each individual agree with himself?
ALCIBIADES: The same.
SOCRATES: And what art makes each of us agree with himself about the comparative length of the span and of the cubit? Does not the art of measure?
ALCIBIADES: Yes.
SOCRATES: Individuals are agreed with one another about this; and states, equally?
ALCIBIADES: Yes.
SOCRATES: And the same holds of the balance?
ALCIBIADES: True.
SOCRATES: But what is the other agreement of which you speak, and about what? What art can give that agreement? And does that which gives it to the state give it also to the individual, so as to make him consistent with himself and with another?
ALCIBIADES: I should suppose so.
SOCRATES: But what is the nature of the agreement? Answer, and faint not.
ALCIBIADES: I mean to say that there should be such friendship and agreement as exists between an affectionate father and mother and their son, or between brothers, or between husband and wife.
SOCRATES: But can a man, Alcibiades, agree with a woman about the spinning of wool, which she understands and he does not?
ALCIBIADES: No, truly.
SOCRATES: Nor has he any need, for spinning is a female accomplishment.
ALCIBIADES: Yes.
SOCRATES: And would a woman agree with a man about the science of arms, which she has never learned?
ALCIBIADES: Certainly not.
SOCRATES: I suppose that the use of arms would be regarded by you as a male accomplishment?
ALCIBIADES: It would.
SOCRATES: Then, upon your view, women and men have two sorts of knowledge?
ALCIBIADES: Certainly.
SOCRATES: Then in their knowledge there is no agreement of women and men?
ALCIBIADES: There is not.
SOCRATES: Nor can there be friendship, if friendship is agreement?

ALCIBIADES: Plainly not.
SOCRATES: Then women are not loved by men when they do their own work?
ALCIBIADES: I suppose not.
SOCRATES: Nor men by women when they do their own work?
ALCIBIADES: No.
SOCRATES: Nor are states well administered, when individuals do their own work?
ALCIBIADES: I should rather think, Socrates, that the reverse is the truth. (Compare Republic.)
SOCRATES: What! do you mean to say that states are well administered when friendship is absent, the presence of which, as we were saying, alone secures their good order?
ALCIBIADES: But I should say that there is friendship among them, for this very reason, that the two parties respectively do their own work.
SOCRATES: That was not what you were saying before; and what do you mean now by affirming that friendship exists when there is no agreement? How can there be agreement about matters which the one party knows, and of which the other is in ignorance?
ALCIBIADES: Impossible.
SOCRATES: And when individuals are doing their own work, are they doing what is just or unjust?
ALCIBIADES: What is just, certainly.
SOCRATES: And when individuals do what is just in the state, is there no friendship among them?
ALCIBIADES: I suppose that there must be, Socrates.
SOCRATES: Then what do you mean by this friendship or agreement about which we must be wise and discreet in order that we may be good men? I cannot make out where it exists or among whom; according to you, the same persons may sometimes have it, and sometimes not.
ALCIBIADES: But, indeed, Socrates, I do not know what I am saying; and I have long been, unconsciously to myself, in a most disgraceful state.
SOCRATES: Nevertheless, cheer up; at fifty, if you had discovered your deficiency, you would have been too old, and the time for taking care of yourself would have passed away, but yours is just the age at which the discovery should be made.
ALCIBIADES: And what should he do, Socrates, who would make the discovery?
SOCRATES: Answer questions, Alcibiades; and that is a process which,

by the grace of God, if I may put any faith in my oracle, will be very improving to both of us.

ALCIBIADES: If I can be improved by answering, I will answer.

SOCRATES: And first of all, that we may not peradventure be deceived by appearances, fancying, perhaps, that we are taking care of ourselves when we are not, what is the meaning of a man taking care of himself? and when does he take care? Does he take care of himself when he takes care of what belongs to him?

ALCIBIADES: I should think so.

SOCRATES: When does a man take care of his feet? Does he not take care of them when he takes care of that which belongs to his feet?

ALCIBIADES: I do not understand.

SOCRATES: Let me take the hand as an illustration; does not a ring belong to the finger, and to the finger only?

ALCIBIADES: Yes.

SOCRATES: And the shoe in like manner to the foot?

ALCIBIADES: Yes.

SOCRATES: And when we take care of our shoes, do we not take care of our feet?

ALCIBIADES: I do not comprehend, Socrates.

SOCRATES: But you would admit, Alcibiades, that to take proper care of a thing is a correct expression?

ALCIBIADES: Yes.

SOCRATES: And taking proper care means improving?

ALCIBIADES: Yes.

SOCRATES: And what is the art which improves our shoes?

ALCIBIADES: Shoemaking.

SOCRATES: Then by shoemaking we take care of our shoes?

ALCIBIADES: Yes.

SOCRATES: And do we by shoemaking take care of our feet, or by some other art which improves the feet?

ALCIBIADES: By some other art.

SOCRATES: And the same art improves the feet which improves the rest of the body?

ALCIBIADES: Very true.

SOCRATES: Which is gymnastic?

ALCIBIADES: Certainly.

SOCRATES: Then by gymnastic we take care of our feet, and by shoemaking of that which belongs to our feet?

ALCIBIADES: Very true.
SOCRATES: And by gymnastic we take care of our hands, and by the art of graving rings of that which belongs to our hands?
ALCIBIADES: Yes.
SOCRATES: And by gymnastic we take care of the body, and by the art of weaving and the other arts we take care of the things of the body?
ALCIBIADES: Clearly.
SOCRATES: Then the art which takes care of each thing is different from that which takes care of the belongings of each thing?
ALCIBIADES: True.
SOCRATES: Then in taking care of what belongs to you, you do not take care of yourself?
ALCIBIADES: Certainly not.
SOCRATES: For the art which takes care of our belongings appears not to be the same as that which takes care of ourselves?
ALCIBIADES: Clearly not.
SOCRATES: And now let me ask you what is the art with which we take care of ourselves?
ALCIBIADES: I cannot say.
SOCRATES: At any rate, thus much has been admitted, that the art is not one which makes any of our possessions, but which makes ourselves better?
ALCIBIADES: True.
SOCRATES: But should we ever have known what art makes a shoe better, if we did not know a shoe?
ALCIBIADES: Impossible.
SOCRATES: Nor should we know what art makes a ring better, if we did not know a ring?
ALCIBIADES: That is true.
SOCRATES: And can we ever know what art makes a man better, if we do not know what we are ourselves?
ALCIBIADES: Impossible.
SOCRATES: And is self-knowledge such an easy thing, and was he to be lightly esteemed who inscribed the text on the temple at Delphi? Or is self-knowledge a difficult thing, which few are able to attain?
ALCIBIADES: At times I fancy, Socrates, that anybody can know himself; at other times the task appears to be very difficult.
SOCRATES: But whether easy or difficult, Alcibiades, still there is no other way; knowing what we are, we shall know how to take care of ourselves, and if we are ignorant we shall not know.

ALCIBIADES: That is true.

SOCRATES: Well, then, let us see in what way the self-existent can be discovered by us; that will give us a chance of discovering our own existence, which otherwise we can never know.

ALCIBIADES: You say truly.

SOCRATES: Come, now, I beseech you, tell me with whom you are conversing—with whom but with me?

ALCIBIADES: Yes.

SOCRATES: As I am, with you?

ALCIBIADES: Yes.

SOCRATES: That is to say, I, Socrates, am talking?

ALCIBIADES: Yes.

SOCRATES: And Alcibiades is my hearer?

ALCIBIADES: Yes.

SOCRATES: And I in talking use words?

ALCIBIADES: Certainly.

SOCRATES: And talking and using words have, I suppose, the same meaning?

ALCIBIADES: To be sure.

SOCRATES: And the user is not the same as the thing which he uses?

ALCIBIADES: What do you mean?

SOCRATES: I will explain; the shoemaker, for example, uses a square tool, and a circular tool, and other tools for cutting?

ALCIBIADES: Yes.

SOCRATES: But the tool is not the same as the cutter and user of the tool?

ALCIBIADES: Of course not.

SOCRATES: And in the same way the instrument of the harper is to be distinguished from the harper himself?

ALCIBIADES: It is.

SOCRATES: Now the question which I asked was whether you conceive the user to be always different from that which he uses?

ALCIBIADES: I do.

SOCRATES: Then what shall we say of the shoemaker? Does he cut with his tools only or with his hands?

ALCIBIADES: With his hands as well.

SOCRATES: He uses his hands too?

ALCIBIADES: Yes.

SOCRATES: And does he use his eyes in cutting leather?

ALCIBIADES: He does.

SOCRATES: And we admit that the user is not the same with the things which he uses?
ALCIBIADES: Yes.
SOCRATES: Then the shoemaker and the harper are to be distinguished from the hands and feet which they use?
ALCIBIADES: Clearly.
SOCRATES: And does not a man use the whole body?
ALCIBIADES: Certainly.
SOCRATES: And that which uses is different from that which is used?
ALCIBIADES: True.
SOCRATES: Then a man is not the same as his own body?
ALCIBIADES: That is the inference.
SOCRATES: What is he, then?
ALCIBIADES: I cannot say.
SOCRATES: Nay, you can say that he is the user of the body.
ALCIBIADES: Yes.
SOCRATES: And the user of the body is the soul?
ALCIBIADES: Yes, the soul.
SOCRATES: And the soul rules?
ALCIBIADES: Yes.
SOCRATES: Let me make an assertion which will, I think, be universally admitted.
ALCIBIADES: What is it?
SOCRATES: That man is one of three things.
ALCIBIADES: What are they?
SOCRATES: Soul, body, or both together forming a whole.
ALCIBIADES: Certainly.
SOCRATES: But did we not say that the actual ruling principle of the body is man?
ALCIBIADES: Yes, we did.
SOCRATES: And does the body rule over itself?
ALCIBIADES: Certainly not.
SOCRATES: It is subject, as we were saying?
ALCIBIADES: Yes.
SOCRATES: Then that is not the principle which we are seeking?
ALCIBIADES: It would seem not.
SOCRATES: But may we say that the union of the two rules over the body, and consequently that this is man?
ALCIBIADES: Very likely.

SOCRATES: The most unlikely of all things; for if one of the members is subject, the two united cannot possibly rule.
ALCIBIADES: True.
SOCRATES: But since neither the body, nor the union of the two, is man, either man has no real existence, or the soul is man?
ALCIBIADES: Just so.
SOCRATES: Is anything more required to prove that the soul is man?
ALCIBIADES: Certainly not; the proof is, I think, quite sufficient.
SOCRATES: And if the proof, although not perfect, be sufficient, we shall be satisfied; more precise proof will be supplied when we have discovered that which we were led to omit, from a fear that the inquiry would be too much protracted.
ALCIBIADES: What was that?
SOCRATES: What I meant, when I said that absolute existence must be first considered; but now, instead of absolute existence, we have been considering the nature of individual existence, and this may, perhaps, be sufficient; for surely there is nothing which may be called more properly ourselves than the soul?
ALCIBIADES: There is nothing.
SOCRATES: Then we may truly conceive that you and I are conversing with one another, soul to soul?
ALCIBIADES: Very true.
SOCRATES: And that is just what I was saying before—that I, Socrates, am not arguing or talking with the face of Alcibiades, but with the real Alcibiades; or in other words, with his soul.
ALCIBIADES: True.
SOCRATES: Then he who bids a man know himself, would have him know his soul?
ALCIBIADES: That appears to be true.
SOCRATES: He whose knowledge only extends to the body, knows the things of a man, and not the man himself?
ALCIBIADES: That is true.
SOCRATES: Then neither the physician regarded as a physician, nor the trainer regarded as a trainer, knows himself?
ALCIBIADES: He does not.
SOCRATES: The husbandmen and the other craftsmen are very far from knowing themselves, for they would seem not even to know their own belongings? When regarded in relation to the arts which they practice

they are even further removed from self-knowledge, for they only know the belongings of the body, which minister to the body.

ALCIBIADES: That is true.

SOCRATES: Then if temperance is the knowledge of self, in respect of his art none of them is temperate?

ALCIBIADES: I agree.

SOCRATES: And this is the reason why their arts are accounted vulgar, and are not such as a good man would practice?

ALCIBIADES: Quite true.

SOCRATES: Again, he who cherishes his body cherishes not himself, but what belongs to him?

ALCIBIADES: That is true.

SOCRATES: But he who cherishes his money, cherishes neither himself nor his belongings, but is in a stage yet further removed from himself?

ALCIBIADES: I agree.

SOCRATES: Then the money-maker has really ceased to be occupied with his own concerns?

ALCIBIADES: True.

SOCRATES: And if anyone has fallen in love with the person of Alcibiades, he loves not Alcibiades, but the belongings of Alcibiades?

ALCIBIADES: True.

SOCRATES: But he who loves your soul is the true lover?

ALCIBIADES: That is the necessary inference.

SOCRATES: The lover of the body goes away when the flower of youth fades?

ALCIBIADES: True.

SOCRATES: But he who loves the soul goes not away, as long as the soul follows after virtue?

ALCIBIADES: Yes.

SOCRATES: And I am the lover who goes not away, but remains with you, when you are no longer young and the rest are gone?

ALCIBIADES: Yes, Socrates; and therein you do well, and I hope that you will remain.

SOCRATES: Then you must try to look your best.

ALCIBIADES: I will.

SOCRATES: The fact is, that there is only one lover of Alcibiades the son of Cleinias; there neither is nor ever has been seemingly any other; and he is his darling—Socrates, the son of Sophroniscus and Phaenarete.

ALCIBIADES: True.

SOCRATES: And did you not say, that if I had not spoken first, you were on the point of coming to me, and inquiring why I only remained?

ALCIBIADES: That is true.

SOCRATES: The reason was that I loved you for your own sake, whereas other men love what belongs to you; and your beauty, which is not you, is fading away, just as your true self is beginning to bloom. And I will never desert you, if you are not spoiled and deformed by the Athenian people; for the danger which I most fear is that you will become a lover of the people and will be spoiled by them. Many a noble Athenian has been ruined in this way. For the demus of the great-hearted Erechteus is of a fair countenance, but you should see him naked; wherefore observe the caution which I give you.

ALCIBIADES: What caution?

SOCRATES: Practice yourself, sweet friend, in learning what you ought to know, before you enter on politics; and then you will have an antidote which will keep you out of harm's way.

ALCIBIADES: Good advice, Socrates, but I wish that you would explain to me in what way I am to take care of myself.

SOCRATES: Have we not made an advance? for we are at any rate tolerably well agreed as to what we are, and there is no longer any danger, as we once feared, that we might be taking care not of ourselves, but of something which is not ourselves.

ALCIBIADES: That is true.

SOCRATES: And the next step will be to take care of the soul, and look to that?

ALCIBIADES: Certainly.

SOCRATES: Leaving the care of our bodies and of our properties to others?

ALCIBIADES: Very good.

SOCRATES: But how can we have a perfect knowledge of the things of the soul? For if we know them, then I suppose we shall know ourselves. Can we really be ignorant of the excellent meaning of the Delphian inscription, of which we were just now speaking?

ALCIBIADES: What have you in your thoughts, Socrates?

SOCRATES: I will tell you what I suspect to be the meaning and lesson of that inscription. Let me take an illustration from sight, which I imagine to be the only one suitable to my purpose.

ALCIBIADES: What do you mean?

SOCRATES: Consider; if someone were to say to the eye, "See thyself,"

as you might say to a man, "Know thyself," what is the nature and meaning of this precept? Would not his meaning be: That the eye should look at that in which it would see itself?
ALCIBIADES: Clearly.
SOCRATES: And what are the objects in looking at which we see ourselves?
ALCIBIADES: Clearly, Socrates, in looking at mirrors and the like.
SOCRATES: Very true; and is there not something of the nature of a mirror in our own eyes?
ALCIBIADES: Certainly.
SOCRATES: Did you ever observe that the face of the person looking into the eye of another is reflected as in a mirror; and in the visual organ which is over against him, and which is called the pupil, there is a sort of image of the person looking?
ALCIBIADES: That is quite true.
SOCRATES: Then the eye, looking at another eye, and at that in the eye which is most perfect, and which is the instrument of vision, will there see itself?
ALCIBIADES: That is evident.
SOCRATES: But looking at anything else either in man or in the world, and not to what resembles this, it will not see itself?
ALCIBIADES: Very true.
SOCRATES: Then if the eye is to see itself, it must look at the eye, and at that part of the eye where sight which is the virtue of the eye resides?
ALCIBIADES: True.
SOCRATES: And if the soul, my dear Alcibiades, is ever to know herself, must she not look at the soul; and especially at that part of the soul in which her virtue resides, and to any other which is like this?
ALCIBIADES: I agree, Socrates.
SOCRATES: And do we know of any part of our souls more divine than that which has to do with wisdom and knowledge?
ALCIBIADES: There is none.
SOCRATES: Then this is that part of the soul which resembles the divine; and he who looks at this and at the whole class of things divine, will be most likely to know himself?
ALCIBIADES: Clearly.
SOCRATES: And self-knowledge we agree to be wisdom?
ALCIBIADES: True.
SOCRATES: But if we have no self-knowledge and no wisdom, can we ever know our own good and evil?

ALCIBIADES: How can we, Socrates?
SOCRATES: You mean, that if you did not know Alcibiades, there would be no possibility of your knowing that what belonged to Alcibiades was really his?
ALCIBIADES: It would be quite impossible.
SOCRATES: Nor should we know that we were the persons to whom anything belonged, if we did not know ourselves?
ALCIBIADES: How could we?
SOCRATES: And if we did not know our own belongings, neither should we know the belongings of our belongings?
ALCIBIADES: Clearly not.
SOCRATES: Then we were not altogether right in acknowledging just now that a man may know what belongs to him and yet not know himself; nay, rather he cannot even know the belongings of his belongings; for the discernment of the things of self, and of the things which belong to the things of self, appear all to be the business of the same man, and of the same art.
ALCIBIADES: So much may be supposed.
SOCRATES: And he who knows not the things which belong to himself, will in like manner be ignorant of the things which belong to others?
ALCIBIADES: Very true.
SOCRATES: And if he knows not the affairs of others, he will not know the affairs of states?
ALCIBIADES: Certainly not.
SOCRATES: Then such a man can never be a statesman?
ALCIBIADES: He cannot.
SOCRATES: Nor an economist?
ALCIBIADES: He cannot.
SOCRATES: He will not know what he is doing?
ALCIBIADES: He will not.
SOCRATES: And will not he who is ignorant fall into error?
ALCIBIADES: Assuredly.
SOCRATES: And if he falls into error will he not fail both in his public and private capacity?
ALCIBIADES: Yes, indeed.
SOCRATES: And failing, will he not be miserable?
ALCIBIADES: Very.
SOCRATES: And what will become of those for whom he is acting?

ALCIBIADES: They will be miserable also.
SOCRATES: Then he who is not wise and good cannot be happy?
ALCIBIADES: He cannot.
SOCRATES: The bad, then, are miserable?
ALCIBIADES: Yes, very.
SOCRATES: And if so, not he who has riches, but he who has wisdom, is delivered from his misery?
ALCIBIADES: Clearly.
SOCRATES: Cities, then, if they are to be happy, do not want walls, or triremes, or docks, or numbers, or size, Alcibiades, without virtue? (Compare Arist. Pol.)
ALCIBIADES: Indeed they do not.
SOCRATES: And you must give the citizens virtue, if you mean to administer their affairs rightly or nobly?
ALCIBIADES: Certainly.
SOCRATES: But can a man give that which he has not?
ALCIBIADES: Impossible.
SOCRATES: Then you or anyone who means to govern and superintend, not only himself and the things of himself, but the state and the things of the state, must in the first place acquire virtue.
ALCIBIADES: That is true.
SOCRATES: You have not therefore to obtain power or authority, in order to enable you to do what you wish for yourself and the state, but justice and wisdom.
ALCIBIADES: Clearly.
SOCRATES: You and the state, if you act wisely and justly, will act according to the will of God?
ALCIBIADES: Certainly.
SOCRATES: As I was saying before, you will look only at what is bright and divine, and act with a view to them?
ALCIBIADES: Yes.
SOCRATES: In that mirror you will see and know yourselves and your own good?
ALCIBIADES: Yes.
SOCRATES: And so you will act rightly and well?
ALCIBIADES: Yes.
SOCRATES: In which case, I will be security for your happiness.
ALCIBIADES: I accept the security.

SOCRATES: But if you act unrighteously, your eye will turn to the dark and godless, and being in darkness and ignorance of yourselves, you will probably do deeds of darkness.

ALCIBIADES: Very possibly.

SOCRATES: For if a man, my dear Alcibiades, has the power to do what he likes, but has no understanding, what is likely to be the result, either to him as an individual or to the state—for example, if he be sick and is able to do what he likes, not having the mind of a physician—having moreover tyrannical power, and no one daring to reprove him, what will happen to him? Will he not be likely to have his constitution ruined?

ALCIBIADES: That is true.

SOCRATES: Or again, in a ship, if a man having the power to do what he likes, has no intelligence or skill in navigation, do you see what will happen to him and to his fellow sailors?

ALCIBIADES: Yes; I see that they will all perish.

SOCRATES: And in like manner, in a state, and where there is any power and authority which is wanting in virtue, will not misfortune, in like manner, ensue?

ALCIBIADES: Certainly.

SOCRATES: Not tyrannical power, then, my good Alcibiades, should be the aim either of individuals or states, if they would be happy, but virtue.

ALCIBIADES: That is true.

SOCRATES: And before they have virtue, to be commanded by a superior is better for men as well as for children? (Compare Arist. Pol.)

ALCIBIADES: That is evident.

SOCRATES: And that which is better is also nobler?

ALCIBIADES: True.

SOCRATES: And what is nobler is more becoming?

ALCIBIADES: Certainly.

SOCRATES: Then to the bad man slavery is more becoming, because better?

ALCIBIADES: True.

SOCRATES: Then vice is only suited to a slave?

ALCIBIADES: Yes.

SOCRATES: And virtue to a freeman?

ALCIBIADES: Yes.

SOCRATES: And, O my friend, is not the condition of a slave to be avoided?

ALCIBIADES: Certainly, Socrates.

SOCRATES: And are you now conscious of your own state? And do you know whether you are a freeman or not?
ALCIBIADES: I think that I am very conscious indeed of my own state.
SOCRATES: And do you know how to escape out of a state which I do not even like to name to my beauty?
ALCIBIADES: Yes, I do.
SOCRATES: How?
ALCIBIADES: By your help, Socrates.
SOCRATES: That is not well said, Alcibiades.
ALCIBIADES: What ought I to have said?
SOCRATES: By the help of God.
ALCIBIADES: I agree; and I further say, that our relations are likely to be reversed. From this day forward, I must and will follow you as you have followed me; I will be the disciple, and you shall be my master.
SOCRATES: O that is rare! My love breeds another love: and so like the stork I shall be cherished by the bird whom I have hatched.
ALCIBIADES: Strange, but true; and henceforward I shall begin to think about justice.
SOCRATES: And I hope that you will persist; although I have fears, not because I doubt you; but I see the power of the state, which may be too much for both of us.

APOLOGY

By Plato

Translated by Benjamin Jowett

INTRODUCTION

In what relation the Apology of Plato stands to the real defense of Socrates, there are no means of determining. It certainly agrees in tone and character with the description of Xenophon, who says in the Memorabilia that Socrates might have been acquitted "if in any moderate degree he would have conciliated the favor of the dicasts"; and who informs us in another passage, on the testimony of Hermogenes, the friend of Socrates, that he had no wish to live; and that the divine sign refused to allow him to prepare a defense, and also that Socrates himself declared this to be unnecessary, on the ground that all his life long he had been preparing against that hour. For the speech breathes throughout a spirit of defiance ("ut non supplex aut reus sed magister aut dominus videretur esse judicum," Cic. de Orat.); and the loose and desultory style is an imitation of the "accustomed manner" in which Socrates spoke in "the agora and among the tables of the money-changers." The allusion in the Crito may, perhaps, be adduced as a further evidence of the literal accuracy of some parts. But in the main it must be regarded as the ideal of Socrates, according to Plato's conception of him, appearing in the greatest and most public scene of his life, and in the height of his triumph, when he is weakest, and yet his mastery over mankind is greatest, and his habitual irony acquires a new meaning and a sort of tragic pathos in the face of death. The facts of his life are summed up, and the features of his character are brought out as if by accident in the course of the defense. The conversational manner, the seeming want of arrangement, the ironical simplicity, are found to result in a perfect work of art, which is the portrait of Socrates.

Yet some of the topics may have been actually used by Socrates; and the recollection of his very words may have rung in the ears of his disciple.

The Apology of Plato may be compared generally with those speeches of Thucydides in which he has embodied his conception of the lofty character and policy of the great Pericles, and which at the same time furnish a commentary on the situation of affairs from the point of view of the historian. So in the Apology there is an ideal rather than a literal truth; much is said which was not said, and is only Plato's view of the situation. Plato was not, like Xenophon, a chronicler of facts; he does not appear in any of his writings to have aimed at literal accuracy. He is not therefore to be supplemented from the Memorabilia and Symposium of Xenophon, who belongs to an entirely different class of writers. The Apology of Plato is not the report of what Socrates said, but an elaborate composition, quite as much so in fact as one of the Dialogues. And we may perhaps even indulge in the fancy that the actual defense of Socrates was as much greater than the Platonic defense as the master was greater than the disciple. But in any case, some of the words used by him must have been remembered, and some of the facts recorded must have actually occurred. It is significant that Plato is said to have been present at the defense (Apol.), as he is also said to have been absent at the last scene in the Phaedo. Is it fanciful to suppose that he meant to give the stamp of authenticity to the one and not to the other?—especially when we consider that these two passages are the only ones in which Plato makes mention of himself. The circumstance that Plato was to be one of his sureties for the payment of the fine which he proposed has the appearance of truth. More suspicious is the statement that Socrates received the first impulse to his favorite calling of cross-examining the world from the Oracle of Delphi; for he must already have been famous before Chaerephon went to consult the Oracle (Riddell), and the story is of a kind which is very likely to have been invented. On the whole we arrive at the conclusion that the Apology is true to the character of Socrates, but we cannot show that any single sentence in it was actually spoken by him. It breathes the spirit of Socrates, but has been cast anew in the mold of Plato.

There is not much in the other Dialogues which can be compared with the Apology. The same recollection of his master may have been present to the mind of Plato when depicting the sufferings of the Just in the Republic. The Crito may also be regarded as a sort of appendage to the Apology, in which Socrates, who has defied the judges, is nevertheless represented as scrupulously obedient to the laws. The idealization of the sufferer is carried still further in the Gorgias, in which the thesis is maintained, that "to suffer is better than to do evil"; and the art of rhetoric is described as only useful for the purpose of self-accusation. The parallelisms which occur in the so-called Apology of Xenophon are not worth noticing, because the writing in which they are contained is manifestly spurious. The statements of the Memorabilia respecting the trial and death of Socrates agree generally with Plato; but they have lost the flavor of Socratic irony in the narrative of Xenophon.

The Apology or Platonic defense of Socrates is divided into three parts: (1) the defense properly so called; (2) the shorter address in mitigation of the penalty; (3) the last words of prophetic rebuke and exhortation.

The first part commences with an apology for his colloquial style; he is, as he has always been, the enemy of rhetoric, and knows of no rhetoric but truth; he will not falsify his character by making a speech. Then he proceeds to divide his accusers into two classes; first, there is the nameless accuser—public opinion. All the world from their earliest years had heard that he was a corrupter of youth, and had seen him caricatured in the Clouds of Aristophanes. Secondly, there are the professed accusers, who are but the mouthpiece of the others. The accusations of both might be summed up in a formula. The first say, "Socrates is an evil-doer and a curious person, searching into things under the earth and above the heaven; and making the worse appear the better cause, and teaching all this to others." The second, "Socrates is an evil-doer and corrupter of the youth, who does not receive the gods whom the state receives, but introduces other new divinities." These last words appear to have been the actual indictment (compare Xen. Mem.); and the previous formula, which is a summary of public opinion, assumes the same legal style.

The answer begins by clearing up a confusion. In the representations of the Comic poets, and in the opinion of the multitude, he had been identified with the teachers of physical science and with the Sophists. But this was an error. For both of them he professes a respect in the open court, which contrasts with his manner of speaking about them in other places. (Compare for Anaxagoras, Phaedo, Laws; for the Sophists, Meno, Republic, Tim., Theaet., Soph., etc.) But at the same time he shows that he is not one of them. Of natural philosophy he knows nothing; not that he despises such pursuits, but the fact is that he is ignorant of them, and never says a word about them. Nor is he paid for giving instruction—that is another mistaken notion; he has nothing to teach. But he commends Evenus for teaching virtue at such a "moderate" rate as five minae. Something of the "accustomed irony," which may perhaps be expected to sleep in the ear of the multitude, is lurking here.

He then goes on to explain the reason why he is in such an evil name.

That had arisen out of a peculiar mission which he had taken upon himself. The enthusiastic Chaerephon (probably in anticipation of the answer which he received) had gone to Delphi and asked the oracle if there was any man wiser than Socrates; and the answer was, that there was no man wiser. What could be the meaning of this—that he who knew nothing, and knew that he knew nothing, should be declared by the oracle to be the wisest of men? Reflecting upon the answer, he determined to refute it by finding "a wiser"; and first he went to the politicians, and then to the poets, and then to the craftsmen, but always with the same result—he found that they knew nothing, or hardly anything more than himself; and that the little advantage which in some cases they possessed was more than counter-balanced by their conceit of knowledge. He knew nothing, and knew that he knew nothing: they knew little or nothing, and imagined that they knew all things. Thus he had passed his life as a sort of missionary in detecting the pretended wisdom of mankind; and this occupation had quite absorbed him and taken him away both from public and private affairs. Young men of the richer sort had made a pastime of the same pursuit, "which was not unamusing." And hence bitter enmities had arisen; the professors of knowledge had revenged themselves by calling him a villainous corrupter of youth, and by repeating the commonplaces about atheism and materialism and sophistry, which are the stock-accusations against all philosophers when there is nothing else to be said of them.

The second accusation he meets by interrogating Meletus, who is present and can be interrogated. "If he is the corrupter, who is the improver of the citizens?" (Compare Meno.) "All men everywhere." But how absurd, how contrary to analogy is this! How inconceivable too, that he should make the citizens worse when he has to live with them. This surely cannot be intentional; and if unintentional, he ought to have been instructed by Meletus, and not accused in the court.

But there is another part of the indictment which says that he teaches men not to receive the gods whom the city receives, and has other new gods. "Is that the way in which he is supposed to corrupt the youth?" "Yes, it is." "Has he only new gods, or none at all?" "None at all." "What, not even the sun and moon?" "No; why, he says that the sun is a stone, and the moon earth." That, replies Socrates, is the old confusion about Anaxagoras; the Athenian people are not so ignorant as to attribute to the influence of Socrates notions which have found their way into the drama, and may be learned at the theatre. Socrates undertakes to show that Meletus (rather unjustifiably) has been compounding a riddle in this part of the indictment:

"There are no gods, but Socrates believes in the existence of the sons of gods, which is absurd."

Leaving Meletus, who has had enough words spent upon him, he returns to the original accusation. The question may be asked, Why will he persist in following a profession which leads him to death? Why? Because he must remain at his post where the god has placed him, as he remained at Potidaea, and Amphipolis, and Delium, where the generals placed him. Besides, he is not so overwise as to imagine that he knows whether death is a good or an evil; and he is certain that desertion of his duty is an evil. Anytus is quite right in saying that they should never have indicted him if they meant to let him go. For he will certainly obey God rather than man; and will continue to preach to all men of all ages the necessity of virtue and improvement; and if they refuse to listen to him he will still persevere and reprove them. This is his way of corrupting the youth, which he will not cease to follow in obedience to the god, even if a thousand deaths await him.

He is desirous that they should let him live—not for his own sake, but for theirs; because he is their heaven-sent friend (and they will never have such another), or, as he may be ludicrously described, he is the gadfly who stirs the generous steed into motion. Why then has he never taken part in public affairs? Because the familiar divine voice has hindered him; if he had been a public man, and had fought for the right, as he would certainly have fought against the many, he would not have lived, and could therefore have done no good. Twice in public matters he has risked his life for the sake of justice—once at the trial of the generals; and again in resistance to the tyrannical commands of the Thirty.

But, though not a public man, he has passed his days in instructing the citizens without fee or reward—this was his mission. Whether his disciples have turned out well or ill, he cannot justly be charged with the result, for he never promised to teach them anything. They might come if they liked, and they might stay away if they liked: and they did come, because they found an amusement in hearing the pretenders to wisdom detected. If they have been corrupted, their elder relatives (if not themselves) might surely come into court and witness against him, and there is an opportunity still for them to appear. But their fathers and brothers all appear in court (including "this" Plato), to witness on his behalf; and if their relatives are corrupted, at least they are uncorrupted; "and they are my witnesses. For they know that I am speaking the truth, and that Meletus is lying."

This is about all that he has to say. He will not entreat the judges to spare his life; neither will he present a spectacle of weeping children, although he, too, is not made of "rock or oak." Some of the judges themselves may have complied with this practice on similar occasions, and he trusts that they will not be angry with him for not following their example. But he feels that such conduct brings discredit on the name of Athens: he feels too, that the judge has sworn not to give away justice; and he cannot be guilty of the impiety of asking the judge to break his oath, when he is himself being tried for impiety.

As he expected, and probably intended, he is convicted. And now the tone of the speech, instead of being more conciliatory, becomes more lofty and commanding. Anytus proposes death as the penalty: And what counter-proposition shall he make? He, the benefactor of the Athenian people, whose whole life has been spent in doing them good, should at least have the Olympic victor's reward of maintenance in the Prytaneum. Or why should he propose any counter-penalty when he does not know whether death, which Anytus proposes, is a good or an evil? And he is certain that imprisonment is an evil, exile is an evil. Loss of money might be an evil, but then he has none to give; perhaps he can make up a mina. Let that be the penalty, or, if his friends wish, thirty minae; for which they will be excellent securities.

(He is condemned to death.)

He is an old man already, and the Athenians will gain nothing but disgrace by depriving him of a few years of life. Perhaps he could have escaped, if he had chosen to throw down his arms and entreat for his life. But he does not at all repent of the manner of his defense; he would rather die in his own fashion than live in theirs. For the penalty of unrighteousness is swifter than death; that penalty has already overtaken his accusers as death will soon overtake him.

And now, as one who is about to die, he will prophesy to them. They have put him to death in order to escape the necessity of giving an account of their lives. But his death "will be the seed" of many disciples who will convince them of their evil ways, and will come forth to reprove them in harsher terms, because they are younger and more inconsiderate.

He would like to say a few words, while there is time, to those who would have acquitted him. He wishes them to know that the divine sign never interrupted him in the course of his defense; the reason of which, as he conjectures, is that the death to which he is going is a good and not an evil. For either death is a long sleep, the best of sleeps, or a journey to another world in which the souls of the dead are gathered together, and in which there may be a hope of seeing the heroes of old—in which, too, there are just judges; and as all are immortal, there can be no fear of anyone suffering death for his opinions.

Nothing evil can happen to the good man either in life or death, and his own death has been permitted by the gods, because it was better for him to depart; and therefore he forgives his judges because they have done him no harm, although they never meant to do him any good.

He has a last request to make to them—that they will trouble his sons as he has troubled them, if they appear to prefer riches to virtue, or to think themselves something when they are nothing.

* * * * *

"Few persons will be found to wish that Socrates should have defended himself otherwise," if, as we must add, his defense was that with which Plato has provided him. But leaving this question, which does not admit of a precise solution, we may go on to ask what was the impression which Plato in the Apology intended to give of the character and conduct of his master in the last great scene? Did he intend to represent him (1) as employing sophistries; (2) as designedly irritating the judges? Or are these sophistries to be regarded as belonging to the age in which he lived and to his personal character, and this apparent haughtiness as flowing from the natural elevation of his position?

For example, when he says that it is absurd to suppose that one man is the corrupter and all the rest of the world the improvers of the youth; or, when he argues that he never could have corrupted the men with whom he had to live; or, when he proves his belief in the gods because he believes in the sons of gods, is he serious or jesting? It may be observed that these sophisms all occur in his cross-examination of Meletus, who is easily foiled and mastered in the hands of the great dialectician. Perhaps he regarded these answers as good enough for his accuser, of whom he makes very light. Also there is a touch of irony in them, which takes them out of the category of sophistry. (Compare Euthyph.)

That the manner in which he defends himself about the lives of his disciples is not satisfactory, can hardly be denied. Fresh in the memory of the Athenians, and detestable as they deserved to be to the newly restored democracy, were the names of Alcibiades, Critias, Charmides. It is obviously not a sufficient answer that Socrates had never professed to teach them anything, and is therefore not justly chargeable with their crimes. Yet the defense, when taken out of this ironical form, is doubtless sound: that his teaching had nothing to do with their evil lives. Here, then, the sophistry is rather in form than in substance, though we might desire that to such a serious charge Socrates had given a more serious answer.

Truly characteristic of Socrates is another point in his answer, which may also be regarded as sophistical. He says that "if he has corrupted the youth, he must have corrupted them involuntarily." But if, as Socrates argues, all evil is involuntary, then all criminals ought to be admonished and not punished. In these words the Socratic doctrine of the involuntariness of evil is clearly intended to be conveyed. Here again, as in the former instance, the defense of Socrates is untrue practically, but may be true in some ideal or transcendental sense. The commonplace reply, that if he had been guilty of corrupting the youth their relations would surely have witnessed against him, with which he concludes this part of his defense, is more satisfactory.

Again, when Socrates argues that he must believe in the gods because he believes in the sons of gods, we must remember that this is a refutation not of the original indictment, which is consistent enough—"Socrates does not receive the gods whom the city receives, and has other new divinities"— but of the interpretation put upon the words by Meletus, who has affirmed that he is a downright atheist. To this Socrates fairly answers, in accordance with the ideas of the time, that a downright atheist cannot believe in the sons of gods or in divine things. The notion that demons or lesser divinities are the sons of gods is not to be regarded as ironical or sceptical. He is arguing "ad hominem" according to the notions of mythology current in his age. Yet he abstains from saying that he believed in the gods whom the State approved. He does not defend himself, as Xenophon has defended him, by appealing to his practice of religion. Probably he neither wholly believed, nor disbelieved, in the existence of the popular gods; he had no means of knowing about them. According to Plato (compare Phaedo; Symp.), as well as Xenophon (Memor.), he was punctual in the performance of the least religious duties; and he must have believed in his own oracular sign, of which he seemed to have an internal witness. But the existence of Apollo or Zeus, or the other gods whom the State approves, would have appeared to him both uncertain and unimportant in comparison of the duty of self-examination, and of those principles of truth and right which he deemed to be the foundation of religion. (Compare Phaedr.; Euthyph.; Republic.)

The second question, whether Plato meant to represent Socrates as braving or irritating his judges, must also be answered in the negative. His irony, his superiority, his audacity, "regarding not the person of man," necessarily flow out of the loftiness of his situation. He is not acting a part upon a great occasion, but he is what he has been all his life long, "a king of men." He would rather not appear insolent, if he could avoid it (ouch os authadizomenos touto lego). Neither is he desirous of hastening his own end, for life and death are simply indifferent to him. But such a defense as would be acceptable to his judges and might procure an acquittal, it is not in his nature to make. He will not say or do anything that might pervert the course of justice; he cannot have his tongue bound even "in the throat of death." With his accusers he will only fence and play, as he had fenced with other "improvers of youth," answering the Sophist according to his sophistry all his life long. He is serious when he is speaking of his own mission, which seems to distinguish him from all other reformers of mankind, and originates in an accident. The dedication of himself to the improvement of his fellow citizens is not so remarkable as the ironical spirit in which he goes about doing good only in vindication of the credit of the oracle, and in the vain hope of finding a wiser man than himself. Yet this singular and almost accidental character of his mission agrees with the divine sign which, according to our notions, is equally accidental and irrational, and is nevertheless accepted by him as the guiding principle of his life. Socrates is nowhere represented to us as a freethinker or sceptic. There is no reason to doubt his sincerity when he speculates on the possibility of seeing and knowing the heroes of the Trojan war in another world. On the other hand, his hope of immortality is uncertain—he also conceives of death as a long sleep (in this respect differing from the Phaedo), and at last falls back on resignation to the divine will, and the certainty that no evil can happen to the good man either in life or death. His absolute truthfulness seems to hinder him from asserting positively more than this; and he makes no attempt to veil his ignorance in mythology and figures of speech. The gentleness of the first part of the speech contrasts with the aggravated, almost threatening, tone of the conclusion. He characteristically remarks that he will not speak as a rhetorician, that is to say, he will not make a regular defense such as Lysias or one of the orators might have composed for him, or, according to some accounts, did compose for him. But he first procures himself a hearing by conciliatory words. He does not attack the Sophists; for they were open to the same charges as himself; they were equally ridiculed by the Comic poets, and almost equally hateful to Anytus and Meletus. Yet incidentally the antagonism between Socrates and the Sophists is allowed to appear. He is poor and they are rich; his profession that he teaches nothing is opposed to their readiness to teach all things; his talking in the marketplace to their private instructions; his tarry-at-home life to their wandering from city to city. The tone which he assumes toward them is one of real friendliness, but also of concealed irony. Toward Anaxagoras, who had disappointed him in his hopes of learning about mind and nature, he shows a less kindly feeling, which is also the feeling of Plato in other passages (Laws). But Anaxagoras had been dead thirty years, and was beyond the reach of persecution.

It has been remarked that the prophecy of a new generation of teachers who would rebuke and exhort the Athenian people in harsher and more violent terms was, as far as we know, never fulfillled. No inference can be drawn from this circumstance as to the probability of the words attributed to him having been actually uttered. They express the aspiration of the first martyr of philosophy, that he would leave behind him many followers, accompanied by the not unnatural feeling that they would be fiercer and more inconsiderate in their words when emancipated from his control.

The above remarks must be understood as applying with any degree of certainty to the Platonic Socrates only. For, although these or similar words may have been spoken by Socrates himself, we cannot exclude the possibility, that like so much else, e.g. the wisdom of Critias, the poem of Solon, the virtues of Charmides, they may have been due only to the imagination of Plato. The arguments of those who maintain that the Apology was composed during the process, resting on no evidence, do not require a serious refutation. Nor are the reasonings of Schleiermacher, who argues that the Platonic defense is an exact or nearly exact reproduction of the words of Socrates, partly because Plato would not have been guilty of the impiety of altering them, and also because many points of the defense might have been improved and strengthened, at all more conclusive. (See English Translation.) What effect the death of Socrates produced on the mind of Plato, we cannot certainly determine; nor can we say how he would or must have written under the circumstances. We observe that the enmity of Aristophanes to Socrates does not prevent Plato from introducing them together in the Symposium engaged in friendly intercourse. Nor is there any trace in the Dialogues of an attempt to make Anytus or Meletus personally odious in the eyes of the Athenian public.

APOLOGY

How you, O Athenians, have been affected by my accusers, I cannot tell; but I know that they almost made me forget who I was—so persuasively did they speak; and yet they have hardly uttered a word of truth. But of the many falsehoods told by them, there was one which quite amazed me;—I mean when they said that you should be upon your guard and not allow yourselves to be deceived by the force of my eloquence. To say this, when they were certain to be detected as soon as I opened my lips and proved myself to be anything but a great speaker, did indeed appear to me most shameless—unless by the force of eloquence they mean the force of truth; for it such is their meaning, I admit that I am eloquent. But in how different a way from theirs! Well, as I was saying, they have scarcely spoken the truth at all; but from me you shall hear the whole truth; not, however, delivered after their manner in a set oration duly ornamented with words and phrases. No, by heaven! but I shall use the words and arguments which occur to me at the moment; for I am confident in the justice of my cause (or, I am certain that I am right in taking this course): At my time of life I ought not to be appearing before you, O men of Athens, in the character of a juvenile orator—let no one expect it of me. And I must beg of you to grant me a favor: If I defend myself in my accustomed manner, and you hear me using the words which I have been in the habit of using in the agora, at the tables of the money-changers, or anywhere else, I would ask you not to be surprised, and not to interrupt me on this account. For I am more than seventy years of age, and appearing now for the first time in a court of law, I am quite a stranger to the language of the place; and therefore I would have you regard me as if I were really a stranger, whom you would excuse if he spoke in his native tongue, and after the fashion of his country: Am I making an unfair request of you? Never mind the manner, which may or may not be good; but think only of the truth of my words, and give heed to that: Let the speaker speak truly and the judge decide justly.

And first, I have to reply to the older charges and to my first accusers, and then I will go on to the later ones. For of old I have had many accusers, who have accused me falsely to you during many years; and I am more afraid of them than of Anytus and his associates, who are dangerous, too, in their own way. But far more dangerous are the others, who began when you were children, and took possession of your minds with their falsehoods, telling of one Socrates, a wise man, who speculated about the heaven above, and searched into the earth beneath, and made the worse appear the better cause. The disseminators of this tale are the accusers whom I dread; for their hearers are apt to fancy that such inquirers do not believe in the existence of the gods. And they are many, and their charges against me are of ancient date, and they were made by them in the days when you were more impressible than you are now—in childhood, or it may have been in youth—and the cause when heard went by default, for there was none to answer. And hardest of all, I do not know and cannot tell the names of my accusers; unless in the chance case of a Comic poet. All who from envy and malice have persuaded you—some of them having first convinced themselves—all this class of men are most difficult to deal with; for I cannot have them up here, and cross-examine them, and therefore I must simply fight with shadows in my own defense, and argue when there is no one who answers. I will ask you then to assume with me, as I was saying, that my opponents are of two kinds; one recent, the other ancient; and I hope that you will see the propriety of my answering the latter first, for these accusations you heard long before the others, and much oftener.

Well, then, I must make my defense, and endeavor to clear away in a short time, a slander which has lasted a long time. May I succeed, if to succeed be for my good and yours, or likely to avail me in my cause! The task is not an easy one; I quite understand the nature of it. And so leaving the event with God, in obedience to the law I will now make my defense.

I will begin at the beginning, and ask what is the accusation which has given rise to the slander of me, and in fact has encouraged Meletus to proof this charge against me. Well, what do the slanderers say? They shall be my prosecutors, and I will sum up their words in an affidavit: "Socrates is an evil-doer, and a curious person, who searches into things under the earth and in heaven, and he makes the worse appear the better cause; and he teaches the aforesaid doctrines to others." Such is the nature of the accusation: it is just what you have yourselves seen in the comedy of Aristophanes (Aristoph., Clouds.), who has introduced a man whom he calls Socrates, going about and saying that he walks in air, and talking a deal of nonsense concerning matters of which I do not pretend to know either much or little—not that I mean to speak disparagingly of anyone who is a student of natural philosophy. I should be very sorry if Meletus could bring so grave a charge against me. But the simple truth is, O Athenians, that I have nothing to do with physical speculations. Very many of those here present are witnesses to the truth of this, and to them I appeal. Speak then, you who have heard me, and tell your neighbors whether any of you have ever known me hold forth in few words or in many upon such matters....You hear their answer. And from what they say of this part of the charge you will be able to judge of the truth of the rest.

As little foundation is there for the report that I am a teacher, and take money; this accusation has no more truth in it than the other. Although, if a man were really able to instruct mankind, to receive money for giving instruction would, in my opinion, be an honor to him. There is Gorgias of

Leontium, and Prodicus of Ceos, and Hippias of Elis, who go the round of the cities, and are able to persuade the young men to leave their own citizens by whom they might be taught for nothing, and come to them whom they not only pay, but are thankful if they may be allowed to pay them. There is at this time a Parian philosopher residing in Athens, of whom I have heard; and I came to hear of him in this way: I came across a man who has spent a world of money on the Sophists, Callias, the son of Hipponicus, and knowing that he had sons, I asked him: "Callias," I said, "if your two sons were foals or calves, there would be no difficulty in finding someone to put over them; we should hire a trainer of horses, or a farmer probably, who would improve and perfect them in their own proper virtue and excellence; but as they are human beings, whom are you thinking of placing over them? Is there anyone who understands human and political virtue? You must have thought about the matter, for you have sons; is there anyone?" "There is," he said. "Who is he?" said I; "and of what country? and what does he charge?" "Evenus the Parian," he replied; "he is the man, and his charge is five minae." Happy is Evenus, I said to myself, if he really has this wisdom, and teaches at such a moderate charge. Had I the same, I should have been very proud and conceited; but the truth is that I have no knowledge of the kind.

I dare say, Athenians, that someone among you will reply, "Yes, Socrates, but what is the origin of these accusations which are brought against you; there must have been something strange which you have been doing? All these rumours and this talk about you would never have arisen if you had been like other men: Tell us, then, what is the cause of them, for we should be sorry to judge hastily of you." Now I regard this as a fair challenge, and I will endeavor to explain to you the reason why I am called wise and have such an evil fame. Please to attend then. And although some of you may think that I am joking, I declare that I will tell you the entire truth. Men of Athens, this reputation of mine has come of a certain sort of wisdom which I possess. If you ask me what kind of wisdom, I reply, wisdom such as may perhaps be attained by man, for to that extent I am inclined to believe that I am wise; whereas the persons of whom I was speaking have a superhuman wisdom which I may fail to describe, because I have it not myself; and he who says that I have, speaks falsely, and is taking away my character. And here, O men of Athens, I must beg you not to interrupt me, even if I seem to say something extravagant. For the word which I will speak is not mine. I will refer you to a witness who is worthy of credit; that witness shall be the God of Delphi—he will tell you about my wisdom, if I have any, and of what sort it is. You must have known Chaerephon; he was early a friend of mine, and also a friend of yours, for he shared in the recent exile of the people, and returned with you. Well, Chaerephon, as you know, was very impetuous in all his doings, and he went to Delphi and boldly asked the oracle to tell him whether—as I was saying, I must beg you not to interrupt—he asked the oracle to tell him whether anyone was wiser than I was, and the Pythian prophetess answered, that there was no man wiser. Chaerephon is dead himself; but his brother, who is in court, will confirm the truth of what I am saying.

Why do I mention this? Because I am going to explain to you why I have such an evil name. When I heard the answer, I said to myself, What can the god mean? and what is the interpretation of his riddle? for I know that I have no wisdom, small or great. What then can he mean when he says that I am the wisest of men? And yet he is a god, and cannot lie; that would be against his nature. After long consideration, I thought of a method of trying the question. I reflected that if I could only find a man wiser than myself, then I might go to the god with a refutation in my hand. I should say to him, "Here is a man who is wiser than I am; but you said that I was the wisest." Accordingly I went to one who had the reputation of wisdom, and observed him—his name I need not mention; he was a politician whom I selected for examination—and the result was as follows: When I began to talk with him, I could not help thinking that he was not really wise, although he was thought wise by many, and still wiser by himself; and thereupon I tried to explain to him that he thought himself wise, but was not really wise; and the consequence was that he hated me, and his enmity was shared by several who were present and heard me. So I left him, saying to myself, as I went away: Well, although I do not suppose that either of us knows anything really beautiful and good, I am better off than he is, for he knows nothing, and thinks that he knows; I neither know nor think that I know. In this latter particular, then, I seem to have slightly the advantage of him. Then I went to another who had still higher pretensions to wisdom, and my conclusion was exactly the same. Whereupon I made another enemy of him, and of many others besides him.

Then I went to one man after another, being not unconscious of the enmity which I provoked, and I lamented and feared this; but necessity was laid upon me, the word of God, I thought, ought to be considered first. And I said to myself, Go I must to all who appear to know, and find out the meaning of the oracle. And I swear to you, Athenians, by the dog I swear!—for I must tell you the truth—the result of my mission was just this: I found that the men most in repute were all but the most foolish; and that others less esteemed were really wiser and better. I will tell you the tale of my wanderings and of the "Herculean" labors, as I may call them, which I endured only to find at last the oracle irrefutable. After the politicians, I went to the poets; tragic, dithyrambic, and all sorts. And there, I said to myself, you will be instantly detected; now you will find out that you are more ignorant than they are. Accordingly, I took them some of the most elaborate passages in their own writings, and asked what was the meaning of them—thinking that they would teach me something. Will you believe me? I am almost ashamed to confess the truth, but I must say that there is hardly a person present who would not have talked better about their poetry than they did themselves. Then I knew that not by wisdom do poets write poetry, but by a sort of genius and inspiration; they are like diviners or soothsayers who also say many fine things, but do not understand the meaning of them. The poets appeared to me to be much in the same case; and I further observed that upon the strength of their poetry they believed themselves to be the wisest of men in other things in which they were not wise. So I departed, conceiving myself to be superior to them for the same reason that I was superior to the politicians.

At last I went to the artisans. I was conscious that I knew nothing at all, as I may say, and I was sure that they knew many fine things; and here I was not mistaken, for they did know many things of which I was ignorant, and in this they certainly were wiser than I was. But I observed that even the good artisans fell into the same error as the poets; because they were good workmen they thought that they also knew all sorts of high matters, and this defect in them overshadowed their wisdom; and therefore I asked myself on behalf of the oracle, whether I would like to be as I was, neither having their knowledge nor their ignorance, or like them in both; and I made answer to myself and to the oracle that I was better off as I was.

This inquisition has led to my having many enemies of the worst and most dangerous kind, and has given occasion also to many calumnies. And I am called wise, for my hearers always imagine that I myself possess the wisdom which I find wanting in others: but the truth is, O men of Athens, that God only is wise; and by his answer he intends to show that the wisdom of men is worth little or nothing; he is not speaking of Socrates, he is only using my name by way of illustration, as if he said, He, O men, is the wisest, who, like Socrates, knows that his wisdom is in truth worth nothing. And so I go about the world, obedient to the god, and search and make inquiry into the wisdom of anyone, whether citizen or stranger, who appears to be wise;

and if he is not wise, then in vindication of the oracle I show him that he is not wise; and my occupation quite absorbs me, and I have no time to give either to any public matter of interest or to any concern of my own, but I am in utter poverty by reason of my devotion to the god.

There is another thing:—young men of the richer classes, who have not much to do, come about me of their own accord; they like to hear the pretenders examined, and they often imitate me, and proceed to examine others; there are plenty of persons, as they quickly discover, who think that they know something, but really know little or nothing; and then those who are examined by them instead of being angry with themselves are angry with me: This confounded Socrates, they say; this villainous misleader of youth!—and then if somebody asks them, "Why, what evil does he practice or teach?" They do not know, and cannot tell; but in order that they may not appear to be at a loss, they repeat the ready-made charges which are used against all philosophers about teaching things up in the clouds and under the earth, and having no gods, and making the worse appear the better cause; for they do not like to confess that their pretence of knowledge has been detected—which is the truth; and as they are numerous and ambitious and energetic, and are drawn up in battle array and have persuasive tongues, they have filled your ears with their loud and inveterate calumnies. And this is the reason why my three accusers, Meletus and Anytus and Lycon, have set upon me; Meletus, who has a quarrel with me on behalf of the poets; Anytus, on behalf of the craftsmen and politicians; Lycon, on behalf of the rhetoricians: and as I said at the beginning, I cannot expect to get rid of such a mass of calumny all in a moment. And this, O men of Athens, is the truth and the whole truth; I have concealed nothing, I have dissembled nothing. And yet, I know that my plainness of speech makes them hate me, and what is their hatred but a proof that I am speaking the truth? Hence has arisen the prejudice against me; and this is the reason of it, as you will find out either in this or in any future inquiry.

I have said enough in my defense against the first class of my accusers; I turn to the second class. They are headed by Meletus, that good man and true lover of his country, as he calls himself. Against these, too, I must try to make a defense: Let their affidavit be read; it contains something of this kind: It says that Socrates is a doer of evil, who corrupts the youth; and who does not believe in the gods of the state, but has other new divinities of his own. Such is the charge; and now let us examine the particular counts. He says that I am a doer of evil, and corrupt the youth; but I say, O men of Athens, that Meletus is a doer of evil, in that he pretends to be in earnest when he is only in jest, and is so eager to bring men to trial from a pretended zeal and interest about matters in which he really never had the smallest interest. And the truth of this I will endeavor to prove to you.

Come hither, Meletus, and let me ask a question of you. You think a great deal about the improvement of youth?

Yes, I do.

Tell the judges, then, who is their improver; for you must know, as you have taken the pains to discover their corrupter, and are citing and accusing me before them. Speak, then, and tell the judges who their improver is. Observe, Meletus, that you are silent, and have nothing to say. But is not this rather disgraceful, and a very considerable proof of what I was saying, that you have no interest in the matter? Speak up, friend, and tell us who their improver is.

The laws.

But that, my good sir, is not my meaning. I want to know who the person is, who, in the first place, knows the laws.

The judges, Socrates, who are present in court.

What, do you mean to say, Meletus, that they are able to instruct and improve youth?

Certainly they are.

What, all of them, or some only and not others?

All of them.

By the goddess: Here, that is good news! There are plenty of improvers, then. And what do you say of the audience—do they improve them?

Yes, they do.

And the senators?

Yes, the senators improve them.

But perhaps the members of the assembly corrupt them? or do they too improve them?

They improve them.

Then every Athenian improves and elevates them; all with the exception of myself; and I alone am their corrupter? Is that what you affirm?

That is what I stoutly affirm.

I am very unfortunate if you are right. But suppose I ask you a question: How about horses? Does one man do them harm and all the world good? Is not the exact opposite the truth? One man is able to do them good, or at least not many—the trainer of horses, that is to say, does them good, and others who have to do with them rather injure them? Is not that true, Meletus, of horses, or of any other animals? Most assuredly it is; whether you and Anytus say yes or no. Happy indeed would be the condition of youth if they had one corrupter only, and all the rest of the world were their improvers. But you, Meletus, have sufficiently shown that you never had a thought about the young; your carelessness is seen in your not caring about the very things which you bring against me.

And now, Meletus, I will ask you another question—by Zeus I will: Which is better, to live among bad citizens, or among good ones? Answer, friend, I say; the question is one which may be easily answered. Do not the good do their neighbors good, and the bad do them evil?

Certainly.

And is there anyone who would rather be injured than benefited by those who live with him? Answer, my good friend, the law requires you to answer—does anyone like to be injured?

Certainly not.

And when you accuse me of corrupting and deteriorating the youth, do you allege that I corrupt them intentionally or unintentionally?

Intentionally, I say.

But you have just admitted that the good do their neighbors good, and the evil do them evil. Now, is that a truth which your superior wisdom has recognized thus early in life, and am I, at my age, in such darkness and ignorance as not to know that if a man with whom I have to live is corrupted by me, I am very likely to be harmed by him; and yet I corrupt him, and intentionally, too—so you say, although neither I nor any other human being is ever likely to be convinced by you. But either I do not corrupt them, or I corrupt them unintentionally; and on either view of the case you lie. If my offense is unintentional, the law has no cognizance of unintentional offenses; you ought to have taken me privately, and warned and admonished me; for if I had been better advised, I should have left off doing what I only did unintentionally—no doubt I should; but you would have nothing to say to me and refused to teach me. And now you bring me up in this court, which is a place not of instruction, but of punishment.

It will be very clear to you, Athenians, as I was saying, that Meletus has no care at all, great or small, about the matter. But still I should like to know, Meletus, in what I am affirmed to corrupt the young. I suppose you mean, as I infer from your indictment, that I teach them not to acknowledge the gods which the state acknowledges, but some other new divinities or spiritual agencies in their stead. These are the lessons by which I corrupt the youth, as you say.

Yes, that I say emphatically.

Then, by the gods, Meletus, of whom we are speaking, tell me and the court, in somewhat plainer terms, what you mean! for I do not as yet understand whether you affirm that I teach other men to acknowledge some gods, and therefore that I do believe in gods, and am not an entire atheist—this you do not lay to my charge, but only you say that they are not the same gods which the city recognizes—the charge is that they are different gods. Or, do you mean that I am an atheist simply, and a teacher of atheism?

I mean the latter—that you are a complete atheist.

What an extraordinary statement! Why do you think so, Meletus? Do you mean that I do not believe in the godhead of the sun or moon, like other men?

I assure you, judges, that he does not, for he says that the sun is stone, and the moon earth.

Friend Meletus, you think that you are accusing Anaxagoras; and you have but a bad opinion of the judges, if you fancy them illiterate to such a degree as not to know that these doctrines are found in the books of Anaxagoras the Clazomenian, which are full of them. And so, forsooth, the youth are said to be taught them by Socrates, when there are not unfrequently exhibitions of them at the theatre (Probably in allusion to Aristophanes who caricatured, and to Euripides who borrowed the notions of Anaxagoras, as well as to other dramatic poets.) (price of admission one drachma at the most); and they might pay their money, and laugh at Socrates if he pretends to father these extraordinary views. And so, Meletus, you really think that I do not believe in any god?

I swear by Zeus that you believe absolutely in none at all.

Nobody will believe you, Meletus, and I am pretty sure that you do not believe yourself. I cannot help thinking, men of Athens, that Meletus is reckless and impudent, and that he has written this indictment in a spirit of mere wantonness and youthful bravado. Has he not compounded a riddle, thinking to try me? He said to himself: I shall see whether the wise Socrates will discover my facetious contradiction, or whether I shall be able to deceive him and the rest of them. For he certainly does appear to me to contradict himself in the indictment as much as if he said that Socrates is guilty of not believing in the gods, and yet of believing in them—but this is not like a person who is in earnest.

I should like you, O men of Athens, to join me in examining what I conceive to be his inconsistency; and do you, Meletus, answer. And I must remind the audience of my request that they would not make a disturbance if I speak in my accustomed manner.

Did ever man, Meletus, believe in the existence of human things, and not of human beings? ... I wish, men of Athens, that he would answer, and not be always trying to get up an interruption. Did ever any man believe in horsemanship, and not in horses? or in flute playing, and not in flute players? No, my friend; I will answer to you and to the court, as you refuse to answer for yourself. There is no man who ever did. But now please to answer the next question: Can a man believe in spiritual and divine agencies, and not in spirits or demigods?

He cannot.

How lucky I am to have extracted that answer, by the assistance of the court! But then you swear in the indictment that I teach and believe in divine or spiritual agencies (new or old, no matter for that); at any rate, I believe in spiritual agencies, so you say and swear in the affidavit; and yet if I believe in divine beings, how can I help believing in spirits or demigods— must I not? To be sure I must; and therefore I may assume that your silence gives consent. Now what are spirits or demigods? Are they not either gods or the sons of gods?

Certainly they are.

But this is what I call the facetious riddle invented by you: The demigods or spirits are gods, and you say first that I do not believe in gods, and then again that I do believe in gods; that is, if I believe in demigods. For if the demigods are the illegitimate sons of gods, whether by the nymphs or by any other mothers, of whom they are said to be the sons—what human being will ever believe that there are no gods if they are the sons of gods? You might as well affirm the existence of mules, and deny that of horses and asses. Such nonsense, Meletus, could only have been intended by you to make trial of me. You have put this into the indictment because you had nothing real of which to accuse me. But no one who has a particle of understanding will ever be convinced by you that the same men can believe in divine and superhuman things, and yet not believe that there are gods and demigods and heroes.

I have said enough in answer to the charge of Meletus: Any elaborate defense is unnecessary, but I know only too well how many are the enmities which I have incurred, and this is what will be my destruction if I am destroyed—not Meletus, nor yet Anytus, but the envy and detraction of the world, which has been the death of many good men, and will probably be the death of many more; there is no danger of my being the last of them.

Someone will say: And are you not ashamed, Socrates, of a course of life which is likely to bring you to an untimely end? To him I may fairly answer: There you are mistaken. A man who is good for anything ought not to calculate the chance of living or dying; he ought only to consider whether in doing anything he is doing right or wrong—acting the part of a good man or of a bad. Whereas, upon your view, the heroes who fell at Troy were not good for much, and the son of Thetis above all, who altogether despised danger in comparison with disgrace; and when he was so eager to slay Hector, his goddess mother said to him, that if he avenged his companion Patroclus, and slew Hector, he would die himself—"Fate," she said, in these or the like words, "waits for you next after Hector"; he, receiving this warning, utterly despised danger and death, and instead of fearing them, feared rather to live in dishonor, and not to avenge his friend. "Let me die forthwith," he replies, "and be avenged of my enemy, rather than abide here by the beaked ships, a laughing-stock and a burden of the Earth." Had Achilles any thought of death and danger? For wherever a man's place is, whether the place which he has chosen or that in which he has been placed by a commander, there he ought to remain in the hour of danger; he should not think of death or of anything but of disgrace. And this, O men of Athens, is a true saying.

Strange, indeed, would be my conduct, O men of Athens, if I who, when I was ordered by the generals whom you chose to command me at Potidaea and Amphipolis and Delium, remained where they placed me, like any other man, facing death—if now, when, as I conceive and imagine, God orders me to fulfill the philosopher's mission of searching into myself and other men, I were to desert my post through fear of death, or any other fear; that would indeed be strange, and I might justly be arraigned in court for denying the existence of the gods, if I disobeyed the oracle because I was afraid of death, fancying that I was wise when I was not wise. For the fear of death is indeed the pretence of wisdom, and not real wisdom, being a pretence of knowing the unknown; and no one knows whether death, which men in their fear apprehend to be the greatest evil, may not be the greatest good. Is not this ignorance of a disgraceful sort, the ignorance which is the conceit that a man knows what he does not know? And in this respect only I believe myself to differ from men in general, and may perhaps claim to be wiser than they are—that whereas I know but little of the world below, I do not suppose that I know: but I do know that injustice and disobedience to a better, whether God or man, is evil and dishonorable, and I will never fear or avoid a possible good rather than a certain evil. And therefore if you let me go now, and are not convinced by Anytus, who said that since I had been prosecuted I must be put to death (or if not that, I ought never to have been prosecuted at all); and that if I escape now, your sons will all be utterly ruined by listening to my words—if you say to me, Socrates, this time we will not mind Anytus, and you shall be let off, but upon one condition, that you are not to inquire and speculate in this way anymore, and that if you are caught doing so again you shall die—if this was the condition on which you let me go, I should reply: Men of Athens, I honor and love you; but I shall obey God rather than you, and while I have life and strength I shall never cease from the practice and teaching of philosophy, exhorting anyone whom I meet and saying to him after my manner: You, my friend, a citizen of the great and mighty and wise city of Athens, are you not ashamed of heaping up the greatest amount of money and honor and reputation, and caring so little about wisdom and truth and the greatest improvement of the soul, which you never regard or heed at all? And if the person with whom I am arguing, says: Yes, but I do care; then I do not leave him or let him go at once; but I proceed to interrogate and examine and cross-examine him, and if I think that he has no virtue in him, but only says that he has, I reproach him with undervaluing the greater, and overvaluing the less. And I shall repeat the same words to everyone whom I meet, young and old, citizen and alien, but especially to the citizens, inasmuch as they are my brethren. For know that this is the command of God; and I believe that no greater good has ever happened in the state than my service to the God. For I do nothing but go about persuading you all, old and young alike, not to take thought for your persons or your properties, but first and chiefly to care about the greatest improvement of the soul. I tell you that virtue is not given by money, but that from virtue comes money and every other good of man, public as well as private. This is my teaching, and if this is the doctrine which corrupts the youth, I am a mischievous person. But if anyone says that this is not my teaching, he is speaking an untruth. Wherefore, O men of Athens, I say to you, do as Anytus bids or not as Anytus bids, and either acquit me or not; but whichever you do, understand that I shall never alter my ways, not even if I have to die many times.

 Men of Athens, do not interrupt, but hear me; there was an understanding between us that you should hear me to the end: I have something more to say, at which you may be inclined to cry out; but I believe that to hear me will be good for you, and therefore I beg that you will not cry out. I would have you know, that if you kill such an one as I am, you will injure yourselves more than you will injure me. Nothing will injure me, not Meletus nor yet Anytus—they cannot, for a bad man is not permitted to injure a better than himself. I do not deny that Anytus may, perhaps, kill him, or drive him into exile, or deprive him of civil rights; and he may imagine, and others may imagine, that he is inflicting a great injury upon him: but there I do not agree. For the evil of doing as he is doing—the evil of unjustly taking away the life of another—is greater far.

And now, Athenians, I am not going to argue for my own sake, as you may think, but for yours, that you may not sin against the God by condemning me, who am his gift to you. For if you kill me you will not easily find a successor to me, who, if I may use such a ludicrous figure of speech, am a sort of gadfly, given to the state by God; and the state is a great and noble steed who is tardy in his motions owing to his very size, and requires to be stirred into life. I am that gadfly which God has attached to the state, and all day long and in all places am always fastening upon you, arousing and persuading and reproaching you. You will not easily find another like me, and therefore I would advise you to spare me. I dare say that you may feel out of temper (like a person who is suddenly awakened from sleep), and you think that you might easily strike me dead as Anytus advises, and then you would sleep on for the remainder of your lives, unless God in his care of you sent you another gadfly. When I say that I am given to you by God, the proof of my mission is this: If I had been like other men, I should not have neglected all my own concerns or patiently seen the neglect of them during all these years, and have been doing yours, coming to you individually like a father or elder brother, exhorting you to regard virtue; such conduct, I say, would be unlike human nature. If I had gained anything, or if my exhortations had been paid, there would have been some sense in my doing so; but now, as you will perceive, not even the impudence of my accusers dares to say that I have ever exacted or sought pay of anyone; of that they have no witness. And I have a sufficient witness to the truth of what I say—my poverty.

Someone may wonder why I go about in private giving advice and busying myself with the concerns of others, but do not venture to come forward in public and advise the state. I will tell you why. You have heard me speak at sundry times and in diverse places of an oracle or sign which comes to me, and is the divinity which Meletus ridicules in the indictment. This sign, which is a kind of voice, first began to come to me when I was a child; it always forbids but never commands me to do anything which I am going to do. This is what deters me from being a politician. And rightly, as I think. For I am certain, O men of Athens, that if I had engaged in politics, I should have perished long ago, and done no good either to you or to myself. And do not be offended at my telling you the truth: For the truth is, that no man who goes to war with you or any other multitude, honestly striving against the many lawless and unrighteous deeds which are done in a state, will save his life; he who will fight for the right, if he would live even for a brief space, must have a private station and not a public one.

I can give you convincing evidence of what I say, not words only, but what you value far more—actions. Let me relate to you a passage of my own life which will prove to you that I should never have yielded to injustice from any fear of death, and that "as I should have refused to yield" I must have died at once. I will tell you a tale of the courts, not very interesting perhaps, but nevertheless true. The only office of state which I ever held, O men of Athens, was that of senator: The tribe Antiochis, which is my tribe, had the presidency at the trial of the generals who had not taken up the bodies of the slain after the battle of Arginusae; and you proposed to try them in a body, contrary to law, as you all thought afterward; but at the time I was the only one of the Prytanes who was opposed to the illegality, and I gave my vote against you; and when the orators threatened to impeach and arrest me, and you called and shouted, I made up my mind that I would run the risk, having law and justice with me, rather than take part in your injustice because I feared imprisonment and death. This happened in the days of the democracy. But when the oligarchy of the Thirty was in power, they sent for me and four others into the rotunda, and bade us bring Leon the Salaminian from Salamis, as they wanted to put him to death. This was a specimen of the sort of commands which they were always giving with the view of implicating as many as possible in their crimes; and then I showed, not in word only but in deed, that, if I may be allowed to use such an expression, I cared not a straw for death, and that my great and only care was lest I should do an unrighteous or unholy thing. For the strong arm of that oppressive power did not frighten me into doing wrong; and when we came out of the rotunda the other four went to Salamis and fetched Leon, but I went quietly home. For which I might have lost my life, had not the power of the Thirty shortly afterward come to an end. And many will witness to my words.

Now do you really imagine that I could have survived all these years, if I had led a public life, supposing that like a good man I had always maintained the right and had made justice, as I ought, the first thing? No indeed, men of Athens, neither I nor any other man. But I have been always the same in all my actions, public as well as private, and never have I yielded any base compliance to those who are slanderously termed my disciples, or to any other. Not that I have any regular disciples. But if anyone likes to come and hear me while I am pursuing my mission, whether he be young or old, he is not excluded. Nor do I converse only with those who pay; but anyone, whether he be rich or poor, may ask and answer me and listen to my words; and whether he turns out to be a bad man or a good one, neither result can be justly imputed to me; for I never taught or professed to teach him anything. And if anyone says that he has ever learned or heard anything from me in private which all the world has not heard, let me tell you that he is lying.

But I shall be asked, Why do people delight in continually conversing with you? I have told you already, Athenians, the whole truth about this matter: They like to hear the cross-examination of the pretenders to wisdom; there is amusement in it. Now this duty of cross-examining other men has been imposed upon me by God; and has been signified to me by oracles, visions, and in every way in which the will of divine power was ever intimated to anyone. This is true, O Athenians, or, if not true, would be soon refuted. If I am or have been corrupting the youth, those of them who are now grown up and have become sensible that I gave them bad advice in the days of their youth should come forward as accusers, and take their revenge; or if they do not like to come themselves, some of their relatives, fathers, brothers, or other kinsmen, should say what evil their families have suffered at my hands. Now is their time. Many of them I see in the court. There is Crito, who is of the same age and of the same deme with myself, and there is Critobulus his son, whom I also see. Then again there is Lysanias of Sphettus, who is the father of Aeschines—he is present; and also there is Antiphon of Cephisus, who is the father of Epigenes; and there are the brothers of several who have associated with me. There is Nicostratus the son of Theosdotides, and the brother of Theodotus (now Theodotus himself is dead, and therefore he, at any rate, will not seek to stop him); and there is Paralus the son of Demodocus, who had a brother Theages; and Adeimantus the son of Ariston, whose brother Plato is present; and Aeantodorus, who is the brother of Apollodorus, whom I also see. I might mention a great many others, some of whom Meletus should have produced as witnesses in the course of his speech; and let him still produce them, if he has forgotten—I will make way for him. And let him say, if he has any testimony of the sort which he can produce. Nay, Athenians, the very opposite is the truth. For all these are ready to witness on behalf of the corrupter, of the injurer of their kindred, as Meletus and Anytus call me; not the corrupted youth only—there might have been a motive for that—but their uncorrupted elder relatives. Why should they too support me with their testimony? Why, indeed, except for the sake of truth and justice, and because they know that I am speaking the truth, and that Meletus is a liar.

Well, Athenians, this and the like of this is all the defense which I have to offer. Yet a word more. Perhaps there may be someone who is offended at me, when he calls to mind how he himself on a similar, or even a less serious occasion, prayed and entreated the judges with many tears, and how he produced his children in court, which was a moving spectacle, together with a host of relations and friends; whereas I, who am probably in danger of my life, will do none of these things. The contrast may occur to his mind, and he may be set against me, and vote in anger because he is displeased at me on this account. Now if there be such a person among you—mind, I do not say that there is—to him I may fairly reply: My friend, I am a man, and like other men, a creature of flesh and blood, and not "of wood or stone," as Homer says; and I have a family, yes, and sons, O Athenians, three in number, one almost a man, and two others who are still young; and yet I will not bring any of them hither in order to petition you for an acquittal. And why not? Not from any self-assertion or want of respect for you. Whether I am or am not afraid of death is another question, of which I will not now speak. But, having regard to public opinion, I feel that such conduct would be discreditable to myself, and to you, and to the whole state. One who has reached my years, and who has a name for wisdom, ought not to demean himself. Whether this opinion of me be deserved or not, at any rate the world has decided that Socrates is in some way superior to other men. And if those among you who are said to be superior in wisdom and courage, and any other virtue, demean themselves in this way, how shameful is their conduct! I have seen men of reputation, when they have been condemned, behaving in the strangest manner: They seemed to fancy that they were going to suffer something dreadful if they died, and that they could be immortal if you only allowed them to live; and I think that such are a dishonor to the state, and that any stranger coming in would have said of them that the most eminent men of Athens, to whom the Athenians themselves give honor and command, are no better than women. And I say that these things ought not to be done by those of us who have a reputation; and if they are done, you ought not to permit them; you ought rather to show that you are far more disposed to condemn the man who gets up a doleful scene and makes the city ridiculous, than him who holds his peace.

But, setting aside the question of public opinion, there seems to be something wrong in asking a favor of a judge, and thus procuring an acquittal, instead of informing and convincing him. For his duty is, not to make a present of justice, but to give judgment; and he has sworn that he will judge according to the laws, and not according to his own good pleasure; and we ought not to encourage you, nor should you allow yourselves to be encouraged, in this habit of perjury—there can be no piety in that. Do not then require me to do what I consider dishonorable and impious and wrong, especially now, when I am being tried for impiety on the indictment of Meletus. For if, O men of Athens, by force of persuasion and entreaty I could overpower your oaths, then I should be teaching you to believe that there are no gods, and in defending should simply convict myself of the charge of not believing in them. But that is not so—far otherwise. For I do believe that there are gods, and in a sense higher than that in which any of my accusers believe in them. And to you and to God I commit my cause, to be determined by you as is best for you and me.

* * * * *

There are many reasons why I am not grieved, O men of Athens, at the vote of condemnation. I expected it, and am only surprised that the votes are so nearly equal; for I had thought that the majority against me would have been far larger; but now, had thirty votes gone over to the other side, I should have been acquitted. And I may say, I think, that I have escaped Meletus. I may say more; for without the assistance of Anytus and Lycon, anyone may see that he would not have had a fifth part of the votes, as the law requires, in which case he would have incurred a fine of a thousand drachmae.

And so he proposes death as the penalty. And what shall I propose on my part, O men of Athens? Clearly that which is my due. And what is my due? What return shall be made to the man who has never had the wit to be idle during his whole life; but has been careless of what the many care for—wealth, and family interests, and military offices, and speaking in the assembly, and magistracies, and plots, and parties. Reflecting that I was really too honest a man to be a politician and live, I did not go where I could do no good to you or to myself; but where I could do the greatest good privately to every one of you, thither I went, and sought to persuade every man among you that he must look to himself, and seek virtue and wisdom before he looks to his private interests, and look to the state before he looks to the interests of the state; and that this should be the order which he observes in all his actions. What shall be done to such an one? Doubtless some good thing, O men of Athens, if he has his reward; and the good should be of a kind suitable to him. What would be a reward suitable to a poor man who is your benefactor, and who desires leisure that he may instruct you? There can be no reward so fitting as maintenance in the Prytaneum, O men of Athens, a reward which he deserves far more than the citizen who has won the prize at Olympia in the horse or chariot race, whether the chariots were drawn by two horses or by many. For I am in want, and he has enough; and he only gives you the appearance of happiness, and I give you the reality. And if I am to estimate the penalty fairly, I should say that maintenance in the Prytaneum is the just return.

Perhaps you think that I am braving you in what I am saying now, as in what I said before about the tears and prayers. But this is not so. I speak rather because I am convinced that I never intentionally wronged anyone, although I cannot convince you—the time has been too short; if there were a law at Athens, as there is in other cities, that a capital cause should not be decided in one day, then I believe that I should have convinced you. But I cannot in a moment refute great slanders; and, as I am convinced that I never wronged another, I will assuredly not wrong myself. I will not say of myself that I deserve any evil, or propose any penalty. Why should I? because I am afraid of the penalty of death which Meletus proposes? When I do not know whether death is a good or an evil, why should I propose a penalty which would certainly be an evil? Shall I say imprisonment? And why should I live in prison, and be the slave of the magistrates of the year—of the Eleven? Or shall the penalty be a fine, and imprisonment until the fine is paid? There is the same objection. I should have to lie in prison, for money I have none, and cannot pay. And if I say exile (and this may possibly be the penalty which you will affix), I must indeed be blinded by the love of life, if I am so irrational as to expect that when you, who are my own citizens, cannot endure my discourses and words, and have found them so grievous and odious that you will have no more of them, others are likely to endure me. No indeed, men of Athens, that is not very likely. And what a life should I lead, at my age, wandering from city to city, ever changing my place of exile, and always being driven out! For I am quite sure that wherever I go, there, as here, the young men will flock to me; and if I drive them away, their elders will drive me out at their request; and if I let them come, their fathers and friends will drive me out for their sakes.

Someone will say: Yes, Socrates, but cannot you hold your tongue, and then you may go into a foreign city, and no one will interfere with you? Now I have great difficulty in making you understand my answer to this. For if I tell you that to do as you say would be a disobedience to the God, and therefore that I cannot hold my tongue, you will not believe that I am serious; and if I say again that daily to discourse about virtue, and of those other things about which you hear me examining myself and others, is the greatest good of man, and that the unexamined life is not worth living, you are still less likely to believe me. Yet I say what is true, although a thing of which it is hard for me to persuade you. Also, I have never been accustomed to think that I deserve to suffer any harm. Had I money I might have estimated the offense at what I was able to pay, and not have been much the worse. But I have none, and therefore I must ask you to proportion the fine to my means. Well, perhaps I could afford a mina, and therefore I propose that penalty: Plato, Crito, Critobulus, and Apollodorus, my friends here, bid me say thirty minae, and they will be the sureties. Let thirty minae be the penalty; for which sum they will be ample security to you.

* * * * *

Not much time will be gained, O Athenians, in return for the evil name which you will get from the detractors of the city, who will say that you killed Socrates, a wise man; for they will call me wise, even although I am not wise, when they want to reproach you. If you had waited a little while, your desire would have been fulfillled in the course of nature. For I am far advanced in years, as you may perceive, and not far from death. I am speaking now not to all of you, but only to those who have condemned me to death. And I have another thing to say to them: You think that I was convicted because I had no words of the sort which would have procured my acquittal—I mean, if I had thought fit to leave nothing undone or unsaid. Not so; the deficiency which led to my conviction was not of words—certainly not. But I had not the boldness or impudence or inclination to address you as you would have liked me to do, weeping and wailing and lamenting, and saying and doing many things which you have been accustomed to hear from others, and which, as I maintain, are unworthy of me. I thought at the time that I ought not to do anything common or mean when in danger: nor do I now repent of the style of my defense; I would rather die having spoken after my manner, than speak in your manner and live. For neither in war nor yet at law ought I or any man to use every way of escaping death. Often in battle there can be no doubt that if a man will throw away his arms, and fall on his knees before his pursuers, he may escape death; and in other dangers there are other ways of escaping death, if a man is willing to say and do anything. The difficulty, my friends, is not to avoid death, but to avoid unrighteousness; for that runs faster than death. I am old and move slowly, and the slower runner has overtaken me, and my accusers are keen and quick, and the faster runner, who is unrighteousness, has overtaken them. And now I depart hence condemned by you to suffer the penalty of death,—they too go their ways condemned by the truth to suffer the penalty of villainy and wrong; and I must abide by my award—let them abide by theirs. I suppose that these things may be regarded as fated,—and I think that they are well.

And now, O men who have condemned me, I would fain prophesy to you; for I am about to die, and in the hour of death men are gifted with prophetic power. And I prophesy to you who are my murderers, that immediately after my departure punishment far heavier than you have inflicted on me will surely await you. Me you have killed because you wanted to escape the accuser, and not to give an account of your lives. But that will not be as you suppose; far otherwise. For I say that there will be more accusers of you than there are now; accusers whom hitherto I have restrained: and as they are younger they will be more inconsiderate with you, and you will be more offended at them. If you think that by killing men you can prevent someone from censuring your evil lives, you are mistaken; that is not a way of escape which is either possible or honorable; the easiest and the noblest way is not to be disabling others, but to be improving yourselves. This is the prophecy which I utter before my departure to the judges who have condemned me.

Friends, who would have acquitted me, I would like also to talk with you about the thing which has come to pass, while the magistrates are busy, and before I go to the place at which I must die. Stay then a little, for we may as well talk with one another while there is time. You are my friends, and I should like to show you the meaning of this event which has happened to me. O my judges—for you I may truly call judges—I should like to tell you of a wonderful circumstance. Hitherto the divine faculty of which the internal oracle is the source has constantly been in the habit of opposing me even about trifles, if I was going to make a slip or error in any matter; and now as you see there has come upon me that which may be thought, and is generally believed to be, the last and worst evil. But the oracle made no sign of opposition, either when I was leaving my house in the morning, or when I was on my way to the court, or while I was speaking, at anything which I was going to say; and yet I have often been stopped in the middle of a speech, but now in nothing I either said or did touching the matter in hand has the oracle opposed me. What do I take to be the explanation of this silence? I will tell you. It is an intimation that what has happened to me is a good, and that those of us who think that death is an evil are in error. For the customary sign would surely have opposed me had I been going to evil and not to good.

Let us reflect in another way, and we shall see that there is great reason to hope that death is a good; for one of two things—either death is a state of nothingness and utter unconsciousness, or, as men say, there is a change and migration of the soul from this world to another. Now if you suppose that there is no consciousness, but a sleep like the sleep of him who is undisturbed even by dreams, death will be an unspeakable gain. For if a person were to select the night in which his sleep was undisturbed even by dreams, and were to compare with this the other days and nights of his life, and then were to tell us how many days and nights he had passed in the course of his life better and more pleasantly than this one, I think that any man, I will not say a private man, but even the great king will not find many such days or nights, when compared with the others. Now if death be of such a nature, I say that to die is gain; for eternity is then only a single night. But if death is the journey to another place, and there, as men say, all the dead abide, what good, O my friends and judges, can be greater than this? If indeed when the pilgrim arrives in the world below, he is delivered from the professors of justice in this world, and finds the true judges who are said to give judgment there, Minos and Rhadamanthus and Aeacus and Triptolemus, and other sons of God who were righteous in their own life, that pilgrimage will be worth making. What would not a man give if he might converse with Orpheus and Musaeus and Hesiod and Homer? Nay, if this be true, let me die again and again. I myself, too, shall have a wonderful interest in there meeting and conversing with Palamedes, and Ajax the son of Telamon, and any other ancient hero who has suffered death through an unjust judgment; and there will be no small pleasure, as I think, in comparing my own sufferings with theirs. Above all, I shall then be able to continue my search into true and false knowledge; as in this world, so also in the next; and I shall find out who is wise, and who pretends to be wise, and is not. What would not a man give, O judges, to be able to examine the leader of the great Trojan expedition; or Odysseus or Sisyphus, or numberless others, men and women too! What infinite delight would there be in conversing with them and asking them questions! In another world they do not put a man to death for asking questions; assuredly not. For besides being happier than we are, they will be immortal, if what is said is true.

Wherefore, O judges, be of good cheer about death, and know of a certainty, that no evil can happen to a good man, either in life or after death. He and his are not neglected by the gods; nor has my own approaching end happened by mere chance. But I see clearly that the time had arrived when it was better for me to die and be released from trouble; wherefore the oracle gave no sign. For which reason, also, I am not angry with my condemners, or with my accusers; they have done me no harm, although they did not mean to do me any good; and for this I may gently blame them.

Still I have a favor to ask of them. When my sons are grown up, I would ask you, O my friends, to punish them; and I would have you trouble them, as I have troubled you, if they seem to care about riches, or anything, more than about virtue; or if they pretend to be something when they are really nothing, then reprove them, as I have reproved you, for not caring about that for which they ought to care, and thinking that they are something when they are really nothing. And if you do this, both I and my sons will have received justice at your hands.

The hour of departure has arrived, and we go our ways—I to die, and you to live. Which is better God only knows.

CRITO

BY PLATO

Translated by Benjamin Jowett

INTRODUCTION

The Crito seems intended to exhibit the character of Socrates in one light only, not as the philosopher, fulfilling a divine mission and trusting in the will of heaven, but simply as the good citizen, who having been unjustly condemned is willing to give up his life in obedience to the laws of the state.

The days of Socrates are drawing to a close; the fatal ship has been seen off Sunium, as he is informed by his aged friend and contemporary Crito, who visits him before the dawn has broken; he himself has been warned in a dream that on the third day he must depart. Time is precious, and Crito has come early in order to gain his consent to a plan of escape. This can be easily accomplished by his friends, who will incur no danger in making the attempt to save him, but will be disgraced forever if they allow him to perish. He should think of his duty to his children, and not play into the hands of his enemies. Money is already provided by Crito as well as by Simmias and others, and he will have no difficulty in finding friends in Thessaly and other places.

Socrates is afraid that Crito is but pressing upon him the opinions of the many: whereas, all his life long he has followed the dictates of reason only and the opinion of the one wise or skilled man. There was a time when Crito himself had allowed the propriety of this. And although someone will say "the many can kill us," that makes no difference; but a good life, in other words, a just and honorable life, is alone to be valued. All considerations of loss of reputation or injury to his children should be dismissed: The only question is whether he would be right in attempting to escape. Crito, who is a disinterested person not having the fear of death before his eyes, shall answer this for him. Before he was condemned they had often held discussions, in which they agreed that no man should either do evil, or return evil for evil, or betray the right. Are these principles to be altered because the circumstances of Socrates are altered? Crito admits that they remain the same. Then is his escape consistent with the maintenance of them? To this Crito is unable or unwilling to reply.

Socrates proceeds: Suppose the Laws of Athens to come and remonstrate with him; they will ask, "Why does he seek to overturn them?" and if he replies, "They have injured him," will not the Laws answer, "Yes, but was that the agreement? Has he any objection to make to them which would justify him in overturning them? Was he not brought into the world and educated by their help, and are they not his parents? He might have left Athens and gone where he pleased, but he has lived there for seventy years more constantly than any other citizen." Thus he has clearly shown that he acknowledged the agreement, which he cannot now break without dishonor to himself and danger to his friends. Even in the course of the trial he might have proposed exile as the penalty, but then he declared that he preferred death to exile. And whither will he direct his footsteps? In any well-ordered state the Laws will consider him as an enemy. Possibly in a land of misrule like Thessaly he may be welcomed at first, and the unseemly narrative of his escape will be regarded by the inhabitants as an amusing tale. But if he offends them he will have to learn another sort of lesson. Will he continue to give lectures in virtue? That would hardly be decent. And how will his children be the gainers if he takes them into Thessaly, and deprives them of Athenian citizenship? Or if he leaves them behind, does he expect that they will be better taken care of by his friends because he is in Thessaly? Will not true friends care for them equally whether he is alive or dead?

Finally, they exhort him to think of justice first, and of life and children afterward. He may now depart in peace and innocence, a sufferer and not a doer of evil. But if he breaks agreements, and returns evil for evil, they will be angry with him while he lives; and their brethren the Laws of the world below will receive him as an enemy. Such is the mystic voice which is always murmuring in his ears.

That Socrates was not a good citizen was a charge made against him during his lifetime, which has been often repeated in later ages. The crimes of Alcibiades, Critias, and Charmides, who had been his pupils, were still recent in the memory of the now restored democracy. The fact that he had been neutral in the death-struggle of Athens was not likely to conciliate popular goodwill. Plato, writing probably in the next generation, undertakes the defense of his friend and master in this particular, not to the Athenians of his day, but to posterity and the world at large.

Whether such an incident ever really occurred as the visit of Crito and the proposal of escape is uncertain: Plato could easily have invented far more than that (Phaedr.); and in the selection of Crito, the aged friend, as the fittest person to make the proposal to Socrates, we seem to recognize the hand of the artist. Whether anyone who has been subjected by the laws of his country to an unjust judgment is right in attempting to escape, is a thesis about which casuists might disagree. Shelley (Prose Works) is of opinion that Socrates "did well to die," but not for the "sophistical" reasons which Plato has put into his mouth. And there would be no difficulty in arguing that Socrates should have lived and preferred to a glorious death the good which he might still be able to perform. "A rhetorician would have had much to say upon that point." It may be observed however that Plato never intended to answer the question of casuistry, but only to exhibit the ideal of patient virtue which refuses to do the least evil in order to avoid the greatest, and to show his master maintaining in death the opinions which he had professed in his life. Not "the world," but the "one wise man," is still the paradox of Socrates in his last hours. He must be guided by reason, although her conclusions may be fatal to him. The remarkable sentiment that the wicked can do neither good nor evil is true, if taken in the sense, which he means, of moral evil; in his own words, "they cannot make a man wise or foolish."

This little dialogue is a perfect piece of dialectic, in which granting the "common principle," there is no escaping from the conclusion. It is anticipated at the beginning by the dream of Socrates and the parody of Homer. The personification of the Laws, and of their brethren the Laws in the world below, is one of the noblest and boldest figures of speech which occur in Plato.

Persons of the dialogue: Socrates, Crito

Scene: The Prison of Socrates

SOCRATES: Why have you come at this hour, Crito? it must be quite early.
CRITO: Yes, certainly.
SOCRATES: What is the exact time?
CRITO: The dawn is breaking.

SOCRATES: I wonder that the keeper of the prison would let you in.

CRITO: He knows me because I often come, Socrates; moreover, I have done him a kindness.

SOCRATES: And are you only just arrived?

CRITO: No, I came some time ago.

SOCRATES: Then why did you sit and say nothing, instead of at once awakening me?

CRITO: I should not have liked myself, Socrates, to be in such great trouble and unrest as you are—indeed I should not: I have been watching with amazement your peaceful slumbers; and for that reason I did not awake you, because I wished to minimize the pain. I have always thought you to be of a happy disposition; but never did I see anything like the easy, tranquil manner in which you bear this calamity.

SOCRATES: Why, Crito, when a man has reached my age he ought not to be repining at the approach of death.

CRITO: And yet other old men find themselves in similar misfortunes, and age does not prevent them from repining.

SOCRATES: That is true. But you have not told me why you come at this early hour.

CRITO: I come to bring you a message which is sad and painful; not, as I believe, to yourself, but to all of us who are your friends, and saddest of all to me.

SOCRATES: What? Has the ship come from Delos, on the arrival of which I am to die?

CRITO: No, the ship has not actually arrived, but she will probably be here today, as persons who have come from Sunium tell me that they have left her there; and therefore tomorrow, Socrates, will be the last day of your life.

SOCRATES: Very well, Crito; if such is the will of God, I am willing; but my belief is that there will be a delay of a day.

CRITO: Why do you think so?

SOCRATES: I will tell you. I am to die on the day after the arrival of the ship?

CRITO: Yes; that is what the authorities say.

SOCRATES: But I do not think that the ship will be here until tomorrow; this I infer from a vision which I had last night, or rather only just now, when you fortunately allowed me to sleep.

CRITO: And what was the nature of the vision?

SOCRATES: There appeared to me the likeness of a woman, fair and comely, clothed in bright raiment, who called to me and said: O Socrates, "The third day hence to fertile Phthia shalt thou go." (Homer, Il.)

CRITO: What a singular dream, Socrates!

SOCRATES: There can be no doubt about the meaning, Crito, I think.

CRITO: Yes; the meaning is only too clear. But, oh! my beloved Socrates, let me entreat you once more to take my advice and escape. For if you die I shall not only lose a friend who can never be replaced, but there is another evil: People who do not know you and me will believe that I might have saved you if I had been willing to give money, but that I did not care. Now, can there be a worse disgrace than this—that I should be thought to value money more than the life of a friend? For the many will not be persuaded that I wanted you to escape, and that you refused.

SOCRATES: But why, my dear Crito, should we care about the opinion of the many? Good men, and they are the only persons who are worth considering, will think of these things truly as they occurred.

CRITO: But you see, Socrates, that the opinion of the many must be regarded, for what is now happening shows that they can do the greatest evil to anyone who has lost their good opinion.

SOCRATES: I only wish it were so, Crito; and that the many could do the greatest evil; for then they would also be able to do the greatest good—and what a fine thing this would be! But in reality they can do neither; for they cannot make a man either wise or foolish; and whatever they do is the result of chance.

CRITO: Well, I will not dispute with you; but please to tell me, Socrates, whether you are not acting out of regard to me and your other friends: Are you not afraid that if you escape from prison we may get into trouble with the informers for having stolen you away, and lose either the whole or a great part of our property; or that even a worse evil may happen to us? Now, if you fear on our account, be at ease; for in order to save you, we ought surely to run this, or even a greater risk; be persuaded, then, and do as I say.

SOCRATES: Yes, Crito, that is one fear which you mention, but by no means the only one.

CRITO: Fear not—there are persons who are willing to get you out of prison at no great cost; and as for the informers they are far from being exorbitant in their demands—a little money will satisfy them. My means, which are certainly ample, are at your service, and if you have a scruple about spending all mine, here are strangers who will give you the use of theirs; and one of them, Simmias the Theban, has brought a large sum of

money for this very purpose; and Cebes and many others are prepared to spend their money in helping you to escape. I say, therefore, do not hesitate on our account, and do not say, as you did in the court (compare Apol.), that you will have a difficulty in knowing what to do with yourself anywhere else. For men will love you in other places to which you may go, and not in Athens only; there are friends of mine in Thessaly, if you like to go to them, who will value and protect you, and no Thessalian will give you any trouble. Nor can I think that you are at all justified, Socrates, in betraying your own life when you might be saved; in acting thus you are playing into the hands of your enemies, who are hurrying on your destruction. And further I should say that you are deserting your own children; for you might bring them up and educate them; instead of which you go away and leave them, and they will have to take their chance; and if they do not meet with the usual fate of orphans, there will be small thanks to you. No man should bring children into the world who is unwilling to persevere to the end in their nurture and education. But you appear to be choosing the easier part, not the better and manlier, which would have been more becoming in one who professes to care for virtue in all his actions, like yourself. And indeed, I am ashamed not only of you, but of us who are your friends, when I reflect that the whole business will be attributed entirely to our want of courage. The trial need never have come on, or might have been managed differently; and this last act, or crowning folly, will seem to have occurred through our negligence and cowardice, who might have saved you, if we had been good for anything; and you might have saved yourself, for there was no difficulty at all. See now, Socrates, how sad and discreditable are the consequences, both to us and you. Make up your mind then, or rather have your mind already made up, for the time of deliberation is over, and there is only one thing to be done, which must be done this very night, and if we delay at all will be no longer practicable or possible; I beseech you therefore, Socrates, be persuaded by me, and do as I say.
SOCRATES: Dear Crito, your zeal is invaluable, if a right one; but if wrong, the greater the zeal the greater the danger; and therefore we ought to consider whether I shall or shall not do as you say. For I am and always have been one of those natures who must be guided by reason, whatever the reason may be which upon reflection appears to me to be the best; and now that this chance has befallen me, I cannot repudiate my own words: the principles which I have hitherto honored and revered I still honor, and unless we can at once find other and better principles, I am certain not

to agree with you; no, not even if the power of the multitude could inflict many more imprisonments, confiscations, deaths, frightening us like children with hobgoblin terrors (compare Apol.). What will be the fairest way of considering the question? Shall I return to your old argument about the opinions of men?—We were saying that some of them are to be regarded, and others not. Now were we right in maintaining this before I was condemned? And has the argument which was once good now proved to be talk for the sake of talking—mere childish nonsense? That is what I want to consider with your help, Crito—whether, under my present circumstances, the argument appears to be in any way different or not; and is to be allowed by me or disallowed. That argument, which, as I believe, is maintained by many persons of authority, was to the effect, as I was saying, that the opinions of some men are to be regarded, and of other men not to be regarded. Now you, Crito, are not going to die tomorrow—at least, there is no human probability of this, and therefore you are disinterested and not liable to be deceived by the circumstances in which you are placed. Tell me then, whether I am right in saying that some opinions, and the opinions of some men only, are to be valued, and that other opinions, and the opinions of other men, are not to be valued. I ask you whether I was right in maintaining this?

CRITO: Certainly.

SOCRATES: The good are to be regarded, and not the bad?

CRITO: Yes.

SOCRATES: And the opinions of the wise are good, and the opinions of the unwise are evil?

CRITO: Certainly.

SOCRATES: And what was said about another matter? Is the pupil who devotes himself to the practice of gymnastics supposed to attend to the praise and blame and opinion of every man, or of one man only—his physician or trainer, whoever he may be?

CRITO: Of one man only.

SOCRATES: And he ought to fear the censure and welcome the praise of that one only, and not of the many?

CRITO: Clearly so.

SOCRATES: And he ought to act and train, and eat and drink in the way which seems good to his single master who has understanding, rather than according to the opinion of all other men put together?

CRITO: True.

SOCRATES: And if he disobeys and disregards the opinion and approval of the one, and regards the opinion of the many who have no understanding, will he not suffer evil?

CRITO: Certainly he will.

SOCRATES: And what will the evil be, whither tending and what affecting, in the disobedient person?

CRITO: Clearly, affecting the body; that is what is destroyed by the evil.

SOCRATES: Very good; and is not this true, Crito, of other things which we need not separately enumerate? In questions of just and unjust, fair and foul, good and evil, which are the subjects of our present consultation, ought we to follow the opinion of the many and to fear them; or the opinion of the one man who has understanding? Ought we not to fear and reverence him more than all the rest of the world? and if we desert him shall we not destroy and injure that principle in us which may be assumed to be improved by justice and deteriorated by injustice—there is such a principle?

CRITO: Certainly there is, Socrates.

SOCRATES: Take a parallel instance:—if, acting under the advice of those who have no understanding, we destroy that which is improved by health and is deteriorated by disease, would life be worth having? And that which has been destroyed is—the body?

CRITO: Yes.

SOCRATES: Could we live, having an evil and corrupted body?

CRITO: Certainly not.

SOCRATES: And will life be worth having, if that higher part of man be destroyed, which is improved by justice and depraved by injustice? Do we suppose that principle, whatever it may be in man, which has to do with justice and injustice, to be inferior to the body?

CRITO: Certainly not.

SOCRATES: More honorable than the body?

CRITO: Far more.

SOCRATES: Then, my friend, we must not regard what the many say of us, but what he, the one man who has understanding of just and unjust, will say, and what the truth will say. And therefore you begin in error when you advise that we should regard the opinion of the many about just and unjust, good and evil, honorable and dishonorable. "Well," someone will say, "but the many can kill us."

CRITO: Yes, Socrates; that will clearly be the answer.

SOCRATES: And it is true; but still I find with surprise that the old argument is unshaken as ever. And I should like to know whether I may say the same of another proposition—that not life, but a good life, is to be chiefly valued?

CRITO: Yes, that also remains unshaken.

SOCRATES: And a good life is equivalent to a just and honorable one—that holds also?

CRITO: Yes, it does.

SOCRATES: From these premises I proceed to argue the question whether I ought or ought not to try and escape without the consent of the Athenians: and if I am clearly right in escaping, then I will make the attempt; but if not, I will abstain. The other considerations which you mention, of money and loss of character and the duty of educating one's children, are, I fear, only the doctrines of the multitude, who would be as ready to restore people to life, if they were able, as they are to put them to death—and with as little reason. But now, since the argument has thus far prevailed, the only question which remains to be considered is, whether we shall do rightly either in escaping or in suffering others to aid in our escape and paying them in money and thanks, or whether in reality we shall not do rightly; and if the latter, then death or any other calamity which may ensue on my remaining here must not be allowed to enter into the calculation.

CRITO: I think that you are right, Socrates; how then shall we proceed?

SOCRATES: Let us consider the matter together, and do you either refute me if you can, and I will be convinced; or else cease, my dear friend, from repeating to me that I ought to escape against the wishes of the Athenians: for I highly value your attempts to persuade me to do so, but I may not be persuaded against my own better judgment. And now please to consider my first position, and try how you can best answer me.

CRITO: I will.

SOCRATES: Are we to say that we are never intentionally to do wrong, or that in one way we ought and in another way we ought not to do wrong, or is doing wrong always evil and dishonorable, as I was just now saying, and as has been already acknowledged by us? Are all our former admissions which were made within a few days to be thrown away? And have we, at our age, been earnestly discoursing with one another all our life long only to discover that we are no better than children? Or, in spite of the opinion of the many, and in spite of consequences whether better or worse, shall we insist on the truth of what was then said, that injustice is always an evil and dishonor to him who acts unjustly? Shall we say so or not?

CRITO: Yes.

SOCRATES: Then we must do no wrong?

CRITO: Certainly not.
SOCRATES: Nor when injured injure in return, as the many imagine; for we must injure no one at all? (E.g. compare Rep.)
CRITO: Clearly not.
SOCRATES: Again, Crito, may we do evil?
CRITO: Surely not, Socrates.
SOCRATES: And what of doing evil in return for evil, which is the morality of the many—is that just or not?
CRITO: Not just.
SOCRATES: For doing evil to another is the same as injuring him?
CRITO: Very true.
SOCRATES: Then we ought not to retaliate or render evil for evil to anyone, whatever evil we may have suffered from him. But I would have you consider, Crito, whether you really mean what you are saying. For this opinion has never been held, and never will be held, by any considerable number of persons; and those who are agreed and those who are not agreed upon this point have no common ground, and can only despise one another when they see how widely they differ. Tell me, then, whether you agree with and assent to my first principle, that neither injury nor retaliation nor warding off evil by evil is ever right. And shall that be the premise of our argument? Or do you decline and dissent from this? For so I have ever thought, and continue to think; but, if you are of another opinion, let me hear what you have to say. If, however, you remain of the same mind as formerly, I will proceed to the next step.
CRITO: You may proceed, for I have not changed my mind.
SOCRATES: Then I will go on to the next point, which may be put in the form of a question: Ought a man to do what he admits to be right, or ought he to betray the right?
CRITO: He ought to do what he thinks right.
SOCRATES: But if this is true, what is the application? In leaving the prison against the will of the Athenians, do I wrong any? or rather do I not wrong those whom I ought least to wrong? Do I not desert the principles which were acknowledged by us to be just—what do you say?
CRITO: I cannot tell, Socrates, for I do not know.
SOCRATES: Then consider the matter in this way: Imagine that I am about to play truant (you may call the proceeding by any name which you like), and the laws and the government come and interrogate me: "Tell us, Socrates," they say, "what are you about? Are you not going by an act of yours to overturn us—the laws, and the whole state, as far as in you lies?

Do you imagine that a state can subsist and not be overthrown, in which the decisions of law have no power, but are set aside and trampled upon by individuals?" What will be our answer, Crito, to these and the like words? Anyone, and especially a rhetorician, will have a good deal to say on behalf of the law which requires a sentence to be carried out. He will argue that this law should not be set aside; and shall we reply, "Yes; but the state has injured us and given an unjust sentence." Suppose I say that?
CRITO: Very good, Socrates.
SOCRATES: "And was that our agreement with you?" the law would answer, "or were you to abide by the sentence of the state?" And if I were to express my astonishment at their words, the law would probably add: "Answer, Socrates, instead of opening your eyes—you are in the habit of asking and answering questions. Tell us, what complaint have you to make against us which justifies you in attempting to destroy us and the state? In the first place did we not bring you into existence? Your father married your mother by our aid and begat you. Say whether you have any objection to urge against those of us who regulate marriage?" None, I should reply. "Or against those of us who after birth regulate the nurture and education of children, in which you also were trained? Were not the laws, which have the charge of education, right in commanding your father to train you in music and gymnastic?" Right, I should reply. "Well then, since you were brought into the world and nurtured and educated by us, can you deny in the first place that you are our child and slave, as your fathers were before you? And if this is true you are not on equal terms with us; nor can you think that you have a right to do to us what we are doing to you. Would you have any right to strike or revile or do any other evil to your father or your master, if you had one, because you have been struck or reviled by him, or received some other evil at his hands? You would not say this? And because we think right to destroy you, do you think that you have any right to destroy us in return, and your country as far as in you lies? Will you, O professor of true virtue, pretend that you are justified in this? Has a philosopher like you failed to discover that our country is more to be valued and higher and holier far than mother or father or any ancestor, and more to be regarded in the eyes of the gods and of men of understanding? Also to be soothed, and gently and reverently entreated when angry, even more than a father, and either to be persuaded, or if not persuaded, to be obeyed? And when we are punished by her, whether with imprisonment or stripes, the punishment is to be endured in silence; and if she lead us to wounds or death in battle, thither we follow as is right; neither may anyone yield or

retreat or leave his rank, but whether in battle or in a court of law, or in any other place, he must do what his city and his country order him; or he must change their view of what is just: and if he may do no violence to his father or mother, much less may he do violence to his country." What answer shall we make to this, Crito? Do the laws speak truly, or do they not?

CRITO: I think that they do.

SOCRATES: Then the laws will say: "Consider, Socrates, if we are speaking truly that in your present attempt you are going to do us an injury. For, having brought you into the world, and nurtured and educated you, and given you and every other citizen a share in every good which we had to give, we further proclaim to any Athenian by the liberty which we allow him, that if he does not like us when he has become of age and has seen the ways of the city, and made our acquaintance, he may go where he pleases and take his goods with him. None of us laws will forbid him or interfere with him. Anyone who does not like us and the city, and who wants to emigrate to a colony or to any other city, may go where he likes, retaining his property. But he who has experience of the manner in which we order justice and administer the state, and still remains, has entered into an implied contract that he will do as we command him. And he who disobeys us is, as we maintain, thrice wrong: first, because in disobeying us he is disobeying his parents; secondly, because we are the authors of his education; thirdly, because he has made an agreement with us that he will duly obey our commands; and he neither obeys them nor convinces us that our commands are unjust; and we do not rudely impose them, but give him the alternative of obeying or convincing us; that is what we offer, and he does neither.

"These are the sort of accusations to which, as we were saying, you, Socrates, will be exposed if you accomplish your intentions; you, above all other Athenians." Suppose now I ask, why I rather than anybody else? They will justly retort upon me that I above all other men have acknowledged the agreement. "There is clear proof," they will say, "Socrates, that we and the city were not displeasing to you. Of all Athenians you have been the most constant resident in the city, which, as you never leave, you may be supposed to love (compare Phaedr.). For you never went out of the city either to see the games, except once when you went to the Isthmus, or to any other place unless when you were on military service; nor did you travel as other men do. Nor had you any curiosity to know other states or their laws: Your affections did not go beyond us and our state; we were your especial favorites, and you acquiesced in our government of you; and here in this city you begat your children, which is a proof of your satisfaction. Moreover, you might in the course of the trial, if you had liked, have fixed the penalty at banishment; the state which refuses to let you go now would have let you go then. But you pretended that you preferred death to exile (compare Apol.), and that you were not unwilling to die. And now you have forgotten these fine sentiments, and pay no respect to us the laws, of whom you are the destroyer; and are doing what only a miserable slave would do, running away and turning your back upon the compacts and agreements which you made as a citizen. And first of all answer this very question: Are we right in saying that you agreed to be governed according to us in deed, and not in word only? Is that true or not?" How shall we answer, Crito? Must we not assent?

CRITO: We cannot help it, Socrates.

SOCRATES: Then will they not say: "You, Socrates, are breaking the covenants and agreements which you made with us at your leisure, not in any haste or under any compulsion or deception, but after you have had seventy years to think of them, during which time you were at liberty to leave the city, if we were not to your mind, or if our covenants appeared to you to be unfair. You had your choice, and might have gone either to Lacedaemon or Crete, both which states are often praised by you for their good government, or to some other Hellenic or foreign state. Whereas you, above all other Athenians, seemed to be so fond of the state, or, in other words, of us her laws (and who would care about a state which has no laws?), that you never stirred out of her; the halt, the blind, the maimed, were not more stationary in her than you were. And now you run away and forsake your agreements. Not so, Socrates, if you will take our advice; do not make yourself ridiculous by escaping out of the city.

"For just consider, if you transgress and err in this sort of way, what good will you do either to yourself or to your friends? That your friends will be driven into exile and deprived of citizenship, or will lose their property, is tolerably certain; and you yourself, if you fly to one of the neighboring cities, as, for example, Thebes or Megara, both of which are well governed, will come to them as an enemy, Socrates, and their government will be against you, and all patriotic citizens will cast an evil eye upon you as a subverter of the laws, and you will confirm in the minds of the judges the justice of their own condemnation of you. For he who is a corrupter of the laws is more than likely to be a corrupter of the young and foolish portion of mankind. Will you then flee from well-ordered cities and virtuous men? and is existence worth having on these terms? Or will you go to them without shame, and talk to them, Socrates? And what will you say to them? What you say here about virtue and justice and institutions and laws being the best things among men? Would that be decent of you? Surely not. But if you go away from well-governed states to Crito's friends in Thessaly, where there is great disorder and licence, they will be charmed to hear the tale of your escape from prison, set off with ludicrous particulars of the manner in which you were wrapped in a goatskin or some other disguise, and metamorphosed as the manner is of runaways; but will there be no one to remind you that in your old age you were not ashamed to violate the most sacred laws from a miserable desire of a little more life? Perhaps not, if you keep them in a good temper; but if they are out of temper you will hear many degrading things; you will live, but how? as the flatterer of all men, and the servant of all men; and doing what? eating and drinking in Thessaly, having gone abroad in order that you may get a dinner. And where will be your fine sentiments about justice and virtue? Say that you wish to live for the sake of your children—you want to bring them up and educate them—will you take them into Thessaly and deprive them of Athenian citizenship? Is this the benefit which you will confer upon them? Or are you under the impression that they will be better cared for and educated here if you are still alive, although absent from them; for your friends will take care of them? Do you fancy that if you are an inhabitant of Thessaly they will take care of them, and if you are an inhabitant of the other world that they will not take care of them? Nay; but if they who call themselves friends are good for anything, they will—to be sure they will.

"Listen, then, Socrates, to us who have brought you up. Think not of life and children first, and of justice afterward, but of justice first, that you may be justified before the princes of the world below. For neither will you nor any that belong to you be happier or holier or juster in this life, or happier in another, if you do as Crito bids. Now you depart in innocence, a sufferer and not a doer of evil; a victim, not of the laws, but of men. But if you go forth, returning evil for evil, and injury for injury, breaking the covenants and agreements which you have made with us, and wronging those whom you ought least of all to wrong, that is to say, yourself, your friends, your country, and us, we shall be angry with you while you live, and our brethren, the laws in the world below, will receive you as an enemy; for they will know that you have done your best to destroy us. Listen, then, to us and not to Crito."

This, dear Crito, is the voice which I seem to hear murmuring in my ears, like the sound of the flute in the ears of the mystic; that voice, I say, is humming in my ears, and prevents me from hearing any other. And I know that anything more which you may say will be vain. Yet speak, if you have anything to say.

CRITO: I have nothing to say, Socrates.

SOCRATES: Leave me then, Crito, to fulfill the will of God, and to follow whither he leads.

SYMPOSIUM

BY PLATO

Translated by Benjamin Jowett

INTRODUCTION

Of all the works of Plato the Symposium is the most perfect in form, and may be truly thought to contain more than any commentator has ever dreamed of; or, as Goethe said of one of his own writings, more than the author himself knew. For in philosophy as in prophecy glimpses of the future may often be conveyed in words which could hardly have been understood or interpreted at the time when they were uttered (compare Symp.)—which were wiser than the writer of them meant, and could not have been expressed by him if he had been interrogated about them. Yet Plato was not a mystic, nor in any degree affected by the Eastern influences which afterward overspread the Alexandrian world. He was not an enthusiast or a sentimentalist, but one who aspired only to see reasoned truth, and whose thoughts are clearly explained in his language. There is no foreign element either of Egypt or of Asia to be found in his writings. And more than any other Platonic work the Symposium is Greek both in style and subject, having a beauty "as of a statue," while the companion Dialogue of the Phaedrus is marked by a sort of Gothic irregularity. More too than in any other of his Dialogues, Plato is emancipated from former philosophies. The genius of Greek art seems to triumph over the traditions of Pythagorean, Eleatic, or Megarian systems, and "the old quarrel of poetry and philosophy" has at least a superficial reconcilement. (Rep.)

An unknown person who had heard of the discourses in praise of love spoken by Socrates and others at the banquet of Agathon is desirous of having an authentic account of them, which he thinks that he can obtain from Apollodorus, the same excitable, or rather "mad" friend of Socrates, who is afterward introduced in the Phaedo. He had imagined that the discourses were recent. There he is mistaken: but they are still fresh in the memory of his informant, who had just been repeating them to Glaucon, and is quite prepared to have another rehearsal of them in a walk from the Piraeus to Athens. Although he had not been present himself, he had heard them from the best authority. Aristodemus, who is described as having been in past times a humble but inseparable attendant of Socrates, had reported them to him (compare Xen. Mem.).

The narrative which he had heard was as follows:

Aristodemus meeting Socrates in holiday attire, is invited by him to a banquet at the house of Agathon, who had been sacrificing in thanksgiving for his tragic victory on the day previous. But no sooner has he entered the house than he finds that he is alone; Socrates has stayed behind in a fit of abstraction, and does not appear until the banquet is half over. On his appearing he and the host jest a little; the question is then asked by Pausanias, one of the guests, "What shall they do about drinking? As they had been all well drunk on the day before, and drinking on two successive days is such a bad thing." This is confirmed by the authority of Eryximachus the physician, who further proposes that instead of listening to the flute girl and her "noise" they shall make speeches in honor of love, one after another, going from left to right in the order in which they are reclining at the table. All of them agree to this proposal, and Phaedrus, who is the "father" of the idea, which he has previously communicated to Eryximachus, begins as follows:

He descants first of all upon the antiquity of love, which is proved by the authority of the poets; secondly upon the benefits which love gives to man. The greatest of these is the sense of honor and dishonor. The lover is ashamed to be seen by the beloved doing or suffering any cowardly or mean act. And a state or army which was made up only of lovers and their loves would be invincible. For love will convert the veriest coward into an inspired hero.

And there have been true loves not only of men but of women also. Such was the love of Alcestis, who dared to die for her husband, and in recompense of her virtue was allowed to come again from the dead. But Orpheus, the miserable harper, who went down to Hades alive, that he might bring back his wife, was mocked with an apparition only, and the gods afterward contrived his death as the punishment of his cowardliness. The love of Achilles, like that of Alcestis, was courageous and true; for he was willing to avenge his lover Patroclus, although he knew that his own death would immediately follow; and the gods, who honor the love of the beloved above that of the lover, rewarded him, and sent him to the islands of the blessed.

Pausanias, who was sitting next, then takes up the tale: He says that Phaedrus should have distinguished the heavenly love from the earthly, before he praised either. For there are two loves, as there are two Aphrodites—one the daughter of Uranus, who has no mother and is the elder and wiser goddess, and the other, the daughter of Zeus and Dione, who is popular and common. The first of the two loves has a noble purpose, and delights only in the intelligent nature of man, and is faithful to the end, and has no shadow of wantonness or lust. The second is the coarser kind of love, which is a love of the body rather than of the soul, and is of women and boys as well as of men. Now the actions of lovers vary, like every other sort of action, according to the manner of their performance. And in different countries there is a difference of opinion about male loves. Some, like the Boeotians, approve of them; others, like the Ionians, and most of the barbarians, disapprove of them; partly because they are aware of the political dangers which ensue from them, as may be seen in the instance of Harmodius and Aristogeiton. At Athens and Sparta there is an apparent contradiction about them. For at times they are encouraged, and then the lover is allowed to play all sorts of fantastic tricks; he may swear and forswear himself (and "at lovers" perjuries they say Jove laughs); he may be a servant, and lie on a mat at the door of his love, without any loss of character; but there are also times when elders look grave and guard their young relations, and personal remarks are made. The truth is that some of these loves are disgraceful and others honorable. The vulgar love of the body which takes wing and flies away when the bloom of youth is over, is disgraceful, and so is the interested love of power or wealth; but the love of the noble mind is lasting. The lover should be tested, and the beloved should not be too ready to yield. The rule in our country is that the beloved may do the same service to the lover in the way of virtue which the lover may do to him.

A voluntary service to be rendered for the sake of virtue and wisdom is permitted among us; and when these two customs—one the love of youth, the other the practice of virtue and philosophy—meet in one, then the lovers may lawfully unite. Nor is there any disgrace to a disinterested lover in being deceived; but the interested lover is doubly disgraced, for if he loses his love he loses his character; whereas the noble love of the other remains the same, although the object of his love is unworthy: For nothing can be nobler than love for the sake of virtue. This is that love of the heavenly goddess which is of great price to individuals and cities, making them work together for their improvement.

The turn of Aristophanes comes next; but he has the hiccups, and therefore proposes that Eryximachus the physician shall cure him or speak in his turn. Eryximachus is ready to do both, and after prescribing for the hiccups, speaks as follows:

He agrees with Pausanias in maintaining that there are two kinds of love; but his art has led him to the further conclusion that the empire of this double love extends over all things, and is to be found in animals and plants as well as in man. In the human body also there are two loves; and the art of medicine shows which is the good and which is the bad love, and persuades the body to accept the good and reject the bad, and reconciles conflicting elements and makes them friends. Every art, gymnastic and husbandry as well as medicine, is the reconciliation of opposites; and this is what Heracleitus meant, when he spoke of a harmony of opposites: but in strictness he should rather have spoken of a harmony which succeeds opposites, for an agreement of disagreements there cannot be. Music too is concerned with the principles of love in their application to harmony and rhythm. In the abstract, all is simple, and we are not troubled with the twofold love; but when they are applied in education with their accompaniments of song and meter, then the discord begins. Then the old tale has to be repeated of fair Urania and the coarse Polyhymnia, who must be indulged sparingly, just as in my own art of medicine care must be taken that the taste of the epicure be gratified without inflicting upon him the attendant penalty of disease.

There is a similar harmony or disagreement in the course of the seasons and in the relations of moist and dry, hot and cold, hoar frost and blight; and diseases of all sorts spring from the excesses or disorders of the element of love. The knowledge of these elements of love and discord in the heavenly bodies is termed astronomy, in the relations of men toward gods and parents is called divination. For divination is the peacemaker of gods and men, and works by a knowledge of the tendencies of merely human loves to piety and impiety. Such is the power of love; and that love which is just and temperate has the greatest power, and is the source of all our happiness and friendship with the gods and with one another. I dare say that I have omitted to mention many things which you, Aristophanes, may supply, as I perceive that you are cured of the hiccups.

Aristophanes is the next speaker:

He professes to open a new vein of discourse, in which he begins by treating of the origin of human nature. The sexes were originally three, men, women, and the union of the two; and they were made round—having four hands, four feet, two faces on a round neck, and the rest to correspond. Terrible was their strength and swiftness; and they were essaying to scale heaven and attack the gods. Doubt reigned in the celestial councils; the gods were divided between the desire of quelling the pride of man and the fear of losing the sacrifices. At last Zeus hit upon an expedient. Let us cut them in two, he said; then they will only have half their strength, and we shall have twice as many sacrifices. He spake, and split them as you might split an egg with a hair; and when this was done, he told Apollo to give their faces a twist and re-arrange their persons, taking out the wrinkles and tying the skin in a knot about the navel. The two halves went about looking for one another, and were ready to die of hunger in one another's arms. Then Zeus invented an adjustment of the sexes, which enabled them to marry and go their way to the business of life. Now the characters of men differ accordingly as they are derived from the original man or the original woman, or the original man-woman. Those who come from the man-woman are lascivious and adulterous; those who come from the woman form female attachments; those who are a section of the male follow the male and embrace him, and in him all their desires center. The pair are inseparable and live together in pure and manly affection; yet they cannot tell what they want of one another. But if Hephaestus were to come to them with his instruments and propose that they should be melted into one and remain one here and hereafter, they would acknowledge that this was the very expression of their want. For love is the desire of the whole, and the pursuit of the whole is called love. There was a time when the two sexes were only one, but now God has halved them—much as the Lacedaemonians have cut up the Arcadians—and if they do not behave themselves he will divide them again, and they will hop about with half a nose and face in basso relievo. Wherefore let us exhort all men to piety, that we may obtain the goods of which love is the author, and be reconciled to God, and find our own true loves, which rarely happens in this world. And now I must beg you not to suppose that I am alluding to Pausanias and Agathon (compare Protag.), for my words refer to all mankind everywhere.

 Some raillery ensues first between Aristophanes and Eryximachus, and then between Agathon, who fears a few select friends more than any number of spectators at the theatre, and Socrates, who is disposed to begin an argument. This is speedily repressed by Phaedrus, who reminds the disputants of their tribute to the god. Agathon's speech follows:

He will speak of the god first and then of his gifts: He is the fairest and blessedest and best of the gods, and also the youngest, having had no existence in the old days of Iapetus and Cronos when the gods were at war. The things that were done then were done of necessity and not of love. For love is young and dwells in soft places,—not like Ate in Homer, walking on the skulls of men, but in their hearts and souls, which are soft enough. He is all flexibility and grace, and his habitation is among the flowers, and he cannot do or suffer wrong; for all men serve and obey him of their own free will, and where there is love there is obedience, and where obedience, there is justice; for none can be wronged of his own free will. And he is temperate as well as just, for he is the ruler of the desires, and if he rules them he must be temperate. Also he is courageous, for he is the conqueror of the lord of war. And he is wise too; for he is a poet, and the author of poesy in others. He created the animals; he is the inventor of the arts; all the gods are his subjects; he is the fairest and best himself, and the cause of what is fairest and best in others; he makes men to be of one mind at a banquet, filling them with affection and emptying them of disaffection; the pilot, helper, defender, savior of men, in whose footsteps let every man follow, chanting a strain of love. Such is the discourse, half playful, half serious, which I dedicate to the god.

The turn of Socrates comes next. He begins by remarking satirically that he has not understood the terms of the original agreement, for he fancied that they meant to speak the true praises of love, but now he finds that they only say what is good of him, whether true or false. He begs to be absolved from speaking falsely, but he is willing to speak the truth, and proposes to begin by questioning Agathon. The result of his questions may be summed up as follows:

Love is of something, and that which love desires is not that which love is or has; for no man desires that which he is or has. And love is of the beautiful, and therefore has not the beautiful. And the beautiful is the good, and therefore, in wanting and desiring the beautiful, love also wants and desires the good. Socrates professes to have asked the same questions and to have obtained the same answers from Diotima, a wise woman of Mantinea, who, like Agathon, had spoken first of love and then of his works. Socrates, like Agathon, had told her that Love is a mighty god and also fair, and she had shown him in return that Love was neither, but in a mean between fair and foul, good and evil, and not a god at all, but only a great demon or intermediate power (compare the speech of Eryximachus) who conveys to the gods the prayers of men, and to men the commands of the gods.

Socrates asks: Who are his father and mother? To this Diotima replies that he is the son of Plenty and Poverty, and partakes of the nature of both, and is full and starved by turns. Like his mother he is poor and squalid, lying on mats at doors (compare the speech of Pausanias); like his father he is bold and strong, and full of arts and resources. Further, he is in a mean between ignorance and knowledge:—in this he resembles the philosopher who is also in a mean between the wise and the ignorant. Such is the nature of Love, who is not to be confused with the beloved.

But Love desires the beautiful; and then arises the question, What does he desire of the beautiful? He desires, of course, the possession of the beautiful; but what is given by that? For the beautiful let us substitute the good, and we have no difficulty in seeing the possession of the good to be happiness, and Love to be the desire of happiness, although the meaning of the word has been too often confined to one kind of love. And Love desires not only the good, but the everlasting possession of the good. Why then is there all this flutter and excitement about love? Because all men and women at a certain age are desirous of bringing to the birth. And love is not of beauty only, but of birth in beauty; this is the principle of immortality in a mortal creature. When beauty approaches, then the conceiving power is benign and diffuse; when foulness, she is averted and morose.

But why again does this extend not only to men but also to animals? Because they too have an instinct of immortality. Even in the same individual there is a perpetual succession as well of the parts of the material body as of the thoughts and desires of the mind; nay, even knowledge comes and goes. There is no sameness of existence, but the new mortality is always taking the place of the old. This is the reason why parents love their children—for the sake of immortality; and this is why men love the immortality of fame. For the creative soul creates not children, but conceptions of wisdom and virtue, such as poets and other creators have invented. And the noblest creations of all are those of legislators, in honor of whom temples have been raised. Who would not sooner have these children of the mind than the ordinary human ones? (Compare Bacon's Essays, 8: "Certainly the best works and of greatest merit for the public have proceeded from the unmarried or childless men; which both in affection and means have married and endowed the public.")

I will now initiate you, she said, into the greater mysteries; for he who would proceed in due course should love first one fair form, and then many, and learn the connection of them; and from beautiful bodies he should proceed to beautiful minds, and the beauty of laws and institutions, until he perceives that all beauty is of one kindred; and from institutions he should go on to the sciences, until at last the vision is revealed to him of a single science of universal beauty, and then he will behold the everlasting nature which is the cause of all, and will be near the end. In the contemplation of that supreme being of love he will be purified of earthly leaven, and will behold beauty, not with the bodily eye, but with the eye of the mind, and will bring forth true creations of virtue and wisdom, and be the friend of God and heir of immortality.

Such, Phaedrus, is the tale which I heard from the stranger of Mantinea, and which you may call the encomium of love, or what you please.

The company applaud the speech of Socrates, and Aristophanes is about to say something, when suddenly a band of revellers breaks into the court, and the voice of Alcibiades is heard asking for Agathon. He is led in drunk, and welcomed by Agathon, whom he has come to crown with a garland. He is placed on a couch at his side, but suddenly, on recognizing Socrates, he starts up, and a sort of conflict is carried on between them, which Agathon is requested to appease. Alcibiades then insists that they shall drink, and has a large wine-cooler filled, which he first empties himself, and then fills again and passes on to Socrates. He is informed of the nature of the entertainment; and is ready to join, if only in the character of a drunken and disappointed lover he may be allowed to sing the praises of Socrates:

He begins by comparing Socrates first to the busts of Silenus, which have images of the gods inside them; and, secondly, to Marsyas the flute player. For Socrates produces the same effect with the voice which Marsyas did with the flute. He is the great speaker and enchanter who ravishes the souls of men; the convincer of hearts too, as he has convinced Alcibiades, and made him ashamed of his mean and miserable life. Socrates at one time seemed about to fall in love with him; and he thought that he would thereby gain a wonderful opportunity of receiving lessons of wisdom. He narrates the failure of his design. He has suffered agonies from him, and is at his wit's end. He then proceeds to mention some other particulars of the life of Socrates; how they were at Potidaea together, where Socrates showed his superior powers of enduring cold and fatigue; how on one occasion he had stood for an entire day and night absorbed in reflection amid the wonder of the spectators; how on another occasion he had saved Alcibiades's life; how at the battle of Delium, after the defeat, he might be seen stalking about like a pelican, rolling his eyes as Aristophanes had described him in the Clouds. He is the most wonderful of human beings, and absolutely unlike anyone but a satyr. Like the satyr in his language too; for he uses the commonest words as the outward mask of the divinest truths.

When Alcibiades has done speaking, a dispute begins between him and Agathon and Socrates. Socrates piques Alcibiades by a pretended affection for Agathon. Presently a band of revellers appears, who introduce disorder into the feast; the sober part of the company, Eryximachus, Phaedrus, and others, withdraw; and Aristodemus, the follower of Socrates, sleeps during the whole of a long winter's night. When he wakes at cockcrow the revellers are nearly all asleep. Only Socrates, Aristophanes, and Agathon hold out; they are drinking from a large goblet, which they pass round, and Socrates is explaining to the two others, who are half-asleep, that the genius of tragedy is the same as that of comedy, and that the writer of tragedy ought to be a writer of comedy also. And first Aristophanes drops, and then, as the day is dawning, Agathon. Socrates, having laid them to rest, takes a bath and goes to his daily avocations until the evening. Aristodemus follows.

* * * * *

If it be true that there are more things in the Symposium of Plato than any commentator has dreamed of, it is also true that many things have been imagined which are not really to be found there. Some writings hardly admit of a more distinct interpretation than a musical composition; and every reader may form his own accompaniment of thought or feeling to the strain which he hears. The Symposium of Plato is a work of this character, and can with difficulty be rendered in any words but the writer's own. There are so many half-lights and cross-lights, so much of the color of mythology, and of the manner of sophistry adhering—rhetoric and poetry, the playful and the serious, are so subtly intermingled in it, and vestiges of old philosophy so curiously blend with germs of future knowledge, that agreement among interpreters is not to be expected. The expression "poema magis putandum quam comicorum poetarum," which has been applied to all the writings of Plato, is especially applicable to the Symposium.

The power of love is represented in the Symposium as running through all nature and all being: at one end descending to animals and plants, and attaining to the highest vision of truth at the other. In an age when man was seeking for an expression of the world around him, the conception of love greatly affected him. One of the first distinctions of language and of mythology was that of gender; and at a later period the ancient physicist, anticipating modern science, saw, or thought that he saw, a sex in plants; there were elective affinities among the elements, marriages of earth and heaven. (Aesch. Frag. Dan.) Love became a mythic personage whom philosophy, borrowing from poetry, converted into an efficient cause of creation. The traces of the existence of love, as of number and figure, were everywhere discerned; and in the Pythagorean list of opposites male and female were ranged side by side with odd and even, finite and infinite.

But Plato seems also to be aware that there is a mystery of love in man as well as in nature, extending beyond the mere immediate relation of the sexes. He is conscious that the highest and noblest things in the world are not easily severed from the sensual desires, or may even be regarded as a spiritualized form of them. We may observe that Socrates himself is not represented as originally unimpassioned, but as one who has overcome his passions; the secret of his power over others partly lies in his passionate but self-controlled nature. In the Phaedrus and Symposium love is not merely the feeling usually so called, but the mystical contemplation of the beautiful and the good. The same passion which may wallow in the mire is capable of rising to the loftiest heights—of penetrating the inmost secret of philosophy. The highest love is the love not of a person, but of the highest and purest abstraction. This abstraction is the far-off heaven on which the eye of the mind is fixed in fond amazement. The unity of truth, the consistency of the warring elements of the world, the enthusiasm for knowledge when first beaming upon mankind, the relativity of ideas to the human mind, and of the human mind to ideas, the faith in the invisible, the adoration of the eternal nature, are all included, consciously or unconsciously, in Plato's doctrine of love.

The successive speeches in praise of love are characteristic of the speakers, and contribute in various degrees to the final result; they are all designed to prepare the way for Socrates, who gathers up the threads anew, and skims the highest points of each of them. But they are not to be regarded as the stages of an idea, rising above one another to a climax. They are fanciful, partly facetious performances, "yet also having a certain measure of seriousness," which the successive speakers dedicate to the god. All of them are rhetorical and poetical rather than dialectical, but glimpses of truth appear in them. When Eryximachus says that the principles of music are simple in themselves, but confused in their application, he touches lightly upon a difficulty which has troubled the moderns as well as the ancients in music, and may be extended to the other applied sciences.

That confusion begins in the concrete, was the natural feeling of a mind dwelling in the world of ideas. When Pausanias remarks that personal attachments are inimical to despots. The experience of Greek history confirms the truth of his remark. When Aristophanes declares that love is the desire of the whole, he expresses a feeling not unlike that of the German philosopher, who says that "philosophy is home sickness." When Agathon says that no man "can be wronged of his own free will," he is alluding playfully to a serious problem of Greek philosophy (compare Arist. Nic. Ethics). So naturally does Plato mingle jest and earnest, truth and opinion in the same work.

The characters—of Phaedrus, who has been the cause of more philosophical discussions than any other man, with the exception of Simmias the Theban (Phaedrus); of Aristophanes, who disguises under comic imagery a serious purpose; of Agathon, who in later life is satirized by Aristophanes in the Thesmophoriazusae, for his effeminate manners and the feeble rhythms of his verse; of Alcibiades, who is the same strange contrast of great powers and great vices, which meets us in history—are drawn to the life; and we may suppose the less-known characters of Pausanias and Eryximachus to be also true to the traditional recollection of them (compare Phaedr., Protag.; and compare Sympos. with Phaedr.). We may also remark that Aristodemus is called "the little" in Xenophon's Memorabilia (compare Symp.).

The speeches have been said to follow each other in pairs: Phaedrus and Pausanias being the ethical, Eryximachus and Aristophanes the physical speakers, while in Agathon and Socrates poetry and philosophy blend together. The speech of Phaedrus is also described as the mythological, that of Pausanias as the political, that of Eryximachus as the scientific, that of Aristophanes as the artistic (!), that of Socrates as the philosophical. But these and similar distinctions are not found in Plato; they are the points of view of his critics, and seem to impede rather than to assist us in understanding him.

When the turn of Socrates comes round he cannot be allowed to disturb the arrangement made at first. With the leave of Phaedrus he asks a few questions, and then he throws his argument into the form of a speech (compare Gorg., Protag.). But his speech is really the narrative of a dialogue between himself and Diotima. And as at a banquet good manners would not allow him to win a victory either over his host or any of the guests, the superiority which he gains over Agathon is ingeniously represented as having been already gained over himself by her. The artifice has the further advantage of maintaining his accustomed profession of ignorance (compare Menex.). Even his knowledge of the mysteries of love, to which he lays claim here and elsewhere (Lys.), is given by Diotima.

The speeches are attested to us by the very best authority. The madman Apollodorus, who for three years past has made a daily study of the actions of Socrates—to whom the world is summed up in the words "Great is Socrates"—he has heard them from another "madman," Aristodemus, who was the "shadow" of Socrates in days of old, like him going about barefooted, and who had been present at the time. "Would you desire better witness?" The extraordinary narrative of Alcibiades is ingeniously represented as admitted by Socrates, whose silence when he is invited to contradict gives consent to the narrator. We may observe, by the way, (1) how the very appearance of Aristodemus by himself is a sufficient indication to Agathon that Socrates has been left behind; also, (2) how the courtesy of Agathon anticipates the excuse which Socrates was to have made on Aristodemus's behalf for coming uninvited; (3) how the story of the fit or trance of Socrates is confirmed by the mention which Alcibiades makes of a similar fit of abstraction occurring when he was serving with the army at Potidaea; like (4) the drinking powers of Socrates and his love of the fair, which receive a similar attestation in the concluding scene; or the attachment of Aristodemus, who is not forgotten when Socrates takes his departure. (5) We may notice the manner in which Socrates himself regards the first five speeches, not as true, but as fanciful and exaggerated encomiums of the god Love; (6) the satirical character of them, shown especially in the appeals to mythology, in the reasons which are given by Zeus for reconstructing the frame of man, or by the Boeotians and Eleans for encouraging male loves; (7) the ruling passion of Socrates for dialectics, who will argue with Agathon instead of making a speech, and will only speak at all upon the condition that he is allowed to speak the truth. We may note also the touch of Socratic irony, (8) which admits of a wide application and reveals a deep insight into the world: that in speaking of holy things and persons there is a general understanding that you should praise them, not that you should speak the truth about them—this is the sort of praise which Socrates is unable to give. Lastly, (9) we may remark that the banquet is a real banquet after all, at which love is the theme of discourse, and huge quantities of wine are drunk.

The discourse of Phaedrus is half-mythical, half-ethical; and he himself, true to the character which is given him in the Dialogue bearing his name, is half-sophist, half-enthusiast. He is the critic of poetry also, who compares

Homer and Aeschylus in the insipid and irrational manner of the schools of the day, characteristically reasoning about the probability of matters which do not admit of reasoning. He starts from a noble text: "That without the sense of honor and dishonor neither states nor individuals ever do any good or great work." But he soon passes on to more common-place topics. The antiquity of love, the blessing of having a lover, the incentive which love offers to daring deeds, the examples of Alcestis and Achilles, are the chief themes of his discourse. The love of women is regarded by him as almost on an equality with that of men; and he makes the singular remark that the gods favor the return of love which is made by the beloved more than the original sentiment, because the lover is of a nobler and diviner nature.

There is something of a sophistical ring in the speech of Phaedrus, which recalls the first speech in imitation of Lysias, occurring in the Dialogue called the Phaedrus. This is still more marked in the speech of Pausanias which follows; and which is at once hyperlogical in form and also extremely confused and pedantic. Plato is attacking the logical feebleness of the sophists and rhetoricians, through their pupils, not forgetting by the way to satirize the monotonous and unmeaning rhythms which Prodicus and others were introducing into Attic prose (compare Protag.). Of course, he is "playing both sides of the game," as in the Gorgias and Phaedrus; but it is not necessary in order to understand him that we should discuss the fairness of his mode of proceeding. The love of Pausanias for Agathon has already been touched upon in the Protagoras, and is alluded to by Aristophanes. Hence he is naturally the upholder of male loves, which, like all the other affections or actions of men, he regards as varying according to the manner of their performance. Like the sophists and like Plato himself, though in a different sense, he begins his discussion by an appeal to mythology, and distinguishes between the elder and younger love. The value which he attributes to such loves as motives to virtue and philosophy is at variance with modern and Christian notions, but is in accordance with Hellenic sentiment. The opinion of Christendom has not altogether condemned passionate friendships between persons of the same sex, but has certainly not encouraged them, because though innocent in themselves in a few temperaments they are liable to degenerate into fearful evil. Pausanias is very earnest in the defense of such loves; and he speaks of them as generally approved among Hellenes and disapproved by barbarians. His speech is "more words than matter," and might have been composed by a pupil of Lysias or of Prodicus, although there is no hint given that Plato is specially referring to them. As Eryximachus says, "he makes a fair beginning, but a lame ending."

Plato transposes the two next speeches, as in the Republic he would transpose the virtues and the mathematical sciences. This is done partly to avoid monotony, partly for the sake of making Aristophanes "the cause of wit in others," and also in order to bring the comic and tragic poet into juxtaposition, as if by accident. A suitable "expectation" of Aristophanes is raised by the ludicrous circumstance of his having the hiccups, which is appropriately cured by his substitute, the physician Eryximachus. To Eryximachus Love is the good physician; he sees everything as an intelligent physicist, and, like many professors of his art in modern times, attempts to reduce the moral to the physical; or recognizes one law of love which pervades them both. There are loves and strifes of the body as well as of the mind. Like Hippocrates the Asclepiad, he is a disciple of Heracleitus, whose conception of the harmony of opposites he explains in a new way as the harmony after discord; to his common sense, as to that of many moderns as well as ancients, the identity of contradictories is an absurdity. His notion of love may be summed up as the harmony of man with himself in soul as well as body, and of all things in heaven and earth with one another.

Aristophanes is ready to laugh and make laugh before he opens his mouth, just as Socrates, true to his character, is ready to argue before he begins to speak. He expresses the very genius of the old comedy, its coarse and forcible imagery, and the licence of its language in speaking about the gods. He has no sophistical notions about love, which is brought back by him to its common-sense meaning of love between intelligent beings. His account of the origin of the sexes has the greatest (comic) probability and verisimilitude. Nothing in Aristophanes is more truly Aristophanic than the description of the human monster whirling round on four arms and four legs, eight in all, with incredible rapidity. Yet there is a mixture of earnestness in this jest; three serious principles seem to be insinuated—first, that man cannot exist in isolation, he must be reunited if he is to be perfected; secondly, that love is the mediator and reconciler of poor, divided human nature; thirdly, that the loves of this world are an indistinct anticipation of an ideal union which is not yet realized.

The speech of Agathon is conceived in a higher strain, and receives the real, if half-ironical, approval of Socrates. It is the speech of the tragic poet and a sort of poem, like tragedy, moving among the gods of Olympus, and not among the elder or Orphic deities. In the idea of the antiquity of love he cannot agree; love is not of the olden time, but present and youthful ever. The speech may be compared with that speech of Socrates in the Phaedrus in which he describes himself as talking dithyrambs. It is at once a preparation for Socrates and a foil to him. The rhetoric of Agathon elevates the soul to "sunlit heights," but at the same time contrasts with the natural and necessary eloquence of Socrates. Agathon contributes the distinction between love and the works of love, and also hints incidentally that love is always of beauty, which Socrates afterward raises into a principle. While the consciousness of discord is stronger in the comic poet Aristophanes, Agathon, the tragic poet, has a deeper sense of harmony and reconciliation, and speaks of Love as the creator and artist.

All the earlier speeches embody common opinions colored with a tinge of philosophy. They furnish the material out of which Socrates proceeds to form his discourse, starting, as in other places, from mythology and the opinions of men. From Phaedrus he takes the thought that love is stronger than death; from Pausanias, that the true love is akin to intellect and political activity; from Eryximachus, that love is a universal phenomenon and the great power of nature; from Aristophanes, that love is the child of want, and is not merely the love of the congenial or of the whole, but (as he adds) of the good; from Agathon, that love is of beauty, not however of beauty only, but of birth in beauty. As it would be out of character for Socrates to make a lengthened harangue, the speech takes the form of a dialogue between Socrates and a mysterious woman of foreign extraction. She elicits the final truth from one who knows nothing, and who, speaking by the lips of another, and himself a despiser of rhetoric, is proved also to be the most consummate of rhetoricians (compare Menexenus).

The last of the six discourses begins with a short argument which overthrows not only Agathon but all the preceding speakers by the help of a distinction which has escaped them. Extravagant praises have been ascribed to Love as the author of every good; no sort of encomium was too high for him, whether deserved and true or not. But Socrates has no talent for speaking anything but the truth, and if he is to speak the truth of Love he must honestly confess that he is not a good at all: for love is of the good, and no man can desire that which he has. This piece of dialectics is ascribed to Diotima, who has already urged upon Socrates the argument which he urges against Agathon. That the distinction is a fallacy is obvious; it is almost acknowledged to be so by Socrates himself. For he who has beauty or good may desire more of them; and he who has beauty or good in himself may desire beauty and good in others. The fallacy seems to arise out of a confusion between the abstract ideas of good and beauty, which do not admit of degrees, and their partial realization in individuals.

But Diotima, the prophetess of Mantineia, whose sacred and superhuman character raises her above the ordinary proprieties of women, has taught Socrates far more than this about the art and mystery of love. She has taught him that love is another aspect of philosophy. The same want in the human soul which is satisfied in the vulgar by the procreation of children, may become the highest aspiration of intellectual desire. As the Christian might speak of hungering and thirsting after righteousness; or of divine loves under the figure of human (compare Eph. "This is a great mystery, but I speak concerning Christ and the church"); as the medieval saint might speak of the "fruitio Dei"; as Dante saw all things contained in his love of Beatrice, so Plato would have us absorb all other loves and desires in the love of knowledge. Here is the beginning of Neoplatonism, or rather, perhaps, a proof (of which there are many) that the so-called mysticism of the East was not strange to the Greek of the fifth century before Christ. The first tumult of the affections was not wholly subdued; there were longings of a creature moving about in worlds not realized, which no art could satisfy. To most men reason and passion appear to be antagonistic both in idea and fact. The union of the greatest comprehension of knowledge and the burning intensity of love is a contradiction in nature, which may have existed in a far-off primeval age in the mind of some Hebrew prophet or other Eastern sage, but has now become an imagination only. Yet this "passion of the reason" is the theme of the Symposium of Plato. And as there is no impossibility in supposing that "one king, or son of a king, may be a philosopher," so also there is a probability that there may be some few—perhaps one or two in a whole generation—in whom the light of truth may not lack the warmth of desire. And if there be such natures, no one will be disposed to deny that "from them flow most of the benefits of individuals and states"; and even from imperfect combinations of the two elements in teachers or statesmen great good may often arise.

Yet there is a higher region in which love is not only felt, but satisfied, in the perfect beauty of eternal knowledge, beginning with the beauty of earthly things, and at last reaching a beauty in which all existence is seen to be harmonious and one. The limited affection is enlarged, and enabled to behold the ideal of all things. And here the highest summit which is reached in the Symposium is seen also to be the highest summit which is attained in the Republic, but approached from another side; and there is "a way upwards and downwards," which is the same and not the same in both.

The ideal beauty of the one is the ideal good of the other; regarded not with the eye of knowledge, but of faith and desire; and they are respectively the source of beauty and the source of good in all other things. And by the steps of a "ladder reaching to heaven" we pass from images of visible beauty (Greek), and from the hypotheses of the Mathematical sciences, which are not yet based upon the idea of good, through the concrete to the abstract, and, by different paths arriving, behold the vision of the eternal (compare Symp. (Greek) Republic (Greek) also Phaedrus). Under one aspect "the idea is love"; under another, "truth." In both the lover of wisdom is the "spectator of all time and of all existence." This is a "mystery" in which Plato also obscurely intimates the union of the spiritual and fleshly, the interpenetration of the moral and intellectual faculties.

The divine image of beauty which resides within Socrates has been revealed; the Silenus, or outward man, has now to be exhibited. The description of Socrates follows immediately after the speech of Socrates; one is the complement of the other. At the height of divine inspiration, when the force of nature can no further go, by way of contrast to this extreme idealism, Alcibiades, accompanied by a troop of revellers and a flute girl, staggers in, and being drunk is able to tell of things which he would have been ashamed to make known if he had been sober. The state of his affections toward Socrates, unintelligible to us and perverted as they appear, affords an illustration of the power ascribed to the loves of man in the speech of Pausanias. He does not suppose his feelings to be peculiar to himself: There are several other persons in the company who have been equally in love with Socrates, and like himself have been deceived by him. The singular part of this confession is the combination of the most degrading passion with the desire of virtue and improvement. Such a union is not wholly untrue to human nature, which is capable of combining good and evil in a degree beyond what we can easily conceive. In imaginative persons, especially, the God and beast in man seem to part asunder more than is natural in a well-regulated mind. The Platonic Socrates (for of the real Socrates this may be doubted—compare his public rebuke of Critias for his shameful love of Euthydemus in Xenophon, Memorabilia) does not regard the greatest evil of Greek life as a thing not to be spoken of; but it has a ridiculous element (Plato's Symp.), and is a subject for irony, no less than for moral reprobation (compare Plato's Symp.). It is also used as a figure of speech which no one interpreted literally (compare Xen. Symp.). Nor does Plato feel any repugnance, such as would be felt in modern times, at bringing his great master and hero into connection with nameless crimes. He is contented with representing him as a saint, who has won "the Olympian victory" over the temptations of human nature. The fault of taste, which to us is so glaring and which was recognized by the Greeks of a later age (Athenaeus), was not perceived by Plato himself. We are still more surprised to find that the philosopher is incited to take the first step in his upward progress (Symp.) by the beauty of young men and boys, which was alone capable of inspiring the modern feeling of romance in the Greek mind. The passion of love took the spurious form of an enthusiasm for the ideal of beauty—a worship as of some godlike image of an Apollo or Antinous. But the love of youth when not depraved was a love of virtue and modesty as well as of beauty, the one being the expression of the other; and in certain Greek states, especially at Sparta and Thebes, the honorable attachment of a youth to an elder man was a part of his education. The "army of lovers and their beloved who would be invincible if they could be united by such a tie" (Symp.), is not a mere fiction of Plato's, but seems actually to have existed at Thebes in the days of Epaminondas and Pelopidas, if we may believe writers cited anonymously by Plutarch, Pelop. Vit. It is observable that Plato never in the least degree excuses the depraved love of the body (compare Charm.; Rep.; Laws; Symp.; and once more Xenophon, Mem.), nor is there any Greek writer of mark who condones or approves such connexions. But owing partly to the puzzling nature of the subject these friendships are spoken of by Plato in a manner different from that customary among ourselves. To most of them we should hesitate to ascribe, any more than to the attachment of Achilles and Patroclus in Homer, an immoral or licentious character. There were many, doubtless, to whom the love of the fair mind was the noblest form of friendship (Rep.), and who deemed the friendship of man with man to be higher than the love of woman, because altogether separated from the bodily appetites. The existence of such attachments may be reasonably attributed to the inferiority and seclusion of woman, and the want of a real family or social life and parental influence in Hellenic cities; and they were encouraged by the practice of gymnastic exercises, by the meetings of political clubs, and by the tie of military companionship. They were also an educational institution: A young person was specially entrusted by his parents to some elder friend who was expected by them to train their son in manly exercises and in virtue. It is not likely that a Greek parent committed him to a lover, any more than we should to a schoolmaster, in the expectation that he would be corrupted by him, but rather in the hope that his morals would be better cared for than was possible in a great household of slaves.

It is difficult to adduce the authority of Plato either for or against such practices or customs, because it is not always easy to determine whether he is speaking of "the heavenly and philosophical love, or of the coarse Polyhymnia;" and he often refers to this (e.g. in the Symposium) half in jest, yet "with a certain degree of seriousness." We observe that they entered into one part of Greek literature, but not into another, and that the larger part is free from such associations. Indecency was an element of the ludicrous in the old Greek Comedy, as it has been in other ages and countries. But effeminate love was always condemned as well as ridiculed by the Comic poets; and in the New Comedy the allusions to such topics have disappeared. They seem to have been no longer tolerated by the greater refinement of the age. False sentiment is found in the Lyric and Elegiac poets; and in mythology "the greatest of the Gods" (Rep.) is not exempt from evil imputations. But the morals of a nation are not to be judged of wholly by its literature. Hellas was not necessarily more corrupted in the days of the Persian and Peloponnesian wars, or of Plato and the Orators, than England in the time of Fielding and Smollett, or France in the nineteenth century. No one supposes certain French novels to be a representation of ordinary French life. And the greater part of Greek literature, beginning with Homer and including the tragedians, philosophers, and, with the exception of the Comic poets (whose business was to raise a laugh by whatever means), all the greater writers of Hellas who have been preserved to us, are free from the taint of indecency.

Some general considerations occur to our mind when we begin to reflect on this subject. (1) That good and evil are linked together in human nature, and have often existed side by side in the world and in man to an extent hardly credible. We cannot distinguish them, and are therefore unable to part them; as in the parable "they grow together unto the harvest;" it is only a rule of external decency by which society can divide them. Nor should we be right in inferring from the prevalence of any one vice or corruption that a state or individual was demoralized in their whole character. Not only has the corruption of the best been sometimes thought to be the worst, but it may be remarked that this very excess of evil has been the stimulus to good (compare Plato, Laws, where he says that in the most corrupt cities individuals are to be found beyond all praise). (2) It may be observed that evils which admit of degrees can seldom be rightly estimated, because under the same name actions of the most different degrees of culpability may be included. No charge is more easily set going than the imputation of secret wickedness (which cannot be either proved or disproved and often cannot be defined) when directed against a person of whom the world, or a section of it, is predisposed to think evil. And it is quite possible that the malignity of Greek scandal, aroused by some personal jealousy or party enmity, may have converted the innocent friendship of a great man for a noble youth into a connection of another kind. Such accusations were brought against several of the leading men of Hellas, e.g. Cimon, Alcibiades, Critias, Demosthenes, Epaminondas: Several of the Roman emperors were assailed by similar weapons which have been used even in our own day against statesmen of the highest character. (3) While we know that in this matter there is a great gulf fixed between Greek and Christian Ethics, yet, if we would do justice to the Greeks, we must also acknowledge that there was a greater outspokenness among them than among ourselves about the things which nature hides, and that the more frequent mention of such topics is not to be taken as the measure of the prevalence of offenses, or as a proof of the general corruption of society. It is likely that every religion in the world has used words or practiced rites in one age, which have become distasteful or repugnant to another. We cannot, though for different reasons, trust the representations either of Comedy or Satire; and still less of Christian Apologists. (4) We observe that at Thebes and Lacedemon the attachment of an elder friend to a beloved youth was often deemed to be a part of his education; and was encouraged by his parents— it was only shameful if it degenerated into licentiousness. Such we may believe to have been the tie which united Asophychus and Cephisodorus with the great Epaminondas in whose companionship they fell (Plutarch, Amat.; Athenaeus on the authority of Theopompus). (5) A small matter: There appears to be a difference of custom among the Greeks and among ourselves, as between ourselves and continental nations at the present time, in modes of salutation. We must not suspect evil in the hearty kiss or embrace of a male friend "returning from the army at Potidaea" any more than in a similar salutation when practiced by members of the same family. But those who make these admissions, and who regard, not without pity, the victims of such illusions in our own day, whose life has been blasted by them, may be nonetheless resolved that the natural and healthy instincts of mankind shall alone be tolerated (Greek); and that the lesson of manliness which we have inherited from our fathers shall not degenerate into sentimentalism or effeminacy. The possibility of an honorable connection of this kind seems to have died out with Greek civilization. Among the Romans, and also among barbarians, such as the Celts and Persians, there is no trace of such attachments existing in any noble or virtuous form.

(Compare Hoeck's Creta and the admirable and exhaustive article of Meier in Ersch and Grueber's Cyclopedia on this subject; Plutarch, Amatores; Athenaeus; Lysias contra Simonem; Aesch. c. Timarchum.)

The character of Alcibiades in the Symposium is hardly less remarkable than that of Socrates, and agrees with the picture given of him in the first of the two Dialogues which are called by his name, and also with the slight sketch of him in the Protagoras. He is the impersonation of lawlessness—"the lion's whelp, who ought not to be reared in the city," yet not without a certain generosity which gained the hearts of men strangely fascinated by Socrates, and possessed of a genius which might have been either the destruction or salvation of Athens. The dramatic interest of the character is heightened by the recollection of his after history. He seems to have been present to the mind of Plato in the description of the democratic man of the Republic (compare also Alcibiades 1).

There is no criterion of the date of the Symposium, except that which is furnished by the allusion to the division of Arcadia after the destruction of Mantinea. This took place in the year 384 BC, which is the forty-fourth year of Plato's life. The Symposium cannot therefore be regarded as a youthful work. As Mantinea was restored in the year 369, the composition of the Dialogue will probably fall between 384 and 369. Whether the recollection of the event is more likely to have been renewed at the destruction or restoration of the city, rather than at some intermediate period, is a consideration not worth raising.

The Symposium is connected with the Phaedrus both in style and subject; they are the only Dialogues of Plato in which the theme of love is discussed at length. In both of them philosophy is regarded as a sort of enthusiasm or madness; Socrates is himself "a prophet new inspired" with Bacchanalian revelry, which, like his philosophy, he characteristically pretends to have derived not from himself but from others. The Phaedo also presents some points of comparison with the Symposium. For there, too, philosophy might be described as "dying for love"; and there are not wanting many touches of humor and fancy, which remind us of the Symposium. But while the Phaedo and Phaedrus look backward and forward to past and future states of existence, in the Symposium there is no break between this world and another; and we rise from one to the other by a regular series of steps or stages, proceeding from the particulars of sense to the universal of reason, and from one universal to many, which are finally reunited in a single science (compare Rep.). At first immortality means only the succession of existences; even knowledge comes and goes. Then follows, in the language of the mysteries, a higher and a higher degree of initiation; at last we arrive at the perfect vision of beauty, not relative or changing, but eternal and absolute; not bounded by this world, or in or out of this world, but an aspect of the divine, extending over all things, and having no limit of space or time: This is the highest knowledge of which the human mind is capable. Plato does not go on to ask whether the individual is absorbed in the sea of light and beauty or retains his personality. Enough for him to have attained the true beauty or good, without inquiring precisely into the relation in which human beings stood to it. That the soul has such a reach of thought, and is capable of partaking of the eternal nature, seems to imply that she too is eternal (compare Phaedrus). But Plato does not distinguish the eternal in man from the eternal in the world or in God. He is willing to rest in the contemplation of the idea, which to him is the cause of all things (Rep.), and has no strength to go further.

The Symposium of Xenophon, in which Socrates describes himself as a pander, and also discourses of the difference between sensual and sentimental love, likewise offers several interesting points of comparison. But the suspicion which hangs over other writings of Xenophon, and the numerous minute references to the Phaedrus and Symposium, as well as to some of the other writings of Plato, throw a doubt on the genuineness of the work. The Symposium of Xenophon, if written by him at all, would certainly show that he wrote against Plato, and was acquainted with his works. Of this hostility there is no trace in the Memorabilia. Such a rivalry is more characteristic of an imitator than of an original writer. The (so-called) Symposium of Xenophon may therefore have no more title to be regarded as genuine than the confessedly spurious Apology.

There are no means of determining the relative order in time of the Phaedrus, Symposium, Phaedo. The order which has been adopted in this translation rests on no other principle than the desire to bring together in a series the memorials of the life of Socrates.

SYMPOSIUM

Persons of the dialogue: Apollodorus, who repeats to his companion the dialogue which he had heard from Aristodemus, and had already once narrated to Glaucon. Phaedrus, Pausanias, Eryximachus, Aristophanes, Agathon, Socrates, Alcibiades, A Troop of Revellers.

Scene: The House of Agathon.

Concerning the things about which you ask to be informed I believe that I am not ill-prepared with an answer. For the day before yesterday I was coming from my own home at Phalerum to the city, and one of my acquaintance, who had caught a sight of me from behind, calling out playfully in the distance, said: Apollodorus, O thou Phalerian (Probably a play of words on (Greek), "bald-headed.") man, halt! So I did as I was bid; and then he said, I was looking for you, Apollodorus, only just now, that I might ask you about the speeches in praise of love, which were delivered by Socrates, Alcibiades, and others, at Agathon's supper. Phoenix, the son of Philip, told another person who told me of them; his narrative was very indistinct, but he said that you knew, and I wish that you would give me an account of them. Who, if not you, should be the reporter of the words of your friend? And first tell me, he said, were you present at this meeting?

Your informant, Glaucon, I said, must have been very indistinct indeed, if you imagine that the occasion was recent; or that I could have been of the party.

Why, yes, he replied, I thought so.

Impossible, I said. Are you ignorant that for many years Agathon has not resided at Athens; and not three have elapsed since I became acquainted with Socrates, and have made it my daily business to know all that he says and does. There was a time when I was running about the world, fancying myself to be well employed, but I was really a most wretched being, no better than you are now. I thought that I ought to do anything rather than be a philosopher.

Well, he said, jesting apart, tell me when the meeting occurred.

In our boyhood, I replied, when Agathon won the prize with his first tragedy, on the day after that on which he and his chorus offered the sacrifice of victory.

Then it must have been a long while ago, he said; and who told you—did Socrates?

No indeed, I replied, but the same person who told Phoenix—he was a little fellow, who never wore any shoes, Aristodemus, of the deme of Cydathenaeum. He had been at Agathon's feast; and I think that in those days there was no one who was a more devoted admirer of Socrates. Moreover, I have asked Socrates about the truth of some parts of his narrative, and he confirmed them. Then, said Glaucon, let us have the tale over again; is not the road to Athens just made for conversation? And so we walked, and talked of the discourses on love; and therefore, as I said at first, I am not ill-prepared to comply with your request, and will have another rehearsal of them if you like. For to speak or to hear others speak of philosophy always gives me the greatest pleasure, to say nothing of the profit. But when I hear another strain, especially that of you rich men and traders, such conversation displeases me; and I pity you who are my companions, because you think that you are doing something when in reality you are doing nothing. And I dare say that you pity me in return, whom you regard as an unhappy creature, and very probably you are right. But I certainly know of you what you only think of me—there is the difference.

COMPANION: I see, Apollodorus, that you are just the same—always speaking evil of yourself, and of others; and I do believe that you pity all mankind, with the exception of Socrates, yourself first of all, true in this to your old name, which, however deserved, I know not how you acquired, of Apollodorus the madman; for you are always raging against yourself and everybody but Socrates.

APOLLODORUS: Yes, friend, and the reason why I am said to be mad, and out of my wits, is just because I have these notions of myself and you; no other evidence is required.

COMPANION: No more of that, Apollodorus; but let me renew my request that you would repeat the conversation.

APOLLODORUS: Well, the tale of love was on this wise—but perhaps I had better begin at the beginning, and endeavor to give you the exact words of Aristodemus.

He said that he met Socrates fresh from the bath and sandalled; and as the sight of the sandals was unusual, he asked him whither he was going that he had been converted into such a beau.

To a banquet at Agathon's, he replied, whose invitation to his sacrifice of victory I refused yesterday, fearing a crowd, but promising that I would come today instead; and so I have put on my finery, because he is such a fine man. What say you to going with me unasked?

I will do as you bid me, I replied.

Follow then, he said, and let us demolish the proverb:

"To the feasts of inferior men the good unbidden go";

instead of which our proverb will run:

"To the feasts of the good the good unbidden go";

and this alteration may be supported by the authority of Homer himself, who not only demolishes but literally outrages the proverb. For, after picturing Agamemnon as the most valiant of men, he makes Menelaus, who is but a fainthearted warrior, come unbidden (Iliad) to the banquet of Agamemnon, who is feasting and offering sacrifices, not the better to the worse, but the worse to the better.

I rather fear, Socrates, said Aristodemus, lest this may still be my case; and that, like Menelaus in Homer, I shall be the inferior person, who "To the feasts of the wise unbidden goes."

But I shall say that I was bidden of you, and then you will have to make an excuse.

"Two going together," he replied, in Homeric fashion, one or other of them may invent an excuse by the way (Iliad).

This was the style of their conversation as they went along. Socrates dropped behind in a fit of abstraction, and desired Aristodemus, who was waiting, to go on before him. When he reached the house of Agathon he found the doors wide open, and a comical thing happened. A servant coming out met him, and led him at once into the banqueting-hall in which the guests were reclining, for the banquet was about to begin. Welcome, Aristodemus, said Agathon, as soon as he appeared—you are just in time to sup with us; if you come on any other matter put it off, and make one of us, as I was looking for you yesterday and meant to have asked you, if I could have found you. But what have you done with Socrates?

I turned around, but Socrates was nowhere to be seen; and I had to explain that he had been with me a moment before, and that I came by his invitation to the supper.

You were quite right in coming, said Agathon; but where is he himself?

He was behind me just now, as I entered, he said, and I cannot think what has become of him.

Go and look for him, boy, said Agathon, and bring him in; and do you, Aristodemus, meanwhile take the place by Eryximachus.

The servant then assisted him to wash, and he lay down, and presently another servant came in and reported that our friend Socrates had retired into the portico of the neighboring house. "There he is fixed," said he, "and when I call to him he will not stir."

How strange, said Agathon; then you must call him again, and keep calling him.

Let him alone, said my informant; he has a way of stopping anywhere and losing himself without any reason. I believe that he will soon appear; do not therefore disturb him.

Well, if you think so, I will leave him, said Agathon. And then, turning to the servants, he added, "Let us have supper without waiting for him. Serve up whatever you please, for there is no one to give you orders; hitherto I have never left you to yourselves. But on this occasion imagine that you are our hosts, and that I and the company are your guests; treat us well, and then we shall commend you." After this, supper was served, but still no Socrates; and during the meal Agathon several times expressed a wish to send for him, but Aristodemus objected; and at last when the feast was about half over—for the fit, as usual, was not of long duration—Socrates entered. Agathon, who was reclining alone at the end of the table, begged that he would take the place next to him; that "I may touch you," he said, "and have the benefit of that wise thought which came into your mind in the portico, and is now in your possession; for I am certain that you would not have come away until you had found what you sought."

How I wish, said Socrates, taking his place as he was desired, that wisdom could be infused by touch, out of the fuller into the emptier man, as water runs through wool out of a fuller cup into an emptier one; if that were so, how greatly should I value the privilege of reclining at your side! For you would have filled me full with a stream of wisdom plenteous and fair; whereas my own is of a very mean and questionable sort, no better than a dream. But yours is bright and full of promise, and was manifested forth in all the splendour of youth the day before yesterday, in the presence of more than thirty thousand Hellenes.

You are mocking, Socrates, said Agathon, and ere long you and I will have to determine who bears off the palm of wisdom—of this Dionysus shall be the judge; but at present you are better occupied with supper.

Socrates took his place on the couch, and supped with the rest; and then libations were offered, and after a hymn had been sung to the god, and there had been the usual ceremonies, they were about to commence drinking, when Pausanias said, And now, my friends, how can we drink with least injury to ourselves? I can assure you that I feel severely the effect of yesterday's potations, and must have time to recover; and I suspect that most of you are in the same predicament, for you were of the party yesterday. Consider then: How can the drinking be made easiest?

I entirely agree, said Aristophanes, that we should, by all means, avoid hard drinking, for I was myself one of those who were yesterday drowned in drink.

I think that you are right, said Eryximachus, the son of Acumenus; but I should still like to hear one other person speak: Is Agathon able to drink hard?

I am not equal to it, said Agathon.

Then, said Eryximachus, the weak heads like myself, Aristodemus, Phaedrus, and others who never can drink, are fortunate in finding that the stronger ones are not in a drinking mood. (I do not include Socrates, who is able either to drink or to abstain, and will not mind, whichever we do.) Well, as of none of the company seem disposed to drink much, I may be forgiven for saying, as a physician, that drinking deep is a bad practice, which I never follow, if I can help, and certainly do not recommend to another, least of all to anyone who still feels the effects of yesterday's carouse.

I always do what you advise, and especially what you prescribe as a physician, rejoined Phaedrus the Myrrhinusian, and the rest of the company, if they are wise, will do the same.

It was agreed that drinking was not to be the order of the day, but that they were all to drink only so much as they pleased.

Then, said Eryximachus, as you are all agreed that drinking is to be voluntary, and that there is to be no compulsion, I move, in the next place, that the flute girl, who has just made her appearance, be told to go away and play to herself, or, if she likes, to the women who are within (compare Prot.). Today let us have conversation instead; and, if you will allow me, I will tell you what sort of conversation. This proposal having been accepted, Eryximachus proceeded as follows:

I will begin, he said, after the manner of Melanippe in Euripides,

"Not mine the word"

which I am about to speak, but that of Phaedrus. For often he says to me in an indignant tone: "What a strange thing it is, Eryximachus, that, whereas other gods have poems and hymns made in their honor, the great and glorious god, Love, has no encomiast among all the poets who are so many. There are the worthy sophists too—the excellent Prodicus for example, who have descanted in prose on the virtues of Heracles and other heroes; and, what is still more extraordinary, I have met with a philosophical work in which the utility of salt has been made the theme of an eloquent discourse; and many other like things have had a like honor bestowed upon them. And only to think that there should have been an eager interest created about them, and yet that to this day no one has ever dared worthily to hymn Love's praises! So entirely has this great deity been neglected." Now in this Phaedrus seems to me to be quite right, and therefore I want to offer him a contribution; also I think that at the present moment we who are here assembled cannot do better than honor the god Love. If you agree with me, there will be no lack of conversation; for I mean to propose that each of us in turn, going from left to right, shall make a speech in honor of Love. Let him give us the best which he can; and Phaedrus, because he is sitting first on the left hand, and because he is the father of the thought, shall begin.

No one will vote against you, Eryximachus, said Socrates. How can I oppose your motion, who profess to understand nothing but matters of love; nor, I presume, will Agathon and Pausanias; and there can be no doubt of Aristophanes, whose whole concern is with Dionysus and Aphrodite; nor will anyone disagree of those whom I see around me. The proposal, as I am aware, may seem rather hard upon us whose place is last; but we shall be contented if we hear some good speeches first. Let Phaedrus begin the praise of Love, and good luck to him. All the company expressed their assent, and desired him to do as Socrates bade him.

Aristodemus did not recollect all that was said, nor do I recollect all that he related to me; but I will tell you what I thought most worthy of remembrance, and what the chief speakers said.

Phaedrus began by affirming that Love is a mighty god, and wonderful among gods and men, but especially wonderful in his birth. For he is the eldest of the gods, which is an honor to him; and a proof of his claim to this honor is, that of his parents there is no memorial; neither poet nor prose writer has ever affirmed that he had any. As Hesiod says:

> "First Chaos came, and then broad-bosomed Earth, The everlasting seat of all that is, And Love."

In other words, after Chaos, the Earth and Love, these two, came into being. Also Parmenides sings of Generation:

"First in the train of gods, he fashioned Love."

And Acusilaus agrees with Hesiod. Thus numerous are the witnesses who acknowledge Love to be the eldest of the gods. And not only is he the eldest, he is also the source of the greatest benefits to us. For I know not any greater blessing to a young man who is beginning life than a virtuous lover, or to the lover than a beloved youth. For the principle which ought to be the guide of men who would nobly live—that principle, I say, neither kindred, nor honor, nor wealth, nor any other motive is able to implant so well as love. Of what am I speaking? Of the sense of honor and dishonor, without which neither states nor individuals ever do any good or great work. And I say that a lover who is detected in doing any dishonorable act, or submitting through cowardice when any dishonor is done to him by another, will be more pained at being detected by his beloved than at being seen by his father, or by his companions, or by anyone else. The beloved too, when he is found in any disgraceful situation, has the same feeling about his lover. And if there were only some way of contriving that a state or an army should be made up of lovers and their loves (compare Rep.), they would be the very best governors of their own city, abstaining from all dishonor, and emulating one another in honor; and when fighting at each other's side, although a mere handful, they would overcome the world. For what lover would not choose rather to be seen by all mankind than by his beloved, either when abandoning his post or throwing away his arms? He would be ready to die a thousand deaths rather than endure this. Or who would desert his beloved or fail him in the hour of danger? The veriest coward would become an inspired hero, equal to the bravest, at such a time; Love would inspire him. That courage which, as Homer says, the god breathes into the souls of some heroes, Love of his own nature infuses into the lover.

Love will make men dare to die for their beloved—love alone; and women as well as men. Of this, Alcestis, the daughter of Pelias, is a monument to all Hellas; for she was willing to lay down her life on behalf of her husband, when no one else would, although he had a father and mother; but the tenderness of her love so far exceeded theirs, that she made them seem to be strangers in blood to their own son, and in name only related to him; and so noble did this action of hers appear to the gods, as well as to men, that among the many who have done virtuously she is one of the very few to whom, in admiration of her noble action, they have granted the privilege of returning alive to Earth; such exceeding honor is paid by the gods to the devotion and virtue of love. But Orpheus, the son of Oeagrus, the harper, they sent empty away, and presented to him an apparition only of her whom he sought, but herself they would not give up, because he showed no spirit; he was only a harp-player, and did not dare like Alcestis to die for love, but was contriving how he might enter Hades alive; moreover, they afterward caused him to suffer death at the hands of women, as the punishment of his cowardliness. Very different was the reward of the true love of Achilles toward his lover Patroclus—his lover and not his love (the notion that Patroclus was the beloved one is a foolish error into which Aeschylus has fallen, for Achilles was surely the fairer of the two, fairer also than all the other heroes; and, as Homer informs us, he was still beardless, and younger far). And greatly as the gods honor the virtue of love, still the return of love on the part of the beloved to the lover is more admired and valued and rewarded by them, for the lover is more divine; because he is inspired by God. Now Achilles was quite aware, for he had been told by his mother, that he might avoid death and return home, and live to a good old age, if he abstained from slaying Hector. Nevertheless he gave his life to revenge his friend, and dared to die, not only in his defense, but after he was dead. Wherefore the gods honored him even above Alcestis, and sent him to the Islands of the Blessed. These are my reasons for affirming that Love is the eldest and noblest and mightiest of the gods; and the chiefest author and giver of virtue in life, and of happiness after death.

 This, or something like this, was the speech of Phaedrus; and some other speeches followed which Aristodemus did not remember; the next which he repeated was that of Pausanias. Phaedrus, he said, the argument has not been set before us, I think, quite in the right form; we should not be called upon to praise Love in such an indiscriminate manner. If there were only one Love, then what you said would be well enough; but since there are more Loves than one, should have begun by determining which of them was to be the theme of our praises. I will amend this defect; and first of all I will tell you which Love is deserving of praise, and then try to hymn the praiseworthy one in a manner worthy of him. For we all know that Love is inseparable from Aphrodite, and if there were only one Aphrodite there would be only one Love; but as there are two goddesses there must be two Loves. And am I not right in asserting that there are two goddesses? The elder one, having no mother, who is called the heavenly Aphrodite—she is the daughter of Uranus; the younger, who is the daughter of Zeus and Dione—her we call common; and the Love who is her fellow worker is rightly named common, as the other love is called heavenly. All the gods ought to have praise given to them, but not without distinction of their natures; and therefore I must try to distinguish the characters of the two Loves. Now actions vary according to the manner of their performance. Take, for example, that which we are now doing, drinking, singing and talking—these actions are not in themselves either good or evil, but they turn out in this or that way according to the mode of performing them; and when well done they are good, and when wrongly done they are evil; and in like manner not every love, but only that which has a noble purpose, is noble and worthy of praise. The Love who is the offspring of the common Aphrodite is essentially common, and has no discrimination, being such as the meaner sort of men feel, and is apt to be of women as well as of youths, and is of the body rather than of the soul—the most foolish beings are the objects of this love which desires only to gain an end, but never thinks of accomplishing the end nobly, and therefore does good and evil quite indiscriminately. The goddess who is his mother is far younger than the other, and she was born of the union of the male and female, and partakes of both. But the offspring of the heavenly Aphrodite is derived from a mother in whose birth the female has no part—she is from the male only; this is that love which is of youths, and the goddess being older, there is nothing of wantonness in her. Those who are inspired by this love turn to the male, and delight in him who is the more valiant and intelligent nature; anyone may recognize the pure enthusiasts in the very character of their attachments. For they love not boys, but intelligent beings whose reason is beginning to be developed, much about the time at which their beards begin to grow. And in choosing young men to be their companions, they mean to be faithful to them, and pass their whole life in company with them, not to take them in their inexperience, and deceive them, and play the fool with them, or run away from one to another of them. But the love of young boys should be forbidden by law, because their future is uncertain; they may turn out good or bad, either in body or soul, and much noble enthusiasm may be thrown away upon them; in this matter the good are a law to themselves, and the coarser sort of lovers ought to be restrained by force; as we restrain or attempt to restrain them from fixing their affections on women of free birth. These are the persons who bring a reproach on love; and some have been led to deny the lawfulness of such attachments because they see the impropriety and evil of them; for surely nothing that is decorously and lawfully done can justly be censured. Now here and in Lacedaemon the rules about love are perplexing, but in most cities they are simple and easily intelligible; in Elis and Boeotia, and in countries having no gifts of eloquence, they are very straightforward; the law is simply in favor of these connexions, and no one, whether young or old, has anything to say to their discredit; the reason being, as I suppose, that they are men of few words in those parts, and therefore the lovers do not like the trouble of pleading their suit. In Ionia and other places, and generally in countries which are subject to the barbarians, the custom is held to be dishonorable; loves of youths share the evil repute in which philosophy and gymnastics are held, because they are inimical to tyranny; for the interests of rulers require that their subjects should be poor in spirit (compare Arist. Politics), and that there should be no strong bond of friendship or society among them, which love, above all other motives, is likely to inspire, as our Athenian tyrants learned by experience; for the love of Aristogeiton and the constancy of Harmodius had a strength which undid their power. And, therefore, the ill-repute into which these attachments have fallen is to be ascribed to the evil condition of those who make them to be ill-reputed; that is to say, to the self-seeking of the governors and the cowardice of the governed; on the other hand, the indiscriminate honor which is given to them in some countries is attributable to the laziness of those who hold this opinion of them. In our own country a far better principle prevails, but, as I was saying, the explanation of it is rather perplexing. For, observe that open loves are held to be more honorable than secret ones, and that the love of the noblest and highest, even if their persons are less beautiful than others, is especially honorable. Consider, too, how great is the encouragement which all the world gives to the lover; neither is he supposed to be doing anything dishonorable; but if he succeeds he is praised, and if he fail he is blamed. And in the pursuit of his love the custom of mankind allows him to do many strange things, which philosophy would bitterly censure if they were done from any motive of interest, or wish for office or power. He may pray, and entreat, and supplicate, and swear, and lie on a mat at the door, and endure a slavery worse than that of any slave—in any other case friends and enemies would be equally ready to prevent him, but now there is no friend who will be ashamed of him and admonish him, and no enemy will charge him with meanness or flattery; the actions of a lover have a grace which ennobles them; and custom has decided that they are highly commendable and that there no loss of character in them; and, what is strangest of all, he only may swear and forswear himself (so men say), and the gods will forgive his transgression, for there is no such thing as a lover's oath. Such is the entire liberty which gods and men have allowed the lover, according to the custom which prevails in our part of the world. From this point of view a man fairly argues that in Athens to love and to be loved is held to be a very honorable thing. But when parents forbid their sons to talk with their lovers, and place them under a tutor's care, who is appointed to see to these things, and their companions and equals cast in their teeth anything of the sort which they may observe, and their elders refuse to silence the reprovers and do not rebuke them—anyone who reflects on all this will, on the contrary, think that we hold these practices to be most disgraceful. But, as I was saying at first, the truth as I imagine is, that whether such practices are honorable or whether they are dishonorable is not a simple question; they are honorable to him who follows them honorably, dishonorable to him who follows them dishonorably. There is dishonor in yielding to the evil, or in an evil manner; but there is honor in yielding to the good, or in an honorable manner. Evil is the vulgar lover who loves the body rather than the soul, inasmuch as he is not even stable, because he loves a thing which is in itself unstable, and therefore when the bloom of youth which he was desiring is over, he takes wing and flies away, in spite of all his words and promises; whereas the love of the noble disposition is life-long, for it becomes one with the everlasting. The custom of our country would have both of them proven well and truly, and would have us yield to the one sort of lover and avoid the other, and therefore encourages some to pursue, and others to fly; testing both the lover and beloved in contests and trials, until they show to which of the two classes they respectively belong. And this is the reason why, in the first place, a hasty attachment is held to be dishonorable, because time is the true test of this as of most other things; and secondly there is a dishonor in being overcome by the love of money, or of wealth, or of political power, whether a man is frightened into surrender by the loss of them, or, having experienced the benefits of money and political corruption, is unable to rise above the seductions of them. For none of these things are of a permanent or lasting nature; not to mention that no generous friendship ever sprang from them. There remains, then, only one way of honorable attachment which custom allows in the beloved, and this is the way of virtue; for as we admitted that any service which the lover does to him is not to be accounted flattery or a dishonor to himself, so the beloved has one way only of voluntary service which is not dishonorable, and this is virtuous service.

For we have a custom, and according to our custom anyone who does service to another under the idea that he will be improved by him either in wisdom, or in some other particular of virtue—such a voluntary service, I say, is not to be regarded as a dishonor, and is not open to the charge of flattery. And these two customs, one the love of youth, and the other the practice of philosophy and virtue in general, ought to meet in one, and then the beloved may honorably indulge the lover. For when the lover and beloved come together, having each of them a law, and the lover thinks that he is right in doing any service which he can to his gracious loving one; and the other that he is right in showing any kindness which he can to him who is making him wise and good; the one capable of communicating wisdom and virtue, the other seeking to acquire them with a view to education and wisdom, when the two laws of love are fulfillled and meet in one—then, and then only, may the beloved yield with honor to the lover. Nor when love is of this disinterested sort is there any disgrace in being deceived, but in every other case there is equal disgrace in being or not being deceived. For he who is gracious to his lover under the impression that he is rich, and is disappointed of his gains because he turns out to be poor, is disgraced all the same: for he has done his best to show that he would give himself up to anyone's "uses base" for the sake of money; but this is not honorable. And on the same principle he who gives himself to a lover because he is a good man, and in the hope that he will be improved by his company, shows himself to be virtuous, even though the object of his affection turn out to be a villain, and to have no virtue; and if he is deceived he has committed a noble error. For he has proved that for his part he will do anything for anybody with a view to virtue and improvement, than which there can be nothing nobler. Thus noble in every case is the acceptance of another for the sake of virtue. This is that love which is the love of the heavenly godess, and is heavenly, and of great price to individuals and cities, making the lover and the beloved alike eager in the work of their own improvement. But all other loves are the offspring of the other, who is the common goddess. To you, Phaedrus, I offer this my contribution in praise of love, which is as good as I could make extempore.

Pausanias came to a pause—this is the balanced way in which I have been taught by the wise to speak; and Aristodemus said that the turn of Aristophanes was next, but either he had eaten too much, or from some other cause he had the hiccups, and was obliged to change turns with Eryximachus the physician, who was reclining on the couch below him.

Eryximachus, he said, you ought either to stop my hiccups, or to speak in my turn until I have left off.

I will do both, said Eryximachus: I will speak in your turn, and do you speak in mine; and while I am speaking let me recommend you to hold your breath, and if after you have done so for some time the hiccups are no better, then gargle with a little water; and if it still continues, tickle your nose with something and sneeze; and if you sneeze once or twice, even the most violent hiccups is sure to go. I will do as you prescribe, said Aristophanes, and now get on.

Eryximachus spoke as follows: Seeing that Pausanias made a fair beginning, and but a lame ending, I must endeavor to supply his deficiency. I think that he has rightly distinguished two kinds of love. But my art further informs me that the double love is not merely an affection of the soul of man toward the fair, or toward anything, but is to be found in the bodies of all animals and in productions of the earth, and I may say in all that is; such is the conclusion which I seem to have gathered from my own art of medicine, whence I learn how great and wonderful and universal is the deity of love, whose empire extends over all things, divine as well as human. And from medicine I will begin that I may do honor to my art. There are in the human body these two kinds of love, which are confessedly different and unlike, and being unlike, they have loves and desires which are unlike; and the desire of the healthy is one, and the desire of the diseased is another; and as Pausanias was just now saying that to indulge good men is honorable, and bad men dishonorable:—so too in the body the good and healthy elements are to be indulged, and the bad elements and the elements of disease are not to be indulged, but discouraged. And this is what the physician has to do, and in this the art of medicine consists: for medicine may be regarded generally as the knowledge of the loves and desires of the body, and how to satisfy them or not; and the best physician is he who is able to separate fair love from foul, or to convert one into the other; and he who knows how to eradicate and how to implant love, whichever is required, and can reconcile the most hostile elements in the constitution and make them loving friends, is a skilful practitioner. Now the most hostile are the most opposite, such as hot and cold, bitter and sweet, moist and dry, and the like. And my ancestor, Asclepius, knowing how to implant friendship and accord in these elements, was the creator of our art, as our friends the poets here tell us, and I believe them; and not only medicine in every branch but the arts of gymnastic and husbandry are under his dominion. Any one who pays the least attention to the subject will also perceive that in music there is the same reconciliation of opposites; and I suppose that this must have been the meaning of Heracleitus, although his words are not accurate; for he says that The One is united by disunion, like the harmony of the bow and the lyre. Now there is an absurdity saying that harmony is discord or is composed of elements which are still in a state of discord. But what he probably meant was, that harmony is composed of differing notes of higher or lower pitch which disagreed once, but are now reconciled by the art of music; for if the higher and lower notes still disagreed, there could be no harmony,—clearly not. For harmony is a symphony, and symphony is an agreement; but an agreement of disagreements while they disagree there cannot be; you cannot harmonize that which disagrees. In like manner rhythm is compounded of elements short and long, once differing and now in accord; which accordance, as in the former instance, medicine, so in all these other cases, music implants, making love and unison to grow up among them; and thus music, too, is concerned with the principles of love in their application to harmony and rhythm. Again, in the essential nature of harmony and rhythm there is no difficulty in discerning love which has not yet become double. But when you want to use them in actual life, either in the composition of songs or in the correct performance of airs or meters composed already, which latter is called education, then the difficulty begins, and the good artist is needed. Then the old tale has to be repeated of fair and heavenly love—the love of Urania the fair and heavenly muse, and of the duty of accepting the temperate, and those who are as yet intemperate only that they may become temperate, and of preserving their love; and again, of the vulgar Polyhymnia, who must be used with circumspection that the pleasure be enjoyed, but may not generate licentiousness; just as in my own art it is a great matter so to regulate the desires of the epicure that he may gratify his tastes without the attendant evil of disease. Whence I infer that in music, in medicine, in all other things human as well as divine, both loves ought to be noted as far as may be, for they are both present.

The course of the seasons is also full of both these principles; and when, as I was saying, the elements of hot and cold, moist and dry, attain the harmonious love of one another and blend in temperance and harmony, they bring to men, animals, and plants health and plenty, and do them no harm; whereas the wanton love, getting the upper hand and affecting the seasons of the year, is very destructive and injurious, being the source of pestilence, and bringing many other kinds of diseases on animals and plants; for hoar-frost and hail and blight spring from the excesses and disorders of these elements of love, which to know in relation to the revolutions of the heavenly bodies and the seasons of the year is termed astronomy. Furthermore all sacrifices and the whole province of divination, which is the art of communion between gods and men—these, I say, are concerned only with the preservation of the good and the cure of the evil love. For all manner of impiety is likely to ensue if, instead of accepting and honoring and reverencing the harmonious love in all his actions, a man honors the other love, whether in his feelings toward gods or parents, toward the living or the dead. Wherefore the business of divination is to see to these loves and to heal them, and divination is the peacemaker of gods and men, working by a knowledge of the religious or irreligious tendencies which exist in human loves. Such is the great and mighty, or rather omnipotent force of love in general. And the love, more especially, which is concerned with the good, and which is perfected in company with temperance and justice, whether among gods or men, has the greatest power, and is the source of all our happiness and harmony, and makes us friends with the gods who are above us, and with one another. I dare say that I too have omitted several things which might be said in praise of Love, but this was not intentional, and you, Aristophanes, may now supply the omission or take some other line of commendation; for I perceive that you are rid of the hiccups.

Yes, said Aristophanes, who followed, the hiccups are gone; not, however, until I applied the sneezing; and I wonder whether the harmony of the body has a love of such noises and ticklings, for I no sooner applied the sneezing than I was cured.

Eryximachus said: Beware, friend Aristophanes, although you are going to speak, you are making fun of me; and I shall have to watch and see whether I cannot have a laugh at your expense, when you might speak in peace.

You are right, said Aristophanes, laughing. I will unsay my words; but do you please not to watch me, as I fear that in the speech which I am about to make, instead of others laughing with me, which is to the manner born of our muse and would be all the better, I shall only be laughed at by them.

Do you expect to shoot your bolt and escape, Aristophanes? Well, perhaps if you are very careful and bear in mind that you will be called to account, I may be induced to let you off.

Aristophanes professed to open another vein of discourse; he had a mind to praise Love in another way, unlike that either of Pausanias or Eryximachus. Mankind, he said, judging by their neglect of him, have never, as I think, at all understood the power of Love. For if they had understood him they would surely have built noble temples and altars, and offered solemn sacrifices in his honor; but this is not done, and most certainly ought to be done: since of all the gods he is the best friend of men, the helper and the healer of the ills which are the great impediment to the happiness of the race. I will try to describe his power to you, and you shall teach the rest of the world what I am teaching you. In the first place, let me treat of the nature of man and what has happened to it; for the original human nature was not like the present, but different. The sexes were not two as they are now, but originally three in number; there was man, woman, and the union of the two, having a name corresponding to this double nature, which had once a real existence, but is now lost, and the word "androgynous" is only preserved as a term of reproach. In the second place, the primeval man was round, his back and sides forming a circle; and he had four hands and four feet, one head with two faces, looking opposite ways, set on a round neck and precisely alike; also four ears, two privy members, and the remainder to correspond. He could walk upright as men now do, backward or forward as he pleased, and he could also roll over and over at a great pace, turning on his four hands and four feet, eight in all, like tumblers going over and over with their legs in the air; this was when he wanted to run fast. Now the sexes were three, and such as I have described them; because the sun, moon, and Earth are three; and the man was originally the child of the sun, the woman of the Earth, and the man-woman of the moon, which is made up of sun and earth, and they were all round and moved round and round like their parents. Terrible was their might and strength, and the thoughts of their hearts were great, and they made an attack upon the gods; of them is told the tale of Otys and Ephialtes who, as Homer says, dared to scale heaven, and would have laid hands upon the gods. Doubt reigned in the celestial councils. Should they kill them and annihilate the race with thunderbolts, as they had done the giants, then there would be an end of the sacrifices and worship which men offered to them; but, on the other hand, the gods could not suffer their insolence to be unrestrained. At last, after a good deal of reflection, Zeus discovered a way. He said: "Methinks I have a plan which will humble their pride and improve their manners; men shall continue to exist, but I will cut them in two and then they will be diminished in strength and increased in numbers; this will have the advantage of making them more profitable to us. They shall walk upright on two legs, and if they continue insolent and will not be quiet, I will split them again and they shall hop about on a single leg." He spoke and cut men in two, like a sorb-apple which is halved for pickling, or as you might divide an egg with a hair; and as he cut them one after another, he bade Apollo give the face and the half of the neck a turn in order that the man might contemplate the section of himself: he would thus learn a lesson of humility. Apollo was also bidden to heal their wounds and compose their forms. So he gave a turn to the face and pulled the skin from the sides all over that which in our language is called the belly, like the purses which draw in, and he made one mouth at the center, which he fastened in a knot (the same which is called the navel); he also moulded the breast and took out most of the wrinkles, much as a shoemaker might smooth leather upon a last; he left a few, however, in the region of the belly and navel, as a memorial of the primeval state. After the division the two parts of man, each desiring his other half, came together, and throwing their arms about one another, entwined in mutual embraces, longing to grow into one, they were on the point of dying from hunger and self-neglect, because they did not like to do anything apart; and when one of the halves died and the other survived, the survivor sought another mate, man or woman as we call them—being the sections of entire men or women—and clung to that. They were being destroyed, when Zeus in pity of them invented a new plan: He turned the parts of generation round to the front, for this had not been always their position, and they sowed the seed no longer as hitherto like grasshoppers in the ground, but in one another; and after the transposition the male generated in the female in order that by the mutual embraces of man and woman they might breed, and the race might continue; or if man came to man they might be satisfied, and rest, and go their ways to the business of life; so ancient is the desire of one another which is implanted in us, reuniting our original nature, making one of two, and healing the state of man. Each of us when separated, having one side only, like a flat fish, is but the indenture of a man, and he is always looking for his other half. Men who are a section of that double nature which was once called Androgynous are lovers of women; adulterers are generally of this breed, and also adulterous women who lust after men: The women who are a section of the woman do not care for men, but have female attachments; the female companions are of this sort. But they who are a section of the male follow the male, and while they are young, being slices of the original man, they hang about men and embrace them, and they are themselves the best of boys and youths, because they have the most manly nature. Some indeed assert that they are shameless, but this is not true; for they do not act thus from any want of shame, but because they are valiant and manly, and have a manly countenance, and they embrace that which is like them. And these when they grow up become our statesmen, and these only, which is a great proof of the truth of what I am saying. When they reach manhood they are lovers of youth, and are not naturally inclined to marry or beget children—if at all, they do so only in obedience to the law; but they are satisfied if they may be allowed to live with one another unwedded; and such a nature is prone to love and ready to return love, always embracing that which is akin to him. And when one of them meets with his other half, the actual half of himself, whether he be a lover of youth or a lover of another sort, the pair are lost in an amazement of love and friendship and intimacy, and one will not be out of the other's sight, as I may say, even for a moment: these are the people who pass their whole lives together; yet they could not explain what they desire of one another. For the intense yearning which each of them has toward the other does not appear to be the desire of lover's intercourse, but of something else which the soul of either evidently desires and cannot tell, and of which she has only a dark and doubtful presentiment. Suppose Hephaestus, with his instruments, to come to the pair who are lying side by side and to say to them, "What do you people want of one another?" they would be unable to explain. And suppose further, that when he saw their perplexity he said: "Do you desire to be wholly one; always day and night to be in one another's company? For if this is what you desire, I am ready to melt you into one and let you grow together, so that being two you shall become one, and while you live a common life as if you were a single man, and after your death in the world below still be one departed soul instead of two—I ask whether this is what you lovingly desire, and whether you are satisfied to attain this?"—there is not a man of them who when he heard the proposal would deny or would not acknowledge that this meeting and melting into one another, this becoming one instead of two, was the very expression of his ancient need (compare Arist. Pol.). And the reason is that human nature was originally one and we were a whole, and the desire and pursuit of the whole is called love. There was a time, I say, when we were one, but now because of the wickedness of mankind God has dispersed us, as the Arcadians were dispersed into villages by the Lacedaemonians (compare Arist. Pol.). And if we are not obedient to the gods, there is a danger that we shall be split up again and go about in basso-relievo, like the profile figures having only half a nose which are sculptured on monuments, and that we shall be like tallies. Wherefore let us exhort all men to piety, that we may avoid evil, and obtain the good, of which Love is to us the lord and minister; and let no one oppose him—he is the enemy of the gods who opposes him. For if we are friends of the God and at peace with him we shall find our own true loves, which rarely happens in this world at present. I am serious, and therefore I must beg Eryximachus not to make fun or to find any allusion in what I am saying to Pausanias and Agathon, who, as I suspect, are both of the manly nature, and belong to the class which I have been describing. But my words have a wider application—they include men and women everywhere; and I believe that if our loves were perfectly accomplished, and each one returning to his primeval nature had his original true love, then our race would be happy. And if this would be best of all, the best in the next degree and under present circumstances must be the nearest approach to such an union; and that will be the attainment of a congenial love. Wherefore, if we would praise him who has given to us the benefit, we must praise the god Love, who is our greatest benefactor, both leading us in this life back to our own nature, and giving us high hopes for the future, for he promises that if we are pious, he will restore us to our original state, and heal us and make us happy and blessed. This, Eryximachus, is my discourse of love, which, although different to yours, I must beg you to leave unassailed by the shafts of your ridicule, in order that each may have his turn; each, or rather either, for Agathon and Socrates are the only ones left.

Indeed, I am not going to attack you, said Eryximachus, for I thought your speech charming, and did I not know that Agathon and Socrates are masters in the art of love, I should be really afraid that they would have nothing to say, after the world of things which have been said already. But, for all that, I am not without hopes.

Socrates said: You played your part well, Eryximachus; but if you were as I am now, or rather as I shall be when Agathon has spoken, you would, indeed, be in a great strait.

You want to cast a spell over me, Socrates, said Agathon, in the hope that I may be disconcerted at the expectation raised among the audience that I shall speak well.

I should be strangely forgetful, Agathon replied Socrates, of the courage and magnanimity which you showed when your own compositions were about to be exhibited, and you came upon the stage with the actors and faced the vast theatre altogether undismayed, if I thought that your nerves could be fluttered at a small party of friends.

Do you think, Socrates, said Agathon, that my head is so full of the theatre as not to know how much more formidable to a man of sense a few good judges are than many fools?

Nay, replied Socrates, I should be very wrong in attributing to you, Agathon, that or any other want of refinement. And I am quite aware that if you happened to meet with any whom you thought wise, you would care for their opinion much more than for that of the many. But then we, having been a part of the foolish many in the theatre, cannot be regarded as the select wise; though I know that if you chanced to be in the presence, not of one of ourselves, but of some really wise man, you would be ashamed of disgracing yourself before him—would you not?

Yes, said Agathon.

But before the many you would not be ashamed, if you thought that you were doing something disgraceful in their presence?

Here Phaedrus interrupted them, saying: do not answer him, my dear Agathon; for if he can only get a partner with whom he can talk, especially a good-looking one, he will no longer care about the completion of our plan. Now I love to hear him talk; but just at present I must not forget the encomium on Love which I ought to receive from him and from everyone. When you and he have paid your tribute to the god, then you may talk.

Very good, Phaedrus, said Agathon; I see no reason why I should not proceed with my speech, as I shall have many other opportunities of conversing with Socrates. Let me say first how I ought to speak, and then speak.

The previous speakers, instead of praising the god Love, or unfolding his nature, appear to have congratulated mankind on the benefits which he confers upon them. But I would rather praise the god first, and then speak of his gifts; this is always the right way of praising everything. May I say without impiety or offense, that of all the blessed gods he is the most blessed because he is the fairest and best? And he is the fairest: for, in the first place, he is the youngest, and of his youth he is himself the witness, fleeing out of the way of age, who is swift enough, swifter truly than most of us like:—Love hates him and will not come near him; but youth and love live and move together—like to like, as the proverb says. Many things were said by Phaedrus about Love in which I agree with him; but I cannot agree that he is older than Iapetus and Kronos:—not so; I maintain him to be the youngest of the gods, and youthful ever. The ancient doings among the gods of which Hesiod and Parmenides spoke, if the tradition of them be true, were done of Necessity and not of Love; had Love been in those days, there would have been no chaining or mutilation of the gods, or other violence, but peace and sweetness, as there is now in heaven, since the rule of Love began. Love is young and also tender; he ought to have a poet like Homer to describe his tenderness, as Homer says of Ate, that she is a goddess and tender:

> "Her feet are tender, for she sets her steps,
> Not on the ground but on the heads of men."

Herein is an excellent proof of her tenderness—that she walks not upon the hard but upon the soft. Let us adduce a similar proof of the tenderness of Love; for he walks not upon the Earth, nor yet upon the skulls of men, which are not so very soft, but in the hearts and souls of both gods and men, which are of all things the softest: in them he walks and dwells and makes his home. Not in every soul without exception, for where there is hardness he departs, where there is softness there he dwells; and nestling always with his feet and in all manner of ways in the softest of soft places, how can he be other than the softest of all things? Of a truth he is the tenderest as well as the youngest, and also he is of flexile form; for if he were hard and without flexure he could not enfold all things, or wind his way into and out of every soul of man undiscovered. And a proof of his flexibility and symmetry of form is his grace, which is universally admitted to be in an especial manner the attribute of Love; ungrace and love are always at war with one another. The fairness of his complexion is revealed by his habitation among the flowers; for he dwells not amid bloomless or fading beauties, whether of body or soul or aught else, but in the place of flowers and scents, there he sits and abides. Concerning the beauty of the god I have said enough; and yet there remains much more which I might say. Of his virtue I have now to speak: his greatest glory is that he can neither do nor suffer wrong to or from any god or any man; for he suffers not by force if he suffers; force comes not near him, neither when he acts does he act by force. For all men in all things serve him of their own free will, and where there is voluntary agreement, there, as the laws which are the lords of the city say, is justice. And not only is he just but exceedingly temperate, for Temperance is the acknowledged ruler of the pleasures and desires, and no pleasure ever masters Love; he is their master and they are his servants; and if he conquers them he must be temperate indeed. As to courage, even the God of War is no match for him; he is the captive and Love is the lord, for love, the love of Aphrodite, masters him, as the tale runs; and the master is stronger than the servant. And if he conquers the bravest of all others, he must be himself the bravest. Of his courage and justice and temperance I have spoken, but I have yet to speak of his wisdom; and according to the measure of my ability I must try to do my best. In the first place he is a poet (and here, like Eryximachus, I magnify my art), and he is also the source of poesy in others, which he could not be if he were not himself a poet. And at the touch of him everyone becomes a poet, even though he had no music in him before (A fragment of the Sthenoaoea of Euripides.); this also is a proof that Love is a good poet and accomplished in all the fine arts; for no one can give to another that which he has not himself, or teach that of which he has no knowledge. Who will deny that the creation of the animals is his doing? Are they not all the works of his wisdom, born and begotten of him? And as to the artists, do we not know that he only of them whom love inspires has the light of fame? He whom Love touches not, walks in darkness. The arts of medicine and archery and divination were discovered by Apollo, under the guidance of love and desire; so that he, too, is a disciple of Love. Also the melody of the Muses, the metallurgy of Hephaestus, the weaving of Athene, the empire of Zeus over gods and men, are all due to Love, who was the inventor of them. And so Love set in order the empire of the gods—the love of beauty, as is evident, for with deformity Love has no concern. In the days of old, as I began by saying, dreadful deeds were done among the gods, for they were ruled by Necessity; but now since the birth of Love, and from the Love of the beautiful, has sprung every good in heaven and earth. Therefore, Phaedrus, I say of Love that he is the fairest and best in himself, and the cause of what is fairest and best in all other things. And there comes into my mind a line of poetry in which he is said to be the god who

> "Gives peace on Earth and calms the stormy deep,
> Who stills the winds and bids the sufferer sleep."

This is he who empties men of disaffection and fills them with affection, who makes them to meet together at banquets such as these: in sacrifices, feasts, dances, he is our lord—who sends courtesy and sends away discourtesy, who gives kindness ever and never gives unkindness; the friend of the good, the wonder of the wise, the amazement of the gods; desired by those who have no part in him, and precious to those who have the better part in him; parent of delicacy, luxury, desire, fondness, softness, grace; regardful of the good, regardless of the evil; in every word, work, wish, fear—savior, pilot, comrade, helper; glory of gods and men, leader best and brightest; in whose footsteps let every man follow, sweetly singing in his honor and joining in that sweet strain with which love charms the souls of gods and men. Such is the speech, Phaedrus, half-playful, yet having a certain measure of seriousness, which, according to my ability, I dedicate to the god.

When Agathon had done speaking, Aristodemus said that there was a general cheer; the young man was thought to have spoken in a manner worthy of himself, and of the god. And Socrates, looking at Eryximachus, said: Tell me, son of Acumenus, was there not reason in my fears? And was I not a true prophet when I said that Agathon would make a wonderful oration, and that I should be in a strait?

The part of the prophecy which concerns Agathon, replied Eryximachus, appears to me to be true; but not the other part—that you will be in a strait.

Why, my dear friend, said Socrates, must not I or anyone be in a strait who has to speak after he has heard such a rich and varied discourse? I am especially struck with the beauty of the concluding words—who could listen to them without amazement? When I reflected on the immeasurable inferiority of my own powers, I was ready to run away for shame, if there had been a possibility of escape. For I was reminded of Gorgias, and at the end of his speech I fancied that Agathon was shaking at me the Gorginian or Gorgonian head of the great master of rhetoric, which was simply to turn me and my speech into stone, as Homer says (Odyssey), and strike me dumb. And then I perceived how foolish I had been in consenting to take my turn with you in praising love, and saying that I too was a master of the art, when I really had no conception how anything ought to be praised. For in my simplicity I imagined that the topics of praise should be true, and that this being presupposed, out of the true the speaker was to choose the best and set them forth in the best manner. And I felt quite proud, thinking that I knew the nature of true praise, and should speak well. Whereas I now see that the intention was to attribute to Love every species of greatness and glory, whether really belonging to him or not, without regard to truth or falsehood—that was no matter; for the original proposal seems to have been not that each of you should really praise Love, but only that you should appear to praise him. And so you attribute to Love every imaginable form of praise which can be gathered anywhere; and you say that "he is all this," and "the cause of all that," making him appear the fairest and best of all to those who know him not, for you cannot impose upon those who know him. And a noble and solemn hymn of praise have you rehearsed. But as I misunderstood the nature of the praise when I said that I would take my turn, I must beg to be absolved from the promise which I made in ignorance, and which (as Euripides would say [Eurip. Hyppolytus]) was a promise of the lips and not of the mind. Farewell then to such a strain: for I do not praise in that way; no, indeed, I cannot. But if you like to hear the truth about love, I am ready to speak in my own manner, though I will not make myself ridiculous by entering into any rivalry with you. Say then, Phaedrus, whether you would like to have the truth about love, spoken in any words and in any order which may happen to come into my mind at the time. Will that be agreeable to you?

Aristodemus said that Phaedrus and the company bid him speak in any manner which he thought best. Then, he added, let me have your permission first to ask Agathon a few more questions, in order that I may take his admissions as the premises of my discourse.

I grant the permission, said Phaedrus; put your questions. Socrates then proceeded as follows:

In the magnificent oration which you have just uttered, I think that you were right, my dear Agathon, in proposing to speak of the nature of Love first and afterward of his works—that is a way of beginning which I very much approve. And as you have spoken so eloquently of his nature, may I ask you further, Whether love is the love of something or of nothing? And here I must explain myself: I do not want you to say that love is the love of a father or the love of a mother—that would be ridiculous; but to answer as you would, if I asked is a father a father of something? to which you would find no difficulty in replying, of a son or daughter; and the answer would be right.

Very true, said Agathon.

And you would say the same of a mother?

He assented.

Yet let me ask you one more question in order to illustrate my meaning: Is not a brother to be regarded essentially as a brother of something?

Certainly, he replied.

That is, of a brother or sister?

Yes, he said.

And now, said Socrates, I will ask about Love: Is Love of something or of nothing?

Of something, surely, he replied.

Keep in mind what this is, and tell me what I want to know—whether Love desires that of which love is.

Yes, surely.

And does he possess, or does he not possess, that which he loves and desires?

Probably not, I should say.

Nay, replied Socrates, I would have you consider whether "necessarily" is not rather the word. The inference that he who desires something is in want of something, and that he who desires nothing is in want of nothing, is in my judgment, Agathon, absolutely and necessarily true. What do you think?

I agree with you, said Agathon.

Very good. Would he who is great, desire to be great, or he who is strong, desire to be strong?

That would be inconsistent with our previous admissions.

True. For he who is anything cannot want to be that which he is?

Very true.

And yet, added Socrates, if a man being strong desired to be strong, or being swift desired to be swift, or being healthy desired to be healthy, in that case he might be thought to desire something which he already has or is. I give the example in order that we may avoid misconception. For the possessors of these qualities, Agathon, must be supposed to have their respective advantages at the time, whether they choose or not; and who can desire that which he has? Therefore, when a person says, I am well and wish to be well, or I am rich and wish to be rich, and I desire simply to have what I have—to him we shall reply: "You, my friend, having wealth and health and strength, want to have the continuance of them; for at this moment, whether you choose or no, you have them. And when you say, I desire that which I have and nothing else, is not your meaning that you want to have what you now have in the future?" He must agree with us—must he not?

He must, replied Agathon.

Then, said Socrates, he desires that what he has at present may be preserved to him in the future, which is equivalent to saying that he desires something which is non-existent to him, and which as yet he has not got.

Very true, he said.

Then he and everyone who desires, desires that which he has not already, and which is future and not present, and which he has not, and is not, and of which he is in want—these are the sort of things which love and desire seek?

Very true, he said.

Then now, said Socrates, let us recapitulate the argument. First, is not love of something, and of something, too, which is wanting to a man?

Yes, he replied.

Remember further what you said in your speech, or if you do not remember I will remind you: You said that the love of the beautiful set in order the empire of the gods, for that of deformed things there is no love—did you not say something of that kind?

Yes, said Agathon.

Yes, my friend, and the remark was a just one. And if this is true, Love is the love of beauty and not of deformity?

He assented.

And the admission has been already made that Love is of something which a man wants and has not?

True, he said.

Then Love wants and has not beauty?

Certainly, he replied.

And would you call that beautiful which wants and does not possess beauty?

Certainly not.

Then would you still say that love is beautiful?

Agathon replied: I fear that I did not understand what I was saying.

You made a very good speech, Agathon, replied Socrates; but there is yet one small question which I would fain ask: Is not the good also the beautiful?

Yes.

Then in wanting the beautiful, love wants also the good?

I cannot refute you, Socrates, said Agathon:—Let us assume that what you say is true.

Say rather, beloved Agathon, that you cannot refute the truth; for Socrates is easily refuted.

And now, taking my leave of you, I would rehearse a tale of love which I heard from Diotima of Mantineia (compare 1 Alcibiades), a woman wise in this and in many other kinds of knowledge, who in the days of old, when the Athenians offered sacrifice before the coming of the plague, delayed the disease ten years. She was my instructress in the art of love, and I shall repeat to you what she said to me, beginning with the admissions made by Agathon, which are nearly if not quite the same which I made to the wise woman when she questioned me: I think that this will be the easiest way, and I shall take both parts myself as well as I can (compare Gorgias). As you, Agathon, suggested (supra), I must speak first of the being and nature of Love, and then of his works. First I said to her in nearly the same words which he used to me, that Love was a mighty god, and likewise fair; and she proved to me as I proved to him that, by my own showing, Love was neither fair nor good. "What do you mean, Diotima," I said, "is love then evil and foul?" "Hush," she cried; "must that be foul which is not fair?" "Certainly," I said. "And is that which is not wise, ignorant? do you not see that there is a mean between wisdom and ignorance?" "And what may that be?" I said. "Right opinion," she replied; "which, as you know, being incapable of giving a reason, is not knowledge (for how can knowledge be devoid of reason? nor again, ignorance, for neither can ignorance attain the truth), but is clearly something which is a mean between ignorance and wisdom." "Quite true," I replied. "Do not then insist," she said, "that what is not fair is of necessity foul, or what is not good evil; or infer that because love is not fair and good he is therefore foul and evil; for he is in a mean between them." "Well," I said, "Love is surely admitted by all to be a great god." "By those who know or by those who do not know?" "By all." "And how, Socrates," she said with a smile, "can Love be acknowledged to be a great god by those who say that he is not a god at all?" "And who are they?" I said. "You and I are two of them," she replied. "How can that be?" I said. "It is quite intelligible," she replied; "for you yourself would acknowledge that the gods are happy and fair—of course you would—would you dare to say that any god was not?" "Certainly not," I replied. "And you mean by the happy, those who are the possessors of things good or fair?" "Yes." "And you admitted that Love, because he was in want, desires those good and fair things of which he is in want?" "Yes, I did." "But how can he be a god who has no portion in what is either good or fair?" "Impossible." "Then you see that you also deny the divinity of Love."

"What then is Love?" I asked; "Is he mortal?" "No." "What then?" "As in the former instance, he is neither mortal nor immortal, but in a mean between the two." "What is he, Diotima?" "He is a great spirit (daimon), and like all spirits he is intermediate between the divine and the mortal." "And what," I said, "is his power?" "He interprets," she replied, "between gods and men, conveying and taking across to the gods the prayers and sacrifices of men, and to men the commands and replies of the gods; he is the mediator who spans the chasm which divides them, and therefore in him all is bound together, and through him the arts of the prophet and the priest, their sacrifices and mysteries and charms, and all prophecy and incantation, find their way. For God mingles not with man; but through Love all the intercourse and converse of God with man, whether awake or asleep, is carried on. The wisdom which understands this is spiritual; all other wisdom, such as that of arts and handicrafts, is mean and vulgar. Now these spirits or intermediate powers are many and diverse, and one of them is Love." "And who," I said, "was his father, and who his mother?" "The tale," she said, "will take time; nevertheless I will tell you. On the birthday of Aphrodite there was a feast of the gods, at which the god Poros or Plenty, who is the son of Metis or Discretion, was one of the guests. When the feast was over, Penia or Poverty, as the manner is on such occasions, came about the doors to beg. Now Plenty who was the worse for nectar (there was no wine in those days), went into the garden of Zeus and fell into a heavy sleep, and Poverty, considering her own straitened circumstances, plotted to have a child by him, and accordingly she lay down at his side and conceived Love, who partly because he is naturally a lover of the beautiful, and because Aphrodite is herself beautiful, and also because he was born on her birthday, is her follower and attendant. And as his parentage is, so also are his fortunes. In the first place he is always poor, and anything but tender and fair, as the many imagine him; and he is rough and squalid, and has no shoes, nor a house to dwell in; on the bare earth exposed he lies under the open heaven, in the streets, or at the doors of houses, taking his rest; and like his mother he is always in distress. Like his father too, whom he also partly resembles, he is always plotting against the fair and good; he is bold, enterprising, strong, a mighty hunter, always weaving some intrigue or other, keen in the pursuit of wisdom, fertile in resources; a philosopher at all times, terrible as an enchanter, sorcerer, sophist. He is by nature neither mortal nor immortal, but alive and flourishing at one moment when he is in plenty, and dead at another moment, and again alive by reason of his father's nature. But that which is always flowing in is always flowing out, and so he is never in want and never in wealth; and, further, he is in a mean between ignorance and knowledge. The truth of the matter is this: No god is a philosopher or seeker after wisdom, for he is wise already; nor does any man who is wise seek after wisdom. Neither do the ignorant seek after wisdom. For herein is the evil of ignorance, that he who is neither good nor wise is nevertheless satisfied with himself; he has no desire for that of which he feels no want." "But who then, Diotima," I said, "are the lovers of wisdom, if they are neither the wise nor the foolish?" "A child may answer that question," she replied; "they are those who are in a mean between the two; Love is one of them. For wisdom is a most beautiful thing, and Love is of the beautiful; and therefore Love is also a philosopher or lover of wisdom, and being a lover of wisdom is in a mean between the wise and the ignorant. And of this too his birth is the cause; for his father is wealthy and wise, and his mother poor and foolish. Such, my dear Socrates, is the nature of the spirit Love. The error in your conception of him was very natural, and as I imagine from what you say, has arisen out of a confusion of love and the beloved, which made you think that love was all beautiful. For the beloved is the truly beautiful, and delicate, and perfect, and blessed; but the principle of love is of another nature, and is such as I have described."

I said, "O thou stranger woman, thou sayest well; but, assuming Love to be such as you say, what is the use of him to men?" "That, Socrates," she replied, "I will attempt to unfold: of his nature and birth I have already spoken; and you acknowledge that love is of the beautiful. But someone will say: Of the beautiful in what, Socrates and Diotima?—or rather let me put the question more clearly, and ask: When a man loves the beautiful, what does he desire?" I answered her "That the beautiful may be his." "Still," she said, "the answer suggests a further question: What is given by the possession of beauty?" "To what you have asked," I replied, "I have no answer ready." "Then," she said, "let me put the word "good" in the place of the beautiful, and repeat the question once more: If he who loves loves the good, what is it then that he loves?" "The possession of the good," I said. "And what does he gain who possesses the good?" "Happiness," I replied; "there is less difficulty in answering that question." "Yes," she said, "the happy are made happy by the acquisition of good things. Nor is there any need to ask why a man desires happiness; the answer is already final." "You are right." I said. "And is this wish and this desire common to all? and do all men always desire their own good, or only some men?—what say you?" "All men," I replied; "the desire is common to all." "Why, then," she rejoined, "are not all men, Socrates, said to love, but only some of them? whereas you say that all men are always loving the same things." "I myself wonder," I said, "why this is." "There is nothing to wonder at," she replied; "the reason is that one part of love is separated off and receives the name of the whole, but the other parts have other names." "Give an illustration," I said. She answered me as follows: "There is poetry, which, as you know, is complex and manifold. All creation or passage of non-being into being is poetry or making, and the processes of all art are creative; and the masters of arts are all poets or makers." "Very true." "Still," she said, "you know that they are not called poets, but have other names; only that portion of the art which is separated off from the rest, and is concerned with music and meter, is termed poetry, and they who possess poetry in this sense of the word are called poets." "Very true," I said. "And the same holds of love. For you may say generally that all desire of good and happiness is only the great and subtle power of love; but they who are drawn toward him by any other path, whether the path of money-making or gymnastics or philosophy, are not called lovers—the name of the whole is appropriated to those whose affection takes one form only—they alone are said to love, or to be lovers." "I dare say," I replied, "that you are right." "Yes," she added, "and you hear people say that lovers are seeking for their other half; but I say that they are seeking neither for the half of themselves, nor for the whole, unless the half or the whole be also a good. And they will cut off their own hands and feet and cast them away, if they are evil; for they love not what is their own, unless perchance there be someone who calls what belongs to him the good, and what belongs to another the evil. For there is nothing which men love but the good. Is there anything?" "Certainly, I should say, that there is nothing." "Then," she said, "the simple truth is, that men love the good." "Yes," I said. "To which must be added that they love the possession of the good?" "Yes, that must be added." "And not only the possession, but the everlasting possession of the good?" "That must be added too." "Then love," she said, "may be described generally as the love of the everlasting possession of the good?" "That is most true."

"Then if this be the nature of love, can you tell me further," she said, "what is the manner of the pursuit? what are they doing who show all this eagerness and heat which is called love? and what is the object which they have in view? Answer me." "Nay, Diotima," I replied, "if I had known, I should not have wondered at your wisdom, neither should I have come to learn from you about this very matter." "Well," she said, "I will teach you: The object which they have in view is birth in beauty, whether of body or soul." "I do not understand you," I said; "the oracle requires an explanation." "I will make my meaning clearer," she replied. "I mean to say, that all men are bringing to the birth in their bodies and in their souls. There is a certain age at which human nature is desirous of procreation—procreation which must be in beauty and not in deformity; and this procreation is the union of man and woman, and is a divine thing; for conception and generation are an immortal principle in the mortal creature, and in the inharmonious they can never be. But the deformed is always inharmonious with the divine, and the beautiful harmonious. Beauty, then, is the destiny or goddess of parturition who presides at birth, and therefore, when approaching beauty, the conceiving power is propitious, and diffusive, and benign, and begets and bears fruit: at the sight of ugliness she frowns and contracts and has a sense of pain, and turns away, and shrivels up, and not without a pang refrains from conception. And this is the reason why, when the hour of conception arrives, and the teeming nature is full, there is such a flutter and ecstasy about beauty whose approach is the alleviation of the pain of travail. For love, Socrates, is not, as you imagine, the love of the beautiful only." "What then?" "The love of generation and of birth in beauty." "Yes," I said. "Yes, indeed," she replied. "But why of generation?" "Because to the mortal creature, generation is a sort of eternity and immortality," she replied; "and if, as has been already admitted, love is of the everlasting possession of the good, all men will necessarily desire immortality together with good: Wherefore love is of immortality."

All this she taught me at various times when she spoke of love. And I remember her once saying to me, "What is the cause, Socrates, of love, and the attendant desire? See you not how all animals, birds, as well as beasts, in their desire of procreation, are in agony when they take the infection of love, which begins with the desire of union; whereto is added the care of offspring, on whose behalf the weakest are ready to battle against the strongest even to the uttermost, and to die for them, and will let themselves be tormented with hunger or suffer anything in order to maintain their young. Man may be supposed to act thus from reason; but why should animals have these passionate feelings? Can you tell me why?" Again I replied that I did not know. She said to me: "And do you expect ever to become a master in the art of love, if you do not know this?" "But I have told you already, Diotima, that my ignorance is the reason why I come to you; for I am conscious that I want a teacher; tell me then the cause of this and of the other mysteries of love." "Marvel not," she said, "if you believe that love is of the immortal, as we have several times acknowledged; for here again, and on the same principle too, the mortal nature is seeking as far as is possible to be everlasting and immortal: and this is only to be attained by generation, because generation always leaves behind a new existence in the place of the old. Nay even in the life of the same individual there is succession and not absolute unity: a man is called the same, and yet in the short interval which elapses between youth and age, and in which every animal is said to have life and identity, he is undergoing a perpetual process of loss and reparation—hair, flesh, bones, blood, and the whole body are always changing. Which is true not only of the body, but also of the soul, whose habits, tempers, opinions, desires, pleasures, pains, fears, never remain the same in any one of us, but are always coming and going; and equally true of knowledge, and what is still more surprising to us mortals, not only do the sciences in general spring up and decay, so that in respect of them we are never the same; but each of them individually experiences a like change. For what is implied in the word "recollection," but the departure of knowledge, which is ever being forgotten, and is renewed and preserved by recollection, and appears to be the same although in reality new, according to that law of succession by which all mortal things are preserved, not absolutely the same, but by substitution, the old worn-out mortality leaving another new and similar existence behind—unlike the divine, which is always the same and not another? And in this way, Socrates, the mortal body, or mortal anything, partakes of immortality; but the immortal in another way. Marvel not then at the love which all men have of their offspring; for that universal love and interest is for the sake of immortality."

I was astonished at her words, and said: "Is this really true, O thou wise Diotima?" And she answered with all the authority of an accomplished sophist: "Of that, Socrates, you may be assured—think only of the ambition of men, and you will wonder at the senselessness of their ways, unless you consider how they are stirred by the love of an immortality of fame. They are ready to run all risks greater far than they would have run for their children, and to spend money and undergo any sort of toil, and even to die, for the sake of leaving behind them a name which shall be eternal. Do you imagine that Alcestis would have died to save Admetus, or Achilles to avenge Patroclus, or your own Codrus in order to preserve the kingdom for his sons, if they had not imagined that the memory of their virtues, which still survives among us, would be immortal? Nay," she said, "I am persuaded that all men do all things, and the better they are the more they do them, in hope of the glorious fame of immortal virtue; for they desire the immortal.

"Those who are pregnant in the body only, betake themselves to women and beget children—this is the character of their love; their offspring, as they hope, will preserve their memory and giving them the blessedness and immortality which they desire in the future. But souls which are pregnant—for there certainly are men who are more creative in their souls than in their bodies—conceive that which is proper for the soul to conceive or contain. And what are these conceptions?—wisdom and virtue in general. And such creators are poets and all artists who are deserving of the name inventor. But the greatest and fairest sort of wisdom by far is that which is concerned with the ordering of states and families, and which is called temperance and justice. And he who in youth has the seed of these implanted in him and is himself inspired, when he comes to maturity desires to beget and generate. He wanders about seeking beauty that he may beget offspring—for in deformity he will beget nothing—and naturally embraces the beautiful rather than the deformed body; above all when he finds a fair and noble and well-nurtured soul, he embraces the two in one person, and to such an one he is full of speech about virtue and the nature and pursuits of a good man; and he tries to educate him; and at the touch of the beautiful which is ever present to his memory, even when absent, he brings forth that which he had conceived long before, and in company with him tends that which he brings forth; and they are married by a far nearer tie and have a closer friendship than those who beget mortal children, for the children who are their common offspring are fairer and more immortal. Who, when he thinks of Homer and Hesiod and other great poets, would not rather have their children than ordinary human ones? Who would not emulate them in the creation of children such as theirs, which have preserved their memory and given them everlasting glory? Or who would not have such children as Lycurgus left behind him to be the saviours, not only of Lacedaemon, but of Hellas, as one may say? There is Solon, too, who is the revered father of Athenian laws; and many others there are in many other places, both among Hellenes and barbarians, who have given to the world many noble works, and have been the parents of virtue of every kind; and many temples have been raised in their honor for the sake of children such as theirs; which were never raised in honor of anyone, for the sake of his mortal children.

"These are the lesser mysteries of love, into which even you, Socrates, may enter; to the greater and more hidden ones which are the crown of these, and to which, if you pursue them in a right spirit, they will lead, I know not whether you will be able to attain. But I will do my utmost to inform you, and do you follow if you can. For he who would proceed aright in this matter should begin in youth to visit beautiful forms; and first, if he be guided by his instructor aright, to love one such form only— out of that he should create fair thoughts; and soon he will of himself perceive that the beauty of one form is akin to the beauty of another; and then if beauty of form in general is his pursuit, how foolish would he be not to recognize that the beauty in every form is and the same! And when he perceives this he will abate his violent love of the one, which he will despise and deem a small thing, and will become a lover of all beautiful forms; in the next stage he will consider that the beauty of the mind is more honorable than the beauty of the outward form. So that if a virtuous soul have but a little comeliness, he will be content to love and tend him, and will search out and bring to the birth thoughts which may improve the young, until he is compelled to contemplate and see the beauty of institutions and laws, and to understand that the beauty of them all is of one family, and that personal beauty is a trifle; and after laws and institutions he will go on to the sciences, that he may see their beauty, being not like a servant in love with the beauty of one youth or man or institution, himself a slave mean and narrow-minded, but drawing toward and contemplating the vast sea of beauty, he will create many fair and noble thoughts and notions in boundless love of wisdom; until on that shore he grows and waxes strong, and at last the vision is revealed to him of a single science, which is the science of beauty everywhere. To this I will proceed; please to give me your very best attention:

"He who has been instructed thus far in the things of love, and who has learned to see the beautiful in due order and succession, when he comes toward the end will suddenly perceive a nature of wondrous beauty (and this, Socrates, is the final cause of all our former toils)—a nature which in the first place is everlasting, not growing and decaying, or waxing and waning; secondly, not fair in one point of view and foul in another, or at one time or in one relation or at one place fair, at another time or in another relation or at another place foul, as if fair to some and foul to others, or in the likeness of a face or hands or any other part of the bodily frame, or in any form of speech or knowledge, or existing in any other being, as for example, in an animal, or in heaven, or in earth, or in any other place; but beauty absolute, separate, simple, and everlasting, which without diminution and without increase, or any change, is imparted to the ever-growing and perishing beauties of all other things. He who from these ascending under the influence of true love, begins to perceive that beauty, is not far from the end. And the true order of going, or being led by another, to the things of love, is to begin from the beauties of Earth and mount upwards for the sake of that other beauty, using these as steps only, and from one going on to two, and from two to all fair forms, and from fair forms to fair practices, and from fair practices to fair notions, until from fair notions he arrives at the notion of absolute beauty, and at last knows what the essence of beauty is. This, my dear Socrates," said the stranger of Mantineia, "is that life above all others which man should live, in the contemplation of beauty absolute; a beauty which if you once beheld, you would see not to be after the measure of gold, and garments, and fair boys and youths, whose presence now entrances you; and you and many a one would be content to live seeing them only and conversing with them without meat or drink, if that were possible—you only want to look at them and to be with them. But what if man had eyes to see the true beauty—the divine beauty, I mean, pure and clear and unalloyed, not clogged with the pollutions of mortality and all the colors and vanities of human life—thither looking, and holding converse with the true beauty simple and divine? Remember how in that communion only, beholding beauty with the eye of the mind, he will be enabled to bring forth, not images of beauty, but realities (for he has hold not of an image but of a reality), and bringing forth and nourishing true virtue to become the friend of God and be immortal, if mortal man may. Would that be an ignoble life?"

Such, Phaedrus—and I speak not only to you, but to all of you—were the words of Diotima; and I am persuaded of their truth. And being persuaded of them, I try to persuade others, that in the attainment of this end human nature will not easily find a helper better than love: And therefore, also, I say that every man ought to honor him as I myself honor him, and walk in his ways, and exhort others to do the same, and praise the power and spirit of love according to the measure of my ability now and ever.

The words which I have spoken, you, Phaedrus, may call an encomium of love, or anything else which you please.

When Socrates had done speaking, the company applauded, and Aristophanes was beginning to say something in answer to the allusion which Socrates had made to his own speech, when suddenly there was a great knocking at the door of the house, as of revellers, and the sound of a flute girl was heard. Agathon told the attendants to go and see who were the intruders. "If they are friends of ours," he said, "invite them in, but if not, say that the drinking is over." A little while afterward they heard the voice of Alcibiades resounding in the court; he was in a great state of intoxication, and kept roaring and shouting "Where is Agathon? Lead me to Agathon," and at length, supported by the flute girl and some of his attendants, he found his way to them. "Hail, friends," he said, appearing at the door crowned with a massive garland of ivy and violets, his head flowing with ribands. "Will you have a very drunken man as a companion of your revels? Or shall I crown Agathon, which was my intention in coming, and go away? For I was unable to come yesterday, and therefore I am here today, carrying on my head these ribands, that taking them from my own head, I may crown the head of this fairest and wisest of men, as I may be allowed to call him. Will you laugh at me because I am drunk? Yet I know very well that I am speaking the truth, although you may laugh. But first tell me; if I come in shall we have the understanding of which I spoke (supra Will you have a very drunken man? etc.)? Will you drink with me or not?"

The company were vociferous in begging that he would take his place among them, and Agathon specially invited him. Thereupon he was led in by the people who were with him; and as he was being led, intending to crown Agathon, he took the ribands from his own head and held them in front of his eyes; he was thus prevented from seeing Socrates, who made way for him, and Alcibiades took the vacant place between Agathon and Socrates, and in taking the place he embraced Agathon and crowned him. Take off his sandals, said Agathon, and let him make a third on the same couch.

By all means; but who makes the third partner in our revels? said Alcibiades, turning round and starting up as he caught sight of Socrates. By Heracles, he said, what is this? here is Socrates always lying in wait for me, and always, as his way is, coming out at all sorts of unsuspected places: and now, what have you to say for yourself, and why are you lying here, where I perceive that you have contrived to find a place, not by a joker or lover of jokes, like Aristophanes, but by the fairest of the company?

Socrates turned to Agathon and said: I must ask you to protect me, Agathon; for the passion of this man has grown quite a serious matter to me. Since I became his admirer I have never been allowed to speak to any other fair one, or so much as to look at them. If I do, he goes wild with envy and jealousy, and not only abuses me but can hardly keep his hands off me, and at this moment he may do me some harm. Please to see to this, and either reconcile me to him, or, if he attempts violence, protect me, as I am in bodily fear of his mad and passionate attempts.

There can never be reconciliation between you and me, said Alcibiades; but for the present I will defer your chastisement. And I must beg you, Agathon, to give me back some of the ribands that I may crown the marvellous head of this universal despot—I would not have him complain of me for crowning you, and neglecting him, who in conversation is the conqueror of all mankind; and this not only once, as you were the day before yesterday, but always. Whereupon, taking some of the ribands, he crowned Socrates, and again reclined.

Then he said: You seem, my friends, to be sober, which is a thing not to be endured; you must drink—for that was the agreement under which I was admitted—and I elect myself master of the feast until you are well drunk. Let us have a large goblet, Agathon, or rather, he said, addressing the attendant, bring me that wine-cooler. The wine-cooler which had caught his eye was a vessel holding more than two quarts—this he filled and emptied, and bade the attendant fill it again for Socrates. Observe, my friends, said Alcibiades, that this ingenious trick of mine will have no effect on Socrates, for he can drink any quantity of wine and not be at all nearer being drunk. Socrates drank the cup which the attendant filled for him.

Eryximachus said: What is this, Alcibiades? Are we to have neither conversation nor singing over our cups; but simply to drink as if we were thirsty?

Alcibiades replied: Hail, worthy son of a most wise and worthy sire!

The same to you, said Eryximachus; but what shall we do?

That I leave to you, said Alcibiades.

The wise physician skilled our wounds to heal (from Pope's Homer, Il.) shall prescribe and we will obey. What do you want?

Well, said Eryximachus, before you appeared we had passed a resolution that each one of us in turn should make a speech in praise of love, and as good a one as he could: the turn was passed round from left to right; and as all of us have spoken, and you have not spoken but have well drunken, you ought to speak, and then impose upon Socrates any task which you please, and he on his right hand neighbor, and so on.

That is good, Eryximachus, said Alcibiades; and yet the comparison of a drunken man's speech with those of sober men is hardly fair; and I should like to know, sweet friend, whether you really believe what Socrates was just now saying; for I can assure you that the very reverse is the fact, and that if I praise anyone but himself in his presence, whether God or man, he will hardly keep his hands off me.

For shame, said Socrates.

Hold your tongue, said Alcibiades, for by Poseidon, there is no one else whom I will praise when you are of the company.

Well then, said Eryximachus, if you like praise Socrates.

What do you think, Eryximachus? said Alcibiades: shall I attack him and inflict the punishment before you all?

What are you about? said Socrates; are you going to raise a laugh at my expense? Is that the meaning of your praise?

I am going to speak the truth, if you will permit me.

I not only permit, but exhort you to speak the truth.

Then I will begin at once, said Alcibiades, and if I say anything which is not true, you may interrupt me if you will, and say "that is a lie," though my intention is to speak the truth. But you must not wonder if I speak any how as things come into my mind; for the fluent and orderly enumeration of all your singularities is not a task which is easy to a man in my condition.

And now, my boys, I shall praise Socrates in a figure which will appear to him to be a caricature, and yet I speak, not to make fun of him, but only for the truth's sake. I say, that he is exactly like the busts of Silenus, which are set up in the statuaries' shops, holding pipes and flutes in their mouths; and they are made to open in the middle, and have images of gods inside them. I say also that he is like Marsyas the satyr. You yourself will not deny, Socrates, that your face is like that of a satyr. Aye, and there is a resemblance in other points too. For example, you are a bully, as I can prove by witnesses, if you will not confess. And are you not a flute player? That you are, and a performer far more wonderful than Marsyas. He indeed with instruments used to charm the souls of men by the power of his breath, and the players of his music do so still: for the melodies of Olympus (compare Arist. Pol.) are derived from Marsyas who taught them, and these, whether they are played by a great master or by a miserable flute girl, have a power which no others have; they alone possess the soul and reveal the wants of those who have need of gods and mysteries, because they are divine. But you produce the same effect with your words only, and do not require the flute: that is the difference between you and him. When we hear any other speaker, even a very good one, he produces absolutely no effect upon us, or not much, whereas the mere fragments of you and your words, even at second-hand, and however imperfectly repeated, amaze and possess the souls of every man, woman, and child who comes within hearing of them. And if I were not afraid that you would think me hopelessly drunk, I would have sworn as well as spoken to the influence which they have always had and still have over me. For my heart leaps within me more than that of any Corybantian reveller, and my eyes rain tears when I hear them. And I observe that many others are affected in the same manner. I have heard Pericles and other great orators, and I thought that they spoke well, but I never had any similar feeling; my soul was not stirred by them, nor was I angry at the thought of my own slavish state. But this Marsyas has often brought me to such a pass, that I have felt as if I could hardly endure the life which I am leading (this, Socrates, you will admit); and I am conscious that if I did not shut my ears against him, and fly as from the voice of the siren, my fate would be like that of others,—he would transfix me, and I should grow old sitting at his feet. For he makes me confess that I ought not to live as I do, neglecting the wants of my own soul, and busying myself with the concerns of the Athenians; therefore I hold my ears and tear myself away from him. And he is the only person who ever made me ashamed, which you might think not to be in my nature, and there is no one else who does the same. For I know that I cannot answer him or say that I ought not to do as he bids, but when I leave his presence the love of popularity gets the better of me. And therefore I run away and fly from him, and when I see him I am ashamed of what I have confessed to him. Many a time have I wished that he were dead, and yet I know that I should be much more sorry than glad, if he were to die: so that I am at my wit's end.

And this is what I and many others have suffered from the flute playing of this satyr. Yet hear me once more while I show you how exact the image is, and how marvellous his power. For let me tell you; none of you know him; but I will reveal him to you; having begun, I must go on. See you how fond he is of the fair? He is always with them and is always being smitten by them, and then again he knows nothing and is ignorant of all things—such is the appearance which he puts on. Is he not like a Silenus in this? To be sure he is: his outer mask is the carved head of the Silenus; but, O my companions in drink, when he is opened, what temperance there is residing within! Know you that beauty and wealth and honor, at which the many wonder, are of no account with him, and are utterly despised by him: he regards not at all the persons who are gifted with them; mankind are nothing to him; all his life is spent in mocking and flouting at them. But when I opened him, and looked within at his serious purpose, I saw in him divine and golden images of such fascinating beauty that I was ready to do in a moment whatever Socrates commanded: they may have escaped the observation of others, but I saw them. Now I fancied that he was seriously enamoured of my beauty, and I thought that I should therefore have a grand opportunity of hearing him tell what he knew, for I had a wonderful opinion of the attractions of my youth. In the prosecution of this design, when I next went to him, I sent away the attendant who usually accompanied me (I will confess the whole truth, and beg you to listen; and if I speak falsely, do you, Socrates, expose the falsehood). Well, he and I were alone together, and I thought that when there was nobody with us, I should hear him speak the language which lovers use to their loves when they are by themselves, and I was delighted. Nothing of the sort; he conversed as usual, and spent the day with me and then went away. Afterward I challenged him to the palaestra; and he wrestled and closed with me several times when there was no one present; I fancied that I might succeed in this manner. Not a bit; I made no way with him. Lastly, as I had failed hitherto, I thought that I must take stronger measures and attack him boldly, and, as I had begun, not give him up, but see how matters stood between him and me. So I invited him to sup with me, just as if he were a fair youth, and I a designing lover. He was not easily persuaded to come; he did, however, after a while accept the invitation, and when he came the first time, he wanted to go away at once as soon as supper was over, and I had not the face to detain him. The second time, still in pursuance of my design, after we had supped, I went on conversing far into the night, and when he wanted to go away, I pretended that the hour was late and that he had much better remain. So he lay down on the couch next to me, the same on which he had supped, and there was no one but ourselves sleeping in the apartment. All this may be told without shame to anyone. But what follows I could hardly tell you if I were sober. Yet as the proverb says, "In vino veritas," whether with boys, or without them (In allusion to two proverbs.); and therefore I must speak. Nor, again, should I be justified in concealing the lofty actions of Socrates when I come to praise him. Moreover I have felt the serpent's sting; and he who has suffered, as they say, is willing to tell his fellow sufferers only, as they alone will be likely to understand him, and will not be extreme in judging of the sayings or doings which have been wrung from his agony. For I have been bitten by a more than viper's tooth; I have known in my soul, or in my heart, or in some other part, that worst of pangs, more violent in ingenuous youth than any serpent's tooth, the pang of philosophy, which will make a man say or do anything. And you whom I see around me, Phaedrus and Agathon and Eryximachus and Pausanias and Aristodemus and Aristophanes, all of you, and I need not say Socrates himself, have had experience of the same madness and passion in your longing after wisdom. Therefore listen and excuse my doings then and my sayings now. But let the attendants and other profane and unmannered persons close up the doors of their ears.

 When the lamp was put out and the servants had gone away, I thought that I must be plain with him and have no more ambiguity. So I gave him a shake, and I said: "Socrates, are you asleep?" "No," he said. "Do you know what I am meditating?" "What are you meditating?" he said. "I think," I replied, "that of all the lovers whom I have ever had you are the only one who is worthy of me, and you appear to be too modest to speak. Now I feel that I should be a fool to refuse you this or any other favor, and therefore I come to lay at your feet all that I have and all that my friends have, in the hope that you will assist me in the way of virtue, which I desire above all things, and in which I believe that you can help me better than anyone else. And I should certainly have more reason to be ashamed of what wise men would say if I were to refuse a favor to such as you, than of what the world, who are mostly fools, would say of me if I granted it." To these words he replied in the ironical manner which is so characteristic of him—"Alcibiades, my friend, you have indeed an elevated aim if what you say is true, and if there really is in me any power by which you may become better; truly you must see in me some rare beauty of a kind infinitely higher than any which I see in you. And therefore, if you mean to share with me and to exchange beauty for beauty, you will have greatly the advantage of me; you will gain true beauty in return for appearance—like Diomede, gold in exchange for brass. But look again, sweet friend, and see whether you are not deceived in me. The mind begins to grow critical when the bodily eye fails, and it will be a long time before you get old." Hearing this, I said: "I have told you my purpose, which is quite serious, and do you consider what you think best for you and me." "That is good," he said; "at some other time then we will consider and act as seems best about this and about other matters." Whereupon, I fancied that he was smitten, and that the words which I had uttered like arrows had wounded him, and so without waiting to hear more I got up, and throwing my coat about him crept under his threadbare cloak, as the time of year was winter, and there I lay during the whole night having this wonderful monster in my arms. This again, Socrates, will not be denied by you. And yet, notwithstanding all, he was so superior to my solicitations, so contemptuous and derisive and disdainful of my beauty—which really, as I fancied, had some attractions—hear, O judges; for judges you shall be of the haughty virtue of Socrates—nothing more happened, but in the morning when I awoke (let all the gods and goddesses be my witnesses) I arose as from the couch of a father or an elder brother.

What do you suppose must have been my feelings, after this rejection, at the thought of my own dishonor? And yet I could not help wondering at his natural temperance and self-restraint and manliness. I never imagined that I could have met with a man such as he is in wisdom and endurance. And therefore I could not be angry with him or renounce his company, any more than I could hope to win him. For I well knew that if Ajax could not be wounded by steel, much less he by money; and my only chance of captivating him by my personal attractions had failed. So I was at my wit's end; no one was ever more hopelessly enslaved by another. All this happened before he and I went on the expedition to Potidaea; there we messed together, and I had the opportunity of observing his extraordinary power of sustaining fatigue. His endurance was simply marvellous when, being cut off from our supplies, we were compelled to go without food—on such occasions, which often happen in time of war, he was superior not only to me but to everybody; there was no one to be compared to him. Yet at a festival he was the only person who had any real powers of enjoyment; though not willing to drink, he could if compelled beat us all at that—

wonderful to relate! no human being had ever seen Socrates drunk; and his powers, if I am not mistaken, will be tested before long. His fortitude in enduring cold was also surprising. There was a severe frost, for the winter in that region is really tremendous, and everybody else either remained indoors, or if they went out had on an amazing quantity of clothes, and were well shod, and had their feet swathed in felt and fleeces: in the midst of this, Socrates with his bare feet on the ice and in his ordinary dress marched better than the other soldiers who had shoes, and they looked daggers at him because he seemed to despise them.

 I have told you one tale, and now I must tell you another, which is worth hearing, "of the doings and sufferings of the enduring man" while he was on the expedition. One morning he was thinking about something which he could not resolve; he would not give it up, but continued thinking from early dawn until noon—there he stood fixed in thought; and at noon attention was drawn to him, and the rumor ran through the wondering crowd that Socrates had been standing and thinking about something ever since the break of day. At last, in the evening after supper, some Ionians out of curiosity (I should explain that this was not in winter but in summer), brought out their mats and slept in the open air that they might watch him and see whether he would stand all night. There he stood until the following morning; and with the return of light he offered up a prayer to the sun, and went his way (compare supra). I will also tell, if you please—and indeed I am bound to tell—of his courage in battle; for who but he saved my life? Now this was the engagement in which I received the prize of valour: for I was wounded and he would not leave me, but he rescued me and my arms; and he ought to have received the prize of valour which the generals wanted to confer on me partly on account of my rank, and I told them so, (this, again, Socrates will not impeach or deny), but he was more eager than the generals that I and not he should have the prize. There was another occasion on which his behavior was very remarkable—in the flight of the army after the battle of Delium, where he served among the heavy-armed, I had a better opportunity of seeing him than at Potidaea, for I was myself on horseback, and therefore comparatively out of danger. He and Laches were retreating, for the troops were in flight, and I met them and told them not to be discouraged, and promised to remain with them; and there you might see him, Aristophanes, as you describe (Aristoph. Clouds), just as he is in the streets of Athens, stalking like a pelican, and rolling his eyes, calmly contemplating enemies as well as friends, and making very intelligible to anybody, even from a distance, that whoever attacked him would be likely to meet with a stout resistance; and in this way he and his companion escaped—for this is the sort of man who is never touched in war; those only are pursued who are running away headlong. I particularly observed how superior he was to Laches in presence of mind. Many are the marvels which I might narrate in praise of Socrates; most of his ways might perhaps be paralleled in another man, but his absolute unlikeness to any human being that is or ever has been is perfectly astonishing. You may imagine Brasidas and others to have been like Achilles; or you may imagine Nestor and Antenor to have been like Pericles; and the same may be said of other famous men, but of this strange being you will never be able to find any likeness, however remote, either among men who now are or who ever have been—other than that which I have already suggested of Silenus and the satyrs; and they represent in a figure not only himself, but his words. For, although I forgot to mention this to you before, his words are like the images of Silenus which open; they are ridiculous when you first hear them; he clothes himself in language that is like the skin of the wanton satyr—for his talk is of pack-asses and smiths and cobblers and curriers, and he is always repeating the same things in the same words (compare Gorg.), so that any ignorant or inexperienced person might feel disposed to laugh at him; but he who opens the bust and sees what is within will find that they are the only words which have a meaning in them, and also the most divine, abounding in fair images of virtue, and of the widest comprehension, or rather extending to the whole duty of a good and honorable man.

This, friends, is my praise of Socrates. I have added my blame of him for his ill-treatment of me; and he has ill-treated not only me, but Charmides the son of Glaucon, and Euthydemus the son of Diocles, and many others in the same way—beginning as their lover he has ended by making them pay their addresses to him. Wherefore I say to you, Agathon, "Be not deceived by him; learn from me and take warning, and do not be a fool and learn by experience, as the proverb says."

When Alcibiades had finished, there was a laugh at his outspokenness; for he seemed to be still in love with Socrates. You are sober, Alcibiades, said Socrates, or you would never have gone so far about to hide the purpose of your satyr's praises, for all this long story is only an ingenious circumlocution, of which the point comes in by the way at the end; you want to get up a quarrel between me and Agathon, and your notion is that I ought to love you and nobody else, and that you and you only ought to love Agathon. But the plot of this Satyric or Silenic drama has been detected, and you must not allow him, Agathon, to set us at variance.

I believe you are right, said Agathon, and I am disposed to think that his intention in placing himself between you and me was only to divide us; but he shall gain nothing by that move; for I will go and lie on the couch next to you.

Yes, yes, replied Socrates, by all means come here and lie on the couch below me.

Alas, said Alcibiades, how I am fooled by this man; he is determined to get the better of me at every turn. I do beseech you, allow Agathon to lie between us.

Certainly not, said Socrates, as you praised me, and I in turn ought to praise my neighbor on the right, he will be out of order in praising me again when he ought rather to be praised by me, and I must entreat you to consent to this, and not be jealous, for I have a great desire to praise the youth.

Hurrah! cried Agathon, I will rise instantly, that I may be praised by Socrates.

The usual way, said Alcibiades; where Socrates is, no one else has any chance with the fair; and now how readily has he invented a specious reason for attracting Agathon to himself.

Agathon arose in order that he might take his place on the couch by Socrates, when suddenly a band of revellers entered, and spoiled the order of the banquet. Someone who was going out, having left the door open, they had found their way in, and made themselves at home; great confusion ensued, and everyone was compelled to drink large quantities of wine. Aristodemus said that Eryximachus, Phaedrus, and others went away—he himself fell asleep, and as the nights were long took a good rest: he was awakened toward daybreak by a crowing of cocks, and when he awoke, the others were either asleep, or had gone away; there remained only Socrates, Aristophanes, and Agathon, who were drinking out of a large goblet which they passed round, and Socrates was discoursing to them. Aristodemus was only half awake, and he did not hear the beginning of the discourse; the chief thing which he remembered was Socrates compelling the other two to acknowledge that the genius of comedy was the same with that of tragedy, and that the true artist in tragedy was an artist in comedy also. To this they were constrained to assent, being drowsy, and not quite following the argument. And first of all Aristophanes dropped off, then, when the day was already dawning, Agathon. Socrates, having laid them to sleep, rose to depart; Aristodemus, as his manner was, following him. At the Lyceum he took a bath, and passed the day as usual. In the evening he retired to rest at his own home.

PHAEDRUS

BY PLATO

Translated by Benjamin Jowett

INTRODUCTION

The Phaedrus is closely connected with the Symposium, and may be regarded either as introducing or following it. The two Dialogues together contain the whole philosophy of Plato on the nature of love, which in the Republic and in the later writings of Plato is only introduced playfully or as a figure of speech. But in the Phaedrus and Symposium love and philosophy join hands, and one is an aspect of the other. The spiritual and emotional part is elevated into the ideal, to which in the Symposium mankind are described as looking forward, and which in the Phaedrus, as well as in the Phaedo, they are seeking to recover from a former state of existence. Whether the subject of the Dialogue is love or rhetoric, or the union of the two, or the relation of philosophy to love and to art in general, and to the human soul, will be hereafter considered. And perhaps we may arrive at some conclusion such as the following—that the dialogue is not strictly confined to a single subject, but passes from one to another with the natural freedom of conversation.

Phaedrus has been spending the morning with Lysias, the celebrated rhetorician, and is going to refresh himself by taking a walk outside the wall, when he is met by Socrates, who professes that he will not leave him until he has delivered up the speech with which Lysias has regaled him, and which he is carrying about in his mind, or more probably in a book hidden under his cloak, and is intending to study as he walks. The imputation is not denied, and the two agree to direct their steps out of the public way along the stream of the Ilissus toward a plane-tree which is seen in the distance. There, lying down amidst pleasant sounds and scents, they will read the speech of Lysias. The country is a novelty to Socrates, who never goes out of the town; and hence he is full of admiration for the beauties of nature, which he seems to be drinking in for the first time.

As they are on their way, Phaedrus asks the opinion of Socrates respecting the local tradition of Boreas and Oreithyia. Socrates, after a satirical allusion to the "rationalizers" of his day, replies that he has no time for these "nice" interpretations of mythology, and he pities anyone who has. When you once begin there is no end of them, and they spring from an uncritical philosophy after all. "The proper study of mankind is man"; and he is a far more complex and wonderful being than the serpent Typho. Socrates as yet does not know himself; and why should he care to know about unearthly monsters? Engaged in such conversation, they arrive at the plane-tree; when they have found a convenient resting-place, Phaedrus pulls out the speech and reads:

The speech consists of a foolish paradox which is to the effect that the non-lover ought to be accepted rather than the lover—because he is more rational, more agreeable, more enduring, less suspicious, less hurtful, less boastful, less engrossing, and because there are more of them, and for a great many other reasons which are equally unmeaning. Phaedrus is captivated with the beauty of the periods, and wants to make Socrates say that nothing was or ever could be written better. Socrates does not think much of the matter, but then he has only attended to the form, and in that he has detected several repetitions and other marks of haste. He cannot agree with Phaedrus in the extreme value which he sets upon this performance, because he is afraid of doing injustice to Anacreon and Sappho and other great writers, and is almost inclined to think that he himself, or rather some power residing within him, could make a speech better than that of Lysias on the same theme, and also different from his, if he may be allowed the use of a few commonplaces which all speakers must equally employ.

Phaedrus is delighted at the prospect of having another speech, and promises that he will set up a golden statue of Socrates at Delphi, if he keeps his word. Some raillery ensues, and at length Socrates, conquered by the threat that he shall never again hear a speech of Lysias unless he fulfills his promise, veils his face and begins.

First, invoking the Muses and assuming ironically the person of the non-lover (who is a lover all the same), he will inquire into the nature and power of love. For this is a necessary preliminary to the other question— How is the non-lover to be distinguished from the lover? In all of us there are two principles—a better and a worse—reason and desire, which are generally at war with one another; and the victory of the rational is called temperance, and the victory of the irrational intemperance or excess. The latter takes many forms and has many bad names—gluttony, drunkenness, and the like. But of all the irrational desires or excesses the greatest is that which is led away by desires of a kindred nature to the enjoyment of personal beauty. And this is the master power of love.

Here Socrates fancies that he detects in himself an unusual flow of eloquence—this newly-found gift he can only attribute to the inspiration of the place, which appears to be dedicated to the nymphs. Starting again from the philosophical basis which has been laid down, he proceeds to show how many advantages the non-lover has over the lover. The one encourages softness and effeminacy and exclusiveness; he cannot endure any superiority in his beloved; he will train him in luxury, he will keep him out of society, he will deprive him of parents, friends, money, knowledge, and of every other good, that he may have him all to himself. Then again his ways are not ways of pleasantness; he is mighty disagreeable; "crabbed age and youth cannot live together." At every hour of the night and day he is intruding upon him; there is the same old withered face and the remainder to match—and he is always repeating, in season or out of season, the praises or dispraises of his beloved, which are bad enough when he is sober, and published all over the world when he is drunk. At length his love ceases; he is converted into an enemy, and the spectacle may be seen of the lover running away from the beloved, who pursues him with vain reproaches, and demands his reward which the other refuses to pay. Too late the beloved learns, after all his pains and disagreeables, that "As wolves love lambs so lovers love their loves." (Compare Char.) Here is the end; the "other" or "non-lover" part of the speech had better be understood, for if in the censure of the lover Socrates has broken out in verse, what will he not do in his praise of the non-lover? He has said his say and is preparing to go away.

Phaedrus begs him to remain, at any rate until the heat of noon has passed; he would like to have a little more conversation before they go. Socrates, who has risen, recognizes the oracular sign which forbids him to depart until he has done penance. His conscious has been awakened, and like Stesichorus when he had reviled the lovely Helen he will sing a palinode for having blasphemed the majesty of love. His palinode takes the form of a myth.

Socrates begins his tale with a glorification of madness, which he divides into four kinds: first, there is the art of divination or prophecy—this, in a vein similar to that pervading the Cratylus and Io, he connects with madness by an etymological explanation (mantike, manike—compare oionoistike, oionistike, "'tis all one reckoning, save the phrase is a little variation"); secondly, there is the art of purification by mysteries; thirdly, poetry or the inspiration of the Muses (compare Ion), without which no man can enter their temple. All this shows that madness is one of heaven's blessings, and may sometimes be a great deal better than sense. There is also a fourth kind of madness—that of love—which cannot be explained without inquiring into the nature of the soul.

All soul is immortal, for she is the source of all motion both in herself and in others. Her form may be described in a figure as a composite nature made up of a charioteer and a pair of winged steeds. The steeds of the gods are immortal, but ours are one mortal and the other immortal. The immortal soul soars upwards into the heavens, but the mortal drops her plumes and settles upon the earth.

Now the use of the wing is to rise and carry the downward element into the upper world—there to behold beauty, wisdom, goodness, and the other things of God by which the soul is nourished. On a certain day Zeus the lord of heaven goes forth in a winged chariot; and an array of gods and demi-gods and of human souls in their train, follows him. There are glorious and blessed sights in the interior of heaven, and he who will may freely behold them. The great vision of all is seen at the feast of the gods, when they ascend the heights of the empyrean—all but Hestia, who is left at home to keep house. The chariots of the gods glide readily upwards and stand upon the outside; the revolution of the spheres carries them round, and they have a vision of the world beyond. But the others labor in vain; for the mortal steed, if he has not been properly trained, keeps them down and sinks them toward the earth. Of the world which is beyond the heavens, who can tell? There is an essence formless, colorless, intangible, perceived by the mind only, dwelling in the region of true knowledge. The divine mind in her revolution enjoys this fair prospect, and beholds justice, temperance, and knowledge in their everlasting essence. When fulfilled with the sight of them she returns home, and the charioteer puts up the horses in their stable, and gives them ambrosia to eat and nectar to drink. This is the life of the gods; the human soul tries to reach the same heights, but hardly succeeds; and sometimes the head of the charioteer rises above, and sometimes sinks below, the fair vision, and he is at last obliged, after much contention, to turn away and leave the plain of truth. But if the soul has followed in the train of her god and once beheld truth she is preserved from harm, and is carried round in the next revolution of the spheres; and if always following, and always seeing the truth, is then forever unharmed. If, however, she drops her wings and falls to the earth, then she takes the form of man, and the soul which has seen most of the truth passes into a philosopher or lover; that which has seen truth in the second degree, into a king or warrior; the third, into a householder or money-maker; the fourth, into a gymnast; the fifth, into a prophet or mystic; the sixth, into a poet or imitator; the seventh, into a husbandman or craftsman; the eighth, into a sophist or demagogue; the ninth, into a tyrant. All these are states of probation, wherein he who lives righteously is improved, and he who lives unrighteously deteriorates. After death comes the judgment; the bad depart to houses of correction under the earth, the good to places of joy in heaven. When a thousand years have elapsed the souls meet together and choose the lives which they will lead for another period of existence. The soul which three times in succession has chosen the life of a philosopher or of a lover who is not without philosophy receives her wings at the close of the third millennium; the remainder have to complete a cycle of ten thousand years before their wings are restored to them. Each time there is full liberty of choice. The soul of a man may descend into a beast, and return again into the form of man. But the form of man will only be taken by the soul which has once seen truth and acquired some conception of the universal—this is the recollection of the knowledge which she attained when in the company of the Gods. And men in general recall only with difficulty the things of another world, but the mind of the philosopher has a better remembrance of them. For when he beholds the visible beauty of Earth his enraptured soul passes in thought to those glorious sights of justice and wisdom and temperance and truth which she once gazed upon in heaven. Then she celebrated holy mysteries and beheld blessed apparitions shining in pure light, herself pure, and not as yet entombed in the body. And still, like a bird eager to quit its cage, she flutters and looks upwards, and is therefore deemed mad. Such a recollection of past days she receives through sight, the keenest of our senses, because beauty, alone of the ideas, has any representation on Earth: wisdom is invisible to mortal eyes. But the corrupted nature, blindly excited by this vision of beauty, rushes on to enjoy, and would fain wallow like a brute beast in sensual pleasures. Whereas the true mystic, who has seen the many sights of bliss, when he beholds a godlike form or face is amazed with delight, and if he were not afraid of being thought mad he would fall down and worship. Then the stiffened wing begins to relax and grow again; desire which has been imprisoned pours over the soul of the lover; the germ of the wing unfolds, and stings, and pangs of birth, like the cutting of teeth, are everywhere felt. (Compare Symp.) Father and mother, and goods and laws and proprieties are nothing to him; his beloved is his physician, who can alone cure his pain. An apocryphal sacred writer says that the power which thus works in him is by mortals called love, but the immortals call him dove, or the winged one, in order to represent the force of his wings—such at any rate is his nature. Now the characters of lovers depend upon the god whom they followed in the other world; and they choose their loves in this world accordingly. The followers of Ares are fierce and violent; those of Zeus seek out some philosophical and imperial nature; the attendants of Hera find a royal love; and in like manner the followers of every god seek a love who is like their god; and to him they communicate the nature which they have received from their god. The manner in which they take their love is as follows:

I told you about the charioteer and his two steeds, the one a noble animal who is guided by word and admonition only, the other an ill-looking villain who will hardly yield to blow or spur. Together all three, who are a figure of the soul, approach the vision of love. And now a fierce conflict begins. The ill-conditioned steed rushes on to enjoy, but the charioteer, who beholds the beloved with awe, falls back in adoration, and forces both the steeds on their haunches; again the evil steed rushes forward and pulls shamelessly. The conflict grows more and more severe; and at last the charioteer, throwing himself backward, forces the bit out of the clenched teeth of the brute, and pulling harder than ever at the reins, covers his tongue and jaws with blood, and forces him to rest his legs and haunches with pain upon the ground. When this has happened several times, the villain is tamed and humbled, and from that time forward the soul of the lover follows the beloved in modesty and holy fear. And now their bliss is consummated; the same image of love dwells in the breast of either, and if they have self-control, they pass their lives in the greatest happiness which is attainable by man—they continue masters of themselves, and conquer in one of the three heavenly victories. But if they choose the lower life of ambition they may still have a happy destiny, though inferior, because they have not the approval of the whole soul. At last they leave the body and proceed on their pilgrim's progress, and those who have once begun can never go back. When the time comes they receive their wings and fly away, and the lovers have the same wings.

Socrates concludes: These are the blessings of love, and thus have I made my recantation in finer language than before; I did so in order to please Phaedrus. If I said what was wrong at first, please to attribute my error to Lysias, who ought to study philosophy instead of rhetoric, and then he will not mislead his disciple Phaedrus.

Phaedrus is afraid that he will lose conceit of Lysias, and that Lysias will be out of conceit with himself, and leave off making speeches, for the politicians have been deriding him. Socrates is of opinion that there is small danger of this; the politicians are themselves the great rhetoricians of the age, who desire to attain immortality by the authorship of laws. And therefore there is nothing with which they can reproach Lysias in being a writer; but there may be disgrace in being a bad one.

And what is good or bad writing or speaking? While the sun is hot in the sky above us, let us ask that question: since by rational conversation man lives, and not by the indulgence of bodily pleasures. And the grasshoppers who are chirruping around may carry our words to the Muses, who are their patronesses; for the grasshoppers were human beings themselves in a world before the Muses, and when the Muses came they died of hunger for the love of song. And they carry to them in heaven the report of those who honor them on Earth.

The first rule of good speaking is to know and speak the truth; as a Spartan proverb says, "true art is truth"; whereas rhetoric is an art of enchantment, which makes things appear good and evil, like and unlike, as the speaker pleases. Its use is not confined, as people commonly suppose, to arguments in the law courts and speeches in the assembly; it is rather a part of the art of disputation, under which are included both the rules of Gorgias and the eristic of Zeno. But it is not wholly devoid of truth. Superior knowledge enables us to deceive another by the help of resemblances, and to escape from such a deception when employed against ourselves. We see therefore that even in rhetoric an element of truth is required. For if we do not know the truth, we can neither make the gradual departures from truth by which men are most easily deceived, nor guard ourselves against deception.

Socrates then proposes that they shall use the two speeches as illustrations of the art of rhetoric; first distinguishing between the debatable and undisputed class of subjects. In the debatable class there ought to be a definition of all disputed matters. But there was no such definition in the speech of Lysias; nor is there any order or connection in his words any more than in a nursery rhyme. With this he compares the regular divisions of the other speech, which was his own (and yet not his own, for the local deities must have inspired him). Although only a playful composition, it will be found to embody two principles: first, that of synthesis or the comprehension of parts in a whole; secondly, analysis, or the resolution of the whole into parts. These are the processes of division and generalization which are so dear to the dialectician, that king of men. They are affected by dialectic, and not by rhetoric, of which the remains are but scanty after order and arrangement have been subtracted. There is nothing left but a heap of "ologies" and other technical terms invented by Polus, Theodorus, Evenus, Tisias, Gorgias, and others, who have rules for everything, and who teach how to be short or long at pleasure. Prodicus showed his good sense when he said that there was a better thing than either to be short or long, which was to be of convenient length.

Still, notwithstanding the absurdities of Polus and others, rhetoric has great power in public assemblies. This power, however, is not given by any technical rules, but is the gift of genius. The real art is always being confused by rhetoricians with the preliminaries of the art. The perfection of oratory is like the perfection of anything else; natural power must be aided by art. But the art is not that which is taught in the schools of rhetoric; it is nearer akin to philosophy. Pericles, for instance, who was the most accomplished of all speakers, derived his eloquence not from rhetoric but from the philosophy of nature which he learned of Anaxagoras. True rhetoric is like medicine, and the rhetorician has to consider the natures of men's souls as the physician considers the natures of their bodies. Such and such persons are to be affected in this way, such and such others in that; and he must know the times and the seasons for saying this or that. This is not an easy task, and this, if there be such an art, is the art of rhetoric.

I know that there are some professors of the art who maintain probability to be stronger than truth. But we maintain that probability is engendered by likeness of the truth which can only be attained by the knowledge of it, and that the aim of the good man should not be to please or persuade his fellow servants, but to please his good masters who are the gods. Rhetoric has a fair beginning in this.

Enough of the art of speaking; let us now proceed to consider the true use of writing. There is an old Egyptian tale of Theuth, the inventor of writing, showing his invention to the god Thamus, who told him that he would only spoil men's memories and take away their understandings. From this tale, of which young Athens will probably make fun, may be gathered the lesson that writing is inferior to speech. For it is like a picture, which can give no answer to a question, and has only a deceitful likeness of a living creature. It has no power of adaptation, but uses the same words for all. It is not a legitimate son of knowledge, but a bastard, and when an attack is made upon this bastard neither parent nor anyone else is there to defend it. The husbandman will not seriously incline to sow his seed in such a hotbed or garden of Adonis; he will rather sow in the natural soil of the human soul which has depth of earth; and he will anticipate the inner growth of the mind, by writing only, if at all, as a remedy against old age. The natural process will be far nobler, and will bring forth fruit in the minds of others as well as in his own.

The conclusion of the whole matter is just this,—that until a man knows the truth, and the manner of adapting the truth to the natures of other men, he cannot be a good orator; also, that the living is better than the written word, and that the principles of justice and truth when delivered by word of mouth are the legitimate offspring of a man's own bosom, and their lawful descendants take up their abode in others. Such an orator as he is who is possessed of them, you and I would fain become. And to all composers in the world, poets, orators, legislators, we hereby announce that if their compositions are based upon these principles, then they are not only poets, orators, legislators, but philosophers. All others are mere flatterers and putters together of words. This is the message which Phaedrus undertakes to carry to Lysias from the local deities, and Socrates himself will carry a similar message to his favorite Isocrates, whose future distinction as a great rhetorician he prophesies. The heat of the day has passed, and after offering up a prayer to Pan and the nymphs, Socrates and Phaedrus depart.

There are two principal controversies which have been raised about the Phaedrus; the first relates to the subject, the second to the date of the Dialogue.

There seems to be a notion that the work of a great artist like Plato cannot fail in unity, and that the unity of a dialogue requires a single subject. But the conception of unity really applies in very different degrees and ways to different kinds of art; to a statue, for example, far more than to any kind of literary composition, and to some species of literature far more than to others. Nor does the dialogue appear to be a style of composition in which the requirement of unity is most stringent; nor should the idea of unity derived from one sort of art be hastily transferred to another. The double titles of several of the Platonic Dialogues are a further proof that the severer rule was not observed by Plato. The Republic is divided between the search after justice and the construction of the ideal state; the Parmenides between the criticism of the Platonic ideas and of the Eleatic one or being; the Gorgias between the art of speaking and the nature of the good; the Sophist between the detection of the Sophist and the correlation of ideas. The Theaetetus, the Politicus, and the Philebus have also digressions which are but remotely connected with the main subject.

Thus the comparison of Plato's other writings, as well as the reason of the thing, lead us to the conclusion that we must not expect to find one idea pervading a whole work, but one, two, or more, as the invention of the writer may suggest, or his fancy wander. If each dialogue were confined to the development of a single idea, this would appear on the face of the dialogue, nor could any controversy be raised as to whether the Phaedrus treated of love or rhetoric. But the truth is that Plato subjects himself to no rule of this sort. Like every great artist he gives unity of form to the different and apparently distracting topics which he brings together. He works freely and is not to be supposed to have arranged every part of the dialogue before he begins to write. He fastens or weaves together the frame of his discourse loosely and imperfectly, and which is the warp and which is the woof cannot always be determined.

The subjects of the Phaedrus (exclusive of the short introductory passage about mythology which is suggested by the local tradition) are first the false or conventional art of rhetoric; secondly, love or the inspiration of beauty and knowledge, which is described as madness; thirdly, dialectic or the art of composition and division; fourthly, the true rhetoric, which is based upon dialectic, and is neither the art of persuasion nor knowledge of the truth alone, but the art of persuasion founded on knowledge of truth and knowledge of character; fifthly, the superiority of the spoken over the written word. The continuous thread which appears and reappears throughout is rhetoric; this is the ground into which the rest of the Dialogue is worked, in parts embroidered with fine words which are not in Socrates's manner, as he says, "in order to please Phaedrus." The speech of Lysias which has thrown Phaedrus into an ecstacy is adduced as an example of the false rhetoric; the first speech of Socrates, though an improvement, partakes of the same character; his second speech, which is full of that higher element said to have been learned of Anaxagoras by Pericles, and which in the midst of poetry does not forget order, is an illustration of the higher or true rhetoric. This higher rhetoric is based upon dialectic, and dialectic is a sort of inspiration akin to love (compare Symp.); in these two aspects of philosophy the technicalities of rhetoric are absorbed. And so the example becomes also the deeper theme of discourse. The true knowledge of things in heaven and earth is based upon enthusiasm or love of the ideas going before us and ever present to us in this world and in another; and the true order of speech or writing proceeds accordingly. Love, again, has three degrees: first, of interested love corresponding to the conventionalities of rhetoric; secondly, of disinterested or mad love, fixed on objects of sense, and answering, perhaps, to poetry; thirdly, of disinterested love directed toward the unseen, answering to dialectic or the science of the ideas. Lastly, the art of rhetoric in the lower sense is found to rest on a knowledge of the natures and characters of men, which Socrates at the commencement of the Dialogue has described as his own peculiar study.

Thus amid discord a harmony begins to appear; there are many links of connection which are not visible at first sight. At the same time the Phaedrus, although one of the most beautiful of the Platonic Dialogues, is also more irregular than any other. For insight into the world, for sustained irony, for depth of thought, there is no Dialogue superior, or perhaps equal to it. Nevertheless the form of the work has tended to obscure some of Plato's higher aims.

The first speech is composed "in that balanced style in which the wise love to talk" (Symp.). The characteristics of rhetoric are insipidity, mannerism, and monotonous parallelism of clauses. There is more rhythm than reason; the creative power of imagination is wanting.

"'Tis Greece, but living Greece no more."

Plato has seized by anticipation the spirit which hung over Greek literature for a thousand years afterward. Yet doubtless there were some who, like Phaedrus, felt a delight in the harmonious cadence and the pedantic reasoning of the rhetoricians newly imported from Sicily, which had ceased to be awakened in them by really great works, such as the odes of Anacreon or Sappho or the orations of Pericles. That the first speech was really written by Lysias is improbable. Like the poem of Solon, or the story of Thamus and Theuth, or the funeral oration of Aspasia (if genuine), or the pretence of Socrates in the Cratylus that his knowledge of philology is derived from Euthyphro, the invention is really due to the imagination of Plato, and may be compared to the parodies of the Sophists in the Protagoras. Numerous fictions of this sort occur in the Dialogues, and the gravity of Plato has sometimes imposed upon his commentators. The introduction of a considerable writing of another would seem not to be in keeping with a great work of art, and has no parallel elsewhere.

In the second speech Socrates is exhibited as beating the rhetoricians at their own weapons; he "an unpracticed man and they masters of the art." True to his character, he must, however, profess that the speech which he makes is not his own, for he knows nothing of himself. (Compare Symp.) Regarded as a rhetorical exercise, the superiority of his speech seems to consist chiefly in a better arrangement of the topics; he begins with a definition of love, and he gives weight to his words by going back to general maxims; a lesser merit is the greater liveliness of Socrates, which hurries him into verse and relieves the monotony of the style.

But Plato had doubtless a higher purpose than to exhibit Socrates as the rival or superior of the Athenian rhetoricians. Even in the speech of Lysias there is a germ of truth, and this is further developed in the parallel oration of Socrates. First, passionate love is overthrown by the sophistical or interested, and then both yield to that higher view of love which is afterward revealed to us. The extreme of commonplace is contrasted with the most ideal and imaginative of speculations. Socrates, half in jest and to satisfy his own wild humor, takes the disguise of Lysias, but he is also in profound earnest and in a deeper vein of irony than usual. Having improvised his own speech, which is based upon the model of the preceding, he condemns them both. Yet the condemnation is not to be taken seriously, for he is evidently trying to express an aspect of the truth. To understand him, we must make abstraction of morality and of the Greek manner of regarding the relation of the sexes. In this, as in his other discussions about love, what Plato says of the loves of men must be transferred to the loves of women before we can attach any serious meaning to his words. Had he lived in our times he would have made the transposition himself. But seeing in his own age the impossibility of woman being the intellectual helpmate or friend of man (except in the rare instances of a Diotima or an Aspasia), seeing that, even as to personal beauty, her place was taken by young mankind instead of womankind, he tries to work out the problem of love without regard to the distinctions of nature. And full of the evils which he recognized as flowing from the spurious form of love, he proceeds with a deep meaning, though partly in joke, to show that the "non-lover's" love is better than the "lover's."

We may raise the same question in another form: Is marriage preferable with or without love? "Among ourselves," as we may say, a little parodying the words of Pausanias in the Symposium, "there would be one answer to this question: the practice and feeling of some foreign countries appears to be more doubtful." Suppose a modern Socrates, in defiance of the received notions of society and the sentimental literature of the day, alone against all the writers and readers of novels, to suggest this inquiry, would not the younger "part of the world be ready to take off its coat and run at him might and main?" (Republic.) Yet, if like Peisthetaerus in Aristophanes, he could persuade the "birds" to hear him, retiring a little behind a rampart, not of pots and dishes, but of unreadable books, he might have something to say for himself. Might he not argue, "that a rational being should not follow the dictates of passion in the most important act of his or her life"? Who would willingly enter into a contract at first sight, almost without thought, against the advice and opinion of his friends, at a time when he acknowledges that he is not in his right mind? And yet they are praised by the authors of romances, who reject the warnings of their friends or parents, rather than those who listen to them in such matters. Two inexperienced persons, ignorant of the world and of one another, how can they be said to choose?—they draw lots, whence also the saying, "marriage is a lottery." Then he would describe their way of life after marriage; how they monopolize one another's affections to the exclusion of friends and relations; how they pass their days in unmeaning fondness or trivial conversation; how the inferior of the two drags the other down to his or her level; how the cares of a family "breed meanness in their souls." In the fulfillment of military or public duties, they are not helpers but hinderers of one another: they cannot undertake any noble enterprise, such as makes the names of men and women famous, from domestic considerations. Too late their eyes are opened; they were taken unawares and desire to part company. Better, he would say, a "little love at the beginning," for heaven might have increased it; but now their foolish fondness has changed into mutual dislike. In the days of their honeymoon they never understood that they must provide against offenses, that they must have interests, that they must learn the art of living as well as loving. Our misogamist will not appeal to Anacreon or Sappho for a confirmation of his view, but to the universal experience of mankind. How much nobler, in conclusion, he will say, is friendship, which does not receive unmeaning praises from novelists and poets, is not exacting or exclusive, is not impaired by familiarity, is much less expensive, is not so likely to take offense, seldom changes, and may be dissolved from time to time without the assistance of the courts. Besides, he will remark that there is a much greater choice of friends than of wives—you may have more of them and they will be far more improving to your mind. They will not keep you dawdling at home, or dancing attendance upon them; or withdraw you from the great world and stirring scenes of life and action which would make a man of you.

In such a manner, turning the seamy side outwards, a modern Socrates might describe the evils of married and domestic life. They are evils which mankind in general have agreed to conceal, partly because they are compensated by greater goods. Socrates or Archilochus would soon have to sing a palinode for the injustice done to lovely Helen, or some misfortune worse than blindness might be fall them. Then they would take up their parable again and say that there were two loves, a higher and a lower, holy and unholy, a love of the mind and a love of the body.

> "Let me not to the marriage of true minds
> Admit impediments. Love is not love
> Which alters when it alteration finds.
>
> . . . . .
>
> Love's not time's fool, though rosy lips and cheeks
> Within his bending sickle's compass come;
> Love alters not with his brief hours and weeks,
> But bears it out even to the edge of doom."

But this true love of the mind cannot exist between two souls, until they are purified from the grossness of earthly passion: they must pass through a time of trial and conflict first; in the language of religion they must be converted or born again. Then they would see the world transformed into a scene of heavenly beauty; a divine idea would accompany them in all their thoughts and actions. Something too of the recollections of childhood might float about them still; they might regain that old simplicity which had been theirs in other days at their first entrance on life. And although their love of one another was ever present to them, they would acknowledge also a higher love of duty and of God, which united them. And their happiness would depend upon their preserving in them this principle—not losing the ideals of justice and holiness and truth, but renewing them at the fountain of light. When they have attained to this exalted state, let them marry (something, too, may be conceded to the animal nature of man), or live together in holy and innocent friendship. The poet might describe in eloquent words the nature of such a union; how after many struggles the true love was found: how the two passed their lives together in the service of God and man; how their characters were reflected upon one another, and seemed to grow more like year by year; how they read in one another's eyes the thoughts, wishes, actions of the other; how they saw each other in God; how in a figure they grew wings like doves, and were "ready to fly away together and be at rest." And lastly, he might tell how, after a time at no long intervals, first one and then the other fell asleep, and "appeared to the unwise" to die, but were reunited in another state of being, in which they saw justice and holiness and truth, not according to the imperfect copies of them which are found in this world, but justice absolute in existence absolute, and so of the rest. And they would hold converse not only with each other, but with blessed souls everywhere; and would be employed in the service of God, every soul fulfillling his own nature and character, and would see into the wonders of earth and heaven, and trace the works of creation to their author.

So, partly in jest but also "with a certain degree of seriousness," we may appropriate to ourselves the words of Plato. The use of such a parody, though very imperfect, is to transfer his thoughts to our sphere of religion and feeling, to bring him nearer to us and us to him. Like the Scriptures, Plato admits of endless applications, if we allow for the difference of times and manners; and we lose the better half of him when we regard his Dialogues merely as literary compositions. Any ancient work which is worth reading has a practical and speculative as well as a literary interest. And in Plato, more than in any other Greek writer, the local and transitory is inextricably blended with what is spiritual and eternal. Socrates is necessarily ironical; for he has to withdraw from the received opinions and beliefs of mankind. We cannot separate the transitory from the permanent; nor can we translate the language of irony into that of plain reflection and common sense. But we can imagine the mind of Socrates in another age and country; and we can interpret him by analogy with reference to the errors and prejudices which prevail among ourselves. To return to the Phaedrus—

Both speeches are strongly condemned by Socrates as sinful and blasphemous toward the god Love, and as worthy only of some haunt of sailors to which good manners were unknown. The meaning of this and other wild language to the same effect, which is introduced by way of contrast to the formality of the two speeches (Socrates has a sense of relief when he has escaped from the trammels of rhetoric), seems to be that the two speeches proceed upon the supposition that love is and ought to be interested, and that no such thing as a real or disinterested passion, which would be at the same time lasting, could be conceived. "But did I call this "love"? O God, forgive my blasphemy. This is not love. Rather it is the love of the world. But there is another kingdom of love, a kingdom not of this world, divine, eternal. And this other love I will now show you in a mystery."

Then follows the famous myth, which is a sort of parable, and like other parables ought not to receive too minute an interpretation. In all such allegories there is a great deal which is merely ornamental, and the interpreter has to separate the important from the unimportant. Socrates himself has given the right clue when, in using his own discourse afterward as the text for his examination of rhetoric, he characterizes it as a "partly true and tolerably credible mythus," in which amid poetical figures, order and arrangement were not forgotten.

The soul is described in magnificent language as the self-moved and the source of motion in all other things. This is the philosophical theme or proem of the whole. But ideas must be given through something, and under the pretext that to realize the true nature of the soul would be not only tedious but impossible, we at once pass on to describe the souls of gods as well as men under the figure of two winged steeds and a charioteer. No connection is traced between the soul as the great motive power and the triple soul which is thus imaged. There is no difficulty in seeing that the charioteer represents the reason, or that the black horse is the symbol of the sensual or concupiscent element of human nature. The white horse also represents rational impulse, but the description, "a lover of honor and modesty and temperance, and a follower of true glory," though similar, does not at once recall the "spirit" (thumos) of the Republic. The two steeds really correspond in a figure more nearly to the appetitive and moral or semi-rational soul of Aristotle. And thus, for the first time perhaps in the history of philosophy, we have represented to us the threefold division of psychology. The image of the charioteer and the steeds has been compared with a similar image which occurs in the verses of Parmenides; but it is important to remark that the horses of Parmenides have no allegorical meaning, and that the poet is only describing his own approach in a chariot to the regions of light and the house of the goddess of truth.

The triple soul has had a previous existence, in which following in the train of some god, from whom she derived her character, she beheld partially and imperfectly the vision of absolute truth. All her after existence, passed in many forms of men and animals, is spent in regaining this. The stages of the conflict are many and various; and she is sorely let and hindered by the animal desires of the inferior or concupiscent steed. Again and again she beholds the flashing beauty of the beloved. But before that vision can be finally enjoyed the animal desires must be subjected.

The moral or spiritual element in man is represented by the immortal steed which, like thumos in the Republic, always sides with the reason. Both are dragged out of their course by the furious impulses of desire. In the end something is conceded to the desires, after they have been finally humbled and overpowered. And yet the way of philosophy, or perfect love of the unseen, is total abstinence from bodily delights. "But all men cannot receive this saying": in the lower life of ambition they may be taken off their guard and stoop to folly unawares, and then, although they do not attain to the highest bliss, yet if they have once conquered they may be happy enough.

The language of the Meno and the Phaedo as well as of the Phaedrus seems to show that at one time of his life Plato was quite serious in maintaining a former state of existence. His mission was to realize the abstract; in that, all good and truth, all the hopes of this and another life seemed to center. To him abstractions, as we call them, were another kind of knowledge—an inner and unseen world, which seemed to exist far more truly than the fleeting objects of sense which were without him. When we are once able to imagine the intense power which abstract ideas exercised over the mind of Plato, we see that there was no more difficulty to him in realizing the eternal existence of them and of the human minds which were associated with them, in the past and future than in the present. The difficulty was not how they could exist, but how they could fail to exist. In the attempt to regain this "saving" knowledge of the ideas, the sense was found to be as great an enemy as the desires; and hence two things which to us seem quite distinct are inextricably blended in the representation of Plato.

Thus far we may believe that Plato was serious in his conception of the soul as a motive power, in his reminiscence of a former state of being, in his elevation of the reason over sense and passion, and perhaps in his doctrine of transmigration. Was he equally serious in the rest? For example, are we to attribute his tripartite division of the soul to the gods? Or is this merely assigned to them by way of parallelism with men? The latter is the more probable; for the horses of the gods are both white, i.e. their every impulse is in harmony with reason; their dualism, on the other hand, only carries out the figure of the chariot. Is he serious, again, in regarding love as "a madness"? That seems to arise out of the antithesis to the former conception of love. At the same time he appears to intimate here, as in the Ion, Apology, Meno, and elsewhere, that there is a faculty in man, whether to be termed in modern language genius, or inspiration, or imagination, or idealism, or communion with God, which cannot be reduced to rule and measure. Perhaps, too, he is ironically repeating the common language of mankind about philosophy, and is turning their jest into a sort of earnest (Compare Phaedo, Symp.). Or is he serious in holding that each soul bears the character of a god? He may have had no other account to give of the differences of human characters to which he afterward refers. Or, again, in his absurd derivation of mantike and oionistike and imeros (compare Cratylus)? It is characteristic of the irony of Socrates to mix up sense and nonsense in such a way that no exact line can be drawn between them. And allegory helps to increase this sort of confusion.

As is often the case in the parables and prophecies of Scripture, the meaning is allowed to break through the figure, and the details are not always consistent. When the charioteers and their steeds stand upon the dome of heaven they behold the intangible invisible essences which are not objects of sight. This is because the force of language can no further go. Nor can we dwell much on the circumstance, that at the completion of ten thousand years all are to return to the place from whence they came; because he represents their return as dependent on their own good conduct in the successive stages of existence. Nor again can we attribute anything to the accidental inference which would also follow, that even a tyrant may live righteously in the condition of life to which fate has called him ("he aiblins might, I dinna ken"). But to suppose this would be at variance with Plato himself and with Greek notions generally. He is much more serious in distinguishing men from animals by their recognition of the universal which they have known in a former state, and in denying that this gift of reason can ever be obliterated or lost. In the language of some modern theologians he might be said to maintain the "final perseverance" of those who have entered on their pilgrim's progress. Other intimations of a "metaphysic" or "theology" of the future may also be discerned in him: (1) The moderate predestinarianism which here, as in the Republic, acknowledges the element of chance in human life, and yet asserts the freedom and responsibility of man; (2) The recognition of a moral as well as an intellectual principle in man under the image of an immortal steed; (3) The notion that the divine nature exists by the contemplation of ideas of virtue and justice—or, in other words, the assertion of the essentially moral nature of God; (4) Again, there is the hint that human life is a life of aspiration only, and that the true ideal is not to be found in art; (5) There occurs the first trace of the distinction between necessary and contingent matter; (6) The conception of the soul itself as the motive power and reason of the universe.

The conception of the philosopher, or the philosopher and lover in one, as a sort of madman, may be compared with the Republic and Theaetetus, in both of which the philosopher is regarded as a stranger and monster upon the Earth. The whole myth, like the other myths of Plato, describes in a figure things which are beyond the range of human faculties, or inaccessible to the knowledge of the age. That philosophy should be represented as the inspiration of love is a conception that has already become familiar to us in the Symposium, and is the expression partly of Plato's enthusiasm for the idea, and is also an indication of the real power exercised by the passion of friendship over the mind of the Greek. The master in the art of love knew that there was a mystery in these feelings and their associations, and especially in the contrast of the sensible and permanent which is afforded by them; and he sought to explain this, as he explained universal ideas, by a reference to a former state of existence. The capriciousness of love is also derived by him from an attachment to some god in a former world. The singular remark that the beloved is more affected than the lover at the final consummation of their love, seems likewise to hint at a psychological truth.

It is difficult to exhaust the meanings of a work like the Phaedrus, which indicates so much more than it expresses; and is full of inconsistencies and ambiguities which were not perceived by Plato himself. For example, when he is speaking of the soul does he mean the human or the divine soul? and are they both equally self-moving and constructed on the same threefold principle? We should certainly be disposed to reply that the self-motive is to be attributed to God only; and on the other hand that the appetitive and passionate elements have no place in His nature. So we should infer from the reason of the thing, but there is no indication in Plato's own writings that this was his meaning. Or, again, when he explains the different characters of men by referring them back to the nature of the God whom they served in a former state of existence, we are inclined to ask whether he is serious: Is he not rather using a mythological figure, here as elsewhere, to draw a veil over things which are beyond the limits of mortal knowledge? Once more, in speaking of beauty is he really thinking of some external form such as might have been expressed in the works of Phidias or Praxiteles; and not rather of an imaginary beauty, of a sort which extinguishes rather than stimulates vulgar love—a heavenly beauty like that which flashed from time to time before the eyes of Dante or Bunyan? Surely the latter. But it would be idle to reconcile all the details of the passage: it is a picture, not a system, and a picture which is for the greater part an allegory, and an allegory which allows the meaning to come through. The image of the charioteer and his steeds is placed side by side with the absolute forms of justice, temperance, and the like, which are abstract ideas only, and which are seen with the eye of the soul in her heavenly journey. The first impression of such a passage, in which no attempt is made to separate the substance from the form, is far truer than an elaborate philosophical analysis.

It is too often forgotten that the whole of the second discourse of Socrates is only an allegory, or figure of speech. For this reason, it is unnecessary to inquire whether the love of which Plato speaks is the love of men or of women. It is really a general idea which includes both, and in which the sensual element, though not wholly eradicated, is reduced to order and measure. We must not attribute a meaning to every fanciful detail. Nor is there any need to call up revolting associations, which as a matter of good taste should be banished, and which were far enough away from the mind of Plato. These and similar passages should be interpreted by the Laws. Nor is there anything in the Symposium, or in the Charmides, in reality inconsistent with the sterner rule which Plato lays down in the Laws. At the same time it is not to be denied that love and philosophy are described by Socrates in figures of speech which would not be used in Christian times; or that nameless vices were prevalent at Athens and in other Greek cities; or that friendships between men were a more sacred tie, and had a more important social and educational influence than among ourselves (See note on Symposium.).

In the Phaedrus, as well as in the Symposium, there are two kinds of love, a lower and a higher, the one answering to the natural wants of the animal, the other rising above them and contemplating with religious awe the forms of justice, temperance, holiness, yet finding them also "too dazzling bright for mortal eye," and shrinking from them in amazement. The opposition between these two kinds of love may be compared to the opposition between the flesh and the spirit in the Epistles of St. Paul. It would be unmeaning to suppose that Plato, in describing the spiritual combat, in which the rational soul is finally victor and master of both the steeds, condescends to allow any indulgence of unnatural lusts.

Two other thoughts about love are suggested by this passage. First of all, love is represented here, as in the Symposium, as one of the great powers of nature, which takes many forms and two principal ones, having a predominant influence over the lives of men. And these two, though opposed, are not absolutely separated the one from the other. Plato, with his great knowledge of human nature, was well aware how easily one is transformed into the other, or how soon the noble but fleeting aspiration may return into the nature of the animal, while the lower instinct which is latent always remains. The intermediate sentimentalism, which has exercised so great an influence on the literature of modern Europe, had no place in the classical times of Hellas; the higher love, of which Plato speaks, is the subject, not of poetry or fiction, but of philosophy.

Secondly, there seems to be indicated a natural yearning of the human mind that the great ideas of justice, temperance, wisdom, should be expressed in some form of visible beauty, like the absolute purity and goodness which Christian art has sought to realize in the person of the Madonna. But although human nature has often attempted to represent outwardly what can be only "spiritually discerned," men feel that in pictures and images, whether painted or carved, or described in words only, we have not the substance but the shadow of the truth which is in heaven. There is no reason to suppose that in the fairest works of Greek art, Plato ever conceived himself to behold an image, however faint, of ideal truths. "Not in that way was wisdom seen."

We may now pass on to the second part of the Dialogue, which is a criticism on the first. Rhetoric is assailed on various grounds: first, as desiring to persuade, without a knowledge of the truth; and secondly, as ignoring the distinction between certain and probable matter. The three speeches are then passed in review: the first of them has no definition of the nature of love, and no order in the topics (being in these respects far inferior to the second); while the third of them is found (though a fancy of the hour) to be framed upon real dialectical principles. But dialectic is not rhetoric; nothing on that subject is to be found in the endless treatises of rhetoric, however prolific in hard names. When Plato has sufficiently put them to the test of ridicule he touches, as with the point of a needle, the real error, which is the confusion of preliminary knowledge with creative power. No attainments will provide the speaker with genius; and the sort of attainments which can alone be of any value are the higher philosophy and the power of psychological analysis, which is given by dialectic, but not by the rules of the rhetoricians.

In this latter portion of the Dialogue there are many texts which may help us to speak and to think. The names dialectic and rhetoric are passing out of use; we hardly examine seriously into their nature and limits, and probably the arts both of speaking and of conversation have been unduly neglected by us. But the mind of Socrates pierces through the differences of times and countries into the essential nature of man; and his words apply equally to the modern world and to the Athenians of old. Would he not have asked of us, or rather is he not asking of us, whether we have ceased to prefer appearances to reality? Let us take a survey of the professions to which he refers and try them by his standard. Is not all literature passing into criticism, just as Athenian literature in the age of Plato was degenerating into sophistry and rhetoric? We can discourse and write about poems and paintings, but we seem to have lost the gift of creating them. Can we wonder that few of them "come sweetly from nature," while ten thousand reviewers (mala murioi) are engaged in dissecting them? Young men, like Phaedrus, are enamoured of their own literary clique and have but a feeble sympathy with the master-minds of former ages. They recognize "a *poetical* necessity in the writings of their favorite author, even when he boldly wrote off just what came in his head." They are beginning to think that Art is enough, just at the time when Art is about to disappear from the world. And would not a great painter, such as Michael Angelo, or a great poet, such as Shakespeare, returning to Earth, "courteously rebuke" us—would he not say that we are putting "in the place of Art the preliminaries of Art," confusing Art the expression of mind and truth with Art the composition of colors and forms; and perhaps he might more severely chastise some of us for trying to invent "a new shudder" instead of bringing to the birth living and healthy creations? These he would regard as the signs of an age wanting in original power.

Turning from literature and the arts to law and politics, again we fall under the lash of Socrates. For do we not often make "the worse appear the better cause"; and do not "both parties sometimes agree to tell lies"? Is not pleading "an art of speaking unconnected with the truth"? There is another text of Socrates which must not be forgotten in relation to this subject. In the endless maze of English law is there any "dividing the whole into parts or reuniting the parts into a whole"—any semblance of an organized being "having hands and feet and other members"? Instead of a system there is the Chaos of Anaxagoras (omou panta chremata) and no Mind or Order. Then again in the noble art of politics, who thinks of first principles and of true ideas? We avowedly follow not the truth but the will of the many (compare Republic). Is not legislation too a sort of literary effort, and might not statesmanship be described as the "art of enchanting" the house? While there are some politicians who have no knowledge of the truth, but only of what is likely to be approved by "the many who sit in judgment," there are others who can give no form to their ideal, neither having learned "the art of persuasion," nor having any insight into the "characters of men." Once more, has not medical science become a professional routine, which many "practice without being able to say who were their instructors"—the application of a few drugs taken from a book instead of a life-long study of the natures and constitutions of human beings? Do we see as clearly as Hippocrates "that the nature of the body can only be understood as a whole"? (Compare Charm.) And are not they held to be the wisest physicians who have the greatest distrust of their art? What would Socrates think of our newspapers, of our theology? Perhaps he would be afraid to speak of them—the one vox populi, the other vox Dei, he might hesitate to attack them; or he might trace a fanciful connection between them, and ask doubtfully, whether they are not equally inspired? He would remark that we are always searching for a belief and deploring our unbelief, seeming to prefer popular opinions unverified and contradictory to unpopular truths which are assured to us by the most certain proofs: that our preachers are in the habit of praising God "without regard to truth and falsehood, attributing to Him every species of greatness and glory, saying that He is all this and the cause of all that, in order that we may exhibit Him as the fairest and best of all" (Symp.) without any consideration of His real nature and character or of the laws by which He governs the world—seeking for a "private judgment" and not for the truth or "God's judgment." What would he say of the Church, which we praise in like manner, "meaning ourselves," without regard to history or experience? Might he not ask, whether we "care more for the truth of religion, or for the speaker and the country from which the truth comes"? or, whether the "select wise" are not "the many" after all? (Symp.) So we may fill up the sketch of Socrates, lest, as Phaedrus says, the argument should be too "abstract and barren of illustrations." (Compare Symp., Apol., Euthyphro.)

He next proceeds with enthusiasm to define the royal art of dialectic as the power of dividing a whole into parts, and of uniting the parts in a whole, and which may also be regarded (compare Soph.) as the process of the mind talking with herself. The latter view has probably led Plato to the paradox that speech is superior to writing, in which he may seem also to be doing an injustice to himself. For the two cannot be fairly compared in the manner which Plato suggests. The contrast of the living and dead word, and the example of Socrates, which he has represented in the form of the Dialogue, seem to have misled him. For speech and writing have really different functions; the one is more transitory, more diffuse, more elastic and capable of adaptation to moods and times; the other is more permanent, more concentrated, and is uttered not to this or that person or audience, but to all the world. In the Politicus the paradox is carried further; the mind or will of the king is preferred to the written law; he is supposed to be the Law personified, the ideal made Life.

Yet in both these statements there is also contained a truth; they may be compared with one another, and also with the other famous paradox, that "knowledge cannot be taught." Socrates means to say, that what is truly written is written in the soul, just as what is truly taught grows up in the soul from within and is not forced upon it from without. When planted in a congenial soil the little seed becomes a tree, and "the birds of the air build their nests in the branches." There is an echo of this in the prayer at the end of the Dialogue, "Give me beauty in the inward soul, and may the inward and outward man be at one." We may further compare the words of St. Paul, "Written not on tables of stone, but on fleshly tables of the heart"; and again, "Ye are my epistles known and read of all men." There may be a use in writing as a preservative against the forgetfulness of old age, but to live is higher far, to be ourselves the book, or the epistle, the truth embodied in a person, the Word made flesh. Something like this we may believe to have passed before Plato's mind when he affirmed that speech was superior to writing. So in other ages, weary of literature and criticism, of making many books, of writing articles in reviews, some have desired to live more closely in communion with their fellow men, to speak heart to heart, to speak and act only, and not to write, following the example of Socrates and of Christ.

Some other touches of inimitable grace and art and of the deepest wisdom may be also noted; such as the prayer or "collect" which has just been cited, "Give me beauty," etc.; or "the great name which belongs to God alone"; or "the saying of wiser men than ourselves that a man of sense should try to please not his fellow servants, but his good and noble masters," like St. Paul again; or the description of the "heavenly originals."

The chief criteria for determining the date of the Dialogue are (1) the ages of Lysias and Isocrates; (2) the character of the work.

Lysias was born in the year 458; Isocrates in the year 436, about seven years before the birth of Plato. The first of the two great rhetoricians is described as in the zenith of his fame; the second is still young and full of promise. Now it is argued that this must have been written in the youth of Isocrates, when the promise was not yet fulfillled. And thus we should have to assign the Dialogue to a year not later than 406, when Isocrates was thirty and Plato twenty-three years of age, and while Socrates himself was still alive.

Those who argue in this way seem not to reflect how easily Plato can "invent Egyptians or anything else," and how careless he is of historical truth or probability. Who would suspect that the wise Critias, the virtuous

Charmides, had ended their lives among the thirty tyrants? Who would imagine that Lysias, who is here assailed by Socrates, is the son of his old friend Cephalus? Or that Isocrates himself is the enemy of Plato and his school? No arguments can be drawn from the appropriateness or inappropriateness of the characters of Plato. (Else, perhaps, it might be further argued that, judging from their extant remains, insipid rhetoric is far more characteristic of Isocrates than of Lysias.) But Plato makes use of names which have often hardly any connection with the historical characters to whom they belong. In this instance the comparative favor shown to Isocrates may possibly be accounted for by the circumstance of his belonging to the aristocratical, as Lysias to the democratical party.

Few persons will be inclined to suppose, in the superficial manner of some ancient critics, that a dialogue which treats of love must necessarily have been written in youth. As little weight can be attached to the argument that Plato must have visited Egypt before he wrote the story of Theuth and Thamus. For there is no real proof that he ever went to Egypt; and even if he did, he might have known or invented Egyptian traditions before he went there. The late date of the Phaedrus will have to be established by other arguments than these: the maturity of the thought, the perfection of the style, the insight, the relation to the other Platonic Dialogues, seem to contradict the notion that it could have been the work of a youth of twenty or twenty-three years of age. The cosmological notion of the mind as the primum mobile, and the admission of impulse into the immortal nature, also afford grounds for assigning a later date. (Compare Tim., Soph., Laws.) Add to this that the picture of Socrates, though in some lesser particulars—e.g. his going without sandals, his habit of remaining within the walls, his emphatic declaration that his study is human nature—an exact resemblance, is in the main the Platonic and not the real Socrates. Can we suppose "the young man to have told such lies" about his master while he was still alive? Moreover, when two Dialogues are so closely connected as the Phaedrus and Symposium, there is great improbability in supposing that one of them was written at least twenty years after the other. The conclusion seems to be, that the Dialogue was written at some comparatively late but unknown period of Plato's life, after he had deserted the purely Socratic point of view, but before he had entered on the more abstract speculations of the Sophist or the Philebus. Taking into account the divisions of the soul, the doctrine of transmigration, the contemplative nature of the philosophic life, and the character of the style, we shall not be far wrong in placing the Phaedrus in the neighborhood of the Republic; remarking only that allowance must be made for the poetical element in the Phaedrus, which, while falling short of the Republic in definite philosophic results, seems to have glimpses of a truth beyond.

Two short passages, which are unconnected with the main subject of the Dialogue, may seem to merit a more particular notice: (1) the locus classicus about mythology; (2) the tale of the grasshoppers.

The first passage is remarkable as showing that Plato was entirely free from what may be termed the Euhemerism of his age. For there were Euhemerists in Hellas long before Euhemerus. Early philosophers, like Anaxagoras and Metrodorus, had found in Homer and mythology hidden meanings. Plato, with a truer instinct, rejects these attractive interpretations; he regards the inventor of them as "unfortunate"; and they draw a man off from the knowledge of himself. There is a latent criticism, and also a poetical sense in Plato, which enable him to discard them, and yet in another way to make use of poetry and mythology as a vehicle of thought and feeling. What would he have said of the discovery of Christian doctrines in these old Greek legends? While acknowledging that such interpretations are "very nice," would he not have remarked that they are found in all sacred literatures? They cannot be tested by any criterion of truth, or used to establish any truth; they add nothing to the sum of human knowledge; they are "what we please," and if employed as "peacemakers" between the new and old are liable to serious misconstruction, as he elsewhere remarks (Republic). And therefore he would have "bid Farewell to them; the study of them would take up too much of his time; and he has not as yet learned the true nature of religion." The "sophistical" interest of Phaedrus, the little touch about the two versions of the story, the ironical manner in which these explanations are set aside—"the common opinion about them is enough for me"—the allusion to the serpent Typho may be noted in passing; also the general agreement between the tone of this speech and the remark of Socrates which follows afterward, "I am a diviner, but a poor one."

The tale of the grasshoppers is naturally suggested by the surrounding scene. They are also the representatives of the Athenians as children of the soil. Under the image of the lively chirruping grasshoppers who inform the Muses in heaven about those who honor them on Earth, Plato intends to represent an Athenian audience (tettigessin eoikotes). The story is introduced, apparently, to mark a change of subject, and also, like several other allusions which occur in the course of the Dialogue, in order to preserve the scene in the recollection of the reader.

* * * * *

No one can duly appreciate the dialogues of Plato, especially the Phaedrus, Symposium, and portions of the Republic, who has not a sympathy with mysticism. To the uninitiated, as he would himself have acknowledged, they will appear to be the dreams of a poet who is disguised as a philosopher. There is a twofold difficulty in apprehending this aspect of the Platonic writings. First, we do not immediately realize that under the marble exterior of Greek literature was concealed a soul thrilling with spiritual emotion. Secondly, the forms or figures which the Platonic philosophy assumes, are not like the images of the prophet Isaiah, or of the Apocalypse, familiar to us in the days of our youth. By mysticism we mean, not the extravagance of an erring fancy, but the concentration of reason in feeling, the enthusiastic love of the good, the true, the one, the sense of the infinity of knowledge and of the marvel of the human faculties. When feeding upon such thoughts the "wing of the soul" is renewed and gains strength; she is raised above "the manikins of Earth" and their opinions, waiting in wonder to know, and working with reverence to find out what God in this or in another life may reveal to her.

ON THE DECLINE OF GREEK LITERATURE

One of the main purposes of Plato in the Phaedrus is to satirize Rhetoric, or rather the Professors of Rhetoric who swarmed at Athens in the fourth century before Christ. As in the opening of the Dialogue he ridicules the interpreters of mythology; as in the Protagoras he mocks at the Sophists; as in the Euthydemus he makes fun of the word-splitting Eristics; as in the Cratylus he ridicules the fancies of Etymologers; as in the Meno and Gorgias and some other dialogues he makes reflections and casts sly imputation upon the higher classes at Athens; so in the Phaedrus, chiefly in the latter part, he aims his shafts at the rhetoricians. The profession of rhetoric was the greatest and most popular in Athens, necessary "to a man's salvation," or at any rate to his attainment of wealth or power; but Plato finds nothing wholesome or genuine in the purpose of it. It is a veritable "sham," having no relation to fact, or to truth of any kind. It is antipathetic to him not only as a philosopher, but also as a great writer. He cannot abide the tricks of the rhetoricians, or the pedantries and mannerisms which they introduce into speech and writing. He sees clearly how far removed they are from the ways of simplicity and truth, and how ignorant of the very elements of the art which they are professing to teach. The thing which is most necessary of all, the knowledge of human nature, is hardly if at all considered by them. The true rules of composition, which are very few, are not to be found in their voluminous systems. Their pretentiousness, their omniscience, their large fortunes, their impatience of argument, their indifference to first principles, their stupidity, their progresses through Hellas accompanied by a troop of their disciples—these things were very distasteful to Plato, who esteemed genius far above art, and was quite sensible of the interval which separated them (Phaedrus). It is the interval which separates Sophists and rhetoricians from ancient famous men and women such as Homer and Hesiod, Anacreon and Sappho, Aeschylus and Sophocles; and the Platonic Socrates is afraid that, if he approves the former, he will be disowned by the latter. The spirit of rhetoric was soon to overspread all Hellas; and Plato with prophetic insight may have seen, from afar, the great literary waste or dead level, or interminable marsh, in which Greek literature was soon to disappear. A similar vision of the decline of the Greek drama and of the contrast of the old literature and the new was present to the mind of Aristophanes after the death of the three great tragedians (Frogs). After about a hundred, or at most two hundred years if we exclude Homer, the genius of Hellas had ceased to flower or blossom. The dreary waste which follows, beginning with the Alexandrian writers and even before them in the platitudes of Isocrates and his school, spreads over much more than a thousand years. And from this decline the Greek language and literature, unlike the Latin, which has come to life in new forms and been developed into the great European languages, never recovered.

This monotony of literature, without merit, without genius and without character, is a phenomenon which deserves more attention than it has hitherto received; it is a phenomenon unique in the literary history of the world. How could there have been so much cultivation, so much diligence in writing, and so little mind or real creative power? Why did a thousand years invent nothing better than Sibylline books, Orphic poems, Byzantine imitations of classical histories, Christian reproductions of Greek plays, novels like the silly and obscene romances of Longus and Heliodorus, innumerable forged epistles, a great many epigrams, biographies of the meanest and most meagre description, a sham philosophy which was the bastard progeny of the union between Hellas and the East? Only in Plutarch, in Lucian, in Longinus, in the Roman emperors Marcus Aurelius and Julian, in some of the Christian fathers are there any traces of good sense or originality, or any power of arousing the interest of later ages.

And when new books ceased to be written, why did hosts of grammarians and interpreters flock in, who never attain to any sound notion either of grammar or interpretation? Why did the physical sciences never arrive at any true knowledge or make any real progress? Why did poetry droop and languish? Why did history degenerate into fable? Why did words lose their power of expression? Why were ages of external greatness and magnificence attended by all the signs of decay in the human mind which are possible?

To these questions many answers may be given, which if not the true causes, are at least to be reckoned among the symptoms of the decline. There is the want of method in physical science, the want of criticism in history, the want of simplicity or delicacy in poetry, the want of political freedom, which is the true atmosphere of public speaking, in oratory. The ways of life were luxurious and commonplace. Philosophy had become extravagant, eclectic, abstract, devoid of any real content. At length it ceased to exist. It had spread words like plaster over the whole field of knowledge. It had grown ascetic on one side, mystical on the other. Neither of these tendencies was favorable to literature. There was no sense of beauty either in language or in art. The Greek world became vacant, barbaric, oriental. No one had anything new to say, or any conviction of truth. The age had no remembrance of the past, no power of understanding what other ages thought and felt. The Catholic faith had degenerated into dogma and controversy. For more than a thousand years not a single writer of first-rate, or even of second-rate, reputation has a place in the innumerable rolls of Greek literature.

If we seek to go deeper, we can still only describe the outward nature of the clouds or darkness which were spread over the heavens during so many ages without relief or light. We may say that this, like several other long periods in the history of the human race, was destitute, or deprived of the moral qualities which are the root of literary excellence. It had no life or aspiration, no national or political force, no desire for consistency, no love of knowledge for its own sake. It did not attempt to pierce the mists which surrounded it. It did not propose to itself to go forward and scale the heights of knowledge, but to go backward and seek at the beginning what can only be found toward the end. It was lost in doubt and ignorance. It rested upon tradition and authority. It had none of the higher play of fancy which creates poetry; and where there is no true poetry, neither can there be any good prose. It had no great characters, and therefore it had no great writers. It was incapable of distinguishing between words and things.

It was so hopelessly below the ancient standard of classical Greek art and literature that it had no power of understanding or of valuing them. It is doubtful whether any Greek author was justly appreciated in antiquity except by his own contemporaries; and this neglect of the great authors of the past led to the disappearance of the larger part of them, while the Greek fathers were mostly preserved. There is no reason to suppose that, in the century before the taking of Constantinople, much more was in existence than the scholars of the Renaissance carried away with them to Italy.

The character of Greek literature sank lower as time went on. It consisted more and more of compilations, of scholia, of extracts, of commentaries, forgeries, imitations. The commentator or interpreter had no conception of his author as a whole, and very little of the context of any passage which he was explaining. The least things were preferred by him to the greatest. The question of a reading, or a grammatical form, or an accent, or the uses of a word, took the place of the aim or subject of the book. He had no sense of the beauties of an author, and very little light is thrown by him on real difficulties. He interprets past ages by his own. The greatest classical writers are the least appreciated by him. This seems to be the reason why so many of them have perished, why the lyric poets have almost wholly disappeared; why, out of the eighty or ninety tragedies of Aeschylus and Sophocles, only seven of each had been preserved.

Such an age of sciolism and scholasticism may possibly once more get the better of the literary world. There are those who prophesy that the signs of such a day are again appearing among us, and that at the end of the present century no writer of the first class will be still alive. They think that the Muse of Literature may transfer herself to other countries less dried up or worn out than our own. They seem to see the withering effect of criticism on original genius. No one can doubt that such a decay or decline of literature and of art seriously affects the manners and character of a nation. It takes away half the joys and refinements of life; it increases its dulness and grossness. Hence it becomes a matter of great interest to consider how, if at all, such a degeneracy may be averted. Is there any elixir which can restore life and youth to the literature of a nation, or at any rate which can prevent it becoming unmanned and enfeebled?

First there is the progress of education. It is possible, and even probable, that the extension of the means of knowledge over a wider area and to persons living under new conditions may lead to many new combinations of thought and language. But, as yet, experience does not favor the realization of such a hope or promise. It may be truly answered that at present the training of teachers and the methods of education are very imperfect, and therefore that we cannot judge of the future by the present. When more of our youth are trained in the best literatures, and in the best parts of them, their minds may be expected to have a larger growth. They will have more interests, more thoughts, more material for conversation; they will have a higher standard and begin to think for themselves. The number of persons who will have the opportunity of receiving the highest education through the cheap press, and by the help of high schools and colleges, may increase tenfold. It is likely that in every thousand persons there is at least one who is far above the average in natural capacity, but the seed which is in him dies for want of cultivation. It has never had any stimulus to grow, or any field in which to blossom and produce fruit. Here is a great reservoir or treasure-house of human intelligence out of which new waters may flow and cover the Earth. If at any time the great men of the world should die out, and originality or genius appear to suffer a partial eclipse, there is a boundless hope in the multitude of intelligences for future generations. They may bring gifts to men such as the world has never received before. They may begin at a higher point and yet take with them all the results of the past. The cooperation of many may have effects not less striking, though different in character from those which the creative genius of a single man, such as Bacon or Newton, formerly produced. There is also great hope to be derived, not merely from the extension of education over a wider area, but from the continuance of it during many generations. Educated parents will have children fit to receive education; and these again will grow up under circumstances far more favorable to the growth of intelligence than any which have hitherto existed in our own or in former ages.

Even if we were to suppose no more men of genius to be produced, the great writers of ancient or of modern times will remain to furnish abundant materials of education to the coming generation. Now that every nation holds communication with every other, we may truly say in a fuller sense than formerly that "the thoughts of men are widened with the process of the suns." They will not be "cribbed, cabined, and confined" within a province or an island. The East will provide elements of culture to the West as well as the West to the East. The religions and literatures of the world will be open books, which he who wills may read. The human race may not be always ground down by bodily toil, but may have greater leisure for the improvement of the mind. The increasing sense of the greatness and infinity of nature will tend to awaken in men larger and more liberal thoughts. The love of mankind may be the source of a greater development of literature than nationality has ever been. There may be a greater freedom from prejudice and party; we may better understand the whereabouts of truth, and therefore there may be more success and fewer failures in the search for it. Lastly, in the coming ages we shall carry with us the recollection of the past, in which are necessarily contained many seeds of revival and renaissance in the future. So far is the world from becoming exhausted, so groundless is the fear that literature will ever die out.

PHAEDRUS

Persons of the dialogue: Socrates, Phaedrus

Scene: Under a plane-tree, by the banks of the Ilissus

SOCRATES: My dear Phaedrus, whence come you, and whither are you going?
PHAEDRUS: I come from Lysias the son of Cephalus, and I am going to take a walk outside the wall, for I have been sitting with him the whole morning; and our common friend Acumenus tells me that it is much more refreshing to walk in the open air than to be shut up in a cloister.
SOCRATES: There he is right. Lysias then, I suppose, was in the town?
PHAEDRUS: Yes, he was staying with Epicrates, here at the house of Morychus; that house which is near the temple of Olympian Zeus.
SOCRATES: And how did he entertain you? Can I be wrong in supposing that Lysias gave you a feast of discourse?
PHAEDRUS: You shall hear, if you can spare time to accompany me.
SOCRATES: And should I not deem the conversation of you and Lysias "a thing of higher import," as I may say in the words of Pindar, "than any business"?
PHAEDRUS: Will you go on?
SOCRATES: And will you go on with the narration?
PHAEDRUS: My tale, Socrates, is one of your sort, for love was the theme which occupied us—love after a fashion: Lysias has been writing about a fair youth who was being tempted, but not by a lover; and this was the point: he ingeniously proved that the non-lover should be accepted rather than the lover.
SOCRATES: O that is noble of him! I wish that he would say the poor

man rather than the rich, and the old man rather than the young one—then he would meet the case of me and of many a man; his words would be quite refreshing, and he would be a public benefactor. For my part, I do so long to hear his speech, that if you walk all the way to Megara, and when you have reached the wall come back, as Herodicus recommends, without going in, I will keep you company.
PHAEDRUS: What do you mean, my good Socrates? How can you imagine that my unpracticed memory can do justice to an elaborate work, which the greatest rhetorician of the age spent a long time in composing. Indeed, I cannot; I would give a great deal if I could.
SOCRATES: I believe that I know Phaedrus about as well as I know myself, and I am very sure that the speech of Lysias was repeated to him, not once only, but again and again; he insisted on hearing it many times over and Lysias was very willing to gratify him; at last, when nothing else would do, he got hold of the book, and looked at what he most wanted to see—this occupied him during the whole morning—and then when he was tired with sitting, he went out to take a walk, not until, by the dog, as I believe, he had simply learned by heart the entire discourse, unless it was unusually long, and he went to a place outside the wall that he might practice his lesson. There he saw a certain lover of discourse who had a similar weakness—he saw and rejoiced; now thought he, "I shall have a partner in my revels." And he invited him to come and walk with him. But when the lover of discourse begged that he would repeat the tale, he gave himself airs and said, "No I cannot," as if he were indisposed; although, if the hearer had refused, he would sooner or later have been compelled by him to listen whether he would or no. Therefore, Phaedrus, bid him do at once what he will soon do whether bidden or not.
PHAEDRUS: I see that you will not let me off until I speak in some fashion or other; verily therefore my best plan is to speak as I best can.
SOCRATES: A very true remark, that of yours.
PHAEDRUS: I will do as I say; but believe me, Socrates, I did not learn the very words—O no; nevertheless I have a general notion of what he said, and will give you a summary of the points in which the lover differed from the non-lover. Let me begin at the beginning.
SOCRATES: Yes, my sweet one; but you must first of all show what you have in your left hand under your cloak, for that roll, as I suspect, is the actual discourse. Now, much as I love you, I would not have you suppose that I am going to have your memory exercised at my expense, if you have Lysias himself here.

PHAEDRUS: Enough; I see that I have no hope of practicing my art upon you. But if I am to read, where would you please to sit?

SOCRATES: Let us turn aside and go by the Ilissus; we will sit down at some quiet spot.

PHAEDRUS: I am fortunate in not having my sandals, and as you never have any, I think that we may go along the brook and cool our feet in the water; this will be the easiest way, and at midday and in the summer is far from being unpleasant.

SOCRATES: Lead on, and look out for a place in which we can sit down.

PHAEDRUS: Do you see the tallest plane-tree in the distance?

SOCRATES: Yes.

PHAEDRUS: There are shade and gentle breezes, and grass on which we may either sit or lie down.

SOCRATES: Move forward.

PHAEDRUS: I should like to know, Socrates, whether the place is not somewhere here at which Boreas is said to have carried off Orithyia from the banks of the Ilissus?

SOCRATES: Such is the tradition.

PHAEDRUS: And is this the exact spot? The little stream is delightfully clear and bright; I can fancy that there might be maidens playing near.

SOCRATES: I believe that the spot is not exactly here, but about a quarter of a mile lower down, where you cross to the temple of Artemis, and there is, I think, some sort of an altar of Boreas at the place.

PHAEDRUS: I have never noticed it; but I beseech you to tell me, Socrates, do you believe this tale?

SOCRATES: The wise are doubtful, and I should not be singular if, like them, I too doubted. I might have a rational explanation that Orithyia was playing with Pharmacia, when a northern gust carried her over the neighboring rocks; and this being the manner of her death, she was said to have been carried away by Boreas. There is a discrepancy, however, about the locality; according to another version of the story she was taken from Areopagus, and not from this place. Now I quite acknowledge that these allegories are very nice, but he is not to be envied who has to invent them; much labor and ingenuity will be required of him; and when he has once begun, he must go on and rehabilitate Hippocentaurs and chimeras dire. Gorgons and winged steeds flow in apace, and numberless other inconceivable and portentous natures. And if he is sceptical about them, and would fain reduce them one after another to the rules of probability, this sort of crude philosophy will take up a great deal of time. Now I have no leisure for such enquiries; shall I tell you why? I must first know myself, as the Delphian inscription says; to be curious about that which is not my concern, while I am still in ignorance of my own self, would be ridiculous. And therefore I bid farewell to all this; the common opinion is enough for me. For, as I was saying, I want to know not about this, but about myself: am I a monster more complicated and swollen with passion than the serpent Typho, or a creature of a gentler and simpler sort, to whom Nature has given a diviner and lowlier destiny? But let me ask you, friend: have we not reached the plane-tree to which you were conducting us?

PHAEDRUS: Yes, this is the tree.

SOCRATES: By Hera, a fair resting place, full of summer sounds and scents. Here is this lofty and spreading plane-tree, and the agnus castus high and clustering, in the fullest blossom and the greatest fragrance; and the stream which flows beneath the plane-tree is deliciously cold to the feet. Judging from the ornaments and images, this must be a spot sacred to Achelous and the Nymphs. How delightful is the breeze—so very sweet; and there is a sound in the air shrill and summerlike which makes answer to the chorus of the cicadae. But the greatest charm of all is the grass, like a pillow gently sloping to the head. My dear Phaedrus, you have been an admirable guide.

PHAEDRUS: What an incomprehensible being you are, Socrates: when you are in the country, as you say, you really are like some stranger who is led about by a guide. Do you ever cross the border? I rather think that you never venture even outside the gates.

SOCRATES: Very true, my good friend; and I hope that you will excuse me when you hear the reason, which is, that I am a lover of knowledge, and the men who dwell in the city are my teachers, and not the trees or the country. Though I do indeed believe that you have found a spell with which to draw me out of the city into the country, like a hungry cow before whom a bough or a bunch of fruit is waved. For only hold up before me in like manner a book, and you may lead me all round Attica, and over the wide world. And now having arrived, I intend to lie down, and do you choose any posture in which you can read best. Begin.

PHAEDRUS: Listen. You know how matters stand with me; and how, as I conceive, this affair may be arranged for the advantage of both of us. And I maintain that I ought not to fail in my suit, because I am not your lover: for lovers repent of the kindnesses which they have shown when their passion ceases, but to the non-lovers who are free and not under any compulsion, no time of repentance ever comes; for they confer their benefits according to the measure of their ability, in the way which is most conducive to their own interest. Then again, lovers consider how by reason of their love they have neglected their own concerns and rendered service to others: and when to these benefits conferred they add on the troubles which they have endured, they think that they have long ago made to the beloved a very ample return. But the non-lover has no such tormenting recollections; he has never neglected his affairs or quarrelled with his relations; he has no troubles to add up or excuses to invent; and being well rid of all these evils, why should he not freely do what will gratify the beloved? If you say that the lover is more to be esteemed, because his love is thought to be greater; for he is willing to say and do what is hateful to other men, in order to please his beloved—that, if true, is only a proof that he will prefer any future love to his present, and will injure his old love at the pleasure of the new. And how, in a matter of such infinite importance, can a man be right in trusting himself to one who is afflicted with a malady which no experienced person would attempt to cure, for the patient himself admits that he is not in his right mind, and acknowledges that he is wrong in his mind, but says that he is unable to control himself? And if he came to his right mind, would he ever imagine that the desires were good which he conceived when in his wrong mind? Once more, there are many more non-lovers than lovers; and if you choose the best of the lovers, you will not have many to choose from; but if from the non-lovers, the choice will be larger, and you will be far more likely to find among them a person who is worthy of your friendship. If public opinion be your dread, and you would avoid reproach, in all probability the lover, who is always thinking that other men are as emulous of him as he is of them, will boast to someone of his successes, and make a show of them openly in the pride of his heart—he wants others to know that his labor has not been lost; but the non-lover is more his own master, and is desirous of solid good, and not of the opinion of mankind. Again, the lover may be generally noted or seen following the beloved (this is his regular occupation), and whenever they are observed to exchange two words they are supposed to meet about some affair of love either past or in contemplation; but when non-lovers meet, no one asks the reason why, because people know that talking to another is natural, whether friendship or mere pleasure be the motive. Once more, if you fear the fickleness of friendship, consider that in any other case a quarrel might be a mutual calamity; but now, when you have given up what is most precious to you, you will be the greater loser, and therefore, you will have more reason in being afraid of the lover, for his vexations are many, and he is always fancying that everyone is leagued against him. Wherefore also he debars his beloved from society; he will not have you intimate with the wealthy, lest they should exceed him in wealth, or with men of education, lest they should be his superiors in understanding; and he is equally afraid of anybody's influence who has any other advantage over himself. If he can persuade you to break with them, you are left without a friend in the world; or if, out of a regard to your own interest, you have more sense than to comply with his desire, you will have to quarrel with him. But those who are non-lovers, and whose success in love is the reward of their merit, will not be jealous of the companions of their beloved, and will rather hate those who refuse to be his associates, thinking that their favorite is slighted by the latter and benefited by the former; for more love than hatred may be expected to come to him out of his friendship with others. Many lovers too have loved the person of a youth before they knew his character or his belongings; so that when their passion has passed away, there is no knowing whether they will continue to be his friends; whereas, in the case of non-lovers who were always friends, the friendship is not lessened by the favors granted; but the recollection of these remains with them, and is an earnest of good things to come.

Further, I say that you are likely to be improved by me, whereas the lover will spoil you. For they praise your words and actions in a wrong way; partly, because they are afraid of offending you, and also, their judgment is weakened by passion. Such are the feats which love exhibits; he makes things painful to the disappointed which give no pain to others; he compels the successful lover to praise what ought not to give him pleasure, and therefore the beloved is to be pitied rather than envied. But if you listen to me, in the first place, I, in my intercourse with you, shall not merely regard present enjoyment, but also future advantage, being not mastered by love, but my own master; nor for small causes taking violent dislikes, but even when the cause is great, slowly laying up little wrath—unintentional offenses I shall forgive, and intentional ones I shall try to prevent; and these are the marks of a friendship which will last.

Do you think that a lover only can be a firm friend? reflect: if this were true, we should set small value on sons, or fathers, or mothers; nor should we ever have loyal friends, for our love of them arises not from passion, but from other associations. Further, if we ought to shower favors on those who are the most eager suitors—on that principle, we ought always to do good, not to the most virtuous, but to the most needy; for they are the persons who will be most relieved, and will therefore be the most grateful;

and when you make a feast you should invite not your friend, but the beggar and the empty soul; for they will love you, and attend you, and come about your doors, and will be the best pleased, and the most grateful, and will invoke many a blessing on your head. Yet surely you ought not to be granting favors to those who besiege you with prayer, but to those who are best able to reward you; nor to the lover only, but to those who are worthy of love; nor to those who will enjoy the bloom of your youth, but to those who will share their possessions with you in age; nor to those who, having succeeded, will glory in their success to others, but to those who will be modest and tell no tales; nor to those who care about you for a moment only, but to those who will continue your friends through life; nor to those who, when their passion is over, will pick a quarrel with you, but rather to those who, when the charm of youth has left you, will show their own virtue. Remember what I have said; and consider yet this further point: friends admonish the lover under the idea that his way of life is bad, but no one of his kindred ever yet censured the non-lover, or thought that he was ill-advised about his own interests.

"Perhaps you will ask me whether I propose that you should indulge every non-lover. To which I reply that not even the lover would advise you to indulge all lovers, for the indiscriminate favor is less esteemed by the rational recipient, and less easily hidden by him who would escape the censure of the world. Now love ought to be for the advantage of both parties, and for the injury of neither.

"I believe that I have said enough; but if there is anything more which you desire or which in your opinion needs to be supplied, ask and I will answer."

Now, Socrates, what do you think? Is not the discourse excellent, more especially in the matter of the language?

SOCRATES: Yes, quite admirable; the effect on me was ravishing. And this I owe to you, Phaedrus, for I observed you while reading to be in an ecstasy, and thinking that you are more experienced in these matters than I am, I followed your example, and, like you, my divine darling, I became inspired with a frenzy.

PHAEDRUS: Indeed, you are pleased to be merry.

SOCRATES: Do you mean that I am not in earnest?

PHAEDRUS: Now don't talk in that way, Socrates, but let me have your real opinion; I adjure you, by Zeus, the god of friendship, to tell me whether you think that any Hellene could have said more or spoken better on the same subject.

SOCRATES: Well, but are you and I expected to praise the sentiments of the author, or only the clearness, and roundness, and finish, and tournure of the language? As to the first I willingly submit to your better judgment, for I am not worthy to form an opinion, having only attended to the rhetorical manner; and I was doubting whether this could have been defended even by Lysias himself; I thought, though I speak under correction, that he repeated himself two or three times, either from want of words or from want of pains; and also, he appeared to me ostentatiously to exult in showing how well he could say the same thing in two or three ways.

PHAEDRUS: Nonsense, Socrates; what you call repetition was the especial merit of the speech; for he omitted no topic of which the subject rightly allowed, and I do not think that anyone could have spoken better or more exhaustively.

SOCRATES: There I cannot go along with you. Ancient sages, men and women, who have spoken and written of these things, would rise up in judgment against me, if out of complaisance I assented to you.

PHAEDRUS: Who are they, and where did you hear anything better than this?

SOCRATES: I am sure that I must have heard; but at this moment I do not remember from whom; perhaps from Sappho the fair, or Anacreon the wise; or, possibly, from a prose writer. Why do I say so? Why, because I perceive that my bosom is full, and that I could make another speech as good as that of Lysias, and different. Now I am certain that this is not an invention of my own, who am well aware that I know nothing, and therefore I can only infer that I have been filled through the ears, like a pitcher, from the waters of another, though I have actually forgotten in my stupidity who was my informant.

PHAEDRUS: That is grand—but never mind where you heard the discourse or from whom; let that be a mystery not to be divulged even at my earnest desire. Only, as you say, promise to make another and better oration, equal in length and entirely new, on the same subject; and I, like the nine Archons, will promise to set up a golden image at Delphi, not only of myself, but of you, and as large as life.

SOCRATES: You are a dear golden ass if you suppose me to mean that Lysias has altogether missed the mark, and that I can make a speech from which all his arguments are to be excluded. The worst of authors will say something which is to the point. Who, for example, could speak on this thesis of yours without praising the discretion of the non-lover and blaming the indiscretion of the lover? These are the commonplaces of the subject which must come in (for what else is there to be said?) and must be allowed and excused; the only merit is in the arrangement of them, for there can be none in the invention; but when you leave the commonplaces, then there may be some originality.

PHAEDRUS: I admit that there is reason in what you say, and I too will be reasonable, and will allow you to start with the premise that the lover is more disordered in his wits than the non-lover; if in what remains you make a longer and better speech than Lysias, and use other arguments, then I say again, that a statue you shall have of beaten gold, and take your place by the colossal offerings of the Cypselids at Olympia.

SOCRATES: How profoundly in earnest is the lover, because to tease him I lay a finger upon his love! And so, Phaedrus, you really imagine that I am going to improve upon the ingenuity of Lysias?

PHAEDRUS: There I have you as you had me, and you must just speak "as you best can." Do not let us exchange "tu quoque" as in a farce, or compel me to say to you as you said to me, "I know Socrates as well as I know myself, and he was wanting to speak, but he gave himself airs." Rather I would have you consider that from this place we stir not until you have unbosomed yourself of the speech; for here are we all alone, and I am stronger, remember, and younger than you: Wherefore perpend, and do not compel me to use violence.

SOCRATES: But, my sweet Phaedrus, how ridiculous it would be of me to compete with Lysias in an extempore speech! He is a master in his art and I am an untaught man.

PHAEDRUS: You see how matters stand; and therefore let there be no more pretences; for, indeed, I know the word that is irresistible.

SOCRATES: Then don't say it.

PHAEDRUS: Yes, but I will; and my word shall be an oath. "I say, or rather swear"—but what god will be witness of my oath?—"By this plane-tree I swear, that unless you repeat the discourse here in the face of this very plane-tree, I will never tell you another; never let you have word of another!"

SOCRATES: Villain! I am conquered; the poor lover of discourse has no more to say.

PHAEDRUS: Then why are you still at your tricks?

SOCRATES: I am not going to play tricks now that you have taken the oath, for I cannot allow myself to be starved.

PHAEDRUS: Proceed.

SOCRATES: Shall I tell you what I will do?

PHAEDRUS: What?
SOCRATES: I will veil my face and gallop through the discourse as fast as I can, for if I see you I shall feel ashamed and not know what to say.
PHAEDRUS: Only go on and you may do anything else which you please.
SOCRATES: Come, O ye Muses, melodious, as ye are called, whether you have received this name from the character of your strains, or because the Melians are a musical race, help, O help me in the tale which my good friend here desires me to rehearse, in order that his friend whom he always deemed wise may seem to him to be wiser than ever.

Once upon a time there was a fair boy, or, more properly speaking, a youth; he was very fair and had a great many lovers; and there was one special cunning one, who had persuaded the youth that he did not love him, but he really loved him all the same; and one day when he was paying his addresses to him, he used this very argument—that he ought to accept the non-lover rather than the lover; his words were as follows:

"All good counsel begins in the same way; a man should know what he is advising about, or his counsel will all come to nought. But people imagine that they know about the nature of things, when they don't know about them, and, not having come to an understanding at first because they think that they know, they end, as might be expected, in contradicting one another and themselves. Now you and I must not be guilty of this fundamental error which we condemn in others; but as our question is whether the lover or non-lover is to be preferred, let us first of all agree in defining the nature and power of love, and then, keeping our eyes upon the definition and to this appealing, let us further inquire whether love brings advantage or disadvantage.

"Every one sees that love is a desire, and we know also that non-lovers desire the beautiful and good. Now in what way is the lover to be distinguished from the non-lover? Let us note that in every one of us there are two guiding and ruling principles which lead us whither they will; one is the natural desire of pleasure, the other is an acquired opinion which aspires after the best; and these two are sometimes in harmony and then again at war, and sometimes the one, sometimes the other conquers. When opinion by the help of reason leads us to the best, the conquering principle is called temperance; but when desire, which is devoid of reason, rules in us and drags us to pleasure, that power of misrule is called excess. Now excess has many names, and many members, and many forms, and any of these forms when very marked gives a name, neither honorable nor creditable, to the bearer of the name. The desire of eating, for example, which gets the better of the higher reason and the other desires, is called gluttony, and he who is possessed by it is called a glutton; the tyrannical desire of drink, which inclines the possessor of the desire to drink, has a name which is only too obvious, and there can be as little doubt by what name any other appetite of the same family would be called; it will be the name of that which happens to be dominant. And now I think that you will perceive the drift of my discourse; but as every spoken word is in a manner plainer than the unspoken, I had better say further that the irrational desire which overcomes the tendency of opinion toward right, and is led away to the enjoyment of beauty, and especially of personal beauty, by the desires which are her own kindred—that supreme desire, I say, which by leading conquers and by the force of passion is reinforced, from this very force, receiving a name, is called love (erromenos eros)."

And now, dear Phaedrus, I shall pause for an instant to ask whether you do not think me, as I appear to myself, inspired?
PHAEDRUS: Yes, Socrates, you seem to have a very unusual flow of words.
SOCRATES: Listen to me, then, in silence; for surely the place is holy; so that you must not wonder, if, as I proceed, I appear to be in a divine fury, for already I am getting into dithyrambics.
PHAEDRUS: Nothing can be truer.
SOCRATES: The responsibility rests with you. But hear what follows, and perhaps the fit may be averted; all is in their hands above. I will go on talking to my youth. Listen:

Thus, my friend, we have declared and defined the nature of the subject. Keeping the definition in view, let us now inquire what advantage or disadvantage is likely to ensue from the lover or the non-lover to him who accepts their advances.

He who is the victim of his passions and the slave of pleasure will of course desire to make his beloved as agreeable to himself as possible. Now to him who has a mind diseased anything is agreeable which is not opposed to him, but that which is equal or superior is hateful to him, and therefore the lover will not brook any superiority or equality on the part of his beloved; he is always employed in reducing him to inferiority. And the ignorant is the inferior of the wise, the coward of the brave, the slow of speech of the speaker, the dull of the clever. These, and not these only, are the mental defects of the beloved—defects which, when implanted by nature, are necessarily a delight to the lover, and when not implanted, he must contrive to implant them in him, if he would not be deprived of his fleeting joy. And therefore he cannot help being jealous, and will debar his beloved from the advantages of society which would make a man of him, and especially from that society which would have given him wisdom, and thereby he cannot fail to do him great harm. That is to say, in his excessive fear lest he should come to be despised in his eyes he will be compelled to banish from him divine philosophy; and there is no greater injury which he can inflict upon him than this. He will contrive that his beloved shall be wholly ignorant, and in everything shall look to him; he is to be the delight of the lover's heart, and a curse to himself. Verily, a lover is a profitable guardian and associate for him in all that relates to his mind.

Let us next see how his master, whose law of life is pleasure and not good, will keep and train the body of his servant. Will he not choose a beloved who is delicate rather than sturdy and strong? One brought up in shady bowers and not in the bright sun, a stranger to manly exercises and the sweat of toil, accustomed only to a soft and luxurious diet, instead of the hues of health having the colors of paint and ornament, and the rest of a piece?—such a life as anyone can imagine and which I need not detail at length. But I may sum up all that I have to say in a word, and pass on. Such a person in war, or in any of the great crises of life, will be the anxiety of his friends and also of his lover, and certainly not the terror of his enemies; which nobody can deny.

And now let us tell what advantage or disadvantage the beloved will receive from the guardianship and society of his lover in the matter of his property; this is the next point to be considered. The lover will be the first to see what, indeed, will be sufficiently evident to all men, that he desires above all things to deprive his beloved of his dearest and best and holiest possessions, father, mother, kindred, friends, of all whom he thinks may be hinderers or reprovers of their most sweet converse; he will even cast a jealous eye upon his gold and silver or other property, because these make him a less easy prey, and when caught less manageable; hence he is of necessity displeased at his possession of them and rejoices at their loss; and he would like him to be wifeless, childless, homeless, as well; and the longer the better, for the longer he is all this, the longer he will enjoy him.

There are some sort of animals, such as flatterers, who are dangerous and mischievous enough, and yet nature has mingled a temporary pleasure and grace in their composition. You may say that a courtesan is hurtful, and disapprove of such creatures and their practices, and yet for the time they are very pleasant. But the lover is not only hurtful to his love; he is also an extremely disagreeable companion. The old proverb says that "birds of a feather flock together"; I suppose that equality of years inclines them to the same pleasures, and similarity begets friendship; yet you may have more than enough even of this; and verily constraint is always said to be grievous. Now the lover is not only unlike his beloved, but he forces himself upon him. For he is old and his love is young, and neither day nor night will he leave him if he can help; necessity and the sting of desire drive him on, and allure him with the pleasure which he receives from seeing, hearing, touching, perceiving him in every way. And therefore he is delighted to fasten upon him and to minister to him. But what pleasure or consolation can the beloved be receiving all this time? Must he not feel the extremity of disgust when he looks at an old shrivelled face and the remainder to match, which even in a description is disagreeable, and quite detestable when he is forced into daily contact with his lover; moreover he is jealously watched and guarded against everything and everybody, and has to hear misplaced and exaggerated praises of himself, and censures equally inappropriate, which are intolerable when the man is sober, and, besides being intolerable, are published all over the world in all their indelicacy and wearisomeness when he is drunk.

And not only while his love continues is he mischievous and unpleasant, but when his love ceases he becomes a perfidious enemy of him on whom he showered his oaths and prayers and promises, and yet could hardly prevail upon him to tolerate the tedium of his company even from motives of interest. The hour of payment arrives, and now he is the servant of another master; instead of love and infatuation, wisdom and temperance are his bosom's lords; but the beloved has not discovered the change which has taken place in him, when he asks for a return and recalls to his recollection former sayings and doings; he believes himself to be speaking to the same person, and the other, not having the courage to confess the truth, and not knowing how to fulfill the oaths and promises which he made when under the dominion of folly, and having now grown wise and temperate, does not want to do as he did or to be as he was before. And so he runs away and is constrained to be a defaulter; the oyster shell (in allusion to a game in which two parties fled or pursued according as an oyster shell which was thrown into the air fell with the dark or light side uppermost) has fallen with the other side uppermost—he changes pursuit into flight, while the other is compelled to follow him with passion and imprecation, not knowing that he ought never from the first to have accepted a demented lover instead of a sensible non-lover; and that in making such a choice he was giving himself up to a faithless, morose, envious, disagreeable being, hurtful to his estate, hurtful to his bodily health, and still more hurtful to the cultivation of his mind, than which there neither is nor ever will be anything more honored in the eyes both of gods and men. Consider this, fair youth, and know that in the friendship of the lover there is no real kindness; he has an appetite and wants to feed upon you:

"As wolves love lambs so lovers love their loves."

But I told you so, I am speaking in verse, and therefore I had better make an end; enough.

PHAEDRUS: I thought that you were only halfway and were going to make a similar speech about all the advantages of accepting the non-lover. Why do you not proceed?

SOCRATES: Does not your simplicity observe that I have got out of dithyrambics into heroics, when only uttering a censure on the lover? And if I am to add the praises of the non-lover what will become of me? Do you not perceive that I am already overtaken by the Nymphs to whom you have mischievously exposed me? And therefore I will only add that the non-lover has all the advantages in which the lover is accused of being deficient. And now I will say no more; there has been enough of both of them. Leaving the tale to its fate, I will cross the river and make the best of my way home, lest a worse thing be inflicted upon me by you.

PHAEDRUS: Not yet, Socrates; not until the heat of the day has passed; do you not see that the hour is almost noon? there is the midday sun standing still, as people say, in the meridian. Let us rather stay and talk over what has been said, and then return in the cool.

SOCRATES: Your love of discourse, Phaedrus, is superhuman, simply marvellous, and I do not believe that there is any one of your contemporaries who has either made or in one way or another has compelled others to make an equal number of speeches. I would except Simmias the Theban, but all the rest are far behind you. And now I do verily believe that you have been the cause of another.

PHAEDRUS: That is good news. But what do you mean?

SOCRATES: I mean to say that as I was about to cross the stream the usual sign was given to me—that sign which always forbids, but never bids, me to do anything which I am going to do; and I thought that I heard a voice saying in my ear that I had been guilty of impiety, and that I must not go away until I had made an atonement. Now I am a diviner, though not a very good one, but I have enough religion for my own use, as you might say of a

bad writer—his writing is good enough for him; and I am beginning to see that I was in error. O my friend, how prophetic is the human soul! At the time I had a sort of misgiving, and, like Ibycus, "I was troubled; I feared that I might be buying honor from men at the price of sinning against the gods." Now I recognize my error.
PHAEDRUS: What error?
SOCRATES: That was a dreadful speech which you brought with you, and you made me utter one as bad.
PHAEDRUS: How so?
SOCRATES: It was foolish, I say, to a certain extent, impious; can anything be more dreadful?
PHAEDRUS: Nothing, if the speech was really such as you describe.
SOCRATES: Well, and is not Eros the son of Aphrodite, and a god?
PHAEDRUS: So men say.
SOCRATES: But that was not acknowledged by Lysias in his speech, nor by you in that other speech which you by a charm drew from my lips. For if love be, as he surely is, a divinity, he cannot be evil. Yet this was the error of both the speeches. There was also a simplicity about them which was refreshing; having no truth or honesty in them, nevertheless they pretended to be something, hoping to succeed in deceiving the manikins of Earth and gain celebrity among them. Wherefore I must have a purgation. And I bethink me of an ancient purgation of mythological error which was devised, not by Homer, for he never had the wit to discover why he was blind, but by Stesichorus, who was a philosopher and knew the reason why; and therefore, when he lost his eyes, for that was the penalty which was inflicted upon him for reviling the lovely Helen, he at once purged himself. And the purgation was a recantation, which began thus—

> "False is that word of mine—the truth is that thou didst not embark in ships, nor ever go to the walls of Troy";

and when he had completed his poem, which is called "the recantation," immediately his sight returned to him. Now I will be wiser than either Stesichorus or Homer, in that I am going to make my recantation for reviling love before I suffer; and this I will attempt, not as before, veiled and ashamed, but with forehead bold and bare.
PHAEDRUS: Nothing could be more agreeable to me than to hear you say so.
SOCRATES: Only think, my good Phaedrus, what an utter want of

delicacy was shown in the two discourses; I mean, in my own and in that which you recited out of the book. Would not anyone who was himself of a noble and gentle nature, and who loved or ever had loved a nature like his own, when we tell of the petty causes of lovers' jealousies, and of their exceeding animosities, and of the injuries which they do to their beloved, have imagined that our ideas of love were taken from some haunt of sailors to which good manners were unknown—he would certainly never have admitted the justice of our censure?

PHAEDRUS: I dare say not, Socrates.

SOCRATES: Therefore, because I blush at the thought of this person, and also because I am afraid of Love himself, I desire to wash the brine out of my ears with water from the spring; and I would counsel Lysias not to delay, but to write another discourse, which shall prove that "ceteris paribus" the lover ought to be accepted rather than the non-lover.

PHAEDRUS: Be assured that he shall. You shall speak the praises of the lover, and Lysias shall be compelled by me to write another discourse on the same theme.

SOCRATES: You will be true to your nature in that, and therefore I believe you.

PHAEDRUS: Speak, and fear not.

SOCRATES: But where is the fair youth whom I was addressing before, and who ought to listen now; lest, if he hear me not, he should accept a non-lover before he knows what he is doing?

PHAEDRUS: He is close at hand, and always at your service.

SOCRATES: Know then, fair youth, that the former discourse was the word of Phaedrus, the son of Vain Man, who dwells in the city of Myrrhina (Myrrhinusius). And this which I am about to utter is the recantation of Stesichorus the son of Godly Man (Euphemus), who comes from the town of Desire (Himera), and is to the following effect: "I told a lie when I said" that the beloved ought to accept the non-lover when he might have the lover, because the one is sane, and the other mad. It might be so if madness were simply an evil; but there is also a madness which is a divine gift, and the source of the chiefest blessings granted to men. For prophecy is a madness, and the prophetess at Delphi and the priestesses at Dodona when out of their senses have conferred great benefits on Hellas, both in public and private life, but when in their senses few or none. And I might also tell you how the Sibyl and other inspired persons have given to many an one many an intimation of the future which has saved them from falling. But it would be tedious to speak of what everyone knows.

There will be more reason in appealing to the ancient inventors of names (compare Cratylus), who would never have connected prophecy (mantike) which foretells the future and is the noblest of arts, with madness (manike), or called them both by the same name, if they had deemed madness to be a disgrace or dishonor—they must have thought that there was an inspired madness which was a noble thing; for the two words, mantike and manike, are really the same, and the letter tau is only a modern and tasteless insertion. And this is confirmed by the name which was given by them to the rational investigation of futurity, whether made by the help of birds or of other signs—this, for as much as it is an art which supplies from the reasoning faculty mind (nous) and information (istoria) to human thought (oiesis) they originally termed oionoistike, but the word has been lately altered and made sonorous by the modern introduction of the letter Omega (oionoistike and oionistike), and in proportion as prophecy (mantike) is more perfect and august than augury, both in name and fact, in the same proportion, as the ancients testify, is madness superior to a sane mind (sophrosune) for the one is only of human, but the other of divine origin. Again, where plagues and mightiest woes have bred in certain families, owing to some ancient blood-guiltiness, there madness has entered with holy prayers and rites, and by inspired utterances found a way of deliverance for those who are in need; and he who has part in this gift, and is truly possessed and duly out of his mind, is by the use of purifications and mysteries made whole and exempt from evil, future as well as present, and has a release from the calamity which was afflicting him. The third kind is the madness of those who are possessed by the Muses; which taking hold of a delicate and virgin soul, and there inspiring frenzy, awakens lyrical and all other numbers; with these adorning the myriad actions of ancient heroes for the instruction of posterity. But he who, having no touch of the Muses' madness in his soul, comes to the door and thinks that he will get into the temple by the help of art—he, I say, and his poetry are not admitted; the sane man disappears and is nowhere when he enters into rivalry with the madman.

I might tell of many other noble deeds which have sprung from inspired madness. And therefore, let no one frighten or flutter us by saying that the temperate friend is to be chosen rather than the inspired, but let him further show that love is not sent by the gods for any good to lover or beloved; if he can do so we will allow him to carry off the palm. And we, on our part, will prove in answer to him that the madness of love is the greatest of heaven's blessings, and the proof shall be one which the wise will receive, and the witling disbelieve. But first of all, let us view the affections and actions of the soul divine and human, and try to ascertain the truth about them. The beginning of our proof is as follows:

(Translated by Cic. Tus. Quaest.) The soul through all her being is immortal, for that which is ever in motion is immortal; but that which moves another and is moved by another, in ceasing to move ceases also to live. Only the self-moving, never leaving self, never ceases to move, and is the fountain and beginning of motion to all that moves besides. Now, the beginning is unbegotten, for that which is begotten has a beginning; but the beginning is begotten of nothing, for if it were begotten of something, then the begotten would not come from a beginning. But if unbegotten, it must also be indestructible; for if beginning were destroyed, there could be no beginning out of anything, nor anything out of a beginning; and all things must have a beginning. And therefore the self-moving is the beginning of motion; and this can neither be destroyed nor begotten, else the whole heavens and all creation would collapse and stand still, and never again have motion or birth. But if the self-moving is proved to be immortal, he who affirms that self-motion is the very idea and essence of the soul will not be put to confusion. For the body which is moved from without is soulless; but that which is moved from within has a soul, for such is the nature of the soul. But if this be true, must not the soul be the self-moving, and therefore of necessity unbegotten and immortal? Enough of the soul's immortality.

Of the nature of the soul, though her true form be ever a theme of large and more than mortal discourse, let me speak briefly, and in a figure. And let the figure be composite—a pair of winged horses and a charioteer. Now the winged horses and the charioteers of the gods are all of them noble and of noble descent, but those of other races are mixed; the human charioteer drives his in a pair; and one of them is noble and of noble breed, and the other is ignoble and of ignoble breed; and the driving of them of necessity gives a great deal of trouble to him. I will endeavor to explain to you in what way the mortal differs from the immortal creature. The soul in her totality has the care of inanimate being everywhere, and traverses the whole heaven in diverse forms appearing—when perfect and fully winged she soars upward, and orders the whole world; whereas the imperfect soul, losing her wings and drooping in her flight at last settles on the solid ground—there, finding a home, she receives an earthly frame which appears to be self-moved, but is really moved by her power; and this composition of soul and body is called a living and mortal creature. For immortal no such union can be reasonably believed to be; although fancy, not having seen nor surely known the nature of God, may imagine an immortal creature having both a body and also a soul which are united throughout all time. Let that, however, be as God wills, and be spoken of acceptably to him. And now let us ask the reason why the soul loses her wings!

The wing is the corporeal element which is most akin to the divine, and which by nature tends to soar aloft and carry that which gravitates downwards into the upper region, which is the habitation of the gods. The divine is beauty, wisdom, goodness, and the like; and by these the wing of the soul is nourished, and grows apace; but when fed upon evil and foulness and the opposite of good, wastes and falls away. Zeus, the mighty lord, holding the reins of a winged chariot, leads the way in heaven, ordering all and taking care of all; and there follows him the array of gods and demigods, marshalled in eleven bands; Hestia alone abides at home in the house of heaven; of the rest they who are reckoned among the princely twelve march in their appointed order. They see many blessed sights in the inner heaven, and there are many ways to and fro, along which the blessed gods are passing, everyone doing his own work; he may follow who will and can, for jealousy has no place in the celestial choir. But when they go to banquet and festival, then they move up the steep to the top of the vault of heaven. The chariots of the gods in even poise, obeying the rein, glide rapidly; but the others labor, for the vicious steed goes heavily, weighing down the charioteer to the Earth when his steed has not been thoroughly trained—and this is the hour of agony and extremest conflict for the soul. For the immortals, when they are at the end of their course, go forth and stand upon the outside of heaven, and the revolution of the spheres carries them round, and they behold the things beyond. But of the heaven which is above the heavens, what earthly poet ever did or ever will sing worthily? It is such as I will describe; for I must dare to speak the truth, when truth is my theme. There abides the very being with which true knowledge is concerned; the colorless, formless, intangible essence, visible only to mind, the pilot of the soul. The divine intelligence, being nurtured upon mind and pure knowledge, and the intelligence of every soul which is capable of receiving the food proper to it, rejoices at beholding reality, and once more gazing upon truth, is replenished and made glad, until the revolution of the worlds brings her round again to the same place. In the revolution she beholds justice, and temperance, and knowledge absolute, not in the form of generation or of relation, which men call existence, but knowledge absolute in existence absolute; and beholding the other true existences in like manner, and feasting upon them, she passes down into the interior of the heavens and returns home; and there the charioteer putting up his horses at the stall, gives them ambrosia to eat and nectar to drink.

Such is the life of the gods; but of other souls, that which follows God best and is likest to him lifts the head of the charioteer into the outer world, and is carried round in the revolution, troubled indeed by the steeds, and with difficulty beholding true being; while another only rises and falls, and sees, and again fails to see by reason of the unruliness of the steeds. The rest of the souls are also longing after the upper world and they all follow, but not being strong enough they are carried round below the surface, plunging, treading on one another, each striving to be first; and there is confusion and perspiration and the extremity of effort; and many of them are lamed or have their wings broken through the ill-driving of the charioteers; and all of them after a fruitless toil, not having attained to the mysteries of true being, go away, and feed upon opinion. The reason why the souls exhibit this exceeding eagerness to behold the plain of truth is that pasturage is found there, which is suited to the highest part of the soul; and the wing on which the soul soars is nourished with this. And there is a law of Destiny, that the soul which attains any vision of truth in company with a god is preserved from harm until the next period, and if attaining always is always unharmed. But when she is unable to follow, and fails to behold the truth, and through some ill-hap sinks beneath the double load of forgetfulness and vice, and her wings fall from her and she drops to the ground, then the law ordains that this soul shall at her first birth pass, not into any other animal, but only into man; and the soul which has seen most of truth shall come to the birth as a philosopher, or artist, or some musical and loving nature; that which has seen truth in the second degree shall be some righteous king or warrior chief; the soul which is of the third class shall be a politician, or economist, or trader; the fourth shall be a lover of gymnastic toils, or a physician; the fifth shall lead the life of a prophet or hierophant; to the sixth the character of poet or some other imitative artist will be assigned; to the seventh the life of an artisan or husbandman; to the eighth that of a sophist or demagogue; to the ninth that of a tyrant—all these are states of probation, in which he who does righteously improves, and he who does unrighteously, deteriorates his lot.

Ten thousand years must elapse before the soul of each one can return to the place from whence she came, for she cannot grow her wings in less; only the soul of a philosopher, guileless and true, or the soul of a lover, who is not devoid of philosophy, may acquire wings in the third of the recurring periods of a thousand years; he is distinguished from the ordinary good man who gains wings in three thousand years—and they who choose this life three times in succession have wings given them, and go away at the end of three thousand years. But the others (the philosopher alone is not subject to judgment [krisis], for he has never lost the vision of truth) receive judgment when they have completed their first life, and after the judgment they go, some of them to the houses of correction which are under the earth, and are punished; others to some place in heaven whither they are lightly borne by justice, and there they live in a manner worthy of the life which they led here when in the form of men. And at the end of the first thousand years the good souls and also the evil souls both come to draw lots and choose their second life, and they may take any which they please. The soul of a man may pass into the life of a beast, or from the beast return again into the man. But the soul which has never seen the truth will not pass into the human form. For a man must have intelligence of universals, and be able to proceed from the many particulars of sense to one conception of reason—this is the recollection of those things which our soul once saw while following God, when regardless of that which we now call being she raised her head up toward the true being. And therefore the mind of the philosopher alone has wings; and this is just, for he is always, according to the measure of his abilities, clinging in recollection to those things in which God abides, and in beholding which He is what He is. And he who employs aright these memories is ever being initiated into perfect mysteries and alone becomes truly perfect. But, as he forgets earthly interests and is rapt in the divine, the vulgar deem him mad, and rebuke him; they do not see that he is inspired.

Thus far I have been speaking of the fourth and last kind of madness, which is imputed to him who, when he sees the beauty of Earth, is transported with the recollection of the true beauty; he would like to fly away, but he cannot; he is like a bird fluttering and looking upward and careless of the world below; and he is therefore thought to be mad. And I have shown this of all inspirations to be the noblest and highest and the offspring of the highest to him who has or shares in it, and that he who loves the beautiful is called a lover because he partakes of it. For, as has been already said, every soul of man has in the way of nature beheld true being; this was the condition of her passing into the form of man. But all souls do not easily recall the things of the other world; they may have seen them for a short time only, or they may have been unfortunate in their earthly lot, and, having had their hearts turned to unrighteousness through some corrupting influence, they may have lost the memory of the holy things which once they saw. Few only retain an adequate remembrance of them; and they, when they behold here any image of that other world, are rapt in amazement; but they are ignorant of what this rapture means, because they do not clearly perceive. For there is no light of justice or temperance or any of the higher ideas which are precious to souls in the earthly copies of them: they are seen through a glass dimly; and there are few who, going to the images, behold in them the realities, and these only with difficulty. There was a time when with the rest of the happy band they saw beauty shining in brightness—we philosophers following in the train of Zeus, others in company with other gods; and then we beheld the beatific vision and were initiated into a mystery which may be truly called most blessed, celebrated by us in our state of innocence, before we had any experience of evils to come, when we were admitted to the sight of apparitions innocent and simple and calm and happy, which we beheld shining in pure light, pure ourselves and not yet enshrined in that living tomb which we carry about, now that we are imprisoned in the body, like an oyster in his shell. Let me linger over the memory of scenes which have passed away.

But of beauty, I repeat again that we saw her there shining in company with the celestial forms; and coming to Earth we find her here too, shining in clearness through the clearest aperture of sense. For sight is the most piercing of our bodily senses; though not by that is wisdom seen; her loveliness would have been transporting if there had been a visible image of her, and the other ideas, if they had visible counterparts, would be equally lovely. But this is the privilege of beauty, that being the loveliest she is also the most palpable to sight. Now he who is not newly initiated or who has become corrupted, does not easily rise out of this world to the sight of true beauty in the other; he looks only at her earthly namesake, and instead of being awed at the sight of her, he is given over to pleasure, and like a brutish beast he rushes on to enjoy and beget; he consorts with wantonness, and is not afraid or ashamed of pursuing pleasure in violation of nature. But he whose initiation is recent, and who has been the spectator of many glories in the other world, is amazed when he sees anyone having a godlike face or form, which is the expression of divine beauty; and at first a shudder runs through him, and again the old awe steals over him; then looking upon the face of his beloved as of a god he reverences him, and if he were not afraid of being thought a downright madman, he would sacrifice to his beloved as to the image of a god; then while he gazes on him there is a sort of reaction, and the shudder passes into an unusual heat and perspiration; for, as he receives the effluence of beauty through the eyes, the wing moistens and he warms. And as he warms, the parts out of which the wing grew, and which had been hitherto closed and rigid, and had prevented the wing from shooting forth, are melted, and as nourishment streams upon him, the lower end of the wing begins to swell and grow from the root upwards; and the growth extends under the whole soul—for once the whole was winged. During this process the whole soul is all in a state of ebullition and effervescence—which may be compared to the irritation and uneasiness in the gums at the time of cutting teeth—bubbles up, and has a feeling of uneasiness and tickling; but when in like manner the soul is beginning to grow wings, the beauty of the beloved meets her eye and she receives the sensible warm motion of particles which flow toward her, therefore called emotion (imeros), and is refreshed and warmed by them, and then she ceases from her pain with joy. But when she is parted from her beloved and her moisture fails, then the orifices of the passage out of which the wing shoots dry up and close, and intercept the germ of the wing; which, being shut up with the emotion, throbbing as with the pulsations of an artery, pricks the aperture which is nearest, until at length the entire soul is pierced and maddened and pained, and at the recollection of beauty is again delighted. And from both of them together the soul is oppressed at the strangeness of her condition, and is in a great strait and excitement, and in her madness can neither sleep by night nor abide in her place by day. And wherever she thinks that she will behold the beautiful one, thither in her desire she runs. And when she has seen him, and bathed herself in the waters of beauty, her constraint is loosened, and she is refreshed, and has no more pangs and pains; and this is the sweetest of all pleasures at the time, and is the reason why the soul of the lover will never forsake his beautiful one, whom he esteems above all; he has forgotten mother and brethren and companions, and he thinks nothing of the neglect and loss of his property; the rules and proprieties of life, on which he formerly prided himself, he now despises, and is ready to sleep like a servant, wherever he is allowed, as near as he can to his desired one, who is the object of his worship, and the physician who can alone assuage the greatness of his pain. And this state, my dear imaginary youth to whom I am talking, is by men called love, and among the gods has a name at which you, in your simplicity, may be inclined to mock; there are two lines in the apocryphal writings of Homer in which the name occurs. One of them is rather outrageous, and not altogether metrical. They are as follows:

"Mortals call him fluttering love, But the immortals call him winged one, Because the growing of wings (or, reading pterothoiton, "the movement of wings") is a necessity to him."

You may believe this, but not unless you like. At any rate the loves of lovers and their causes are such as I have described.

Now the lover who is taken to be the attendant of Zeus is better able to bear the winged god, and can endure a heavier burden; but the attendants and companions of Ares, when under the influence of love, if they fancy that they have been at all wronged, are ready to kill and put an end to themselves and their beloved. And he who follows in the train of any other god, while he is unspoiled and the impression lasts, honors and imitates him, as far as he is able; and after the manner of his God he behaves in his intercourse with his beloved and with the rest of the world during the first period of his earthly existence. Every one chooses his love from the ranks of beauty according to his character, and this he makes his god, and fashions and adorns as a sort of image which he is to fall down and worship. The followers of Zeus desire that their beloved should have a soul like him; and therefore they seek out someone of a philosophical and imperial nature, and when they have found him and loved him, they do all they can to confirm such a nature in him, and if they have no experience of such a disposition hitherto, they learn of anyone who can teach them, and themselves follow in the same way. And they have the less difficulty in finding the nature of their own god in themselves, because they have been compelled to gaze intensely on him; their recollection clings to him, and they become possessed of him, and receive from him their character and disposition, so far as man can participate in God. The qualities of their god they attribute to the beloved, wherefore they love him all the more, and if, like the Bacchic Nymphs, they draw inspiration from Zeus, they pour out their own fountain upon him, wanting to make him as like as possible to their own god. But those who are the followers of Hera seek a royal love, and when they have found him they do just the same with him; and in like manner the followers of Apollo, and of every other god walking in the ways of their god, seek a love who is to be made like him whom they serve, and when they have found him, they themselves imitate their god, and persuade their love to do the same, and educate him into the manner and nature of the god as far as they each can; for no feelings of envy or jealousy are entertained by them toward their beloved, but they do their utmost to create in him the greatest likeness of themselves and of the god whom they honor. Thus fair and blissful to the beloved is the desire of the inspired lover, and the initiation of which I speak into the mysteries of true love, if he be captured by the lover and their purpose is effected. Now the beloved is taken captive in the following manner:

As I said at the beginning of this tale, I divided each soul into three—two horses and a charioteer; and one of the horses was good and the other bad: the division may remain, but I have not yet explained in what the goodness or badness of either consists, and to that I will now proceed. The right-hand horse is upright and cleanly made; he has a lofty neck and an aquiline nose; his color is white, and his eyes dark; he is a lover of honor and modesty and temperance, and the follower of true glory; he needs no touch of the whip, but is guided by word and admonition only. The other is a crooked lumbering animal, put together anyhow; he has a short thick neck; he is flat-faced and of a dark color, with grey eyes and blood-red complexion (or with grey and bloodshot eyes); the mate of insolence and pride, shag-eared and deaf, hardly yielding to whip and spur. Now when the charioteer beholds the vision of love, and has his whole soul warmed through sense, and is full of the prickings and ticklings of desire, the obedient steed, then as always under the government of shame, refrains from leaping on the beloved; but the other, heedless of the pricks and of the blows of the whip, plunges and runs away, giving all manner of trouble to his companion and the charioteer, whom he forces to approach the beloved and to remember the joys of love. They at first indignantly oppose him and will not be urged on to do terrible and unlawful deeds; but at last, when he persists in plaguing them, they yield and agree to do as he bids them. And now they are at the spot and behold the flashing beauty of the beloved; which when the charioteer sees, his memory is carried to the true beauty, whom he beholds in company with Modesty like an image placed upon a holy pedestal. He sees her, but he is afraid and falls backward in adoration, and by his fall is compelled to pull back the reins with such violence as to bring both the steeds on their haunches, the one willing and unresisting, the unruly one very unwilling; and when they have gone back a little, the one is overcome with shame and wonder, and his whole soul is bathed in perspiration; the other, when the pain is over which the bridle and the fall had given him, having with difficulty taken breath, is full of wrath and reproaches, which he heaps upon the charioteer and his fellow steed, for want of courage and manhood, declaring that they have been false to their agreement and guilty of desertion. Again they refuse, and again he urges them on, and will scarce yield to their prayer that he would wait until another time. When the appointed hour comes, they make as if they had forgotten, and he reminds them, fighting and neighing and dragging them on, until at length he on the same thoughts intent, forces them to draw near again. And when they are near he stoops his head and puts up his tail, and takes the bit in his teeth and pulls shamelessly. Then the charioteer is worse off than ever; he falls back like a racer at the barrier, and with a still more violent wrench drags the bit out of the teeth of the wild steed and covers his abusive tongue and jaws with blood, and forces his legs and haunches to the ground and punishes him sorely. And when this has happened several times and the villain has ceased from his wanton way, he is tamed and humbled, and follows the will of the charioteer, and when he sees the beautiful one he is ready to die of fear. And from that time forward the soul of the lover follows the beloved in modesty and holy fear.

And so the beloved who, like a god, has received every true and loyal service from his lover, not in pretence but in reality, being also himself of a nature friendly to his admirer, if in former days he has blushed to own his passion and turned away his lover, because his youthful companions or others slanderously told him that he would be disgraced, now as years advance, at the appointed age and time, is led to receive him into communion. For fate which has ordained that there shall be no friendship among the evil has also ordained that there shall ever be friendship among the good. And the beloved when he has received him into communion and intimacy, is quite amazed at the goodwill of the lover; he recognizes that the inspired friend is worth all other friends or kinsmen; they have nothing of friendship in them worthy to be compared with his. And when this feeling continues and he is nearer to him and embraces him, in gymnastic exercises and at other times of meeting, then the fountain of that stream, which Zeus when he was in love with Ganymede named Desire, overflows upon the lover, and some enters into his soul, and some when he is filled flows out again; and as a breeze or an echo rebounds from the smooth rocks and returns whence it came, so does the stream of beauty, passing through the eyes which are the windows of the soul, come back to the beautiful one; there arriving and quickening the passages of the wings, watering them and inclining them to grow, and filling the soul of the beloved also with love. And thus he loves, but he knows not what; he does not understand and cannot explain his own state; he appears to have caught the infection of blindness from another; the lover is his mirror in whom he is beholding himself, but he is not aware of this. When he is with the lover, both cease from their pain, but when he is away then he longs as he is longed for, and has love's image, love for love (Anteros) lodging in his breast, which he calls and believes to be not love but friendship only, and his desire is as the desire of the other, but weaker; he wants to see him, touch him, kiss him, embrace him, and probably not long afterward his desire is accomplished. When they meet, the wanton steed of the lover has a word to say to the charioteer; he would like to have a little pleasure in return for many pains, but the wanton steed of the beloved says not a word, for he is bursting with passion which he understands not; he throws his arms around the lover and embraces him as his dearest friend; and, when they are side by side, he is not in a state in which he can refuse the lover anything, if he ask him; although his fellow steed and the charioteer oppose him with the arguments of shame and reason. After this their happiness depends upon their self-control; if the better elements of the mind which lead to order and philosophy prevail, then they pass their life here in happiness and harmony—masters of themselves and orderly—enslaving the vicious and emancipating the virtuous elements of the soul; and when the end comes, they are light and winged for flight, having conquered in one of the three heavenly or truly Olympian victories; nor can human discipline or divine inspiration confer any greater blessing on man than this. If, on the other hand, they leave philosophy and lead the lower life of ambition, then probably, after wine or in some other careless hour, the two wanton animals take the two souls when off their guard and bring them together, and they accomplish that desire of their hearts which to the many is bliss; and this having once enjoyed they continue to enjoy, yet rarely because they have not the approval of the whole soul. They too are dear, but not so dear to one another as the others, either at the time of their love or afterward. They consider that they have given and taken from each other the most sacred pledges, and they may not break them and fall into enmity. At last they pass out of the body, unwinged, but eager to soar, and thus obtain no mean reward of love and madness. For those who have once begun the heavenward pilgrimage may not go down again to darkness and the journey beneath the earth, but they live in light always; happy companions in their pilgrimage, and when the time comes at which they receive their wings they have the same plumage because of their love.

   Thus great are the heavenly blessings which the friendship of a lover will confer upon you, my youth. Whereas the attachment of the non-lover, which is alloyed with a worldly prudence and has worldly and niggardly ways of doling out benefits, will breed in your soul those vulgar qualities which the populace applaud, will send you bowling round the Earth during a period of nine thousand years, and leave you a fool in the world below.

And thus, dear Eros, I have made and paid my recantation, as well and as fairly as I could; more especially in the matter of the poetical figures which I was compelled to use, because Phaedrus would have them. And now forgive the past and accept the present, and be gracious and merciful to me, and do not in thine anger deprive me of sight, or take from me the art of love which thou hast given me, but grant that I may be yet more esteemed in the eyes of the fair. And if Phaedrus or I myself said anything rude in our first speeches, blame Lysias, who is the father of the brat, and let us have no more of his progeny; bid him study philosophy, like his brother Polemarchus; and then his lover Phaedrus will no longer halt between two opinions, but will dedicate himself wholly to love and to philosophical discourses.

PHAEDRUS: I join in the prayer, Socrates, and say with you, if this be for my good, may your words come to pass. But why did you make your second oration so much finer than the first? I wonder why. And I begin to be afraid that I shall lose conceit of Lysias, and that he will appear tame in comparison, even if he be willing to put another as fine and as long as yours into the field, which I doubt. For quite lately one of your politicians was abusing him on this very account; and called him a "speech writer" again and again. So that a feeling of pride may probably induce him to give up writing speeches.

SOCRATES: What a very amusing notion! But I think, my young man, that you are much mistaken in your friend if you imagine that he is frightened at a little noise; and, possibly, you think that his assailant was in earnest?

PHAEDRUS: I thought, Socrates, that he was. And you are aware that the greatest and most influential statesmen are ashamed of writing speeches and leaving them in a written form, lest they should be called Sophists by posterity.

SOCRATES: You seem to be unconscious, Phaedrus, that the "sweet elbow" (A proverb, like "the grapes are sour," applied to pleasures which cannot be had, meaning sweet things which, like the elbow, are out of the reach of the mouth. The promised pleasure turns out to be a long and tedious affair.) of the proverb is really the long arm of the Nile. And you appear to be equally unaware of the fact that this sweet elbow of theirs is also a long arm. For there is nothing of which our great politicians are so fond as of writing speeches and bequeathing them to posterity. And they add their admirers' names at the top of the writing, out of gratitude to them.

PHAEDRUS: What do you mean? I do not understand.

SOCRATES: Why, do you not know that when a politician writes, he begins with the names of his approvers?

PHAEDRUS: How so?

SOCRATES: Why, he begins in this manner: "Be it enacted by the senate, the people, or both, on the motion of a certain person," who is our author; and so putting on a serious face, he proceeds to display his own wisdom to his admirers in what is often a long and tedious composition. Now what is that sort of thing but a regular piece of authorship?
PHAEDRUS: True.
SOCRATES: And if the law is finally approved, then the author leaves the theatre in high delight; but if the law is rejected and he is done out of his speech-making, and not thought good enough to write, then he and his party are in mourning.
PHAEDRUS: Very true.
SOCRATES: So far are they from despising, or rather so highly do they value the practice of writing.
PHAEDRUS: No doubt.
SOCRATES: And when the king or orator has the power, as Lycurgus or Solon or Darius had, of attaining an immortality or authorship in a state, is he not thought by posterity, when they see his compositions, and does he not think himself, while he is yet alive, to be a god?
PHAEDRUS: Very true.
SOCRATES: Then do you think that anyone of this class, however ill-disposed, would reproach Lysias with being an author?
PHAEDRUS: Not upon your view; for according to you he would be casting a slur upon his own favorite pursuit.
SOCRATES: Any one may see that there is no disgrace in the mere fact of writing.
PHAEDRUS: Certainly not.
SOCRATES: The disgrace begins when a man writes not well, but badly.
PHAEDRUS: Clearly.
SOCRATES: And what is well and what is badly—need we ask Lysias, or any other poet or orator, who ever wrote or will write either a political or any other work, in meter or out of meter, poet or prose writer, to teach us this?
PHAEDRUS: Need we? For what should a man live if not for the pleasures of discourse? Surely not for the sake of bodily pleasures, which almost always have previous pain as a condition of them, and therefore are rightly called slavish.
SOCRATES: There is time enough. And I believe that the grasshoppers chirruping after their manner in the heat of the sun over our heads are talking to one another and looking down at us. What would they say if they

saw that we, like the many, are not conversing, but slumbering at midday, lulled by their voices, too indolent to think? Would they not have a right to laugh at us? They might imagine that we were slaves, who, coming to rest at a place of resort of theirs, like sheep lie asleep at noon around the well. But if they see us discoursing, and like Odysseus sailing past them, deaf to their siren voices, they may perhaps, out of respect, give us of the gifts which they receive from the gods that they may impart them to men.

PHAEDRUS: What gifts do you mean? I never heard of any.

SOCRATES: A lover of music like yourself ought surely to have heard the story of the grasshoppers, who are said to have been human beings in an age before the Muses. And when the Muses came and song appeared they were ravished with delight; and singing always, never thought of eating and drinking, until at last in their forgetfulness they died. And now they live again in the grasshoppers; and this is the return which the Muses make to them—they neither hunger, nor thirst, but from the hour of their birth are always singing, and never eating or drinking; and when they die they go and inform the Muses in heaven who honors them on Earth. They win the love of Terpsichore for the dancers by their report of them; of Erato for the lovers, and of the other Muses for those who do them honor, according to the several ways of honoring them—of Calliope the eldest Muse and of Urania who is next to her, for the philosophers, of whose music the grasshoppers make report to them; for these are the Muses who are chiefly concerned with heaven and thought, divine as well as human, and they have the sweetest utterance. For many reasons, then, we ought always to talk and not to sleep at midday.

PHAEDRUS: Let us talk.

SOCRATES: Shall we discuss the rules of writing and speech as we were proposing?

PHAEDRUS: Very good.

SOCRATES: In good speaking should not the mind of the speaker know the truth of the matter about which he is going to speak?

PHAEDRUS: And yet, Socrates, I have heard that he who would be an orator has nothing to do with true justice, but only with that which is likely to be approved by the many who sit in judgment; nor with the truly good or honorable, but only with opinion about them, and that from opinion comes persuasion, and not from the truth.

SOCRATES: The words of the wise are not to be set aside; for there is probably something in them; and therefore the meaning of this saying is not hastily to be dismissed.

PHAEDRUS: Very true.

SOCRATES: Let us put the matter thus: Suppose that I persuaded you to buy a horse and go to the wars. Neither of us knew what a horse was like, but I knew that you believed a horse to be of tame animals the one which has the longest ears.

PHAEDRUS: That would be ridiculous.

SOCRATES: There is something more ridiculous coming: Suppose, further, that in sober earnest I, having persuaded you of this, went and composed a speech in honor of an ass, whom I entitled a horse beginning: "A noble animal and a most useful possession, especially in war, and you may get on his back and fight, and he will carry baggage or anything."

PHAEDRUS: How ridiculous!

SOCRATES: Ridiculous! Yes; but is not even a ridiculous friend better than a cunning enemy?

PHAEDRUS: Certainly.

SOCRATES: And when the orator instead of putting an ass in the place of a horse, puts good for evil, being himself as ignorant of their true nature as the city on which he imposes is ignorant; and having studied the notions of the multitude, falsely persuades them not about "the shadow of an ass," which he confounds with a horse, but about good which he confounds with evil, what will be the harvest which rhetoric will be likely to gather after the sowing of that seed?

PHAEDRUS: The reverse of good.

SOCRATES: But perhaps rhetoric has been getting too roughly handled by us, and she might answer: What amazing nonsense you are talking! As if I forced any man to learn to speak in ignorance of the truth! Whatever my advice may be worth, I should have told him to arrive at the truth first, and then come to me. At the same time I boldly assert that mere knowledge of the truth will not give you the art of persuasion.

PHAEDRUS: There is reason in the lady's defense of herself.

SOCRATES: Quite true; if only the other arguments which remain to be brought up bear her witness that she is an art at all. But I seem to hear them arraying themselves on the opposite side, declaring that she speaks falsely, and that rhetoric is a mere routine and trick, not an art. Lo! a Spartan appears, and says that there never is nor ever will be a real art of speaking which is divorced from the truth.

PHAEDRUS: And what are these arguments, Socrates? Bring them out that we may examine them.

SOCRATES: Come out, fair children, and convince Phaedrus, who is the father of similar beauties, that he will never be able to speak about anything as he ought to speak unless he have a knowledge of philosophy. And let Phaedrus answer you.

PHAEDRUS: Put the question.

SOCRATES: Is not rhetoric, taken generally, a universal art of enchanting the mind by arguments; which is practiced not only in courts and public assemblies, but in private houses also, having to do with all matters, great as well as small, good and bad alike, and is in all equally right, and equally to be esteemed—that is what you have heard?

PHAEDRUS: Nay, not exactly that; I should say rather that I have heard the art confined to speaking and writing in lawsuits, and to speaking in public assemblies—not extended farther.

SOCRATES: Then I suppose that you have only heard of the rhetoric of Nestor and Odysseus, which they composed in their leisure hours when at Troy, and never of the rhetoric of Palamedes?

PHAEDRUS: No more than of Nestor and Odysseus, unless Gorgias is your Nestor, and Thrasymachus or Theodorus your Odysseus.

SOCRATES: Perhaps that is my meaning. But let us leave them. And do you tell me, instead, what are plaintiff and defendant doing in a law court—are they not contending?

PHAEDRUS: Exactly so.

SOCRATES: About the just and unjust—that is the matter in dispute?

PHAEDRUS: Yes.

SOCRATES: And a professor of the art will make the same thing appear to the same persons to be at one time just, at another time, if he is so inclined, to be unjust?

PHAEDRUS: Exactly.

SOCRATES: And when he speaks in the assembly, he will make the same things seem good to the city at one time, and at another time the reverse of good?

PHAEDRUS: That is true.

SOCRATES: Have we not heard of the Eleatic Palamedes (Zeno), who has an art of speaking by which he makes the same things appear to his hearers like and unlike, one and many, at rest and in motion?

PHAEDRUS: Very true.

SOCRATES: The art of disputation, then, is not confined to the courts and the assembly, but is one and the same in every use of language;

this is the art, if there be such an art, which is able to find a likeness of everything to which a likeness can be found, and draws into the light of day the likenesses and disguises which are used by others?

PHAEDRUS: How do you mean?

SOCRATES: Let me put the matter thus: When will there be more chance of deception—when the difference is large or small?

PHAEDRUS: When the difference is small.

SOCRATES: And you will be less likely to be discovered in passing by degrees into the other extreme than when you go all at once?

PHAEDRUS: Of course.

SOCRATES: He, then, who would deceive others, and not be deceived, must exactly know the real likenesses and differences of things?

PHAEDRUS: He must.

SOCRATES: And if he is ignorant of the true nature of any subject, how can he detect the greater or less degree of likeness in other things to that of which by the hypothesis he is ignorant?

PHAEDRUS: He cannot.

SOCRATES: And when men are deceived and their notions are at variance with realities, it is clear that the error slips in through resemblances?

PHAEDRUS: Yes, that is the way.

SOCRATES: Then he who would be a master of the art must understand the real nature of everything; or he will never know either how to make the gradual departure from truth into the opposite of truth which is affected by the help of resemblances, or how to avoid it?

PHAEDRUS: He will not.

SOCRATES: He then, who being ignorant of the truth aims at appearances, will only attain an art of rhetoric which is ridiculous and is not an art at all?

PHAEDRUS: That may be expected.

SOCRATES: Shall I propose that we look for examples of art and want of art, according to our notion of them, in the speech of Lysias which you have in your hand, and in my own speech?

PHAEDRUS: Nothing could be better; and indeed I think that our previous argument has been too abstract and wanting in illustrations.

SOCRATES: Yes; and the two speeches happen to afford a very good example of the way in which the speaker who knows the truth may, without any serious purpose, steal away the hearts of his hearers. This piece of good fortune I attribute to the local deities; and, perhaps, the prophets of the Muses who are singing over our heads may have imparted their inspiration to me. For I do not imagine that I have any rhetorical art of my own.

PHAEDRUS: Granted; if you will only please to get on.
SOCRATES: Suppose that you read me the first words of Lysias's speech.
PHAEDRUS: "You know how matters stand with me, and how, as I conceive, they might be arranged for our common interest; and I maintain that I ought not to fail in my suit, because I am not your lover. For lovers repent—"
SOCRATES: Enough—Now, shall I point out the rhetorical error of those words?
PHAEDRUS: Yes.
SOCRATES: Every one is aware that about some things we are agreed, whereas about other things we differ.
PHAEDRUS: I think that I understand you; but will you explain yourself?
SOCRATES: When anyone speaks of iron and silver, is not the same thing present in the minds of all?
PHAEDRUS: Certainly.
SOCRATES: But when anyone speaks of justice and goodness we part company and are at odds with one another and with ourselves?
PHAEDRUS: Precisely.
SOCRATES: Then in some things we agree, but not in others?
PHAEDRUS: That is true.
SOCRATES: In which are we more likely to be deceived, and in which has rhetoric the greater power?
PHAEDRUS: Clearly, in the uncertain class.
SOCRATES: Then the rhetorician ought to make a regular division, and acquire a distinct notion of both classes, as well of that in which the many err, as of that in which they do not err?
PHAEDRUS: He who made such a distinction would have an excellent principle.
SOCRATES: Yes; and in the next place he must have a keen eye for the observation of particulars in speaking, and not make a mistake about the class to which they are to be referred.
PHAEDRUS: Certainly.
SOCRATES: Now to which class does love belong—to the debatable or to the undisputed class?
PHAEDRUS: To the debatable, clearly; for if not, do you think that love would have allowed you to say as you did, that he is an evil both to the lover and the beloved, and also the greatest possible good?
SOCRATES: Capital. But will you tell me whether I defined love at the beginning of my speech? for, having been in an ecstasy, I cannot well remember.

PHAEDRUS: Yes, indeed; that you did, and no mistake.
SOCRATES: Then I perceive that the Nymphs of Achelous and Pan the son of Hermes, who inspired me, were far better rhetoricians than Lysias the son of Cephalus. Alas! how inferior to them he is! But perhaps I am mistaken; and Lysias at the commencement of his lover's speech did insist on our supposing love to be something or other which he fancied him to be, and according to this model he fashioned and framed the remainder of his discourse. Suppose we read his beginning over again:
PHAEDRUS: If you please; but you will not find what you want.
SOCRATES: Read, that I may have his exact words.
PHAEDRUS: "You know how matters stand with me, and how, as I conceive, they might be arranged for our common interest; and I maintain I ought not to fail in my suit because I am not your lover, for lovers repent of the kindnesses which they have shown, when their love is over."
SOCRATES: Here he appears to have done just the reverse of what he ought; for he has begun at the end, and is swimming on his back through the flood to the place of starting. His address to the fair youth begins where the lover would have ended. Am I not right, sweet Phaedrus?
PHAEDRUS: Yes, indeed, Socrates; he does begin at the end.
SOCRATES: Then as to the other topics—are they not thrown down anyhow? Is there any principle in them? Why should the next topic follow next in order, or any other topic? I cannot help fancying in my ignorance that he wrote off boldly just what came into his head, but I dare say that you would recognize a rhetorical necessity in the succession of the several parts of the composition?
PHAEDRUS: You have too good an opinion of me if you think that I have any such insight into his principles of composition.
SOCRATES: At any rate, you will allow that every discourse ought to be a living creature, having a body of its own and a head and feet; there should be a middle, beginning, and end, adapted to one another and to the whole?
PHAEDRUS: Certainly.
SOCRATES: Can this be said of the discourse of Lysias? See whether you can find any more connection in his words than in the epitaph which is said by some to have been inscribed on the grave of Midas the Phrygian.
PHAEDRUS: What is there remarkable in the epitaph?
SOCRATES: It is as follows:

"I am a maiden of bronze and lie on the tomb of Midas; So long as water flows and tall trees grow, So long here on this spot by his sad tomb abiding, I shall declare to passers-by that Midas sleeps below."

Now in this rhyme whether a line comes first or comes last, as you will perceive, makes no difference.

PHAEDRUS: You are making fun of that oration of ours.

SOCRATES: Well, I will say no more about your friend's speech lest I should give offense to you; although I think that it might furnish many other examples of what a man ought rather to avoid. But I will proceed to the other speech, which, as I think, is also suggestive to students of rhetoric.

PHAEDRUS: In what way?

SOCRATES: The two speeches, as you may remember, were unlike; the one argued that the lover and the other that the non-lover ought to be accepted.

PHAEDRUS: And right manfully.

SOCRATES: You should rather say "madly"; and madness was the argument of them, for, as I said, "love is a madness."

PHAEDRUS: Yes.

SOCRATES: And of madness there were two kinds; one produced by human infirmity, the other was a divine release of the soul from the yoke of custom and convention.

PHAEDRUS: True.

SOCRATES: The divine madness was subdivided into four kinds, prophetic, initiatory, poetic, erotic, having four gods presiding over them; the first was the inspiration of Apollo, the second that of Dionysus, the third that of the Muses, the fourth that of Aphrodite and Eros. In the description of the last kind of madness, which was also said to be the best, we spoke of the affection of love in a figure, into which we introduced a tolerably credible and possibly true though partly erring myth, which was also a hymn in honor of Love, who is your lord and also mine, Phaedrus, and the guardian of fair children, and to him we sung the hymn in measured and solemn strain.

PHAEDRUS: I know that I had great pleasure in listening to you.

SOCRATES: Let us take this instance and note how the transition was made from blame to praise.

PHAEDRUS: What do you mean?

SOCRATES: I mean to say that the composition was mostly playful. Yet in these chance fancies of the hour were involved two principles of which we should be too glad to have a clearer description if art could give us one.

PHAEDRUS: What are they?

SOCRATES: First, the comprehension of scattered particulars in one idea; as in our definition of love, which whether true or false certainly gave clearness and consistency to the discourse, the speaker should define his several notions and so make his meaning clear.

PHAEDRUS: What is the other principle, Socrates?

SOCRATES: The second principle is that of division into species according to the natural formation, where the joint is, not breaking any part as a bad carver might. Just as our two discourses, alike assumed, first of all, a single form of unreason; and then, as the body which from being one becomes double and may be divided into a left side and right side, each having parts right and left of the same name—after this manner the speaker proceeded to divide the parts of the left side and did not desist until he found in them an evil or left-handed love which he justly reviled; and the other discourse leading us to the madness which lay on the right side, found another love, also having the same name, but divine, which the speaker held up before us and applauded and affirmed to be the author of the greatest benefits.

PHAEDRUS: Most true.

SOCRATES: I am myself a great lover of these processes of division and generalization; they help me to speak and to think. And if I find any man who is able to see "a One and Many" in nature, him I follow, and "walk in his footsteps as if he were a god." And those who have this art, I have hitherto been in the habit of calling dialecticians; but God knows whether the name is right or not. And I should like to know what name you would give to your or to Lysias's disciples, and whether this may not be that famous art of rhetoric which Thrasymachus and others teach and practice? Skilful speakers they are, and impart their skill to any who is willing to make kings of them and to bring gifts to them.

PHAEDRUS: Yes, they are royal men; but their art is not the same with the art of those whom you call, and rightly, in my opinion, dialecticians—still we are in the dark about rhetoric.

SOCRATES: What do you mean? The remains of it, if there be anything remaining which can be brought under rules of art, must be a fine thing; and, at any rate, is not to be despised by you and me. But how much is left?

PHAEDRUS: There is a great deal surely to be found in books of rhetoric?

SOCRATES: Yes; thank you for reminding me: There is the exordium, showing how the speech should begin, if I remember rightly; that is what you mean—the niceties of the art?

PHAEDRUS: Yes.

SOCRATES: Then follows the statement of facts, and upon that witnesses; thirdly, proofs; fourthly, probabilities are to come; the great Byzantian word-maker also speaks, if I am not mistaken, of confirmation and further confirmation.

PHAEDRUS: You mean the excellent Theodorus.

SOCRATES: Yes; and he tells how refutation or further refutation is to be managed, whether in accusation or defense. I ought also to mention the illustrious Parian, Evenus, who first invented insinuations and indirect praises; and also indirect censures, which according to some he put into verse to help the memory. But shall I "to dumb forgetfulness consign" Tisias and Gorgias, who are not ignorant that probability is superior to truth, and who by force of argument make the little appear great and the great little, disguise the new in old fashions and the old in new fashions, and have discovered forms for everything, either short or going on to infinity. I remember Prodicus laughing when I told him of this; he said that he had himself discovered the true rule of art, which was to be neither long nor short, but of a convenient length.

PHAEDRUS: Well done, Prodicus!

SOCRATES: Then there is Hippias the Elean stranger, who probably agrees with him.

PHAEDRUS: Yes.

SOCRATES: And there is also Polus, who has treasuries of diplasiology, and gnomology, and eikonology, and who teaches in them the names of which Licymnius made him a present; they were to give a polish.

PHAEDRUS: Had not Protagoras something of the same sort?

SOCRATES: Yes, rules of correct diction and many other fine precepts; for the "sorrows of a poor old man," or any other pathetic case, no one is better than the Chalcedonian giant; he can put a whole company of people into a passion and out of one again by his mighty magic, and is first-rate at inventing or disposing of any sort of calumny on any grounds or none. All of them agree in asserting that a speech should end in a recapitulation, though they do not all agree to use the same word.

PHAEDRUS: You mean that there should be a summing up of the arguments in order to remind the hearers of them.

SOCRATES: I have now said all that I have to say of the art of rhetoric: have you anything to add?

PHAEDRUS: Not much; nothing very important.

SOCRATES: Leave the unimportant and let us bring the really important question into the light of day, which is: What power has this art of rhetoric, and when?

PHAEDRUS: A very great power in public meetings.

SOCRATES: It has. But I should like to know whether you have the same feeling as I have about the rhetoricians? To me there seem to be a great many holes in their web.

PHAEDRUS: Give an example.

SOCRATES: I will. Suppose a person to come to your friend Eryximachus, or to his father Acumenus, and to say to him: "I know how to apply drugs which shall have either a heating or a cooling effect, and I can give a vomit and also a purge, and all that sort of thing; and knowing all this, as I do, I claim to be a physician and to make physicians by imparting this knowledge to others"—what do you suppose that they would say?

PHAEDRUS: They would be sure to ask him whether he knew "to whom" he would give his medicines, and "when," and "how much."

SOCRATES: And suppose that he were to reply: "No; I know nothing of all that; I expect the patient who consults me to be able to do these things for himself"?

PHAEDRUS: They would say in reply that he is a madman or a pedant who fancies that he is a physician because he has read something in a book, or has stumbled on a prescription or two, although he has no real understanding of the art of medicine.

SOCRATES: And suppose a person were to come to Sophocles or Euripides and say that he knows how to make a very long speech about a small matter, and a short speech about a great matter, and also a sorrowful speech, or a terrible, or threatening speech, or any other kind of speech, and in teaching this fancies that he is teaching the art of tragedy—?

PHAEDRUS: They too would surely laugh at him if he fancies that tragedy is anything but the arranging of these elements in a manner which will be suitable to one another and to the whole.

SOCRATES: But I do not suppose that they would be rude or abusive to him: Would they not treat him as a musician a man who thinks that he is a harmonist because he knows how to pitch the highest and lowest note; happening to meet such an one he would not say to him savagely, "Fool, you are mad!" But like a musician, in a gentle and harmonious tone of voice, he would answer: "My good friend, he who would be a harmonist must certainly know this, and yet he may understand nothing of harmony if he has not got beyond your stage of knowledge, for you only know the preliminaries of harmony and not harmony itself."

PHAEDRUS: Very true.

SOCRATES: And will not Sophocles say to the display of the would-be tragedian, that this is not tragedy but the preliminaries of tragedy? and

will not Acumenus say the same of medicine to the would-be physician?
PHAEDRUS: Quite true.
SOCRATES: And if Adrastus the mellifluous or Pericles heard of these wonderful arts, brachylogies and eikonologies and all the hard names which we have been endeavouring to draw into the light of day, what would they say? Instead of losing temper and applying uncomplimentary epithets, as you and I have been doing, to the authors of such an imaginary art, their superior wisdom would rather censure us, as well as them. "Have a little patience, Phaedrus and Socrates, they would say; you should not be in such a passion with those who from some want of dialectical skill are unable to define the nature of rhetoric, and consequently suppose that they have found the art in the preliminary conditions of it, and when these have been taught by them to others, fancy that the whole art of rhetoric has been taught by them; but as to using the several instruments of the art effectively, or making the composition a whole, an application of it such as this is they regard as an easy thing which their disciples may make for themselves."
PHAEDRUS: I quite admit, Socrates, that the art of rhetoric which these men teach and of which they write is such as you describe—there I agree with you. But I still want to know where and how the true art of rhetoric and persuasion is to be acquired.
SOCRATES: The perfection which is required of the finished orator is, or rather must be, like the perfection of anything else; partly given by nature, but may also be assisted by art. If you have the natural power and add to it knowledge and practice, you will be a distinguished speaker; if you fall short in either of these, you will be to that extent defective. But the art, as far as there is an art, of rhetoric does not lie in the direction of Lysias or Thrasymachus.
PHAEDRUS: In what direction then?
SOCRATES: I conceive Pericles to have been the most accomplished of rhetoricians.
PHAEDRUS: What of that?
SOCRATES: All the great arts require discussion and high speculation about the truths of nature; hence come loftiness of thought and completeness of execution. And this, as I conceive, was the quality which, in addition to his natural gifts, Pericles acquired from his intercourse with Anaxagoras whom he happened to know. He was thus imbued with the higher philosophy, and attained the knowledge of Mind and the negative of Mind, which were favorite themes of Anaxagoras, and applied what suited his purpose to the art of speaking.

PHAEDRUS: Explain.
SOCRATES: Rhetoric is like medicine.
PHAEDRUS: How so?
SOCRATES: Why, because medicine has to define the nature of the body and rhetoric of the soul—if we would proceed, not empirically but scientifically, in the one case to impart health and strength by giving medicine and food, in the other to implant the conviction or virtue which you desire, by the right application of words and training.
PHAEDRUS: There, Socrates, I suspect that you are right.
SOCRATES: And do you think that you can know the nature of the soul intelligently without knowing the nature of the whole?
PHAEDRUS: Hippocrates the Asclepiad says that the nature even of the body can only be understood as a whole. (Compare Charmides.)
SOCRATES: Yes, friend, and he was right—still, we ought not to be content with the name of Hippocrates, but to examine and see whether his argument agrees with his conception of nature.
PHAEDRUS: I agree.
SOCRATES: Then consider what truth as well as Hippocrates says about this or about any other nature. Ought we not to consider first whether that which we wish to learn and to teach is a simple or multiform thing, and if simple, then to inquire what power it has of acting or being acted upon in relation to other things, and if multiform, then to number the forms; and see first in the case of one of them, and then in the case of all of them, what is that power of acting or being acted upon which makes each and all of them to be what they are?
PHAEDRUS: You may very likely be right, Socrates.
SOCRATES: The method which proceeds without analysis is like the groping of a blind man. Yet, surely, he who is an artist ought not to admit of a comparison with the blind, or deaf. The rhetorician, who teaches his pupil to speak scientifically, will particularly set forth the nature of that being to which he addresses his speeches; and this, I conceive, to be the soul.
PHAEDRUS: Certainly.
SOCRATES: His whole effort is directed to the soul; for in that he seeks to produce conviction.
PHAEDRUS: Yes.
SOCRATES: Then clearly, Thrasymachus or anyone else who teaches rhetoric in earnest will give an exact description of the nature of the soul; which will enable us to see whether she be single and same, or, like

the body, multiform. That is what we should call showing the nature of the soul.

PHAEDRUS: Exactly.

SOCRATES: He will explain, secondly, the mode in which she acts or is acted upon.

PHAEDRUS: True.

SOCRATES: Thirdly, having classified men and speeches, and their kinds and affections, and adapted them to one another, he will tell the reasons of his arrangement, and show why one soul is persuaded by a particular form of argument, and another not.

PHAEDRUS: You have hit upon a very good way.

SOCRATES: Yes, that is the true and only way in which any subject can be set forth or treated by rules of art, whether in speaking or writing. But the writers of the present day, at whose feet you have sat, craftily conceal the nature of the soul which they know quite well. Nor, until they adopt our method of reading and writing, can we admit that they write by rules of art?

PHAEDRUS: What is our method?

SOCRATES: I cannot give you the exact details; but I should like to tell you generally, as far as is in my power, how a man ought to proceed according to rules of art.

PHAEDRUS: Let me hear.

SOCRATES: Oratory is the art of enchanting the soul, and therefore he who would be an orator has to learn the differences of human souls—they are so many and of such a nature, and from them come the differences between man and man. Having proceeded thus far in his analysis, he will next divide speeches into their different classes: "Such and such persons," he will say, "are affected by this or that kind of speech in this or that way," and he will tell you why. The pupil must have a good theoretical notion of them first, and then he must have experience of them in actual life, and be able to follow them with all his senses about him, or he will never get beyond the precepts of his masters. But when he understands what persons are persuaded by what arguments, and sees the person about whom he was speaking in the abstract actually before him, and knows that it is he, and can say to himself, "This is the man or this is the character who ought to have a certain argument applied to him in order to convince him of a certain opinion"—he who knows all this, and knows also when he should speak and when he should refrain, and when he should use pithy sayings, pathetic appeals, sensational effects, and all the other modes of speech which he has learned; when, I say, he knows the times and seasons of all these things, then, and not till then, he is a perfect master of his art; but if he fail in any of these points, whether in speaking or teaching or writing them, and yet declares that he speaks by rules of art, he who says "I don't believe you" has the better of him. Well, the teacher will say, is this, Phaedrus and Socrates, your account of the so-called art of rhetoric, or am I to look for another?

PHAEDRUS: He must take this, Socrates, for there is no possibility of another, and yet the creation of such an art is not easy.

SOCRATES: Very true; and therefore let us consider this matter in every light, and see whether we cannot find a shorter and easier road; there is no use in taking a long rough roundabout way if there be a shorter and easier one. And I wish that you would try and remember whether you have heard from Lysias or anyone else anything which might be of service to us.

PHAEDRUS: If trying would avail, then I might; but at the moment I can think of nothing.

SOCRATES: Suppose I tell you something which somebody who knows told me.

PHAEDRUS: Certainly.

SOCRATES: May not "the wolf," as the proverb says, "claim a hearing"?

PHAEDRUS: Do you say what can be said for him.

SOCRATES: He will argue that there is no use in putting a solemn face on these matters, or in going round and round, until you arrive at first principles; for, as I said at first, when the question is of justice and good, or is a question in which men are concerned who are just and good, either by nature or habit, he who would be a skilful rhetorician has no need of truth— for that in courts of law men literally care nothing about truth, but only about conviction: and this is based on probability, to which he who would be a skilful orator should therefore give his whole attention. And they say also that there are cases in which the actual facts, if they are improbable, ought to be withheld, and only the probabilities should be told either in accusation or defense, and that always in speaking, the orator should keep probability in view, and say good-bye to the truth. And the observance of this principle throughout a speech furnishes the whole art.

PHAEDRUS: That is what the professors of rhetoric do actually say, Socrates. I have not forgotten that we have quite briefly touched upon this matter already; with them the point is all-important.

SOCRATES: I dare say that you are familiar with Tisias. Does he not define probability to be that which the many think?

PHAEDRUS: Certainly, he does.

SOCRATES: I believe that he has a clever and ingenious case of this sort: He supposes a feeble and valiant man to have assaulted a strong and cowardly one, and to have robbed him of his coat or of something or other; he is brought into court, and then Tisias says that both parties should tell lies: the coward should say that he was assaulted by more men than one; the other should prove that they were alone, and should argue thus: "How could a weak man like me have assaulted a strong man like him?" The complainant will not like to confess his own cowardice, and will therefore invent some other lie which his adversary will thus gain an opportunity of refuting. And there are other devices of the same kind which have a place in the system. Am I not right, Phaedrus?

PHAEDRUS: Certainly.

SOCRATES: Bless me, what a wonderfully mysterious art is this which Tisias or some other gentleman, in whatever name or country he rejoices, has discovered. Shall we say a word to him or not?

PHAEDRUS: What shall we say to him?

SOCRATES: Let us tell him that, before he appeared, you and I were saying that the probability of which he speaks was engendered in the minds of the many by the likeness of the truth, and we had just been affirming that he who knew the truth would always know best how to discover the resemblances of the truth. If he has anything else to say about the art of speaking we should like to hear him; but if not, we are satisfied with our own view, that unless a man estimates the various characters of his hearers and is able to divide all things into classes and to comprehend them under single ideas, he will never be a skilful rhetorician even within the limits of human power. And this skill he will not attain without a great deal of trouble, which a good man ought to undergo, not for the sake of speaking and acting before men, but in order that he may be able to say what is acceptable to God and always to act acceptably to Him as far as in him lies; for there is a saying of wiser men than ourselves, that a man of sense should not try to please his fellow servants (at least this should not be his first object) but his good and noble masters; and therefore if the way is long and circuitous, marvel not at this, for, where the end is great, there we may take the longer road, but not for lesser ends such as yours. Truly, the argument may say, Tisias, that if you do not mind going so far, rhetoric has a fair beginning here.

PHAEDRUS: I think, Socrates, that this is admirable, if only practicable.

SOCRATES: But even to fail in an honorable object is honorable.

PHAEDRUS: True.
SOCRATES: Enough appears to have been said by us of a true and false art of speaking.
PHAEDRUS: Certainly.
SOCRATES: But there is something yet to be said of propriety and impropriety of writing.
PHAEDRUS: Yes.
SOCRATES: Do you know how you can speak or act about rhetoric in a manner which will be acceptable to God?
PHAEDRUS: No, indeed. Do you?
SOCRATES: I have heard a tradition of the ancients, whether true or not they only know; although if we had found the truth ourselves, do you think that we should care much about the opinions of men?
PHAEDRUS: Your question needs no answer; but I wish that you would tell me what you say that you have heard.
SOCRATES: At the Egyptian city of Naucratis, there was a famous old god, whose name was Theuth; the bird which is called the Ibis is sacred to him, and he was the inventor of many arts, such as arithmetic and calculation and geometry and astronomy and draughts and dice, but his great discovery was the use of letters. Now in those days the god Thamus was the king of the whole country of Egypt; and he dwelt in that great city of Upper Egypt which the Hellenes call Egyptian Thebes, and the god himself is called by them Ammon. To him came Theuth and showed his inventions, desiring that the other Egyptians might be allowed to have the benefit of them; he enumerated them, and Thamus inquired about their several uses, and praised some of them and censured others, as he approved or disapproved of them. It would take a long time to repeat all that Thamus said to Theuth in praise or blame of the various arts. But when they came to letters, This, said Theuth, will make the Egyptians wiser and give them better memories; it is a specific both for the memory and for the wit. Thamus replied: O most ingenious Theuth, the parent or inventor of an art is not always the best judge of the utility or inutility of his own inventions to the users of them. And in this instance, you who are the father of letters, from a paternal love of your own children have been led to attribute to them a quality which they cannot have; for this discovery of yours will create forgetfulness in the learners' souls, because they will not use their memories; they will trust to the external written characters and not remember of themselves. The specific which you have discovered is an aid not to memory, but to reminiscence, and you give your disciples not

truth, but only the semblance of truth; they will be hearers of many things and will have learned nothing; they will appear to be omniscient and will generally know nothing; they will be tiresome company, having the show of wisdom without the reality.

PHAEDRUS: Yes, Socrates, you can easily invent tales of Egypt, or of any other country.

SOCRATES: There was a tradition in the temple of Dodona that oaks first gave prophetic utterances. The men of old, unlike in their simplicity to young philosophy, deemed that if they heard the truth even from "oak or rock," it was enough for them; whereas you seem to consider not whether a thing is or is not true, but who the speaker is and from what country the tale comes.

PHAEDRUS: I acknowledge the justice of your rebuke; and I think that the Theban is right in his view about letters.

SOCRATES: He would be a very simple person, and quite a stranger to the oracles of Thamus or Ammon, who should leave in writing or receive in writing any art under the idea that the written word would be intelligible or certain; or who deemed that writing was at all better than knowledge and recollection of the same matters?

PHAEDRUS: That is most true.

SOCRATES: I cannot help feeling, Phaedrus, that writing is unfortunately like painting; for the creations of the painter have the attitude of life, and yet if you ask them a question they preserve a solemn silence. And the same may be said of speeches. You would imagine that they had intelligence, but if you want to know anything and put a question to one of them, the speaker always gives one unvarying answer. And when they have been once written down they are tumbled about anywhere among those who may or may not understand them, and know not to whom they should reply, to whom not: and, if they are maltreated or abused, they have no parent to protect them; and they cannot protect or defend themselves.

PHAEDRUS: That again is most true.

SOCRATES: Is there not another kind of word or speech far better than this, and having far greater power—a son of the same family, but lawfully begotten?

PHAEDRUS: Whom do you mean, and what is his origin?

SOCRATES: I mean an intelligent word graven in the soul of the learner, which can defend itself, and knows when to speak and when to be silent.

PHAEDRUS: You mean the living word of knowledge which has a soul, and of which the written word is properly no more than an image?

SOCRATES: Yes, of course that is what I mean. And now may I be allowed to ask you a question: Would a husbandman, who is a man of sense, take the seeds, which he values and which he wishes to bear fruit, and in sober seriousness plant them during the heat of summer, in some garden of Adonis, that he may rejoice when he sees them in eight days appearing in beauty? at least he would do so, if at all, only for the sake of amusement and pastime. But when he is in earnest he sows in fitting soil, and practices husbandry, and is satisfied if in eight months the seeds which he has sown arrive at perfection?

PHAEDRUS: Yes, Socrates, that will be his way when he is in earnest; he will do the other, as you say, only in play.

SOCRATES: And can we suppose that he who knows the just and good and honorable has less understanding, than the husbandman, about his own seeds?

PHAEDRUS: Certainly not.

SOCRATES: Then he will not seriously incline to "write" his thoughts "in water" with pen and ink, sowing words which can neither speak for themselves nor teach the truth adequately to others?

PHAEDRUS: No, that is not likely.

SOCRATES: No, that is not likely—in the garden of letters he will sow and plant, but only for the sake of recreation and amusement; he will write them down as memorials to be treasured against the forgetfulness of old age, by himself, or by any other old man who is treading the same path. He will rejoice in beholding their tender growth; and while others are refreshing their souls with banqueting and the like, this will be the pastime in which his days are spent.

PHAEDRUS: A pastime, Socrates, as noble as the other is ignoble, the pastime of a man who can be amused by serious talk, and can discourse merrily about justice and the like.

SOCRATES: True, Phaedrus. But nobler far is the serious pursuit of the dialectician, who, finding a congenial soul, by the help of science sows and plants therein words which are able to help themselves and him who planted them, and are not unfruitful, but have in them a seed which others brought up in different soils render immortal, making the possessors of it happy to the utmost extent of human happiness.

PHAEDRUS: Far nobler, certainly.

SOCRATES: And now, Phaedrus, having agreed upon the premises we may decide about the conclusion.

PHAEDRUS: About what conclusion?

SOCRATES: About Lysias, whom we censured, and his art of writing, and his discourses, and the rhetorical skill or want of skill which was shown in them—these are the questions which we sought to determine, and they brought us to this point. And I think that we are now pretty well informed about the nature of art and its opposite.
PHAEDRUS: Yes, I think with you; but I wish that you would repeat what was said.
SOCRATES: Until a man knows the truth of the several particulars of which he is writing or speaking, and is able to define them as they are, and having defined them again to divide them until they can be no longer divided, and until in like manner he is able to discern the nature of the soul, and discover the different modes of discourse which are adapted to different natures, and to arrange and dispose them in such a way that the simple form of speech may be addressed to the simpler nature, and the complex and composite to the more complex nature—until he has accomplished all this, he will be unable to handle arguments according to rules of art, as far as their nature allows them to be subjected to art, either for the purpose of teaching or persuading—such is the view which is implied in the whole preceding argument.
PHAEDRUS: Yes, that was our view, certainly.
SOCRATES: Secondly, as to the censure which was passed on the speaking or writing of discourses, and how they might be rightly or wrongly censured—did not our previous argument show—?
PHAEDRUS: Show what?
SOCRATES: That whether Lysias or any other writer that ever was or will be, whether private man or statesman, proposes laws and so becomes the author of a political treatise, fancying that there is any great certainty and clearness in his performance, the fact of his so writing is only a disgrace to him, whatever men may say. For not to know the nature of justice and injustice, and good and evil, and not to be able to distinguish the dream from the reality, cannot in truth be otherwise than disgraceful to him, even though he have the applause of the whole world.
PHAEDRUS: Certainly.
SOCRATES: But he who thinks that in the written word there is necessarily much which is not serious, and that neither poetry nor prose, spoken or written, is of any great value, if, like the compositions of the rhapsodes, they are only recited in order to be believed, and not with any view to criticism or instruction; and who thinks that even the best of writings are but a reminiscence of what we know, and that only in principles of justice

and goodness and nobility taught and communicated orally for the sake of instruction and graven in the soul, which is the true way of writing, is there clearness and perfection and seriousness, and that such principles are a man's own and his legitimate offspring—being, in the first place, the word which he finds in his own bosom; secondly, the brethren and descendants and relations of his idea which have been duly implanted by him in the souls of others;—and who cares for them and no others—this is the right sort of man; and you and I, Phaedrus, would pray that we may become like him.

PHAEDRUS: That is most assuredly my desire and prayer.

SOCRATES: And now the play is played out; and of rhetoric enough. Go and tell Lysias that to the fountain and school of the Nymphs we went down, and were bidden by them to convey a message to him and to other composers of speeches—to Homer and other writers of poems, whether set to music or not; and to Solon and others who have composed writings in the form of political discourses which they would term laws—to all of them we are to say that if their compositions are based on knowledge of the truth, and they can defend or prove them, when they are put to the test, by spoken arguments, which leave their writings poor in comparison of them, then they are to be called, not only poets, orators, legislators, but are worthy of a higher name, befitting the serious pursuit of their life.

PHAEDRUS: What name would you assign to them?

SOCRATES: Wise, I may not call them; for that is a great name which belongs to God alone; lovers of wisdom or philosophers is their modest and befitting title.

PHAEDRUS: Very suitable.

SOCRATES: And he who cannot rise above his own compilations and compositions, which he has been long patching and piecing, adding some and taking away some, may be justly called poet or speech-maker or law-maker.

PHAEDRUS: Certainly.

SOCRATES: Now go and tell this to your companion.

PHAEDRUS: But there is also a friend of yours who ought not to be forgotten.

SOCRATES: Who is he?

PHAEDRUS: Isocrates the fair: What message will you send to him, and how shall we describe him?

SOCRATES: Isocrates is still young, Phaedrus; but I am willing to hazard a prophecy concerning him.

PHAEDRUS: What would you prophesy?

SOCRATES: I think that he has a genius which soars above the orations of Lysias, and that his character is cast in a finer mold. My impression of him is that he will marvellously improve as he grows older, and that all former rhetoricians will be as children in comparison of him. And I believe that he will not be satisfied with rhetoric, but that there is in him a divine inspiration which will lead him to things higher still. For he has an element of philosophy in his nature. This is the message of the gods dwelling in this place, and which I will myself deliver to Isocrates, who is my delight; and do you give the other to Lysias, who is yours.

PHAEDRUS: I will; and now as the heat is abated let us depart.

SOCRATES: Should we not offer up a prayer first of all to the local deities?

PHAEDRUS: By all means.

SOCRATES: Beloved Pan, and all ye other gods who haunt this place, give me beauty in the inward soul; and may the outward and inward man be at one. May I reckon the wise to be the wealthy, and may I have such a quantity of gold as a temperate man and he only can bear and carry. Anything more? The prayer, I think, is enough for me.

PHAEDRUS: Ask the same for me, for friends should have all things in common.

SOCRATES: Let us go.

PHAEDO

BY PLATO

Translated by Benjamin Jowett

INTRODUCTION

After an interval of some months or years, and at Phlius, a town of Peloponnesus, the tale of the last hours of Socrates is narrated to Echecrates and other Phliasians by Phaedo the "beloved disciple." The Dialogue necessarily takes the form of a narrative, because Socrates has to be described acting as well as speaking. The minutest particulars of the event are interesting to distant friends, and the narrator has an equal interest in them.

During the voyage of the sacred ship to and from Delos, which has occupied thirty days, the execution of Socrates has been deferred. (Compare Xen. Mem.) The time has been passed by him in conversation with a select company of disciples. But now the holy season is over, and the disciples meet earlier than usual in order that they may converse with Socrates for the last time. Those who were present, and those who might have been expected to be present, are mentioned by name. There are Simmias and Cebes (Crito), two disciples of Philolaus whom Socrates "by his enchantments has attracted from Thebes" (Mem.), Crito the aged friend, the attendant of the prison, who is as good as a friend—these take part in the conversation. There are present also, Hermogenes, from whom Xenophon derived his information about the trial of Socrates (Mem.), the "madman" Apollodorus (Symp.), Euclid and Terpsion from Megara (compare Theaet.), Ctesippus, Antisthenes, Menexenus, and some other less-known members of the Socratic circle, all of whom are silent auditors. Aristippus, Cleombrotus, and Plato are noted as absent. Almost as soon as the friends of Socrates enter the prison Xanthippe and her children are sent home in the care of one of Crito's servants. Socrates himself has just been released from chains, and is led by this circumstance to make the natural remark that "pleasure follows pain." (Observe that Plato is preparing the way for his doctrine of the alternation of opposites.) "Aesop would have represented them in a fable as a two-headed creature of the gods." The mention of Aesop reminds Cebes of a question which had been asked by Evenus the poet (compare Apol.): "Why Socrates, who was not a poet, while in prison had been putting Aesop into verse?"—"Because several times in his life he had been warned in dreams that he should practice music; and as he was about to die and was not certain of what was meant, he wished to fulfill the admonition in the letter as well as in the spirit, by writing verses as well as by cultivating philosophy. Tell this to Evenus; and say that I would have him follow me in death." "He is not at all the sort of man to comply with your request, Socrates." "Why, is he not a philosopher?" "Yes." "Then he will be willing to die, although he will not take his own life, for that is held to be unlawful."

Cebes asks why suicide is thought not to be right, if death is to be accounted a good? Well, (1) according to one explanation, because man is a prisoner, who must not open the door of his prison and run away—this is the truth in a "mystery." Or (2) rather, because he is not his own property, but a possession of the gods, and has no right to make away with that which does not belong to him. But why, asks Cebes, if he is a possession of the gods, should he wish to die and leave them? For he is under their protection; and surely he cannot take better care of himself than they take of him. Simmias explains that Cebes is really referring to Socrates, whom they think too unmoved at the prospect of leaving the gods and his friends. Socrates answers that he is going to other gods who are wise and good, and perhaps to better friends; and he professes that he is ready to defend himself against the charge of Cebes. The company shall be his judges, and he hopes that he will be more successful in convincing them than he had been in convincing the court.

The philosopher desires death—which the wicked world will insinuate that he also deserves: and perhaps he does, but not in any sense which they are capable of understanding. Enough of them: the real question is, What is the nature of that death which he desires? Death is the separation of soul and body—and the philosopher desires such a separation. He would like to be freed from the dominion of bodily pleasures and of the senses, which are always perturbing his mental vision. He wants to get rid of eyes and ears, and with the light of the mind only to behold the light of truth. All the evils and impurities and necessities of men come from the body. And death separates him from these corruptions, which in life he cannot wholly lay aside. Why then should he repine when the hour of separation arrives? Why, if he is dead while he lives, should he fear that other death, through which alone he can behold wisdom in her purity?

Besides, the philosopher has notions of good and evil unlike those of other men. For they are courageous because they are afraid of greater dangers, and temperate because they desire greater pleasures. But he disdains this balancing of pleasures and pains, which is the exchange of commerce and not of virtue. All the virtues, including wisdom, are regarded by him only as purifications of the soul. And this was the meaning of the founders of the mysteries when they said, "Many are the wand-bearers but few are the mystics." (Compare Matt. xxii.: "Many are called but few are chosen.") And in the hope that he is one of these mystics, Socrates is now departing. This is his answer to anyone who charges him with indifference at the prospect of leaving the gods and his friends.

Still, a fear is expressed that the soul upon leaving the body may vanish away like smoke or air. Socrates in answer appeals first of all to the old Orphic tradition that the souls of the dead are in the world below, and that the living come from them. This he attempts to found on a philosophical assumption that all opposites—e.g. less, greater; weaker, stronger; sleeping, waking; life, death—are generated out of each other. Nor can the process of generation be only a passage from living to dying, for then all would end in death. The perpetual sleeper (Endymion) would be no longer distinguished from the rest of mankind. The circle of nature is not complete unless the living come from the dead as well as pass to them.

The Platonic doctrine of reminiscence is then adduced as a confirmation of the pre-existence of the soul. Some proofs of this doctrine are demanded. One proof given is the same as that of the Meno, and is derived from the latent knowledge of mathematics, which may be elicited from an unlearned person when a diagram is presented to him. Again, there is a power of association, which from seeing Simmias may remember Cebes, or from seeing a picture of Simmias may remember Simmias. The lyre may recall the player of the lyre, and equal pieces of wood or stone may be associated with the higher notion of absolute equality. But here observe that material equalities fall short of the conception of absolute equality with which they are compared, and which is the measure of them. And the measure or standard must be prior to that which is measured, the idea of equality prior to the visible equals. And if prior to them, then prior also to the perceptions of the senses which recall them, and therefore either given before birth or at birth. But all men have not this knowledge, nor have any without a process of reminiscence; which is a proof that it is not innate or given at birth, unless indeed it was given and taken away at the same instant. But if not given to men in birth, it must have been given before birth—this is the only alternative which remains. And if we had ideas in a former state, then our souls must have existed and must have had intelligence in a former state. The pre-existence of the soul stands or falls with the doctrine of ideas.

It is objected by Simmias and Cebes that these arguments only prove a former and not a future existence. Socrates answers this objection by recalling the previous argument, in which he had shown that the living come from the dead. But the fear that the soul at departing may vanish into air (especially if there is a wind blowing at the time) has not yet been charmed away. He proceeds: When we fear that the soul will vanish away, let us ask ourselves what is that which we suppose to be liable to dissolution? Is it the simple or the compound, the unchanging or the changing, the invisible idea or the visible object of sense? Clearly the latter and not the former; and therefore not the soul, which in her own pure thought is unchangeable, and only when using the senses descends into the region of change. Again, the soul commands, the body serves: in this respect too the soul is akin to the divine, and the body to the mortal. And in every point of view the soul is the image of divinity and immortality, and the body of the human and mortal. And whereas the body is liable to speedy dissolution, the soul is almost if not quite indissoluble. (Compare Tim.) Yet even the body may be preserved for ages by the embalmer's art: how unlikely, then, that the soul will perish and be dissipated into air while on her way to the good and wise God! She has been gathered into herself, holding aloof from the body, and practicing death all her life long, and she is now finally released from the errors and follies and passions of men, and forever dwells in the company of the gods.

But the soul which is polluted and engrossed by the corporeal, and has no eye except that of the senses, and is weighed down by the bodily appetites, cannot attain to this abstraction. In her fear of the world below she lingers about the sepulchre, loath to leave the body which she loved, a ghostly apparition, saturated with sense, and therefore visible. At length entering into some animal of a nature congenial to her former life of sensuality or violence, she takes the form of an ass, a wolf or a kite. And of these earthly souls the happiest are those who have practiced virtue without philosophy; they are allowed to pass into gentle and social natures, such as bees and ants. (Compare Republic, Meno.) But only the philosopher who departs pure is permitted to enter the company of the gods. (Compare Phaedrus.) This is the reason why he abstains from fleshly lusts, and not because he fears loss or disgrace, which is the motive of other men. He too has been a captive, and the willing agent of his own captivity. But philosophy has spoken to him, and he has heard her voice; she has gently entreated him, and brought him out of the "miry clay," and purged away the mists of passion and the illusions of sense which envelope him; his soul has escaped from the influence of pleasures and pains, which are like nails fastening her to the body. To that prison-house she will not return; and therefore she abstains from bodily pleasures—not from a desire of having more or greater ones, but because she knows that only when calm and free from the dominion of the body can she behold the light of truth.

Simmias and Cebes remain in doubt; but they are unwilling to raise objections at such a time. Socrates wonders at their reluctance. Let them regard him rather as the swan, who, having sung the praises of Apollo all his life long, sings at his death more lustily than ever. Simmias acknowledges that there is cowardice in not probing truth to the bottom. "And if truth divine and inspired is not to be had, then let a man take the best of human notions, and upon this frail bark let him sail through life." He proceeds to state his difficulty: It has been argued that the soul is invisible and incorporeal, and therefore immortal, and prior to the body. But is not the soul acknowledged to be a harmony, and has she not the same relation to the body, as the harmony—which like her is invisible—has to the lyre? And yet the harmony does not survive the lyre. Cebes has also an objection, which like Simmias he expresses in a figure. He is willing to admit that the soul is more lasting than the body. But the more lasting nature of the soul does not prove her immortality; for after having worn out many bodies in a single life, and many more in successive births and deaths, she may at last perish, or, as Socrates afterward restates the objection, the very act of birth may be the beginning of her death, and her last body may survive her, just as the coat of an old weaver is left behind him after he is dead, although a man is more lasting than his coat. And he who would prove the immortality of the soul, must prove not only that the soul outlives one or many bodies, but that she outlives them all.

The audience, like the chorus in a play, for a moment interpret the feelings of the actors; there is a temporary depression, and then the inquiry is resumed. It is a melancholy reflection that arguments, like men, are apt to be deceivers; and those who have been often deceived become distrustful both of arguments and of friends. But this unfortunate experience should not make us either haters of men or haters of arguments. The want of health and truth is not in the argument, but in ourselves. Socrates, who is about to die, is sensible of his own weakness; he desires to be impartial, but he cannot help feeling that he has too great an interest in the truth of the argument. And therefore he would have his friends examine and refute him, if they think that he is in error.

At his request Simmias and Cebes repeat their objections. They do not go to the length of denying the pre-existence of ideas. Simmias is of opinion that the soul is a harmony of the body. But the admission of the pre-existence of ideas, and therefore of the soul, is at variance with this. (Compare a parallel difficulty in Theaet.) For a harmony is an effect, whereas the soul is not an effect, but a cause; a harmony follows, but the soul leads; a harmony admits of degrees, and the soul has no degrees. Again, upon the supposition that the soul is a harmony, why is one soul better than another? Are they more or less harmonized, or is there one harmony within another? But the soul does not admit of degrees, and cannot therefore be more or less harmonized. Further, the soul is often engaged in resisting the affections of the body, as Homer describes Odysseus "rebuking his heart." Could he have written this under the idea that the soul is a harmony of the body? Nay rather, are we not contradicting Homer and ourselves in affirming anything of the sort?

The goddess Harmonia, as Socrates playfully terms the argument of Simmias, has been happily disposed of; and now an answer has to be given to the Theban Cadmus. Socrates recapitulates the argument of Cebes, which, as he remarks, involves the whole question of natural growth or causation; about this he proposes to narrate his own mental experience. When he was young he had puzzled himself with physics: he had inquired into the growth and decay of animals, and the origin of thought, until at last he began to doubt the self-evident fact that growth is the result of eating and drinking; and so he arrived at the conclusion that he was not meant for such enquiries. Nor was he less perplexed with notions of comparison and number. At first he had imagined himself to understand differences of greater and less, and to know that ten is two more than eight, and the like. But now those very notions appeared to him to contain a contradiction. For how can one be divided into two? Or two be compounded into one? These are difficulties which Socrates cannot answer. Of generation and destruction he knows nothing. But he has a confused notion of another method in which matters of this sort are to be investigated. (Compare Republic; Charm.)

Then he heard someone reading out of a book of Anaxagoras, that mind is the cause of all things. And he said to himself: If mind is the cause of all things, surely mind must dispose them all for the best. The new teacher will show me this "order of the best" in man and nature. How great had been his hopes and how great his disappointment! For he found that his new friend was anything but consistent in his use of mind as a cause, and that he soon introduced winds, waters, and other eccentric notions. (Compare Arist. Metaph.) It was as if a person had said that Socrates is sitting here because he is made up of bones and muscles, instead of telling the true reason—that he is here because the Athenians have thought good to sentence him to death, and he has thought good to await his sentence. Had his bones and muscles been left by him to their own ideas of right, they would long ago have taken themselves off. But surely there is a great confusion of the cause and condition in all this. And this confusion also leads people into all sorts of erroneous theories about the position and motions of the Earth. None of them know how much stronger than any Atlas is the power of the best. But this "best" is still undiscovered; and in inquiring after the cause, we can only hope to attain the second best.

Now there is a danger in the contemplation of the nature of things, as there is a danger in looking at the sun during an eclipse, unless the precaution is taken of looking only at the image reflected in the water, or in a glass. (Compare Laws; Republic.) "I was afraid," says Socrates, "that I might injure the eye of the soul. I thought that I had better return to the old and safe method of ideas. Though I do not mean to say that he who contemplates existence through the medium of ideas sees only through a glass darkly, any more than he who contemplates actual effects."

If the existence of ideas is granted to him, Socrates is of opinion that he will then have no difficulty in proving the immortality of the soul. He will only ask for a further admission:—that beauty is the cause of the beautiful, greatness the cause of the great, smallness of the small, and so on of other things. This is a safe and simple answer, which escapes the contradictions of greater and less (greater by reason of that which is smaller!), of addition and subtraction, and the other difficulties of relation. These subtleties he is for leaving to wiser heads than his own; he prefers to test ideas by the consistency of their consequences, and, if asked to give an account of them, goes back to some higher idea or hypothesis which appears to him to be the best, until at last he arrives at a resting place. (Republic; Phil.)

The doctrine of ideas, which has long ago received the assent of the Socratic circle, is now affirmed by the Phliasian auditor to command the assent of any man of sense. The narrative is continued; Socrates is desirous of explaining how opposite ideas may appear to co-exist but do not really co-exist in the same thing or person. For example, Simmias may be said to have greatness and also smallness, because he is greater than Socrates and less than Phaedo. And yet Simmias is not really great and also small, but only when compared to Phaedo and Socrates. I use the illustration, says Socrates, because I want to show you not only that ideal opposites exclude one another, but also the opposites in us. I, for example, having the attribute of smallness remain small, and cannot become great: the smallness which is in me drives out greatness.

One of the company here remarked that this was inconsistent with the old assertion that opposites generated opposites. But that, replies Socrates, was affirmed, not of opposite ideas either in us or in nature, but of opposition in the concrete—not of life and death, but of individuals living and dying. When this objection has been removed, Socrates proceeds: This doctrine of the mutual exclusion of opposites is not only true of the opposites themselves, but of things which are inseparable from them. For example, cold and heat are opposed; and fire, which is inseparable from heat, cannot co-exist with cold, or snow, which is inseparable from cold, with heat. Again, the number three excludes the number four, because three is an odd number and four is an even number, and the odd is opposed to the even. Thus we are able to proceed a step beyond "the safe and simple answer." We may say, not only that the odd excludes the even, but that the number three, which participates in oddness, excludes the even. And in like manner, not only does life exclude death, but the soul, of which life is the inseparable attribute, also excludes death. And that of which life is the inseparable attribute is by the force of the terms imperishable. If the odd principle were imperishable, then the number three would not perish but remove, on the approach of the even principle. But the immortal is imperishable; and therefore the soul on the approach of death does not perish but removes.

Thus all objections appear to be finally silenced. And now the application has to be made: If the soul is immortal, "what manner of persons ought we to be?" having regard not only to time but to eternity. For death is not the end of all, and the wicked is not released from his evil by death; but everyone carries with him into the world below that which he is or has become, and that only.

For after death the soul is carried away to judgment, and when she has received her punishment returns to Earth in the course of ages. The wise soul is conscious of her situation, and follows the attendant angel who guides her through the windings of the world below; but the impure soul wanders hither and thither without companion or guide, and is carried at last to her own place, as the pure soul is also carried away to hers. "In order that you may understand this, I must first describe to you the nature and conformation of the Earth."

Now the whole Earth is a globe placed in the center of the heavens, and is maintained there by the perfection of balance. That which we call the Earth is only one of many small hollows, wherein collect the mists and waters and the thick lower air; but the true Earth is above, and is in a finer and subtler element. And if, like birds, we could fly to the surface of the air, in the same manner that fishes come to the top of the sea, then we should behold the true Earth and the true heaven and the true stars. Our Earth is everywhere corrupted and corroded; and even the land which is fairer than the sea, for that is a mere chaos or waste of water and mud and sand, has nothing to show in comparison of the other world. But the heavenly earth is of diverse colors, sparkling with jewels brighter than gold and whiter than any snow, having flowers and fruits innumerable. And the inhabitants dwell some on the shore of the sea of air, others in "islets of the blessed," and they hold converse with the gods, and behold the sun, moon and stars as they truly are, and their other blessedness is of a piece with this.

The hollows on the surface of the globe vary in size and shape from that which we inhabit: but all are connected by passages and perforations in the interior of the Earth. And there is one huge chasm or opening called Tartarus, into which streams of fire and water and liquid mud are ever flowing; of these small portions find their way to the surface and form seas and rivers and volcanoes. There is a perpetual inhalation and exhalation of the air rising and falling as the waters pass into the depths of the earth and return again, in their course forming lakes and rivers, but never descending below the center of the Earth; for on either side the rivers flowing either way are stopped by a precipice. These rivers are many and mighty, and there are four principal ones, Oceanus, Acheron, Pyriphlegethon, and Cocytus. Oceanus is the river which encircles the Earth; Acheron takes an opposite direction, and after flowing under the earth through desert places, at last reaches the Acherusian lake—this is the river at which the souls of the dead await their return to Earth. Pyriphlegethon is a stream of fire, which coils round the Earth and flows into the depths of Tartarus. The fourth river, Cocytus, is that which is called by the poets the Stygian river, and passes into and forms the lake Styx, from the waters of which it gains new and strange powers. This river, too, falls into Tartarus.

The dead are first of all judged according to their deeds, and those who are incurable are thrust into Tartarus, from which they never come out. Those who have only committed venial sins are first purified of them, and then rewarded for the good which they have done. Those who have committed crimes, great indeed, but not unpardonable, are thrust into Tartarus, but are cast forth at the end of a year by way of Pyriphlegethon or Cocytus, and these carry them as far as the Acherusian lake, where they call upon their victims to let them come out of the rivers into the lake. And if they prevail, then they are let out and their sufferings cease: if not, they are borne unceasingly into Tartarus and back again, until they at last obtain mercy. The pure souls also receive their reward, and have their abode in the upper Earth, and a select few in still fairer "mansions."

Socrates is not prepared to insist on the literal accuracy of this description, but he is confident that something of the kind is true. He who has sought after the pleasures of knowledge and rejected the pleasures of the body, has reason to be of good hope at the approach of death; whose voice is already speaking to him, and who will one day be heard calling all men.

The hour has come at which he must drink the poison, and not much remains to be done. How shall they bury him? That is a question which he refuses to entertain, for they are burying, not him, but his dead body. His friends had once been sureties that he would remain, and they shall now be sureties that he has run away. Yet he would not die without the customary ceremonies of washing and burial. Shall he make a libation of the poison? In the spirit he will, but not in the letter. One request he utters in the very act of death, which has been a puzzle to after ages. With a sort of irony he remembers that a trifling religious duty is still unfulfillled, just as above he desires before he departs to compose a few verses in order to satisfy a scruple about a dream—unless, indeed, we suppose him to mean, that he was now restored to health, and made the customary offering to Asclepius in token of his recovery.

* * * * *

1. The doctrine of the immortality of the soul has sunk deep into the heart of the human race; and men are apt to rebel against any examination of the nature or grounds of their belief. They do not like to acknowledge that this, as well as the other "eternal ideas" of man, has a history in time, which may be traced in Greek poetry or philosophy, and also in the Hebrew Scriptures. They convert feeling into reasoning, and throw a network of dialectics over that which is really a deeply-rooted instinct. In the same

temper which Socrates reproves in himself they are disposed to think that even fallacies will do no harm, for they will die with them, and while they live they will gain by the delusion. And when they consider the numberless bad arguments which have been pressed into the service of theology, they say, like the companions of Socrates, "What argument can we ever trust again?" But there is a better and higher spirit to be gathered from the Phaedo, as well as from the other writings of Plato, which says that first principles should be most constantly reviewed (Phaedo and Crat.), and that the highest subjects demand of us the greatest accuracy (Republic); also that we must not become misologists because arguments are apt to be deceivers.

2. In former ages there was a customary rather than a reasoned belief in the immortality of the soul. It was based on the authority of the Church, on the necessity of such a belief to morality and the order of society, on the evidence of an historical fact, and also on analogies and figures of speech which filled up the void or gave an expression in words to a cherished instinct. The mass of mankind went on their way busy with the affairs of this life, hardly stopping to think about another. But in our own day the question has been reopened, and it is doubtful whether the belief which in the first ages of Christianity was the strongest motive of action can survive the conflict with a scientific age in which the rules of evidence are stricter and the mind has become more sensitive to criticism. It has faded into the distance by a natural process as it was removed further and further from the historical fact on which it has been supposed to rest. Arguments derived from material things such as the seed and the ear of corn or transitions in the life of animals from one state of being to another (the chrysalis and the butterfly) are not "in pari materia" with arguments from the visible to the invisible, and are therefore felt to be no longer applicable. The evidence to the historical fact seems to be weaker than was once supposed: it is not consistent with itself, and is based upon documents which are of unknown origin. The immortality of man must be proved by other arguments than these if it is again to become a living belief. We must ask ourselves afresh why we still maintain it, and seek to discover a foundation for it in the nature of God and in the first principles of morality.

3. At the outset of the discussion we may clear away a confusion. We certainly do not mean by the immortality of the soul the immortality of fame, which whether worth having or not can only be ascribed to a very select class of the whole race of mankind, and even the interest in these few is comparatively short-lived. To have been a benefactor to the world,

whether in a higher or a lower sphere of life and thought, is a great thing: to have the reputation of being one, when men have passed out of the sphere of earthly praise or blame, is hardly worthy of consideration. The memory of a great man, so far from being immortal, is really limited to his own generation:—so long as his friends or his disciples are alive, so long as his books continue to be read, so long as his political or military successes fill a page in the history of his country. The praises which are bestowed upon him at his death hardly last longer than the flowers which are strewed upon his coffin or the "immortelles" which are laid upon his tomb. Literature makes the most of its heroes, but the true man is well aware that far from enjoying an immortality of fame, in a generation or two, or even in a much shorter time, he will be forgotten and the world will get on without him.

4. Modern philosophy is perplexed at this whole question, which is sometimes fairly given up and handed over to the realm of faith. The perplexity should not be forgotten by us when we attempt to submit the Phaedo of Plato to the requirements of logic. For what idea can we form of the soul when separated from the body? Or how can the soul be united with the body and still be independent? Is the soul related to the body as the ideal to the real, or as the whole to the parts, or as the subject to the object, or as the cause to the effect, or as the end to the means? Shall we say with Aristotle, that the soul is the entelechy or form of an organized living body? or with Plato, that she has a life of her own? Is the Pythagorean image of the harmony, or that of the monad, the truer expression? Is the soul related to the body as sight to the eye, or as the boatman to his boat? (Arist. de Anim.) And in another state of being is the soul to be conceived of as vanishing into infinity, hardly possessing an existence which she can call her own, as in the pantheistic system of Spinoza: or as an individual informing another body and entering into new relations, but retaining her own character? (Compare Gorgias.) Or is the opposition of soul and body a mere illusion, and the true self neither soul nor body, but the union of the two in the "I" which is above them? And is death the assertion of this individuality in the higher nature, and the falling away into nothingness of the lower? Or are we vainly attempting to pass the boundaries of human thought? The body and the soul seem to be inseparable, not only in fact, but in our conceptions of them; and any philosophy which too closely unites them, or too widely separates them, either in this life or in another, disturbs the balance of human nature. No thinker has perfectly adjusted them, or been entirely consistent with himself in describing their relation to one another. Nor can we wonder that Plato in the infancy of human thought

should have confused mythology and philosophy, or have mistaken verbal arguments for real ones.

5. Again, believing in the immortality of the soul, we must still ask the question of Socrates, "What is that which we suppose to be immortal?" Is it the personal and individual element in us, or the spiritual and universal? Is it the principle of knowledge or of goodness, or the union of the two? Is it the mere force of life which is determined to be, or the consciousness of self which cannot be got rid of, or the fire of genius which refuses to be extinguished? Or is there a hidden being which is allied to the Author of all existence, who is because he is perfect, and to whom our ideas of perfection give us a title to belong? Whatever answer is given by us to these questions, there still remains the necessity of allowing the permanence of evil, if not forever, at any rate for a time, in order that the wicked "may not have too good a bargain." For the annihilation of evil at death, or the eternal duration of it, seem to involve equal difficulties in the moral government of the universe. Sometimes we are led by our feelings, rather than by our reason, to think of the good and wise only as existing in another life. Why should the mean, the weak, the idiot, the infant, the herd of men who have never in any proper sense the use of reason, reappear with blinking eyes in the light of another world? But our second thought is that the hope of humanity is a common one, and that all or none will be partakers of immortality. Reason does not allow us to suppose that we have any greater claims than others, and experience may often reveal to us unexpected flashes of the higher nature in those whom we had despised. Why should the wicked suffer any more than ourselves? had we been placed in their circumstances should we have been any better than they? The worst of men are objects of pity rather than of anger to the philanthropist; must they not be equally such to divine benevolence? Even more than the good they have need of another life; not that they may be punished, but that they may be educated. These are a few of the reflections which arise in our minds when we attempt to assign any form to our conceptions of a future state.

There are some other questions which are disturbing to us because we have no answer to them. What is to become of the animals in a future state? Have we not seen dogs more faithful and intelligent than men, and men who are more stupid and brutal than any animals? Does their life cease at death, or is there some "better thing reserved" also for them? They may be said to have a shadow or imitation of morality, and imperfect moral claims upon the benevolence of man and upon the justice of God. We cannot think of the least or lowest of them, the insect, the bird, the inhabitants of the sea or the desert, as having any place in a future world, and if not all, why should those who are specially attached to man be deemed worthy of any exceptional privilege? When we reason about such a subject, almost at once we degenerate into nonsense. It is a passing thought which has no real hold on the mind. We may argue for the existence of animals in a future state from the attributes of God, or from texts of Scripture ("Are not two sparrows sold for one farthing?" etc.), but the truth is that we are only filling up the void of another world with our own fancies. Again, we often talk about the origin of evil, that great bugbear of theologians, by which they frighten us into believing any superstition. What answer can be made to the old commonplace, "Is not God the author of evil, if he knowingly permitted, but could have prevented it?" Even if we assume that the inequalities of this life are rectified by some transposition of human beings in another, still the existence of the very least evil if it could have been avoided, seems to be at variance with the love and justice of God. And so we arrive at the conclusion that we are carrying logic too far, and that the attempt to frame the world according to a rule of divine perfection is opposed to experience and had better be given up. The case of the animals is our own. We must admit that the Divine Being, although perfect himself, has placed us in a state of life in which we may work together with him for good, but we are very far from having attained to it.

6. Again, ideas must be given through something; and we are always prone to argue about the soul from analogies of outward things which may serve to embody our thoughts, but are also partly delusive. For we cannot reason from the natural to the spiritual, or from the outward to the inward. The progress of physiological science, without bringing us nearer to the great secret, has tended to remove some erroneous notions respecting the relations of body and mind, and in this we have the advantage of the ancients. But no one imagines that any seed of immortality is to be discerned in our mortal frames. Most people have been content to rest their belief in another life on the agreement of the more enlightened part of mankind, and on the inseparable connection of such a doctrine with the existence of a God—also in a less degree on the impossibility of doubting about the continued existence of those whom we love and reverence in this world. And after all has been said, the figure, the analogy, the argument, are felt to be only approximations in different forms to an expression of the common sentiment of the human heart. That we shall live again is far more certain than that we shall take any particular form of life.

7. When we speak of the immortality of the soul, we must ask further what we mean by the word immortality. For of the duration of a living being in countless ages we can form no conception; far less than a three years" old child of the whole of life. The naked eye might as well try to see the furthest star in the infinity of heaven. Whether time and space really exist when we take away the limits of them may be doubted; at any rate the thought of them when unlimited us so overwhelming to us as to lose all distinctness. Philosophers have spoken of them as forms of the human mind, but what is the mind without them? As then infinite time, or an existence out of time, which are the only possible explanations of eternal duration, are equally inconceivable to us, let us substitute for them a hundred or a thousand years after death, and ask not what will be our employment in eternity, but what will happen to us in that definite portion of time; or what is now happening to those who passed out of life a hundred or a thousand years ago. Do we imagine that the wicked are suffering torments, or that the good are singing the praises of God, during a period longer than that of a whole life, or of ten lives of men? Is the suffering physical or mental? And does the worship of God consist only of praise, or of many forms of service? Who are the wicked, and who are the good, whom we venture to divide by a hard and fast line; and in which of the two classes should we place ourselves and our friends? May we not suspect that we are making differences of kind, because we are unable to imagine differences of degree?—putting the whole human race into heaven or hell for the greater convenience of logical division? Are we not at the same time describing them both in superlatives, only that we may satisfy the demands of rhetoric? What is that pain which does not become deadened after a thousand years? or what is the nature of that pleasure or happiness which never wearies by monotony? Earthly pleasures and pains are short in proportion as they are keen; of any others which are both intense and lasting we have no experience, and can form no idea. The words or figures of speech which we use are not consistent with themselves. For are we not imagining heaven under the similitude of a church, and hell as a prison, or perhaps a madhouse or chamber of horrors? And yet to beings constituted as we are, the monotony of singing psalms would be as great an infliction as the pains of hell, and might be even pleasantly interrupted by them. Where are the actions worthy of rewards greater than those which are conferred on the greatest benefactors of mankind? And where are the crimes which according to Plato's merciful reckoning,—more merciful, at any rate, than the eternal damnation of so-called Christian

teachers,—for every ten years in this life deserve a hundred of punishment in the life to come? We should be ready to die of pity if we could see the least of the sufferings which the writers of Infernos and Purgatorios have attributed to the damned. Yet these joys and terrors seem hardly to exercise an appreciable influence over the lives of men. The wicked man when old, is not, as Plato supposes (Republic), more agitated by the terrors of another world when he is nearer to them, nor the good in an ecstasy at the joys of which he is soon to be the partaker. Age numbs the sense of both worlds; and the habit of life is strongest in death. Even the dying mother is dreaming of her lost children as they were forty or fifty years before, "pattering over the boards," not of reunion with them in another state of being. Most persons when the last hour comes are resigned to the order of nature and the will of God. They are not thinking of Dante's Inferno or Paradiso, or of the Pilgrim's Progress. Heaven and hell are not realities to them, but words or ideas; the outward symbols of some great mystery, they hardly know what. Many noble poems and pictures have been suggested by the traditional representations of them, which have been fixed in forms of art and can no longer be altered. Many sermons have been filled with descriptions of celestial or infernal mansions. But hardly even in childhood did the thought of heaven and hell supply the motives of our actions, or at any time seriously affect the substance of our belief.

8. Another life must be described, if at all, in forms of thought and not of sense. To draw pictures of heaven and hell, whether in the language of Scripture or any other, adds nothing to our real knowledge, but may perhaps disguise our ignorance. The truest conception which we can form of a future life is a state of progress or education—a progress from evil to good, from ignorance to knowledge. To this we are led by the analogy of the present life, in which we see different races and nations of men, and different men and women of the same nation, in various states or stages of cultivation; some more and some less developed, and all of them capable of improvement under favorable circumstances. There are punishments too of children when they are growing up inflicted by their parents, of elder offenders which are imposed by the law of the land, of all men at all times of life, which are attached by the laws of nature to the performance of certain actions. All these punishments are really educational; that is to say, they are not intended to retaliate on the offender, but to teach him a lesson. Also there is an element of chance in them, which is another name for our ignorance of the laws of nature. There is evil too inseparable from good (compare Lysis); not always punished here, as good is not always

rewarded. It is capable of being indefinitely diminished; and as knowledge increases, the element of chance may more and more disappear.

For we do not argue merely from the analogy of the present state of this world to another, but from the analogy of a probable future to which we are tending. The greatest changes of which we have had experience as yet are due to our increasing knowledge of history and of nature. They have been produced by a few minds appearing in three or four favored nations, in a comparatively short period of time. May we be allowed to imagine the minds of men everywhere working together during many ages for the completion of our knowledge? May not the science of physiology transform the world? Again, the majority of mankind have really experienced some moral improvement; almost everyone feels that he has tendencies to good, and is capable of becoming better. And these germs of good are often found to be developed by new circumstances, like stunted trees when transplanted to a better soil. The differences between the savage and the civilized man, or between the civilized man in old and new countries, may be indefinitely increased. The first difference is the effect of a few thousand, the second of a few hundred years. We congratulate ourselves that slavery has become industry; that law and constitutional government have superseded despotism and violence; that an ethical religion has taken the place of fetishism. There may yet come a time when the many may be as well off as the few; when no one will be weighed down by excessive toil; when the necessity of providing for the body will not interfere with mental improvement; when the physical frame may be strengthened and developed; and the religion of all men may become a reasonable service.

Nothing therefore, either in the present state of man or in the tendencies of the future, as far as we can entertain conjecture of them, would lead us to suppose that God governs us vindictively in this world, and therefore we have no reason to infer that he will govern us vindictively in another. The true argument from analogy is not, "This life is a mixed state of justice and injustice, of great waste, of sudden casualties, of disproportionate punishments, and therefore the like inconsistencies, irregularities, injustices are to be expected in another"; but "This life is subject to law, and is in a state of progress, and therefore law and progress may be believed to be the governing principles of another." All the analogies of this world would be against unmeaning punishments inflicted a hundred or a thousand years after an offense had been committed. Suffering there might be as a part of education, but not hopeless or protracted; as there might be a retrogression of individuals or of bodies of men, yet not such as to interfere with a plan for the improvement of the whole (compare Laws).

9. But someone will say: That we cannot reason from the seen to the unseen, and that we are creating another world after the image of this, just as men in former ages have created gods in their own likeness. And we, like the companions of Socrates, may feel discouraged at hearing our favorite "argument from analogy" thus summarily disposed of. Like himself, too, we may adduce other arguments in which he seems to have anticipated us, though he expresses them in different language. For we feel that the soul partakes of the ideal and invisible; and can never fall into the error of confusing the external circumstances of man with his higher self; or his origin with his nature. It is as repugnant to us as it was to him to imagine that our moral ideas are to be attributed only to cerebral forces. The value of a human soul, like the value of a man's life to himself, is inestimable, and cannot be reckoned in earthly or material things. The human being alone has the consciousness of truth and justice and love, which is the consciousness of God. And the soul becoming more conscious of these, becomes more conscious of her own immortality.

10. The last ground of our belief in immortality, and the strongest, is the perfection of the divine nature. The mere fact of the existence of God does not tend to show the continued existence of man. An evil God or an indifferent God might have had the power, but not the will, to preserve us. He might have regarded us as fitted to minister to his service by a succession of existences,—like the animals, without attributing to each soul an incomparable value. But if he is perfect, he must will that all rational beings should partake of that perfection which he himself is. In the words of the Timaeus, he is good, and therefore he desires that all other things should be as like himself as possible. And the manner in which he accomplishes this is by permitting evil, or rather degrees of good, which are otherwise called evil. For all progress is good relatively to the past, and yet may be comparatively evil when regarded in the light of the future. Good and evil are relative terms, and degrees of evil are merely the negative aspect of degrees of good. Of the absolute goodness of any finite nature we can form no conception; we are all of us in process of transition from one degree of good or evil to another. The difficulties which are urged about the origin or existence of evil are mere dialectical puzzles, standing in the same relation to Christian philosophy as the puzzles of the Cynics and Megarians to the philosophy of Plato. They arise out of the tendency of the human mind to regard good and evil both as relative and absolute; just

as the riddles about motion are to be explained by the double conception of space or matter, which the human mind has the power of regarding either as continuous or discrete.

In speaking of divine perfection, we mean to say that God is just and true and loving, the author of order and not of disorder, of good and not of evil. Or rather, that he is justice, that he is truth, that he is love, that he is order, that he is the very progress of which we were speaking; and that wherever these qualities are present, whether in the human soul or in the order of nature, there is God. We might still see him everywhere, if we had not been mistakenly seeking for him apart from us, instead of in us; away from the laws of nature, instead of in them. And we become united to him not by mystical absorption, but by partaking, whether consciously or unconsciously, of that truth and justice and love which he himself is.

Thus the belief in the immortality of the soul rests at last on the belief in God. If there is a good and wise God, then there is a progress of mankind toward perfection; and if there is no progress of men toward perfection, then there is no good and wise God. We cannot suppose that the moral government of God of which we see the beginnings in the world and in ourselves will cease when we pass out of life.

11. Considering the "feebleness of the human faculties and the uncertainty of the subject," we are inclined to believe that the fewer our words the better. At the approach of death there is not much said; good men are too honest to go out of the world professing more than they know. There is perhaps no important subject about which, at any time, even religious people speak so little to one another. In the fulness of life the thought of death is mostly awakened by the sight or recollection of the death of others rather than by the prospect of our own. We must also acknowledge that there are degrees of the belief in immortality, and many forms in which it presents itself to the mind. Some persons will say no more than that they trust in God, and that they leave all to Him. It is a great part of true religion not to pretend to know more than we do. Others when they quit this world are comforted with the hope "That they will see and know their friends in heaven." But it is better to leave them in the hands of God and to be assured that "no evil shall touch them." There are others again to whom the belief in a divine personality has ceased to have any longer a meaning; yet they are satisfied that the end of all is not here, but that something still remains to us, "and some better thing for the good than for the evil." They are persuaded, in spite of their theological nihilism, that the ideas of justice and truth and holiness and love are

realities. They cherish an enthusiastic devotion to the first principles of morality. Through these they see, or seem to see, darkly, and in a figure, that the soul is immortal.

But besides differences of theological opinion which must ever prevail about things unseen, the hope of immortality is weaker or stronger in men at one time of life than at another; it even varies from day to day. It comes and goes; the mind, like the sky, is apt to be overclouded. Other generations of men may have sometimes lived under an "eclipse of faith," to us the total disappearance of it might be compared to the "sun falling from heaven." And we may sometimes have to begin again and acquire the belief for ourselves; or to win it back again when it is lost. It is really weakest in the hour of death. For Nature, like a kind mother or nurse, lays us to sleep without frightening us; physicians, who are the witnesses of such scenes, say that under ordinary circumstances there is no fear of the future. Often, as Plato tells us, death is accompanied "with pleasure." (Tim.) When the end is still uncertain, the cry of many a one has been, "Pray, that I may be taken." The last thoughts even of the best men depend chiefly on the accidents of their bodily state. Pain soon overpowers the desire of life; old age, like the child, is laid to sleep almost in a moment. The long experience of life will often destroy the interest which mankind have in it. So various are the feelings with which different persons draw near to death; and still more various the forms in which imagination clothes it. For this alternation of feeling compare the Old Testament,—Psalm vi.; Isaiah; Eccles.

12. When we think of God and of man in his relation to God; of the imperfection of our present state and yet of the progress which is observable in the history of the world and of the human mind; of the depth and power of our moral ideas which seem to partake of the very nature of God Himself; when we consider the contrast between the physical laws to which we are subject and the higher law which raises us above them and is yet a part of them; when we reflect on our capacity of becoming the "spectators of all time and all existence," and of framing in our own minds the ideal of a perfect Being; when we see how the human mind in all the higher religions of the world, including Buddhism, notwithstanding some aberrations, has tended toward such a belief—we have reason to think that our destiny is different from that of animals; and though we cannot altogether shut out the childish fear that the soul upon leaving the body may "vanish into thin air," we have still, so far as the nature of the subject admits, a hope of immortality with which we comfort ourselves on sufficient grounds. The denial of the belief takes the heart out of human

life; it lowers men to the level of the material. As Goethe also says, "He is dead even in this world who has no belief in another."

13. It is well also that we should sometimes think of the forms of thought under which the idea of immortality is most naturally presented to us. It is clear that to our minds the risen soul can no longer be described, as in a picture, by the symbol of a creature half-bird, half-human, nor in any other form of sense. The multitude of angels, as in Milton, singing the Almighty's praises, are a noble image, and may furnish a theme for the poet or the painter, but they are no longer an adequate expression of the kingdom of God which is within us. Neither is there any mansion, in this world or another, in which the departed can be imagined to dwell and carry on their occupations. When this earthly tabernacle is dissolved, no other habitation or building can take them in: it is in the language of ideas only that we speak of them.

First of all there is the thought of rest and freedom from pain; they have gone home, as the common saying is, and the cares of this world touch them no more. Secondly, we may imagine them as they were at their best and brightest, humbly fulfillling their daily round of duties—selfless, childlike, unaffected by the world; when the eye was single and the whole body seemed to be full of light; when the mind was clear and saw into the purposes of God. Thirdly, we may think of them as possessed by a great love of God and man, working out His will at a further stage in the heavenly pilgrimage. And yet we acknowledge that these are the things which eye hath not seen nor ear heard and therefore it hath not entered into the heart of man in any sensible manner to conceive them. Fourthly, there may have been some moments in our own lives when we have risen above ourselves, or been conscious of our truer selves, in which the will of God has superseded our wills, and we have entered into communion with Him, and been partakers for a brief season of the Divine truth and love, in which like Christ we have been inspired to utter the prayer, "I in them, and thou in me, that we may be all made perfect in one." These precious moments, if we have ever known them, are the nearest approach which we can make to the idea of immortality.

14. Returning now to the earlier stage of human thought which is represented by the writings of Plato, we find that many of the same questions have already arisen: there is the same tendency to materialism; the same inconsistency in the application of the idea of mind; the same doubt whether the soul is to be regarded as a cause or as an effect; the same falling back on moral convictions. In the Phaedo the soul is conscious

of her divine nature, and the separation from the body which has been commenced in this life is perfected in another. Beginning in mystery, Socrates, in the intermediate part of the Dialogue, attempts to bring the doctrine of a future life into connection with his theory of knowledge. In proportion as he succeeds in this, the individual seems to disappear in a more general notion of the soul; the contemplation of ideas "under the form of eternity" takes the place of past and future states of existence. His language may be compared to that of some modern philosophers, who speak of eternity, not in the sense of perpetual duration of time, but as an ever-present quality of the soul. Yet at the conclusion of the Dialogue, having "arrived at the end of the intellectual world" (Republic), he replaces the veil of mythology, and describes the soul and her attendant genius in the language of the mysteries or of a disciple of Zoroaster. Nor can we fairly demand of Plato a consistency which is wanting among ourselves, who acknowledge that another world is beyond the range of human thought, and yet are always seeking to represent the mansions of heaven or hell in the colors of the painter, or in the descriptions of the poet or rhetorician.

15. The doctrine of the immortality of the soul was not new to the Greeks in the age of Socrates, but, like the unity of God, had a foundation in the popular belief. The old Homeric notion of a gibbering ghost flitting away to Hades; or of a few illustrious heroes enjoying the isles of the blessed; or of an existence divided between the two; or the Hesiodic, of righteous spirits, who become guardian angels,—had given place in the mysteries and the Orphic poets to representations, partly fanciful, of a future state of rewards and punishments. (Laws.) The reticence of the Greeks on public occasions and in some part of their literature respecting this "underground" religion, is not to be taken as a measure of the diffusion of such beliefs. If Pericles in the funeral oration is silent on the consolations of immortality, the poet Pindar and the tragedians on the other hand constantly assume the continued existence of the dead in an upper or under world. Darius and Laius are still alive; Antigone will be dear to her brethren after death; the way to the palace of Cronos is found by those who "have thrice departed from evil." The tragedy of the Greeks is not "rounded" by this life, but is deeply set in decrees of fate and mysterious workings of powers beneath the earth. In the caricature of Aristophanes there is also a witness to the common sentiment. The Ionian and Pythagorean philosophies arose, and some new elements were added to the popular belief. The individual must find an expression as well as the world. Either the soul was supposed to exist in the form of a magnet, or of a particle of fire, or of light, or air, or

water; or of a number or of a harmony of number; or to be or have, like the stars, a principle of motion (Arist. de Anim.). At length Anaxagoras, hardly distinguishing between life and mind, or between mind human and divine, attained the pure abstraction; and this, like the other abstractions of Greek philosophy, sank deep into the human intelligence. The opposition of the intelligible and the sensible, and of God to the world, supplied an analogy which assisted in the separation of soul and body. If ideas were separable from phenomena, mind was also separable from matter; if the ideas were eternal, the mind that conceived them was eternal too. As the unity of God was more distinctly acknowledged, the conception of the human soul became more developed. The succession, or alternation of life and death, had occurred to Heracleitus. The Eleatic Parmenides had stumbled upon the modern thesis, that "thought and being are the same." The Eastern belief in transmigration defined the sense of individuality; and some, like Empedocles, fancied that the blood which they had shed in another state of being was crying against them, and that for thirty thousand years they were to be "fugitives and vagabonds upon the Earth." The desire of recognizing a lost mother or love or friend in the world below (Phaedo) was a natural feeling which, in that age as well as in every other, has given distinctness to the hope of immortality. Nor were ethical considerations wanting, partly derived from the necessity of punishing the greater sort of criminals, whom no avenging power of this world could reach. The voice of conscience, too, was heard reminding the good man that he was not altogether innocent. (Republic.) To these indistinct longings and fears an expression was given in the mysteries and Orphic poets: a "heap of books" (Republic), passing under the names of Musaeus and Orpheus in Plato's time, were filled with notions of an under-world.

16. Yet after all the belief in the individuality of the soul after death had but a feeble hold on the Greek mind. Like the personality of God, the personality of man in a future state was not inseparably bound up with the reality of his existence. For the distinction between the personal and impersonal, and also between the divine and human, was far less marked to the Greek than to ourselves. And as Plato readily passes from the notion of the good to that of God, he also passes almost imperceptibly to himself and his reader from the future life of the individual soul to the eternal being of the absolute soul. There has been a clearer statement and a clearer denial of the belief in modern times than is found in early Greek philosophy, and hence the comparative silence on the whole subject which is often remarked in ancient writers, and particularly in Aristotle. For Plato and Aristotle are

not further removed in their teaching about the immortality of the soul than they are in their theory of knowledge.

17. Living in an age when logic was beginning to mold human thought, Plato naturally cast his belief in immortality into a logical form. And when we consider how much the doctrine of ideas was also one of words, it is not surprising that he should have fallen into verbal fallacies: early logic is always mistaking the truth of the form for the truth of the matter. It is easy to see that the alternation of opposites is not the same as the generation of them out of each other; and that the generation of them out of each other, which is the first argument in the Phaedo, is at variance with their mutual exclusion of each other, whether in themselves or in us, which is the last. For even if we admit the distinction which he draws between the opposites and the things which have the opposites, still individuals fall under the latter class; and we have to pass out of the region of human hopes and fears to a conception of an abstract soul which is the impersonation of the ideas. Such a conception, which in Plato himself is but half expressed, is unmeaning to us, and relative only to a particular stage in the history of thought. The doctrine of reminiscence is also a fragment of a former world, which has no place in the philosophy of modern times. But Plato had the wonders of psychology just opening to him, and he had not the explanation of them which is supplied by the analysis of language and the history of the human mind. The question, "Whence come our abstract ideas?" he could only answer by an imaginary hypothesis. Nor is it difficult to see that his crowning argument is purely verbal, and is but the expression of an instinctive confidence put into a logical form:—"The soul is immortal because it contains a principle of imperishableness." Nor does he himself seem at all to be aware that nothing is added to human knowledge by his "safe and simple answer," that beauty is the cause of the beautiful; and that he is merely reasserting the Eleatic being "divided by the Pythagorean numbers," against the Heracleitean doctrine of perpetual generation. The answer to the "very serious question" of generation and destruction is really the denial of them. For this he would substitute, as in the Republic, a system of ideas, tested, not by experience, but by their consequences, and not explained by actual causes, but by a higher, that is, a more general notion. Consistency with themselves is the only test which is to be applied to them. (Republic, and Phaedo.)

18. To deal fairly with such arguments, they should be translated as far as possible into their modern equivalents. "If the ideas of men are eternal, their souls are eternal, and if not the ideas, then not the souls." Such an

argument stands nearly in the same relation to Plato and his age, as the argument from the existence of God to immortality among ourselves. "If God exists, then the soul exists after death; and if there is no God, there is no existence of the soul after death." For the ideas are to his mind the reality, the truth, the principle of permanence, as well as of intelligence and order in the world. When Simmias and Cebes say that they are more strongly persuaded of the existence of ideas than they are of the immortality of the soul, they represent fairly enough the order of thought in Greek philosophy. And we might say in the same way that we are more certain of the existence of God than we are of the immortality of the soul, and are led by the belief in the one to a belief in the other. The parallel, as Socrates would say, is not perfect, but agrees in as far as the mind in either case is regarded as dependent on something above and beyond herself. The analogy may even be pressed a step further: "We are more certain of our ideas of truth and right than we are of the existence of God, and are led on in the order of thought from one to the other." Or more correctly: "The existence of right and truth is the existence of God, and can never for a moment be separated from Him."

19. The main argument of the Phaedo is derived from the existence of eternal ideas of which the soul is a partaker; the other argument of the alternation of opposites is replaced by this. And there have not been wanting philosophers of the idealist school who have imagined that the doctrine of the immortality of the soul is a theory of knowledge, and that in what has preceded Plato is accommodating himself to the popular belief. Such a view can only be elicited from the Phaedo by what may be termed the transcendental method of interpretation, and is obviously inconsistent with the Gorgias and the Republic. Those who maintain it are immediately compelled to renounce the shadow which they have grasped, as a play of words only. But the truth is, that Plato in his argument for the immortality of the soul has collected many elements of proof or persuasion, ethical and mythological as well as dialectical, which are not easily to be reconciled with one another; and he is as much in earnest about his doctrine of retribution, which is repeated in all his more ethical writings, as about his theory of knowledge. And while we may fairly translate the dialectical into the language of Hegel, and the religious and mythological into the language of Dante or Bunyan, the ethical speaks to us still in the same voice, and appeals to a common feeling.

20. Two arguments of this ethical character occur in the Phaedo. The first may be described as the aspiration of the soul after another state of

being. Like the Oriental or Christian mystic, the philosopher is seeking to withdraw from impurities of sense, to leave the world and the things of the world, and to find his higher self. Plato recognizes in these aspirations the foretaste of immortality; as Butler and Addison in modern times have argued, the one from the moral tendencies of mankind, the other from the progress of the soul toward perfection. In using this argument Plato has certainly confused the soul which has left the body, with the soul of the good and wise. (Compare Republic.) Such a confusion was natural, and arose partly out of the antithesis of soul and body. The soul in her own essence, and the soul "clothed upon" with virtues and graces, were easily interchanged with one another, because on a subject which passes expression the distinctions of language can hardly be maintained.

21. The ethical proof of the immortality of the soul is derived from the necessity of retribution. The wicked would be too well off if their evil deeds came to an end. It is not to be supposed that an Ardiaeus, an Archelaus, an Ismenias could ever have suffered the penalty of their crimes in this world. The manner in which this retribution is accomplished Plato represents under the figures of mythology. Doubtless he felt that it was easier to improve than to invent, and that in religion especially the traditional form was required in order to give verisimilitude to the myth. The myth too is far more probable to that age than to ours, and may fairly be regarded as "one guess among many" about the nature of the Earth, which he cleverly supports by the indications of geology. Not that he insists on the absolute truth of his own particular notions: "No man of sense will be confident in such matters; but he will be confident that something of the kind is true." As in other passages (Gorg., Tim., compare Crito), he wins belief for his fictions by the moderation of his statements; he does not, like Dante or Swedenborg, allow himself to be deceived by his own creations.

The Dialogue must be read in the light of the situation. And first of all we are struck by the calmness of the scene. Like the spectators at the time, we cannot pity Socrates; his mien and his language are so noble and fearless. He is the same that he ever was, but milder and gentler, and he has in no degree lost his interest in dialectics; he will not forego the delight of an argument in compliance with the jailer's intimation that he should not heat himself with talking. At such a time he naturally expresses the hope of his life, that he has been a true mystic and not a mere retainer or wand-bearer: and he refers to passages of his personal history. To his old enemies the Comic poets, and to the proceedings on the trial, he alludes playfully; but he vividly remembers the disappointment which he felt in reading the books of Anaxagoras. The return of Xanthippe and his children indicates that the philosopher is not "made of oak or rock." Some other traits of his character may be noted; for example, the courteous manner in which he inclines his head to the last objector, or the ironical touch, "Me already, as the tragic poet would say, the voice of fate calls"; or the depreciation of the arguments with which "he comforted himself and them"; or his fear of "misology"; or his references to Homer; or the playful smile with which he "talks like a book" about greater and less; or the allusion to the possibility of finding another teacher among barbarous races (compare Polit.); or the mysterious reference to another science (mathematics?) of generation and destruction for which he is vainly feeling. There is no change in him; only now he is invested with a sort of sacred character, as the prophet or priest of Apollo the God of the festival, in whose honor he first of all composes a hymn, and then like the swan pours forth his dying lay. Perhaps the extreme elevation of Socrates above his own situation, and the ordinary interests of life (compare his jeu d'esprit about his burial, in which for a moment he puts on the "Silenus mask"), create in the mind of the reader an impression stronger than could be derived from arguments that such a one has in him "a principle which does not admit of death."

The other persons of the dialogue may be considered under two heads: (1) private friends; (2) the respondents in the argument.

First there is Crito, who has been already introduced to us in the Euthydemus and the Crito; he is the equal in years of Socrates, and stands in quite a different relation to him from his younger disciples. He is a man of the world who is rich and prosperous (compare the jest in the Euthydemus), the best friend of Socrates, who wants to know his commands, in whose presence he talks to his family, and who performs the last duty of closing his eyes. It is observable too that, as in the Euthydemus, Crito shows no aptitude for philosophical discussions. Nor among the friends of Socrates must the jailer be forgotten, who seems to have been introduced by Plato in order to show the impression made by the extraordinary man on the common. The gentle nature of the man is indicated by his weeping at the announcement of his errand and then turning away, and also by the words of Socrates to his disciples: "How charming the man is! Since I have been in prison he has been always coming to me, and is as good as could be to me." We are reminded too that he has retained this gentle nature amid scenes of death and violence by the contrasts which he draws between the behavior of Socrates and of others when about to die.

Another person who takes no part in the philosophical discussion is the excitable Apollodorus, the same who, in the Symposium, of which he is the narrator, is called "the madman," and who testifies his grief by the most violent emotions. Phaedo is also present, the "beloved disciple" as he may be termed, who is described, if not "leaning on his bosom," as seated next to Socrates, who is playing with his hair. He too, like Apollodorus, takes no part in the discussion, but he loves above all things to hear and speak of Socrates after his death. The calmness of his behavior, veiling his face when he can no longer restrain his tears, contrasts with the passionate outcries of the other. At a particular point the argument is described as falling before the attack of Simmias. A sort of despair is introduced in the minds of the company. The effect of this is heightened by the description of Phaedo, who has been the eye-witness of the scene, and by the sympathy of his Phliasian auditors who are beginning to think "that they too can never trust an argument again." And the intense interest of the company is communicated not only to the first auditors, but to us who in a distant country read the narrative of their emotions after more than two thousand years have passed away.

The two principal interlocutors are Simmias and Cebes, the disciples of Philolaus the Pythagorean philosopher of Thebes. Simmias is described in the Phaedrus as fonder of an argument than any man living; and Cebes, although finally persuaded by Socrates, is said to be the most incredulous of human beings. It is Cebes who at the commencement of the Dialogue asks why "suicide is held to be unlawful," and who first supplies the doctrine of recollection in confirmation of the pre-existence of the soul. It is Cebes who urges that the pre-existence does not necessarily involve the future existence of the soul, as is shown by the illustration of the weaver and his coat. Simmias, on the other hand, raises the question about harmony and the lyre, which is naturally put into the mouth of a Pythagorean disciple. It is Simmias, too, who first remarks on the uncertainty of human knowledge, and only at last concedes to the argument such a qualified approval as is consistent with the feebleness of the human faculties. Cebes is the deeper and more consecutive thinker, Simmias more superficial and rhetorical; they are distinguished in much the same manner as Adeimantus and Glaucon in the Republic.

Other persons, Menexenus, Ctesippus, Lysis, are old friends; Evenus has been already satirized in the Apology; Aeschines and Epigenes were present at the trial; Euclid and Terpsion will reappear in the Introduction to the Theaetetus, Hermogenes has already appeared in the Cratylus. No inference can fairly be drawn from the absence of Aristippus, nor from the omission of Xenophon, who at the time of Socrates" death was in Asia. The mention of Plato's own absence seems like an expression of sorrow, and may, perhaps, be an indication that the report of the conversation is not to be taken literally.

The place of the Dialogue in the series is doubtful. The doctrine of ideas is certainly carried beyond the Socratic point of view; in no other of the writings of Plato is the theory of them so completely developed. Whether the belief in immortality can be attributed to Socrates or not is uncertain; the silence of the Memorabilia, and of the earlier Dialogues of Plato, is an argument to the contrary. Yet in the Cyropaedia Xenophon has put language into the mouth of the dying Cyrus which recalls the Phaedo, and may have been derived from the teaching of Socrates. It may be fairly urged that the greatest religious interest of mankind could not have been wholly ignored by one who passed his life in fulfillling the commands of an oracle, and who recognized a Divine plan in man and nature. (Xen. Mem.) And the language of the Apology and of the Crito confirms this view.

The Phaedo is not one of the Socratic Dialogues of Plato; nor, on the other hand, can it be assigned to that later stage of the Platonic writings at which the doctrine of ideas appears to be forgotten. It belongs rather to the intermediate period of the Platonic philosophy, which roughly corresponds to the Phaedrus, Gorgias, Republic, Theaetetus. Without pretending to determine the real time of their composition, the Symposium, Meno, Euthyphro, Apology, Phaedo may be conveniently read by us in this order as illustrative of the life of Socrates. Another chain may be formed of the Meno, Phaedrus, Phaedo, in which the immortality of the soul is connected with the doctrine of ideas. In the Meno the theory of ideas is based on the ancient belief in transmigration, which reappears again in the Phaedrus as well as in the Republic and Timaeus, and in all of them is connected with a doctrine of retribution. In the Phaedrus the immortality of the soul is supposed to rest on the conception of the soul as a principle of motion, whereas in the Republic the argument turns on the natural continuance of the soul, which, if not destroyed by her own proper evil, can hardly be destroyed by any other. The soul of man in the Timaeus is derived from the Supreme Creator, and either returns after death to her kindred star, or descends into the lower life of an animal. The Apology expresses the same view as the Phaedo, but with less confidence; there the probability of death being a long sleep is not excluded. The Theaetetus also describes, in a digression, the desire of the soul to fly away and be with God—"and to fly to him is to be like him." The Symposium may be observed to resemble as well as to differ from the Phaedo. While the first notion of immortality is only in the way of natural procreation or of posthumous fame and glory, the higher revelation of beauty, like the good in the Republic, is the vision of the eternal idea. So deeply rooted in Plato's mind is the belief in immortality; so various are the forms of expression which he employs.

As in several other Dialogues, there is more of system in the Phaedo than appears at first sight. The succession of arguments is based on previous philosophies; beginning with the mysteries and the Heracleitean alternation of opposites, and proceeding to the Pythagorean harmony and transmigration; making a step by the aid of Platonic reminiscence, and a further step by the help of the nous of Anaxagoras; until at last we rest in the conviction that the soul is inseparable from the ideas, and belongs to the world of the invisible and unknown. Then, as in the Gorgias or Republic, the curtain falls, and the veil of mythology descends upon the argument. After the confession of Socrates that he is an interested party, and the acknowledgment that no man of sense will think the details of his narrative true, but that something of the kind is true, we return from speculation to practice. He is himself more confident of immortality than he is of his own arguments; and the confidence which he expresses is less strong than that which his cheerfulness and composure in death inspire in us.

Difficulties of two kinds occur in the Phaedo—one kind to be explained out of contemporary philosophy, the other not admitting of an entire solution. (1) The difficulty which Socrates says that he experienced in explaining generation and corruption; the assumption of hypotheses which proceed from the less general to the more general, and are tested by their consequences; the puzzle about greater and less; the resort to the method of ideas, which to us appear only abstract terms,—these are to be explained out of the position of Socrates and Plato in the history of philosophy. They were living in a twilight between the sensible and the intellectual world, and saw no way of connecting them. They could neither explain the relation of ideas to phenomena, nor their correlation to one another. The very idea of relation or comparison was embarrassing to them. Yet in this intellectual uncertainty they had a conception of a proof from results, and of a moral truth, which remained unshaken amid the questionings of philosophy. (2) The other is a difficulty which is touched upon in the Republic as well as in the Phaedo, and is common to modern and ancient philosophy. Plato is not altogether satisfied with his safe and simple method of ideas. He wants to have proved to him by facts that all things are for the best, and that there is one mind or design which pervades them all. But this "power of the best" he is unable to explain; and therefore takes refuge in universal ideas. And are not we at this day seeking to discover that which Socrates in a glass darkly foresaw?

Some resemblances to the Greek drama may be noted in all the Dialogues of Plato. The Phaedo is the tragedy of which Socrates is the protagonist and Simmias and Cebes the secondary performers, standing to them in the same relation as to Glaucon and Adeimantus in the Republic. No Dialogue has a greater unity of subject and feeling. Plato has certainly fulfillled the condition of Greek, or rather of all art, which requires that scenes of death and suffering should be clothed in beauty. The gathering of the friends at the commencement of the Dialogue, the dismissal of Xanthippe, whose presence would have been out of place at a philosophical discussion, but who returns again with her children to take a final farewell, the dejection of the audience at the temporary overthrow of the argument, the picture of Socrates playing with the hair of Phaedo, the final scene in which Socrates alone retains his composure—are masterpieces of art. And the chorus at the end might have interpreted the feeling of the play: "There can no evil happen to a good man in life or death."

"The art of concealing art" is nowhere more perfect than in those writings of Plato which describe the trial and death of Socrates. Their charm is their simplicity, which gives them verisimilitude; and yet they touch, as if incidentally, and because they were suitable to the occasion, on some of the deepest truths of philosophy. There is nothing in any tragedy, ancient or modern, nothing in poetry or history (with one exception), like the last hours of Socrates in Plato. The master could not be more fitly occupied at such a time than in discoursing of immortality; nor the disciples more divinely consoled. The arguments, taken in the spirit and not in the letter, are our arguments; and Socrates by anticipation may be even thought to refute some "eccentric notions" current in our own age. For there are philosophers among ourselves who do not seem to understand how much stronger is the power of intelligence, or of the best, than of Atlas, or mechanical force. How far the words attributed to Socrates were actually uttered by him we forbear to ask; for no answer can be given to this question. And it is better to resign ourselves to the feeling of a great work, than to linger among critical uncertainties.

PHAEDO

Persons of the dialogue: Phaedo, who is the narrator of the dialogue to Echecrates of Phlius. Socrates, Apollodorus, Simmias, Cebes, Crito, and an Attendant of the Prison

Scene: The Prison of Socrates

Place of the narration: Phlius

ECHECRATES: Were you yourself, Phaedo, in the prison with Socrates on the day when he drank the poison?
PHAEDO: Yes, Echecrates, I was.
ECHECRATES: I should so like to hear about his death. What did he say in his last hours? We were informed that he died by taking poison, but no one knew anything more; for no Phliasian ever goes to Athens now, and it is a long time since any stranger from Athens has found his way hither; so that we had no clear account.
PHAEDO: Did you not hear of the proceedings at the trial?
ECHECRATES: Yes; someone told us about the trial, and we could not understand why, having been condemned, he should have been put to death, not at the time, but long afterward. What was the reason of this?
PHAEDO: An accident, Echecrates: the stern of the ship which the Athenians send to Delos happened to have been crowned on the day before he was tried.
ECHECRATES: What is this ship?
PHAEDO: It is the ship in which, according to Athenian tradition, Theseus went to Crete when he took with him the fourteen youths, and was the savior of them and of himself. And they were said to have vowed to Apollo at the time, that if they were saved they would send a yearly mission to Delos. Now this custom still continues, and the whole period of the voyage to and from Delos, beginning when the priest of Apollo crowns the stern of the ship, is a holy season, during which the city is not allowed to be polluted by public executions; and when the vessel is detained by contrary winds, the time spent in going and returning is very considerable. As I was saying, the ship was crowned on the day before the trial, and this was the reason why Socrates lay in prison and was not put to death until long after he was condemned.
ECHECRATES: What was the manner of his death, Phaedo? What

was said or done? And which of his friends were with him? Or did the authorities forbid them to be present—so that he had no friends near him when he died?

PHAEDO: No; there were several of them with him.

ECHECRATES: If you have nothing to do, I wish that you would tell me what passed, as exactly as you can.

PHAEDO: I have nothing at all to do, and will try to gratify your wish. To be reminded of Socrates is always the greatest delight to me, whether I speak myself or hear another speak of him.

ECHECRATES: You will have listeners who are of the same mind with you, and I hope that you will be as exact as you can.

PHAEDO: I had a singular feeling at being in his company. For I could hardly believe that I was present at the death of a friend, and therefore I did not pity him, Echecrates; he died so fearlessly, and his words and bearing were so noble and gracious, that to me he appeared blessed. I thought that in going to the other world he could not be without a divine call, and that he would be happy, if any man ever was, when he arrived there, and therefore I did not pity him as might have seemed natural at such an hour. But I had not the pleasure which I usually feel in philosophical discourse (for philosophy was the theme of which we spoke). I was pleased, but in the pleasure there was also a strange admixture of pain; for I reflected that he was soon to die, and this double feeling was shared by us all; we were laughing and weeping by turns, especially the excitable Apollodorus—you know the sort of man?

ECHECRATES: Yes.

PHAEDO: He was quite beside himself; and I and all of us were greatly moved.

ECHECRATES: Who were present?

PHAEDO: Of native Athenians there were, besides Apollodorus, Critobulus and his father Crito, Hermogenes, Epigenes, Aeschines, Antisthenes; likewise Ctesippus of the deme of Paeania, Menexenus, and some others; Plato, if I am not mistaken, was ill.

ECHECRATES: Were there any strangers?

PHAEDO: Yes, there were; Simmias the Theban, and Cebes, and Phaedondes; Euclid and Terpison, who came from Megara.

ECHECRATES: And was Aristippus there, and Cleombrotus?

PHAEDO: No, they were said to be in Aegina.

ECHECRATES: Any one else?

PHAEDO: I think that these were nearly all.

ECHECRATES: Well, and what did you talk about?

PHAEDO: I will begin at the beginning, and endeavor to repeat the entire conversation. On the previous days we had been in the habit of assembling early in the morning at the court in which the trial took place, and which is not far from the prison. There we used to wait talking with one another until the opening of the doors (for they were not opened very early); then we went in and generally passed the day with Socrates. On the last morning we assembled sooner than usual, having heard on the day before when we quitted the prison in the evening that the sacred ship had come from Delos, and so we arranged to meet very early at the accustomed place. On our arrival the jailer who answered the door, instead of admitting us, came out and told us to stay until he called us. "For the Eleven," he said, "are now with Socrates; they are taking off his chains, and giving orders that he is to die today." He soon returned and said that we might come in. On entering we found Socrates just released from chains, and Xanthippe, whom you know, sitting by him, and holding his child in her arms. When she saw us she uttered a cry and said, as women will: "O Socrates, this is the last time that either you will converse with your friends, or they with you." Socrates turned to Crito and said: "Crito, let someone take her home." Some of Crito's people accordingly led her away, crying out and beating herself. And when she was gone, Socrates, sitting up on the couch, bent and rubbed his leg, saying, as he was rubbing: How singular is the thing called pleasure, and how curiously related to pain, which might be thought to be the opposite of it; for they are never present to a man at the same instant, and yet he who pursues either is generally compelled to take the other; their bodies are two, but they are joined by a single head. And I cannot help thinking that if Aesop had remembered them, he would have made a fable about God trying to reconcile their strife, and how, when he could not, he fastened their heads together; and this is the reason why when one comes the other follows, as I know by my own experience now, when after the pain in my leg which was caused by the chain pleasure appears to succeed.

Upon this Cebes said: I am glad, Socrates, that you have mentioned the name of Aesop. For it reminds me of a question which has been asked by many, and was asked of me only the day before yesterday by Evenus the poet—he will be sure to ask it again, and therefore if you would like me to have an answer ready for him, you may as well tell me what I should say to him:—he wanted to know why you, who never before wrote a line of poetry, now that you are in prison are turning Aesop's fables into verse, and also composing that hymn in honor of Apollo.

Tell him, Cebes, he replied, what is the truth—that I had no idea of rivalling him or his poems; to do so, as I knew, would be no easy task. But I wanted to see whether I could purge away a scruple which I felt about the meaning of certain dreams. In the course of my life I have often had intimations in dreams "that I should compose music." The same dream came to me sometimes in one form, and sometimes in another, but always saying the same or nearly the same words: "Cultivate and make music," said the dream. And hitherto I had imagined that this was only intended to exhort and encourage me in the study of philosophy, which has been the pursuit of my life, and is the noblest and best of music. The dream was bidding me do what I was already doing, in the same way that the competitor in a race is bidden by the spectators to run when he is already running. But I was not certain of this, for the dream might have meant music in the popular sense of the word, and being under sentence of death, and the festival giving me a respite, I thought that it would be safer for me to satisfy the scruple, and, in obedience to the dream, to compose a few verses before I departed. And first I made a hymn in honor of the god of the festival, and then considering that a poet, if he is really to be a poet, should not only put together words, but should invent stories, and that I have no invention, I took some fables of Aesop, which I had ready at hand and which I knew—they were the first I came upon—and turned them into verse. Tell this to Evenus, Cebes, and bid him be of good cheer; say that I would have him come after me if he be a wise man, and not tarry; and that today I am likely to be going, for the Athenians say that I must.

Simmias said: What a message for such a man! having been a frequent companion of his I should say that, as far as I know him, he will never take your advice unless he is obliged.

Why, said Socrates,—is not Evenus a philosopher?

I think that he is, said Simmias.

Then he, or any man who has the spirit of philosophy, will be willing to die, but he will not take his own life, for that is held to be unlawful.

Here he changed his position, and put his legs off the couch on to the ground, and during the rest of the conversation he remained sitting.

Why do you say, inquired Cebes, that a man ought not to take his own life, but that the philosopher will be ready to follow the dying?

Socrates replied: And have you, Cebes and Simmias, who are the disciples of Philolaus, never heard him speak of this?

Yes, but his language was obscure, Socrates.

My words, too, are only an echo; but there is no reason why I should not repeat what I have heard: and indeed, as I am going to another place, it is very meet for me to be thinking and talking of the nature of the pilgrimage which I am about to make. What can I do better in the interval between this and the setting of the sun?

Then tell me, Socrates, why is suicide held to be unlawful? as I have certainly heard Philolaus, about whom you were just now asking, affirm when he was staying with us at Thebes: and there are others who say the same, although I have never understood what was meant by any of them.

Do not lose heart, replied Socrates, and the day may come when you will understand. I suppose that you wonder why, when other things which are evil may be good at certain times and to certain persons, death is to be the only exception, and why, when a man is better dead, he is not permitted to be his own benefactor, but must wait for the hand of another.

Very true, said Cebes, laughing gently and speaking in his native Boeotian.

I admit the appearance of inconsistency in what I am saying; but there may not be any real inconsistency after all. There is a doctrine whispered in secret that man is a prisoner who has no right to open the door and run away; this is a great mystery which I do not quite understand. Yet I too believe that the gods are our guardians, and that we are a possession of theirs. Do you not agree?

Yes, I quite agree, said Cebes.

And if one of your own possessions, an ox or an ass, for example, took the liberty of putting himself out of the way when you had given no intimation of your wish that he should die, would you not be angry with him, and would you not punish him if you could?

Certainly, replied Cebes.

Then, if we look at the matter thus, there may be reason in saying that a man should wait, and not take his own life until God summons him, as he is now summoning me.

Yes, Socrates, said Cebes, there seems to be truth in what you say. And yet how can you reconcile this seemingly true belief that God is our guardian and we his possessions, with the willingness to die which we were just now attributing to the philosopher? That the wisest of men should be willing to leave a service in which they are ruled by the gods who are the best of rulers, is not reasonable; for surely no wise man thinks that when set at liberty he can take better care of himself than the gods take of him. A fool may perhaps think so—he may argue that he had better run away from his master, not considering that his duty is to remain to the end, and not to run away from the good, and that there would be no sense in his running away. The wise man will want to be ever with him who is better than himself. Now this, Socrates, is the reverse of what was just now said; for upon this view the wise man should sorrow and the fool rejoice at passing out of life.

The earnestness of Cebes seemed to please Socrates. Here, said he, turning to us, is a man who is always inquiring, and is not so easily convinced by the first thing which he hears.

And certainly, added Simmias, the objection which he is now making does appear to me to have some force. For what can be the meaning of a truly wise man wanting to fly away and lightly leave a master who is better than himself? And I rather imagine that Cebes is referring to you; he thinks that you are too ready to leave us, and too ready to leave the gods whom you acknowledge to be our good masters.

Yes, replied Socrates; there is reason in what you say. And so you think that I ought to answer your indictment as if I were in a court?

We should like you to do so, said Simmias.

Then I must try to make a more successful defense before you than I did when before the judges. For I am quite ready to admit, Simmias and Cebes, that I ought to be grieved at death, if I were not persuaded in the first place that I am going to other gods who are wise and good (of which I am as certain as I can be of any such matters), and secondly (though I am not so sure of this last) to men departed, better than those whom I leave behind; and therefore I do not grieve as I might have done, for I have good hope that there is yet something remaining for the dead, and as has been said of old, some far better thing for the good than for the evil.

But do you mean to take away your thoughts with you, Socrates? said Simmias. Will you not impart them to us?—for they are a benefit in which we too are entitled to share. Moreover, if you succeed in convincing us, that will be an answer to the charge against yourself.

I will do my best, replied Socrates. But you must first let me hear what Crito wants; he has long been wishing to say something to me.

Only this, Socrates, replied Crito:—the attendant who is to give you the poison has been telling me, and he wants me to tell you, that you are not to talk much, talking, he says, increases heat, and this is apt to interfere with the action of the poison; persons who excite themselves are sometimes obliged to take a second or even a third dose.

Then, said Socrates, let him mind his business and be prepared to give the poison twice or even thrice if necessary; that is all.

I knew quite well what you would say, replied Crito; but I was obliged to satisfy him.

Never mind him, he said.

And now, O my judges, I desire to prove to you that the real philosopher has reason to be of good cheer when he is about to die, and that after death he may hope to obtain the greatest good in the other world. And how this may be, Simmias and Cebes, I will endeavor to explain. For I deem that the true votary of philosophy is likely to be misunderstood by other men; they do not perceive that he is always pursuing death and dying; and if this be so, and he has had the desire of death all his life long, why when his time comes should he repine at that which he has been always pursuing and desiring?

Simmias said laughingly: Though not in a laughing humor, you have made me laugh, Socrates; for I cannot help thinking that the many when they hear your words will say how truly you have described philosophers, and our people at home will likewise say that the life which philosophers desire is in reality death, and that they have found them out to be deserving of the death which they desire.

And they are right, Simmias, in thinking so, with the exception of the words "they have found them out"; for they have not found out either what is the nature of that death which the true philosopher deserves, or how he deserves or desires death. But enough of them:—let us discuss the matter among ourselves: Do we believe that there is such a thing as death?

To be sure, replied Simmias.

Is it not the separation of soul and body? And to be dead is the completion of this; when the soul exists in herself, and is released from the body and the body is released from the soul, what is this but death?

Just so, he replied.

There is another question, which will probably throw light on our present inquiry if you and I can agree about it:—Ought the philosopher to care about the pleasures—if they are to be called pleasures—of eating and drinking?

Certainly not, answered Simmias.

And what about the pleasures of love—should he care for them?

By no means.

And will he think much of the other ways of indulging the body, for example, the acquisition of costly raiment, or sandals, or other adornments of the body? Instead of caring about them, does he not rather despise anything more than nature needs? What do you say?

I should say that the true philosopher would despise them.

Would you not say that he is entirely concerned with the soul and not with the body? He would like, as far as he can, to get away from the body and to turn to the soul.

Quite true.

In matters of this sort philosophers, above all other men, may be observed in every sort of way to dissever the soul from the communion of the body.

Very true.

Whereas, Simmias, the rest of the world are of opinion that to him who has no sense of pleasure and no part in bodily pleasure, life is not worth having; and that he who is indifferent about them is as good as dead.

That is also true.

What again shall we say of the actual acquirement of knowledge?—is the body, if invited to share in the inquiry, a hinderer or a helper? I mean to say, have sight and hearing any truth in them? Are they not, as the poets are always telling us, inaccurate witnesses? and yet, if even they are inaccurate and indistinct, what is to be said of the other senses?—for you will allow that they are the best of them?

Certainly, he replied.

Then when does the soul attain truth?—for in attempting to consider anything in company with the body she is obviously deceived.

True.

Then must not true existence be revealed to her in thought, if at all?

Yes.

And thought is best when the mind is gathered into herself and none of these things trouble her—neither sounds nor sights nor pain nor any pleasure,—when she takes leave of the body, and has as little as possible to do with it, when she has no bodily sense or desire, but is aspiring after true being?

Certainly.

And in this the philosopher dishonors the body; his soul runs away from his body and desires to be alone and by herself?

That is true.

Well, but there is another thing, Simmias: Is there or is there not an absolute justice?

Assuredly there is.

And an absolute beauty and absolute good?

Of course.

But did you ever behold any of them with your eyes?

Certainly not.

Or did you ever reach them with any other bodily sense?—and I speak not of these alone, but of absolute greatness, and health, and strength, and of the essence or true nature of everything. Has the reality of them ever been perceived by you through the bodily organs? or rather, is not the nearest approach to the knowledge of their several natures made by him who so orders his intellectual vision as to have the most exact conception of the essence of each thing which he considers?

Certainly.

And he attains to the purest knowledge of them who goes to each with the mind alone, not introducing or intruding in the act of thought sight or any other sense together with reason, but with the very light of the mind in her own clearness searches into the very truth of each; he who has got rid, as far as he can, of eyes and ears and, so to speak, of the whole body, these being in his opinion distracting elements which when they infect the soul hinder her from acquiring truth and knowledge—who, if not he, is likely to attain the knowledge of true being?

What you say has a wonderful truth in it, Socrates, replied Simmias.

And when real philosophers consider all these things, will they not be led to make a reflection which they will express in words something like the following? "Have we not found," they will say, "a path of thought which seems to bring us and our argument to the conclusion, that while we are in the body, and while the soul is infected with the evils of the body, our desire will not be satisfied? and our desire is of the truth. For the body is a source of endless trouble to us by reason of the mere requirement of food; and is liable also to diseases which overtake and impede us in the search after true being: it fills us full of loves, and lusts, and fears, and fancies of all kinds, and endless foolery, and in fact, as men say, takes away from us the power of thinking at all. Whence come wars, and fightings, and factions? whence but from the body and the lusts of the body? Wars are occasioned by the love of money, and money has to be acquired for the sake and in the service of the body; and by reason of all these impediments we have no time to give to philosophy; and, last and worst of all, even if we are at leisure and betake ourselves to some speculation, the body is always breaking in upon us, causing turmoil and confusion in our enquiries, and so amazing us that we are prevented from seeing the truth. It has been proved to us by experience that if we would have pure knowledge of anything we must be quit of the body—the soul in herself must behold things in themselves: and then we shall attain the wisdom which we desire, and of which we say that we are lovers, not while we live, but after death; for if while in company with the body, the soul cannot have pure knowledge, one of two things follows—either knowledge is not to be attained at all, or, if at all, after death. For then, and not till then, the soul will be parted from the body and exist in herself alone. In this present life, I reckon that we make the nearest approach to knowledge when we have the least possible intercourse or communion with the body, and are not surfeited with the bodily nature, but keep ourselves pure until the hour when God himself is pleased to release us. And thus having got rid of the foolishness of the body we shall be pure and hold converse with the pure, and know of ourselves the clear light everywhere, which is no other than the light of truth." For the impure are not permitted to approach the pure. These are the sort of words, Simmias, which the true lovers of knowledge cannot help saying to one another, and thinking. You would agree; would you not?

Undoubtedly, Socrates.

But, O my friend, if this is true, there is great reason to hope that, going whither I go, when I have come to the end of my journey, I shall attain that which has been the pursuit of my life. And therefore I go on my way rejoicing, and not I only, but every other man who believes that his mind has been made ready and that he is in a manner purified.

Certainly, replied Simmias.

And what is purification but the separation of the soul from the body, as I was saying before; the habit of the soul gathering and collecting herself into herself from all sides out of the body; the dwelling in her own place alone, as in another life, so also in this, as far as she can;—the release of the soul from the chains of the body?

Very true, he said.

And this separation and release of the soul from the body is termed death?

To be sure, he said.

And the true philosophers, and they only, are ever seeking to release the soul. Is not the separation and release of the soul from the body their especial study?

That is true.

And, as I was saying at first, there would be a ridiculous contradiction in men studying to live as nearly as they can in a state of death, and yet repining when it comes upon them.

Clearly.

And the true philosophers, Simmias, are always occupied in the practice of dying, wherefore also to them least of all men is death terrible. Look at the matter thus:—if they have been in every way the enemies of the body, and are wanting to be alone with the soul, when this desire of theirs is granted, how inconsistent would they be if they trembled and repined, instead of rejoicing at their departure to that place where, when they arrive, they hope to gain that which in life they desired—and this was wisdom—and at the same time to be rid of the company of their enemy. Many a man has been willing to go to the world below animated by the hope of seeing there an earthly love, or wife, or son, and conversing with them. And will he who is a true lover of wisdom, and is strongly persuaded in like manner that only in the world below he can worthily enjoy her, still repine at death? Will he not depart with joy? Surely he will, O my friend, if he be a true philosopher. For he will have a firm conviction that there and there only, he can find wisdom in her purity. And if this be true, he would be very absurd, as I was saying, if he were afraid of death.

He would, indeed, replied Simmias.

And when you see a man who is repining at the approach of death, is not his reluctance a sufficient proof that he is not a lover of wisdom, but a lover of the body, and probably at the same time a lover of either money or power, or both?

Quite so, he replied.

And is not courage, Simmias, a quality which is specially characteristic of the philosopher?

Certainly.

There is temperance again, which even by the vulgar is supposed to consist in the control and regulation of the passions, and in the sense of superiority to them—is not temperance a virtue belonging to those only who despise the body, and who pass their lives in philosophy?

Most assuredly.

For the courage and temperance of other men, if you will consider them, are really a contradiction.

How so?

Well, he said, you are aware that death is regarded by men in general as a great evil.

Very true, he said.

And do not courageous men face death because they are afraid of yet greater evils?

That is quite true.

Then all but the philosophers are courageous only from fear, and because they are afraid; and yet that a man should be courageous from fear, and because he is a coward, is surely a strange thing.

Very true.

And are not the temperate exactly in the same case? They are temperate because they are intemperate—which might seem to be a contradiction, but is nevertheless the sort of thing which happens with this foolish temperance. For there are pleasures which they are afraid of losing; and in their desire to keep them, they abstain from some pleasures, because they are overcome by others; and although to be conquered by pleasure is called by men intemperance, to them the conquest of pleasure consists in being conquered by pleasure. And that is what I mean by saying that, in a sense, they are made temperate through intemperance.

Such appears to be the case.

Yet the exchange of one fear or pleasure or pain for another fear or pleasure or pain, and of the greater for the less, as if they were coins, is not the exchange of virtue. O my blessed Simmias, is there not one true coin for which all things ought to be exchanged?—and that is wisdom; and only in exchange for this, and in company with this, is anything truly bought or sold, whether courage or temperance or justice. And is not all true virtue the companion of wisdom, no matter what fears or pleasures or other similar goods or evils may or may not attend her? But the virtue which is made up of these goods, when they are severed from wisdom and exchanged with one another, is a shadow of virtue only, nor is there any freedom or health or truth in her; but in the true exchange there is a purging away of all these things, and temperance, and justice, and courage, and wisdom herself are the purgation of them. The founders of the mysteries would appear to have had a real meaning, and were not talking nonsense when they intimated in a figure long ago that he who passes unsanctified and uninitiated into the world below will lie in a slough, but that he who arrives there after initiation and purification will dwell with the gods. For "many," as they say in the mysteries, "are the thyrsus-bearers, but few are the mystics,"—meaning, as I interpret the words, "the true philosophers." In the number of whom, during my whole life, I have been seeking, according to my ability, to find a place;—whether I have sought in a right way or not, and whether I have succeeded or not, I shall truly know in a little while, if God will, when I myself arrive in the other world—such is my belief. And therefore I maintain that I am right, Simmias and Cebes, in not grieving or repining at parting from you and my masters in this world, for I believe that

I shall equally find good masters and friends in another world. But most men do not believe this saying; if then I succeed in convincing you by my defense better than I did the Athenian judges, it will be well.

Cebes answered: I agree, Socrates, in the greater part of what you say. But in what concerns the soul, men are apt to be incredulous; they fear that when she has left the body her place may be nowhere, and that on the very day of death she may perish and come to an end—immediately on her release from the body, issuing forth dispersed like smoke or air and in her flight vanishing away into nothingness. If she could only be collected into herself after she has obtained release from the evils of which you are speaking, there would be good reason to hope, Socrates, that what you say is true. But surely it requires a great deal of argument and many proofs to show that when the man is dead his soul yet exists, and has any force or intelligence.

True, Cebes, said Socrates; and shall I suggest that we converse a little of the probabilities of these things?

I am sure, said Cebes, that I should greatly like to know your opinion about them.

I reckon, said Socrates, that no one who heard me now, not even if he were one of my old enemies, the Comic poets, could accuse me of idle talking about matters in which I have no concern:—If you please, then, we will proceed with the inquiry.

Suppose we consider the question whether the souls of men after death are or are not in the world below. There comes into my mind an ancient doctrine which affirms that they go from hence into the other world, and returning hither, are born again from the dead. Now if it be true that the living come from the dead, then our souls must exist in the other world, for if not, how could they have been born again? And this would be conclusive, if there were any real evidence that the living are only born from the dead; but if this is not so, then other arguments will have to be adduced.

Very true, replied Cebes.

Then let us consider the whole question, not in relation to man only, but in relation to animals generally, and to plants, and to everything of which there is generation, and the proof will be easier. Are not all things which have opposites generated out of their opposites? I mean such things as good and evil, just and unjust—and there are innumerable other opposites which are generated out of opposites. And I want to show that in all opposites there is of necessity a similar alternation; I mean to say, for example, that anything which becomes greater must become greater after being less.

True.

And that which becomes less must have been once greater and then have become less.

Yes.

And the weaker is generated from the stronger, and the swifter from the slower.

Very true.

And the worse is from the better, and the more just is from the more unjust.

Of course.

And is this true of all opposites? and are we convinced that all of them are generated out of opposites?

Yes.

And in this universal opposition of all things, are there not also two intermediate processes which are ever going on, from one to the other opposite, and back again; where there is a greater and a less there is also an intermediate process of increase and diminution, and that which grows is said to wax, and that which decays to wane?

Yes, he said.

And there are many other processes, such as division and composition, cooling and heating, which equally involve a passage into and out of one another. And this necessarily holds of all opposites, even though not always expressed in words—they are really generated out of one another, and there is a passing or process from one to the other of them?

Very true, he replied.

Well, and is there not an opposite of life, as sleep is the opposite of waking?

True, he said.

And what is it?

Death, he answered.

And these, if they are opposites, are generated the one from the other, and have there their two intermediate processes also?

Of course.

Now, said Socrates, I will analyze one of the two pairs of opposites which I have mentioned to you, and also its intermediate processes, and you shall analyze the other to me. One of them I term sleep, the other waking. The state of sleep is opposed to the state of waking, and out of sleeping waking is generated, and out of waking, sleeping; and the process of generation is in the one case falling asleep, and in the other waking up. Do you agree?

I entirely agree.

Then, suppose that you analyze life and death to me in the same manner. Is not death opposed to life?

Yes.

And they are generated one from the other?

Yes.

What is generated from the living?

The dead.

And what from the dead?

I can only say in answer—the living.

Then the living, whether things or persons, Cebes, are generated from the dead?

That is clear, he replied.

Then the inference is that our souls exist in the world below?

That is true.

And one of the two processes or generations is visible—for surely the act of dying is visible?

Surely, he said.

What then is to be the result? Shall we exclude the opposite process? And shall we suppose nature to walk on one leg only? Must we not rather assign to death some corresponding process of generation?

Certainly, he replied.

And what is that process?

Return to life.

And return to life, if there be such a thing, is the birth of the dead into the world of the living?

Quite true.

Then here is a new way by which we arrive at the conclusion that the living come from the dead, just as the dead come from the living; and this, if true, affords a most certain proof that the souls of the dead exist in some place out of which they come again.

Yes, Socrates, he said; the conclusion seems to flow necessarily out of our previous admissions.

And that these admissions were not unfair, Cebes, he said, may be shown, I think, as follows: If generation were in a straight line only, and there were no compensation or circle in nature, no turn or return of elements into their opposites, then you know that all things would at last have the same form and pass into the same state, and there would be no more generation of them.

What do you mean? he said.

A simple thing enough, which I will illustrate by the case of sleep, he replied. You know that if there were no alternation of sleeping and waking, the tale of the sleeping Endymion would in the end have no meaning, because all other things would be asleep, too, and he would not be distinguishable from the rest. Or if there were composition only, and no division of substances, then the chaos of Anaxagoras would come again. And in like manner, my dear Cebes, if all things which partook of life were to die, and after they were dead remained in the form of death, and did not come to life again, all would at last die, and nothing would be alive—what other result could there be? For if the living spring from any other things, and they too die, must not all things at last be swallowed up in death? (But compare Republic.)

There is no escape, Socrates, said Cebes; and to me your argument seems to be absolutely true.

Yes, he said, Cebes, it is and must be so, in my opinion; and we have not been deluded in making these admissions; but I am confident that there truly is such a thing as living again, and that the living spring from the dead, and that the souls of the dead are in existence, and that the good souls have a better portion than the evil.

Cebes added: Your favorite doctrine, Socrates, that knowledge is simply recollection, if true, also necessarily implies a previous time in which we have learned that which we now recollect. But this would be impossible unless our soul had been in some place before existing in the form of man; here then is another proof of the soul's immortality.

But tell me, Cebes, said Simmias, interposing, what arguments are urged in favor of this doctrine of recollection. I am not very sure at the moment that I remember them.

One excellent proof, said Cebes, is afforded by questions. If you put a question to a person in a right way, he will give a true answer of himself, but how could he do this unless there were knowledge and right reason already in him? And this is most clearly shown when he is taken to a diagram or to anything of that sort. (Compare Meno.)

But if, said Socrates, you are still incredulous, Simmias, I would ask you whether you may not agree with me when you look at the matter in another way;—I mean, if you are still incredulous as to whether knowledge is recollection.

Incredulous, I am not, said Simmias; but I want to have this doctrine of recollection brought to my own recollection, and, from what Cebes has said, I am beginning to recollect and be convinced; but I should still like to hear what you were going to say.

This is what I would say, he replied:—We should agree, if I am not mistaken, that what a man recollects he must have known at some previous time.

Very true.

And what is the nature of this knowledge or recollection? I mean to ask, Whether a person who, having seen or heard or in any way perceived anything, knows not only that, but has a conception of something else which is the subject, not of the same but of some other kind of knowledge, may not be fairly said to recollect that of which he has the conception?

What do you mean?

I mean what I may illustrate by the following instance:—The knowledge of a lyre is not the same as the knowledge of a man?

True.

And yet what is the feeling of lovers when they recognize a lyre, or a garment, or anything else which the beloved has been in the habit of using? Do not they, from knowing the lyre, form in the mind's eye an image of the youth to whom the lyre belongs? And this is recollection. In like manner anyone who sees Simmias may remember Cebes; and there are endless examples of the same thing.

Endless, indeed, replied Simmias.

And recollection is most commonly a process of recovering that which has been already forgotten through time and inattention.

Very true, he said.

Well; and may you not also from seeing the picture of a horse or a lyre remember a man? and from the picture of Simmias, you may be led to remember Cebes?

True.

Or you may also be led to the recollection of Simmias himself?

Quite so.

And in all these cases, the recollection may be derived from things either like or unlike?

It may be.

And when the recollection is derived from like things, then another consideration is sure to arise, which is—whether the likeness in any degree falls short or not of that which is recollected?

Very true, he said.

And shall we proceed a step further, and affirm that there is such a thing as equality, not of one piece of wood or stone with another, but that, over and above this, there is absolute equality? Shall we say so?

Say so, yes, replied Simmias, and swear to it, with all the confidence in life.

And do we know the nature of this absolute essence?

To be sure, he said.

And whence did we obtain our knowledge? Did we not see equalities of material things, such as pieces of wood and stones, and gather from them the idea of an equality which is different from them? For you will acknowledge that there is a difference. Or look at the matter in another way:—Do not the same pieces of wood or stone appear at one time equal, and at another time unequal?

That is certain.

But are real equals ever unequal? or is the idea of equality the same as of inequality?

Impossible, Socrates.

Then these (so-called) equals are not the same with the idea of equality?

I should say, clearly not, Socrates.

And yet from these equals, although differing from the idea of equality, you conceived and attained that idea?

Very true, he said.

Which might be like, or might be unlike them?

Yes.

But that makes no difference; whenever from seeing one thing you conceived another, whether like or unlike, there must surely have been an act of recollection?

Very true.

But what would you say of equal portions of wood and stone, or other material equals? and what is the impression produced by them? Are they equals in the same sense in which absolute equality is equal? or do they fall short of this perfect equality in a measure?

Yes, he said, in a very great measure too.

And must we not allow, that when I or anyone, looking at any object, observes that the thing which he sees aims at being some other thing, but falls short of, and cannot be, that other thing, but is inferior, he who makes this observation must have had a previous knowledge of that to which the other, although similar, was inferior?

Certainly.

And has not this been our own case in the matter of equals and of absolute equality?

Precisely.

Then we must have known equality previously to the time when we first saw the material equals, and reflected that all these apparent equals strive to attain absolute equality, but fall short of it?

Very true.

And we recognize also that this absolute equality has only been known, and can only be known, through the medium of sight or touch, or of some other of the senses, which are all alike in this respect?

Yes, Socrates, as far as the argument is concerned, one of them is the same as the other.

From the senses then is derived the knowledge that all sensible things aim at an absolute equality of which they fall short?

Yes.

Then before we began to see or hear or perceive in any way, we must have had a knowledge of absolute equality, or we could not have referred to that standard the equals which are derived from the senses?—for to that they all aspire, and of that they fall short.

No other inference can be drawn from the previous statements.

And did we not see and hear and have the use of our other senses as soon as we were born?

Certainly.

Then we must have acquired the knowledge of equality at some previous time?

Yes.

That is to say, before we were born, I suppose?

True.

And if we acquired this knowledge before we were born, and were born having the use of it, then we also knew before we were born and at the instant of birth not only the equal or the greater or the less, but all other ideas; for we are not speaking only of equality, but of beauty, goodness, justice, holiness, and of all which we stamp with the name of essence in the dialectical process, both when we ask and when we answer questions. Of all this we may certainly affirm that we acquired the knowledge before birth?

We may.

But if, after having acquired, we have not forgotten what in each case we acquired, then we must always have come into life having knowledge, and shall always continue to know as long as life lasts—for knowing is the acquiring and retaining knowledge and not forgetting. Is not forgetting, Simmias, just the losing of knowledge?

Quite true, Socrates.

But if the knowledge which we acquired before birth was lost by us at birth, and if afterward by the use of the senses we recovered what we previously knew, will not the process which we call learning be a recovering of the knowledge which is natural to us, and may not this be rightly termed recollection?

Very true.

So much is clear—that when we perceive something, either by the help of sight, or hearing, or some other sense, from that perception we are able to obtain a notion of some other thing like or unlike which is associated with it but has been forgotten. Whence, as I was saying, one of two alternatives follows:—either we had this knowledge at birth, and continued to know through life; or, after birth, those who are said to learn only remember, and learning is simply recollection.

Yes, that is quite true, Socrates.

And which alternative, Simmias, do you prefer? Had we the knowledge at our birth, or did we recollect the things which we knew previously to our birth?

I cannot decide at the moment.

At any rate you can decide whether he who has knowledge will or will not be able to render an account of his knowledge? What do you say?

Certainly, he will.

But do you think that every man is able to give an account of these very matters about which we are speaking?

Would that they could, Socrates, but I rather fear that tomorrow, at this time, there will no longer be anyone alive who is able to give an account of them such as ought to be given.

Then you are not of opinion, Simmias, that all men know these things?

Certainly not.

They are in process of recollecting that which they learned before?

Certainly.

But when did our souls acquire this knowledge?—not since we were born as men?

Certainly not.

And therefore, previously?

Yes.

Then, Simmias, our souls must also have existed without bodies before they were in the form of man, and must have had intelligence.

Unless indeed you suppose, Socrates, that these notions are given us at the very moment of birth; for this is the only time which remains.

Yes, my friend, but if so, when do we lose them? for they are not in us when we are born—that is admitted. Do we lose them at the moment of receiving them, or if not at what other time?

No, Socrates, I perceive that I was unconsciously talking nonsense.

Then may we not say, Simmias, that if, as we are always repeating, there is an absolute beauty, and goodness, and an absolute essence of all things; and if to this, which is now discovered to have existed in our former state, we refer all our sensations, and with this compare them, finding these ideas to be pre-existent and our inborn possession—then our souls must have had a prior existence, but if not, there would be no force in the argument? There is the same proof that these ideas must have existed before we were born, as that our souls existed before we were born; and if not the ideas, then not the souls.

Yes, Socrates; I am convinced that there is precisely the same necessity for the one as for the other; and the argument retreats successfully to the position that the existence of the soul before birth cannot be separated from the existence of the essence of which you speak. For there is nothing which to my mind is so patent as that beauty, goodness, and the other notions of which you were just now speaking, have a most real and absolute existence; and I am satisfied with the proof.

Well, but is Cebes equally satisfied? for I must convince him too.

I think, said Simmias, that Cebes is satisfied: although he is the most incredulous of mortals, yet I believe that he is sufficiently convinced of the existence of the soul before birth. But that after death the soul will continue to exist is not yet proven even to my own satisfaction. I cannot get rid of the feeling of the many to which Cebes was referring—the feeling that when the man dies the soul will be dispersed, and that this may be the extinction of her. For admitting that she may have been born elsewhere, and framed out of other elements, and was in existence before entering the human body, why after having entered in and gone out again may she not herself be destroyed and come to an end?

Very true, Simmias, said Cebes; about half of what was required has been proven; to wit, that our souls existed before we were born:—that the soul will exist after death as well as before birth is the other half of which the proof is still wanting, and has to be supplied; when that is given the demonstration will be complete.

But that proof, Simmias and Cebes, has been already given, said Socrates, if you put the two arguments together—I mean this and the former one, in which we admitted that everything living is born of the dead. For if the soul exists before birth, and in coming to life and being born can be born only from death and dying, must she not after death continue to exist, since she has to be born again?—Surely the proof which you desire has been already furnished. Still I suspect that you and Simmias would be glad to probe the argument further. Like children, you are haunted with a fear that when the soul leaves the body, the wind may really blow her away and scatter her; especially if a man should happen to die in a great storm and not when the sky is calm.

Cebes answered with a smile: Then, Socrates, you must argue us out of our fears—and yet, strictly speaking, they are not our fears, but there is a child within us to whom death is a sort of hobgoblin; him too we must persuade not to be afraid when he is alone in the dark.

Socrates said: Let the voice of the charmer be applied daily until you have charmed away the fear.

And where shall we find a good charmer of our fears, Socrates, when you are gone?

Hellas, he replied, is a large place, Cebes, and has many good men, and there are barbarous races not a few: seek for him among them all, far and wide, sparing neither pains nor money; for there is no better way of spending your money. And you must seek among yourselves too; for you will not find others better able to make the search.

The search, replied Cebes, shall certainly be made. And now, if you please, let us return to the point of the argument at which we digressed.

By all means, replied Socrates; what else should I please?

Very good.

Must we not, said Socrates, ask ourselves what that is which, as we imagine, is liable to be scattered, and about which we fear? and what again is that about which we have no fear? And then we may proceed further to inquire whether that which suffers dispersion is or is not of the nature of soul—our hopes and fears as to our own souls will turn upon the answers to these questions.

Very true, he said.

Now the compound or composite may be supposed to be naturally capable, as of being compounded, so also of being dissolved; but that which is uncompounded, and that only, must be, if anything is, indissoluble.

Yes; I should imagine so, said Cebes.

And the uncompounded may be assumed to be the same and unchanging, whereas the compound is always changing and never the same.

I agree, he said.

Then now let us return to the previous discussion. Is that idea or essence, which in the dialectical process we define as essence or true existence—whether essence of equality, beauty, or anything else—are these essences, I say, liable at times to some degree of change? or are they each of them always what they are, having the same simple self-existent and unchanging forms, not admitting of variation at all, or in any way, or at any time?

They must be always the same, Socrates, replied Cebes.

And what would you say of the many beautiful—whether men or horses or garments or any other things which are named by the same names and may be called equal or beautiful,—are they all unchanging and the same always, or quite the reverse? May they not rather be described as almost always changing and hardly ever the same, either with themselves or with one another?

The latter, replied Cebes; they are always in a state of change.

And these you can touch and see and perceive with the senses, but the unchanging things you can only perceive with the mind—they are invisible and are not seen?

That is very true, he said.

Well, then, added Socrates, let us suppose that there are two sorts of existences—one seen, the other unseen.

Let us suppose them.

The seen is the changing, and the unseen is the unchanging?

That may be also supposed.

And, further, is not one part of us body, another part soul?

To be sure.

And to which class is the body more alike and akin?

Clearly to the seen—no one can doubt that.

And is the soul seen or not seen?

Not by man, Socrates.

And what we mean by "seen" and "not seen" is that which is or is not visible to the eye of man?

Yes, to the eye of man.

And is the soul seen or not seen?

Not seen.

Unseen then?

Yes.

Then the soul is more like to the unseen, and the body to the seen?

That follows necessarily, Socrates.

And were we not saying long ago that the soul when using the body as an instrument of perception, that is to say, when using the sense of sight or hearing or some other sense (for the meaning of perceiving through the body is perceiving through the senses)—were we not saying that the soul too is then dragged by the body into the region of the changeable, and wanders and is confused; the world spins round her, and she is like a drunkard, when she touches change?

Very true.

But when returning into herself she reflects, then she passes into the other world, the region of purity, and eternity, and immortality, and unchangeableness, which are her kindred, and with them she ever lives, when she is by herself and is not let or hindered; then she ceases from her erring ways, and being in communion with the unchanging is unchanging. And this state of the soul is called wisdom?

That is well and truly said, Socrates, he replied.

And to which class is the soul more nearly alike and akin, as far as may be inferred from this argument, as well as from the preceding one?

I think, Socrates, that, in the opinion of everyone who follows the argument, the soul will be infinitely more like the unchangeable—even the most stupid person will not deny that.

And the body is more like the changing?

Yes.

Yet once more consider the matter in another light: When the soul and the body are united, then nature orders the soul to rule and govern, and the body to obey and serve. Now which of these two functions is akin to the divine? and which to the mortal? Does not the divine appear to you to be that which naturally orders and rules, and the mortal to be that which is subject and servant?

True.

And which does the soul resemble?

The soul resembles the divine, and the body the mortal—there can be no doubt of that, Socrates.

Then reflect, Cebes: of all which has been said is not this the conclusion?—that the soul is in the very likeness of the divine, and immortal, and intellectual, and uniform, and indissoluble, and unchangeable; and that the body is in the very likeness of the human, and mortal, and unintellectual, and multiform, and dissoluble, and changeable. Can this, my dear Cebes, be denied?

It cannot.

But if it be true, then is not the body liable to speedy dissolution? and is not the soul almost or altogether indissoluble?

Certainly.

And do you further observe, that after a man is dead, the body, or visible part of him, which is lying in the visible world, and is called a corpse, and would naturally be dissolved and decomposed and dissipated, is not dissolved or decomposed at once, but may remain for a for some time, nay even for a long time, if the constitution be sound at the time of death, and the season of the year favorable? For the body when shrunk and embalmed, as the manner is in Egypt, may remain almost entire through infinite ages; and even in decay, there are still some portions, such as the bones and ligaments, which are practically indestructible:—Do you agree?

Yes.

And is it likely that the soul, which is invisible, in passing to the place of the true Hades, which like her is invisible, and pure, and noble, and on her way to the good and wise God, whither, if God will, my soul is also soon to go,—that the soul, I repeat, if this be her nature and origin, will be blown away and destroyed immediately on quitting the body, as the many say? That can never be, my dear Simmias and Cebes. The truth rather is, that the soul which is pure at departing and draws after her no bodily taint, having never voluntarily during life had connection with the body, which she is ever avoiding, herself gathered into herself;—and making such abstraction her perpetual study—which means that she has been a true disciple of philosophy; and therefore has in fact been always engaged in the practice of dying? For is not philosophy the practice of death?—

Certainly—

That soul, I say, herself invisible, departs to the invisible world—to the divine and immortal and rational: thither arriving, she is secure of bliss and is released from the error and folly of men, their fears and wild passions and all other human ills, and forever dwells, as they say of the initiated, in company with the gods (compare Apol.). Is not this true, Cebes?

Yes, said Cebes, beyond a doubt.

But the soul which has been polluted, and is impure at the time of her departure, and is the companion and servant of the body always, and is in love with and fascinated by the body and by the desires and pleasures of the body, until she is led to believe that the truth only exists in a bodily form, which a man may touch and see and taste, and use for the purposes of his lusts,—the soul, I mean, accustomed to hate and fear and avoid the intellectual principle, which to the bodily eye is dark and invisible, and can be attained only by philosophy;—do you suppose that such a soul will depart pure and unalloyed?

Impossible, he replied.

She is held fast by the corporeal, which the continual association and constant care of the body have wrought into her nature.

Very true.

And this corporeal element, my friend, is heavy and weighty and earthy, and is that element of sight by which a soul is depressed and dragged down again into the visible world, because she is afraid of the invisible and of the world below—prowling about tombs and sepulchres, near which, as they tell us, are seen certain ghostly apparitions of souls which have not departed pure, but are cloyed with sight and therefore visible.

(Compare Milton, Comus:—

> "But when lust,
> By unchaste looks, loose gestures, and foul talk,
> But most by lewd and lavish act of sin,
> Lets in defilement to the inward parts,
> The soul grows clotted by contagion,
> Imbodies, and imbrutes, till she quite lose,
> The divine property of her first being.
> Such are those thick and gloomy shadows damp
> Oft seen in charnel vaults and sepulchres,
> Lingering, and sitting by a new made grave,
> As loath to leave the body that it lov'd,
> And linked itself by carnal sensuality
> To a degenerate and degraded state.")

That is very likely, Socrates.

Yes, that is very likely, Cebes; and these must be the souls, not of the good, but of the evil, which are compelled to wander about such places in payment of the penalty of their former evil way of life; and they continue to wander until through the craving after the corporeal which never leaves them, they are imprisoned finally in another body. And they may be supposed to find their prisons in the same natures which they have had in their former lives.

What natures do you mean, Socrates?

What I mean is that men who have followed after gluttony, and wantonness, and drunkenness, and have had no thought of avoiding them, would pass into asses and animals of that sort. What do you think?

I think such an opinion to be exceedingly probable.

And those who have chosen the portion of injustice, and tyranny, and violence, will pass into wolves, or into hawks and kites;—whither else can we suppose them to go?

Yes, said Cebes; with such natures, beyond question.

And there is no difficulty, he said, in assigning to all of them places answering to their several natures and propensities?

There is not, he said.

Some are happier than others; and the happiest both in themselves and in the place to which they go are those who have practiced the civil and social virtues which are called temperance and justice, and are acquired by habit and attention without philosophy and mind. (Compare Republic.)

Why are they the happiest?

Because they may be expected to pass into some gentle and social kind which is like their own, such as bees or wasps or ants, or back again into the form of man, and just and moderate men may be supposed to spring from them.

Very likely.

No one who has not studied philosophy and who is not entirely pure at the time of his departure is allowed to enter the company of the Gods, but the lover of knowledge only. And this is the reason, Simmias and Cebes, why the true votaries of philosophy abstain from all fleshly lusts, and hold out against them and refuse to give themselves up to them,—not because they fear poverty or the ruin of their families, like the lovers of money, and the world in general; nor like the lovers of power and honor, because they dread the dishonor or disgrace of evil deeds.

No, Socrates, that would not become them, said Cebes.

No indeed, he replied; and therefore they who have any care of their own souls, and do not merely live moulding and fashioning the body, say farewell to all this; they will not walk in the ways of the blind: and when philosophy offers them purification and release from evil, they feel that they ought not to resist her influence, and whither she leads they turn and follow.

What do you mean, Socrates?

I will tell you, he said. The lovers of knowledge are conscious that the soul was simply fastened and glued to the body—until philosophy received her, she could only view real existence through the bars of a prison, not in and through herself; she was wallowing in the mire of every sort of ignorance; and by reason of lust had become the principal accomplice in her own captivity. This was her original state; and then, as I was saying, and as the lovers of knowledge are well aware, philosophy, seeing how terrible was her confinement, of which she was to herself the cause, received and gently comforted her and sought to release her, pointing out that the eye and the ear and the other senses are full of deception, and persuading her to retire from them, and abstain from all but the necessary use of them, and be gathered up and collected into herself, bidding her trust in herself and her own pure apprehension of pure existence, and to mistrust whatever comes to her through other channels and is subject to variation; for such things are visible and tangible, but what she sees in her own nature is intelligible and invisible. And the soul of the true philosopher thinks that she ought not to resist this deliverance, and therefore abstains from pleasures and desires and pains and fears, as far as she is able; reflecting that when a man has great joys or sorrows or fears or desires, he suffers from them, not merely the sort of evil which might be anticipated—as for example, the loss of his health or property which he has sacrificed to his lusts—but an evil greater far, which is the greatest and worst of all evils, and one of which he never thinks.

What is it, Socrates? said Cebes.

The evil is that when the feeling of pleasure or pain is most intense, every soul of man imagines the objects of this intense feeling to be then plainest and truest: but this is not so, they are really the things of sight.

Very true.

And is not this the state in which the soul is most enthralled by the body?

How so?

Why, because each pleasure and pain is a sort of nail which nails and rivets the soul to the body, until she becomes like the body, and believes that to be true which the body affirms to be true; and from agreeing with the body and having the same delights she is obliged to have the same habits and haunts, and is not likely ever to be pure at her departure to the world below, but is always infected by the body; and so she sinks into another body and there germinates and grows, and has therefore no part in the communion of the divine and pure and simple.

Most true, Socrates, answered Cebes.

And this, Cebes, is the reason why the true lovers of knowledge are temperate and brave; and not for the reason which the world gives.

Certainly not.

Certainly not! The soul of a philosopher will reason in quite another way; she will not ask philosophy to release her in order that when released she may deliver herself up again to the thraldom of pleasures and pains, doing a work only to be undone again, weaving instead of unweaving her Penelope's web. But she will calm passion, and follow reason, and dwell in the contemplation of her, beholding the true and divine (which is not matter of opinion), and thence deriving nourishment. Thus she seeks to live while she lives, and after death she hopes to go to her own kindred and to that which is like her, and to be freed from human ills. Never fear, Simmias and Cebes, that a soul which has been thus nurtured and has had these pursuits, will at her departure from the body be scattered and blown away by the winds and be nowhere and nothing.

When Socrates had done speaking, for a considerable time there was silence; he himself appeared to be meditating, as most of us were, on what had been said; only Cebes and Simmias spoke a few words to one another. And Socrates observing them asked what they thought of the argument, and whether there was anything wanting? For, said he, there are many points still open to suspicion and attack, if anyone were disposed to sift the matter thoroughly. Should you be considering some other matter I say no more, but if you are still in doubt do not hesitate to say exactly what you think, and let us have anything better which you can suggest; and if you think that I can be of any use, allow me to help you.

Simmias said: I must confess, Socrates, that doubts did arise in our minds, and each of us was urging and inciting the other to put the question which we wanted to have answered and which neither of us liked to ask, fearing that our importunity might be troublesome under present at such a time.

Socrates replied with a smile: O Simmias, what are you saying? I am not very likely to persuade other men that I do not regard my present situation as a misfortune, if I cannot even persuade you that I am no worse off now than at any other time in my life. Will you not allow that I have as much of the spirit of prophecy in me as the swans? For they, when they perceive that they must die, having sung all their life long, do then sing more lustily than ever, rejoicing in the thought that they are about to go away to the god whose ministers they are. But men, because they are themselves afraid of death, slanderously affirm of the swans that they sing a lament at the last, not considering that no bird sings when cold, or hungry, or in pain, not even the nightingale, nor the swallow, nor yet the hoopoe; which are said indeed to tune a lay of sorrow, although I do not believe this to be true of them any more than of the swans. But because they are sacred to Apollo, they have the gift of prophecy, and anticipate the good things of another world, wherefore they sing and rejoice in that day more than they ever did before. And I too, believing myself to be the consecrated servant of the same God, and the fellow servant of the swans, and thinking that I have received from my master gifts of prophecy which are not inferior to theirs, would not go out of life less merrily than the swans. Never mind then, if this be your only objection, but speak and ask anything which you like, while the eleven magistrates of Athens allow.

Very good, Socrates, said Simmias; then I will tell you my difficulty, and Cebes will tell you his. I feel myself, (and I daresay that you have the same feeling), how hard or rather impossible is the attainment of any certainty about questions such as these in the present life. And yet I should deem him a coward who did not prove what is said about them to the uttermost, or whose heart failed him before he had examined them on every side. For he should persevere until he has achieved one of two things: either he should discover, or be taught the truth about them; or, if this be impossible, I would have him take the best and most irrefragable of human theories, and let this be the raft upon which he sails through life—not without risk, as I admit, if he cannot find some word of God which will more surely and safely carry him. And now, as you bid me, I will venture to question you, and then I shall not have to reproach myself hereafter with not having said at the time what I think. For when I consider the matter, either alone or with Cebes, the argument does certainly appear to me, Socrates, to be not sufficient.

Socrates answered: I dare say, my friend, that you may be right, but I should like to know in what respect the argument is insufficient.

In this respect, replied Simmias:—Suppose a person to use the same argument about harmony and the lyre—might he not say that harmony is a thing invisible, incorporeal, perfect, divine, existing in the lyre which is harmonized, but that the lyre and the strings are matter and material, composite, earthy, and akin to mortality? And when someone breaks the lyre, or cuts and rends the strings, then he who takes this view would argue as you do, and on the same analogy, that the harmony survives and has not perished—you cannot imagine, he would say, that the lyre without the strings, and the broken strings themselves which are mortal remain, and yet that the harmony, which is of heavenly and immortal nature and kindred, has perished—perished before the mortal. The harmony must still be somewhere, and the wood and strings will decay before anything can happen to that. The thought, Socrates, must have occurred to your own mind that such is our conception of the soul; and that when the body is in a manner strung and held together by the elements of hot and cold, wet and dry, then the soul is the harmony or due proportionate admixture of them. But if so, whenever the strings of the body are unduly loosened or overstrained through disease or other injury, then the soul, though most divine, like other harmonies of music or of works of art, of course perishes at once, although the material remains of the body may last for a considerable time, until they are either decayed or burnt. And if anyone maintains that the soul, being the harmony of the elements of the body, is first to perish in that which is called death, how shall we answer him?

Socrates looked fixedly at us as his manner was, and said with a smile: Simmias has reason on his side; and why does not some one of you who is better able than myself answer him? for there is force in his attack upon me. But perhaps, before we answer him, we had better also hear what Cebes has to say that we may gain time for reflection, and when they have both spoken, we may either assent to them, if there is truth in what they say, or if not, we will maintain our position. Please to tell me then, Cebes, he said, what was the difficulty which troubled you?

Cebes said: I will tell you. My feeling is that the argument is where it was, and open to the same objections which were urged before; for I am ready to admit that the existence of the soul before entering into the bodily form has been very ingeniously, and, if I may say so, quite sufficiently proven; but the existence of the soul after death is still, in my judgment, unproven. Now my objection is not the same as that of Simmias; for I am not disposed to deny that the soul is stronger and more lasting than the body, being of opinion that in all such respects the soul very far excels the body. Well, then, says the argument to me, why do you remain unconvinced?—When you see that the weaker continues in existence after the man is dead, will you not admit that the more lasting must also survive during the same period of time? Now I will ask you to consider whether the objection, which, like Simmias, I will express in a figure, is of any weight. The analogy which I will adduce is that of an old weaver, who dies, and after his death somebody says:—He is not dead, he must be alive;—see, there is the coat which he himself wove and wore, and which remains whole and undecayed. And then he proceeds to ask of someone who is incredulous, whether a man lasts longer, or the coat which is in use and wear; and when he is answered that a man lasts far longer, thinks that he has thus certainly demonstrated the survival of the man, who is the more lasting, because the less lasting remains. But that, Simmias, as I would beg you to remark, is a mistake; anyone can see that he who talks thus is talking nonsense. For the truth is, that the weaver aforesaid, having woven and worn many such coats, outlived several of them, and was outlived by the last; but a man is not therefore proved to be slighter and weaker than a coat. Now the relation of the body to the soul may be expressed in a similar figure; and anyone may very fairly say in like manner that the soul is lasting, and the body weak and shortlived in comparison. He may argue in like manner that every soul wears out many bodies, especially if a man live many years. While he is alive the body deliquesces and decays, and the soul always weaves another garment and repairs the waste. But of course, whenever the soul perishes, she must have on her last garment, and this will survive her; and then at length, when the soul is dead, the body will show its native weakness, and quickly decompose and pass away. I would therefore rather not rely on the argument from superior strength to prove the continued existence of the soul after death. For granting even more than you affirm to be possible, and acknowledging not only that the soul existed before birth, but also that the souls of some exist, and will continue to exist after death, and will be born and die again and again, and that there is a natural strength in the soul which will hold out and be born many times—nevertheless, we may be still inclined to think that she will weary in the labors of successive births, and may at last succumb in one of her deaths and utterly perish; and this death and dissolution of the body which brings destruction to the soul may be unknown to any of us, for no one of us can have had any experience of it: and if so, then I maintain that he who is confident about death has but a foolish confidence, unless he is able to prove that the soul is altogether immortal and imperishable. But if he cannot prove the soul's immortality, he who is about to die will always have reason to fear that when the body is disunited, the soul also may utterly perish.

All of us, as we afterward remarked to one another, had an unpleasant feeling at hearing what they said. When we had been so firmly convinced before, now to have our faith shaken seemed to introduce a confusion and uncertainty, not only into the previous argument, but into any future one; either we were incapable of forming a judgment, or there were no grounds of belief.

ECHECRATES: There I feel with you—by heaven I do, Phaedo, and when you were speaking, I was beginning to ask myself the same question: What argument can I ever trust again? For what could be more convincing than the argument of Socrates, which has now fallen into discredit? That the soul is a harmony is a doctrine which has always had a wonderful attraction for me, and, when mentioned, came back to me at once, as my own original conviction. And now I must begin again and find another argument which will assure me that when the man is dead the soul survives. Tell me, I implore you, how did Socrates proceed? Did he appear to share the unpleasant feeling which you mention? or did he calmly meet the attack? And did he answer forcibly or feebly? Narrate what passed as exactly as you can.

PHAEDO: Often, Echecrates, I have wondered at Socrates, but never more than on that occasion. That he should be able to answer was nothing, but what astonished me was, first, the gentle and pleasant and approving manner in which he received the words of the young men, and then his quick sense of the wound which had been inflicted by the argument, and the readiness with which he healed it. He might be compared to a general rallying his defeated and broken army, urging them to accompany him and return to the field of argument.

ECHECRATES: What followed?

PHAEDO: You shall hear, for I was close to him on his right hand, seated on a sort of stool, and he on a couch which was a good deal higher. He stroked my head, and pressed the hair upon my neck—he had a way of playing with my hair; and then he said: Tomorrow, Phaedo, I suppose that these fair locks of yours will be severed.

Yes, Socrates, I suppose that they will, I replied.

Not so, if you will take my advice.

What shall I do with them? I said.

Today, he replied, and not tomorrow, if this argument dies and we cannot bring it to life again, you and I will both shave our locks; and if I were you, and the argument got away from me, and I could not hold my ground against Simmias and Cebes, I would myself take an oath, like the Argives, not to wear hair any more until I had renewed the conflict and defeated them.

Yes, I said, but Heracles himself is said not to be a match for two.

Summon me then, he said, and I will be your Iolaus until the sun goes down.

I summon you rather, I rejoined, not as Heracles summoning Iolaus, but as Iolaus might summon Heracles.

That will do as well, he said. But first let us take care that we avoid a danger.

Of what nature? I said.

Lest we become misologists, he replied, no worse thing can happen to a man than this. For as there are misanthropists or haters of men, there are also misologists or haters of ideas, and both spring from the same cause, which is ignorance of the world. Misanthropy arises out of the too great confidence of inexperience;—you trust a man and think him altogether true and sound and faithful, and then in a little while he turns out to be false and knavish; and then another and another, and when this has happened several times to a man, especially when it happens among those whom he deems to be his own most trusted and familiar friends, and he has often quarreled with them, he at last hates all men, and believes that no one has any good in him at all. You must have observed this trait of character?

I have.

And is not the feeling discreditable? Is it not obvious that such an one having to deal with other men, was clearly without any experience of human nature; for experience would have taught him the true state of the case, that few are the good and few the evil, and that the great majority are in the interval between them.

What do you mean? I said.

I mean, he replied, as you might say of the very large and very small, that nothing is more uncommon than a very large or very small man; and this applies generally to all extremes, whether of great and small, or swift and slow, or fair and foul, or black and white: and whether the instances you select be men or dogs or anything else, few are the extremes, but many are in the mean between them. Did you never observe this?

Yes, I said, I have.

And do you not imagine, he said, that if there were a competition in evil, the worst would be found to be very few?

Yes, that is very likely, I said.

Yes, that is very likely, he replied; although in this respect arguments are unlike men—there I was led on by you to say more than I had intended; but the point of comparison was, that when a simple man who has no skill in dialectics believes an argument to be true which he afterward imagines to be false, whether really false or not, and then another and another, he has no longer any faith left, and great disputers, as you know, come to think at last that they have grown to be the wisest of mankind; for they alone perceive the utter unsoundness and instability of all arguments, or indeed, of all things, which, like the currents in the Euripus, are going up and down in never-ceasing ebb and flow.

That is quite true, I said.

Yes, Phaedo, he replied, and how melancholy, if there be such a thing as truth or certainty or possibility of knowledge—that a man should have lighted upon some argument or other which at first seemed true and then turned out to be false, and instead of blaming himself and his own want of wit, because he is annoyed, should at last be too glad to transfer the blame from himself to arguments in general: and forever afterward should hate and revile them, and lose truth and the knowledge of realities.

Yes, indeed, I said; that is very melancholy.

Let us then, in the first place, he said, be careful of allowing or of admitting into our souls the notion that there is no health or soundness in any arguments at all. Rather say that we have not yet attained to soundness in ourselves, and that we must struggle manfully and do our best to gain health of mind—you and all other men having regard to the whole of your future life, and I myself in the prospect of death. For at this moment I am sensible that I have not the temper of a philosopher; like the vulgar, I am only a partisan. Now the partisan, when he is engaged in a dispute, cares nothing about the rights of the question, but is anxious only to convince his hearers of his own assertions. And the difference between him and me at the present moment is merely this—that whereas he seeks to convince his hearers that what he says is true, I am rather seeking to convince myself; to convince my hearers is a secondary matter with me. And do but see how much I gain by the argument. For if what I say is true, then I do well to be persuaded of the truth, but if there be nothing after death, still, during the short time that remains, I shall not distress my friends with lamentations, and my ignorance will not last, but will die with me, and therefore no harm will be done. This is the state of mind, Simmias and Cebes, in which I approach the argument. And I would ask you to be thinking of the truth and not of Socrates: agree with me, if I seem to you to be speaking the truth; or if not, withstand me might and main, that I may not deceive you as well as myself in my enthusiasm, and like the bee, leave my sting in you before I die.

And now let us proceed, he said. And first of all let me be sure that I have in my mind what you were saying. Simmias, if I remember rightly, has fears and misgivings whether the soul, although a fairer and diviner thing than the body, being as she is in the form of harmony, may not perish first. On the other hand, Cebes appeared to grant that the soul was more lasting than the body, but he said that no one could know whether the soul, after having worn out many bodies, might not perish herself and leave her last body behind her; and that this is death, which is the destruction not of the body but of the soul, for in the body the work of destruction is ever going on. Are not these, Simmias and Cebes, the points which we have to consider?

They both agreed to this statement of them.

He proceeded: And did you deny the force of the whole preceding argument, or of a part only?

Of a part only, they replied.

And what did you think, he said, of that part of the argument in which we said that knowledge was recollection, and hence inferred that the soul must have previously existed somewhere else before she was enclosed in the body?

Cebes said that he had been wonderfully impressed by that part of the argument, and that his conviction remained absolutely unshaken. Simmias agreed, and added that he himself could hardly imagine the possibility of his ever thinking differently.

But, rejoined Socrates, you will have to think differently, my Theban friend, if you still maintain that harmony is a compound, and that the soul is a harmony which is made out of strings set in the frame of the body; for you will surely never allow yourself to say that a harmony is prior to the elements which compose it.

Never, Socrates.

But do you not see that this is what you imply when you say that the soul existed before she took the form and body of man, and was made up of elements which as yet had no existence? For harmony is not like the soul, as you suppose; but first the lyre, and the strings, and the sounds exist in a state of discord, and then harmony is made last of all, and perishes first. And how can such a notion of the soul as this agree with the other?

Not at all, replied Simmias.

And yet, he said, there surely ought to be harmony in a discourse of which harmony is the theme.

There ought, replied Simmias.

But there is no harmony, he said, in the two propositions that knowledge is recollection, and that the soul is a harmony. Which of them will you retain?

I think, he replied, that I have a much stronger faith, Socrates, in the first of the two, which has been fully demonstrated to me, than in the latter, which has not been demonstrated at all, but rests only on probable and plausible grounds; and is therefore believed by the many. I know too well that these arguments from probabilities are impostors, and unless great caution is observed in the use of them, they are apt to be deceptive—in geometry, and in other things too. But the doctrine of knowledge and recollection has been proven to me on trustworthy grounds; and the proof was that the soul must have existed before she came into the body, because to her belongs the essence of which the very name implies existence. Having, as I am convinced, rightly accepted this conclusion, and on sufficient grounds, I must, as I suppose, cease to argue or allow others to argue that the soul is a harmony.

Let me put the matter, Simmias, he said, in another point of view: Do you imagine that a harmony or any other composition can be in a state other than that of the elements, out of which it is compounded?

Certainly not.

Or do or suffer anything other than they do or suffer?

He agreed.

Then a harmony does not, properly speaking, lead the parts or elements which make up the harmony, but only follows them.

He assented.

For harmony cannot possibly have any motion, or sound, or other quality which is opposed to its parts.

That would be impossible, he replied.

And does not the nature of every harmony depend upon the manner in which the elements are harmonized?

I do not understand you, he said.

I mean to say that a harmony admits of degrees, and is more of a harmony, and more completely a harmony, when more truly and fully harmonized, to any extent which is possible; and less of a harmony, and less completely a harmony, when less truly and fully harmonized.

True.

But does the soul admit of degrees? or is one soul in the very least degree more or less, or more or less completely, a soul than another?

Not in the least.

Yet surely of two souls, one is said to have intelligence and virtue, and to be good, and the other to have folly and vice, and to be an evil soul: and this is said truly?

Yes, truly.

But what will those who maintain the soul to be a harmony say of this presence of virtue and vice in the soul?—will they say that here is another harmony, and another discord, and that the virtuous soul is harmonized, and herself being a harmony has another harmony within her, and that the vicious soul is inharmonical and has no harmony within her?

I cannot tell, replied Simmias; but I suppose that something of the sort would be asserted by those who say that the soul is a harmony.

And we have already admitted that no soul is more a soul than another; which is equivalent to admitting that harmony is not more or less harmony, or more or less completely a harmony?

Quite true.

And that which is not more or less a harmony is not more or less harmonized?

True.

And that which is not more or less harmonized cannot have more or less of harmony, but only an equal harmony?

Yes, an equal harmony.

Then one soul not being more or less absolutely a soul than another, is not more or less harmonized?

Exactly.

And therefore has neither more nor less of discord, nor yet of harmony?

She has not.

And having neither more nor less of harmony or of discord, one soul has no more vice or virtue than another, if vice be discord and virtue harmony?

Not at all more.

Or speaking more correctly, Simmias, the soul, if she is a harmony, will never have any vice; because a harmony, being absolutely a harmony, has no part in the inharmonical.

No.

And therefore a soul which is absolutely a soul has no vice?

How can she have, if the previous argument holds?

Then, if all souls are equally by their nature souls, all souls of all living creatures will be equally good?

I agree with you, Socrates, he said.

And can all this be true, think you? he said; for these are the consequences which seem to follow from the assumption that the soul is a harmony?

It cannot be true.

Once more, he said, what ruler is there of the elements of human nature other than the soul, and especially the wise soul? Do you know of any?

Indeed, I do not.

And is the soul in agreement with the affections of the body? or is she at variance with them? For example, when the body is hot and thirsty, does not the soul incline us against drinking? and when the body is hungry, against eating? And this is only one instance out of ten thousand of the opposition of the soul to the things of the body.

Very true.

But we have already acknowledged that the soul, being a harmony, can never utter a note at variance with the tensions and relaxations and vibrations and other affections of the strings out of which she is composed; she can only follow, she cannot lead them?

It must be so, he replied.

And yet do we not now discover the soul to be doing the exact opposite—leading the elements of which she is believed to be composed; almost always opposing and coercing them in all sorts of ways throughout life, sometimes more violently with the pains of medicine and gymnastic; then again more gently; now threatening, now admonishing the desires, passions, fears, as if talking to a thing which is not herself, as Homer in the Odyssee represents Odysseus doing in the words—

"He beat his breast, and thus reproached his heart: Endure, my heart; far worse hast thou endured!"

Do you think that Homer wrote this under the idea that the soul is a harmony capable of being led by the affections of the body, and not rather of a nature which should lead and master them—herself a far diviner thing than any harmony?

Yes, Socrates, I quite think so.

Then, my friend, we can never be right in saying that the soul is a harmony, for we should contradict the divine Homer, and contradict ourselves.

True, he said.

Thus much, said Socrates, of Harmonia, your Theban goddess, who has graciously yielded to us; but what shall I say, Cebes, to her husband Cadmus, and how shall I make peace with him?

I think that you will discover a way of propitiating him, said Cebes; I am sure that you have put the argument with Harmonia in a manner that I could never have expected. For when Simmias was mentioning his difficulty, I quite imagined that no answer could be given to him, and therefore I was surprised at finding that his argument could not sustain the first onset of yours, and not impossibly the other, whom you call Cadmus, may share a similar fate.

Nay, my good friend, said Socrates, let us not boast, lest some evil eye should put to flight the word which I am about to speak. That, however, may be left in the hands of those above, while I draw near in Homeric fashion, and try the mettle of your words. Here lies the point:—You want to have it proven to you that the soul is imperishable and immortal, and the philosopher who is confident in death appears to you to have but a vain and foolish confidence, if he believes that he will fare better in the world below than one who has led another sort of life, unless he can prove this; and you say that the demonstration of the strength and divinity of the soul, and of her existence prior to our becoming men, does not necessarily imply her immortality. Admitting the soul to be longlived, and to have known and done much in a former state, still she is not on that account immortal; and her entrance into the human form may be a sort of disease which is the beginning of dissolution, and may at last, after the toils of life are over, end in that which is called death. And whether the soul enters into the body once only or many times, does not, as you say, make any difference in the fears of individuals. For any man, who is not devoid of sense, must fear, if he has no knowledge and can give no account of the soul's immortality. This, or something like this, I suspect to be your notion, Cebes; and I designedly recur to it in order that nothing may escape us, and that you may, if you wish, add or subtract anything.

But, said Cebes, as far as I see at present, I have nothing to add or subtract: I mean what you say that I mean.

Socrates paused awhile, and seemed to be absorbed in reflection. At length he said: You are raising a tremendous question, Cebes, involving the whole nature of generation and corruption, about which, if you like, I will give you my own experience; and if anything which I say is likely to avail toward the solution of your difficulty you may make use of it.

I should very much like, said Cebes, to hear what you have to say.

Then I will tell you, said Socrates. When I was young, Cebes, I had a prodigious desire to know that department of philosophy which is called the investigation of nature; to know the causes of things, and why a thing is and is created or destroyed appeared to me to be a lofty profession; and I was always agitating myself with the consideration of questions such as these:—Is the growth of animals the result of some decay which the hot and cold principle contracts, as some have said? Is the blood the element with which we think, or the air, or the fire? or perhaps nothing of the kind—but the brain may be the originating power of the perceptions of hearing and sight and smell, and memory and opinion may come from them, and science may be based on memory and opinion when they have attained fixity. And then I went on to examine the corruption of them, and then to the things of heaven and earth, and at last I concluded myself to be utterly and absolutely incapable of these enquiries, as I will satisfactorily prove to you. For I was fascinated by them to such a degree that my eyes grew blind to things which I had seemed to myself, and also to others, to know quite well; I forgot what I had before thought self-evident truths; e.g.

such a fact as that the growth of man is the result of eating and drinking; for when by the digestion of food flesh is added to flesh and bone to bone, and whenever there is an aggregation of congenial elements, the lesser bulk becomes larger and the small man great. Was not that a reasonable notion?

Yes, said Cebes, I think so.

Well; but let me tell you something more. There was a time when I thought that I understood the meaning of greater and less pretty well; and when I saw a great man standing by a little one, I fancied that one was taller than the other by a head; or one horse would appear to be greater than another horse: and still more clearly did I seem to perceive that ten is two more than eight, and that two cubits are more than one, because two is the double of one.

And what is now your notion of such matters? said Cebes.

I should be far enough from imagining, he replied, that I knew the cause of any of them, by heaven I should; for I cannot satisfy myself that, when one is added to one, the one to which the addition is made becomes two, or that the two units added together make two by reason of the addition. I cannot understand how, when separated from the other, each of them was one and not two, and now, when they are brought together, the mere juxtaposition or meeting of them should be the cause of their becoming two: neither can I understand how the division of one is the way to make two; for then a different cause would produce the same effect,—as in the former instance the addition and juxtaposition of one to one was the cause of two, in this the separation and subtraction of one from the other would be the cause. Nor am I any longer satisfied that I understand the reason why one or anything else is either generated or destroyed or is at all, but I have in my mind some confused notion of a new method, and can never admit the other.

Then I heard someone reading, as he said, from a book of Anaxagoras, that mind was the disposer and cause of all, and I was delighted at this notion, which appeared quite admirable, and I said to myself: If mind is the disposer, mind will dispose all for the best, and put each particular in the best place; and I argued that if anyone desired to find out the cause of the generation or destruction or existence of anything, he must find out what state of being or doing or suffering was best for that thing, and therefore a man had only to consider the best for himself and others, and then he would also know the worse, since the same science comprehended both. And I rejoiced to think that I had found in Anaxagoras a teacher of the causes of existence such as I desired, and I imagined that he would tell me first whether the Earth is flat or round; and whichever was true, he would proceed to explain the cause and the necessity of this being so, and then he would teach me the nature of the best and show that this was best; and if he said that the Earth was in the center, he would further explain that this position was the best, and I should be satisfied with the explanation given, and not want any other sort of cause. And I thought that I would then go on and ask him about the sun and moon and stars, and that he would explain to me their comparative swiftness, and their returnings and various states, active and passive, and how all of them were for the best. For I could not imagine that when he spoke of mind as the disposer of them, he would give any other account of their being as they are, except that this was best; and I thought that when he had explained to me in detail the cause of each and the cause of all, he would go on to explain to me what was best for each and what was good for all. These hopes I would not have sold for a large sum of money, and I seized the books and read them as fast as I could in my eagerness to know the better and the worse.

What expectations I had formed, and how grievously was I disappointed! As I proceeded, I found my philosopher altogether forsaking mind or any other principle of order, but having recourse to air, and ether, and water, and other eccentricities. I might compare him to a person who began by maintaining generally that mind is the cause of the actions of Socrates, but who, when he endeavoured to explain the causes of my several actions in detail, went on to show that I sit here because my body is made up of bones and muscles; and the bones, as he would say, are hard and have joints which divide them, and the muscles are elastic, and they cover the bones, which have also a covering or environment of flesh and skin which contains them; and as the bones are lifted at their joints by the contraction or relaxation of the muscles, I am able to bend my limbs, and this is why I am sitting here in a curved posture—that is what he would say, and he would have a similar explanation of my talking to you, which he would attribute to sound, and air, and hearing, and he would assign ten thousand other causes of the same sort, forgetting to mention the true cause, which is, that the Athenians have thought fit to condemn me, and accordingly I have thought it better and more right to remain here and undergo my sentence; for I am inclined to think that these muscles and bones of mine would have gone off long ago to Megara or Boeotia—by the dog they would, if they had been moved only by their own idea of what was best, and if I had not chosen the better and nobler part, instead of playing truant and running away, of enduring any punishment which the state inflicts. There is surely a strange confusion of causes and conditions in all this. It may be said, indeed, that without bones and muscles and the other parts of the body I cannot execute my purposes. But to say that I do as I do because of them, and that this is the way in which mind acts, and not from the choice of the best, is a very careless and idle mode of speaking. I wonder that they cannot distinguish the cause from the condition, which the many, feeling about in the dark, are always mistaking and misnaming. And thus one man makes a vortex all round and steadies the earth by the heaven; another gives the air as a support to the Earth, which is a sort of broad trough. Any power which in arranging them as they are arranges them for the best never enters into their minds; and instead of finding any superior strength in it, they rather expect to discover another Atlas of the world who is stronger and more everlasting and more containing than the good;—of the obligatory and containing power of the good they think nothing; and yet this is the principle which I would fain learn if anyone would teach me. But as I have failed either to discover myself, or to learn of anyone else, the nature of the best, I will exhibit to you, if you like, what I have found to be the second best mode of inquiring into the cause.

I should very much like to hear, he replied.

Socrates proceeded:—I thought that as I had failed in the contemplation of true existence, I ought to be careful that I did not lose the eye of my soul; as people may injure their bodily eye by observing and gazing on the sun during an eclipse, unless they take the precaution of only looking at the image reflected in the water, or in some similar medium. So in my own case, I was afraid that my soul might be blinded altogether if I looked at things with my eyes or tried to apprehend them by the help of the senses. And I thought that I had better have recourse to the world of mind and seek there the truth of existence. I dare say that the simile is not perfect—for I am very far from admitting that he who contemplates existences through the medium of thought, sees them only "through a glass darkly," any more than he who considers them in action and operation. However, this was the method which I adopted: I first assumed some principle which I judged to be the strongest, and then I affirmed as true whatever seemed to agree with this, whether relating to the cause or to anything else; and that which disagreed I regarded as untrue. But I should like to explain my meaning more clearly, as I do not think that you as yet understand me.

No indeed, replied Cebes, not very well.

There is nothing new, he said, in what I am about to tell you; but only what I have been always and everywhere repeating in the previous discussion and on other occasions: I want to show you the nature of that cause which has occupied my thoughts. I shall have to go back to those familiar words which are in the mouth of everyone, and first of all assume that there is an absolute beauty and goodness and greatness, and the like; grant me this, and I hope to be able to show you the nature of the cause, and to prove the immortality of the soul.

Cebes said: You may proceed at once with the proof, for I grant you this.

Well, he said, then I should like to know whether you agree with me in the next step; for I cannot help thinking, if there be anything beautiful other than absolute beauty should there be such, that it can be beautiful only in as far as it partakes of absolute beauty—and I should say the same of everything. Do you agree in this notion of the cause?

Yes, he said, I agree.

He proceeded: I know nothing and can understand nothing of any other of those wise causes which are alleged; and if a person says to me that the bloom of color, or form, or any such thing is a source of beauty, I leave all that, which is only confusing to me, and simply and singly, and perhaps foolishly, hold and am assured in my own mind that nothing makes a thing beautiful but the presence and participation of beauty in whatever way or manner obtained; for as to the manner I am uncertain, but I stoutly contend that by beauty all beautiful things become beautiful. This appears to me to be the safest answer which I can give, either to myself or to another, and to this I cling, in the persuasion that this principle will never be overthrown, and that to myself or to anyone who asks the question, I may safely reply, That by beauty beautiful things become beautiful. Do you not agree with me?

I do.

And that by greatness only great things become great and greater, and by smallness the less become less?

True.

Then if a person were to remark that A is taller by a head than B, and B less by a head than A, you would refuse to admit his statement, and would stoutly contend that what you mean is only that the greater is greater by, and by reason of, greatness, and the less is less only by, and by reason of, smallness; and thus you would avoid the danger of saying that the greater is greater and the less less by the measure of the head, which is the same in both, and would also avoid the monstrous absurdity of supposing that the greater man is greater by reason of the head, which is small. You would be afraid to draw such an inference, would you not?

Indeed, I should, said Cebes, laughing.

In like manner you would be afraid to say that ten exceeded eight by, and by reason of, two; but would say by, and by reason of, number; or you would say that two cubits exceed one cubit not by a half, but by magnitude?—for there is the same liability to error in all these cases.

Very true, he said.

Again, would you not be cautious of affirming that the addition of one to one, or the division of one, is the cause of two? And you would loudly asseverate that you know of no way in which anything comes into existence except by participation in its own proper essence, and consequently, as far as you know, the only cause of two is the participation in duality—this is the way to make two, and the participation in one is the way to make one. You would say: I will let alone puzzles of division and addition—wiser heads than mine may answer them; inexperienced as I am, and ready to start, as the proverb says, at my own shadow, I cannot afford to give up the sure ground of a principle. And if anyone assails you there, you would not mind him, or answer him, until you had seen whether the consequences which follow agree with one another or not, and when you are further required to give an explanation of this principle, you would go on to assume a higher principle, and a higher, until you found a resting-place in the best of the higher; but you would not confuse the principle and the consequences in your reasoning, like the Eristics—at least if you wanted to discover real existence. Not that this confusion signifies to them, who never care or think about the matter at all, for they have the wit to be well pleased with themselves however great may be the turmoil of their ideas. But you, if you are a philosopher, will certainly do as I say.

What you say is most true, said Simmias and Cebes, both speaking at once.

ECHECRATES: Yes, Phaedo; and I do not wonder at their assenting. Any one who has the least sense will acknowledge the wonderful clearness of Socrates's reasoning.

PHAEDO: Certainly, Echecrates; and such was the feeling of the whole company at the time.

ECHECRATES: Yes, and equally of ourselves, who were not of the company, and are now listening to your recital. But what followed?

PHAEDO: After all this had been admitted, and they had that ideas exist, and that other things participate in them and derive their names from them, Socrates, if I remember rightly, said:—

This is your way of speaking; and yet when you say that Simmias is greater than Socrates and less than Phaedo, do you not predicate of Simmias both greatness and smallness?

Yes, I do.

But still you allow that Simmias does not really exceed Socrates, as the words may seem to imply, because he is Simmias, but by reason of the size which he has; just as Simmias does not exceed Socrates because he is Simmias, any more than because Socrates is Socrates, but because he has smallness when compared with the greatness of Simmias?

True.

And if Phaedo exceeds him in size, this is not because Phaedo is Phaedo, but because Phaedo has greatness relatively to Simmias, who is comparatively smaller?

That is true.

And therefore Simmias is said to be great, and is also said to be small, because he is in a mean between them, exceeding the smallness of the one by his greatness, and allowing the greatness of the other to exceed his smallness. He added, laughing, I am speaking like a book, but I believe that what I am saying is true.

Simmias assented.

I speak as I do because I want you to agree with me in thinking, not only that absolute greatness will never be great and also small, but that greatness in us or in the concrete will never admit the small or admit of being exceeded: instead of this, one of two things will happen, either the greater will fly or retire before the opposite, which is the less, or at the approach of the less has already ceased to exist; but will not, if allowing or admitting of smallness, be changed by that; even as I, having received and admitted smallness when compared with Simmias, remain just as I was, and am the same small person. And as the idea of greatness cannot condescend ever to be or become small, in like manner the smallness in us cannot be or become great; nor can any other opposite which remains the same ever be or become its own opposite, but either passes away or perishes in the change.

That, replied Cebes, is quite my notion.

Hereupon one of the company, though I do not exactly remember which of them, said: In heaven's name, is not this the direct contrary of what was admitted before—that out of the greater came the less and out of the less the greater, and that opposites were simply generated from opposites; but now this principle seems to be utterly denied.

Socrates inclined his head to the speaker and listened. I like your courage, he said, in reminding us of this. But you do not observe that there is a difference in the two cases. For then we were speaking of opposites in the concrete, and now of the essential opposite which, as is affirmed, neither in us nor in nature can ever be at variance with itself: then, my friend, we were speaking of things in which opposites are inherent and which are called after them, but now about the opposites which are inherent in them and which give their name to them; and these essential opposites will never, as we maintain, admit of generation into or out of one another. At the same time, turning to Cebes, he said: Are you at all disconcerted, Cebes, at our friend's objection?

No, I do not feel so, said Cebes; and yet I cannot deny that I am often disturbed by objections.

Then we are agreed after all, said Socrates, that the opposite will never in any case be opposed to itself?

To that we are quite agreed, he replied.

Yet once more let me ask you to consider the question from another point of view, and see whether you agree with me:—There is a thing which you term heat, and another thing which you term cold?

Certainly.

But are they the same as fire and snow?

Most assuredly not.

Heat is a thing different from fire, and cold is not the same with snow?

Yes.

And yet you will surely admit, that when snow, as was before said, is under the influence of heat, they will not remain snow and heat; but at the advance of the heat, the snow will either retire or perish?

Very true, he replied.

And the fire too at the advance of the cold will either retire or perish; and when the fire is under the influence of the cold, they will not remain as before, fire and cold.

That is true, he said.

And in some cases the name of the idea is not only attached to the idea in an eternal connection, but anything else which, not being the idea, exists only in the form of the idea, may also lay claim to it. I will try to make this clearer by an example:—The odd number is always called by the name of odd?

Very true.

But is this the only thing which is called odd? Are there not other things which have their own name, and yet are called odd, because, although not the same as oddness, they are never without oddness?—that is what I mean to ask—whether numbers such as the number three are not of the class of odd. And there are many other examples: would you not say, for example, that three may be called by its proper name, and also be called odd, which is not the same with three? and this may be said not only of three but also of five, and of every alternate number—each of them without being oddness is odd, and in the same way two and four, and the other series of alternate numbers, has every number even, without being evenness. Do you agree?

Of course.

Then now mark the point at which I am aiming:—not only do essential opposites exclude one another, but also concrete things, which, although not in themselves opposed, contain opposites; these, I say, likewise reject the idea which is opposed to that which is contained in them, and when it approaches them they either perish or withdraw. For example: Will not the number three endure annihilation or anything sooner than be converted into an even number, while remaining three?

Very true, said Cebes.

And yet, he said, the number two is certainly not opposed to the number three?

It is not.

Then not only do opposite ideas repel the advance of one another, but also there are other natures which repel the approach of opposites.

Very true, he said.

Suppose, he said, that we endeavor, if possible, to determine what these are.

By all means.

Are they not, Cebes, such as compel the things of which they have possession, not only to take their own form, but also the form of some opposite?

What do you mean?

I mean, as I was just now saying, and as I am sure that you know, that those things which are possessed by the number three must not only be three in number, but must also be odd.

Quite true.

And on this oddness, of which the number three has the impress, the opposite idea will never intrude?

No.

And this impress was given by the odd principle?

Yes.

And to the odd is opposed the even?

True.

Then the idea of the even number will never arrive at three?

No.

Then three has no part in the even?

None.

Then the triad or number three is uneven?

Very true.

To return then to my distinction of natures which are not opposed, and yet do not admit opposites—as, in the instance given, three, although not opposed to the even, does not any the more admit of the even, but always brings the opposite into play on the other side; or as two does not receive the odd, or fire the cold—from these examples (and there are many more of them) perhaps you may be able to arrive at the general conclusion, that not only opposites will not receive opposites, but also that nothing which brings the opposite will admit the opposite of that which it brings, in that to which it is brought. And here let me recapitulate—for there is no harm in repetition. The number five will not admit the nature of the even, any more than ten, which is the double of five, will admit the nature of the odd. The double has another opposite, and is not strictly opposed to the odd, but nevertheless rejects the odd altogether. Nor again will parts in the ratio 3:2, nor any fraction in which there is a half, nor again in which there is a third, admit the notion of the whole, although they are not opposed to the whole: You will agree?

Yes, he said, I entirely agree and go along with you in that.

And now, he said, let us begin again; and do not you answer my question in the words in which I ask it: let me have not the old safe answer of which I spoke at first, but another equally safe, of which the truth will be inferred by you from what has been just said. I mean that if anyone asks you "what that is, of which the inherence makes the body hot," you will reply not heat (this is what I call the safe and stupid answer), but fire, a far superior answer, which we are now in a condition to give. Or if anyone asks you "why a body is diseased," you will not say from disease, but from fever; and instead of saying that oddness is the cause of odd numbers, you will say that the monad is the cause of them: and so of things in general, as I dare say that you will understand sufficiently without my adducing any further examples.

Yes, he said, I quite understand you.

Tell me, then, what is that of which the inherence will render the body alive?

The soul, he replied.
And is this always the case?
Yes, he said, of course.
Then whatever the soul possesses, to that she comes bearing life?
Yes, certainly.
And is there any opposite to life?
There is, he said.
And what is that?
Death.
Then the soul, as has been acknowledged, will never receive the opposite of what she brings.
Impossible, replied Cebes.
And now, he said, what did we just now call that principle which repels the even?
The odd.
And that principle which repels the musical, or the just?
The unmusical, he said, and the unjust.
And what do we call the principle which does not admit of death?
The immortal, he said.
And does the soul admit of death?
No.
Then the soul is immortal?
Yes, he said.
And may we say that this has been proven?
Yes, abundantly proven, Socrates, he replied.
Supposing that the odd were imperishable, must not three be imperishable?
Of course.
And if that which is cold were imperishable, when the warm principle came attacking the snow, must not the snow have retired whole and unmelted—for it could never have perished, nor could it have remained and admitted the heat?
True, he said.
Again, if the uncooling or warm principle were imperishable, the fire when assailed by cold would not have perished or have been extinguished, but would have gone away unaffected?
Certainly, he said.
And the same may be said of the immortal: if the immortal is also imperishable, the soul when attacked by death cannot perish; for the

preceding argument shows that the soul will not admit of death, or ever be dead, any more than three or the odd number will admit of the even, or fire or the heat in the fire, of the cold. Yet a person may say: "But although the odd will not become even at the approach of the even, why may not the odd perish and the even take the place of the odd?" Now to him who makes this objection, we cannot answer that the odd principle is imperishable; for this has not been acknowledged, but if this had been acknowledged, there would have been no difficulty in contending that at the approach of the even the odd principle and the number three took their departure; and the same argument would have held good of fire and heat and any other thing.

Very true.

And the same may be said of the immortal: if the immortal is also imperishable, then the soul will be imperishable as well as immortal; but if not, some other proof of her imperishableness will have to be given.

No other proof is needed, he said; for if the immortal, being eternal, is liable to perish, then nothing is imperishable.

Yes, replied Socrates, and yet all men will agree that God, and the essential form of life, and the immortal in general, will never perish.

Yes, all men, he said—that is true; and what is more, gods, if I am not mistaken, as well as men.

Seeing then that the immortal is indestructible, must not the soul, if she is immortal, be also imperishable?

Most certainly.

Then when death attacks a man, the mortal portion of him may be supposed to die, but the immortal retires at the approach of death and is preserved safe and sound?

True.

Then, Cebes, beyond question, the soul is immortal and imperishable, and our souls will truly exist in another world!

I am convinced, Socrates, said Cebes, and have nothing more to object; but if my friend Simmias, or anyone else, has any further objection to make, he had better speak out, and not keep silence, since I do not know to what other season he can defer the discussion, if there is anything which he wants to say or to have said.

But I have nothing more to say, replied Simmias; nor can I see any reason for doubt after what has been said. But I still feel and cannot help feeling uncertain in my own mind, when I think of the greatness of the subject and the feebleness of man.

Yes, Simmias, replied Socrates, that is well said: and I may add that first principles, even if they appear certain, should be carefully considered; and when they are satisfactorily ascertained, then, with a sort of hesitating confidence in human reason, you may, I think, follow the course of the argument; and if that be plain and clear, there will be no need for any further inquiry.

Very true.

But then, O my friends, he said, if the soul is really immortal, what care should be taken of her, not only in respect of the portion of time which is called life, but of eternity! And the danger of neglecting her from this point of view does indeed appear to be awful. If death had only been the end of all, the wicked would have had a good bargain in dying, for they would have been happily quit not only of their body, but of their own evil together with their souls. But now, inasmuch as the soul is manifestly immortal, there is no release or salvation from evil except the attainment of the highest virtue and wisdom. For the soul when on her progress to the world below takes nothing with her but nurture and education; and these are said greatly to benefit or greatly to injure the departed, at the very beginning of his journey thither.

For after death, as they say, the genius of each individual, to whom he belonged in life, leads him to a certain place in which the dead are gathered together, whence after judgment has been given they pass into the world below, following the guide, who is appointed to conduct them from this world to the other: and when they have there received their due and remained their time, another guide brings them back again after many revolutions of ages. Now this way to the other world is not, as Aeschylus says in the Telephus, a single and straight path—if that were so no guide would be needed, for no one could miss it; but there are many partings of the road, and windings, as I infer from the rites and sacrifices which are offered to the gods below in places where three ways meet on Earth. The wise and orderly soul follows in the straight path and is conscious of her surroundings; but the soul which desires the body, and which, as I was relating before, has long been fluttering about the lifeless frame and the world of sight, is after many struggles and many sufferings hardly and with violence carried away by her attendant genius, and when she arrives at the place where the other souls are gathered, if she be impure and have done impure deeds, whether foul murders or other crimes which are the brothers of these, and the works of brothers in crime—from that soul everyone flees and turns away; no one will be her companion, no one her guide, but alone she wanders in extremity of evil until certain times are fulfillled, and when they are fulfillled, she is borne irresistibly to her own fitting habitation; as every pure and just soul which has passed through life in the company and under the guidance of the gods has also her own proper home.

Now the Earth has diverse wonderful regions, and is indeed in nature and extent very unlike the notions of geographers, as I believe on the authority of one who shall be nameless.

What do you mean, Socrates? said Simmias. I have myself heard many descriptions of the Earth, but I do not know, and I should very much like to know, in which of these you put faith.

And I, Simmias, replied Socrates, if I had the art of Glaucus would tell you; although I know not that the art of Glaucus could prove the truth of my tale, which I myself should never be able to prove, and even if I could, I fear, Simmias, that my life would come to an end before the argument was completed. I may describe to you, however, the form and regions of the Earth according to my conception of them.

That, said Simmias, will be enough.

Well, then, he said, my conviction is, that the Earth is a round body in the center of the heavens, and therefore has no need of air or any similar force to be a support, but is kept there and hindered from falling or inclining any way by the equability of the surrounding heaven and by her own equipoise. For that which, being in equipoise, is in the center of that which is equably diffused, will not incline any way in any degree, but will always remain in the same state and not deviate. And this is my first notion.

Which is surely a correct one, said Simmias.

Also I believe that the Earth is very vast, and that we who dwell in the region extending from the river Phasis to the Pillars of Heracles inhabit a small portion only about the sea, like ants or frogs about a marsh, and that there are other inhabitants of many other like places; for everywhere on the face of the Earth there are hollows of various forms and sizes, into which the water and the mist and the lower air collect. But the true Earth is pure and situated in the pure heaven—there are the stars also; and it is the heaven which is commonly spoken of by us as the ether, and of which our own earth is the sediment gathering in the hollows beneath. But we who live in these hollows are deceived into the notion that we are dwelling above on the surface of the Earth; which is just as if a creature who was at the bottom of the sea were to fancy that he was on the surface of the water, and that the sea was the heaven through which he saw the sun and the other stars, he having never come to the surface by reason of his feebleness and sluggishness, and having never lifted up his head and seen, nor ever heard from one who had seen, how much purer and fairer the world above is than his own. And such is exactly our case: for we are dwelling in a hollow of the Earth, and fancy that we are on the surface; and the air we call the heaven, in which we imagine that the stars move. But the fact is, that owing to our feebleness and sluggishness we are prevented from reaching the surface of the air: for if any man could arrive at the exterior limit, or take the wings of a bird and come to the top, then like a fish who puts his head out of the water and sees this world, he would see a world beyond; and, if the nature of man could sustain the sight, he would acknowledge that this other world was the place of the true heaven and the true light and the true Earth. For our earth, and the stones, and the entire region which surrounds us, are spoiled and corroded, as in the sea all things are corroded by the brine, neither is there any noble or perfect growth, but caverns only, and sand, and an endless slough of mud: and even the shore is not to be compared to the fairer sights of this world. And still less is this our world to be compared with the other. Of that upper earth which is under the heaven, I can tell you a charming tale, Simmias, which is well worth hearing.

And we, Socrates, replied Simmias, shall be charmed to listen to you.

The tale, my friend, he said, is as follows:—In the first place, the Earth, when looked at from above, is in appearance streaked like one of those balls which have leather coverings in twelve pieces, and is decked with various colors, of which the colors used by painters on Earth are in a manner samples. But there the whole Earth is made up of them, and they are brighter far and clearer than ours; there is a purple of wonderful luster, also the radiance of gold, and the white which is in the earth is whiter than any chalk or snow. Of these and other colors the Earth is made up, and they are more in number and fairer than the eye of man has ever seen; the very hollows (of which I was speaking) filled with air and water have a color of their own, and are seen like light gleaming amid the diversity of the other colors, so that the whole presents a single and continuous appearance of variety in unity. And in this fair region everything that grows—trees, and flowers, and fruits—are in a like degree fairer than any here; and there are hills, having stones in them in a like degree smoother, and more transparent, and fairer in color than our highly-valued emeralds and sardonyxes and jaspers, and other gems, which are but minute fragments of them: for there all the stones are like our precious stones, and fairer still (compare Republic). The reason is, that they are pure, and not, like our precious stones, infected or corroded by the corrupt briny elements which coagulate among us, and which breed foulness and disease both in earth and stones, as well as in animals and plants. They are the jewels of the upper earth, which also shines with gold and silver and the like, and they are set in the light of day and are large and abundant and in all places, making the Earth a sight to gladden the beholder's eye. And there are animals and men, some in a middle region, others dwelling about the air as we dwell about the sea; others in islands which the air flows round, near the continent: and in a word, the air is used by them as the water and the sea are by us, and the ether is to them what the air is to us. Moreover, the temperament of their seasons is such that they have no disease, and live much longer than we do, and have sight and hearing and smell, and all the other senses, in far greater perfection, in the same proportion that air is purer than water or the ether than air. Also they have temples and sacred places in which the gods really dwell, and they hear their voices and receive their answers, and are conscious of them and hold converse with them, and they see the sun, moon, and stars as they truly are, and their other blessedness is of a piece with this.

Such is the nature of the whole Earth, and of the things which are around the Earth; and there are diverse regions in the hollows on the face of the globe everywhere, some of them deeper and more extended than that which we inhabit, others deeper but with a narrower opening than ours, and some are shallower and also wider. All have numerous perforations, and there are passages broad and narrow in the interior of the Earth, connecting them with one another; and there flows out of and into them, as into basins, a vast tide of water, and huge subterranean streams of perennial rivers, and springs hot and cold, and a great fire, and great rivers of fire, and streams of liquid mud, thin or thick (like the rivers of mud in Sicily, and the lava streams which follow them), and the regions about which they happen to flow are filled up with them. And there is a swinging or seesaw in the interior of the Earth which moves all this up and down, and is due to the following cause:—There is a chasm which is the vastest of them all, and pierces right through the whole Earth; this is that chasm which Homer describes in the words,—

"Far off, where is the inmost depth beneath the Earth";

and which he in other places, and many other poets, have called Tartarus. And the seesaw is caused by the streams flowing into and out of this chasm, and they each have the nature of the soil through which they flow. And the reason why the streams are always flowing in and out, is that the watery element has no bed or bottom, but is swinging and surging up and down, and the surrounding wind and air do the same; they follow the water up and down, hither and thither, over the earth—just as in the act of respiration the air is always in process of inhalation and exhalation;—and the wind swinging with the water in and out produces fearful and irresistible blasts: when the waters retire with a rush into the lower parts of the Earth, as they are called, they flow through the Earth in those regions, and fill them up like water raised by a pump, and then when they leave those regions and rush back hither, they again fill the hollows here, and when these are filled, flow through subterranean channels and find their way to their several places, forming seas, and lakes, and rivers, and springs. Thence they again enter the Earth, some of them making a long circuit into many lands, others going to a few places and not so distant; and again fall into Tartarus, some at a point a good deal lower than that at which they rose, and others not much lower, but all in some degree lower than the point from which they came. And some burst forth again on the opposite side, and some on the same side, and some wind round the Earth with one or many folds like the coils of a serpent, and descend as far as they can, but always return and fall into the chasm. The rivers flowing in either direction can descend only to the center and no further, for opposite to the rivers is a precipice.

Now these rivers are many, and mighty, and diverse, and there are four principal ones, of which the greatest and outermost is that called Oceanus, which flows round the Earth in a circle; and in the opposite direction flows Acheron, which passes under the earth through desert places into the Acherusian lake: this is the lake to the shores of which the souls of the many go when they are dead, and after waiting an appointed time, which is to some a longer and to some a shorter time, they are sent back to be born again as animals. The third river passes out between the two, and near the place of outlet pours into a vast region of fire, and forms a lake larger than the Mediterranean Sea, boiling with water and mud; and proceeding muddy and turbid, and winding about the earth, comes, among other places, to the extremities of the Acherusian Lake, but mingles not with the waters of the lake, and after making many coils about the earth plunges into Tartarus at a deeper level. This is that Pyriphlegethon, as the stream is called, which throws up jets of fire in different parts of the Earth. The fourth river goes out on the opposite side, and falls first of all into a wild and savage region, which is all of a dark-blue color, like lapis lazuli; and this is that river which is called the Stygian river, and falls into and forms the Lake Styx, and after falling into the lake and receiving strange powers in the waters, passes under the earth, winding round in the opposite direction, and comes near the Acherusian lake from the opposite side to Pyriphlegethon. And the water of this river too mingles with no other, but flows round in a circle and falls into Tartarus over against Pyriphlegethon; and the name of the river, as the poets say, is Cocytus.

Such is the nature of the other world; and when the dead arrive at the place to which the genius of each severally guides them, first of all, they have sentence passed upon them, as they have lived well and piously or not. And those who appear to have lived neither well nor ill, go to the river Acheron, and embarking in any vessels which they may find, are carried in them to the lake, and there they dwell and are purified of their evil deeds, and having suffered the penalty of the wrongs which they have done to others, they are absolved, and receive the rewards of their good deeds, each of them according to his deserts. But those who appear to be incurable by reason of the greatness of their crimes—who have committed many and terrible deeds of sacrilege, murders foul and violent, or the like—such are hurled into Tartarus which is their suitable destiny, and they never come out. Those again who have committed crimes, which, although great, are not irremediable—who in a moment of anger, for example, have done violence to a father or a mother, and have repented for the remainder of their lives, or, who have taken the life of another under the like extenuating circumstances—these are plunged into Tartarus, the pains of which they are compelled to undergo for a year, but at the end of the year the wave casts them forth—mere homicides by way of Cocytus, parricides and matricides by Pyriphlegethon—and they are borne to the Acherusian lake, and there they lift up their voices and call upon the victims whom they have slain or wronged, to have pity on them, and to be kind to them, and let them come out into the lake. And if they prevail, then they come forth and cease from their troubles; but if not, they are carried back again into Tartarus and from thence into the rivers unceasingly, until they obtain mercy from those whom they have wronged: for that is the sentence inflicted upon them by their judges. Those too who have been preeminent for holiness of life are released from this earthly prison, and go to their pure home which is above, and dwell in the purer Earth; and of these, such as have duly purified themselves with philosophy live henceforth altogether without the body, in mansions fairer still which may not be described, and of which the time would fail me to tell.

Wherefore, Simmias, seeing all these things, what ought not we to do that we may obtain virtue and wisdom in this life? Fair is the prize, and the hope great!

A man of sense ought not to say, nor will I be very confident, that the description which I have given of the soul and her mansions is exactly true. But I do say that, inasmuch as the soul is shown to be immortal, he may venture to think, not improperly or unworthily, that something of the kind is true. The venture is a glorious one, and he ought to comfort himself with words like these, which is the reason why I lengthen out the tale. Wherefore, I say, let a man be of good cheer about his soul, who having cast away the pleasures and ornaments of the body as alien to him and working harm rather than good, has sought after the pleasures of knowledge; and has arrayed the soul, not in some foreign attire, but in her own proper jewels, temperance, and justice, and courage, and nobility, and truth—in these adorned she is ready to go on her journey to the world below, when her hour comes. You, Simmias and Cebes, and all other men, will depart at some time or other. Me already, as the tragic poet would say, the voice of fate calls. Soon I must drink the poison; and I think that I had better repair to the bath first, in order that the women may not have the trouble of washing my body after I am dead.

When he had done speaking, Crito said: And have you any commands for us, Socrates—anything to say about your children, or any other matter in which we can serve you?

Nothing particular, Crito, he replied: only, as I have always told you, take care of yourselves; that is a service which you may be ever rendering to me and mine and to all of us, whether you promise to do so or not. But if you have no thought for yourselves, and care not to walk according to the rule which I have prescribed for you, not now for the first time, however much you may profess or promise at the moment, it will be of no avail.

We will do our best, said Crito: And in what way shall we bury you?

In any way that you like; but you must get hold of me, and take care that I do not run away from you. Then he turned to us, and added with a smile:—I cannot make Crito believe that I am the same Socrates who have been talking and conducting the argument; he fancies that I am the other Socrates whom he will soon see, a dead body—and he asks, How shall he bury me? And though I have spoken many words in the endeavor to show that when I have drunk the poison I shall leave you and go to the joys of the blessed,—these words of mine, with which I was comforting you and myself, have had, as I perceive, no effect upon Crito. And therefore I want you to be surety for me to him now, as at the trial he was surety to the judges for me: but let the promise be of another sort; for he was surety for me to the judges that I would remain, and you must be my surety to him that I shall not remain, but go away and depart; and then he will suffer less at my death, and not be grieved when he sees my body being burned or buried. I would not have him sorrow at my hard lot, or say at the burial, Thus we lay out Socrates, or, Thus we follow him to the grave or bury him; for false words are not only evil in themselves, but they infect the soul with evil. Be of good cheer, then, my dear Crito, and say that you are burying my body only, and do with that whatever is usual, and what you think best.

When he had spoken these words, he arose and went into a chamber to bathe; Crito followed him and told us to wait. So we remained behind, talking and thinking of the subject of discourse, and also of the greatness of our sorrow; he was like a father of whom we were being bereaved, and we were about to pass the rest of our lives as orphans. When he had taken the bath his children were brought to him—(he had two young sons and an elder one); and the women of his family also came, and he talked to them and gave them a few directions in the presence of Crito; then he dismissed them and returned to us.

Now the hour of sunset was near, for a good deal of time had passed while he was within. When he came out, he sat down with us again after his bath, but not much was said. Soon the jailer, who was the servant of the Eleven, entered and stood by him, saying:—To you, Socrates, whom I know to be the noblest and gentlest and best of all who ever came to this place, I will not impute the angry feelings of other men, who rage and swear at me, when, in obedience to the authorities, I bid them drink the poison—indeed, I am sure that you will not be angry with me; for others, as you are aware, and not I, are to blame. And so fare you well, and try to bear lightly what must needs be—you know my errand. Then bursting into tears he turned away and went out.

Socrates looked at him and said: I return your good wishes, and will do as you bid. Then turning to us, he said, How charming the man is: since I have been in prison he has always been coming to see me, and at times he would talk to me, and was as good to me as could be, and now see how generously he sorrows on my account. We must do as he says, Crito; and therefore let the cup be brought, if the poison is prepared: if not, let the attendant prepare some.

Yet, said Crito, the sun is still upon the hill-tops, and I know that many a one has taken the draught late, and after the announcement has been made to him, he has eaten and drunk, and enjoyed the society of his beloved; do not hurry—there is time enough.

Socrates said: Yes, Crito, and they of whom you speak are right in so acting, for they think that they will be gainers by the delay; but I am right in not following their example, for I do not think that I should gain anything by drinking the poison a little later; I should only be ridiculous in my own eyes for sparing and saving a life which is already forfeit. Please then to do as I say, and not to refuse me.

 Crito made a sign to the servant, who was standing by; and he went out, and having been absent for some time, returned with the jailer carrying the cup of poison. Socrates said: You, my good friend, who are experienced in these matters, shall give me directions how I am to proceed. The man answered: You have only to walk about until your legs are heavy, and then to lie down, and the poison will act. At the same time he handed the cup to Socrates, who in the easiest and gentlest manner, without the least fear or change of color or feature, looking at the man with all his eyes, Echecrates, as his manner was, took the cup and said: What do you say about making a libation out of this cup to any god? May I, or not? The man answered: We only prepare, Socrates, just so much as we deem enough. I understand, he said: but I may and must ask the gods to prosper my journey from this to the other world—even so—and so be it according to my prayer. Then raising the cup to his lips, quite readily and cheerfully he drank off the poison. And hitherto most of us had been able to control our sorrow; but now when we saw him drinking, and saw too that he had finished the draught, we could no longer forbear, and in spite of myself my own tears were flowing fast; so that I covered my face and wept, not for him, but at the thought of my own calamity in having to part from such a friend. Nor was I the first; for Crito, when he found himself unable to restrain his tears, had got up, and I followed; and at that moment, Apollodorus, who had been weeping all the time, broke out in a loud and passionate cry which made cowards of us all. Socrates alone retained his calmness: What is this strange outcry? he said. I sent away the women mainly in order that they might not misbehave in this way, for I have been told that a man should die in peace. Be quiet, then, and have patience. When we heard his words we were ashamed, and refrained our tears; and he walked about until, as he said, his legs began to fail, and then he lay on his back, according to the directions, and the man who gave him the poison now and then looked at his feet and legs; and after a while he pressed his foot hard, and asked him if he could feel; and he said, No; and then his leg, and so upwards and upwards, and showed us that he was cold and stiff. And he felt them himself, and said: When the poison reaches the heart, that will be the end. He was beginning to grow cold about the groin, when he uncovered his face, for he had covered himself up, and said—they were his last words—he said: Crito, I owe a cock to Asclepius;

will you remember to pay the debt? The debt shall be paid, said Crito; is there anything else? There was no answer to this question; but in a minute or two a movement was heard, and the attendants uncovered him; his eyes were set, and Crito closed his eyes and mouth.

    Such was the end, Echecrates, of our friend; concerning whom I may truly say, that of all the men of his time whom I have known, he was the wisest and justest and best.

ARISTOTLE

POETICS

BY ARISTOTLE

Translated by S. H. Butcher

SECTION 1

Part I

I propose to treat of Poetry in itself and of its various kinds, noting the essential quality of each, to inquire into the structure of the plot as requisite to a good poem; into the number and nature of the parts of which a poem is composed; and similarly into whatever else falls within the same inquiry. Following, then, the order of nature, let us begin with the principles which come first.

Epic poetry and Tragedy, Comedy also and Dithyrambic poetry, and the music of the flute and of the lyre in most of their forms, are all in their general conception modes of imitation. They differ, however, from one another in three respects: the medium, the objects, the manner or mode of imitation, being in each case distinct.

For as there are persons who, by conscious art or mere habit, imitate and represent various objects through the medium of color and form, or again by the voice; so in the arts above mentioned, taken as a whole, the imitation is produced by rhythm, language, or "harmony," either singly or combined.

Thus in the music of the flute and of the lyre, "harmony" and rhythm alone are employed; also in other arts, such as that of the shepherd's pipe, which are essentially similar to these. In dancing, rhythm alone is used without "harmony"; for even dancing imitates character, emotion, and action, by rhythmical movement.

There is another art which imitates by means of language alone, and that either in prose or verse—which verse, again, may either combine different meters or consist of but one kind, but this has hitherto been without a name. For there is no common term we could apply to the mimes of Sophron and Xenarchus and the Socratic dialogues on the one hand; and, on the other, to poetic imitations in iambic, elegiac, or any similar meter. People do, indeed, add the word "maker" or "poet" to the name of the meter, and speak of elegiac poets, or epic (that is, hexameter) poets, as if it were not the imitation that makes the poet, but the verse that entitles them all to the name. Even when a treatise on medicine or natural science is brought out in verse, the name of poet is by custom given to the author; and yet Homer and Empedocles have nothing in common but the meter, so that it would be right to call the one poet, the other physicist rather than poet. On the same principle, even if a writer in his poetic imitation were to combine all meters, as Chaeremon did in his Centaur, which is a medley composed of meters of all kinds, we should bring him too under the general term poet.

So much then for these distinctions. There are, again, some arts which employ all the means above mentioned—namely, rhythm, tune, and meter. Such are Dithyrambic and Nomic poetry, and also Tragedy and Comedy; but between them originally the difference is, that in the first two cases these means are all employed in combination, in the latter, now one means is employed, now another.

Such, then, are the differences of the arts with respect to the medium of imitation

Part II

Since the objects of imitation are men in action, and these men must be either of a higher or a lower type (for moral character mainly answers to these divisions, goodness and badness being the distinguishing marks of moral differences), it follows that we must represent men either as better than in real life, or as worse, or as they are. It is the same in painting. Polygnotus depicted men as nobler than they are, Pauson as less noble, Dionysius drew them true to life.

Now it is evident that each of the modes of imitation above mentioned will exhibit these differences, and become a distinct kind in imitating objects that are thus distinct. Such diversities may be found even in dancing, flute playing, and lyre-playing. So again in language, whether prose or verse unaccompanied by music. Homer, for example, makes men better than they are; Cleophon as they are; Hegemon the Thasian, the inventor of parodies, and Nicochares, the author of the Deiliad, worse than they are. The same thing holds good of Dithyrambs and Nomes; here too one may portray different types, as Timotheus and Philoxenus differed in representing their Cyclopes. The same distinction marks off Tragedy from Comedy;

for Comedy aims at representing men as worse, Tragedy as better than in actual life.

Part III

There is still a third difference—the manner in which each of these objects may be imitated. For the medium being the same, and the objects the same, the poet may imitate by narration—in which case he can either take another personality as Homer does, or speak in his own person, unchanged—or he may present all his characters as living and moving before us.

These, then, as we said at the beginning, are the three differences which distinguish artistic imitation: the medium, the objects, and the manner. So that from one point of view, Sophocles is an imitator of the same kind as Homer—for both imitate higher types of character; from another point of view, of the same kind as Aristophanes—for both imitate persons acting and doing. Hence, some say, the name of "drama" is given to such poems, as representing action. For the same reason the Dorians claim the invention both of Tragedy and Comedy. The claim to Comedy is put forward by the Megarians—not only by those of Greece proper, who allege that it originated under their democracy, but also by the Megarians of Sicily, for the poet Epicharmus, who is much earlier than Chionides and Magnes, belonged to that country. Tragedy too is claimed by certain Dorians of the Peloponnese. In each case they appeal to the evidence of language. The outlying villages, they say, are by them called komai, by the Athenians demoi: and they assume that comedians were so named not from komazein, "to revel," but because they wandered from village to village (kata komas), being excluded contemptuously from the city. They add also that the Dorian word for "doing" is dran, and the Athenian, prattein.

This may suffice as to the number and nature of the various modes of imitation.

Part IV

Poetry in general seems to have sprung from two causes, each of them lying deep in our nature. First, the instinct of imitation is implanted in man from childhood, one difference between him and other animals being that he is the most imitative of living creatures, and through imitation learns his earliest lessons; and no less universal is the pleasure felt in things imitated. We have evidence of this in the facts of experience. Objects which in themselves we view with pain, we delight to contemplate when reproduced with minute fidelity: such as the forms of the most ignoble animals and of dead bodies. The cause of this again is, that to learn gives the liveliest pleasure, not only to philosophers but to men in general; whose capacity, however, of learning is more limited. Thus the reason why men enjoy seeing a likeness is, that in contemplating it they find themselves learning or inferring, and saying perhaps, "Ah, that is he." For if you happen not to have seen the original, the pleasure will be due not to the imitation as such, but to the execution, the coloring, or some such other cause.

Imitation, then, is one instinct of our nature. Next, there is the instinct for "harmony" and rhythm, meters being manifestly sections of rhythm. Persons, therefore, starting with this natural gift developed by degrees their special aptitudes, till their rude improvisations gave birth to Poetry.

Poetry now diverged in two directions, according to the individual character of the writers. The graver spirits imitated noble actions, and the actions of good men. The more trivial sort imitated the actions of meaner persons, at first composing satires, as the former did hymns to the gods and the praises of famous men. A poem of the satirical kind cannot indeed be put down to any author earlier than Homer; though many such writers probably there were. But from Homer onward, instances can be cited—his own Margites, for example, and other similar compositions. The appropriate meter was also here introduced; hence the measure is still called the iambic or lampooning measure, being that in which people lampooned one another. Thus the older poets were distinguished as writers of heroic or of lampooning verse.

As, in the serious style, Homer is preeminent among poets, for he alone combined dramatic form with excellence of imitation so he too first laid down the main lines of comedy, by dramatizing the ludicrous instead of writing personal satire. His Margites bears the same relation to comedy that the Iliad and Odyssey do to tragedy. But when Tragedy and Comedy came to light, the two classes of poets still followed their natural bent: the lampooners became writers of Comedy, and the Epic poets were succeeded by Tragedians, since the drama was a larger and higher form of art.

Whether Tragedy has as yet perfected its proper types or not; and whether it is to be judged in itself, or in relation also to the audience, this raises another question. Be that as it may, Tragedy—as also Comedy—was at first mere improvisation. The one originated with the authors of the Dithyramb, the other with those of the phallic songs, which are still in use in many of our cities. Tragedy advanced by slow degrees; each new element that showed itself was in turn developed. Having passed through many changes, it found its natural form, and there it stopped.

Aeschylus first introduced a second actor; he diminished the importance of the Chorus, and assigned the leading part to the dialogue. Sophocles raised the number of actors to three, and added scene-painting. Moreover, it was not till late that the short plot was discarded for one of greater compass, and the grotesque diction of the earlier satyric form for the stately manner of Tragedy. The iambic measure then replaced the trochaic tetrameter, which was originally employed when the poetry was of the satyric order, and had greater with dancing. Once dialogue had come in, Nature herself discovered the appropriate measure. For the iambic is, of all measures, the most colloquial we see it in the fact that conversational speech runs into iambic lines more frequently than into any other kind of verse; rarely into hexameters, and only when we drop the colloquial intonation. The additions to the number of "episodes" or acts, and the other accessories of which tradition tells, must be taken as already described; for to discuss them in detail would, doubtless, be a large undertaking.

Part V

Comedy is, as we have said, an imitation of characters of a lower type—not, however, in the full sense of the word bad, the ludicrous being merely a subdivision of the ugly. It consists in some defect or ugliness which is not painful or destructive. To take an obvious example, the comic mask is ugly and distorted, but does not imply pain.

The successive changes through which Tragedy passed, and the authors of these changes, are well known, whereas Comedy has had no history, because it was not at first treated seriously. It was late before the Archon granted a comic chorus to a poet; the performers were till then voluntary. Comedy had already taken definite shape when comic poets, distinctively so called, are heard of. Who furnished it with masks, or prologues, or increased the number of actors—these and other similar details remain unknown. As for the plot, it came originally from Sicily; but of Athenian writers Crates was the first who abandoning the "iambic" or lampooning form, generalized his themes and plots.

Epic poetry agrees with Tragedy in so far as it is an imitation in verse of characters of a higher type. They differ in that Epic poetry admits but one kind of meter and is narrative in form. They differ, again, in their length: for Tragedy endeavors, as far as possible, to confine itself to a single revolution of the sun, or but slightly to exceed this limit, whereas the Epic action has no limits of time. This, then, is a second point of difference;

though at first the same freedom was admitted in Tragedy as in Epic poetry.

Of their constituent parts some are common to both, some peculiar to Tragedy: whoever, therefore knows what is good or bad Tragedy, knows also about Epic poetry. All the elements of an Epic poem are found in Tragedy, but the elements of a Tragedy are not all found in the Epic poem.

Part VI

Of the poetry which imitates in hexameter verse, and of Comedy, we will speak hereafter. Let us now discuss Tragedy, resuming its formal definition, as resulting from what has been already said.

Tragedy, then, is an imitation of an action that is serious, complete, and of a certain magnitude; in language embellished with each kind of artistic ornament, the several kinds being found in separate parts of the play; in the form of action, not of narrative; through pity and fear effecting the proper purgation of these emotions. By "language embellished," I mean language into which rhythm, "harmony" and song enter. By "the several kinds in separate parts," I mean, that some parts are rendered through the medium of verse alone, others again with the aid of song.

Now as tragic imitation implies persons acting, it necessarily follows in the first place, that Spectacular equipment will be a part of Tragedy. Next, Song and Diction, for these are the media of imitation. By "Diction" I mean the mere metrical arrangement of the words: as for "Song," it is a term whose sense everyone understands.

Again, Tragedy is the imitation of an action; and an action implies personal agents, who necessarily possess certain distinctive qualities both of character and thought; for it is by these that we qualify actions themselves, and these—thought and character—are the two natural causes from which actions spring, and on actions again all success or failure depends. Hence, the Plot is the imitation of the action—for by plot I here mean the arrangement of the incidents. By Character I mean that in virtue of which we ascribe certain qualities to the agents. Thought is required wherever a statement is proved, or, it may be, a general truth enunciated. Every Tragedy, therefore, must have six parts, which parts determine its quality—namely, Plot, Character, Diction, Thought, Spectacle, Song. Two of the parts constitute the medium of imitation, one the manner, and three the objects of imitation. And these complete the fist. These elements have been employed, we may say, by the poets to a man; in fact, every play contains Spectacular elements as well as Character, Plot, Diction, Song, and Thought.

But most important of all is the structure of the incidents. For Tragedy is an imitation, not of men, but of an action and of life, and life consists in action, and its end is a mode of action, not a quality. Now character determines men's qualities, but it is by their actions that they are happy or the reverse. Dramatic action, therefore, is not with a view to the representation of character: character comes in as subsidiary to the actions. Hence the incidents and the plot are the end of a tragedy; and the end is the chief thing of all. Again, without action there cannot be a tragedy; there may be without character. The tragedies of most of our modern poets fail in the rendering of character; and of poets in general this is often true. It is the same in painting; and here lies the difference between Zeuxis and Polygnotus. Polygnotus delineates character well; the style of Zeuxis is devoid of ethical quality. Again, if you string together a set of speeches expressive of character, and well finished in point of diction and thought, you will not produce the essential tragic effect nearly so well as with a play which, however deficient in these respects, yet has a plot and artistically constructed incidents. Besides which, the most powerful elements of emotional interest in Tragedy—Peripeteia or Reversal of the Situation, and Recognition scenes—are parts of the plot. A further proof is, that novices in the art attain to finish of diction and precision of portraiture before they can construct the plot. It is the same with almost all the early poets.

The plot, then, is the first principle, and, as it were, the soul of a tragedy; Character holds the second place. A similar fact is seen in painting. The most beautiful colors, laid on confusedly, will not give as much pleasure as the chalk outline of a portrait. Thus Tragedy is the imitation of an action, and of the agents mainly with a view to the action.

Third in order is Thought—that is, the faculty of saying what is possible and pertinent in given circumstances. In the case of oratory, this is the function of the political art and of the art of rhetoric: and so indeed the older poets make their characters speak the language of civic life; the poets of our time, the language of the rhetoricians. Character is that which reveals moral purpose, showing what kind of things a man chooses or avoids. Speeches, therefore, which do not make this manifest, or in which the speaker does not choose or avoid anything whatever, are not expressive of character. Thought, on the other hand, is found where something is proved to be or not to be, or a general maxim is enunciated.

Fourth among the elements enumerated comes Diction; by which I mean, as has been already said, the expression of the meaning in words; and its essence is the same both in verse and prose.

Of the remaining elements Song holds the chief place among the embellishments

The Spectacle has, indeed, an emotional attraction of its own, but, of all the parts, it is the least artistic, and connected least with the art of poetry. For the power of Tragedy, we may be sure, is felt even apart from representation and actors. Besides, the production of spectacular effects depends more on the art of the stage machinist than on that of the poet.

Part VII

These principles being established, let us now discuss the proper structure of the Plot, since this is the first and most important thing in Tragedy.

Now, according to our definition Tragedy is an imitation of an action that is complete, and whole, and of a certain magnitude; for there may be a whole that is wanting in magnitude. A whole is that which has a beginning, a middle, and an end. A beginning is that which does not itself follow anything by causal necessity, but after which something naturally is or comes to be. An end, on the contrary, is that which itself naturally follows some other thing, either by necessity, or as a rule, but has nothing following it. A middle is that which follows something as some other thing follows it. A well constructed plot, therefore, must neither begin nor end at haphazard, but conform to these principles.

Again, a beautiful object, whether it be a living organism or any whole composed of parts, must not only have an orderly arrangement of parts, but must also be of a certain magnitude; for beauty depends on magnitude and order. Hence a very small animal organism cannot be beautiful; for the view of it is confused, the object being seen in an almost imperceptible moment of time. Nor, again, can one of vast size be beautiful; for as the eye cannot take it all in at once, the unity and sense of the whole is lost for the spectator; as for instance if there were one a thousand miles long. As, therefore, in the case of animate bodies and organisms a certain magnitude is necessary, and a magnitude which may be easily embraced in one view; so in the plot, a certain length is necessary, and a length which can be easily embraced by the memory. The limit of length in relation to dramatic competition and sensuous presentment is no part of artistic theory. For had it been the rule for a hundred tragedies to compete together, the performance would have been regulated by the water-clock—as indeed we are told was formerly done. But the limit as fixed by the nature of the drama itself is this: the greater the length, the more beautiful will the piece be by reason of its size, provided that the whole be perspicuous.

And to define the matter roughly, we may say that the proper magnitude is comprised within such limits, that the sequence of events, according to the law of probability or necessity, will admit of a change from bad fortune to good, or from good fortune to bad.

Part VIII

Unity of plot does not, as some persons think, consist in the unity of the hero. For infinitely various are the incidents in one man's life which cannot be reduced to unity; and so, too, there are many actions of one man out of which we cannot make one action. Hence the error, as it appears, of all poets who have composed a Heracleid, a Theseid, or other poems of the kind. They imagine that as Heracles was one man, the story of Heracles must also be a unity. But Homer, as in all else he is of surpassing merit, here too—whether from art or natural genius—seems to have happily discerned the truth. In composing the Odyssey he did not include all the adventures of Odysseus, such as his wound on Parnassus, or his feigned madness at the mustering of the host, incidents between which there was no necessary or probable connection: but he made the Odyssey, and likewise the Iliad, to center round an action that in our sense of the word is one. As therefore, in the other imitative arts, the imitation is one when the object imitated is one, so the plot, being an imitation of an action, must imitate one action and that a whole, the structural union of the parts being such that, if any one of them is displaced or removed, the whole will be disjointed and disturbed. For a thing whose presence or absence makes no visible difference, is not an organic part of the whole.

Part IX

It is, moreover, evident from what has been said, that it is not the function of the poet to relate what has happened, but what may happen—what is possible according to the law of probability or necessity. The poet and the historian differ not by writing in verse or in prose. The work of Herodotus might be put into verse, and it would still be a species of history, with meter no less than without it. The true difference is that one relates what has happened, the other what may happen. Poetry, therefore, is a more philosophical and a higher thing than history: for poetry tends to express the universal, history the particular. By the universal I mean how a person of a certain type on occasion speak or act, according to the law of probability or necessity; and it is this universality at which poetry aims in the names she attaches to the personages. The particular is, for example, what Alcibiades did or suffered. In Comedy this is already apparent: for here the poet first constructs the plot on the lines of probability, and then inserts characteristic names, unlike the lampooners who write about particular individuals. But tragedians still keep to real names, the reason being that what is possible is credible: what has not happened we do not at once feel sure to be possible; but what has happened is manifestly possible: otherwise it would not have happened. Still there are even some tragedies in which there are only one or two well-known names, the rest being fictitious. In others, none are well known, as in Agathon's Antheus, where incidents and names alike are fictitious, and yet they give none the less pleasure. We must not, therefore, at all costs keep to the received legends, which are the usual subjects of Tragedy. Indeed, it would be absurd to attempt it; for even subjects that are known are known only to a few, and yet give pleasure to all. It clearly follows that the poet or "maker" should be the maker of plots rather than of verses; since he is a poet because he imitates, and what he imitates are actions. And even if he chances to take a historical subject, he is none the less a poet; for there is no reason why some events that have actually happened should not conform to the law of the probable and possible, and in virtue of that quality in them he is their poet or maker.

Of all plots and actions the episodic are the worst. I call a plot "episodic" in which the episodes or acts succeed one another without probable or necessary sequence. Bad poets compose such pieces by their own fault, good poets, to please the players; for, as they write show pieces for competition, they stretch the plot beyond its capacity, and are often forced to break the natural continuity.

But again, Tragedy is an imitation not only of a complete action, but of events inspiring fear or pity. Such an effect is best produced when the events come on us by surprise; and the effect is heightened when, at the same time, they follow as cause and effect. The tragic wonder will then be greater than if they happened of themselves or by accident; for even coincidences are most striking when they have an air of design. We may instance the statue of Mitys at Argos, which fell upon his murderer while he was a spectator at a festival, and killed him. Such events seem not to be due to mere chance. Plots, therefore, constructed on these principles are necessarily the best.

Part X

Plots are either Simple or Complex, for the actions in real life, of which the plots are an imitation, obviously show a similar distinction. An action which is one and continuous in the sense above defined, I call Simple, when the change of fortune takes place without Reversal of the Situation and without Recognition.

A Complex action is one in which the change is accompanied by such Reversal, or by Recognition, or by both. These last should arise from the internal structure of the plot, so that what follows should be the necessary or probable result of the preceding action. It makes all the difference whether any given event is a case of propter hoc or post hoc.

PART XI

Reversal of the Situation is a change by which the action veers round to its opposite, subject always to our rule of probability or necessity. Thus in the Oedipus, the messenger comes to cheer Oedipus and free him from his alarms about his mother, but by revealing who he is, he produces the opposite effect. Again in the Lynceus, Lynceus is being led away to his death, and Danaus goes with him, meaning to slay him; but the outcome of the preceding incidents is that Danaus is killed and Lynceus saved.

Recognition, as the name indicates, is a change from ignorance to knowledge, producing love or hate between the persons destined by the poet for good or bad fortune. The best form of recognition is coincident with a Reversal of the Situation, as in the Oedipus. There are indeed other forms. Even inanimate things of the most trivial kind may in a sense be objects of recognition. Again, we may recognize or discover whether a person has done a thing or not. But the recognition which is most intimately connected with the plot and action is, as we have said, the recognition of persons. This recognition, combined with Reversal, will produce either pity or fear; and actions producing these effects are those which, by our definition, Tragedy represents. Moreover, it is upon such situations that the issues of good or bad fortune will depend. Recognition, then, being between persons, it may happen that one person only is recognized by the other when the latter is already known, or it may be necessary that the recognition should be on both sides. Thus Iphigenia is revealed to Orestes by the sending of the letter; but another act of recognition is required to make Orestes known to Iphigenia.

Two parts, then, of the Plot—Reversal of the Situation and Recognition—turn upon surprises. A third part is the Scene of Suffering. The Scene of Suffering is a destructive or painful action, such as death on the stage, bodily agony, wounds, and the like.

SECTION 2

PART XII

The parts of Tragedy which must be treated as elements of the whole have been already mentioned. We now come to the quantitative parts—the separate parts into which Tragedy is divided—namely, Prologue, Episode, Exode, Choric song; this last being divided into Parode and Stasimon. These are common to all plays: peculiar to some are the songs of actors from the stage and the Commoi.

The Prologue is that entire part of a tragedy which precedes the Parode of the Chorus. The Episode is that entire part of a tragedy which is between complete choric songs. The Exode is that entire part of a tragedy which has no choric song after it. Of the Choric part the Parode is the first undivided utterance of the Chorus: the Stasimon is a Choric ode without anapaests or trochaic tetrameters: the Commos is a joint lamentation of Chorus and actors. The parts of Tragedy which must be treated as elements of the whole have been already mentioned. The quantitative parts—the separate parts into which it is divided—are here enumerated.

PART XIII

As the sequel to what has already been said, we must proceed to consider what the poet should aim at, and what he should avoid, in constructing his plots; and by what means the specific effect of Tragedy will be produced.

A perfect tragedy should, as we have seen, be arranged not on the simple but on the complex plan. It should, moreover, imitate actions which excite pity and fear, this being the distinctive mark of tragic imitation. It follows plainly, in the first place, that the change of fortune presented must not be the spectacle of a virtuous man brought from prosperity to adversity: for this moves neither pity nor fear; it merely shocks us. Nor, again, that of a bad man passing from adversity to prosperity: for nothing can be more alien to the spirit of Tragedy; it possesses no single tragic quality; it neither satisfies the moral sense nor calls forth pity or fear. Nor, again, should the downfall of the utter villain be exhibited. A plot of this kind would, doubtless, satisfy the moral sense, but it would inspire neither pity nor fear; for pity is aroused by unmerited misfortune, fear by the misfortune of a man like ourselves. Such an event, therefore, will be neither pitiful nor terrible. There remains, then, the character between these two extremes—that of a man who is not eminently good and just, yet whose misfortune is brought about not by vice or depravity, but by some error or frailty. He must be one who is highly renowned and prosperous—a personage like Oedipus, Thyestes, or other illustrious men of such families.

A well-constructed plot should, therefore, be single in its issue, rather than double as some maintain. The change of fortune should be not from bad to good, but, reversely, from good to bad. It should come about as the result not of vice, but of some great error or frailty, in a character either such as we have described, or better rather than worse. The practice of the stage bears out our view. At first the poets recounted any legend that came in their way. Now, the best tragedies are founded on the story of a few houses—on the fortunes of Alcmaeon, Oedipus, Orestes, Meleager, Thyestes, Telephus, and those others who have done or suffered something terrible. A tragedy, then, to be perfect according to the rules of art should be of this construction. Hence they are in error who censure Euripides just because he follows this principle in his plays, many of which end unhappily. It is, as we have said, the right ending. The best proof is that on the stage and in dramatic competition, such plays, if well worked out, are the most tragic in effect; and Euripides, faulty though he may be in the general management of his subject, yet is felt to be the most tragic of the poets.

In the second rank comes the kind of tragedy which some place first. Like the Odyssey, it has a double thread of plot, and also an opposite catastrophe for the good and for the bad. It is accounted the best because of the weakness of the spectators; for the poet is guided in what he writes by the wishes of his audience. The pleasure, however, thence derived is not the true tragic pleasure. It is proper rather to Comedy, where those who, in the piece, are the deadliest enemies—like Orestes and Aegisthus—quit the stage as friends at the close, and no one slays or is slain.

Part XIV

Fear and pity may be aroused by spectacular means; but they may also result from the inner structure of the piece, which is the better way, and indicates a superior poet. For the plot ought to be so constructed that, even without the aid of the eye, he who hears the tale told will thrill with horror and melt to pity at what takes place. This is the impression we should receive from hearing the story of the Oedipus. But to produce this effect by the mere spectacle is a less artistic method, and dependent on extraneous aids. Those who employ spectacular means to create a sense not of the terrible but only of the monstrous, are strangers to the purpose of Tragedy; for we must not demand of Tragedy any and every kind of pleasure, but only that which is proper to it. And since the pleasure which the poet should afford is that which comes from pity and fear through imitation, it is evident that this quality must be impressed upon the incidents.

Let us then determine what are the circumstances which strike us as terrible or pitiful.

Actions capable of this effect must happen between persons who are either friends or enemies or indifferent to one another. If an enemy kills an enemy, there is nothing to excite pity either in the act or the intention—except so far as the suffering in itself is pitiful. So again with indifferent persons. But when the tragic incident occurs between those who are near or dear to one another—if, for example, a brother kills, or intends to kill, a brother, a son his father, a mother her son, a son his mother, or any other deed of the kind is done—these are the situations to be looked for by the poet. He may not indeed destroy the framework of the received legends—the fact, for instance, that Clytemnestra was slain by Orestes and Eriphyle by Alcmaeon—but he ought to show of his own, and skilfully handle the traditional. material. Let us explain more clearly what is meant by skilful handling.

The action may be done consciously and with knowledge of the persons, in the manner of the older poets. It is thus too that Euripides makes Medea slay her children. Or, again, the deed of horror may be done, but done in ignorance, and the tie of kinship or friendship be discovered afterward. The Oedipus of Sophocles is an example. Here, indeed, the incident is outside the drama proper; but cases occur where it falls within the action of the play: one may cite the Alcmaeon of Astydamas, or Telegonus in the Wounded Odysseus. Again, there is a third case—to be about to act with knowledge of the persons and then not to act. The fourth case is when someone is about to do an irreparable deed through ignorance, and makes the discovery before it is done. These are the only possible ways. For the deed must either be done or not done—and that wittingly or unwittingly. But of all these ways, to be about to act knowing the persons, and then not to act, is the worst. It is shocking without being tragic, for no disaster follows It is, therefore, never, or very rarely, found in poetry. One instance, however, is in the Antigone, where Haemon threatens to kill Creon. The next and better way is that the deed should be perpetrated. Still better, that it should be perpetrated in ignorance, and the discovery made afterward. There is then nothing to shock us, while the discovery produces a startling effect. The last case is the best, as when in the Cresphontes Merope is about to slay her son, but, recognizing who he is, spares his life. So in the Iphigenia, the sister recognizes the brother just in time. Again in the Helle, the son recognizes the mother when on the point of giving her up. This, then, is why a few families only, as has been already observed, furnish the subjects of tragedy. It was not art, but happy chance, that led the poets in search of subjects to impress the tragic quality upon their plots. They are compelled, therefore, to have recourse to those houses whose history contains moving incidents like these.

Enough has now been said concerning the structure of the incidents, and the right kind of plot.

Part XV

In respect of Character there are four things to be aimed at. First, and most important, it must be good. Now any speech or action that manifests moral purpose of any kind will be expressive of character: the character will be good if the purpose is good. This rule is relative to each class. Even a woman may be good, and also a slave; though the woman may be said to be an inferior being, and the slave quite worthless. The second thing to aim at is propriety. There is a type of manly valor; but valor in a woman, or unscrupulous cleverness is inappropriate. Thirdly, character must be true to life: for this is a distinct thing from goodness and propriety, as here described. The fourth point is consistency: for though the subject of the imitation, who suggested the type, be inconsistent, still he must be consistently inconsistent. As an example of motiveless degradation of character, we have Menelaus in the Orestes; of character indecorous and inappropriate, the lament of Odysseus in the Scylla, and the speech of Melanippe; of inconsistency, the Iphigenia at Aulis—for Iphigenia the suppliant in no way resembles her later self.

As in the structure of the plot, so too in the portraiture of character, the poet should always aim either at the necessary or the probable. Thus a person of a given character should speak or act in a given way, by the rule either of necessity or of probability; just as this event should follow that by necessary or probable sequence. It is therefore evident that the unraveling of the plot, no less than the complication, must arise out of the plot itself, it must not be brought about by the Deus ex Machina—as in the Medea, or in the return of the Greeks in the Iliad. The Deus ex Machina should be employed only for events external to the drama—for antecedent or subsequent events, which lie beyond the range of human knowledge, and which require to be reported or foretold; for to the gods we ascribe the power of seeing all things. Within the action there must be nothing irrational. If the irrational cannot be excluded, it should be outside the scope of the tragedy. Such is the irrational element the Oedipus of Sophocles.

Again, since Tragedy is an imitation of persons who are above the common level, the example of good portrait painters should be followed. They, while reproducing the distinctive form of the original, make a likeness which is true to life and yet more beautiful. So too the poet, in representing men who are irascible or indolent, or have other defects of character, should preserve the type and yet ennoble it. In this way Achilles is portrayed by Agathon and Homer.

These then are rules the poet should observe. Nor should he neglect those appeals to the senses, which, though not among the essentials, are the concomitants of poetry; for here too there is much room for error. But of this enough has been said in our published treatises.

PART XVI

What Recognition is has been already explained. We will now enumerate its kinds.

First, the least artistic form, which, from poverty of wit, is most commonly employed—recognition by signs. Of these some are congenital—such as "the spear which the Earth-born race bear on their bodies," or the stars introduced by Carcinus in his Thyestes. Others are acquired after birth; and of these some are bodily marks, as scars; some external tokens, as necklaces, or the little ark in the Tyro by which the discovery is effected. Even these admit of more or less skilful treatment. Thus in the recognition of Odysseus by his scar, the discovery is made in one way by the nurse, in another by the swineherds. The use of tokens for the express purpose of proof—and, indeed, any formal proof with or without tokens—is a less artistic mode of recognition. A better kind is that which comes about by a turn of incident, as in the Bath Scene in the Odyssey.

Next come the recognitions invented at will by the poet, and on that account wanting in art. For example, Orestes in the Iphigenia reveals the fact that he is Orestes. She, indeed, makes herself known by the letter; but he, by speaking himself, and saying what the poet, not what the plot requires. This, therefore, is nearly allied to the fault above mentioned, for Orestes might as well have brought tokens with him. Another similar instance is the "voice of the shuttle" in the Tereus of Sophocles.

The third kind depends on memory when the sight of some object awakens a feeling: as in the Cyprians of Dicaeogenes, where the hero breaks into tears on seeing the picture; or again in the Lay of Alcinous, where Odysseus, hearing the minstrel play the lyre, recalls the past and weeps; and hence the recognition.

The fourth kind is by process of reasoning. Thus in the Choephori: "Someone resembling me has come: no one resembles me but Orestes: therefore Orestes has come." Such too is the discovery made by Iphigenia in the play of Polyidus the Sophist. It was a natural reflection for Orestes to make, "So I too must die at the altar like my sister." So, again, in the Tydeus of Theodectes, the father says, "I came to find my son, and I lose my own life." So too in the Phineidae: the women, on seeing the place, inferred their fate: "Here we are doomed to die, for here we were cast forth." Again, there is a composite kind of recognition involving false inference on the part of one of the characters, as in the Odysseus Disguised as a Messenger. A said [that no one else was able to bend the bow; hence, B (the disguised Odysseus) imagined that A would] recognize the bow which, in fact, he had not seen; and to bring about a recognition by this means—the expectation that A would recognize the bow—is false inference.

But, of all recognitions, the best is that which arises from the incidents themselves, where the startling discovery is made by natural means. Such is that in the Oedipus of Sophocles, and in the Iphigenia; for it was natural that Iphigenia should wish to dispatch a letter. These recognitions alone dispense with the artificial aid of tokens or amulets. Next come the recognitions by process of reasoning.

Part XVII

In constructing the plot and working it out with the proper diction, the poet should place the scene, as far as possible, before his eyes. In this way, seeing everything with the utmost vividness, as if he were a spectator of the action, he will discover what is in keeping with it, and be most unlikely to overlook inconsistencies. The need of such a rule is shown by the fault found in Carcinus. Amphiaraus was on his way from the temple. This fact escaped the observation of one who did not see the situation. On the stage, however, the Piece failed, the audience being offended at the oversight.

Again, the poet should work out his play, to the best of his power, with appropriate gestures; for those who feel emotion are most convincing through natural sympathy with the characters they represent; and one who is agitated storms, one who is angry rages, with the most lifelike reality. Hence poetry implies either a happy gift of nature or a strain of madness. In the one case a man can take the mold of any character; in the other, he is lifted out of his proper self.

As for the story, whether the poet takes it ready made or constructs it for himself, he should first sketch its general outline, and then fill in the episodes and amplify in detail. The general plan may be illustrated by the Iphigenia. A young girl is sacrificed; she disappears mysteriously from the eyes of those who sacrificed her; she is transported to another country, where the custom is to offer up an strangers to the goddess. To this ministry she is appointed. Some time later her own brother chances to arrive. The fact that the oracle for some reason ordered him to go there, is outside the general plan of the play. The purpose, again, of his coming is outside the action proper. However, he comes, he is seized, and, when on the point of being sacrificed, reveals who he is. The mode of recognition may be either that of Euripides or of Polyidus, in whose play he exclaims very naturally: "So it was not my sister only, but I too, who was doomed to be sacrificed"; and by that remark he is saved.

After this, the names being once given, it remains to fill in the episodes. We must see that they are relevant to the action. In the case of Orestes, for example, there is the madness which led to his capture, and his deliverance by means of the purificatory rite. In the drama, the episodes are short, but it is these that give extension to Epic poetry. Thus the story of the Odyssey can be stated briefly. A certain man is absent from home for many years; he is jealously watched by Poseidon, and left desolate. Meanwhile his home is in a wretched plight—suitors are wasting his substance and plotting against his son. At length, tempest-tost, he himself arrives; he makes certain persons acquainted with him; he attacks the suitors with his own hand, and is himself preserved while he destroys them. This is the essence of the plot; the rest is episode.

Part XVIII

Every tragedy falls into two parts—Complication, and Unraveling or Denouement. Incidents extraneous to the action are frequently combined with a portion of the action proper, to form the Complication; the rest is the Unraveling. By the Complication I mean all that extends from the beginning of the action to the part which marks the turning-point to good or bad fortune. The Unraveling is that which extends from the beginning of the change to the end. Thus, in the Lynceus of Theodectes, the Complication consists of the incidents presupposed in the drama, the seizure of the child, and then again ... [the Unraveling] extends from the accusation of murder to the end.

There are four kinds of Tragedy: the Complex, depending entirely on

Reversal of the Situation and Recognition; the Pathetic (where the motive is passion), such as the tragedies on Ajax and Ixion; the Ethical (where the motives are ethical), such as the Phthiotides and the Peleus. The fourth kind is the Simple. [We here exclude the purely spectacular element], exemplified by the Phorcides, the Prometheus, and scenes laid in Hades. The poet should endeavor, if possible, to combine all poetic elements; or failing that, the greatest number and those the most important; the more so, in face of the caviling criticism of the day. For whereas there have hitherto been good poets, each in his own branch, the critics now expect one man to surpass all others in their several lines of excellence.

In speaking of a tragedy as the same or different, the best test to take is the plot. Identity exists where the Complication and Unraveling are the same. Many poets tie the knot well, but unravel it Both arts, however, should always be mastered.

Again, the poet should remember what has been often said, and not make an Epic structure into a tragedy—by an Epic structure I mean one with a multiplicity of plots—as if, for instance, you were to make a tragedy out of the entire story of the Iliad. In the Epic poem, owing to its length, each part assumes its proper magnitude. In the drama the result is far from answering to the poet's expectation. The proof is that the poets who have dramatized the whole story of the Fall of Troy, instead of selecting portions, like Euripides; or who have taken the whole tale of Niobe, and not a part of her story, like Aeschylus, either fail utterly or meet with poor success on the stage. Even Agathon has been known to fail from this one defect. In his Reversals of the Situation, however, he shows a marvelous skill in the effort to hit the popular taste—to produce a tragic effect that satisfies the moral sense. This effect is produced when the clever rogue, like Sisyphus, is outwitted, or the brave villain defeated. Such an event is probable in Agathon's sense of the word: "is probable," he says, "that many things should happen contrary to probability."

The Chorus too should be regarded as one of the actors; it should be an integral part of the whole, and share in the action, in the manner not of Euripides but of Sophocles. As for the later poets, their choral songs pertain as little to the subject of the piece as to that of any other tragedy. They are, therefore, sung as mere interludes—a practice first begun by Agathon. Yet what difference is there between introducing such choral interludes, and transferring a speech, or even a whole act, from one play to another.

Part XIX

It remains to speak of Diction and Thought, the other parts of Tragedy having been already discussed. concerning Thought, we may assume what is said in the Rhetoric, to which inquiry the subject more strictly belongs. Under Thought is included every effect which has to be produced by speech, the subdivisions being: proof and refutation; the excitation of the feelings, such as pity, fear, anger, and the like; the suggestion of importance or its opposite. Now, it is evident that the dramatic incidents must be treated from the same points of view as the dramatic speeches, when the object is to evoke the sense of pity, fear, importance, or probability. The only difference is that the incidents should speak for themselves without verbal exposition; while effects aimed at in should be produced by the speaker, and as a result of the speech. For what were the business of a speaker, if the Thought were revealed quite apart from what he says?

Next, as regards Diction. One branch of the inquiry treats of the Modes of Utterance. But this province of knowledge belongs to the art of Delivery and to the masters of that science. It includes, for instance: what is a command, a prayer, a statement, a threat, a question, an answer, and so forth. To know or not to know these things involves no serious censure upon the poet's art. For who can admit the fault imputed to Homer by Protagoras—that in the words, "Sing, goddess, of the wrath," he gives a command under the idea that he utters a prayer? For to tell someone to do a thing or not to do it is, he says, a command. We may, therefore, pass this over as an inquiry that belongs to another art, not to poetry.

Part XX

Language in general includes the following parts: Letter, Syllable, Connecting Word, Noun, Verb, Inflection or Case, Sentence or Phrase.

A Letter is an indivisible sound, yet not every such sound, but only one which can form part of a group of sounds. For even brutes utter indivisible sounds, none of which I call a letter. The sound I mean may be either a vowel, a semivowel, or a mute. A vowel is that which without impact of tongue or lip has an audible sound. A semivowel that which with such impact has an audible sound, as S and R. A mute, that which with such impact has by itself no sound, but joined to a vowel sound becomes audible, as G and D. These are distinguished according to the form assumed by the mouth and the place where they are produced; according as they are aspirated or smooth, long or short; as they are acute, grave, or of an intermediate tone; which inquiry belongs in detail to the writers on meter.

A Syllable is a nonsignificant sound, composed of a mute and a vowel: for GR without A is a syllable, as also with A—GRA. But the investigation of these differences belongs also to metrical science.

A Connecting Word is a nonsignificant sound, which neither causes nor hinders the union of many sounds into one significant sound; it may be placed at either end or in the middle of a sentence. Or, a nonsignificant sound, which out of several sounds, each of them significant, is capable of forming one significant sound, as amphi, peri, and the like. Or, a nonsignificant sound, which marks the beginning, end, or division of a sentence; such, however, that it cannot correctly stand by itself at the beginning of a sentence, as men, etoi, de.

A Noun is a composite significant sound, not marking time, of which no part is in itself significant: for in double or compound words we do not employ the separate parts as if each were in itself significant. Thus in Theodorus, "god-given," the doron or "gift" is not in itself significant.

A Verb is a composite significant sound, marking time, in which, as in the noun, no part is in itself significant. For "man" or "white" does not express the idea of "when"; but "he walks" or "he has walked" does connote time, present or past.

Inflection belongs both to the noun and verb, and expresses either the relation "of," "to," or the like; or that of number, whether one or many, as "man" or "men"; or the modes or tones in actual delivery, e.g. a question or a command. "Did he go?" and "go" are verbal inflections of this kind.

A Sentence or Phrase is a composite significant sound, some at least of whose parts are in themselves significant; for not every such group of words consists of verbs and nouns—"the definition of man," for example—but it may dispense even with the verb. Still it will always have some significant part, as "in walking," or "Cleon son of Cleon." A sentence or phrase may form a unity in two ways, either as signifying one thing, or as consisting of several parts linked together. Thus the Iliad is one by the linking together of parts, the definition of man by the unity of the thing signified.

SECTION 3

Part XXI

Words are of two kinds, simple and double. By simple I mean those composed of nonsignificant elements, such as γη, "earth." By double or compound, those composed either of a significant and nonsignificant element (though within the whole word no element is significant), or of elements that are both significant. A word may likewise be triple, quadruple, or multiple in form, like so many Massilian expressions, e.g. "Hermo-caico-xanthus [who prayed to Father Zeus]."

Every word is either current, or strange, or metaphorical, or ornamental, or newly-coined, or lengthened, or contracted, or altered.

By a current or proper word I mean one which is in general use among a people; by a strange word, one which is in use in another country. Plainly, therefore, the same word may be at once strange and current, but not in relation to the same people. The word sigynon, "lance," is to the Cyprians a current term but to us a strange one.

Metaphor is the application of an alien name by transference either from genus to species, or from species to genus, or from species to species, or by analogy, that is, proportion. Thus from genus to species, as: "There lies my ship"; for lying at anchor is a species of lying. From species to genus, as: "Verily ten thousand noble deeds hath Odysseus wrought"; for ten thousand is a species of large number, and is here used for a large number generally. From species to species, as: "With blade of bronze drew away the life," and "Cleft the water with the vessel of unyielding bronze." Here arusai, "to draw away" is used for tamein, "to cleave," and tamein, again for arusai, each being a species of taking away. Analogy or proportion is when the second term is to the first as the fourth to the third. We may then use the fourth for the second, or the second for the fourth. Sometimes too we qualify the metaphor by adding the term to which the proper word is relative. Thus the cup is to Dionysus as the shield to Ares. The cup may, therefore, be called "the shield of Dionysus," and the shield "the cup of Ares." Or, again, as old age is to life, so is evening to day. Evening may therefore be called, "the old age of the day," and old age, "the evening of life," or, in the phrase of Empedocles, "life's setting sun." For some of the terms of the proportion there is at times no word in existence; still the metaphor may be used. For instance, to scatter seed is called sowing: but the action of the sun in scattering his rays is nameless. Still this process bears to the sun the same relation as sowing to the seed. Hence the expression of the poet "sowing the god-created light." There is another way in which this kind of metaphor may be employed. We may apply an alien term, and then deny of that term one of its proper attributes; as if we were to call the shield, not "the cup of Ares," but "the wineless cup."

A newly-coined word is one which has never been even in local use, but is adopted by the poet himself. Some such words there appear to be:

as ernyges, "sprouters," for kerata, "horns"; and areter, "supplicator," for hiereus, "priest."

A word is lengthened when its own vowel is exchanged for a longer one, or when a syllable is inserted. A word is contracted when some part of it is removed. Instances of lengthening are: poleos for poleos, Peleiadeo for Peleidou; of contraction: kri, do, and ops, as in mia ginetai amphoteron ops, "the appearance of both is one."

An altered word is one in which part of the ordinary form is left unchanged, and part is recast: as in dexiteron kata mazon, "on the right breast," dexiteron is for dexion.

Nouns in themselves are either masculine, feminine, or neuter. Masculine are such as end in N, R, S, or in some letter compounded with S—these being two, PS and X. Feminine, such as end in vowels that are always long, namely E and O, and—of vowels that admit of lengthening—those in A. Thus the number of letters in which nouns masculine and feminine end is the same; for PS and X are equivalent to endings in S. No noun ends in a mute or a vowel short by nature. Three only end in I—meli, "honey"; kommi, "gum"; peperi, "pepper"; five end in U. Neuter nouns end in these two latter vowels; also in N and S.

Part XXII

The perfection of style is to be clear without being mean. The clearest style is that which uses only current or proper words; at the same time it is mean—witness the poetry of Cleophon and of Sthenelus. That diction, on the other hand, is lofty and raised above the commonplace which employs unusual words. By unusual, I mean strange (or rare) words, metaphorical, lengthened—anything, in short, that differs from the normal idiom. Yet a style wholly composed of such words is either a riddle or a jargon; a riddle, if it consists of metaphors; a jargon, if it consists of strange (or rare) words. For the essence of a riddle is to express true facts under impossible combinations. Now this cannot be done by any arrangement of ordinary words, but by the use of metaphor it can. Such is the riddle: "A man I saw who on another man had glued the bronze by aid of fire," and others of the same kind. A diction that is made up of strange (or rare) terms is a jargon. A certain infusion, therefore, of these elements is necessary to style; for the strange (or rare) word, the metaphorical, the ornamental, and the other kinds above mentioned, will raise it above the commonplace and mean, while the use of proper words will make it perspicuous. But nothing contributes more to produce a cleanness of diction that is remote from commonness than the lengthening, contraction, and alteration of words. For by deviating in exceptional cases from the normal idiom, the language will gain distinction; while, at the same time, the partial conformity with usage will give perspicuity. The critics, therefore, are in error who censure these licenses of speech, and hold the author up to ridicule. Thus Eucleides, the elder, declared that it would be an easy matter to be a poet if you might lengthen syllables at will. He caricatured the practice in the very form of his diction, as in the verse:

> "Epicharen eidon Marathonade badizonta,
> "I saw Epichares walking to Marathon,"

or,

> "ouk an g'eramenos ton ekeinou elleboron.
> "Not if you desire his hellebore."

To employ such license at all obtrusively is, no doubt, grotesque; but in any mode of poetic diction there must be moderation. Even metaphors, strange (or rare) words, or any similar forms of speech, would produce the like effect if used without propriety and with the express purpose of being ludicrous. How great a difference is made by the appropriate use of lengthening, may be seen in Epic poetry by the insertion of ordinary forms in the verse. So, again, if we take a strange (or rare) word, a metaphor, or any similar mode of expression, and replace it by the current or proper term, the truth of our observation will be manifest. For example, Aeschylus and Euripides each composed the same iambic line. But the alteration of a single word by Euripides, who employed the rarer term instead of the ordinary one, makes one verse appear beautiful and the other trivial. Aeschylus in his Philoctetes says:

> "phagedaina d'he mou sarkas esthiei podos.
> "The tumor which is eating the flesh of my foot."

Euripides substitutes thoinatai, "feasts on," for esthiei, "feeds on." Again, in the line,

> "nun de m'eon oligos te kai outidanos kai aeikes,
> "Yet a small man, worthless and unseemly,"

the difference will be felt if we substitute the common words,

"nun de m'eon mikros te kai asthenikos kai aeides.
"Yet a little fellow, weak and ugly."

Or, if for the line,

"diphron aeikelion katatheis oligen te trapezan,
"Setting an unseemly couch and a meager table,"

we read,

"diphron mochtheron katatheis mikran te trapezan.
"Setting a wretched couch and a puny table."

Or, for eiones booosin, "the sea shores roar," eiones krazousin, "the sea shores screech."

Again, Ariphrades ridiculed the tragedians for using phrases which no one would employ in ordinary speech: for example, domaton apo, "from the house away," instead of apo domaton, "away from the house"; sethen, ego de nin, "to thee, and I to him"; Achilleos peri, "Achilles about," instead of peri Achilleos, "about Achilles"; and the like. It is precisely because such phrases are not part of the current idiom that they give distinction to the style. This, however, he failed to see.

It is a great matter to observe propriety in these several modes of expression, as also in compound words, strange (or rare) words, and so forth. But the greatest thing by far is to have a command of metaphor. This alone cannot be imparted by another; it is the mark of genius, for to make good metaphors implies an eye for resemblances.

Of the various kinds of words, the compound are best adapted to dithyrambs, rare words to heroic poetry, metaphors to iambic. In heroic poetry, indeed, all these varieties are serviceable. But in iambic verse, which reproduces, as far as may be, familiar speech, the most appropriate words are those which are found even in prose. These are the current or proper, the metaphorical, the ornamental.

Concerning Tragedy and imitation by means of action this may suffice.

Part XXIII

As to that poetic imitation which is narrative in form and employs a single meter, the plot manifestly ought, as in a tragedy, to be constructed on dramatic principles. It should have for its subject a single action, whole and complete, with a beginning, a middle, and an end. It will thus resemble a living organism in all its unity, and produce the pleasure proper to it. It will differ in structure from historical compositions, which of necessity present not a single action, but a single period, and all that happened within that period to one person or to many, little connected together as the events may be. For as the sea-fight at Salamis and the battle with the Carthaginians in Sicily took place at the same time, but did not tend to any one result, so in the sequence of events, one thing sometimes follows another, and yet no single result is thereby produced. Such is the practice, we may say, of most poets. Here again, then, as has been already observed, the transcendent excellence of Homer is manifest. He never attempts to make the whole war of Troy the subject of his poem, though that war had a beginning and an end. It would have been too vast a theme, and not easily embraced in a single view. If, again, he had kept it within moderate limits, it must have been over-complicated by the variety of the incidents. As it is, he detaches a single portion, and admits as episodes many events from the general story of the war—such as the Catalogue of the ships and others—thus diversifying the poem. All other poets take a single hero, a single period, or an action single indeed, but with a multiplicity of parts. Thus did the author of the Cypria and of the Little Iliad. For this reason the Iliad and the Odyssey each furnish the subject of one tragedy, or, at most, of two; while the Cypria supplies materials for many, and the Little Iliad for eight—the Award of the Arms, the Philoctetes, the Neoptolemus, the Eurypylus, the Mendicant Odysseus, the Laconian Women, the Fall of Ilium, the Departure of the Fleet.

Part XXIV

Again, Epic poetry must have as many kinds as Tragedy: it must be simple, or complex, or "ethical," or "pathetic." The parts also, with the exception of song and spectacle, are the same; for it requires Reversals of the Situation, Recognitions, and Scenes of Suffering. Moreover, the thoughts and the diction must be artistic. In all these respects Homer is our earliest and sufficient model. Indeed each of his poems has a twofold character. The Iliad is at once simple and "pathetic," and the Odyssey complex (for Recognition scenes run through it), and at the same time "ethical." Moreover, in diction and thought they are supreme.

Epic poetry differs from Tragedy in the scale on which it is constructed, and in its meter. As regards scale or length, we have already laid down an adequate limit: the beginning and the end must be capable of being brought within a single view. This condition will be satisfied by poems on a smaller scale than the old epics, and answering in length to the group of tragedies presented at a single sitting.

Epic poetry has, however, a great—a special—capacity for enlarging its dimensions, and we can see the reason. In Tragedy we cannot imitate several lines of actions carried on at one and the same time; we must confine ourselves to the action on the stage and the part taken by the players. But in Epic poetry, owing to the narrative form, many events simultaneously transacted can be presented; and these, if relevant to the subject, add mass and dignity to the poem. The Epic has here an advantage, and one that conduces to grandeur of effect, to diverting the mind of the hearer, and relieving the story with varying episodes. For sameness of incident soon produces satiety, and makes tragedies fail on the stage.

As for the meter, the heroic measure has proved its fitness by hexameter test of experience. If a narrative poem in any other meter or in many meters were now composed, it would be found incongruous. For of all measures the heroic is the stateliest and the most massive; and hence it most readily admits rare words and metaphors, which is another point in which the narrative form of imitation stands alone. On the other hand, the iambic and the trochaic tetrameter are stirring measures, the latter being akin to dancing, the former expressive of action. Still more absurd would it be to mix together different meters, as was done by Chaeremon. Hence no one has ever composed a poem on a great scale in any other than heroic verse. Nature herself, as we have said, teaches the choice of the proper measure.

Homer, admirable in all respects, has the special merit of being the only poet who rightly appreciates the part he should take himself. The poet should speak as little as possible in his own person, for it is not this that makes him an imitator. Other poets appear themselves upon the scene throughout, and imitate but little and rarely. Homer, after a few prefatory words, at once brings in a man, or woman, or other personage; none of them wanting in characteristic qualities, but each with a character of his own.

The element of the wonderful is required in Tragedy. The irrational, on which the wonderful depends for its chief effects, has wider scope in Epic poetry, because there the person acting is not seen. Thus, the pursuit of Hector would be ludicrous if placed upon the stage—the Greeks standing still and not joining in the pursuit, and Achilles waving them back. But in the Epic poem the absurdity passes unnoticed. Now the wonderful is pleasing, as may be inferred from the fact that everyone tells a story with some addition of his knowing that his hearers like it. It is Homer who has chiefly taught other poets the art of telling lies skilfully. The secret of it lies in a fallacy For, assuming that if one thing is or becomes, a second is or becomes, men imagine that, if the second is, the first likewise is or becomes. But this is a false inference. Hence, where the first thing is untrue, it is quite unnecessary, provided the second be true, to add that the first is or has become. For the mind, knowing the second to be true, falsely infers the truth of the first. There is an example of this in the Bath Scene of the Odyssey.

Accordingly, the poet should prefer probable impossibilities to improbable possibilities. The tragic plot must not be composed of irrational parts. Everything irrational should, if possible, be excluded; or, at all events, it should lie outside the action of the play (as, in the Oedipus, the hero's ignorance as to the manner of Laius's death); not within the drama, as in the Electra, the messenger's account of the Pythian games; or, as in the Mysians, the man who has come from Tegea to Mysia and is still speechless. The plea that otherwise the plot would have been ruined, is ridiculous; such a plot should not in the first instance be constructed. But once the irrational has been introduced and an air of likelihood imparted to it, we must accept it in spite of the absurdity. Take even the irrational incidents in the Odyssey, where Odysseus is left upon the shore of Ithaca. How intolerable even these might have been would be apparent if an inferior poet were to treat the subject. As it is, the absurdity is veiled by the poetic charm with which the poet invests it.

The diction should be elaborated in the pauses of the action, where there is no expression of character or thought. For, conversely, character and thought are merely obscured by a diction that is over-brilliant

Part XXV

With respect to critical difficulties and their solutions, the number and nature of the sources from which they may be drawn may be thus exhibited.

The poet being an imitator, like a painter or any other artist, must of necessity imitate one of three objects: things as they were or are, things as they are said or thought to be, or things as they ought to be. The vehicle of expression is language—either current terms or, it may be, rare words or metaphors. There are also many modifications of language, which we concede to the poets. Add to this, that the standard of correctness is not the same in poetry and politics, any more than in poetry and any other art. Within the art of poetry itself there are two kinds of faults: those which touch its essence, and those which are accidental. If a poet has chosen to imitate something, [but has imitated it incorrectly] through want of capacity, the error is inherent in the poetry. But if the failure is due to a wrong choice—if he has represented a horse as throwing out both his off legs at once, or introduced technical inaccuracies in medicine, for example, or in any other art—the error is not essential to the poetry. These are the points of view from which we should consider and answer the objections raised by the critics.

First as to matters which concern the poet's own art. If he describes the impossible, he is guilty of an error; but the error may be justified, if the end of the art be thereby attained (the end being that already mentioned)—if, that is, the effect of this or any other part of the poem is thus rendered more striking. A case in point is the pursuit of Hector. if, however, the end might have been as well, or better, attained without violating the special rules of the poetic art, the error is not justified: for every kind of error should, if possible, be avoided.

Again, does the error touch the essentials of the poetic art, or some accident of it? For example, not to know that a hind has no horns is a less serious matter than to paint it inartistically.

Further, if it be objected that the description is not true to fact, the poet may perhaps reply, "But the objects are as they ought to be"; just as Sophocles said that he drew men as they ought to be; Euripides, as they are. In this way the objection may be met. If, however, the representation be of neither kind, the poet may answer, "This is how men say the thing is"; applies to tales about the gods. It may well be that these stories are not higher than fact nor yet true to fact: they are, very possibly, what Xenophanes says of them. But anyhow, "this is what is said." Again, a description may be no better than the fact: "Still, it was the fact"; as in the passage about the arms: "Upright upon their butt-ends stood the spears." This was the custom then, as it now is among the Illyrians.

Again, in examining whether what has been said or done by someone is poetically right or not, we must not look merely to the particular act or saying, and ask whether it is poetically good or bad. We must also consider by whom it is said or done, to whom, when, by what means, or for what end; whether, for instance, it be to secure a greater good, or avert a greater evil.

Other difficulties may be resolved by due regard to the usage of language. We may note a rare word, as in oureas men proton, "the mules first [he killed]," where the poet perhaps employs oureas not in the sense of mules, but of sentinels. So, again, of Dolon: "ill-favored indeed he was to look upon." It is not meant that his body was ill-shaped but that his face was ugly; for the Cretans use the word eueides, "well-flavored" to denote a fair face. Again, zoroteron de keraie, "mix the drink livelier" does not mean "mix it stronger" as for hard drinkers, but "mix it quicker."

Sometimes an expression is metaphorical, as "Now all gods and men were sleeping through the night," while at the same time the poet says: "Often indeed as he turned his gaze to the Trojan plain, he marveled at the sound of flutes and pipes." "All" is here used metaphorically for "many," all being a species of many. So in the verse, "alone she hath no part…," oie, "alone" is metaphorical; for the best known may be called the only one.

Again, the solution may depend upon accent or breathing. Thus Hippias of Thasos solved the difficulties in the lines, didomen (didomen) de hoi, and to men hou (ou) kataputhetai ombro.

Or again, the question may be solved by punctuation, as in Empedocles: "Of a sudden things became mortal that before had learned to be immortal, and things unmixed before mixed."

Or again, by ambiguity of meaning, as parocheken de pleo nux, where the word "pleo" is ambiguous.

Or by the usage of language. Thus any mixed drink is called oinos, "wine." Hence Ganymede is said "to pour the wine to Zeus," though the gods do not drink wine. So too workers in iron are called chalkeas, or "workers in bronze." This, however, may also be taken as a metaphor.

Again, when a word seems to involve some inconsistency of meaning, we should consider how many senses it may bear in the particular passage. For example: "there was stayed the spear of bronze"—we should ask in how many ways we may take "being checked there." The true mode of interpretation is the precise opposite of what Glaucon mentions. Critics, he says, jump at certain groundless conclusions; they pass adverse judgement and then proceed to reason on it; and, assuming that the poet has said whatever they happen to think, find fault if a thing is inconsistent with their own fancy.

The question about Icarius has been treated in this fashion. The critics imagine he was a Lacedaemonian. They think it strange, therefore, that Telemachus should not have met him when he went to Lacedaemon. But the Cephallenian story may perhaps be the true one. They allege that Odysseus took a wife from among themselves, and that her father was Icadius, not Icarius. It is merely a mistake, then, that gives plausibility to the objection.

In general, the impossible must be justified by reference to artistic requirements, or to the higher reality, or to received opinion. With respect to the requirements of art, a probable impossibility is to be preferred to a thing improbable and yet possible. Again, it may be impossible that there should be men such as Zeuxis painted. "Yes," we say, "but the impossible is the higher thing; for the ideal type must surpass the realty." To justify the irrational, we appeal to what is commonly said to be. In addition to which, we urge that the irrational sometimes does not violate reason; just as "it is probable that a thing may happen contrary to probability."

Things that sound contradictory should be examined by the same rules as in dialectical refutation—whether the same thing is meant, in the same relation, and in the same sense. We should therefore solve the question by reference to what the poet says himself, or to what is tacitly assumed by a person of intelligence.

The element of the irrational, and, similarly, depravity of character, are justly censured when there is no inner necessity for introducing them. Such is the irrational element in the introduction of Aegeus by Euripides and the badness of Menelaus in the Orestes.

Thus, there are five sources from which critical objections are drawn. Things are censured either as impossible, or irrational, or morally hurtful, or contradictory, or contrary to artistic correctness. The answers should be sought under the twelve heads above mentioned.

Part XXVI

The question may be raised whether the Epic or Tragic mode of imitation is the higher. If the more refined art is the higher, and the more refined in every case is that which appeals to the better sort of audience, the art which imitates anything and everything is manifestly most unrefined. The audience is supposed to be too dull to comprehend unless something of their own is thrown by the performers, who therefore indulge in restless movements. Bad flute-players twist and twirl, if they have to represent "the quoit-throw," or hustle the coryphaeus when they perform the Scylla. Tragedy, it is said, has this same defect. We may compare the opinion that the older actors entertained of their successors. Mynniscus used to call Callippides "ape" on account of the extravagance of his action, and the same view was held of Pindarus. Tragic art, then, as a whole, stands to Epic in the same relation as the younger to the elder actors. So we are told that Epic poetry is addressed to a cultivated audience, who do not need gesture; Tragedy, to an inferior public. Being then unrefined, it is evidently the lower of the two.

Now, in the first place, this censure attaches not to the poetic but to the histrionic art; for gesticulation may be equally overdone in epic recitation, as by Sosistratus, or in lyrical competition, as by Mnasitheus the Opuntian. Next, all action is not to be condemned—any more than all dancing—but only that of bad performers. Such was the fault found in Callippides, as also in others of our own day, who are censured for representing degraded women. Again, Tragedy like Epic poetry produces its effect even without action; it reveals its power by mere reading. If, then, in all other respects it is superior, this fault, we say, is not inherent in it.

And superior it is, because it has an the epic elements—it may even use the epic meter—with the music and spectacular effects as important accessories; and these produce the most vivid of pleasures. Further, it has vividness of impression in reading as well as in representation. Moreover, the art attains its end within narrower limits for the concentrated effect is more pleasurable than one which is spread over a long time and so diluted. What, for example, would be the effect of the Oedipus of Sophocles, if it were cast into a form as long as the Iliad? Once more, the Epic imitation has less unity; as is shown by this, that any Epic poem will furnish subjects for several tragedies. Thus if the story adopted by the poet has a strict unity, it must either be concisely told and appear truncated; or, if it conforms to the Epic canon of length, it must seem weak and watery. [Such length implies some loss of unity,] if, I mean, the poem is constructed out of several actions, like the Iliad and the Odyssey, which have many such parts, each with a certain magnitude of its own. Yet these poems are as perfect as possible in structure; each is, in the highest degree attainable, an imitation of a single action.

If, then, tragedy is superior to epic poetry in all these respects, and, moreover, fulfills its specific function better as an art—for each art ought to produce, not any chance pleasure, but the pleasure proper to it, as already stated—it plainly follows that tragedy is the higher art, as attaining its end more perfectly.

Thus much may suffice concerning Tragic and Epic poetry in general; their several kinds and parts, with the number of each and their differences; the causes that make a poem good or bad; the objections of the critics and the answers to these objections....

RHETORIC

BY ARISTOTLE

Translated by W. Rhys Roberts

BOOK I

Part I

Rhetoric is the counterpart of Dialectic. Both alike are concerned with such things as come, more or less, within the general ken of all men and belong to no definite science. Accordingly all men make use, more or less, of both; for to a certain extent all men attempt to discuss statements and to maintain them, to defend themselves and to attack others. Ordinary people do this either at random or through practice and from acquired habit. Both ways being possible, the subject can plainly be handled systematically, for it is possible to inquire the reason why some speakers succeed through practice and others spontaneously; and everyone will at once agree that such an inquiry is the function of an art.

Now, the framers of the current treatises on rhetoric have constructed but a small portion of that art. The modes of persuasion are the only true constituents of the art: everything else is merely accessory. These writers, however, say nothing about enthymemes, which are the substance of rhetorical persuasion, but deal mainly with non-essentials. The arousing of prejudice, pity, anger, and similar emotions has nothing to do with the essential facts, but is merely a personal appeal to the man who is judging the case. Consequently if the rules for trials which are now laid down some states—especially in well-governed states—were applied everywhere, such people would have nothing to say. All men, no doubt, think that the laws should prescribe such rules, but some, as in the court of Areopagus, give practical effect to their thoughts and forbid talk about non-essentials.

This is sound law and custom. It is not right to pervert the judge by moving him to anger or envy or pity—one might as well warp a carpenter's rule before using it. Again, a litigant has clearly nothing to do but to show that the alleged fact is so or is not so, that it has or has not happened. As to whether a thing is important or unimportant, just or unjust, the judge must surely refuse to take his instructions from the litigants: he must decide for himself all such points as the law-giver has not already defined for him.

Now, it is of great moment that well-drawn laws should themselves define all the points they possibly can and leave as few as may be to the decision of the judges; and this for several reasons. First, to find one man, or a few men, who are sensible persons and capable of legislating and administering justice is easier than to find a large number. Next, laws are made after long consideration, whereas decisions in the courts are given at short notice, which makes it hard for those who try the case to satisfy the claims of justice and expediency. The weightiest reason of all is that the decision of the lawgiver is not particular but prospective and general, whereas members of the assembly and the jury find it their duty to decide on definite cases brought before them. They will often have allowed themselves to be so much influenced by feelings of friendship or hatred or self-interest that they lose any clear vision of the truth and have their judgement obscured by considerations of personal pleasure or pain. In general, then, the judge should, we say, be allowed to decide as few things as possible. But questions as to whether something has happened or has not happened, will be or will not be, is or is not, must of necessity be left to the judge, since the lawgiver cannot foresee them. If this is so, it is evident that anyone who lays down rules about other matters, such as what must be the contents of the "introduction" or the "narration" or any of the other divisions of a speech, is theorizing about non-essentials as if they belonged to the art. The only question with which these writers here deal is how to put the judge into a given frame of mind. About the orator's proper modes of persuasion they have nothing to tell us; nothing, that is, about how to gain skill in enthymemes.

Hence it comes that, although the same systematic principles apply to political as to forensic oratory, and although the former is a nobler business, and fitter for a citizen, than that which concerns the relations of private individuals, these authors say nothing about political oratory, but try, one and all, to write treatises on the way to plead in court. The reason for this is that in political oratory there is less inducement to talk about nonessentials. Political oratory is less given to unscrupulous practices than forensic, because it treats of wider issues. In a political debate the man who is forming a judgement is making a decision about his own vital interests. There is no need, therefore, to prove anything except that the facts are what the supporter of a measure maintains they are. In forensic oratory this is not enough; to conciliate the listener is what pays here. It is other people's affairs that are to be decided, so that the judges, intent on their own satisfaction and listening with partiality, surrender themselves to the disputants instead of judging between them. Hence in many places, as we have said already, irrelevant speaking is forbidden in the law courts: in the public assembly those who have to form a judgement are themselves well able to guard against that.

It is clear, then, that rhetorical study, in its strict sense, is concerned with the modes of persuasion. Persuasion is clearly a sort of demonstration, since we are most fully persuaded when we consider a thing to have been demonstrated. The orator's demonstration is an enthymeme, and this is, in general, the most effective of the modes of persuasion. The enthymeme is a sort of syllogism, and the consideration of syllogisms of all kinds, without distinction, is the business of dialectic, either of dialectic as a whole or of one of its branches. It follows plainly, therefore, that he who is best able to see how and from what elements a syllogism is produced will also be best skilled in the enthymeme, when he has further learned what its subject matter is and in what respects it differs from the syllogism of strict logic. The true and the approximately true are apprehended by the same faculty; it may also be noted that men have a sufficient natural instinct for what is true, and usually do arrive at the truth. Hence the man who makes a good guess at truth is likely to make a good guess at probabilities.

It has now been shown that the ordinary writers on rhetoric treat of non-essentials; it has also been shown why they have inclined more toward the forensic branch of oratory.

Rhetoric is useful (1) because things that are true and things that are just have a natural tendency to prevail over their opposites, so that if the decisions of judges are not what they ought to be, the defeat must be due to the speakers themselves, and they must be blamed accordingly. Moreover, (2) before some audiences not even the possession of the exactest knowledge will make it easy for what we say to produce conviction. For argument based on knowledge implies instruction, and there are people whom one cannot instruct. Here, then, we must use, as our modes of persuasion and argument, notions possessed by everybody, as we observed in the Topics when dealing with the way to handle a popular audience. Further, (3) we must be able to employ persuasion, just as strict reasoning can be employed, on opposite sides of a question, not in order that we may in practice employ it in both ways (for we must not make people believe what is wrong), but in order that we may see clearly what the facts are, and that, if another man argues unfairly, we on our part may be able to confute him. No other of the arts draws opposite conclusions: dialectic and rhetoric alone do this. Both these arts draw opposite conclusions impartially. Nevertheless, the underlying facts do not lend themselves equally well to the contrary views. No; things that are true and things that are better are, by their nature, practically always easier to prove and easier to believe in. Again, (4) it is absurd to hold that a man ought to be ashamed of being unable to defend himself with his limbs, but not of being unable to defend himself with speech and reason, when the use of rational speech is more distinctive of a human being than the use of his limbs. And if it be objected that one who uses such power of speech unjustly might do great harm, that is a charge which may be made in common against all good things except virtue, and above all against the things that are most useful, as strength, health, wealth, generalship. A man can confer the greatest of benefits by a right use of these, and inflict the greatest of injuries by using them wrongly.

It is clear, then, that rhetoric is not bound up with a single definite class of subjects, but is as universal as dialectic; it is clear, also, that it is useful. It is clear, further, that its function is not simply to succeed in persuading, but rather to discover the means of coming as near such success as the circumstances of each particular case allow. In this it resembles all other arts. For example, it is not the function of medicine simply to make a man quite healthy, but to put him as far as may be on the road to health; it is possible to give excellent treatment even to those who can never enjoy sound health. Furthermore, it is plain that it is the function of one and the same art to discern the real and the apparent means of persuasion, just as it is the function of dialectic to discern the real and the apparent syllogism. What makes a man a "sophist" is not his faculty, but his moral purpose. In rhetoric, however, the term "rhetorician" may describe either the speaker's knowledge of the art, or his moral purpose. In dialectic it is different: a man is a "sophist" because he has a certain kind of moral purpose, a "dialectician" in respect, not of his moral purpose, but of his faculty.

Let us now try to give some account of the systematic principles of Rhetoric itself—of the right method and means of succeeding in the object we set before us. We must make as it were a fresh start, and before going further define what rhetoric is.

Part II

Rhetoric may be defined as the faculty of observing in any given case the available means of persuasion. This is not a function of any other art. Every other art can instruct or persuade about its own particular subject matter; for instance, medicine about what is healthy and unhealthy, geometry about the properties of magnitudes, arithmetic about numbers, and the same is true of the other arts and sciences. But rhetoric we look upon as the power of observing the means of persuasion on almost any subject presented to us; and that is why we say that, in its technical character, it is not concerned with any special or definite class of subjects.

Of the modes of persuasion some belong strictly to the art of rhetoric and some do not. By the latter I mean such things as are not supplied by the speaker but are there at the outset—witnesses, evidence given under torture, written contracts, and so on. By the former I mean such as we can ourselves construct by means of the principles of rhetoric. The one kind has merely to be used, the other has to be invented.

Of the modes of persuasion furnished by the spoken word there are three kinds. The first kind depends on the personal character of the speaker; the second on putting the audience into a certain frame of mind; the third on the proof, or apparent proof, provided by the words of the speech itself. Persuasion is achieved by the speaker's personal character when the speech is so spoken as to make us think him credible. We believe good men more fully and more readily than others: this is true generally whatever the question is, and absolutely true where exact certainty is impossible and opinions are divided. This kind of persuasion, like the others, should be achieved by what the speaker says, not by what people think of his character before he begins to speak. It is not true, as some writers assume in their treatises on rhetoric, that the personal goodness revealed by the speaker contributes nothing to his power of persuasion; on the contrary, his character may almost be called the most effective means of persuasion he possesses. Secondly, persuasion may come through the hearers, when the speech stirs their emotions. Our judgements when we are pleased and friendly are not the same as when we are pained and hostile. It is toward producing these effects, as we maintain, that present-day writers on rhetoric direct the whole of their efforts. This subject shall be treated in detail when we come to speak of the emotions. Thirdly, persuasion is effected through the speech itself when we have proved a truth or an apparent truth by means of the persuasive arguments suitable to the case in question.

There are, then, these three means of effecting persuasion. The man who is to be in command of them must, it is clear, be able (1) to reason logically, (2) to understand human character and goodness in their various forms, and (3) to understand the emotions—that is, to name them and describe them, to know their causes and the way in which they are excited. It thus appears that rhetoric is an offshoot of dialectic and also of ethical studies. Ethical studies may fairly be called political; and for this reason rhetoric masquerades as political science, and the professors of it as political experts-sometimes from want of education, sometimes from ostentation, sometimes owing to other human failings. As a matter of fact, it is a branch of dialectic and similar to it, as we said at the outset. Neither rhetoric nor dialectic is the scientific study of any one separate subject: both are faculties for providing arguments. This is perhaps a sufficient account of their scope and of how they are related to each other.

With regard to the persuasion achieved by proof or apparent proof: just as in dialectic there is induction on the one hand and syllogism or apparent syllogism on the other, so it is in rhetoric. The example is an induction, the enthymeme is a syllogism, and the apparent enthymeme is an apparent syllogism. I call the enthymeme a rhetorical syllogism, and the example a rhetorical induction. Every one who effects persuasion through proof does in fact use either enthymemes or examples: there is no other way. And since everyone who proves anything at all is bound to use either syllogisms or inductions (and this is clear to us from the Analytics), it must follow that enthymemes are syllogisms and examples are inductions. The difference between example and enthymeme is made plain by the passages in the Topics where induction and syllogism have already been discussed. When we base the proof of a proposition on a number of similar cases, this is induction in dialectic, example in rhetoric; when it is shown that, certain propositions being true, a further and quite distinct proposition must also be true in consequence, whether invariably or usually, this is called syllogism in dialectic, enthymeme in rhetoric. It is plain also that each of these types of oratory has its advantages. Types of oratory, I say: for what has been said in the Methodics applies equally well here; in some oratorical styles examples prevail, in others enthymemes; and in like manner, some orators are better at the former and some at the latter. Speeches that rely on examples are as persuasive as the other kind, but those which rely on enthymemes excite the louder applause. The sources of examples and enthymemes, and their proper uses, we will discuss later. Our next step is to define the processes themselves more clearly.

A statement is persuasive and credible either because it is directly self-evident or because it appears to be proved from other statements that are so. In either case it is persuasive because there is somebody whom it persuades. But none of the arts theorize about individual cases. Medicine, for instance, does not theorize about what will help to cure Socrates or Callias, but only about what will help to cure any or all of a given class of patients: this alone is business: individual cases are so infinitely various that no systematic knowledge of them is possible. In the same way the theory of rhetoric is concerned not with what seems probable to a given individual like Socrates or Hippias, but with what seems probable to men of a given type; and this is true of dialectic also. Dialectic does not construct its syllogisms out of any haphazard materials, such as the fancies of crazy people, but out of materials that call for discussion; and rhetoric, too, draws upon the regular subjects of debate. The duty of rhetoric is to deal with such matters as we deliberate upon without arts or systems to guide us, in the hearing of persons who cannot take in at a glance a complicated argument, or follow a long chain of reasoning. The subjects of our deliberation are such as seem to present us with alternative possibilities: about things that could not have been, and cannot now or in the future be, other than they are, nobody who takes them to be of this nature wastes his time in deliberation.

It is possible to form syllogisms and draw conclusions from the results of previous syllogisms; or, on the other hand, from premises which have not been thus proved, and at the same time are so little accepted that they call for proof. Reasonings of the former kind will necessarily be hard to follow owing to their length, for we assume an audience of untrained thinkers; those of the latter kind will fail to win assent, because they are based on premises that are not generally admitted or believed.

The enthymeme and the example must, then, deal with what is in the main contingent, the example being an induction, and the enthymeme a syllogism, about such matters. The enthymeme must consist of few propositions, fewer often than those which make up the normal syllogism. For if any of these propositions is a familiar fact, there is no need even to mention it; the hearer adds it himself. Thus, to show that Dorieus has been victor in a contest for which the prize is a crown, it is enough to say "For he has been victor in the Olympic games," without adding "And in the Olympic games the prize is a crown," a fact which everybody knows.

There are few facts of the "necessary" type that can form the basis of rhetorical syllogisms. Most of the things about which we make decisions, and into which therefore we inquire, present us with alternative possibilities.

For it is about our actions that we deliberate and inquire, and all our actions have a contingent character; hardly any of them are determined by necessity. Again, conclusions that state what is merely usual or possible must be drawn from premises that do the same, just as "necessary" conclusions must be drawn from "necessary" premises; this too is clear to us from the Analytics. It is evident, therefore, that the propositions forming the basis of enthymemes, though some of them may be "necessary," will most of them be only usually true. Now the materials of enthymemes are Probabilities and Signs, which we can see must correspond respectively with the propositions that are generally and those that are necessarily true. A Probability is a thing that usually happens; not, however, as some definitions would suggest, anything whatever that usually happens, but only if it belongs to the class of the "contingent" or "variable." It bears the same relation to that in respect of which it is probable as the universal bears to the particular. Of Signs, one kind bears the same relation to the statement it supports as the particular bears to the universal, the other the same as the universal bears to the particular. The infallible kind is a "complete proof" (tekmerhiou); the fallible kind has no specific name. By infallible signs I mean those on which syllogisms proper may be based: and this shows us why this kind of Sign is called "complete proof": when people think that what they have said cannot be refuted, they then think that they are bringing forward a "complete proof," meaning that the matter has now been demonstrated and completed (peperhasmeuou); for the word "perhas" has the same meaning (of "end" or "boundary") as the word "tekmarh" in the ancient tongue. Now the one kind of Sign (that which bears to the proposition it supports the relation of particular to universal) may be illustrated thus. Suppose it were said, "The fact that Socrates was wise and just is a sign that the wise are just." Here we certainly have a Sign; but even though the proposition be true, the argument is refutable, since it does not form a syllogism. Suppose, on the other hand, it were said, "The fact that he has a fever is a sign that he is ill," or, "The fact that she is giving milk is a sign that she has lately borne a child." Here we have the infallible kind of Sign, the only kind that constitutes a complete proof, since it is the only kind that, if the particular statement is true, is irrefutable. The other kind of Sign, that which bears to the proposition it supports the relation of universal to particular, might be illustrated by saying, "The fact that he breathes fast is a sign that he has a fever." This argument also is refutable, even if the statement about the fast breathing be true, since a man may breathe hard without having a fever.

It has, then, been stated above what is the nature of a Probability, of a Sign, and of a complete proof, and what are the differences between them. In the Analytics a more explicit description has been given of these points; it is there shown why some of these reasonings can be put into syllogisms and some cannot.

The "example" has already been described as one kind of induction; and the special nature of the subject matter that distinguishes it from the other kinds has also been stated above. Its relation to the proposition it supports is not that of part to whole, nor whole to part, nor whole to whole, but of part to part, or like to like. When two statements are of the same order, but one is more familiar than the other, the former is an "example." The argument may, for instance, be that Dionysius, in asking as he does for a bodyguard, is scheming to make himself a despot. For in the past Peisistratus kept asking for a bodyguard in order to carry out such a scheme, and did make himself a despot as soon as he got it; and so did Theagenes at Megara; and in the same way all other instances known to the speaker are made into examples, in order to show what is not yet known, that Dionysius has the same purpose in making the same request: all these being instances of the one general principle, that a man who asks for a bodyguard is scheming to make himself a despot. We have now described the sources of those means of persuasion which are popularly supposed to be demonstrative.

There is an important distinction between two sorts of enthymemes that has been wholly overlooked by almost everybody—one that also subsists between the syllogisms treated of in dialectic. One sort of enthymeme really belongs to rhetoric, as one sort of syllogism really belongs to dialectic; but the other sort really belongs to other arts and faculties, whether to those we already exercise or to those we have not yet acquired. Missing this distinction, people fail to notice that the more correctly they handle their particular subject the further they are getting away from pure rhetoric or dialectic. This statement will be clearer if expressed more fully. I mean that the proper subjects of dialectical and rhetorical syllogisms are the things with which we say the regular or universal Lines of Argument are concerned, that is to say those lines of argument that apply equally to questions of right conduct, natural science, politics, and many other things that have nothing to do with one another. Take, for instance, the line of argument concerned with "the more or less." On this line of argument it is equally easy to base a syllogism or enthymeme about any of what nevertheless are essentially disconnected subjects—right conduct, natural science, or anything else whatever. But there are also those special Lines of

Argument which are based on such propositions as apply only to particular groups or classes of things. Thus there are propositions about natural science on which it is impossible to base any enthymeme or syllogism about ethics, and other propositions about ethics on which nothing can be based about natural science. The same principle applies throughout. The general Lines of Argument have no special subject matter, and therefore will not increase our understanding of any particular class of things. On the other hand, the better the selection one makes of propositions suitable for special Lines of Argument, the nearer one comes, unconsciously, to setting up a science that is distinct from dialectic and rhetoric. One may succeed in stating the required principles, but one's science will be no longer dialectic or rhetoric, but the science to which the principles thus discovered belong. Most enthymemes are in fact based upon these particular or special Lines of Argument; comparatively few on the common or general kind. As in the therefore, so in this work, we must distinguish, in dealing with enthymemes, the special and the general Lines of Argument on which they are to be founded. By special Lines of Argument I mean the propositions peculiar to each several class of things, by general those common to all classes alike. We may begin with the special Lines of Argument. But, first of all, let us classify rhetoric into its varieties. Having distinguished these we may deal with them one by one, and try to discover the elements of which each is composed, and the propositions each must employ.

Part III

Rhetoric falls into three divisions, determined by the three classes of listeners to speeches. For of the three elements in speech-making—speaker, subject, and person addressed—it is the last one, the hearer, that determines the speech's end and object. The hearer must be either a judge, with a decision to make about things past or future, or an observer. A member of the assembly decides about future events, a juryman about past events: while those who merely decide on the orator's skill are observers. From this it follows that there are three divisions of oratory: (1) political, (2) forensic, and (3) the ceremonial oratory of display.

Political speaking urges us either to do or not to do something: one of these two courses is always taken by private counsellors, as well as by men who address public assemblies. Forensic speaking either attacks or defends somebody: one or other of these two things must always be done by the parties in a case. The ceremonial oratory of display either praises or censures somebody. These three kinds of rhetoric refer to three different kinds of time. The political orator is concerned with the future: it is about things to be done hereafter that he advises, for or against. The party in a case at law is concerned with the past; one man accuses the other, and the other defends himself, with reference to things already done. The ceremonial orator is, properly speaking, concerned with the present, since all men praise or blame in view of the state of things existing at the time, though they often find it useful also to recall the past and to make guesses at the future.

Rhetoric has three distinct ends in view, one for each of its three kinds. The political orator aims at establishing the expediency or the harmfulness of a proposed course of action; if he urges its acceptance, he does so on the ground that it will do good; if he urges its rejection, he does so on the ground that it will do harm; and all other points, such as whether the proposal is just or unjust, honorable or dishonorable, he brings in as subsidiary and relative to this main consideration. Parties in a law case aim at establishing the justice or injustice of some action, and they too bring in all other points as subsidiary and relative to this one. Those who praise or attack a man aim at proving him worthy of honor or the reverse, and they too treat all other considerations with reference to this one.

That the three kinds of rhetoric do aim respectively at the three ends we have mentioned is shown by the fact that speakers will sometimes not try to establish anything else. Thus, the litigant will sometimes not deny that a thing has happened or that he has done harm. But that he is guilty of injustice he will never admit; otherwise there would be no need of a trial. So too, political orators often make any concession short of admitting that they are recommending their hearers to take an inexpedient course or not to take an expedient one. The question whether it is not unjust for a city to enslave its innocent neighbors often does not trouble them at all. In like manner those who praise or censure a man do not consider whether his acts have been expedient or not, but often make it a ground of actual praise that he has neglected his own interest to do what was honorable. Thus, they praise Achilles because he championed his fallen friend Patroclus, though he knew that this meant death, and that otherwise he need not die; yet while to die thus was the nobler thing for him to do, the expedient thing was to live on.

It is evident from what has been said that it is these three subjects, more than any others, about which the orator must be able to have propositions at his command. Now the propositions of Rhetoric are Complete Proofs, Probabilities, and Signs. Every kind of syllogism is composed of propositions, and the enthymeme is a particular kind of syllogism composed of the aforesaid propositions.

Since only possible actions, and not impossible ones, can ever have been done in the past or the present, and since things which have not occurred, or will not occur, also cannot have been done or be going to be done, it is necessary for the political, the forensic, and the ceremonial speaker alike to be able to have at their command propositions about the possible and the impossible, and about whether a thing has or has not occurred, will or will not occur. Further, all men, in giving praise or blame, in urging us to accept or reject proposals for action, in accusing others or defending themselves, attempt not only to prove the points mentioned but also to show that the good or the harm, the honor or disgrace, the justice or injustice, is great or small, either absolutely or relatively; and therefore it is plain that we must also have at our command propositions about greatness or smallness and the greater or the lesser-propositions both universal and particular. Thus, we must be able to say which is the greater or lesser good, the greater or lesser act of justice or injustice; and so on.

Such, then, are the subjects regarding which we are inevitably bound to master the propositions relevant to them. We must now discuss each particular class of these subjects in turn, namely those dealt with in political, in ceremonial, and lastly in legal, oratory.

Part IV

First, then, we must ascertain what are the kinds of things, good or bad, about which the political orator offers counsel. For he does not deal with all things, but only with such as may or may not take place. Concerning things which exist or will exist inevitably, or which cannot possibly exist or take place, no counsel can be given. Nor, again, can counsel be given about the whole class of things which may or may not take place; for this class includes some good things that occur naturally, and some that occur by accident; and about these it is useless to offer counsel. Clearly counsel can only be given on matters about which people deliberate; matters, namely, that ultimately depend on ourselves, and which we have it in our power to set going. For we turn a thing over in our mind until we have reached the point of seeing whether we can do it or not.

Now to enumerate and classify accurately the usual subjects of public business, and further to frame, as far as possible, true definitions of them is a task which we must not attempt on the present occasion. For it does not belong to the art of rhetoric, but to a more instructive art and a more real branch of knowledge; and as it is, rhetoric has been given a far wider subject matter than strictly belongs to it. The truth is, as indeed we have said already, that rhetoric is a combination of the science of logic and of the ethical branch of politics; and it is partly like dialectic, partly like sophistical reasoning. But the more we try to make either dialectic rhetoric not, what they really are, practical faculties, but sciences, the more we shall inadvertently be destroying their true nature; for we shall be refashioning them and shall be passing into the region of sciences dealing with definite subjects rather than simply with words and forms of reasoning. Even here, however, we will mention those points which it is of practical importance to distinguish, their fuller treatment falling naturally to political science.

The main matters on which all men deliberate and on which political speakers make speeches are some five in number: ways and means, war and peace, national defense, imports and exports, and legislation.

As to Ways and Means, then, the intending speaker will need to know the number and extent of the country's sources of revenue, so that, if any is being overlooked, it may be added, and, if any is defective, it may be increased. Further, he should know all the expenditure of the country, in order that, if any part of it is superfluous, it may be abolished, or, if any is too large, it may be reduced. For men become richer not only by increasing their existing wealth but also by reducing their expenditure. A comprehensive view of these questions cannot be gained solely from experience in home affairs; in order to advise on such matters a man must be keenly interested in the methods worked out in other lands.

As to Peace and War, he must know the extent of the military strength of his country, both actual and potential, and also the mature of that actual and potential strength; and further, what wars his country has waged, and how it has waged them. He must know these facts not only about his own country, but also about neighbouring countries; and also about countries with which war is likely, in order that peace may be maintained with those stronger than his own, and that his own may have power to make war or not against those that are weaker. He should know, too, whether the military power of another country is like or unlike that of his own; for this is a matter that may affect their relative strength. With the same end in view he must, besides, have studied the wars of other countries as well as those of his own, and the way they ended; similar causes are likely to have similar results.

With regard to National Defense: he ought to know all about the methods of defense in actual use, such as the strength and character of the defensive force and the positions of the forts—this last means that he must be well acquainted with the lie of the country—in order that a garrison may be increased if it is too small or removed if it is not wanted, and that the strategic points may be guarded with special care.

With regard to the Food Supply, he must know what outlay will meet the needs of his country; what kinds of food are produced at home and what imported; and what articles must be exported or imported. This last he must know in order that agreements and commercial treaties may be made with the countries concerned. There are, indeed, two sorts of state to which he must see that his countrymen give no cause for offense, states stronger than his own, and states with which it is advantageous to trade.

But while he must, for security's sake, be able to take all this into account, he must before all things understand the subject of legislation; for it is on a country's laws that its whole welfare depends. He must, therefore, know how many different forms of constitution there are; under what conditions each of these will prosper and by what internal developments or external attacks each of them tends to be destroyed. When I speak of destruction through internal developments I refer to the fact that all constitutions, except the best one of all, are destroyed both by not being pushed far enough and by being pushed too far. Thus, democracy loses its vigor, and finally passes into oligarchy, not only when it is not pushed far enough, but also when it is pushed a great deal too far; just as the aquiline and the snub nose not only turn into normal noses by not being aquiline or snub enough, but also by being too violently aquiline or snub arrive at a condition in which they no longer look like noses at all. It is useful, in framing laws, not only to study the past history of one's own country, in order to understand which constitution is desirable for it now, but also to have a knowledge of the constitutions of other nations, and so to learn for what kinds of nation the various kinds of constitution are suited. From this we can see that books of travel are useful aids to legislation, since from these we may learn the laws and customs of different races. The political speaker will also find the researches of historians useful. But all this is the business of political science and not of rhetoric.

These, then, are the most important kinds of information which the political speaker must possess. Let us now go back and state the premises from which he will have to argue in favor of adopting or rejecting measures regarding these and other matters.

Part V

It may be said that every individual man and all men in common aim at a certain end which determines what they choose and what they avoid. This end, to sum it up briefly, is happiness and its constituents. Let us, then, by way of illustration only, ascertain what is in general the nature of happiness, and what are the elements of its constituent parts. For all advice to do things or not to do them is concerned with happiness and with the things that make for or against it; whatever creates or increases happiness or some part of happiness, we ought to do; whatever destroys or hampers happiness, or gives rise to its opposite, we ought not to do.

We may define happiness as prosperity combined with virtue; or as independence of life; or as the secure enjoyment of the maximum of pleasure; or as a good condition of property and body, together with the power of guarding one's property and body and making use of them. That happiness is one or more of these things, pretty well everybody agrees.

From this definition of happiness it follows that its constituent parts are:-good birth, plenty of friends, good friends, wealth, good children, plenty of children, a happy old age, also such bodily excellences as health, beauty, strength, large stature, athletic powers, together with fame, honor, good luck, and virtue. A man cannot fail to be completely independent if he possesses these internal and these external goods; for besides these there are no others to have. (Goods of the soul and of the body are internal. Good birth, friends, money, and honor are external.) Further, we think that he should possess resources and luck, in order to make his life really secure. As we have already ascertained what happiness in general is, so now let us try to ascertain what of these parts of it is.

Now good birth in a race or a state means that its members are indigenous or ancient: that its earliest leaders were distinguished men, and that from them have sprung many who were distinguished for qualities that we admire.

The good birth of an individual, which may come either from the male or the female side, implies that both parents are free citizens, and that, as in the case of the state, the founders of the line have been notable for virtue or wealth or something else which is highly prized, and that many distinguished persons belong to the family, men and women, young and old.

The phrases "possession of good children" and "of many children" bear a quite clear meaning. Applied to a community, they mean that its young men are numerous and of a good quality: good in regard to bodily excellences, such as stature, beauty, strength, athletic powers; and also in regard to the excellences of the soul, which in a young man are temperance and courage. Applied to an individual, they mean that his own children are numerous and have the good qualities we have described. Both male and female are here included; the excellences of the latter are, in body, beauty and stature; in soul, self-command and an industry that is not sordid. Communities as well as individuals should lack none of these perfections, in their women as well as in their men. Where, as among the Lacedaemonians, the state of women is bad, almost half of human life is spoiled.

 The constituents of wealth are: plenty of coined money and territory; the ownership of numerous, large, and beautiful estates; also the ownership of numerous and beautiful implements, live stock, and slaves. All these kinds of property are our own, are secure, gentlemanly, and useful. The useful kinds are those that are productive, the gentlemanly kinds are those that provide enjoyment. By "productive" I mean those from which we get our income; by "enjoyable," those from which we get nothing worth mentioning except the use of them. The criterion of "security" is the ownership of property in such places and under such Conditions that the use of it is in our power; and it is "our own" if it is in our own power to dispose of it or keep it. By "disposing of it" I mean giving it away or selling it. Wealth as a whole consists in using things rather than in owning them; it is really the activity—that is, the use—of property that constitutes wealth.

 Fame means being respected by everybody, or having some quality that is desired by all men, or by most, or by the good, or by the wise.

 Honor is the token of a man's being famous for doing good. It is chiefly and most properly paid to those who have already done good; but also to the man who can do good in future. Doing good refers either to the preservation of life and the means of life, or to wealth, or to some other of the good things which it is hard to get either always or at that particular place or time—for many gain honor for things which seem small, but the place and the occasion account for it. The constituents of honor are: sacrifices; commemoration, in verse or prose; privileges; grants of land; front seats at civic celebrations; state burial; statues; public maintenance; among foreigners, obeisances and giving place; and such presents as are among various bodies of men regarded as marks of honor. For a present is not only the bestowal of a piece of property, but also a token of honor; which explains why honor-loving as well as money-loving persons desire it. The present brings to both what they want; it is a piece of property, which is what the lovers of money desire; and it brings honor, which is what the lovers of honor desire.

The excellence of the body is health; that is, a condition which allows us, while keeping free from disease, to have the use of our bodies; for many people are "healthy" as we are told Herodicus was; and these no one can congratulate on their "health," for they have to abstain from everything or nearly everything that men do. Beauty varies with the time of life. In a young man beauty is the possession of a body fit to endure the exertion of running and of contests of strength; which means that he is pleasant to look at; and therefore all-around athletes are the most beautiful, being naturally adapted both for contests of strength and for speed also. For a man in his prime, beauty is fitness for the exertion of warfare, together with a pleasant but at the same time formidable appearance. For an old man, it is to be strong enough for such exertion as is necessary, and to be free from all those deformities of old age which cause pain to others. Strength is the power of moving someone else at will; to do this, you must either pull, push, lift, pin, or grip him; thus you must be strong in all of those ways or at least in some. Excellence in size is to surpass ordinary people in height, thickness, and breadth by just as much as will not make one's movements slower in consequence. Athletic excellence of the body consists in size, strength, and swiftness; swiftness implying strength. He who can fling forward his legs in a certain way, and move them fast and far, is good at running; he who can grip and hold down is good at wrestling; he who can drive an adversary from his ground with the right blow is a good boxer: he who can do both the last is a good pancratiast, while he who can do all is an "all-around" athlete.

Happiness in old age is the coming of old age slowly and painlessly; for a man has not this happiness if he grows old either quickly, or tardily but painfully. It arises both from the excellences of the body and from good luck. If a man is not free from disease, or if he is strong, he will not be free from suffering; nor can he continue to live a long and painless life unless he has good luck. There is, indeed, a capacity for long life that is quite independent of health or strength; for many people live long who lack the excellences of the body; but for our present purpose there is no use in going into the details of this.

The terms "possession of many friends" and "possession of good friends" need no explanation; for we define a "friend" as one who will always try, for your sake, to do what he takes to be good for you. The man toward whom many feel thus has many friends; if these are worthy men, he has good friends.

"Good luck" means the acquisition or possession of all or most, or the most important, of those good things which are due to luck. Some of the things that are due to luck may also be due to artificial contrivance; but many are independent of art, as for example those which are due to nature—though, to be sure, things due to luck may actually be contrary to nature. Thus health may be due to artificial contrivance, but beauty and stature are due to nature. All such good things as excite envy are, as a class, the outcome of good luck. Luck is also the cause of good things that happen contrary to reasonable expectation: as when, for instance, all your brothers are ugly, but you are handsome yourself; or when you find a treasure that everybody else has overlooked; or when a missile hits the next man and misses you; or when you are the only man not to go to a place you have gone to regularly, while the others go there for the first time and are killed. All such things are reckoned pieces of good luck.

As to virtue, it is most closely connected with the subject of Eulogy, and therefore we will wait to define it until we come to discuss that subject.

Part VI

It is now plain what our aims, future or actual, should be in urging, and what in depreciating, a proposal; the latter being the opposite of the former. Now the political or deliberative orator's aim is utility: deliberation seeks to determine not ends but the means to ends, i.e. what it is most useful to do. Further, utility is a good thing. We ought therefore to assure ourselves of the main facts about Goodness and Utility in general.

We may define a good thing as that which ought to be chosen for its own sake; or as that for the sake of which we choose something else; or as that which is sought after by all things, or by all things that have sensation or reason, or which will be sought after by any things that acquire reason; or as that which must be prescribed for a given individual by reason generally, or is prescribed for him by his individual reason, this being his individual good; or as that whose presence brings anything into a satisfactory and self-sufficing condition; or as self-sufficiency; or as what produces, maintains, or entails characteristics of this kind, while preventing and destroying their opposites. One thing may entail another in either of two ways: (1) simultaneously, (2) subsequently. Thus learning entails knowledge subsequently, health entails life simultaneously. Things are productive of other things in three senses: first as being healthy produces health; secondly, as food produces health; and thirdly, as exercise does—i.e. it does so usually. All this being settled, we now see that both the acquisition of good things and the removal of bad things must be good; the latter entails freedom from the evil things simultaneously, while the former entails possession of the good things subsequently. The acquisition of a greater in place of a lesser good, or of a lesser in place of a greater evil, is also good, for in proportion as the greater exceeds the lesser there is acquisition of good or removal of evil. The virtues, too, must be something good; for it is by possessing these that we are in a good condition, and they tend to produce good works and good actions. They must be severally named and described elsewhere. Pleasure, again, must be a good thing, since it is the nature of all animals to aim at it. Consequently both pleasant and beautiful things must be good things, since the former are productive of pleasure, while of the beautiful things some are pleasant and some desirable in and for themselves.

The following is a more detailed list of things that must be good. Happiness, as being desirable in itself and sufficient by itself, and as being that for whose sake we choose many other things. Also justice, courage, temperance, magnanimity, magnificence, and all such qualities, as being excellences of the soul. Further, health, beauty, and the like, as being bodily excellences and productive of many other good things: for instance, health is productive both of pleasure and of life, and therefore is thought the greatest of goods, since these two things which it causes, pleasure and life, are two of the things most highly prized by ordinary people. Wealth, again: for it is the excellence of possession, and also productive of many other good things. Friends and friendship: for a friend is desirable in himself and also productive of many other good things. So, too, honor and reputation, as being pleasant, and productive of many other good things, and usually accompanied by the presence of the good things that cause them to be bestowed. The faculty of speech and action; since all such qualities are productive of what is good. Further—good parts, strong memory, receptiveness, quickness of intuition, and the like, for all such faculties are productive of what is good. Similarly, all the sciences and arts. And life: since, even if no other good were the result of life, it is desirable in itself. And justice, as the cause of good to the community.

The above are pretty well all the things admittedly good. In dealing with things whose goodness is disputed, we may argue in the following ways:-That is good of which the contrary is bad. That is good the contrary of which is to the advantage of our enemies; for example, if it is to the particular advantage of our enemies that we should be cowards, clearly courage is of particular value to our countrymen. And generally, the contrary of that which our enemies desire, or of that at which they rejoice, is evidently valuable. Hence the passage beginning:

"Surely would Priam exult."

This principle usually holds good, but not always, since it may well be that our interest is sometimes the same as that of our enemies. Hence it is said that "evils draw men together"; that is, when the same thing is hurtful to them both.

Further, that which is not in excess is good, and that which is greater than it should be is bad. That also is good on which much labor or money has been spent; the mere fact of this makes it seem good, and such a good is assumed to be an end—an end reached through a long chain of means; and any end is a good. Hence the lines beginning:

"And for Priam (and Troy-town's folk) should
"they leave behind them a boast";
and
"Oh, it were shame
"To have tarried so long and return empty-handed
"as erst we came";
and there is also the proverb about "breaking the pitcher at the door."

That which most people seek after, and which is obviously an object of contention, is also a good; for, as has been shown, that is good which is sought after by everybody, and "most people" is taken to be equivalent to "everybody." That which is praised is good, since no one praises what is not good. So, again, that which is praised by our enemies [or by the worthless] for when even those who have a grievance think a thing good, it is at once felt that everyone must agree with them; our enemies can admit the fact only because it is evident, just as those must be worthless whom their friends censure and their enemies do not. (For this reason the Corinthians conceived themselves to be insulted by Simonides when he wrote:

"Against the Corinthians hath Ilium no complaint.")

Again, that is good which has been distinguished by the favor of a discerning or virtuous man or woman, as Odysseus was distinguished by Athena, Helen by Theseus, Paris by the goddesses, and Achilles by Homer. And, generally speaking, all things are good which men deliberately choose to do; this will include the things already mentioned, and also whatever may be bad for their enemies or good for their friends, and at the same time practicable. Things are "practicable" in two senses: (1) it is possible to do them, (2) it is easy to do them. Things are done "easily" when they are done either without pain or quickly: the "difficulty" of an act lies either in its painfulness or in the long time it takes. Again, a thing is good if it is as men wish; and they wish to have either no evil at an or at least a balance of good over evil. This last will happen where the penalty is either imperceptible or slight. Good, too, are things that are a man's very own, possessed by no one else, exceptional; for this increases the credit of having them. So are things which befit the possessors, such as whatever is appropriate to their birth or capacity, and whatever they feel they ought to have but lack—such things may indeed be trifling, but none the less men deliberately make them the goal of their action. And things easily effected; for these are practicable (in the sense of being easy); such things are those in which everyone, or most people, or one's equals, or one's inferiors have succeeded. Good also are the things by which we shall gratify our friends or annoy our enemies; and the things chosen by those whom we admire: and the things for which we are fitted by nature or experience, since we think we shall succeed more easily in these: and those in which no worthless man can succeed, for such things bring greater praise: and those which we do in fact desire, for what we desire is taken to be not only pleasant but also better. Further, a man of a given disposition makes chiefly for the corresponding things: lovers of victory make for victory, lovers of honor for honor, money-loving men for money, and so with the rest. These, then, are the sources from which we must derive our means of persuasion about Good and Utility.

Part VII

Since, however, it often happens that people agree that two things are both useful but do not agree about which is the more so, the next step will be to treat of relative goodness and relative utility.

A thing which surpasses another may be regarded as being that other thing plus something more, and that other thing which is surpassed as being what is contained in the first thing. Now to call a thing "greater" or "more" always implies a comparison of it with one that is "smaller" or "less," while "great" and "small," "much" and "little," are terms used in comparison with normal magnitude. The "great" is that which surpasses the normal, the "small" is that which is surpassed by the normal; and so with "many" and "few."

Now we are applying the term "good" to what is desirable for its own sake and not for the sake of something else; to that at which all things aim; to what they would choose if they could acquire understanding and practical wisdom; and to that which tends to produce or preserve such goods, or is always accompanied by them. Moreover, that for the sake of which things are done is the end (an end being that for the sake of which all else is done), and for each individual that thing is a good which fulfills these conditions in regard to himself. It follows, then, that a greater number of goods is a greater good than one or than a smaller number, if that one or that smaller number is included in the count; for then the larger number surpasses the smaller, and the smaller quantity is surpassed as being contained in the larger.

Again, if the largest member of one class surpasses the largest member of another, then the one class surpasses the other; and if one class surpasses another, then the largest member of the one surpasses the largest member of the other. Thus, if the tallest man is taller than the tallest woman, then men in general are taller than women. Conversely, if men in general are taller than women, then the tallest man is taller than the tallest woman. For the superiority of class over class is proportionate to the superiority possessed by their largest specimens. Again, where one good is always accompanied by another, but does not always accompany it, it is greater than the other, for the use of the second thing is implied in the use of the first. A thing may be accompanied by another in three ways, either simultaneously, subsequently, or potentially. Life accompanies health simultaneously (but not health life), knowledge accompanies the act of learning subsequently, cheating accompanies sacrilege potentially, since a man who has committed sacrilege is always capable of cheating. Again, when two things each surpass a third, that which does so by the greater amount is the greater of the two; for it must surpass the greater as well as the less of the other two. A thing productive of a greater good than another is productive of is itself a greater good than that other. For this conception of "productive of a greater" has been implied in our argument. Likewise, that which is produced by a greater good is itself a greater good; thus, if what is wholesome is more desirable and a greater good than what gives pleasure, health too must be a greater good than pleasure. Again, a thing which is desirable in itself is a greater good than a thing which is not desirable in itself, as for example bodily strength than what is wholesome, since the latter is not pursued for its own sake, whereas the former is; and this was our definition of the good. Again, if one of two things is an end, and the other is not, the former is the greater good, as being chosen for its own sake and not for the sake of something else; as, for example, exercise is chosen for the sake of physical well-being. And of two things that which stands less in need of the other, or of other things, is the greater good, since it is more self-sufficing. (That which stands "less" in need of others is that which needs either fewer or easier things.) So when one thing does not exist or cannot come into existence without a second, while the second can exist without the first, the second is the better. That which does not need something else is more self-sufficing than that which does, and presents itself as a greater good for that reason. Again, that which is a beginning of other things is a greater good than that which is not, and that which is a cause is a greater good than that which is not; the reason being the same in each case, namely that without a cause and a beginning nothing can exist or come into existence. Again, where there are two sets of consequences arising from two different beginnings or causes, the consequences of the more important beginning or cause are themselves the more important; and conversely, that beginning or cause is itself the more important which has the more important consequences. Now it is plain, from all that has been said, that one thing may be shown to be more important than another from two opposite points of view: it may appear the more important (1) because it is a beginning and the other thing is not, and also (2) because it is not a beginning and the other thing is, on the ground that the end is more important and is not a beginning. So Leodamas, when accusing Callistratus, said that the man who prompted the deed was more guilty than the doer, since it would not have been done if he had not planned it. On the other hand, when accusing Chabrias he said that the doer was worse than the prompter, since there would have been no deed without someone to do it; men, said he, plot a thing only in order to carry it out.

Further, what is rare is a greater good than what is plentiful. Thus, gold is a better thing than iron, though less useful: it is harder to get, and therefore better worth getting. Reversely, it may be argued that the plentiful is a better thing than the rare, because we can make more use of it. For what is often useful surpasses what is seldom useful, whence the saying:

"The best of things is water."

More generally: the hard thing is better than the easy, because it is rarer: and reversely, the easy thing is better than the hard, for it is as we wish it to be. That is the greater good whose contrary is the greater evil, and whose loss affects us more. Positive goodness and badness are more important than the mere absence of goodness and badness: for positive goodness and badness are ends, which the mere absence of them cannot be. Further, in proportion as the functions of things are noble or base, the things themselves are good or bad: conversely, in proportion as the things themselves are good or bad, their functions also are good or bad; for the nature of results corresponds with that of their causes and beginnings, and conversely the nature of causes and beginnings corresponds with that of their results. Moreover, those things are greater goods, superiority in which is more desirable or more honorable. Thus, keenness of sight is more desirable than keenness of smell, sight generally being more desirable than smell generally; and similarly, unusually great love of friends being more honorable than unusually great love of money, ordinary love of friends is more honorable than ordinary love of money. Conversely, if one of two normal things is better or nobler than the other, an unusual degree of that thing is better or nobler than an unusual degree of the other. Again, one thing is more honorable or better than another if it is more honorable or better to desire it; the importance of the object of a given instinct corresponds to the importance of the instinct itself; and for the same reason, if one thing is more honorable or better than another, it is more honorable and better to desire it. Again, if one science is more honorable and valuable than another, the activity with which it deals is also more honorable and valuable; as is the science, so is the reality that is its object, each science being authoritative in its own sphere. So, also, the more valuable and honorable the object of a science, the more valuable and honorable the science itself is—in consequence. Again, that which would be judged, or which has been judged, a good thing, or a better thing than something else, by all or most people of understanding, or by the majority of men, or by the ablest, must be so; either without qualification, or in so far as they use their understanding to form their judgement. This is indeed a general principle, applicable to all other judgements also; not only the goodness of things, but their essence, magnitude, and general nature are in fact just what knowledge and understanding will declare them to be. Here the principle is applied to judgements of goodness, since one definition of "good" was "what beings that acquire understanding will choose in any given case": from which it clearly follows that that thing is better which understanding declares to be so. That, again, is a better thing which attaches to better men, either absolutely, or in virtue of their being better; as courage is better than strength. And that is a greater good which would be chosen by a better man, either absolutely, or in virtue of his being better: for instance, to suffer wrong rather than to do wrong, for that would be the choice of the juster man. Again, the pleasanter of two things is the better, since all things pursue pleasure, and things instinctively desire pleasurable sensation for its own sake; and these are two of the characteristics by which the "good" and the "end" have been defined. One pleasure is greater than another if it is more unmixed with pain, or more lasting. Again, the nobler thing is better than the less noble, since the noble is either what is pleasant or what is desirable in itself. And those things also are greater goods which men desire more earnestly to bring about for themselves or for their friends, whereas those things which they least desire to bring about are greater evils. And those things which are more lasting are better than those which are more fleeting, and the more secure than the less; the enjoyment of the lasting has the advantage of being longer, and that of the secure has the advantage of suiting our wishes, being there for us whenever we like. Further, in accordance with the rule of coordinate terms and inflections of the same stem, what is true of one such related word is true of all. Thus if the action qualified by the term "brave" is more noble and desirable than the action qualified by the term "temperate," then "bravery" is more desirable than "temperance" and "being brave" than "being temperate." That, again, which is chosen by all is a greater good than that which is not, and that chosen by the majority than that chosen by the minority. For that which all desire is good, as we have said"; and so, the more a thing is desired, the better it is. Further, that is the better thing which is considered so by competitors or enemies, or, again, by authorized judges or those whom they select to represent them. In the first two cases the decision is virtually that of everyone, in the last two that of authorities and experts. And sometimes it may be argued that what all share is the better thing, since it is a dishonor not to share in it; at other times, that what none or few share is better, since it is rarer. The more praiseworthy things are, the nobler and therefore the better they are. So with the things that earn greater honors than others—honor is, as it were, a measure of value; and the things whose absence involves comparatively heavy penalties; and the things that are better than others admitted or believed to be good. Moreover, things look better merely by being divided into their parts, since they then seem to surpass a greater number of things than before. Hence Homer says that Meleager was roused to battle by the thought of

> "All horrors that light on a folk whose city
> is ta'en of their foes,
> When they slaughter the men, when the burg is
> wasted with ravening flame,
> When strangers are haling young children to thraldom,
> (fair women to shame.)"

The same effect is produced by piling up facts in a climax after the manner of Epicharmus. The reason is partly the same as in the case of division (for combination too makes the impression of great superiority), and partly that the original thing appears to be the cause and origin of important results. And since a thing is better when it is harder or rarer than other things, its superiority may be due to seasons, ages, places, times, or one's natural powers. When a man accomplishes something beyond his natural power, or beyond his years, or beyond the measure of people like him, or in a special way, or at a special place or time, his deed will have a high degree of nobleness, goodness, and justice, or of their opposites. Hence the epigram on the victor at the Olympic games:

> "In time past, hearing a Yoke on my shoulders,
> of wood unshaven,
> I carried my loads of fish from, Argos to Tegea town."

So Iphicrates used to extol himself by describing the low estate from which he had risen. Again, what is natural is better than what is acquired, since it is harder to come by. Hence the words of Homer:

> "I have learned from none but myself."

And the best part of a good thing is particularly good; as when Pericles in his funeral oration said that the country's loss of its young men in battle was "as if the spring were taken out of the year." So with those things which are of service when the need is pressing; for example, in old age and times of sickness. And of two things that which leads more directly to the end in view is the better. So too is that which is better for people generally as well as for a particular individual. Again, what can be got is better than what cannot, for it is good in a given case and the other thing is not. And what is at the end of life is better than what is not, since those things are ends in a greater degree which are nearer the end. What aims at reality is better than what aims at appearance. We may define what aims at appearance as what a man will not choose if nobody is to know of his having it. This would seem to show that to receive benefits is more desirable than to confer them, since a man will choose the former even if nobody is to know of it, but it is not the general view that he will choose the latter if nobody knows of it. What a man wants to be is better than what a man wants to seem, for in aiming at that he is aiming more at reality. Hence men say that justice is of small value, since it is more desirable to seem just than to be just, whereas with health it is not so. That is better than other things which is more useful than they are for a number of different purposes; for example, that which promotes life, good life, pleasure, and noble conduct. For this reason wealth and health are commonly thought to be of the highest value, as possessing all these advantages. Again, that is better than other things which is accompanied both with less pain and with actual pleasure; for here there is more than one advantage; and so here we have the good of feeling pleasure and also the good of not feeling pain. And of two good things that is the better whose addition to a third thing makes a better whole than the addition of the other to the same thing will make. Again, those things which we are seen to possess are better than those which we are not seen to possess, since the former have the air of reality. Hence wealth may be regarded as a greater good if its existence is known to others. That which is dearly prized is better than what is not—the sort of thing that some people have only one of, though others have more like it. Accordingly, blinding a one-eyed man inflicts worse injury than half-blinding a man with two eyes; for the one-eyed man has been robbed of what he dearly prized.

The grounds on which we must base our arguments, when we are speaking for or against a proposal, have now been set forth more or less completely.

Part VIII

The most important and effective qualification for success in persuading audiences and speaking well on public affairs is to understand all the forms of government and to discriminate their respective customs, institutions, and interests. For all men are persuaded by considerations of their interest, and their interest lies in the maintenance of the established order. Further, it rests with the supreme authority to give authoritative decisions, and this varies with each form of government; there are as many different supreme authorities as there are different forms of government. The forms of government are four: democracy, oligarchy, aristocracy, monarchy. The supreme right to judge and decide always rests, therefore, with either a part or the whole of one or other of these governing powers.

A Democracy is a form of government under which the citizens distribute the offices of state among themselves by lot, whereas under oligarchy there is a property qualification, under aristocracy one of education. By education I mean that education which is laid down by the law; for it is those who have been loyal to the national institutions that hold office under an aristocracy. These are bound to be looked upon as "the best men," and it is from this fact that this form of government has derived its name ("the rule of the best"). Monarchy, as the word implies, is the constitution a in which one man has authority over all. There are two forms of monarchy: kingship, which is limited by prescribed conditions, and "tyranny," which is not limited by anything.

We must also notice the ends which the various forms of government pursue, since people choose in practice such actions as will lead to the realization of their ends. The end of democracy is freedom; of oligarchy, wealth; of aristocracy, the maintenance of education and national institutions; of tyranny, the protection of the tyrant. It is clear, then, that we must distinguish those particular customs, institutions, and interests which tend to realize the ideal of each constitution, since men choose their means with reference to their ends. But rhetorical persuasion is effected not only by demonstrative but by ethical argument; it helps a speaker to convince us, if we believe that he has certain qualities himself, namely, goodness, or goodwill toward us, or both together. Similarly, we should know the moral qualities characteristic of each form of government, for the special moral character of each is bound to provide us with our most effective means of persuasion in dealing with it. We shall learn the qualities of governments in the same way as we learn the qualities of individuals, since they are revealed in their deliberate acts of choice; and these are determined by the end that inspires them.

We have now considered the objects, immediate or distant, at which we are to aim when urging any proposal, and the grounds on which we are to base our arguments in favor of its utility. We have also briefly considered the means and methods by which we shall gain a good knowledge of the moral qualities and institutions peculiar to the various forms of government—only, however, to the extent demanded by the present occasion; a detailed account of the subject has been given in the Politics.

Part IX

We have now to consider Virtue and Vice, the Noble and the Base, since these are the objects of praise and blame. In doing so, we shall at the same time be finding out how to make our hearers take the required view of our own characters—our second method of persuasion. The ways in which to make them trust the goodness of other people are also the ways in which to make them trust our own. Praise, again, may be serious or frivolous; nor is it always of a human or divine being but often of inanimate things, or of the humblest of the lower animals. Here too we must know on what grounds to argue, and must, therefore, now discuss the subject, though by way of illustration only.

The Noble is that which is both desirable for its own sake and also worthy of praise; or that which is both good and also pleasant because good. If this is a true definition of the Noble, it follows that virtue must be noble, since it is both a good thing and also praiseworthy. Virtue is, according to the usual view, a faculty of providing and preserving good things; or a faculty of conferring many great benefits, and benefits of all kinds on all occasions. The forms of Virtue are justice, courage, temperance, magnificence, magnanimity, liberality, gentleness, prudence, wisdom. If virtue is a faculty of beneficence, the highest kinds of it must be those which are most useful to others, and for this reason men honor most the just and the courageous, since courage is useful to others in war, justice both in war and in peace. Next comes liberality; liberal people let their money go instead of fighting for it, whereas other people care more for money than for anything else. Justice is the virtue through which everybody enjoys his own possessions in accordance with the law; its opposite is injustice, through which men enjoy the possessions of others in defiance of the law. Courage is the virtue that disposes men to do noble deeds in situations of danger, in accordance with the law and in obedience to its commands; cowardice is the opposite. Temperance is the virtue that disposes us to obey the law where physical pleasures are concerned; incontinence is the opposite. Liberality disposes us to spend money for others' good; illiberality is the opposite. Magnanimity is the virtue that disposes us to do good to others on a large scale; [its opposite is meanness of spirit]. Magnificence is a virtue productive of greatness in matters involving the spending of money. The opposites of these two are smallness of spirit and meanness respectively. Prudence is that virtue of the understanding which enables men to come to wise decisions about the relation to happiness of the goods and evils that have been previously mentioned.

The above is a sufficient account, for our present purpose, of virtue and vice in general, and of their various forms. As to further aspects of the subject, it is not difficult to discern the facts; it is evident that things productive of virtue are noble, as tending toward virtue; and also the effects of virtue, that is, the signs of its presence and the acts to which it leads. And since the signs of virtue, and such acts as it is the mark of a virtuous man to do or have done to him, are noble, it follows that all deeds or signs of courage, and everything done courageously, must be noble things; and so with what is just and actions done justly. (Not, however, actions justly done to us; here justice is unlike the other virtues; "justly" does not always mean "nobly"; when a man is punished, it is more shameful that this should be justly than unjustly done to him.) The same is true of the other virtues. Again, those actions are noble for which the reward is simply honor, or honor more than money. So are those in which a man aims at something desirable for someone else's sake; actions good absolutely, such as those a man does for his country without thinking of himself; actions good in their own nature; actions that are not good simply for the individual, since individual interests are selfish. Noble also are those actions whose advantage may be enjoyed after death, as opposed to those whose advantage is enjoyed during one's lifetime: for the latter are more likely to be for one's own sake only. Also, all actions done for the sake of others, since less than other actions are done for one's own sake; and all successes which benefit others and not oneself; and services done to one's benefactors, for this is just; and good deeds generally, since they are not directed to one's own profit. And the opposites of those things of which men feel ashamed, for men are ashamed of saying, doing, or intending to do shameful things. So when Alcaeus said

> "Something I fain would say to thee,
> Only shame restraineth me,"

Sappho wrote

> "If for things good and noble thou wert yearning,
> If to speak baseness were thy tongue not burning,
> No load of shame would on thine eyelids weigh;
> What thou with honor wishest thou wouldst say."

Those things, also, are noble for which men strive anxiously, without feeling fear; for they feel thus about the good things which lead to fair fame. Again, one quality or action is nobler than another if it is that of a naturally finer being: thus a man's will be nobler than a woman's. And those qualities are noble which give more pleasure to other people than to their possessors; hence the nobleness of justice and just actions. It is noble to avenge oneself on one's enemies and not to come to terms with them; for requital is just, and the just is noble; and not to surrender is a sign of courage. Victory, too, and honor belong to the class of noble things, since they are desirable even when they yield no fruits, and they prove our superiority in good qualities. Things that deserve to be remembered are noble, and the more they deserve this, the nobler they are. So are the things that continue even after death; those which are always attended by honor; those which are exceptional; and those which are possessed by one person alone-these last are more readily remembered than others. So again are possessions that bring no profit, since they are more fitting than others for a gentleman. So are the distinctive qualities of a particular people, and the symbols of what it specially admires, like long hair in Sparta, where this is a mark of a free man, as it is not easy to perform any menial task when one's hair is long. Again, it is noble not to practice any sordid craft, since it is the mark of a free man not to live at another's beck and call. We are also to assume when we wish either to praise a man or blame him that qualities closely allied to those which he actually has are identical with them; for instance, that the cautious man is cold-blooded and treacherous, and that the stupid man is an honest fellow or the thick-skinned man a good-tempered one. We can always idealize any given man by drawing on the virtues akin to his actual qualities; thus we may say that the passionate and excitable man is "outspoken"; or that the arrogant man is "superb" or "impressive." Those who run to extremes will be said to possess the corresponding good qualities; rashness will be called courage, and extravagance generosity. That will be what most people think; and at the same time this method enables an advocate to draw a misleading inference from the motive, arguing that if a man runs into danger needlessly, much more will he do so in a noble cause; and if a man is open-handed to anyone and everyone, he will be so to his friends also, since it is the extreme form of goodness to be good to everybody.

We must also take into account the nature of our particular audience when making a speech of praise; for, as Socrates used to say, "it is not difficult to praise the Athenians to an Athenian audience." If the audience esteems a given quality, we must say that our hero has that quality, no matter whether we are addressing Scythians or Spartans or philosophers. Everything, in fact, that is esteemed we are to represent as noble. After all, people regard the two things as much the same.

All actions are noble that are appropriate to the man who does them: if, for instance, they are worthy of his ancestors or of his own past career. For it makes for happiness, and is a noble thing, that he should add to the honor he already has. Even inappropriate actions are noble if they are better and nobler than the appropriate ones would be; for instance, if one who was just an average person when all went well becomes a hero in adversity, or if he becomes better and easier to get on with the higher he rises. Compare the saying of Iphicrates, "Think what I was and what I am"; and the epigram on the victor at the Olympic games,

> "In time past, bearing a yoke on my shoulders,
> of wood unshaven,"

and the encomium of Simonides,

> "A woman whose father, whose husband, whose
> brethren were princes all."

Since we praise a man for what he has actually done, and fine actions are distinguished from others by being intentionally good, we must try to prove that our hero's noble acts are intentional. This is all the easier if we can make out that he has often acted so before, and therefore we must assert coincidences and accidents to have been intended. Produce a number of good actions, all of the same kind, and people will think that they must have been intended, and that they prove the good qualities of the man who did them.

Praise is the expression in words of the eminence of a man's good qualities, and therefore we must display his actions as the product of such qualities. Encomium refers to what he has actually done; the mention of accessories, such as good birth and education, merely helps to make our story credible—good fathers are likely to have good sons, and good training is likely to produce good character. Hence it is only when a man has already done something that we bestow encomiums upon him. Yet the actual deeds are evidence of the doer's character: even if a man has not actually done a given good thing, we shall bestow praise on him, if we are sure that he is the sort of man who would do it. To call anyone blessed is, it may be added, the same thing as to call him happy; but these are not the same thing as to bestow praise and encomium upon him; the two latter are a part of "calling happy," just as goodness is a part of happiness.

To praise a man is in one respect akin to urging a course of action. The suggestions which would be made in the latter case become encomiums when differently expressed. When we know what action or character is required, then, in order to express these facts as suggestions for action, we have to change and reverse our form of words. Thus the statement "A man should be proud not of what he owes to fortune but of what he owes to himself," if put like this, amounts to a suggestion; to make it into praise we must put it thus, "Since he is proud not of what he owes to fortune but of what he owes to himself." Consequently, whenever you want to praise anyone, think what you would urge people to do; and when you want to urge the doing of anything, think what you would praise a man for having done. Since suggestion may or may not forbid an action, the praise into which we convert it must have one or other of two opposite forms of expression accordingly.

There are, also, many useful ways of heightening the effect of praise. We must, for instance, point out that a man is the only one, or the first, or almost the only one who has done something, or that he has done it better than anyone else; all these distinctions are honorable. And we must, further, make much of the particular season and occasion of an action, arguing that we could hardly have looked for it just then. If a man has often achieved the same success, we must mention this; that is a strong point; he himself, and not luck, will then be given the credit. So, too, if it is on his account that observances have been devised and instituted to encourage or honor such achievements as his own: thus we may praise Hippolochus because the first encomium ever made was for him, or Harmodius and Aristogeiton because their statues were the first to be put up in the marketplace. And we may censure bad men for the opposite reason.

Again, if you cannot find enough to say of a man himself, you may pit him against others, which is what Isocrates used to do owing to his want of familiarity with forensic pleading. The comparison should be with famous men; that will strengthen your case; it is a noble thing to surpass men who are themselves great. It is only natural that methods of "heightening the effect" should be attached particularly to speeches of praise; they aim at proving superiority over others, and any such superiority is a form of nobleness. Hence if you cannot compare your hero with famous men, you should at least compare him with other people generally, since any superiority is held to reveal excellence. And, in general, of the lines of argument which are common to all speeches, this "heightening of effect" is most suitable for declamations, where we take our hero's actions as admitted facts, and our business is simply to invest these with dignity and nobility. "Examples" are most suitable to deliberative speeches; for we judge of future events by divination from past events. Enthymemes are most suitable to forensic speeches; it is our doubts about past events that most admit of arguments showing why a thing must have happened or proving that it did happen.

The above are the general lines on which all, or nearly all, speeches of praise or blame are constructed. We have seen the sort of thing we must bear in mind in making such speeches, and the materials out of which encomiums and censures are made. No special treatment of censure and vituperation is needed. Knowing the above facts, we know their contraries; and it is out of these that speeches of censure are made.

Part X

We have next to treat of Accusation and Defense, and to enumerate and describe the ingredients of the syllogisms used therein. There are three things we must ascertain first, the nature and number of the incentives to wrongdoing; second, the state of mind of wrongdoers; third, the kind of persons who are wronged, and their condition. We will deal with these questions in order. But before that let us define the act of "wrongdoing."

We may describe "wrongdoing" as injury voluntarily inflicted contrary to law. "Law" is either special or general. By special law I mean that written law which regulates the life of a particular community; by general law, all those unwritten principles which are supposed to be acknowledged everywhere. We do things "voluntarily" when we do them consciously and without constraint. (Not all voluntary acts are deliberate, but all deliberate acts are conscious—no one is ignorant of what he deliberately intends.) The causes of our deliberately intending harmful and wicked acts contrary to law are (1) vice, (2) lack of self-control. For the wrongs a man does to others will correspond to the bad quality or qualities that he himself possesses. Thus it is the mean man who will wrong others about money, the profligate in matters of physical pleasure, the effeminate in matters of comfort, and the coward where danger is concerned—his terror makes him abandon those who are involved in the same danger. The ambitious man does wrong for sake of honor, the quick-tempered from anger, the lover of victory for the sake of victory, the embittered man for the sake of revenge, the stupid man because he has misguided notions of right and wrong, the shameless man because he does not mind what people think of him; and so with the rest—any wrong that anyone does to others corresponds to his particular faults of character.

However, this subject has already been cleared up in part in our discussion of the virtues and will be further explained later when we treat of the emotions. We have now to consider the motives and states of mind of wrongdoers, and to whom they do wrong.

Let us first decide what sort of things people are trying to get or avoid when they set about doing wrong to others. For it is plain that the prosecutor must consider, out of all the aims that can ever induce us to do wrong to our neighbors, how many, and which, affect his adversary; while the defendant must consider how many, and which, do not affect him. Now every action of every person either is or is not due to that person himself. Of those not due to himself some are due to chance, the others to necessity; of these latter, again, some are due to compulsion, the others to nature. Consequently all actions that are not due to a man himself are due either to chance or to nature or to compulsion. All actions that are due to a man himself and caused by himself are due either to habit or to rational or irrational craving. Rational craving is a craving for good, i.e. a wish—nobody wishes for anything unless he thinks it good. Irrational craving is twofold, viz. anger and appetite.

Thus every action must be due to one or other of seven causes: chance, nature, compulsion, habit, reasoning, anger, or appetite. It is superfluous further to distinguish actions according to the doers' ages, moral states, or the like; it is of course true that, for instance, young men do have hot tempers and strong appetites; still, it is not through youth that they act accordingly, but through anger or appetite. Nor, again, is action due to wealth or poverty; it is of course true that poor men, being short of money, do have an appetite for it, and that rich men, being able to command needless pleasures, do have an appetite for such pleasures; but here, again, their actions will be due not to wealth or poverty but to appetite. Similarly, with just men, and unjust men, and all others who are said to act in accordance with their moral qualities, their actions will really be due to one of the causes mentioned—either reasoning or emotion: due, indeed, sometimes to good dispositions and good emotions, and sometimes to bad; but that good qualities should be followed by good emotions, and bad by bad, is merely an accessory fact-it is no doubt true that the temperate man, for instance, because he is temperate, is always and at once attended by healthy opinions and appetites in regard to pleasant things, and the intemperate man by unhealthy ones. So we must ignore such distinctions. Still we must consider what kinds of actions and of people usually go together; for while there are no definite kinds of action associated with the fact that a man is fair or dark, tall or short, it does make a difference if he is young or old, just or unjust. And, generally speaking, all those accessory qualities that cause distinctions of human character are important: e.g. the sense of wealth or poverty, of being lucky or unlucky. This shall be dealt with later—let us now deal first with the rest of the subject before us.

The things that happen by chance are all those whose cause cannot be determined, that have no purpose, and that happen neither always nor usually nor in any fixed way. The definition of chance shows just what they are. Those things happen by nature which have a fixed and internal cause; they take place uniformly, either always or usually. There is no need to discuss in exact detail the things that happen contrary to nature, nor to ask whether they happen in some sense naturally or from some other cause; it would seem that chance is at least partly the cause of such events. Those things happen through compulsion which take place contrary to the desire or reason of the doer, yet through his own agency. Acts are done from habit which men do because they have often done them before. Actions are due to reasoning when, in view of any of the goods already mentioned, they appear useful either as ends or as means to an end, and are performed for that reason: "for that reason," since even licentious persons perform a certain number of useful actions, but because they are pleasant and not because they are useful. To passion and anger are due all acts of revenge. Revenge and punishment are different things. Punishment is inflicted for the sake of the person punished; revenge for that of the punisher, to satisfy his feelings. (What anger is will be made clear when we come to discuss the emotions.) Appetite is the cause of all actions that appear pleasant. Habit, whether acquired by mere familiarity or by effort, belongs to the class of pleasant things, for there are many actions not naturally pleasant which men perform with pleasure, once they have become used to them. To sum up then, all actions due to ourselves either are or seem to be either good or pleasant. Moreover, as all actions due to ourselves are done voluntarily and actions not due to ourselves are done involuntarily, it follows that all voluntary actions must either be or seem to be either good or pleasant; for I reckon among goods escape from evils or apparent evils and the exchange of a greater evil for a less (since these things are in a sense positively desirable), and likewise I count among pleasures escape from painful or apparently painful things and the exchange of a greater pain for a less. We must ascertain, then, the number and nature of the things that are useful and pleasant. The useful has been previously examined in connection with political oratory; let us now proceed to examine the pleasant. Our various definitions must be regarded as adequate, even if they are not exact, provided they are clear.

Part XI

We may lay it down that Pleasure is a movement, a movement by which the soul as a whole is consciously brought into its normal state of being; and that Pain is the opposite. If this is what pleasure is, it is clear that the pleasant is what tends to produce this condition, while that which tends to destroy it, or to cause the soul to be brought into the opposite state, is painful. It must therefore be pleasant as a rule to move toward a natural state of being, particularly when a natural process has achieved the complete recovery of that natural state. Habits also are pleasant; for as soon as a thing has become habitual, it is virtually natural; habit is a thing not unlike nature; what happens often is akin to what happens always, natural events happening always, habitual events often. Again, that is pleasant which is not forced on us; for force is unnatural, and that is why what is compulsory, painful, and it has been rightly said

"All that is done on compulsion is bitterness unto the soul."

So all acts of concentration, strong effort, and strain are necessarily painful; they all involve compulsion and force, unless we are accustomed to them, in which case it is custom that makes them pleasant. The opposites to these are pleasant; and hence ease, freedom from toil, relaxation, amusement, rest, and sleep belong to the class of pleasant things; for these are all free from any element of compulsion. Everything, too, is pleasant for which we have the desire within us, since desire is the craving for pleasure. Of the desires some are irrational, some associated with reason. By irrational I mean those which do not arise from any opinion held by the mind. Of this kind are those known as "natural"; for instance, those originating in the body, such as the desire for nourishment, namely hunger and thirst, and a separate kind of desire answering to each kind of nourishment; and the desires connected with taste and sex and sensations of touch in general; and those of smell, hearing, and vision. Rational desires are those which we are induced to have; there are many things we desire to see or get because we have been told of them and induced to believe them good. Further, pleasure is the consciousness through the senses of a certain kind of emotion; but imagination is a feeble sort of sensation, and there will always be in the mind of a man who remembers or expects something an image or picture of what he remembers or expects. If this is so, it is clear that memory and expectation also, being accompanied by sensation, may be accompanied by pleasure. It follows that anything pleasant is either present and perceived, past and remembered, or future and expected, since we perceive present pleasures, remember past ones, and expect future ones. Now the things that are pleasant to remember are not only those that, when actually perceived as present, were pleasant, but also some things that were not, provided that their results have subsequently proved noble and good. Hence the words

"Sweet 'tis when rescued to remember pain,"

and

> "Even his griefs are a joy long after to one that remembers
> All that he wrought and endured."

The reason of this is that it is pleasant even to be merely free from evil. The things it is pleasant to expect are those that when present are felt to afford us either great delight or great but not painful benefit. And in general, all the things that delight us when they are present also do so, as a rule, when we merely remember or expect them. Hence even being angry is pleasant—Homer said of wrath that

> "Sweeter it is by far than the honeycomb dripping with
> sweetness—"

for no one grows angry with a person on whom there is no prospect of taking vengeance, and we feel comparatively little anger, or none at all, with those who are much our superiors in power. Some pleasant feeling is associated with most of our appetites we are enjoying either the memory of a past pleasure or the expectation of a future one, just as persons down with fever, during their attacks of thirst, enjoy remembering the drinks they have had and looking forward to having more. So also a lover enjoys talking or writing about his loved one, or doing any little thing connected with him; all these things recall him to memory and make him actually present to the eye of imagination. Indeed, it is always the first sign of love, that besides enjoying someone's presence, we remember him when he is gone, and feel pain as well as pleasure, because he is there no longer. Similarly there is an element of pleasure even in mourning and lamentation for the departed. There is grief, indeed, at his loss, but pleasure in remembering him and as it were seeing him before us in his deeds and in his life. We can well believe the poet when he says

> "He spake, and in each man's heart he awakened
> the love of lament."

Revenge, too, is pleasant; it is pleasant to get anything that it is painful to fail to get, and angry people suffer extreme pain when they fail to get their revenge; but they enjoy the prospect of getting it. Victory also is pleasant, and not merely to "bad losers," but to everyone; the winner sees himself in the light of a champion, and everybody has a more or less keen appetite for being that. The pleasantness of victory implies of course that combative sports and intellectual contests are pleasant (since in these it often happens that someone wins) and also games like knuckle-bones, ball, dice, and draughts. And similarly with the serious sports; some of these become pleasant when one is accustomed to them; while others are pleasant from the first, like hunting with hounds, or indeed any kind of hunting. For where there is competition, there is victory. That is why forensic pleading and debating contests are pleasant to those who are accustomed to them and have the capacity for them. Honor and good repute are among the most pleasant things of all; they make a man see himself in the character of a fine fellow, especially when he is credited with it by people whom he thinks good judges. His neighbors are better judges than people at a distance; his associates and fellow countrymen better than strangers; his contemporaries better than posterity; sensible persons better than foolish ones; a large number of people better than a small number: those of the former class, in each case, are the more likely to be good judges of him. Honor and credit bestowed by those whom you think much inferior to yourself—e.g. children or animals—you do not value: not for its own sake, anyhow: if you do value it, it is for some other reason. Friends belong to the class of pleasant things; it is pleasant to love—if you love wine, you certainly find it delightful: and it is pleasant to be loved, for this too makes a man see himself as the possessor of goodness, a thing that every being that has a feeling for it desires to possess: to be loved means to be valued for one's own personal qualities. To be admired is also pleasant, simply because of the honor implied. Flattery and flatterers are pleasant: the flatterer is a man who, you believe, admires and likes to do the same thing often is pleasant, since, as we saw, anything habitual is pleasant. And to change is also pleasant: change means an approach to nature, whereas invariable repetition of anything causes the excessive prolongation of a settled condition: therefore, says the poet,

> "Change is in all things sweet."

That is why what comes to us only at long intervals is pleasant, whether it be a person or a thing; for it is a change from what we had before, and, besides, what comes only at long intervals has the value of rarity. Learning things and wondering at things are also pleasant as a rule; wondering implies the desire of learning, so that the object of wonder is an object of desire; while in learning one is brought into one's natural condition. Conferring and receiving benefits belong to the class of pleasant things; to receive a benefit is to get what one desires; to confer a benefit implies both posses sion and superiority, both of which are things we try to attain.

It is because beneficent acts are pleasant that people find it pleasant to put their neighbors straight again and to supply what they lack. Again, since learning and wondering are pleasant, it follows that such things as acts of imitation must be pleasant—for instance, painting, sculpture, poetry and every product of skilful imitation; this latter, even if the object imitated is not itself pleasant; for it is not the object itself which here gives delight; the spectator draws inferences ("That is a so-and-so") and thus learns something fresh. Dramatic turns of fortune and hairbreadth escapes from perils are pleasant, because we feel all such things are wonderful.

And since what is natural is pleasant, and things akin to each other seem natural to each other, therefore all kindred and similar things are usually pleasant to each other; for instance, one man, horse, or young person is pleasant to another man, horse, or young person. Hence the proverbs "mate delights mate," "like to like," "beast knows beast," "jackdaw to jackdaw," and the rest of them. But since everything like and akin to oneself is pleasant, and since every man is himself more like and akin to himself than anyone else is, it follows that all of us must be more or less fond of ourselves. For all this resemblance and kinship is present particularly in the relation of an individual to himself. And because we are all fond of ourselves, it follows that what is our own is pleasant to all of us, as for instance our own deeds and words. That is why we are usually fond of our flatterers, [our lovers,] and honor; also of our children, for our children are our own work. It is also pleasant to complete what is defective, for the whole thing thereupon becomes our own work. And since power over others is very pleasant, it is pleasant to be thought wise, for practical wisdom secures us power over others. (Scientific wisdom is also pleasant, because it is the knowledge of many wonderful things.) Again, since most of us are ambitious, it must be pleasant to disparage our neighbors as well as to have power over them. It is pleasant for a man to spend his time over what he feels he can do best; just as the poet says,

> "To that he bends himself,
> To that each day allots most time, wherein
> He is indeed the best part of himself."

Similarly, since amusement and every kind of relaxation and laughter too belong to the class of pleasant things, it follows that ludicrous things are pleasant, whether men, words, or deeds. We have discussed the ludicrous separately in the treatise on the Art of Poetry.

So much for the subject of pleasant things: by considering their opposites we can easily see what things are unpleasant.

Part XII

The above are the motives that make men do wrong to others; we are next to consider the states of mind in which they do it, and the persons to whom they do it.

They must themselves suppose that the thing can be done, and done by them: either that they can do it without being found out, or that if they are found out they can escape being punished, or that if they are punished the disadvantage will be less than the gain for themselves or those they care for. The general subject of apparent possibility and impossibility will be handled later on, since it is relevant not only to forensic but to all kinds of speaking. But it may here be said that people think that they can themselves most easily do wrong to others without being punished for it if they possess eloquence, or practical ability, or much legal experience, or a large body of friends, or a great deal of money. Their confidence is greatest if they personally possess the advantages mentioned: but even without them they are satisfied if they have friends or supporters or partners who do possess them: they can thus both commit their crimes and escape being found out and punished for committing them. They are also safe, they think, if they are on good terms with their victims or with the judges who try them. Their victims will in that case not be on their guard against being wronged, and will make some arrangement with them instead of prosecuting; while their judges will favor them because they like them, either letting them off altogether or imposing light sentences. They are not likely to be found out if their appearance contradicts the charges that might be brought against them: for instance, a weakling is unlikely to be charged with violent assault, or a poor and ugly man with adultery. Public and open injuries are the easiest to do, because nobody could at all suppose them possible, and therefore no precautions are taken. The same is true of crimes so great and terrible that no man living could be suspected of them: here too no precautions are taken. For all men guard against ordinary offenses, just as they guard against ordinary diseases; but no one takes precautions against a disease that nobody has ever had. You feel safe, too, if you have either no enemies or a great many; if you have none, you expect not to be watched and therefore not to be detected; if you have a great many, you will be watched, and therefore people will think you can never risk an attempt on them, and you can defend your innocence by pointing out that you could never have taken such a risk. You may also trust to hide your crime by the way you do it or the place you do it in, or by some convenient means of disposal.

You may feel that even if you are found out you can stave off a trial, or have it postponed, or corrupt your judges: or that even if you are sentenced you can avoid paying damages, or can at least postpone doing so for a long time: or that you are so badly off that you will have nothing to lose. You may feel that the gain to be got by wrongdoing is great or certain or immediate, and that the penalty is small or uncertain or distant. It may be that the advantage to be gained is greater than any possible retribution: as in the case of despotic power, according to the popular view. You may consider your crimes as bringing you solid profit, while their punishment is nothing more than being called bad names. Or the opposite argument may appeal to you: your crimes may bring you some credit (thus you may, incidentally, be avenging your father or mother, like Zeno), whereas the punishment may amount to a fine, or banishment, or something of that sort. People may be led on to wrong others by either of these motives or feelings; but no man by both—they will affect people of quite opposite characters. You may be encouraged by having often escaped detection or punishment already; or by having often tried and failed; for in crime, as in war, there are men who will always refuse to give up the struggle. You may get your pleasure on the spot and the pain later, or the gain on the spot and the loss later. That is what appeals to weak-willed persons—and weakness of will may be shown with regard to all the objects of desire. It may on the contrary appeal to you as it does appeal to self-controlled and sensible people—that the pain and loss are immediate, while the pleasure and profit come later and last longer. You may feel able to make it appear that your crime was due to chance, or to necessity, or to natural causes, or to habit: in fact, to put it generally, as if you had failed to do right rather than actually done wrong. You may be able to trust other people to judge you equitably. You may be stimulated by being in want: which may mean that you want necessaries, as poor people do, or that you want luxuries, as rich people do. You may be encouraged by having a particularly good reputation, because that will save you from being suspected: or by having a particularly bad one, because nothing you are likely to do will make it worse.

The above, then, are the various states of mind in which a man sets about doing wrong to others. The kind of people to whom he does wrong, and the ways in which he does it, must be considered next. The people to whom he does it are those who have what he wants himself, whether this means necessities or luxuries and materials for enjoyment. His victims may be far off or near at hand. If they are near, he gets his profit quickly; if they are far off, vengeance is slow, as those think who plunder the Carthaginians. They may be those who are trustful instead of being cautious and watchful, since all such people are easy to elude. Or those who are too easy-going to have enough energy to prosecute an offender. Or sensitive people, who are not apt to show fight over questions of money. Or those who have been wronged already by many people, and yet have not prosecuted; such men must surely be the proverbial "Mysian prey." Or those who have either never or often been wronged before; in neither case will they take precautions; if they have never been wronged they think they never will, and if they have often been wronged they feel that surely it cannot happen again. Or those whose character has been attacked in the past, or is exposed to attack in the future: they will be too much frightened of the judges to make up their minds to prosecute, nor can they win their case if they do: this is true of those who are hated or unpopular. Another likely class of victim is those who their injurer can pretend have, themselves or through their ancestors or friends, treated badly, or intended to treat badly, the man himself, or his ancestors, or those he cares for; as the proverb says, "wickedness needs but a pretext." A man may wrong his enemies, because that is pleasant: he may equally wrong his friends, because that is easy. Then there are those who have no friends, and those who lack eloquence and practical capacity; these will either not attempt to prosecute, or they will come to terms, or failing that they will lose their case. There are those whom it does not pay to waste time in waiting for trial or damages, such as foreigners and small farmers; they will settle for a trifle, and always be ready to leave off. Also those who have themselves wronged others, either often, or in the same way as they are now being wronged themselves—for it is felt that next to no wrong is done to people when it is the same wrong as they have often themselves done to others: if, for instance, you assault a man who has been accustomed to behave with violence to others. So too with those who have done wrong to others, or have meant to, or mean to, or are likely to do so; there is something fine and pleasant in wronging such persons, it seems as though almost no wrong were done. Also those by doing wrong to whom we shall be gratifying our friends, or those we admire or love, or our masters, or in general the people by reference to whom we mold our lives. Also those whom we may wrong and yet be sure of equitable treatment. Also those against whom we have had any grievance, or any previous differences with them, as Callippus had when he behaved as he did to Dion: here too it seems as if almost no wrong were being done. Also those who are on the point of being wronged by others if we fail to wrong them ourselves, since here we feel we have no time left for thinking the matter over. So Aenesidemus is said to have sent the "cottabus" prize to Gelon, who had just reduced a town to slavery, because Gelon had got there first and forestalled his own attempt. Also those by wronging whom we shall be able to do many righteous acts; for we feel that we can then easily cure the harm done. Thus Jason the Thessalian said that it is a duty to do some unjust acts in order to be able to do many just ones.

Among the kinds of wrong done to others are those that are done universally, or at least commonly: one expects to be forgiven for doing these. Also those that can easily be kept dark, as where things that can rapidly be consumed like eatables are concerned, or things that can easily be changed in shape, color, or combination, or things that can easily be stowed away almost anywhere—portable objects that you can stow away in small corners, or things so like others of which you have plenty already that nobody can tell the difference. There are also wrongs of a kind that shame prevents the victim speaking about, such as outrages done to the women in his household or to himself or to his sons. Also those for which you would be thought very litigious to prosecute any one—trifling wrongs, or wrongs for which people are usually excused.

The above is a fairly complete account of the circumstances under which men do wrong to others, of the sort of wrongs they do, of the sort of persons to whom they do them, and of their reasons for doing them.

Part XIII

It will now be well to make a complete classification of just and unjust actions. We may begin by observing that they have been defined relatively to two kinds of law, and also relatively to two classes of persons. By the two kinds of law I mean particular law and universal law. Particular law is that which each community lays down and applies to its own members: this is partly written and partly unwritten. Universal law is the law of Nature. For there really is, as everyone to some extent divines, a natural justice and injustice that is binding on all men, even on those who have no association or covenant with each other. It is this that Sophocles's Antigone clearly means when she says that the burial of Polyneices was a just act in spite of the prohibition: she means that it was just by nature.

> "Not of today or yesterday it is,
> But lives eternal: none can date its birth."

And so Empedocles, when he bids us kill no living creature, says that doing this is not just for some people while unjust for others,

> "Nay, but, an all-embracing law, through the realms of
>   the sky
> Unbroken it stretcheth, and over the Earth's immensity."

And as Alcidamas says in his Messeniac Oration....[1]

The actions that we ought to do or not to do have also been divided into two classes as affecting either the whole community or some one of its members. From this point of view we can perform just or unjust acts in either of two ways-toward one definite person, or toward the community. The man who is guilty of adultery or assault is doing wrong to some definite person; the man who avoids service in the army is doing wrong to the community.

Thus the whole class of unjust actions may be divided into two classes, those affecting the community, and those affecting one or more other persons. We will next, before going further, remind ourselves of what "being wronged" means. Since it has already been settled that "doing a wrong" must be intentional, "being wronged" must consist in having an injury done to you by someone who intends to do it. In order to be wronged, a man must (1) suffer actual harm, (2) suffer it against his will. The various possible forms of harm are clearly explained by our previous, separate discussion of goods and evils. We have also seen that a voluntary action is one where the doer knows what he is doing. We now see that every accusation must be of an action affecting either the community or some individual. The doer of the action must either understand and intend the action, or not understand and intend it. In the former case, he must be acting either from deliberate choice or from passion. (Anger will be discussed when we speak of the passions the motives for crime and the state of mind of the criminal have already been discussed.) Now it often happens that a man will admit an act, but will not admit the prosecutor's label for the act nor the facts which that label implies. He will admit that he took a thing but not that he "stole" it; that he struck someone first, but not that he committed "outrage"; that he had intercourse with a woman, but not that he committed "adultery"; that he is guilty of theft, but not that

---

[1] What Alcidamas said is not identified in surviving manuscripts. [Ed.]

he is guilty of "sacrilege," the object stolen not being consecrated; that he has encroached, but not that he has "encroached on State lands"; that he has been in communication with the enemy, but not that he has been guilty of "treason." Here therefore we must be able to distinguish what is theft, outrage, or adultery, from what is not, if we are to be able to make the justice of our case clear, no matter whether our aim is to establish a man's guilt or to establish his innocence. Wherever such charges are brought against a man, the question is whether he is or is not guilty of a criminal offense. It is deliberate purpose that constitutes wickedness and criminal guilt, and such names as "outrage" or "theft" imply deliberate purpose as well as the mere action. A blow does not always amount to "outrage," but only if it is struck with some such purpose as to insult the man struck or gratify the striker himself. Nor does taking a thing without the owner's knowledge always amount to "theft," but only if it is taken with the intention of keeping it and injuring the owner. And as with these charges, so with all the others.

We saw that there are two kinds of right and wrong conduct toward others, one provided for by written ordinances, the other by unwritten. We have now discussed the kind about which the laws have something to say. The other kind has itself two varieties. First, there is the conduct that springs from exceptional goodness or badness, and is visited accordingly with censure and loss of honor, or with praise and increase of honor and decorations: for instance, gratitude to, or requital of, our benefactors, readiness to help our friends, and the like. The second kind makes up for the defects of a community's written code of law. This is what we call equity; people regard it as just; it is, in fact, the sort of justice which goes beyond the written law. Its existence partly is and partly is not intended by legislators; not intended, where they have noticed no defect in the law; intended, where find themselves unable to define things exactly, and are obliged to legislate as if that held good always which in fact only holds good usually; or where it is not easy to be complete owing to the endless possible cases presented, such as the kinds and sizes of weapons that may be used to inflict wounds—a lifetime would be too short to make out a complete list of these. If, then, a precise statement is impossible and yet legislation is necessary, the law must be expressed in wide terms; and so, if a man has no more than a finger-ring on his hand when he lifts it to strike or actually strikes another man, he is guilty of a criminal act according to the unwritten words of the law; but he is innocent really, and it is equity that declares him to be so. From this definition of equity it is plain what sort of actions, and what sort of persons, are equitable or the reverse. Equity must be applied to forgivable actions; and it must make us distinguish between criminal acts on the one hand, and errors of judgement, or misfortunes, on the other. (A "misfortune" is an act, not due to moral badness, that has unexpected results: an "error of judgement" is an act, also not due to moral badness, that has results that might have been expected: a "criminal act" has results that might have been expected, but is due to moral badness, for that is the source of all actions inspired by our appetites.) Equity bids us be merciful to the weakness of human nature; to think less about the laws than about the man who framed them, and less about what he said than about what he meant; not to consider the actions of the accused so much as his intentions, nor this or that detail so much as the whole story; to ask not what a man is now but what he has always or usually been. It bids us remember benefits rather than injuries, and benefits received rather than benefits conferred; to be patient when we are wronged; to settle a dispute by negotiation and not by force; to prefer arbitration to motion—for an arbitrator goes by the equity of a case, a judge by the strict law, and arbitration was invented with the express purpose of securing full power for equity.

The above may be taken as a sufficient account of the nature of equity.

Part XIV

The worse of two acts of wrong done to others is that which is prompted by the worse disposition. Hence the most trifling acts may be the worst ones; as when Callistratus charged Melanopus with having cheated the temple-builders of three consecrated half-obols. The converse is true of just acts. This is because the greater is here potentially contained in the less: there is no crime that a man who has stolen three consecrated half-obols would shrink from committing. Sometimes, however, the worse act is reckoned not in this way but by the greater harm that it does. Or it may be because no punishment for it is severe enough to be adequate; or the harm done may be incurable—a difficult and even hopeless crime to defend; or the sufferer may not be able to get his injurer legally punished, a fact that makes the harm incurable, since legal punishment and chastisement are the proper cure. Or again, the man who has suffered wrong may have inflicted some fearful punishment on himself; then the doer of the wrong ought in justice to receive a still more fearful punishment. Thus Sophocles, when pleading for retribution to Euctemon, who had cut his own throat because of the outrage done to him, said he would not fix a penalty less than the victim had fixed for himself. Again, a man's crime is worse if he has been the first man, or the only man, or almost the only man, to commit it: or if it is by no means the first time he has gone seriously wrong in the same way: or if his crime has led to the thinking out and invention of measures to prevent and punish similar crimes—thus in Argos a penalty is inflicted on a man on whose account a law is passed, and also on those on whose account the prison was built: or if a crime is specially brutal, or specially deliberate: or if the report of it awakes more terror than pity. There are also such rhetorically effective ways of putting it as the following: That the accused has disregarded and broken not one but many solemn obligations like oaths, promises, pledges, or rights of intermarriage between states— here the crime is worse because it consists of many crimes; and that the crime was committed in the very place where criminals are punished, as for example perjurers do—it is argued that a man who will commit a crime in a law court would commit it anywhere. Further, the worse deed is that which involves the doer in special shame; that whereby a man wrongs his benefactors—for he does more than one wrong, by not merely doing them harm but failing to do them good; that which breaks the unwritten laws of justice—the better sort of man will be just without being forced to be so, and the written laws depend on force while the unwritten ones do not. It may however be argued otherwise, that the crime is worse which breaks the written laws: for the man who commits crimes for which terrible penalties are provided will not hesitate over crimes for which no penalty is provided at all. So much, then, for the comparative badness of criminal actions.

Part XV

There are also the so-called "non-technical" means of persuasion; and we must now take a cursory view of these, since they are specially characteristic of forensic oratory. They are five in number: laws, witnesses, contracts, tortures, oaths.

First, then, let us take laws and see how they are to be used in persuasion and dissuasion, in accusation and defense. If the written law tells against our case, clearly we must appeal to the universal law, and insist on its greater equity and justice. We must argue that the juror's oath "I will give my verdict according to honest opinion" means that one will not simply follow the letter of the written law. We must urge that the principles of equity are permanent and changeless, and that the universal law does not change either, for it is the law of nature, whereas written laws often do change. This is the bearing the lines in Sophocles's *Antigone*, where Antigone pleads that in burying her brother she had broken Creon's law, but not the unwritten law:

> "Not of today or yesterday they are,
> But live eternal: (none can date their birth.)
> Not I would fear the wrath of any man
> (And brave God's vengeance) for defying these."

We shall argue that justice indeed is true and profitable, but that sham justice is not, and that consequently the written law is not, because it does not fulfill the true purpose of law. Or that justice is like silver, and must be assayed by the judges, if the genuine is to be distinguished from the counterfeit. Or that the better a man is, the more he will follow and abide by the unwritten law in preference to the written. Or perhaps that the law in question contradicts some other highly-esteemed law, or even contradicts itself. Thus it may be that one law will enact that all contracts must be held binding, while another forbids us ever to make illegal contracts. Or if a law is ambiguous, we shall turn it about and consider which construction best fits the interests of justice or utility, and then follow that way of looking at it. Or if, though the law still exists, the situation to meet which it was passed exists no longer, we must do our best to prove this and to combat the law thereby. If however the written law supports our case, we must urge that the oath "to give my verdict according to my honest opinion" not meant to make the judges give a verdict that is contrary to the law, but to save them from the guilt of perjury if they misunderstand what the law really means. Or that no one chooses what is absolutely good, but everyone what is good for himself. Or that not to use the laws is as ahas to have no laws at all. Or that, as in the other arts, it does not pay to try to be cleverer than the doctor: for less harm comes from the doctor's mistakes than from the growing habit of disobeying authority. Or that trying to be cleverer than the laws is just what is forbidden by those codes of law that are accounted best. So far as the laws are concerned, the above discussion is probably sufficient.

As to witnesses, they are of two kinds, the ancient and the recent; and these latter, again, either do or do not share in the risks of the trial. By "ancient" witnesses I mean the poets and all other notable persons whose judgements are known to all. Thus the Athenians appealed to Homer as a witness about Salamis; and the men of Tenedos not long ago appealed to Periander of Corinth in their dispute with the people of Sigeum; and Cleophon supported his accusation of Critias by quoting the elegiac verse of Solon, maintaining that discipline had long been slack in the family of Critias, or Solon would never have written,

> "Pray thee, bid the red-haired Critias do what
> his father commands him."

These witnesses are concerned with past events. As to future events we shall also appeal to soothsayers: thus Themistocles quoted the oracle about "the wooden wall" as a reason for engaging the enemy's fleet. Further, proverbs are, as has been said, one form of evidence. Thus if you are urging somebody not to make a friend of an old man, you will appeal to the proverb,

> "Never show an old man kindness."

Or if you are urging that he who has made away with fathers should also make away with their sons, quote,

> "Fool, who slayeth the father and leaveth his sons to
> avenge him."

"Recent" witnesses are well-known people who have expressed their opinions about some disputed matter: such opinions will be useful support for subsequent disputants on the same oints: thus Eubulus used in the law-courts against the reply Plato had made to Archibius, "It has become the regular custom in this country to admit that one is a scoundrel." There are also those witnesses who share the risk of punishment if their evidence is pronounced false. These are valid witnesses to the fact that an action was or was not done, that something is or is not the case; they are not valid witnesses to the quality of an action, to its being just or unjust, useful or harmful. On such questions of quality the opinion of detached persons is highly trustworthy. Most trustworthy of all are the "ancient" witnesses, since they cannot be corrupted.

In dealing with the evidence of witnesses, the following are useful arguments. If you have no witnesses on your side, you will argue that the judges must decide from what is probable; that this is meant by "giving a verdict in accordance with one's honest opinion"; that probabilities cannot be bribed to mislead the court; and that probabilities are never convicted of perjury. If you have witnesses, and the other man has not, you will argue that probabilities cannot be put on their trial, and that we could do without the evidence of witnesses altogether if we need do no more than balance the pleas advanced on either side.

The evidence of witnesses may refer either to ourselves or to our opponent; and either to questions of fact or to questions of personal character: so, clearly, we need never be at a loss for useful evidence. For if we have no evidence of fact supporting our own case or telling against that of our opponent, at least we can always find evidence to prove our own worth or our opponent's worthlessness. Other arguments about a witness—that he is a friend or an enemy or neutral, or has a good, bad, or indifferent reputation, and any other such distinctions—we must construct upon the same general lines as we use for the regular rhetorical proofs.

Concerning contracts argument can be so far employed as to increase or diminish their importance and their credibility; we shall try to increase both if they tell in our favor, and to diminish both if they tell in favor of our opponent. Now for confirming or upsetting the credibility of contracts the procedure is just the same as for dealing with witnesses, for the credit to be attached to contracts depends upon the character of those who have signed them or have the custody of them. The contract being once admitted genuine, we must insist on its importance, if it supports our case. We may argue that a contract is a law, though of a special and limited kind; and that, while contracts do not of course make the law binding, the law does make any lawful contract binding, and that the law itself as a whole is a of contract, so that anyone who disregards or repudiates any contract is repudiating the law itself. Further, most business relations—those, namely, that are voluntary—are regulated by contracts, and if these lose their binding force, human intercourse ceases to exist. We need not go very deep to discover the other appropriate arguments of this kind. If, however, the contract tells against us and for our opponents, in the first place those arguments are suitable which we can use to fight a law that tells against us. We do not regard ourselves as bound to observe a bad law which it was a mistake ever to pass: and it is ridiculous to suppose that we are bound to observe a bad and mistaken contract. Again, we may argue that the duty of the judge as umpire is to decide what is just, and therefore he must ask where justice lies, and not what this or that document means. And that it is impossible to pervert justice by fraud or by force, since it is founded on nature, but a party to a contract may be the victim of either fraud or force. Moreover, we must see if the contract contravenes either universal law or any written law of our own or another country; and also if it contradicts any other previous or subsequent contract; arguing that the subsequent is the binding contract, or else that the previous one was right and the subsequent one fraudulent—whichever way suits us. Further, we must consider the question of utility, noting whether the contract is against the interest of the judges or not; and so on—these arguments are as obvious as the others.

Examination by torture is one form of evidence, to which great weight is often attached because it is in a sense compulsory. Here again it is not hard to point out the available grounds for magnifying its value, if it happens to tell in our favor, and arguing that it is the only form of evidence that is infallible; or, on the other hand, for refuting it if it tells against us and for our opponent, when we may say what is true of torture of every kind alike, that people under its compulsion tell lies quite as often as they tell the truth, sometimes persistently refusing to tell the truth, sometimes recklessly making a false charge in order to be let off sooner. We ought to be able to quote cases, familiar to the judges, in which this sort of thing has actually happened. [We must say that evidence under torture is not trustworthy, the fact being that many men whether thick-witted, tough-skinned, or stout of heart endure their ordeal nobly, while cowards and timid men are full of boldness till they see the ordeal of these others: so that no trust can be placed in evidence under torture.]

In regard to oaths, a fourfold division can be made. A man may either both offer and accept an oath, or neither, or one without the other—that is, he may offer an oath but not accept one, or accept an oath but not offer one. There is also the situation that arises when an oath has already been sworn either by himself or by his opponent.

If you refuse to offer an oath, you may argue that men do not hesitate to perjure themselves; and that if your opponent does swear, you lose your money, whereas, if he does not, you think the judges will decide against him; and that the risk of an unfavourable verdict is prefer, able, since you trust the judges and do not trust him.

If you refuse to accept an oath, you may argue that an oath is always paid for; that you would of course have taken it if you had been a rascal, since if you are a rascal you had better make something by it, and you would in that case have to swear in order to succeed. Thus your refusal, you argue, must be due to high principle, not to fear of perjury: and you may aptly quote the saying of Xenophanes,

> " 'Tis not fair that he who fears not God
> should challenge him who doth."

It is as if a strong man were to challenge a weakling to strike, or be struck by, him.

If you agree to accept an oath, you may argue that you trust yourself but not your opponent; and that (to invert the remark of Xenophanes) the fair thing is for the impious man to offer the oath and for the pious man to accept it; and that it would be monstrous if you yourself were unwilling to accept an oath in a case where you demand that the judges should do so before giving their verdict. If you wish to offer an oath, you may argue that piety disposes you to commit the issue to the gods; and that your opponent ought not to want other judges than himself, since you leave the decision with him; and that it is outrageous for your opponents to refuse to swear about this question, when they insist that others should do so.

Now that we see how we are to argue in each case separately, we see also how we are to argue when they occur in pairs, namely, when you are willing to accept the oath but not to offer it; to offer it but not to accept it; both to accept and to offer it; or to do neither. These are of course combinations of the cases already mentioned, and so your arguments also must be combinations of the arguments already mentioned.

If you have already sworn an oath that contradicts your present one, you must argue that it is not perjury, since perjury is a crime, and a crime must be a voluntary action, whereas actions due to the force or fraud of others are involuntary. You must further reason from this that perjury depends on the intention and not on the spoken words. But if it is your opponent who has already sworn an oath that contradicts his present one, you must say that if he does not abide by his oaths he is the enemy of society, and that this is the reason why men take an oath before administering the laws. "My opponents insist that you, the judges, must abide by the oath you have sworn, and yet they are not abiding by their own oaths." And there are other arguments which may be used to magnify the importance of the oath. [So much, then, for the "non-technical" modes of persuasion.]

BOOK II

Part I

We have now considered the materials to be used in supporting or opposing a political measure, in pronouncing eulogies or censures, and for prosecution and defense in the law courts. We have considered the received opinions on which we may best base our arguments so as to convince our hearers—those opinions with which our enthymemes deal, and out of which they are built, in each of the three kinds of oratory, according to what may be called the special needs of each.

But since rhetoric exists to affect the giving of decisions—the hearers decide between one political speaker and another, and a legal verdict is a decision—the orator must not only try to make the argument of his speech demonstrative and worthy of belief; he must also make his own character look right and put his hearers, who are to decide, into the right frame of mind. Particularly in political oratory, but also in lawsuits, it adds much to an orator's influence that his own character should look right and that he should be thought to entertain the right feelings toward his hearers; and also that his hearers themselves should be in just the right frame of mind. That the orator's own character should look right is particularly important in political speaking: that the audience should be in the right frame of mind, in lawsuits. When people are feeling friendly and placable, they think one sort of thing; when they are feeling angry or hostile, they think either something totally different or the same thing with a different intensity: when they feel friendly to the man who comes before them for judgement, they regard him as having done little wrong, if any; when they feel hostile, they take the opposite view. Again, if they are eager for, and have good hopes of, a thing that will be pleasant if it happens, they think that it certainly will happen and be good for them: whereas if they are indifferent or annoyed, they do not think so.

There are three things which inspire confidence in the orator's own character—the three, namely, that induce us to believe a thing apart from any proof of it: good sense, good moral character, and goodwill. False statements and bad advice are due to one or more of the following three causes. Men either form a false opinion through want of good sense; or they form a true opinion, but because of their moral badness do not say what they really think; or finally, they are both sensible and upright, but not well disposed to their hearers, and may fail in consequence to recommend what they know to be the best course. These are the only possible cases. It follows that anyone who is thought to have all three of these good qualities will inspire trust in his audience. The way to make ourselves thought to be sensible and morally good must be gathered from the analysis of goodness already given: the way to establish your own goodness is the same as the way to establish that of others. Good will and friendliness of disposition will form part of our discussion of the emotions, to which we must now turn.

The Emotions are all those feelings that so change men as to affect their judgements, and that are also attended by pain or pleasure. Such are anger, pity, fear and the like, with their opposites. We must arrange what we have to say about each of them under three heads. Take, for instance, the emotion of anger: here we must discover (1) what the state of mind of angry people is, (2) who the people are with whom they usually get angry, and (3) on what grounds they get angry with them. It is not enough to know one or even two of these points; unless we know all three, we shall be unable to arouse anger in anyone. The same is true of the other emotions. So just as earlier in this work we drew up a list of useful propositions for the orator, let us now proceed in the same way to analyse the subject before us.

Part II

Anger may be defined as an impulse, accompanied by pain, to a conspicuous revenge for a conspicuous slight directed without justification toward what concerns oneself or toward what concerns one's friends. If this is a proper definition of anger, it must always be felt toward some particular individual, e.g. Cleon, and not "man" in general. It must be felt because the other has done or intended to do something to him or one of his friends. It must always be attended by a certain pleasure—that which arises from the expectation of revenge. For since nobody aims at what he thinks he cannot attain, the angry man is aiming at what he can attain, and the belief that you will attain your aim is pleasant. Hence it has been well said about wrath,

> "Sweeter it is by far than the honeycomb
>   dripping with sweetness,
> And spreads through the hearts of men."

It is also attended by a certain pleasure because the thoughts dwell upon the act of vengeance, and the images then called up cause pleasure, like the images called up in dreams.

Now slighting is the actively entertained opinion of something as obviously of no importance. We think bad things, as well as good ones, have serious importance; and we think the same of anything that tends to produce such things, while those which have little or no such tendency we consider unimportant. There are three kinds of slighting—contempt, spite, and insolence. (1) Contempt is one kind of slighting: you feel contempt for what you consider unimportant, and it is just such things that you slight. (2) Spite is another kind; it is a thwarting another man's wishes, not to get something yourself but to prevent his getting it. The slight arises just from the fact that you do not aim at something for yourself: clearly you do not think that he can do you harm, for then you would be afraid of him instead of slighting him, nor yet that he can do you any good worth mentioning, for then you would be anxious to make friends with him. (3) Insolence is also a form of slighting, since it consists in doing and saying things that cause shame to the victim, not in order that anything may happen to yourself, or because anything has happened to yourself, but simply for the pleasure involved. (Retaliation is not "insolence," but vengeance.) The cause of the pleasure thus enjoyed by the insolent man is that he thinks himself greatly superior to others when ill-treating them. That is why youths and rich men are insolent; they think themselves superior when they show insolence. One sort of insolence is to rob people of the honor due to them; you certainly slight them thus; for it is the unimportant, for good or evil, that has no honor paid to it. So Achilles says in anger:

> "He hath taken my prize for himself
> and hath done me dishonor,"

and

> "Like an alien honored by none,"

meaning that this is why he is angry. A man expects to be specially respected by his inferiors in birth, in capacity, in goodness, and generally in anything in which he is much their superior: as where money is concerned a wealthy man looks for respect from a poor man; where speaking is concerned, the man with a turn for oratory looks for respect from one who cannot speak; the ruler demands the respect of the ruled, and the man who thinks he ought to be a ruler demands the respect of the man whom he thinks he ought to be ruling. Hence it has been said

> "Great is the wrath of kings, whose father is Zeus almighty,"

and

> "Yea, but his rancour abideth long afterward also,"

their great resentment being due to their great superiority. Then again a man looks for respect from those who he thinks owe him good treatment, and these are the people whom he has treated or is treating well, or means or has meant to treat well, either himself, or through his friends, or through others at his request.

It will be plain by now, from what has been said, (1) in what frame of mind, (2) with what persons, and (3) on what grounds people grow angry. The frame of mind is that of one in which any pain is being felt. In that condition, a man is always aiming at something. Whether, then, another man opposes him either directly in any way, as by preventing him from drinking when he is thirsty, or indirectly, the act appears to him just the same; whether someone works against him, or fails to work with him, or otherwise vexes him while he is in this mood, he is equally angry in all these cases. Hence people who are afflicted by sickness or poverty or love or thirst or any other unsatisfied desires are prone to anger and easily roused: especially against those who slight their present distress. Thus a sick man is angered by disregard of his illness, a poor man by disregard of his poverty, a man waging war by disregard of the war he is waging, a lover by disregard of his love, and so throughout, any other sort of slight being enough if special slights are wanting. Each man is predisposed, by the emotion now controlling him, to his own particular anger. Further, we are angered if we happen to be expecting a contrary result: for a quite unexpected evil is specially painful, just as the quite unexpected fulfillment of our wishes is specially pleasant. Hence it is plain what seasons, times, conditions, and periods of life tend to stir men easily to anger, and where and when this will happen; and it is plain that the more we are under these conditions the more easily we are stirred.

These, then, are the frames of mind in which men are easily stirred to anger. The persons with whom we get angry are those who laugh, mock, or jeer at us, for such conduct is insolent. Also those who inflict injuries upon us that are marks of insolence. These injuries must be such as are neither retaliatory nor profitable to the doers: for only then will they be felt to be due to insolence. Also those who speak ill of us, and show contempt for us, in connection with the things we ourselves most care about: thus those who are eager to win fame as philosophers get angry with those who show contempt for their philosophy; those who pride themselves upon their appearance get angry with those who show contempt for their appearance and so on in other cases. We feel particularly angry on this account if we suspect that we are in fact, or that people think we are, lacking completely or to any effective extent in the qualities in question. For when we are convinced that we excel in the qualities for which we are jeered at, we can ignore the jeering. Again, we are angrier with our friends than with other people, since we feel that our friends ought to treat us well and not badly. We are angry with those who have usually treated us with honor or regard, if a change comes and they behave to us otherwise: for we think that they feel contempt for us, or they would still be behaving as they did before. And with those who do not return our kindnesses or fail to return them adequately, and with those who oppose us though they are our inferiors: for all such persons seem to feel contempt for us; those who oppose us seem to think us inferior to themselves, and those who do not return our kindnesses seem to think that those kindnesses were conferred by inferiors. And we feel particularly angry with men of no account at all, if they slight us. For, by our hypothesis, the anger caused by the slight is felt toward people who are not justified in slighting us, and our inferiors are not thus justified. Again, we feel angry with friends if they do not speak well of us or treat us well; and still more, if they do the contrary; or if they do not perceive our needs, which is why Plexippus is angry with Meleager in Antiphon's play; for this want of perception shows that they are slighting us—we do not fail to perceive the needs of those for whom we care. Again we are angry with those who rejoice at our misfortunes or simply keep cheerful in the midst of our misfortunes, since this shows that they either hate us or are slighting us. Also with those who are indifferent to the pain they give us: this is why we get angry with bringers of bad news. And with those who listen to stories about us or keep on looking at our weaknesses; this seems like either slighting us or hating us; for those who love us share in all our distresses and it must distress anyone to keep on looking at his own weaknesses. Further, with those who slight us before five classes of people: namely, (1) our rivals, (2) those whom we admire, (3) those whom we wish to admire us, (4) those for whom we feel reverence, (5) those who feel reverence for us: if anyone slights us before such persons, we feel particularly angry. Again, we feel angry with those who slight us in connection with what we are as honorable men bound to champion—our parents, children, wives, or subjects. And with those who do not return a favor, since such a slight is unjustifiable. Also with those who reply with humorous levity when we are speaking seriously, for such behavior indicates contempt. And with those who treat us less well than they treat everybody else; it is another mark of contempt that they should think we do not deserve what everyone else deserves. Forgetfulness, too, causes anger, as when our own names are forgotten, trifling as this may be; since forgetfulness is felt to be another sign that we are being slighted; it is due to negligence, and to neglect us is to slight us.

The persons with whom we feel anger, the frame of mind in which we feel it, and the reasons why we feel it, have now all been set forth. Clearly the orator will have to speak so as to bring his hearers into a frame of mind that will dispose them to anger, and to represent his adversaries as open to such charges and possessed of such qualities as do make people angry.

Part III

Since growing calm is the opposite of growing angry, and calmness the opposite of anger, we must ascertain in what frames of mind men are calm, toward whom they feel calm, and by what means they are made so. Growing calm may be defined as a settling down or quieting of anger. Now we get angry with those who slight us; and since slighting is a voluntary act, it is plain that we feel calm toward those who do nothing of the kind, or who do or seem to do it involuntarily. Also toward those who intended to do the opposite of what they did do. Also toward those who treat themselves as they have treated us: since no one can be supposed to slight himself. Also toward those who admit their fault and are sorry: since we accept their grief at what they have done as satisfaction, and cease to be angry. The punishment of servants shows this: those who contradict us and deny their offense we punish all the more, but we cease to be incensed against those who agree that they deserved their punishment. The reason is that it is shameless to deny what is obvious, and those who are shameless toward us slight us and show contempt for us: anyhow, we do not feel shame before those of whom we are thoroughly contemptuous. Also we feel calm toward those who humble themselves before us and do not gainsay us; we feel that they thus admit themselves our inferiors, and inferiors feel fear, and nobody can slight anyone so long as he feels afraid of him. That our anger ceases toward those who humble themselves before us is shown even by dogs, who do not bite people when they sit down. We also feel calm toward those who are serious when we are serious, because then we feel that we are treated seriously and not contemptuously. Also toward those who have done us more kindnesses than we have done them. Also toward those who pray to us and beg for mercy, since they humble themselves by doing so. Also toward those who do not insult or mock at or slight anyone at all, or not any worthy person or anyone like ourselves. In general, the things that make us calm may be inferred by seeing what the opposites are of those that make us angry. We are not angry with people we fear or respect, as long as we fear or respect them; you cannot be afraid of a person and also at the same time angry with him. Again, we feel no anger, or comparatively little, with those who have done what they did through anger: we do not feel that they have done it from a wish to slight us, for no one slights people when angry with them, since slighting is painless, and anger is painful. Nor do we grow angry with those who reverence us.

As to the frame of mind that makes people calm, it is plainly the opposite to that which makes them angry, as when they are amusing themselves or laughing or feasting; when they are feeling prosperous or successful or satisfied; when, in fine, they are enjoying freedom from pain, or inoffensive pleasure, or justifiable hope. Also when time has passed and their anger is no longer fresh, for time puts an end to anger. And vengeance previously taken on one person puts an end to even greater anger felt against another person. Hence Philocrates, being asked by someone, at a time when the public was angry with him, "Why don't you defend yourself?" did right to reply, "The time is not yet." "Why, when is the time?" "When I see someone else calumniated." For men become calm when they have spent their anger on somebody else. This happened in the case of Ergophilus: though the people were more irritated against him than against Callisthenes, they acquitted him because they had condemned Callisthenes to death the day before. Again, men become calm if they have convicted the offender; or if he has already suffered worse things than they in their anger would have themselves inflicted upon him; for they feel as if they were already avenged. Or if they feel that they themselves are in the wrong and are suffering justly (for anger is not excited by what is just), since men no longer think then that they are suffering without justification; and anger, as we have seen, means this. Hence we ought always to inflict a preliminary punishment in words: if that is done, even slaves are less aggrieved by the actual punishment. We also feel calm if we think that the offender will not see that he is punished on our account and because of the way he has treated us. For anger has to do with individuals. This is plain from the definition. Hence the poet has well written:

> "Say that it was Odysseus, sacker of cities,"

implying that Odysseus would not have considered himself avenged unless the Cyclops perceived both by whom and for what he had been blinded. Consequently we do not get angry with anyone who cannot be aware of our anger, and in particular we cease to be angry with people once they are dead, for we feel that the worst has been done to them, and that they will neither feel pain nor anything else that we in our anger aim at making them feel. And therefore the poet has well made Apollo say, in order to put a stop to the anger of Achilles against the dead Hector,

> "For behold in his fury he doeth despite to the senseless clay."

It is now plain that when you wish to calm others you must draw upon these lines of argument; you must put your hearers into the corresponding frame of mind, and represent those with whom they are angry as formidable, or as worthy of reverence, or as benefactors, or as involuntary agents, or as much distressed at what they have done.

Part IV

Let us now turn to Friendship and Enmity, and ask toward whom these feelings are entertained, and why. We will begin by defining and friendly feeling. We may describe friendly feeling toward anyone as wishing for him what you believe to be good things, not for your own sake but for his, and being inclined, so far as you can, to bring these things about. A friend is one who feels thus and excites these feelings in return: those who think they feel thus toward each other think themselves friends. This being assumed, it follows that your friend is the sort of man who shares your pleasure in what is good and your pain in what is unpleasant, for your sake and for no other reason. This pleasure and pain of his will be the token of his good wishes for you, since we all feel glad at getting what we wish for, and pained at getting what we do not. Those, then, are friends to whom the same things are good and evil; and those who are, moreover, friendly or unfriendly to the same people; for in that case they must have the same wishes, and thus by wishing for each other what they wish for themselves, they show themselves each other's friends. Again, we feel friendly to those who have treated us well, either ourselves or those we care for, whether on a large scale, or readily, or at some particular crisis; provided it was for our own sake. And also to those who we think wish to treat us well. And also to our friends" friends, and to those who like, or are liked by, those whom we like ourselves. And also to those who are enemies to those whose enemies we are, and dislike, or are disliked by, those whom we dislike. For all such persons think the things good which we think good, so that they wish what is good for us; and this, as we saw, is what friends must do. And also to those who are willing to treat us well where money or our personal safety is concerned: and therefore we value those who are liberal, brave, or just. The just we consider to be those who do not live on others; which means those who work for their living, especially farmers and others who work with their own hands. We also like temperate men, because they are not unjust to others; and, for the same reason, those who mind their own business. And also those whose friends we wish to be, if it is plain that they wish to be our friends: such are the morally good, and those well thought of by everyone, by the best men, or by those whom we admire or who admire us. And also those with whom it is pleasant to live and spend our days:

such are the good-tempered, and those who are not too ready to show us our mistakes, and those who are not cantankerous or quarrelsome—such people are always wanting to fight us, and those who fight us we feel wish for the opposite of what we wish for ourselves—and those who have the tact to make and take a joke; here both parties have the same object in view, when they can stand being made fun of as well as do it prettily themselves. And we also feel friendly toward those who praise such good qualities as we possess, and especially if they praise the good qualities that we are not too sure we do possess. And toward those who are cleanly in their person, their dress, and all their way of life. And toward those who do not reproach us with what we have done amiss to them or they have done to help us, for both actions show a tendency to criticize us. And toward those who do not nurse grudges or store up grievances, but are always ready to make friends again; for we take it that they will behave to us just as we find them behaving to everyone else. And toward those who are not evil speakers and who are aware of neither their neighbors' bad points nor our own, but of our good ones only, as a good man always will be. And toward those who do not try to thwart us when we are angry or in earnest, which would mean being ready to fight us. And toward those who have some serious feeling toward us, such as admiration for us, or belief in our goodness, or pleasure in our company; especially if they feel like this about qualities in us for which we especially wish to be admired, esteemed, or liked. And toward those who are like ourselves in character and occupation, provided they do not get in our way or gain their living from the same source as we do—for then it will be a case of "potter against potter":

> "Potter to potter and builder to builder begrudge their reward."

And those who desire the same things as we desire, if it is possible for us both to share them together; otherwise the same trouble arises here too. And toward those with whom we are on such terms that, while we respect their opinions, we need not blush before them for doing what is conventionally wrong: as well as toward those before whom we should be ashamed to do anything really wrong. Again, our rivals, and those whom we should like to envy us—though without ill-feeling—either we like these people or at least we wish them to like us. And we feel friendly toward those whom we help to secure good for themselves, provided we are not likely to suffer heavily by it ourselves. And those who feel as friendly to us when we are not with them as when we are—which is why all men feel friendly toward those who are faithful to their dead friends. And, speaking generally, toward those who are really fond of their friends and do not desert them in trouble; of all good men, we feel most friendly to those who show their goodness as friends. Also toward those who are honest with us, including those who will tell us of their own weak points: it has just said that with our friends we are not ashamed of what is conventionally wrong, and if we do have this feeling, we do not love them; if therefore we do not have it, it looks as if we did love them. We also like those with whom we do not feel frightened or uncomfortable—nobody can like a man of whom he feels frightened. Friendship has various forms—comradeship, intimacy, kinship, and so on.

Things that cause friendship are: doing kindnesses; doing them unasked; and not proclaiming the fact when they are done, which shows that they were done for our own sake and not for some other reason.

Enmity and Hatred should clearly be studied by reference to their opposites. Enmity may be produced by anger or spite or calumny. Now whereas anger arises from offenses against oneself, enmity may arise even without that; we may hate people merely because of what we take to be their character. Anger is always concerned with individuals—a Callias or a Socrates—whereas hatred is directed also against classes: we all hate any thief and any informer. Moreover, anger can be cured by time; but hatred cannot. The one aims at giving pain to its object, the other at doing him harm; the angry man wants his victims to feel; the hater does not mind whether they feel or not. All painful things are felt; but the greatest evils, injustice and folly, are the least felt, since their presence causes no pain. And anger is accompanied by pain, hatred is not; the angry man feels pain, but the hater does not. Much may happen to make the angry man pity those who offend him, but the hater under no circumstances wishes to pity a man whom he has once hated: for the one would have the offenders suffer for what they have done; the other would have them cease to exist.

It is plain from all this that we can prove people to be friends or enemies; if they are not, we can make them out to be so; if they claim to be so, we can refute their claim; and if it is disputed whether an action was due to anger or to hatred, we can attribute it to whichever of these we prefer.

Part V

To turn next to Fear, what follows will show things and persons of which, and the states of mind in which, we feel afraid. Fear may be defined as a pain or disturbance due to a mental picture of some destructive or painful evil in the future. Of destructive or painful evils only; for there are some evils, e.g. wickedness or stupidity, the prospect of which does not frighten us: I mean only such as amount to great pains or losses. And even these only if they appear not remote but so near as to be imminent: we do not fear things that are a very long way off: for instance, we all know we shall die, but we are not troubled thereby, because death is not close at hand. From this definition it will follow that fear is caused by whatever we feel has great power of destroying or of harming us in ways that tend to cause us great pain. Hence the very indications of such things are terrible, making us feel that the terrible thing itself is close at hand; the approach of what is terrible is just what we mean by "danger." Such indications are the enmity and anger of people who have power to do something to us; for it is plain that they have the will to do it, and so they are on the point of doing it. Also injustice in possession of power; for it is the unjust man's will to do evil that makes him unjust. Also outraged virtue in possession of power; for it is plain that, when outraged, it always has the will to retaliate, and now it has the power to do so. Also fear felt by those who have the power to do something to us, since such persons are sure to be ready to do it. And since most men tend to be bad—slaves to greed, and cowards in danger—it is, as a rule, a terrible thing to be at another man's mercy; and therefore, if we have done anything horrible, those in the secret terrify us with the thought that they may betray or desert us. And those who can do us wrong are terrible to us when we are liable to be wronged; for as a rule men do wrong to others whenever they have the power to do it. And those who have been wronged, or believe themselves to be wronged, are terrible; for they are always looking out for their opportunity. Also those who have done people wrong, if they possess power, since they stand in fear of retaliation: we have already said that wickedness possessing power is terrible. Again, our rivals for a thing cause us fear when we cannot both have it at once; for we are always at war with such men. We also fear those who are to be feared by stronger people than ourselves: if they can hurt those stronger people, still more can they hurt us; and, for the same reason, we fear those whom those stronger people are actually afraid of. Also those who have destroyed people stronger than we are. Also those who are attacking people weaker than we are: either they are already formidable, or they will be so when they have thus grown stronger. Of those we have wronged, and of our enemies or rivals, it is not the passionate and outspoken whom we have to fear, but the quiet, dissembling, unscrupulous; since we never know when they are upon us, we can never be sure they are at a safe distance. All terrible things are more terrible if they give us no chance of retrieving a blunder either no chance at all, or only one that depends on our enemies and not ourselves. Those things are also worse which we cannot, or cannot easily, help. Speaking generally, anything causes us to feel fear that when it happens to, or threatens, others cause us to feel pity.

The above are, roughly, the chief things that are terrible and are feared. Let us now describe the conditions under which we ourselves feel fear. If fear is associated with the expectation that something destructive will happen to us, plainly nobody will be afraid who believes nothing can happen to him; we shall not fear things that we believe cannot happen to us, nor people who we believe cannot inflict them upon us; nor shall we be afraid at times when we think ourselves safe from them. It follows therefore that fear is felt by those who believe something to be likely to happen to them, at the hands of particular persons, in a particular form, and at a particular time. People do not believe this when they are, or think they a are, in the midst of great prosperity, and are in consequence insolent, contemptuous, and reckless—the kind of character produced by wealth, physical strength, abundance of friends, power: nor yet when they feel they have experienced every kind of horror already and have grown callous about the future, like men who are being flogged and are already nearly dead—if they are to feel the anguish of uncertainty, there must be some faint expectation of escape. This appears from the fact that fear sets us thinking what can be done, which of course nobody does when things are hopeless. Consequently, when it is advisable that the audience should be frightened, the orator must make them feel that they really are in danger of something, pointing out that it has happened to others who were stronger than they are, and is happening, or has happened, to people like themselves, at the hands of unexpected people, in an unexpected form, and at an unexpected time.

Having now seen the nature of fear, and of the things that cause it, and the various states of mind in which it is felt, we can also see what confidence is, about what things we feel it, and under what conditions. It is the opposite of fear, and what causes it is the opposite of what causes fear; it is, therefore, the expectation associated with a mental picture of the nearness of what keeps us safe and the absence or remoteness of what is terrible: it may be due either to the near presence of what inspires confidence or to the absence of what causes alarm. We feel it if we can take steps—many, or important, or both—to cure or prevent trouble; if we have neither wronged others nor been wronged by them; if we have either no rivals at all or no strong ones; if our rivals who are strong are our friends or have treated us well or been treated well by us; or if those whose interest is the same as ours are the more numerous party, or the stronger, or both.

As for our own state of mind, we feel confidence if we believe we have often succeeded and never suffered reverses, or have often met danger and escaped it safely. For there are two reasons why human beings face danger calmly: they may have no experience of it, or they may have means to deal with it: thus when in danger at sea people may feel confident about what will happen either because they have no experience of bad weather, or because their experience gives them the means of dealing with it. We also feel confident whenever there is nothing to terrify other people like ourselves, or people weaker than ourselves, or people than whom we believe ourselves to be stronger—and we believe this if we have conquered them, or conquered others who are as strong as they are, or stronger. Also if we believe ourselves superior to our rivals in the number and importance of the advantages that make men formidable—wealth, physical strength, strong bodies of supporters, extensive territory, and the possession of all, or the most important, appliances of war. Also if we have wronged no one, or not many, or not those of whom we are afraid; and generally, if our relations with the gods are satisfactory, as will be shown especially by signs and oracles. The fact is that anger makes us confident—that anger is excited by our knowledge that we are not the wrongers but the wronged, and that the divine power is always supposed to be on the side of the wronged. Also when, at the outset of an enterprise, we believe that we cannot and shall not fail, or that we shall succeed completely. So much for the causes of fear and confidence.

Part VI

We now turn to Shame and Shamelessness; what follows will explain the things that cause these feelings, and the persons before whom, and the states of mind under which, they are felt. Shame may be defined as pain or disturbance in regard to bad things, whether present, past, or future, which seem likely to involve us in discredit; and shamelessness as contempt or indifference in regard to these same bad things. If this definition be granted, it follows that we feel shame at such bad things as we think are disgraceful to ourselves or to those we care for. These evils are, in the first place, those due to moral badness. Such are throwing away one's shield or taking to flight; for these bad things are due to cowardice. Also, withholding a deposit or otherwise wronging people about money; for these acts are due to injustice.

Also, having carnal intercourse with forbidden persons, at wrong times, or in wrong places; for these things are due to licentiousness. Also, making profit in petty or disgraceful ways, or out of helpless persons, e.g. the poor, or the dead—whence the proverb "He would pick a corpse's pocket"; for all this is due to low greed and meanness. Also, in money matters, giving less help than you might, or none at all, or accepting help from those worse off than yourself; so also borrowing when it will seem like begging; begging when it will seem like asking the return of a favor; asking such a return when it will seem like begging; praising a man in order that it may seem like begging; and going on begging in spite of failure: all such actions are tokens of meanness. Also, praising people to their face, and praising extravagantly a man's good points and glozing over his weaknesses, and showing extravagant sympathy with his grief when you are in his presence, and all that sort of thing; all this shows the disposition of a flatterer. Also, refusing to endure hardships that are endured by people who are older, more delicately brought up, of higher rank, or generally less capable of endurance than ourselves: for all this shows effeminacy. Also, accepting benefits, especially accepting them often, from another man, and then abusing him for conferring them: all this shows a mean, ignoble disposition. Also, talking incessantly about yourself, making loud professions, and appropriating the merits of others; for this is due to boastfulness. The same is true of the actions due to any of the other forms of badness of moral character, of the tokens of such badness, etc.: they are all disgraceful and shameless. Another sort of bad thing at which we feel shame is, lacking a share in the honorable things shared by everyone else, or by all or nearly all who are like ourselves. By "those like ourselves" I mean those of our own race or country or age or family, and generally those who are on our own level. Once we are on a level with others, it is a disgrace to be, say, less well educated than they are; and so with other advantages: all the more so, in each case, if it is seen to be our own fault: wherever we are ourselves to blame for our present, past, or future circumstances, it follows at once that this is to a greater extent due to our moral badness. We are moreover ashamed of having done to us, having had done, or being about to have done to us acts that involve us in dishonor and reproach; as when we surrender our persons, or lend ourselves to vile deeds, e.g. when we submit to outrage. And acts of yielding to the lust of others are shameful whether willing or unwilling (yielding to force being an instance of unwillingness), since unresisting submission to them is due to unmanliness or cowardice.

These things, and others like them, are what cause the feeling of shame.

Now since shame is a mental picture of disgrace, in which we shrink from the disgrace itself and not from its consequences, and we only care what opinion is held of us because of the people who form that opinion, it follows that the people before whom we feel shame are those whose opinion of us matters to us. Such persons are: those who admire us, those whom we admire, those by whom we wish to be admired, those with whom we are competing, and those whose opinion of us we respect. We admire those, and wish those to admire us, who possess any good thing that is highly esteemed; or from whom we are very anxious to get something that they are able to give us—as a lover feels. We compete with our equals. We respect, as true, the views of sensible people, such as our elders and those who have been well educated. And we feel more shame about a thing if it is done openly, before all men's eyes. Hence the proverb, "shame dwells in the eyes." For this reason we feel most shame before those who will always be with us and those who notice what we do, since in both cases eyes are upon us. We also feel it before those not open to the same imputation as ourselves: for it is plain that their opinions about it are the opposite of ours. Also before those who are hard on anyone whose conduct they think wrong; for what a man does himself, he is said not to resent when his neighbors do it: so that of course he does resent their doing what he does not do himself. And before those who are likely to tell everybody about you; not telling others is as good as not believing you wrong. People are likely to tell others about you if you have wronged them, since they are on the look out to harm you; or if they speak evil of everybody, for those who attack the innocent will be still more ready to attack the guilty. And before those whose main occupation is with their neighbors' failings—people like satirists and writers of comedy; these are really a kind of evil—speakers and tell-tales. And before those who have never yet known us come to grief, since their attitude to us has amounted to admiration so far: that is why we feel ashamed to refuse those a favor who ask one for the first time—we have not as yet lost credit with them. Such are those who are just beginning to wish to be our friends; for they have seen our best side only (hence the appropriateness of Euripides's reply to the Syracusans): and such also are those among our old acquaintances who know nothing to our discredit. And we are ashamed not merely of the actual shameful conduct mentioned, but also of the evidences of it: not merely, for example, of actual sexual intercourse, but also of its evidences; and not merely of disgraceful acts but also of disgraceful talk. Similarly we feel shame not merely in presence of the persons mentioned but also of those who will tell them what we have done, such as their servants or friends. And, generally, we feel no shame before those upon whose opinions we quite look down as untrustworthy (no one feels shame before small children or animals); nor are we ashamed of the same things before intimates as before strangers, but before the former of what seem genuine faults, before the latter of what seem conventional ones.

The conditions under which we shall feel shame are these: first, having people related to us like those before whom, as has been said, we feel shame. These are, as was stated, persons whom we admire, or who admire us, or by whom we wish to be admired, or from whom we desire some service that we shall not obtain if we forfeit their good opinion. These persons may be actually looking on (as Cydias represented them in his speech on land assignments in Samos, when he told the Athenians to imagine the Greeks to be standing all around them, actually seeing the way they voted and not merely going to hear about it afterward): or again they may be near at hand, or may be likely to find out about what we do. This is why in misfortune we do not wish to be seen by those who once wished themselves like us; for such a feeling implies admiration. And men feel shame when they have acts or exploits to their credit on which they are bringing dishonor, whether these are their own, or those of their ancestors, or those of other persons with whom they have some close connection. Generally, we feel shame before those for whose own misconduct we should also feel it—those already mentioned; those who take us as their models; those whose teachers or advisers we have been; or other people, it may be, like ourselves, whose rivals we are. For there are many things that shame before such people makes us do or leave undone. And we feel more shame when we are likely to be continually seen by, and go about under the eyes of, those who know of our disgrace. Hence, when Antiphon the poet was to be cudgelled to death by order of Dionysius, and saw those who were to perish with him covering their faces as they went through the gates, he said, "Why do you cover your faces? Is it lest some of these spectators should see you tomorrow?"

So much for Shame; to understand Shamelessness, we need only consider the converse cases, and plainly we shall have all we need.

Part VII

To take Kindness next: the definition of it will show us toward whom it is felt, why, and in what frames of mind. Kindness—under the influence of which a man is said to "be kind"—may be defined as helpfulness toward someone in need, not in return for anything, nor for the advantage of the helper himself, but for that of the person helped. Kindness is great if shown to one who is in great need, or who needs what is important and hard to get, or who needs it at an important and difficult crisis; or if the helper is the only, the first, or the chief person to give the help. Natural cravings constitute such needs; and in particular cravings, accompanied by pain, for what is not being attained. The appetites are cravings for this kind: sexual desire, for instance, and those which arise during bodily injuries and in dangers; for appetite is active both in danger and in pain. Hence those who stand by us in poverty or in banishment, even if they do not help us much, are yet really kind to us, because our need is great and the occasion pressing; for instance, the man who gave the mat in the Lyceum. The helpfulness must therefore meet, preferably, just this kind of need; and failing just this kind, some other kind as great or greater. We now see to whom, why, and under what conditions kindness is shown; and these facts must form the basis of our arguments. We must show that the persons helped are, or have been, in such pain and need as has been described, and that their helpers gave, or are giving, the kind of help described, in the kind of need described. We can also see how to eliminate the idea of kindness and make our opponents appear unkind: we may maintain that they are being or have been helpful simply to promote their own interest—this, as has been stated, is not kindness; or that their action was accidental, or was forced upon them; or that they were not doing a favor, but merely returning one, whether they know this or not—in either case the action is a mere return, and is therefore not a kindness even if the doer does not know how the case stands. In considering this subject we must look at all the categories: an act may be an act of kindness because (1) it is a particular thing, (2) it has a particular magnitude or (3) quality, or (4) is done at a particular time or (5) place. As evidence of the want of kindness, we may point out that a smaller service had been refused to the man in need; or that the same service, or an equal or greater one, has been given to his enemies; these facts show that the service in question was not done for the sake of the person helped. Or we may point out that the thing desired was worthless and that the helper knew it: no one will admit that he is in need of what is worthless.

Part VIII

So much for Kindness and Unkindness. Let us now consider Pity, asking ourselves what things excite pity, and for what persons, and in what states of our mind pity is felt. Pity may be defined as a feeling of pain caused by the sight of some evil, destructive or painful, which befalls one who does not deserve it, and which we might expect to befall ourselves or some friend of ours, and moreover to befall us soon. In order to feel pity, we must obviously be capable of supposing that some evil may happen to us or some friend of ours, and moreover some such evil as is stated in our definition or is more or less of that kind. It is therefore not felt by those completely ruined, who suppose that no further evil can befall them, since the worst has befallen them already; nor by those who imagine themselves immensely fortunate—their feeling is rather presumptuous insolence, for when they think they possess all the good things of life, it is clear that the impossibility of evil befalling them will be included, this being one of the good things in question. Those who think evil may befall them are such as have already had it befall them and have safely escaped from it; elderly men, owing to their good sense and their experience; weak men, especially men inclined to cowardice; and also educated people, since these can take long views. Also those who have parents living, or children, or wives; for these are our own, and the evils mentioned above may easily befall them. And those who neither moved by any courageous emotion such as anger or confidence (these emotions take no account of the future), nor by a disposition to presumptuous insolence (insolent men, too, take no account of the possibility that something evil will happen to them), nor yet by great fear (panic-stricken people do not feel pity, because they are taken up with what is happening to themselves); only those feel pity who are between these two extremes. In order to feel pity we must also believe in the goodness of at least some people; if you think nobody good, you will believe that everybody deserves evil fortune. And, generally, we feel pity whenever we are in the condition of remembering that similar misfortunes have happened to us or ours, or expecting them to happen in the future.

So much for the mental conditions under which we feel pity. What we pity is stated clearly in the definition. All unpleasant and painful things excite pity if they tend to destroy pain and annihilate; and all such evils as are due to chance, if they are serious. The painful and destructive evils are: death in its various forms, bodily injuries and afflictions, old age, diseases, lack of food. The evils due to chance are: friendlessness, scarcity of friends (it is a pitiful thing to be torn away from friends and companions), deformity, weakness, mutilation; evil coming from a source from which good ought to have come; and the frequent repetition of such misfortunes. Also the coming of good when the worst has happened: e.g. the arrival of the Great King's gifts for Diopeithes after his death. Also that either no good should have befallen a man at all, or that he should not be able to enjoy it when it has.

The grounds, then, on which we feel pity are these or like these. The people we pity are: those whom we know, if only they are not very closely related to us—in that case we feel about them as if we were in danger ourselves. For this reason Amasis did not weep, they say, at the sight of his son being led to death, but did weep when he saw his friend begging: the latter sight was pitiful, the former terrible, and the terrible is different from the pitiful; it tends to cast out pity, and often helps to produce the opposite of pity. Again, we feel pity when the danger is near ourselves. Also we pity those who are like us in age, character, disposition, social standing, or birth; for in all these cases it appears more likely that the same misfortune may befall us also. Here too we have to remember the general principle that what we fear for ourselves excites our pity when it happens to others. Further, since it is when the sufferings of others are close to us that they excite our pity (we cannot remember what disasters happened a hundred centuries ago, nor look forward to what will happen a hundred centuries hereafter, and therefore feel little pity, if any, for such things): it follows that those who heighten the effect of their words with suitable gestures, tones, dress, and dramatic action generally, are especially successful in exciting pity: they thus put the disasters before our eyes, and make them seem close to us, just coming or just past. Anything that has just happened, or is going to happen soon, is particularly piteous: so too therefore are the tokens and the actions of sufferers—the garments and the like of those who have already suffered; the words and the like of those actually suffering—of those, for instance, who are on the point of death. Most piteous of all is it when, in such times of trial, the victims are persons of noble character: whenever they are so, our pity is especially excited, because their innocence, as well as the setting of their misfortunes before our eyes, makes their misfortunes seem close to ourselves.

Part IX

Most directly opposed to pity is the feeling called Indignation. Pain at unmerited good fortune is, in one sense, opposite to pain at unmerited bad fortune, and is due to the same moral qualities. Both feelings are associated with good moral character; it is our duty both to feel sympathy and pity for unmerited distress, and to feel indignation at unmerited prosperity; for whatever is undeserved is unjust, and that is why we ascribe indignation even to the gods. It might indeed be thought that envy is similarly opposed to pity, on the ground that envy it closely akin to indignation, or even the same thing. But it is not the same. It is true that it also is a disturbing pain excited by the prosperity of others. But it is excited not by the prosperity of the undeserving but by that of people who are like us or equal with us. The two feelings have this in common, that they must be due not to some untoward thing being likely to befall ourselves, but only to what is happening to our neighbor. The feeling ceases to be envy in the one case and indignation in the other, and becomes fear, if the pain and disturbance are due to the prospect of something bad for ourselves as the result of the other man's good fortune. The feelings of pity and indignation will obviously be attended by the converse feelings of satisfaction. If you are pained by the unmerited distress of others, you will be pleased, or at least not pained, by their merited distress. Thus no good man can be pained by the punishment of parricides or murderers. These are things we are bound to rejoice at, as we must at the prosperity of the deserving; both these things are just, and both give pleasure to any honest man, since he cannot help expecting that what has happened to a man like him will happen to him too. All these feelings are associated with the same type of moral character. And their contraries are associated with the contrary type; the man who is delighted by others' misfortunes is identical with the man who envies others" prosperity. For anyone who is pained by the occurrence or existence of a given thing must be pleased by that thing's non-existence or destruction. We can now see that all these feelings tend to prevent pity (though they differ among themselves, for the reasons given), so that all are equally useful for neutralizing an appeal to pity.

We will first consider Indignation—reserving the other emotions for subsequent discussion—and ask with whom, on what grounds, and in what states of mind we may be indignant. These questions are really answered by what has been said already. Indignation is pain caused by the sight of undeserved good fortune. It is, then, plain to begin with that there are some forms of good the sight of which cannot cause it. Thus a man may be just or brave, or acquire moral goodness: but we shall not be indignant with him for that reason, any more than we shall pity him for the contrary reason. Indignation is roused by the sight of wealth, power, and the like—by all those things, roughly speaking, which are deserved by good men and by those who possess the goods of nature—noble birth, beauty, and so on. Again, what is long established seems akin to what exists by nature; and therefore we feel more indignation at those possessing a given good if they have as a matter of fact only just got it and the prosperity it brings with it. The newly rich give more offense than those whose wealth is of long standing and inherited. The same is true of those who have office or power, plenty of friends, a fine family, etc. We feel the same when these advantages of theirs secure them others. For here again, the newly rich give us more offense by obtaining office through their riches than do those whose wealth is of long standing; and so in all other cases. The reason is that what the latter have is felt to be really their own, but what the others have is not; what appears to have been always what it is is regarded as real, and so the possessions of the newly rich do not seem to be really their own. Further, it is not any and every man that deserves any given kind of good; there is a certain correspondence and appropriateness in such things; thus it is appropriate for brave men, not for just men, to have fine weapons, and for men of family, not for parvenus, to make distinguished marriages. Indignation may therefore properly be felt when anyone gets what is not appropriate for him, though he may be a good man enough. It may also be felt when anyone sets himself up against his superior, especially against his superior in some particular respect—whence the lines

> "Only from battle he shrank with Aias Telamon's son;
> Zeus had been angered with him,
> had he fought with a mightier one";

but also, even apart from that, when the inferior in any sense contends with his superior; a musician, for instance, with a just man, for justice is a finer thing than music.

Enough has been said to make clear the grounds on which, and the persons against whom, Indignation is felt—they are those mentioned, and others like him. As for the people who feel it; we feel it if we do ourselves deserve the greatest possible goods and moreover have them, for it is an injustice that those who are not our equals should have been held to deserve as much as we have. Or, secondly, we feel it if we are really good and honest people; our judgement is then sound, and we loathe any kind of injustice. Also if we are ambitious and eager to gain particular ends, especially if we are ambitious for what others are getting without deserving to get it. And, generally, if we think that we ourselves deserve a thing and that others do not, we are disposed to be indignant with those others so far as that thing is concerned. Hence servile, worthless, unambitious persons are not inclined to Indignation, since there is nothing they can believe themselves to deserve.

From all this it is plain what sort of men those are at whose misfortunes, distresses, or failures we ought to feel pleased, or at least not pained: by considering the facts described we see at once what their contraries are. If therefore our speech puts the judges in such a frame of mind as that indicated and shows that those who claim pity on certain definite grounds do not deserve to secure pity but do deserve not to secure it, it will be impossible for the judges to feel pity.

Part X

To take Envy next: we can see on what grounds, against what persons, and in what states of mind we feel it. Envy is pain at the sight of such good fortune as consists of the good things already mentioned; we feel it toward our equals; not with the idea of getting something for ourselves, but because the other people have it. We shall feel it if we have, or think we have, equals; and by "equals" I mean equals in birth, relationship, age, disposition, distinction, or wealth. We feel envy also if we fall but a little short of having everything; which is why people in high place and prosperity feel it—they think everyone else is taking what belongs to themselves. Also if we are exceptionally distinguished for some particular thing, and especially if that thing is wisdom or good fortune. Ambitious men are more envious than those who are not. So also those who profess wisdom; they are ambitious to be thought wise. Indeed, generally, those who aim at a reputation for anything are envious on this particular point. And small-minded men are envious, for everything seems great to them. The good things which excite envy have already been mentioned. The deeds or possessions which arouse the love of reputation and honor and the desire for fame, and the various gifts of fortune, are almost all subject to envy; and particularly if we desire the thing ourselves, or think we are entitled to it, or if having it puts us a little above others, or not having it a little below them. It is clear also what kind of people we envy; that was included in what has been said already: we envy those who are near us in time, place, age, or reputation. Hence the line:

"Ay, kin can even be jealous of their kin."

Also our fellow competitors, who are indeed the people just mentioned—we do not compete with men who lived a hundred centuries ago, or those not yet born, or the dead, or those who dwell near the Pillars of Hercules, or those whom, in our opinion or that of others, we take to be far below us or far above us. So too we compete with those who follow the same ends as ourselves: we compete with our rivals in sport or in love, and generally with those who are after the same things; and it is therefore these whom we are bound to envy beyond all others. Hence the saying:

"Potter against potter."

We also envy those whose possession of or success in a thing is a reproach to us: these are our neighbors and equals; for it is clear that it is our own fault we have missed the good thing in question; this annoys us, and excites envy in us. We also envy those who have what we ought to have, or have got what we did have once. Hence old men envy younger men, and those who have spent much envy those who have spent little on the same thing. And men who have not got a thing, or not got it yet, envy those who have got it quickly. We can also see what things and what persons give pleasure to envious people, and in what states of mind they feel it: the states of mind in which they feel pain are those under which they will feel pleasure in the contrary things. If therefore we ourselves with whom the decision rests are put into an envious state of mind, and those for whom our pity, or the award of something desirable, is claimed are such as have been described, it is obvious that they will win no pity from us.

Part XI

We will next consider Emulation, showing in what follows its causes and objects, and the state of mind in which it is felt. Emulation is pain caused by seeing the presence, in persons whose nature is like our own, of good things that are highly valued and are possible for ourselves to acquire; but it is felt not because others have these goods, but because we have not got them ourselves. It is therefore a good feeling felt by good persons, whereas envy is a bad feeling felt by bad persons. Emulation makes us take steps to secure the good things in question, envy makes us take steps to stop our neighbor having them. Emulation must therefore tend to be felt by persons who believe themselves to deserve certain good things that they have not got, it being understood that no one aspires to things which appear impossible. It is accordingly felt by the young and by persons of lofty disposition. Also by those who possess such good things as are deserved by men held in honor—these are wealth, abundance of friends, public office, and the like; on the assumption that they ought to be good men, they are emulous to gain such goods because they ought, in their belief, to belong to men whose state of mind is good. Also by those whom all others think deserving. We also feel it about anything for which our ancestors, relatives, personal friends, race, or country are specially honored, looking upon that thing as really our own, and therefore feeling that we deserve to have it. Further, since all good things that are highly honored are objects of emulation, moral goodness in its various forms must be such an object, and also all those good things that are useful and serviceable to others: for men honor those who are morally good, and also those who do them service. So with those good things our possession of which can give enjoyment to our neighbors—wealth and beauty rather than health. We can see, too, what persons are the objects of the feeling. They are those who have these and similar things—those already mentioned, as courage, wisdom, public office. Holders of public office—generals, orators, and all who possess such powers—can do many people a good turn. Also those whom many people wish to be like; those who have many acquaintances or friends; those whom admire, or whom we ourselves admire; and those who have been praised and eulogized by poets or prose-writers. Persons of the contrary sort are objects of contempt: for the feeling and notion of contempt are opposite to those of emulation. Those who are such as to emulate or be emulated by others are inevitably disposed to be contemptuous of all such persons as are subject to those bad things which are contrary to the good things that are the objects of emulation: despising them for just that reason. Hence we often despise the fortunate, when luck comes to them without their having those good things which are held in honor.

This completes our discussion of the means by which the several emotions may be produced or dissipated, and upon which depend the persuasive arguments connected with the emotions.

Part XII

Let us now consider the various types of human character, in relation to the emotions and moral qualities, showing how they correspond to our various ages and fortunes. By emotions I mean anger, desire, and the like; these we have discussed already. By moral qualities I mean virtues and vices; these also have been discussed already, as well as the various things that various types of men tend to will and to do. By ages I mean youth, the prime of life, and old age. By fortune I mean birth, wealth, power, and their opposites—in fact, good fortune and ill fortune.

To begin with the Youthful type of character. Young men have strong passions, and tend to gratify them indiscriminately. Of the bodily desires, it is the sexual by which they are most swayed and in which they show absence of self-control. They are changeable and fickle in their desires, which are violent while they last, but quickly over: their impulses are keen but not deep-rooted, and are like sick people's attacks of hunger and thirst. They are hot-tempered, and quick-tempered, and apt to give way to their anger; bad temper often gets the better of them, for owing to their love of honor they cannot bear being slighted, and are indignant if they imagine themselves unfairly treated. While they love honor, they love victory still more; for youth is eager for superiority over others, and victory is one form of this. They love both more than they love money, which indeed they love very little, not having yet learned what it means to be without it—this is the point of Pittacus's remark about Amphiaraus. They look at the good side rather than the bad, not having yet witnessed many instances of wickedness. They trust others readily, because they have not yet often been cheated. They are sanguine; nature warms their blood as though with excess of wine; and besides that, they have as yet met with few disappointments. Their lives are mainly spent not in memory but in expectation; for expectation refers to the future, memory to the past, and youth has a long future before it and a short past behind it: on the first day of one's life one has nothing at all to remember, and can only look forward. They are easily cheated, owing to the sanguine disposition just mentioned. Their hot tempers and hopeful dispositions make them more courageous than older men are; the hot temper prevents fear, and the hopeful disposition creates confidence; we cannot feel fear so long as we are feeling angry, and any expectation of good makes us confident. They are shy, accepting the rules of society in which they have been trained, and not yet believing in any other standard of honor. They have exalted notions, because they have not yet been humbled by life or learned its necessary limitations; moreover, their hopeful disposition makes them think themselves equal to great things—and that means having exalted notions. They would always rather do noble deeds than useful ones: their lives are regulated more by moral feeling than by reasoning; and whereas reasoning leads us to choose what is useful, moral goodness leads us to choose what is noble. They are fonder of their friends, intimates, and companions than older men are, because they like spending their days in the company of others, and have not yet come to value either their friends or anything else by their usefulness to themselves. All their mistakes are in the direction of doing things excessively and vehemently. They disobey Chilon's precept by overdoing everything, they love too much and hate too much, and the same thing with everything else. They think they know everything, and are always quite sure about it; this, in fact, is why they overdo everything. If they do wrong to others, it is because they mean to insult them, not to do them actual harm. They are ready to pity others, because they think everyone an honest man, or anyhow better than he is: they judge their neighbor by their own harmless natures, and so cannot think he deserves to be treated in that way. They are fond of fun and therefore witty, wit being well-bred insolence.

Part XIII

Such, then is the character of the Young. The character of Elderly Men— men who are past their prime—may be said to be formed for the most part of elements that are the contrary of all these. They have lived many years; they have often been taken in, and often made mistakes; and life on the whole is a bad business. The result is that they are sure about nothing and under-do everything. They "think," but they never "know"; and because of their hesitation they always add a "possibly" or a "perhaps," putting everything this way and nothing positively. They are cynical; that is, they tend to put the worse construction on everything. Further, their experience makes them distrustful and therefore suspicious of evil. Consequently they neither love warmly nor hate bitterly, but following the hint of Bias they love as though they will some day hate and hate as though they will some day love. They are small-minded, because they have been humbled by life: their desires are set upon nothing more exalted or unusual than what will help them to keep alive. They are not generous, because money is one of the things they must have, and at the same time their experience has taught them how hard it is to get and how easy to lose. They are cowardly, and are always anticipating danger; unlike that of the young, who are warm-blooded, their temperament is chilly; old age has paved the way for cowardice; fear is, in fact, a form of chill. They love life; and all the more when their last day has come, because the object of all desire is something we have not got, and also because we desire most strongly that which we need most urgently. They are too fond of themselves; this is one form that small-mindedness takes. Because of this, they guide their lives too much by considerations of what is useful and too little by what is noble—for the useful is what is good for oneself, and the noble what is good absolutely. They are not shy, but shameless rather; caring less for what is noble than for what is useful, they feel contempt for what people may think of them. They lack confidence in the future; partly through experience—for most things go wrong, or anyhow turn out worse than one expects; and partly because of their cowardice. They live by memory rather than by hope; for what is left to them of life is but little as compared with the long past; and hope is of the future, memory of the past. This, again, is the cause of their loquacity; they are continually talking of the past, because they enjoy remembering it. Their fits of anger are sudden but feeble. Their sensual passions have either altogether gone or have lost their vigor: consequently they do not feel their passions much, and their actions are inspired less by what they do feel than by the love of gain. Hence men at this time of life are often supposed to have a self-controlled character; the fact is that their passions have slackened, and they are slaves to the love of gain. They guide their lives by reasoning more than by moral feeling; reasoning being directed to utility and moral feeling to moral goodness. If they wrong others, they mean to injure them, not to insult them. Old men may feel pity, as well as young men, but not for the same reason. Young men feel it out of kindness; old men out of weakness, imagining that anything that befalls anyone else might easily happen to them, which, as we saw, is a thought that excites pity. Hence they are querulous, and not disposed to jesting or laughter—the love of laughter being the very opposite of querulousness.

Such are the characters of Young Men and Elderly Men. People always think well of speeches adapted to, and reflecting, their own character: and we can now see how to compose our speeches so as to adapt both them and ourselves to our audiences.

Part XIV

As for Men in their Prime, clearly we shall find that they have a character between that of the young and that of the old, free from the extremes of either. They have neither that excess of confidence which amounts to rashness, nor too much timidity, but the right amount of each. They neither trust everybody nor distrust everybody, but judge people correctly. Their lives will be guided not by the sole consideration either of what is noble or of what is useful, but by both; neither by parsimony nor by prodigality, but by what is fit and proper. So, too, in regard to anger and desire; they will be brave as well as temperate, and temperate as well as brave; these virtues are divided between the young and the old; the young are brave but intemperate, the old temperate but cowardly. To put it generally, all the valuable qualities that youth and age divide between them are united in the prime of life, while all their excesses or defects are replaced by moderation and fitness. The body is in its prime from thirty to five-and-thirty; the mind about forty-nine.

Part XV

So much for the types of character that distinguish youth, old age, and the prime of life. We will now turn to those Gifts of Fortune by which human character is affected. First let us consider Good Birth. Its effect on character is to make those who have it more ambitious; it is the way of all men who have something to start with to add to the pile, and good birth implies ancestral distinction. The well-born man will look down even on those who are as good as his own ancestors, because any far-off distinction is greater than the same thing close to us, and better to boast about. Being well-born, which means coming of a fine stock, must be distinguished from nobility, which means being true to the family nature—a quality not usually found in the well-born, most of whom are poor creatures. In the generations of men as in the fruits of the earth, there is a varying yield; now and then, where the stock is good, exceptional men are produced for a while, and then decadence sets in. A clever stock will degenerate toward the insane type of character, like the descendants of Alcibiades or of the elder Dionysius; a steady stock toward the fatuous and torpid type, like the descendants of Cimon, Pericles, and Socrates.

Part XVI

The type of character produced by Wealth lies on the surface for all to see. Wealthy men are insolent and arrogant; their possession of wealth affects their understanding; they feel as if they had every good thing that exists; wealth becomes a sort of standard of value for everything else, and therefore they imagine there is nothing it cannot buy. They are luxurious and ostentatious; luxurious, because of the luxury in which they live and the prosperity which they display; ostentatious and vulgar, because, like other people's, their minds are regularly occupied with the object of their love and admiration, and also because they think that other people's idea of happiness is the same as their own. It is indeed quite natural that they should be affected thus; for if you have money, there are always plenty of people who come begging from you. Hence the saying of Simonides about wise men and rich men, in answer to Hiero's wife, who asked him whether it was better to grow rich or wise. "Why, rich," he said; "for I see the wise men spending their days at the rich men's doors." Rich men also consider themselves worthy to hold public office; for they consider they already have the things that give a claim to office. In a word, the type of character produced by wealth is that of a prosperous fool. There is indeed one difference between the type of the newly enriched and those who have long been rich: the newly enriched have all the bad qualities mentioned in an exaggerated and worse form—to be newly enriched means, so to speak, no education in riches. The wrongs they do others are not meant to injure their victims, but spring from insolence or self-indulgence, e.g. those that end in assault or in adultery.

Part XVII

As to Power: here too it may fairly be said that the type of character it produces is mostly obvious enough. Some elements in this type it shares with the wealthy type, others are better. Those in power are more ambitious and more manly in character than the wealthy, because they aspire to do the great deeds that their power permits them to do. Responsibility makes them more serious: they have to keep paying attention to the duties their position involves. They are dignified rather than arrogant, for the respect in which they are held inspires them with dignity and therefore with moderation—dignity being a mild and becoming form of arrogance. If they wrong others, they wrong them not on a small but on a great scale.

Good fortune in certain of its branches produces the types of character belonging to the conditions just described, since these conditions are in fact more or less the kinds of good fortune that are regarded as most important. It may be added that good fortune leads us to gain all we can in the way of family happiness and bodily advantages. It does indeed make men more supercilious and more reckless; but there is one excellent quality that goes with it—piety, and respect for the divine power, in which they believe because of events which are really the result of chance.

This account of the types of character that correspond to differences of age or fortune may end here; for to arrive at the opposite types to those described, namely, those of the poor, the unfortunate, and the powerless, we have only to ask what the opposite qualities are.

Part XVIII

The use of persuasive speech is to lead to decisions. (When we know a thing, and have decided about it, there is no further use in speaking about it.) This is so even if one is addressing a single person and urging him to do or not to do something, as when we scold a man for his conduct or try to change his views: the single person is as much your "judge" as if he were one of many; we may say, without qualification, that any one is your judge whom you have to persuade. Nor does it matter whether we are arguing against an actual opponent or against a mere proposition; in the latter case we still have to use speech and overthrow the opposing arguments, and we attack these as we should attack an actual opponent. Our principle holds good of ceremonial speeches also; the "onlookers" for whom such a speech is put together are treated as the judges of it. Broadly speaking, however, the only sort of person who can strictly be called a judge is the man who decides the issue in some matter of public controversy; that is, in law suits and in political debates, in both of which there are issues to be decided. In the section on political oratory an account has already been given of the types of character that mark the different constitutions.

The manner and means of investing speeches with moral character may now be regarded as fully set forth.

Each of the main divisions of oratory has, we have seen, its own distinct purpose. With regard to each division, we have noted the accepted views and propositions upon which we may base our arguments—for political, for ceremonial, and for forensic speaking. We have further determined completely by what means speeches may be invested with the required moral character. We are now to proceed to discuss the arguments common to all oratory. All orators, besides their special lines of argument, are bound to use, for instance, the topic of the Possible and Impossible; and to try to show that a thing has happened, or will happen in future. Again, the topic of Size is common to all oratory; all of us have to argue that things are bigger or smaller than they seem, whether we are making political speeches, speeches of eulogy or attack, or prosecuting or defending in the law-courts. Having analized these subjects, we will try to say what we can about the general principles of arguing by "enthymeme" and "example," by the addition of which we may hope to complete the project with which we set out. Of the above-mentioned general lines of argument, that concerned with Amplification is—as has been already said—most appropriate to ceremonial speeches; that concerned with the Past, to forensic speeches, where the required decision is always about the past; that concerned with Possibility and the Future, to political speeches.

Part XIX

Let us first speak of the Possible and Impossible. It may plausibly be argued: That if it is possible for one of a pair of contraries to be or happen, then it is possible for the other: e.g. if a man can be cured, he can also fall ill; for any two contraries are equally possible, in so far as they are contraries. That if of two similar things one is possible, so is the other. That if the harder of two things is possible, so is the easier. That if a thing can come into existence in a good and beautiful form, then it can come into existence generally; thus a house can exist more easily than a beautiful house. That if the beginning of a thing can occur, so can the end; for nothing impossible occurs or begins to occur; thus the commensurability of the diagonal of a square with its side neither occurs nor can begin to occur. That if the end is possible, so is the beginning; for all things that occur have a beginning. That if that which is posterior in essence or in order of generation can come into being, so can that which is prior: thus if a man can come into being, so can a boy, since the boy comes first in order of generation; and if a boy can, so can a man, for the man also is first. That those things are possible of which the love or desire is natural; for no one, as a rule, loves or desires impossibilities. That things which are the object of any kind of science or art are possible and exist or come into existence. That anything is possible the first step in whose production depends on men or things which we can compel or persuade to produce it, by our greater strength, our control of them, or our friendship with them. That where the parts are possible, the whole is possible; and where the whole is possible, the parts are usually possible. For if the slit in front, the toe-piece, and the upper leather can be made, then shoes can be made; and if shoes, then also the front slit and toe-piece. That if a whole genus is a thing that can occur, so can the species; and if the species can occur, so can the genus: thus, if a sailing vessel can be made, so also can a trireme; and if a trireme, then a sailing vessel also. That if one of two things whose existence depends on each other is possible, so is the other; for instance, if "double," then "half," and if "half," then "double." That if a thing can be produced without art or preparation, it can be produced still more certainly by the careful application of art to it. Hence Agathon has said:

> "To some things we by art must needs attain,
> Others by destiny or luck we gain."

That if anything is possible to inferior, weaker, and stupider people, it is more so for their opposites; thus Isocrates said that it would be a strange thing if he could not discover a thing that Euthynus had found out. As for Impossibility, we can clearly get what we want by taking the contraries of the arguments stated above.

Questions of Past Fact may be looked at in the following ways: First, that if the less likely of two things has occurred, the more likely must have occurred also. That if one thing that usually follows another has happened, then that other thing has happened; that, for instance, if a man has forgotten a thing, he has also once learned it. That if a man had the power and the wish to do a thing, he has done it; for everyone does do whatever he intends to do whenever he can do it, there being nothing to stop him. That, further, he has done the thing in question either if he intended it and nothing external prevented him; or if he had the power to do it and was angry at the time; or if he had the power to do it and his heart was set upon it—for people as a rule do what they long to do, if they can; bad people through lack of self-control; good people, because their hearts are set upon good things. Again, that if a thing was "going to happen," it has happened; if a man was "going to do something," he has done it, for it is likely that the intention was carried out. That if one thing has happened which naturally happens before another or with a view to it, the other has happened; for instance, if it has lightened, it has also thundered; and if an action has been attempted, it has been done. That if one thing has happened which naturally happens after another, or with a view to which that other happens, then that other (that which happens first, or happens with a view to this thing) has also happened; thus, if it has thundered it has lightened, and if an action has been done it has been attempted. Of all these sequences some are inevitable and some merely usual. The arguments for the non-occurrence of anything can obviously be found by considering the opposites of those that have been mentioned.

How questions of Future Fact should be argued is clear from the same considerations: That a thing will be done if there is both the power and the wish to do it; or if along with the power to do it there is a craving for the result, or anger, or calculation, prompting it. That the thing will be done, in these cases, if the man is actually setting about it, or even if he means to do it later—for usually what we mean to do happens rather than what we do not mean to do. That a thing will happen if another thing which naturally happens before it has already happened; thus, if it is clouding over, it is likely to rain. That if the means to an end have occurred, then the end is likely to occur; thus, if there is a foundation, there will be a house.

For arguments about the Greatness and Smallness of things, the greater and the lesser, and generally great things and small, what we have already said will show the line to take. In discussing deliberative oratory we have spoken about the relative greatness of various goods, and about the greater and lesser in general. Since therefore in each type oratory the object under discussion is some kind of good—whether it is utility, nobleness, or justice—it is clear that every orator must obtain the materials of amplification through these channels. To go further than this, and try to establish abstract laws of greatness and superiority, is to argue without an object; in practical life, particular facts count more than generalizations.

Enough has now been said about these questions of possibility and the reverse, of past or future fact, and of the relative greatness or smallness of things.

Part XX

The special forms of oratorical argument having now been discussed, we have next to treat of those which are common to all kinds of oratory. These are of two main kinds, "Example" and "Enthymeme"; for the "Maxim" is part of an enthymeme.

We will first treat of argument by Example, for it has the nature of induction, which is the foundation of reasoning. This form of argument has two varieties; one consisting in the mention of actual past facts, the other in the invention of facts by the speaker. Of the latter, again, there are two varieties, the illustrative parallel and the fable (e.g. the fables of Aesop, those from Libya). As an instance of the mention of actual facts, take the following. The speaker may argue thus: "We must prepare for war against the king of Persia and not let him subdue Egypt. For Darius of old did not cross the Aegean until he had seized Egypt; but once he had seized it, he did cross. And Xerxes, again, did not attack us until he had seized Egypt; but once he had seized it, he did cross. If therefore the present king seizes Egypt, he also will cross, and therefore we must not let him."

The illustrative parallel is the sort of argument Socrates used: e.g. "Public officials ought not to be selected by lot. That is like using the lot to select athletes, instead of choosing those who are fit for the contest; or using the lot to select a steersman from among a ship's crew, as if we ought to take the man on whom the lot falls, and not the man who knows most about it."

Instances of the fable are that of Stesichorus about Phalaris, and that of Aesop in defense of the popular leader. When the people of Himera had made Phalaris military dictator, and were going to give him a bodyguard, Stesichorus wound up a long talk by telling them the fable of the horse who had a field all to himself. Presently there came a stag and began to spoil his pasturage. The horse, wishing to revenge himself on the stag, asked a man if he could help him to do so. The man said, "Yes, if you will let me bridle you and get on to your back with javelins in my hand." The horse agreed, and the man mounted; but instead of getting his revenge on the stag, the horse found himself the slave of the man. "You too," said Stesichorus, "take care lest your desire for revenge on your enemies, you meet the same fate as the horse. By making Phalaris military dictator, you have already let yourselves be bridled. If you let him get on to your backs by giving him a bodyguard, from that moment you will be his slaves."

Aesop, defending before the assembly at Samos a poular leader who was being tried for his life, told this story: A fox, in crossing a river, was swept into a hole in the rocks; and, not being able to get out, suffered miseries for a long time through the swarms of fleas that fastened on her. A hedgehog, while roaming around, noticed the fox; and feeling sorry for her asked if he might remove the fleas. But the fox declined the offer; and when the hedgehog asked why, she replied, "These fleas are by this time full of me and not sucking much blood; if you take them away, others will come with fresh appetites and drink up all the blood I have left." "So, men of Samos," said Aesop, "my client will do you no further harm; he is wealthy already. But if you put him to death, others will come along who are not rich, and their peculations will empty your treasury completely."

Fables are suitable for addresses to popular assemblies; and they have one advantage—they are comparatively easy to invent, whereas it is hard to find parallels among actual past events. You will in fact frame them just as you frame illustrative parallels: all you require is the power of thinking out your analogy, a power developed by intellectual training. But while it is easier to supply parallels by inventing fables, it is more valuable for the political speaker to supply them by quoting what has actually happened, since in most respects the future will be like what the past has been.

Where we are unable to argue by Enthymeme, we must try to demonstrate our point by this method of Example, and to convince our hearers thereby. If we can argue by Enthymeme, we should use our Examples as subsequent supplementary evidence. They should not precede the Enthymemes: that will give the argument an inductive air, which only rarely suits the conditions of speech-making. If they follow the Enthymemes, they have the effect of witnesses giving evidence, and this alway tells. For the same reason, if you put your examples first you must give a large number of them; if you put them last, a single one is sufficient; even a single witness will serve if he is a good one. It has now been stated how many varieties of argument by Example there are, and how and when they are to be employed.

Part XXI

We now turn to the use of Maxims, in order to see upon what subjects and occasions, and for what kind of speaker, they will appropriately form part of a speech. This will appear most clearly when we have defined a maxim. It is a statement; not a particular fact, such as the character of Iphicrates, but of a general kind; nor is it about any and every subject—e.g. "straight is the contrary of curved" is not a maxim—but only about questions of practical conduct, courses of conduct to be chosen or avoided. Now an Enthymeme is a syllogism dealing with such practical subjects. It is therefore roughly true that the premises or conclusions of Enthymemes, considered apart from the rest of the argument, are Maxims: e.g.

> "Never should any man whose wits are sound
> Have his sons taught more wisdom than their fellows."

Here we have a Maxim; add the reason or explanation, and the whole thing is an Enthymeme; thus—

> "It makes them idle; and therewith they earn
> Ill-will and jealousy throughout the city."

Again,

> "There is no man in all things prosperous,"

and

> "There is no man among us all is free,"

are maxims; but the latter, taken with what follows it, is an Enthymeme—

> "For all are slaves of money or of chance."

From this definition of a maxim it follows that there are four kinds of maxims. In the first Place, the maxim may or may not have a supplement. Proof is needed where the statement is paradoxical or disputable; no supplement is wanted where the statement contains nothing paradoxical, either because the view expressed is already a known truth, e.g.

> "Chiefest of blessings is health for a man, as it seemeth to me,"

this being the general opinion: or because, as soon as the view is stated, it is clear at a glance, e.g.

> "No love is true save that which loves forever."

Of the Maxims that do have a supplement attached, some are part of an Enthymeme, e.g.

"Never should any man whose wits are sound, etc."

Others have the essential character of Enthymemes, but are not stated as parts of Enthymemes; these latter are reckoned the best; they are those in which the reason for the view expressed is simply implied, e.g.

"O mortal man, nurse not immortal wrath."

To say "it is not right to nurse immortal wrath" is a maxim; the added words "mortal man" give the reason. Similarly, with the words Mortal creatures ought to cherish mortal, not immortal thoughts.

What has been said has shown us how many kinds of Maxims there are, and to what subjects the various kinds are appropriate. They must not be given without supplement if they express disputed or paradoxical views: we must, in that case, either put the supplement first and make a maxim of the conclusion, e.g. you might say, "For my part, since both unpopularity and idleness are undesirable, I hold that it is better not to be educated"; or you may say this first, and then add the previous clause. Where a statement, without being paradoxical, is not obviously true, the reason should be added as concisely as possible. In such cases both laconic and enigmatic sayings are suitable: thus one might say what Stesichorus said to the Locrians, "Insolence is better avoided, lest the cicalas chirp on the ground."

The use of Maxims is appropriate only to elderly men, and in handling subjects in which the speaker is experienced. For a young man to use them is—like telling stories—unbecoming; to use them in handling things in which one has no experience is silly and ill-bred: a fact sufficiently proved by the special fondness of country fellows for striking out maxims, and their readiness to air them.

To declare a thing to be universally true when it is not is most appropriate when working up feelings of horror and indignation in our hearers; especially by way of preface, or after the facts have been proved. Even hackneyed and commonplace maxims are to be used, if they suit one's purpose: just because they are commonplace, everyone seems to agree with them, and therefore they are taken for truth. Thus, anyone who is calling on his men to risk an engagement without obtaining favorable omens may quote

"One omen of all is best, that we fight for our fatherland."

Or, if he is calling on them to attack a stronger force—

> "The War God showeth no favor."

Or, if he is urging people to destroy the innocent children of their enemies—

> "Fool, who slayeth the father and leaveth his sons to avenge him."

Some proverbs are also maxims, e.g. the proverb "an attic neighbor." You are not to avoid uttering maxims that contradict such sayings as have become public property (I mean such sayings as "know thyself" and "nothing in excess") if doing so will raise your hearers' opinion of your character, or convey an effect of strong emotion—e.g. an angry speaker might well say, "It is not true that we ought to know ourselves: anyhow, if this man had known himself, he would never have thought himself fit for an army command." It will raise people's opinion of our character to say, for instance, "We ought not to follow the saying that bids us treat our friends as future enemies: much better to treat our enemies as future friends." The moral purpose should be implied partly by the very wording of our maxim. Failing this, we should add our reason: e.g. having said "We should treat our friends, not as the saying advises, but as if they were going to be our friends always," we should add "for the other behavior is that of a traitor": or we might put it, "I disapprove of that saying. A true friend will treat his friend as if he were going to be his friend forever"; and again, "Nor do I approve of the saying 'nothing in excess': we are bound to hate bad men excessively." One great advantage of Maxims to a speaker is due to the want of intelligence in his hearers, who love to hear him succeed in expressing as a universal truth the opinions which they hold themselves about particular cases. I will explain what I mean by this, indicating at the same time how we are to hunt down the maxims required. The maxim, as has been already said, a general statement and people love to hear stated in general terms what they already believe in some particular connection: e.g. if a man happens to have bad neighbors or bad children, he will agree with anyone who tells him, "Nothing is more annoying than having neighbors," or, "Nothing is more foolish than to be the parent of children." The orator has therefore to guess the subjects on which his hearers really hold views already, and what those views are, and then must express, as general truths, these same views on these same subjects. This is one advantage of using maxims. There is another which is more important—it invests a speech with moral character. There is moral character in every speech in which the moral purpose is conspicuous: and maxims always produce this effect, because the utterance of them amounts to a general declaration of moral principles: so that, if the maxims are sound, they display the speaker as a man of sound moral character. So much for the Maxim—its nature, varieties, proper use, and advantages.

Part XXII

We now come to the Enthymemes, and will begin the subject with some general consideration of the proper way of looking for them, and then proceed to what is a distinct question, the lines of argument to be embodied in them. It has already been pointed out that the Enthymeme is a syllogism, and in what sense it is so. We have also noted the differences between it and the syllogism of dialectic. Thus we must not carry its reasoning too far back, or the length of our argument will cause obscurity: nor must we put in all the steps that lead to our conclusion, or we shall waste words in saying what is manifest. It is this simplicity that makes the uneducated more effective than the educated when addressing popular audiences—makes them, as the poets tell us, "charm the crowd's ears more finely." Educated men lay down broad general principles; uneducated men argue from common knowledge and draw obvious conclusions. We must not, therefore, start from any and every accepted opinion, but only from those we have defined—those accepted by our judges or by those whose authority they recognize: and there must, moreover, be no doubt in the minds of most, if not all, of our judges that the opinions put forward really are of this sort. We should also base our arguments upon probabilities as well as upon certainties.

The first thing we have to remember is this. Whether our argument concerns public affairs or some other subject, we must know some, if not all, of the facts about the subject on which we are to speak and argue. Otherwise we can have no materials out of which to construct arguments. I mean, for instance, how could we advise the Athenians whether they should go to war or not, if we did not know their strength, whether it was naval or military or both, and how great it is; what their revenues amount to; who their friends and enemies are; what wars, too, they have waged, and with what success; and so on? Or how could we eulogize them if we knew nothing about the sea-fight at Salamis, or the battle of Marathon, or what they did for the Heracleidae, or any other facts like that? All eulogy is based upon the noble deeds—real or imaginary—that stand to the credit of those eulogized. On the same principle, invectives are based on facts of the opposite kind: the orator looks to see what base deeds—real or imaginary—stand to the discredit of those he is attacking, such as treachery to the cause of Hellenic freedom, or the enslavement of their gallant allies against the barbarians (Aegina, Potidaea, etc.), or any other misdeeds of this kind that are recorded against them. So, too, in a court of law: whether we are prosecuting or defending, we must pay attention to the existing facts of the case. It makes no difference whether the subject is the Lacedaemonians or the Athenians, a man or a god; we must do the same thing. Suppose it to be Achilles whom we are to advise, to praise or blame, to accuse or defend; here too we must take the facts, real or imaginary; these must be our material, whether we are to praise or blame him for the noble or base deeds he has done, to accuse or defend him for his just or unjust treatment of others, or to advise him about what is or is not to his interest. The same thing applies to any subject whatever. Thus, in handling the question whether justice is or is not a good, we must start with the real facts about justice and goodness. We see, then, that this is the only way in which anyone ever proves anything, whether his arguments are strictly cogent or not: not all facts can form his basis, but only those that bear on the matter in hand: nor, plainly, can proof be effected otherwise by means of the speech. Consequently, as appears in the Topics, we must first of all have by us a selection of arguments about questions that may arise and are suitable for us to handle; and then we must try to think out arguments of the same type for special needs as they emerge; not vaguely and indefinitely, but by keeping our eyes on the actual facts of the subject we have to speak on, and gathering in as many of them as we can that bear closely upon it: for the more actual facts we have at our command, the more easily we prove our case; and the more closely they bear on the subject, the more they will seem to belong to that speech only instead of being commonplaces. By "commonplaces" I mean, for example, eulogy of Achilles because he is a human being or a demi-god, or because he joined the expedition against Troy: these things are true of many others, so that this kind of eulogy applies no better to Achilles than to Diomede. The special facts here needed are those that are true of Achilles alone; such facts as that he slew Hector, the bravest of the Trojans, and Cycnus the invulnerable, who prevented all the Greeks from landing, and again that he was the youngest man who joined the expedition, and was not bound by oath to join it, and so on.

Here, again, we have our first principle of selection of Enthymemes—

that which refers to the lines of argument selected. We will now consider the various elementary classes of enthymemes. (By an "elementary class" of enthymeme I mean the same thing as a "line of argument.") We will begin, as we must begin, by observing that there are two kinds of enthymemes. One kind proves some affirmative or negative proposition; the other kind disproves one. The difference between the two kinds is the same as that between syllogistic proof and disproof in dialectic. The demonstrative enthymeme is formed by the conjunction of compatible propositions; the refutative, by the conjunction of incompatible propositions.

We may now be said to have in our hands the lines of argument for the various special subjects that it is useful or necessary to handle, having selected the propositions suitable in various cases. We have, in fact, already ascertained the lines of argument applicable to enthymemes about good and evil, the noble and the base, justice and injustice, and also to those about types of character, emotions, and moral qualities. Let us now lay hold of certain facts about the whole subject, considered from a different and more general point of view. In the course of our discussion we will take note of the distinction between lines of proof and lines of disproof: and also of those lines of argument used in what seems to be enthymemes, but are not, since they do not represent valid syllogisms. Having made all this clear, we will proceed to classify Objections and Refutations, showing how they can be brought to bear upon enthymemes.

Part XXIII

1. One line of positive proof is based upon consideration of the opposite of the thing in question. Observe whether that opposite has the opposite quality. If it has not, you refute the original proposition; if it has, you establish it. E.g. "Temperance is beneficial; for licentiousness is hurtful." Or, as in the Messenian speech, "If war is the cause of our present troubles, peace is what we need to put things right again." Or—

> "For if not even evil-doers should
> Anger us if they meant not what they did,
> Then can we owe no gratitude to such
> As were constrained to do the good they did us."

Or—

> "Since in this world liars may win belief,
> Be sure of the opposite likewise—that this world
> Hears many a true word and believes it not."

2. Another line of proof is got by considering some modification of the keyword, and arguing that what can or cannot be said of the one, can or cannot be said of the other: e.g. "just" does not always mean "beneficial," or "justly" would always mean "beneficially," whereas it is not desirable to be justly put to death.

3. Another line of proof is based upon correlative ideas. If it is true that one man noble or just treatment to another, you argue that the other must have received noble or just treatment; or that where it is right to command obedience, it must have been right to obey the command. Thus Diomedon, the tax farmer, said of the taxes: "If it is no disgrace for you to sell them, it is no disgrace for us to buy them." Further, if "well" or "justly" is true of the person to whom a thing is done, you argue that it is true of the doer. But it is possible to draw a false conclusion here. It may be just that A should be treated in a certain way, and yet not just that he should be so treated by B. Hence you must ask yourself two distinct questions: (1) Is it right that A should be thus treated? (2) Is it right that B should thus treat him? and apply your results properly, according as your answers are Yes or No. Sometimes in such a case the two answers differ: you may quite easily have a position like that in the Alcmaeon of Theodectes:

> "And was there none to loathe thy mother's crime?"

to which question Alcmaeon in reply says,

> "Why, there are two things to examine here."

And when Alphesiboea asks what he means, he rejoins:

> "They judged her fit to die, not me to slay her."

Again there is the lawsuit about Demosthenes and the men who killed Nicanor; as they were judged to have killed him justly, it was thought that he was killed justly. And in the case of the man who was killed at Thebes, the judges were requested to decide whether it was unjust that he should be killed, since if it was not, it was argued that it could not have been unjust to kill him.

4. Another line of proof is the "*a fortiori*." Thus it may be argued that

if even the gods are not omniscient, certainly human beings are not. The principle here is that, if a quality does not in fact exist where it is more likely to exist, it clearly does not exist where it is less likely. Again, the argument that a man who strikes his father also strikes his neighbors follows from the principle that, if the less likely thing is true, the more likely thing is true also; for a man is less likely to strike his father than to strike his neighbors. The argument, then, may run thus. Or it may be urged that, if a thing is not true where it is more likely, it is not true where it is less likely; or that, if it is true where it is less likely, it is true where it is more likely: according as we have to show that a thing is or is not true. This argument might also be used in a case of parity, as in the lines:

> "Thou hast pity for thy sire, who has lost his sons:
> Hast none for Oeneus, whose brave son is dead?"

And, again, "if Theseus did no wrong, neither did Paris"; or "the sons of Tyndareus did no wrong, neither did Paris"; or "if Hector did well to slay Patroclus, Paris did well to slay Achilles." And "if other followers of an art are not bad men, neither are philosophers." And "if generals are not bad men because it often happens that they are condemned to death, neither are sophists." And the remark that "if each individual among you ought to think of his own city's reputation, you ought all to think of the reputation of Greece as a whole."

5. Another line of argument is based on considerations of time. Thus Iphicrates, in the case against Harmodius, said, "if before doing the deed I had bargained that, if I did it, I should have a statue, you would have given me one. Will you not give me one now that I have done the deed? You must not make promises when you are expecting a thing to be done for you, and refuse to fulfill them when the thing has been done." And, again, to induce the Thebans to let Philip pass through their territory into Attica, it was argued that "if he had insisted on this before he helped them against the Phocians, they would have promised to do it. It is monstrous, therefore, that just because he threw away his advantage then, and trusted their honor, they should not let him pass through now."

6. Another line is to apply to the other speaker what he has said against yourself. It is an excellent turn to give to a debate, as may be seen in the Teucer. It was employed by Iphicrates in his reply to Aristophon. "Would you," he asked, "take a bribe to betray the fleet?" "No," said Aristophon; and Iphicrates replied, "Very good: if you, who are Aristophon, would not

betray the fleet, would I, who am Iphicrates?" Only, it must be recognized beforehand that the other man is more likely than you are to commit the crime in question. Otherwise you will make yourself ridiculous; it is Aristeides who is prosecuting, you cannot say that sort of thing to him. The purpose is to discredit the prosecutor, who as a rule would have it appear that his character is better than that of the defendant, a pretension which it is desirable to upset. But the use of such an argument is in all cases ridiculous if you are attacking others for what you do or would do yourself, or are urging others to do what you neither do nor would do yourself.

7. Another line of proof is secured by defining your terms. Thus, "What is the supernatural? Surely it is either a god or the work of a god. Well, anyone who believes that the work of a god exists, cannot help also believing that gods exist." Or take the argument of Iphicrates, "Goodness is true nobility; neither Harmodius nor Aristogeiton had any nobility before they did a noble deed." He also argued that he himself was more akin to Harmodius and Aristogeiton than his opponent was. "At any rate, my deeds are more akin to those of Harmodius and Aristogeiton than yours are." Another example may be found in the Alexander. "Every one will agree that by incontinent people we mean those who are not satisfied with the enjoyment of one love." A further example is to be found in the reason given by Socrates for not going to the court of Archelaus. He said that "one is insulted by being unable to requite benefits, as well as by being unable to requite injuries." All the persons mentioned define their term and get at its essential meaning, and then use the result when reasoning on the point at issue.

8. Another line of argument is founded upon the various senses of a word. Such a word is "rightly," as has been explained in the Topics.

9. Another line is based upon logical division. Thus, "All men do wrong from one of three motives, A, B, or C: in my case A and B are out of the question, and even the accusers do not allege C."

10. Another line is based upon induction. Thus from the case of the woman of Peparethus it might be argued that women everywhere can settle correctly the facts about their children. Another example of this occurred at Athens in the case between the orator Mantias and his son, when the boy's mother revealed the true facts: and yet another at Thebes, in the case between Ismenias and Stilbon, when Dodonis proved that it was Ismenias who was the father of her son Thettaliscus, and he was in consequence always regarded as being so. A further instance of induction may be taken from the Law of Theodectes: "If we do not hand over our

horses to the care of men who have mishandled other people's horses, nor ships to those who have wrecked other people's ships, and if this is true of everything else alike, then men who have failed to secure other people's safety are not to be employed to secure our own." Another instance is the argument of Alcidamas: "Every one honors the wise." Thus the Parians have honored Archilochus, in spite of his bitter tongue; the Chians Homer, though he was not their countryman; the Mytilenaeans Sappho, though she was a woman; the Lacedaemonians actually made Chilon a member of their senate, though they are the least literary of men; the Italian Greeks honored Pythagoras; the inhabitants of Lampsacus gave public burial to Anaxagoras, though he was an alien, and honor him even to this day. (It may be argued that peoples for whom philosophers legislate are always prosperous) on the ground that the Athenians became prosperous under Solon's laws and the Lacedaemonians under those of Lycurgus, while at Thebes no sooner did the leading men become philosophers than the country began to prosper.

11. Another line of argument is founded upon some decision already pronounced, whether on the same subject or on one like it or contrary to it. Such a proof is most effective if everyone has always decided thus; but if not everyone, then at any rate most people; or if all, or most, wise or good men have thus decided, or the actual judges of the present question, or those whose authority they accept, or anyone whose decision they cannot gainsay because he has complete control over them, or those whom it is not seemly to gainsay, as the gods, or one's father, or one's teachers. Thus Autocles said, when attacking Mixidemides, that it was a strange thing that the Dread Goddesses could without loss of dignity submit to the judgement of the Areopagus, and yet Mixidemides could not. Or as Sappho said, "Death is an evil thing; the gods have so judged it, or they would die." Or again as Aristippus said in reply to Plato when he spoke somewhat too dogmatically, as Aristippus thought: "Well, anyhow, our friend," meaning Socrates, "never spoke like that." And Hegesippus, having previously consulted Zeus at Olympia, asked Apollo at Delphi "whether his opinion was the same as his father's," implying that it would be shameful for him to contradict his father. Thus too Isocrates argued that Helen must have been a good woman, because Theseus decided that she was; and Paris a good man, because the goddesses chose him before all others; and Evagoras also, says Isocrates, was good, since when Conon met with his misfortune he betook himself to Evagoras without trying anyone else on the way.

12. Another line of argument consists in taking separately the parts of

a subject. Such is that given in the Topics: "What sort of motion is the soul? for it must be this or that." The Socrates of Theodectes provides an example: "What temple has he profaned? What gods recognized by the state has he not honored?"

13. Since it happens that any given thing usually has both good and bad consequences, another line of argument consists in using those consequences as a reason for urging that a thing should or should not be done, for prosecuting or defending anyone, for eulogy or censure. E.g. education leads both to unpopularity, which is bad, and to wisdom, which is good. Hence you either argue, "It is therefore not well to be educated, since it is not well to be unpopular": or you answer, "No, it is well to be educated, since it is well to be wise." The Art of Rhetoric of Callippus is made up of this line of argument, with the addition of those of Possibility and the others of that kind already described.

14. Another line of argument is used when we have to urge or discourage a course of action that may be done in either of two opposite ways, and have to apply the method just mentioned to both. The difference between this one and the last is that, whereas in the last any two things are contrasted, here the things contrasted are opposites. For instance, the priestess enjoined upon her son not to take to public speaking: "For," she said, "if you say what is right, men will hate you; if you say what is wrong, the gods will hate you." The reply might be, "On the contrary, you ought to take to public speaking: for if you say what is right the gods will love you; if you say what is wrong, men will love you." This amounts to the proverbial "buying the marsh with the salt." It is just this situation, viz. when each of two opposites has both a good and a bad consequence opposite respectively to each other, that has been termed divarication.

15. Another line of argument is this: The things people approve of openly are not those which they approve of secretly: openly, their chief praise is given to justice and nobleness; but in their hearts they prefer their own advantage. Try, in face of this, to establish the point of view which your opponent has not adopted. This is the most effective of the forms of argument that contradict common opinion.

16. Another line is that of rational correspondence. E.g. Iphicrates, when they were trying to compel his son, a youth under the prescribed age, to perform one of the state duties because he was tall, said "If you count tall boys men, you will next be voting short men boys." And Theodectes in his Law said, "You make citizens of such mercenaries as Strabax and Charidemus, as a reward of their merits; will you not make exiles of such

citizens as those who have done irreparable harm among the mercenaries?"

17. Another line is the argument that if two results are the same their antecedents are also the same. For instance, it was a saying of Xenophanes that to assert that the gods had birth is as impious as to say that they die; the consequence of both statements is that there is a time when the gods do not exist. This line of proof assumes generally that the result of any given thing is always the same: e.g. "you are going to decide not about Isocrates, but about the value of the whole profession of philosophy." Or, "to give earth and water" means slavery; or, "to share in the Common Peace" means obeying orders. We are to make either such assumptions or their opposite, as suits us best.

18. Another line of argument is based on the fact that men do not always make the same choice on a later as on an earlier occasion, but reverse their previous choice, e.g. the following enthymeme: "When we were exiles, we fought in order to return; now we have returned, it would be strange to choose exile in order not to have to fight." On one occasion, that is, they chose to be true to their homes at the cost of fighting, and on the other to avoid fighting at the cost of deserting their homes.

19. Another line of argument is the assertion that some possible motive for an event or state of things is the real one: e.g. that a gift was given in order to cause pain by its withdrawal. This notion underlies the lines:

> "God gives to many great prosperity,
> Not of good God toward them, but to make
> The ruin of them more conspicuous."

Or take the passage from the Meleager of Antiphon:

> "To slay no boar, but to be witnesses
> Of Meleager's prowess unto Greece."

Or the argument in the Ajax of Theodectes, that Diomede chose out Odysseus not to do him honor, but in order that his companion might be a lesser man than himself—such a motive for doing so is quite possible.

20. Another line of argument is common to forensic and deliberative oratory, namely, to consider inducements and deterrents, and the motives people have for doing or avoiding the actions in question. These are the conditions which make us bound to act if they are for us, and to refrain from action if they are against us: that is, we are bound to act if the action is possible, easy, and useful to ourselves or our friends or hurtful to our

enemies; this is true even if the action entails loss, provided the loss is outweighed by the solid advantage. A speaker will urge action by pointing to such conditions, and discourage it by pointing to the opposite. These same arguments also form the materials for accusation or defense—the deterrents being pointed out by the defense, and the inducements by the prosecution. As for the defense, this topic forms the whole Art of Rhetoric both of Pamphilus and of Callippus.

21. Another line of argument refers to things which are supposed to happen and yet seem incredible. We may argue that people could not have believed them, if they had not been true or nearly true: even that they are the more likely to be true because they are incredible. For the things which men believe are either facts or probabilities: if, therefore, a thing that is believed is improbable and even incredible, it must be true, since it is certainly not believed because it is at all probable or credible. An example is what Androcles of the deme Pitthus said in his well-known arraignment of the law. The audience tried to shout him down when he observed that the laws required a law to set them right. "Why," he went on, "fish need salt, improbable and incredible as this might seem for creatures reared in salt water; and olive cakes need oil, incredible as it is that what produces oil should need it."

22. Another line of argument is to refute our opponent's case by noting any contrasts or contradictions of dates, acts, or words that it anywhere displays; and this in any of the three following connexions. (1) Referring to our opponent's conduct, e.g. "He says he is devoted to you, yet he conspired with the Thirty." (2) Referring to our own conduct, e.g. "He says I am litigious, and yet he cannot prove that I have been engaged in a single lawsuit." (3) Referring to both of us together, e.g. "He has never even lent anyone a penny, but I have ransomed quite a number of you."

23. Another line that is useful for men and causes that have been really or seemingly slandered, is to show why the facts are not as supposed; pointing out that there is a reason for the false impression given. Thus a woman, who had palmed off her son on another woman, was thought to be the lad's mistress because she embraced him; but when her action was explained the charge was shown to be groundless. Another example is from the Ajax of Theodectes, where Odysseus tells Ajax the reason why, though he is really braver than Ajax, he is not thought so.

24. Another line of argument is to show that if the cause is present, the effect is present, and if absent, absent. For by proving the cause you at once prove the effect, and conversely nothing can exist without its cause. Thus Thrasybulus accused Leodamas of having had his name recorded as a

criminal on the slab in the Acropolis, and of erasing the record in the time of the Thirty Tyrants: to which Leodamas replied, "Impossible: for the Thirty would have trusted me all the more if my quarrel with the commons had been inscribed on the slab."

25. Another line is to consider whether the accused person can take or could have taken a better course than that which he is recommending or taking, or has taken. If he has not taken this better course, it is clear that he is not guilty, since no one deliberately and consciously chooses what is bad. This argument is, however, fallacious, for it often becomes clear after the event how the action could have been done better, though before the event this was far from clear.

26. Another line is, when a contemplated action is inconsistent with any past action, to examine them both together. Thus, when the people of Elea asked Xenophanes if they should or should not sacrifice to Leucothea and mourn for her, he advised them not to mourn for her if they thought her a goddess, and not to sacrifice to her if they thought her a mortal woman.

27. Another line is to make previous mistakes the grounds of accusation or defense. Thus, in the Medea of Carcinus the accusers allege that Medea has slain her children; "at all events," they say, "they are not to be seen"—Medea having made the mistake of sending her children away. In defense she argues that it is not her children, but Jason, whom she would have slain; for it would have been a mistake on her part not to do this if she had done the other. This special line of argument for enthymeme forms the whole of the Art of Rhetoric in use before Theodorus.

"Another line is to draw meanings from names. Sophocles, for instance, says,

"O steel in heart as thou art steel in name."

This line of argument is common in praises of the gods. Thus, too, Conon called Thrasybulus rash in counsel. And Herodicus said of Thrasymachus, "You are always bold in battle"; of Polus, "you are always a colt"; and of the legislator Draco that his laws were those not of a human being but of a dragon, so savage were they. And, in Euripides, Hecuba says of Aphrodite,

"Her name and Folly's (aphrosuns) lightly begin alike,"

and Chaeremon writes

"Pentheus—a name foreshadowing grief (penthos) to come."

The Refutative Enthymeme has a greater reputation than the Demonstrative, because within a small space it works out two opposing arguments, and arguments put side by side are clearer to the audience. But of all syllogisms, whether refutative or demonstrative, those are most applauded of which we foresee the conclusions from the beginning, so long as they are not obvious at first sight—for part of the pleasure we feel is at our own intelligent anticipation; or those which we follow well enough to see the point of them as soon as the last word has been uttered.

Part XXIV

Besides genuine syllogisms, there may be syllogisms that look genuine but are not; and since an enthymeme is merely a syllogism of a particular kind, it follows that, besides genuine enthymemes, there may be those that look genuine but are not.

1. Among the lines of argument that form the Spurious Enthymeme the first is that which arises from the particular words employed.

(a) One variety of this is when—as in dialectic, without having gone through any reasoning process, we make a final statement as if it were the conclusion of such a process, "Therefore so-and-so is not true," "Therefore also so-and-so must be true"—so too in rhetoric a compact and antithetical utterance passes for an enthymeme, such language being the proper province of enthymeme, so that it is seemingly the form of wording here that causes the illusion mentioned. In order to produce the effect of genuine reasoning by our form of wording it is useful to summarize the results of a number of previous reasonings: as "some he saved—others he avenged—the Greeks he freed." Each of these statements has been previously proved from other facts; but the mere collocation of them gives the impression of establishing some fresh conclusion.

(b) Another variety is based on the use of similar words for different things; e.g. the argument that the mouse must be a noble creature, since it gives its name to the most august of all religious rites—for such the Mysteries are. Or one may introduce, into a eulogy of the dog, the dog-star; or Pan, because Pindar said:

> "O thou blessed one!
> Thou whom they of Olympus call
> The hound of manifold shape
> That follows the Mother of Heaven:"

or we may argue that, because there is much disgrace in there not being a dog about, there is honor in being a dog. Or that Hermes is readier than any other god to go shares, since we never say "shares all round" except of him. Or that speech is a very excellent thing, since good men are not said to be worth money but to be worthy of esteem—the phrase "worthy of esteem" also having the meaning of "worth speech."

2. Another line is to assert of the whole what is true of the parts, or of the parts what is true of the whole. A whole and its parts are supposed to be identical, though often they are not. You have therefore to adopt whichever of these two lines better suits your purpose. That is how Euthydemus argues: e.g. that anyone knows that there is a trireme in the Peiraeus, since he knows the separate details that make up this statement. There is also the argument that one who knows the letters knows the whole word, since the word is the same thing as the letters which compose it; or that, if a double portion of a certain thing is harmful to health, then a single portion must not be called wholesome, since it is absurd that two good things should make one bad thing. Put thus, the enthymeme is refutative; put as follows; demonstrative: "For one good thing cannot be made up of two bad things." The whole line of argument is fallacious. Again, there is Polycrates" saying that Thrasybulus put down thirty tyrants, where the speaker adds them up one by one. Or the argument in the Orestes of Theodectes, where the argument is from part to whole:

" 'Tis right that she who slays her lord should die."

"It is right, too, that the son should avenge his father. Very good: these two things are what Orestes has done." Still, perhaps the two things, once they are put together, do not form a right act. The fallacy might also be said to be due to omission, since the speaker fails to say by whose hand a husband-slayer should die.

3. Another line is the use of indignant language, whether to support your own case or to overthrow your opponent's. We do this when we paint a highly colored picture of the situation without having proved the facts of it: if the defendant does so, he produces an impression of his innocence; and if the prosecutor goes into a passion, he produces an impression of the defendant's guilt. Here there is no genuine enthymeme: the hearer infers guilt or innocence, but no proof is given, and the inference is fallacious accordingly.

4. Another line is to use a "Sign," or single instance, as certain evidence; which, again, yields no valid proof. Thus, it might be said that lovers are

useful to their countries, since the love of Harmodius and Aristogeiton caused the downfall of the tyrant Hipparchus. Or, again, that Dionysius is a thief, since he is a vicious man—there is, of course, no valid proof here; not every vicious man is a thief, though every thief is a vicious man.

5. Another line represents the accidental as essential. An instance is what Polycrates says of the mice, that they "came to the rescue" because they gnawed through the bowstrings. Or it might be maintained that an invitation to dinner is a great honor, for it was because he was not invited that Achilles was "angered" with the Greeks at Tenedos? As a fact, what angered him was the insult involved; it was a mere accident that this was the particular form that the insult took.

6. Another is the argument from consequence. In the Alexander, for instance, it is argued that Paris must have had a lofty disposition, since he despised society and lived by himself on Mount Ida: because lofty people do this kind of thing, therefore Paris too, we are to suppose, had a lofty soul. Or, if a man dresses fashionably and roams around at night, he is a rake, since that is the way rakes behave. Another similar argument points out that beggars sing and dance in temples, and that exiles can live wherever they please, and that such privileges are at the disposal of those we account happy and therefore everyone might be regarded as happy if only he has those privileges. What matters, however, is the circumstances under which the privileges are enjoyed. Hence this line too falls under the head of fallacies by omission.

7. Another line consists in representing as causes things which are not causes, on the ground that they happened along with or before the event in question. They assume that, because B happens after A, it happens because of A. Politicians are especially fond of taking this line. Thus Demades said that the policy of Demosthenes was the cause of all the mischief, "for after it the war occurred."

8. Another line consists in leaving out any mention of time and circumstances. E.g. the argument that Paris was justified in taking Helen, since her father left her free to choose: here the freedom was presumably not perpetual; it could only refer to her first choice, beyond which her father's authority could not go. Or again, one might say that to strike a free man is an act of wanton outrage; but it is not so in every case—only when it is unprovoked.

9. Again, a spurious syllogism may, as in "eristical" discussions, be based on the confusion of the absolute with that which is not absolute but particular. As, in dialectic, for instance, it may be argued that what-is-not

is, on the ground that what-is-not is what-is-not: or that the unknown can be known, on the ground that it can be known to he unknown: so also in rhetoric a spurious enthymeme may be based on the confusion of some particular probability with absolute probability. Now no particular probability is universally probable: as Agathon says,

> "One might perchance say that was probable—
> That things improbable oft will hap to men."

For what is improbable does happen, and therefore it is probable that improbable things will happen. Granted this, one might argue that "what is improbable is probable." But this is not true absolutely. As, in eristic, the imposture comes from not adding any clause specifying relationship or reference or manner; so here it arises because the probability in question is not general but specific. It is of this line of argument that Corax's Art of Rhetoric is composed. If the accused is not open to the charge—for instance if a weakling be tried for violent assault—the defense is that he was not likely to do such a thing. But if he is open to the charge—i.e. if he is a strong man—the defense is still that he was not likely to do such a thing, since he could be sure that people would think he was likely to do it. And so with any other charge: the accused must be either open or not open to it: there is in either case an appearance of probable innocence, but whereas in the latter case the probability is genuine, in the former it can only be asserted in the special sense mentioned. This sort of argument illustrates what is meant by making the worse argument seem the better. Hence people were right in objecting to the training Protagoras undertook to give them. It was a fraud; the probability it handled was not genuine but spurious, and has a place in no art except Rhetoric and Eristic.

Part XXV

Enthymemes, genuine and apparent, have now been described; the next subject is their Refutation.

An argument may be refuted either by a counter-syllogism or by bringing an objection. It is clear that counter-syllogisms can be built up from the same lines of arguments as the original syllogisms: for the materials of syllogisms are the ordinary opinions of men, and such opinions often contradict each other. Objections, as appears in the Topics, may be raised in four ways—either by directly attacking your opponent's own statement, or by putting forward another statement like it, or by putting forward a statement contrary to it, or by quoting previous decisions.

1. By "attacking your opponent's own statement" I mean, for instance, this: if his enthymeme should assert that love is always good, the objection can be brought in two ways, either by making the general statement that "all want is an evil," or by making the particular one that there would be no talk of "Caunian love" if there were not evil loves as well as good ones.

2. An objection "from a contrary statement" is raised when, for instance, the opponent's enthymeme having concluded that a good man does good to all his friends, you object, "That proves nothing, for a bad man does not do evil to all his friends."

3. An example of an objection "from a like statement" is, the enthymeme having shown that ill-used men always hate their ill-users, to reply, "That proves nothing, for well-used men do not always love those who used them well."

4. The "decisions" mentioned are those proceeding from well-known men; for instance, if the enthymeme employed has concluded that "that allowance ought to be made for drunken offenders, since they did not know what they were doing," the objection will be, "Pittacus, then, deserves no approval, or he would not have prescribed specially severe penalties for offenses due to drunkenness."

Enthymemes are based upon one or other of four kinds of alleged fact: (1) Probabilities, (2) Examples, (3) Infallible Signs, (4) Ordinary Signs. (1) Enthymemes based upon Probabilities are those which argue from what is, or is supposed to be, usually true. (2) Enthymemes based upon Example are those which proceed by induction from one or more similar cases, arrive at a general proposition, and then argue deductively to a particular inference. (3) Enthymemes based upon Infallible Signs are those which argue from the inevitable and invariable. (4) Enthymemes based upon Ordinary Signs are those which argue from some universal or particular proposition, true or false.

Now (1) as a Probability is that which happens usually but not always, Enthymemes founded upon Probabilities can, it is clear, always be refuted by raising some objection. The refutation is not always genuine: it may be spurious: for it consists in showing not that your opponent's premise is not probable, but only in showing that it is not inevitably true. Hence it is always in defense rather than in accusation that it is possible to gain an advantage by using this fallacy. For the accuser uses probabilities to prove his case: and to refute a conclusion as improbable is not the same thing as to refute it as not inevitable. Any argument based upon what usually happens is always open to objection: otherwise it would not be a probability but an invariable and necessary truth. But the judges think, if the refutation takes this form, either that the accuser's case is not probable or that they must not decide it; which, as we said, is a false piece of reasoning. For they ought to decide by considering not merely what must be true but also what is likely to be true: this is, indeed, the meaning of "giving a verdict in accordance with one's honest opinion." Therefore it is not enough for the defendant to refute the accusation by proving that the charge is not hound to be true: he must do so by showing that it is not likely to be true. For this purpose his objection must state what is more usually true than the statement attacked. It may do so in either of two ways: either in respect of frequency or in respect of exactness. It will be most convincing if it does so in both respects; for if the thing in question both happens oftener as we represent it and happens more as we represent it, the probability is particularly great.

(2) Fallible Signs, and Enthymemes based upon them, can be refuted even if the facts are correct, as was said at the outset. For we have shown in the Analytics that no Fallible Sign can form part of a valid logical proof.

(3) Enthymemes depending on Examples may be refuted in the same way as Probabilities. If we have a negative instance, the argument is refuted, in so far as it is proved not inevitable, even though the positive examples are more similar and more frequent. And if the positive examples are more numerous and more frequent, we must contend that the present case is dissimilar, or that its conditions are dissimilar, or that it is different in some way or other.

(4) It will be impossible to refute Infallible Signs, and Enthymemes resting on them, by showing in any way that they do not form a valid logical proof: this, too, we see from the Analytics. All we can do is to show that the fact alleged does not exist. If there is no doubt that it does, and that it is an Infallible Sign, refutation now becomes impossible: for this is equivalent to a demonstration which is clear in every respect.

Part XXVI

Amplification and Depreciation are not an element of Enthymeme. By "an element of enthymeme" I mean the same thing as a line of enthymematic argument—a general class embracing a large number of particular kinds of Enthymeme. Amplification and Depreciation are one kind of Enthymeme, viz. the kind used to show that a thing is great or small; just as there are other kinds used to show that a thing is good or bad, just or unjust, and anything else of the sort. All these things are the subject matter of syllogisms and enthymemes; none of these is the line of argument of an

Enthymeme; no more, therefore, are Amplification and Depreciation. Nor are Refutative Enthymemes a different species from Constructive. For it is clear that refutation consists either in offering positive proof or in raising an objection. In the first case we prove the opposite of our adversary's statements. Thus, if he shows that a thing has happened, we show that it has not; if he shows that it has not happened, we show that it has. This, then, could not be the distinction if there were one, since the same means are employed by both parties, Enthymemes being adduced to show that the fact is or is not so-and-so. An objection, on the other hand, is not an Enthymeme at all, as was said in the Topics, consists in stating some accepted opinion from which it will be clear that our opponent has not reasoned correctly or has made a false assumption.

Three points must be studied in making a speech; and we have now completed the account of (1) Examples, Maxims, Enthymemes, and in general the thought-element the way to invent and refute arguments. We have next to discuss (2) Style, and (3) Arrangement.

BOOK III

Part I

In making a speech one must study three points: first, the means of producing persuasion; second, the style, or language, to be used; third, the proper arrangement of the various parts of the speech. We have already specified the sources of persuasion. We have shown that these are three in number; what they are; and why there are only these three: for we have shown that persuasion must in every case be effected either (1) by working on the emotions of the judges themselves, (2) by giving them the right impression of the speakers' character, or (3) by proving the truth of the statements made.

Enthymemes also have been described, and the sources from which they should be derived; there being both special and general lines of argument for enthymemes.

Our next subject will be the style of expression. For it is not enough to know what we ought to say; we must also say it as we ought; much help is thus afforded toward producing the right impression of a speech. The first question to receive attention was naturally the one that comes first naturally—how persuasion can be produced from the facts themselves.

The second is how to set these facts out in language. A third would be the proper method of delivery; this is a thing that affects the success of a speech greatly; but hitherto the subject has been neglected. Indeed, it was long before it found a way into the arts of tragic drama and epic recitation: at first poets acted their tragedies themselves. It is plain that delivery has just as much to do with oratory as with poetry. (In connection with poetry, it has been studied by Glaucon of Teos among others.) It is, essentially, a matter of the right management of the voice to express the various emotions—of speaking loudly, softly, or between the two; of high, low, or intermediate pitch; of the various rhythms that suit various subjects. These are the three things—volume of sound, modulation of pitch, and rhythm—that a speaker bears in mind. It is those who do bear them in mind who usually win prizes in the dramatic contests; and just as in drama the actors now count for more than the poets, so it is in the contests of public life, owing to the defects of our political institutions. No systematic treatise upon the rules of delivery has yet been composed; indeed, even the study of language made no progress till late in the day. Besides, delivery is—very properly—not regarded as an elevated subject of inquiry. Still, the whole business of rhetoric being concerned with appearances, we must pay attention to the subject of delivery, unworthy though it is, because we cannot do without it. The right thing in speaking really is that we should be satisfied not to annoy our hearers, without trying to delight them: we ought in fairness to fight our case with no help beyond the bare facts: nothing, therefore, should matter except the proof of those facts. Still, as has been already said, other things affect the result considerably, owing to the defects of our hearers. The arts of language cannot help having a small but real importance, whatever it is we have to expound to others: the way in which a thing is said does affect its intelligibility. Not, however, so much importance as people think. All such arts are fanciful and meant to charm the hearer. Nobody uses fine language when teaching geometry.

When the principles of delivery have been worked out, they will produce the same effect as on the stage. But only very slight attempts to deal with them have been made and by a few people, as by Thrasymachus in his "Appeals to Pity." Dramatic ability is a natural gift, and can hardly be systematically taught. The principles of good diction can be so taught, and therefore we have men of ability in this direction too, who win prizes in their turn, as well as those speakers who excel in delivery—speeches of the written or literary kind owe more of their effect to their direction than to their thought.

It was naturally the poets who first set the movement going; for words represent things, and they had also the human voice at their disposal, which of all our organs can best represent other things. Thus the arts of recitation and acting were formed, and others as well. Now it was because poets seemed to win fame through their fine language when their thoughts were simple enough, that the language of oratorical prose at first took a poetical color, e.g. that of Gorgias. Even now most uneducated people think that poetical language makes the finest discourses. That is not true: the language of prose is distinct from that of poetry. This is shown by the state of things today, when even the language of tragedy has altered its character. Just as iambics were adopted, instead of tetrameters, because they are the most prose-like of all meters, so tragedy has given up all those words, not used in ordinary talk, which decorated the early drama and are still used by the writers of hexameter poems. It is therefore ridiculous to imitate a poetical manner which the poets themselves have dropped; and it is now plain that we have not to treat in detail the whole question of style, but may confine ourselves to that part of it which concerns our present subject, rhetoric. The other—the poetical—part of it has been discussed in the treatise on the Art of Poetry.

Part II

We may, then, start from the observations there made, including the definition of style. Style to be good must be clear, as is proved by the fact that speech which fails to convey a plain meaning will fail to do just what speech has to do. It must also be appropriate, avoiding both meanness and undue elevation; poetical language is certainly free from meanness, but it is not appropriate to prose. Clearness is secured by using the words (nouns and verbs alike) that are current and ordinary. Freedom from meanness, and positive adornment too, are secured by using the other words mentioned in the Art of Poetry. Such variation from what is usual makes the language appear more stately. People do not feel toward strangers as they do toward their own countrymen, and the same thing is true of their feeling for language. It is therefore well to give to everyday speech an unfamiliar air: people like what strikes them, and are struck by what is out of the way. In verse such effects are common, and there they are fitting: the persons and things there spoken of are comparatively remote from ordinary life. In prose passages they are far less often fitting because the subject matter is less exalted. Even in poetry, it is not quite appropriate that fine language should be used by a slave or a very young man, or about very trivial subjects: even in poetry the style, to be appropriate, must sometimes be toned down, though at other times heightened. We can now see that a writer must disguise his art and give the impression of speaking naturally and not artificially. Naturalness is persuasive, artificiality is the contrary; for our hearers are prejudiced and think we have some design against them, as if we were mixing their wines for them. It is like the difference between the quality of Theodorus's voice and the voices of all other actors: his really seems to be that of the character who is speaking, theirs do not. We can hide our purpose successfully by taking the single words of our composition from the speech of ordinary life. This is done in poetry by Euripides, who was the first to show the way to his successors.

Language is composed of nouns and verbs. Nouns are of the various kinds considered in the treatise on Poetry. Strange words, compound words, and invented words must be used sparingly and on few occasions: on what occasions we shall state later. The reason for this restriction has been already indicated: they depart from what is suitable, in the direction of excess. In the language of prose, besides the regular and proper terms for things, metaphorical terms only can be used with advantage. This we gather from the fact that these two classes of terms, the proper or regular and the metaphorical—these and no others—are used by everybody in conversation. We can now see that a good writer can produce a style that is distinguished without being obtrusive, and is at the same time clear, thus satisfying our definition of good oratorical prose. Words of ambiguous meaning are chiefly useful to enable the sophist to mislead his hearers. Synonyms are useful to the poet, by which I mean words whose ordinary meaning is the same, e.g. "porheueseai" (advancing) and "badizein" (proceeding); these two are ordinary words and have the same meaning.

In the Art of Poetry, as we have already said, will be found definitions of these kinds of words; a classification of Metaphors; and mention of the fact that metaphor is of great value both in poetry and in prose. Prose writers must, however, pay specially careful attention to metaphor, because their other resources are scantier than those of poets. Metaphor, moreover, gives style clearness, charm, and distinction as nothing else can: and it is not a thing whose use can be taught by one man to another. Metaphors, like epithets, must be fitting, which means that they must fairly correspond to the thing signified: failing this, their inappropriateness will be conspicuous: the want of harmony between two things is emphasized by their being placed side by side. It is like having to ask ourselves what dress will suit an old man; certainly not the crimson cloak that suits a young man. And if you wish to pay a compliment, you must take your metaphor from something better in the same line; if to disparage, from something worse. To illustrate my meaning: since opposites are in the same class, you do what I have suggested if you say that a man who begs "prays," and a man who prays "begs"; for praying and begging are both varieties of asking. So Iphicrates called Callias a "mendicant priest" instead of a "torch-bearer," and Callias replied that Iphicrates must be uninitiated or he would have called him not a "mendicant priest" but a "torch-bearer." Both are religious titles, but one is honorable and the other is not. Again, somebody calls actors "hangers-on of Dionysus," but they call themselves "artists": each of these terms is a metaphor, the one intended to throw dirt at the actor, the other to dignify him. And pirates now call themselves "purveyors." We can thus call a crime a mistake, or a mistake a crime. We can say that a thief "took" a thing, or that he "plundered" his victim. An expression like that of Euripides" Telephus,

> "King of the oar, on Mysia's coast he landed,"

is inappropriate; the word "king" goes beyond the dignity of the subject, and so the art is not concealed. A metaphor may be amiss because the very syllables of the words conveying it fail to indicate sweetness of vocal utterance. Thus Dionysius the Brazen in his elegies calls poetry "Calliope's screech." Poetry and screeching are both, to be sure, vocal utterances. But the metaphor is bad, because the sounds of "screeching," unlike those of poetry, are discordant and unmeaning. Further, in using metaphors to give names to nameless things, we must draw them not from remote but from kindred and similar things, so that the kinship is clearly perceived as soon as the words are said. Thus in the celebrated riddle

> "I marked how a man glued bronze with fire to another man's body,"

the process is nameless; but both it and gluing are a kind of application, and that is why the application of the cupping-glass is here called a "gluing." Good riddles do, in general, provide us with satisfactory metaphors: for metaphors imply riddles, and therefore a good riddle can furnish a good metaphor. Further, the materials of metaphors must be beautiful; and the beauty, like the ugliness, of all words may, as Licymnius says, lie in their sound or in their meaning. Further, there is a third consideration—one that upsets the fallacious argument of the sophist Bryson, that there is no such thing as foul language, because in whatever words you put a given thing your meaning is the same. This is untrue. One term may describe a thing more truly than another, may be more like it, and set it more intimately before our eyes. Besides, two different words will represent a thing in two different lights; so on this ground also one term must be held fairer or fouler than another. For both of two terms will indicate what is fair, or what is foul, but not simply their fairness or their foulness, or if so, at any rate not in an equal degree. The materials of metaphor must be beautiful to the ear, to the understanding, to the eye or some other physical sense. It is better, for instance, to say "rosy-fingered morn," than "crimson-fingered" or, worse still, "red-fingered morn." The epithets that we apply, too, may have a bad and ugly aspect, as when Orestes is called a "mother-slayer"; or a better one, as when he is called his "father's avenger." Simonides, when the victor in the mule race offered him a small fee, refused to write him an ode, because, he said, it was so unpleasant to write odes to half-asses: but on receiving an adequate fee, he wrote

"Hail to you, daughters of storm-footed steeds?"

though of course they were daughters of asses too. The same effect is attained by the use of diminutives, which make a bad thing less bad and a good thing less good. Take, for instance, the banter of Aristophanes in the Babylonians where he uses "goldlet" for "gold," "cloaklet" for "cloak," "scoffiet" for "scoff, and "plaguelet." But alike in using epithets and in using diminutives we must be wary and must observe the mean.

Part III

Bad taste in language may take any of four forms: (1) The misuse of compound words. Lycophron, for instance, talks of the "many visaged heaven" above the "giant-crested earth," and again the "straight-pathed shore"; and Gorgias of the "pauper-poet flatterer" and "oath-breaking and over-oath-keeping." Alcidamas uses such expressions as "the soul filling with rage and face becoming flame-flushed," and "he thought their enthusiasm would be issue-fraught" and "issue-fraught he made the persuasion of his words," and "sombre-hued is the floor of the sea." The way all these words are compounded makes them, we feel, fit for verse only. This, then, is one form in which bad taste is shown.

(2) Another is the employment of strange words. For instance, Lycophron talks of "the prodigious Xerxes" and "spoliative Sciron"; Alcidamas of "a toy for poetry" and "the witlessness of nature," and says

"whetted with the unmitigated temper of his spirit."

(3) A third form is the use of long, unseasonable, or frequent epithets. It is appropriate enough for a poet to talk of "white milk," in prose such epithets are sometimes lacking in appropriateness or, when spread too thickly, plainly reveal the author turning his prose into poetry. Of course we must use some epithets, since they lift our style above the usual level and give it an air of distinction. But we must aim at the due mean, or the result will be worse than if we took no trouble at all; we shall get something actually bad instead of something merely not good. That is why the epithets of Alcidamas seem so tasteless; he does not use them as the seasoning of the meat, but as the meat itself, so numerous and swollen and aggressive are they. For instance, he does not say "sweat," but "the moist sweat"; not "to the Isthmian games," but "to the world—concourse of the Isthmian games"; not "laws," but "the laws that are monarchs of states"; not "at a run," but "his heart impelling him to speed of foot"; not "a school of the Muses," but "Nature's school of the Muses had he inherited"; and so "frowning care of heart," and "achiever" not of "popularity" but of "universal popularity," and "dispenser of pleasure to his audience," and "he concealed it" not "with boughs" but "with boughs of the forest trees," and "he clothed" not "his body" but "his body's nakedness," and "his soul's desire was counter imitative" (this's at one and the same time a compound and an epithet, so that it seems a poet's effort), and "so extravagant the excess of his wickedness." We thus see how the inappropriateness of such poetical language imports absurdity and tastelessness into speeches, as well as the obscurity that comes from all this verbosity—for when the sense is plain, you only obscure and spoil its clearness by piling up words.

The ordinary use of compound words is where there is no term for a thing and some compound can be easily formed, like "pastime" (chronotribein); but if this is much done, the prose character disappears entirely. We now see why the language of compounds is just the thing for writers of dithyrambs, who love sonorous noises; strange words for writers of epic poetry, which is a proud and stately affair; and metaphor for iambic verse, the meter which (as has been already said) is widely used today.

(4) There remains the fourth region in which bad taste may be shown, metaphor. Metaphors like other things may be inappropriate. Some are so because they are ridiculous; they are indeed used by comic as well as tragic poets. Others are too grand and theatrical; and these, if they are far-fetched, may also be obscure. For instance, Gorgias talks of "events that are green and full of sap," and says "foul was the deed you sowed and evil

the harvest you reaped." That is too much like poetry. Alcidamas, again, called philosophy "a fortress that threatens the power of law," and the Odyssey "a goodly looking-glass of human life," talked about "offering no such toy to poetry": all these expressions fail, for the reasons given, to carry the hearer with them. The address of Gorgias to the swallow, when she had let her droppings fall on him as she flew overhead, is in the best tragic manner. He said, "Nay, shame, O Philomela." Considering her as a bird, you could not call her act shameful; considering her as a girl, you could; and so it was a good gibe to address her as what she was once and not as what she is.

Part IV

The Simile also is a metaphor; the difference is but slight. When the poet says of Achilles that he

"Leapt on the foe as a lion,"

this is a simile; when he says of him "the lion leapt," it is a metaphor—here, since both are courageous, he has transferred to Achilles the name of "lion." Similes are useful in prose as well as in verse; but not often, since they are of the nature of poetry. They are to be employed just as metaphors are employed, since they are really the same thing except for the difference mentioned.

The following are examples of similes. Androtion said of Idrieus that he was like a terrier let off the chain, that flies at you and bites you—Idrieus too was savage now that he was let out of his chains. Theodamas compared Archidamus to an Euxenus who could not do geometry—a proportional simile, implying that Euxenus is an Archidamus who can do geometry. In Plato's Republic those who strip the dead are compared to curs which bite the stones thrown at them but do not touch the thrower, and there is the simile about the Athenian people, who are compared to a ship's captain who is strong but a little deaf; and the one about poets' verses, which are likened to persons who lack beauty but possess youthful freshness—when the freshness has faded the charm perishes, and so with verses when broken up into prose. Pericles compared the Samians to children who take their pap but go on crying; and the Boeotians to holm-oaks, because they were ruining one another by civil wars just as one oak causes another oak's fall. Demosthenes said that the Athenian people were like seasick men on board ship. Again, Demosthenes compared the political orators to nurses who swallow the bit of food themselves and then smear the children's lips with the spittle. Antisthenes compared the lean Cephisodotus to frankincense, because it was his consumption that gave one pleasure. All these ideas may be expressed either as similes or as metaphors; those which succeed as metaphors will obviously do well also as similes, and similes, with the explanation omitted, will appear as metaphors. But the proportional metaphor must always apply reciprocally to either of its coordinate terms. For instance, if a drinking-bowl is the shield of Dionysus, a shield may fittingly be called the drinking-bowl of Ares.

Part V

Such, then, are the ingredients of which speech is composed. The foundation of good style is correctness of language, which falls under five heads. (1) First, the proper use of connecting words, and the arrangement of them in the natural sequence which some of them require. For instance, the connective "men" (e.g. ego men) requires the correlative de (e.g. o de). The answering word must be brought in before the first has been forgotten, and not be widely separated from it; nor, except in the few cases where this is appropriate, is another connective to be introduced before the one required. Consider the sentence, "But as soon as he told me (for Cleon had come begging and praying), took them along and set out." In this sentence many connecting words are inserted in front of the one required to complete the sense; and if there is a long interval before "set out," the result is obscurity. One merit, then, of good style lies in the right use of connecting words. (2) The second lies in calling things by their own special names and not by vague general ones. (3) The third is to avoid ambiguities; unless, indeed, you definitely desire to be ambiguous, as those do who have nothing to say but are pretending to mean something. Such people are apt to put that sort of thing into verse. Empedocles, for instance, by his long circumlocutions imposes on his hearers; these are affected in the same way as most people are when they listen to diviners, whose ambiguous utterances are received with nods of acquiescence—

"Croesus by crossing the Halys will ruin a mighty realm."

Diviners use these vague generalities about the matter in hand because their predictions are thus, as a rule, less likely to be falsified. We are more likely to be right, in the game of "odd and even," if we simply guess "even" or "odd" than if we guess at the actual number; and the oracle-monger is more likely to be right if he simply says that a thing will happen than if he says when it will happen, and therefore he refuses to add a definite date. All these ambiguities have the same sort of effect, and are to be avoided unless we have some such object as that mentioned. (4) A fourth rule is to observe Protagoras" classification of nouns into male, female, and inanimate; for these distinctions also must be correctly given. "Upon her arrival she said her say and departed (e d elthousa kai dialechtheisa ocheto)." (5) A fifth rule is to express plurality, fewness, and unity by the correct wording, e.g. "Having come, they struck me (oi d elthontes etupton me)."

It is a general rule that a written composition should be easy to read and therefore easy to deliver. This cannot be so where there are many connecting words or clauses, or where punctuation is hard, as in the writings of Heracleitus. To punctuate Heracleitus is no easy task, because we often cannot tell whether a particular word belongs to what precedes or what follows it. Thus, at the outset of his treatise he says, "Though this truth is always men understand it not," where it is not clear with which of the two clauses the word "always" should be joined by the punctuation. Further, the following fact leads to solecism, viz. that the sentence does not work out properly if you annex to two terms a third which does not suit them both. Thus either "sound" or "color" will fail to work out properly with some verbs: "perceive" will apply to both, "see" will not. Obscurity is also caused if, when you intend to insert a number of details, you do not first make your meaning clear; for instance, if you say, "I meant, after telling him this, that and the other thing, to set out," rather than something of this kind "I meant to set out after telling him; then this, that, and the other thing occurred."

Part VI

The following suggestions will help to give your language impressiveness. (1) Describe a thing instead of naming it: do not say "circle," but "that surface which extends equally from the middle every way." To achieve conciseness, do the opposite—put the name instead of the description. When mentioning anything ugly or unseemly, use its name if it is the description that is ugly, and describe it if it is the name that is ugly. (2) Represent things with the help of metaphors and epithets, being careful to avoid poetical effects. (3) Use plural for singular, as in poetry, where one finds

"Unto havens Achaean,"

though only one haven is meant, and

"Here are my letter's many-leaved folds."

(4) Do not bracket two words under one article, but put one article with each; e.g. "that wife of ours." The reverse to secure conciseness; e.g. "our wife." Use plenty of connecting words; conversely, to secure conciseness, dispense with connectives, while still preserving connection; e.g. "having gone and spoken," and "having gone, I spoke," respectively. (6) And the practice of Antimachus, too, is useful—to describe a thing by mentioning attributes it does not possess, as he does in talking of Teumessus:

"There is a little wind-swept knoll..."

A subject can be developed indefinitely along these lines. You may apply this method of treatment by negation either to good or to bad qualities, according to which your subject requires. It is from this source that the poets draw expressions such as the "stringless" or "lyreless" melody, thus forming epithets out of negations. This device is popular in proportional metaphors, as when the trumpet's note is called "a lyreless melody."

Part VII

Your language will be appropriate if it expresses emotion and character, and if it corresponds to its subject. "Correspondence to subject" means that we must neither speak casually about weighty matters, nor solemnly about trivial ones; nor must we add ornamental epithets to commonplace nouns, or the effect will be comic, as in the works of Cleophon, who can use phrases as absurd as "O queenly fig tree." To express emotion, you will employ the language of anger in speaking of outrage; the language of disgust and discreet reluctance to utter a word when speaking of impiety or foulness; the language of exultation for a tale of glory, and that of humiliation for a tale of and so in all other cases.

This aptness of language is one thing that makes people believe in the truth of your story: their minds draw the false conclusion that you are to be trusted from the fact that others behave as you do when things are as you describe them; and therefore they take your story to be true, whether it is so or not. Besides, an emotional speaker always makes his audience feel with him, even when there is nothing in his arguments; which is why many speakers try to overwhelm their audience by mere noise.

Furthermore, this way of proving your story by displaying these signs of its genuineness expresses your personal character. Each class of men, each type of disposition, will have its own appropriate way of letting the truth appear. Under "class" I include differences of age, as boy, man, or old man; of sex, as man or woman; of nationality, as Spartan or Thessalian.

By "dispositions" I here mean those dispositions only which determine the character of a man's for it is not every disposition that does this. If, then, a speaker uses the very words which are in keeping with a particular disposition, he will reproduce the corresponding character; for a rustic and an educated man will not say the same things nor speak in the same way. Again, some impression is made upon an audience by a device which speechwriters employ to nauseous excess, when they say "Who does not know this?" or "It is known to everybody." The hearer is ashamed of his ignorance, and agrees with the speaker, so as to have a share of the knowledge that everybody else possesses.

All the variations of oratorical style are capable of being used in season or out of season. The best way to counteract any exaggeration is the well-worn device by which the speaker puts in some criticism of himself; for then people feel it must be all right for him to talk thus, since he certainly knows what he is doing. Further, it is better not to have everything always just corresponding to everything else—your hearers will see through you less easily thus. I mean for instance, if your words are harsh, you should not extend this harshness to your voice and your countenance and have everything else in keeping. If you do, the artificial character of each detail becomes apparent; whereas if you adopt one device and not another, you are using art all the same and yet nobody notices it. (To be sure, if mild sentiments are expressed in harsh tones and harsh sentiments in mild tones, you become comparatively unconvincing.) Compound words, fairly plentiful epithets, and strange words best suit an emotional speech. We forgive an angry man for talking about a wrong as "heaven-high" or "colossal"; and we excuse such language when the speaker has his hearers already in his hands and has stirred them deeply either by praise or blame or anger or affection, as Isocrates, for instance, does at the end of his Panegyric, with his "name and fame" and "in that they brooked." Men do speak in this strain when they are deeply stirred, and so, once the audience is in a like state of feeling, approval of course follows. This is why such language is fitting in poetry, which is an inspired thing. This language, then, should be used either under stress of emotion, or ironically, after the manner of Gorgias and of the passages in the Phaedrus.

Part VIII

The form of a prose composition should be neither metrical nor destitute of rhythm. The metrical form destroys the hearer's trust by its artificial appearance, and at the same time it diverts his attention, making him watch for metrical recurrences, just as children catch up the herald's question, "Whom does the freedman choose as his advocate?", with the answer "Cleon!" On the other hand, unrhythmical language is too unlimited; we do not want the limitations of meter, but some limitation we must have, or the effect will be vague and unsatisfactory. Now it is number that limits all things; and it is the numerical limitation of the forms of a composition that constitutes rhythm, of which meters are definite sections. Prose, then, is to be rhythmical, but not metrical, or it will become not prose but verse. It should not even have too precise a prose rhythm, and therefore should only be rhythmical to a certain extent.

Of the various rhythms, the heroic has dignity, but lacks the tones of the spoken language. The iambic is the very language of ordinary people, so that in common talk iambic lines occur oftener than any others: but in a speech we need dignity and the power of taking the hearer out of his ordinary self. The trochee is too much akin to wild dancing: we can see this in tetrameter verse, which is one of the trochaic rhythms.

There remains the paean, which speakers began to use in the time of Thrasymachus, though they had then no name to give it. The paean is a third class of rhythm, closely akin to both the two already mentioned; it has in it the ratio of three to two, whereas the other two kinds have the ratio of one to one, and two to one respectively. Between the two last ratios comes the ratio of one-and-a-half to one, which is that of the paean.

Now the other two kinds of rhythm must be rejected in writing prose, partly for the reasons given, and partly because they are too metrical; and the paean must be adopted, since from this alone of the rhythms mentioned no definite meter arises, and therefore it is the least obtrusive of them. At present the same form of paean is employed at the beginning a at the end of sentences, whereas the end should differ from the beginning. There are two opposite kinds of paean, one of which is suitable to the beginning of a sentence, where it is indeed actually used; this is the kind that begins with a long syllable and ends with three short ones, as

"Dalogenes | eite Luki | an,"

and

"Chruseokom | a Ekate | pai Dios."

The other paean begins, conversely, with three short syllables and ends with a long one, as

"meta de lan | udata t ok | eanon e | oanise nux."

This kind of paean makes a real close: a short syllable can give no effect of finality, and therefore makes the rhythm appear truncated. A sentence should break off with the long syllable: the fact that it is over should be indicated not by the scribe, or by his period-mark in the margin, but by the rhythm itself.

We have now seen that our language must be rhythmical and not destitute of rhythm, and what rhythms, in what particular shape, make it so.

Part IX

The language of prose must be either free-running, with its parts united by nothing except the connecting words, like the preludes in dithyrambs; or compact and antithetical, like the strophes of the old poets. The free-running style is the ancient one, e.g. "Herein is set forth the inquiry of Herodotus the Thurian." Every one used this method formerly; not many do so now. By "free-running" style I mean the kind that has no natural stopping places, and comes to a stop only because there is no more to say of that subject. This style is unsatisfying just because it goes on indefinitely—one always likes to sight a stopping place in front of one: it is only at the goal that men in a race faint and collapse; while they see the end of the course before them, they can keep on going. Such, then, is the free-running kind of style; the compact is that which is in periods. By a period I mean a portion of speech that has in itself a beginning and an end, being at the same time not too big to be taken in at a glance. Language of this kind is satisfying and easy to follow. It is satisfying, because it is just the reverse of indefinite; and moreover, the hearer always feels that he is grasping something and has reached some definite conclusion; whereas it is unsatisfactory to see nothing in front of you and get nowhere. It is easy to follow, because it can easily be remembered; and this because language when in periodic form can be numbered, and number is the easiest of all things to remember. That is why verse, which is measured, is always more easily remembered than prose, which is not: the measures of verse can be numbered. The period must, further, not be completed until the sense is complete: it must not be capable of breaking off abruptly, as may happen with the following iambic lines of Sophocles—

> "Calydon's soil is this; of Pelops" land
> (The smiling plains face us across the strait.)"

By a wrong division of the words the hearer may take the meaning to be the reverse of what it is: for instance, in the passage quoted, one might imagine that Calydon is in the Peloponnesus.

A Period may be either divided into several members or simple. The period of several members is a portion of speech (1) complete in itself, (2) divided into parts, and (3) easily delivered at a single breath—as a whole, that is; not by fresh breath being taken at the division. A member is one of the two parts of such a period. By a "simple" period, I mean that which has only one member. The members, and the whole periods, should be neither curt nor long. A member which is too short often makes the listener stumble; he is still expecting the rhythm to go on to the limit his mind has fixed for it; and if meanwhile he is pulled back by the speaker's stopping, the shock is bound to make him, so to speak, stumble. If, on the other hand, you go on too long, you make him feel left behind, just as people who when walking pass beyond the boundary before turning back leave their companions behind So too if a period is too long you turn it into a speech, or something like a dithyrambic prelude. The result is much like the preludes that Democritus of Chios jeered at Melanippides for writing instead of antistrophic stanzas—

> "He that sets traps for another man's feet
> Is like to fall into them first;
> And long-winded preludes do harm to us all,
> But the preluder catches it worst."

Which applies likewise to long-membered orators. Periods whose members are altogether too short are not periods at all; and the result is to bring the hearer down with a crash.

The periodic style which is divided into members is of two kinds. It is either simply divided, as in "I have often wondered at the conveners of national gatherings and the founders of athletic contests"; or it is antithetical, where, in each of the two members, one of one pair of opposites is put along with one of another pair, or the same word is used to bracket two opposites, as "They aided both parties—not only those who stayed behind but those who accompanied them: for the latter they acquired new territory larger than that at home, and to the former they left territory at home that was large enough." Here the contrasted words are "staying behind" and "accompanying," "enough" and "larger." So in the example, "Both to those who want to get property and to those who desire to enjoy it" where "enjoyment" is contrasted with "getting." Again, "it often happens in such enterprises that the wise men fail and the fools succeed"; "they were awarded the prize of valour immediately, and won the command of the sea not long afterward"; "to sail through the mainland and march through the sea, by bridging the Hellespont and cutting through Athos"; "nature gave them their country and law took it away again"; "of them perished in misery, others were saved in disgrace"; "Athenian citizens keep foreigners in their houses as servants, while the city of Athens allows her allies by thousands to live as the foreigner's slaves"; and "to possess in life or to bequeath at death." There is also what someone said about Peitholaus and Lycophron in a law court, "These men used to sell you when they were at home, and now they have come to you here and bought you." All these passages have the structure described above. Such a form of speech is satisfying, because the significance of contrasted ideas is easily felt, especially when they are thus put side by side, and also because it has the effect of a logical argument; it is by putting two opposing conclusions side by side that you prove one of them false.

Such, then, is the nature of antithesis. Parisosis is making the two members of a period equal in length. Paromoeosis is making the extreme words of both members like each other. This must happen either at the beginning or at the end of each member. If at the beginning, the resemblance must always be between whole words; at the end, between final syllables or inflections of the same word or the same word repeated. Thus, at the beginning

> "agron gar elaben arlon par' autou"

and

> "dorhetoi t epelonto pararretoi t epeessin".

At the end

> "ouk wethesan auton paidion tetokenai,
> all autou aitlon lelonenai";

and

> "en pleiotals de opontisi kai en elachistais elpisin".

An example of inflections of the same word is

> "axios de staoenai chalkous ouk axios on chalkou";

of the same word repeated,

"su d' auton kai zonta eleges kakos kai nun grafeis kakos";

of one syllable,

"ti d' an epaoes deinon, ei andrh' eides arhgon".

It is possible for the same sentence to have all these features together—antithesis, parison, and homoeoteleuton. (The possible beginnings of periods have been pretty fully enumerated in the Theodectea.) There are also spurious antitheses, like that of Epicharmus—

"There one time I as their guest did stay,
And they were my hosts on another day."

Part X

We may now consider the above points settled, and pass on to say something about the way to devise lively and taking sayings. Their actual invention can only come through natural talent or long practice; but this treatise may indicate the way it is done. We may deal with them by enumerating the different kinds of them. We will begin by remarking that we all naturally find it agreeable to get hold of new ideas easily: words express ideas, and therefore those words are the most agreeable that enable us to get hold of new ideas. Now strange words simply puzzle us; ordinary words convey only what we know already; it is from metaphor that we can best get hold of something fresh. When the poet calls "old age a withered stalk," he conveys a new idea, a new fact, to us by means of the general notion of bloom, which is common to both things. The similes of the poets do the same, and therefore, if they are good similes, give an effect of brilliance. The simile, as has been said before, is a metaphor, differing from it only in the way it is put; and just because it is longer it is less attractive. Besides, it does not say outright that "this" is "that," and therefore the hearer is less interested in the idea. We see, then, that both speech and reasoning are lively in proportion as they make us seize a new idea promptly. For this reason people are not much taken either by obvious arguments (using the word "obvious" to mean what is plain to everybody and needs no investigation), nor by those which puzzle us when we hear them stated, but only by those which convey their information to us as soon as we hear them, provided we had not the information already; or which the mind only just fails to keep up with. These two kinds do convey to us a sort of information: but the obvious and the obscure kinds convey nothing, either at once or later on. It is these qualities, then, that, so far as the meaning of what is said is concerned, make an argument acceptable. So far as the style is concerned, it is the antithetical form that appeals to us, e.g. "judging that the peace common to all the rest was a war upon their own private interests," where there is an antithesis between war and peace. It is also good to use metaphorical words; but the metaphors must not be far-fetched, or they will be difficult to grasp, nor obvious, or they will have no effect. The words, too, ought to set the scene before our eyes; for events ought to be seen in progress rather than in prospect. So we must aim at these three points: Antithesis, Metaphor, and Actuality.

Of the four kinds of Metaphor, the most taking is the proportional kind. Thus Pericles, for instance, said that the vanishing from their country of the young men who had fallen in the war was "as if the spring were taken out of the year." Leptines, speaking of the Lacedaemonians, said that he would not have the Athenians let Greece "lose one of her two eyes." When Chares was pressing for leave to be examined upon his share in the Olynthiac war, Cephisodotus was indignant, saying that he wanted his examination to take place "while he had his fingers upon the people's throat." The same speaker once urged the Athenians to march to Euboea, "with Miltiades' decree as their rations. Iphicrates, indignant at the truce made by the Athenians with Epidaurus and the neighboring seaboard, said that they had stripped themselves of their travelling money for the journey of war. Peitholaus called the state-galley "the people's big stick," and Sestos "the corn-bin of the Peiraeus." Pericles bade his countrymen remove Aegina, "that eyesore of the Peiraeus." And Moerocles said he was no more a rascal than was a certain respectable citizen he named, "whose rascality was worth over thirty per cent per annum to him, instead of a mere ten like his own." There is also the iambic line of Anaxandrides about the way his daughters put off marrying—

"My daughters' marriage-bonds are overdue."

Polyeuctus said of a paralytic man named Speusippus that he could not keep quiet, "though fortune had fastened him in the pillory of disease." Cephisodotus called warships "painted millstones." Diogenes the Dog called taverns "the mess-rooms of Attica." Aesion said that the Athenians had "emptied" their town into Sicily: this is a graphic metaphor. "Till all Hellas shouted aloud" may be regarded as a metaphor, and a graphic one again. Cephisodotus bade the Athenians take care not to hold too many "parades." Isocrates used the same word of those who "parade at the national festivals." Another example occurs in the Funeral Speech: "It is fitting that Greece should cut off her hair beside the tomb of those who fell at Salamis, since her freedom and their valour are buried in the same grave." Even if the speaker here had only said that it was right to weep when valour was being buried in their grave, it would have been a metaphor, and a graphic one; but the coupling of "their valour" and "her freedom" presents a kind of antithesis as well. "The course of my words," said Iphicrates, "lies straight through the middle of Chares' deeds": this is a proportional metaphor, and the phrase "straight through the middle" makes it graphic. The expression "to call in one danger to rescue us from another" is a graphic metaphor. Lycoleon said, defending Chabrias, "They did not respect even that bronze statue of his that intercedes for him yonder." This was a metaphor for the moment, though it would not always apply; a vivid metaphor, however; Chabrias is in danger, and his statue intercedes for him—that lifeless yet living thing which records his services to his country. "Practicing in every way littleness of mind" is metaphorical, for practicing a quality implies increasing it. So is "God kindled our reason to be a lamp within our soul," for both reason and light reveal things. So is "we are not putting an end to our wars, but only postponing them," for both literal postponement and the making of such a peace as this apply to future action. So is such a saying as "This treaty is a far nobler trophy than those we set up on fields of battle; they celebrate small gains and single successes; it celebrates our triumph in the war as a whole"; for both trophy and treaty are signs of victory. So is "A country pays a heavy reckoning in being condemned by the judgement of mankind," for a reckoning is damage deservedly incurred.

Part XI

It has already been mentioned that liveliness is got by using the proportional type of metaphor and being making (ie. making your hearers see things). We have still to explain what we mean by their "seeing things," and what must be done to effect this. By "making them see things" I mean using expressions that represent things as in a state of activity. Thus, to say that a good man is "four-square" is certainly a metaphor; both the good man and the square are perfect; but the metaphor does not suggest activity. On the other hand, in the expression "with his vigor in full bloom" there is a notion of activity; and so in "But you must roam as free as a sacred victim"; and in

> "Thereas up sprang the Hellenes to their feet,"

where "up sprang" gives us activity as well as metaphor, for it at once suggests swiftness. So with Homer's common practice of giving metaphorical life to lifeless things: all such passages are distinguished by the effect of activity they convey. Thus,

> "Downward anon to the valley rebounded the boulder remorseless";

and

> "The (bitter) arrow flew";

and

> "Flying on eagerly";

and

> "Stuck in the earth, still panting to feed on the flesh of the heroes";

and

> "And the point of the spear in its fury drove full through his breastbone."

In all these examples the things have the effect of being active because they are made into living beings; shameless behavior and fury and so on are all forms of activity. And the poet has attached these ideas to the things by means of proportional metaphors: as the stone is to Sisyphus, so is the shameless man to his victim. In his famous similes, too, he treats inanimate things in the same way:

> "Curving and crested with white, host following host without ceasing."

Here he represents everything as moving and living; and activity is movement.

Metaphors must be drawn, as has been said already, from things that are related to the original thing, and yet not obviously so related—just as in philosophy also an acute mind will perceive resemblances even in things far apart. Thus Archytas said that an arbitrator and an altar were the same, since the injured fly to both for refuge. Or you might say that an anchor and an overhead hook were the same, since both are in a way the same, only the one secures things from below and the other from above. And to speak of states as "levelled" is to identify two widely different things, the equality of a physical surface and the equality of political powers.

Liveliness is specially conveyed by metaphor, and by the further power of surprising the hearer; because the hearer expected something different, his acquisition of the new idea impresses him all the more. His mind seems to say, "Yes, to be sure; I never thought of that." The liveliness of epigrammatic remarks is due to the meaning not being just what the words say: as in the saying of Stesichorus that "the cicalas will chirp to themselves on the ground." Well-constructed riddles are attractive for the same reason; a new idea is conveyed, and there is metaphorical expression. So with the "novelties" of Theodorus. In these the thought is startling, and, as Theodorus puts it, does not fit in with the ideas you already have. They are like the burlesque words that one finds in the comic writers. The effect is produced even by jokes depending upon changes of the letters of a word; this too is a surprise. You find this in verse as well as in prose. The word which comes is not what the hearer imagined; thus:

"Onward he came, and his feet were shod with his chilblains,"

where one imagined the word would be "sandals." But the point should be clear the moment the words are uttered. Jokes made by altering the letters of a word consist in meaning, not just what you say, but something that gives a twist to the word used; e.g. the remark of Theodorus about Nicon the harpist Thratt' ei su ("you Thracian slavey"), where he pretends to mean Thratteis su ("you harpplayer"), and surprises us when we find he means something else. So you enjoy the point when you see it, though the remark will fall flat unless you are aware that Nicon is Thracian. Or again: Boulei auton persai. In both these cases the saying must fit the facts. This is also true of such lively remarks as the one to the effect that to the Athenians their empire (arche) of the sea was not the beginning (arche) of their troubles, since they gained by it. Or the opposite one of Isocrates, that their empire (arche) was the beginning (arche) of their troubles. Either way, the speaker says something unexpected, the soundness of which is thereupon recognized. There would be nothing clever is saying "empire is empire." Isocrates means more than that, and uses the word with a new meaning. So too with the former saying, which denies that arche in one sense was arche in another sense. In all these jokes, whether a word is used in a second sense or metaphorically, the joke is good if it fits the facts. For instance, Anaschetos (proper name) ouk anaschetos: where you say that what is so-and-so in one sense is not so-and-so in another; well, if the man is unpleasant, the joke fits the facts. Again, take—

"Thou must not be a stranger stranger than Thou should'st."

Do not the words "thou must not be," etc., amount to saying that the stranger must not always be strange? Here again is the use of one word in different senses. Of the same kind also is the much-praised verse of Anaxandrides:

"Death is most fit before you do
Deeds that would make death fit for you."

This amounts to saying "it is a fit thing to die when you are not fit to die," or "it is a fit thing to die when death is not fit for you," i.e. when death is not the fit return for what you are doing. The type of language employed is the same in all these examples; but the more briefly and antithetically such sayings can be expressed, the more taking they are, for antithesis impresses the new idea more firmly and brevity more quickly. They should always have either some personal application or some merit of expression, if they are to be true without being commonplace—two requirements not always satisfied simultaneously. Thus "a man should die having done no wrong" is true but dull: "the right man should marry the right woman" is also true but dull. No, there must be both good qualities together, as in "it is fitting to die when you are not fit for death." The more a saying has these qualitis, the livelier it appears: if, for instance, its wording is metaphorical, metaphorical in the right way, antithetical, and balanced, and at the same time it gives an idea of activity.

Successful similes also, as has been said above, are in a sense metaphors, since they always involve two relations like the proportional metaphor. Thus: a shield, we say, is the "drinking-bowl of Ares," and a bow is the "chordless lyre." This way of putting a metaphor is not "simple," as it would be if we called the bow a lyre or the shield a drinking-bowl. There are "simple" similes also: we may say that a flute player is like a monkey, or that a shortsighted man's eyes are like a lamp-flame with water dropping on it, since both eyes and flame keep winking. A simile succeeds best when it is a converted metaphor, for it is possible to say that a shield is like the drinking-bowl of Ares, or that a ruin is like a house in rags, and to say that Niceratus is like a Philoctetes stung by Pratys—the simile made by Thrasyniachus when he saw Niceratus, who had been beaten by Pratys in a recitation competition, still going about unkempt and unwashed. It is in these respects that poets fail worst when they fail, and succeed best when they succeed, i.e. when they give the resemblance pat, as in

> "Those legs of his curl just like parsley leaves";

and

> "Just like Philammon struggling with his punchball."

These are all similes; and that similes are metaphors has been stated often already.

Proverbs, again, are metaphors from one species to another. Suppose, for instance, a man to start some undertaking in hope of gain and then to lose by it later on, "Here we have once more the man of Carpathus and his hare," says he. For both alike went through the said experience.

It has now been explained fairly completely how liveliness is secured and why it has the effect it has. Successful hyperboles are also metaphors, e.g. the one about the man with a black eye, "you would have thought he was a basket of mulberries"; here the "black eye" is compared to a mulberry because of its color, the exaggeration lying in the quantity of mulberries suggested. The phrase "like so-and-so" may introduce a hyperbole under the form of a simile. Thus "Just like Philammon struggling with his punchball" is equivalent to "you would have thought he was Philammon struggling with his punchball"; and "Those legs of his curl just like parsley leaves" is equivalent to "his legs are so curly that you would have thought they were not legs but parsley leaves." Hyperboles are for young men to use; they show vehemence of character; and this is why angry people use them more than other people.

> "Not though he gave me as much as the dust
> or the sands of the sea...
> But her, the daughter of Atreus' son, I never will marry,
> Nay, not though she were fairer than Aphrodite the Golden,
> Defter of hand than Athene..."

(The Attic orators are particularly fond of this method of speech.) Consequently it does not suit an elderly speaker.

Part XII

It should be observed that each kind of rhetoric has its own appropriate style. The style of written prose is not that of spoken oratory, nor are those of political and forensic speaking the same. Both written and spoken have to be known. To know the latter is to know how to speak good Greek. To know the former means that you are not obliged, as otherwise you are, to hold your tongue when you wish to communicate something to the general public.

The written style is the more finished: the spoken better admits of dramatic delivery—like the kind of oratory that reflects character and the kind that reflects emotion. Hence actors look out for plays written in the latter style, and poets for actors competent to act in such plays. Yet poets whose plays are meant to be read are read and circulated: Chaeremon, for instance, who is as finished as a professional speechwriter; and Licymnius among the dithyrambic poets. Compared with those of others, the speeches of professional writers sound thin in actual contests. Those of the orators, on the other hand, are good to hear spoken, but look amateurish enough when they pass into the hands of a reader. This is just because they are so well suited for an actual tussle, and therefore contain many dramatic touches, which, being robbed of all dramatic rendering, fail to do their own proper work, and consequently look silly. Thus strings of unconnected words, and constant repetitions of words and phrases, are very properly condemned in written speeches: but not in spoken speeches—speakers use them freely, for they have a dramatic effect. In this repetition there must be variety of tone, paving the way, as it were, to dramatic effect; e.g. "This is the villain among you who deceived you, who cheated you, who meant to betray you completely." This is the sort of thing that Philemon the actor used to do in the Old Men's Madness of Anaxandrides whenever he spoke the words "Rhadamanthus and Palamedes," and also in the prologue to the Saints whenever he pronounced the pronoun "I." If one does not deliver such things cleverly, it becomes a case of "the man who swallowed a poker." So too with strings of unconnected words, e.g. "I came to him; I met him; I besought him." Such passages must be acted, not delivered with the same quality and pitch of voice, as though they had only one idea in them. They have the further peculiarity of suggesting that a number of separate statements have been made in the time usually occupied by one. Just as the use of conjunctions makes many statements into a single one, so the omission of conjunctions acts in the reverse way and makes a single one into many. It thus makes everything more important: e.g. "I came to him; I talked to him; I entreated him"—what a lot of facts! the hearer thinks—"he paid no attention to anything I said." This is the effect which Homer seeks when he writes,

> "Nireus likewise from Syme (three well-fashioned ships did bring),
> Nireus, the son of Aglaia (and Charopus, bright-faced king),
> Nireus, the comeliest man (of all that to Ilium's strand)."

If many things are said about a man, his name must be mentioned many times; and therefore people think that, if his name is mentioned many times, many things have been said about him. So that Homer, by means of this illusion, has made a great deal of though he has mentioned him only in this one passage, and has preserved his memory, though he nowhere says a word about him afterward.

Now the style of oratory addressed to public assemblies is really just like scene-painting. The bigger the throng, the more distant is the point of view: so that, in the one and the other, high finish in detail is superfluous and seems better away. The forensic style is more highly finished; still more so is the style of language addressed to a single judge, with whom there is very little room for rhetorical artifices, since he can take the whole thing in better, and judge of what is to the point and what is not; the struggle is less intense and so the judgement is undisturbed. This is why the same speakers do not distinguish themselves in all these branches at once; high finish is wanted least where dramatic delivery is wanted most, and here the speaker must have a good voice, and above all, a strong one. It is ceremonial oratory that is most literary, for it is meant to be read; and next to it forensic oratory.

To analyse style still further, and add that it must be agreeable or magnificent, is useless; for why should it have these traits any more than "restraint," "liberality," or any other moral excellence? Obviously agreeableness will be produced by the qualities already mentioned, if our definition of excellence of style has been correct. For what other reason should style be "clear," and "not mean" but "appropriate"? If it is prolix, it is not clear; nor yet if it is curt. Plainly the middle way suits best. Again, style will be made agreeable by the elements mentioned, namely by a good blending of ordinary and unusual words, by the rhythm, and by the persuasiveness that springs from appropriateness.

This concludes our discussion of style, both in its general aspects and in its special applications to the various branches of rhetoric. We have now to deal with Arrangement.

Part XIII

A speech has two parts. You must state your case, and you must prove it. You cannot either state your case and omit to prove it, or prove it without having first stated it; since any proof must be a proof of something, and the only use of a preliminary statement is the proof that follows it. Of these two parts the first part is called the Statement of the case, the second part the Argument, just as we distinguish between Enunciation and Demonstration. The current division is absurd. For "narration" surely is part of a forensic speech only: how in a political speech or a speech of display can there be "narration" in the technical sense? or a reply to a forensic opponent? or an epilogue in closely reasoned speeches? Again, introduction, comparison of conflicting arguments, and recapitulation are only found in political speeches when there is a struggle between two policies. They may occur then; so may even accusation and defense, often enough; but they form no essential part of a political speech. Even forensic speeches do not always need epilogues; not, for instance, a short speech, nor one in which the facts are easy to remember, the effect of an epilogue being always a reduction in the apparent length. It follows, then, that the only necessary parts of a speech are the Statement and the Argument. These are the essential features of a speech; and it cannot in any case have more than Introduction, Statement, Argument, and Epilogue. "Refutation of the Opponent" is part of the arguments: so is "Comparison" of the opponent's case with your own, for that process is a magnifying of your own case and therefore a part of the arguments, since one who does this proves something. The Introduction does nothing like this; nor does the Epilogue—it merely reminds us of what has been said already. If we make such distinctions we shall end, like Theodorus and his followers, by distinguishing "narration" proper from "post-narration" and "pre-narration," and "refutation" from "final refutation." But we ought only to bring in a new name if it indicates a real species with distinct specific qualities; otherwise the practice is pointless and silly, like the way Licymnius invented names in his Art of Rhetoric—"Secundation," "Divagation," "Ramification."

Part XIV

The Introduction is the beginning of a speech, corresponding to the prologue in poetry and the prelude in flute music; they are all beginnings, paving the way, as it were, for what is to follow. The musical prelude resembles the introduction to speeches of display; as flute players play first some brilliant passage they know well and then fit it on to the opening notes of the piece itself, so in speeches of display the writer should proceed in the same way; he should begin with what best takes his fancy, and then strike up his theme and lead into it; which is indeed what is always done. (Take as an example the introduction to the Helen of Isocrates—there is nothing in common between the "eristics" and Helen.) And here, even if you travel far from your subject, it is fitting, rather than that there should be sameness in the entire speech.

The usual subject for the introductions to speeches of display is some piece of praise or censure. Thus Gorgias writes in his Olympic Speech, "You deserve widespread admiration, men of Greece," praising thus those who start,ed the festival gatherings." Isocrates, on the other hand, censures them for awarding distinctions to fine athletes but giving no prize for intellectual ability. Or one may begin with a piece of advice, thus: "We ought to honor good men and so I myself am praising Aristeides" or "We ought to honor those who are unpopular but not bad men, men whose good qualities have never been noticed, like Alexander son of Priam." Here the orator gives advice. Or we may begin as speakers do in the law courts; that is to say, with appeals to the audience to excuse us if our speech is about something paradoxical, difficult, or hackneyed; like Choerilus in the lines—

"But now when allotment of all has been made..."

Introductions to speeches of display, then, may be composed of some piece of praise or censure, of advice to do or not to do something, or of appeals to the audience; and you must choose between making these preliminary passages connected or disconnected with the speech itself.

Introductions to forensic speeches, it must be observed, have the same value as the prologues of dramas and the introductions to epic poems; the dithyrambic prelude resembling the introduction to a speech of display, as

"For thee, and thy gilts, and thy battle spoils...."

In prologues, and in epic poetry, a foretaste of the theme is given, intended to inform the hearers of it in advance instead of keeping their minds in suspense. Anything vague puzzles them: so give them a grasp of the beginning, and they can hold fast to it and follow the argument. So we find—

> "Sing, O goddess of song, of the Wrath...
> Tell me, O Muse, of the hero...
> Lead me to tell a new tale, how there came great warfare
>   to Europe
> Out of the Asian land..."

The tragic poets, too, let us know the pivot of their play; if not at the outset like Euripides, at least somewhere in the preface to a speech like Sophocles—

> "Polybus was my father...";

and so in Comedy. This, then, is the most essential function and distinctive property of the introduction, to show what the aim of the speech is; and therefore no introduction ought to be employed where the subject is not long or intricate.

The other kinds of introduction employed are remedial in purpose, and may be used in any type of speech. They are concerned with the speaker, the hearer, the subject, or the speaker's opponent. Those concerned with the speaker himself or with his opponent are directed to removing or exciting prejudice. But whereas the defendant will begin by dealing with this sort of thing, the prosecutor will take quite another line and deal with such matters in the closing part of his speech. The reason for this is not far to seek. The defendant, when he is going to bring himself on the stage, must clear away any obstacles, and therefore must begin by removing any prejudice felt against him. But if you are to excite prejudice, you must do so at the close, so that the judges may more easily remember what you have said.

The appeal to the hearer aims at securing his goodwill, or at arousing his resentment, or sometimes at gaining his serious attention to the case, or even at distracting it—for gaining it is not always an advantage, and speakers will often for that reason try to make him laugh.

You may use any means you choose to make your hearer receptive; among others, giving him a good impression of your character, which always helps to secure his attention. He will be ready to attend to anything that touches himself and to anything that is important, surprising, or agreeable; and you should accordingly convey to him the impression that what you have to say is of this nature. If you wish to distract his attention, you should imply that the subject does not affect him, or is trivial or disagreeable. But observe, all this has nothing to do with the speech itself. It merely has to do with the weak-minded tendency of the hearer to listen to what is beside the point. Where this tendency is absent, no introduction wanted beyond a summary statement of your subject, to put a sort of head on the main body of your speech. Moreover, calls for attention, when required, may come equally well in any part of a speech; in fact, the beginning of it is just where there is least slackness of interest; it is therefore ridiculous to put this kind of thing at the beginning, when everyone is listening with most attention. Choose therefore any point in the speech where such an appeal is needed, and then say "Now I beg you to note this point—it concerns you quite as much as myself"; or

"I will tell you that whose like you have never yet"

heard for terror, or for wonder. This is what Prodicus called "slipping in a bit of the fifty-drachma show-lecture for the audience whenever they began to nod." It is plain that such introductions are addressed not to ideal hearers, but to hearers as we find them. The use of introductions to excite prejudice or to dispel misgivings is universal—

"My lord, I will not say that eagerly…"

or

"Why all this preface?"

Introductions are popular with those whose case is weak, or looks weak; it pays them to dwell on anything rather than the actual facts of it. That is why slaves, instead of answering the questions put to them, make indirect replies with long preambles. The means of exciting in your hearers goodwill and various other feelings of the same kind have already been described. The poet finely says "May I find in Phaeacian hearts, at my coming, goodwill and compassion"; and these are the two things we should aim at. In speeches of display we must make the hearer feel that the eulogy includes either himself or his family or his way of life or something or other of the kind. For it is true, as Socrates says in the Funeral Speech, that "the difficulty is not to praise the Athenians at Athens but at Sparta."

The introductions of political oratory will be made out of the same materials as those of the forensic kind, though the nature of political oratory makes them very rare. The subject is known already, and therefore the facts of the case need no introduction; but you may have to say something on account of yourself or to your opponents; or those present may be inclined to treat the matter either more or less seriously than you wish them to. You may accordingly have to excite or dispel some prejudice, or to make the matter under discussion seem more or less important than before: for either of which purposes you will want an introduction. You may also want one to add elegance to your remarks, feeling that otherwise they will have a casual air, like Gorgias" eulogy of the Eleans, in which, without any preliminary sparring or fencing, he begins straight off with "Happy city of Elis!"

Part XV

In dealing with prejudice, one class of argument is that whereby you can dispel objectionable suppositions about yourself. It makes no practical difference whether such a supposition has been put into words or not, so that this distinction may be ignored. Another way is to meet any of the issues directly: to deny the alleged fact; or to say that you have done no harm, or none to him, or not as much as he says; or that you have done him no injustice, or not much; or that you have done nothing disgraceful, or nothing disgraceful enough to matter: these are the sort of questions on which the dispute hinges. Thus Iphicrates replying to Nausicrates, admitted that he had done the deed alleged, and that he had done Nausicrates harm, but not that he had done him wrong. Or you may admit the wrong, but balance it with other facts, and say that, if the deed harmed him, at any rate it was honorable; or that, if it gave him pain, at least it did him good; or something else like that. Another way is to allege that your action was due to mistake, or bad luck, or necessity as Sophocles said he was not trembling, as his traducer maintained, in order to make people think him an old man, but because he could not help it; he would rather not be eighty years old. You may balance your motive against your actual deed; saying, for instance, that you did not mean to injure him but to do so-and-so; that you did not do what you are falsely charged with doing—the damage was accidental—"I should indeed be a detestable person if I had deliberately intended this result." Another way is open when your calumniator, or any of his connexions, is or has been subject to the same grounds for suspicion. Yet another, when others are subject to the same grounds for suspicion but are admitted to be in fact innocent of the charge: e.g. "Must I be a profligate because I am well-groomed? Then so-and-so must be one too." Another, if other people have been calumniated by the same man or someone else, or, without being calumniated, have been suspected, like yourself now, and yet have been proved innocent. Another way is to return calumny for calumny and say, "It is monstrous to trust the man's statements when you cannot trust the man himself." Another is when the question has been already decided. So with Euripides" reply to Hygiaenon, who, in the action for an exchange of properties, accused him of impiety in having written a line encouraging perjury—

"My tongue hath sworn: no oath is on my soul."

Euripides said that his opponent himself was guilty in bringing into the law courts cases whose decision belonged to the Dionysiac contests. "If I have not already answered for my words there, I am ready to do so if you choose to prosecute me there." Another method is to denounce calumny, showing what an enormity it is, and in particular that it raises false issues, and that it means a lack of confidence in the merits of his case. The argument from evidential circumstances is available for both parties: thus in the Teucer Odysseus says that Teucer is closely bound to Priam, since his mother Hesione was Priam's sister. Teucer replies that Telamon his father was Priam's enemy, and that he himself did not betray the spies to Priam. Another method, suitable for the calumniator, is to praise some trifling merit at great length, and then attack some important failing concisely; or after mentioning a number of good qualities to attack one bad one that really bears on the question. This is the method of thoroughly skilful and unscrupulous prosecutors. By mixing up the man's merits with what is bad, they do their best to make use of them to damage him.

There is another method open to both calumniator and apologist. Since a given action can be done from many motives, the former must try to disparage it by selecting the worse motive of two, the latter to put the better construction on it. Thus one might argue that Diomedes chose Odysseus as his companion because he supposed Odysseus to be the best man for the purpose; and you might reply to this that it was, on the contrary, because he was the only hero so worthless that Diomedes need not fear his rivalry.

Part XVI

We may now pass from the subject of calumny to that of Narration.

Narration in ceremonial oratory is not continuous but intermittent. There must, of course, be some survey of the actions that form the subject matter of the speech. The speech is a composition containing two parts.

One of these is not provided by the orator's art, viz. the actions themselves, of which the orator is in no sense author. The other part is provided by his namely, the proof (where proof is needed) that the actions were done, the description of their quality or of their extent, or even all these three things together. Now the reason why sometimes it is not desirable to make the whole narrative continuous is that the case thus expounded is hard to keep in mind. Show, therefore, from one set of facts that your hero is, e.g. brave, and from other sets of facts that he is able, just, etc. A speech thus arranged is comparatively simple, instead of being complicated and elaborate. You will have to recall well-known deeds among others; and because they are well-known, the hearer usually needs no narration of them; none, for instance, if your object is the praise of Achilles; we all know the facts of his life—what you have to do is to apply those facts. But if your object is the praise of Critias, you must narrate his deeds, which not many people know of...

Nowadays it is said, absurdly enough, that the narration should be rapid. Remember what the man said to the baker who asked whether he was to make the cake hard or soft: "What, can't you make it right?" Just so here. We are not to make long narrations, just as we are not to make long introductions or long arguments. Here, again, rightness does not consist either in rapidity or in conciseness, but in the happy mean; that is, in saying just so much as will make the facts plain, or will lead the hearer to believe that the thing has happened, or that the man has caused injury or wrong to someone, or that the facts are really as important as you wish them to be thought: or the opposite facts to establish the opposite arguments.

You may also narrate as you go anything that does credit to yourself, e.g. "I kept telling him to do his duty and not abandon his children"; or discredit to your adversary, e.g. "But he answered me that, wherever he might find himself, there he would find other children," the answer Herodotus's records of the Egyptian mutineers. Slip in anything else that the judges will enjoy.

The defendant will make less of the narration. He has to maintain that the thing has not happened, or did no harm, or was not unjust, or not so bad as is alleged. He must therefor snot waste time about what is admitted fact, unless this bears on his own contention; e.g. that the thing was done, but was not wrong. Further, we must speak of events as past and gone, except where they excite pity or indignation by being represented as present. The Story told to Alcinous is an example of a brief chronicle, when it is repeated to Penelope in sixty lines. Another instance is the Epic Cycle as treated by Phayllus, and the prologue to the Oeneus.

The narration should depict character; to which end you must know what makes it do so. One such thing is the indication of moral purpose; the quality of purpose indicated determines the quality of character depicted and is itself determined by the end pursued. Thus it is that mathematical discourses depict no character; they have nothing to do with moral purpose, for they represent nobody as pursuing any end. On the other hand, the Socratic dialogues do depict character, being concerned with moral questions. This end will also be gained by describing the manifestations of various types of character, e.g. "he kept walking along as he talked," which shows the man's recklessness and rough manners. Do not let your words seem inspired so much by intelligence, in the manner now current, as by moral purpose: e.g. "I willed this; aye, it was my moral purpose; true, I gained nothing by it, still it is better thus." For the other way shows good sense, but this shows good character; good sense making us go after what is useful, and good character after what is noble. Where any detail may appear incredible, then add the cause of it; of this Sophocles provides an example in the Antigone, where Antigone says she had cared more for her brother than for husband or children, since if the latter perished they might be replaced,

> "But since my father and mother in their graves
> Lie dead, no brother can be born to me."

If you have no such cause to suggest, just say that you are aware that no one will believe your words, but the fact remains that such is our nature, however hard the world may find it to believe that a man deliberately does anything except what pays him.

Again, you must make use of the emotions. Relate the familiar manifestations of them, and those that distinguish yourself and your opponent; for instance, "he went away scowling at me." So Aeschines described Cratylus as "hissing with fury and shaking his fists." These details carry conviction: the audience take the truth of what they know as so much evidence for the truth of what they do not. Plenty of such details may be found in Homer:

> "Thus did she say: but the old woman buried her face in
> her hands"

a true touch—people beginning to cry do put their hands over their eyes.

Bring yourself on the stage from the first in the right character, that people may regard you in that light; and the same with your adversary;

but do not let them see what you are about. How easily such impressions may be conveyed we can see from the way in which we get some inkling of things we know nothing of by the mere look of the messenger bringing news of them. Have some narrative in many different parts of your speech; and sometimes let there be none at the beginning of it.

In political oratory there is very little opening for narration; nobody can "narrate" what has not yet happened. If there is narration at all, it will be of past events, the recollection of which is to help the hearers to make better plans for the future. Or it may be employed to attack someone's character, or to eulogize him—only then you will not be doing what the political speaker, as such, has to do.

If any statement you make is hard to believe, you must guarantee its truth, and at once offer an explanation, and then furnish it with such particulars as will be expected. Thus Carcinus's Jocasta, in his Oedipus, keeps guaranteeing the truth of her answers to the inquiries of the man who is seeking her son; and so with Haemon in Sophocles.

Part XVII

The duty of the Arguments is to attempt demonstrative proofs. These proofs must bear directly upon the question in dispute, which must fall under one of four heads. (1) If you maintain that the act was not committed, your main task in court is to prove this. (2) If you maintain that the act did no harm, prove this. If you maintain that (3) the act was less than is alleged, or (4) justified, prove these facts, just as you would prove the act not to have been committed if you were maintaining that.

It should be noted that only where the question in dispute falls under the first of these heads can it be true that one of the two parties is necessarily a rogue. Here ignorance cannot be pleaded, as it might if the dispute were whether the act was justified or not. This argument must therefore be used in this case only, not in the others.

In ceremonial speeches you will develop your case mainly by arguing that what has been done is, e.g. noble and useful. The facts themselves are to be taken on trust; proof of them is only submitted on those rare occasions when they are not easily credible or when they have been set down to someone else.

In political speeches you may maintain that a proposal is impracticable; or that, though practicable, it is unjust, or will do no good, or is not so important as its proposer thinks. Note any falsehoods about irrelevant matters—they will look like proof that his other statements also are false.

Argument by "example" is highly suitable for political oratory, argument by "enthymeme" better suits forensic. Political oratory deals with future events, of which it can do no more than quote past events as examples. Forensic oratory deals with what is or is not now true, which can better be demonstrated, because not contingent—there is no contingency in what has now already happened. Do not use a continuous succession of enthymemes: intersperse them with other matter, or they will spoil one another's effect. There are limits to their number—

"Friend, you have spoken as much as a sensible man would have spoken." "As much" says Homer, not "as well." Nor should you try to make enthymemes on every point; if you do, you will be acting just like some students of philosophy, whose conclusions are more familiar and believable than the premises from which they draw them. And avoid the enthymeme form when you are trying to rouse feeling; for it will either kill the feeling or will itself fall flat: all simultaneous motions tend to cancel each other either completely or partially. Nor should you go after the enthymeme form in a passage where you are depicting character—the process of demonstration can express neither moral character nor moral purpose. Maxims should be employed in the Arguments—and in the Narration too—since these do express character: "I have given him this, though I am quite aware that one should 'Trust no man.'" Or if you are appealing to the emotions: "I do not regret it, though I have been wronged; if he has the profit on his side, I have justice on mine."

Political oratory is a more difficult task than forensic; and naturally so, since it deals with the future, whereas the pleader deals with the past, which, as Epimenides of Crete said, even the diviners already know. (Epimenides did not practice divination about the future; only about the obscurities of the past.) Besides, in forensic oratory you have a basis in the law; and once you have a starting point, you can prove anything with comparative ease. Then again, political oratory affords few chances for those leisurely digressions in which you may attack your adversary, talk about yourself, or work on your hearers' emotions; fewer chances indeed, than any other affords, unless your set purpose is to divert your hearers' attention. Accordingly, if you find yourself in difficulties, follow the lead of the Athenian speakers, and that of Isocrates, who makes regular attacks upon people in the course of a political speech, e.g. upon the Lacedaemonians in the Panegyricus, and upon Chares in the speech about the allies. In ceremonial oratory, intersperse your speech with bits of episodic eulogy, like Isocrates, who is always bringing someone forward for this purpose.

And this is what Gorgias meant by saying that he always found something to talk about. For if he speaks of Achilles, he praises Peleus, then Aeacus, then Zeus; and in like manner the virtue of valour, describing its good results, and saying what it is like.

Now if you have proofs to bring forward, bring them forward, and your moral discourse as well; if you have no enthymemes, then fall back upon moral discourse: after all, it is more fitting for a good man to display himself as an honest fellow than as a subtle reasoner. Refutative enthymemes are more popular than demonstrative ones: their logical cogency is more striking: the facts about two opposites always stand out clearly when the two are put side by side.

The "Reply to the Opponent" is not a separate division of the speech; it is part of the Arguments to break down the opponent's case, whether by objection or by counter-syllogism. Both in political speaking and when pleading in court, if you are the first speaker you should put your own arguments forward first, and then meet the arguments on the other side by refuting them and pulling them to pieces beforehand. If, however, the case for the other side contains a great variety of arguments, begin with these, like Callistratus in the Messenian assembly, when he demolished the arguments likely to be used against him before giving his own. If you speak later, you must first, by means of refutation and counter-syllogism, attempt some answer to your opponent's speech, especially if his arguments have been well received. For just as our minds refuse a favorable reception to a person against whom they are prejudiced, so they refuse it to a speech when they have been favorably impressed by the speech on the other side. You should, therefore, make room in the minds of the audience for your coming speech; and this will be done by getting your opponent's speech out of the way. So attack that first—either the whole of it, or the most important, successful, or vulnerable points in it, and thus inspire confidence in what you have to say yourself—

> "First, champion will I be of Goddesses...
> Never, I ween, would Hera..."

where the speaker has attacked the silliest argument first. So much for the Arguments.

With regard to the element of moral character: there are assertions which, if made about yourself, may excite dislike, appear tedious, or expose you to the risk of contradiction; and other things which you cannot say about your opponent without seeming abusive or ill-bred. Put such remarks, therefore, into the mouth of some third person. This is what Isocrates does in the Philippus and in the Antidosis, and Archilochus in his satires. The latter represents the father himself as attacking his daughter in the lampoon

> "Think nought impossible at all,
> Nor swear that it shall not befall..."

and puts into the mouth of Charon the carpenter the lampoon which begins

> "Not for the wealth of Gyes..."

So too Sophocles makes Haemon appeal to his father on behalf of Antigone as if it were others who were speaking.

Again, sometimes you should restate your enthymemes in the form of maxims; e.g. "Wise men will come to terms in the hour of success; for they will gain most if they do." Expressed as an enthymeme, this would run, "If we ought to come to terms when doing so will enable us to gain the greatest advantage, then we ought to come to terms in the hour of success."

Part XVIII

Next as to Interrogation. The best moment to a employ this is when your opponent has so answered one question that the putting of just one more lands him in absurdity. Thus Pericles questioned Lampon about the way of celebrating the rites of the Savior Goddess. Lampon declared that no uninitiated person could be told of them. Pericles then asked, "Do you know them yourself?" "Yes," answered Lampon. "Why," said Pericles, "how can that be, when you are uninitiated?"

Another good moment is when one premise of an argument is obviously true, and you can see that your opponent must say "yes" if you ask him whether the other is true. Having first got this answer about the other, do not go on to ask him about the obviously true one, but just state the conclusion yourself. Thus, when Meletus denied that Socrates believed in the existence of gods but admitted that he talked about a supernatural power, Socrates proceeded to to ask whether "supernatural beings were not either children of the gods or in some way divine?" "Yes," said Meletus. "Then," replied Socrates, "is there anyone who believes in the existence of children of the gods and yet not in the existence of the gods themselves?" Another good occasion is when you expect to show that your opponent is contradicting either his own words or what everyone believes. A fourth is when it is impossible for him to meet your question except by an evasive answer. If he answers "True, and yet not true," or "Partly true and partly not true," or "True in one sense but not in another," the audience thinks he is in difficulties, and applauds his discomfiture. In other cases do not attempt interrogation; for if your opponent gets in an objection, you are felt to have been worsted. You cannot ask a series of questions owing to the incapacity of the audience to follow them; and for this reason you should also make your enthymemes as compact as possible.

In replying, you must meet ambiguous questions by drawing reasonable distinctions, not by a curt answer. In meeting questions that seem to involve you in a contradiction, offer the explanation at the outset of your answer, before your opponent asks the next question or draws his conclusion. For it is not difficult to see the drift of his argument in advance. This point, however, as well as the various means of refutation, may be regarded as known to us from the Topics.

When your opponent in drawing his conclusion puts it in the form of a question, you must justify your answer. Thus when Sophocles was asked by Peisander whether he had, like the other members of the Board of Safety, voted for setting up the Four Hundred, he said "Yes." "Why, did you not think it wicked?" "Yes." "So you committed this wickedness?" "Yes," said Sophocles, "for there was nothing better to do." Again, the Lacedaemonian, when he was being examined on his conduct as ephor, was asked whether he thought that the other ephors had been justly put to death. "Yes," he said. "Well then," asked his opponent, "did not you propose the same measures as they?" "Yes." "Well then, would not you too be justly put to death?" "Not at all," said he; "they were bribed to do it, and I did it from conviction." Hence you should not ask any further questions after drawing the conclusion, nor put the conclusion itself in the form of a further question, unless there is a large balance of truth on your side.

As to jests. These are supposed to be of some service in controversy. Gorgias said that you should kill your opponents' earnestness with jesting and their jesting with earnestness; in which he was right. Jests have been classified in the Poetics. Some are becoming to a gentleman, others are not; see that you choose such as become you. Irony better befits a gentleman than buffoonery; the ironical man jokes to amuse himself, the buffoon to amuse other people.

Part XIX

The Epilogue has four parts. You must (1) make the audience well-disposed toward yourself and ill-disposed toward your opponent, (2) magnify or minimize the leading facts, (3) excite the required state of emotion in your hearers, and (4) refresh their memories.

(1) Having shown your own truthfulness and the untruthfulness of your opponent, the natural thing is to commend yourself, censure him, and hammer in your points. You must aim at one of two objects—you must make yourself out a good man and him a bad one either in yourselves or in relation to your hearers. How this is to be managed? by what lines of argument you are to represent people as good or bad? This has been already explained.

(2) The facts having been proved, the natural thing to do next is to magnify or minimize their importance. The facts must be admitted before you can discuss how important they are; just as the body cannot grow except from something already present. The proper lines of argument to be used for this purpose of amplification and depreciation have already been set forth.

(3) Next, when the facts and their importance are clearly understood, you must excite your hearers' emotions. These emotions are pity, indignation, anger, hatred, envy, emulation, pugnacity. The lines of argument to be used for these purposes also have been previously mentioned.

(4) Finally you have to review what you have already said. Here you may properly do what some wrongly recommend doing in the introduction—repeat your points frequently so as to make them easily understood. What you should do in your introduction is to state your subject, in order that the point to be judged may be quite plain; in the epilogue you should summarize the arguments by which your case has been proved. The first step in this reviewing process is to observe that you have done what you undertook to do. You must, then, state what you have said and why you have said it. Your method may be a comparison of your own case with that of your opponent; and you may compare either the ways you have both handled the same point or make your comparison less direct: "My opponent said so-and-so on this point; I said so-and-so, and this is why I said it." Or with modest irony, e.g. "He certainly said so-and-so, but I said so-and-so." Or "How vain he would have been if he had proved all this instead of that!" Or put it in the form of a question. "What has not been proved by me?" or "What has my opponent proved?" You may proceed then, either in this way by setting point against point, or by following the natural order of the arguments as spoken, first giving your own, and then separately, if you wish, those of your opponent.

For the conclusion, the disconnected style of language is appropriate, and will mark the difference between the oration and the peroration. "I have done. You have heard me. The facts are before you. I ask for your judgement."

XENOPHON

MEMORABILIA: RECOLLECTIONS OF SOCRATES

BY XENOPHON

Translated by H. G. Dakyns

Xenophon the Athenian was born 431 BC. He was a pupil of Socrates. He marched with the Spartans, and was exiled from Athens. Sparta gave him land and property in Scillus, where he lived for many years before having to move once more, to settle in Corinth. He died in 354 BC.

The Memorabilia is a recollection of Socrates in word and deed, to show his character as the best and happiest of men.

Preparer's Note:
First Published 1897 by Macmillan and Co. This was typed from Dakyns' series, "The Works of Xenophon," a four-volume set. Text in brackets "{}" is my transliteration of Greek text into English using an Oxford English Dictionary alphabet table. The diacritical marks have been lost.

BOOK I

I

I have often wondered by what arguments those who indicted[1] Socrates could have persuaded the Athenians that his life was justly forfeit to the state. The indictment was to this effect: "Socrates is guilty of crime in refusing to recognize the gods acknowledged by the state, and importing strange divinities of his own; he is further guilty of corrupting the young."

In the first place, what evidence did they produce that Socrates refused to recognize the gods acknowledged by the state? Was it that he did not sacrifice? or that he dispensed with divination? On the contrary, he was

---

1 {oi grapsamenoi} = Meletus (below, IV. iv. 4, viii. 4; "Apol." 11, 19), Anytus ("Apol." 29), and Lycon. See Plat. "Apol." II. v. 18; Diog. Laert. II. v. (Socr.); M. Schanz, "Plat. Apol. mit deutschen Kemmentar, Einleitung," S. 5 foll.

often to be seen engaged in sacrifice, at home or at the common altars of the state. Nor was his dependence on divination less manifest. Indeed that saying of his, "A divinity[1] gives me a sign," was on everybody's lips. So much so that, if I am not mistaken, it lay at the root of the imputation that he imported novel divinities; though there was no greater novelty in his case than in that of other believers in oracular help, who commonly rely on omens of all sorts: the flight or cry of birds, the utterances of man, chance meetings,[2] or a victim's entrails. Even according to the popular conception, it is not the mere fowl, it is not the chance individual one meets, who knows what things are profitable for a man, but it is the gods who vouchsafe by such instruments to signify the same. This was also the tenet of Socrates. Only, whereas men ordinarily speak of being turned aside, or urged onward by birds, or other creatures encountered on the path, Socrates suited his language to his conviction. "The divinity," said he, "gives me a sign." Further, he would constantly advise his associates to do this, or beware of doing that, upon the authority of this same divine voice; and, as a matter of fact, those who listened to his warnings prospered, whilst he who turned a deaf ear to them repented afterward.[3] Yet, it will be readily conceded, he would hardly desire to present himself to his everyday companions in the character of either knave or fool. Whereas he would have appeared to be both, supposing[4] the God-given revelations had but revealed his own proneness to deception. It is plain he would not have ventured on forecast at all, but for his belief that the words he spoke would in fact be verified. Then on whom, or what, was the assurance rooted, if not upon God? And if he had faith in the gods, how could he fail to recognize them?

But his mode of dealing with his intimates has another aspect. As regards the ordinary necessities of life,[5] his advice was, "Act as you believe[6] these

---

1 Or, "A divine something." See "Encyc. Brit." "Socrates." Dr. H. Jackson; "The Daemon of Socrates," F. W. H. Myers; K. Joel, "Der echte und der Xenophontische Sokrates," i. p. 70 foll.; cf. Aristot. "M. M." 1182 a 10.
2 See Aesch. "P. V." 487, {enodious te sombolous}, "and pathway tokens," L. Campbell; Arist. "Birds," 721, {sombolon ornin}: "Frogs," 196, {to sometukhon exion}; "Eccl." 792; Hor. "Od." iii. 27, 1-7.
3 See "Anab." III. i. 4; "Symp." iv. 48.
4 Or, "if his vaunted manifestations from heaven had but manifested the falsity of his judgment."
5 Or, "in the sphere of the determined," {ta anagkaia} = certa, quorum eventus est necessarius; "things positive, the law-ordained department of life," as we might say. See Grote, "H. G." i. ch. xvi. 500 and passim.
6 Reading {os nomizoien}, or if {os enomizen}, translate "As to things with certain results, he advised them to do them in the way in which he believed they would be done best"; i.e. he did not say, "follow your conscience," but, "this course seems best to me under the circumstances."

things may best be done." But in the case of those darker problems, the issues of which are incalculable, he directed his friends to consult the oracle, whether the business should be undertaken or not. "No one," he would say, "who wishes to manage a house or city with success: no one aspiring to guide the helm of state aright, can afford to dipense with aid from above." Doubtless, skill in carpentering, building, smithying, farming, of the art of governing men, together with the theory of these processes, and the sciences of arithmetic, economy, strategy, are affairs of study, and within the grasp of human intelligence. Yet there is a side even of these, and that not the least important, which the gods reserve to themselves, the bearing of which is hidden from mortal vision. Thus, let a man sow a field or plant a farm never so well, yet he cannot foretell who will gather in the fruits: another may build him a house of fairest proportion, yet he knows not who will inhabit it. Neither can a general foresee whether it will profit him to conduct a campaign, nor a politician be certain whether his leadership will turn to evil or good. Nor can the man who weds a fair wife, looking forward to joy, know whether through her he shall not reap sorrow. Neither can he who has built up a powerful connection in the state know whether he shall not by means of it be cast out of his city. To suppose that all these matters lay within the scope of human judgment, to the exclusion of the preternatural, was preternatural folly. Nor was it less extravagant to go and consult the will of Heaven on any questions which it is given to us to decide by dint of learning. As though a man should inquire, "Am I to choose an expert driver as my coachman, or one who has never handled the reins?" "Shall I appoint a mariner to be skipper of my vessel, or a landsman?" And so with respect to all we may know by numbering, weighing, and measuring. To seek advice from Heaven on such points was a sort of profanity. "Our duty is plain," he would observe; "where we are permitted to work through our natural faculties, there let us by all means apply them. But in things which are hidden, let us seek to gain knowledge from above, by divination; for the gods," he added, "grant signs to those to whom they will be gracious."

Again, Socrates ever lived in the public eye; at early morning he was to be seen betaking himself to one of the promenades, or wrestling-grounds; at noon he would appear with the gathering crowds in the marketplace; and as day declined, wherever the largest throng might be encountered, there was he to be found, talking for the most part, while anyone who chose might stop and listen. Yet no one ever heard him say, or saw him do anything impious or irreverent. Indeed, in contrast to others he set his face against all discussion of such high matters as the nature of the Universe;

how the "kosmos," as the savants[1] phrase it, came into being;[2] or by what forces the celestial phenomena arise. To trouble one's brain about such matters was, he argued, to play the fool. He would ask first: Did these investigators feel their knowledge of things human so complete that they betook themselves to these lofty speculations? Or did they maintain that they were playing their proper parts in thus neglecting the affairs of man to speculate on the concerns of God? He was astonished they did not see how far these problems lay beyond mortal ken; since even those who pride themselves most on their discussion of these points differ from each other, as madmen do. For just as some madmen, he said, have no apprehension of what is truly terrible, others fear where no fear is; some are ready to say and do anything in public without the slightest symptom of shame;[3] others think they ought not so much as to set foot among their fellow men; some honor neither temple, nor altar, nor aught else sacred to the name of God; others bow down to stocks and stones and worship the very beasts:—so is it with those thinkers whose minds are cumbered with cares[4] concerning the Universal Nature. One sect[5] has discovered that Being is one and indivisible. Another[6] that it is infinite in number. If one[7] proclaims that all things are in a continual flux, another[8] replies that nothing can possibly be moved at any time. The theory of the universe as a process of birth and death is met by the counter theory, that nothing ever could be born or ever will die.

But the questioning of Socrates on the merits of these speculators sometimes took another form. The student of human learning expects, he said, to make something of his studies for the benefit of himself or others, as he likes. Do these explorers into the divine operations hope that when they have discovered by what forces the various phenomena occur, they will create winds and waters at will and fruitful seasons? Will they manipulate these and the like to suit their needs? or has no such notion perhaps ever entered their heads, and will they be content simply to know how such things come into existence? But if this was his mode of

---

1 Lit. "the sophists." See H. Sidgwick, "J. of Philol." iv. 1872; v. 1874.
2 Reading {ephu}. Cf. Lucian, "Icaromenip." xlvi. 4, in imitation of this passage apparently; or if {ekhei}, translate "is arranged." See Grote, "H. G." viii. 573.
3 See "Anab." V. iv. 30.
4 See Arist. "Clouds," 101, {merimnophrontistai kaloi te kagathoi}.
5 E.g. Xenophanes and, see Grote, "Plato," I. i. 16 foll.
6 E.g. Leucippus and Democritus, ib. 63 foll.
7 E.g. Heraclitus, ib. 27 foll.
8 E.g. Zeno, ib. ii. 96.

describing those who meddle with such matters as these, he himself never wearied of discussing human topics. What is piety? what is impiety? What is the beautiful? what the ugly? What the noble? what the base? What are meant by just and unjust? what by sobriety and madness? what by courage and cowardice? What is a state? what is a statesman? what is a ruler over men? what is a ruling character? and other like problems, the knowledge of which, as he put it, conferred a patent of nobility on the possessor,[1] whereas those who lacked the knowledge might deservedly be stigmatised as slaves.

Now, in so far as the opinions of Socrates were unknown to the world at large, it is not surprising that the court should draw false conclusions respecting them; but that facts patent to all should have been ignored is indeed astonishing.

At one time Socrates was a member of the Council,[2] he had taken the senatorial oath, and sworn "as a member of that house to act in conformity with the laws." It was thus he chanced to be President of the Popular Assembly,[3] when that body was seized with a desire to put the nine[4] generals, Thrasyllus, Erasinides, and the rest, to death by a single inclusive vote. Whereupon, in spite of the bitter resentment of the people, and the menaces of several influential citizens, he refused to put the question, esteeming it of greater importance faithfully to abide by the oath which he had taken, than to gratify the people wrongfully, or to screen himself from the menaces of the mighty. The fact being, that with regard to the care bestowed by the gods upon men, his belief differed widely from that of the multitude. Whereas most people seem to imagine that the gods know in part, and are ignorant in part, Socrates believed firmly that the gods know all things—both the things that are said and the things that are done, and the things that are counselled in the silent chambers of the heart. Moreover, they are present everywhere, and bestow signs upon man concerning all the things of man.

I can, therefore, but repeat my former words. It is a marvel to me how the Athenians came to be persuaded that Socrates fell short of sober-mindedness as touching the gods. A man who never ventured one impious word or deed against the gods we worship, but whose whole language concerning them, and his every act, closely coincided, word for word, and deed for deed, with all we deem distinctive of devoutest piety.

---

1 Or, "was distinctive of the 'beautiful and good.'" For the phrase see below, ii. 2 et passim.
2 Or "Senate." Lit. "the Boule."
3 Lit. "Epistates of the Ecclesia." See Grote, "H. G." viii. 271; Plat. "Apol." 32 B.
4 {ennea} would seem to be a slip of the pen for {okto}, eight. See "Hell." I. v. 16; vi. 16; vi. 29; vii. 1 foll.

II

No less surprising to my mind is the belief that Socrates corrupted the young. This man, who, beyond what has been already stated, kept his appetites and passions under strict control, who was pre-eminently capable of enduring winter's cold and summer's heat and every kind of toil, who was so schooled to curtail his needs that with the scantiest of means he never lacked sufficiency—is it credible that such a man could have made others irreverent or lawless, or licentious, or effeminate in face of toil? Was he not rather the saving of many through the passion for virtue which he roused in them, and the hope he infused that through careful management of themselves they might grow to be truly beautiful and good—not indeed that he ever undertook to be a teacher of virtue, but being evidently virtuous himself he made those who associated with him hope that by imitating they might at last resemble him.

But let it not be inferred that he was negligent of his own body or approved of those who neglected theirs. If excess of eating, counteracted by excess of toil, was a dietary of which he disapproved,[1] to gratify the natural claim of appetite in conjunction with moderate exercise was a system he favored, as tending to a healthy condition of the body without trammelling the cultivation of the spirit. On the other hand, there was nothing dandified or pretentious about him; he indulged in no foppery of shawl or shoes, or other effeminacy of living.

Least of all did he tend to make his companions greedy of money. He would not, while restraining passion generally, make capital out of the one passion which attached others to himself; and by this abstinence, he believed, he was best consulting his own freedom; in so much that he stigmatised those who condescended to take wages for their society as vendors of their own persons, because they were compelled to discuss for the benefits of their paymasters. What surprised him was that anyone possessing virtue should deign to ask money as its price instead of simply finding his reward in the acquisition of an honest friend, as if the new-fledged soul of honor could forget her debt of gratitude to her greatest benefactor.

For himself, without making any such profession, he was content to believe that those who accepted his views would play their parts as good and true friends to himself and one another their lives long. Once more then: how should a man of this character corrupt the young, unless the careful cultivation of virtue be corruption?

---

1 See (Plat.) "Erast." 132 C.

But, says the accuser,[1] by all that's sacred! did not Socrates cause his associates to despise the established laws when he dwelt on the folly of appointing state officers by ballot?[2] a principle which, he said, no one would care to apply in selecting a pilot or a flute player or in any similar case, where a mistake would be far less disastrous than in matters political. Words like these, according to the accuser, tended to incite the young to contemn the established constitution, rendering them violent and headstrong. But for myself I think that those who cultivate wisdom and believe themselves able to instruct their fellow citizens as to their interests are least likely to become partisans of violence. They are too well aware that to violence attach enmities and dangers, whereas results as good may be obtained by persuasion safely and amicably. For the victim of violence hates with vindictiveness as one from whom something precious has been stolen, while the willing subject of persuasion is ready to kiss the hand which has done him a service. Hence compulsion is not the method of him who makes wisdom his study, but of him who wields power untempered by reflection. Once more: the man who ventures on violence needs the support of many to fight his battles, while he whose strength lies in persuasiveness triumphs single-handed, for he is conscious of a cunning to compel consent unaided. And what has such a one to do with the spilling of blood? since how ridiculous it were to do men to death rather than turn to account the trusty service of the living.

But, the accuser answers, the two men[3] who wrought the greatest evils to the state at any time—to wit, Critias and Alcibiades—were both companions of Socrates—Critias the oligarch, and Alcibiades the democrat. Where would you find a more arrant thief, savage, and murderer[4] than the one? where such a portent of insolence, incontinence, and high-handedness as the other? For my part, in so far as these two wrought evil to the state, I have no desire to appear as the apologist of either. I confine myself to explaining what this intimacy of theirs with Socrates really was.

Never were two more ambitious citizens seen at Athens. Ambition was in their blood. If they were to have their will, all power was to be in their

---

1 {o kategoros} = *Polycrates possibly. See M. Schantz, op. cit., "Einleitun," S. 6: "Die Anklagerede des Polykrates"; Introduction, p. xxxii. foll.*
2 *I.e. staking the election of a magistrate on the color of a bean. See Aristot. "Ath. Pol." viii. 2, and Dr. Sandys ad loc.*
3 *See "Hell." I. and II. passim.*
4 *Reading {kleptistatos te kai biaiotatos kai phonikotatos}, or if {pleonektistatos te kai biaiotatis}, translate "such a manner of greed and violence as the one, of insolence, etc., as the other?" See Grote, "H. G." viii. 337.*

hands; their fame was to eclipse all other. Of Socrates they knew—first that he lived an absolutely independent life on the scantiest means; next that he was self-disciplined to the last degree in respect of pleasures; lastly that he was so formidable in debate that there was no antagonist he could not twist round his little finger. Such being their views, and such the character of the pair, which is the more probable: that they sought the society of Socrates because they felt the fascination of his life, and were attracted by the bearing of the man? or because they thought, if only we are leagued with him we shall become adepts in statecraft and unrivalled in the arts of speech and action? For my part I believe that if the choice from Heaven had been given them to live such a life as they saw Socrates living to its close, or to die, they would both have chosen death.

Their acts are a conclusive witness to their characters. They no sooner felt themselves to be the masters of those they came in contact with than they sprang aside from Socrates and plunged into that whirl of politics but for which they might never have sought his society.

It may be objected: before giving his companions lessons in politics Socrates had better have taught them sobriety.[1] Without disputing the principle, I would point out that a teacher cannot fail to discover to his pupils his method of carrying out his own precepts, and this along with argumentative encouragement. Now I know that Socrates disclosed himself to his companions as a beautiful and noble being, who would reason and debate with them concerning virtue and other human interests in the noblest manner. And of these two I know that as long as they were companions of Socrates even they were temperate, not assuredly from fear of being fined or beaten by Socrates, but because they were persuaded for the nonce of the excellence of such conduct.

Perhaps some self-styled philosophers[2] may here answer: "Nay, the man truly just can never become unjust, the temperate man can never become intemperate, the man who has learned any subject of knowledge can never be as though he had learned it not." That, however, is not my own conclusion. It is with the workings of the soul as with those of the body; want of exercise of the organ leads to inability of function, here bodily, there spiritual, so that we can neither do the things that we should nor abstain from the things we should not. And that is why fathers keep

---

1 {sophrosune} = "sound-mindedness," "temperence." See below, IV. iii. 1.
2 In reference to some such tenet as that of Antisthenes ap. Diog. Laert. VI. ix. 30, {areskei d" autois kai ten areten didakten einai, katha phesin "Antisthenes en to "Rraklei kai anapobleton uparkhein}. Cf. Plat. "Protag." 340 D, 344 D.

their sons, however temperate they may be, out of the reach of wicked men, considering that if the society of the good is a training in virtue so also is the society of the bad its dissolution.

To this the poet[1] is a witness, who says:

> "From the noble thou shalt be instructed in nobleness; but, and if thou minglest with the base thou wilt destroy what wisdom thou hast now";

And he[2] who says:

> "But the good man has his hour of baseness as well as his hour of virtue"—

to whose testimony I would add my own. For I see that it is impossible to remember a long poem without practice and repetition; so is forgetfulness of the words of instruction engendered in the heart that has ceased to value them. With the words of warning fades the recollection of the very condition of mind in which the soul yearned after holiness; and once forgetting this, what wonder that the man should let slip also the memory of virtue itself! Again I see that a man who falls into habits of drunkenness or plunges headlong into licentious love, loses his old power of practicing the right and abstaining from the wrong. Many a man who has found frugality easy whilst passion was cold, no sooner falls in love than he loses the faculty at once, and in his prodigal expenditure of riches he will no longer withhold his hand from gains which in former days were too base to invite his touch. Where then is the difficulty of supposing that a man may be temperate today, and tomorrow the reverse; or that he who once has had it in his power to act virtuously may not quite lose that power?[3] To myself, at all events, it seems that all beautiful and noble things are the result of constant practice and training; and pre-eminently the virtue of temperance, seeing that in one and the same bodily frame pleasures are planted and spring up side by side with the soul and keep whispering in her ear, "Have done with self-restraint, make haste to gratify us and the body."[4]

But to return to Critias and Alcibiades, I repeat that as long as they lived with Socrates they were able by his support to dominate their ignoble

---

1 Theognis, 35, 36. See "Symp." ii. 4; Plat. "Men." 95 D.
2 The author is unknown. See Plat. "Protag." l.c.
3 Cf. "Cyrop." V. i. 9 foll.; VI. i. 41.
4 See my remarks, "Hellenica Essays," p. 371 foll.

appetites;[1] but being separated from him, Critias had to fly to Thessaly,[2] where he consorted with fellows better versed in lawlessness than justice. And Alcibiades fared no better. His personal beauty on the one hand incited bevies of fine ladies[3] to hunt him down as fair spoil, while on the other hand his influence in the state and among the allies exposed him to the corruption of many an adept in the arts of flattery; honored by the democracy and stepping easily to the front rank he behaved like an athlete who in the games of the Palaestra is so assured of victory that he neglects his training; thus he presently forgot the duty which he owed himself.

Such were the misadventures of these two. Is the sequel extraordinary? Inflated with the pride of ancestry,[4] exalted by their wealth, puffed up by power, sapped to the soul's core by a host of human tempters, separate moreover for many a long day from Socrates—what wonder that they reached the full stature of arrogancy! And for the offenses of these two Socrates is to be held responsible! The accuser will have it so. But for the fact that in early days, when they were both young and of an age when dereliction from good feeling and self-restraint might have been expected, this same Socrates kept them modest and well-behaved, not one word of praise is uttered by the accuser for all this. That is not the measure of justice elsewhere meted. Would a master of the harp or flute, would a teacher of any sort who has turned out proficient pupils, be held to account because one of them goes away to another teacher and turns out to be a failure? Or what father, if he have a son who in the society of a certain friend remains an honest lad, but falling into the company of some other becomes a good-for-nothing, will that father straightway accuse the earlier instructor? Will not he rather, in proportion as the boy deteriorates in the company of the latter, bestow more heartfelt praise upon the former? What father, himself sharing the society of his own children, is held to blame for their transgressions, if only his own goodness be established? Here would have been a fair test to apply to Socrates: Was he guilty of any base conduct himself? If so let him be set down as a knave, but if, on the contrary, he never faltered in sobriety from beginning to end, how in the name of justice is he to be held to account for a baseness which was not in him?

I go further: if, short of being guilty of any wrong himself, he saw

---

1 *Cf. (Plat.) "Theag." 130 A.*
2 *See "Hell." II. iii. 36.*
3 *Cf. Plut. "Ages.," "Alcib."*
4 *Or, "became overweening in arrogance." Cf. "Henry VIII. II. iv. 110": "But your heart is crammed with arrogancy, spleen, and pride."*

the evil doings of others with approval, reason were he should be held blameworthy. Listen then: Socrates was well aware that Critias was attached to Euthydemus,[1] aware too that he was endeavouring to deal by him after the manner of those wantons whose love is carnal of the body. From this endeavor he tried to deter him, pointing out how illiberal a thing it was, how ill befitting a man of honor to appear as a beggar before him whom he loved, in whose eyes he would fain be precious, ever petitioning for something base to give and base to get.

But when this reasoning fell on deaf ears and Critias refused to be turned aside, Socrates, as the story goes, took occasion of the presence of a whole company and of Euthydemus to remark that Critias appeared to be suffering from a swinish affection, or else why this desire to rub himself against Euthydemus like a herd of piglings scraping against stones.

The hatred of Critias to Socrates doubtless dates from this incident. He treasured it up against him, and afterward, when he was one of the Thirty and associated with Charicles as their official lawgiver,[2] he framed the law against teaching the art of words[3] merely from a desire to vilify Socrates. He was at a loss to know how else to lay hold of him except by levelling against him the vulgar charge[4] against philosophers, by which he hoped to prejudice him with the public. It was a charge quite unfounded as regards Socrates, if I may judge from anything I ever heard fall from his lips myself or have learned about him from others. But the animus of Critias was clear. At the time when the Thirty were putting citizens, highly respectable citizens, to death wholesale, and when they were egging on one man after another to the commission of crime, Socrates let fall an observation: "It would be sufficiently extraordinary if the keeper of a herd of cattle[5] who was continually thinning and impoverishing his cattle did not admit himself to be a sorry sort of herdsman, but that a ruler of the state who was continually thinning and impoverishing the citizens should neither be ashamed nor admit himself to be a sorry sort of ruler was more extraordinary still." The remark being reported to the government, Socrates was summoned by Critias and Charicles, who proceeded to point out the law and forbade him to converse with the young. "Was it open to

---

1 See below, IV. ii. 1 (if the same person).
2 Lit. "Nomothetes." See "Hell." II. iii. 2; Dem. 706. For Charicles see Lys. "c. Eratosth." S. 56; Aristot. "Pol." v. 6. 6.
3 See Diog. Laert. II. v. ("Socr.")
4 I.e. {to ton etto logon kreitto poiein}, "of making the worse appear the better cause." Cf. Arist. "Clouds."
5 See Dio Chrys. "Or." 43.

him," Socrates inquired of the speaker, "in case he failed to understand their commands in any point, to ask for an explanation?"

"Certainly," the two assented.

Then Socrates: I am prepared to obey the laws, but to avoid transgression of the law through ignorance I need instruction: is it on the supposition that the art of words tends to correctness of statement or to incorrectness that you bid us abstain from it? for if the former, it is clear we must abstain from speaking correctly, but if the latter, our endeavor should be to amend our speech.

To which Charicles, in a fit of temper, retorted: In consideration of your ignorance,[1] Socrates, we will frame the prohibition in language better suited to your intelligence: we forbid you to hold any conversation whatsoever with the young.

Then Socrates: To avoid all ambiguity then, or the possibility of my doing anything else than what you are pleased to command, may I ask you to define up to what age a human being is to be considered young?

For just so long a time (Charicles answered) as he is debarred from sitting as a member of the Council,[2] as not having attained to the maturity of wisdom; accordingly you will not hold converse with anyone under the age of thirty.

Soc. In making a purchase even, I am not to ask, what is the price of this? if the vendor is under the age of thirty?

Cha. Tut, things of that sort: but you know, Socrates, that you have a way of asking questions, when all the while you know how the matter stands. Let us have no questions of that sort.

Soc. Nor answers either, I suppose, if the inquiry concerns what I know, as, for instance, where does Charicles live? or where is Critias to be found?

Oh yes, of course, things of that kind (replied Charicles), while Critias added: But at the same time you had better have done with your shoemakers, carpenters, and coppersmiths.[3] These must be pretty well trodden out at heel by this time, considering the circulation you have given them.

Soc. And am I to hold away from their attendant topics also—the just, the holy, and the like?

Most assuredly (answered Charicles), and from cowherds in particular; or else see that you do not lessen the number of the herd yourself.

---

1 See Aristot. "de Soph. El." 183 b7.
2 The Boule or Senate. See W. L. Newman, "Pol. Aristot." i. 326.
3 Cf. Plat. "Gorg." 491 A; "Symp." 221 E; Dio Chrys. "Or." 55, 560 D, 564 A.

Thus the secret was out. The remark of Socrates about the cattle had come to their ears, and they could not forgive the author of it.

Perhaps enough has been said to explain the kind of intimacy which had subsisted between Critias and Socrates, and their relation to one another. But I will venture to maintain that where the teacher is not pleasing to the pupil there is no education. Now it cannot be said of Critias and Alcibiades that they associated with Socrates because they found him pleasing to them. And this is true of the whole period. From the first their eyes were fixed on the headship of the state as their final goal. During the time of their intimacy with Socrates there were no disputants whom they were more eager to encounter than professed politicians.

Thus the story is told of Alcibiades—how before the age of twenty he engaged his own guardian, Pericles, at that time prime minister of the state, in a discussion concerning laws.

Alc. Please, Pericles, can you teach me what a law is?

Per. To be sure I can.

Alc. I should be so much obliged if you would do so. One so often hears the epithet "law-abiding" applied in a complimentary sense; yet, it strikes me, one hardly deserves the compliment, if one does not know what a law is.

Per. Fortunately there is a ready answer to your difficulty. You wish to know what a law is? Well, those are laws which the majority, being met together in conclave, approve and enact as to what it is right to do, and what it is right to abstain from doing.

Alc. Enact on the hypothesis that it is right to do what is good? or to do what is bad?

Per. What is good, to be sure, young sir, not what is bad.

Alc. Supposing it is not the majority, but, as in the case of an oligarchy, the minority, who meet and enact the rules of conduct, what are these?

Per. Whatever the ruling power of the state after deliberation enacts as our duty to do, goes by the name of laws.

Alc. Then if a tyrant, holding the chief power in the state, enacts rules of conduct for the citizens, are these enactments law?

Per. Yes, anything which a tyrant as head of the state enacts, also goes by the name of law.

Alc. But, Pericles, violence and lawlessness—how do we define them? Is it not when a stronger man forces a weaker to do what seems right to him—not by persuasion but by compulsion?

Per. I should say so.

Alc. It would seem to follow that if a tyrant, without persuading the citizens, drives them by enactment to do certain things—that is lawlessness?

Per. You are right; and I retract the statement that measures passed by a tyrant without persuasion of the citizens are law.

Alc. And what of measures passed by a minority, not by persuasion of the majority, but in the exercise of its power only? Are we, or are we not, to apply the term violence to these?

Per. I think that anything which anyone forces another to do without persuasion, whether by enactment or not, is violence rather than law.

Alc. It would seem that everything which the majority, in the exercise of its power over the possessors of wealth, and without persuading them, chooses to enact, is of the nature of violence rather than of law?

To be sure (answered Pericles), adding: At your age we were clever hands at such quibbles ourselves. It was just such subtleties which we used to practice our wits upon; as you do now, if I mistake not.

To which Alcibiades replied: Ah, Pericles, I do wish we could have met in those days when you were at your cleverest in such matters.

Well, then, as soon as the desired superiority over the politicians of the day seemed to be attained, Critias and Alcibiades turned their backs on Socrates. They found his society unattractive, not to speak of the annoyance of being cross-questioned on their own shortcomings. Forthwith they devoted themselves to those affairs of state but for which they would never have come near him at all.

No; if one would seek to see true companions of Socrates, one must look to Crito,[1] and Chaerephon, and Chaerecrates, to Hermogenes, to Simmias and Cebes, to Phaedondes and others, who clung to him not to excel in the rhetoric of the Assembly or the law-courts, but with the nobler ambition of attaining to such beauty and goodliness of soul as would enable them to discharge the various duties of life to house and family, to relatives and friends, to fellow citizens, and to the state at large. Of these true followers not one in youth or old age was ever guilty, or thought guilty, of committing any evil deed.

"But for all that," the accuser insists, "Socrates taught sons to pour contumely upon their fathers[2] by persuading his young friends that he could make them wiser than their sires, or by pointing out that the law

---

[1] For these true followers, familiar to us in the pages of Plato, ("Crito," "Apol.," "Phaedo," etc.) see Cobet, "Pros. Xen."

[2] See "Apol." 20; Arist. "Clouds," 1407, where Pheidippides "drags his father Strepsiades through the mire."

allowed a son to sue his father for aberration of mind, and to imprison him, which legal ordinance he put in evidence to prove that it might be well for the wiser to imprison the more ignorant."

Now what Socrates held was, that if a man may with justice incarcerate another for no better cause than a form of folly or ignorance, this same person could not justly complain if he in his turn were kept in bonds by his superiors in knowledge; and to come to the bottom of such questions, to discover the difference between madness and ignorance was a problem which he was perpetually working at. His opinion came to this: If a madman may, as a matter of expediency to himself and his friends, be kept in prison, surely, as a matter of justice, the man who knows not what he ought to know should be content to sit at the feet of those who know, and be taught.

But it was the rest of their kith and kin, not fathers only (according to the accuser), whom Socrates dishonored in the eyes of his circle of followers, when he said that "the sick man or the litigant does not derive assistance from his relatives,[1] but from his doctor in the one case, and his legal adviser in the other." "Listen further to his language about friends," says the accuser: "What is the good of their being kindly disposed, unless they can be of some practical use to you? Mere goodness of disposition is nothing; those only are worthy of honor who combine with the knowledge of what is right the faculty of expounding it";[2] and so by bringing the young to look upon himself as a superlatively wise person gifted with an extraordinary capacity for making others wise also, he so worked on the dispositions of those who consorted with him that in their esteem the rest of the world counted for nothing by comparison with Socrates."

Now I admit the language about fathers and the rest of a man's relations. I can go further, and add some other sayings of his, that "when the soul (which is alone the indwelling center of intelligence) is gone out of a man, be he our nearest and dearest friend, we carry the body forth and bury it out of sight." "Even in life," he used to say, "each of us is ready to part with any portion of his best possession—to wit, his own body—if it be useless and unprofitable. He will remove it himself, or suffer another to do so in his stead. Thus men cut off their own nails, hair, or corns; they allow surgeons to cut and cauterise them, not without pains and aches, and are so grateful to the doctor for his services that they further give him a fee.

---

1 See Grote, "H. G." v. 535.
2 Cf. Thuc. ii. 60. Pericles says, "Yet I with whom you are so angry venture to say of myself, that I am as capable as anyone of devising and explaining a sound policy."—Jowett.

Or again, a man ejects the spittle from his mouth as far as possible.[1] Why? Because it is of no use while it stays within the system, but is detrimental rather."

Now by these instances his object was not to inculcate the duty of burying one's father alive or of cutting oneself to bits, but to show that lack of intelligence means lack of worth;[2] and so he called upon his hearers to be as sensible and useful as they could be, so that, be it father or brother or anyone else whose esteem he would deserve, a man should not hug himself in careless self-interest, trusting to mere relationship, but strive to be useful to those whose esteem he coveted.

But (pursues the accuser) by carefully culling the most immoral passages of the famous poets, and using them as evidences, he taught his associates to be evildoers and tyrranical: the line of Hesiod[3] for instance—

> No work is a disgrace; slackness of work is the disgrace—

"interpreted," says the accuser, "by Socrates as if the poet enjoined us to abstain from no work wicked or ignoble; do everything for the sake of gain."

Now while Socrates would have entirely admitted the propositions that "it is a blessing and a benefit to a man to be a worker," and that "a lazy do-nothing is a pestilent evil," that "work is good and idleness a curse," the question arises, whom did he mean by workers? In his vocabulary only those were good workmen[4] who were engaged on good work; dicers and gamblers and others engaged on any other base and ruinous business he stigmatised as the "idle drones"; and from this point of view the quotation from Hesiod is unimpeachable—

> No work is a disgrace; only idlesse is disgrace.

But there was a passage from Homer[5] forever on his lips, as the accuser tells us—the passage which says concerning Odysseus,

> What prince, or man of name, He found flight-giv'n, he
> would restrain with words of gentlest blame:
> Good sir, it fits you not to fly, or fare as one afraid
> You should not only stay yourself, but see the people stayed.

---

1 See Aristot. "Eth. Eud." vii. 1.
2 I.e. "witless and worthless are synonymous."
3 "Works and Days," 309 {"Ergon d" ouden oneidos}. Cf. Plat. "Charm." 163 C.
4 See below, III. ix. 9.
5 "Il." ii. 188 foll., 199 foll. (so Chapman).

> Thus he the best sort us'd; the worst, whose spirits brake out
>   in noise,[1]
> He cudgell'd with his sceptre, chid, and said: Stay, wretch,
>   be still,
> And hear thy betters; thou art base, and both in power
>   and skill.
> Poor and unworthy, without name in counsel or in war.
> We must not all be kings."

The accuser informs us that Socrates interpreted these lines as though the poet approved the giving of blows to commoners and poor folk. Now no such remark was ever made by Socrates; which indeed would have been tantamount to maintaining that he ought to be beaten himself. What he did say was, that those who were useful neither in word nor deed, who were incapable of rendering assistance in time of need to the army or the state or the people itself, be they never so wealthy, ought to be restrained, and especially if to incapacity they added effrontery.

As to Socrates, he was the very opposite of all this—he was plainly a lover of the people, and indeed of all mankind. Though he had many ardent admirers among citizens and strangers alike, he never demanded any fee for his society from anyone,[2] but bestowed abundantly upon all alike of the riches of his sould—good things, indeed, of which fragments accepted gratis at his hands were taken and sold at high prices to the rest of the community by some,[3] who were not, as he was, lovers of the people, since with those who had not money to give in return they refused to discourse. But of Socrates be it said that in the eyes of the whole world he reflected more honor on the state and a richer luster than ever Lichas,[4] whose fame is proverbial, shed on Lacedaemon. Lichas feasted and entertained the foreign residents in Lacedaemon at the Gymnopaediae most handsomely. Socrates gave a lifetime to the outpouring of his substance in the shape of the greatest benefits bestowed on all who cared to receive them. In other words, he made those who lived in his society better men, and sent them on their way rejoicing.

To no other conclusion, therefore, can I come but that, being so good a man, Socrates was worthier to have received honor from the state than

---

1 Lit. "But whatever man of the people he saw and found him shouting."—W. Leaf.
2 See "Symp." iv. 43; Plat. "Hipp. maj." 300 D; "Apol." 19 E.
3 See Diog. Laert. II. viii. 1.
4 See "Hell." III. ii. 21; Thuc. v. 50; Plut. "Cim." 284 C. For the Gymnopaediae, see Paus. III. xi. 9; Athen. xiv. p. 631.

death. And this I take to be the strictly legal view of the case, for what does the law require?[1] "If a man be proved to be a thief, a filcher of clothes, a cut-purse, a housebreaker, a man-stealer, a robber of temples, the penalty is death." Even so; and of all men Socrates stood most aloof from such crimes.

To the state he was never the cause of any evil—neither disaster in war, nor faction, nor treason, nor any other mischief whatsoever. And if his public life was free from all offense, so was his private. He never hurt a single soul either by deprivation of good or infliction of evil, nor did he ever lie under the imputation of any of those misdoings. WHere then is his liability to the indictment to be found? Who, so far from disbelieving in the gods, as set forth in the indictment, was conspicuous beyond all men for service to heaven; so far from corrupting the young—a charge alleged with insistence by the prosecutor—was notorious for the zeal with which he strove not only to stay his associates from evil desires, but to foster in them a passionate desire for that loveliest and queenliest of virtues without which states and families crumble to decay.[2] Such being his conduct, was he not worthy of high honor from the state of Athens?

III

It may serve to illustrate the assertion that he benefited his associates partly by the display of his own virtue and partly by verbal discourse and argument, if I set down my various recollections[3] on these heads. And first with regard to religion and the concerns of heaven. In conduct and language his behavior conformed to the rule laid down by the Pythia[4] in reply to the question, "How shall we act?" as touching a sacrifice or the worship of ancestors, or any similar point. Her answer is: "Act according to the law and custom of your state, and you will act piously." After this pattern Socrates behaved himself, and so he exhorted others to behave, holding them to be but busybodies and vain fellows who acted on any different principle.

His formula or prayer was simple: "Give me that which is best for me," for, said he, the gods know best what good things are—to pray for gold or silver or despotic power were no better than to make some particular

---

1 See "Symp." iv. 36; Plat. "Rep." 575 B; "Gorg." 508 E.
2 Or, "the noblest and proudest virtue by means of which states and families are prosperously directed."
3 Hence the title of the work, {"*Apomoneumata*"}, "Recollections, Memoirs, Memorabilia." See Diog. Laert. "Xen." II. vi. 48.
4 The Pythia at Delphi.

throw at dice or stake in battle or any such thing the subject of prayer, of which the future consequences are manifestly uncertain.[1]

If with scant means he offered but small sacrifices he believed that he was in no wise inferior to those who make frequent and large sacrifices from an ampler store. It were ill surely for the very gods themselves, could they take delight in large sacrifices rather than in small, else oftentimes must the offerings of bad men be found acceptable rather than of good; nor from the point of view of men themselves would life be worth living if the offerings of a villain rather than of a righteous man found favor in the sight of Heaven. His belief was that the joy of the gods is greater in proportion to the holiness of the giver, and he was ever an admirer of that line of Hesiod which says,

> According to thine ability do sacrifice to the immortal gods.[2]

"Yes," he would say, "in our dealings with friends and strangers alike, and in reference to the demands of life in general, there is no better motto for a man than that: "let a man do according to his ability."

Or to take another point. If it appeared to him that a sign from heaven had been given him, nothing would have induced him to go against heavenly warning: he would as soon have been persuaded to accept the guidance of a blind man ignorant of the path to lead him on a journey in place of one who knew the road and could see; and so he denounced the folly of others who do things contrary to the warnings of God in order to avoid some disrepute among men. For himself he despised all human aids by comparison with counsel from above.

The habit and style of living to which he subjected his soul and body was one which under ordinary circumstances[3] would enable anyone adopting it to look existence cheerily in the face and to pass his days serenely: it would certainly entail no difficulties as regards expense. So frugal was it that a man must work little indeed who could not earn the quantum which contented Socrates. Of food he took just enough to make eating a pleasure—the appetite he brought to it was sauce sufficient; while as to drinks, seeing that he only drank when thirsty, any draught refreshed.[4] If he accepted an invitation to dinner, he had no difficulty in avoiding the

---

1 See (Plat.) "Alcib. II." 142 foll.; Valerius Max. vii. 2; "Spectator," No. 207.
2 Hesiod, "Works and Days," 336. See "Anab." III. ii. 9.
3 {ei me ti daimonion eie}, "save under some divinely-ordained calamity." Cf. "Cyrop." I. vi. 18; "Symp." viii. 43.
4 See "Ages." ix; Cic. "Tusc." v. 34, 97; "de Fin." ii. 28, 90.

common snare of over-indulgence, and his advice to people who could not equally control their appetite was to avoid taking what would allure them to eat if not hungry or to drink if not thirsty.[1] Such things are ruinous to the constitution, he said, bad for stomachs, brains, and soul alike; or as he used to put it, with a touch of sarcasm,[2] "It must have been by feasting men on so many dainty dishes that Circe produced her pigs; only Odysseus through his continency and the "promptings[3] of Hermes" abstained from touching them immoderately, and by the same token did not turn into a swine." So much for this topic, which he touched thus lightly and yet seriously.

But as to the concerns of Aphrodite, his advice was to hold strongly aloof from the fascination of fair forms: once lay finger on these and it is not easy to keep a sound head and a sober mind. To take a particular case. It was a mere kiss which, as he had heard, Critobulus[4] had some time given to a fair youth, the son of Alcibiades.[5] Accordingly Critobulus being present, Socrates propounded the question.

Soc. Tell me, Xenophon, have you not always believed Critobulus to be a man of sound sense, not wild and self-willed? Should you not have said that he was remarkable for his prudence rather than thoughtless or foolhardy?

Xen. Certainly that is what I should have said of him.

Soc. Then you are now to regard him as quite the reverse—a hot-blooded, reckless libertine: this is the sort of man to throw somersaults into knives,[6] or to leap into the jaws of fire.

Xen. And what have you seen him doing, that you give him so bad a character?

Soc. Doing? Why, has not the fellow dared to steal a kiss from the son of Alcibiades, most fair of youths and in the golden prime?

Xen. Nay, then, if that is the foolhardy adventure, it is a danger which I could well encounter myself.

Soc. Pour soul! and what do you expect your fate to be after that kiss? Let me tell you. On the instant you will lose your freedom, the indenture of your bondage will be signed; it will be yours on compulsion to spend large sums on hurtful pleasures; you will have scarcely a moment's leisure left for any noble study; you will be driven to concern yourself most zealously

---

1 Cf. Plut. "Mor." 128 D; Clement, "Paedag." 2. 173, 33; "Strom." 2, 492, 24; Aelian, "N. A." 8, 9.
2 "Half in gibe and half in jest," in ref. to "Od." x. 233 foll.: "So she let them in..."
3 {upothemosune}, "inspiration." Cf. "Il." xv. 412; "Od." xvi. 233.
4 For Critobulus (the son of Crito) see "Econ." i. 1 foll.; "Symp." i. 3 foll.
5 See Isocr. "Or." xvi. Cobet conj. {ton tou "Axiokhou uion"}, i.e. Clinias.
6 Cf. "Symp." ii. 10, iv. 16. See Schneider ad loc.

with things which no man, not even a madman, would choose to make an object of concern.

Xen. O Heracles! how fell a power to reside in a kiss!

Soc. Does it surprise you? Do you not know that the tarantula, which is no bigger than a threepenny bit,[1] has only to touch the mouth and it will afflict its victim with pains and drive him out of his senses.

Xen. Yes, but then the creature injects something with its bite.

Soc. Ah, fool! and do you imagine that these lovely creatures infuse nothing with their kiss, simply because you do not see the poison? Do you not know that this wild beast which men call beauty in its bloom is all the more terrible than the tarantula in that the insect must first touch its victim, but this at a mere glance of the beholder, without even contact, will inject something into him—yards away—which will make him mad. And may be that is why the Loves are called "archers," because these beauties wound so far off.[2] But my advice to you, Xenophon, is, whenever you catch sight of one of these fair forms, to run helter-skelter for bare life without a glance behind; and to you, Critobulus, I would say, "Go abroad for a year: so long time will it take to heal you of this wound."

Such (he said), in the affairs of Aphrodite, as in meats and drinks, should be the circumspection of all whose footing is insecure. At least they should confine themselves to such diet as the soul would dispense with, save for some necessity of the body; and which even so ought to set up no disturbance.[3] But for himself, it was clear, he was prepared at all points and invulnerable. He found less difficulty in abstaining from beauty's fairest and fullest bloom than many others from weeds and garbage. To sum up:[4] with regard to eating and drinking and these other temptations of the sense, the equipment of his soul made him independent; he could boast honestly that in his moderate fashion[5] his pleasures were no less than theirs who take such trouble to procure them, and his pains far fewer.

IV

A belief is current, in accordance with views maintained concerning Socrates in speech and writing, and in either case conjecturally, that, however powerful he may have been in stimulating men to virtue as a

---

1 Lit. "a half-obol piece." For the {phalaggion} see Aristot. "H. A." ix. 39, 1.
2 L. Dindorf, etc. regard the sentence as a gloss. Cf. "Symp." iv. 26 ({isos de kai... entimoteron estin}).
3 Cf. "Symp." iv. 38.
4 L. Dindorf (brackets) this passage as spurious.
5 On the principle "enough is as good as a feast," {arkountos}.

theorist, he was incapable of acting as their guide himself.[1] (1) It would be well for those who adopt this view to weigh carefully not only what Socrates effected "by way of castigation" in cross-questioning whose who conceived themselves to be possessed of all knowledge, but also his everyday conversation with those who spent their time in close intercourse with himself. Having done this, let them decide whether he was incapable of making his companions better.

I will first state what I once heard fall from his lips in a discussion with Aristodemus,[2] "the little," as he was called, on the topic of divinity.[3] Socrates had observed that Aristodemus neither sacrificed nor gave heed to divination, but on the contrary was disposed to ridicule those who did.

So tell me, Aristodemus (he began), are there any human beings who have won your admiration for their wisdom?

Ar. There are.

Soc. Would you mention to us their names?

Ar. In the writings of epic poetry I have the greatest admiration for Homer.... And as a dithyrambic poet for Melanippides.[4] I admire also Sophocles as a tragedian, Polycleitus as a sculptor, and Zeuxis as a painter.

Soc. Which would you consider the more worthy of admiration, a fashioner of senseless images devoid of motion or one who could fashion living creatures endowed with understanding and activity?

Ar. Decidedly the latter, provided his living creatures owed their birth to design and were not the offspring of some chance.

Soc. But now if you had two sorts of things, the one of which presents no clue as to what it is for, and the other is obviously for some useful purpose—which would you judge to be the result of chance, which of design?

Ar. Clearly that which is produced for some useful end is the work of design.

Soc. Does it not strike you then that he who made man from the beginning[5] did for some useful end furnish him with his several senses—

---

1 Al. "If anyone believes that Socrates, as represented in certain dialogues (e.g. of Plato, Antisthenes, etc.) of an imaginary character, was an adept ({protrepsasthai}) in the art of stimulating people to virtue negatively but scarcely the man to guide ({proagein}) his hearers on the true path himself." Cf. (Plat.) "Clitophon," 410 B; Cic. "de Or." I. xlvii. 204; Plut. "Mor." 798 B. See Grote, "Plato," iii. 21; K. Joel, op. cit. p. 51 foll.; Cf. below, IV. iii. 2.

2 See Plat. "Symp." 173 B: "He was a little fellow who never wore any shoes, Aristodemus, of the deme of Cydathenaeum."—Jowett.

3 Or, "the divine element."

4 Melanippides, 430 BC See Cobet, "Pros. Xen." s.n.

5 Cf. Aristot. "de Part. Animal." 1. For the "teleological" views see IV. iii. 2 foll.

giving him eyes to behold the visible word, and ears to catch the intonations of sound? Or again, what good would there be in odors if nostrils had not been bestowed upon us? what perception of sweet things and pungent, and of all the pleasures of the palate, had not a tongue been fashioned in us as an interpreter of the same? And besides all this, do you not think this looks like a matter of foresight, this closing of the delicate orbs of sight with eyelids as with folding doors, which, when there is need to use them for any purpose, can be thrown wide open and firmly closed again in sleep? and, that even the winds of heaven may not visit them too roughly, this planting of the eyelashes as a protecting screen?[1] this coping of the region above the eyes with cornice-work of eyebrow so that no drop of sweat fall from the head and injure them? again this readiness of the ear to catch all sounds and yet not to be surcharged? this capacity of the front teeth of all animals to cut and of the "grinders" to receive the food and reduce it to pulp? the position of the mouth again, close to the eyes and nostrils as a portal of ingress for all the creature's supplies? and lastly, seeing that matter passing out[2] of the body is unpleasant, this hindward direction of the passages, and their removal to a distance from the avenues of sense? I ask you, when you see all these things constructed with such show of foresight can you doubt whether they are products of chance or intelligence?

Ar. To be sure not! Viewed in this light they would seem to be the handiwork of some wise artificer,[3] full of love for all things living.[4]

Soc. What shall we say of this passion implanted in man to beget offspring, this passion in the mother to rear her babe, and in the creature itself, once born, this deep desire of life and fear of death?

Ar. No doubt these do look like the contrivances of someone deliberately planning the existence of living creatures.

Soc. Well, and doubtless you feel to have a spark of wisdom yourself?

Ar. Put your questions, and I will answer.

Soc. And yet you imagine that elsewhere no spark of wisdom is to be found? And that, too, when you know that you have in your body a tiny fragment only of the mighty Earth, a little drop of the great waters, and of the other elements, vast in their extent, you got, I presume, a particle of each toward the compacting of your bodily frame? Mind alone, it would

---

1 *"Like a sieve"* or *"colander."*
2 *"That which goeth out of a man."*
3 *"Demiurge."*
4 Passage referred to by Epictetus ap. Stob. *"Flor."* 121, 29.

seem, which is nowhere to be found,[1] you had the lucky chance to snatch up and make off with, you cannot tell how. And these things around and about us, enormous in size, infinite in number, owe their orderly arrangement, as you suppose, to some vacuity of wit?

Ar. It may be, for my eyes fail to see the master agents of these, as one sees the fabricators of things produced on Earth.

Soc. No more do you see your own soul, which is the master agent of your body; so that, as far as that goes, you may maintain, if you like, that you do nothing with intelligence,[2] but everything by chance.

At this point Aristodemus: I assure you, Socrates, that I do not disdain the Divine power. On the contrary, my belief is that the Divinity is too grand to need any service which I could render.

Soc. But the grander that power is, which deigns to tend and wait upon you, the more you are called upon to honor it.

Ar. Be well assured, if I could believe the gods take thought for all men, I would not neglect them.

Soc. How can you suppose that they do not so take thought? Who, in the first place, gave to man alone of living creatures his erect posture, enabling him to see farther in front of him and to contemplate more freely the height above, and to be less subject to distress than other creatures (endowed like himself with eyes and ears and mouth).[3] Consider next how they gave to the beast of the field[4] feet as a means of progression only, but to man they gave in addition hands—those hands which have achieved so much to raise us in the scale of happiness above all animals. Did they not make the tongue also? which belongs indeed alike to man and beast, but in man they fashioned it so as to play on different parts of the mouth at different times, whereby we can produce articulate speech, and have a code of signals to express our every want to one another. Or consider the pleasures of the sexual appetite; limited in the rest of the animal kingdom to certain seasons, but in the case of man a series prolonged unbroken to old age. Nor did it content the Godhead merely to watch over the interests of man's body. What is of far higher import, he implanted in man the noblest and most excellent type of soul. For what other creature, to begin with, has a soul

---

1 Cf. Plat. "Phileb." 30 B: "Soc. May our body be said to have a soul? Pro. Clearly. Soc. And whence comes that soul, my dear Protarchus, unless the body of the universe, which contains elements similar to our bodies but finer, has also a soul? Can there be any other source?"—Jowett. Cic. "de N. D." ii. 6; iii. 11.
2 Or, "by your wit," {gnome}.
3 See Kuhner for an attempt to cure the text.
4 {erpetois}, a "poetical" word. Cf. "Od." iv. 418; Herod. i. 140.

to appreciate the existence of the gods who have arranged this grand and beauteous universe? What other tribe of animals save man can render service to the gods? How apt is the spirit of man to take precautions against hunger and thirst, cold and heat, to alleviate disease and foster strength! how suited to labor with a view to learning! how capable of garnering in the storehouse of his memory all that he has heard or seen or understood! Is it not most evident to you that by the side of other animals men live and move a race of gods—by nature excellent, in beauty of body and of soul supreme? For, mark you, had a creature of man's wit been encased in the body of an ox,[1] he would have been powerless to carry out his wishes, just as the possession of hands divorced from human wit is profitless. And then you come, you who have obtained these two most precious attributes, and give it as your opinion, that the gods take no thought or care for you. Why, what will you have them to do, that you may believe and be persuaded that you too are in their thoughts?

Ar. When they treat me as you tell us they treat you, and send me counsellors to warn me what I am to do and what abstain from doing,[2] I will believe.

Soc. Send you counsellors! Come now, what when the people of Athens make inquiry by oracle, and the gods" answer comes? Are you not an Athenian? Think you not that to you also the answer is given? What when they send portents to forewarn the states of Hellas? or to all mankind? Are you not a man? a Hellene? Are not these intended for you also? Can it be that you alone are excepted as a signal instance of Divine neglect? Again, do you suppose that the gods could have implanted in the heart of man the belief in their capacity to work him weal or woe had they not the power? Would not men have discovered the imposture in all this lapse of time? Do you not perceive that the wisest and most perdurable of human institutions—be they cities or tribes of men—are ever the most God-fearing; and in the individual man the riper his age and judgment, the deeper his religousness? Ay, my good sir (he broke forth), lay to heart and understand that even as your own mind within you can turn and dispose of your body as it lists, so ought we to think that the wisdom which abides within the universal frame does so dispose of all things as it finds agreeable to itself; for hardly may it be that your eye is able to range over many a league, but that the eye of God is powerless to embrace all things at a glance; or that to your soul it is given to dwell in thought on matters here or far away in Egypt or in

---

1 See Aristot. "de Part. Animal." iv. 10.
2 See IV. iii. 12.

Sicily, but that the wisdom and thought of God is not sufficient to include all things at one instant under His care. If only you would copy your own behavior[1] where human beings are concerned. It is by acts of service and of kindness that you discover which of your fellows are willing to requite you in kind. It is by taking another into your counsel that you arrive at the secret of his wisdom. If, on like principle, you will but make trial of the gods by acts of service, whether they will choose to give you counsel in matters obscure to mortal vision, you shall discover the nature and the greatness of Godhead to be such that they are able at once to see all things and to hear all things and to be present everywhere, nor does the least thing escape their watchful care.

To my mind the effect of words like these was to cause those about him to hold aloof from unholiness, baseness, and injustice, not only whilst they were seen of men, but even in the solitary place, since they must believe that no part of their conduct could escape the eye of Heaven.

V

I suppose it may be taken as admitted that self-control is a noble acquirement for a man.[2] If so, let us turn and consider whether by language like the following he was likely to lead his listeners onward[3] to the attainment of this virtue. "Sirs," he would say, "if a war came upon us and we wished to choose a man who would best help us to save ourselves and to subdue our enemy, I suppose we should scarcely select one whom we knew to be a slave to his belly, to wine, or lust, and prone to succumb to toil or sleep. Could we expect such an one to save us or to master our foes? Or if one of us were nearing the end of his days, and he wished to discover someone to whom he might entrust his sons for education, his maiden daughters for protection, and his property in general for preservation, would he deem a libertine worthy of such offices? Why, no one would dream of entrusting his flocks and herds, his storehouses and barns, or the superintendence of his works to the tender mercies of an intemperate slave. If a butler or an errand boy with such a character were offered to us we would not take him as a free gift. And if he would not accept an intemperate slave, what pains should the master himself take to avoid that imputation.[4] For with the incontinent man it is not as with the self-seeker and the covetous. These

---

1 Or, *"reason as you are wont to do."*
2 Lit. *"a beautiful and brave possession."*
3 {proubibaze}.
4 Or, *"how should the master himself beware lest he fall into that category."*

may at any rate be held to enrich themselves in depriving others. But the intemperate man cannot claim in like fashion to be a blessing to himself if a curse to his neighbors; nay, the mischief which he may cause to others is nothing by comparison with that which redounds against himself, since it is the height of mischief to ruin—I do not say one's own house and property—but one's own body and one's own soul. Or to take an example from social intercourse, no one cares for a guest who evidently takes more pleasure in the wine and the viands than in the friends beside him—who stints his comrades of the affection due to them to dote upon a mistress. Does it not come to this, that every honest man is bound to look upon self-restraint as the very cornerstone of virtue:[1] which he should seek to lay down as the basis and foundation of his soul? Without self-restraint who can lay any good lesson to heart or practice it when learned in any degree worth speaking of? Or, to put it conversely, what slave of pleasure will not suffer degeneracy of soul and body? By Hera,[2] well may every free man pray to be saved from the service of such a slave; and well too may he who is in bondage to such pleasures supplicate Heaven to send him good masters, seeing that is the one hope of salvation left him."

Well-tempered words: yet his self-restraint shone forth even more in his acts than in his language. Not only was he master over the pleasures which flow from the body, but of those also which are fed by riches, his belief being that he who receives money from this or that chance donor sets up over himself a master, and binds himself to an abominable slavery.

VI

In this context some discussions with Antiphon the sophist[3] deserve record. Antiphon approaches Socrates in hope of drawing away his associates, and in their presence thus accosts him.

Antiphon. Why, Socrates, I always thought it was expected of students of philosophy to grow in happiness daily; but you seem to have reaped other fruits from your philosophy. At any rate, you exist, I do not say live, in a style such as no slave serving under a master would put up with. Your meat and your drink are of the cheapest sort, and as to clothes, you cling to one wretched cloak which serves you for summer and winter alike; and so you go the whole year round, without shoes to your feet or a shirt to your back.

---

1 {krepida}. See Pind. "Pyth." iv. 138; ib. vii. 3; ib. fr. 93.
2 See below, III. x. 9, xi. 5; IV. ii. 9, iv. 8; "Econ." x. 1; "Cyrop." I. iv. 12; Plat. "Phaedr." 230 B. Cf. Shakesp. "by'r Lakin."
3 {o teratoskopos}, "jealous of Socrates," according to Aristotle ap. Diog. Laert. II. v. 25. See Cobet, "Pros. Xen."

Then again, you are not for taking or making money, the mere seeking of which is a pleasure, even as the possession of it adds to the sweetness and independence of existence. I do not know whether you follow the common rule of teachers, who try to fashion their pupils in imitation of themselves,[1] and propose to mold the characters of your companions; but if you do you ought to dub yourself professor of the art of wretchedness.[2]

Thus challenged, Socrates replied: One thing to me is certain, Antiphon; you have conceived so vivid an idea of my life of misery that for yourself you would choose death sooner than live as I do. Suppose now we turn and consider what it is you find so hard in my life. Is it that he who takes payment must as a matter of contract finish the work for which he is paid, whereas I, who do not take it, lie under no constraint to discourse except with whom I choose? Do you despise my dietary on the ground that the food which I eat is less wholesome and less stengthening than yours, or that the articles of my consumption are so scarce and so much costlier to procure than yours? Or have the fruits of your marketing a flavor denied to mine? Do you not know the sharper the appetite the less the need of sauces, the keener the thirst the less the desire for out-of-the-way drinks? And as to raiment, clothes, you know, are changed on account of cold or else of heat. People only wear boots and shoes in order not to gall their feet and be prevented walking. Now I ask you, have you ever noticed that I keep more within doors than others on account of the cold? Have you ever seen me battling with anyone for shade on account of the heat? Do you not know that even a weakling by nature may, by dint of exercise and practice, come to outdo a giant who neglects his body? He will beat him in the particular point of training, and bear the strain more easily. But you apparently will not have it that I, who am forever training myself to endure this, that, and the other thing which may befall the body, can brave all hardships more easily than yourself for instance, who perhaps are not so practiced. And to escape slavery to the belly or to sleep or lechery, can you suggest more effective means than the possession of some powerful attraction, some counter-charm which shall gladden not only in the using, but by the hope enkindled of its lasting usefulness? And yet this you do know; joy is not to him who feels that he is doing well in nothing—it belongs to one who is persuaded that things are progressing with him, be it tillage or the working of a vessel,[3] or any of the thousand and one things on which a man may

---

1 Or, *"try to turn out their pupils as copies of themselves."*
2 See Arist. *"Clouds,"* {*on o kakodaimon Sokrates kai Khairephon*}.
3 *"The business of a shipowner or skipper."*

chance to be employed. To him it is given to rejoice as he reflects, "I am doing well." But is the pleasured derived from all these put together half as joyous as the consciousness of becoming better oneself, of acquiring better and better friends? That, for my part, is the belief I continue to cherish.

Again, if it be a question of helping one's friends or country, which of the two will have the larger leisure to devote to these objects—he who leads the life which I lead today, or he who lives in the style which you deem so fortunate? Which of the two will adopt a soldier's life more easily—the man who cannot get on without expensive living, or he to whom whatever comes to hand suffices? Which will be the readier to capitulate and cry "mercy" in a siege—the man of elaborate wants, or he who can get along happily with the readiest things to hand? You, Antiphon, would seem to suggest that happiness consists of luxury and extravagance; I hold a different creed. To have no wants at all is, to my mind, an attribute of Godhead;[1] to have as few wants as possible the nearest approach to Godhead; and as that which is divine is mightiest, so that is next mightiest which comes closest to the divine.

Returning to the charge at another time, this same Antiphon engaged Socrates in conversation thus.

Ant. Socrates, for my part, I believe you to be a good and upright man; but for your wisdom I cannot say much. I fancy you would hardly dispute the verdict yourself, since, as I remark, you do not ask a money payment for your society; and yet if it were your cloak now, or your house, or any other of your possessions, you would set some value upon it, and never dream, I will not say of parting with it gratis, but of exchanging it for less than its worth. A plain proof, to my mind, that if you thought your society worth anything, you would ask for it not less than its equivalent in gold.[2] Hence the conclusion to which I have come, as already stated: good and upright you may be, since you do not cheat people from pure selfishness; but wise you cannot be, since your knowledge is not worth a cent.

To this onslaught Socrates: Antiphon, it is a tenet which we cling to that beauty and wisdom have this in common, that there is a fair way and a foul way in which to dispose of them. The vendor of beauty purchases an evil name, but supposing the same person has discerned a soul of beauty in his lover and makes that man his friend, we regard his choice as sensible.[3] So is it with wisdom; he who sells it for money to the first bidder we name a

---

1 Cf. Aristot. "Eth. N." x. viii. 1.
2 Or rather "money," lit. "silver."
3 Add "and a sign of modesty," {sophrona nomizomen}.

sophist,[1] as though one should say a man who prostitutes his wisdom; but if the same man, discerning the noble nature of another, shall teach that other every good thing, and make him his friend, of such a one we say he does that which it is the duty of every good citizen of gentle soul to do. In accordance with this theory, I too, Antiphon, having my tastes, even as another finds pleasure in his horse and his hounds,[2] and another in his fighting cocks, so I too take my pleasure in good friends; and if I have any good thing myself I teach it them, or I commend them to others by whom I think they will be helped forward on the path of virtue. The treasures also of the wise of old, written and bequeathed in their books,[3] I unfold and peruse in common with my friends. If our eye light upon any good thing we cull it eagerly, and regard it as great gain if we may but grow in friendship with one another.

As I listened to this talk I could not but reflect that he, the master, was a person to be envied, and that we, his hearers, were being led by him to beauty and nobility of soul.

Again on some occasion the same Antiphon asked Socrates how he expected to make politicians of others when, even if he had the knowledge, he did not engage in politics himself.

Socrates replied: I will put to you a question, Antiphon: Which were the more statesmanlike proceeding, to practice politics myself single-handed, or to devote myself to making as many others as possible fit to engage in that pursuit?

VII

Let us here turn and consider whether by deterring his associates from quackery and false seeming he did not directly stimulate them to the pursuit of virtue.[4] He used often to say there was no better road to renown than the one by which a man became good at that wherein he desired to be reputed good.[5] The truth of the concept he enforced as follows: "Let us reflect on what a man would be driven to do who wanted to be thought a good flute player, without really being so. He would be forced to imitate the good flute player in the externals of his art, would he not? and first of all, seeing that these artists always have a splendid equipment,[6] and travel about with a

---

1 {*sophistas*}. See Grote, "H. G." viii. 482 foll.; "Hunting," xi. foll.
2 Cf. Plat. "Lys." 211 E.
3 Cf. "Symp." iv. 27.
4 {*apotrepon proutrepen*}. See K. Joel, op. cit. p. 450 foll.
5 Cf. "Cyrop." I. vi. 22.
6 Or, "furniture of the finest," like Arion's in Herod. i. 24. Schneid. cf. Demosth. 565. 6.

long train of attendants, he must have the same; in the next place, they can command the plaudits of a multitude, he therefore must pack a conclave of clackers. But one thing is clear: nothing must induce him to give a performance, or he will be exposed at once, and find himself a laughing-stock not only as a sorry sort of flute player, but as a wretched imposter. And now he has a host of expenses to meet; and not one advantage to be reaped; and worse than all his evil reputation. What is left him but to lead a life stale and unprofitable, the scorn and mockery of men? Let us try another case. Suppose a man wished to be thought a good general or a good pilot, though he were really nothing of the sort, let us picture to our minds how it will fare with him. Of two misfortunes one: either with a strong desire to be thought proficient in these matters, he will fail to get others to agree with him, which will be bad enough; or he will succeed, with worse result; since it stands to reason that anyone appointed to work a vessel or lead an army without the requisite knowledge will speedily ruin a number of people whom he least desires to hurt, and will make but a sorry exit from the stage himself." Thus first by one instance and then another would he demonstrate the unprofitableness of trying to appear rich, or courageous, or strong, without really being the thing pretended. "You are sure sooner or later to have commands laid upon you beyond your power to execute, and failing just where you are credited with capacity, the world will give you no commiseration." "I call that man a cheat, and a great cheat too," he would say, "who gets money or goods out of someone by persuasion, and defrauds him; but of all imposters he surely is the biggest who can delude people into thinking that he is fit to lead the state, when all the while he is a worthless creature."[1]

BOOK II

I

Now, if the effect of such discourses was, as I imagine, to deter his hearers from the paths of quackery and false-seeming,[2] so I am sure that language like the following was calculated to stimulate his followers to

---

[1] Here follows the sentence ({emoi men oun edokei kai tou alazoneuesthai apotrepein tous sunontas toiade dialegomenos}), which, for the sake of convenience, I have attached to the first sentence of Bk. II. ch. i. ({edokei de moi... ponou.}) I believe that the commentators are right in bracketing both one and the other as editorial interpolations.

[2] This sentence in the Greek concludes Bk. I. There is something wrong or very awkward in the text here.

practice self-control and endurance: self-control in the matters of eating, drinking, sleeping, and the cravings of lust; endurance of cold and heat and toil and pain. He had noticed the undue licence which one of his acquaintances allowed himself in all such matters.[1] Accordingly he thus addressed him:

Tell me, Aristippus (Socrates said), supposing you had two children entrusted to you to educate, one of them must be brought up with an aptitude for government, and the other without the faintest propensity to rule—how would you educate them? What do you say? Shall we begin our inquiry from the beginning, as it were, with the bare elements of food and nutriment?

Ar. Yes, food to begin with, by all means, being a first principle,[2] without which there is no man living but would perish.

Soc. Well, then, we may expect, may we not, that a desire to grasp food at certain seasons will exhibit itself in both the children?

Ar. It is to be expected.

Soc. Which, then, of the two must be trained, of his own free will,[3] to prosecute a pressing business rather than gratify the belly?

Ar. No doubt the one who is being trained to govern, if we would not have affairs of state neglected during[4] his government.

Soc. And the same pupil must be furnished with a power of holding out against thirst also when the craving to quench it comes upon him?

Ar. Certainly he must.

Soc. And on which of the two shall we confer such self-control in regard to sleep as shall enable him to rest late and rise early, or keep vigil, if the need arise?

Ar. To the same one of the two must be given that endurance also.

Soc. Well, and a continence in regard to matters sexual so great that nothing of the sort shall prevent him from doing his duty? Which of them claims that?

Ar. The same one of the pair again.

Soc. Well, and on which of the two shall be bestowed, as a further gift, the voluntary resolution to face toils rather than turn and flee from them?

Ar. This, too, belongs of right to him who is being trained for government.

---

1 Cf. Grote, "Plato," III. xxxviii. p. 530.
2 Aristippus plays upon the word {arkhe}.
3 {proairesis}.
4 Lit. "along of."

Soc. Well, and to which of them will it better accord to be taught all knowledge necessary toward the mastery of antagonists?

Ar. To our future ruler certainly, for without these parts of learning all his other capacities will be merely waste.

Soc. [1]Will not a man so educated be less liable to be entrapped by rival powers, and so escape a common fate of living creatures, some of which (as we all know) are hooked through their own greediness, and often even in spite of a native shyness; but through appetite for food they are drawn toward the bait, and are caught; while others are similarly ensnared by drink?

Ar. Undoubtedly.

Soc. And others again are victims of amorous heat, as quails, for instance, or partridges, which, at the cry of the hen-bird, with lust and expectation of such joys grow wild, and lose their power of computing dangers: on they rush, and fall into the snare of the hunter?

Aristippus assented.

Soc. And would it not seem to be a base thing for a man to be affected like the silliest bird or beast? as when the adulterer invades the innermost sanctum[2] of the house, though he is well aware of the risks which his crime involves,[3] the formidable penalties of the law, the danger of being caught in the toils, and then suffering the direst contumely. Considering all the hideous penalties which hang over the adulterer's head, considering also the many means at hand to release him from the thraldom of his passion, that a man should so drive headlong on to the quicksands of perdition[4] —what are we to say of such frenzy? The wretch who can so behave must surely be tormented by an evil spirit?[5]

Ar. So it strikes me.

Soc. And does it not strike you as a sign of strange indifference that, whereas the greater number of the indispensable affairs of men, as for instance, those of war and agriculture, and more than half the rest, need to be conducted under the broad canopy of heaven,[6] yet the majority of men are quite untrained to wrestle with cold and heat?

Aristippus again assented.

---

1 (SS. 4, 5, L. Dind. ed Lips.)
2 {eis as eirktas}. The penetralia.
3 Or, "he knows the risks he runs of suffering those penalties with which the law threatens his crime should he fall into the snare, and being caught, be mutilated."
4 Or, "leap headlong into the jaws of danger."
5 {kakodaimonontos}.
6 Or, "in the open air."

Soc. And do you not agree that he who is destined to rule must train himself to bear these things lightly?

Ar. Most certainly.

Soc. And whilst we rank those who are self-disciplined in all these matters among persons fit to rule, we are bound to place those incapable of such conduct in the category of persons without any pretension whatsoever to be rulers?

Ar. I assent.

Soc. Well, then, since you know the rank peculiar to either section of mankind, did it ever strike you to consider to which of the two you are best entitled to belong?

Yes I have (replied Aristippus). I do not dream for a moment of ranking myself in the class of those who wish to rule. In fact, considering how serious a business it is to cater for one's own private needs, I look upon it as the mark of a fool not to be content with that, but to further saddle oneself with the duty of providing the rest of the community with whatever they may be pleased to want. That, at the cost of much personal enjoyment, a man should put himself at the head of a state, and then, if he fail to carry through every jot and tittle of that state's desire, be held to criminal account, does seem to me the very extravagance of folly. Why, bless me! States claim to treat their rulers precisely as I treat my domestic slaves. I expect my attendants to furnish me with an abundance of necessaries, but not to lay a finger on one of them themselves. So these states regard it as the duty of a ruler to provide them with all the good things imaginable, but to keep his own hands off them all the while.[1] So then, for my part, if anybody desires to have a heap of pother himself,[2] and be a nuisance to the rest of the world, I will educate him in the manner suggested, and he shall take his place among those who are fit to rule; but for myself, I beg to be enrolled among those who wish to spend their days as easily and pleasantly as possible.

Soc. Shall we then at this point turn and inquire which of the two are likely to lead the pleasanter life, the rulers or the ruled?

Ar. By all means let us do so.

Soc. To begin then with the nations and races known to ourselves.[3] In Asia the Persians are the rulers, while the Syrians, Phrygians, Lydians are ruled; and in Europe we find the Scythians ruling, and the Maeotians being

---

1 Or, "but he must have no finger in the pie himself."
2 See Kuhner ad loc.
3 Or, "the outer world, the non-Hellenic races and nationalities of which we have any knowledge."

ruled. In Africa[1] the Carthaginians are rulers, the Libyans ruled. Which of these two sets respectively leads the happier life, in your opinion? Or, to come nearer home—you are yourself a Hellene—which among Hellenes enjoy the happier existence, think you, the dominant or the subject states?

Nay,[2] I would have you to understand (exclaimed Aristippus) that I am just as far from placing myself in the ranks of slavery; there is, I take it, a middle path between the two which it is my ambition to tread, avoiding rule and slavery alike; it lies through freedom—the high road which leads to happiness.

Soc. True, if only your path could avoid human beings, as it avoids rule and slavery, there would be something in what you say. But being placed as you are amidst human beings, if you purpose neither to rule nor to be ruled, and do not mean to dance attendance, if you can help it, on those who rule, you must surely see that the stronger have an art to seat the weaker on the stool of repentance[3] both in public and in private, and to treat them as slaves. I daresay you have not failed to note this common case: a set of people has sown and planted, whereupon in comes another set and cuts their corn and fells their fruit-trees, and in every way lays siege to them because, though weaker, they refuse to pay them proper court, till at length they are persuaded to accept slavery rather than war against their betters. And in private life also, you will bear me out, the brave and powerful are known to reduce the helpless and cowardly to bondage, and to make no small profit out of their victims.

Ar. Yes, but I must tell you I have a simple remedy against all such misadventures. I do not confine myself to any single civil community. I roam the wide world a foreigner.

Soc. Well, now, that is a masterly stroke, upon my word![4] Of course, ever since the decease of Sinis, and Sciron, and Procrustes,[5] foreign travellers have had an easy time of it. But still, if I bethink me, even in these modern days the members of free communities do pass laws in their respective countries for self-protection against wrongdoing. Over and above their personal connections, they provide themselves with a host of friends; they gird their cities about with walls and battlements; they collect

---

1 Lit. "Libya."
2 Or, "Pardon me interrupting you, Socrates; but I have not the slightest intention of placing myself." See W. L. Newman, op. cit. i. 306.
3 See "Symp." iii. 11; "Cyrop." II. ii. 14; Plat. "Ion," 535 E; L. Dindorf ad loc.
4 Or, "Well foiled!" "A masterly fall! my prince of wrestlers."
5 For these mythical highway robbers, see Diod. iv. 59; and for Sciron in particular, Plut. "Theseus," 10.

armaments to ward off evil-doers; and to make security doubly sure, they furnish themselves with allies from foreign states. In spite of all which defensive machinery these same free citizens do occasionally fall victims to injustice. But you, who are without any of these aids; you, who pass half your days on the high roads where iniquity is rife;[1] you, who, into whatever city you enter, are less than the least of its free members, and moreover are just the sort of person whom anyone bent on mischief would single out for attack—yet you, with your foreigner's passport, are to be exempt from injury? So you flatter yourself. And why? Will the state authorities cause proclamation to be made on your behalf: "The person of this man Aristippus is secure; let his going out and his coming in be free from danger"? Is that the ground of your confidence? or do you rather rest secure in the consciousness that you would prove such a slave as no master would care to keep? For who would care to have in his house a fellow with so slight a disposition to work and so strong a propensity to extravagance? Suppose we stop and consider that very point: how do masters deal with that sort of domestic? If I am not mistaken, they chastise his wantonness by starvation; they balk his thieving tendencies by bars and bolts where there is anything to steal; they hinder him from running away by bonds and imprisonment; they drive the sluggishness out of him with the lash. Is it not so? Or how do you proceed when you discover the like tendency in one of your domestics?

Ar. I correct them with all the plagues, till I force them to serve me properly. But, Socrates, to return to your pupil educated in the royal art,[2] which, if I mistake not, you hold to be happiness: how, may I ask, will he be better off than others who lie in evil case, in spite of themselves, simply because they suffer perforce, but in his case the hunger and the thirst, the cold shivers and the lying awake at nights, with all the changes he will ring on pain, are of his own choosing? For my part I cannot see what difference it makes, provided it is one and the same bare back which receives the stripes, whether the whipping be self-appointed or unasked for; nor indeed does it concern my body in general, provided it be my body, whether I am beleaguered by a whole armament of such evils[3] of my own will or against my will—except only for the folly which attaches to self-appointed suffering.

---

1 Or, "where so many suffer wrong."
2 Cf. below, IV. ii. 11; Plat. "Statesm." 259 B; "Euthyd." 291 C; K. Joel, op. cit. p. 387 foll. "Aristippus anticipates Adeimantus" ("Rep." 419), W. L. Newman, op. cit. i. 395.
3 Cf. "suffers the slings and arrows of outrageous fortune."

Soc. What, Aristippus, does it not seem to you that, as regards such matters, there is all the difference between voluntary and involuntary suffering, in that he who starves of his own accord can eat when he chooses, and he who thirsts of his own free will can drink, and so for the rest; but he who suffers in these ways perforce cannot desist from the suffering when the humor takes him? Again, he who suffers hardship voluntarily, gaily confronts his troubles, being buoyed on hope[1]—just as a hunter in pursuit of wild beasts, through hope of capturing his quarry, finds toil a pleasure—and these are but prizes of little worth in return for their labors; but what shall we say of their reward who toil to obtain to themselves good friends, or to subdue their enemies, or that through strength of body and soul they may administer their households well, befriend their friends, and benefit the land which gave them birth? Must we not suppose that these too will take their sorrows lightly, looking to these high ends? Must we not suppose that they too will gaily confront existence, who have to support them not only their conscious virtue, but the praise and admiration of the world?[2] And once more, habits of indolence, along with the fleeting pleasures of the moment, are incapable, as gymnastic trainers say, of setting up[3] a good habit of body, or of implanting in the soul any knowledge worthy of account; whereas by painstaking endeavor in the pursuit of high and noble deeds, as good men tell us, through endurance we shall in the end attain the goal. So Hesiod somewhere says:[4]

> Wickedness may a man take wholesale with ease, smooth is the way and her dwelling-place is very nigh; but in front of virtue the immortal gods have placed toil and sweat, long is the path and steep that leads to her, and rugged at the first, but when the summit of the pass is reached, then for all its roughness the path grows easy.

And Ephicharmus[5] bears his testimony when he says:

> The gods sell us all good things in return for our labors.

And again in another passage he exclaims:

---

1 Cf. above, I. vi. 8.
2 Or, "in admiration of themselves, the praise and envy of the world at large."
3 See Hippocrates, "V. Med." 18.
4 Hesiod, "Works and Days," 285. See Plat. "Prot." 340 C; "Rep." ii. 364 D; "Laws," iv. 718 E.
5 Epicharmus of Cos, the chief comic poet among the Dorians, fl. 500 BC Cf. Plat. "Theaet." 152 E, "the prince of comedy"; "Gorg." 505 D.

> Set not thine heart on soft things, thou knave, lest thou light upon the hard.

And that wise man Prodicus[1] delivers himself in a like strain concerning virtue in that composition of his about Heracles, which crowds have listened to.[2] This, as far as I can recollect it, is the substance at least of what he says:

> "When Heracles was emerging from boyhood into the bloom of youth, having reached that season in which the young man, now standing upon the verge of independence, shows plainly whether he will enter upon the path of virtue or of vice, he went forth into a quiet place, and sat debating with himself which of those two paths he should pursue; and as he there sat musing, there appeared to him two women of great stature which drew nigh to him. The one was fair to look upon, frank and free by gift of nature,[3] her limbs adorned with purity and her eyes with bashfulness; sobriety set the rhythm of her gait, and she was clad in white apparel. The other was of a different type; the fleshy softness of her limbs betrayed her nurture, while the complexion of her skin was embellished that she might appear whiter and rosier than she really was, and her figure that she might seem taller than nature made her; she stared with wide-open eyes, and the raiment wherewith she was clad served but to reveal the ripeness of her bloom. With frequent glances she surveyed her person, or looked to see if others noticed her; while ever and anon she fixed her gaze upon the shadow of herself intently.

> "Now when these two had drawn near to Heracles, she who was first named advanced at an even pace[4] toward him, but the other, in her eagerness to outstrip her, ran forward to the youth, exclaiming, 'I see you, Heracles, in doubt and

---

1 Prodicus of Ceos. See Plat. "Men." 24; "Cratyl." 1; Philostr. "Vit. Soph." i. 12.
2 Or, "which he is fond of reciting as a specimen of style." The title of the {epideixis} was {"Orai"} according to Suidas, {Prodikos}.
3 Reading {eleutherion phusei,...} or if {eleutherion, phusei...} translate "nature had adorned her limbs..."
4 Or, "without change in her demeanor."

difficulty what path of life to choose; make me your friend, and I will lead you to the pleasantest road and easiest. This I promise you: you shall taste all of life's sweets and escape all bitters. In the first place, you shall not trouble your brain with war or business; other topics shall engage your mind;[1] your only speculation, what meat or drink you shall find agreeable to your palate; what delight[2] of ear or eye; what pleasure of smell or touch; what darling lover's intercourse shall most enrapture you; how you shall pillow your limbs in softest slumber; how cull each individual pleasure without alloy of pain; and if ever the suspicion steal upon you that the stream of joys will one day dwindle, trust me I will not lead you where you shall replenish the store by toil of body and trouble of soul. No! Others shall labor, but you shall reap the fruit of their labors; you shall withhold your hand from nought which shall bring you gain. For to all my followers I give authority and power to help themselves freely from every side."

Heracles hearing these words made answer: "What, O lady, is the name you bear?" To which she: "Know that my friends call be Happiness, but they that hate me have their own nicknames[3] for me, Vice and Naughtiness."

But just then the other of those fair women approached and spoke: "Heracles, I too am come to you, seeing that your parents are well known to me, and in your nurture I have gauged your nature; wherefore I entertain good hope that if you choose the path which leads to me, you shall greatly bestir yourself to be the doer of many a doughty deed of noble emprise; and that I too shall be held in even higher honor for your sake, lit with the luster shed by valorous deeds.[4] I will not cheat you with preludings of pleasure,[5] but I will relate to you the things that are according to the ordinances of God in very truth. Know then that among things that are lovely and of good report, not one have the gods bestowed upon mortal men apart from toil and pains. Would you obtain the favor of the gods,

---

1 Reading {diese}, or {dioisei}, "you shall continue speculating solely."
2 It will be recollected that Prodicus prided himself on {orthotes onomaton}. Possibly Xenophon is imitating (caricaturing?) his style. {terphtheies, estheies, euphrantheies}.
3 So the vulg. {upokorizomenoi} is interpreted. Cobet ("Pros. Xen." p. 36) suggests {upoknizomenoi} = "quippe qui desiderio pungantur."
4 Or, "bathed in the splendour of thy virtues."
5 Or, "honeyed overtures of pleasure."

then must you pay these same gods service; would you be loved by your friends, you must benefit these friends; do you desire to be honored by the state, you must give the state your aid; do you claim admiration for your virtue from all Hellas, you must strive to do some good to Hellas; do you wish Earth to yield her fruits to you abundantly, to Earth must you pay your court; do you seek to amass riches from your flocks and herds, on them must you bestow your labor; or is it your ambition to be potent as a warrior, able to save your friends and to subdue your foes, then must you learn the arts of war from those who have the knowledge, and practice their application in the field when learned; or would you e'en be powerful of limb and body, then must you habituate limbs and body to obey the mind, and exercise yourself with toil and sweat."

At this point, (as Prodicus relates) Vice broke in exclaiming: "See you, Heracles, how hard and long the road is by which yonder woman would escort you to her festal joys.[1] But I will guide you by a short and easy road to happiness."

Then spoke Virtue: "Nay, wretched one, what good thing hast thou? or what sweet thing art thou acquainted with—that wilt stir neither hand nor foot to gain it? Thou, that mayest not even await the desire of pleasure, but, or ever that desire springs up, art already satiated; eating before thou hungerest, and drinking before thou thirsteth; who to eke out an appetite must invent an army of cooks and confectioners; and to whet thy thirst must lay down costliest wines, and run up and down in search of ice in summer-time; to help thy slumbers soft coverlets suffice not, but couches and feather-beds must be prepared thee and rockers to rock thee to rest; since desire for sleep in thy case springs not from toil but from vacuity and nothing in the world to do. Even the natural appetite of love thou forcest prematurely by every means thou mayest devise, confounding the sexes in thy service. Thus thou educatest thy friends: with insult in the night season and drowse of slumber during the precious hours of the day. Immortal, thou art cast forth from the company of gods, and by good men art dishonored: that sweetest sound of all, the voice of praise, has never thrilled thine ears; and the fairest of all fair visions is hidden from thine eyes that have never beheld one bounteous deed wrought by thine own hand. If thou openest thy lips in speech, who will believe thy word? If thou hast need of aught, none shall satisfy thee. What sane man will venture to join thy rablle rout? Ill indeed are thy revellers to look upon, young men impotent of body, and old men witless in mind: in the heyday of life they batten in sleek idleness,

---

1 Hesiod, *"Theog."* 909; Milton, *"L'Allegro,"* 12.

and wearily do they drag through an age of wrinkled wretchedness: and why? they blush with shame at the thought of deeds done in the past, and groan for weariness at what is left to do. During their youth they ran riot through their sweet things, and laid up for themselves large store of bitterness against the time of eld. But my companionship is with the gods; and with the good among men my conversation; no bounteous deed, divine or human, is wrought without my aid. Therefore am I honored in Heaven pre-eminently, and upon Earth among men whose right it is to honor me;[1] as a beloved fellow worker of all craftsmen; a faithful guardian of house and lands, whom the owners bless; a kindly helpmeet of servants;[2] a brave assistant in the labors of peace; an unflinching ally in the deeds of war; a sharer in all friendships indispensable. To my friends is given an enjoyment of meats and drinks, which is sweet in itself and devoid of trouble, in that they can endure until desire ripens, and sleep more delicious visits them than those who toil not. Yet they are not pained to part with it; nor for the sake of slumber do they let slip the performance of their duties. Among my followers the youth delights in the praises of his elders, and the old man glories in the honor of the young; with joy they call to memory their deeds of old, and in today's well-doing are well pleased. For my sake they are dear in the sight of God, beloved of their friends and honored by the country of their birth. When the appointed goal is reached they lie not down in oblivion with dishonor, but bloom afresh—their praise resounded on the lips of men forever.[3] Toils like these, O son of noble parents, Heracles, it is yours to meet with, and having endured, to enter into the heritage assured you of transcendant happiness."

This, Aristippus, in rough sketch is the theme which Prodicus pursues[4] in his "Education of Heracles by Virtue," only he decked out his sentiments, I admit, in far more magnificent phrases than I have ventured on. Were it not well, Aristippus, to lay to heart these sayings, and to strive to bethink you somewhat of that which touches the future of our life?

II

At another time, he had noticed the angry temper shown by Lamprocles, the elder of his sons, toward their mother, and thus addressed himself to the lad.

---

1 Reading {ois prosekei}, or if {proseko}, translate "to whom I am attached."
2 Cf. "Econ." v. 8.
3 Or, "so true is it, a branch is left them; undying honor to their name!"
4 Reading {diokei}, al. {diokei} = "so Prodicus arranged the parts of his discourse."

Soc. Pray, my son, did you ever hear of certain people being called ungrateful?

That I have (replied the young man).

Soc. And have you understood what it is they do to get that bad name?

Lamp. Yes, I have: when anyone has been kindly treated, and has it in his power to requite the kindness but neglects to do so, men call him ungrateful.

Soc. And you admit that people reckon the ungrateful among wrongdoers?

Lamp. I do.

Soc. And has it ever struck you to inquire whether, as regards the right or wrong of it, ingratitude may not perhaps resemble some such conduct as the enslavement, say, of prisoners, which is accounted wrong toward friends but justifiable toward enemies?

Lamp. Yes, I have put that question to myself. In my opinion, no matter who confers the kindness, friend or foe, the recipient should endeavor to requite it, failing which he is a wrongdoer.

Soc. Then if that is how the matter stands, ingratitude would be an instance of pure unadulterate wrongdoing?

Lamprocles assented to the proposition.

Soc. It follows, then, that in proportion to the greatness of the benefit conferred, the greater his misdoing who fails to requite the kindness?

Lamprocles again assented.

Socrates continued: And where can we hope to find greater benefits than those which children derive from their parents—their father and mother who brought them out of nothingness into being, who granted them to look upon all these fair sights, and to partake of all those blessings which the gods bestow on man, things so priceless in our eyes that one and all we shudder at the thought of leaving them, and states have made death the penalty for the greatest crimes, because there is no greater evil through fear of which to stay iniquity.

You do not suppose that human beings produce children for the sake of carnal pleasure[1] merely; were this the motive, street and bordell are full of means to quit them of that thrall; whereas nothing is plainer than the pains we take to seek out wives who shall bear us the finest children.[2] With these we wed, and carry on the race. The man has a twofold duty to perform: partly in cherishing her who is to raise up children along with him, and partly toward the children yet unborn in providing them with things that

---

1 Lit. *"the joys of Aphrodite."*
2 *"For the procreation of children."* See below, IV. iv. 22; *"Pol. Lac."* i.

he thinks will contribute to their well-being—and of these as large a store as possible. The woman, conceiving, bears her precious burthen with travail and pain, and at the risk of life itself—sharing with that within her womb the food on which she herself is fed. And when with much labor she has borne to the end and brought forth her offspring, she feeds it and watches over it with tender care—not in return for any good thing previously received, for indeed the babe itself is little conscious of its benefactor and cannot even signify its wants; only she, the mother, making conjecture of what is good for it, and what will please it, essays to satisfy it;[1] and for many months she feeds it night and day, enduring the toil nor recking what return she shall receive for all her trouble. Nor does the care and kindness of parents end with nurture; but when the children seem of an age to learn, they teach them themselves whatever cunning they possess, as a guide to life, or where they feel that another is more competent, to him they send them to be taught at their expense. Thus they watch over their children, doing all in their power to enable them to grow up to be as good as possible.

So be it (the youth answered); but even if she have done all that, and twenty times as much, no soul on Earth could endure my mother's cross-grained temper.

Then Socrates: Which, think you, would be harder to bear—a wild beast's savagery or a mother's?

Lamp. To my mind, a mother's—at least if she be such as mine.

Soc. Dear me! And has this mother ever done you any injury—such as people frequently receive from beasts, by bite or kick?

Lamp. If she has not done quite that, she uses words which anyone would sooner sell his life than listen to.

Soc. And how many annoyances have you caused your mother, do you suppose, by fretfulness and peevishness in word and deed, night and day, since you were a little boy? How much sorrow and pain, when you were ill?

Lamp. Well, I never said or did anything to bring a blush to her cheeks.

Soc. No, come now! Do you suppose it is harder for you to listen to your mother's speeches than for actor to listen to actor on the tragic stage,[2] when the floodgates of abuse are opened?

Lamp. Yes; for the simple reason that they know it is all talk on their parts. The inquisitor may cross-question, but he will not inflict a fine; the threatener may hurl his menaces, but he will do no mischief—that is why they take it all so easily.

---

1 Lit. "to leave nought lacking."
2 See Grote, "H. G." viii. 457; Plut. "Solon," xxix.

Soc. Then ought you to fly into a passion, who know well enough that, whatever your mother says, she is so far from meaning you mischief that she is actually wishing blessings to descend upon you beyond all others? Or do you believe that your mother is really ill disposed toward you?

Lamp. No, I do not think that.

Soc. Then this mother, who is kindly disposed to you, and takes such tender care of you when you are ill to make you well again, and to see that you want for nothing which may help you; and, more than all, who is perpetually pleading for blessings in your behalf and offering her vows to Heaven[1]—can you say of her that she is cross-grained and harsh? For my part, I think, if you cannot away with such a mother, you cannot away with such blessings either.

But tell me (he proceeded), do you owe service to any living being, think you? or are you prepared to stand alone? Prepared not to please or try to please a single soul? to follow none? To obey neither general nor ruler of any sort? Is that your attitude, or do you admit that you owe allegiance to somebody?

Lamp. Yes; certainly I owe allegiance.

Soc. May I take it that you are willing to please at any rate your neighbor, so that he may kindle a fire for you in your need, may prove himself a ready helpmate in good fortune, or if you chance on evil and are stumbling, may friendlily stand by your side to aid?

Lamp. I am willing.

Soc. Well, and what of that other chance companion—your fellow traveller by land or sea? what of any others, you may light upon? is it indifferent to you whether these be friends or not, or do you admit that the goodwill of these is worth securing by some pains on your part?

Lamp. I do.

Soc. It stands thus then: you are prepared to pay attention to this, that, and the other stranger, but to your mother who loves you more than all else, you are bound to render no service, no allegiance? Do you not know that whilst the state does not concern itself with ordinary ingratitude or pass judicial sentence on it; whilst it overlooks the thanklessness of those who fail to make return for kindly treatment, it reserves its pains and penalties for the special case? If a man render not the service and allegiance due to his parents, on him the finger of the law is laid; his name is struck off the roll; he is forbidden to hold the archonship—which is as much as to say, "Sacrifices in behalf of the state offered by such a man would be no

---

1 Or, "paying vows."

offerings, being tainted with impiety; nor could aught else be "well and justly" performed of which he is the doer." Heaven help us! If a man fail to adorn the sepulchre of his dead parents the state takes cognizance of the matter, and inquisition is made in the scrutiny of the magistrates.[1] And as for you, my son, if you are in your sober senses, you will earnestly entreat your mother, lest the very gods take you to be an ungrateful being, and on their side also refuse to do you good; and you will beware of men also, lest they should perceive your neglect of your parents, and with one consent hold you in dishonor;[2] and so you find yourself in a desert devoid of friends. For if once the notion be entertained that here is a man ungrateful to his parents, no one will believe that any kindness shown you would be other than thrown away.

III

At another time the differences between two brothers named Chaerephon and Chaerecrates, both well known to him, had drawn his attention; and on seeing the younger of the two he thus addressed him.

Soc. Tell me, Chaerecrates, you are not, I take it, one of those strange people who believe that goods are better and more precious than a brother;[3] and that too although the former are but senseless chattels which need protection, the latter a sensitive and sensible being who can afford it; and what is more, he is himself alone, whilst as for them their name is legion. And here again is a marvellous thing: that a man should count his brother a loss, because the goods of his brother are not his; but he does not count his fellow citizens loss, and yet their possessions are not his; only it seems in their case he has wits to see that to dwell securely with many and have enough is better than to own the whole wealth of a community and to live in dangerous isolation; but this same doctrine as applied to brothers they ignore. Again, if a man have the means, he will purchase domestic slaves, because he wants assistants in his work; he will acquire friends, because he needs their support; but this brother of his—who cares about brothers? It seems a friend may be discovered in an ordinary citizen, but not in a blood relation who is also a brother. And yet it is a great vantage-ground toward friendship to have sprung from the same loins and to have been suckled at the same breasts, since even among beasts a certain natural craving, and

---

1 Lit. "the docimasia." See Gow, "Companion," xiv.
2 "Visiti with atimia."
3 Cf. "Merchant of Venice," II. viii. 17: "Justice! the law! my ducats, and my daughter!"

sympathy springs up between creatures reared together.[1] Added to which, a man who has brothers commands more respect from the rest of the world than the man who has none, and who must fight his own battles.[2]

Chaer. I daresay, Socrates, where the differences are not profound, reason would a man should bear with his brother, and not avoid him for some mere trifle's sake, for a brother of the right sort is, as you say, a blessing; but if he be the very antithesis of that, why should a man lay his hand to achieve the impossible?

Soc. Well now, tell me, is there nobody whom Chaerephon can please any more than he can please yourself; or do some people find him agreeable enough?

Chaer. Nay, there you hit it. That is just why I have a right to detest him. He can be pleasing enough to others, but to me, whenever he appears on the scene, he is not a blessing—no! but by every manner of means the reverse.

Soc. May it not happen that just as a horse is no gain to the inexpert rider who essays to handle him, so in like manner, if a man tries to deal with his brother after an ignorant fashion, this same brother will kick?

Chaer. But is it likely now? How should I be ignorant of the art of dealing with my brother if I know the art of repaying kind words and good deeds in kind? But a man who tries all he can to annoy me by word and deed, I can neither bless nor benefit, and, what is more, I will not try.

Soc. Well now, that is a marvellous statement, Chaerecrates. Your dog, the serviceable guardian of your flocks, who will fawn and lick the hand of your shepherd, when you come near him can only growl and show his teeth. Well; you take no notice of the dog's ill-temper, you try to propitiate him by kindness; but your brother? If your brother were what he ought to be, he would be a great blessing to you—that you admit; and, as you further confess, you know the secret of kind acts and words, yet you will not set yourself to apply means to make him your best of friends.

Chaer. I am afraid, Socrates, that I have no wisdom or cunning to make Chaerephon bear himself toward me as he should.

Soc. Yet there is no need to apply any recondite or novel machinery. Only bait your hook in the way best known to yourself, and you will capture him; whereupon he will become your devoted friend.

Chaer. If you are aware that I know some love-charm, Socrates, of

---

1 Or, "a yearning after their foster-brothers manifests itself in animals." See "Cyrop." *VIII. vii.* 14 foll. for a parallel to this discussion.
2 Lit. "and is less liable to hostility."

which I am the happy but unconscious possessor, pray make haste and enlighten me.

Soc. Answer me then. Suppose you wanted to get some acquaintance to invite you to dinner when he next keeps holy day,[1] what steps would you take?

Chaer. No doubt I should set him a good example by inviting him myself on a like occasion.

Soc. And if you wanted to induce some friend to look after your affairs during your absence abroad, how would you achieve your purpose?

Chaer. No doubt I should present a precedent in undertaking to look after his in like circumstances.

Soc. And if you wished to get some foreign friend to take you under his roof while visiting his country, what would you do?

Chaer. No doubt I should begin by offering him the shelter of my own roof when he came to Athens, in order to enlist his zeal in furthering the objects of my visit; it is plain I should first show my readiness to do as much for him in a like case.

Soc. Why, it seems you are an adept after all in all the philtres known to man, only you chose to conceal your knowledge all the while; or is it that you shrink from taking the first step because of the scandal you will cause by kindly advances to your brother? And yet it is commonly held to redound to a man's praise to have outstripped an enemy in mischief or a friend in kindness. Now if it seemed to me that Chaerephon were better fitted to lead the way toward this friendship,[2] I should have tried to persuade him to take the first step in winning your affection, but now I am persuaded the first move belongs to you, and to you the final victory.

Chaer. A startling announcement, Socrates, from your lips, and most unlike you, to bid me the younger take precedence of my elder brother. Why, it is contrary to the universal custom of mankind, who look to the elder to take the lead in everything, whether as a speaker or an actor.

Soc. How so? Is it not the custom everywhere for the younger to step aside when he meets his elder in the street and to give him place? Is he not expected to get up and offer him his seat, to pay him the honor of a soft couch,[3] to yield him precedence in argument?

---

1 *"When he next does sacrifice"*; see *"Hiero,"* viii. 3. Cf. Theophr. *"Char."* xv. 2, and Prof. Jebb's note ad loc.
2 Reading {pros ten philian}, or if {phusin}, transl. *"natural disposition."*
3 Lit. *"with a soft bed,"* or, as we say, *"the best bedroom."*

My good fellow, do not stand shilly-shallying,[1] but put out your hand caressingly, and you will see the worthy soul will respond at once with alacrity. Do you not note your brother's character, proud and frank and sensitive to honor? He is not a mean and sorry rascal to be caught by a bribe—no better way indeed for such riff-raff. No! gentle natures need a finer treatment. You can best hope to work on them by affection.

Chaer. But suppose I do, and suppose that, for all my attempts, he shows no change for the better?

Soc. At the worst you will have shown yourself to be a good, honest, brotherly man, and he will appear as a sorry creature on whom kindness is wasted. But nothing of the sort is going to happen, as I conjecture. My belief is that as soon as he hears your challenge, he will embrace the contest; pricked on by emulous pride, he will insist upon getting the better of you in kindness of word and deed.

At present you two are in the condition of two hands formed by God to help each other, but which have let go their business and have turned to hindering one another all they can. You are a pair of feet fashioned on the Divine plan to work together, but which have neglected this in order to trammel each other's gait. Now is it not insensate stupidity[2] to use for injury what was meant for advantage? And yet in fashioning two brothers God intends them, methinks, to be of more benefit to one another than either two hands, or two feet, or two eyes, or any other of those pairs which belong to man from his birth.[3] Consider how powerless these hands of ours if called upon to combine their action at two points more than a single fathom's length apart;[4] and these feet could not stretch asunder[5] even a bare fathom; and these eyes, for all the wide-reaching range we claim for them, are incapable of seeing simultaneously the back and front of an object at even closer quarters. But a pair of brothers, linked in bonds of amity, can work each for the other's good, though seas divide them.[6]

IV

I have at another time heard him discourse on the kindred theme of friendship in language well calculated, as it seemed to me, to help a man to choose and also to use his friends aright.

---

1 Or, "have no fears, essay a soothing treatment."
2 "Boorishness verging upon monomania."
3 "With which man is endowed at birth."
4 "More than an 'arms' stretch" asunder."
5 Lit. "reach at one stretch two objects, even over that small distance."
6 "Though leagues separate them."

He (Socrates) had often heard the remark made that of all possessions there is none equal to that of a good and sincere friend; but, in spite of this assertion, the mass of people, as far as he could see, concerned themselves about nothing so little as the acquisition of friends. Houses, and fields, and slaves, and cattle, and furniture of all sorts (he said) they were at pains to acquire, and they strove hard to keep what they had got; but to procure for themselves this greatest of all blessings, as they admitted a friend to be, or to keep the friends whom they already possessed, not one man in a hundred ever gave himself a thought. It was noticeable, in the case of a sickness befalling a man's friend and one of his own household simultaneously, the promptness with which the master would fetch the doctor to his domestic, and take every precaution necessary for his recovery, with much expenditure of pains; but meanwhile little account would be taken of the friend in like condition, and if both should die, he will show signs of deep annoyance at the death of his domestic, which, as he reflects, is a positive loss to him; but as regards his friend his position is in no wise materially affected, and thus, though he would never dream of leaving his other possessions disregarded and ill cared for, friendship's mute appeal is met with flat indifference.[1]

Or to take (said he) a crowning instance:[2] with regard to ordinary possessions, however multifarious these may be, most people are at least acquainted with their number, but if you ask a man to enumerate his friends, who are not so very many after all perhaps, he cannot; or if, to oblige the inquirer, he essays to make a list, he will presently retract the names of some whom he had previously included.[3] Such is the amount of thought which people bestow upon their friends.

And yet what thing else may a man call his own is comparable to this one best possession! what rather will not serve by contrast to enhance the value of an honest friend! Think of a horse or a yoke of oxen; they have their worth; but who shall gauge the worth of a worthy friend? Kindlier and more constant than the faithfullest of slaves—this is that possession best named all-serviceable.[4] Consider what the post is that he assigns himself! to meet and supplement what is lacking to the welfare of his friends, to promote their private and their public interests, is his concern. Is there need of kindly action in any quarter? he will throw in the full weight of

---
1 Or, "the cry of a friend for careful tending falls on deaf ears."
2 Or, "Nor had he failed to observe another striking contrast." Cf. Cic. "Lael." 17; Diog. Laert. ii. 30.
3 I.e. "like a chess-player recalling a move."
4 "A vessel fit for all work indeed is this friend." Cf. Ar. "Ach." 936, {pagkhreston aggos estai}, like the "leather bottel."

his support. Does some terror confound? he is at hand to help and defend by expenditure of money and of energy,[1] by appeals to reason or resort to force. His the privilege alike to gladden the prosperous in the hour of success and to sustain their footing who have well-nigh slipped. All that the hands of a man may minister, all that the eyes of each are swift to see, the ears to hear, and the feet to compass, he with his helpful arts will not fall short of. Nay, not seldom that which a man has failed to accomplish for himself, has missed seeing or hearing or attaining, a friend acting in behalf of friend will achieve vicariously. And yet, albeit to try and tend a tree for the sake of its fruit is not uncommon, this copious mine of wealth—this friend—attracts only a lazy and listless attention on the part of more than half the world.

V

I remember listening to another argument of his, the effect of which would be to promote self-examination. The listener must needs be brought to ask himself, "Of what worth am I to my friends?" It happened thus. One of those who were with him was neglectful, as he noted, of a friend who was at the pinch of poverty (Antisthenes).[2] Accordingly, in the presence of the negligent person and of several others, he proceeded to question the sufferer.

Soc. What say you, Antisthenes?—have friends their values like domestic slaves? One of these latter may be worth perhaps two minae,[3] another only half a mina, a third five, and a fourth as much as ten; while they do say that Nicias,[4] the son of Niceratus, paid a whole talent for a superintendent of his silver mines. And so I propound the question to myself as follows: "Have friends, like slaves, their market values?"

Not a doubt of it (replied Antisthenes). At any rate, I know that I would rather have such a one as my friend than be paid two minae, and there is such another whose worth I would not estimate at half a mina, and a third with whom I would not part for ten, and then again a fourth whose friendship would be cheap if it cost me all the wealth and pains in the world to purchase it.

Well then (continued Socrates), if that be so, would it not be well if

---

1 Or, *"by dint of his diplomacy."*
2 Antisthenes, *"cynicorum et stoicorum parens."* Cic. *"de Or."* iii. 17; *"ad Att."* xii. 38. See below, III. iii. 17; *"Symp."* passim; Diog. Laert. II. v.; VI. i.
3 A mina = L4 circ.
4 For Nicias see Thuc. vii. 77 foll.; *"Revenues,"* iv. 14; Plut. *"Nic."* IV. v.; Lys. *"de bon. Aristoph."* 648.

everyone were to examine himself: "What after all may I chance to be worth to my friends?" Should he not try to become as dear as possible, so that his friends will not care to give him up? How often do I hear the complaint: "My friend So-and-so has given me up"; or "Such an one, whom I looked upon as a friend, has sacrificed me for a mina." And every time I hear these remarks, the question arises in my mind: If the vendor of a worthless slave is ready to part with him to a purchaser for what he will fetch—is there not at least a strong temptation to part with a base friend when you have a chance of making something on the exchange? Good slaves, as far as I can see, are not so knocked down to the hammer; no, nor good friends so lightly parted with.

VI

Again, in reference to the test to be applied, if we would gauge the qualifications of a friend worth the winning, the following remarks of Socrates could not fail, I think, to prove instructive.[1]

Tell me (said Socrates, addressing Critobulus), supposing we stood in need of a good friend, how should we set about his discovery? We must, in the first place, I suppose, seek out one who is master of his appetites, not under the dominion, that is, of his belly, not addicted to the wine-cup or to lechery or sleep or idleness, since no one enslaved to such tyrants could hope to do his duty either by himself or by his friends, could he?

Certainly not (Critobulus answered).

SOCRATES: Do you agree, then, that we must hold aloof from everyone so dominated?

CRITOBULUS: Most assuredly.

Well then (proceeded Socrates), what shall we say of the spendthrift who has lost his independence and is forever begging of his neighbors; if he gets anything out of them he cannot repay, but if he fails to get anything, he hates you for not giving—do you not think that this man too would prove but a disagreeable friend?

CRITOBULUS: Certainly.

SOCRATES: Then we must keep away from him too?

CRITOBULUS: That we must.

SOCRATES: Well! and what of the man whose strength lies in monetary transactions?[2] His one craving is to amass money; and for that reason he is

---

[1] Or, "Again, as to establishing a test of character, since a friend worth having must be of a particular type, I cannot but think that the following remarks would prove instructive."
[2] Or, "the money-lender? He has a passion for big money-bags."

an adept at driving a hard bargain[1]—glad enough to take in, but loath to pay out.

CRITOBULUS: In my opinion he will prove even a worse fellow than the last.

SOCRATES: Well! and what of that other whose passion for money-making is so absorbing that he has no leisure for anything else, save how he may add to his gains?

CRITOBULUS: Hold aloof from him, say I, since there is no good to be got out of him or his society.

SOCRATES: Well! what of the quarrelsome and factious person[2] whose main object is to saddle his friends with a host of enemies?

CRITOBULUS: For God's sake let us avoid him also.

SOCRATES: But now we will imagine a man exempt indeed from all the above defects—a man who has no objection to receive kindnesses, but it never enters into his head to do a kindness in return.

CRITOBULUS: There will be no good in him either. But, Socrates, what kind of man shall we endeavor to make our friend? what is he like?

SOCRATES: I should say he must be just the converse of the above: he has control over the pleasures of the body, he is kindly disposed,[3] upright in all his dealings,[4] very zealous is he not to be outdone in kindness by his benefactors, if only his friends may derive some profit from his acquaintance.

CRITOBULUS: But how are we to test these qualities, Socrates, before acquaintance?

SOCRATES: How do we test the merits of a sculptor?—not by inferences drawn from the talk of the artist merely. No, we look to what he has already achieved. These former statues of his were nobly executed, and we trust he will do equally well with the rest.

CRITOBULUS: You mean that if we find a man whose kindness to older friends is established, we may take it as proved that he will treat his newer friends as amiably?

SOCRATES: Why, certainly, if I see a man who has shown skill in the handling of horses previously, I argue that he will handle others no less skilfully again.

CRITOBULUS: Good! and when we have discovered a man whose friendship is worth having, how ought we to make him our friend?

---

1 Or, "hard in all his dealings."
2 "The partisan."
3 Reading {eunous}, or if {euorkos}, transl. "a man of his word."
4 Or, "easy to deal with."

SOCRATES: First we ought to ascertain the will of Heaven whether it be advisable to make him our friend.

CRITOBULUS: Well! and how are we to effect the capture of this friend of our choice, whom the gods approve? will you tell me that?

Not, in good sooth (replied Socrates), by running him down like a hare, nor by decoying him like a bird, or by force like a wild boar.[1] To capture a friend against his will is a toilsome business, and to bind him in fetters like a slave by no means easy. Those who are so treated are apt to become foes instead of friends.[2]

CRITOBULUS: But how convert them into friends?

SOCRATES: There are certain incantations, we are told, which those who know them have only to utter, and they can make friends of whom they list; and there are certain philtres also which those who have the secret of them may administer to whom they like and win their love.

CRITOBULUS: From what source shall we learn them?

SOCRATES: You need not go farther than Homer to learn that which the Sirens sang to Odysseus,[3] the first words of which run, I think, as follows:

Hither, come hither, thou famous man, Odysseus, great glory of the Achaeans!

CRITOBULUS: And did the magic words of this spell serve for all men alike? Had the Sirens only to utter this one incantation, and was every listener constrained to stay?

SOCRATES: No; this was the incantation reserved for souls athirst for fame, of virtue emulous.

CRITOBULUS: Which is as much as to say, we must suit the incantation to the listener, so that when he hears the words he shall not think that the enchanter is laughing at him in his sleeve. I cannot certainly conceive a method better calculated to excite hatred and repulsion than to go to someone who knows that he is small and ugly and a weakling, and to breathe in his ears the flattering tale that he is beautiful and tall and stalwart. But do you know any other love-charms, Socrates?

SOCRATES: I cannot say that I do; but I have heard that Pericles[4] was skilled in not a few, which he poured into the ear of our city and won her love.

---

1 Reading {kaproi}, al. {ekhthroi}, "an enemy."
2 Or, "Hate rather than friendship is the outcome of these methods."
3 "Od." xii. 184.
4 See above, I. ii. 40; "Symp." viii. 39.

CRITOBULUS: And how did Themistocles[1] win our city's love?

SOCRATES: Ah, that was not by incantation at all. What he did was to encircle our city with an amulet of saving virtue.[2]

CRITOBULUS: You would imply, Socrates, would you not, that if we want to win the love of any good man we need to be good ourselves in speech and action?

And did you imagine (replied Socrates) that it was possible for a bad man to make good friends?

CRITOBULUS: Why, I could fancy I had seen some sorry speech-monger who was fast friends with a great and noble statesman; or again, some born commander and general who was boon companion with fellows quite incapable of generalship.[3]

SOCRATES: But in reference to the point we were discussing, may I ask whether you know of anyone who can attach a useful friend to himself without being of use in return?[4] Can service ally in friendship with disservice?

CRITOBULUS: In good sooth no. But now, granted it is impossible for a base man to be friends with the beautiful and noble,[5] I am concerned at once to discover if one who is himself of a beautiful and noble character can, with a wave of the hand, as it were, attach himself in friendship to every other beautiful and noble nature.

SOCRATES: What perplexes and confounds you, Critobulus, is the fact that so often men of noble conduct, with souls aloof from baseness, are not friends but rather at strife and discord with one another, and deal more harshly by one another than they would by the most good-for-nothing of mankind.

CRITOBULUS: Yes, and this holds true not of private persons only, but states, the most eager to pursue a noble policy and to repudiate a base one, are frequently in hostile relation to one another. As I reason on these things my heart fails me, and the question, how friends are to be acquired, fills me with despondency. The bad, as I see, cannot be friends with one another. For how can such people, the ungrateful, or reckless, or covetous, or faithless, or incontinent, adhere together as friends? Without hesitation I

---

1 See below, III. vi. 2; IV. ii. 2.
2 See Herod. vii. 143, "the wooden wall"; Thuc. i. 93, "the walls of Athens."
3 Or, "Why, yes, when I see some base orator fast friends with a great leader of the people; or, again, some fellow incapable of generalship a comrade to the greatest captains of his age."
4 Add, "Can service ally in friendship with disservice? Must there not be a reciprocity of service to make friendship lasting?"
5 {kalous kagathous}.

set down the bad as born to be foes not friends, and as bearing the birthmark of internecine hate. But then again, as you suggest, no more can these same people harmonise in friendship with the good. For how should they who do evil be friends with those who hate all evil-doing? And if, last of all, they that cultivate virtue are torn by party strife in their struggle for the headship of the states, envying one another, hating one another, who are left to be friends? where shall goodwill and faithfulness be found among men?

SOCRATES: The fact is there is some subtlety in the texture of these things.[1] Seeds of love are implanted in man by nature. Men have need of one another, feel pity, help each other by united efforts, and in recognition of the fact show mutual gratitude. But there are seeds of war implanted also. The same objects being regarded as beautiful or agreeable by all alike, they do battle for their possession; a spirit of disunion[2] enters, and the parties range themselves in adverse camps. Discord and anger sound a note of war: the passion of more-having, staunchless avarice, threatens hostility; and envy is a hateful fiend.[3]

But nevertheless, through all opposing barriers friendship steals her way and binds together the beautiful and good among mankind.[4] Such is their virtue that they would rather possess scant means painlessly than wield an empire won by war. In spite of hunger and thirst they will share their meat and drink without a pang. Not bloom of lusty youth, nor love's delights can warp their self-control; nor will they be tempted to cause pain where pain should be unknown. It is theirs not merely to eschew all greed of riches, not merely to make a just and lawful distribution of wealth, but to supply what is lacking to the needs of one another. Theirs it is to compose strife and discord not in painless oblivion simply, but to the general advantage. Theirs also to hinder such extravagance of anger as shall entail remorse hereafter. And as to envy they will make a clean sweep and clearance of it: the good things which a man possesses shall be also the property of his friends, and the goods which they possess are to be looked upon as his. Where then is the improbability that the beautiful and noble should be sharers in the honors[5] of the state not only without injury, but even to their mutual advantage?

---

1 I.e. a cunning intertwining of the threads of warp and woof.
2 Cf. Shelley, "The devil of disunion in their souls."
3 The diction is poetical.
4 Or, as we say, "the elite of human kind."
5 "And the offices."

They indeed who covet and desire the honors and offices in a state for the sake of the liberty thereby given them to embezzle the public moneys, to deal violently by their fellow creatures, and to batten in luxury themselves, may well be regarded as unjust and villainous persons incapable of harmony with one another. But if a man desire to obtain these selfsame honors in order that, being himself secure against wrongdoing, he may be able to assist his friends in what is right, and, raised to a high position,[1] may essay to confer some blessing on the land of his fathers, what is there to hinder him from working in harmony with some other of a like spirit? Will he, with the "beautiful and noble" at his side, be less able to aid his friends? or will his power to benefit the community be shortened because the flower of that community are fellow workers in that work? Why, even in the contests of the games it is obvious that if it were possible for the stoutest combatants to combine against the weakest, the chosen band would come off victors in every bout, and would carry off all the prizes. This indeed is against the rules of the actual arena; but in the field of politics, where the beautiful and good hold empery, and there is nought to hinder any from combining with whomsoever a man may choose to benefit the state, it will be a clear gain, will it not, for anyone engaged in state affairs to make the best men his friends, whereby he will find partners and co-operators in his aims instead of rivals and antagonists? And this at least is obvious: in case of foreign war a man will need allies, but all the more if in the ranks opposed to him should stand the flower of the enemy.[2] Moreover, those who are willing to fight your battles must be kindly dealt with, that goodwill may quicken to enthusiasm; and one good man[3] is better worth your benefiting that a dozen knaves, since a little kindness goes a long way with the good, but with the base the more you give them the more they ask for.

So keep a good heart, Critobulus; only try to become good yourself, and when you have attained, set to your hand to capture the beautiful and good. Perhaps I may be able to give you some help in this quest, being myself an adept in Love's lore.[4] No matter who it is for whom my heart is aflame; in an instant my whole soul is eager to leap forth. With vehemence I speed to the mark. I, who love, demand to be loved again; this desire in me must be met by counter desire in him; this thirst for his society by thirst reciprocal for mine. And these will be your needs also, I foresee, whenever

---

1 "As archon," or "raised to rule."
2 Lit. "the beautiful and good."
3 Or, "the best, though few, are better worth your benefiting than the many base."
4 "An authority in matters of love." Cf. Plat. "Symp." 177 D; Xen. "Symp." viii. 2.

you are seized with longing to contract a friendship. Do not hide from me, therefore, whom you would choose as a friend, since, owing to the pains I take to please him who pleases me, I am not altogether unversed, I fancy, in the art of catching men.[1]

Critobulus replied: Why, these are the very lessons of instruction, Socrates, for which I have been long athirst, and the more particularly if this same love's lore will enable me to capture those who are good of soul and those who are beautiful of person.

SOCRATES: Nay, now I warn you, Critobulus, it is not within the province of my science to make the beautiful endure him who would lay hands upon them. And that is why men fled from Scylla, I am persuaded, because she laid hands upon them; but the Sirens were different—they laid hands on nobody, but sat afar off and chanted their spells in the ears of all; and therefore, it is said, all men endured to listen, and were charmed.

CRITOBULUS: I promise I will not lay violent hands on any; therefore, if you have any good device for winning friends, instruct your pupil.

SOCRATES: And if there is to be no laying on of the hands, there must be no application either of the lips; is it agreed?

CRITOBULUS: No, nor application of the lips to anyone—not beautiful.

SOCRATES: See now! you cannot open your mouth without some luckless utterance. Beauty suffers no such liberty, however eagerly the ugly may invite it, making believe some quality of soul must rank them with the beautiful.

CRITOBULUS: Be of good cheer then; let the compact stand thus: "Kisses for the beautiful, and for the good a rain of kisses." So now teach us the art of catching friends.

SOCRATES: Well then, when you wish to win someone's affection, you will allow me to lodge information against you to the effect that you admire him and desire to be his friend?

CRITOBULUS: Lodge the indictment, with all my heart. I never heard of anyone who hated his admirers.

SOCRATES: And if I add to the indictment the further charge that through your admiration you are kindly disposed toward him, you will not feel I am taking away your character?

CRITOBULUS: Why, no; for myself I know a kindly feeling springs up in my heart toward anyone whom I conceive to be kindly disposed to me.

SOCRATES: All this I shall feel empowered to say about you to those

---

1 See below, III. xi. 7; cf. Plat. "Soph." 222; N. T. Matt. iv. 19, {alieis anthropon}.

whose friendship you seek, and I can promise further help; only there is a comprehensive "if" to be considered: if you will further authorize me to say that you are devoted to your friends; that nothing gives you so much joy as a good friend; that you pride yourself no less on the fine deeds of those you love than on your own; and on their good things equally with your own; that you never weary of plotting and planning to procure them a rich harvest of the same; and lastly, that you have discovered a man's virtue is to excel his friends in kindness and his foes in hostility. If I am authorized thus to report of you, I think you will find me a serviceable fellow hunter in the quest of friends, which is the conquest of the good.

CRITOBULUS: Why this appeal to me?—as if you had not free permission to say exactly what you like about me.

SOCRATES: No; that I deny, on the authority of Aspasia.[1] I have it from her own lips. "Good matchmakers," she said tome, "were clever hands at cementing alliances between people, provided the good qualities they vouched for were truthfully reported; but when it came to their telling lies, for her part she could not compliment them.[2] Their poor deluded dupes ended by hating each other and the go-betweens as well." Now I myself am so fully persuaded of the truth of this that I feel it is not in my power to say aught in your praise which I cannot say with truth.

CRITOBULUS: Really, Socrates, you are a wonderfully good friend to me—in so far as I have any merit which will entitle me to win a friend, you will lend me a helping hand, it seems; otherwise you would rather not forge any petty fiction for my benefit.

SOCRATES: But tell me, how shall I assist you best, think you? By praising you falsely or by persuading you to try to be a good man? Or if it is not plain to you thus, look at the matter by the light of some examples. I wish to introduce you to a shipowner, or to make him your friend: I begin by singing your praises to him falsely thus, "You will find him a good pilot"; he catches at the phrase, and entrusts his ship to you, who have no notion of guiding a vessel. What can you expect but to make shipwreck of the craft and yourself together? or suppose by similar false assertions I can persuade the state at large to entrust her destinies to you—"a man with a fine genius for command," I say, "a practiced lawyer," "a politician born," and so

---

1 Aspasia, daughter of Axiochus, of Miletus. See "Econ." iii. 14; Plat. "Menex." 235 E; Aesch. Socrat. ap. Cic. "de Invent." I. xxxi. 51. See Grote, "H. G." vi. 132 foll.; Cobet, "Pros. Xen."

2 Reading {ouk ethelein epainein}, or if {ouk ophelein epainousas} with Kuhner transl. "Good matchmakers, she told me, have to consult truth when reporting favorably of anyone: then indeed they are terribly clever at bringing people together: whereas false flatterers do no good; their dupes," etc.

forth. The odds are, the state and you may come to grief through you. Or to take an instance from everyday life. By my falsehoods I persuade some private person to entrust his affairs to you as "a really careful and business-like person with a head for economy." When put to the test would not your administration prove ruinous, and the figure you cut ridiculous? No, my dear friend, there is but one road, the shortest, safest, best, and it is simply this: In whatsoever you desire to be deemed good, endeavor to be good. For of all the virtues namable among men, consider, and you will find there is not one but may be increased by learning and practice. For my part then, Critobulus, these are the principles on which we ought to go a-hunting; but if you take a different view, I am all attention, please instruct me.

Then Critobulus: Nay, Socrates, I should be ashamed to gainsay what you have said; if I did, it would neither be a noble statement nor a true.[1]

VII

He had two ways of dealing with the difficulties of his friends: where ignorance was the cause, he tried to meet the trouble by a dose of common sense; or where want and poverty were to blame, by lessoning them that they should assist one another according to their ability; and here I may mention certain incidents which occurred within my own knowledge. How, for instance, he chanced upon Aristarchus wearing the look of one who suffered from a fit of the "sullens," and thus accosted him.

SOCRATES: You seem to have some trouble on your mind, Aristarchus; if so, you should share it with your friends. Perhaps together we might lighten the weight of it a little.

Aristarchus answered: Yes, Socrates, I am in sore straits indeed. Ever since the party strife declared itself in the city,[2] what with the rush of people to Piraeus, and the wholesale banishments, I have been fairly at the mercy of my poor deserted female relatives. Sisters, nieces, cousins, they have all come flocking to me for protection. I have fourteen free-born souls, I tell you, under my single roof, and how are we to live? We can get nothing out of the soil—that is in the hands of the enemy; nothing from my house property, for there is scarcely a living soul left in the city; my furniture? no one will buy it; money? there is none to be borrowed—you would have a better chance to find it by looking for it on the road than to borrow it from a banker. Yes, Socrates, to stand by and see one's relatives die of hunger is hard indeed, and yet to feed so many at such a pinch impossible.

---

1 {kala... alethe}.
2 I.e. circa 404–403 BC See "Hell." II. iv.

After he listened to the story, Socrates asked: How comes it that Ceramon,[1] with so many mouths to feed, not only contrives to furnish himself and them with the necessaries of life, but to realize a handsome surplus, whilst you being in like plight[2] are afraid you will one and all perish of starvation for want of the necessaries of life?

ARISTARCHUS: Why, bless your soul, do you not see he has only slaves and I have free-born souls to feed?

SOCRATES: And which should you say were the better human beings, the free-born members of your household or Ceramon's slaves?

ARISTARCHUS: The free souls under my roof without a doubt.

SOCRATES: Is it not a shame, then, that he with his baser folk to back him should be in easy circumstances, while you and your far superior household are in difficulties?

ARISTARCHUS: To be sure it is, when he has only a set of handicraftsmen to feed, and I my liberally-educated household.

SOCRATES: What is a handicraftsman? Does not the term apply to all who can make any sort of useful product or commodity?

ARISTARCHUS: Certainly.

SOCRATES: Barley meal is a useful product, is it not?

ARISTARCHUS: Pre-eminently so.

SOCRATES: And loaves of bread?

ARISTARCHUS: No less.

SOCRATES: Well, and what do you say to cloaks for men and for women—tunics, mantles, vests?[3]

ARISTARCHUS: Yes, they are all highly useful commodities.

SOCRATES: Then your household do not know how to make any of these?

ARISTARCHUS: On the contrary, I believe they can make them all.

SOCRATES: Then you are not aware that by means of the manufacture of one of these alone—his barley meal store—Nausicydes[4] not only maintains himself and his domestics, but many pigs and cattle besides, and realises such large profits that he frequently contributes to the state benevolences;[5] while there is Cyrebus, again, who, out of a bread factory,

---

1 An employer of labor, apparently, on a grand scale.
2 Lit. "with your large family to feed." L. Dindorf would like to read {su de oligous}, "you with your small family."
3 For these articles of dress see Becker's "Charicles," Exc. i. to Sc. xi. "Dress."
4 Nausicydes. Cobet, "Pros. Xen." cf. Aristoph. "Eccles." 426.
5 Lit. "state liturgies," or "to the burden of the public services." For these see Gow, "Companion," xviii. "Athenian Finance."

more than maintains the whole of his establishment, and lives in the lap of luxury; and Demeas of Collytus gets a livelihood out of a cloak business, and Menon as a mantua-maker, and so, again, more than half the Megarians[1] by the making of vests.

ARISTARCHUS: Bless me, yes! They have got a set of barbarian fellows, whom they purchase and keep, to manufacture by forced labor whatever takes their fancy. My kinswomen, I need not tell you, are free-born ladies.

SOCRATES: Then, on the ground that they are free-born and your kinswomen, you think that they ought to do nothing but eat and sleep? Or is it your opinion that people who live in this way—I speak of free-born people in general—lead happier lives, and are more to be congratulated, than those who give their time and attention to such useful arts of life as they are skilled in? Is this what you see in the world, that for the purpose of learning what it is well to know, and of recollecting the lessons taught, or with a view to health and strength of body, or for the sake of acquiring and preserving all that gives life its charm, idleness and inattention are found to be helpful, whilst work and study are simply a dead loss? Pray, when those relatives of yours were taught what you tell me they know, did they learn it as barren information which they would never turn to practical account, or, on the contrary, as something with which they were to be seriously concerned some day, and from which they were to reap advantage? Do human beings in general attain to well-tempered manhood by a course of idling, or by carefully attending to what will be of use? Which will help a man the more to grow in justice and uprightness, to be up and doing, or to sit with folded hands revolving the ways and means of existence? As things now stand, if I am not mistaken, there is no love lost between you. You cannot help feeling that they are costly to you, and they must see that you find them a burthen? This is a perilous state of affairs, in which hatred and bitterness have every prospect of increasing, whilst the pre-existing bond of affection[2] is likely to be snapped.

But now, if only you allow them free scope for their energies, when you come to see how useful they can be, you will grow quite fond of them, and they, when they perceive that they can please you, will cling to their benefactor warmly. Thus, with the memory of former kindnesses made sweeter, you will increase the grace which flows from kindnesses tenfold; you will in consequence be knit in closer bonds of love and domesticity. If,

---

1 Cf. Arist. "Acharnians," 519, {esukophantei Megareon ta khlaniskia}. See Dr. Merry's note ad loc.

2 Or, "the original stock of kindliness will be used up."

indeed, they were called upon to do any shameful work, let them choose death rather than that; but now they know, it would seem, the very arts and accomplishments which are regarded as the loveliest and the most suitable for women; and the things which we know, any of us, are just those which we can best perform, that is to say, with ease and expedition; it is a joy to do them, and the result is beautiful.[1] Do not hesitate, then, to initiate your friends in what will bring advantage to them and you alike; probably they will gladly respond to your summons.

Well, upon my word (Aristarchus answered), I like so well what you say, Socrates, that though hitherto I have not been disposed to borrow, knowing that when I had spent what I got I should not be in a condition to repay, I think I can now bring myself to do so in order to raise a fund for these works.

Thereupon a capital was provided; wools were purchased; the good man's relatives set to work, and even whilst they breakfasted they worked, and on and on till work was ended and they supped. Smiles took the place of frowns; they no longer looked askance with suspicion, but full into each other's eyes with happiness. They loved their kinsman for his kindness to them. He became attached to them as helpmates; and the end of it all was, he came to Socrates and told him with delight how matters fared; "and now," he added, "they tax me with being the only drone in the house, who sit and eat the bread of idleness."

To which Socrates: Why do not you tell them the fable of the dog?[2] Once on a time, so goes the story, when beasts could speak, the sheep said to her master, "What a marvel is this, master, that to us, your own sheep, who provide you with fleeces and lambs and cheese, you give nothing, save only what we may nibble off Earth's bosom; but with this dog of yours, who provides you with nothing of the sort, you share the very meat out of your mouth." When the dog heard these words, he answered promptly, "Ay, in good sooth, for is it not I who keep you safe and sound, you sheep, so that you are not stolen by man nor harried by wolves; since, if I did not keep watch over you, you would not be able so much as to graze afield, fearing to be destroyed." And so, says the tale, the sheep had to admit that the dog was rightly preferred to themselves in honor. And so do you tell your flock yonder that like the dog in the fable you are their guardian and overseer,

---

1 Or, "with ease, rapidity, pleasure and effect."
2 See Joseph Jacobs, "The Fables of Aesop," vol. i. p. 26 foll., for "a complete list of the Fables given in Greek literature up to the fall of Greek independence." Cf. Hesiod, "Works and Days," 202 foll.; Archilochus, 89 (60), Bergk; Herod. i. 141; Aesch. "Myrmid." fr. 123; Aristot. "Rhet." II. xx.

and it is thanks to you that they are protected from evil and evildoers, so that they work their work and live their lives in blissful security.

VIII

At another time chancing upon an old friend whom he had not seen for a long while, he greeted him thus.

SOCRATES: What quarter of the world do you hail from, Eutherus?

The other answered: From abroad, just before the close of the war; but at present from the city itself.[1] You see, since we have been denuded of our possessions across the frontier,[2] and my father left me nothing in Attica, I must needs bide at home, and provide myself with the necessaries of life by means of bodily toil, which seems preferable to begging from another, especially as I have no security on which to raise a loan.

SOCRATES: And how long do you expect your body to be equal to providing the necessaries of life for hire?

EUTHERUS: Goodness knows, Socrates—not for long.

SOCRATES: And when you find yourself an old man, expenses will not diminish, and yet no one will care to pay you for the labor of your hands.

EUTHERUS: That is true.

SOCRATES: Would it not be better then to apply yourself at once to such work as will stand you in good stead when you are old—that is, address yourself to some large proprietor who needs an assistant in managing his estate?[3] By superintending his works, helping to get in his crops, and guarding his property in general, you will be a benefit to the estate and be benefited in return.

I could not endure the yoke of slavery, Socrates! (he exclaimed).

SOCRATES: And yet the heads of departments in a state are not regarded as adopting the badge of slavery because they manage the public property, but as having attained a higher degree of freedom rather.

EUTHERUS: In a word, Socrates, the idea of being held to account to another is not at all to my taste.

SOCRATES: And yet, Eutherus, it would be hard to find a work which did not involve some liability to account; in fact it is difficult to do anything without some mistake or other, and no less difficult, if you should succeed in doing it immaculately, to escape all unfriendly criticism. I wonder now whether you find it easy to get through your

---

1 Lit. *"from here."* The conversation perhaps takes place in Piraeus 404 BC
2 Or, *"colonial possession."* Cf. *"Symp."* iv. 31.
3 Cf. *"Cyrop."* VIII. iii. 48.

present occupations entirely without reproach. No? Let me tell you what you should do. You should avoid censorious persons and attach yourself to the considerate and kind-hearted, and in all your affairs accept with a good grace what you can and decline what you feel you cannot do. Whatever it be, do it heart and soul, and make it your finest work.[1] There lies the method at once to silence fault-finders and to minister help to your own difficulties. Life will flow smoothly, risks will be diminished, provision against old age secured.

IX

At another time, as I am aware, he had heard a remark made by Crito[2] that life at Athens was no easy matter for a man who wished to mind his own affairs.

As, for instance, at this moment (Crito proceeded) there are a set of fellows threatening me with lawsuits, not because they have any misdemeanour to allege against me, but simply under the conviction that I will sooner pay a sum of money than be troubled further.

To which Socrates replied: Tell me, Crito, you keep dogs, do you not, to ward off wolves from your flocks?

CRITO: Certainly; it pays to do so.

SOCRATES: Then why do you not keep a watchman willing and competent to ward off this pack of people who seek to injure you?

I should not at all mind (he answered), if I were not afraid he might turn again and rend his keeper.

What! (rejoined Socrates), do you not see that to gratify a man like yourself is far pleasanter as a matter of self-interest than to quarrel with you? You may be sure there are plenty of people here who will take the greatest pride in making you their friend.

Accordingly, they sought out Archedemus,[3] a practical man with a clever tongue in his head[4] but poor; the fact being, he was not the sort to make gain by hook or by crook, but a lover of honesty and of too

---

1 Or, "study to make it your finest work, the expression of a real enthusiasm."
2 Crito. See above, I. ii. 48; Cobet, "P. X."; cf. Plat. "Rep." viii. 549 C.
3 Archedemus, possibly the demagogue, "Hell." I. vii. 2. So Cobet, "P. X.," but see Grote, "H. G." viii. 245.
4 Lit. "very capable of speech and action"—the writer's favorite formula for the well-trained Athenian who can speak fluently and reason clearly, and act energetically and opportunely.

good a nature himself to make his living as a pettifogger.[1] Crito would then take the opportunity of times of harvesting and put aside small presents for Achedemus of corn and oil, or wine, or wool, or any other of the farm produce forming the staple commodities of life, or he would invite him to a sacrificial feast, and otherwise pay him marked attention. Archedemus, feeling that he had in Crito's house a harbor of refuge, could not make too much of his patron, and ere long he had hunted up a long list of iniquities which could be lodged against Crito's pettifogging persecutors themselves, and not only their numerous crimes but their numerous enemies; and presently he prosecuted one of them in a public suit, where sentence would be given against him "what to suffer or what to pay."[2] The accused, conscious as he was of many rascally deeds, did all he could to be quit of Archedemus, but Archedemus was not to be got rid of. He held on until he had made the informer not only loose his hold of Crito but pay himself a sum of money; and now that Archedemus had achieved this and other similar victories, it is easy to guess what followed.[3] It was just as when some shepherd has got a very good dog, all the other shepherds wish to lodge their flocks in his neighborhood that they too may reap the benefit of him. So a number of Crito's friends came begging him to allow Archedemus to be their guardian also, and Archedemus was overjoyed to do something to gratify Crito, and so it came about that not only Crito abode in peace, but his friends likewise. If any of those people with whom Archedemus was not on the best of terms were disposed to throw it in his teeth that he accepted his patron's benefits and paid in flatteries, he had a ready retort: "Answer me this question—which is the more scandalous, to accept kindnesses from honest folk and to repay them, with the result that I make such people my friends but quarrel with knaves, or to make enemies of honorable gentlemen[4] by attempts to do them wrong, with the off-chance indeed of winning the friendship of some scamps in return for my cooperation, but the certainty of losing in the tone of my acquaintances?"[5]

---

1 Reading {kai euphuesteros on} (or {e os})... {apo sukophanton} (or {sukophantion}), after Cobet, "P. X." s.v. Archedemus. The MSS. give {kai ephe raston einai}—"nothing is easier," he said, "than recovering from sycophants."
2 For this formula cf. "Econ." vi. 24. Cf. Plat. "Statesm." 299 A.
3 {ede tote}. Cf. Plat. "Laws," vi. 778 C.
4 Lit. the {kaloi kagathoi}, which like {khrestous} and {ponerous} has a political as well as an ethical meaning.
5 Lit. "must associate with these (the {ponerois}) instead of those (the {kalois te kagathois})."

The net result of the whole proceedings was that Archedemus was now Crito's right hand,[1] and by the rest of Crito's friends he was held in honor.

X

Again I may cite, as known to myself,[2] the following discussion; the arguments were addressed to Diodorus, one of his companions. The master said:

Tell me, Diodorus, if one of your slaves runs away, are you at pains to recover him?

More than that (Diodorus answered), I summon others to my aid and I have a reward cried for his recovery.

SOCRATES: Well, if one of your domestics is sick, do you tend him and call in the doctors to save his life?

DIODORUS: Decidedly I do.

SOCRATES: And if an intimate acquaintance who is far more precious to you than any of your household slaves is about to perish of want, you would think it incumbent on you to take pains to save his life? Well! now you know without my telling you that Hermogenes[3] is not made of wood or stone. If you helped him he would be ashamed not to pay you in kind. And yet—the opportunity of possessing a willing, kindly, and trusty assistant well fitted to do your bidding, and not merely that, but capable of originating useful ideas himself, with a certain forecast of mind and judgment—I say such a man is worth dozens of slaves. Good economists tell us that when a precious article may be got at a low price we ought to buy. And nowadays when times are so bad it is possible to get good friends exceedingly cheap.

Diodorus answered: You are quite right, Socrates; bid Hermogenes come to me.

SOCRATES: Bid Hermogenes come to you!—not I indeed! since for aught I can understand you are no better entitled to summon him that to go to him yourself, nor is the advantage more on his side than your own.

Thus Diodorus went off in a trice to seek Hermogenes, and at no great outlay won to himself a friend—a friend whose one concern it now was to discover how, by word or deed, he might help and gladden Diodorus.

---

1 *He was No. 1—{eis}.*
2 *Or, "for which I can personally vouch."*
3 *Hermogenes, presumably the son of Hipponicus. See I. ii. 48.*

BOOK III

I

Aspirants to honor and distinction[1] derived similar help from Socrates, who in each case stimulated in them a persevering assiduity toward their several aims, as the following narratives tend to show. He had heard on one occasion of the arrival in Athens of Dionysodorus,[2] who professed to teach the whole duty of a general.[3] Accordingly he remarked to one of those who were with him—a young man whose anxiety to obtain the office of Strategos[4] was no secret to him:

SOCRATES: It would be monstrous on the part of anyone who sought to become a general[5] to throw away the slightest opportunity of learning the duties of the office. Such a person, I should say, would deserve to be fined and punished by the state far more than the charlatan who without having learned the art of a sculptor undertakes a contract to carve a statue. Considering that the whole fortunes of the state are entrusted to the general during a war, with all its incidental peril, it is only reasonable to anticipate that great blessings or great misfortunes will result in proportion to the success or bungling of that officer. I appeal to you, young sir, do you not agree that a candidate who, while taking pains to be elected neglects to learn the duties of the office, would richly deserve to be fined?

With arguments like these he persuaded the young man to go and take lessons. After he had gone through the course he came back, and Socrates proceeded playfully to banter him.

SOCRATES: Behold our young friend, sirs, as Homer says of Agamemnon, of mein majestical,[6] so he; does he not seem to move more majestically, like one who has studied to be a general? Of course, just as a man who has learned to play the harp is a harper, even if he never touch the instrument, or as one who has studied medicine is a physician, though he does not practice, so our friend here from this time forward is now and ever shall be a general, even though he does not receive a vote at the elections. But the dunce who has not the science is neither general nor doctor, no, not even if the whole world appointed him. But (he proceeded, turning to

---

1 {ton kalon} = *everything which the* {kalos te kagathos} *should aim at, but especially the honorable offices of state such as the Archonship, Strategia, Hipparchia, etc. See Plat. "Laches."*
2 *Dionysodorus of Chios, presumably. See Plat. "Euthyd." 271 C foll.*
3 *A professor of the science and art of strategy.*
4 *Lit. "that honor," sc. the Strategia.*
5 *I.e. "head of the war department, and commander-in-chief," etc.*
6 *"Il." iii. 169, 170.*

the youth), in case any of us should ever find ourselves captain or colonel[1] under you, to give us some smattering of the science of war, what did the professor take as the starting-point of his instruction in generalship? Please inform us.

Then the young man: He began where he ended; he taught me tactics[2]—tactics and nothing else.

Yet surely (replied Socrates) that is only an infinitesimal part of generalship. A general[3] must be ready in furnishing the material of war: in providing the commissariat for his troops; quick in devices, he must be full of practical resource; nothing must escape his eye or tax his endurance; he must be shrewd, and ready of wit, a combination at once of clemency and fierceness, of simplicity and of insidious craft; he must play the part of watchman, of robber; now prodigal as a spendthrift, and again close-fisted as a miser, the bounty of his munificence must be equalled by the narrowness of his greed; impregnable in defense, a very dare-devil in attack—these and many other qualities must he possess who is to make a good general and minister of war; they must come to him by gift of nature or through science. No doubt it is a grand thing also to be a tactician, since there is all the difference in the world between an army properly handled in the field and the same in disorder; just as stones and bricks, woodwork and tiles, tumbled together in a heap are of no use at all, but arrange them in a certain order—at bottom and atop materials which will not crumble or rot, such as stones and earthen tiles, and in the middle between the two put bricks and woodwork, with an eye to architectural principle,[4] and finally you get a valuable possession—to wit, a dwelling-place.

The simile is very apt, Socrates[5] (replied the youth), for in battle, too, the rule is to draw up the best men in front and rear, with those of inferior quality between, where they may be led on by the former and pushed on by the hinder.

SOCRATES: Very good, no doubt, if the professor taught you to distinguish good and bad; but if not, where is the use of your learning? It would scarcely help you, would it, to be told to arrange coins in piles, the best coins at top and bottom and the worst in the middle, unless you were first taught to distinguish real from counterfeit.

---

1 Or, *"brigadier or captain,"* lit. *taxiarch* or *lochagos.*
2 Cf. *"Cyrop." I. vi. 12 foll.; VIII. v. 15.*
3 *A strategos.* For the duties and spheres of action of this officer, see Gow, op. cit. xiv. 58.
4 *"As in the building of a house."* See *Vitrivius, ii. 3; Plin. xxv. 14.*
5 Cf. *"Il." iv. 297 foll.; "Cyrop." VI. iii. 25; Polyb. x. 22.*

THE YOUTH: Well no, upon my word, he did not teach us that, so that the task of distinguishing between good and bad must devolve on ourselves.

Soc. Well, shall we see, then, how we may best avoid making blunders between them?

I am ready (replied the youth).

SOCRATES: Well then! Let us suppose we are marauders, and the task imposed upon us is to carry off some bullion; it will be a right disposition of our forces if we place in the vanguard those who are the greediest of gain?[1]

THE YOUTH: I should think so.

SOCRATES: Then what if there is danger to be faced? Shall the vanguard consist of men who are greediest of honor?

The Youth. It is these, at any rate, who will face danger for the sake of praise and glory.[2] Fortunately such people are not hid away in a corner; they shine forth conspicuous everywhere, and are easy to be discovered.

SOCRATES: But tell me, did he teach you how to draw up troops in general, or specifically where and how to apply each particular kind of tactical arrangement?

THE YOUTH: Nothing of the sort.

SOCRATES: And yet there are and must be innumerable circumstances in which the same ordering of march or battle will be out of place.

THE YOUTH: I assure you he did not draw any of these fine distinctions.

He did not, did not he? (he answered). Bless me! Go back to him again, then, and ply him with questions; if he really has the science, and is not lost to all sense of shame, he will blush to have taken your money and then to have sent you away empty.

II

At another time he fell in with a man who had been chosen general and minister of war, and thus accosted him.

SOCRATES: Why did Homer, think you, designate Agamemnon "shepherd of the peoples"?[3] Was it possibly to show that, even as a shepherd must care for his sheep and see that they are safe and have all things needful, and that the objects of their rearing be secured, so also must a general take care that his soldiers are safe and have their supplies, and attain the objects of their soldiering? Which last is that they may get the mastery of their

---

1 *"Whose fingers itch for gold."*
2 Cf. Shakesp. *"seeking the bubble reputation even in the cannon's mouth."*
3 *"Il."* ii. 243. *"The People's Paster,"* Chapman.

enemies, and so add to their own good fortune and happiness; or tell me, what made him praise Agamemnon, saying—

He is both a good king and a warrior bold?[1]

Did he mean, perhaps, to imply that he would be a "warrior bold," not merely in standing alone and bravely battling against the foe, but as inspiring the whole of his host with like prowess; and by a "good king," not merely one who should stand forth gallantly to protect his own life, but who should be the source of happiness to all over whom he reigns? Since a man is not chosen king in order to take heed to himself, albeit nobly, but that those who chose him may attain to happiness through him. And why do men go soldiering except to ameliorate existence?[2] and to this end they choose their generals that they may find in them guides to the goal in question. He, then, who undertakes that office is bound to procure for those who choose him the thing they seek for. And indeed it were not easy to find any nobler ambition than this, or aught ignobler than its opposite.

After such sort he handled the question, what is the virtue of a good leader? and by shredding off all superficial qualities, laid bare as the kernel of the matter that it is the function of every leader to make those happy whom he may be called upon to lead.[3]

III

The following conversation with a youth who had just been elected hipparch[4] (or commandant of cavalry), I can also vouch for.[5]

SOCRATES: Can you tell us what set you wishing to be a general of cavalry, young sir? What was your object? I suppose it was not simply to ride at the head of the "knights," an honor not denied to the mounted archers,[6] who ride even in front of the generals themselves?

HIPPARCH: You are right.

SOCRATES: No more was it for the sake merely of public notoriety, since a madman might boast of that fatal distinction.[7]

HIPPARCH: You are right again.

SOCRATES: Is this possibly the explanation? you think to improve the

---

1 "Il." iii. 179; cf. "Symp." iv. 6. A favorite line of Alexander the Great's, it is said.
2 Of, "that life may reach some flower of happiness."
3 Cf. Plat. "Rep." 342.
4 Cf. "Hipparch."
5 Lit. "I know he once held."
6 Lit. "Hippotoxotai." See Boeckh, "P. E. A." II. xxi. p. 264 (Eng. tr.)
7 Or, "as we all know, "Tom Fool" can boast," etc.

cavalry—your aim would be to hand it over to the state in better condition than you find it; and, if the cavalry chanced to be called out, you at their head would be the cause of some good thing to Athens?

HIPPARCH: Most certainly.

SOCRATES: Well, and a noble ambition too, upon my word—if you can achieve your object. The command to which you are appointed concerns horses and riders, does it not?

HIPPARCH: It does, no doubt.

SOCRATES: Come then, will you explain to us first how you propose to improve the horses.

HIPPARCH: Ah, that will scarcely form part of my business, I fancy. Each trooper is personally responsible for the condition of his horse.

SOCRATES: But suppose, when they present themselves and their horses,[1] you find that some have brought beasts with bad feet or legs or otherwise infirm, and others such ill-fed jades that they cannot keep up on the march; others, again, brutes so ill broken and unmanageable that they will not keep their place in the ranks, and others such desperate plungers that they cannot be got to any place in the ranks at all. What becomes of your cavalry force then? How will you charge at the head of such a troop, and win glory for the state?

HIPPARCH: You are right. I will try to look after the horses to my utmost.

SOCRATES: Well, and will you not lay your hand to improve the men themselves?

HIPPARCH: I will.

SOCRATES: The first thing will be to make them expert in mounting their chargers?

HIPPARCH: That certainly, for if any of them were dismounted he would then have a better chance of saving himself.

SOCRATES: Well, but when it comes to the hazard of engagement, what will you do then? Give orders to draw the enemy down to the sandy ground[2] where you are accustomed to manouvre, or endeavor beforehand to put your men through their practice on ground resembling a real battlefield?

HIPPARCH: That would be better, no doubt.

SOCRATES: Well, shall you regard it as a part of your duty to see that as many of your men as possible can take aim and shoot on horseback?[3]

---

1 For this phrase, see Schneider and Kuhner ad loc.
2 E.g. the hippodrome at Phaleron.
3 Cf. "Hipparch," i. 21.

HIPPARCH: It will be better, certainly.

SOCRATES: And have you thought how to whet the courage of your troopers? to kindle in them rage to meet the enemy?—which things are but stimulants to make stout hearts stouter?

HIPPARCH: If I have not done so hitherto, I will try to make up for lost time now.

SOCRATES: And have you troubled your head at all to consider how you are to secure the obedience of your men? for without that not one particle of good will you get, for all your horses and troopers so brave and so stout.

HIPPARCH: That is a true saying; but how, Socrates, should a man best bring them to this virtue?[1]

SOCRATES: I presume you know that in any business whatever, people are more apt to follow the lead of those whom they look upon as adepts; thus in case of sickness they are readiest to obey him whom they regard as the cleverest physician; and so on a voyage the most skilful pilot; in matters agricultural the best farmer, and so forth.

HIPPARCH: Yes, certainly.

SOCRATES: Then in this matter of cavalry also we may reasonably suppose that he who is looked upon as knowing his business best will command the readiest obedience.

HIPPARCH: If, then, I can prove to my troopers that I am better than all of them, will that suffice to win their obedience?

SOCRATES: Yes, if along with that you can teach them that obedience to you brings greater glory and surer safety to themselves.

HIPPARCH: How am I to teach them that?

SOCRATES: Upon my word! How are you to teach them that? Far more easily, I take it, than if you had to teach them that bad things are better than good, and more advantageous to boot.

HIPPARCH: I suppose you mean that, besides his other qualifications a commandant of cavalry must have command of speech and argument?[2]

SOCRATES: Were you under the impression that the commandant was not to open his mouth? Did it never occur to you that all the noblest things which custom[3] compels us to learn, and to which indeed we owe our

---

1 {protrepsasthai}. See above, I. ii. 64; below, IV. v. 1.
2 Or, "practice the art of oratory"; "express himself clearly and rationally." See Grote, "H. G." VIII. lxvii. p. 463 note; "Hipparch," i. 24; viii. 22.
3 Cf Arist. "Rhet." ii. 12, {oi neoi pepaideuntai upo tou nomou monon}.

knowledge of life, have all been learned by means of speech[1] and reason; and if there be any other noble learning which a man may learn, it is this same reason whereby he learns it; and the best teachers are those who have the freest command of thought and language, and those that have the best knowledge of the most serious things are the most brilliant masters of disputation. Again, have you not observed that whenever this city of ours fits out one of her choruses—such as that, for instance, which is sent to Delos[2]—there is nothing elsewhere from any quarter of the world which can compete with it; nor will you find in any other state collected so fair a flower of manhood as in Athens?[3]

HIPPARCH: You say truly.

SOCRATES: But for all that, it is not in sweetness of voice that the Athenians differ from the rest of the world so much, nor in stature of body or strength of limb, but in ambition and that love of honor[4] which most of all gives a keen edge to the spirit in the pursuit of things lovely and of high esteem.

HIPPARCH: That, too, is a true saying.

SOCRATES: Do you not think, then, that if a man devoted himself to our cavalry also, here in Athens, we should far outstrip the rest of the world, whether in the furnishing of arms and horses, or in orderliness of battle-array, or in eager hazardous encounter with the foe, if only we could persuade ourselves that by so doing we should obtain honor and distinction?

HIPPARCH: It is reasonable to think so.

SOCRATES: Have no hesitation, therefore, but try to guide your men into this path,[5] whence you yourself, and through you your fellow citizens, will reap advantage.

Yes, in good sooth, I will try (he answered).

IV

At another time, seeing Nicomachides on his way back from the elections (of magistrates),[6] he asked him: Who are elected generals, Nicomachides?

And he: Is it not just like them, these citizens of Athens—just like them, I say—to go and elect, not me, who ever since my name first appeared on

---

1 {dia logou}.
2 See Thuc. iii. 104; and below, IV. viii. 2.
3 See references ap. Schneider and Kuhner; "Symp." iv. 17.
4 See below, v. 3; Dem. "de Cor." 28 foll.
5 Or, "to conduct which will not certainly fail of profit to yourself or through you to..."
6 Cf. "Pol. Ath." i. 3; Aristot. "Ath. Pol." 44. 4; and Dr. Sandys" note ad loc. p. 165 of his edition.

the muster-roll have literally worn myself out with military service—now as a captain, now as a colonel—and have received all these wounds from the enemy, look you! (at the same time, and suiting the action to the word, he bared his arms and proceeded to show the scars of ancient wounds)—they elect not me (he went on), but, if you please, Antisthenes! who never served as a hoplite[1] in his life nor in the cavalry ever made a brilliant stroke, that I ever heard tell of; no! in fact, he has got no science at all, I take it, except to amass stores of wealth.

But still (returned Socrates), surely that is one point in his favor—he ought to be able to provide the troops with supplies.

NICOMACHIDES: Well, for the matter of that, merchants are good hands at collecting stores; but it does not follow that a merchant or trader will be able to command an army.

But (rejoined Socrates) Antisthenes is a man of great pertinacity, who insists on winning, and that is a very necessary quality in a general.[2] Do not you see how each time he has been choragos[3] he has been successful with one chorus after another?

NICOMACHIDES: Bless me! yes; but there is a wide difference between standing at the head of a band of singers and dancers and a troop of soldiers.

SOCRATES: Still, without any practical skill in singing or in the training of a chorus, Antisthenes somehow had the art to select the greatest proficients in both.

NICOMACHIDES: Yes, and by the same reasoning we are to infer that on a campaign he will find proficients, some to marshal the troops for him and others to fight his battles?

SOCRATES: Just so. If in matters military he only exhibits the same skill in selecting the best hands as he has shown in matters of the chorus, it is highly probable he will here also bear away the palm of victory; and we may presume that if he expended so much to win a choric victory with a single tribe,[4] he will be ready to expend more to secure a victory in war with the whole state to back him.

NICOMACHIDES: Do you really mean, Socrates, that it is the function

---

1 Cf. *Lys.* xiv. 10.
2 See Grote, "Plato," i. 465 foll.
3 Choir-master, or Director of the Chorus. It was his duty to provide and preside over a chorus to sing, dance, or play at any of the public festivals, defraying the cost as a state service of {leitourgia}. See "Pol. Ath." iii. 4; "Hiero," ix. 4; Aristot. "Pol. Ath." 28. 3.
4 See Dem. "against Lept." 496. 26. Each tribe nominated such of its members as were qualified to undertake the burden.

of the same man to provide efficient choruses and to act as commander-in-chief?

SOCRATES: I mean this, that, given a man knows what he needs to provide, and has the skill to do so, no matter what the department of things may be—house or city or army—you will find him a good chief and director[1] of the same.

Then Nicomachides: Upon my word, Socrates, I should never have expected to hear you say that a good housekeeper[2] and steward of an estate would make a good general.

SOCRATES: Come then, suppose we examine their respective duties, and so determine[3] whether they are the same or different.

NICOMACHIDES: Let us do so.

SOCRATES: Well then, is it not a common duty of both to procure the ready obedience of those under them to their orders?

NICOMACHIDES: Certainly.

SOCRATES: And also to assign to those best qualified to perform them their distinctive tasks?

That, too, belongs to both alike (he answered).

SOCRATES: Again, to chastise the bad and reward the good belongs to both alike, methinks?

NICOMACHIDES: Decidedly.

SOCRATES: And to win the kindly feeling of their subordinates must surely be the noble ambition of both?

That too (he answered).

SOCRATES: And do you consider it to the interest of both alike to win the adherence of supporters and allies?[4]

NICOMACHIDES: Without a doubt.

SOCRATES: And does it not closely concern them both to be good guardians of their respective charges?

NICOMACHIDES: Very much so.

SOCRATES: Then it equally concerns them both to be painstaking and prodigal of toil in all their doings?

NICOMACHIDES: Yes, all these duties belong to both alike, but the parallel ends when you come to actual fighting.

---

1 Or, "representative."
2 Or, "economist"; cf. "Cyrop." I. vi. 12.
3 Lit. "get to know."
4 In reference to the necessity of building up a family connection or political alliances cf. Arist. "Pol." iii. 9, 13.

SOCRATES: Yet they are both sure to meet with enemies?

NICOMACHIDES: There is no doubt about that.

SOCRATES: Then is it not to the interest of both to get the upper hand of these?

NICOMACHIDES: Certainly; but you omit to tell us what service organization and the art of management will render when it comes to actual fighting.

SOCRATES: Why, it is just then, I presume, it will be of most service, for the good economist knows that nothing is so advantageous or so lucrative as victory in battle, or to put it negatively, nothing so disastrous and expensive as defeat. He will enthusiastically seek out and provide everything conducive to victory, he will painstakingly discover and guard against all that tends to defeat, and when satisfied that all is ready and ripe for victory he will deliver battle energetically, and what is equally important, until the hour of final preparation has arrived,[1] he will be cautious to deliver battle. Do not despise men of economic genius, Nicomachides; the difference between the devotion requisite to private affairs and to affairs of state is merely one of quantity. For the rest the parallel holds strictly, and in this respect pre-eminently, that both are concerned with human instruments: which human beings, moreover, are of one type and temperament, whether we speak of devotion to public affairs or of the administration of private property. To fare well in either case is given to those who know the secret of dealing with humanity, whereas the absence of that knowledge will as certainly imply in either case a fatal note of discord.[2]

V

A conversation held with Pericles the son of the great statesman may here be introduced.[3] Socrates began:

I am looking forward, I must tell you, Pericles, to a great improvement in our military affairs when you are minister of war.[4] The prestige of Athens, I hope, will rise; we shall gain the mastery over our enemies.

Pericles replied: I devoutly wish your words might be fulfillled, but how this happy result is to be obtained, I am at a loss to discover.

---

1 Lit. "as long as he is unprepared."
2 L. Dindorf, "Index Graec." Ox. ed.; cf. Hor. "Ep." II. ii. 144, "sed verae numerosque modosque ediscere vitae," "the harmony of life," Conington.
3 Or, "On one occasion Pericles was the person addressed in conversation." For Pericles see "Hell." I. v. 16; vii. 15; Plut. "Pericl." 37 (Clough, i. 368).
4 "Strategos."

Shall we (Socrates continued), shall we balance the arguments for and against, and consider to what extent the possibility does exist?

Pray let us do so (he answered).

SOCRATES: Well then, you know that in point of numbers the Athenians are not inferior to the Boeotians?

PERICLES: Yes, I am aware of that.

SOCRATES: And do you think the Boeotians could furnish a better pick of fine healthy men than the Athenians?

PERICLES: I think we should very well hold our own in that respect.

SOCRATES: And which of the two would you take to be the more united people—the friendlier among themselves?

PERICLES: The Athenians, I should say, for so many sections of the Boeotians, resenting the selfish policy[1] of Thebes, are ill disposed to that power, but at Athens I see nothing of the sort.

SOCRATES: But perhaps you will say that there is no people more jealous of honor or haughtier in spirit.[2] And these feelings are no weak spurs to quicken even a dull spirit to hazard all for glory's sake and fatherland.

PERICLES: Nor is there much fault to find with Athenians in these respects.

SOCRATES: And if we turn to consider the fair deeds of ancestry,[3] to no people besides ourselves belongs so rich a heritage of stimulating memories, whereby so many of us are stirred to pursue virtue with devotion and to show ourselves in our turn also men of valour like our sires.

PERICLES: All that you say, Socrates, is most true, but do you observe that ever since the disaster of the thousand under Tolmides at Lebadeia, coupled with that under Hippocrates at Delium,[4] the prestige of Athens by comparison with the Boeotians has been lowered, whilst the spirit of Thebes as against Athens had been correspondingly exalted, so that those Boeotians who in old days did not venture to give battle to the Athenians even in their own territory unless they had the Lacedaemonians and the rest of the Peloponnesians to help them, do nowadays threaten to make an incursion into Attica single-handed; and the Athenians, who formerly, if they had to deal with the Boeotians[5] only, made havoc of their territory,

---

1 *"The self-aggrandisement."*

2 Reading {megalophronestatoi}, after Cobet. See *"Hipparch,"* vii. 3; or if as vulg. {philophronestatoi}, transl. *"more affable."*

3 See Wesley's anthem, Eccles. xliv. 1, *"Let us now praise famous men and our fathers that begat us."*

4 Lebadeia, 447 BC; Delium, 424 BC For Tolmides and Hippocrates see Thuc. i. 113; iv. 100 foll.; Grote, *"H. G."* v. 471; vi. 533.

5 Reading {ote B. monoi}, al. {ou monoi}, *"when the Boeotians were not unaided."*

are now afraid the Boeotians may some day harry Attica.

To which Socrates: Yes, I perceive that this is so, but it seems to me that the state was never more tractably disposed, never so ripe for a really good leader, as today. For if boldness be the parent of carelessness, laxity, and insubordination, it is the part of fear to make people more disposed to application, obedience, and good order. A proof of which you may discover in the behavior of people on ship-board. It is in seasons of calm weather when there is nothing to fear that disorder may be said to reign, but as soon as there is apprehension of a storm, or an enemy in sight, the scene changes; not only is each word of command obeyed, but there is a hush of silent expectation; the mariners wait to catch the next signal like an orchestra with eyes upon the leader.

PERICLES: But indeed, given that now is the opportunity to take obedience at the flood, it is high time also to explain by what means we are to rekindle in the hearts of our countrymen[1] the old fires—the passionate longing for antique valour, for the glory and the wellbeing of the days of old.

Well (proceeded Socrates), supposing we wished them to lay claim to certain material wealth now held by others, we could not better stimulate them to lay hands on the objects coveted than by showing them that these were ancestral possessions[2] to which they had a natural right. But since our object is that they should set their hearts on virtuous pre-eminence, we must prove to them that such headship combined with virtue is an old time-honored heritage which pertains to them beyond all others, and that if they strive earnestly after it they will soon out-top the world.

Por. How are we to inculcate this lesson?

SOCRATES: I think by reminding them of a fact already registered in their minds,[3] that the oldest of our ancestors whose names are known to us were also the bravest of heroes.

PERICLES: I suppose you refer to that judgment of the gods which, for their virtue's sake, Cecrops and his followers were called on to decide?[4]

SOCRATES: Yes, I refer to that and to the birth and rearing of Erectheus,[5] and also to the war[6] which in his days was waged to stay the

---

1 Reading {anerasthenai}, Schneider's emendation of the vulg. {aneristhenai}.
2 Cf. Solon in the matter of Salamis, Plut. "Sol." 8; Bergk. "Poet. Lyr. Gr. Solon," SALAMIS, i. 2, 3.
3 Or, "to which their ears are already opened."
4 See Apollodorus, iii. 14.
5 Cf. "Il." ii. 547, {"Erekhtheos megaletoros k.t.l.}
6 Cf. Isoc. "Paneg." 19, who handles all the topics.

tide of invasion from the whole adjoining continent; and that other war in the days of the Heraclidae[1] against the men of Peloponnese; and that series of battles fought in the days of Theseus[2]—in all which the virtuous pre-eminence of our ancestry above the men of their own times was made manifest. Or, if you please, we may come down to things of a later date, which their descendants and the heroes of days not so long anterior to our own wrought in the struggle with the lords of Asia,[3] nay of Europe also, as far as Macedonia: a people possessing a power and means of attack far exceeding any who had gone before—who, moreover, had accomplished the doughtiest deeds. These things the men of Athens wrought partly single-handed,[4] and partly as sharers with the Peloponnesians in laurels won by land and sea. Heroes were these men also, far outshining, as tradition tells us, the peoples of their time.

PERICLES: Yes, so runs the story of their heroism.

SOCRATES: Therefore it is that, amidst the many changes of inhabitants, and the migrations which have, wave after wave, swept over Hellas, these maintained themselves in their own land, unmoved; so that it was a common thing for others to turn to them as to a court of appeal on points of right, or to flee to Athens as a harbor of refuge from the hand of the oppressor.[5]

Then Pericles: And the wonder to me, Socrates, is how our city ever came to decline.

SOCRATES: I think we are victims of our own success. Like some athlete,[6] whose facile preponderance in the arena has betrayed him into laxity until he eventually succumbs to punier antagonists, so we Athenians, in the plenitude of our superiority, have neglected ourselves and are become degenerate.

PERICLES: What then ought we to do now to recover our former virtue?

SOCRATES: There need be no mystery about that, I think. We can rediscover the institutions of our forefathers—applying them to the regulation of our lives with something of their precision, and not improbably with like success; or we can imitate those who stand at the front

---

1 Commonly spoken of as "the Return." See Grote, "H. G." II. ch. xviii.
2 Against the Amazons and Thracians; cf. Herod. ix. 27; Plut. "Thes." 27.
3 The "Persian" wars; cf. Thucyd. I. i.
4 He omits the Plataeans.
5 Cf. (Plat.) "Menex."; Isocr. "Paneg."
6 Reading {athletai tines}, or if {alloi tines}, translate "anyone else."

of affairs today,[1] adapting to ourselves their rule of life, in which case, if we live up to the standard of our models, we may hope at least to rival their excellence, or, by a more conscientious adherence to what they aim at, rise superior.

You would seem to suggest (he answered) that the spirit of beautiful and brave manhood has taken wings and left our city;[2] as, for instance, when will Athenians, like the Lacedaemonians, reverence old age—the Athenian, who takes his own father as a starting-point for the contempt he pours upon grey hairs? When will he pay as strict an attention to the body, who is not content with neglecting a good habit,[3] but laughs to scorn those who are careful in this matter? When shall we Athenians so obey our magistrates—we who take a pride, as it were, in despising authority? When, once more, shall we be united as a people—we who, instead of combining to promote common interests, delight in blackening each other's characters,[4] envying one another more than we envy all the world besides; and—which is our worst failing—who, in private and public intercourse alike, are torn by dissension and are caught in a maze of litigation, and prefer to make capital out of our neighbor's difficulties rather than to render natural assistance? To make our conduct consistent, indeed, we treat our national interests no better than if they were the concerns of some foreign state; we make them bones of contention to wrangle over, and rejoice in nothing so much as in possessing means and ability to indulge these tastes. From this hotbed is engendered in the state a spirit of blind folly[5] and cowardice, and in the hearts of the citizens spreads a tangle of hatred and mutual hostility which, as I often shudder to think, will some day cause some disaster to befall the state greater than it can bear.[6]

Do not (replied Socrates), do not, I pray you, permit yourself to believe that Athenians are smitten with so incurable a depravity. Do you not observe their discipline in all naval matters? Look at their prompt and orderly obedience to the superintendents at the gymnastic contests,[7] their quite unrivalled subservience to their teachers in the training of our choruses.

---

1 Sc. the Lacedaemonians. See W. L. Newman, op. cit. i. 396.
2 Or, "is far enough away from Athens."
3 See below, III. xii. 5; "Pol. Ath." i. 13; "Rev." iv. 52.
4 Or, "to deal despitefully with one another."
5 Reading {ateria}. See L. Dindorf ad loc., Ox. ed. lxii. Al. {apeiria}, a want of skill, or {ataxia}, disorderliness. Cf. "Pol. Ath." i. 5.
6 Possibly the author is thinking of the events of 406, 405 BC (see "Hell." I. vii. and II.), and history may repeat itself.
7 Epistatoi, i.e. stewards and training-masters.

Yes (he answered), there's the wonder of it; to think that all those good people should so obey their leaders, but that our hoplites and our cavalry, who may be supposed to rank before the rest of the citizens in excellence of manhood,[1] should be so entirely unamenable to discipline.

Then Socrates: Well, but the council which sits on Areopagos is composed of citizens of approved[2] character, is it not?

Certainly (he answered).

SOCRATES: Then can you name any similar body, judicial or executive, trying cases or transacting other business with greater honor, stricter legality, higher dignity, or more impartial justice?

No, I have no fault to find on that score (he answered).

SOCRATES: Then we ought not to despair as though all sense of orderliness and good discipline had died out of our countrymen.

Still (he answered), if it is not to harp upon one string, I maintain that in military service, where, if anywhere, sobreity and temperance, orderliness and good discipline are needed, none of these essentials receives any attention.

May it not perhaps be (asked Socrates) that in this department they are officered by those who have the least knowledge?[3] Do you not notice, to take the case of harp-players, choric performers, dancers, and the like, that no one would ever dream of leading if he lacked the requisite knowledge? and the same holds of wrestlers or pancratiasts.

Moreover, while in these cases anyone in command can tell you where he got the elementary knowledge of what he presides over, most generals are amateurs and improvisers.[4] I do not at all suppose that you are one of that sort. I believe you could give as clear an account of your schooling in strategy as you could in the matter of wrestling. No doubt you have got at first hand many of your father's "rules for generalship," which you carefully preserve, besides having collected many others from every quarter whence it was possible to pick up any knowledge which would be of use to a future general. Again, I feel sure you are deeply concerned to escape even unconscious ignorance of anything which will be serviceable to you in so high an office; and if you detect in yourself any ignorance, you turn to those who have knowledge in these matters (sparing neither gifts

---

1 {kalokagathia}.
2 Technically, they must have passed the {dokimasia}. And for the "Aeropagos" see Grote, "H. G." v. 498; Aristot. "Pol." ii. 12; "Ath. Pol." 4. 4, where see Dr. Sandys" note, p. 18.
3 {episteme}. See below, III. ix. 10.
4 Cf. "Pol. Lac." xiii. 5.

nor gratitude) to supplement your ignorance by their knowledge and to secure their help.

To which Pericles: I am not so blind, Socrates, as to imagine you say these words under the idea that I am truly so careful in these matters; but rather your object is to teach me that the would-be general must make such things his care. I admit in any case all you say.

Socrates proceeded: Has it ever caught your observation, Pericles, that a high mountain barrier stretches like a bulwark in front of our country down toward Boeotia—cleft, moreover, by narrow and precipitous passes, the only avenues into the heart of Attica, which lies engirdled by a ring of natural fortresses?[1]

PERICLES: Certainly I have.

SOCRATES: Well, and have you ever heard tell of the Mysians and Pisidians living within the territory of the great king,[2] who, inside their mountain fortresses, lightly armed, are able to rush down and inflict much injury on the king's territory by their raids, while preserving their own freedom?

PERICLES: Yes, the circumstance is not new to me.

And do you not think (added Socrates) that a corps of young able-bodied Athenians, accoutred with lighter arms,[3] and holding our natural mountain rampart in possession, would prove at once a thorn in the enemy's side offensively, whilst defensively they would form a splendid bulwark to protect the country?

To which Pericles: I think, Socrates, these would be all useful measures, decidedly.

If, then (replied Socrates), these suggestions meet your approbation, try, O best of men, to realizethem—if you can carry out a portion of them, it will be an honor to yourself and a blessing to the state; while, if you fail in any point, there will be no damage done to the city nor discredit to yourself.

VI

Glaucon,[4] the son of Ariston, had conceived such an ardour to gain the headship of the state that nothing could hinder him but he must deliver a course of public speeches,[5] though he had not yet reached the age of

---

1 *The mountains are Cithaeron and Parnes N., and Cerata N.W.*
2 *For this illustration see "Anab." III. ii. 23; cf. "Econ." iv. 18, where Socrates ({XS}) refers to Cyrus's expedition and death.*
3 *Cf. the reforms of Iphicrates.*
4 *Glaucon, Plato's brother. Grote, "Plato," i. 508.*
5 *"Harangue the People."*

twenty. His friends and relatives tried in vain to stop him making himself ridiculous and being dragged down from the bema.[1] Socrates, who took a kindly interest in the youth for the sake of Charmides[2] the son of Glaucon, and of Plato, alone succeeded in restraining him. It happened thus. He fell in with him, and first of all, to get him to listen, detained him by some such remarks as the following:[3]

Ah, Glaucon (he exclaimed), so you have determined to become prime minister?[4]

GLAUCON: Yes, Socrates, I have.

SOCRATES: And what a noble aim! if aught human ever deserved to be called noble; since if you succeed in your design, it follows, as the night the day, you will be able not only to gratify your every wish, but you will be in a position to benefit your friends, you will raise up your father's house, you will exalt your fatherland, you will become a name thrice famous in the city first, and next in Hellas, and lastly even among barbarians perhaps, like Themistocles; but be it here or be it there, wherever you be, you will be the observed of all beholders.[5]

The heart of Glaucon swelled with pride as he drank in the words, and gladly he stayed to listen.

Presently Socrates proceeded: Then this is clear, Glaucon, is it not? that you must needs benefit the city, since you desire to reap her honors?

GLAUCON: Undoubtedly.

Then, by all that is sacred (Socrates continued), do not keep us in the dark, but tell us in what way do you propose first to benefit the state? what is your starting-point?[6] When Glaucon remained with sealed lips, as if he were now for the first time debating what this starting-point should be, Socrates continued: I presume, if you wished to improve a friend's estate, you would endeavor to do so by adding to its wealth, would you not? So here, maybe, you will try to add to the wealth of the state?

---

1 See Plat. "Protag." 319 C: "And if some person offers to give them advice who is not supposed by them to have any skill in the art (sc. of politics), even though he be good-looking, and rich, and noble, they will not listen to him, but laugh at him, and hoot at him, until he is either clamored down and retires of himself; or if he persists, he is dragged away or put out by the constables at the command of the prytanes" (Jowett). Cf. Aristoph. "Knights," 665, {kath eilkon auton oi prutaneis kai toxotai}.
2 For Charmides (maternal uncle of Plato and Glaucon, cousin of Critias) see ch. vii. below; Plato the philosopher, Glaucon's brother, see Cobet, "Pros. Xen." p. 28.
3 Or, "and in the first instance addressing him in such terms he could not choose but hear, detained him." See above, II. vi. 11. Socrates applies his own theory.
4 {prostateuein}.
5 "The center of attraction—the cynosure of neighboring eyes."
6 Or, "tell us what your starting-point will be in the path of benefaction."

Most decidedly (he answered).

SOCRATES: And we may take it the state will grow wealthier in proportion as her revenues increase?

GLAUCON: That seems probable, at any rate.

SOCRATES: Then would you kindly tell us from what sources the revenues of the state are at present derived, and what is their present magnitude? No doubt you have gone carefully into the question, so that if any of these are failing you may make up the deficit, or if neglected for any reason, make some new provision.[1]

GLAUCON: Nay, to speak the truth, these are matters I have not thoroughly gone into.

Never mind (he said) if you have omitted the point; but you might oblige us by running through the items or heads of expenditure. Obviously you propose to remove all those which are superfluous?

GLAUCON: Well, no. Upon my word I have not had time to look into that side of the matter either as yet.

SOCRATES: Then we will postpone for the present the problem of making the state wealthier; obviously without knowing the outgoings and the incomings it would be impossible to deal with the matter seriously.

But, Socrates (Glaucon remarked), it is possible to enrich the state out of the pockets of her enemies!

Yes, to be sure, considerably (answered Socrates), in the event of getting the better of them; but in the event of being worsted, it is also possible to lose what we have got.

A true observation (he replied).

And therefore (proceeded Socrates), before he makes up his mind with what enemy to go to war, a statesman should know the relative powers of his own city and the adversary's, so that, in case the superiority be on his own side, he may throw the weight of his advice into the scale of undertaking war; but if the opposite he may plead in favor of exercising caution.

You are right (he answered).

SOCRATES: Then would you for our benefit enumerate the land and naval forces first of Athens and then of our opponents?

GLAUCON: Pardon me. I could not tell you them off-hand at a moment's notice.

Or (added Socrates), if you have got the figures on paper, you might produce them. I cannot tell how anxious I am to hear your statement.

---

1 Or, "or if others have dropped out or been negligently overlooked, you may replace them."

GLAUCON: No, I assure you, I have not got them even on paper yet.

SOCRATES: Well then, we will defer tending advice on the topic of peace or war, in a maiden speech at any rate.[1] I can understand that, owing to the magnitude of the questions, in these early days of your ministry you have not yet fully examined them. But come, I am sure that you have studied the defenses of the country, at all events, and you know exactly how many forts and outposts are serviceable[2] and how many are not; you can tell us which garrisons are strong enough and which defective; and you are prepared to throw in the weight of your advice in favor of increasing the serviceable outposts and sweeping away those that are superfluous?

GLAUCON: Yes, sweep them all away, that's my advice; for any good that is likely to come of them! Defences indeed! so maintained that the property of the rural districts is simply pilfered.

But suppose you sweep away the outposts (he asked), may not something worse, think you, be the consequence? will not sheer plundering be free to any ruffian who likes?... But may I ask is this judgment the result of personal inspection? have you gone yourself and examined the defenses? or how do you know that they are all maintained as you say?

GLAUCON: I conjecture that it is so.

SOCRATES: Well then, until we have got beyond the region of conjecture shall we defer giving advice on the matter? (It will be time enough when we know the facts.)

Possibly it would be better to wait till then (replied Glaucon).

SOCRATES: Then there are the mines,[3] but, of course, I am aware that you have not visited them in person, so as to be able to say why they are less productive than formerly.

Well, no; I have never been there myself (he answered).

SOCRATES: No, Heaven help us! an unhealthy district by all accounts; so that, when the moment for advice on that topic arrives, you will have an excuse ready to hand.

I see you are making fun of me (Glaucon answered).

SOCRATES: Well, but here is a point, I am sure, which you have not neglected. No, you will have thoroughly gone into it, and you can tell us. For how long a time could the corn supplies from the country districts support the city? how much is requisite for a single year, so that the city may not run short of this prime necessary, before you are well aware; but

---

1 See "Econ." xi. 1.
2 Or, "advantageously situated." See the author's own tract on "Revenues."
3 Again the author's tract on "Revenues" is a comment on the matter.

on the contrary you with your full knowledge will be in a position to give advice on so vital a question, to the aid or may be the salvation of your country?

It is a colossal business this (Glaucon answered), if I am to be obliged to give attention to all these details.

SOCRATES: On the other hand, a man could not even manage his own house or his estate well, without, in the first place, knowing what he requires, and, in the second place, taking pains, item by item, to supply his wants. But since this city consists of more than ten thousand houses, and it is not easy to pay minute attention to so many all at once, how is it you did not practice yourself by trying to augment the resources of one at any rate of these—I mean your own uncle's? The service would not be thrown away. Then if your strength suffices in the single case you might take in hand a larger number; but if you fail to relieve one, how could you possibly hope to succeed with many? How absurd for a man, if he cannot carry half a hundredweight, to attempt to carry a whole![1]

GLAUCON: Nay, for my part, I am willing enough to assist my uncle's house, if my uncle would only be persuaded to listen to my advice.

SOCRATES: Then, when you cannot persuade your uncle, do you imagine you will be able to make the whole Athenian people, uncle and all, obey you? Be careful, Glaucon (he added), lest in your thirst for glory and high repute you come to the opposite. Do you not see how dangerous it is for a man to speak or act beyond the range[2] of his knowledge? To take the cases known to you of people whose conversation or conduct clearly transcends these limits: should you say they gain more praise or more blame on that account? Are they admired the rather or despised? Or, again, consider those who do know what they say and what they do; and you will find, I venture to say, that in every sort of undertaking those who enjoy repute and admiration belong to the class of those endowed with the highest knowledge; whilst conversely the people of sinister reputation, the mean and the contemptible, emanate from some depth of ignorance and dulness. If therefore what you thirst for is repute and admiration as a statesman, try to make sure of one accomplishment: in other words, the knowledge as far as in you lies of what you wish to do.[3] If, indeed, with this to distinguish you from the rest of the world you venture to concern

---

1 Lit. "a single talent's weight... to carry two."
2 Or, "to talk of things which he does not know, or to meddle with them."
3 Or, "try as far as possible to achieve one thing, and that is to know the business which you propose to carry out."

yourself with state affairs, it would not surprise me but that you might reach the goal of your ambition easily.

VII

Now Charmides,[1] the son of Glaucon, was, as Socrates observed, a man of mark and influence: a much more powerful person in fact than the mass of those devoted to politics at that date, but at the same time he was a man who shrank from approaching the people or busying himself with the concerns of the state. Accordingly Socrates addressed him thus:

Tell me, Charmides, supposing someone competent to win a victory in the arena and to receive a crown,[2] whereby he will gain honor himself and make the land of his fathers more glorious in Hellas,[3] were to refuse to enter the lists—what kind of person should you set him down to be?

Clearly an effeminate and cowardly fellow (he answered).

SOCRATES: And what if another man, who had it in him, by devotion to affairs of state, to exalt his city and win honor himself thereby, were to shrink and hesitate and hang back—would he too not reasonably be regarded as a coward?

Possibly (he answered); but why do you address these questions to me?

Because (replied Socrates) I think that you, who have this power, do hesitate to devote yourself to matters which, as being a citizen, if for no other reason, you are bound to take part in.[4]

CHARMIDES: And wherein have you detected in me this power, that you pass so severe a sentence upon me?

SOCRATES: I have detected it plainly enough in those gatherings[5] in which you meet the politicians of the day, when, as I observe, each time they consult you on any point you have always good advice to offer, and when they make a blunder you lay your finger on the weak point immediately.

CHARMIDES: To discuss and reason in private is one thing, Socrates, to battle in the throng of the assembly is another.

SOCRATES: And yet a man who can count, counts every bit as well in a crowd as when seated alone by himself; and it is the best performer on the harp in private who carries off the palm of victory in public.

---

1 *See last chapter for his relationship to Glaucon (the younger) and Plato; for a conception of his character, Plato's dialogue "Charmides"; "Theag." 128 E; "Hell." II. iv. 19; "Symp." iv. 31; Grote, "Plato," i. 480.*
2 *In some conquest (e.g. of the Olympic games) where the prize is a mere wreath.*
3 *Cf. Pindar passim.*
4 *Or add, "and cannot escape from."*
5 *See above, I. v. 4; here possibly of political club conversation.*

CHARMIDES: But do you not see that modesty and timidity are feelings implanted in man's nature? and these are much more powerfully present to us in a crowd than within the circle of our intimates.

SOCRATES: Yes, but what I am bent on teaching you is that while you feel no such bashfulness and timidity before the wisest and strongest of men, you are ashamed of opening your lips in the midst of weaklings and dullards.[1] Is it the fullers among them of whom you stand in awe, or the cobblers, or the carpenters, or the coppersmiths, or the merchants, or the farmers, or the hucksters of the marketplace exchanging their wares, and bethinking them how they are to buy this thing cheap, and to sell the other dear—is it before these you are ashamed, for these are the individual atoms out of which the Public Assembly is composed?[2] And what is the difference, pray, between your behavior and that of a man who, being the superior of trained athletes, quails before a set of amateurs? Is it not the case that you who can argue so readily with the foremost statesmen in the city, some of whom affect to look down upon you—you, with your vast superiority over practiced popular debaters—are no sooner confronted with a set of folk who never in their lives gave politics a thought, and into whose heads certainly it never entered to look down upon you—than you are afraid to open your lips in mortal terror of being laughed at?

Well, but you would admit (he answered) that sound argument does frequently bring down the ridicule of the Popular Assembly.

SOCRATES: Which is equally true of the others.[3] And that is just what rouses my astonishment, that you who can cope so easily with these lordly people (when guilty of ridicule) should persuade yourself that you cannot stand up against a set of commoners.[4] My good fellow, do not be ignorant of yourself![5] do not fall into that commonest of errors—theirs who rush off to investigate the concerns of the rest of the world, and have no time to turn and examine themselves. Yet that is a duty which you must not in cowardly sort draw back from: rather must you brace ourself to give good heed to your own self; and as to public affairs, if by any manner of means they may be improved through you, do not neglect them. Success in the sphere of politics means that not only the mass of your fellow citizens, but your personal friends and you yourself last but not least, will profit by your action.

---

1 Cf. Cic. "Tusc." v. 36, 104; Plat. "Gorg." 452 E, 454 B.
2 Cf. Plat. "Protag." 319 C. See W. L. Newman, op. cit. i. 103.
3 {oi eteroi}, i.e. "the foremost statesmen" mentioned before. Al. "the opposite party," the "Tories," if one may so say, of the political clubs.
4 Lit. "those... these."
5 Ernesti aptly cf. Cic. "ad Quint." iii. 6. See below, III. ix. 6; IV. ii. 24.

MEMORABILIA

VIII

Once when Aristippus[1] set himself to subject Socrates to a cross-examination, such as he had himself undergone at the hands of Socrates on a former occasion,[2] Socrates, being minded to benefit those who were with him, gave his answers less in the style of a debater guarding against perversions of his argument, than of a man persuaded of the supreme importance of right conduct.[3]

Aristippus asked him "if he knew of anything good,"[4] intending in case he assented and named any particular good thing, like food or drink, or wealth, or health, or strength, or courage, to point out that the thing named was sometimes bad. But he, knowing that if a thing troubles us, we immediately want that which will put an end to our trouble, answered precisely as it was best to do.[5]

SOCRATES: Do I understand you to ask me whether I know anything good for fever?

No (he replied), that is not my question.

SOCRATES: Then for inflammation of the eyes?

ARISTIPPUS: No, nor yet that.

SOCRATES: Well then, for hunger?

ARISTIPPUS: No, nor yet for hunger.

Well, but (answered Socrates) if you ask me whether I know of any good thing which is good for nothing, I neither know of it nor want to know.

And when Aristippus, returning to the charge, asked him "if he knew of any thing beautiful."

He answered: Yes, many things.

ARISTIPPUS: Are they all like each other?

SOCRATES: On the contrary, they are often as unlike as possible.

How then (he asked) can that be beautiful which is unlike the beautiful?

SOCRATES: Bless me! for the simple reason that it is possible for a man who is a beautiful runner to be quite unlike another man who is a beautiful boxer,[6] or for a shield, which is a beautiful weapon for the purpose of

---

1 For Aristippus see above, p. 38; for the connection, {boulomenos tous sunontas ophelein}, between this and the preceeding chapter, see above, Conspectus, p. xxvi.
2 Possibly in reference to the conversation above. In reference to the present dialogue see Grote, "Plato," I. xi. p. 380 foll.
3 For {prattein ta deonta} cf. below, III. ix. 4, 11; Plat. "Charm." 164 B; but see J. J. Hartman, "An. Xen." p. 141.
4 See Grote, "Plato," ii. 585, on Philebus.
5 Or, "made the happiest answer."
6 See Grote, "H. G." x. 164, in reference to Epaminondas and his gymnastic training; below, III. x. 6.

defense, to be absolutely unlike a javelin, which is a beautiful weapon of swift and sure discharge.

ARISTIPPUS: Your answers are no better now than[1] when I asked you whether you knew any good thing. They are both of a pattern.

SOCRATES: And so they should be. Do you imagine that one thing is good and another beautiful? Do not you know that relatively to the same standard all things are at once beautiful and good?[2] In the first place, virtue is not a good thing relatively to one standard and a beautiful thing relatively to another standard; and in the next place, human beings, on the same principle[3] and relatively to the same standard, are called "beautiful and good"; and so the bodily frames of men relatively to the same standards are seen to be "beautiful and good," and in general all things capable of being used by man are regarded as at once beautiful and good relatively to the same standard—the standing being in each case what the thing happens to be useful for.[4]

ARISTIPPUS: Then I presume even a basket for carrying dung[5] is a beautiful thing?

SOCRATES: To be sure, and a spear of gold an ugly thing, if for their respective uses—the former is well and the latter ill adapted.

ARISTIPPUS: Do you mean to assert that the same things may be beautiful and ugly?

SOCRATES: Yes, to be sure; and by the same showing things may be good and bad: as, for instance, what is good for hunger may be bad for fever, and what is good for fever bad for hunger; or again, what is beautiful for wrestling is often ugly for running; and in general everything is good and beautiful when well adapted for the end in view, bad and ugly when ill adapted for the same.

Similarly when he spoke about houses,[6] and argued that "the same house must be at once beautiful and useful"—I could not help feeling that he was giving a good lesson on the problem: "how a house ought to be built." He investigated the matter thus:

SOCRATES: "Do you admit that anyone purposing to build a perfect

---

1 Or, "You answer precisely as you did when…"
2 Or, "good and beautiful are convertible terms: whatever is good is beautiful, or whatever is beautiful is good."
3 Or, "in the same breath." Cf. Plat. "Hipp. maj." 295 D; "Gorg." 474 D.
4 Or, "and this standard is the serviceableness of the thing in question."
5 Cf. Plat. "Hipp. maj." 288 D, 290 D; and Grote's note, loc. cit. p. 381: "in regard to the question wherein consists {to kalon}?"
6 See K. Joel, op. cit. p. 488; "Classical Review," vii. 262.

house[1] will plan to make it at once as pleasant and as useful to live in as possible?" and that point being admitted,[2] the next question would be:

"It is pleasant to have one's house cool in summer and warm in winter, is it not?" and this proposition also having obtained assent, "Now, supposing a house to have a southern aspect, sunshine during winter will steal in under the verandah,[3] but in summer, when the sun traverses a path right over our heads, the roof will afford an agreeable shade, will it not? If, then, such an arrangement is desirable, the southern side of a house should be built higher to catch the rays of the winter sun, and the northern side lower to prevent the cold winds finding ingress; in a word, it is reasonable to suppose that the pleasantest and most beautiful dwelling place will be one in which the owner can at all seasons of the year find the pleasantest retreat, and stow away his goods with the greatest security."

Paintings[4] and ornamental mouldings are apt (he said) to deprive one of more joy[5] than they confer.

The fittest place for a temple or an altar (he maintained) was some site visible from afar, and untrodden by foot of man:[6] since it was a glad thing for the worshipper to lift up his eyes afar off and offer up his orison; glad also to wend his way peaceful to prayer unsullied.[7]

IX

Being again asked by someone: could courage be taught,[8] or did it come by nature? he answered: I imagine that just as one body is by nature stronger than another body to encounter toils, so one soul by nature grows more robust than another soul in face of dangers. Certainly I do note that people brought up under the same condition of laws and customs differ greatly in respect of daring. Still my belief is that by learning and practice the natural aptitude may always be strengthened toward courage. It is clear, for instance, that Scythians or Thracians would not venture to take shield

---

1 Or, "the ideal house"; lit. "a house as it should be."
2 See below, IV. vi. 15.
3 Or, "porticoes" or "collonades."
4 See "Econ." ix. 2; Plat. "Hipp. maj." 298 A; "Rep." 529; Becker, "Charicles," 268 (Engl. trans.)
5 {euphrosunas}, archaic or "poetical" = "joyance." See "Hiero," vi. 1.
6 E.g. the summit of Lycabettos, or the height on which stands the temple of Phygaleia. Cf. Eur. "Phoen." 1372, {Pallados khrusaspidos blepsas pros oikon euxato} of Eteocles.
7 See Vitruvius, i. 7, iv. 5, ap. Schneid. ad loc.; W. L. Newman, op. cit. i. 338.
8 Or, "When someone retorted upon him with the question: 'Can courage be taught?'" and for this problem see IV. vi. 10, 11; "Symp." ii. 12; Plat. "Lach."; "Protag." 349; "Phaedr." 269 D; K. Joel, op. cit. p. 325 foll.; Grote, "Plato," i. 468 foll., ii. 60; Jowett, "Plato," i. 77, 119; Newman, op. cit. i. 343.

and spear and contend with Lacedaemonians; and it is equally evident that Lacedaemonians would demur to entering the lists of battle against Thracians if limited to their light shields and javelins, or against Scythians without some weapon more familiar than their bows and arrows.[1] And as far as I can see, this principle holds generally: the natural differences of one man from another may be compensated by artificial progress, the result of care and attention. All which proves clearly that whether nature has endowed us with keener or blunter sensibilities, the duty of all alike is to learn and practice those things in which we would fain achieve distinction.

Between wisdom and sobriety of soul (which is temperance) he drew no distinction.[2] Was a man able on the one hand to recognize things beautiful and good sufficiently to live in them? Had he, on the other hand, knowledge of the "base and foul" so as to beware of them? If so, Socrates judged him to be wise at once and sound of soul (or temperate).[3]

And being further questioned whether "he considered those who have the knowledge of right action, but do not apply it, to be wise and self-controlled?"—"Not a whit more," he answered, "than I consider them to be unwise and intemperate.[4] Every one, I conceive, deliberately chooses what, within the limits open to him, he considers most conducive to his interest, and acts accordingly. I must hold therefore that those who act against rule and crookedly[5] are neither wise nor self-controlled.

He said that justice, moreover, and all other virtue is wisdom. That is to say, things just, and all things else that are done with virtue, are "beautiful and good"; and neither will those who know these things deliberately choose aught else in their stead, nor will he who lacks the special knowledge of them be able to do them, but even if he makes the attempt he will miss the mark and fail. So the wise alone can perform the things which are "beautiful and good"; they that are unwise cannot, but even if they try they

---

1 Or, "against Thracians with light shields and javelins, or against Scythians with bows and arrows"; and for the national arms of these peoples respectively see Arist. "Lysistr." 563; "Anab." III. iv. 15; VI. VII. passim.
2 But cf. IV. vi. 7; K. Joel, op. cit. p. 363.
3 Reading {alla to... kai to}, or more lit. "he discovered the wise man and sound of soul in his power not only to recognize things 'beautiful and good,' but to live and move and have his being in them; as also in his gift of avoiding consciously things base." Or if {alla ton... kai ton...} transl. "The man who not only could recognize the beautiful and good, but lived, etc., in that world, and who moreover consciously avoided things base, in the judgment of Socrates was wise and sound of soul." Cf. Plat. "Charm."
4 For the phrase "not a whit the more" see below, III. xii. 1; "Econ." xii. 18. Al. "I should by no means choose to consider them wise and self-controlled rather than foolish and intemperate."
5 "Who cannot draw a straight line, ethically speaking."

fail. Therefore, since all things just, and generally all things "beautiful and good," are wrought with virtue, it is clear that justice and all other virtue is wisdom.

On the other hand, madness (he maintained) was the opposite to wisdom; not that he regarded simple ignorance as madness,[1] but he put it thus: for a man to be ignorant of himself, to imagine and suppose that he knows what he knows not, was (he argued), if not madness itself, yet something very like it. The mass of men no doubt hold a different language: if a man is all abroad on some matter of which the mass of mankind are ignorant, they do not pronounce him "mad";[2] but a like aberration of mind, if only it be about matters within the scope of ordinary knowledge, they call madness. For instance, anyone who imagined himself too tall to pass under a gateway of the Long Wall without stooping, or so strong as to try to lift a house, or to attempt any other obvious impossibility, is a madman according to them; but in the popular sense he is not mad, if his obliquity is confined to small matters. In fact, just as strong desire goes by the name of passion in popular parlance, so mental obliquity on a grand scale is entitled madness.

In answer to the question: what is envy? he discovered it to be a certain kind of pain; not certainly the sorrow felt at the misfortunes of a friend or the good fortune of an enemy—that is not envy; but, as he said, "envy is felt by those alone who are annoyed at the successes of their friends." And when some one or other expressed astonishment that anyone friendlily disposed to another should be pained at his well-doing, he reminded him of a common tendency in people: when anyone is faring ill their sympathies are touched, they rush to the aid of the unfortunate; but when fortune smiles on others, they are somehow pained. "I do not say," he added, "this could happen to a thoughtful person; but it is no uncommon condition of a silly mind."[3]

In answer to the question: what is leisure? I discover (he said) that most men do something:[4] for instance, the dice player,[5] the gambler, the buffoon, do something, but these have leisure; they can, if they like, turn and do something better; but nobody has leisure to turn from the better to the worse, and if he does so turn, when he has no leisure, he does but ill in that.

(To pass to another definition.) They are not kings or rulers (he said)

---

1 See K. Joel, op. cit. p. 346; Grote, "Plato," i. 400.
2 Or, "they resent the term "mad" being applied to people who are all abroad," etc. See Comte, "Pos. Pol." i. 575; ii. 373 (Engl. trans.).
3 Or, "a man in his senses... a simpleton"; for the sentiment L. Dind. cf. Isocr. "ad Demonic." 7 D.
4 See above, I. ii. 57; and in ref. to these definitions, K. Joel, op. cit. p. 347 foll.
5 For "dice-playing" see Becker, "Charicl." 354 (Engl. trans.); for "buffoonery," ib. 98; "Symp."

who hold the sceptre merely, or are chosen by fellows out of the street,[1] or are appointed by lot, or have stepped into office by violence or by fraud; but those who have the special knowledge[2] how to rule. Thus having won the admission that it is the function of a ruler to enjoin what ought to be done, and of those who are ruled to obey, he proceeded to point out by instances that in a ship the ruler or captain is the man of special knowledge, to whom, as an expert, the shipowner himself and all the others on board obey. So likewise, in the matter of husbandry, the proprietor of an estate; in that of sickness, the patient; in that of physical training of the body, the youthful athlete going through a course; and, in general, everyone directly concerned in any matter needing attention and care will either attend to this matter personally, if he thinks he has the special knowledge; or, if he mistrusts his own science, will be eager to obey any expert on the spot, or will even send and fetch one from a distance. The guidance of this expert he will follow, and do what he has to do at his dictation.

And thus, in the art of spinning wool, he liked to point out that women are the rulers of men—and why? because they have the knowledge of the art, and men have not.

And if anyone raised the objection that a tyrant has it in his power not to obey good and correct advice, he would retort: "Pray, how has he the option not to obey, considering the penalty hanging over him who disobeys the words of wisdom? for whatever the matter be in which he disobeys the word of good advice, he will fall into error, I presume, and falling into error, be punished." And to the suggestion that the tyrant could, if he liked, cut off the head of the man of wisdom, his answer was: "Do you think that he who destroys his best ally will go scot free, or suffer a mere slight and passing loss? Is he more likely to secure his salvation that way, think you, or to compass his own swift destruction?"[3]

When someone asked him: "What he regarded as the best pursuit or business[4] for a man?" he answered: "Successful conduct";[5] and to a second question: "Did he then regard good fortune as an end to be pursued?"—"On the contrary," he answered, "for myself, I consider fortune and conduct to be diametrically opposed. For instance, to succeed in some desirable course

---

1 *Tom, Dick, and Harry (as we say).*
2 *The {episteme}. See above, III. v. 21; Newman, op. cit. i. 256.*
3 *Or, "Is that to choose the path of safety, think you? Is it not rather to sign his own death-warrant?" L. Dind. cf. Hesiod, "Works and Days," 293. See Newman, op. cit. i. 393-397.*
4 *Or, "the noblest study."*
5 *{eupraxia, eu prattein}—to do well, in the sense both of well or right doing, and of welfare, and is accordingly opposed to {eutukhia}, mere good luck or success. Cf. Plat. "Euthyd." 281 B.*

of action without seeking to do so, I hold to be good fortune; but to do a thing well by dint of learning and practice, that according to my creed is successful conduct,[1] and those who make this the serious business of their life seem to me to do well."

They are at once the best and the dearest in the sight of God[2] (he went on to say) who for instance in husbandry do well the things of farming, or in the art of healing all that belongs to healing, or in statecraft the affairs of state; whereas a man who does nothing well—nor well in anything—is (he added) neither good for anything nor dear to God.

X

But indeed,[3] if chance brought him into conversation with anyone possessed of an art, and using it for daily purposes of business, he never failed to be useful to this kind of person. For instance, stepping one time into the studio of Parrhasius[4] the painter, and getting into conversation with him—

I suppose, Parrhasius (said he), painting may be defined as "a representation of visible objects," may it not?[5] That is to say, by means of colors and palette you painters represent and reproduce as closely as possible the ups and downs, lights and shadows, hard and soft, rough and smooth surfaces, the freshness of youth and the wrinkles of age, do you not?

You are right (he answered), that is so.

Soc. Further, in portraying ideal types of beauty, seeing it is not easy to light upon any one human being who is absolutely devoid of blemish, you cull from many models the most beautiful traits of each, and so make your figures appear completely beautiful?[6]

Parrh. Yes, that is how we do.[7]

Well, but stop (Socrates continued); do you also pretend to represent in similar perfection the characteristic moods of the soul, its captivating charm and sweetness, with its deep wells of love, its intensity of yearning, its burning point of passion? or is all this quite incapable of being depicted?

---

1 Lit. "well-doing"; and for the Socratic view see Newman, op. cit. i. 305, 401.
2 Or, "most divinely favored." Cf. Plat. "Euthyphro," 7 A.
3 {alla men kai}... "But indeed the sphere of his helpfulness was not circumscribed; if," etc.
4 For Parrhasius of Ephesus, the son of Evenor and rival of Zeuxis, see Woltmann and Woermann, "Hist. of Painting," p. 47 foll.; Cobet, "Pros. Xen." p. 50 (cf. in particular Quint. XII. x. 627). At the date of conversation (real or ideal) he may be supposed to have been a young man.
5 Reading with Schneider, L. Dind., etc., after Stobaeus, {e graphike estin eikasia}, or if the vulg. {graphike estin e eikasia}, trans. "Painting is the term applied to a particular representation," etc.
6 Cf. Cic. "de Invent." ii. 1 ad in. of Zeuxis; Max. Tur. "Dissert." 23, 3, ap. Schneider ad loc.
7 Or, "that is the secret of our creations," or "our art of composition."

Nay (he answered), how should a mood be other than inimitable, Socrates, when it possesses neither linear proportion[1] nor color, nor any of those qualities which you named just now; when, in a word, it is not even visible?

Soc. Well, but the kindly look of love, the angry glance of hate at anyone, do find expression in the human subject, do they not?[2]

Parrh. No doubt they do.

Soc. Then this look, this glance, at any rate may be imitated in the eyes, may it not?

Undoubtedly (he answered).

Soc. And do anxiety and relief of mind occasioned by the good or evil fortune of those we love both wear the same expression?

By no means (he answered); at the thought of good we are radiant, at that of evil a cloud hangs on the brow.

Soc. Then here again are looks with it is possible to represent?

Parrh. Decidedly.

Soc. Furthermore, as through some chink or crevice, there pierces through the countenance of a man, through the very posture of his body as he stands or moves, a glimpse of his nobility and freedom, or again of something in him low and grovelling—the calm of self-restraint, and wisdom, or the swagger of insolence and vulgarity?

You are right (he answered).

Soc. Then these too may be imitated?

No doubt (he said).

Soc. And which is the pleasanter type of face to look at, do you think— one on which is imprinted the characteristics of a beautiful, good, and lovable disposition, or one which bears the impress of what is ugly, and bad, and hateful?[3]

Parrh. Doubtless, Socrates, there is a vast distinction between the two.

At another time he entered the workshop of the sculptor Cleiton,[4] and in course of conversation with him said:

You have a gallery of handsome people here,[5] Cleiton, runners, and

---

1 Lit. "symmetry." Cf. Plin. xxxv. 10, "primus symmetriam picturae dedit," etc.
2 Or, "the glance of love, the scowl of hate, which one directs toward another, are recognized expressions of human feeling." Cf. the description of Parrhasius's own portrait of Demos, ap. Plin. loc. cit.
3 For this theory cp. Ruskin, "Mod. P." ii. 94 foll. and indeed passim.
4 An unknown artist. Coraes conj. {Kleona}. Cf. Plin. xxxiv. 19; Paus. v. 17, vi. 3. He excelled in portrait statues. See Jowett, "Plato," iv.; "Laws," p. 123.
5 Reading after L. Dind. {kaloi ous}, or if vulg. {alloious}, translate "You have a variety of types, Cleiton, not all of one mold, but runners," etc.; al. "I see quite well how you give the diversity of form to your runners," etc.

wrestlers, and boxers, and pancratiasts—that I see and know; but how do you give the magic touch of life to your creations, which most of all allures the soul of the beholder through his sense of vision?

As Cleiton stood perplexed, and did not answer at once, Socrates added: Is it by closely imitating the forms of living beings that you succeed in giving that touch of life to your statues?

No doubt (he answered).

Soc. It is, is it not, by faithfully copying the various muscular contractions of the body in obedience to the play of gesture and poise, the wrinklings of flesh and the sprawl of limbs, the tensions and the relaxations, that you succeed in making your statues like real beings—make them "breathe" as people say?

Cleit. Without a doubt.

Soc. And does not the faithful imitation of the various affections of the body when engaged in any action impart a particular pleasure to the beholder?

Cleit. I should say so.

Soc. Then the threatenings in the eyes of warriors engaged in battle should be carefully copied, or again you should imitate the aspect of a conqueror radiant with success?

Cleit. Above all things.

Soc. It would seem then that the sculptor is called upon to incorporate in his ideal form the workings and energies also of the soul?

Paying a visit to Pistias,[1] the corselet maker, when that artist showed him some exquisite samples of his work, Socrates exclaimed:

By Hera! a pretty invention this, Pistias, by which you contrive that the corselet should cover the parts of the person which need protection, and at the same time leave free play to the arms and hands.... But tell me, Pistias (he added), why do you ask a higher price for these corselets of yours if they are not stouter or made of costlier material than the others?

Because, Socrates (he answered), mine are of much finer proportion.

Soc. Proportion! Then how do you make this quality apparent to the customer so as to justify the higher price—by measure or weight? For I presume you cannot make them all exactly equal and of one pattern—if you make them fit, as of course you do?

Fit indeed! that I most distinctly do (he answered), take my word for it: no use in a corselet without that.

---

1 Cf. *Athen.* iv. 20, *where the same artist is referred to apparently as* {Piston}, *and for the type of person see the "Portrait of a Tailor" by Moroni in the National Gallery—see "Handbook," Edw. T. Cook, p. 152.*

But then are not the wearer's bodies themselves (asked Socrates) some well proportioned and others ill?

Decidedly so (he answered).

Soc. Then how do you manage to make the corselet well proportioned if it is to fit an ill-proportioned body?[1]

Pist. To the same degree exactly as I make it fit. What fits is well proportioned.

Soc. It seems you use the term "well-proportioned" not in an absolute sense, but in reference to the wearer, just as you might describe a shield as well proportioned to the individual it suits; and so of a military cloak, and so of the rest of things, in your terminology? But maybe there is another considerable advantage in this "fitting"?

Pist. Pray instruct me, Socrates, if you have got an idea.

Soc. A corselet which fits is less galling by its weight than one which does not fit, for the latter must either drag from the shoulders with a dead weight or press upon some other part of the body, and so it becomes troublesome and uncomfortable; but that which fits, having its weight distributed partly along the collar-bone and shoulder-blade, partly over the shoulders and chest, and partly the back and belly, feels like another natural integument rather than an extra load to carry.[2]

Pist. You have named the very quality which gives my work its exceptional value, as I consider; still there are customers, I am bound to say, who look for something else in a corselet—they must have them ornamental or inlaid with gold.

For all that (replied Socrates), if they end by purchasing an ill-fitting article, they only become the proprietors of a curiously-wrought and gilded nuisance, as it seems to me. But (he added), as the body is never in one fixed position, but is at one time curved, at another raised erect how can an exactly modelled corselet fit?

Pist. It cannot fit at all.

You mean (Socrates continued) that it is not the exactly-modelled corselet which fits, but that which does not gall the wearer in the using?

Pist. There, Socrates, you have hit the very point. I see you understand the matter most precisely.[3]

---

1 Or, "how do you make a well-proportioned corselet fit an ill-proportioned body? how well proportioned?"

2 Schneider ad loc. cf Eur. "Electr." 192, {prosthemata aglaias}, and for the weight cf. Aristoph. "Peace," 1224.

3 Or, "There, Socrates, you have hit the very phrase. I could not state the matter more explicitly myself."

XI

There was once in the city a fair woman named Theodote.[1] She was not only fair, but ready to consort with any suitor who might win her favor. Now it chanced that someone of the company mentioned her, saying that her beauty beggared description. "So fair is she," he added, "that painters flock to draw her portrait, to whom, within the limits of decorum, she displays the marvels of her beauty." "Then there is nothing for it but to go and see her," answered Socrates, "since to comprehend by hearsay what is beyond description is clearly impossible." Then he who had introduced the matter replied: "Be quick then to follow me"; and on this wise they set off to seek Theodote. They found her "posing" to a certain painter; and they took their stand as spectators. Presently the painter had ceased his work; whereupon Socrates:

"Do you think, sirs, that we ought to thank Theodote for displaying her beauty to us, or she us for coming to gaze at her?... It would seem, would it not, that if the exhibition of her charms is the more profitable to her, the debt is on her side; but if the spectacle of her beauty confers the greater benefit on us, then we are her debtors."

Someone answered that "was an equitable statement of the case."

Well then (he continued), as far as she is concerned, the praise we bestow on her is an immediate gain; and presently, when we have spread her fame abroad, she will be further benefited; but for ourselves the immediate effect on us is a strong desire to touch what we have seen; by and by, too, we shall go away with a sting inside us, and when we are fairly gone we shall be consumed with longing. Consequently it seems that we should do her service and she accept our court.

Whereupon Theodote: Oh dear! if that is how the matter stands, it is I who am your debtor for the spectacle.[2]

At this point, seeing that the lady herself was expensively attired, and that she had with her her mother also, whose dress and style of attendance[3] were out of the common, not to speak of the waiting-women—many and fair to look upon, who presented anything but a forlorn appearance; while in every respect the whole house itself was sumptuously furnished—

---

1 For Theodote see Athen. v. 200 F, xiii. 574 F; Liban. i. 582. Some say that it was Theodote who stood by Alcibiades to the last, though there are apparently other better claimants to the honor. Plut. "Alc." (Clough, ii. p. 50).

2 In reference to the remark of Socrates above; or, "have to thank you for coming to look at me."

3 Or, "her mother there with her in a dress and general get-up ({therapeia}) which was out of the common." See Becker, "Charicles," p. 247 (Eng. tr.)

Socrates put a question:

Pray tell me, Theodote, have you an estate in the country?

Theod. Not I indeed.

Soc. Then perhaps you possess a house and large revenues along with it?

Theod. No, nor yet a house.

Soc. You are not an employer of labor on a large scale?[1]

Theod. No, nor yet an employer of labor.

Soc. From what source, then, do you get your means of subsistence?[2]

Theod. My friends are my life and fortune, when they care to be kind to me.

Soc. By heaven, Theodote, a very fine property indeed, and far better worth possessing than a multitude of sheep or goats or cattle. A flock of friends!... But (he added) do you leave it to fortune whether a friend lights like a fly on your hand at random, or do you use any artifice[3] yourself to attract him?

Theod. And how might I hit upon any artifice to attract him?

Soc. Bless me! far more naturally than any spider. You know how they capture the creatures on which they live;[4] by weaving webs of gossamer, is it not? and woe betide the fly that tumbles into their toils! They eat him up.

Theod. So then you would counsel me to weave myself some sort of net?

Soc. Why, surely you do not suppose you are going to ensnare that noblest of all game—a lover, to wit—in so artless a fashion? Do you not see (to speak of a much less noble sort of game) what a number of devices are needed to bag a hare?[5] The creatures range for their food at night; therefore the hunter must provide himself with night dogs. At peep of dawn they are off as fast as they can run. He must therefore have another pack of dogs to scent out and discover which way they betake them from their grazing ground to their forms;[6] and as they are so fleet of foot that they run and are out of sight in no time, he must once again be provided with other fleet-footed dogs to follow their tracks and overtake them;[7] and as some of them will give even these the slip, he must, last of all, set up nets on the paths at the points of escape, so that they may fall into the meshes and be caught.

---

1 Lit. "You have not (in your employ) a body of handicraftsmen of any sort?"
2 Or, Anglice, "derive your income."
3 Or, "means and appliances," "machinery."
4 Lit. "the creatures on which they live."
5 See the author's own treatise on "Hunting," vi. 6 foll.
6 Lit. "from pasture to bed."
7 Or, "close at their heels and run them down." See "Hunting"; cf. "Cyrop." I. vi. 40.

Theod. And by what like contrivance would you have me catch my lovers?

Soc. Well now! what if in place of a dog you can get a man who will hunt up your wealthy lover of beauty and discover his lair, and having found him, will plot and plan to throw him into your meshes?

Theod. Nay, what sort of meshes have I?

Soc. One you have, and a close-folding net it is,[1] I trow; to wit, your own person; and inside it sits a soul that teaches you[2] with what looks to please and with what words to cheer; how, too, with smiles you are to welcome true devotion, but to exclude all wantons from your presence.[3] It tells you, you are to visit your beloved in sickness with solicitude, and when he has wrought some noble deed you are greatly to rejoice with him; and to one who passionately cares for you, you are to make surrender of yourself with heart and soul. The secret of true love I am sure you know: not to love softly merely, but devotedly.[4] And of this too I am sure: you can convince your lovers of your fondness for them not by lip phrases, but by acts of love.

Theod. No, upon my word, I have none of these devices.

Soc. And yet it makes all the difference whether you approach a human being in the natural and true way, since it is not by force certainly that you can either catch or keep a friend. Kindness and pleasure are the only means to capture this fearful wild-fowl man and keep him constant.

Theod. You are right.

Soc. In the first place you must make such demands only of your well-wisher as he can grant without repentance; and in the next place you must make requital, dispensing your favors with a like economy. Thus you will best make friends whose love shall last the longest and their generosity know no stint.[5] And for your favors you will best win your friends if you suit your largess to their penury; for, mark you, the sweetest viands presented to a man before he wants them are apt to prove insipid, or, to one already sated, even nauseous; but create hunger, and even coarser stuff seems honey-sweet.

Theod. How then shall I create this hunger in the heart of my friends?

Soc. In the first place you must not offer or make suggestion of your

---

1 Or, "right well woven."
2 Lit. "by which you understand."
3 Or, "with what smiles to lie in wait for (cf. "Cyrop." II. iv. 20; Herod. vi. 104) the devoted admirer, and how to banish from your presence the voluptary."
4 Or, "that it should be simply soft, but full of tender goodwill."
5 Or, "This is the right road to friendship—permanent and open-handed friendship."

dainties to jaded appetites until satiety has ceased and starvation cries for alms. Even then shall you make but a faint suggestion to their want, with modest converse—like one who would fain bestow a kindness... and lo! the vision fades and she is gone—until the very pinch of hunger; for the same gifts have then a value unknown before the moment of supreme desire.

Then Theodote: Oh why, Socrates, why are you not by my side (like the huntsman's assistant) to help me catch my friends and lovers?

Soc. That will I be in good sooth if only you can woo and win me.

Theod. How shall I woo and win you?

Soc. Seek and you will find means, if you truly need me.

Theod. Come then in hither and visit me often.

And Socrates, poking sly fun at his own lack of business occupation, answered: Nay, Theodote, leisure is not a commodity in which I largely deal. I have a hundred affairs of my own too, private or public, to occupy me; and then there are my lady-loves, my dear friends, who will not suffer me day or night to leave them, forever studying to learn love-charms and incantations at my lips.

Theod. Why, are you really versed in those things, Socrates?

Soc. Of course, or else how is it, do you suppose, that Apollodorus[1] here and Antisthenes never leave me; or why have Cebes and Simmias come all the way from Thebes to stay with me? Be assured these things cannot happen without diverse love-charms and incantations and magic wheels.

Theod. I wish you would lend me your magic-wheel,[2] then, and I will set it spinning first of all for you.

Soc. Ah! but I do not wish to be drawn to you. I wish you to come to me.

Theod. Then I will come. Only, will you be "at home" to me?

Soc. Yes, I will welcome you, unless someone still dearer holds me engaged, and I must needs be "not at home."

XII

Seeing one of those who were with him, a young man, but feeble of body, named Epigenes,[3] he addressed him.

Soc. You have not the athletic appearance of a youth in training,[4] Epigenes.

---

1 For Apollodorus see "Apol." 28; Plat. "Symp." 172 A; "Phaed." 59 A, 117 D. For Antisthenes see above. For Cebes and Simmias see above, I. ii. 48; Plat. "Crit." 45 B; "Phaed." passim.

2 Cf. Theocr. ii. 17; Schneider ad loc.

3 Epigenes, possibly the son of Antiphon. See Plat. "Apol." 33 E; "Phaed." 59 B.

4 {idiotikos}, lit. of the person untrained in gymnastics. See A. R. Cluer ad loc. Cf. Plat. "Laws," 839 E; I. ii. 4; III. v. 15; "Symp." ii. 17.

And he: That may well be, seeing I am an amateur and not in training.

Soc. As little of an amateur, I take it, as anyone who ever entered the lists of Olympia, unless you are prepared to make light of that contest for life and death against the public foe which the Athenians will institute when the day comes.[1] And yet they are not a few who, owing to a bad habit of body, either perish outright in the perils of war, or are ignobly saved. Many are they who for the self-same cause are taken prisoners, and being taken must, if it so betide, endure the pains of slavery for the rest of their days; or, after falling into dolorous straits,[2] when they have paid to the uttermost farthing of all, or may be more than the worth of all, that they possess, must drag on a miserable existence in want of the barest necessaries until death release them. Many also are they who gain an evil repute through infirmity of body, being thought to play the coward. Can it be that you despise these penalties affixed to an evil habit? Do you think you could lightly endure them? Far lighter, I imagine, nay, pleasant even by comparison, are the toils which he will undergo who duly cultivates a healthy bodily condition. Or do you maintain that the evil habit is healthier, and in general more useful than the good? Do you pour contempt upon those blessings which flow from the healthy state? And yet the very opposite of that which befalls the ill attends the sound condition. Does not the very soundness imply at once health and strength?[3] Many a man with no other talisman than this has passed safely through the ordeal of war; stepping, not without dignity,[4] through all its horrors unscathed. Many with no other support than this have come to the rescue of friends, or stood forth as benefactors of their fatherland; whereby they were thought worthy of gratitude, and obtained a great renown and received as a recompense the highest honors of the State; to whom is also reserved a happier and brighter passage through what is left to them of life, and at their death they leave to their children the legacy of a fairer starting-point in the race of life.

Because our city does not practice military training in public,[5] that is no reason for neglecting it in private, but rather a reason for making it a foremost care. For be you assured that there is no contest of any sort, nor any transaction, in which you will be the worse off for being well

---

1 Or, "should chance betide." Is the author thinking of a life-and-death struggle with Thebes?
2 E.g. the prisoners in the Latomiae. Thuc. vii. 87.
3 It is almost a proverb—"Sound of body and limb is hale and strong." "Qui valet praevalebit."
4 E.g. Socrates himself, according to Alcibiades, ap. Plat. "Symp." 221 B; and for the word {euskhemonos} see Arist. "Wasps," 1210, "like a gentleman"; L. and S.; "Cyr." I. iii. 8; Aristot. "Eth. N." i. 10, 13, "gracefully."
5 Cf. "Pol. Ath." i. 13; and above, III. v. 15.

prepared in body; and in fact there is nothing which men do for which the body is not a help. In every demand, therefore, which can be laid upon the body it is much better that it should be in the best condition; since, even where you might imagine the claims upon the body to be slightest—in the act of reasoning—who does not know the terrible stumbles which are made through being out of health? It suffices to say that forgetfulness, and despondency, and moroseness, and madness take occasion often of ill-health to visit the intellectual faculties so severely as to expel all knowledge[1] from the brain. But he who is in good bodily plight has large security. He runs no risk of incurring any such catastrophe through ill-health at any rate; he has the expectation rather that a good habit must procure consequences the opposite to those of an evil habit;[2] and surely to this end there is nothing a man in his senses would not undergo.... It is a base thing for a man to wax old in careless self-neglect before he has lifted up his eyes and seen what manner of man he was made to be, in the full perfection of bodily strength and beauty. But these glories are withheld from him who is guilty of self-neglect, for they are not wont to blaze forth unbidden.[3]

XIII

Once when someone was in a fury of indignation because he had bidden a passerby good-day and the salutation was not returned, Socrates said: "It is enough to make one laugh! If you met a man in a wretched condition of body, you would not fall into a rage; but because you stumble upon a poor soul somewhat boorishly disposed, you feel annoyed."

To the remark of another who complained that he did not take his food with pleasure, he said: "Acumenus[4] has a good prescription for that." And when the other asked: "And what may that be?" "To stop eating," he said. "On the score of pleasure, economy, and health, total abstinence has much in its favor."[5]

And when someone else lamented that "the drinking-water in his house was hot," he replied: "Then when you want a warm bath you will not have to wait."

The Other. But for bathing purposes it is cold.

---

1 Or, "whole branches of knowledge" ({tas epistemas}).
2 Or, "he may well hope to be insured by his good habit against the evils attendant on its opposite."
3 Or, "to present themselves spontaneously."
4 A well-known physician. See Plat. "Phaedr." 227 A, 269 A; "Symp." 176 B. A similar story is told of Dr. Abernethy, I think.
5 Lit. "he would live a happier, thriftier, and healthier life, if he stopped eating."

Soc. Do you find that your domestics seem to mind drinking it or washing in it?

The Other. Quite the reverse; it is a constant marvel to me how contentedly they use it for either purpose.

Soc. Which is hotter to the taste—the water in your house or the hot spring in the temple of Asclepius?[1]

The Other. The water in the temple of Asclepius.

Soc. And which is colder for bathing—yours or the cold spring in the cave of Amphiaraus?[2]

The Other. The water in the cave of Amphiaraus.

Soc. Then please to observe: if you do not take care, they will set you down as harder to please than a domestic servant or an invalid.[3]

A man had administered a severe whipping to the slave in attendance on him, and when Socrates asked: "Why he was so wroth with his own serving-man?" excused himself on the ground that "the fellow was a lazy, gourmandising, good-for-nothing dolt—fonder of money than of work." To which Socrates: "Did it ever strike you to consider which of the two in that case the more deserves a whipping—the master or the man?"

When someone was apprehending the journey to Olympia, "Why are you afraid of the long distance?" he asked. "Here at home you spend nearly all your day in taking walks.[4] Well, on your road to Olympia you will take a walk and breakfast, and then you will take another walk and dine, and go to bed. Do you not see, if you take and tack together five or six days" length of walks, and stretch them out in one long line, it will soon reach from Athens to Olympia? I would recommend you, however, to set off a day too soon rather than a day too late. To be forced to lengthen the day's journey beyond a reasonable amount may well be a nuisance; but to take one day's journey beyond what is necessary is pure relaxation. Make haste to start, I say, and not while on the road."[5]

When someone else remarked "he was utterly prostrated after a long journey," Socrates asked him: "Had he had any baggage to carry?"

"Not I," replied the complainer; "only my cloak."

Soc. Were you travelling alone, or was your man-servant with you?

He. Yes, I had my man.

---

1 *In the Hieron at Epidauros probably. See Baedeker, "Greece," p. 240 foll.*
2 *Possibly at Oropos. Cf. Paus. i. 34. 3.*
3 *I.e. "the least and the most fastidious of men."*
4 *{peripateis}, "promenading up and down."*
5 *"Festina lente"—that is your motto.*

Soc. Empty-handed, or had he something to carry?

He. Of course; carrying my rugs and other baggage.

Soc. And how did he come off on the journey?

He. Better than I did myself, I take it.

Soc. Well, but now suppose you had had to carry his baggage, what would your condition have been like?

He. Sorry enough, I can tell you; or rather, I could not have carried it at all.

Soc. What a confession! Fancy being capable of so much less toil than a poor slave boy! Does that sound like the perfection of athletic training?

XIV

On the occasion of a common dinner-party[1] where some of the company would present themselves with a small, and others with a large supply of viands, Socrates would bid the servants[2] throw the small supplies into the general stock, or else to help each of the party to a share all round. Thus the grand victuallers were ashamed in the one case not to share in the common stock, and in the other not to throw in their supplies also.[3] Accordingly in went the grand supplies into the common stock. And now, being no better off than the small contributors, they soon ceased to cater for expensive delicacies.

At a supper-party one member of the company, as Socrates chanced to note, had put aside the plain fare and was devoting himself to certain dainties.[4] A discussion was going on about names and definitions, and the proper applications of terms to things.[5] Whereupon Socrates, appealing to the company: "Can we explain why we call a man a "dainty fellow"? What is the particular action to which the term applies?[6]—since everyone adds some dainty to his food when he can get it.[7] But we have not quite hit the definition yet, I think. Are we to be called dainty eaters because we like our bread buttered?"[8]

---

1 For the type of entertainment see Becker, "Charicles," p. 315 (Eng. tr.)

2 "The boy."

3 Or, "were ashamed not to follow suit by sharing in the common stock and contributing their own portion."

4 For the distinction between {sitos} and {opson} see Plat. "Rep." 372 C.

5 Or, "The conversation had fallen upon names: what is the precise thing denoted under such and such a term? Define the meaning of so and so."

6 {opsophagos} = {opson} (or relish) eater, and so a "gourmand" or "epicure"; but how to define a gourmand?

7 Lit. "takes some {opson} (relish) to his {sitos} (food)."

8 Lit. "simply for that" (sc. the taking of some sort of {opson}. For {epi touto} cf. Plat. "Soph." 218 C; "Parmen." 147 D.)

No! hardly! (some member of the company replied).

Soc. Well, but now suppose a man confine himself to eating venison or other dainty without any plain food at all, not as a matter of training,[1] but for the pleasure of it: has such a man earned the title? "The rest of the world would have a poor chance against him,"[2] someone answered. "Or," interposed another, "what if the dainty dishes he devours are out of all proportion to the rest of his meal—what of him?"[3]

Soc. He has established a very fair title at any rate to the appellation, and when the rest of the world pray to heaven for a fine harvest: "May our corn and oil increase!" he may reasonably ejaculate, "May my fleshpots multiply!"

At this last sally the young man, feeling that the conversation set somewhat in his direction, did not desist indeed from his savoury viands, but helped himself generously to a piece of bread. Socrates was all-observant, and added: Keep an eye on our friend yonder, you others next him, and see fair play between the sop and the sauce.[4]

Another time, seeing one of the company using but one sop of bread[5] to test several savoury dishes, he remarked: Could there be a more extravagant style of cookery, or more murderous to the dainty dishes themselves, than this wholesale method of taking so many dishes together?—why, bless me, twenty different sorts of seasoning at one swoop![6] First of all he mixes up actually more ingredients than the cook himself prescribes, which is extravagant; and secondly, he has the audacity to commingle what the chef holds incongruous, whereby if the cooks are right in their method he is wrong in his, and consequently the destroyer of their art. Now is it not ridiculous first to procure the greatest virtuosi to cook for us, and then without any claim to their skill to take and alter their procedure? But there is a worse thing in store for the bold man who habituates himself to eat a

---

1 Lit. "{opson} (relish) by itself, not for the sake of training," etc. The English reader wil bear in mind that a raw beefsteak or other meat prescribed by the gymnastic trainer in preference to farinaceous food ({sitos}) would be {opson}.
2 Or, more lit. "Hardly anyone could deserve the appellation better."
3 Lit. "and what of the man who eats much {opson} on the top of a little ({sitos})?" {epesthion} = follows up one course by another, like the man in a fragment of Euripides, "Incert." 98: {kreasi boeiois khlora suk" epesthien}, who "followed up his beefsteak with a garnish of green figs."
4 Lit. "see whether he will make a relish of the staple or a staple of the relish" ("butter his bread or bread his butter").
5 {psomos}, a sop or morsel of bread (cf. {psomion}, N. T., in mod. Greek = "bread").
6 Huckleberry Finn (p. 2 of that young person's "Adventures") propounds the rationale of the system: "In a barrel of odds and ends it is different; things get mixed up, and the juice kind of swaps around, and the things go better."

dozen dishes at once: when there are but few dishes served, out of pure habit he will feel himself half starved, whilst his neighbor, accustomed to send his sop down by help of a single relish, will feast merrily, be the dishes never so few.

He had a saying that {euokheisthai}, to "make good cheer,"[1] was in Attic parlance a synonym for "eating," and the affix {eu} (the attributive "good") connoted the eating of such things as would not trouble soul or body, and were not far to seek or hard to find. So that to "make good cheer" in his vocabulary applied to a modest and well-ordered style of living.[2]

BOOK IV

I

Such was Socrates; so helpful under all circumstances and in every way that no observer, gifted with ordinary sensibility, could fail to appreciate the fact, that to be with Socrates, and to spend long time in his society (no matter where or what the circumstances), was indeed a priceless gain. Even the recollection of him, when he was no longer present, was felt as no small benefit by those who had grown accustomed to be with him, and who accepted him. Nor indeed was he less helpful to his acquaintance in his lighter than in his graver moods.

Let us take as an example that saying of his, so often on his lips: "I am in love with so and so"; and all the while it was obvious the going-forth of his soul was not toward excellence of body in the bloom of beauty, but rather toward faculties of the soul unfolding in virtue.[3] And these "good natures" he detected by certain tokens: a readiness to learn that to which the attention was directed; a power of retaining in the memory the lessons learned; and a passionate predilection for those studies in particular which serve to good administration of a house or of a state,[4] and in general to the proper handling of man and human affairs. Such beings, he maintained,

---

1 {euokheisthai}, cf. "Cyrop." IV. v. 7; "Pol. Ath." ii. 9; Kuhner cf. Eustah. "ad Il." ii. p. 212, 37, {"Akhaioi ten trophen okhen legousin oxutonos}. Athen. viii. 363 B. See "Hipparch," viii. 4, of horses. Cf. Arist. "H. A." viii. 6.
2 See "Symp." vi. 7; and for similar far-fetched etymologies, Plat. "Crat." passim.
3 Or, "not excellence of body in respect of beauty, but of the soul as regards virtue; and this good natural disposition might be detected by the readiness of its possessor to learn," etc. Cf. Plat. "Rep." 535 B.
4 Cf. above, I. i. 7.

needed only to be educated[1] to become not only happy themselves and happy administrators of their private households, but to be capable of rendering other human beings as states or individuals happy also.

He had indeed a different way of dealing with different kinds of people.[2] Those who thought they had good natural ability and despised learning he instructed that the most highly-gifted nature stands most in need of training and education;[3] and he would point out how in the case of horses it is just the spirited and fiery thoroughbred which, if properly broken in as a colt, will develop into a serviceable and superb animal, but if left unbroken will turn out utterly intractable and good for nothing. Or take the case of dogs: a puppy exhibiting that zest for toil and eagerness to attack wild creatures which are the marks of high breeding,[4] will, if well brought up, prove excellent for the chase or for any other useful purpose; but neglect his education and he will turn out a stupid, crazy brute, incapable of obeying the simplest command. It is just the same with human beings; here also the youth of best natural endowments—that is to say, possessing the most robust qualities of spirit and a fixed determination to carry out whatever he has laid his hand to—will, if trained and taught what it is right to do, prove a superlatively good and useful man. He achieves, in fact, what is best upon the grandest scale. But leave him in boorish ignorance untrained, and he will prove not only very bad but very mischievous,[5] and for this reason, that lacking the knowledge to discern what is right to do, he will frequently lay his hand to villainous practices; whilst the very magnificence and vehemence of his character render it impossible either to rein him in or to turn him aside from his evil courses. Hence in his case also his achievements are on the grandest scale but of the worst.[6]

Or to take the type of person so eaten up with the pride of riches that he conceives himself dispensed from any further need of education—since it is "money makes the man," and his wealth will amply suffice him to carry out his desires and to win honors from admiring humanity.[7] Socrates would

---

1 Or, "A person of this type would, if educated, not only prove a fortune-favored individual himself and," etc. Al. Kuhner, "Eos, qui ita instituti sunt, ut tales sint."
2 Or, "His method of attack was not indeed uniformly the same. It varied with the individual."
3 Or, "If anyone was disposed to look down upon learning and study in reliance upon his own natural ability, he tried to lesson him that it is just the highly-gifted nature which stands," etc. See Newman, op. cit. i. 397.
4 Cf. Aristot. "H. A." ix. 1; and "Hunting," iii. 11.
5 Or, "and the same man may easily become a master villain of the most dangerous sort."
6 Kuhner ad loc. after Fr. Hermann cf. Plato. "Crito," 44 E; "Hipp. min." 375 E; "Rep." vi. 491 E; "Gorg." 526 A; "Polit." 303 A.
7 Or, "and to be honored by mankind."

bring such people to their senses by pointing out the folly of supposing that without instruction it was possible to draw the line of demarcation[1] (10) between what is gainful and what is hurtful in conduct; and the further folly of supposing that, apart from such discrimination, a man could help himself by means of wealth alone to whatever he liked or find the path of expediency plain before him; and was it not the veriest simplicity to suppose that, without the power of laboring profitably, a man can either be doing well or be in any sort of way sufficiently equipped for the battle of life? and again, the veriest simplicity to suppose that by mere wealth without true knowledge it was possible either to purchase a reputation for some excellence, or without such reputation to gain distinction and celebrity?

II

Or to come to a third kind—the class of people who are persuaded that they have received the best education, and are proud of their wisdom: his manner of dealing with these I will now describe.

Euthydemus[2] "the beautiful" had (Socrates was given to understand) collected a large library, consisting of the most celebrated poets and philosophers,[3] by help of which he already believed himself to be more than a match for his fellows in wisdom, and indeed might presently expect to out-top them all in capacity of speech and action.[4] At first, as Socrates noted, the young man by reason of his youth had not as yet set foot in the agora,[5] but if he had anything to transact, his habit was to seat himself in a saddler's shop hard by. Accordingly to this same saddler's shop Socrates betook himself with some of those who were with him. And first the question was started by someone: "Was it through consorting with the wise,[6] or by his own unaided talent, that Themistocles came so to surpass his fellow citizens that when the services of a capable man were needed the eyes of the whole community instinctively turned to him?" Socrates, with a view to stirring[7] Euthydemus, answered: There was certainly an

---

1 Or, "that without learning the distinction it was possible to distinguish between," etc.
2 Euthydemus, the son of Diocles perhaps. See Plat. "Symp." 222 B, and Jowet ad loc.; Cobet, "Prosop. Xen." s.n.; K. Joel, op. cit. p. 372 foll. For {ton kalon} cf. "Phaedr." 278 E, "Isocrates the fair." For the whole chapter cf. Plat. "Alc." i.; "Lys." 210 E. See above, "Mem." I. ii. 29; Grote, "Plato," i. ch. x. passim.
3 Lit. "sophists." See Grote, "H. G." viii. p. 480, note. For private libraries see Becker, "Char." p. 272 foll. (Eng. tr.)
4 See "Hipparch," i. 24; "Cyrop." V. v. 46.
5 See above, III. vi. 1; Schneid. cf. Isocr. "Areop." 149 C.
6 Cf. Soph. fr. 12, {sophoi turannoi ton sophon xunousia}.
7 L. and S. cf. Plat. "Lys." 223 A; "Rep." 329 B: "Wishing to draw him out."

ingenuous simplicity in the belief that superiority in arts of comparatively little worth could only be attained by aid of qualified teachers, but that the leadership of the state, the most important concern of all, was destined to drop into the lap of anybody, no matter whom, like an accidental windfall.[1]

On a subsequent occasion, Euthydemus being present, though, as was plain to see, somewhat disposed to withdraw from the friendly concourse,[2] as if he would choose anything rather than appear to admire Socrates on the score of wisdom, the latter made the following remarks.

Soc. It is clear from his customary pursuits, is it not, sirs, that when our friend Euthydemus here is of full age, and the state propounds some question for solution, he will not abstain from offering the benefit of his advice? One can imagine the pretty exordium to his parliamentary speeches which, in his anxiety not to be thought to have learned anything from anybody, he has ready for the occasion.[3] Clearly at the outset he will deliver himself thus: "Men of Athens, I have never at any time learned anything from anybody; nor, if I have ever heard of anyone as being an able statesman, well versed in speech and capable of action, have I sought to come across him individually. I have not so much as been at pains to provide myself with a teacher from among those who have knowledge;[4] on the contrary, I have persistently avoided, I will not say learning from others, but the very faintest suspicion of so doing. However, anything that occurs to me by the light of nature I shall be glad to place at your disposal." How appropriate[5] would such a preface sound on the lips of anyone seeking, say, the office of state physician,[6] would it not? How advantageously he might begin an address on this wise: "Men of Athens, I have never learned the art of healing by help of anybody, nor have I sought to provide myself with any teacher among medical men. Indeed, to put it briefly, I have been ever on my guard not only against learning anything from the profession, but against the very notion of having studied medicine at all. If, however, you will be so good as to confer on me this post, I promise I will do my

---

1 Cf. Plat. "Alc." i. 118 C: "And Pericles is said not to have got his wisdom by the light of nature, but to have associated with several of the philosophers" (Jowett).

2 {sunedrias}, "the council."

3 Or, "the pretty exordium... now in course of composition. He must at all hazards avoid the suspicion of having picked up any crumb of learning from anybody; how can he help therefore beginning his speech thus?"

4 Or, "scientific experts."

5 Al. "Just as if one seeking the office of state physician were to begin with a like exordium." {armoseie} = "it would be consistent (with what has gone before)."

6 Schneider cf. Plat. "Laws," iv. 720 A; "Gorg." 456 A; and for "the parish doctor," "Polit." 259 A; Arist. "Acharn." 1030.

best to acquire skill by experimenting on your persons." Every one present laughed at the exordium (and there the matter dropped).

Presently, when it became apparent that Euthydemus had got so far that he was disposed to pay attention to what was said, though he was still at pains not to utter a sound himself, as if he hoped by silence to attach to himself some reputation for sagacity, Socrates, wishing to cure him of that defect, proceeded.

Soc. Is it not surprising that people anxious to learn to play the harp or the flute, or to ride, or to become proficient in any like accomplishment, are not content to work unremittingly in private by themselves at whatever it is in which they desire to excel, but they must sit at the feet of the best-esteemed teachers, doing all things and enduring all things for the sake of following the judgment of those teachers in everything, as though they themselves could not otherwise become famous; whereas, among those who aspire to become eminent politically as orators and statesmen,[1] there are some who cannot see why they should not be able to do all that politics demand, at a moment's notice, by inspiration as it were, without any preliminary pains or preparations whatever? And yet it would appear that the latter concerns must be more difficult of achievement than the former, in proportion as there are more competitors in the field but fewer who reach the goal of their ambition, which is as much as to say that a more sustained effort of attention is needed on the part of those who embark upon the sea of politics than is elsewhere called for.

Such were the topics on which Socrates was wont in the early days of their association to dilate in the hearing of Euthydemus; but when the philosopher perceived that the youth not only could tolerate the turns of the discussion more readily but was now become a somewhat eager listener, he went to the saddler's shop alone,[2] and when Euthydemus was seated by his side the following conversation took place.

Soc. Pray tell me, Euthydemus, is it really true what people tell me, that you have made a large collection of the writings of "the wise," as they are called?[3]

Euthydemus answered: Quite true, Socrates, and I mean to go on collecting until I possess all the books I can possibly lay hold of.

Soc. By Hera! I admire you for wishing to possess treasures of wisdom rather than of gold and silver, which shows that you do not believe gold

---

1 Or, more lit. "powerful in speech and action within the sphere of politics."
2 The question arises: how far is the conversation historical or imaginary?
3 Or, "have collected several works of our classical authors and philosophers."

and silver to be the means of making men better, but that the thoughts[1] of the wise alone enrich with virtue their possessions.

And Euthydemus was glad when he heard that saying, for, thought he to himself, "In the eyes of Socrates I am on the high road to the acquisition of wisdom." But the latter, perceiving him to be pleased with the praise, continued.

Soc. And what is it in which you desire to excel, Euthydemus, that you collect books?

And when Euthydemus was silent, considering what answer he should make, Socrates added: Possibly you want to be a great doctor? Why, the prescriptions[2] of the Pharmacopoeia would form a pretty large library by themselves.

No, indeed, not I! (answered Euthydemus).

Soc. Then do you wish to be an architect? That too implies a man of well-stored wit and judgment.[3]

I have no such ambition (he replied).

Soc. Well, do you wish to be a mathematician, like Theodorus?[4]

Euth. No, nor yet a mathematician.

Soc. Then do you wish to be an astronomer?[5] or (as the youth signified dissent) possibly a rhapsodist?[6] (he asked), for I am told you have the entire works of Homer in your possession.[7]

Nay, God forbid! not I! (ejaculated the youth). Rhapsodists have a very exact acquaintance with epic poetry, I know, of course; but they are empty-pated creatures enough themselves.[8]

At last Socrates said: Can it be, Euthydemus, that you are an aspirant to that excellence through which men become statesmen and administrators fit to rule and apt to benefit[9] the rest of the world and themselves?

Yes (replied he), that is the excellence I desire—beyond measure.

Upon my word (said Socrates), then you have indeed selected as the object of your ambition the noblest of virtues and the greatest of the arts, for this is the property of kings, and is entitled "royal"; but (he continued)

---

1 Lit. "gnomes," maxims, sententiae. Cf. Aristot. "Rhet." ii. 21.
2 {suggrammata}, "medical treatises." See Aristot. "Eth." x. 9, 21.
3 Or, "To be that implies a considerable store of well-packed wisdom.
4 Of Cyrene (cf. Plat. "Theaet.") taught Plato. Diog. Laert. ii. 8, 19.
5 Cf. below, IV. vii. 4.
6 See "Symp." iii. 6; Plat. "Ion."
7 See Jowett, "Plato," i. 229; Grote, "Plato," i. 455.
8 Or, "are simply perfect in the art of reciting epic poetry, but are apt to be the veriest simpletons themselves."
9 Or, "statesmen, and economists, and rules, and benefactors of the rest of the world and themselves."

have you considered whether it is possible to excel in these matters without being just and upright?[1]

Euth. Certainly I have, and I say that without justice and uprightness it is impossible to be a good citizen.

No doubt (replied Socrates) you have accomplished that initial step?

Euth. Well, Socrates, I think I could hold my own against all comers as an upright man.

And have upright men (continued Socrates) their distinctive and appropriate works like those of carpenters or shoe-makers?

Euth. To be sure they have.

Soc. And just as the carpenter is able to exhibit his works and products, the righteous man should be able to expound and set forth his, should he not?

I see (replied Euthydemus) you are afraid I cannot expound the works of righteousness! Why, bless me! of course I can, and the works of unrighteousness into the bargain, since there are not a few of that sort within reach of eye and ear every day.

Shall we then (proceeded Socrates) write the letter R on this side,[2] and on that side the letter W; and then anything that appears to us to be the product of righteousness we will place to the R account, and anything which appears to be the product of wrongdoing and iniquity to the account of W?

By all means do so (he answered), if you think that it assists matters.

Accordingly Socrates drew the letters, as he had suggested, and continued.

Soc. Lying exists among men, does it not?

Euth. Certainly.

To which side of the account then shall we place it? (he asked).

Euth. Clearly on the side of wrong and injustice.

Soc. Deceit too is not uncommon?

Euth. By no means.

Soc. To which side shall we place deceit?

Euth. Deceit clearly on the side of wrong.

Soc. Well, and chicanery[3] or mischief of any sort?

---

[1] Just, {dikaios} = upright, righteous. Justice, {dikaiosune} = social uprightness = righteousness, N.T. To quote a friend: "The Greek {dikaios} combines the active dealing out of justice with the self-reflective idea of preserving justice in our conduct, which is what we mean by 'upright.'"

[2] The letter R (to stand for Right, Righteous, Upright, Just). The letter W (to stand for Wrong, Unrighteous, Unjust).

[3] Reading {to kakourgein} (= furari, Sturz); al. {kleptein}, Stob.

Euth. That too.

Soc. And the enslavement of free-born men?[1]

Euth. That too.

Soc. And we cannot allow any of these to lie on the R side of the account, to the side of right and justice, can we, Euthydemus?

It would be monstrous (he replied).

Soc. Very good. But supposing a man to be elected general, and he succeeds in enslaving an unjust, wicked, and hostile state, are we to say that he is doing wrong?

Euth. By no means.

Soc. Shall we not admit that he is doing what is right?

Euth. Certainly.

Soc. Again, suppose he deceives the foe while at war with them?

Euth. That would be all fair and right also.

Soc. Or steals and pillages their property? would he not be doing what is right?

Euth. Certainly; when you began I thought you were limiting the question to the case of friends.

Soc. So then everything which we set down on the side of Wrong will now have to be placed to the credit of Right?

Euth. Apparently.

Soc. Very well then, let us so place them; and please, let us make a new definition—that while it is right to do such things to a foe, it is wrong to do them to a friend, but in dealing with the latter it behoves us to be as straightforward as possible.[2]

I quite assent (replied Euthydemus).

So far so good (remarked Socrates); but if a general, seeing his troops demoralised, were to invent a tale to the effect that reinforcements were coming, and by means of this false statement should revive the courage of his men, to which of the two accounts shall we place that act of fraud?[3]

On the side of right, to my notion (he replied).

Soc. Or again, if a man chanced to have a son ill and in need of medicine, which the child refused to take, and supposing the father by an act of deceit to administer it under the guise of something nice to eat, and by service of that lie to restore the boy to health, to which account shall we set down this fraud?

---

1 Or, "the kidnapping of men into slavery." {to andrapodizesthai} = the reduction of a free-born man to a state of slavery. Slavery itself ({douleia}) being regarded as the normal condition of a certain portion of the human race and not in itself immoral.

2 Or, "an absolutely straightforward course is necessary."

3 Cf. "Hell." IV. iii. 10; "Cyrop." I. vi. 31.

Euth. In my judgment it too should be placed to the same account.

Soc. Well, supposing you have a friend in deplorably low spirits, and you are afraid he will make away with himself—accordingly you rob him of his knife or other such instrument: to which side ought we to set the theft?

Euth. That too must surely be placed to the score of right behavior.

Soc. I understand you to say that a straightforward course is not in every case to be pursued even in dealing with friends?

Heaven forbid! (the youth exclaimed). If you will allow me, I rescind my former statement.[1]

Soc. Allow you! Of course you may—anything rather than make a false entry on our lists.... But there is just another point we ought not to leave uninvestigated. Let us take the case of deceiving a friend to his detriment: which is the more wrongful—to do so voluntarily or unintentionally?

Euth. Really, Socrates, I have ceased to believe in my own answers, for all my former admissions and conceptions seem to me other than I first supposed them.[2] Still, if I may hazard one more opinion, the intentional deceiver, I should say, is worse than the involuntary.

Soc. And is it your opinion that there is a lore and science of Right and Justice just as there is of letters and grammar?[3]

Euth. That is my opinion.

Soc. And which should you say was more a man of letters[4]—he who intentionally misspells or misreads, or he who does so unconsciously?

Euth. He who does so intentionally, I should say, because he can spell or read correctly whenever he chooses.

Soc. Then the voluntary misspeller may be a lettered person, but the involuntary offender is an illiterate?[5]

Euth. True, he must be. I do not see how to escape from that conclusion.

Soc. And which of the two knows what is right—he who intentionally lies and deceives, or he who lies and deceives unconsciously?[6]

Euth. The intentional and conscious liar clearly.

---

1 See above, I. ii. 44 ({anatithemai}).
2 Or, "*all my original positions seem to me now other than I first conceived them*"; or, "*everything I first asserted seems now to be twisted topsy-turvy.*"
3 {mathesis kai episteme tou dikaiou}—*a doctrine and a knowledge of the Just.*
4 Or, "*more grammatical*"; "*the better grammarian.*"
5 Or, "*In fact, he who sins against the lore of grammer intentionally may be a good grammarian and a man of letters, but he who does so involuntarily is illiterate and a bad grammarian?*"
6 Or, Soc. *And does he who lies and deceives with intent know what is right rather than he who does either or both unconsciously?*
 Euth. *Clearly he does.*

Soc. Well then, your statement is this: on the one hand, the man who has the knowledge of letters is more lettered than he who has no such knowledge?[1]

Euth. Yes.

Soc. And, on the other, he who has the knowledge of what is right is more righteous than he who lacks that knowledge?

Euth. I suppose it is, but for the life of me I cannot make head or tail of my own admission.[2]

Soc. Well (look at it like this). Suppose a man to be anxious to speak the truth, but he is never able to hold the same language about a thing for two minutes together. First he says: "The road is toward the east," and then he says, "No, it's toward the west"; or, running up a column of figures, now he makes the product this, and again he makes it that, now more, now less—what do you think of such a man?

Euth. Heaven help us! clearly he does not know what he thought he knew.

Soc. And you know the appellation given to certain people—"slavish,"[3] or, "little better than a slave?"

Euth. I do.

Soc. Is it a term suggestive of the wisdom or the ignorance of those to whom it is applied?

Euth. Clearly of their ignorance.

Soc. Ignorance, for instance, of smithying?

Euth. No, certainly not.

Soc. Then possibly ignorance of carpentering?

Euth. No, nor yet ignorance of carpentering.

Soc. Well, ignorance of shoemaking?

Euth. No, nor ignorance of any of these: rather the reverse, for the majority of those who do know just these matters are "little better than slaves."

---

1 Or, Soc. *It is a fair inference, is it not, that he who has the {episteme} of grammar is more grammatical than he who has no such {episteme}?*
   Euth. *Yes.*
   Soc. *And he who has the {episteme} of things rightful is more righteous than he who lacks the {episteme}?* See Plat. "Hipp. min."; Arist. "Eth. Eud." VI. v. 7.

2 Lit. "Apparently; but I appear to myself to be saying this also, heaven knows how." See Jowett, "Plato," ii. p. 416 (ed. 2).

3 {andropododeis}, which has the connotation of mental dulness, and a low order of intellect, cf. "boorish," "rustic," "loutish," ("pariah," conceivably). "Slavish," "servile," with us connote moral rather than intellectual deficiency, I suppose. Hence it is impossible to preserve the humor of the Socratic argument. See Newman, op. cit. i. 107.

Soc. You mean it is a title particularly to those who are ignorant of the beautiful, the good, the just?[1]

It is, in my opinion (he replied).

Soc. Then we must in every way strain every nerve to avoid the imputation of being slaves?

Euth. Nay, Socrates, by all that is holy, I did flatter myself that at any rate I was a student of philosophy, and on the right road to be taught everything essential to one who would fain make beauty and goodness his pursuit.[2] So that now you may well imagine my despair when, for all my pains expended, I cannot even answer the questions put to me about what most of all a man should know; and there is no path of progress open to me, no avenue of improvement left.

Thereupon Socrates: Tell me, Euthydemus, have you ever been to Delphi?

Yes, certainly; twice (said he).

Soc. And did you notice an inscription somewhere on the temple:

{Gnomi Seauton}—Know Thyself?

Euth. I did.

Soc. Did you, possibly, pay no regard to the inscription? or did you give it heed and try to discover who and what you were?

I can safely say I did not (he answered). That much I made quite sure I knew, at any rate; since if I did not know even myself, what in the world did I know?

Soc. Can a man be said, do you think, to know himself who knows his own name and nothing more? or must he not rather set to work precisely like the would-be purchaser of a horse, who certainly does not think that he has got the knowledge he requires until he has discovered whether the beast is tractable or stubborn, strong or weak, quick or slow, and how it stands with the other points, serviceable or the reverse, in reference to the use and purpose of a horse? So, I say, must a man in like manner interrogate his own nature in reference to a man's requirements, and learn to know his own capacities, must he not?

Euth. Yes, so it strikes me: he who knows not his own ability knows not himself.

Soc. And this too is plain, is it not: that through self-knowledge men meet with countless blessings, and through ignorance of themselves

---

1 Cf. Goethe's "Im Ganzen Guten Schonen resolut zu leben."
2 {tes kalokagathias}, the virtue of the {kalos te kagathos}— nobility of soul. Cf. above, I. vi. 14.

with many evils? Because, the man who knows himself knows what is advantageous to himself; he discerns the limits of his powers, and by doing what he knows, he provides himself with what he needs and so does well; or, conversely, by holding aloof from what he knows not, he avoids mistakes and thereby mishaps. And having now a test to gauge other human beings he uses their need as a stepping-stone to provide himself with good and to avoid evil. Whereas he who does not know himself, but is mistaken as to his own capacity, is in like predicament to the rest of mankind and all human matters else; he neither knows what he wants, nor what he is doing, nor the people whom he deals with; and being all abroad in these respects, he misses what is good and becomes involved in what is ill.

Again, he that knows what he is doing through the success of his performance attains to fame and honor; his peers and co-mates are glad to make use of him, whilst his less successful neighbors, failing in their affairs, are anxious to secure his advice, his guidance, his protection;[1] they place their hopes of happiness in him, and for all these causes[2] single him out as the chief object of their affection. He, on the contrary, who knows not what he does, who chooses amiss and fails in what he puts his hands to, not only incurs loss and suffers chastisement through his blunders, but step by step loses reputation and becomes a laughing-stock, and in the end is doomed to a life of dishonor and contempt.

What is true of individuals is true also of communities.[3] That state which in ignorance of its power goes to war with a stronger than itself ends by being uprooted or else reduced to slavery.

Thereupon Euthydemus: Be assured I fully concur in your opinion; the precept KNOW THYSELF cannot be too highly valued; but what is the application? What the starting-point of self-examination? I look to you for an explanation, if you would kindly give one.[4]

Well (replied Socrates), I presume you know quite well the distinction between good and bad things: your knowledge may be relied upon so far?

Why, yes, to be sure (replied the youth); for without that much discernment I should indeed be worse than any slave.[5]

Come then (said he), do you give me an explanation of the things so termed.

---

1 Cf. Dante, "Tu duca, tu maestro, tu signore."
2 Reading, {dia panta tauta}, or if {dia tauta}, translate "and therefore."
3 Or, more lit. "A law which applies, you will observe, to bodies politic."
4 Or, "at what point to commence the process of self-inspection?— there is the mystery. I look to you, if you are willing, to interpret it."
5 Lit. "if I did not know even that."

That is fortunately not hard (replied the youth). First of all, health in itself I hold to be a good, and disease in itself an evil; and in the next place the sources of either of those aforenamed, meats and drinks, and habits of life,[1] I regard as good or evil according as they contribute either to health or to disease.

Soc. Then health and disease themselves when they prove to be sources of any good are good, but when of any evil, evil?

And when (asked he), can health be a source of evil, or disease a source of good?

Why, bless me! often enough (replied Socrates). In the event, for instance, of some ill-starred expedition or of some disastrous voyage or other incident of the sort, of which veritably there are enough to spare—when those who owing to their health and strength take a part in the affair are lost; whilst those who were left behind—as hors de combat, on account of ill-health of other feebleness—are saved.

Euth. Yes, you are right; but you will admit that there are advantages to be got from strength and lost through weakness.

Soc. Even so; but ought we to regard those things which at one moment benefit and at another moment injure us in any strict sense good rather than evil?

Euth. No, certainly not, according to that line of argument. But wisdom,[2] Socrates, you must on your side admit, is irrefragably a good; since there is nothing which or in which a wise man would not do better than a fool.

Soc. What say you? Have you never heard of Daedalus,[3] how he was seized by Minos on account of his wisdom, and forced to be his slave, and robbed of fatherland and freedom at one swoop? and how, while endeavouring to make his escape with his son, he caused the boy's death without effecting his own salvation, but was carried off among barbarians and again enslaved?

Yes, I know the old story (he answered).[4]

Soc. Or have you not heard of the "woes of Palamedes,"[5] that commonest theme of song, how for his wisdom's sake Odysseus envied him and slew him?

Euth. That tale also is current.

---

1 Or, "pursuits and occupations"; "manners and customs."
2 See above, III. ix. 5. Here {sophia} is not = {sophrosune}.
3 See Ovid. "Met." viii. 159 foll., 261 foll.; Hygin. "Fab." 39, 40; Diod. Sic. iv. 79; Paus. vii. 4. 6.
4 Or, "Ah yes, of course; the tale is current."
5 See Virg. "Aen." ii. 90; Hygin. 105; Philostr. "Her." x.

Soc. And how many others, pray, do you suppose have been seized on account of their wisdom, and despatched to the great king and at his court enslaved?[1]

Well, prosperity, well-being[2] (he exclaimed), must surely be a blessing, and that the most indisputable, Socrates?

It might be so (replied the philosopher) if it chanced not to be in itself a compound of other questionable blessings.

Euth. And which among the components of happiness and well-being can possibly be questionable?

None (he retorted), unless of course we are to include among these components beauty, or strength, or wealth, or reputation, or anything else of that kind?

Euth. By heaven! of course we are to include these, for what would happiness be without these?

Soc. By heaven! yes; only then we shall be including the commonest sources of mischief which befall mankind. How many are ruined by their fair faces at the hand of admirers driven to distraction[3] by the sight of beauty in its bloom! how many, tempted by their strength to essay deeds beyond their power, are involved in no small evils! how many, rendered effeminate by reason of their wealth, have been plotted against and destroyed![4] how many through fame and political power have suffered a world of woe!

Well (the youth replied) if I am not even right in praising happiness, I must confess I know not for what one ought to supplicate the gods in prayer.[5]

Nay, these are matters (proceeded Socrates) which perhaps, through excessive confidence in your knowledge of them, you have failed to examine into; but since the state, which you are preparing yourself to direct, is democratically constituted,[6] of course you know what a democracy is.

Euth. I presume I do, decidedly.

Soc. Well, now, is it possible to know what a popular state is without knowing who the people are?

Euth. Certainly not.

Soc. And whom do you consider to be the people?

Euth. The poor citizens, I should say.

---

1 Cf. Herod. iii. 129.
2 {to eudaimonein}, "happiness." Cf. Herod. i. 86.
3 Cf. Plat. "Rep." vii. 517 D; "Phaedr." 249 D.
4 E.g. Alcibiades.
5 See above for Socrates's own form of supplication.
6 Or, "popularly governed."

Soc. Then you know who the poor are, of course?

Euth. Of course I do.

Soc. I presume you also know who the rich are?

Euth. As certainly as I know who are the poor.

Soc. Whom do you understand by poor and rich?

Euth. By poor I mean those who have not enough to pay for their necessaries,[1] and by rich those who have more means than sufficient for all their needs.

Soc. Have you noticed that some who possess a mere pittance not only find this sufficient, but actually succeed in getting a surplus out of it; while others do not find a large fortune large enough?

I have, most certainly; and I thank you for the reminder (replied Euthydemus). One has heard of crowned heads and despotic rulers being driven by want to commit misdeeds like the veriest paupers.

Then, if that is how matters stand (continued Socrates), we must class these same crowned heads with the commonalty; and some possessors of scant fortunes, provided they are good economists, with the wealthy?

Then Euthydemus: It is the poverty of my own wit which forces me to this admission. I bethink me it is high time to keep silence altogether; a little more, and I shall be proved to know absolutely nothing. And so he went away crestfallen, in an agony of self-contempt, persuaded that he was verily and indeed no better than a slave.

Among those who were reduced to a like condition by Socrates, many refused to come near him again, whom he for his part looked upon as dolts and dullards.[2] But Euthydemus had the wit to understand that, in order to become worthy of account, his best plan was to associate as much as possible with Socrates; and from that moment, save for some necessity, he never left him—in some points even imitating him in his habits and pursuits. Socrates, on his side, seeing that this was the young man's disposition, disturbed him as little as possible, but in the simplest and plainest manner initiated him into everything which he held to be needful to know or important to practice.

III

It may be inferred that Socrates was in no hurry for those who were with

---

[1] Al. "who cannot contribute their necessary quota to the taxes (according to the census)."
[2] Or, "as people of dull intelligence and sluggish temperament." Cf. Plat. "Gorg." 488 A.

him to discover capacities for speech and action or as inventive geniuses,[1] without at any rate a well-laid foundation of self-control.[2] For those who possessed such abilities without these same saving virtues would, he believed, only become worse men with greater power for mischief. His first object was to instil into those who were with him a wise spirit in their relation to the gods.[3] That such was the tenor of his conversation in dealing with men may be seen from the narratives of others who were present on some particular occasion.[4] I confine myself to a particular discussion with Euthydemus at which I was present.

Socrates said:[5] Tell me, Euthydemus, has it ever struck you to observe what tender pains the gods have taken to furnish man with all his needs?

Euth. No indeed, I cannot say that it has ever struck me.

Well (Socrates continued), you do not need to be reminded that, in the first place, we need light, and with light the gods supply us.

Euth. Most true, and if we had not got it we should, as far as our own eyes could help us, be like men born blind.

Soc. And then, again, seeing that we stand in need of rest and relaxation, they bestow upon us "the blessed balm of silent night."[6]

Yes (he answered), we are much beholden for that boon.

Soc. Then, forasmuch as the sun in his splendour makes manifest to us the hours of the day and bathes all things in brightness, but anon night in her darkness obliterates distinctions, have they not displayed aloft the starry orbs, which inform us of the watches of the night, whereby we can accomplish many of our needs?[7]

It is so (he answered).

Soc. And let us not forget that the moon herself not only makes clear to us the quarters of the night, but of the month also?

Certainly (he answered).

---

1 Or, "as speakers" (see ch. vi. below), "and men of action" (see ch. v. below), "or as masters of invention" (see ch. vii. below).

2 Or, "but as prior to those excellences must be engrafted in them {sophrosune} (the virtues of temperance and sanity of soul)."

3 Lit. "His first object and endeavor was to make those who were with him {sophronas} (sound of soul) as regards the gods."

4 Reading after Herbst, Cobet, etc., {diegountai}, or if vulg. {diegounto}, translate, "from the current accounts penned during his lifetime by the other witnesses." For {alloi} see K. Joel, op. cit. pp. 15, 23; above, "Mem." I. iv. 1.

5 For the subject matter of this "teleological" chapter, see above, I. iv.; K. Joel, op. cit. Appendix, p. 547 foll. in ref. to Dummler's views.

6 {kalliston anapauterion}. The diction throughout is "poetical."

7 E.g. for temple orientation see Dr. Penrose quoted by Norman Lockyer, "Nature," August 31. 1893.

Soc. And what of this: that whereas we need nutriment, this too the heavenly powers yield us? Out of Earth's bosom they cause good to spring up[1] for our benefit; and for our benefit provide appropriate seasons to furnish us in turn not only with the many and diverse objects of need, but with the sources also of our joy and gladness?[2]

Yes (he answered eagerly), these things bear token truly to a love for man.[3]

Soc. Well, and what of another priceless gift, that of water, which conspires with earth and the seasons to give both birth and increase to all things useful to us; nay, which helps to nurture our very selves, and commingling with all that feeds us, renders it more digestible, more wholesome, and more pleasant to the taste; and mark you in proportion to the abundance of our need the superabundance of its supply. What say you concerning such a boon?

Euth. In this again I see a sign of providential care.

Soc. And then the fact that the same heavenly power has provided us with fire[4]—our assistant against cold, our auxiliary in darkness, our fellow workman in every art and every instrument which for the sake of its utility mortal man may invent or furnish himself withal. What of this, since, to put it compendiously, there is nothing serviceable to the life of man worth speaking of but owes its fabrication to fire?[5]

Euth. Yes, a transcendent instance of benevolent design.[6]

Soc. Again, consider the motions of the Sun,[7] how when he has turned him about in winter[8] he again draws nigh to us, ripening some fruits, and causing others whose time is past to dry up; how when he has fulfillled his work he comes no closer, but turns away as if in fear to scorch us to our hurt unduly; and again, when he has reached a point where if he should prolong his retreat we should plainly be frozen to death with cold, note how he turns him about and resumes his approach, traversing that region of the heavens where he may shed his genial influence best upon us.

---

1 *Cf. Plat. "Laws," 747 D.*
2 Or, *"pleasure."*
3 *Cf. Plat. "Laws," 713 D; "Symp." 189 D. "These things are signs of a beneficent regard for man."*
4 Lit. *"and then the fact that they made provision for us of even fire"; the credit of this boon, according to Hesiod, being due to Prometheus.*
5 Or, *"no life-aiding appliance worthy of the name."*
6 Or, *"Yes, that may be called an extreme instance of the divine 'philanthropy.' " Cf. Cic. "de N. D." ii. 62.*
7 *A single MS. inserts a passage {to de kai era... "Anekphraston"}.*
8 *I.e. as we say, "after the winter solstice."*

Yes, upon my word (he answered), these occurrences bear the impress of being so ordered for the sake of man.

Soc. And then, again, it being manifest that we could not endure either scorching heat or freezing cold if they came suddenly upon us, note how gradually the sun approaches, and how gradually recedes, so that we fail to notice how we come at last to either extreme.[1]

For my part (he replied), the question forces itself upon my mind, whether the gods have any other occupation save only to minister to man; and I am only hindered from saying so, because the rest of animals would seem to share these benefits along with man.

Soc. Why, to be sure; and is it not plain that these animals themselves are born and bred for the sake of man? At any rate, no living creature save man derives so many of his enjoyments from sheep and goats, horses and cattle and asses, and other animals. He is more dependent, I should suppose, on these than even on plants and vegetables. At any rate, equally with these latter they serve him as means of subsistence or articles of commerce; indeed, a large portion of the human family do not use the products of the soil as food at all, but live on the milk and cheese and flesh of their flocks and herds, whilst all men everywhere tame and domesticate the more useful kinds of animals, and turn them to account as fellow workers in war and for other purposes.

Yes, I cannot but agree with what you say (he answered), when I see that animals so much stronger than man become so subservient to his hand that he can use them as he lists.

Soc. And as we reflect on the infinite beauty and utility and the variety of nature, what are we to say of the fact that man has been endowed with sensibilities which correspond with this diversity, whereby we take our fill of every blessing;[2] or, again, this implanted faculty of reasoning, which enables us to draw inferences concerning the things which we perceive, and by aid of memory to understand how each set of things may be turned to our good, and to devise countless contrivances with a view to enjoying the good and repelling the evil; or lastly, when we consider the faculty bestowed upon us of interpretative speech, by which we are enabled to instruct one another, and to participate in all the blessings fore-named: to

---

1 Or, "note the gradual approach and gradual recession of the sun-god, so gradual that we reach either extreme in a manner imperceptibly, and before we are aware of its severity."
2 Or, "Again, when we consider how many beautiful objects there are serviceable to man, and yet how unlike they are to one another, the fact that man has been endowed with senses adapted to each class of things, and so has access to a world of happiness."

form societies, to establish laws, and to enter upon a civilised existence[1]—what are we to think?

Euth. Yes, Socrates, decidedly it would appear that the gods do manifest a great regard, nay, a tender care, toward mankind.

Soc. Well, and what do you make of the fact that where we are powerless to take advantageous forethought for our future, at this stage they themselves lend us their cooperation, imparting to the inquirer through divination knowledge of events about to happen, and instructing him by what means they may best be turned to good account?

Euth. Ay, and you, Socrates, they would seem to treat in a more friendly manner still than the rest of men, if, without waiting even to be inquired of by you, they show you by signs beforehand what you must, and what you must not do.[2]

Soc. Yes, and you will discover for yourself the truth of what I say, if, without waiting to behold the outward and visible forms[3] of the gods themselves, you will be content to behold their works; and with these before you, to worship and honor the Divine authors of them.[4] I would have you reflect that the very gods themselves suggest this teaching.[5] Not one of these but gives us freely of his blessings; yet they do not step from behind their veil in order to grant one single boon.[6] And pre-eminently He who orders and holds together the universe,[7] in which are all things beautiful and good;[8] who fashions and refashions it to never-ending use unworn, keeping it free from sickness or decay,[9] so that swifter than thought it ministers to his will unerringly—this God is seen to perform the mightiest operations, but in the actual administration of the same abides himself invisible to mortal ken. Reflect further, this Sun above our heads, so visible to all—as we suppose—will not suffer man to regard him too narrowly, but should any essay to watch him with a shameless stare he will snatch away their power of vision. And if the gods themselves are thus unseen, so too shall you find their ministers to be hidden also; from the height of

---

1 Cf. Aristot. "Pol." III. ix. 5.

2 See above, I. iv. 14, for a parallel to the train of thought on the part of Aristodemus "the little," and of Euthydemus; and for Socrates's {daimonion}, see above; Grote, "Plato," i. 400.

3 Cf. Cic. "de N. D." I. xii. 31; Lactantius, "de Ira," xi. 13.

4 See L. Dindorf ad loc. (ed. Ox. 1862), {theous}; G. Sauppe, vol. iii. "An. crit." p. xxix; R. Kuhner; C. Schenkl.

5 I.e. "that man must walk by faith." For {upodeiknunai} cf. "Econ." xii. 18.

6 Schneid. cf. Plat. "Crat." 396.

7 Or, "the co-ordinator and container of the universe."

8 Or, "in whom all beauty and goodness is."

9 Cf. "Cyrop." VIII. vii. 22; above, I. iv. 13.

heaven above the thunderbolt is plainly hurled, and triumphs over all that it encounters, yet it is all-invisible, no eye may detect its coming or its going at the moment of its swoop. The winds also are themselves unseen, though their works are manifest, and through their approach we are aware of them. And let us not forget, the soul of man himself, which if aught else human shares in the divine—however manifestly enthroned within our bosom, is as wholly as the rest hidden from our gaze. These things you should lay to mind, and not despise the invisible ones, but learn to recognize their power, as revealed in outward things, and to know the divine influence.[1]

Nay, Socrates (replied Euthydemus), there is no danger I shall turn a deaf ear to the divine influence even a little; of that I am not afraid, but I am out of heart to think that no soul of man may ever requite the kindness of the gods with fitting gratitude.

Be not out of heart because of that (he said); you know what answer the god at Delphi makes to each one who comes asking "how shall I return thanks to heaven?"—"According to the law and custom of your city"; and this, I presume, is law and custom everywhere that a man should please the gods with offerings according to the ability which is in him.[2] How then should a man honor the gods with more beautiful or holier honor than by doing what they bid him? but he must in no wise slacken or fall short of his ability, for when a man so does, it is manifest, I presume, that at the moment he is not honoring the gods. You must then honor the gods, not with shortcoming but according to your ability; and having so done, be of good cheer and hope to receive the greatest blessings. For where else should a man of sober sense look to receive great blessings if not from those who are able to help him most, and how else should he hope to obtain them save by seeking to please his helper, and how may he hope to please his helper better than by yielding him the amplest obedience?

By such words—and conduct corresponding to his words—did Socrates mold and fashion the hearts of his companions, making them at once more devout and more virtuous.[3]

IV

But indeed[4] with respect to justice and uprightness he not only made no

---

1 {to daimonion}, the divinity.
2 Or, "and that law, I presume, is universal which says, Let a man," etc.; and for the maxim see above; "Anab." III. ii. 9.
3 Or, "sounder of soul and more temperate as well as more pious."
4 L. Dindorf suspects (SS. 1-6, {'Alla men... pollakis'}), ed. Lips. 1872. See also Praef. to Ox. ed. p. viii.

secret of the opinion he held, but gave practical demonstration of it, both in private by his law-abiding and helpful behavior to all,[1] and in public by obeying the magistrates in all that the laws enjoined, whether in the life of the city or in military service, so that he was a pattern of loyalty to the rest of the world, and on three several occasions in particular: first, when as president (Epistates) of the assembly he would not suffer the sovereign people to take an unconstitutional vote,[2] but ventured, on the side of the laws, to resist a current of popular feeling strong enough, I think, to have daunted any other man. Again, when the Thirty tried to lay some injunction on him contrary to the laws, he refused to obey, as for instance when they forbade his conversing with the young;[3] or again, when they ordered him and certain other citizens to arrest a man to be put to death,[4] he stood out single-handed on the ground that the injunctions laid upon him were contrary to the laws. And lastly, when he appeared as defendant in the suit instituted by Meletus,[5] notwithstanding that it was customary for litigants in the law courts to humor the judges in the conduct of their arguments by flattery and supplications contrary to the laws,[6] notwithstanding also that defendants owed their acquittal by the court to the employment of such methods, he refused to do a single thing however habitual in a court of law which was not strictly legal; and though by only a slight deflection from the strict path he might easily have been acquitted by his judges,[7] he preferred to abide by the laws and die rather than transgress them and live.

These views he frequently maintained in conversation, now with one and now with another, and one particular discussion with Hippias of Elis[8] on the topic of justice and uprightness has come to my knowledge.[9]

Hippias had just arrived at Athens after a long absence, and chanced to be present when Socrates was telling some listeners how astonishing it was that if a man wanted to get another taught to be a shoemaker or carpenter or coppersmith or horseman, he would have no doubt where to send him

---

1 Or, "by his conduct to all, which was not merely innocent in the eye of law and custom but positively helpful."
2 See above, I. i. 18; "Hell." I. vii. 14, 15; Grote, "H. G." viii. 272.
3 See above, I. ii. 35.
4 Leon of Salamis. See "Hell." II. iii. 39; Plat. "Apol." 32 C; Andoc. "de Myst." 46.
5 See above, I. i. 1; Plat. "Apol." 19 C.
6 Kuhner cf. Quintil. VI. i. 7: "Athenis affectus movere etiam per praeconem prohibatur orator"; "Apol." 4; Plat. "Apol." 38 D, E.
7 See Grote, "H. G." viii. p. 663 foll.
8 For this famous person see Cob. "Pros. Xen." s.n.; Plat. "Hipp. maj." 148; Quint. xii. 11, 21; Grote, "H. G." viii. 524.
9 Or, "I can personally vouch for."

for the purpose: "People say,"[1] he added, "that if a man wants to get his horse or his ox taught in the right way,[2] the world is full of instructors; but if he would learn himself, or have his son or his slave taught in the way of right, he cannot tell where to find such instruction."

Hippias, catching the words, exclaimed in a bantering tone: What! still repeating the same old talk,[3] Socrates, which I used to hear from you long ago?

Yes (answered Socrates), and what is still more strange, Hippias, it is not only the same old talk but about the same old subjects. Now you, I daresay, through versatility of knowledge,[4] never say the same thing twice over on the same subject?

To be sure (he answered), my endeavor is to say something new on all occasions.

What (he asked) about things which you know, as for instance in a case of spelling, if anyone asks you, "How many letters in Socrates, and what is their order?"[5] I suppose you try to run off one string of letters today and tomorrow another? or to a question of arithmetic, "Does twice five make ten?" your answer today will differ from that of yesterday?

Hipp. No; on these topics, Socrates, I do as you do and repeat myself. However, to revert to justice (and uprightness),[6] I flatter myself I can at present furnish you with some remarks which neither you nor anyone else will be able to controvert.

By Hera![7] (he exclaimed), what a blessing to have discovered![8] Now we shall have no more divisions of opinion on points of right and wrong; judges will vote unanimously; citizens will cease wrangling; there will be no more litigation, no more party faction, states will reconcile their differences, and wars are ended. For my part I do not know how I can tear myself away from you, until I have heard from your own lips all about the grand discovery you have made.

---

1 L. Dindorf, after Ruhnken and Valckenar, omits this sentence {phasi de tines... didaxonton}. See Kuhner ad loc. For the sentiment see Plat. "Apol." 20 A.
2 Cf. "Cyrop." II. ii. 26; VIII. iii. 38; also "Horsem." iii. 5; "Hunting," vii. 4.
3 This tale is repeated by Dio Chrys. "Or." III. i. 109. Cf. Plat. "Gorg." 490 E.
4 Or, "such is the breadth of your learning," {polumathes}. Cf. Plat. "Hipp. maj."
5 Cf. "Econ." viii. 14; Plat. "Alc." i. 113 A.
6 Or, "on the topic of the just I have something to say at present which," etc.
7 See above, I. v. 5.
8 Or, "what a panacea are you the inventor of"; lit. "By Hera, you have indeed discovered a mighty blessing, if juries are to cease recording their verdicts "aye" and "no"; if citizens are to cease their wranglings on points of justice, their litigations, and their party strifes; if states are to cease differing on matters of right and wrong and appealing to the arbitrament of war."

You shall hear all in good time (Hippias answered), but not until you make a plain statement of your own belief. What is justice? We have had enough of your ridiculing all the rest of the world, questioning and cross-examining first one and then the other, but never a bit will you render an account to anyone yourself or state a plain opinion upon a single topic.[1]

What, Hippias (Socrates retorted), have you not observed that I am in a chronic condition of proclaiming what I regard as just and upright?

Hipp. And pray what is this theory[2] of yours on the subject? Let us have it in words.

Soc. If I fail to proclaim it in words, at any rate I do so in deed and in fact. Or do you not think that a fact is worth more as evidence than a word?[3]

Worth far more, I should say (Hippias answered), for many a man with justice and right on his lips commits injustice and wrong, but no doer of right ever was a misdoer or could possibly be.

Soc. I ask then, have you ever heard or seen or otherwise perceived me bearing false witness or lodging malicious information, or stirring up strife among friends or political dissension in the city, or committing any other unjust and wrongful act?

No, I cannot say that I have (he answered).

Soc. And do you not regard it as right and just to abstain from wrong?[4]

Hipp. Now you are caught, Socrates, plainly trying to escape from a plain statement. When asked what you believe justice to be, you keep telling us not what the just man does, but what he does not do.

Why, I thought for my part (answered Socrates) that the refusal to do wrong and injustice was a sufficient warrent in itself of righteousness and justice, but if you do not agree, see if this pleases you better: I assert that what is "lawful" is "just and righteous."

Do you mean to assert (he asked) that lawful and just are synonymous terms?

Soc. I do.

I ask (Hippias added), for I do not perceive what you mean by lawful, nor what you mean by just.[5]

Soc. You understand what is meant by laws of a city or state?

Yes (he answered).

---

1 See Plat. "Gorg." 465 A.
2 {o logos}.
3 Or, "is of greater evidential value," "ubi res adsunt, quid opus est verbis?"
4 Or, "is not abstinence from wrongdoing synonymous with righteous behavior?"
5 Lit. "what sort of lawful or what sort of just is spoken of."

Soc. What do you take them to be?

Hipp. The several enactments drawn up by the citizens or members of a state in agreement as to what things should be done or left undone.

Then I presume (Socrates continued) that a member of a state who regulates his life in accordance with these enactments will be law-abiding, while the transgressor of the same will be lawless?

Certainly (he answered).

Soc. And I presume the law-loving citizen will do what is just and right, while the lawless man will do what is unjust and wrong?

Hipp. Certainly.

Soc. And I presume that he who does what is just is just, and he who does what is unjust is unjust?

Hipp. Of course.

Soc. It would appear, then, that the law-loving man is just, and the lawless unjust?

Then Hippias: Well, but laws, Socrates, how should anyone regard as a serious matter either the laws themselves, or obedience to them, which laws the very people who made them are perpetually rejecting and altering?

Which is also true of war (Socrates replied); cities are perpetually undertaking war and then making peace again.

Most true (he answered).

Soc. If so, what is the difference between depreciating obedience to law because laws will be repealed, and depreciating good discipline in war because peace will one day be made? But perhaps you object to enthusiasm displayed in defense of one's home and fatherland in war?

No, indeed I do not! I heartily approve of it (he answered).

Soc. Then have you laid to heart the lesson taught by Lycurgus to the Lacedaemonians,[1] and do you understand that if he succeeded in giving Sparta a distinction above other states, it was only by instilling into her, beyond all else, a spirit of obedience to the laws? And among magistrates and rulers in the different states, you would scarcely refuse the palm of superiority to those who best contribute to make their fellow citizens obedient to the laws? And you would admit that any particular state in which obedience to the laws is the paramount distinction of the citizens flourishes most in peace time, and in time of war is irresistible? But, indeed, of all the blessings which a state may enjoy, none stands higher than the blessing of unanimity. "Concord among citizens"—that is the constant theme of

---

1 Cf. "Pol. Lac." viii. See Newman, op. cit. i. 396.

exhortation emphasised by the councils of elders[1] and by the choice spirits of the community;[2] at all times and everywhere through the length and breadth of all Hellas it is an established law that the citizens be bound together by an oath of concord;[3] everywhere they do actually swear this oath; not of course as implying that citizens shall all vote for the same choruses, or give their plaudits to the same flute-players, or choose the same poets, or limit themselves to the same pleasures, but simply that they shall pay obedience to the laws, since in the end that state will prove most powerful and most prosperous in which the citizens abide by these; but without concord neither can a state be well administered nor a household well organized.

And if we turn to private life, what better protection can a man have than obedience to the laws? This shall be his safeguard against penalties, his guarantee of honors at the hands of the community; it shall be a clue to thread his way through the mazes of the law courts unbewildered, secure against defeat, assured of victory.[4] It is to him, the law-loving citizen, that men will turn in confidence when seeking a guardian of the most sacred deposits, be it of money or be it their sons or daughters. He, in the eyes of the state collectively, is trustworthy—he and no other; who alone may be depended on to render to all alike their dues—to parents and kinsmen and servants, to friends and fellow citizens and foreigners. This is he whom the enemy will soonest trust to arrange an armistice, or a truce, or a treaty of peace. They would like to become the allies of this man, and to fight on his side. This is he to whom the allies[5] of his country will most confidently entrust the command of their forces, or of a garrison, or their states themselves. This, again, is he who may be counted on to recompense kindness with gratitude, and who, therefore, is more sure of kindly treatment than another whose sense of gratitude is fuller.[6] The most desirable among friends, the enemy of all others to be avoided, clearly he is not the person whom a foreign state would choose to go to war with; encompassed by a host of friends and exempt from foes, his very character has a charm to compel friendship and alliance, and before him hatred and hostility melt away.

---

1 Lit. "the Gerousiai." {S} or {X S} uses the Spartan phraseology.
2 Lit. "the best men." {S} or {X S} speaks as an "aristocrat."
3 Cf. "Hell." II. iv. 43; Lys. xxv. 21 foll.; Schneid. cf. Lycurg. "u Leocr." 189.
4 Or, "ignorant of hostile, assured of favorable verdict."
5 Lit. "the Allies," e.g. of Sparta or of Athens, etc.
6 Lit. "From whom may the doer of a deed of kindness more confidently expect the recompense of gratitude than from your lover of the law? and whom would one select as the recipient of kindness rather than a man susceptible of gratitude?"

And now, Hippias, I have done my part; that is my proof and demonstration that the "lawful" and "law-observant" are synonymous with the "upright" and the "just"; do you, if you hold a contrary view, instruct us.[1]

Then Hippias: Nay, upon my soul, Socrates, I am not aware of holding any contrary opinion to what you have uttered on the theme of justice.[2]

Soc. But now, are you aware, Hippias, of certain unwritten laws?[3]

Yes (he answered), those held in every part of the world, and in the same sense.

Can you then assert (asked Socrates) of these unwritten laws that men made them?

Nay, how (he answered) should that be, for how could they all have come together from the ends of the Earth? and even if they had so done, men are not all of one speech?[4]

Soc. Whom then do you believe to have been the makers of these laws.

Hipp. For my part, I think that the gods must have made these laws for men, and I take it as proof that first and foremost it is a law and custom everywhere to worship and reverence the gods.

Soc. And, I presume, to honor parents is also customary everywhere?

Yes, that too (he answered).

Soc. And, I presume, also the prohibition of intermarriage between parents and children?

Hipp. No; at that point I stop, Socrates. That does not seem to me to be a law of God.

Now, why? (he asked).

Because I perceive it is not infrequently transgressed (he answered).[5]

Soc. Well, but there are a good many other things which people do contrary to law; only the penalty, I take it, affixed to the transgression of the divine code is certain; there is no escape for the offender after the manner in which a man may transgress the laws of man with impunity, slipping through the fingers of justice by stealth, or avoiding it by violence.

Hipp. And what is the inevitable penalty paid by those who, being related as parents and children, intermingle in marriage?

---

1 *For the style of this enconium (of the {nomimos}) cf. "Ages." i. 36; and for the "Socratic" reverence for law cf. Plat. "Crito."*

2 *Lit. "the just and upright," {tou dikaiou}.*

3 *See Soph. "Antig." "Oed. T." 865, and Prof. Jebb ad loc.; Dem. "de Cor." 317, 23; Aristot. "Rhet." I. xiii.*

4 *Or, "there would be difficulty of understanding each other, and a babel of tongues."*

5 *Or, "as I perceive, it is not of universal application, some transgress it."*

Soc. The greatest of all penalties; for what worse calamity can human beings suffer in the production of offspring than to misbeget?[1]

Hipp. But how or why should they breed them ill where nothing hinders them, being of a good stock themselves and producing from stock as good?

Soc. Because, forsooth, in order to produce good children, it is not simply necessary that the parents should be good and of a good stock, but that both should be equally in the prime and vigor of their bodies.[2] Do you suppose that the seed of those who are at their prime is like theirs who either have not yet reached their prime, or whose prime has passed?

Hipp. No, it is reasonable to expect that the seed will differ.

Soc. And for the better—which?

Hipp. Theirs clearly who are at their prime.

Soc. It would seem that the seed of those who are not yet in their prime or have passed their prime is not good?

Hipp. It seems most improbable it should be.

Soc. Then the right way to produce children is not that way?

Hipp. No, that is not the right way.

Soc. Then children who are so produced are produced not as they ought to be?

Hipp. So it appears to me.

What offspring then (he asked) will be ill produced, ill begotten, and ill born, if not these?

I subscribe to that opinion also (replied Hippias).

Soc. Well, it is a custom universally respected, is it not, to return good for good, and kindness with kindness?

Hipp. Yes, a custom, but one which again is apt to be transgressed.

Soc. Then he that so transgresses it pays penalty in finding himself isolated; bereft of friends who are good, and driven to seek after those who love him not. Or is it not so that he who does me kindness in my intercourse with him is my good friend, but if I requite not this kindness to my benefactor, I am hated by him for my ingratitude, and yet I must needs pursue after him and cling to him because of the great gain to me of his society?

Hipp. Yes, Socrates. In all these cases, I admit, there is an implication of divine authority;[3] that a law should in itself be loaded with the penalty of its transgression does suggest to my mind a higher than human type of legislator.

---

1 Or, "in the propagation of the species than to produce misbegotten children."
2 Cf. Plat. "Laws," viii. 839 A; Herbst, etc., cf. Grotius, "de Jure," ii. 5, xii. 4.
3 Lit. "Yes, upon my word, Socrates, all these cases look very like (would seem to point to) the gods."

Soc. And in your opinion, Hippias, is the legislation of the gods just and righteous, or the reverse of what is just and righteous?

Hipp. Not the reverse of what is just and righteous, Socrates, God forbid! for scarcely could any other legislate aright, of not God himself.

Soc. It would seem then, Hippias, the gods themselves are well pleased that "the lawful" and "the just" should be synonymous?[1]

By such language and by such conduct, through example and precept alike, he helped to make those who approached him more upright and more just.

V

And now I propose to show in what way he made those who were with him more vigorous in action.[2] In the first place, as befitted one whose creed was that a basis of self-command is indispensable to any noble performance, he manifested himself to his companions as one who had pre-eminently disciplined himself;[3] and in the next place by conversation and discussion he encouraged them to a like self-restraint beyond all others.[4] Thus it was that he continued ever mindful himself, and was continually reminding all whom he encountered, of matters conducive to virtue; as the following discussion with Euthydemus, which has come to my knowledge,[5] will serve to illustrate—the topic of the discussion being self-command.

Tell me, Euthydemus (he began), do you believe freedom to be a noble and magnificent acquisition, whether for a man or for a state?

I cannot conceive a nobler or more magnificent (he answered).

Soc. Then do you believe him to be a free man who is ruled by the pleasures of the body, and thereby cannot perform what is best?

Certainly not (he answered).

Soc. No! for possibly to perform what is best appears to you to savour of freedom? And, again, to have someone over you who will prevent you doing the like seems a loss of freedom?

Most decidedly (he answered).

Soc. It would seem you are decidedly of opinion that the incontinent are the reverse of free?[6]

---

1 Or, "it is well pleasing also to the gods that what is lawful is just and what is just is lawful."
2 Lit. "more practical," i.e. more energetic and effective.
3 "If anyone might claim to be a prince of ascetics, it was Socrates; such was the ineffaceable impression left on the minds of his associates."
4 Or, "he stimulated in these same companions a spirit of self-restraint beyond all else."
5 Or, "which I can vouch for."
6 Or, "incontinency is illiberal."

Euth. Upon my word, I much suspect so.

Soc. And does it appear to you that the incontinent man is merely hindered from doing what is noblest, or that further he is impelled to do what is most shameful?

Euth. I think he is as much driven to the one as he is hindered from the other.

Soc. And what sort of lords and masters are those, think you, who at once put a stop to what is best and enforce what is worst?

Euth. Goodness knows, they must be the very worst of masters.

Soc. And what sort of slavery do you take to be the worst?

I should say (he answered) slavery to the worst masters.

It would seem then (pursued Socrates) that the incontinent man is bound over to the worst sort of slavery, would it not?

So it appears to be (the other answered).

Soc. And does it not appear to you that this same beldame incontinence shuts out wisdom, which is the best of all things,[1] from mankind, and plunges them into the opposite? Does it not appear to you that she hinders men from attending to things which will be of use and benefit, and from learning to understand them; that she does so by dragging them away to things which are pleasant; and often though they are well aware of the good and of the evil, she amazes and confounds[2] their wits and makes them choose the worse in place of the better?

Yes, so it comes to pass (he answered).

Soc. And[3] soundness of soul, the spirit of temperate modesty? Who has less claim to this than the incontinent man? The works of the temperate spirit and the works of incontinency are, I take it, diametrically opposed?

That too, I admit (he answered).

Soc. If this then be so concerning these virtues,[4] what with regard to carefulness and devotion to all that ought to occupy us? Can anything more seriously militate against these than this same incontinence?

Nothing that I can think of (he replied).

Soc. And can worse befall a man, think you? Can he be subjected to a more baleful influence than that which induces him to choose what is hurtful in place of what is helpful; which cajoles him to devote himself to

---

1 *"Wisdom, the greatest good which men can possess."*

2 Schneid. cf. Plat. *"Protag."* 355 A; and *"Symp."* iv. 23.

3 *"And if this be so concerning wisdom, {sophia}, what of {sophrasune}, soundness of soul—sobriety?"*

4 Or add, *"If this be so concerning not wisdom only, but concerning temperance and soundness of soul, what,"* etc.

the evil and to neglect the good; which forces him, will he nill he, to do what every man in his sober senses would shrink from and avoid?

I can imagine nothing worse (he replied).

Soc. Self-control, it is reasonable to suppose, will be the cause of opposite effects upon mankind to those of its own opposite, the want of self-control?

Euth. It is to be supposed so.

Soc. And this, which is the source of opposite effects to the very worst, will be the very best of things?

Euth. That is the natural inference.

Soc. It looks, does it not, Euthydemus, as if self-control were the best thing a man could have?

It does indeed, Socrates (he answered).

Soc. But now, Euthydemus, has it ever occurred to you to note one fact? What fact? (he asked).

Soc. That, after all, incontinency is powerless to bring us to that realm of sweetness which some look upon[1] as her peculiar province; it is not incontinency but self-control alone which has the passport to highest pleasures.

In what way? (he asked). How so?

Why, this way (Socrates answered): since incontinency will not suffer us to resist hunger and thirst, or to hold out against sexual appetite, or want of sleep (which abstinences are the only channels to true pleasure in eating and drinking, to the joys of love, to sweet repose and blissful slumber won by those who will patiently abide and endure till each particular happiness is at the flood)[2] —it comes to this: by incontinency we are cut off from the full fruition of the more obvious and constantly recurring pleasures.[3] To self-control, which alone enables us to endure the pains aforesaid, alone belongs the power to give us any pleasure worth remembering in these common cases.

You speak the words of truth[4] (he answered).

Soc. Furthermore,[5] if there be any joy in learning aught "beautiful and good," or in patient application to such rules as may enable a man to manage

---

1 Or, "which we are apt to think of as."
2 Or, "at its season." Lit. "is as sweet as possible."
3 Or, "from tasting to any extent worth speaking of the most necessary and all-pervading sources of happiness."
4 Lit. "What you say is absolutely and entirely true" (the "vraie verite" of the matter).
5 Or, "But indeed, if there be joy in the pursuit of any noble study or of such accomplishments as shall enable," etc.

his body aright, or to administer his household well, or to prove himself useful to his friends and to the state, or to dominate his enemies—which things are the sources not only of advantage but of deepest satisfaction[1]— to the continent and self-controlled it is given to reap the fruits of them in their performance. It is the incontinent who have neither part nor lot in any one of them. Since we must be right in asserting that he is least concerned with such things who has least ability to do them, being tied down to take an interest in the pleasure which is nearest to hand.

Euthydemus replied: Socrates, you would say, it seems to me, that a man who is mastered by the pleasures of the body has no concern at all with virtue.

And what is the distinction, Euthydemus (he asked), between a man devoid of self-control and the dullest of brute beasts? A man who foregoes all height of aim, who gives up searching for the best and strives only to gratify his sense of pleasure,[2] is he better than the silliest of cattle?[3] But to the self-controlled alone is it given to discover the hid treasures. These, by word and by deed, they will pick out and make selection of them according to their kinds, choosing deliberately the good and holding aloof from the evil.[4] Thus (he added) it is that a man reaches the zenith, as it were, of goodness and happiness, thus it is that he becomes most capable of reasoning and discussion.[5] The very name discussion ({dialegesthai}) is got from people coming together and deliberating in common by picking out and selecting things ({dialegein}) according to their kinds.[6] A man then is bound to prepare himself as much as possible for this business, and to pursue it beyond all else with earnest resolution; for this is the right road to excellence, this will make a man fittest to lead his fellows and be a master in debate.[7]

VI

At this point I will endeavor to explain in what way Socrates fostered this greater "dialectic" capacity among his intimates.[8] He held firmly to

---

1 Or, "of the highest pleasures."
2 Or, "and seeks by hook and by crook to do what is pleasantest."
3 I.e. he becomes an animal "feeding a blind life within the brain."
4 Or, "selecting the ore and repudiating the dross." Kuhner cf. Plat. "Laws," v. 735 B.
5 Or, "draws nearer to happiness and perfection, and is most capable of truth-disclosing conversation." Cf. Plat. "Apol." 41: "What would not a man give, O judges, to be able to examine the leaders of the great Trojan expedition, or Odysseus, or Sisyphus, or numberless others, men and women too! What infinite delight would there be in conversing with them and asking them questions!" (Jowett).
6 For {dialegein kata gene} = {dialegesthai}, cf. Grote, "H. G." viii. 590.
7 Cf. Plat. "Rep." 534 D; "Phaedr." 252 E; "Crat." 390 C; "Statesm." 286 D foll.
8 Lit. "essayed to make those who were with him more potent in dialectic."

the opinion that if a man knew what each reality was, he would be able to explain this knowledge to others; but, failing the possession of that knowledge, it did not surprise him that men should stumble themselves and cause others to stumble also.[1] It was for this reason that he never ceased inquiring with those who were with him into the true nature of things that are.[2] It would be a long business certainly to go through in detail all the definitions at which he arrived; I will therefore content myself with such examples as will serve to show his method of procedure. As a first instance I will take the question of piety. The mode of investigation may be fairly represented as follows.

Tell me (said he), Euthydemus, what sort of thing you take piety to be?

Something most fair and excellent, no doubt (the other answered).[3]

Soc. And can you tell me what sort of person the pious man is?[4]

I should say (he answered) he is a man who honors the gods.

Soc. And is it allowable to honor the gods in any mode or fashion one likes?

Euth. No; there are laws in accordance with which one must do that.

Soc. Then he who knows these laws will know how he must honor the gods?

I think so (he answered).

Soc. And he who knows how he must honor the gods conceives that he ought not to do so except in the manner which accords with his knowledge?[5] Is it not so?

Euth. That is so.[6]

Soc. And does any man honor the gods otherwise than he thinks he ought?[7]

I think not (he answered).

Soc. It comes to this then: he who knows what the law requires in reference to the gods will honor the gods in the lawful way?[8]

Euth. Certainly.

---

1 Or, "Socrates believed that anyone who knew the nature of anything would be able to let others into his secret; but, failing that knowledge, he thought the best of men would be but blind leaders of the blind, stumbling themselves and causing others to stumble also."
2 Or add, "'What is this among things? and what is its definition?' —such was the ever-recurrent question for which he sought an answer."
3 Or, "A supreme excellence, no doubt."
4 Or, "can you give me a definition of the pious man?"; "tell me who and what the pious man is."
5 I.e. "his practice must square with his knowledge and be the outward expression of his belief?"
6 "That is so; you rightly describe his frame of mind and persuasion."
7 "As he should and must." See K. Joel, op. cit. p. 322 foll.
8 Or, "he who knows what is lawful with regard to Heaven pays honor to Heaven lawfully."

Soc. But now, he who honors lawfully honors as he ought?[1]

Euth. I see no alternative.

Soc. And he who honors as he ought is a pious man?

Euth. Certainly.

Soc. It would appear that he who knows what the law requires with respect to the gods will correctly be defined as a pious man, and that is our definition?

So it appears to me, at any rate (he replied).[2]

Soc. But now, with regard to human beings; is it allowable to deal with men in any way one pleases?[3]

Euth. No; with regard to men also, he will be a law-observing man[4] who knows what things are lawful as concerning men, in accordance with which our dealings with one another must be conducted.[5]

Soc. Then those who deal with one another in this way, deal with each other as they ought?[6]

Obviously (he answered).

Soc. And they who deal with one another as they ought, deal well and nobly—is it not so?

Certainly (he answered).

Soc. And they who deal well and nobly by mankind are well-doers in respect of human affairs?

That would seem to follow (he replied).

Soc. I presume that those who obey the laws do what is just and right?

Without a doubt, (he answered).

Soc. And by things right and just you know what sort of things are meant?

What the laws ordain (he answered).

Soc. It would seem to follow that they who do what the laws ordain both do what is right and just and what they ought?[7]

---

1 *"As he should and must."*

2 *"I accept it at any rate as mine."* N.B.—*in reference to this definition of Piety, the question is never raised {poion ti esti nomos}; nor yet {poioi tines eisin oi theoi}; but clearly there is a growth in {ta nomima}. Cf. the conversation recorded in St. John iv. 7 foll., and the words (verse 23) {pneuma o Theos kai tous proskunountas auton en pneumati kai aletheia dei proskunein}, which the philosopher Socrates would perhaps readily have assented to.*

3 *Or, "may a man deal with his fellow men arbitrarily according to his fancy?" See above, II. vii. 8.*

4 *Or, "he is a man full of the law (lawful) and law-abiding who knows," etc.*

5 *Reading {kath" a dei pros allelous khresthai}, subaud. {allelois}, or if vulg. {kath" a dei pos allelois khresthai}, translate "must be specifically conducted."*

6 *"As they should and must."*

7 *"What they should and must."*

Euth. I see no alternative.

Soc. But then, he who does what is just and right is upright and just?[1]

I should say so myself (he answered).

Soc. And should you say that anyone obeys the laws without knowing what the laws ordain?

I should not (he answered).

Soc. And do you suppose that anyone who knows what things he ought to do supposes that he ought not to do them?[2]

No, I suppose not (he answered).

Soc. And do you know of anybody doing other than what he feels bound to do?[3]

No, I do not (he answered).

Soc. It would seem that he who knows what things are lawful[4] as concerning men does the things that are just and right?

Without a doubt (he answered).

Soc. But then, he who does what is just and right is upright and just?[5]

Who else, if not? (he replied).

Soc. It would seem, then, we shall have got to a right definition if we name as just and upright those who know the things which are lawful as concerning men?

That is my opinion (he answered).

Soc. And what shall we say that wisdom is? Tell me, does it seem to you that the wise are wise in what they know,[6] or are there any who are wise in what they know not?

---

1 This proposition, as Kuhner argues (ad loc.), is important as being the middle term of the double syllogism (A and B)—

A. Those who do what the law demands concerning men do what is just and right.

Those who do what is just and right are righteous and just.

Ergo—Those who do what the law demands concerning men are righteous and just.

B. Those who know what is just and right ought (and are bound, cf. above, III. ix. 4) to do also what is just and right.

Those who do what is just and right are righteous and just.

Ergo—Righteous and Just ({dikaioi}) may be defined as "Those who know what the law demands (aliter things right and just) concerning men."

2 Or, "and no one who knows what he must and should do imagines that he must and should not do it?"

3 Or, "and nobody that you know of does the contrary of what he thinks he should do?"

4 Or, "of lawful obligation."

5 N.B.—In reference to this definition of justice, see K. Joel, op. cit. p. 323 foll., "Das ist eine Karrikatur des Sokratischen Dialogs."

6 Or, "in that of which they have the knowledge ({episteme})."

Euth. Clearly they are wise in what they know;[1] for how could a man have wisdom in that which he does not know?

Soc. In fact, then, the wise are wise in knowledge?

Euth. Why, in what else should a man be wise save only in knowledge?

Soc. And is wisdom anything else than that by which a man is wise, think you?

Euth. No; that, and that only, I think.

Soc. It would seem to follow that knowledge and wisdom are the same?

Euth. So it appears to me.

Soc. May I ask, does it seem to you possible for a man to know all the things that are?

Euth. No, indeed! not the hundredth part of them, I should say.

Soc. Then it would seem that it is impossible for a man to be all-wise?

Quite impossible (he answered).

Soc. It would seem the wisdom of each is limited to his knowledge; each is wise only in what he knows?

Euth. That is my opinion.[2]

Soc. Well! come now, Euthydemus, as concerning the good: ought we to search for the good in this way?

What way? (he asked).

Soc. Does it seem to you that the same thing is equally advantageous to all?

No, I should say not (he answered).

Soc. You would say that a thing which is beneficial to one is sometimes hurtful to another?

Decidedly (he replied).

Soc. And is there anything else good except that which is beneficial, should you say?[3]

Nothing else (he answered).

Soc. It would seem to follow that the beneficial is good relatively to him to whom it is beneficial?

That is how it appears to me (he answered).

Soc. And the beautiful: can we speak of a thing as beautiful in any other

---

1 Or, "*their wisdom is confined to that of which they have the* {*episteme*}. *How could a man be wise in what he lacks the knowledge of?*"

2 Cf. Plat. "Theaet." 145 D. N.B.—For this definition of wisdom see K. Joel, ib. p. 324 foll.

3 Or reading (1) {allo d' an ti phaies e agathon einai to ophelimon}; or else (2) {allo d' an ti phaies agathon einai to ophelimon}; (in which case {alloti} = {allo ti e};) translate (1) "and what is beneficial is good (or a good), should you not say?" lit. "could you say that the beneficial is anything else than good (or a good)?" or else (2) "and what is beneficial is good (or a good)? or is it anything else?"

way than relatively? or can you name any beautiful thing, body, vessel, or whatever it be, which you know of as universally beautiful?[1]

Euth. I confess I do not know of any such myself.[2]

Soc. I presume to turn a thing to its proper use is to apply it beautifully?

Euth. Undoubtedly it is a beautiful appliance.[3]

Soc. And is this, that, and the other thing beautiful for aught else except that to which it may be beautifully applied?

Euth. No single thing else.

Soc. It would seem that the useful is beautiful relatively to that for which it is of use?

So it appears to me (he answered).

Soc. And what of courage,[4] Euthydemus? I presume you rank courage among things beautiful? It is a noble quality?[5]

Nay, one of the most noble (he answered).

Soc. It seems that you regard courage as useful to no mean end?

Euth. Nay, rather the greatest of all ends, God knows.

Soc. Possibly in face of terrors and dangers you would consider it an advantage to be ignorant of them?

Certainly not (he answered).

Soc. It seems that those who have no fear in face of dangers, simply because they do not know what they are, are not courageous?

Most true (he answered); or, by the same showing, a large proportion of madmen and cowards would be courageous.

Soc. Well, and what of those who are in dread of things which are not dreadful, are they—

Euth. Courageous, Socrates?—still less so than the former, goodness knows.

Soc. Possibly, then, you would deem those who are good in the face of

---

1 I.e. "beautiful in all relations into which it enters." Reading {to de kalon ekhoimen an pos allos eipein e estin onomazein kalon e soma e skeuos e all" otioun, o oistha pros tanta kalon on; Ma Di," ouk egog," ephe}. For other emendations of the vulg., and the many interpretations which have been given to the passage, see R. Kuhner ad loc.

2 Or, adopting the reading {ekhois an} in place of {ekhoimen an} above, translate "I certainly cannot, I confess."

3 Or, "I presume it is well and good and beautiful to use this, that, and the other thing for the purpose for which the particular thing is useful?"—"That nobody can deny (he answered)." It is impossible to convey simply the verbal play and the quasi-argumentative force of the Greek {kalos ekhei pros ti tini khresthai}. See K. Joel, p. 426.

4 Or, perhaps better, "fortitude." See H. Sidgwick, "Hist. of Ethics," p. 43.

5 It is one of {ta kala}. See K. Joel, ib. p. 325, and in reference to the definitions of the Good and of the Beautiful, ib. p. 425 foll.

terrors and dangers to be courageous, and those who are bad in the face of the same to be cowards?

Certainly I should (he answered).

Soc. And can you suppose any other people to be good in respect of such things except those who are able to cope with them and turn them to noble account?[1]

No; these and these alone (he answered).

Soc. And those people who are of a kind to cope but badly with the same occurrences, it would seem, are bad?

Who else, if not they? (he asked).

Soc. May it be that both one and the other class do use these circumstances as they think they must and should?[2]

Why, how else should they deal with them? (he asked).

Soc. Can it be said that those who are unable to cope well with them or to turn them to noble account know how they must and should deal with them?[3]

I presume not (he answered).

Soc. It would seem to follow that those who have the knowledge how to behave are also those who have the power?[4]

Yes; these, and these alone (he said).

Soc. Well, but now, what of those who have made no egregious blunder (in the matter); can it be they cope ill with the things and circumstances we are discussing?

I think not (he answered).

Soc. It would seem, conversely, that they who cope ill have made some egregious blunder?

Euth. Probably; indeed, it would appear to follow.

Soc. It would seem, then, that those who know[5] how to cope with terrors and dangers well and nobly are courageous, and those who fail utterly of this are cowards?

So I judge them to be (he answered).[6]

---

1 {kalos khresthai}, lit. "make a beautiful use of them."
2 Or, "feel bound and constrained to do."
3 Or, "Can it be said that those who are unable to cope nobly with their perilous surroundings know how they ought to deal with them?"
4 "He who kens can."
5 "Who have the {episteme}."
6 N.B.—For this definition of courage see Plat. "Laches," 195 A and passim; K. Joel, op. cit. p. 325 foll.

A kingdom and a tyranny[1] were, he opined, both of them forms of government, but forms which differed from one another, in his belief; a kingdom was a government over willing men in accordance with civil law, whereas a tyranny implied the government over unwilling subjects not according to law, but so as to suit the whims and wishes of the ruler.

There were, moreover, three forms of citizenship or polity; in the case where the magistrates were appointed from those who discharged the obligations prescribed by law, he held the polity to be an aristocracy (or rule of the best);[2] where the title to office depended on rateable property, it was a plutocracy (or rule of wealth); and lastly, where all the citizens without distinction held the reins of office, that was a democracy (or rule of the people).

Let me explain his method of reply where the disputant had no clear statement to make, but without attempt at proof chose to contend that such or such a person named by himself was wiser, or more of a statesman, or more courageous, and so forth, than some other person.[3] Socrates had a way of bringing the whole discussion back to the underlying proposition,[4] as thus:

Soc. You state that so and so, whom you admire, is a better citizen that this other whom I admire?

The Disputant. Yes; I repeat the assertion.

Soc. But would it not have been better to inquire first what is the work or function of a good citizen?

The Disputant. Let us do so.

Soc. To begin, then, with the matter of expenditure: his superiority will be shown by his increasing the resources and lightening the expenditure of the state?[5]

Certainly (the disputant would answer).

Soc. And in the event of war, by rendering his state superior to her antagonists?

The Disputant. Clearly.

---

1 Or, "despotism."
2 Or, "in which the due discharge of lawful (law-appointed) obligations gave the title to magisterial office and government, this form of polity he held to be an aristocracy (or rule of the best)." See Newman, op. cit. i. 212, 235.
3 Or, "if anyone encountered him in argument about any topic or person without any clear statement, but a mere ipse dixit, devoid of demonstration, that so and so," etc.
4 Or, "question at bottom." Cf. Plat. "Laws," 949 B.
5 Or, "In the management of moneys, then, his strength will consist in his rendering the state better provided with ways and means?"

Soc. Or on an embassy as a diplomatist, I presume, by securing friends in place of enemies?

That I should imagine (replies the disputant).

Soc. Well, and in parliamentary debate, by putting a stop to party strife and fostering civic concord?

The Disputant. That is my opinion.

By this method of bringing back the argument to its true starting-point, even the disputant himself would be affected and the truth become manifest to his mind.

His own—that is, the Socratic—method of conducting a rational discussion[1] was to proceed step by step from one point of general agreement to another: "Herein lay the real security of reasoning,"[2] he would say; and for this reason he was more successful in winning the common assent of his hearers than anyone I ever knew. He had a saying that Homer had conferred on Odyesseus the title of a safe, unerring orator,[3] because he had the gift to lead the discussion from one commonly accepted opinion to another.

VII

The frankness and simplicity with which Socrates endeavoured to declare his own opinions, in dealing with those who conversed with him,[4] is, I think, conclusively proved by the above instances; at the same time, as I hope now to show, he was no less eager to cultivate a spirit of independence in others, which would enable them to stand alone in all transactions suited to their powers.

Of all the men I have ever known, he was most anxious to ascertain in what any of those about him was really versed; and within the range of his own knowledge he showed the greatest zeal in teaching everything which it befits the true gentleman[5] to know; or where he was deficient in knowledge himself,[6] he would introduce his friends to those who knew.[7] He did not fail to teach them also up to what point it was proper for an educated man to acquire empiric knowledge of any particular matter.[8]

---

1 Of, "of threading the mazes of an argument."
2 Reading {tauton asphaleian}; aliter. {tauten ten asphaleian} = "that this security was part and parcel of reasoning."
3 "Od." viii. 171, {o d" asphaleos agoreuei}, "and his speech runs surely on its way" (Butcher and Lang), where Odysseus is describing himself. Cf. Dion. Hal. "de Arte Rhet." xi. 8.
4 Or, "who frequented his society, is, I hope, clear from what has been said."
5 Lit. "a beautiful and good man."
6 Or, "where he lacked acquaintance with the matter himself." See, for an instance, "Econ." iii. 14.
7 "To those who had the special knowledge"; "a connoisseur in the matter."
8 Or, "of any particular branch of learning"; "in each department of things."

To take geometry as an instance: Every one (he would say) ought to be taught geometry so far, at any rate, as to be able, if necessary, to take over or part with a piece of land, or to divide it up or assign a portion of it for cultivation,[1] and in every case by geometric rule.[2] That amount of geometry was so simple indeed, and easy to learn, that it only needed ordinary application of the mind to the method of mensuration, and the student could at once ascertain the size of the piece of land, and, with the satisfaction of knowing its measurement, depart in peace. But he was unable to approve of the pursuit of geometry up to the point at which it became a study of unintelligible diagrams.[3] What the use of these might be, he failed, he said, to see; and yet he was not unversed in these recondite matters himself.[4] These things, he would say, were enough to wear out a man's life, and to hinder him from many other more useful studies.[5]

Again, a certain practical knowledge of astronomy, a certain skill in the study of the stars, he strongly insisted on. Every one should know enough of the science to be able to discover the hour of the night or the season of the month or year, for the purposes of travel by land or sea—the march, the voyage, and the regulations of the watch;[6] and in general, with regard to all matters connected with the night season, or with the month, or the year,[7] it was well to have such reliable data to go upon as would serve to distinguish the various times and seasons. But these, again, were pieces of knowledge easily learned from night sportsmen,[8] pilots of vessels, and many others who make it their business to know such things. As to pushing the study of astronomy so far as to include a knowledge of the movements of bodies outside our own orbit, whether planets or stars of eccentric movement,[9] or wearing oneself out endeavouring to discover their distances from the Earth, their periods, and their causes,[10] all this he strongly discountenanced;

---

1 {e ergon apodeixasthai}, or "and to explain the process." Cf. Plat. "Rep." vii. 528 D. See R. Kuhner ad loc. for other interpretations of the phrase. Cf. Max. Tyr. xxxvii. 7.
2 Or, "by correct measurement"; lit. "by measurement of the Earth."
3 Cf. Aristot. "Pol." v. (viii.) 2; Cic. "Acad. Post." I. iv. 15. For the attitude compare the attitude of a philosopher in other respects most unlike Socrates—August Comte, e.g. as to the futility of sidereal astronomy, "Pos. Pol." i. 412 (Bridges).
4 Cf. Isocr. "On the Antidosis," 258-269, as to the true place of "Eristic" in education. See above, IV. ii. 10.
5 Cf. A. Comte as to "perte intellectuelle" in the pursuit of barren studies.
6 Schneid. cf. Plat. "Rep." vii. 527 D.
7 "Occurrences connected with the night, the month, or year." e.g. the festival of the Karneia, the {tekmerion} (point de repere) of which is the full moon of August. Cf. Eur. "Alc." 449.
8 See Plat. "Soph." 220 D; above, III. xi. 8; "Cyrop." I. vi. 40; "Hunting," xii. 6; Hippocr. "Aer." 28.
9 See Lewis, "Astron. of the Ancients"; cf. Diog. Laert. vii. 1. 144.
10 Or, "the causes of these."

for he saw (he said) no advantage in these any more than in the former studies. And yet he was not unversed[1] in the subtleties of astronomy any more than in those of geometry; only these, again, he insisted, were sufficient to wear out a man's lifetime, and to keep him away from many more useful pursuits.

And to speak generally, in regard of things celestial he set his face against attempts to excogitate the machinery by which the divine power formed its several operations.[2] Not only were these matters beyond man's faculties to discover, as he believed, but the attempt to search out what the gods had not chosen to reveal could hardly (he supposed) be well pleasing in their sight. Indeed, the man who tortured his brains about such subjects stood a fair chance of losing his wits entirely, just as Anaxagoras,[3] the headiest speculator of them all, in his attempt to explain the divine mechanism, had somewhat lost his head. Anaxagoras took on himself to assert that sun and fire are identical,[4] ignoring the fact that human beings can easily look at fire, but to gaze steadily into the face of the sun is given to no man; or that under the influence of his rays the color of the skin changes, but under the rays of fire not.[5] He forgot that no plant or vegetation springs from Earth's bosom with healthy growth without the help of sunlight, whilst the influence of fire is to parch up everything, and to destroy life; and when he came to speak of the sun as being a "red-hot stone" he ignored another fact, that a stone in fire neither lights up nor lasts, whereas the sun-god abides forever with intensist brilliancy undimmed.

Socrates inculcated the study of reasoning processes,[6] but in these, equally with the rest, he bade the student beware of vain and idle overoccupation. Up to the limit set by utility, he was ready to join in any investigation, and to follow out an argument with those who were with him; but there he stopped. He particularly urged those who were with him to pay the utmost attention to health. They would learn all it was possible to learn from adepts, and not only so, but each one individually should take

---

1 {oude touton ge anekoos en}. He had "heard," it is said, Archelaus, a pupil of Anaxagoras. Cf. Cic. "Tusc." V. iv. 10.

2 Or, "he tried to divert one from becoming overly-wise in heavenly matters and the "mecanique celeste" of the Godhead in His several operations." See above, I. i. 11. See Grote, "Plato," i. 438.

3 Of Clazomenae. Cf. Plat. "Apol." 14; Diog. Laert. II. vi; Cic. "Tusc." V. iv. 10; Cobet, "Prosop. Xen." s.n.; Grote, "H. G." i. 501.

4 Or, "that the sun was simply a fire, forgetting so simple a fact as that."

5 Or, "the complexion darkens, whereas fire has no such effect."

6 {logismous} = (1) "arithmetic," (2) "calculation," (3) "syllogistic reasoning." See L. Dind. "Index. Gr." s.v., and Kuhner ad loc.; cf. Plat. "Gorg." 451 C. It is important to decide which form of "logism" is meant here.

pains to discover, by a lifelong observation of his own case, what particular regimen, what meat or drink, or what kind of work, best suited him; these he should turn to account with a view to leading the healthiest possible life. It would be no easy matter for anyone who would follow this advice, and study his own idiosyncrasy, to find a doctor to improve either on the diagnosis or the treatment requisite.[1]

Where anyone came seeking for help which no human wisdom could supply, he would counsel him to give heed to "divination." He who has the secret of the means whereby the gods give signs to men touching their affairs can never surely find himself bereft of heavenly guidance.

VIII

Now if anyone should be disposed to set the statement of Socrates touching the divinity[2] which warned him what he ought to do or not to do, against the fact that he was sentenced to death by the board of judges, and argue that thereby Socrates stood convicted of lying and delusion in respect of this "divinity" of his, I would have him to note in the first place that, at the date of his trial, Socrates was already so far advanced in years that had he not died then his life would have reached its natural term soon afterward; and secondly, as matters went, he escaped life's bitterest load[3] in escaping those years which bring a diminution of intellectual force to all—instead of which he was called upon to exhibit the full robustness of his soul and acquire glory in addition,[4] partly by the style of his defense—felicitous alike in its truthfulness, its freedom, and its rectitude[5]—and partly by the manner in which he bore the sentence of condemnation with infinite gentleness and manliness. Since no one within the memory of man, it is admitted, ever bowed his head to death more nobly. After the sentence he must needs live for thirty days, since it was the month of the "Delia,"[6] and the law does not suffer any man to die by the hand of the public executioner until the sacred embassy return from Delos. During the whole of that period (as his acquaintances without exception can testify) his life proceeded as usual. There was nothing to mark the difference between

---

1 Or, "to find a doctor better able than himself to "diagnose" and prescribe a treatment congenial to health." Cf. Tac. "Ann." vi. 46; Plut. "de San." 136 E, ap. Schneid. ad loc.
2 Or, "the words of Socrates with regard to a divine something which warned him," etc.
3 The phraseology is poetical.
4 Or, "in a manner which redounded to his glory."
5 Or, "marvellous alike for the sincerity of its language, the free unbroken spirit of its delivery, and the absolute rectitude of the speaker."
6 I.e. the lesser "Delian" solemnities, an annual festival instituted, it was said, by Theseus. See Plut. "Theseus," 23 (Clough, i. 19); and for the whole matter see Plat. "Phaed." 58 foll.

now and formerly in the even tenour of its courage; and it was a life which at all times had been a marvel of cheerfulness and calm content.[1]

(Let us pause and ask how could man die more nobly and more beautifully than in the way described? or put it thus: dying so, then was his death most noble and most beautiful; and being the most beautiful, then was it also the most fortunate and heaven-blessed; and being most blessed of heaven, then was it also most precious in the sight of God.)[2]

And now I will mention further certain things which I have heard from Hermogenes, the son of Hipponicus,[3] concerning him. He said that even after Meletus[4] had drawn up the indictment, he himself used to hear Socrates conversing and discussing everything rather than the suit impending, and had ventured to suggest that he ought to be considering the line of his defense, to which, in the first instance, the master answered: "Do I not seem to you to have been practicing that my whole life long?" And upon his asking "How?" added in explanation that he had passed his days in nothing else save in distinguishing between what is just and what is unjust (right and wrong), and in doing what is right and abstaining from what is wrong; "which conduct" (he added) "I hold to be the finest possible practice for my defense"; and when he (Hermogenes), returning to the point again, pleaded with Socrates: "Do you not see, Socrates, how commonly it happens that an Athenian jury, under the influence of argument, condemns innocent people to death and acquits real criminals?"—Socrates replied, "I assure you, Hermogenes, that each time I have essayed to give my thoughts to the defense which I am to make before the court, the divinity[5] has opposed me." And when he (Hermogenes) exclaimed, "How strange!"—"Do you find it strange" (he continued), "that to the Godhead it should appear better for me to close my life at once? Do you not know that up to the present moment there is no man whom I can admit to have spent a better or happier life than mine. Since theirs I regard as the best of lives who study best to become as good as may be, and theirs the happiest who have the liveliest sense of growth in goodness; and such, hitherto, is the happy fortune which I perceive to have fallen to my lot. To such conclusion I have come, not only in accidental intercourse with others, but by a strict comparison drawn between myself and others, and in this faith I continue

---

1 Cf. Arist. "Frogs," 82; of Sophocles, {o d' eukolos men enthad', eukolos d' ekei}.
2 This is bracketed as spurious by Sauppe and other commentators. But see "Cyrop." VIII. ii. 7, 8, for similar ineptitude of style. R. Kuhner defends the passage as genuine.
3 See above, II. x. 3; "Symp." i. 3; iii. 14; iv. 47 foll.; vi. 2; "Apol." 2; Plat. "Crat." 384.
4 See above, I. i. 1.
5 {to daimonion}—"the divine (voice)."

to this day; and not I only, but my friends continue in a like persuasion with regard to me, not for the lame reason that they are my friends and love me (or else would others have been in like case as regards their friends), but because they are persuaded that by being with me they will attain to their full height of goodness. But, if I am destined to prolong my days, maybe I shall be enforced to pay in full the penalties of old age—to see and hear less keenly, to fail in intellectual force, and to leave school, as it were, more of a dunce than when I came, less learned and more forgetful—in a word, I shall fall from my high estate, and daily grow worse in that wherein aforetime I excelled. But indeed, were it possible to remain unconscious of the change, the life left would scarcely be worth living; but given that there is a consciousness of the change, then must the existence left to live be found by comparison insipid, joyless, a death in life, devoid of life's charm. But indeed, if it is reserved for me to die unjustly, then on those who unjustly slay me lies the shame (since, given injustice is base, how can any unjust action whatsoever fail of baseness?)[1] But for me what disgrace is it that others should fail of a just decision and right acts concerning me?... I see before me a long line of predecessors on this road, and I mark the reputation also among posterity which they have left.[2] I note how it varies according as they did or suffered wrong, and for myself I know that I too, although I die today, shall obtain from mankind a consideration far different from that which will be accorded to those who put me to death. I know that undying witness will be borne me to this effect, that I never at any time did wrong to any man, or made him a worse man, but ever tried to make those better who were with me."

Such are the words which he spoke in conversation with Hermogenes and the rest. But among those who knew Socrates and recognized what manner of man he was, all who make virtue and perfection their pursuit still to this day cease not to lament his loss with bitterest regret, as for one who helped them in the pursuit of virtue as none else could.

To me, personally, he was what I have myself endeavoured to describe: so pious and devoutly religious[3] that he would take no step apart from the will of heaven; so just and upright that he never did even a trifling injury to any living soul; so self-controlled, so temperate, that he never at any time

---

1 *This passage also may, perhaps, be regarded as spurious.*
2 Or, *"There floats before my eyes a vision of the many who have gone this same gate. I note their legacies of fame among posterity."*
3 Or, *"of such piety and religious devotedness... of such rectitude... of such sobreity and self-control... of such sound sense and wisdom..."*

chose the sweeter in place of the better; so sensible, and wise, and prudent that in distinguishing the better from the worse he never erred; nor had he need of any helper, but for the knowledge of these matters, his judgment was at once infallible and self-sufficing. Capable of reasonably setting forth and defining moral questions,[1] he was also able to test others, and where they erred, to cross-examine and convict them, and so to impel and guide them in the path of virtue and noble manhood. With these characteristics, he seemed to be the very impersonation of human perfection and happiness.[2]

Such is our estimate. If the verdict fail to satisfy I would ask those who disagree with it to place the character of any other side by side with this delineation, and then pass sentence.

---

1 Or, "gifted with an ability logically to set forth and to define moral subtleties."
2 Or, "I look upon him as at once the best and happiest of men."

HELLENICA

BY XENOPHON

Translation by H. G. Dakyns

Xenophon the Athenian was born 431 BC. He was a pupil of Socrates. He marched with the Spartans, and was exiled from Athens. Sparta gave him land and property in Scillus, where he lived for many years before having to move once more, to settle in Corinth. He died in 354 BC.

The Hellenica is his chronicle of the history of the Hellenes from 411 to 359 BC, starting as a continuation of Thucydides, and becoming his own brand of work from Book III onward.

PREPARER'S NOTE:

This was typed from Dakyns' series, "The Works of Xenophon," a four-volume set. Text in brackets "{}" is my transliteration of Greek text into English using an Oxford English Dictionary alphabet table. The diacritical marks have been lost.

BOOK I

I

411 BC. To follow the order of events.[1] A few days later Thymochares arrived from Athens with a few ships, when another sea fight between the Lacedaemonians and Athenians at once took place, in which the former, under the command of Agesandridas, gained the victory.

Another short interval brings us to a morning in early winter, when Dorieus, the son of Diagoras, was entering the Hellespont with fourteen ships from Rhodes at break of day. The Athenian day-watch descrying him, signalled to the generals, and they, with twenty sail, put out to sea to

---

1 Lit. "after these events"; but is hard to conjecture to what events the author refers. For the order of events and the connection between the closing chapter of Thuc. viii. 109, and the opening words of the "Hellenica," see introductory remarks above. The scene of this sea-fight is, I think, the Hellespont.

attack him. Dorieus made good his escape, and, as he shook himself free of the narrows,[1] ran his triremes aground off Rhoeteum. When the Athenians had come to close quarters, the fighting commenced, and was sustained at once from ships and shore, until at length the Athenians retired to their main camp at Madytus, having achieved nothing.

Meanwhile Mindarus, while sacrificing to Athena at Ilium, had observed the battle. He at once hastened to the sea, and getting his own triremes afloat, sailed out to pick up the ships with Dorieus. The Athenians on their side put out to meet him, and engaged him off Abydos. From early morning till the afternoon the fight was kept up close to the shore.[2] Victory and defeat hung still in even balance, when Alcibiades came sailing up with eighteen ships. Thereupon the Peloponnesians fled toward Abydos, where, however, Pharnabazus brought them timely assistance.[3] Mounted on horseback, he pushed forward into the sea as far as his horse would let him, doing battle himself, and encouraging his troopers and the infantry alike to play their parts. Then the Peloponnesians, ranging their ships in close-packed order, and drawing up their battle line in proximity to the land, kept up the fight. At length the Athenians, having captured thirty of the enemy's vessels without their crews, and having recovered those of their own which they had previously lost, set sail for Sestos. Here the fleet, with the exception of forty vessels, dispersed in different directions outside the Hellespont, to collect money; while Thrasylus, one of the generals, sailed to Athens to report what had happened, and to beg for a reinforcement of troops and ships. After the above incidents, Tissaphernes arrived in the Hellespont, and received a visit from Alcibiades, who presented him with a single ship, bringing with him tokens of friendship and gifts, whereupon Tissaphernes seized him and shut him up in Sardis, giving out that the king's orders were to go to war with the Athenians. Thirty days later Alcibiades, accompanied by Mantitheus, who had been captured in Caria, managed to procure horses and escaped by night to Clazomenae.

410 BC. And now the Athenians at Sestos, hearing that Mindarus was meditating an attack upon them with a squadron of sixty sail, gave him the slip, and under cover of night escaped to Cardia. Hither also Alcibiades repaired from Clazomenae, having with him five triremes and a light skiff;

---

1 Lit. "as he opened" {os enoige}. This is still a mariner's phrase in modern Greek, if I am rightly informed.
2 The original has a somewhat more poetical ring. The author uses the old Attic or Ionic word {eona}. This is a mark of style, of which we shall have many instances. One might perhaps produce something of the effect here by translating: "the battle hugged the strand."
3 Or, "came to their aid along the shore."

but on learning that the Peloponnesian fleet had left Abydos and was in full sail for Cyzicus, he set off himself by land to Sestos, giving orders to the fleet to sail round and join him there. Presently the vessels arrived, and he was on the point of putting out to sea with everything ready for action, when Theramenes, with a fleet of twenty ships from Macedonia, entered the port, and at the same instant Thrasybulus, with a second fleet of twenty sail from Thasos, both squadrons having been engaged in collecting money. Bidding these officers also follow him with all speed, as soon as they had taken out their large sails and cleared for action, Alcibiades set sail himself for Parium. During the following night the united squadron, consisting now of eighty-six vessels, stood out to sea from Parium, and reached Proconnesus next morning, about the hour of breakfast. Here they learned that Mindarus was in Cyzicus, and that Pharnabazus, with a body of infantry, was with him. Accordingly they waited the whole of this day at Proconnesus. On the following day Alcibiades summoned an assembly, and addressing the men in terms of encouragement, warned them that a threefold service was expected of them; that they must be ready for a sea fight, a land fight, and a wall fight all at once, "for look you," said he, "we have no money, but the enemy has unlimited supplies from the king."

Now, on the previous day, as soon as they were come to moorings, he had collected all the sea-going craft of the island, big and little alike, under his own control, that no one might report the number of his squadron to the enemy, and he had further caused a proclamation to be made, that anyone caught sailing across to the opposite coast would be punished with death. When the meeting was over, he got his ships ready for action, and stood out to sea toward Cyzicus in torrents of rain. Off Cyzicus the sky cleared, and the sun shone out and revealed to him the spectacle of Mindarus's vessels, sixty in number, exercising at some distance from the harbor, and, in fact, intercepted by himself. The Peloponnesians, perceiving at a glance the greatly increased number of the Athenian galleys, and noting their proximity to the port, made haste to reach the land, where they brought their vessels to anchor in a body, and prepared to engage the enemy as he sailed to the attack. But Alcibiades, sailing round with twenty of his vessels, came to land and disembarked. Seeing this, Mindarus also landed, and in the engagement which ensued he fell fighting, whilst those who were with him took to flight. As for the enemy's ships, the Athenians succeeded in capturing the whole of them (with the exception of the Syracusan vessels, which were burnt by their crews), and made off with their prizes to Proconnesus. From thence on the following day they sailed to attack Cyzicus. The men of that place, seeing that the Peloponnesians and Pharnabazus had evacuated the town, admitted the Athenians. Here Alcibiades remained twenty days, obtaining large sums of money from the Cyzicenes, but otherwise inflicting no sort of mischief on the community. He then sailed back to Proconnesus, and from there to Perinthus and Selybria. The inhabitants of the former place welcomed his troops into their city, but the Selybrians preferred to give money, and so escape the admission of the troops. Continuing the voyage the squadron reached Chrysopolis in Chalcedonia,[1] where they built a fort, and established a custom-house to collect the tithe dues which they levied on all merchantmen passing through the Straights from the Black Sea. Besides this, a detachment of thirty ships was left there under the two generals, Theramenes and Eubulus, with instructions not only to keep a look-out on the port itself and on all traders passing through the channel, but generally to injure the enemy in any way which might present itself. This done, the rest of the generals hastened back to the Hellespont.

Now a despatch from Hippocrates, Mindarus's vice-admiral,[2] had been intercepted on its way to Lacedaemon, and taken to Athens. It ran as follows (in broad Doric):[3] "Ships gone; Mindarus dead; the men starving; at our wits' end what to do."

Pharnabazus, however, was ready to meet with encouragement the despondency which afflicted the whole Peloponnesian army and their allies. "As long as their own bodies were safe and sound, why need they take to heart the loss of a few wooden hulls? Was there not timber enough and to spare in the king's territory?" And so he presented each man with a cloak and maintenance for a couple of months, after which he armed the sailors and formed them into a coastguard for the security of his own seaboard.

He next called a meeting of the generals and trierarchs of the different States, and instructed them to build just as many new ships in the dockyards of Antandrus as they had respectively lost. He himself was to furnish the funds, and he gave them to understand that they might bring down timber from Mount Ida. While the ships were building, the Syracusans helped the

---

1 This is the common spelling, but the coins of Calchedon have the letters {KALKH}, and so the name is written in the best MSS. of Herodotus, Xenophon, and other writers, by whom the place is named. See "Dict. of Greek and Roman Geog." "Chalcedon."

2 "Epistoleus," i.e. secretary or despatch writer, is the Spartan title of the officer second in command to the admiral.

3 Reading {"Errei ta kala} (Bergk's conjecture for {kala}) = "timbers," i.e. "ships" (a Doric word). Cf. Aristoph., "Lys." 1253, {potta kala}. The despatch continues: {Mindaros apessoua} (al. {apessua}), which is much more racy than the simple word "dead." "M. is gone off." I cannot find the right English or "broad Scotch" equivalent. See Thirlwall, "Hist. Gr." IV. xxix. 88 note.

men of Antandrus to finish a section of their walls, and were particularly pleasant on garrison duty; and that is why the Syracusans to this day enjoy the privilege of citizenship, with the title of "benefactors," at Antandrus. Having so arranged these matters, Pharnabazus proceeded at once to the rescue of Chalcedon.

It was at this date that the Syracusan generals received news from home of their banishment by the democratic party. Accordingly they called a meeting of their separate divisions, and putting forward Hermocrates[1] as their spokesman, proceeded to deplore their misfortune, insisting upon the injustice and the illegality of their banishment. "And now let us admonish you," they added, "to be eager and willing in the future, even as in the past: whatever the word of command may be, show yourselves good men and true: let not the memory of those glorious sea fights fade. Think of those victories you have won, those ships you have captured by your own unaided efforts; forget not that long list of achievements shared by yourselves with others, in all which you proved yourselves invincible under our generalship. It was to a happy combination of our merit and your enthusiasm, displayed alike on land and sea, that you owe the strength and perfection of your discipline."

With these words they called upon the men to choose other commanders, who should undertake the duties of their office, until the arrival of their successors. Thereupon the whole assembly, and more particularly the captains and masters of vessels and marines, insisted with loud cries on their continuance in command. The generals replied, "It was not for them to indulge in faction against the State, but rather it was their duty, in case any charges were forthcoming against themselves, at once to render an account." When, however, no one had any kind of accusation to prefer, they yielded to the general demand, and were content to await the arrival of their successors. The names of these were—Demarchus, the son of Epidocus; Myscon, the son of Mencrates; and Potamis, the son of Gnosis.

The captains, for their part, swore to restore the exiled generals as soon as they themselves should return to Syracuse. At present with a general vote

---

1 *Hermocrates, the son of Hermon. We first hear of him in Thuc. iv. 58 foll. as the chief agent in bringing the Sicilian States together in conference at Gela 424 BC, with a view to healing their differences and combining to frustrate the dangerous designs of Athens. In 415 BC, when the attack came, he was again the master spirit in rendering it abortive (Thuc. vi. 72 foll.) In 412 BC it was he who urged the Sicilians to assist in completing the overthrow of Athens, by sending a squadron to co-operate with the Peloponnesian navy—for the relief of Miletus, etc. (Thuc. viii. 26, 27 foll.) At a later date, in 411 BC, when the Peloponnesian sailors were ready to mutiny, and "laid all their grievances to the charge of Astyochus (the Spartan admiral), who humoured Tissaphernes for his own gain" (Thuc. viii. 83), Hermocrates took the men's part, and so incurred the hatred of Tissaphernes.*

of thanks they despatched them to their several destinations. It particular those who had enjoyed the society of Hermocrates recalled his virtues with regret, his thoroughness and enthusiasm, his frankness and affability, the care with which every morning and evening he was wont to gather in his quarters a group of naval captains and mariners whose ability he recognized. These were his confidants, to whom he communicated what he intended to say or do: they were his pupils, to whom he gave lessons in oratory, now calling upon them to speak extempore, and now again after deliberation. By these means Hermocrates had gained a wide reputation at the council board, where his mastery of language was no less felt than the wisdom of his advice. Appearing at Lacedaemon as the accuser of Tissaphernes,[1] he had carried his case, not only by the testimony of Astyochus, but by the obvious sincerity of his statements, and on the strength of this reputation he now betook himself to Pharnabazus. The latter did not wait to be asked, but at once gave him money, which enabled him to collect friends and triremes, with a view to his ultimate recall to Syracuse. Meanwhile the successors of the Syracusans had arrived at Miletus, where they took charge of the ships and the army.

It was at this same season that a revolution occurred in Thasos, involving the expulsion of the philo-Laconian party, with the Laconian governor Eteonicus. The Laconian Pasippidas was charged with having brought the business about in conjunction with Tissaphernes, and was banished from Sparta in consequence. The naval force which he had been collecting from the allies was handed over to Cratesippidas, who was sent out to take his place in Chios.

About the same period, while Thrasylus was still in Athens, Agis[2] made a foraging expedition up to the very walls of the city. But Thrasylus led out the Athenians with the rest of the inhabitants of the city, and drew them up by the side of the Lyceum Gymnasium, ready to engage the enemy if they approached; seeing which, Agis beat a hasty retreat, not however without the loss of some of his supports, a few of whom were cut down by the Athenian light troops. This success disposed the citizens to take a still more favorable view of the objects for which Thrasylus had come; and they passed a decree empowering him to call out a thousand hoplites, one hundred cavalry, and fifty triremes.

---

1 The matter referred to is fully explained Thuc. viii. 85.
2 The reader will recollect that we are giving in "the Deceleian" period of the war, 413–404 BC The Spartan king was in command of the fortress of Deceleia, only fourteen miles distant from Athens, and erected on a spot within sight of the city. See Thuc. vii. 19, 27, 28.

Meanwhile Agis, as he looked out from Deceleia, and saw vessel after vessel laden with corn running down to Piraeus, declared that it was useless for his troops to go on week after week excluding the Athenians from their own land, while no one stopped the source of their corn supply by sea: the best plan would be to send Clearchus,[1] the son of Rhamphius, who was proxenos[2] of the Byzantines, to Chalcedon and Byzantium. The suggestion was approved, and with fifteen vessels duly manned from Megara, or furnished by other allies, Clearchus set out. These were troop-ships rather than swift-sailing men-of-war. Three of them, on reaching the Hellespont, were destroyed by the Athenian ships employed to keep a sharp look-out on all merchant craft in those waters. The other twelve escaped to Sestos, and thence finally reached Byzantium in safety.

So closed the year—a year notable also for the expedition against Sicily of the Carthaginians under Hannibal with one hundred thousand men, and the capture, within three months, of the two Hellenic cities of Selinus and Himera.

II

409 BC. Next year[3]... the Athenians fortified Thoricus; and Thrasylus, taking the vessels lately voted him and five thousand of his seamen armed to serve as peltasts,[4] set sail for Samos at the beginning of summer. At Samos he stayed three days, and then continued his voyage to Pygela, where he proceeded to ravage the territory and attack the fortress. Presently a detachment from Miletus came to the rescue of the men of Pygela, and attacking the scattered bands of the Athenian light troops, put them to flight. But to the aid of the light troops came the naval brigade of peltasts, with two companies of heavy infantry, and all but annihilated the whole detachment from Miletus. They captured about two hundred shields, and

---

1 *Of Clearchus we shall hear more in the sequel, and in the "Anabasis."*

2 *The Proxenus answered pretty nearly to our "Consul," "Agent," "Resident"; but he differed in this respect, that he was always a member of the foreign State. An Athenian represented Sparta at Athens; a Laconian represented Athens at Sparta, and so forth. See Liddell and Scott.*

3 *The MSS. here give a suspected passage, which may be rendered thus: "The first of Olympiad 93, celebrated as the year in which the newly added two-horse race was won by Evagorias the Eleian, and the stadion (200 yards foot-race) by the Cyrenaean Eubotas, when Evarchippus was ephor at Sparta and Euctemon archon at Athens." But Ol. 93, to which these officers, and the addition of the new race at Olympia belong, is the year 408. We must therefore suppose either that this passage has been accidentally inserted in the wrong place by some editor or copyist, or that the author was confused in his dates. The "stadium" is the famous foot-race at Olympia, 606 3/4 English feet in length, run on a course also called the "Stadion," which was exactly a stade long.*

4 *Peltasts, i.e. light infantry armed with the "pelta" or light shield, instead of the heavy {aspis} of the hoplite or heavy infantry soldiers.*

set up a trophy. Next day they sailed to Notium, and from Notium, after due preparation, marched upon Colophon. The Colophonians capitulated without a blow. The following night they made an incursion into Lydia, where the corn crops were ripe, and burnt several villages, and captured money, slaves, and other booty in large quantity. But Stages, the Persian, who was employed in this neighborhood, fell in with a reinforcement of cavalry sent to protect the scattered pillaging parties from the Athenian camp, whilst occupied with their individual plunder, and took one trooper prisoner, killing seven others. After this Thrasylus led his troops back to the sea, intending to sail to Ephesus. Meanwhile Tissaphernes, who had wind of this intention, began collecting a large army and despatching cavalry with a summons to the inhabitants one and all to rally to the defense of the goddess Artemis at Ephesus.

On the seventeenth day after the incursion above mentioned Thrasylus sailed to Ephesus. He disembarked his troops in two divisions, his heavy infantry in the neighborhood of Mount Coressus; his cavalry, peltasts, and marines, with the remainder of his force, near the marsh on the other side of the city. At daybreak he pushed forward both divisions. The citizens of Ephesus, on their side, were not slow to protect themselves. They had to aid them the troops brought up by Tissaphernes, as well as two detachments of Syracusans, consisting of the crews of their former twenty vessels and those of five new vessels which had opportunely arrived quite recently under Eucles, the son of Hippon, and Heracleides, the son of Aristogenes, together with two Selinuntian vessels. All these several forces first attacked the heavy infantry near Coressus; these they routed, killing about one hundred of them, and driving the remainder down into the sea. They then turned to deal with the second division on the marsh. Here, too, the Athenians were put to flight, and as many as three hundred of them perished. On this spot the Ephesians erected a trophy, and another at Coressus. The valour of the Syracusans and Selinuntians had been so conspicuous that the citizens presented many of them, both publicly and privately, with prizes for distinction in the field, besides offering the right of residence in their city with certain immunities to all who at any time might wish to live there. To the Selinuntians, indeed, as their own city had lately been destroyed, they offered full citizenship.

The Athenians, after picking up their dead under a truce, set sail for Notium, and having there buried the slain, continued their voyage toward Lesbos and the Hellespont. Whilst lying at anchor in the harbor of Methymna, in that island, they caught sight of the Syracusan vessels, five-and-twenty in number, coasting along from Ephesus. They put out to sea to attack them, and captured four ships with their crews, and chased the remainder back to Ephesus. The prisoners were sent by Thrasylus to Athens, with one exception. This was an Athenian, Alcibiades, who was a cousin and fellow exile of Alcibiades. Him Thrasylus released. (3) From Methymna Thrasylus set sail to Sestos to join the main body of the army, after which the united forces crossed to Lampsacus. And now winter was approaching. It was the winter in which the Syracusan prisoners who had been immured in the stone quarries of Piraeus dug through the rock and escaped one night, some to Decelia and others to Megara. At Lampsacus Alcibiades was anxious to marshal the whole military force there collected in one body, but the old troops refused to be incorporated with those of Thrasylus. "They, who had never yet been beaten, with these newcomers who had just suffered a defeat." So they devoted the winter to fortifying Lampsacus. They also made an expedition against Abydos, where Pharnabazus, coming to the rescue of the place, encountered them with numerous cavalry, but was defeated and forced to flee, Alcibiades pursuing hard with his cavalry and one hundred and twenty infantry under the command of Menander, till darkness intervened. After this battle the soldiers came together of their own accord, and freely fraternised with the troops of Thrasylus. This expedition was followed by other incursions during the winter into the interior, where they found plenty to do ravaging the king's territory.

(3) Reading {apelusen}. Wolf's conjecture for the MSS. {katelousen} = stoned. See Thirlwall, "Hist. Gr." IV. xxix. 93 note.

It was at this period also that the Lacedaemonians allowed their revolted helots from Malea, who had found an asylum at Coryphasium, to depart under a flag of truce. It was also about the same period that the Achaeans betrayed the colonists of Heracleia Trachinia, when they were all drawn up in battle to meet the hostile Oetaeans, whereby as many as seven hundred of them were lost, together with the governor (4) from Lacedaemon, Labotas. Thus the year came to its close—a year marked further by a revolt of the Medes from Darius, the king of Persia, followed by renewed submission to his authority.

(4) Technically {armostes} (harmost), i.e. administrator.

III

408 BC. The year following is the year in which the temple of Athena,

in Phocaea, was struck by lightning and set on fire.[1] With the cessation of winter, in early spring, the Athenians set sail with the whole of their force to Proconnesus, and thence advanced upon Chalcedon and Byzantium, encamping near the former town. The men of Chalcedon, aware of their approach, had taken the precaution to deposit all their pillageable property with their neighbors, the Bithynian Thracians; whereupon Alcibiades put himself at the head of a small body of heavy infantry with the cavalry, and giving orders to the fleet to follow along the coast, marched against the Bithynians and demanded back the property of the Chalcedonians, threatening them with war in case of refusal. The Bithynians delivered up the property. Returning to camp, not only thus enriched, but with the further satisfaction of having secured pledges of good behavior from the Bithynians, Alcibiades set to work with the whole of his troops to draw lines of circumvallation round Chalcedon from sea to sea, so as to include as much of the river as possible within his wall, which was made of timber. Thereupon the Lacedaemonian governor, Hippocrates, let his troops out of the city and offered battle, and the Athenians, on their side, drew up their forces opposite to receive him; while Pharnabazus, from without the lines of circumvallation, was still advancing with his army and large bodies of horse. Hippocrates and Thrasylus engaged each other with their heavy infantry for a long while, until Alcibiades, with a detachment of infantry and the cavalry, intervened. Presently Hippocrates fell, and the troops under him fled into the city; at the same instant Pharnabazus, unable to effect a junction with the Lacedaemonian leader, owing to the circumscribed nature of the ground and the close proximity of the river to the enemy's lines, retired to the Heracleium,[2] belonging to the Chalcedonians, where his camp lay. After this success Alcibiades set off to the Hellespont and the Chersonese to raise money, and the remaining generals came to terms with Pharnabazus in respect of Chalcedon; according to these, the Persian satrap agreed to pay the Athenians twenty talents[3] in behalf of the town, and to grant their ambassadors a safe conduct up country to the king. It was further stipulated by mutual consent and under oaths provided, that the Chalcedonians should continue the payment of their customary tribute to Athens, being also bound to discharge all outstanding debts. The Athenians, on their side, were bound

---

1 The MSS. here give the words, "in the ephorate of Pantacles and the archonship of Antigenes, two-and-twenty years from the beginning of the war," but the twenty-second year of the war = 410 BC; Antigenes archon, 407 BC = Ol. 93, 2; the passage must be regarded as a note mis-inserted by some editor or copyist (vide supra, I. 11.)

2 I.e. sacred place or temple of Heracles.

3 Twenty talents = 4800 pounds; or, more exactly, 4875 pounds.

to desist from all hostilities until the return of their ambassadors from the king. These oaths were not witnessed by Alcibiades, who was now in the neighborhood of Selybria. Having taken that place, he presently appeared before the walls of Byzantium at the head of the men of Chersonese, who came out with their whole force; he was aided further by troops from Thrace and more than three hundred horse. Accordingly Pharnabazus, insisting that he too must take the oath, decided to remain in Chalcedon, and to await his arrival from Byzantium. Alcibiades came, but was not prepared to bind himself by any oaths, unless Pharnabazus would, on his side, take oaths to himself. After this, oaths were exchanged between them by proxy. Alcibiades took them at Chrysopolis in the presence of two representatives sent by Pharnabazus—namely, Mitrobates and Arnapes. Pharnabazus took them at Chalcedon in the presence of Euryptolemus and Diotimus, who represented Alcibiades. Both parties bound themselves not only by the general oath, but also interchanged personal pledges of good faith.

This done, Pharnabazus left Chalcedon at once, with injunctions that those who were going up to the king as ambassadors should meet him at Cyzicus. The representatives of Athens were Dorotheus, Philodices, Theogenes, Euryptolemus, and Mantitheus; with them were two Argives, Cleostratus and Pyrrholochus. An embassy of the Lacedaemonians was also about to make the journey. This consisted of Pasippidas and his fellows, with whom were Hermocrates, now an exile from Syracuse, and his brother Proxenus. So Pharnabazus put himself at their head. Meanwhile the Athenians prosecuted the siege of Byzantium; lines of circumvallation were drawn; and they diversified the blockade by sharpshooting at long range and occasional assaults upon the walls. Inside the city lay Clearchus, the Lacedaemonian governor, and a body of Perioci with a small detachment of Neodamodes.[1] There was also a body of Megarians

---

[1] According to the constitution of Lacedaemon the whole government was in Dorian hands. The subject population was divided into (1) Helots, who were State serfs. The children of Helots were at times brought up by Spartans and called "Mothakes"; Helots who had received their liberty were called "Neodamodes" ({neodamodeis}). After the conquest of Messenia this class was very numerous. (2) Perioeci. These were the ancient Achaean inhabitants, living in towns and villages, and managing their own affairs, paying tribute, and serving in the army as heavy-armed soldiers. In 458 BC they were said to number thirty thousand. The Spartans themselves were divided, like all Dorians, into three tribes, Hylleis, Dymanes, and Pamphyli, each of which tribes was divided into ten "obes," which were again divided into {oikoi} or families possessed of landed properties. In 458 BC there were said to be nine thousand such families; but in course of time, through alienation of lands, deaths in war, and other causes, their numbers were much diminished; and in many cases there was a loss of status, so that in the time of Agis III., 244 BC, we hear of two orders of Spartans, the {omoioi} and the {upomeiones} (inferiors); seven hundred Spartans (families) proper and one hundred landed proprietors. See Mullers "Dorians," vol. ii. bk. iii. ch. x. S. 3 (Eng. trans.); Arist. "Pol." ii. 9, 15; Plut. ("Agis").

under their general Helixus, a Megarian, and another body of Boeotians, with their general Coeratadas. The Athenians, finding presently that they could effect nothing by force, worked upon some of the inhabitants to betray the place. Clearchus, meanwhile, never dreaming that anyone would be capable of such an act, had crossed over to the opposite coast to visit Pharnabazus; he had left everything in perfect order, entrusting the government of the city to Coeratadas and Helixus. His mission was to obtain pay for the soldiers from the Persian satrap, and to collect vessels from various quarters. Some were already in the Hellespont, where they had been left as guardships by Pasippidas, or else at Antandrus. Others formed the fleet which Agesandridas, who had formerly served as a marine[1] under Mindarus, now commanded on the Thracian coast. Others Clearchus purposed to have built, and with the whole united squadron to so injure the allies of the Athenians as to draw off the besieging army from Byzantium. But no sooner was he fairly gone than those who were minded to betray the city set to work. Their names were Cydon, Ariston, Anaxicrates, Lycurgus, and Anaxilaus. The last-named was afterward impeached for treachery in Lacedaemon on the capital charge, and acquitted on the plea that, to begin with, he was not a Lacedaemonian, but a Byzantine, and, so far from having betrayed the city, he had saved it, when he saw women and children perishing of starvation; for Clearchus had given away all the corn in the city to the Lacedaemonian soldiers. It was for these reasons, as Anaxilaus himself admitted, he had introduced the enemy, and not for the sake of money, nor out of hatred to Lacedaemon.

As soon as everything was ready, these people opened the gates leading to the Thracian Square, as it is called, and admitted the Athenian troops with Alcibiades at their head. Helixus and Coeratadas, in complete ignorance of the plot, hastened to the Agora with the whole of the garrison, ready to confront the danger; but finding the enemy in occupation, they had nothing for it but to give themselves up. They were sent off as prisoners to Athens, where Coeratadas, in the midst of the crowd and confusion of debarkation at Piraeus, gave his guards the slip, and made his way in safety to Decelia.

IV

407 BC. Pharnabazus and the ambassadors were passing the winter at Gordium in Phrygia, when they heard of the occurrences at Byzantium. Continuing their journey to the king's court in the commencement of

---

1 *The greek word is {epibates}, which some think was the title of an inferior naval officer in the Spartan service, but there is no proof of this. Cf. Thuc. viii. 61, and Prof. Jowett's note; also Grote, "Hist. of Greece," viii. 27 (2d ed.)*

spring, they were met by a former embassy, which was now on its return journey. These were the Lacedaemonian ambassadors, Boeotius and his party, with the other envoys; who told them that the Lacedaemonians had obtained from the king all they wanted. One of the company was Cyrus, the new governor of all the seaboard districts, who was prepared to co-operate with the Lacedaemonians in war. He was the bearer, moreover, of a letter with the royal seal attached. It was addressed to all the populations of Lower Asia, and contained the following words: "I send down Cyrus as 'Karanos'"[1]—that is to say, supreme lord—"over all those who muster at Castolus." The ambassadors of the Athenians, even while listening to this announcement, and indeed after they had seen Cyrus, were still desirous, if possible, to continue their journey to the king, or, failing that, to return home. Cyrus, however, urged upon Pharnabazus either to deliver them up to himself, or to defer sending them home at present; his object being to prevent the Athenians learning what was going on. Pharnabazus, wishing to escape all blame, for the time being detained them, telling them, at one time, that he would presently escort them up country to the king, and at another time that he would send them safe home. But when three years had elapsed, he prayed Cyrus to let them go, declaring that he had taken an oath to bring them back to the sea, in default of escorting them up to the king. Then at last they received safe conduct to Ariobarzanes, with orders for their further transportation. The latter conducted them a stage further, to Cius in Mysia; and from Cius they set sail to join their main armament.

Alcibiades, whose chief desire was to return home to Athens with the troops, immediately set sail for Samos; and from that island, taking twenty of the ships, he sailed to the Ceramic Gulf of Caria, where he collected a hundred talents, and so returned to Samos.

Thrasybulus had gone Thrace-wards with thirty ships. In this quarter he reduced various places which had revolted to Lacedaemon, including the island of Thasos, which was in a bad plight, the result of wars, revolutions, and famine.

Thrasylus, with the rest of the army, sailed back straight to Athens. On his arrival he found that the Athenians had already chosen as their general

---

1 {Karanos.} Is this a Greek word, a Doric form, {karanos}, akin to {kara} (cf. {karenon}) = chief? or is it not more likely a Persian or native word, Karanos? and might not the title be akin conceivably to the word {korano}, which occurs on many Indo-Bactrian coins (see A. von Sallet, "Die Nachfolger Alexanders des Grossen," p. 57, etc.)? or is {koiranos} the connecting link? The words translated "that is to say, supreme lord," {to de karanon esti kurion}, look very like a commentator's gloss.

Alcibiades, who was still in exile, and Thrasybulus, who was also absent, and as a third, from among those at home, Conon.

Meanwhile Alcibiades, with the moneys lately collected and his fleet of twenty ships, left Samos and visited Paros. From Paros he stood out to sea across to Gytheum,[1] to keep an eye on the thirty ships of war which, as he was informed, the Lacedaemonians were equipping in that arsenal. Gytheum would also be a favorable point of observation from which to gauge the disposition of his fellow countrymen and the prospects of his recall. When at length their good disposition seemed to him established, not only by his election as general, but by the messages of invitation which he received in private from his friends, he sailed home, and entered Piraeus on the very day of the festival of the Plunteria,[2] when the statue of Athena is veiled and screened from public gaze. This was a coincidence, as some thought, of evil omen, and unpropitious alike to himself and the State, for no Athenian would transact serious business on such a day.

As he sailed into the harbor, two great crowds—one from the Piraeus, the other from the city[3]—flocked to meet the vessels. Wonderment, mixed with a desire to see Alcibiades, was the prevailing sentiment of the multitude. Of him they spoke: some asserting that he was the best of citizens, and that in his sole instance banishment had been ill-deserved. He had been the victim of plots, hatched in the brains of people less able than himself, however much they might excel in pestilent speech; men whose one principle of statecraft was to look to their private gains; whereas this man's policy had ever been to uphold the common weal, as much by his private means as by all the power of the State. His own choice, eight years ago, when the charge of impiety in the matter of the mysteries was still fresh, would have been to submit to trial at once. It was his personal foes, who had succeeded in postponing that undeniably just procedure; who waited till his back was turned, and then robbed him of his fatherland. Then it was that, being made the very slave of circumstance, he was driven to court the men he hated most; and at a time when his own life was in daily peril, he must see his dearest friends and fellow citizens, nay, the very State itself, bent on a suicidal course, and yet, in the exclusion of exile, be unable to lend a helping hand. "It is not men of this stamp," they averred, "who

---

1 *Gytheum, the port and arsenal of Sparta, situated near the head of the Laconian Gulf (now Marathonisi).*

2 *{ta Plunteria}, or feast of washings, held on the 25th of the month Thargelion, when the image of the goddess Athena was stripped in order that her clothes might be washed by the Praxiergidae; neither assembly nor court was held on that day, and the Temple was closed.*

3 *Or, "collected to meet the vessels from curiosity and a desire to see Alcibiades."*

desire changes in affairs and revolution: had he not already guaranteed to him by the Democracy a position higher than that of his equals in age, and scarcely if at all inferior to his seniors? How different was the position of his enemies. It had been the fortune of these, though they were known to be the same men they had always been, to use their lately acquired power for the destruction in the first instance of the better classes; and then, being alone left surviving, to be accepted by their fellow citizens in the absence of better men."

Others, however, insisted that for all their past miseries and misfortunes Alcibiades alone was responsible: "If more trials were still in store for the State, here was the master mischief-maker ready at his post to precipitate them."

When the vessels came to their moorings, close to the land, Alcibiades, from fear of his enemies, was unwilling to disembark at once. Mounting on the quarterdeck, he scanned the multitude,[1] anxious to make certain of the presence of his friends. Presently his eyes lit upon Euryptolemus, the son of Peisianax, who was his cousin, and then on the rest of his relations and other friends. Upon this he landed, and so, in the midst of an escort ready to put down any attempt upon his person, made his way to the city.

In the Senate and Public Assembly[2] he made speeches, defending himself against the charge of impiety, and asserting that he had been the victim of injustice, with other like topics, which in the present temper of the assembly no one ventured to gainsay.

He was then formally declared leader and chief of the State, with irresponsible powers, as being the sole individual capable of recovering the ancient power and prestige of Athens. Armed with this authority, his first act was to institute anew the processional march to Eleusis; for of late years, owing to the war, the Athenians had been forced to conduct the mysteries by sea. Now, at the head of the troops, he caused them to be conducted once again by land. This done, his next step was to muster an armament of one thousand five hundred heavy infantry, one hundred and fifty cavalry, and one hundred ships; and lastly, within three months of his return, he set sail for Andros, which had revolted from Athens.

The generals chosen to co-operate with him on land were Aristocrates and Adeimantus, the son of Leucophilides. He disembarked his troops on the island of Andros at Gaurium, and routed the Andrian citizens who sallied out from the town to resist the invader; forcing them to return and

---

1 Or, "he looked to see if his friends were there."
2 Technically the "Boule" ({Boule}) or Senate, and "Ecclesia" or Popular Assembly.

keep close within their walls, though the number who fell was not large. This defeat was shared by some Lacedaemonians who were in the place. Alcibiades erected a trophy, and after a few days set sail himself for Samos, which became his base of operations in the future conduct of the war.

V

At a date not much earlier than that of the incidents just described, the Lacedaemonians had sent out Lysander as their admiral, in the place of Cratesippidas, whose period of office had expired. The new admiral first visited Rhodes, where he got some ships, and sailed to Cos and Miletus, and from the latter place to Ephesus. At Ephesus he waited with seventy sail, expecting the advent of Cyrus in Sardis, when he at once went up to pay the prince a visit with the ambassadors from Lacedaemon. And now an opportunity was given to denounce the proceedings of Tissaphernes, and at the same time to beg Cyrus himself to show as much zeal as possible in the prosecution of the war. Cyrus replied that not only had he received express injunction from his father to the same effect, but that his own views coincided with their wishes, which he was determined to carry out to the letter. He had, he informed them, brought with him five hundred talents;[1] and if that sum failed, he had still the private revenue, which his father allowed him, to fall back upon, and when this resource was in its turn exhausted, he would coin the gold and silver throne on which he sat, into money for their benefit.[2]

His audience thanked him for what he said, and further begged him to fix the rate of payment for the seamen at one Attic drachma per man,[3] explaining that should this rate of payment be adopted, the sailors of the Athenians would desert, and in the end there would be a saving of expenditure. Cyrus complimented them on the soundness of their arguments, but said that it was not in his power to exceed the injunctions of the king. The terms

---

1 *About 120,000 pounds. One Euboic or Attic talent = sixty minae = six thousand drachmae = 243 pounds 15 shillings of our money.*

2 *Cf. the language of Tissaphernes, Thuc. viii. 81.*

3 *About 9 3/4 pence; a drachma (= six obols) would be very high pay for a sailor—indeed, just double the usual amount. See Thuc. vi. 8 and viii. 29, and Prof. Jowett ad loc. Tissaphernes had, in the winter of 412 BC, distributed one month's pay among the Peloponnesian ships at this high rate of a drachma a day, "as his envoy had promised at Lacedaemon"; but this he proposed to reduce to half a drachma, "until he had asked the king's leave, promising that if he obtained it, he would pay the entire drachma. On the remonstrance, however, of Hermocrates, the Syracusan general, he promised to each man a payment of somewhat more than three obols."*

of agreement were precise, thirty minae[1] a month per vessel to be given, whatever number of vessels the Lacedaemonians might choose to maintain.

To this rejoinder Lysander at the moment said nothing. But after dinner, when Cyrus drank to his health, asking him "What he could do to gratify him most?" Lysander replied, "Add an obol[2] to the sailors" pay." After this the pay was raised to four instead of three obols, as it hitherto had been. Nor did the liberality of Cyrus end here; he not only paid up all arrears, but further gave a month's pay in advance, so that, if the enthusiasm of the army had been great before, it was greater than ever now. The Athenians when they heard the news were proportionately depressed, and by help of Tissaphernes despatched ambassadors to Cyrus. That prince, however, refused to receive them, nor were the prayers of Tissaphernes of any avail, however much he insisted that Cyrus should adopt the policy which he himself, on the advice of Alcibiades, had persistently acted on. This was simply not to suffer any single Hellenic state to grow strong at the expense of the rest, but to keep them all weak alike, distracted by internecine strife.

Lysander, now that the organization of his navy was arranged to his satisfaction, beached his squadron of ninety vessels at Ephesus, and sat with hands folded, whilst the vessels dried and underwent repairs. Alcibiades, being informed that Thrasybulus had come south of the Hellespont and was fortifying Phocaea, sailed across to join him, leaving his own pilot Antiochus in command of the fleet, with orders not to attack Lysander's fleet. Antiochus, however, was tempted to leave Notium and sail into the harbor of Ephesus with a couple of ships, his own and another, past the prows of Lysander's squadron. The Spartan at first contented himself with launching a few of his ships, and started in pursuit of the intruder; but when the Athenians came out with other vessels to assist Antiochus, he formed his whole squadron into line of battle, and bore down upon them, whereupon the Athenians followed suit, and getting their remaining triremes under weigh at Notium, stood out to sea as fast as each vessel could clear the point.[3] Thus it befell in the engagement which ensued, that while the enemy was in due order, the Athenians came up in scattered detachments and without concert, and in the end were put to flight with the loss of fifteen ships of war. Of the crews, indeed, the majority escaped,

---

1 *Nearly 122 pounds; and thirty minae a month to each ship (the crew of each ship being taken at two hundred) = three obols a day to each man. The terms of agreement to which Cyrus refers may have been specified in the convention mentioned above in chap. iv, which Boeotius and the rest were so proud to have obtained. But see Grote, "Hist. of Greece," vol. viii. p. 192 note (2d ed.)*

2 *An obol = one-sixth of a drachma; the Attic obol = rather more than 1 1/2 pence.*

3 *{os ekastos enoixen}, for this nautical term see above.*

though a certain number fell into the hands of the enemy. Then Lysander collected his vessels, and having erected a trophy on Cape Notium, sailed across to Ephesus, whilst the Athenians retired to Samos.

On his return to Samos a little later, Alcibiades put out to sea with the whole squadron in the direction of the harbor of Ephesus. At the mouth of the harbor he marshalled his fleet in battle order, and tried to tempt the enemy to an engagement; but as Lysander, conscious of his inferiority in numbers, refused to accept the challenge, he sailed back again to Samos. Shortly after this the Lacedaemonians captured Delphinium and Eion.[1]

But now the news of the late disaster at Notium had reached the Athenians at home, and in their indignation they turned upon Alcibiades, to whose negligence and lack of self-command they attributed the destruction of the ships. Accordingly they chose ten new generals—namely Conon, Diomedon, Leon, Pericles, Erasinides, Aristocrates, Archestratus, Protomachus, Thrasylus, and Aristogenes. Alcibiades, who was moreover in bad odour in the camp, sailed away with a single trireme to his private fortress in the Chersonese.

After this Conon, in obedience to a decree of the Athenian people, set sail from Andros with the twenty vessels under his command in that island to Samos, and took command of the whole squadron. To fill the place thus vacated by Conon, Phanosthenes was sent to Andros with four ships. That captain was fortunate enough to intercept and capture two Thurian ships of war, crews and all, and these captives were all imprisoned by the Athenians, with the exception of their leader Dorieus. He was the Rhodian, who some while back had been banished from Athens and from his native city by the Athenians, when sentence of death was passed upon him and his family. This man, who had once enjoyed the right of citizenship among them, they now took pity on and released without ransom.

When Conon had reached Samos he found the armament in a state of great despondency. Accordingly his first measure was to man seventy ships with their full complement, instead of the former hundred and odd vessels. With this squadron he put to sea accompanied by the other generals, and confined himself to making descents first at one point and then at another of the enemy's territory, and to collecting plunder.

And so the year drew to its close: a year signalled further by an invasion of Sicily by the Carthaginians, with one hundred and twenty ships of war and a land force of one hundred and twenty thousand men, which resulted

---

1 *This should probably be Teos, in Ionia, in spite of the MSS.* {"*Eiona*"}. *The place referred to cannot at any rate be the well-known Eion at the mouth of the Strymon in Thrace.*

in the capture of Agrigentum. The town was finally reduced to famine after a siege of seven months, the invaders having previously been worsted in battle and forced to sit down before its walls for so long a time.

VI

406 BC. In the following year—the year of the evening eclipse of the moon, and the burning of the old temple of Athena[1] at Athens[2]—the Lacedaemonians sent out Callicratidas to replace Lysander, whose period of office had now expired.[3] Lysander, when surrendering the squadron to his successor, spoke of himself as the winner of a sea fight, which had left him in undisputed mastery of the sea, and with this boast he handed over the ships to Callicratidas, who retorted, "If you will convey the fleet from Ephesus, keeping Samos[4] on your right" (that is, past where the Athenian navy lay), "and hand it over to me at Miletus, I will admit that you are master of the sea." But Lysander had no mind to interfere in the province of another officer. Thus Callicratidas assumed responsibility. He first manned, in addition to the squadron which he received from Lysander, fifty new vessels furnished by the allies from Chios and Rhodes and elsewhere. When all these contingents were assembled, they formed a total of one hundred and forty sail, and with these he began making preparations for engagement with the enemy. But it was impossible for him not to note the strong current of opposition which he encountered from the friends of Lysander. Not only was there lack of zeal in their service, but they openly disseminated an opinion in the States, that it was the greatest possible blunder on the part of the Lacedaemonians so to change their admirals. Of course, they must from time to time get officers altogether unfit for the post—men whose nautical knowledge dated from yesterday, and who, moreover, had no notion of dealing with human beings. It would be very odd if this practice of sending out people ignorant of the sea and unknown to the folk of the country did not lead to some catastrophe. Callicratidas at once summoned the Lacedaemonians there present, and addressed them in the following terms:—

---

1 I.e. as some think, the Erechtheion, which was built partly on the site of the old temple of Athena Polias, destroyed by the Persians. According to Dr. Dorpfeld, a quite separate building of the Doric order, the site of which (S. of the Erechtheion) has lately been discovered.
2 The MSS. here add "in the ephorate of Pityas and the archonship of Callias at Athens"; but though the date is probably correct (cf. Leake, "Topography of Athens," vol. i. p. 576 foll.), the words are almost certainly a gloss.
3 Here the MSS. add "with the twenty-fourth year of the war," probably an annotator's gloss; the correct date should be twenty-fifth. Pel. war 26 = 406 BC. Pel. war 25 ended 407 BC.
4 Lit. on the left (or east) of Samos, looking south from Ephesus.

"For my part," he said, "I am content to stay at home: and if Lysander or anyone else claim greater experience in nautical affairs than I possess, I have no desire to block his path. Only, being sent out by the State to take command of this fleet, I do not know what is left to me, save to carry out my instructions to the best of my ability. For yourselves, all I beg of you, in reference to my personal ambitions and the kind of charges brought against our common city, and of which you are as well aware as I am, is to state what you consider to be the best course: am I to stay where I am, or shall I sail back home, and explain the position of affairs out here?"

No one ventured to suggest any other course than that he should obey the authorities, and do what he was sent to do. Callicratidas then went up to the court of Cyrus to ask for further pay for the sailors, but the answer he got from Cyrus was that he should wait for two days. Callicratidas was annoyed at the rebuff: to dance attendance at the palace gates was little to his taste. In a fit of anger he cried out at the sorry condition of the Hellenes, thus forced to flatter the barbarian for the sake of money. "If ever I get back home," he added, "I will do what in me lies to reconcile the Athenians and the Lacedaemonians." And so he turned and sailed back to Miletus. From Miletus he sent some triremes to Lacedaemon to get money, and convoking the public assembly of the Milesians, addressed them thus:—

"Men of Miletus, necessity is laid upon me to obey the rulers at home; but for yourselves, whose neighborhood to the barbarians has exposed you to many evils at their hands, I only ask you to let your zeal in the war bear some proportion to your former sufferings. You should set an example to the rest of the allies, and show us how to inflict the sharpest and swiftest injury on our enemy, whilst we await the return from Lacedaemon of my envoys with the necessary funds. Since one of the last acts of Lysander, before he left us, was to hand back to Cyrus the funds already on the spot, as though we could well dispense with them. I was thus forced to turn to Cyrus, but all I got from him was a series of rebuffs; he refused me an audience, and, for my part, I could not induce myself to hang about his gates like a mendicant. But I give you my word, men of Miletus, that in return for any assistance which you can render us while waiting for these aids, I will requite you richly. Only by God's help let us show these barbarians that we do not need to worship them, in order to punish our foes."

The speech was effective; many members of the assembly arose, and not the least eagerly those who were accused of opposing him. These, in some terror, proposed a vote of money, backed by offers of further private contributions. Furnished with these sums, and having procured from Chios a further remittance of five drachmas[1] a piece as outfit for each seaman, he set sail to Methyma in Lesbos, which was in the hands of the enemy. But as the Methymnaeans were not disposed to come over to him (since there was an Athenian garrison in the place, and the men at the head of affairs were partisans of Athens), he assaulted and took the place by storm. All the property within accordingly became the spoil of the soldiers. The prisoners were collected for sale by Callicratidas in the marketplace, where, in answer to the demand of the allies, who called upon him to sell the Methymnaeans also, he made answer, that as long as he was in command, not a single Hellene should be enslaved if he could help it. The next day he set at liberty the free-born captives; the Athenian garrison with the captured slaves he sold.[2] To Conon he sent word:—He would put a stop to his strumpeting the sea.[3] And catching sight of him, as he put out to sea, at break of day, he gave chase, hoping to cut him off from his passage to Samos, and prevent his taking refuge there.

But Conon, aided by the sailing qualities of his fleet, the rowers of which were the pick of several ships' companies, concentrated in a few vessels, made good his escape, seeking shelter within the harbor of Mitylene in Lesbos, and with him two of the ten generals, Leon and Erasinides. Callicratidas, pursuing him with one hundred and seventy sail, entered the harbor simultaneously; and Conon thus hindered from further or final escape by the too rapid movements of the enemy, was forced to engage inside the harbor, and lost thirty of his ships, though the crews escaped to land. The remaining, forty in number, he hauled up under the walls of the town. Callicratidas, on his side, came to moorings in the harbor; and, having command of the exit, blocked the Athenian within. His next step was to send for the Methymnaeans in force by land, and to transport his army across from Chios. Money also came to him from Cyrus.

Conon, finding himself besieged by land and sea, without means of providing himself with corn from any quarter, the city crowded with inhabitants, and aid from Athens, whither no news of the late events could

---

1 About 4d.

2 Grote, "Hist. of Greece," vol. viii. p. 224 (2d ed.), thinks that Callicratidas did not even sell the Athenian garrison, as if the sense of the passage were: "The next day he set at liberty the free-born captives with the Athenian garrison, contenting himself with selling the captive slaves." But I am afraid that no ingenuity of stopping will extract that meaning from the Greek words, which are, {te d' usteraia tous men eleutherous apheke tous de ton 'Athenaion phrourous kai ta andrapoda ta doula panta apedoto}. To spare the Athenian garrison would have been too extraordinary a proceeding even for Callicratidas. The idea probably never entered his head. It was sufficiently noble for him to refuse to sell the Methymnaeans. See the remarks of Mr. W. L. Newman, "The Pol. of Aristotle," vol. i. p. 142.

3 I.e. the sea was Sparta's bride.

be conveyed, impossible, launched two of the fastest sailing vessels of his squadron. These he manned, before daybreak, with the best rowers whom he could pick out of the fleet, stowing away the marines at the same time in the hold of the ships and closing the port shutters. Every day for four days they held out in this fashion, but at evening as soon as it was dark he disembarked his men, so that the enemy might not suspect what they were after. On the fifth day, having got in a small stock of provisions, when it was already midday and the blockaders were paying little or no attention, and some of them even were taking their siesta, the two ships sailed out of the harbor: the one directing her course toward the Hellespont, whilst her companion made for the open sea. Then, on the part of the blockaders, there was a rush to the scene of action, as fast as the several crews could get clear of land, in bustle and confusion, cutting away the anchors, and rousing themselves from sleep, for, as chance would have it, they had been breakfasting on shore. Once on board, however, they were soon in hot pursuit of the ship which had started for the open sea, and ere the sun dipped they overhauled her, and after a successful engagement attached her by cables and towed her back into harbor, crew and all. Her comrade, making for the Hellespont, escaped, and eventually reached Athens with news of the blockade. The first relief was brought to the blockaded fleet by Diomedon, who anchored with twelve vessels in the Mitylenaean Narrows.[1] But a sudden attack of Callicratidas, who bore down upon him without warning, cost him ten of his vessels, Diomedon himself escaping with his own ship and one other.

Now that the position of affairs, including the blockade, was fully known at Athens, a vote was passed to send out a reinforcement of one hundred and ten ships. Every man of ripe age,[2] whether slave or free, was impressed for this service, so that within thirty days the whole one hundred and ten vessels were fully manned and weighed anchor. Among those who served in this fleet were also many of the knights.[3] The fleet at once stood out across to Samos, and picked up the Samian vessels in that island. The muster-roll was swelled by the addition of more than thirty others from the rest of the allies, to whom the same principle of conscription applied, as also it did to the ships already engaged on foreign service. The actual total, therefore, when all the contingents were collected, was over one hundred and fifty vessels.

---

1 Or, *"Euripus."*

2 *I.e. from eighteen to sixty years.*

3 See Boeckh. *"P. E. A." Bk. II. chap. xxi. p. 263 (Eng. trans.)*

Callicratidas, hearing that the relief squadron had already reached Samos, left fifty ships, under command of Eteonicus, in the harbor of Mitylene, and setting sail with the other one hundred and twenty, hove to for the evening meal off Cape Malea in Lesbos, opposite Mitylene. It so happened that the Athenians on this day were supping on the islands of Arginusae, which lie opposite Lesbos. In the night the Spartan not only saw their watch-fires, but received positive information that "these were the Athenians"; and about midnight he got under weigh, intending to fall upon them suddenly. But a violent downpour of rain with thunder and lightning prevented him putting out to sea. By daybreak it had cleared, and he sailed toward Arginusae. On their side, the Athenian squadron stood out to meet him, with their left wing facing toward the open sea, and drawn up in the following order:—Aristocrates, in command of the left wing, with fifteen ships, led the van; next came Diomedon with fifteen others, and immediately in rear of Aristocrates and Diomedon respectively, as their supports, came Pericles and Erasinides. Parallel with Diomedon were the Samians, with their ten ships drawn up in single line, under the command of a Samian officer named Hippeus. Next to these came the ten vessels of the taxiarchs, also in single line, and supporting them, the three ships of the navarchs, with any other allied vessels in the squadron. The right wing was entrusted to Protomachus with fifteen ships, and next to him (on the extreme right) was Thrasylus with another division of fifteen. Protomachus was supported by Lysias with an equal number of ships, and Thrasylus by Aristogenes. The object of this formation was to prevent the enemy from manouvring so as to break their line by striking them amidships,[1] since they were inferior in sailing power.

The Lacedaemonians, on the contrary, trusting to their superior seamanship, were formed opposite with their ships all in single line, with the special object of manouvring so as either to break the enemy's line or to wheel round them. Callicratidas commanded the right wing in person. Before the battle the officer who acted as his pilot, the Megarian Hermon, suggested that it might be well to withdraw the fleet as the Athenian ships were far more numerous. But Callicratidas replied that Sparta would be no worse off even if he personally should perish, but to flee would be

---

1 Lit. "by the diekplous." Cf. Thuc. i. 49, and Arnold's note, who says: "The "diecplus" was a breaking through the enemy's line in order by a rapid turning of the vessel to strike the enemy's ship on the side or stern, where it was most defenseless, and so to sink it." So, it seems, "the superiority of nautical skill has passed," as Grote (viii. p. 234) says, "to the Peloponnesians and their allies." Well may the historian add, "How astonished would the Athenian Admiral Phormion have been, if he could have witnessed the fleets and the order of battle at Arginusae!" See Thuc. iv. 11.

disgraceful.[1] And now the fleets approached, and for a long space the battle endured. At first the vessels were engaged in crowded masses, and later on in scattered groups. At length Callicratidas, as his vessel dashed her beak into her antagonist, was hurled off into the sea and disappeared. At the same instant Protomachus, with his division on the right, had defeated the enemy's left, and then the flight of the Peloponnesians began toward Chios, though a very considerable body of them made for Phocaea, whilst the Athenians sailed back again to Arginusae. The losses on the side of the Athenians were twenty-five ships, crews and all, with the exception of the few who contrived to reach dry land. On the Peloponnesian side, nine out of the ten Lacedaemonian ships, and more than sixty belonging to the rest of the allied squadron, were lost.

After consultation the Athenian generals agreed that two captains of triremes, Theramenes and Thrasybulus, accompanied by some of the taxiarchs, should take forty-seven ships and sail to the assistance of the disabled fleet and of the men on board, whilst the rest of the squadron proceeded to attack the enemy's blockading squadron under Eteonicus at Mitylene. In spite of their desire to carry out this resolution, the wind and a violent storm which arose prevented them. So they set up a trophy, and took up their quarters for the night. As to Etenoicus, the details of the engagement ware faithfully reported to him by the express despatch-boat in attendance. On receipt of the news, however, he sent the despatch-boat out again the way she came, with an injunction to those on board of her to sail off quickly without exchanging a word with anyone. Then on a sudden they were to return garlanded with wreaths of victory and shouting "Callicratidas has won a great sea fight, and the whole Athenian squadron is destroyed." This they did, and Eteonicus, on his side, as soon as the despatch-boat came sailing in, proceeded to offer sacrifice of thanksgiving in honor of the good news. Meanwhile he gave orders that the troops were to take their evening meal, and that the masters of the trading ships were silently to stow away their goods on board the merchant ships and make sail as fast as the favorable breeze could speed them to Chios. The ships of war were to follow suit with what speed they might. This done, he set fire to his camp, and led off the land forces to Methymna. Conon, finding

---

1 For the common reading, {oikeitai}, which is ungrammatical, various conjectures have been made, e.g.

   {oikieitai} = "would be none the worse off for citizens,"

   {oikesetai} = "would be just as well administered without him,"

but as the readings and their renderings are alike doubtful, I have preferred to leave the matter vague. Cf. Cicero, "De Offic." i. 24; Plutarch, "Lac. Apophth." p. 832.

the enemy had made off, and the wind had grown comparatively mild,[1] got his ships afloat, and so fell in with the Athenian squadron, which had by this time set out from Arginusae. To these he explained the proceedings of Eteonicus. The squadron put into Mitylene, and from Mitylene stood across to Chios, and thence, without effecting anything further, sailed back to Samos.

VII

All the above-named generals, with the exception of Conon, were presently deposed by the home authorities. In addition to Conon two new generals were chosen, Adeimantus and Philocles. Of those concerned in the late victory two never returned to Athens: these were Protomachus and Aristogenes. The other six sailed home. Their names were Pericles, Diomedon, Lysias, Aristocrates, Thrasylus, and Erasinides. On their arrival Archidemus, the leader of the democracy at that date, who had charge of the two obol fund,[2] inflicted a fine on Erasinides, and accused him before the Dicastery[3] of having appropriated money derived from the Hellespont, which belonged to the people. He brought a further charge against him of misconduct while acting as general, and the court sentenced him to imprisonment.

These proceedings in the law court were followed by the statement of the generals before the senate[4] touching the late victory and the magnitude of the storm. Timocrates then proposed that the other five generals should be put in custody and handed over to the public assembly.[5] Whereupon the senate committed them all to prison. Then came the meeting of the public assembly, in which others, and more particularly Theramenes, formally accused the generals. He insisted that they ought to show cause why they had not picked up the shipwrecked crews. To prove that there had been no attempt on their part to attach blame to others, he might point,

---

1 Or, "had changed to a finer quarter."
2 Reading {tes diobelais}, a happy conjecture for the MSS. {tes diokelias}, which is inexplicable. See Grote, "Hist. of Greece," vol. viii. p. 244 note (2d ed.)
3 I.e. a legal tribunal or court of law. At Athens the free citizens constitutionally sworn and impannelled sat as "dicasts" ("jurymen," or rather as a bench of judges) to hear cases ({dikai}). Any particular board of dicasts formed a "dicastery."
4 This is the Senate or Council of Five Hundred. One of its chief duties was to prepare measures for discussion in the assembly. It had also a certain amount of judicial power, hearing complaints and inflicting fines up to fifty drachmas. It sat daily, a "prytany" of fifty members of each of the ten tribes in rotation holding office for a month in turn.
5 This is the great Public Assembly (the Ecclesia), consisting of all genuine Athenian citizens of more than twenty years of age.

as conclusive testimony, to the despatch sent by the generals themselves to the senate and the people, in which they attributed the whole disaster to the storm, and nothing else. After this the generals each in turn made a defense, which was necessarily limited to a few words, since no right of addressing the assembly at length was allowed by law. Their explanation of the occurrences was that, in order to be free to sail against the enemy themselves, they had devolved the duty of picking up the shipwrecked crews upon certain competent captains of men-of-war, who had themselves been generals in their time, to wit Theramenes and Tharysbulus, and others of like stamp. If blame could attach to anyone at all with regard to the duty in question, those to whom their orders had been given were the sole persons they could hold responsible. "But," they went on to say, "we will not, because these very persons have denounced us, invent a lie, and say that Theramenes and Thrasybulus are to blame, when the truth of the matter is that the magnitude of the storm alone prevented the burial of the dead and the rescue of the living." In proof of their contention, they produced the pilots and numerous other witnesses from among those present at the engagement. By these arguments they were in a fair way to persuade the people of their innocence. Indeed many private citizens rose wishing to become bail for the accused, but it was resolved to defer decision till another meeting of the assembly. It was indeed already so late that it would have been impossible to see to count the show of hands. It was further resolved that the senate meanwhile should prepare a measure, to be introduced at the next assembly, as to the mode in which the accused should take their trial.

Then came the festival of the Aparturia,[1] with its family gatherings of fathers and kinsfolk. Accordingly the party of Theramenes procured numbers of people clad in black apparel, and close-shaven,[2] who were to go in and present themselves before the public assembly in the middle of the festival, as relatives, presumably, of the men who had perished; and they persuaded Callixenus to accuse the generals in the senate. The next step was to convoke the assembly, when the senate laid before it the proposal just passed by their body, at the instance of Callixenus, which ran as follows: "Seeing that both the parties to this case, to wit, the prosecutors of the generals on the one hand, and the accused themselves in their

---

1 An important festival held in October at Athens, and in nearly all Ionic cities. Its objects were (1) the recognition of a common descent from Ion, the son of Apollo Patrous; and (2) the maintenance of the ties of clanship. See Grote, "Hist. of Greece," vol. viii. p. 260 foll. (2d ed.); Jebb, "Theophr." xviii. 5.
2 I.e. in sign of mourning.

defense on the other, have been heard in the late meeting of the assembly; we propose that the people of Athens now record their votes, one and all, by their tribes; that a couple of voting urns be placed for the convenience of each several tribe; and the public crier in the hearing of each several tribe proclaim the mode of voting as follows: 'Let everyone who finds the generals guilty of not rescuing the heroes of the late sea fight deposit his vote in urn No. 1. Let him who is of the contrary opinion deposit his vote in urn No. 2. Further, in the event of the aforesaid generals being found guilty, let death be the penalty. Let the guilty persons be delivered over to the eleven. Let their property be confiscated to the State, with the exception of one tithe, which falls to the goddess.'"

Now there came forward in the assembly a man, who said that he had escaped drowning by clinging to a meal tub. The poor fellows perishing around him had commissioned him, if he succeeded in saving himself, to tell the people of Athens how bravely they had fought for their fatherland, and how the generals had left them there to drown.

Presently Euryptolemus, the son of Peisianax, and others served a notice of indictment on Callixenus, insisting that his proposal was unconstitutional, and this view of the case was applauded by some members of the assembly. But the majority kept crying out that it was monstrous if the people were to be hindered by any stray individual from doing what seemed to them right. And when Lysicus, embodying the spirit of those cries, formally proposed that if these persons would not abandon their action, they should be tried by the same vote along with the generals: a proposition to which the mob gave vociferous assent; and so these were compelled to abandon their summonses. Again, when some of the Prytanes[1] objected to put a resolution to the vote which was in itself unconstitutional, Callixenus again got up and accused them in the same terms, and the shouting began again. "Yes, summons all who refuse," until the Prytanes, in alarm, all agreed with one exception to permit the voting. This obstinate dissentient was Socrates, the son of Sophroniscus, who insisted that he would do nothing except in accordance with the law.[2] After this Euryptolemus rose and spoke in behalf of the generals. He said:—

"I stand here, men of Athens, partly to accuse Pericles, though he is a close and intimate connection of my own, and Diomedon, who is my friend, and partly to urge certain considerations on their behalf, but chiefly

---

[1] *Prytanes*—*the technical term for the senators of the presiding tribe, who acted as presidents of the assembly. Their chairman for the day was called Epistates.*

[2] *For the part played by Socrates see further Xenophon's "Memorabilia," I. i. 18; IV. iv. 2.*

to press upon you what seems to me the best course for the State collectively. I hold them to blame in that they dissuaded their colleagues from their intention to send a despatch to the senate and this assembly, which should have informed you of the orders given to Theramenes and Thrasybulus to take forty-seven ships of war and pick up the shipwrecked crews, and of the neglect of the two officers to carry out those orders. And it follows that though the offense was committed by one or two, the responsibility must be shared by all; and in return for kindness in the past, they are in danger at present of sacrificing their lives to the machinations of these very men, and others whom I could mention. In danger, do I say, of losing their lives? No, not so, if you will suffer me to persuade you to do what is just and right; if you will only adopt such a course as shall enable you best to discover the truth and shall save you from too late repentance, when you find you have transgressed irremediably against heaven and your own selves. In what I urge there is no trap nor plot whereby you can be deceived by me or any other man; it is a straightforward course which will enable you to discover and punish the offender by whatever process you like, collectively or individually. Let them have, if not more, at any rate one whole day to make what defense they can for themselves; and trust to your own unbiased judgment to guide you to the right conclusion.

"You know, men of Athens, the exceeding stringency of the decree of Cannonus,[1] which orders that man, whosoever he be, who is guilty of treason against the people of Athens, to be put in irons, and so to meet the charge against him before the people. If he be convicted, he is to be thrown into the Barathron and perish, and the property of such an one is to be confiscated, with the exception of the tithe which falls to the goddess. I call upon you to try these generals in accordance with this decree. Yes, and so help me God—if it please you, begin with my own kinsman Pericles for base would it be on my part to make him of more account than the whole of the State. Or, if you prefer, try them by that other law, which is directed against robbers of temples and betrayers of their country, which says: if a man betray his city or rob a sacred temple of the gods, he shall be tried before a law court, and if he be convicted, his body shall not be buried in Attica, and his goods shall be confiscated to the State. Take your choice as

---

1 "There was a rule in Attic judicial procedure, called the psephism of Kannonus (originally adopted, we do not know when, on the proposition of a citizen of that name, as a psephism or decree for some particular case, but since generalised into common practice, and grown into great prescriptive reverence), which peremptorily forbade any such collective trial or sentence, and directed that a separate judicial vote should in all cases be taken for or against each accused party." Grote, "Hist. of Greece," vol. viii. p. 266 (2d ed.)

between these two laws, men of Athens, and let the prisoners be tried by one or other. Let three portions of a day be assigned to each respectively, one portion wherein they shall listen to their accusation, a second wherein they shall make their defense, and a third wherein you shall meet and give your votes in due order on the question of their guilt or innocence. By this procedure the malefactors will receive the desert of their misdeeds in full, and those who are innocent will owe you, men of Athens, the recovery of their liberty, in place of unmerited destruction.[1]

"On your side, in trying the accused by recognized legal procedure, you will show that you obey the dictates of pious feeling, and can regard the sanctity of an oath, instead of joining hands with our enemies the Lacedaemonians and fighting their battles. For is it not to fight their battles, if you take their conquerors, the men who deprived them of seventy vessels, and at the moment of victory sent them to perdition untried and in the teeth of the law? What are you afraid of, that you press forward with such hot haste? Do you imagine that you may be robbed of the power of life and death over whom you please, should you condescend to a legal trial? but that you are safe if you take shelter behind an illegality, like the illegality of Callixenus, when he worked upon the senate to propose to this assembly to deal with the accused by a single vote? But consider, you may actually put to death an innocent man, and then repentance will one day visit you too late. Bethink you how painful and unavailing remorse will then be, and more particularly if your error has cost a fellow creature his life. What a travesty of justice it would be if in the case of a man like Aristarchus,[2] who first tried to destroy the democracy and then betrayed Oenoe to our enemy the Thebans, you granted him a day for his defense, consulting his wishes, and conceded to him all the other benefits of the law; whereas now you are proposing to deprive of these same privileges your own generals, who in every way conformed to your views and defeated your enemies. Do not you, of all men, I implore you, men of Athens, act thus. Why, these laws are your own, to them, beyond all else you owe your greatness. Guard them jealously; in nothing, I implore you, act without their sanction.

"But now, turn for a moment and consider with me the actual occurrences which have created the suspicion of misconduct on the part of our late generals. The sea-fight had been fought and won, and the ships had returned to land, when Diomedon urged that the whole squadron should sail out in

---

1 Reading {adikos apolountai}.
2 See below, II. iii; also cf. Thuc. viii. 90, 98.

line and pick up the wrecks and floating crews. Erasinides was in favor of all the vessels sailing as fast as possible to deal with the enemy's forces at Mitylene. And Thrasylus represented that both objects could be effected, by leaving one division of the fleet there, and with the rest sailing against the enemy; and if this resolution were agreed to, he advised that each of the eight generals should leave three ships of his own division with the ten vessels of the taxiarchs, the ten Samian vessels, and the three belonging to the navarchs. These added together make forty-seven, four for each of the lost vessels, twelve in number. Among the taxiarchs left behind, two were Thrasybulus and Theramenes, the men who in the late meeting of this assembly undertook to accuse the generals. With the remainder of the fleet they were to sail to attack the enemy's fleet. Everything, you must admit, was duly and admirably planned. It was only common justice, therefore, that those whose duty it was to attack the enemy should render an account for all miscarriages of operations against the enemy; while those who were commissioned to pick up the dead and dying should, if they failed to carry out the instructions of the generals, be put on trial to explain the reasons of the failure. This indeed I may say in behalf of both parites. It was really the storm which, in spite of what the generals had planned, prevented anything being done. There are witnesses ready to attest the truth of this: the men who escaped as by a miracle, and among these one of these very generals, who was on a sinking ship and was saved. And this man, who needed picking up as much as anybody at that moment, is, they insist, to be tried by one and the same vote as those who neglected to perform their orders! Once more, I beg you, men of Athens, to accept your victory and your good fortune, instead of behaving like the desperate victims of misfortune and defeat. Recognize the finger of divine necessity; do not incur the reproach of stony-heartedness by discovering treason where there was merely powerlessness, and condemning as guilty those who were prevented by the storm from carrying out their instructions. Nay! you will better satisfy the demands of justice by crowning these conquerors with wreaths of victory than by punishing them with death at the instigation of wicked men."

At the conclusion of his speech Euryptolemus proposed, as an amendment, that the prisoners should, in accordance with the decree of Cannonus, be tried each separately, as against the proposal of the senate to try them all by a single vote.

At the show of hands the tellers gave the majority in favor of Euryptolemus's amendment, but upon the application of Menecles, who took formal exception[1] to this decision, the show of hands was gone through again, and now the verdict was in favor of the resolution of the senate. At a later date the balloting was made, and by the votes recorded the eight generals were condemned, and the six who were in Athens were put to death.

Not long after, repentance seized the Athenians, and they passed a decree authorising the public prosecution of those who had deceived the people, and the appointment of proper securities for their persons until the trial was over. Callixenus was one of those committed for trail. There were, besides Callixenus, four others against whom true bills were declared, and they were all five imprisoned by their sureties. But all subsequently effected their escape before the trial, at the time of the sedition in which Cleophon[2] was killed. Callixenus eventually came back when the party in Piraeus returned to the city, at the date of the amnesty,[3] but only to die of hunger, an object of universal detestation.

BOOK II

I

To return to Eteonicus and his troops in Chios. During summer they were well able to support themselves on the fruits of the season, or by laboring for hire in different parts of the island, but with the approach of winter these means of subsistence began to fail. Ill-clad at the same time, and ill-shod, they fell to caballing and arranging plans to attack the city of Chios. It was agreed among them, that in order to gauge their numbers, every member of the conspiracy should carry a reed. Eteonicus got wind of the design, but was at a loss how to deal with it, considering the number of these reed-bearers. To make an open attack upon them seemed dangerous. It would probably lead to a rush to arms, in which the conspirators would seize the city and commence hostilities, and, in the event of their success, everything hitherto achieved would be lost. Or again, the destruction on his part of many fellow creatures and allies was a

---

1 *For this matter cf. Schomann, "De Comitiis Athen." p. 161 foll.; also Grote, "Hist. of Grece," vol. viii. p. 276 note (2d ed.)*
2 *Cleophon, the well-known demagogue. For the occasion of his death see Grote, "Hist. of Greece," vol. viii. pp. 166, 310 (2d ed.); Prof. Jebb, "Attic Orators," i. 266, ii. 288. For his character, as popularly conceived, cf. Aristoph. "Frogs," 677.*
3 *403 BC.*

terrible alternative, which would place the Spartans in an unenviable light with regard to the rest of Hellas, and render the soldiers ill-disposed to the cause in hand. Accordingly he took with him fifteen men, armed with daggers, and marched through the city. Falling in with one of the reed-bearers, a man suffering from ophthalmia, who was returning from the surgeon's house, he put him to death. This led to some uproar, and people asked why the man was thus slain. By Eteonicus's orders the answer was set afloat, "because he carried a reed." As the explanation circulated, one reed-bearer after another threw away the symbol, each one saying to himself, as he heard the reason given, "I have better not be seen with this." After a while Eteonicus called a meeting of the Chians, and imposed upon them a contribution of money, on the ground that with pay in their pockets the sailors would have no temptation to revolutionary projects. The Chians acquiesced. Whereupon Eteonicus promptly ordered his crews to get on board their vessels. He then rowed alongside each ship in turn, and addressed the men at some length in terms of encouragement and cheery admonition, just as though he knew nothing of what had taken place, and so distributed a month's pay to every man on board.

After this the Chians and the other allies held a meeting in Ephesus, and, considering the present posture of affairs, determined to send ambassadors to Lacedaemon with a statement of the facts, and a request that Lysander might be sent out to take command of the fleet. Lysander's high reputation among the allies dated back to his former period of office, when as admiral he had won the naval victory of Notium. The ambassadors accordingly were despatched, accompanied by envoys also from Cyrus, charged with the same message. The Lacedaemonians responded by sending them Lysander as second in command,[1] with Aracus as admiral, since it was contrary to their custom that the same man should be admiral twice. At the same time the fleet was entrusted to Lysander.[2]

It was in this year[3] that Cyrus put Autoboesaces and Mitraeus to death. These were sons of the sister of Dariaeus[4] (the daughter of Xerxes, the father of Darius).[5] He put them to death for neglecting, when they met

---

1 *Epistoleus. See above.*
2 *"At this date the war had lasted five-and-twenty years." So the MSS. read. The words are probably an interpolation.*
3 *406 BC.*
4 *Dariaeus, i.e. Darius, but the spelling of the name is correct, and occurs in Ctesias, though in the "Anabasis" we have the spelling Darius.*
5 *These words look like the note of a foolish and ignorant scribe. He ought to have written, "The daughter of Artaxerxes and own sister of Darius, commonly so called."*

him, to thrust their hands into the sleeve (or "kore") which is a tribute of respect paid to the king alone. This "kore" is longer than the ordinary sleeve, so long in fact that a man with his hand inside is rendered helpless. In consequence of this act on the part of Cyrus, Hieramenes[1] and his wife urged upon Dariaeus the danger of overlooking such excessive insolence on the part of the young prince, and Dariaeus, on the plea of sickness, sent a special embassy to summon Cyrus to his bedside.

405 BC. In the following year[2] Lysander arrived at Ephesus, and sent for Eteonicus with his ships from Chios, and collected all other vessels elsewhere to be found. His time was now devoted to refitting the old ships and having new ones built in Antandrus. He also made a journey to the court of Cyrus with a request for money. All Cyrus could say was, that not only the money sent by the king was spent, but much more besides; and he pointed out the various sums which each of the admirals had received, but at the same time he gave him what he asked for. Furnished with this money, Lysander appointed captains to the different men-of-war, and remitted to the sailors their arrears of pay. Meanwhile the Athenian generals, on their side, were devoting their energies to the improvements of their navy at Samos.

It was now Cyrus's turn to send for Lysander. It was the moment at which the envoy from his father had arrived with the message: "Your father is on his sick-bed and desires your presence." The king lay at Thamneria, in Media, near the territory of the Cadusians, against whom he had marched to put down a revolt. When Lysander presented himself, Cyrus was urgent with him not to engage the Athenians at sea unless he had many more ships than they. "The king," he added, "and I have plenty of wealth, so that, as far as money goes, you can man plenty of vessels." He then consigned to him all the tributes from the several cities which belonged to him personally, and gave him the ready money which he had as a gift; and finally, reminding him of the sincere friendship he entertained toward the state of Lacedaemon, as well as to himself personally, he set out up country to visit his father. Lysander, finding himself thus left with the complete control of the property of Cyrus (during the absence of that prince, so summoned to the bedside of his father), was able to distribute pay to his troops, after which he set sail for the Ceramic Gulf of Caria. Here he stormed a city in alliance with the Athenians named Cedreae, and on the

---

1 For Hieramenes cf. Thuc. viii. 95, and Prof. Jowett ad loc.
2 The MSS. add "during the ephorate of Archytas and the archonship at Athens of Alexias," which, though correct enough, is probably an interpolation.

following day's assault took it, and reduced the inhabitants to slavery. These were of a mixed Hellene and barbaric stock. From Cedreae he continued his voyage to Rhodes. The Athenians meanwhile, using Samos as their base of operations, were employed in devastating the king's territory, or in swooping down upon Chios and Ephesus, and in general were preparing for a naval battle, having but lately chosen three new generals in addition to those already in office, whose names were Menander, Tydeus, and Cephisodotus. Now Lysander, leaving Rhodes, and coasting along Ionia, made his way to the Hellespont, having an eye to the passage of vessels through the Straits, and, in a more hostile sense, on the cities which had revolted from Sparta. The Athenians also set sail from Chios, but stood out to open sea, since the seaboard of Asia was hostile to them.

Lysander was again on the move; leaving Abydos, he passed up channel to Lampsacus, which town was allied with Athens; the men of Abydos and the rest of the troops advancing by land, under the command of the Lacedaemonian Thorax. They then attacked and took by storm the town, which was wealthy, and with its stores of wine and wheat and other commodities was pillaged by the soldiery. All free-born persons, however, were without exception released by Lysander. And now the Athenian fleet, following close on his heels, came to moorings at Elaeus, in the Chersonesus, one hundred and eighty sail in all. It was not until they had reached this place, and were getting their early meal, that the news of what had happened at Lampsacus reached them. Then they instantly set sail again to Sestos, and, having halted long enough merely to take in stores, sailed on further to Aegospotami, a point facing Lampsacus, where the Hellespont is not quite two miles[1] broad. Here they took their evening meal.

The night following, or rather early next morning, with the first streak of dawn, Lysander gave the signal for the men to take their breakfasts and get on board their vessels; and so, having got all ready for a naval engagement, with his ports closed and movable bulwarks attached, he issued the order that no one was to stir from his post or put out to sea. As the sun rose the Athenians drew up their vessels facing the harbor, in line of battle ready for action; but Lysander declining to come out to meet them, as the day advanced they retired again to Aegospotami. Then Lysander ordered the swiftest of his ships to follow the Athenians, and as soon as the crews had disembarked, to watch what they did, sail back, and report to him. Until these look-outs returned he would permit no disembarkation from his

---

1 Lit. fifteen stades.

ships. This performance he repeated for four successive days, and each day the Athenians put out to sea and challenged an engagement.

But now Alcibiades, from one of his fortresses, could espy the position of his fellow countrymen, moored on an open beach beyond reach of any city, and forced to send for supplies to Sestos, which was nearly two miles distant, while their enemies were safely lodged in a harbor, with a city adjoining, and everything within reach. The situation did not please him, and he advised them to shift their anchorage to Sestos, where they would have the advantage of a harbor and a city. "Once there," he concluded, "you can engage the enemy whenever it suits you." But the generals, and more particularly Tydeus and Menander, bade him go about his business. "We are generals now—not you," they said; and so he went away. And now for five days in succession the Athenians had sailed out to offer battle, and for the fifth time retired, followed by the same swift sailors of the enemy. But this time Lysander's orders to the vessels so sent in pursuit were, that as soon as they saw the enemy's crew fairly disembarked and dispersed along the shores of the Chersonesus (a practice, it should be mentioned, which had grown upon them from day to day owing to the distance at which eatables had to be purchased, and out of sheer contempt, no doubt, of Lysander, who refused to accept battle), they were to begin their return voyage, and when in mid-channel to hoist a shield. The orders were punctually carried out, and Lysander at once signalled to his whole squadron to put across with all speed, while Thorax, with the land forces, was to march parallel with the fleet along the coast. Aware of the enemy's fleet, which he could see bearing down upon him, Conon had only time to signal to the crews to join their ships and rally to the rescue with all their might. But the men were scattered far and wide, and some of the vessels had only two out of their three banks of rowers, some only a single one, while others again were completely empty. Conon's own ship, with seven others in attendance on him and the *Paralus*,[1] put out to sea, a little cluster of nine vessels, with their full complement of men; but every one of the remaining one hundred and seventy-one vessels were captured by Lysander on the beach. As to the men themselves, the large majority of them were easily made prisoners on shore, a few only escaping to the small fortresses of the neighborhood. Meanwhile Conon and his nine vessels made good their escape. For himself, knowing that the fortune of Athens was ruined, he put into Abarnis, the promontory of Lampsacus, and there picked up the great sails of Lysander's ships, and then with eight ships set

---

1 The Paralus—*the Athenian sacred vessel; cf. Thuc. iii. 33 et passim.*

sail himself to seek refuge with Evagoras in Cyprus, while the "Paralus" started for Athens with tidings of what had taken place.

    Lysander, on his side, conveyed the ships and prisoners and all other spoil back to Lampsacus, having on board some of the Athenian generals, notably Philocles and Adeimantus. On the very day of these achievements he despatched Theopompus, a Milesian privateersman, to Lacedaemon to report what had taken place. This envoy arrived within three days and delivered his message. Lysander's next step was to convene the allies and bid them deliberate as to the treatment of the prisoners. Many were the accusations here levied against the Athenians. There was talk of crimes committed against the law of Hellas, and of cruelties sanctioned by popular decrees; which, had they conquered in the late sea-fight, would have been carried out; such as the proposal to cut off the right hand of every prisoner taken alive, and lastly the ill-treatment of two captured men-of-war, a Corinthian and an Andrian vessel, when every man on board had been hurled headlong down the cliff. Philocles was the very general of the Athenians who had so ruthlessly destroyed those men. Many other tales were told; and at length a resolution was passed to put all the Athenian prisoners, with the exception of Adeimantus, to death. He alone, it was pleaded, had taken exception to the proposal to cut off the prisoners' hands. On the other hand, he was himself accused by some people of having betrayed the fleet. As to Philocles, Lysander put to him one question, as the officer who had thrown[1] the Corinthians and Andrians down the cliff: What fate did the man deserve to suffer who had embarked on so cruel a course of illegality against Hellenes? and so delivered him to the executioner.

II

    When he had set the affairs of Lampsacus in order, Lysander sailed to Byzantium and Chalcedon, where the inhabitants, having first dismissed the Athenian garrison under a flag of truce, admitted him within their walls. Those citizens of Byzantium, who had betrayed Byzantium into the hands of Alcibiades, fled as exiles into Pontus, but subsequently betaking themselves to Athens, became Athenian citizens. In dealing with the Athenian garrisons, and indeed with all Athenians wheresoever found, Lysander made it a rule to give them safe conduct to Athens, and to Athens only, in the certainty that the larger the number collected within the city and Piraeus, the more quickly the want of necessaries of life would make itself felt. And now, leaving Sthenelaus, a Laconian, as governor-general

---

1 Reading {os... katekremnise}.

of Byzantium and Chalcedon, he sailed back himself to Lampsacus and devoted himself to refitting his ships.

It was night when the *Paralus* reached Athens with her evil tidings, on receipt of which a bitter wail of woe broke forth. From Piraeus, following the line of the long walls up to the heart of the city, it swept and swelled, as each man to his neighbor passed on the news. On that night no man slept. There was mourning and sorrow for those that were lost, but the lamentation for the dead was merged in even deeper sorrow for themselves, as they pictured the evils they were about to suffer, the like of which they themselves had inflicted upon the men of Melos, who were colonists of the Lacedaemonians, when they mastered them by siege. Or on the men of Histiaea; on Scione and Torone; on the Aeginetans, and many another Hellene city.[1] On the following day the public assembly met, and, after debate, it was resolved to block up all the harbors save one, to put the walls in a state of defense, to post guards at various points, and to make all other necessary preparations for a siege. Such were the concerns of the men of Athens.

Lysander presently left the Hellespont with two hundred sail and arrived at Lesbos, where he established a new order of things in Mitylene and the other cities of the island. Meanwhile he despatched Eteonicus with a squadron of ten ships to the northern coasts,[2] where that officer brought about a revolution of affairs which placed the whole region in the hands of Lacedaemon. Indeed, in a moment of time, after the sea-fight, the whole of Hellas had revolted from Athens, with the solitary exception of the men of Samos. These, having massacred the notables,[3] held the state under their control. After a while Lysander sent messages to Agis at Deceleia, and to Lacedaemon, announcing his approach with a squadron of two hundred sail.

In obedience to a general order of Pausanias, the other king of Lacedaemon, a levy in force of the Lacedaemonians and all the rest of

---

1 *With regard to these painful recollections, see (1) for the siege and surrender of Melos (in 416 BC), Thuc. v. 114, 116; and cf. Aristoph. "Birds," 186; Plut. ("Lysander," 14); (2) for the ejection of the Histiaeans, an incident of the recovery of Euboea in 445 BC, see Thuc. i. 14; Plut. ("Pericles," 23); (3) for the matter of Scione, which revolted in 423 BC, and was for a long time a source of disagreement between the Athenians and Lacedaemonians, until finally captured by the former in 421 BC, when the citizens were slain and the city given to the Plataeans, see Thuc. iv. 120-122, 129-133; v. 18, 32; (4) for Torone see Thuc. ib., and also v. 3; (5) for the expulsion of the Aeginetans in 431 BC see Thuc. ii. 27.*
2 *Lit. "the Thraceward districts." See above, p. 16.*
3 *Or, "since they had slain their notables, held the state under popular control." See Grote, "Hist. of Greece," vol. viii. p. 303 note 3 (2d ed.), who thinks that the incident referred to is the violent democratic revolution in Samos described in Thuc. viii. 21, 412 BC.*

Peloponnesus, except the Argives, was set in motion for a campaign. As soon as the several contingents had arrived, the king put himself at their head and marched against Athens, encamping in the gymnasium of the Academy,[1] as it is called. Lysander had now reached Aegina, where, having got together as many of the former inhabitants as possible, he formally reinstated them in their city; and what he did in behalf of the Aeginetans, he did also in behalf of the Melians, and of the rest who had been deprived of their countries. He then pillaged the island of Salamis, and finally came to moorings off Piraeus with one hundred and fifty ships of the line, and established a strict blockade against all merchant ships entering that harbor.

The Athenians, finding themselves besieged by land and sea, were in sore perplexity what to do. Without ships, without allies, without provisions, the belief gained hold upon them that there was no way of escape. They must now, in their turn, suffer what they had themselves inflincted upon others; not in retaliation, indeed, for ills received, but out of sheer insolence, overriding the citizens of petty states, and for no better reason than that these were allies of the very men now at their gates. In this frame of mind they enfranchised those who at any time had lost their civil rights, and schooled themselves to endurance; and, albeit many succumbed to starvation, no thought of truce or reconciliation with their foes was breathed.[2] But when the stock of corn was absolutely insufficient, they sent an embassage to Agis, proposing to become allies of the Lacedaemonians on the sole condition of keeping their fortification walls and Piraeus; and to draw up articles of treaty on these terms. Agis bade them betake themselves to Lacedaemon, seeing that he had no authority to act himself. With this answer the ambassadors returned to Athens, and were forthwith sent on to Lacedaemon. On reaching Sellasia,[3] a town in[4] Laconian territory, they waited till they got their answer from the ephors, who, having learned their terms (which were identical to those already proposed to Agis), bade them instantly to be gone, and, if they really desired peace, to come with other proposals, the fruit of happier reflection. Thus the ambassadors returned home, and reported the result of their embassage, whereupon despondency fell upon all. It was a painful reflection that in the end they would be sold into slavery; and meanwhile,

---

1 For this most illustrious of Athenian gymnasia, which still retains its name, see Leake, "Topography of Athens," i. 195 foll.
2 Or, "they refused to treat for peace."
3 Sellasia, the bulwark of Sparta in the valley of the Oenus.
4 The MSS. have "in the neighborhood of," which words are inappropriate at this date, though they may well have been added by some annotator after the Cleomenic war and the battle of Sellasia, bc 222, when Antigonus of Macedon destroyed the place in the interests of the Achaean League.

pending the return of a second embassy, many must needs fall victims to starvation. The razing of their fortifications was not a solution which anyone cared to recommend. A senator, Archestratus, had indeed put the question in the senate, whether it were not best to make peace with the Lacedaemonians on such terms as they were willing to propose; but he was thrown into prison. The Laconian proposals referred to involved the destruction of both long walls for a space of more than a mile. And a decree had been passed, making it illegal to submit any such proposition about the walls. Things having reached this pass, Theramenes made a proposal in the public assembly as follows: If they chose to send him as an ambassador to Lysander, he would go and find out why the Lacedaemonians were so unyielding about the walls; whether it was they really intended to enslave the city, or merely that they wanted a guarantee of good faith. Despatched accordingly, he lingered on with Lysander for three whole months and more, watching for the time when the Athenians, at the last pinch of starvation, would be willing to accede to any terms that might be offered. At last, in the fourth month, he returned and reported to the public assembly that Lysander had detained him all this while, and had ended by bidding him betake himself to Lacedaemon, since he had no authority himself to answer his questions, which must be addressed directly to the ephors. After this Theramenes was chosen with nine others to go to Lacedaemon as ambassadors with full powers. Meanwhile Lysander had sent an Athenian exile, named Aristoteles, in company of certain Lacedaemonians, to Sparta to report to the board of ephors how he had answered Theramenes, that they, and they alone, had supreme authority in matters of peace and war.

Theramenes and his companions presently reached Sellasia, and being there questioned as to the reason of their visit, replied that they had full powers to treat of peace. After which the ephors ordered them to be summoned to their presence. On their arrival a general assembly was convened, in which the Corinthians and Thebans more particularly, though their views were shared by many other Hellenes also, urged the meeting not to come to terms with the Athenians, but to destroy them. The Lacedaemonians replied that they would never reduce to slavery a city which was itself an integral portion of Hellas, and had performed a great and noble service to Hellas in the most perilous of emergencies. On the contrary, they were willing to offer peace on the terms now specified—namely, "That the long walls and the fortifications of Piraeus should be destroyed; that the Athenian fleet, with the exception of twelve vessels, should be surrendered; that the exiles should be restored; and lastly, that the Athenians should acknowledge the headship of Sparta in peace and war, leaving to her the choice of friends and foes, and following her lead by land and sea." Such were the terms which Theramenes and the rest who acted with him were able to report on their return to Athens. As they entered the city, a vast crowd met them, trembling lest their mission have proved fruitless. For indeed delay was no longer possible, so long already was the list of victims daily perishing from starvation. On the day following, the ambassadors delivered their report, stating the terms upon which the Lacedaemonians were willing to make peace. Theramenes acted as spokesman, insisting that they ought to obey the Lacedaemonians and pull down the walls. A small minority raised their voice in opposition, but the majority were strongly in favor of the proposition, and the resolution was passed to accept the peace. After that, Lysander sailed into the Piraeus, and the exiles were readmitted. And so they fell to levelling the fortifications and walls with much enthusiasm, to the accompaniment of female flute-players, deeming that day the beginning of liberty to Greece.

Thus the year drew to its close[1]—during its middle months took place the accession of Dionysius, the son of Hermocrates the Syracusan, to the tyranny of Syracuse; an incident itself preceded by a victory gained over the Carthaginians by the Syracusans; the reduction of Agrigentum through famine by the Carthaginians themselves; and the exodus of the Sicilian Greeks from that city.

III

404 BC. In the following year[2] the people passed a resolution to choose thirty men who were to draft a constitution based on the ancestral laws of the State. The following were chosen to act on this committee:—Polychares, Critias, Melobius, Hippolochus, Eucleides, Hiero, Mnesilochus, Chremo, Theramenes, Aresias, Diocles, Phaedrias, Chaereleos, Anaetius, Piso, Sophocles, Erastosthenes, Charicles, Onomacles, Theognis, Aeschines, Theogones, Cleomedes, Erasistratus, Pheido, Dracontides, Eumathes, Aristoteles, Hippomachus, Mnesitheides. After these transactions, Lysander

---

1 For the puzzling chronology of this paragraph see Grote, "Hist. of Greece," vol. x. p 619 (2d ed.) If genuine, the words may perhaps have slipt out of their natural place in chapter i. above, in front of the words "in the following year Lysander arrived," etc. L. Dindorf brackets them as spurious. Xen., "Hist. Gr." ed. tertia, Lipsiae, MDCCCLXXII. For the incidents referred to see above; Grote, "Hist. of Greece," vol. x. pp. 582, 598 (2d ed.)

2 The MSS. here add "it was that year of the Olympiad cycle in which Crocinas, a Thessalian, won the Stadium; when Endius was ephor at Sparta, and Pythodorus archon at Athens, though the Athenians indeed do not call the year by that archon's name, since he was elected during the oligarchy, but prefer to speak of the year of 'anarchy'; the aforesaid oligarchy originated thus,"—which, though correct, probably was not written by Xenophon. The year of anarchy might perhaps be better rendered "the year without archons."

set sail for Samos; and Agis withdrew the land force from Deceleia and disbanded the troops, dismissing the contingents to their several cities.

In was at this date, about the time of the solar eclipse,[1] that Lycophron of Pherae, who was ambitious of ruling over the whole of Thessaly, defeated those sections of the Thessalians who opposed him, such as the men of Larissa and others, and slew many of them. It was also about this date that Dionysius, now tyrant of Syracuse, was defeated by the Carthaginians and lost Gela and Camarina. And again, a little later, the men of Leontini, who previously had been amalgamated with the Syracusans, separated themselves from Syracuse and Dionysius, and asserted their independence, and returned to their native city. Another incident of this period was the sudden despatch and introduction of Syracusan horse into Catana by Dionysius.

Now the Samians, though besieged by Lysander on all sides, were at first unwilling to come to terms. But at the last moment, when Lysander was on the point of assaulting the town, they accepted the terms, which allowed every free man to leave the island, but not to carry away any part of his property, except the clothes on his back. On these conditions they marched out. The city and all it contained was then delivered over to its ancient citizens by Lysander, who finally appointed ten governors to garrison the island.[2] After which, he disbanded the allied fleet, dismissing them to their respective cities, while he himself, with the Lacedaemonian squadron, set sail for Laconia, bringing with him the prows of the conquered vessels and the whole navy of Piraeus, with the exception of twelve ships. He also brought the crowns which he had received from the cities as private gifts, and a sum of four hundred and seventy talents[3] in silver (the surplus of the tribute money which Cyrus had assigned to him for the prosecution of the war), besides other property, the fruit of his military exploits. All these things Lysander delivered to the Lacedaemonians in the latter end of summer.[4]

---

1 *This took place on 2d September 404 BC.*

2 *A council of ten, or "decarchy." See Grote, "H. G." viii. 323 (1st ed.)*

3 *About 112,800 pounds.*

4 *The MSS. add "a summer, the close of which coincided with the termination of a war which had lasted twenty-eight and a half years, as the list of annual ephors, appended in order, serves to show. Aenesias is the first name. The war began during his ephorate, in the fifteenth year of the thirty years' truce after the capture of Euboea. His successors were Brasidas, Isanor, Sostratidas, Exarchus, Agesistratus, Angenidas, Onomacles, Zeuxippus, Pityas, Pleistolas, Cleinomachus, Harchus, Leon, Chaerilas, Patesiadas, Cleosthenes, Lycarius, Eperatus, Onomantius, Alexippidas, Misgolaidas, Isias, Aracus, Euarchippus, Pantacles, Pityas, Archytas, and lastly, Endius, during whose year of office Lysander sailed home in triumph, after performing the exploits above recorded,"—the interpolation, probably, of some editor or copyist, the words "twenty-eight and a half" being probably a mistake on his part for "twenty-seven and a half." Cf. Thuc. v. 26; also Buchsenschutz, Einleitung, p. 8 of his school edition of the "Hellenica."*

The Thirty had been chosen almost immediately after the long walls and the fortifications round Piraeus had been razed. They were chosen for the express purpose of compiling a code of laws for the future constitution of the State. The laws were always on the point of being published, yet they were never forthcoming; and the thirty compilers contented themselves meanwhile with appointing a senate and the other magistracies as suited their fancy best. That done, they turned their attention, in the first instance, to such persons as were well known to have made their living as informers[1] under the democracy, and to be thorns in the side of all respectable people. These they laid hold on and prosecuted on the capital charge. The new senate gladly recorded its vote of condemnation against them; and the rest of the world, conscious of bearing no resemblance to them, seemed scarcely vexed. But the Thirty did not stop there. Presently they began to deliberate by what means they could get the city under their absolute control, in order that they might work their will upon it. Here again they proceeded tentatively; in the first instance, they sent (two of their number), Aeschines and Aristoteles, to Lacedaemon, and persuaded Lysander to support them in getting a Lacedaemonian garrison despatched to Athens. They only needed it until they had got the "malignants" out of the way, and had established the constitution; and they would undertake to maintain these troops at their own cost. Lysander was not deaf to their persuasions, and by his cooperation their request was granted. A bodyguard, with Callibius as governor, was sent.

And now that they had got the garrison, they fell to flattering Callibius with all servile flattery, in order that he might give countenance to their doings. Thus they prevailed on him to allow some of the guards, whom they selected, to accompany them, while they proceeded to lay hands on whom they would; no longer confining themselves to base folk and people of no account, but boldly laying hands on those who they felt sure would least easily brook being thrust aside, or, if a spirit of opposition seized them, could command the largest number of partisans.

These were early days; as yet Critias was of one mind with Theramenes, and the two were friends. But the time came when, in proportion as Critias was ready to rush headlong into wholesale carnage, like one who thirsted for the blood of the democracy, which had banished him, Theramenes balked and thwarted him. It was barely reasonable, he argued, to put

---

1 Lit. "by sycophancy," i.e. calumnious accusation—the sycophant's trade. For a description of this pest of Athenian life cf. "Dem." in Arist. 1, S. 52; quoted in Jebb, "Attic Orators," chap. xxix. 14; cf. Aristoph. "Ach." 904; Xen. "Mem." II. ix. 1.

people to death, who had never done a thing wrong to respectable people in their lives, simply because they had enjoyed influence and honor under the democracy. "Why, you and I, Critias," he would add, "have said and done many things ere now for the sake of popularity." To which the other (for the terms of friendly intimacy still subsisted) would retort, "There is no choice left to us, since we intend to take the lion's share, but to get rid of those who are best able to hinder us. If you imagine, because we are thirty instead of one, our government requires one whit the less careful guarding than an actual tyranny, you must be very innocent."

So things went on. Day after day the list of persons put to death for no just reason grew longer. Day after day the signs of resentment were more significant in the groups of citizens banding together and forecasting the character of this future constitution; till at length Theramenes spoke again, protesting:—There was no help for it but to associate with themselves a sufficient number of persons in the conduct of affairs, or the oligarchy would certainly come to an end. Critias and the rest of the Thirty, whose fears had already converted Theramenes into a dangerous popular idol, proceeded at once to draw up a list of three thousand citizens; fit and proper persons to have a share in the conduct of affairs. But Theramenes was not wholly satisfied, "indeed he must say, for himself, he regarded it as ridiculous, that in their effort to associate the better classes with themselves in power, they should fix on just that particular number, three thousand, as if that figure had some necessary connection with the exact number of gentlemen in the State, making it impossible to discover any respectability outside or rascality within the magic number. And in the second place," he continued, "I see we are trying to do two things, diametrically opposed; we are manufacturing a government, which is based on force, and at the same time inferior in strength to those whom we propose to govern." That was what he said, but what his colleagues did, was to institute a military inspection or review. The Three Thousand were drawn up in the Agora, and the rest of the citizens, who were not included in the list, elsewhere in various quarters of the city. The order to take arms was given;[1] but while the men's backs were turned, at the bidding of the Thirty, the Laconian guards, with those of the citizens who shared their views, appeared on the

---

1 Or, "a summons to the "place d'armes" was given; but." Or, "the order to seize the arms was given, and." It is clear from Aristoph. "Acharn." 1050, that the citizens kept their weapons at home. On the other hand, it was a custom not to come to any meeting in arms. See Thuc. vi. 58. It seems probable that while the men were being reviewed in the marketplace and elsewhere, the ruling party gave orders to seize their weapons (which they had left at home), and this was done except in the case of the Three Thousand. Cf. Arnold, "Thuc." II. 2. 5; and IV. 91.

scene and took away the arms of all except the Three Thousand, carried them up to the Acropolis, and safely deposited them in the temple.

The ground being thus cleared, as it were, and feeling that they had it in their power to do what they pleased, they embarked on a course of wholesale butchery, to which many were sacrificed to the merest hatred, many to the accident of possessing riches. Presently the question rose, How they were to get money to pay their guards? and to meet this difficulty a resolution was passed empowering each of the committee to seize on one of the resident aliens apiece, to put his victim to death, and to confiscate his property. Theramenes was invited, or rather told to seize some one or other. "Choose whom you will, only let it be done." To which he made answer, it hardly seemed to him a noble or worthy course on the part of those who claimed to be the elite of society to go beyond the informers[1] in injustice. "Yesterday they, today we; with this difference, the victim of the informer must live as a source of income; our innocents must die that we may get their wealth. Surely their method was innocent in comparison with ours."

The rest of the Thirty, who had come to regard Theramenes as an obstacle to any course they might wish to adopt, proceeded to plot against him. They addressed themselves to the members of the senate in private, here a man and there a man, and denounced him as the marplot of the constitution. Then they issued an order to the young men, picking out the most audacious characters they could find, to be present, each with a dagger hidden in the hollow of the armpit; and so called a meeting of the senate. When Theramenes had taken his place, Critias got up and addressed the meeting:

"If," said he, "any member of this council, here seated, imagines that an undue amount of blood has been shed, let me remind him that with changes of constitution such things can not be avoided. It is the rule everywhere, but more particularly at Athens it was inevitable there should be found a specially large number of persons sworn foes to any constitutional change in the direction of oligarchy, and this for two reasons. First, because the population of this city, compared with other Hellenic cities, is enormously large; and again, owing to the length of time during which the people has battened upon liberty. Now, as to two points we are clear. The first is that democracy is a form of government detestable to persons like ourselves— to us and to you; the next is that the people of Athens could never be got to be friendly to our friends and saviours, the Lacedaemonians. But on the

---

1 *See above.*

loyalty of the better classes the Lacedaemonians can count. And that is our reason for establishing an oligarchical constitution with their concurrence. That is why we do our best to rid us of everyone whom we perceive to be opposed to the oligarchy; and, in our opinion, if one of ourselves should elect to undermine this constitution of ours, he would deserve punishment. Do you not agree? And the case," he continued, "is no imaginary one. The offender is here present—Theramenes. And what we say of him is, that he is bent upon destroying yourselves and us by every means in his power. These are not baseless charges; but if you will consider it, you will find them amply established in this unmeasured censure of the present posture of affairs, and his persistent opposition to us, his colleagues, if ever we seek to get rid of any of these demagogues. Had this been his guiding principle of action from the beginning, in spite of hostility, at least he would have escaped all imputation of villainy. Why, this is the very man who originated our friendly and confidential relations with Lacedaemon. This is the very man who authorized the abolition of the democracy, who urged us on to inflict punishment on the earliest batch of prisoners brought before us. But today all is changed; now you and we are out of odour with the people, and he accordingly has ceased to be pleased with our proceedings. The explanation is obvious. In case of a catastrophe, how much pleasanter for him once again to light upon his legs, and leave us to render account for our past performances.

"I contend that this man is fairly entitled to render his account also, not only as an ordinary enemy, but as a traitor to yourselves and us. And let us add, not only is treason more formidable than open war, in proportion as it is harder to guard against a hidden assassin than an open foe, but it bears the impress of a more enduring hostility, inasmuch as men fight their enemies and come to terms with them again and are fast friends; but whoever heard of reconciliation with a traitor? There he stands unmasked; he has forfeited our confidence for evermore. But to show you that these are no new tactics of his, to prove to you that he is a traitor in grain, I will recall to your memories some points in his past history.

"He began by being held in high honor by the democracy; but taking a leaf out of his father's, Hagnon's, book, he next showed a most headlong anxiety to transform the democracy into the Four Hundred, and, in fact, for a time held the first place in that body. But presently, detecting the formation of rival power to the oligarchs, round he shifted; and we find him next a ringleader of the popular party in assailing them. It must be admitted, he has well earned his nickname "Buskin."[1] Yes, Theramenes! clever you may be, but the man who deserves to live should not show his cleverness in leading on his associates into trouble, and when some obstacle presents itself, at once veer round; but like a pilot on shipboard, he ought then to redouble his efforts, until the wind is fair. Else, how in the name of wonderment are those mariners to reach the haven where they would be, if at the first contrary wind or tide they turn about and sail in the opposite direction? Death and destruction are concomitants of constitutional changes and revolution, no doubt; but you are such an impersonation of change, that, as you twist and turn and double, you deal destruction on all sides. At one swoop you are the ruin of a thousand oligarchs at the hands of the people, and at another of a thousand democrats at the hands of the better classes. Why, sirs, this is the man to whom the orders were given by the generals, in the sea-fight off Lesbos, to pick up the crews of the disabled vessels; and who, neglecting to obey orders, turned round and accused the generals; and to save himself murdered them! What, I ask you, of a man who so openly studied the art of self-seeking, deaf alike to the pleas of honor and to the claims of friendship? Would not leniency toward such a creature be misplaced? Can it be our duty at all to spare him? Ought we not rather, when we know the doublings of his nature, to guard against them, lest we enable him presently to practice on ourselves? The case is clear. We therefore hereby cite this man before you, as a conspirator and traitor against yourselves and us. The reasonableness of our conduct, one further reflection may make clear. No one, I take it, will dispute the splendour, the perfection of the Laconian constitution. Imagine one of the ephors there in Sparta, in lieu of devoted obedience to the majority, taking on himself to find fault with the government and to oppose all measures. Do you not think that the ephors themselves, and the whole commonwealth besides, would hold this renegade worthy of condign punishment? So, too, by the same token, if you are wise, do you spare yourselves, not him. For what does the alternative mean? I will tell you. His preservation will cause the courage of many who hold opposite views to your own to rise; his destruction will cut off the last hopes of all your enemies, whether within or without the city."

With these words he sat down, but Theramenes rose and said: "Sirs, with

---

1 An annotator seems to have added here the words, occurring in the MSS., "the buskin which seems to fit both legs equally, but is constant to neither," unless, indeed, they are an original "marginal note" of the author. For the character of Theramenes, as popularly conceived, cf. Aristoph. "Frogs," 538, 968 foll., and Thuc. viii. 92; and Prof. Jowett, "Thuc." vol. ii. pp. 523, 524.

your permission I will first touch upon the charge against me which Critias has mentioned last. The assertion is that as the accuser of the generals I was their murderer. Now I presume it was not I who began the attack upon them, but it was they who asserted that in spite of the orders given me I had neglected to pick up the unfortunates in the sea-fight off Lesbos. All I did was to defend myself. My defense was that the storm was too violent to permit any vessel to ride at sea, much more therefore to pick up the men, and this defense was accepted by my fellow citizens as highly reasonable, while the generals seemed to be condemned out of their own mouths. For while they kept on asserting that it was possible to save the men, the fact still remained that they abandoned them to their fate, set sail, and were gone.

"However, I am not surprised, I confess, at this grave misconception[1] on the part of Critias, for at the date of these occurrences he was not in Athens. He was away in Thessaly, laying the foundations of a democracy with Prometheus, and arming the Penestae[2] against their masters. Heaven forbid that any of his transactions there should be re-enacted here. However, I must say, I do heartily concur with him on one point. Whoever desires to exclude you from the government, or to strength the hands of your secret foes, deserves and ought to meet with condign punishment; but who is most capable of so doing? That you will best discover, I think, by looking a little more closely into the past and the present conduct of each of us. Well, then! up to the moment at which you were formed into a senatorial body, when the magistracies were appointed, and certain notorious "informers" were brought to trial, we all held the same views. But later on, when our friends yonder began to hale respectable honest folk to prison and to death, I, on my side, began to differ from them. From the moment when Leon of Salamis,[3] a man of high and well-deserved reputation, was put to death, though he had not committed the shadow of a crime, I knew that all his equals must tremble for themselves, and, so trembling, be driven into opposition to the new constitution. In the same way, when Niceratus,[4] the son of Nicias, was arrested; a wealthy man, who, no more than his father, had never done anything that could be called popular or democratic in his life; it did not require much insight to discover that his compeers would be converted

---

1 Reading with Cobet {paranenomikenai}.
2 I.e. serfs—Penestae being the local name in Thessaly for the villein class. Like the {Eilotes} in Laconia, they were originally a conquered tribe, afterward increased by prisoners of war, and formed a link between the freemen and born slaves.
3 Cf. "Mem." IV. iv. 3; Plat. "Apol." 8. 32.
4 Cf. Lysias, "Or." 18. 6.

into our foes. But to go a step further: when it came to Antiphon[1] falling at our hands—Antiphon, who during the war contributed two fast-sailing men-of-war out of his own resources, it was then plain to me, that all who had ever been zealous and patriotic must eye us with suspicion. Once more I could not help speaking out in opposition to my colleagues when they suggested that each of us ought to seize some one resident alien.[2] For what could be more certain than that their death-warrant would turn the whole resident foreign population into enemies of the constitution. I spoke out again when they insisted on depriving the populace of their arms; it being no part of my creed that we ought to take the strength out of the city; nor, indeed, so far as I could see, had the Lacedaemonians stept between us and destruction merely that we might become a handful of people, powerless to aid them in the day of need. Had that been their object, they might have swept us away to the last man. A few more weeks, or even days, would have sufficed to extinguish us quietly by famine. Nor, again, can I say that the importation of mercenary foreign guards was altogether to my taste, when it would have been so easy for us to add to our own body a sufficient number of fellow citizens to ensure our supremacy as governors over those we essayed to govern. But when I saw what an army of malcontents this government had raised up within the city walls, besides another daily increasing host of exiles without, I could not but regard the banishment of people like Thrasybulus and Anytus and Alcibiades[3] as impolitic. Had our object been to strengthen the rival power, we could hardly have set about it better than by providing the populace with the competent leaders whom they needed, and the would-be leaders themselves with an army of willing adherents.

"I ask then is the man who tenders such advice in the full light of day justly to be regarded as a traitor, and not as a benefactor? Surely Critias, the peacemaker, the man who hinders the creation of many enemies, whose counsels tend to the acquistion of yet more friends,[4] cannot be accused of strengthening the hands of the enemy. Much more truly may the imputation

---

1 *Probably the son of Lysidonides. See Thirlwall, "Hist. of Greece," vol. iv. p. 179 (ed. 1847); also Lysias, "Or." 12. contra Eratosth. According to Lysias, Theramenes, when a member of the first Oligarchy, betrayed his own closest friends, Antiphon and Archeptolemus. See Prof. Jebb, "Attic Orators," I. x. p. 266.*
2 *The resident aliens, or {metoikoi}, "metics," so technically called.*
3 *Isocr. "De Bigis," 355; and Prof. Jebb's "Attic Orators," ii. 230. In the defense of his father's career, which the younger Alcibiades, the defendant in this case (397 BC probably) has occasion to make, he reminds the court, that under the Thirty, others were banished from Athens, but his father was driven out of the civilised world of Hellas itself, and finally murdered. See Plutarch, "Alcibiades," ad fin.*
4 *Or, "the peacemaker, the healer of differences, the cementer of new alliances, cannot," etc.*

be retorted on those who wrongfully appropriate their neighbors' goods and put to death those who have done no wrong. These are they who cause our adversaries to grow and multiply, and who in very truth are traitors, not to their friends only, but to themselves, spurred on by sordid love of gain.

"I might prove the truth of what I say in many ways, but I beg you to look at the matter thus. With which condition of affairs here in Athens do you think will Thrasybulus and Anytus and the other exiles be the better pleased? That which I have pictured as desirable, or that which my colleagues yonder are producing? For my part I cannot doubt but that, as things now are, they are saying to themselves, 'Our allies muster thick and fast.' But were the real strength, the pith and fibre of this city, kindly disposed to us, they would find it an uphill task even to get a foothold anywhere in the country.

"Then, with regard to what he said of me and my propensity to be forever changing sides, let me draw your attention to the following facts. Was it not the people itself, the democracy, who voted the constitution of the Four Hundred? This they did, because they had learned to think that the Lacedaemonians would trust any other form of government rather than a democracy. But when the efforts of Lacedaemon were not a whit relaxed, when Aristoteles, Melanthius, and Aristarchus,[1] and the rest of them acting as generals, were plainly minded to construct an intrenched fortress on the mole for the purpose of admitting the enemy, and so getting the city under the power of themselves and their associates;[2] because I got wind of these schemes, and nipped them in the bud, is that to be a traitor to one's friends?

"Then he threw in my teeth the nickname 'Buskin,' as descriptive of an endeavor on my part to fit both parties. But what of the man who pleases neither? What in heaven's name are we to call him? Yes! you—Critias? Under the democracy you were looked upon as the most arrant hater of the people, and under the aristocracy you have proved yourself the bitterest foe of everything respectable. Yes! Critias, I am, and ever have been, a foe of those who think that a democracy cannot reach perfection until slaves and those who, from poverty, would sell the city for a drachma, can get their drachma a day.[3] But not less am I, and ever have been, a pronounced opponent of those who do not think there can possibly exist a perfect

---

1 Cf. Thuc. viii. 90-92, for the behavior of the Lacedaemonian party at Athens and the fortification of Eetioneia in bc 411.
2 I.e. of the political clubs.
3 I.e. may enjoy the senatorial stipend of a drachma a day = 9 3/4 pence.

oligarchy until the State is subjected to the despotism of a few. On the contrary, my own ambition has been to combine with those who are rich enough to possess a horse and shield, and to use them for the benefit of the State.[1] That was my ideal in the old days, and I hold to it without a shadow of turning still. If you can imagine when and where, in conjunction with despots or demagogues, I have set to my hand to deprive honest gentlefolk of their citizenship, pray speak. If you can convict me of such crimes at present, or can prove my perpetration of them in the past, I admit that I deserve to die, and by the worst of deaths."

With these words he ceased, and the loud murmur of the applause which followed marked the favorable impression produced upon the senate. It was plain to Critias, that if he allowed his adversary's fate to be decided by formal voting, Theramenes would escape, and life to himself would become intolerable. Accordingly he stepped forward and spoke a word or two in the ears of the Thirty. This done, he went out and gave an order to the attendants with the daggers to stand close to the bar in full view of the senators. Again he entered and addressed the senate thus: "I hold it to be the duty of a good president, when he sees the friends about him being made the dupes of some delusion, to intervene. That at any rate is what I propose to do. Indeed our friends here standing by the bar say that if we propose to acquit a man so openly bent upon the ruin of the oligarchy, they do not mean to let us do so. Now there is a clause in the new code forbidding any of the Three Thousand to be put to death without your vote; but the Thirty have power of life and death over all outside that list. Accordingly," he proceeded, "I herewith strike this man, Theramenes, off the list; and this with the concurrence of my colleagues. And now," he continued, "we condemn him to death."

Hearing these words Theramenes sprang upon the altar of Hestia, exclaiming: "And I, sirs, supplicate you for the barest forms of law and justice. Let it not be in the power of Critias to strike off either me, or any one of you whom he will. But in my case, in what may be your case, if we are tried, let our trial be in accordance with the law they have made concerning those on the list. I know," he added, "but too well, that this altar will not protect me; but I will make it plain that these men are as impious toward the gods as they are nefarious toward men. Yet I do marvel, good

---

1 See Thuc. viii. 97, for a momentary realisation of that "duly attempered compound of Oligarchy and Democracy" which Thucydides praises, and which Theramenes here refers to. It threw the power into the hands of the wealthier upper classes to the exclusion of the {nautikos okhlos}. See Prof. Jowett, vol. ii. note, ad loc. cit.

sirs and honest gentlemen, for so you are, that you will not help yourselves, and that too when you must see that the name of every one of you is as easily erased as mine."

But when he had got so far, the voice of the herald was heard giving the order to the Eleven to seize Theramenes. They at that instant entered with their satellites—at their head Satyrus, the boldest and most shameless of the body—and Critias exclaimed, addressing the Eleven, "We deliver over to you Theramenes yonder, who has been condemned according to the law. Do you take him and lead him away to the proper place, and do there with him what remains to do." As Critias uttered the words, Satyrus laid hold upon Theramenes to drag him from the altar, and the attendants lent their aid. But he, as was natural, called upon gods and men to witness what was happening. The senators the while kept silence, seeing the companions of Satyrus at the bar, and the whole front of the senate house crowded with the foreign guards, nor did they need to be told that there were daggers in reserve among those present.

And so Theramenes was dragged through the Agora, in vehement and loud tones proclaiming the wrongs that he was suffering. One word, which is said to have fallen from his lips, I cite. It is this: Satyrus, bade him "Be silent, or he would rue the day"; to which he made answer, "And if I be silent, shall I not rue it?" Also, when they brought him the hemlock, and the time was come to drink the fatal draught, they tell how he playfully jerked out the dregs from the bottom of the cup, like one who plays "Cottabos,"[1] with the words, "This to the lovely Critias." These are but "apophthegms"[2] too trivial, it may be thought, to find a place in history. Yet I must deem it an admirable trait in this man's character, if at such a moment, when death confronted him, neither his wits forsook him, nor could the childlike sportiveness vanish from his soul.

IV

So Theramenes met his death; and, now that this obstacle was removed, the Thirty, feeling that they had it in their power to play the tyrant without

---

1 "A Sicilian game much in vogue at the drinking parties of young men at Athens. The simplest mode was when each threw the wine left in his cup so as to strike smartly in a metal basin, at the same time invoking his mistress's name; if all fell into the basin and the sound was clear, it was a sign he stood well with her."— Liddell and Scott, sub. v. For the origin of the game compare curiously enough the first line of the first Elegy of Critias himself, who was a poet and political philosopher, as well as a politician:—
"{Kottabos ek Sikeles esti khthonos, euprepes ergon on skopon es latagon toxa kathistametha.}" Bergk. "Poetae Lyr. Graec." Pars II. xxx.

2 Or, "these are sayings too slight, perhaps, to deserve record; yet," etc. By an "apophthegm" was meant originally a terse (sententious) remark, but the word has somewhat altered in meaning.

fear, issued an order forbidding all, whose names were not on the list, to set foot within the city. Retirement in the country districts was no protection, thither the prosecutor followed them, and thence dragged them, that their farms and properties might fall to the possession of the Thirty and their friends. Even Piraeus was not safe; of those who sought refuge there, many were driven forth in similar fashion, until Megara and Thebes overflowed with the crowd of refugees.

Presently Thrasybulus, with about seventy followers, sallied out from Thebes, and made himself master of the fortress of Phyle.[1] The weather was brilliant, and the Thirty marched out of the city to repel the invader; with them were the Three Thousand and the Knights. When they reached the place, some of the young men, in the foolhardiness of youth, made a dash at the fortress, but without effect; all they got was wounds, and so retired. The intention of the Thirty now was to blockade the place; by shutting off all the avenues of supplies, they thought to force the garrison to capitulate. But this project was interrupted by a steady downfall of snow that night and the following day. Baffled by this all-pervading enemy they beat a retreat to the city, but not without the sacrifice of many of their camp-followers, who fell a prey to the men in Phyle. The next anxiety of the government in Athens was to secure the farms and country houses against the plunderings and forays to which they would be exposed, if there were no armed force to protect them. With this object a protecting force was despatched to the "boundary estates,"[2] about two miles south of Phyle. This corps consisted of the Lacedaemonian guards, or nearly all of them, and two divisions of horse.[3] They encamped in a wild and broken district, and the round of their duties commenced.

But by this time the small garrison above them had increased tenfold, until there were now something like seven hundred men collected in Phyle; and with these Thrasybulus one night descended. When he was not quite half a mile from the enemy's encampment he grounded arms, and a deep silence was maintained until it drew toward day. In a little while the men opposite, one by one, were getting to their legs or leaving the camp for necessary purposes, while a suppressed din and murmur arose, caused by

1 "A strong fortress (the remains of which still exist) commanding the narrow pass across Mount Parnes, through which runs the direct road from Thebes to Athens, past Acharnae. The precipitous rock on which it stands can only be approached by a ridge on the eastern side. The height commands a magnificent view of the whole Athenian plain, of the city itself, of Mount Hymettus, and the Saronic Gulf,"—"Dict. of Geog., The demi of the Diacria and Mount Parnes."
2 Cf. Boeckh, "P. E. A." p. 63, Eng. ed.
3 Lit. tribes, each of the ten tribes furnishing about one hundred horse.

the grooms currying and combing their horses. This was the moment for Thrasybulus and his men to snatch up their arms and make a dash at the enemy's position. Some they felled on the spot; and routing the whole body, pursued them six or seven furlongs, killing one hundred and twenty hoplites and more. Of the cavalry, Nicostratus, "the beautiful," as men called him, and two others besides were slain; they were caught while still in their beds. Returning from the pursuit, the victors set up a trophy, got together all the arms they had taken, besides baggage, and retired again to Phyle. A reinforcement of horse sent from the city could not discover the vestige of a foe; but waited on the scene of battle until the bodies of the slain had been picked up by their relatives, when they withdrew again to the city.

After this the Thirty, who had begun to realizethe insecurity of their position, were anxious to appropriate Eleusis, so that an asylum might be ready for them against the day of need. With this view an order was issued to the Knights; and Critias, with the rest of the Thirty, visited Eleusis. There they held a review of the Eleusians in the presence of the Knights;[1] and, on the pretext of wishing to discover how many they were, and how large a garrison they would further require, they ordered the townsfolk to enter their names. As each man did so he had to retire by a postern leading to the sea. But on the sea-beach this side there were lines of cavalry drawn up in waiting, and as each man appeared he was handcuffed by the satellites of the Thirty. When all had so been seized and secured, they gave orders to Lysimachus, the commander of the cavalry, to take them off to the city and deliver them over to the Eleven. Next day they summoned the heavy armed who were on the list, and the rest of the Knights[2] to the Odeum, and Critias rose and addressed them. He said: "Sirs, the constitution, the lines of which we are laying down, is a work undertaken in your interests no less than ours; it is incumbent on you therefore to participate in its dangers, even as you will partake of its honors. We expect you therefore, in reference to these Eleusians here, who have been seized and secured, to vote their condemnation, so that our hopes and fears may be identical." Then, pointing to a particular spot, he said peremptorily, "You will please deposit your votes there within sight of all." It must be understood that the Laconian guards were present at the time, and armed to the teeth, and

---

1 Or, "in the cavalry quarters," cf. {en tois ikhthusin} = in the fish market. Or, "at the review of the horse."

2 For the various Odeums at Athens vide Prof. Jebb, "Theophr." xviii. 235, 236. The one here named was near the fountain Callirhoe by the Ilissus.

filling one-half of the Odeum. As to the proceedings themselves, they found acceptance with those members of the State, besides the Thirty, who could be satisfied with a simple policy of self-aggrandisement.

But now Thrasybulus at the head of his followers, by this time about one thousand strong, descended from Phyle and reached Piraeus in the night. The Thirty, on their side, informed of this new move, were not slow to rally to the rescue, with the Laconian guards, supported by their own cavalry and hoplites. And so they advanced, marching down along the broad carriage road which leads into Piraeus. The men from Phyle seemed at first inclined to dispute their passage, but as the wide circuit of the walls needed a defense beyond the reach of their still scanty numbers, they fell back in a compact body upon Munychia.[1] Then the troops from the city poured into the Agora of Hippodmus.[2] Here they formed in line, stretching along and filling the street which leads to the temple of Artemis and the Bendideum.[3] This line must have been at least fifty shields deep; and in this formation they at once began to march up. As to the men of Phyle, they too blocked the street at the opposite end, and facing the foe. They presented only a thin line, not more than ten deep, though behind these, certainly, were ranged a body of targeteers and light-armed javelin men, who were again supported by an artillery of stone-throwers—a tolerably numerous division drawn from the population of the port and district itself. While his antagonists were still advancing, Thrasybulus gave the order to ground their heavy shields, and having done so himself, whilst retaining the rest of his arms, he stood in the midst, and thus addressed them: "Men and fellow citizens, I wish to inform some, and to remind others of you, that of the men you see advancing beneath us there, the right division are the very men we routed and pursued only five days ago; while on the extreme left there you see the Thirty. These are the men who have not spared to rob us of our city, though we did no wrong; who have hounded us from our homes; who have set the seal of proscription on our dearest friends. But today the wheel of fortune has revolved; that has come about which least of all they looked for, which most of all we prayed for. Here we stand with our good swords in our hands, face to face with our foes; and the gods themselves are with us, seeing that we were arrested in the midst of our peaceful pursuits; at any

---

1 *The citadel quarter of Piraeus.*
2 *Named after the famous architect Hippodamus, who built the town. It was situated near where the two long walls joined the wall of Piraeus; a broad street led from it up to the citadel of Munychia.*
3 *I.e. the temple of Bendis (the Thracian Artemis). Cf. Plat. "Rep." 327, 354; and Prof. Jowett, "Plato," vol. iii. pp. 193, 226.*

moment, whilst we supped, or slept, or marketed, sentence of banishment was passed upon us: we had done no wrong—nay, many of us were not even resident in the country. Today, therefore, I repeat, the gods do visibly fight upon our side; the great gods, who raise a tempest even in the midst of calm for our benefit, and when we lay to our hand to fight, enable our little company to set up the trophy of victory over the multitude of our foes. On this day they have brought us hither to a place where the steep ascent must needs hinder our foes from reaching with lance or arrow further than our foremost ranks; but we with our volley of spears and arrows and stones cannot fail to reach them with terrible effect. Had we been forced to meet them vanguard to vanguard, on an equal footing, who could have been surprised? But as it is, all I say to you is, let fly your missiles with a will in right brave style. No one can miss his mark when the road is full of them. To avoid our darts they must be forever ducking and skulking beneath their shields; but we will rain blows upon them in their blindness; we will leap upon them and lay them low. But, O sirs! let me call upon you so to bear yourselves that each shall be conscious to himself that victory was won by him and him alone. Victory—which, God willing, shall this day restore to us the land of our fathers, our homes, our freedom, and the rewards of civic life, our children, if children we have, our darlings, and our wives! Thrice happy those among us who as conquerors shall look upon this gladdest of all days. Nor less fortunate the man who falls today. Not all the wealth in the world shall purchase him a monument so glorious. At the right instant I will strike the keynote of the paean; then, with an invocation to the God of battle,[1] and in return for the wanton insults they put upon us, let us with one accord wreak vengeance on yonder men."

Having so spoken, he turned round, facing the foemen, and kept quiet, for the order passed by the soothsayer enjoined on them, not to charge before one of their side was slain or wounded. "As soon as that happens," said the seer, "we will lead you onward, and the victory shall be yours; but for myself, if I err not, death is waiting." And herein he spoke truly, for they had barely resumed their arms when he himself as though he were driven by some fatal hand, leapt out in front of the ranks, and so springing into the midst of the foe, was slain, and lies now buried at the passage of the Cephisus. But the rest were victorious, and pursued the routed enemy down to the level ground. There fell in this engagement, out of the number

---

1 Lit. "Enyalius," in Homer an epithet of Ares; at another date (cf. Aristoph. "Peace," 456) looked upon as a distinct divinity.

of the Thirty, Critias himself and Hippomachus, and with them Charmides,[1] the son of Glaucon, one of the ten archons in Piraeus, and of the rest about seventy men. The arms of the slain were taken; but, as fellow citizens, the conquerors forebore to despoil them of their coats. This being done, they proceeded to give back the dead under cover of a truce, when the men, on either side, in numbers stept forward and conversed with one another. Then Cleocritus (he was the Herald of the Initiated,[2] a truly "sweet-voiced herald," if ever there was), caused a deep silence to reign, and addressed their late combatants as follows: "Fellow citizens—Why do you drive us forth? why would you slay us? what evil have we wrought you at any time? or is it a crime that we have shared with you in the most solemn rites and sacrifices, and in festivals of the fairest: we have been companions in the chorus, the school, the army. We have braved a thousand dangers with you by land and sea in behalf of our common safety, our common liberty. By the gods of our fathers, by the gods of our mothers, by the hallowed names of kinship, intermarriage, comradeship, those three bonds which knit the hearts of so many of us, bow in reverence before God and man, and cease to sin against the land of our fathers: cease to obey these most unhallowed Thirty, who for the sake of private gain have in eight months slain almost more men than the Peloponnesians together in ten years of warfare. See, we have it in our power to live as citizens in peace; it is only these men, who lay upon us this most foul burthen, this hideous horror of fratricidal war, loathed of God and man. Ah! be well assured, for these men slain by our hands this day, ye are not the sole mourners. There are among them some whose deaths have wrung from us also many a bitter tear."

So he spoke, but the officers and leaders of the defeated army who were left, unwilling that their troops should listen to such topics at that moment, led them back to the city. But the next day the Thirty, in deep down-heartedness and desolation, sat in the council chamber. The Three Thousand, wherever their several divisions were posted, were everywhere a prey to discord. Those who were implicated in deeds of violence, and whose fears could not sleep, protested hotly that to yield to the party in Piraeus were preposterous. Those on the other hand who had faith in their own innocence, argued in their own minds, and tried to convince their

---

1 *He was cousin to Critias, and uncle by the mother's side to Plato, who introduces him in the dialogue, which bears his name (and treats of Temperance), as a very young man at the beginning of the Peloponnesian War. We hear more of him also from Xenophon himself in the "Memorabilia," iii. 6. 7; and as one of the interlocutors in the "Symposium."*

2 *I.e. of the Eleusinian mysteries. He had not only a loud voice, but a big body. Cf. Aristoph. "Frogs," 1237.*

neighbors that they could well dispense with most of their present evils. "Why yield obedience to these Thirty?" they asked, "Why assign to them the privilege of destroying the State?" In the end they voted a resolution to depose the government, and to elect another. This was a board of ten, elected one from each tribe.

403 BC. As to the Thirty, they retired to Eleusis; but the Ten, assisted by the cavalry officers, had enough to do to keep watch over the men in the city, whose anarchy and mutual distrust were rampant. The Knights did not return to quarters at night, but slept out in the Odeum, keeping their horses and shields close beside them; indeed the distrust was so great that from evening onward they patrolled the walls on foot with their shields, and at break of day mounted their horses, at every moment fearing some sudden attack upon them by the men in Piraeus. These latter were now so numerous, and of so mixed a company, that it was difficult to find arms for all. Some had to be content with shields of wood, others of wickerwork, which they spent their time in coating with whitening. Before ten days had elapsed guarantees were given, securing full citizenship, with equality of taxation and tribute to all, even foreigners, who would take part in the fighting. Thus they were presently able to take the field, with large detachments both of heavy infantry and light-armed troops, besides a division of cavalry, about seventy in number. Their system was to push forward foraging parties in quest of wood and fruits, returning at nightfall to Piraeus. Of the city party no one ventured to take the field under arms; only, from time to time, the cavalry would capture stray pillagers from Piraeus or inflict some damage on the main body of their opponents. Once they fell in with a party belonging to the deme Aexone,[1] marching to their own farms in search of provisions. These, in spite of many prayers for mercy and the strong disapprobation of many of the knights, were ruthlessly slaughtered by Lysimachus, the general of cavalry. The men of Piraeus retaliated by putting to death a horseman, named Callistratus, of the tribe Leontis, whom they captured in the country. Indeed their courage ran so high at present that they even meditated an assault upon the city walls. And here perhaps the reader will pardon the record of a somewhat ingenious device on the part of the city engineer, who, aware of the enemy's intention to advance his batteries along the racecourse, which slopes from the Lyceum, had all the carts and waggons which were to be found laden with blocks of stone, each one a cartload in itself, and so sent them to deposit their freights "pele-mele" on the course in question. The

---

1 *On the coast south of Phalerum, celebrated for its fisheries. Cf. "Athen." vii. 325.*

annoyance created by these separate blocks of stone was enormous, and quite out of proportion to the simplicity of the contrivance.

But it was to Lacedaemon that men's eyes now turned. The Thirty despatched one set of ambassadors from Eleusis, while another set representing the government of the city, that is to say the men on the list, was despatched to summon the Lacedaemonians to their aid, on the plea that the people had revolted from Sparta. At Sparta, Lysander, taking into account the possibility of speedily reducing the party in Piraeus by blockading them by land and sea, and so cutting them off from all supplies, supported the application, and negotiated the loan of one hundred talents[1] to his clients, backed by the appointment of himself as harmost on land, and of his brother, Libys, as admiral of the fleet. And so proceeding to the scene of action at Eleusis, he got together a large body of Peloponnesian hoplites, whilst his brother, the admiral, kept watch and ward by sea to prevent the importation of supplies into Piraeus by water. Thus the men in Piraeus were soon again reduced to their former helplessness, while the ardour of the city folk rose to a proportionally high pitch under the auspices of Lysander.

Things were progressing after this sort when King Pausanias intervened. Touched by a certain envy of Lysander—(who seemed, by a final stroke of achievement, about to reach the pinnacle of popularity, with Athens laid like a pocket dependency at his feet)—the king persuaded three of the ephors to support him, and forthwith called out the ban. With him marched contingents of all the allied States, except the Boeotians and Corinthians. These maintained, that to undertake such an expedition against the Athenians, in whose conduct they saw nothing contrary to the treaty, was inconsistent with their oaths. But if that was the language held by them, the secret of their behavior lay deeper; they seemed to be aware of a desire on the part of the Lacedaemonians to annex the soil of the Athenians and to reduce the state to vassalage. Pausanias encamped on the Halipedon,[2] as the sandy flat is called, with his right wing resting on Piraeus, and Lysander and his mercenaries forming the left. His first act was to send an embassage to the party in Piraeus, calling upon them to retire peacably to their homes; when they refused to obey, he made, as far as mere noise went, the semblance of an attack, with sufficient show of fight to prevent his kindly disposition being too apparent. But gaining nothing by the feint, he was forced to retire. Next day he took two Laconian regiments, with three tribes

---

1 24,375 pounds, reckoning one tal. = 243 pounds 15 shillings.
2 *The Halipedon is the long stretch of flat sandy land between Piraeus Phalerum and the city.*

of Athenian horse, and crossed over to the Mute[1] Harbor, examining the lie of the ground to discover how and where it would be easiest to draw lines of circumvallation round Piraeus. As he turned his back to retire, a party of the enemy sallied out and caused him annoyance. Nettled at the liberty, he ordered the cavalry to charge at the gallop, supported by the ten-year-service[2] infantry, whilst he himself, with the rest of the troops, followed close, holding quietly back in reserve. They cut down about thirty of the enemy's light troops and pursued the rest hotly to the theatre in Piraeus. Here, as chance would have it, the whole light and heavy infantry of the Piraeus men were getting under arms; and in an instant their light troops rushed out and dashed at the assailants; thick and fast flew missiles of all sorts—javelins, arrows and sling stones. The Lacedaemonians finding the number of their wounded increasing every minute, and sorely called, slowly fell back step by step, eyeing their opponents. These meanwhile resolutely pressed on. Here fell Chaeron and Thibrachus, both polemarchs, here also Lacrates, an Olympic victor, and other Lacedaemonians, all of whom now lie entombed before the city gates in the Ceramicus.[3]

Watching how matters went, Thrasybulus began his advance with the whole of his heavy infantry to support his light troops and quickly fell into line eight deep, acting as a screen to the rest of his troops. Pausanias, on his side, had retired, sorely pressed, about half a mile toward a bit of rising ground, where he sent orders to the Lacedaemonians and the other allied troops to bring up reinforcements. Here, on this slope, he reformed his troops, giving his phalanx the full depth, and advanced against the Athenians, who did not hesitate to receive him at close quarters, but presently had to give way; one portion being forced into the mud and clay at Halae,[4] while the others wavered and broke their line; one hundred and fifty of them were left dead on the field, whereupon Pausanias set up a trophy and retired. Not even so, were his feelings embittered against his adversary. On the contrary he sent secretly and instructed the men of Piraeus, what sort of terms they should propose to himself and the ephors

---

1 Perhaps the landlocked creek just round the promontory of Eetioneia, as Leake conjectures, "Topog. of Athens," p. 389. See also Prof. Jowett's note, "Thuc." v. 2; vol. ii. p. 286.

2 I.e. who had already seen ten years of service, i.e. over twenty-eight, as the Spartan was eligible to serve at eighteen. Cf. Xen. "Hell." III. iv. 23; VI. iv. 176.

3 The outer Ceramicus, "the most beautiful spot outside the walls." Cf. Thuc. ii. 34; through it passes the street of the tombs on the sacred road; and here was the place of burial for all persons honored with a public funeral. Cf. Arist. "Birds," 395.

4 Halae, the salt marshy ground immediately behind the great harbor of Piraeus, but outside the fortification lines.

in attendance. To this advice they listened. He also fostered a division in the party within the city. A deputation, acting on his orders, sought an audience of him and the ephors. It had all the appearance of a mass meeting. In approaching the Spartan authorities, they had no desire or occasion, they stated, to look upon the men of Piraeus as enemies, they would prefer a general reconciliation and the friendship of both sides with Lacedaemon. The propositions were favorably received, and by no less a person than Nauclidas. He was present as ephor, in accordance with the custom which obliges two members of that board to serve on all military expeditions with the king, and with his colleague shared the political views represented by Pausanias, rather than those of Lysander and his party. Thus the authorities were quite ready to despatch to Lacedaemon the representatives of Piraeus, carrying their terms of truce with the Lacedaemonians, as also two private individuals belonging to the city party, whose names were Cephisophon and Meletus. This double deputation, however, had no sooner set out to Lacedaemon than the "de facto" government of the city followed suit, by sending a third set of representatives to state on their behalf: that they were prepared to deliver up themselves and the fortifications in their possession to the Lacedaemonians, to do with them what they liked. "Are the men of Piraeus," they asked, "prepared to surrender Piraeus and Munychia in the same way? If they are sincere in their profession of friendship to Lacedaemon, they ought to do so." The ephors and the members of assembly at Sparta[1] gave audience to these several parties, and sent out fifteen commissioners to Athens empowered, in conjunction with Pausanias, to discover the best settlement possible. The terms[2] arrived at were that a general peace between the rival parties should be established, liberty to return to their own homes being granted to all, with the exception of the Thirty, the Eleven, and the Ten who had been governors in Piraeus; but a proviso was added, enabling any of the city party who feared to remain at Athens to find a home in Eleusis.

And now that everything was happily concluded, Pausanias disbanded his army, and the men from Piraeus marched up under arms into the acropolis and offered sacrifice to Athena. When they were come down, the generals called a meeting of the Ecclesia,[3] and Thrasybulus made a speech

---

1 Cf. "Hell." VI. iii. 3, {oi ekkletoi}.
2 Cf. Prof. Jebb, "Orators," i. 262, note 2.
3 I.e. the Public Assembly, see above; and reading with Sauppe after Cobet {ekklesian epoiesan}, which words are supposed to have dropt out of the MSS. Or, keeping to the MSS., translate "When the generals were come down, Thrasybulus," etc. See next note.

in which, addressing the city party, he said: "Men of the city! I have one piece of advice I would tender to you; it is that you should learn to know yourselves, and toward the attainment of that self-knowledge I would have you make a careful computation of your good qualities and satisfy yourselves on the strength of which of these it is that you claim to rule over us. Is it that you are more just than ourselves? Yet the people, who are poorer—have never wronged you for the purposes of plunder; but you, whose wealth would outweigh the whole of ours, have wrought many a shameful deed for the sake of gain. If, then, you have no monopoly of justice, can it be on the score of courage that you are warranted to hold your heads so high? If so, what fairer test of courage will you propose than the arbitrament of war—the war just ended? Or do you claim superiority of intelligence?—you, who with all your wealth of arms and walls, money and Peloponnesian allies, have been paralysed by men who had none of these things to aid them! Or is it on these Laconian friends of yours that you pride yourselves? What! when these same friends have dealt by you as men deal by vicious dogs. You know how that is. They put a heavy collar round the neck of the brutes and hand them over muzzled to their masters. So too have the Lacedaemonians handed you over to the people, this very people whom you have injured; and now they have turned their backs and are gone. But" (turning to the mass) "do not misconceive me. It is not for me, sirs, coldly to beg of you, in no respect to violate your solemn undertakings. I go further; I beg you, to crown your list of exploits by one final display of virtue. Show the world that you can be faithful to your oaths, and flawless in your conduct." By these and other kindred arguments he impressed upon them that there was no need for anarchy or disorder, seeing that there were the ancient laws ready for use. And so he broke up[1] the assembly.

At this auspicious moment, then, they reappointed the several magistrates; the constitution began to work afresh, and civic life was recommenced. At a subsequent period, on receiving information that the party at Eleusis were collecting a body of mercenaries, they marched out with their whole force against them, and put to death their generals, who came out to parley. These removed, they introduced to the others their friends and connections, and so persuaded them to come to terms and be reconciled. The oath they bound themselves by consisted of a simple

---

1 The Greek words are {antestese ten ekklesian} (an odd phrase for the more technical {eluse} or {dieluse ten ekklesian}). Or, accepting the MSS. reading above (see last note), translate "he set up (i.e. restored) the Assembly." So Mr. J. G. Philpotts, Mr. Herbert Hailstone, and others.

asseveration: "We will remember past offenses no more"; and to this day[1] the two parties live amicably together as good citizens, and the democracy is steadfast to its oaths.

BOOK III

I

403–402 BC. Thus the civil strife at Athens had an end. At a subsequent date Cyrus sent messengers to Lacedaemon, claiming requital in kind for he service which he had lately rendered in the war with Athens.[2] The demand seemed to the ephorate just and reasonable. Accordingly they ordered Samius,[3] who was admiral at the time, to put himself at the disposition of Cyrus for any service which he might require. Samius himself needed no persuasion to carry out the wishes of Cyrus. With his own fleet, accompanied by that of Cyrus, he sailed round to Cilicia, and so made it impossible for Syennesis, the ruler of that province, to oppose Cyrus by land in his advance against the king his brother.

401 BC. The particulars of the expedition are to be found in the pages of the Syracusan Themistogenes,[4] who describes the mustering of the

---

[1] It would be interesting to know the date at which the author penned these words. Was this portion of the "Hellenica" written before the expedition of Cyrus? i.e. in the interval between the formal restoration of the Democracy, September 403 BC, and March 401 BC. The remaining books of the "Hellenica" were clearly written after that expedition, since reference is made to it quite early in Bk. III. i. 2. Practically, then, the first volume of Xenophon's "History of Hellenic Affairs" ends here. This history is resumed in Bk. III. i. 3. after the Cyreian expedition (of which episode we have a detailed account in the "Anabasis" from March 401 BC down to March 399 BC, when the remnant of the Ten Thousand was handed over to the Spartan general Thibron in Asia). Some incidents belonging to 402 BC are referred to in the opening paragraphs of "Hellenica," III. i. 1, 2, but only as an introduction to the new matter; and with regard to the historian himself, it is clear that "a change has come o'er the spirit of his dream." This change of view is marked by a change of style in writing. I have thought it legitimate, under the circumstances, to follow the chronological order of events, and instead of continuing the "Hellenica," at this point to insert the "Anabasis." My next volume will contain the remaining books of the "Hellenica" and the rest of Xenophon's "historical" writings.

[2] Lit. "what Cyrus himself had been to the Lacedaemonians let the Lacedaemonians in their turn be to Cyrus."

[3] Samius (Diod. Sic. xiv. 19). But see "Anab." I. iv. 2, where Pythagoras is named as admiral. Possibly the one officer succeeded the other.

[4] Lit. "as to how then Cyrus collected an army and with it went up against his brother, and how the battle was fought and how he died, and how in the sequel the Hellenes escaped to the sea (all this), is written by (or 'for,' or 'in honor of') Themistogenes the Syracusan." My impression is that Xenophon's "Anabasis," or a portion of the work so named, was edited originally by Themistogenes. See "Philol. Museum," vol. i. p. 489; L. Dindorf, {Xen. Ell.}, Ox. MDCCCLIII., node ad loc. {Themistogenei}. Cf. Diod. Sic. xiv. 19–31, 37, after Ephorus and Theopompus probably.

armament, and the advance of Cyrus at the head of his troops; and then the battle, and death of Cyrus himself, and the consequent retreat of the Hellenes while effecting their escape to the sea.[1]

400 BC. It was in recognition of the service which he had rendered in this affair, that Tissaphernes was despatched to Lower Asia by the king his master. He came as satrap, not only of his own provinces, but of those which had belonged to Cyrus; and he at once demanded the absolute submission of the Ionic cities, without exception, to his authority. These communities, partly from a desire to maintain their freedom, and partly from fear of Tissaphernes himself, whom they had rejected in favor of Cyrus during the lifetime of that prince, were loth to admit the satrap within their gates. They thought it better to send an embassy to the Lacedaemonians, calling upon them as representatives and leaders[2] of the Hellenic world to look to the interests of their petitioners, who were Hellenes also, albeit they lived in Asia, and not to suffer their country to be ravaged and themselves enslaved.

In answer to this appeal, the Lacedaemonians sent out Thibron[3] as governor, providing him with a body of troops, consisting of one thousand neodamodes[4] (i.e. enfranchised helots) and four thousand Peloponnesians. In addition to these, Thibron himself applied to the Athenians for a detachment of three hundred horse, for whose service-money he would hold himself responsible. The Athenians in answer sent him some of the knights who had served under the Thirty,[5] thinking that the people of Athens would be well rid of them if they went abroad and perished there.

400–399 BC. On their arrival in Asia, Thibron further collected contingents from the Hellenic cities on the continent; for at this time the word of a Lacedaemonian was law. He had only to command, and every city must needs obey.[6] But although he had this armament, Thibron, when he saw the cavalry, had no mind to descend into the plain. If he succeeded in protecting from pillage the particular district in which he chanced to be, he was quite content. It was only when the troops[7] who had taken part in the expedition of Cyrus had joined him on their safe return, that he assumed a bolder attitude. He was now ready to confront Tissaphernes,

---

1 *At Trapezus, March 10, 400 BC.*
2 {*Prostatai*}, *"patrons and protectors."*
3 *"As harmost." See "Anab." ad fin.*
4 *See "Hell." I. iii. 15; Thuc. vii. 58.*
5 *See "Hell." II. iv. 2.*
6 *See "Anab." VI. vi. 12.*
7 *March 399 BC. See the final sentence of the "Anabasis."*

army against army, on the level ground, and won over a number of cities. Pergamum came in of her own accord. So did Teuthrania and Halisarna. These were under the government of Eurysthenes and Procles,[1] the descendants of Demaratus the Lacedaemonian, who in days of old had received this territory as a gift from the Persian monarch in return for his share in the campaign against Hellas. Gorgion and Gongylus, two brothers, also gave in their adhesion; they were lords, the one of Gambreum and Palae-Gambreum, the other of Myrina and Gryneum, four cities which, like those above named, had originally been gifts from the king to an earlier Gongylus—the sole Eretrian who "joined the Mede," and in consequence was banished. Other cities which were too weak to resist, Thibron took by force of arms. In the case of one he was not so successful. This was the Egyptian[2] Larisa, as it is called, which refused to capitulate, and was forthwith invested and subjected to a regular siege. When all other attempts to take it failed, he set about digging a tank or reservoir, and in connection with the tank an underground channel, by means of which he proposed to draw off the water supply of the inhabitants. In this he was baffled by frequent sallies of the besieged, and a continual discharge of timber and stones into the cutting. He retaliated by the construction of a wooden tortoise which he erected over the tank; but once more the tortoise was burnt to a cinder in a successful night attack on the part of the men of Larisa. These ineffectual efforts induced the ephors to send a despatch bidding Thibron give up Larisa and march upon Caria.

He had already reached Ephesus, and was on the point of marching into Caria, when Dercylidas arrived to take command of his army. The new general was a man whose genius for invention had won him the nickname of Sisyphus. Thus it was that Thibron returned home, where on his arrival he was fined and banished, the allies accusing him of allowing his troops to plunder their friends.

Dercylidas was not slow to perceive and turn to account the jealousy which subsisted between Tissaphernes and Pharnabazus. Coming to terms with the former, he marched into the territory of the latter, preferring, as he said, to be at war with one of the pair at a time, rather than the two together. His hostility, indeed, to Pharnabazus was an old story, dating back to a period during the naval command[3] of Lysander, when he was

---

1 See "Anab." VII. viii. 8-16.
2 Seventy stades S.E. of Cyme in the Aeolid. See Strabo, xiii. 621. For the origin of the name cf. "Cyrop." VII. i. 45.
3 Technically "navarchy," in 408-407 BC. "Hell." I. v. 1.

himself governor in Abydos; where, thanks to Pharnabazus, he had got into trouble with his superior officer, and had been made to stand "with his shield on his arm"—a stigma on his honor which no true Lacedaemonian would forgive, since this is the punishment of insubordination.[1] For this reason, doubtless, Dercylidas had the greater satisfaction in marching against Pharnabazus. From the moment he assumed command there was a marked difference for the better between his methods and those of his predecessor. Thus he contrived to conduct his troops into that portion of the Aeolid which belonged to Pharnabazus, through the heart of friendly territory without injury to the allies.

This district of Aeolis belonged to Pharnabazus,[2] but had been held as a satrapy under him by a Dardanian named Zenis whilst he was alive; but when Zenis fell sick and died, Pharnabazus made preparation to give the satrapy to another. Then Mania the wife of Zenis, herself also a Dardanian, fitted out an expedition, and taking with her gifts wherewith to make a present to Pharnabazus himself, and to gratify his concubines and those whose power was greatest with Pharnabazus, set forth on her journey. When she had obtained audience with him she spoke as follows: "O Pharnabazus, thou knowest that thy servant my husband was in all respects friendly to thee; moreover, he paid my lord the tributes which were thy due, so that thou didst praise and honor him. Now therefore, if I do thee service as faithfully as my husband, why needest thou to appoint another satrap?—nay but, if in any matter I please thee not, is it not in thy power to take from me the government on that day, and to give it to another?" When he had heard her words, Pharnabazus decided that the woman ought to be satrap. She, as soon as she was mistress of the territory, never ceased to render the tribute in due season, even as her husband before her had done. Moreover, whenever she came to the court of Pharnabazus she brought him gifts continually, and whenever Pharnabazus went down to visit her provinces she welcomed him with all fair and courteous entertainment beyond what his other viceroys were wont to do. The cities also which had been left to her by her husband, she guarded safely for him; while of those cities that owed her no allegiance, she acquired, on the seaboard, Larisa and Hamaxitus and Colonae—attacking their walls by aid of Hellenic mercenaries, whilst she herself sat in her carriage and watched the spectacle. Nor was she sparing of her gifts to those who won her admiration; and thus she furnished herself with a mercenary force of exceptional splendour. She also went

---

1 See Plut. "Aristid." 23 (Clough, ii. p. 309).
2 I.e. as suzerain.

with Pharnabazus on his campaigns, even when, on pretext of some injury done to the king's territory, Mysians or Pisidians were the object of attack. In requital, Pharnabazus paid her magnificent honor, and at times invited her to assist him with her counsel.[1]

Now when Mania was more than forty years old, the husband of her own daughter, Meidias—flustered by the suggestions of certain people who said that it was monstrous a woman should rule and he remain a private person[2]—found his way into her presence, as the story goes, and strangled her. For Mania, albeit she carefully guarded herself against all ordinary comers, as behoved her in the exercise of her "tyranny," trusted in Meidias, and, as a woman might her own son-in-law, was ready to greet him at all times with open arms. He also murdered her son, a youth of marvellous beauty, who was about seventeen years of age. He next seized upon the strong cities of Scepsis and Gergithes, in which lay for the most part the property and wealth of Mania. As for the other cities of the satrapy, they would not receive the usurper, their garrisons keeping them safely for Pharnabazus. Thereupon Meidias sent gifts to Pharnabazus, and claimed to hold the district even as Mania had held it; to whom the other answered, "Keep your gifts and guard them safely until that day when I shall come in person and take both you and them together"; adding, "What care I to live longer if I avenge not myself for the murder of Mania!"

Just at the critical moment Dercylidas arrived, and in a single day received the adhesion of the three seaboard cities Larisa, Hamaxitus, and Colonae—which threw open their gates to him. Then he sent messengers to the cities of the Aeolid also, offering them freedom if they would receive him within their walls and become allies. Accordingly the men of Neandria and Ilium and Cocylium lent willing ears; for since the death of Mania their Hellenic garrisons had been treated but ill. But the commander of the garrison in Cebrene, a place of some strength, bethinking him that if he should succeed in guarding that city for Pharnabazus, he would receive honor at his hands, refused to admit Dercylidas. Whereupon the latter, in a rage, prepared to take the place by force; but when he came to sacrifice, on the first day the victims would not yield good omens; on the second, and again upon the third day, it was the same story. Thus for as many as four days he persevered in sacrificing, cherishing wrath the while—for he was in haste to become master of the whole Aeolid before Pharnabazus came to the succour of the district.

---

1 Grote, "H. G." ix. 292; cf. Herod. viii. 69.
2 Or, "his brains whimsied with insinuations."

Meanwhile a certain Sicyonian captain, Athenadas by name, said to himself: "Dercylidas does but trifle to waste his time here, whilst I with my own hand can draw off their water from the men of Cybrene"; wherewith he ran forward with his division and essayed to choke up the spring which supplied the city. But the garrison sallied out and covered the Sicyonian himself with wounds, besides killing two of his men. Indeed, they plied their swords and missiles with such good effect that the whole company was forced to beat a retreat. Dercylidas was not a little annoyed, thinking that now the spirit of the besiegers would certainly die away; but whilst he was in this mood, behold! there arrived from the beleaguered fortress emissaries of the Hellenes, who stated that the action taken by the commandant was not to their taste; for themselves, they would far rather be joined in bonds of fellowship with Hellenes than with barbarians. While the matter was still under discussion there came a messenger also from the commandant, to say that whatever the former deputation had proposed he, on his side, was ready to endorse. Accordingly Dercylidas, who, it so happened, had at length obtained favorable omens on that day, marched his force without more ado up to the gates of the city, which were flung open by those within; and so he entered.[1] Here, then, he was content to appoint a garrison, and without further stay advanced upon Scepsis and Gergithes.

And now Meidias, partly expecting the hostile advance of Pharnabazus, and partly mistrusting the citizens—for to such a pass things had come—sent to Dercylidas, proposing to meet him in conference provided he might take security of hostages. In answer to this suggestion the other sent him one man from each of the cities of the allies, and bade him take his pick of these, whichsoever and how many soever he chose, as hostages for his own security. Meidias selected ten, and so went out. In conversation with Dercylidas, he asked him on what terms he would accept his alliance. The other answered: "The terms are that you grant the citizens freedom and self-government." The words were scarcely out of his mouth before he began marching upon Scepsis. Whereupon Meidias, perceiving it was vain to hinder him in the teeth of the citizens, suffered him to enter. That done, Dercylidas offered sacrifice to Athena in the citadel of the Scepsians, turned out the bodyguards of Meidias, and handed over the city to the citizens. And so, having admonished them to regulate their civic life as

---

1 Grote ("H. G." ix. 294) says: "The reader will remark how Xenophon shapes the narrative in such a manner as to inculcate the pious duty in a general of obeying the warnings furnished by the sacrifice—either for action or for inaction.... Such an inference is never (I believe) to be found suggested in Thucydides." See Brietenbach, "Xen. Hell." I et II, praef. in alteram ed. p. xvii.

Hellenes and free men ought, he left the place and continued his advance against Gergithes. On this last march he was escorted by many of the Scepsians themselves; such was the honor they paid him and so great their satisfaction at his exploits. Meidias also followed close at his side, petitioning that he would hand over the city of Gergithians to himself. To whom Dercylidas only made reply, that he should not fail to obtain any of his just rights. And whilst the words were yet upon his lips, he was drawing close to the gates, with Meidias at his side. Behind him followed the troops, marching two and two in peaceful fashion. The defenders of Gergithes from their towers—which were extraordinarily high—espied Meidias in company of the Spartan, and abstained from shooting. And Dercylidas said: "Bid them open the gates, Meidias, when you shall lead the way, and I will enter the temple along with you and do sacrifice to Athena." And Meidias, though he shrank from opening the gates, yet in terror of finding himself on a sudden seized, reluctantly gave the order to open the gates. As soon as he was entered in, the Spartan, still taking Meidias with him, marched up to the citadel and there ordered the main body of his soldiers to take up their position round the walls, whilst he with those about him did sacrifice to Athena. When the sacrifice was ended he ordered Meidias's bodyguard to pile arms[1] in the van of his troops. Here for the future they would serve as mercenaries, since Meidias their former master stood no longer in need of their protection. The latter, being at his wits" end what to do, exclaimed: "Look you, I will now leave you; I go to make preparation for my guest." But the other replied: "Heaven forbid! Ill were it that I who have offered sacrifice should be treated as a guest by you. I rather should be the entertainer and you the guest. Pray stay with us, and while the supper is preparing, you and I can consider our obligations, and perform them."

When they were seated Dercylidas put certain questions: "Tell me, Meidias, did your father leave you heir to his estates?" "Certainly he did," answered the other. "And how many dwelling-houses have you? what landed estates? how much pasturage?" The other began running off an inventory, whilst some of the Scepsians who were present kept interposing, "He is lying to you, Dercylidas." "Nay, you take too minute a view of matters," replied the Spartan. When the inventory of the paternal property was completed, he proceeded: "Tell me, Meidias, to whom did Mania belong?" A chorus of voices rejoined, "To Pharnabazus." "Then must her property have belonged to Pharnabazus too." "Certainly," they answered.

---

1 I.e. take up a position, or "to order arms," whilst he addressed them; not probably "to ground arms," as if likely to be mutinous.

"Then it must now be ours," he remarked, "by right of conquest, since Pharnabazus is at war with us. Will some one of you escort me to the place where the property of Mania and Pharnabazus lies?" So the rest led the way to the dwelling-place of Mania which Meidias had taken from her, and Meidias followed too. When he was entered, Dercylidas summoned the stewards, and bidding his attendants seize them, gave them to understand that, if detected stealing anything which belonged to Mania, they would lose their heads on the spot. The stewards proceeded to point out the treasures, and he, when he had looked through the whole store, bolted and barred the doors, affixing his seal, and setting a watch. As he went out he found at the doors certain of the generals[1] and captains, and said to them: "Here, sirs, we have pay ready made for the army—a year's pay nearly for eight thousand men—and if we can win anything besides, there will be so much the more." This he said, knowing that those who heard it would be all the more amenable to discipline, and would yield him a more flattering obedience. Then Meidias asked, "And where am I to live, Dercylidas?" "Where you have the very best right to live," replied the other, "in your native town of Scepsis, and in your father's house."

II

Such were the exploits of Dercylidas: nine cities taken in eight days. Two considerations now began to occupy his mind: how was he to avoid falling into the fatal error of Thibron and becoming a burthen to his allies, whilst wintering in a friendly country? how, again, was he to prevent Pharnabazus from overriding the Hellenic states in pure contempt with his cavalry? Accordingly he sent to Pharnabazus and put it to him point-blank: Which will you have, peace or war? Whereupon Pharnabazus, who could not but perceive that the whole Aeolid had now been converted practically into a fortified base of operations, which threatened his own homestead of Phrygia, chose peace.

399–398 BC. This being so, Dercylidas advanced into Bithynian Thrace, and there spent the winter; nor did Pharnabazus exhibit a shadow of annoyance, since the Bithynians were perpetually at war with himself. For the most part, Dercylidas continued to harry[2] Bithynia in perfect security, and found provisions without stint. Presently he was joined from the other side of the straits by some Odrysian allies sent by Seuthes;[3] they numbered

---

1 Lit. "of the taxiarchs and lochagoi."
2 {Pheson kai agon}, i.e. "there was plenty of live stock to lift and chattels to make away with."
3 For Seuthes see "Anab." VII. i. 5; and below, IV. viii. 26.

two hundred horse and three hundred peltasts. These fellows pitched upon a site a little more than a couple of miles[1] from the Hellenic force, where they entrenched themselves; then having got from Dercylidas some heavy infantry soldiers to act as guards of their encampment, they devoted themselves to plundering, and succeeded in capturing an ample store of slaves and other wealth. Presently their camp was full of prisoners, when one morning the Bithynians, having ascertained the actual numbers of the marauding parties as well as of the Hellenes left as guards behind, collected in large masses of light troops and cavalry, and attacked the garrison, who were not more than two hundred strong. As soon as they came close enough, they began discharging spears and other missiles on the little body, who on their side continued to be wounded and shot down, but were quite unable to retaliate, cooped up as they were within a palisading barely six feet high, until in desperation they tore down their defenses with their own hands, and dashed at the enemy. These had nothing to do but to draw back from the point of egress, and being light troops easily escaped beyond the grasp of heavy-armed men, while ever and again, from one point of vantage or another, they poured their shower of javelins, and at every sally laid many a brave man low, till at length, like sheep penned in a fold, the defenders were shot down almost to a man. A remnant, it is true, did escape, consisting of some fifteen who, seeing the turn affairs were taking, had already made off in the middle of the fighting. Slipping through their assailants' fingers,[2] to the small concern of the Bithynians, they reached the main Hellenic camp in safety. The Bithynians, satisfied with their achievement, part of which consisted in cutting down the tent guards of the Odrysian Thracians and recovering all their prisoners, made off without delay; so that by the time the Hellenes got wind of the affair and rallied to the rescue, they found nothing left in the camp save only the stripped corpses of the slain. When the Odrysians themselves returned, they fell to burying their own dead, quaffing copious draughts of wine in their honor and holding horse-races; but for the future they deemed it advisable to camp along with the Hellenes. Thus they harried and burned Bithynia the winter through.

398 BC. With the commencement of spring Dercylidas turned his back upon the Bithynians and came to Lampsacus. Whilst at this place envoys reached him from the home authorities. These were Aracus, Naubates, and Antisthenes. They were sent to inquire generally into the condition of affairs in Asia, and to inform Dercylidas of the extension of his office

---

1 Lit. "twenty stades."
2 Or, "slipping through the enemy's fingers, who took no heed of them, they," etc.

for another year. They had been further commissioned by the ephors to summon a meeting of the soldiers and inform them that the ephors held them to blame for their former doings, though for their present avoidance of evil conduct they must needs praise them; and for the future they must understand that while no repetition of misdoing would be tolerated, all just and upright dealing by the allies would receive its meed of praise. The soldiers were therefore summoned, and the envoys delivered their message, to which the leader of the Cyreians answered: "Nay, men of Lacedaemon, listen; we are the same today as we were last year; only our general of today is different from our general in the past. If today we have avoided our offense of yesterday, the cause is not far to seek; you may discover it for yourselves."

Aracus and the other envoys shared the hospitality of Dercylidas's tent, and one of the party chanced to mention how they had left an embassy from the men of Chersonese in Lacedaemon. According to their statement, he added, it was impossible for them to till their land nowadays, so perpetually were they robbed and plundered by the Thracians; whereas the peninsula needed only to be walled across from sea to sea, and there would be abundance of good land to cultivate—enough for themselves and as many others from Lacedaemon as cared to come. "So that it would not surprise us," continued the envoys, "if a Lacedaemonian were actually sent out from Sparta with a force to carry out the project." Dercylidas kept his ears open but his counsel close, and so sent forward the commissioners to Ephesus.[1] It pleased him to picture their progress through the Hellenic cities, and the spectacle of peace and prosperity which would everywhere greet their eyes. When he knew that his stay was to be prolonged, he sent again to Pharnabazus and offered him once more as an alternative either the prolongation of the winter truce or war. And once again Pharnabazus chose truce. It was thus that Dercylidas was able to leave the cities in the neighborhood of the satrap[2] in peace and friendship. Crossing the Hellespont himself he brought his army into Europe, and marching through Thrace, which was also friendly, was entertained by Seuthes,[3] and so reached the Chersonese.

This district, he soon discovered, not only contained something like a dozen cities,[4] but was singularly fertile. The soil was of the best, but ruined

---

1 See Grote, "H. G." ix. 301.
2 Or, reading after Cobet, {tas peri ekeina poleis}—"the cities of that neighborhood."
3 See "Anab." VII. vii. 51.
4 Lit. "eleven or twelve cities." For the natural productivity, see "Anab." V. vi. 25.

by the ravages of the Thracians, precisely as he had been told. Accordingly, having measured and found the breadth of the isthmus barely four miles,[1] he no longer hesitated. Having offered sacrifice, he commenced his line of wall, distributing the area to the soldiers in detachments, and promising to award them prizes for their industry—a first prize for the section first completed, and the rest as each detachment of workers might deserve. By this means the whole wall begun in spring was finished before autumn. Within these lines he established eleven cities, with numerous harbors, abundance of good arable land, and plenty of land under plantation, besides magnificent grazing grounds for sheep and cattle of every kind.

Having finished the work, he crossed back again into Asia, and on a tour of inspection, found the cities for the most part in a thriving condition; but when he came to Atarneus he discovered that certain exiles from Chios had got possession of the stronghold, which served them as a convenient base for pillaging and plundering Ionia; and this, in fact, was their means of livelihood. Being further informed of the large supplies of grain which they had inside, he proceeded to draw entrenchments around the place with a view to a regular investment, and by this means he reduced it in eight months. Then having appointed Draco of Pellene[2] commandant, he stocked the fortress with an abundance of provisions of all sorts, to serve him as a halting-place when he chanced to pass that way, and so withdrew to Ephesus, which is three days' journey from Sardis.

397 BC. Up to this date peace had been maintained between Tissaphernes and Dercylidas, as also between the Hellenes and the barbarians in those parts. But the time came when an embassy arrived at Lacedaemon from the Ionic cities, protesting that Tissaphernes might, if he chose, leave the Hellenic cities independent. "Our idea," they added, "is, that if Caria, the home of Tissaphernes, felt the pinch of war, the satrap would very soon agree to grant us independence." The ephors, on hearing this, sent a despatch to Dercylidas, and bade him cross the frontier with his army into Caria, whilst Pharax the admiral coasted round with the fleet. These orders were carried out. Meanwhile a visitor had reached Tissaphernes. This was not less a person than Pharnabazus. His coming was partly owing to the fact that Tissaphernes had been appointed general-in-chief, and party in order to testify his readiness to make common cause with his brother satrap in fighting and expelling the Hellenes from the king's territory; for if his

---

1 Lit. *"thirty-seven stades."* Mod. Gallipoli. See Herod. vi. 36; Plut. *"Pericl."* xix.
2 Cf. Isocr. *"Panegyr."* 70; Jebb. *"Att. Or."* ii. p. 161. Of Pellene (or Pellana) in Laconia, not Pellene in Achaia? though that is the opinion of Grote and Thirlwall.

heart was stirred by jealousy on account of the generalship bestowed upon his rival, he was not the less aggrieved at finding himself robbed of the Aeolid. Tissaphernes, lending willing ears to the proposal, had answered: "First cross over with me in Caria, and then we will take counsel on these matters." But being arrived in Caria, they determined to establish garrisons of some strength in the various fortresses, and so crossed back again into Ionia.

Hearing that the satraps had recrossed the Maeander, Dercylidas grew apprehensive for the district which lay there unprotected. "If Tissaphernes and Pharnabazus," he said to Pharax, "chose to make a descent, they could harry the country right and left." In this mind he followed suit, and recrossed the frontier too. And now as they marched on, preserving no sort of battle order—on the supposition that the enemy had got far ahead of them into the district of Ephesus—suddenly they caught sight of his scouts perched on some monumental structures facing them. To send up scouts into similar edifices and towers on their own side was the work of a few moments, and before them lay revealed the long lines of troops drawn up just where their road lay. These were the Carians, with their white shields, and the whole Persian troops there present, with all the Hellenic contingents belonging to either satrap. Besides these there was a great cloud of cavalry: on the right wing the squadrons of Tissaphernes, and on the left those of Pharnabazus.

Seeing how matters lay, Dercylidas ordered the generals of brigade and captains to form into line as quickly as possible, eight deep, placing the light infantry on the fringe of battle, with the cavalry—such cavalry, that is, and of such numerical strength, as he chanced to have. Meanwhile, as general, he sacrificed.[1] During this interval the troops from Peloponnese kept quiet in preparation as for battle. Not so the troops from Priene and Achilleum, from the islands and the Ionic cities, some of whom left their arms in the corn, which stood thick and deep in the plain of the Maeander, and took to their heels; while those who remained at their posts gave evident signs that their steadiness would not last. Pharnabazus, it was reported, had given orders to engage; but Tissaphernes, who recalled his experience of his own exploits with the Cyreian army, and assumed that all other Hellenes were of similar mettle, had no desire to engage, but sent to Dercylidas saying, he should be glad to meet him in conference. So Dercylidas, attended by the pick of his troops, horse and foot, in personal attendance on himself,[2]

---

1 I.e. according to custom on the eve of battle. See "Pol. Lac." xiii. 8.
2 Lit. "they were splendid fellows to look at." See "Anab." II. iii. 3.

went forward to meet the envoys. He told them that for his own part he had made his preparations to engage, as they themselves might see, but still, if the satraps were minded to meet in conference, he had nothing to say against it—"Only, in that case, there must be mutual exchange of hostages and other pledges."

When this proposal had been agreed to and carried out, the two armies retired for the night—the Asiatics to Tralles in Caria, the Hellenes to Leucophrys, where was a temple[1] of Artemis of great sanctity, and a sandy-bottomed lake more than a furlong in extent, fed by a spring of ever-flowing water fit for drinking and warm. For the moment so much was effected. On the next day they met at the place appointed, and it was agreed that they should mutually ascertain the terms on which either party was willing to make peace. On his side, Dercylidas insisted that the king should grant independence to the Hellenic cities; while Tissaphernes and Pharnabazus demanded the evacuation of the country by the Hellenic army, and the withdrawal of the Lacedaemonian governors from the cities. After this interchange of ideas a truce was entered into, so as to allow time for the reports of the proceedings to be sent by Dercylidas to Lacedaemon, and by Tissaphernes to the king.

401 BC (?). Whilst such was the conduct of affairs in Asia under the guidance of Dercylidas, the Lacedaemonians at home were at the same time no less busily employed with other matters. They cherished a long-standing embitterment against the Eleians, the grounds of which were that the Eleians had once[2] contracted an alliance with the Athenians, Argives, and Mantineans; moreover, on pretence of a sentence registered against the Lacedaemonians, they had excluded them from the horse-race and gymnastic contests. Nor was that the sum of their offending. They had taken and scourged Lichas,[3] under the following circumstances:—Being a Spartan, he had formally consigned his chariot to the Thebans, and when the Thebans were proclaimed victors he stepped forward to crown his charioteer; whereupon, in spite of his grey hairs, the Eleians put those indignities upon him and expelled him from the festival. Again, at a date subsequent to that occurrence, Agis being sent to offer sacrifice to Olympian Zeus in accordance with the bidding of an oracle, the Eleians would not suffer him to offer prayer for victory in war, asserting that the

---

1 Lately unearthed. See "Class. Rev." v. 8, p. 391.
2 In 421 BC (see Thuc. v. 31); for the second charge, see Thuc. v. 49 foll.
3 See "Mem." I. ii. 61; Thuc. v. 50; and Jowett, note ad loc. vol. ii. p. 314.

ancient law and custom[1] forbade Hellenes to consult the god for war with Hellenes; and Agis was forced to go away without offering the sacrifice.

In consequence of all these annoyances the ephors and the Assembly determined "to bring the men of Elis to their senses." Thereupon they sent an embassy to that state, announcing that the authorities of Lacedaemon deemed it just and right that they should leave the country[2] townships in the territory of Elis free and independent. This the Eleians flatly refused to do. The cities in question were theirs by right of war. Thereupon the ephors called out the ban. The leader of the expedition was Agis. He invaded Elis through Achaia[3] by the Larisus; but the army had hardly set foot on the enemy's soil and the work of devastation begun, when an earthquake took place, and Agis, taking this as a sign from Heaven, marched back again out of the country and disbanded his army. Thereat the men of Elis were much more emboldened, and sent embassies to various cities which they knew to be hostile to the Lacedaemonians.

The year had not completed its revolution[4] ere the ephors again called out the ban against Elis, and the invading host of Agis was this time swelled by the rest of the allies, including the Athenians; the Boeotians and Corinthians alone excepted. The Spartan king now entered through Aulon,[5] and the men of Lepreum[6] at once revolted from the Eleians and gave in their adhesion to the Spartan, and simultaneously with these the Macistians and their next-door neighbors the Epitalians. As he crossed the river further adhesions followed, on the part of the Letrinians, the Amphidolians, and the Marganians.

400 BC (?). Upon this he pushed on into Olympian territory and did sacrifice to Olympian Zeus. There was no attempt to stay his proceedings now. After sacrifice he marched against the capital,[7] devastating and burning the country as he went. Multitudes of cattle, multitudes of slaves, were the fruits of conquest yielded, insomuch that the fame thereof spread, and many more Arcadians and Achaeans flocked to join the standard of the invader and to share in the plunder. In fact, the expedition became one enormous foray. Here was the chance to fill all the granaries of Peloponnese with

---

1 See Grote, "H. G." ix. 311 note.
2 Lit. "perioecid."
3 From the north. The Larisus is the frontier stream between Achaia and Elis. See Strabo, viii. 387.
4 Al. "on the coming round of the next year." See Jowett (note to Thuc. i. 31), vol. ii. p. 33.
5 On the south. For the history, see Busolt, "Die Laked." pp. 146-200. "The river" is the Alpheus.
6 See below, VI. v. 11; Paus. IV. xv. 8.
7 I.e. Elis, of which Cyllene is the port town. For the wealth of the district, see Polyb. iv. 73; and below, VII. iv. 33.

corn. When he had reached the capital, the beautiful suburbs and gymnasia became a spoil to the troops; but the city itself, though it lay open before him a defenseless and unwalled town, he kept aloof from. He would not, rather than could not, take it. Such was the explanation given. Thus the country was a prey to devastation, and the invaders massed round Cyllene.

Then the friends of a certain Xenias—a man of whom it was said that he might measure the silver coin, inherited from his father, by the bushel—wishing to be the leading instrument in bringing over the state to Lacedaemon, rushed out of the house, sword in hand, and began a work of butchery. Among other victims they killed a man who strongly resembled the leader of the democratic party, Thrasydaeus.[1] Everyone believed it was really Thrasydaeus who was slain. The popular party were panic-stricken, and stirred neither hand nor foot. On their side, the cut-throats poured their armed bands into the marketplace. But Thrasydaeus was laid asleep the while where the fumes of wine had overpowered him. When the people came to discover that their hero was not dead, they crowded round his house this side and that,[2] like a swarm of bees clinging to their leader; and as soon as Thrasydaeus had put himself in the van, with the people at his back, a battle was fought, and the people won. And those who had laid their hands to deeds of butchery went as exiles to the Lacedaemonians.

After a while Agis himself retired, recrossing the Alpheus; but he was careful to leave a garrison in Epitalium near that river, with Lysippus as governor, and the exiles from Elis along with him. Having done so, he disbanded his army and returned home himself.

400–399 BC (?).[3] During the rest of the summer and the ensuing winter the territory of the Eleians was ravaged and ransacked by Lysippus and his troops, until Thrasydaeus, the following summer, sent to Lacedaemon and agreed to dismantle the walls of Phea and Cyllene, and to grant autonomy to the Triphylian townships[4]—together with Phrixa and Epitalium, the Letrinians, Amphidolians, and Marganians; and besides these to the

---

1 See Paus. III. viii. 4. He was a friend of Lysias ("Vit. X. Orat. 835").
2 The house was filled to overflowing by the clustering close-packed crowd.
3 Grote ("H. G." ix. 316) discusses the date of this war between Elis and Sparta, which he thinks, reaches over three different years, 402–400 BC But Curtius (vol. iv. Eng. tr. p. 196) disagrees: "The Eleian war must have occurred in 401–400 BC, and Grote rightly conjectures that the Eleians were anxious to bring it to a close before the celebration of the festival. But he errs in extending its duration over three years." See Diod. xiv. 17. 24; Paus. III. viii. 2 foll.
4 Grote remarks: "There is something perplexing in Xenophon's description of the Triphylian townships which the Eleians surrendered" ("H. G." ix. 315). I adopt Grote's emend. {kai Phrixan}. See Busolt, op. cit. p. 176.

Acroreians and to Lasion, a place claimed by the Arcadians. With regard to Epeium, a town midway between Heraea and Macistus, the Eleians claimed the right to keep it, on the plea that they had purchased the whole district from its then owners, for thirty talents,[1] which sum they had actually paid. But the Lacedaemonians, acting on the principle "that a purchase which forcibly deprives the weaker party of his possession is no more justifiable than a seizure by violence," compelled them to emancipate Epeium also. From the presidency of the temple of Olympian Zeus, however, they did not oust them; not that it belonged to Elis of ancient right, but because the rival claimants,[2] it was felt, were "villagers," hardly equal to the exercise of the presidency. After these concessions, peace and alliance between the Eleians and the Lacedaemonians were established, and the war between Elis and Sparta ceased.

III

After this Agis came to Delphi and offered as a sacrifice a tenth of the spoil. On his return journey he fell ill at Heraea—being by this time an old man—and was carried back to Lacedaemon. He survived the journey, but being there arrived, death speedily overtook him. He was buried with a sepulchre transcending in solemnity the lot of ordinary mortality.[3]

When the holy days of mourning were accomplished, and it was necessary to choose another king, there were rival claimants to the throne. Leotychides claimed it as the son, Agesilaus as the brother, of Agis. Then Leotychides protested: "Yet consider, Agesilaus, the law bids not 'the king's brother,' but 'the king's son' to be king; only if there chance to be no son, in that case shall the brother of the king be king." Agesilaus: "Then must I needs be king." Leotychides: "How so, seeing that I am not dead?" Agesilaus: "Because he whom you call your father denied you, saying, 'Leotychides is no son of mine.'" Leotychides: "Nay, but my mother, who would know far better than he, said, and still today says, I am." Agesilaus: "Nay, but the god himself, Poteidan, laid his finger on thy falsity when by his earthquake he drove forth thy father from the bridal chamber into the light of day; and time, 'that tells no lies,' as the proverb has it, bare witness to the witness of the god; for just ten months from the moment at which he

---

1 = 7,312 pounds: 10 shillings.
2 I.e. the men of the Pisatid. See below, VII. iv. 28; Busolt, op. cit. p 156.
3 See "Ages." xi. 16; "Pol. Lac." xv. 9.

fled and was no more seen within that chamber, you were born."[1] So they reasoned together.

Diopethes,[2] a great authority upon oracles, supported Leotychides. There was an oracle of Apollo, he urged, which said "Beware of the lame reign." But Diopethes was met by Lysander, who in behalf of Agesilaus demurred to this interpretation put upon the language of the god. If they were to beware of a lame reign, it meant not, beware lest a man stumble and halt, but rather, beware of him in whose veins flows not the blood of Heracles; most assuredly the kingdom would halt, and that would be a lame reign in very deed, whensoever the descendants of Heracles should cease to lead the state. Such were the arguments on either side, after hearing which the city chose Agesilaus to be king.

Now Agesilaus had not been seated on the throne one year when, as he sacrificed one of the appointed sacrifices in behalf of the city,[3] the soothsayer warned him, saying: "The gods reveal a conspiracy of the most fearful character"; and when the king sacrificed a second time, he said: "The aspect of the victims is now even yet more terrible"; but when he had sacrificed for the third time, the soothsayer exclaimed: "O Agesilaus, the sign is given to me, even as though we were in the very midst of the enemy." Thereupon they sacrificed to the deities who avert evil and work salvation, and so barely obtained good omens and ceased sacrificing. Nor had five days elapsed after the sacrifices were ended, ere one came bringing information to the ephors of a conspiracy, and named Cinadon as the ringleader; a young man robust of body as of soul, but not one of the peers.[4] Accordingly the ephors questioned their informant: "How say you the occurrence is to take place?" and he who gave the information answered: "Cinadon took me to the limit of the marketplace, and bade me count how many Spartans there were in the marketplace; and I counted—'king, ephors, and elders, and others—maybe forty. But tell me, Cinadon,' I said to him, 'why have you bidden me count them?' and he answered me: 'Those men, I would have you know, are your sworn foes; and all those others, more than four thousand, congregated there are your natural allies.'

---

1 *I have followed Sauppe as usual, but see Hartman ("Anal. Xen." p. 327) for a discussion of the whole passage. He thinks Xenophon wrote {ex ou gar toi ephugen} ({o sos pater}, i.e. adulterer) {ek to thalamo dekato meni tu ephus}. The Doric {ek to thalamo} was corrupted into {en to thalamo} and {kai ephane} inserted. This corrupt reading Plutarch had before him, and hence his distorted version of the story.*
2 *See Plut. "Ages." ii. 4; "Lys." xxii. (Clough, iv. 3; iii. 129); Paus. III. viii. 5.*
3 *"Pol. Lac." xv. 2.*
4 *For the {omoioi}, see Muller, "Dorians," iii. 5, 7 (vol. ii. p. 84); Grote, "H. G." ix. 345, note 2.*

Then he took and showed me in the streets, here one and there two of 'our enemies,' as we chanced to come across them, and all the rest 'our natural allies'; and so again running through the list of Spartans to be found in the country districts, he still kept harping on that string: 'Look you, on each estate one foeman—the master—and all the rest allies.'" The ephors asked: "How many do you reckon are in the secret of this matter?" The informant answered: "On that point also he gave me to understand that there were by no means many in their secret who were prime movers of the affair, but those few to be depended on; 'and to make up,' said he, 'we ourselves are in their secret, all the rest of them—helots, enfranchised, inferiors, provincials, one and all.[1] Note their demeanor when Spartans chance to be the topic of their talk. Not one of them can conceal the delight it would give him if he might eat up every Spartan raw.'"[2] Then, as the inquiry went on, the question came: "And where did they propose to find arms?" The answer followed: "He explained that those of us, of course, who are enrolled in regiments have arms of our own already, and as for the mass—he led the way to the war foundry, and showed me scores and scores of knives, of swords, of spits, hatchets, and axes, and reaping-hooks. 'Anything or everything,' he told me, 'which men use to delve in earth, cut timber, or quarry stone, would serve our purpose; nay, the instruments used for other arts would in nine cases out of ten furnish weapons enough and to spare, especially when dealing with unarmed antagonists.'" Once more being asked what time the affair was to come off, he replied his orders were "not to leave the city."

As the result of their inquiry the ephors were persuaded that the man's statements were based upon things he had really seen,[3] and they were so alarmed that they did not even venture to summon the Little Assembly,[4] as it was named; but holding informal meetings among themselves—a few senators here and a few there—they determined to send Cinadon and others of the young men to Aulon, with instructions to apprehend certain of the inhabitants and helots, whose names were written on the scytale (or scroll).[5] He had further instructions to capture another resident in Aulon; this was a woman, the fashionable beauty of the place—supposed to be the arch-corruptress of all Lacedaemonians, young and old, who visited Aulon.

---

1 For the neodamodes, hypomeiones, perioeci, see Arnold, "Thuc." v. 34; Muller, "Dorians," ii. 43, 84, 18; Busolt, op. cit. p 16.
2 See "Anab." IV. viii. 14; and Hom. "Il." iv. 34.
3 "And pointed to a well-concerted plan."
4 See Grote, "H. G." ix. 348.
5 See Thuc. i. 131; Plut. "Lys." 19 (Clough, iii. p. 125).

It was not the first mission of the sort on which Cinadon had been employed by the ephors. It was natural, therefore, that the ephors should entrust him with the scytale on which the names of the suspects were inscribed; and in answer to his inquiry which of the young men he was to take with him, they said: "Go and order the eldest of the Hippagretae[1] (or commanders of horse) to let you have six or seven who chance to be there." But they had taken care to let the commander know whom he was to send, and that those sent should also know that their business was to capture Cinadon. Further, the authorities instructed Cinadon that they would send three waggons to save bringing back his captives on foot—concealing as deeply as possible the fact that he, and he alone, was the object of the mission. Their reason for not securing him in the city was that they did not really know the extent of the mischief; and they wished, in the first instance, to learn from Cinadon who his accomplices were before these latter could discover they were informed against and effect their escape. His captors were to secure him first, and having learned from him the names of his confederates, to write them down and send them as quickly as possible to the ephors. The ephors, indeed, were so much concerned about the whole occurrence that they further sent a company of horse to assist their agents at Aulon.[2] As soon as the capture was effected, and one of the horsemen was back with the list of names taken down on the information of Cinadon, they lost no time in apprehending the soothsayer Tisamenus and the rest who were the principals in the conspiracy. When Cinadon[3] himself was brought back and cross-examined, and had made a full confession of the whole plot, his plans, and his accomplices, they put to him one final question: "What was your object in undertaking this business?" He answered: "I wished to be inferior to no man in Lacedaemon." Let that be as it might, his fate was to be taken out forthwith in irons, just as he was, and to be placed with his two hands and his neck in the collar, and so under scourge and goad to be driven, himself and his accomplices, round the city. Thus upon the heads of those was visited the penalty of their offenses.

IV

397 BC.[4] It was after the incidents just recorded that a Syracusan named Herodas brought news to Lacedaemon. He had chanced to be in Phoenicia

---

1 "The Hippagretes (or commander of the three hundred guards called horsemen, though they were not really mounted)." Grote, "H. G." vol. ix. p. 349; see "Pol. Lac." iv. 3.
2 Or, "to those on the way to Aulon."
3 See for Cinadon's case, Arist. "Pol." v. 7, 3.
4 See Grote, "H. G." ix. 353, for chronology, etc.

with a certain shipowner, and was struck by the number of Phoenician triremes which he observed, some coming into harbor from other ports, others already there with their ships' companies complete, while others again were still completing their equipments. Nor was it only what he saw, but he had heard say further that there were to be three hundred of these vessels all told; whereupon he had taken passage on the first sailing ship bound for Hellas. He was in haste to lay this information before the Lacedaemonians, feeling sure that the king and Tissaphernes were concerned in these preparations—though where the fleet was to act, or against whom, he would not venture to predict.

These reports threw the Lacedaemonians into a flutter of expectation and anxiety. They summoned a meeting of the allies, and began to deliberate as to what ought to be done. Lysander, convinced of the enormous superiority of the Hellenic navy, and with regard to land forces drawing an obvious inference from the exploits and final deliverance of the troops with Cyrus, persuaded Agesilaus, to undertake a campaign into Asia, provided the authorities would furnish him with thirty Spartans, two thousand of the enfranchised,[1] and contingents of the allies amounting to six thousand men. Apart from these calculations, Lysander had a personal object: he wished to accompany the king himself, and by his aid to re-establish the decarchies originally set up by himself in the different cities, but at a later date expelled through the action of the ephors, who had issued a fiat re-establishing the old order of constitution.

396 BC. To this offer on the part of Agesilaus to undertake such an expedition the Lacedaemonians responded by presenting him with all he asked for, and six months" provisions besides. When the hour of departure came he offered all such sacrifices as are necessary, and lastly those "before crossing the border,"[2] and so set out. This done, he despatched to the several states[3] messengers with directions as to the numbers to be sent from each, and the points of rendezvous; but for himself he was minded to go and do sacrifice at Aulis, even as Agamemnon had offered sacrifice in that place ere he set sail for Troy. But when he had reached the place and had

---

1 Technically, "neodamodes."
2 "Pol. Lac." xiii. 2 foll.
3 Or, "To the several cities he had already despatched messengers with directions," etc.; see Paus. III. ix. 1-3.

begun to sacrifice, the Boeotarchs[1] being apprised of his design, sent a body of cavalry and bade him desist from further sacrificing;[2] and lighting upon victims already offered, they hurled them from off the altars, scattering the fragments. Then Agesilaus, calling the gods to witness, got on board his trireme in bitter indignation, and sailed away. Arrived at Geraestus, he there collected as large a portion of his troops as possible, and with the armada made sail for Ephesus.

When he had reached that city the first move was made by Tissaphernes, who sent asking, "With what purpose he was come thither?" And the Spartan king made answer: "With the intention that the cities in Asia shall be independent even as are the cities in our quarter of Hellas." In answer to this Tissaphernes said: "If you on your part choose to make a truce whilst I send ambassadors to the king, I think you may well arrange the matter, and sail back home again, if so you will." "Willing enough should I be," replied Agesilaus, "were I not persuaded that you are cheating me." "Nay, but it is open to you," replied the satrap, "to exact a surety for the execution of the terms... 'Provided always that you, Tissaphernes, carry out what you say without deceit, we on our side will abstain from injuring your dominion in any respect whatever during the truce.'"[3] Accordingly in the presence of three commissioners—Herippidas, Dercylidas, and Megillus—Tissaphernes took an oath in the words prescribed: "Verily and indeed, I will effect peace honestly and without guile." To which the commissioners, on behalf of Agesilaus, swore a counter-oath: "Verily and indeed, provided Tissaphernes so acts, we on our side will observe the truce."

Tissaphernes at once gave the lie to what he had sworn. Instead of adhering to peace he sent up to demand a large army from the king, in addition to what he already had. But Agesilaus, though he was fully alive to these proceedings, adhered as rigidly as ever to the truce.

To keep quiet and enjoy leisure was his duty, in the exercise of which he wore away the time at Ephesus. But in reference to the organization of the several states it was a season of vehement constitutional disturbance

---

[1] See Freeman, "Hist. of Federal Government," ch. iv. "Constitution of the Boeotian League," pp. 162, 163. The Boeotarchs, as representatives of the several Boeotian cities, were the supreme military commanders of the League, and, as it would appear, the general administrators of Federal affairs. "The Boeotarchs of course command at Delion, but they also act as administrative magistrates of the League by hindering Agesilaus from sacrificing at Aulis."

[2] Plut. "Ages." vi.; "Pelop." xxi. See Breitenb. op. cit. Praef. p. xvi.; and below, III. v. 5; VI. iv. 23.

[3] For this corrupt passage, see Hartman, "Anal. Xen." p. 332; also Otto Keller's critical edition of the "Hellenica" (Lips, MDCCCLXXX.)

in the several cities; that is to say, there were neither democracies as in the old days of the Athenians, nor yet were there decarchies as in the days of Lysander. But here was Lysander back again. Every one recognized him, and flocked to him with petitions for one favor or another, which he was to obtain for them from Agesilaus. A crowd of suitors danced attendance on his heels, and formed so conspicuous a retinue that Agesilaus, anyone would have supposed, was the private person and Lysander the king. All this was maddening to Agesilaus, as was presently plain. As to the rest of the Thirty, jealousy did not suffer them to keep silence, and they put it plainly to Agesilaus that the super-regal splendour in which Lysander lived was a violation of the constitution. So when Lysander took upon himself to introduce some of his petitioners to Agesilaus, the latter turned them a deaf ear. Their being aided and abetted by Lysander was sufficient; he sent them away discomfited. At length, as time after time things turned out contrary to his wishes, Lysander himself perceived the position of affairs. He now no longer suffered that crowd to follow him, and gave those who asked him help in anything plainly to understand that they would gain nothing, but rather be losers, by his intervention. But being bitterly annoyed at the degradation put upon him, he came to the king and said to him: "Ah, Agesilaus, how well you know the art of humbling your friends!" "Ay, indeed," the king replied; "those of them whose one idea it is to appear greater than myself; if I did not know how also to requite with honor those who work for my good, I should be ashamed." And Lysander said: "maybe there is more reason in your doings than ever guided my conduct"; adding, "Grant me for the rest one favor, so shall I cease to blush at the loss of my influence with you, and you will cease to be embarrassed by my presence. Send me off on a mission somewhere; wherever I am I will strive to be of service to you." Such was the proposal of Lysander. Agesilaus resolved to act upon it, and despatched Lysander to the Hellespont. And this is what befell.[1] Lysander, being made aware of a slight which had been put upon Spithridates the Persian by Pharnabazus, got into conversation with the injured man, and so worked upon him that he was persuaded to bring his children and his personal belongings, and with a couple of hundred troops to revolt. The next step was to deposit all the goods safely in Cyzicus, and the last to get on shipboard with Spithridates and his son, and so to present himself with his Persian friends to Agesilaus. Agesilaus, on his side, was delighted at the transaction, and set himself at once to get information about Pharnabazus, his territory and his government.

---

1 See "Ages." iii. 3; "Anab." VI. v. 7.

Meanwhile Tissaphernes had waxed bolder. A large body of troops had been sent down by the king. On the strength of that he declared war against Agesilaus, if he did not instantly withdraw his troops from Asia. The Lacedaemonians there[1] present, no less than the allies, received the news with profound vexation, persuaded as they were that Agesilaus had no force capable of competing with the king's grand armament. But a smile lit up the face of Agesilaus as he bade the ambassadors return to Tissaphernes and tell him that he was much in his debt for the perjury by which he had won the enmity of Heaven and made the very gods themselves allies of Hellas. He at once issued a general order to the troops to equip themselves for a forward movement. He warned the cities through which he must pass in an advance upon Caria, to have markets in readiness, and lastly, he despatched a message to the Ionian, Aeolian, and Hellespontine communities to send their contingents to join him at Ephesus.

Tissaphernes, putting together the facts that Agesilaus had no cavalry and that Caria was a region unadapted to that arm, and persuaded in his own mind also that the Spartan could not but cherish wrath against himself personally for his chicanery, felt convinced that he was really intending to invade Caria, and that the satrap's palace was his final goal. Accordingly he transferred the whole of his infantry to that province, and proceeded to lead his cavalry round into the plain of the Maeander. Here he conceived himself capable of trampling the Hellenes under foot with his horsemen before they could reach the craggy districts where no cavalry could operate.

But, instead of marching straight into Caria, Agesilaus turned sharp off in the opposite direction toward Phrygia. Picking up various detachments of troops which met him on his march, he steadily advanced, laying cities prostrate before him, and by the unexpectedness of his attack reaping a golden harvest of spoil. As a rule the march was prosecuted safely; but not far from Dascylium his advanced guard of cavalry were pushing on toward a knoll to take a survey of the state of things in front, when, as chance would have it, a detachment of cavalry sent forward by Pharnabazus— the corps, in fact, of Rhathines and his natural brother Bagaeus—just about equal to the Hellenes in number, also came galloping up to the very knoll in question. The two bodies found themselves face to face not one hundred and fifty yards[2] apart, and for the first moment or two stood stock still. The Hellenic horse were drawn up like an ordinary phalanx four deep, the barbarians presenting a narrow front of twelve or thereabouts,

---

1 *I.e. at Ephesus.*
2 *Lit. "four plethra."*

and a very disproportionate depth. There was a moment's pause, and then the barbarians, taking the initiative, charged. There was a hand-to-hand tussle, in which any Hellene who succeeded in striking his man shivered his lance with the blow, while the Persian troopers, armed with cornel-wood javelins, speedily despatched a dozen men and a couple of horses.[1] At this point the Hellenic cavalry turned and fled. But as Agesilaus came up to the rescue with his heavy infantry, the Asiatics were forced in their turn to withdraw, with the loss of one man slain. This cavalry engagement gave them pause. Agesilaus on the day following it offered sacrifice. "Was he to continue his advance?" But the victims proved hopeless.[2] There was nothing for it after this manifestation but to turn and march toward the sea. It was clear enough to his mind that without a proper cavalry force it would be impossible to conduct a campaign in the flat country. Cavalry, therefore, he must get, or be driven to mere guerilla warfare. With this view he drew up a list of all the wealthiest inhabitants belonging to the several cities of those parts. Their duty would be to support a body of cavalry, with the proviso, however, that anyone contributing a horse, arms, and rider, up to the standard, would be exempted from personal service. The effect was instantaneous. The zeal with which the recipients of these orders responded could hardly have been greater if they had been seeking substitutes to die for them.

395 BC. After this, at the first indication of spring, he collected the whole of his army at Ephesus. But the army needed training. With that object he proposed a series of prizes—prizes to the heavy infantry regiments, to be won by those who presented their men in the best condition; prizes for the cavalry regiments which could ride best; prizes for those divisions of peltasts and archers which proved most efficient in their respective duties. And now the gymnasiums were a sight to see, thronged as they were, one and all, with warriors stripping for exercise; or again, the hippodrome crowded with horses and riders performing their evolutions; or the javelin men and archers going through their peculiar drill. In fact, the whole city where he lay presented under his hands a spectacle not to be forgotten. The marketplace literally teemed with horses, arms, and accoutrements of all sorts for sale. The bronze-worker, the carpenter, the smith, the leather-cutter, the painter and embosser, were all busily engaged in fabricating the implements of war; so that the city of Ephesus itself was fairly converted

---

1 See Xenophon's treatise "On Horsemanship," xii. 12.
2 Lit. "lobeless," i.e. with a lobe of the liver wanting—a bad sign.

into a military workshop.¹ It would have done a man's heart good to see those long lines of soldiers with Agesilaus at their head, as they stepped gaily be-garlanded from the gymnasiums to dedicate their wreaths to the goddess Artemis. Nor can I well conceive of elements more fraught with hope than were here combined. Here were reverence and piety toward Heaven; here practice in war and military training; here discipline with habitual obedience to authority. But contempt for one's enemy will infuse a kind of strength in battle. So the Spartan leader argued; and with a view to its production he ordered the quartermasters to put up the prisoners who had been captured by his foraging bands for auction, stripped naked; so that his Hellenic soldiery, as they looked at the white skins which had never been bared to sun and wind, the soft limbs unused to toil through constant riding in carriages, came to the conclusion that war with such adversaries would differ little from a fight with women.

By this date a full year had elapsed since the embarkation of Agesilaus, and the time had come for the Thirty with Lysander to sail back home, and for their successors, with Herippidas, to arrive. Among these Agesilaus appointed Xenocles and another to the command of the cavalry, Scythes to that of the heavy infantry of the enfranchised,² Herippidas to that of the Cyreians, and Migdon to that of the contingents from the states. Agesilaus gave them to understand that he intended to lead them forthwith by the most expeditious route against the stronghold of the country,³ so that without further ceremony they might prepare their minds and bodies for the tug of battle. Tissaphernes, however, was firmly persuaded that this was only talk intended to deceive him; Agesilaus would this time certainly invade Caria. Accordingly he repeated his former tactics, transporting his infantry bodily into Caria and posting his cavalry in the valley of the Maeander. But Agesilaus was as good as his word, and at once invaded the district of Sardis. A three days' march through a region denuded of the enemy threw large supplies into his hands. On the fourth day the cavalry of the enemy approached. Their general ordered the officer in charge of his baggage-train to cross the Pactolus and encamp, while his troopers, catching sight of stragglers from the Hellenic force scattered in pursuit of booty, put several of them to the sword. Perceiving which, Agesilaus ordered his cavalry to the rescue; and the Persians on their side, seeing their advance, collected together in battle order to receive them, with dense squadrons of horse,

---

1 See Plut. "Marc." (Clough, ii. 262); Polyb. "Hist." x. 20.
2 The neodamodes.
3 I.e. Lydia. See Plut. "Ages." x. (Clough, iv. 11).

troop upon troop. The Spartan, reflecting that the enemy had as yet no infantry to support him, whilst he had all branches of the service to depend upon, concluded that the critical moment had arrived at which to risk an engagement. In this mood he sacrificed, and began advancing his main line of battle against the serried lines of cavalry in front of him, at the same time ordering the flower of his heavy infantry—the ten-years-service men[1]—to close with them at a run, and the peltasts to bring up their supports at the double. The order passed to his cavalry was to charge in confidence that he and the whole body of his troops were close behind them. The cavalry charge was received by the Persians without flinching, but presently finding themselves environed by the full tide of war they swerved. Some found a speedy grave within the river, but the mass of them gradually made good their escape. The Hellenes followed close on the heels of the flying foe and captured his camp. here the peltasts not unnaturally fell to pillaging; whereupon Agesilaus planted his troops so as to form a cordon enclosing the property of friends and foes alike. The spoil taken was considerable; it fetched more than seventy talents,[2] not to mention the famous camels, subsequently brought over by Agesilaus into Hellas, which were captured here. At the moment of the battle Tissaphernes lay in Sardis. Hence the Persians argued that they had been betrayed by the satrap. And the king of Persia, coming to a like conclusion himself that Tissaphernes was to blame for the evil turn of his affairs, sent down Tithraustes and beheaded him.[3]

This done, Tithraustes sent an embassy to Agesilaus with a message as follows: "The author of all our trouble, yours and ours, Agesilaus, has paid the penalty of his misdoings; the king therefore asks of you first that you should sail back home in peace; secondly, that the cities in Asia secured in their autonomy should continue to render him the ancient tribute." To this proposition Agesilaus made answer that "without the authorities at home he could do nothing in the matter." "Then do you, at least," replied Tithraustes, "while awaiting advice from Lacedaemon, withdraw into the territory of Pharnabazus. Have I not avenged you of your enemy?" "While, then, I am on my way thither," rejoined Agesilaus, "will you support my army with provisions?" On this wise Tithraustes handed him thirty talents,[4] which the other took, and forthwith began his march into Phrygia (the Phrygia of Pharnabazus). He lay in the plain district above

---

1 See note to "Hell." II. iv. 32.
2 = 17,062 pounds: 10 shillings.
3 See Diod. xiv. 80.
4 = 7,312 pounds: 10 shillings.

Cyme,[1] when a message reached him from the home authorities, giving him absolute disposal of the naval forces,[2] with the right to appoint the admiral of his choice. This course the Lacedaemonians were led to adopt by the following considerations: If, they argued, the same man were in command of both services, the land force would be greatly strengthened through the concentration of the double force at any point necessary; and the navy likewise would be far more useful through the immediate presence and cooperation of the land force where needed. Apprised of these measures, Agesilaus in the first instance sent an order to the cities on the islands and the seaboard to fit out as many ships of war as they severally might deem desirable. The result was a new navy, consisting of the vessels thus voluntarily furnished by the states, with others presented by private persons out of courtesy to their commander, and amounting in all to a fleet of one hundred and twenty sail. The admiral whom he selected was Peisander, his wife's brother, a man of genuine ambition and of a vigorous spirit, but not sufficiently expert in the details of equipment to achieve a great naval success. Thus while Peisander set off to attend to naval matters, Agesilaus continued his march whither he was bound to Phrygia.

V

But now Tithraustes seemed to have discovered in Agesilaus a disposition to despise the fortunes of the Persian monarch—he evidently had no intention to withdraw from Asia; on the contrary, he was cherishing hopes vast enough to include the capture of the king himself. Being at his wits' end how to manage matters, he resolved to send Timocrates the Rhodian to Hellas with a gift of gold worthy fifty silver talents,[3] and enjoined upon him to endeavor to exchange solemn pledges with the leading men in the several states, binding them to undertake a war against Lacedaemon. Timocrates arrived and began to dole out his presents. In Thebes he gave gifts to Androcleidas, Ismenias, and Galaxidorus; in Corinth to Timolaus and Polyanthes; in Argos to Cylon and his party. The Athenians,[4] though they took no share of the gold, were none the less eager for the war, being of opinion that empire was theirs by right.[5] The recipients of the moneys forthwith began covertly to attack the Lacedaemonians in their respective

---

1 See "Cyrop." VII. i. 45.
2 See Grote, "H. G." ix. 327, note 3; Arist. "Pol." ii. 9, 33.
3 = 12,187 pounds: 10 shillings.
4 See Paus. III. ix. 8; Plut. "Ages." xv.
5 Reading {nomizontes auton to arkhein} with Sauppe; or if, as Breitinbach suggests, {enomizon de oukh outon to arkhesthai}, translate "but thought it was not for them to take the initiative."

states, and, when they had brought these to a sufficient pitch of hatred, bound together the most important of them in a confederacy.

But it was clear to the leaders in Thebes that, unless someone struck the first blow, the Lacedaemonians would never be brought to break the truce with their allies. They therefore persuaded the Opuntian Locrians[1] to levy moneys on a debatable district,[2] jointly claimed by the Phocians and themselves, when the Phocians would be sure to retaliate by an attack on Locris. These expectations were fulfillled. The Phocians immediately invaded Locris and seized moneys on their side with ample interest. Then Androcleidas and his friends lost no time in persuading the Thebans to assist the Locrians, on the ground that it was no debatable district which had been entered by the Phocians, but the admittedly friendly and allied territory of Locris itself. The counter-invasion of Phocis and pillage of their country by the Thebans promptly induced the Phocians to send an embassy to Lacedaemon. In claiming assistance they explained that the war was not of their own seeking, but that they had attacked the Locrians in self-defense. On their side the Lacedaemonians were glad enough to seize a pretext for marching upon the Thebans, against whom they cherished a long-standing bitterness. They had not forgotten the claim which the Thebans had set up to a tithe for Apollo in Deceleia,[3] nor yet their refusal to support Lacedaemon in the attack on Piraeus;[4] and they accused them further of having persuaded the Corinthians not to join that expedition. Nor did they fail to call to mind some later proceedings of the Thebans— their refusal to allow Agesilaus to sacrifice in Aulis;[5] their snatching the victims already offered and hurling them from the altars; their refusal to join the same general in a campaign directed even against Asia.[6] The Lacedaemonians further reasoned that now, if ever, was the favorable moment to conduct an expedition against the Thebans, and once for all to put a stop to their insolent behavior toward them. Affairs in Asia were prospering under the strong arm of Agesilaus, and in Hellas they had no other war on hand to trammel their movements. Such, therefore, being the general view of the situation adopted at Lacedaemon, the ephors proceeded to call out the ban. Meanwhile they despatched Lysander to Phocis with orders to put himself at the head of the Phocians along with the Oetaeans,

---

1 For an alliance between Athens and the Locrians, 395 BC, see Hicks, 67; and below, IV. ii. 17.
2 Lit. "the." See Paus. III. ix. 9.
3 See Grote, "H. G." ix. 309, 403; viii. 355.
4 "Hell." II. iv. 30, 403 BC.
5 See above, III. iv. 3; and below, VII. i. 34.
6 See Paus. III. ix. 1-3.

Heracleotes, Melians, and Aenianians, and to march upon Haliartus; before the walls of which place Pausanias, the destined leader of the expedition, undertook to present himself at the head of the Lacedaemonians and other Peloponnesian forces by a specified date. Lysander not only carried out his instructions to the letter, but going a little beyond them, succeeded in detaching Orchomenus from Thebes.[1] Pausanias, on the other hand, after finding the sacrifice for crossing the frontier favorable, sat down at Tegea and set about despatching to and fro the commandants of allied troops whilst contentedly awaiting the soldiers from the provincial[2] districts of Laconia.

And now that it was fully plain to the Thebans that the Lacedaemonians would invade their territory, they sent ambassadors to Athens, who spoke as follows:—

"Men of Athens, it is a mistake on your part to blame us for certain harsh resolutions concerning Athens at the conclusion of the war.[3] That vote was not authorized by the state of Thebes. It was the utterance merely of one man,[4] who was at that time seated in the congress of the allies. A more important fact is that when the Lacedaemonians summoned us to attack Piraeus[5] the collective state of Thebes passed a resolution refusing to join in the campaign. As then you are to a large extent the cause of the resentment which the Lacedaemonians feel toward us, we consider it only fair that you in your turn should render us assistance. Still more do we demand of you, sirs, who were of the city party at that date, to enter heart and soul into war with the Lacedaemonians. For what were their services to you? They first deliberately converted you into an oligarchy and placed you in hostility to the democracy, and then they came with a great force under guise of being your allies, and delivered you over to the majority, so that, for any service they rendered you, you were all dead men; and you owe your lives to our friends here, the people of Athens.[6]

"But to pass on—we all know, men of Athens, that you would like to recover the empire which you formerly possessed; and how can you

---

1 See Freeman, op. cit. p. 167, "Ill feeling between Thebes and other towns."—"Against Thebes, backed by Sparta, resistance was hopeless. It was not till long after that, at last (in 395 BC), on a favorable opportunity during the Corinthian war, Orchomenos openly seceded." And for the prior "state of disaffection toward Thebes on the part of the smaller cities," see "Mem." III. v. 2, in reference to 407 BC.
2 Lit. "perioecid."
3 See "Hell." II. ii. 19; and below, VI. v. 35.
4 Plut. "Lys." xv. "Erianthus the Theban gave his vote to pull down the city, and turn the country into sheep-pasture."—Clough, iii. 121.
5 See "Hell." II. iv. 30.
6 See "Hell." II. iv. 38, 40, 41.

compass your object better than by coming to the aid yourselves of the victims of Lacedaemonian injustice? Is it their wide empire of which you are afraid? Let not that make cowards of you—much rather let it embolden you as you lay to heart and ponder your own case. When your empire was widest then the crop of your enemies was thickest. Only so long as they found no opportunity to revolt did they keep their hatred of you dark; but no sooner had they found a champion in Lacedaemon than they at once showed what they really felt toward you. So too today. Let us show plainly that we mean to stand shoulder to shoulder[1] embattled against the Lacedaemonians; and haters enough of them—whole armies—never fear, will be forthcoming. To prove the truth of this assertion you need only to count upon your fingers. How many friends have they left to them today? The Argives have been, are, and ever will be, hostile to them. Of course. But the Eleians? Why, the Eleians have quite lately[2] been robbed of so much territory and so many cities that their friendship is converted into hatred. And what shall we say of the Corinthians? the Arcadians? the Achaeans? In the war which Sparta waged against you, there was no toil, no danger, no expense, which those peoples did not share, in obedience to the dulcet coaxings[3] and persuasions of that power. The Lacedaemonians gained what they wanted, and then not one fractional portion of empire, honor, or wealth did these faithful followers come in for. That is not all. They have no scruple in appointing their helots[4] as governors, and on the free necks of their alies, in the day of their good fortune, they have planted the tyrant's heel.

"Then again take the case of those whom they have detached from yourselves. In the most patent way they have cajoled and cheated them; in place of freedom they have presented them with a twofold slavery. The allies are tyrannised over by the governor and tyrannised over by the ten commissioners set up by Lysander over every city.[5] And to come lastly to the great king. In spite of all the enormous contributions with which he aided them to gain a mastery over you, is the lord of Asia one whit better

---

1 Lit. "shield to shield."
2 Lit. "today," "nowadays."
3 {mala liparoumenoi}. See Thuc. i. 66 foll.; vi. 88.
4 See "Pol. Lac." xiv.
5 Grote ("H. G." ix. 323), referring to this passage, and to "Hell." VI. iii. 8–11, notes the change in Spartan habits between 405 and 394 BC (i.e. between the victory of Aegospotami and the defeat of Cnidos), when Sparta possessed a large public revenue derived from the tribute of the dependent cities. For her earlier condition, 432 BC, cf. Thuc. i. 80. For her subsequent condition, 334 BC, cf. Arist. "Pol." ii. 6, 23.

off today than if he had taken exactly the opposite course and joined you in reducing them?

"Is it not clear that you have only to step forward once again as the champions of this crowd of sufferers from injustice, and you will attain to a pinnacle of power quite unprecedented? In the days of your old empire you were leaders of the maritime powers merely—that is clear; but your new empire today will be universal. You will have at your backs not only your former subjects, but ourselves, and the Peloponnesians, and the king himself, with all that mighty power which is his. We do not deny that we were serviceable allies enough to Lacedaemon, as you will bear us witness; but this we say:—If we helped the Lacedaemonians vigorously in the past, everything tends to show that we shall help you still more vigorously today; for our swords will be unsheathed, not in behalf of islanders, or Syracusans, or men of alien stock, as happened in the late war, but of ourselves, suffering under a sense of wrong. And there is another important fact which you ought to realise: this selfish system of organized greed which is Sparta's will fall more readily to pieces than your own late empire. Yours was the proud assertion of naval empire over subjects powerless by sea. Theirs is the selfish sway of a minority asserting dominion over states equally well armed with themselves, and many times more numerous. Here our remarks end. Do not forget, however, men of Athens, that as far as we can understand the matter, the field to which we invite you is destined to prove far richer in blessings to your own state of Athens than to ours, Thebes."

With these words the speaker ended. Among the Athenians, speaker after speaker spoke in favor of the proposition,[1] and finally a unanimous resolution was passed voting assistance to the Thebans. Thrasybulus, in an answer communicating the resolution, pointed out with pride that in spite of the unfortified condition of Piraeus, Athens would not shrink from repaying her former debt of gratitude to Thebes with interest. "You," he added, "refused to join in a campaign against us; we are prepared to fight your battles with you against the enemy, if he attacks you." Thus the Thebans returned home and made preparations to defend themselves, whilst the Athenians made ready to assist them.

And now the Lacedaemonians no longer hesitated. Pausanias the king advanced into Boeotia with the home army and the whole of the

---

1 For the alliance between Boeotia and Athens, 395 BC, see Kohler, "C. I. A." ii. 6; Hicks, op. cit. 65; Lys. "pro Man." S. 13; Jebb, "Att. Or." i. p. 247; and the two speeches of the same orator Lysias against Alcibiades (son of the famous Alcibiades), on a Charge of Desertion ("Or." xiv.), and on a Charge of Failure to Serve ("Or." xv.)—Jebb, op. cit. i. p. 256 foll.

Peloponnesian contingents, saving only the Corinthians, who declined to serve. Lysander, at the head of the army supplied by Phocis and Orchomenus and the other strong places in those parts, had already reached Haliartus, in front of Pausanias. Being arrived, he refused to sit down quietly and await the arrival of the army from Lacedaemon, but at once marched with what troops he had against the walls of Haliartus; and in the first instance he tried to persuade the citizens to detach themselves from Thebes and to assume autonomy, but the intention was cut short by certain Thebans within the fortress. Whereupon Lysander attacked the place. The Thebans were made aware,[1] and hurried to the rescue with heavy infantry and cavalry. Then, whether it was that the army of relief fell upon Lysander unawares, or that with clear knowledge of his approach he preferred to await the enemy, with intent to crush him, is uncertain. This only is clear: a battle was fought beside the walls, and a trophy still exists to mark the victory of the townsfolk before the gates of Haliartus. Lysander was slain, and the rest fled to the mountains, the Thebans hotly pursuing. But when the pursuit had led them to some considerable height, and they were fairly environed and hemmed in by difficult ground and narrow space, then the heavy infantry turned to bay, and greeted them with a shower of darts and missiles. First two or three men dropped who had been foremost of the pursuers, and then upon the rest they poured volleys of stones down the precipitous incline, and pressed on their late pursuers with much zeal, until the Thebans turned tail and quitted the deadly slope, leaving behind them more than a couple of hundred corpses.

On this day, thereafter, the hearts of the Thebans failed them as they counted their losses and found them equal to their gains; but the next day they discovered that during the night the Phocians and the rest of them had made off to their several homes, whereupon they fell to pluming themselves highly on their achievement. But presently Pausanias appeared at the head of the Lacedaemonian army, and once more their dangers seemed to thicken round them. Deep, we are told, was the silence and abasement which reigned in their host. It was not until the third day, when the Athenians arrived[2] and were duely drawn up beside them, whilst Pausanias neither attacked nor offered battle, that at length the confidence of the Thebans took a larger range. Pausanias, on his side, having summoned his generals and commanders of fifties,[3] deliberated whether to give battle or to content

---

1 See Plut. "Lys." xxviii. (Clough, iii. 137).
2 See Dem. "On the Crown," 258.
3 Lit. "polemarchs and penteconters"—"colonels and lieutenants." See "Pol. Lac." xi.

himself with picking up the bodies of Lysander and those who fell with him, under cover of a truce.

The considerations which weighed upon the minds of Pausanias and the other high officers of the Lacedaemonians seem to have been that Lysander was dead and his defeated army in retreat; while, as far as they themselves were concerned, the Corinthian contingent was absolutely wanting, and the zeal of the troops there present at the lowest ebb. They further reasoned that the enemy's cavalry was numerous and theirs the reverse; whilst, weightiest of all, there lay the dead right under the walls, so that if they had been ever so much stronger it would have been no easy task to pick up the bodies within range of the towers of Haliartus. On all these grounds they determined to ask for a flag of truce, in order to pick up the bodies of the slain. These, however, the Thebans were not disposed to give back unless they agreed to retire from their territory. The terms were gladly accepted by the Lacedaemonians, who at once picked up the corpses of the slain, and prepared to quit the territory of Boeotia. The preliminaries were transacted, and the retreat commenced. Despondent indeed was the demeanor of the Lacedaemonians, in contrast with the insolent bearing of the Thebans, who visited the slightest attempt to trespass on their private estates with blows and chased the offenders back on to the high roads unflinchingly. Such was the conclusion of the campaign of the Lacedaemonians.

As for Pausanias, on his arrival at home he was tried on the capital charge. The heads of indictment set forth that he had failed to reach Haliartus as soon as Lysander, in spite of his undertaking to be there on the same day: that, instead of using any endeavor to pick up the bodies of the slain by force of arms, he had asked for a flag of truce: that at an earlier date, when he had got the popular government of Athens fairly in his grip at Piraeus, he had suffered it to slip through his fingers and escape. Besides this,[1] he failed to present himself at the trial, and a sentence of death was passed upon him. He escaped to Tegea and there died of an illness whilst still in exile. Thus closes the chapter of events enacted on the soil of Hellas. To return to Asia and Agesilaus.

BOOK IV

I

395 BC. With the fall of the year Agesilaus reached Phrygia—the Phrygia

---

1 Or, add, "as a further gravamen."

of Pharnabazus—and proceeded to burn and harry the district. City after city was taken, some by force and some by voluntary surrender. To a proposal of Spithridates to lead him into Paphlagonia,[1] where he would introduce the king of the country to him in conference and obtain his alliance, he readily acceded. It was a long-cherished ambition of Agesilaus to alienate some one of the subject nations from the Persian monarch, and he pushed forward eagerly.

On his arrival in Paphlagonia, King Otys[2] came, and an alliance was made. (The fact was, he had been summoned by the king to Susa and had not gone up.) More than that, through the persuasion of Spithridates he left behind as a parting gift to Agesilaus one thousand cavalry and a couple of thousand peltasts. Agesilaus was anxious in some way to show his gratitude to Spithridates for such help, and spoke as follows:—"Tell me," he said to Spithridates, "would you not like to give your daughter to King Otys?" "Much more would I like to give her," he answered, "than he to take her—I an outcast wanderer, and he lord of a vast territory and forces." Nothing more was said at the time about the marriage; but when Otys was on the point of departure and came to bid farewell, Agesilaus, having taken care that Spithridates should be out of the way, in the presence of the Thirty broached the subject:[3] "Can you tell me, Otys, to what sort of family Spithridates belongs?" "To one of the noblest in Persia," replied the king. Agesilaus: "Have you observed how beautiful his son is?" Otys: "To be sure; last evening I was supping with him." Agesilaus: "And they tell me his daughter is yet more beautiful." Otys: "That may well be; beautiful she is." Agesilaus: "For my part, as you have proved so good a friend to us, I should like to advise you to take this girl to wife. Not only is she very beautiful—and what more should a husband ask for?—but her father is of noble family, and has a force at his back large enough to retaliate on Pharnabazus for an injury. He has made the satrap, as you see, a fugitive and a vagabond in his own vast territory. I need not tell you," he added, "that a man who can so chastise an enemy is well able to benefit a friend; and of this be assured: by such an alliance you will gain not the connection of Spithridates alone, but of myself and the Lacedaemonians, and, as we are the leaders of Hellas, of the rest of Hellas also. And what a wedding yours will be! Were ever nuptials celebrated on so grand a scale before? Was ever bride led home by such an escort of cavalry and light-armed troops and

---

1 See Hartman ("An. Xen." p. 339), who suggests {Otun auto} for {sun auto}.
2 See "Ages." iii. 4, where he is called Cotys.
3 I.e. "Spartan counsellors."

heavy infantry, as shall escort your wife home to your palace?" Otys asked: "Is Spithridates of one mind with you in this proposal?" and Agesilaus answered: "In good sooth he did not bid me make it for him. And for my own part in the matter, though it is, I admit, a rare pleasure to requite an enemy, yet I had far rather at any time discover some good fortune for my friends." Otys: "Why not ask if your project pleases Spithridates too?" Then Agesilaus, turning to Herippidas and the rest of the Thirty, bade them go to Spithridates; "and give him such good instruction," he added, "that he shall wish what we wish." The Thirty rose and retired to administer their lesson. But they seemed to tarry a long time, and Agesilaus asked: "What say you, King Otys—shall we summon him hither ourselves? You, I feel certain, are better able to persuade him than the whole Thirty put together." Thereupon Agesilaus summoned Spithridates and the others. As they came forward, Herippidas promptly delivered himself thus: "I spare you the details, Agesilaus. To make a long story short, Spithridates says, 'He will be glad to do whatever pleases you.'" Then Agesilaus, turning first to one and then to the other: "What pleases me," said he, "is that you should wed a daughter—and you a wife—so happily.[1] But," he added, "I do not see how we can well bring home the bride by land till spring." "No, not by land," the suitor answered, "but you might, if you chose, conduct her home at once by sea." Thereupon they exchanged pledges to ratify the compact; and so sent Otys rejoicing on his way.

Agesilaus, who had not failed to note the king's impatience, at once fitted out a ship of war and gave orders to Callias, a Lacedaemonian, to escort the maiden to her new home; after which he himself began his march on Dascylium. Here was the palace of Pharnabazus. It lay in the midst of abundant supplies. Here, too, were most fair hunting grounds, offering the hunter choice between enclosed parks[2] and a wide expanse of field and fell; and all around there flowed a river full of fish of every sort; and for the sportsman versed in fowling, winged game in abundance.

In these quarters the Spartan king passed the winter, collecting supplies for the army either on the spot or by a system of forage. On one of these occasions the troops, who had grown reckless and scornful of the enemy through long immunity from attack, whilst engaged in collecting supplies were scattered over the flat country, when Pharnabazus fell upon them with two scythe-chariots and about four hundred horse. Seeing him thus advancing, the Hellenes ran together, mustering possibly seven hundred

---

1 Or, "*and may the wedding be blessed!*"
2 Lit. "*paradises.*" See "*Anab.*" I. ii. 7; "*Cyrop.*" I. iv. 11.

men. The Persian did not hesitate, but placing his chariots in front, supported by himself and the cavalry, he gave the command to charge. The scythe-chariots charged and scattered the compact mass, and speedily the cavalry had laid low in the dust about a hundred men, while the rest retreated hastily, under cover of Agesilaus and his hoplites, who were fortunately near.

It was the third or fourth day after this that Spithridates made a discovery: Pharnabazus lay encamped in Caue, a large village not more than eighteen miles[1] away. This news he lost no time in reporting to Herippidas. The latter, who was longing for some brilliant exploit, begged Agesilaus to furnish him with two thousand hoplites, an equal number of peltasts, and some cavalry—the latter to consist of the horsemen of Spithridates, the Paphlagonians, and as many Hellene troopers as he might perchance persuade to follow him. Having got the promise of them from Agesilaus, he proceeded to take the auspices. Toward late afternoon he obtained favorable omens and broke off the sacrifice. Thereupon he ordered the troops to get their evening meal, after which they were to present themselves in front of the camp. But by the time darkness had closed in, not one half of them had come out. To abandon the project was to call down the ridicule of the rest of the Thirty. So he set out with the force to hand, and about daylight, falling on the camp of Pharnabazus, put many of his advanced guard of Mysians to the sword. The men themselves made good their escape in different directions, but the camp was taken, and with it diverse goblets and other gear such as a man like Pharnabazus would have, not to speak of much baggage and many baggage animals. It was the dread of being surrounded and besieged, if he should establish himself for long at any one spot, which induced Pharnabazus to flee in gipsy fashion from point to point over the country, carefully obliterating his encampments. Now as the Paphlagonians and Spithridates brought back the captured property, they were met by Herippidas with his brigadiers and captains, who stopped them and[2] relieved them of all they had; the object being to have as large a list as possible of captures to deliver over to the officers who superintended the sale of booty.[3] This treatment the Asiatics found intolerable. They deemed themselves at once injured and insulted, got their kit together in the night, and made off in the direction of Sardis to join Ariaeus without mistrust, seeing that he too had revolted and gone to war with the king. On

---

1 Lit. "one hundred and sixty stades."
2 Or, "captains posted to intercept them, who relieved..." See "Anab." IV. i. 14.
3 See "Pol. Lac." xiii. 11, for these officers.

Agesilaus himself no heavier blow fell during the whole campaign than the desertion of Spithridates and Megabates and the Paphlagonians.

Now there was a certain man of Cyzicus, Apollophanes by name; he was an old friend of Pharnabazus, and at this time had become a friend also of Agesilaus.[1] This man informed Agesilaus that he thought he could bring about a meeting between him and Pharnabazus, which might tend to friendship; and having so got ear of him, he obtained pledges of good faith between his two friends, and presented himself with Pharnabazus at the trysting-place, where Agesilaus with the Thirty around him awaited their coming, reclined upon a grassy sward. Pharnabazus presently arrived clad in costliest apparel; but just as his attendants were about to spread at his feet the carpets on which the Persians delicately seat themselves, he was touched with a sense of shame at his own luxury in sight of the simplicity of Agesilaus, and he also without further ceremony seated himself on the bare ground. And first the two bade one another hail, and then Pharnabazus stretched out his right hand and Agesilaus his to meet him, and the conversation began. Pharnabazus, as the elder of the two, spoke first. "Agesilaus," he said, "and all you Lacedaemonians here present, while you were at war with the Athenians I was your friend and ally; it was I who furnished the wealth that made your navy strong on sea; on land I fought on horseback by your side, and pursued your enemies into the sea.[2] As to duplicity like that of Tissaphernes, I challenge you to accuse me of having played you false by word or deed. Such have I ever been; and in return how am I treated by yourselves today?—in such sort that I cannot even sup in my own country unless, like the wild animals, I pick up the scraps you chance to leave. The beautiful palaces which my father left me as an heirloom, the parks[3] full of trees and beasts of the chase in which my heart rejoiced, lie before my eyes hacked to pieces, burnt to ashes. Maybe I do not comprehend the first principles of justice and holiness; do you then explain to me how all this resembles the conduct of men who know how to repay a simple debt of gratitude." He ceased, and the Thirty were ashamed before him and kept silence.[4]

At length, after some pause, Agesilaus spoke. "I think you are aware,"

---

1 "Ages." v. 4; Plut. "Ages." xi. (Clough, iv. p. 14).
2 See "Hell." I. i. 6.
3 Lit. "paradises."
4 Theopompus of Chios, the historian (b. 378 BC, fl. 333 BC), "in the eleventh book (of his {Suntazis Ellenikon}) borrowed Xenophon's lively account of the interview between Agesilaus and Pharnabazus (Apollonius apud Euseb. B, "Praep. Evang." p. 465)." See "Hist. Lit. of Anc. Gr.," Muller and Donaldson, ii. p. 380.

he said, "Pharnabazus, that within the states of Hellas the folk of one community contract relations of friendship and hospitality with one another;[1] but if these states should go to war, then each man will side with his fatherland, and friend will find himself pitted against friend in the field of battle, and, if it so betide, the one may even deal the other his death-blow. So too we today, being at war with your sovereign lord the king, must needs regard as our enemy all that he calls his; not but that with yourself personally we should esteem it our high fortune to be friends. If indeed it were merely an exchange of service—were you asked to give up your lord the king and to take us as your masters in his stead, I could not so advise you; but the fact is, by joining with us it is in your power today to bow your head to no man, to call no man master, to reap the produce of your own domain in freedom—freedom, which to my mind is more precious than all riches. Not that we bid you to become a beggar for the sake of freedom, but rather to use our friendship to increase not the king's authority, but your own, by subduing those who are your fellow slaves today, and who tomorrow shall be your willing subjects. Well, then, freedom given and wealth added—what more would you desire to fill the cup of happiness to overflowing?" Pharnabazus replied: "Shall I tell you plainly what I will do?" "That were but kind and courteous on your part," he answered. "Thus it stands with me, then," said Pharnabazus. "If the king should send another general, and if he should wish to rank me under this new man's orders, I, for my part, am willing to accept your friendship and alliance; but if he offers me the supreme command—why, then, I plainly tell you, there is a certain something in the very name ambition which whispers me that I shall war against you to the best of my ability."[2] When he heard that, Agesilaus seized the satrap's hand, exclaiming: "Ah, best of mortals, may the day arrive which sends us such a friend! Of one thing rest assured. This instant I leave your territory with what haste I may, and for the future—even in case of war—as long as we can find foes elsewhere our hands shall hold aloof from you and yours."

And with these words he broke up the meeting. Pharnabazus mounted his horse and rode away, but his son by Parapita, who was still in the bloom of youth, lingered behind; then, running up to Agesilaus, he exclaimed: "See, I choose you as my friend." "And I accept you," replied the king. "Remember, then," the lad answered, and with the word presented the

---

1 Or, add, "we call them guest friends."
2 Or, "so subtle a force, it seems, is the love of honor that." Grote, "H. G." ix. 386; cf. Herod. iii. 57 for "ambition," {philotimia}.

beautiful javelin in his hand to Agesilaus, who received it, and unclasping a splendid trapping[1] which his secretary, Idaeus, had round the neck of his charger, he gave it in return to the youth; whereupon the boy leapt on his horse's back and galloped after his father.[2] At a later date, during the absence of Pharnabazus abroad, this same youth, the son of Parapita, was deprived of the government by his brother and driven into exile. Then Agesilaus took great interest in him, and as he had a strong attachment to the son of Eualces, an Athenian, Agesilaus did all he could to have this friend of his, who was the tallest of the boys, admitted to the two hundred yards race at Olympia.

394 BC. But to return to the actual moment. Agesilaus was as good as his word, and at once marched out of the territory of Pharnabazus. The season verged on spring. Reaching the plain of Thebe,[3] he encamped in the neighborhood of the temple of Artemis of Astyra,[4] and there employed himself in collecting troops from every side, in addition to those which he already had, so as to form a complete armament. These preparations were pressed forward with a view to penetrating as far as possible into the interior. He was persuaded that every tribe or nation placed in his rear might be considered as alienated from the king.

II

Such were the concerns and projects of Agesilaus. Meanwhile the Lacedaemonians at home were quite alive to the fact that moneys had been sent into Hellas, and that the bigger states were leagued together to declare war against them. It was hard to avoid the conclusion that Sparta herself was in actual danger, and that a campaign was inevitable. While busy, therefore, with preparations themselves, they lost no time in despatching Epicydidas to fetch Agesilaus. That officer, on his arrival, explained the position of affairs, and concluded by delivering a peremptory summons of the state recalling him to the assistance of the fatherland without delay. The announcement could not but come as a grievous blow to Agesilaus, as he reflected on the vanished hopes, and the honors plucked from his

---

1 {phalara}, *bosses of gold, silver, or other metals, cast or chased, with some appropriate device in relief, which were worn as an ornamental trapping for horses, affixed to the head-stall or to a throat-collar, or to a martingale over the chest.—Rich's "Companion to Lat. Dict. and Greek Lex.," s.v.*
2 *See Grote, ix. 387; Plut. "Ages." xiv. (Clough, iv. 15); "Ages." iii. 5. The incident is idealised in the "Cyrop." I. iv. 26 foll. See "Lyra Heroica": CXXV. A Ballad of East and West—the incident of the "turquoise-studded rein."*
3 *"Anab." VII. viii. 7.*
4 *Vide Strab. xiii. 606, 613. Seventy stades from Thebe.*

grasp. Still, he summoned the allies and announced to them the contents of the despatch from home. "To aid our fatherland," he added, "is an imperative duty. If, however, matters turn out well on the other side, rely upon it, friends and allies, I will not forget you, but I shall be back anon to carry out your wishes." When they heard the announcement many wept, and they passed a resolution, one and all, to assist Agesilaus in assisting Lacedaemon; if matters turned out well there, they undertook to take him as their leader and come back again to Asia; and so they fell to making preparations to follow him.

Agesilaus, on his side, determined to leave behind him in Asia Euxenus as governor, and with him a garrison numbering no less than four thousand troops, which would enable him to protect the states in Asia. But for himself, as on the one hand he could see that the majority of the soldiers would far rather stay behind than undertake service against fellow Hellenes, and on the other hand he wished to take as fine and large an army with him as he could, he offered prizes first to that state or city which should continue the best corps of troops, and secondly to that captain of mercenaries who should join the expedition with the best equipped battalion of heavy infantry, archers, and light infantry. On the same principle he informed the chief cavalry officers that the general who succeeded in presenting the best accoutred and best mounted regiment would receive from himself some victorious distinction. "The final adjudication," he said, "would not be made until they had crossed from Asia into Europe and had reached the Chersonese; and this with a view to impress upon them that the prizes were not for show but for real campaigners."[1] These consisted for the most part of infantry or cavalry arms and accoutrements tastefully furnished, besides which there were chaplets of gold. The whole, useful and ornamental alike, must have cost nearly a thousand pounds,[2] but as the result of this outlay, no doubt, arms of great value were procured for the expedition.[3] When the Hellespont was crossed the judges were appointed. The Lacedaemonians were represented by Menascus, Herippidas, and Orsippus, and the allies by one member from each state. As soon as the adjudication was complete, the army commenced its march with Agesilaus at its head, following the very route taken by the great king when he invaded Hellas.

Meanwhile the ephors had called out the ban, and as Agesipolis was

---

1 Or, "that the perfection of equipment was regarded as anticipative of actual service in the field." Cobet suggests for {eukrinein} {dieukrinein}; cf. "Oecon." viii. 6.
2 Lit. "at least four talents" = 975 pounds.
3 Or, "beyond which, the arms and material to equip the expedition were no doubt highly costly."

still a boy, the state called upon Aristodemus, who was of the royal family and guardian of the young king, to lead the expedition; and now that the Lacedaemonians were ready to take the field and the forces of their opponents were duly mustered, the latter met[1] to consider the most advantageous method of doing battle.

Timolaus of Corinth spoke: "Soldiers of the allied forces," he said, "the growth of Lacedaemon seems to me just like that of some mighty river—at its sources small and easily crossed, but as it farther and farther advances, other rivers discharge themselves into its channel, and its stream grows ever more formidable. So is it with the Lacedaemonians. Take them at the starting-point and they are but a single community, but as they advance and attach city after city they grow more numerous and more resistless. I observe that when people wish to take wasps' nests—if they try to capture the creatures on the wing, they are liable to be attacked by half the hive; whereas, if they apply fire to them ere they leave their homes, they will master them without scathe themselves. On this principle I think it best to bring about the battle within the hive itself, or, short of that, as close to Lacedaemon as possible."[2]

The arguments of the speaker were deemed sound, and a resolution was passed in that sense; but before it could be carried out there were various arrangements to be made. There was the question of headship. Then, again, what was the proper depth of line to be given to the different army corps? for if any particular state or states gave too great a depth to their battle line they would enable the enemy to turn their flank. Whilst they were debating these points, the Lacedaemonians had incorporated the men of Tegea and the men of Mantinea, and were ready to debouch into the bimarine region.[3] And as the two armies advanced almost at the same time, the Corinthians and the rest reached the Nemea,[4] and the Lacedaemonians and their allies occupied Sicyon. The Lacedaemonians entered by Epieiceia, and at first were severely handled by the light-armed troops of the enemy, who discharged stones and arrows from the vantage-ground on their right; but as they dropped down upon the Gulf of Corinth they advanced steadily onward through the flat country, felling timber and burning the

---

1 At Corinth. See above, III. iv. 11; below, V. iv. 61, where the victory of Nixos is described but not localised.
2 Or, "if not actually at Lacedaemon, then at least as near as possible to the hornet's nest."
3 I.e. "the shores of the Corinthian Gulf." Or, "upon the strand or coast road or coast land of Achaia" (aliter {ten aigialon}(?) the Strand of the Corinthian Gulf, the old name of this part of Achaia).
4 Or, "the district of Nemea."

fair land. Their rivals, on their side, after a certain forward movement,[1] paused and encamped, placing the ravine in front of them; but still the Lacedaemonians advanced, and it was only when they were within ten furlongs[2] of the hostile position that they followed suit and encamped, and then they remained quiet.

And here I may state the numbers on either side. The Lacedaemonian heavy-armed infantry levies amounted to six thousand men. Of Eleians, Triphylians, Acroreians, and Lasionians, there must have been nearly three thousand, with fifteen hundred Sicyonians, while Epidaurus, Troezen, Hermione, and Halieis[3] contributed at least another three thousand. To these heavy infantry troops must be added six hundred Lacedaemonian cavalry, a body of Cretan archers about three hundred strong, besides another force of slingers, at least four hundred in all, consisting of Marganians, Letrinians, and Amphidolians. The men of Phlius were not represented. Their plea was they were keeping "holy truce." That was the total of the forces on the Lacedaemonian side. There was collected on the enemy's side six thousand Athenian heavy infantry, with about, as was stated, seven thousand Argives, and in the absence of the men of Orchomenus something like five thousand Boeotians. There were besides three thousand Corinthians, and again from the whole of Euboea at least three thousand. These formed the heavy infantry. Of cavalry the Boeotians, again in the absence of the Orchomenians, furnished eight hundred, the Athenians[4] six hundred, the Chalcidians of Euboea one hundred, the Opuntian Locrians[5] fifty. Their light troops, including those of the Corinthians, were more numerous, as the Ozolian Locrians, the Melians, and Arcarnanians[6] helped to swell their numbers.

Such was the strength of the two armies. The Boeotians, as long as they occupied the left wing, showed no anxiety to join battle, but after a rearrangement which gave them the right, placing the Athenians opposite the Lacedaemonians, and themselves opposite the Achaeans, at once, we are told,[7] the victims proved favorable, and the order was passed along

---

1 {epelthontes}, but see Grote ("H. G." ix. 425 note), who prefers {apelthontes} = retreated and encamped.
2 Lit. "ten stades." For the numbers below, see Grote, "H. G." ix. 422, note 1.
3 Halieis, a seafaring people (Strabo, viii. 373) and town on the coast of Hermionis; Herod. vii. 137; Thuc. i. 105, ii. 56, iv. 45; Diod. xi. 78; "Hell." VI. ii. 3.
4 For a treaty between Athens and Eretria, 395 BC, see Hicks, 66; and below, "Hell." IV. iii. 15; Hicks, 68, 69; Diod. xiv. 82.
5 See above, "Hell." III. v. 3.
6 See below, "Hell." IV. vi. 1; ib. vii. 1; VI. v. 23.
7 Or, "then they lost no time in discovering that the victims proved favorable."

the lines to prepare for immediate action. The Boeotians, in the first place, abandoning the rule of sixteen deep, chose to give their division the fullest possible depth, and, moreover, kept veering more and more to their right, with the intention of overlapping their opponent's flank. The consequence was that the Athenians, to avoid being absolutely severed, were forced to follow suit, and edged toward the right, though they recognized the risk they ran of having their flank turned. For a while the Lacedaemonians had no idea of the advance of the enemy, owing to the rough nature of the ground,[1] but the notes of the paean at length announced to them the fact, and without an instant's delay the answering order "prepare for battle" ran along the different sections of their army. As soon as their troops were drawn up, according to the tactical disposition of the various generals of foreign brigades, the order was passed to "follow the lead," and then the Lacedaemonians on their side also began edging to their right, and eventually stretched out their wing so far that only six out of the ten regimental divisions of the Athenians confronted the Lacedaemonians, the other four finding themselves face to face with the men of Tegea. And now when they were less than a furlong[2] apart, the Lacedaemonians sacrificed in customary fashion a kid to the huntress goddess,[3] and advanced upon their opponents, wheeling round their overlapping columns to outflank his left. As the two armies closed, the allies of Lacedaemon were as a rule fairly borne down by their opponents. The men of Pellene alone, steadily confronting the Thespiaeans, held their ground, and the dead of either side strewed the position.[4] As to the Lacedaemonians themselves: crushing that portion of the Athenian troops which lay immediately in front of them, and at the same time encircling them with their overlapping right, they slew man after man of them; and, absolutely unscathed themselves, their unbroken columns continued their march, and so passed behind the four remaining divisions[5] of the Athenians before these latter had returned from their own victorious pursuit. Whereby the four divisions in question also emerged from battle intact, except for the casualties inflicted by the Tegeans in the first clash of the engagement. The troops next encountered by the Lacedaemonians were the Argives retiring. These they fell foul of, and the senior polemarch was just on the point of closing with them "breast

---

1 See Grote, "H. G." ix. 428; cf. Lys. "pro Mant." 20.
2 Lit. "a stade."
3 Lit. "our Lady of the Chase." See "Pol. Lac." xiii. 8.
4 Lit. "men on either side kept dropping at their post."
5 Lit. "tribes."

to breast" when someone, it is said, shouted, "Let their front ranks pass." This was done, and as the Argives raced past, their enemies thrust at their unprotected¹ sides and killed many of them. The Corinthians were caught in the same way as they retired, and when their turn had passed, once more the Lacedaemonians lit upon a portion of the Theban division retiring from the pursuit, and strewed the field with their dead. The end of it all was that the defeated troops in the first instance made for safety to the walls of their city, but the Corinthians within closed the gates, whereupon the troops took up quarters once again in their old encampment. The Lacedaemonians on their side withdrew to the point at which they first closed with the enemy, and there set up a trophy of victory. So the battle ended.

III

Meanwhile Agesilaus was rapidly hastening with his reinforcements from Asia. He had reached Amphipolis when Dercylidas brought the news of this fresh victory of the Lacedaemonians; their own loss had been eight men, that of the enemy considerable. It was his business at the same time to explain that not a few of the allies had fallen also. Agesilaus asked, "Would it not be opportune, Dercylidas, if the cities that have furnished us with contingents could hear of this victory as soon as possible?" And Dercylidas replied: "The news at any rate is likely to put them in better heart." Then said the king: "As you were an eye-witness there could hardly be a better bearer of the news than yourself." To this proposal Dercylidas lent a willing ear—to travel abroad² was his special delight—and he replied, "Yes, under your orders." "Then you have my orders," the king said. "And you may further inform the states from myself that we have not forgotten our promise; if all goes well over here we shall be with them again ere long." So Dercylidas set off on his travels, in the first instance to the Hellespont;³ while Agesilaus crossed Macedonia, and arrived in Thessaly. And now the men of Larissa, Crannon, Scotussa, and Pharsalus, who were allies of the Boeotians—and in fact all the Thessalians except the exiles for the time being—hung on his heels⁴ and did him damage.

For some while he marched his troops in a hollow square,⁵ posting half his cavalry in front and half on his rear; but finding that the Thessalians checked his passage by repeated charges from behind, he strengthened his

---

1 *I.e. "right."*
2 *See "Pol. Lac." xiv. 4.*
3 *See below, "Hell." IV. viii. 3.*
4 *See "Ages." ii. 2; Grote, "H. G." ix. 420, note 2.*
5 *See Rustow and Kochly, S. 187 foll.*

rearguard by sending round the cavalry from his van, with the exception of his own personal escort.[1] The two armies stood confronted in battle order; but the Thessalians, not liking the notion of a cavalry engagement with heavy infantry, turned, and step by step retreated, while the others followed them with considerable caution. Agesilaus, perceiving the error under which both alike labored, now sent his own personal guard of stalwart troopers with orders that both they and the rest of the horsemen should charge at full gallop,[2] and not give the enemy the chance to recoil. The Thessalians were taken aback by this unexpected onslaught, and half of them never thought of wheeling about, whilst those who did essay to do so presented the flanks of their horses to the charge,[3] and were made prisoners. Still Polymarchus of Pharsalus, the general in command of their cavalry, rallied his men for an instant, and fell, sword in hand, with his immediate followers. This was the signal for a flight so precipitate on the part of the Thessalians, that their dead and dying lined the road, and prisoners were taken; nor was any halt made until they reached Mount Narthacius. Here, then, midway between Pras and Narthacius, Agesilaus set up a trophy, halting for the moment, in unfeigned satisfaction at the exploit. It was from antagonists who prided themselves on their cavalry beyond everything that he had wrested victory, with a body of cavalry of his own mustering. Next day he crossed the mountains of Achaea Phthiotis, and for the future continued his march through friendly territory until he reached the confines of Boeotia.

Here, at the entrance of that territory, the sun (in partial eclipse)[4] seemed to appear in a crescent shape, and the news reached him of the defeat of the Lacedaemonians in a naval engagement, and the death of the admiral Peisander. Details of the disaster were not wanting. The engagement of the hostile fleets took place off Cnidus. Pharnabazus, the Persian admiral, was present with the Phoenician fleet, and in front of him were ranged the ships of the Hellenic squadron under Conon. Peisander had ventured to draw out his squadron to meet the combined fleets, though the numerical inferiority of his fleet to that of the Hellenic navy under Conon was conspicuous, and he had the mortification of seeing the allies who formed his left wing take to flight immediately. He himself came to close quarters with the enemy, and was driven on shore, on board his trireme, under

---

1 See Thuc. v. 72; Herod. vi. 56, viii. 124.
2 Lit. "and bids them pass the order to the others and themselves to charge," etc.
3 See "Horsemanship," vii. 16; Polyb. iv. 8.
4 394 BC, August 14.

pressure of the hostile rams. The rest, as many as were driven to shore, deserted their ships and sought safety as best they could in the territory of Cnidus. The admiral alone stuck to his ship, and fell sword in hand.

It was impossible for Agesilaus not to feel depressed by those tidings at first; on further reflection, however, it seemed to him that the moral quality of more than half his troops well entitled them to share in the sunshine of success, but in the day of trouble, when things looked black, he was not bound to take them into his confidence. Accordingly he turned round and gave out that he had received news that Peisander was dead, but that he had fallen in the arms of victory in a sea-fight; and suiting his action to the word, he proceeded to offer sacrifice in return for good tidings,[1] distributing portions of the victims to a large number of recipients. So it befell that in the first skirmish with the enemy the troops of Agesilaus gained the upper hand, in consequence of the report that the Lacedaemonians had won a victory by sea.

To confront Agesilaus stood an army composed of the Boeotians, Athenians, Argives, Corinthians, Aenianians, Euboeans, and both divisions of the Locrians. Agesilaus on his side had with him a division[2] of Lacedaemonians, which had crossed from Corinth, also half the division from Orchomenus; besides which there were the neodamodes[3] from Lacedaemon, on service with him already; and in addition to these the foreign contingent under Herippidas;[4] and again the quota furnished by the Hellenic cities in Asia, with others from the cities in Europe which he had brought over during his progress; and lastly, there were additional levies from the spot—Orchomenian and Phocian heavy infantry. In light-armed troops, it must be admitted, the numbers told heavily in favor of Agesilaus, but the cavalry[5] on both sides were fairly balanced.

Such were the forces of either party. I will describe the battle itself, if only on account of certain features which distinguish it from the battles of our time. The two armies met on the plain of Coronea—the troops of Agesilaus advancing from the Cephisus, the Thebans and their allies from the slopes of Helicon. Agesilaus commanded his own right in person, with the men of Orchomenus on his extreme left. The Thebans formed their own right, while the Argives held their left. As they drew together,

---

1 "*Splendide mendax.*" For the ethics of the matter, see "*Mem.*" IV. ii. 17; "*Cyrop.*" I. vi. 31.
2 Lit. "*a mora*"; for the numbers, see "*Ages.*" ii. 6; Plut. "*Ages.*" 17; Grote, "*H. G.*" ix. 433.
3 I.e. "enfranchised helots."
4 See "*Ages.*" ii. 10, 11; and above, "*Hell.*" III. iv. 20.
5 See Hicks, op. cit. 68.

for a while deep silence reigned on either side; but when they were not more than a furlong[1] apart, with the loud hurrah[2] the Thebans, quickening to a run, rushed furiously[3] to close quarters; and now there was barely a hundred yards[4] breadth between the two armies, when Herippidas with his foreign brigade, and with them the Ionians, Aeolians, and Hellespontines, darted out from the Spartans" battle-lines to greet their onset. One and all of the above played their part in the first rush forward; in another instant they were[5] within spear-thrust of the enemy, and had routed the section immediately before them. As to the Argives, they actually declined to receive the attack of Agesilaus, and betook themselves in flight to Helicon. At this moment some of the foreign division were already in the act of crowning Agesilaus with the wreath of victory, when someone brought him word that the Thebans had cut through the Orchomenians and were in among the baggage train. At this the Spartan general immediately turned his army right about and advanced against them. The Thebans, on their side, catching sight of their allies withdrawn in flight to the base of the Helicon, and anxious to get across to their own friends, formed in close order and tramped forward stoutly.

At this point no one will dispute the valour of Agesilaus, but he certainly did not choose the safest course. It was open to him to make way for the enemy to pass, which done, he might have hung upon his heels and mastered his rear. This, however, he refused to do, preferring to crash full front against the Thebans. Thereupon, with close interlock of shield wedged in with shield, they shoved, they fought, they dealt death,[6] they breathed out life, till at last a portion of the Thebans broke their way through toward Helicon, but paid for that departure by the loss of many lives. And now the victory of Agesilaus was fairly won, and he himself, wounded, had been carried back to the main line, when a party of horse came galloping up to tell him that something like eighty of the enemy,

---

1 Lit. "a stade."
2 Lit. "Alalah."
3 Like a tornado.
4 Lit. "about three plethra."
5 Or, "All these made up the attacking columns... and coming within... routed..."
6 Or, "they slew, they were slain." In illustration of this famous passage, twice again worked up in "Ages." ii. 12, and "Cyrop." VII. i. 38, commented on by Longinus, {peri upsous}, 19, and copied by Dio Cassius, 47, 45, I venture to quote a passage from Mr. Rudyard Kipling, "With the Main Guard," p. 57, Mulvaney loquitur: "The Tyrone was pushin' an' pushin' in, an' our men was sweerin' at thim, an' Crook was workin' away in front av us all, his sword-arm swingin' like a pump-handle an' his revolver spittin' like a cat. But the strange thing av ut was the quiet that lay upon. 'Twas like a fight in a dhrame—excipt for thim that wus dead."

under arms, were sheltering under the temple, and they asked what they ought to do. Agesilaus, though he was covered with wounds, did not, for all that, forget his duty to God. He gave orders to let them retire unscathed, and would not suffer any injury to be done to them. And now, seeing it was already late, they took their suppers and retired to rest.

But with the morning Gylis the polemarch received orders to draw up the troops in battle order, and to set up a trophy, every man crowned with a wreath in honor of the god, and all the pipers piping. Thus they busied themselves in the Spartan camp. On their side the Thebans sent heralds asking to bury their dead, under a truce; and in this wise a truce was made. Agesilaus withdrew to Delphi, where on arrival he offered to the god a tithe of the produce of his spoils—no less than a hundred talents.[1] Gylis the polemarch meanwhile withdrew into Phocis at the head of his troops, and from that district made a hostile advance into Locris. Here nearly a whole day was spent by the men in freely helping themselves to goods and chattels out of the villages and pillaging the corn;[2] but as it drew toward evening the troops began to retire, with the Lacedaemonians in the rear. The Locrians hung upon their heels with a heavy pelt of stones and javelins. Thereupon the Lacedaemonians turned short round and gave chase, laying some of their assailants low. Then the Locrians ceased clinging to their rear, but continued their volleys from the vantage-ground above. The Lacedaemonians again made efforts to pursue their persistent foes even up the slope. At last darkness descended on them, and as they retired man after man dropped, succumbing to the sheer difficulty of the ground; some in their inability to see what lay in front, or else shot down by the enemy's missiles. It was then that Gylis the polemarch met his end, as also Pelles, who was on his personal staff, and the whole of the Spartans present without exception—eighteen or thereabouts—perished, either crushed by stones or succumbing to other wounds. Indeed, except for timely aid brought from the camp where the men were supping, the chances are that not a man would have escaped to tell the tale.

IV

This incident ended the campaign. The army as a whole was disbanded, the contingents retiring to their several cities, and Agesilaus home across the Gulf by sea.

---

1 = 25,000 pounds nearly.
2 Or, "not to speak of provisions."

393 BC. Subsequently[1] the war between the two parties recommenced. The Athenians, Boeotians, Argives, and the other allies made Corinth the base of their operations; the Lacedaemonians and their allies held Sicyon as theirs. As to the Corinthians, they had to face the fact that, owing to their proximity to the seat of war, it was their territory which was ravaged and their people who perished, while the rest of the allies abode in peace and reaped the fruits of their lands in due season. Hence the majority of them, including the better class, desired peace, and gathering into knots they indoctrinated one another with these views.

392 BC.[2] On the other hand, it could hardly escape the notice of the allied powers, the Argives, Athenians, and Boeotians, as also those of the Corinthians themselves who had received a share of the king's moneys, or for whatever reason were most directly interested in the war, that if they did not promptly put the peace party out of the way, ten chances to one the old laconising policy would again hold the field. It seemed there was nothing for it but the remedy of the knife. There was a refinement of wickedness in the plan adopted. With most people the life even of a legally condemned criminal is held sacred during a solemn season, but these men deliberately selected the last day of the Eucleia,[3] when they might reckon on capturing more victims in the crowded marketplace, for their murderous purposes. Their agents were supplied with the names of those to be gotten rid of, the signal was given, and then, drawing their daggers, they fell to work. Here a man was struck down standing in the center of a group of talkers, and there another seated; a third while peacably enjoying himself at the play; a fourth actually whilst officiating as a judge at some dramatic contest.[4] When what was taking place became known, there was a general flight on the part of the better classes. Some fled to the images of the gods in the marketplace, others to the altars; and here these unhallowed miscreants, ringleaders and followers alike, utterly regardless of duty and law, fell to butchering their victims even within the sacred precincts of the gods; so that even some of those against whom no hand was lifted—honest, law-abiding folk—were filled with sore amazement at sight of such impiety. In this way many of the elder citizens, as mustering more thickly in the marketplace, were done to death. The younger men, acting on a suspicion conceived by one of their number, Pasimelus, as to what was going to take place, kept quiet in

---

1 393 BC. See Grote, ix. p. 455, note 2 foll.; "Hell." IV. viii. 7.
2 Others assign the incidents of this whole chapter iv. to 393 BC.
3 The festival of Artemis Eucleia.
4 See Diod. xiv. 86.

the Kraneion;[1] but hearing screams and shouting and being joined anon by some who had escaped from the affair, they took the hint, and, running up along the slope of the Acrocorinthus, succeeded in repelling an attack of the Argives and the rest. While they were still deliberating what they ought to do, down fell a capital from its column—without assignable cause, whether of earthquake or wind. Also, when they sacrificed, the aspect of the victims was such that the soothsayers said it was better to descend from that position.

So they retired, in the first instance prepared to go into exile beyond the territory of Corinth. It was only upon the persuasion of their friends and the earnest entreaties of their mothers and sisters who came out to them, supported by the solemn assurance of the men in power themselves, who swore to guarantee them against evil consequences, that some of them finally consented to return home. Presented to their eyes was the spectacle of a tyranny in full exercise, and to their minds the consciousness of the obliteration of their city, seeing that boundaries were plucked up and the land of their fathers had come to be re-entitled by the name of Argos instead of Corinth; and furthermore, compulsion was put upon them to share in the constitution in vogue at Argos, for which they had little appetite, while in their own city they wielded less power than the resident aliens. So that a party sprang up among them whose creed was, that life was not worth living on such terms: their endeavor must be to make their fatherland once more the Corinth of old days—to restore freedom to their city, purified from the murderer and his pollution and fairly rooted in good order and legality.[2] It was a design worth the venture: if they succeeded they would become the saviours of their country; if not—why, in the effort to grasp the fairest flower of happiness, they would but overreach, and find instead a glorious termination to existence.

It was in furtherance of this design that two men—Pasimelus and Alcimenes—undertook to creep through a watercourse and effect a meeting with Praxitas the polemarch of the Lacedaemonians, who was on garrison duty with his own division in Sicyon. They told him they could give him ingress at a point in the long walls leading to Lechaeum. Praxitas, knowing from previous experience that the two men might be relied upon, believed their statement; and having arranged for the further detention in Sicyon of the division which was on the point of departure, he busied himself with plans for the enterprise. When the two men, partly by chance and partly by

---

1 See Paus. II. ii. 4.
2 {eunomia}. See "Pol. Ath." i. 8; Arist. "Pol." iv. 8, 6; iii. 9, 8; v. 7, 4.

contrivance, came to be on guard at the gate where the tophy now stands, without further ado Praxitas presented himself with his division, taking with him also the men of Sicyon and the whole of the Corinthian exiles. Having reached the gate, he had a qualm of misgiving, and hesitated to step inside until he had first sent in a man on whom he could rely to take a look at things within. The two Corinthians introduced him, and made so simple and straightforward a representation[1] that the visitor was convinced, and reported everything as free of pitfalls as the two had asserted. Then the polemarch entered, but owing to the wide space between the double walls, as soon as they came to form in line within, the intruders were impressed by the paucity of their numbers. They therefore erected a stockade, and dug as good a trench as they could in front of them, pending the arrival of reinforcements from the allies. In their rear, moreover, lay the guard of the Boeotians in the harbor. Thus they passed the whole day which followed the night of ingress without striking a blow.

On the next day, however, the Argive troops arrived in all haste, hurrying to the rescue, and found the enemy duly drawn up. The Lacedaemonians were on their own right, the men of Sicyon next, and leaning against the eastern wall the Corinthian exiles, one hundred and fifty strong.[2] Their opponents marshalled their lines face to face in correspondence: Iphicrates with his mercenaries abutting on the eastern wall; next to them the Argives, whilst the Corinthians of the city held their left. In the pride inspired by numbers they began advancing at once. They overpowered the Sicyonians, and tearing asunder the stockade, pursued them to the sea and here slew numbers of them. At that instant Pasimachus, the cavalry general, at the head of a handful of troopers, seeing the Sicyonians sore presed, made fast the horses of his troops to the trees, and relieving the Sicyonians of their heavy infantry shields, advanced with his volunteers against the Argives. The latter, seeing the Sigmas on the shields and taking them to be "Sicyonians," had not the slightest fear. Whereupon, as the story goes, Pasimachus, exclaiming in his broad Doric, "By the twin gods! these Sigmas will cheat you, you Argives," came to close quarters, and in that battle of a handful against a host, was slain himself with all his followers. In another quarter of the field, however, the Corinthian exiles had got the better of their opponents and worked their way up, so that they were now touching the city circumvallation walls.

The Lacedaemonians, on their side, perceiving the discomfiture of the

---

1 Or, "showed him the place in so straightforward a manner."
2 See Grote, ix. p. 333 foll.

Sicyonians, sprang out with timely aid, keeping the palisade-work on their left. But the Argives, discovering that the Lacedaemonians were behind them, wheeled round and came racing back, pouring out of the palisade at full speed. Their extreme right, with unprotected flanks exposed, fell victims to the Lacedaemonians; the rest, hugging the wall, made good their retreat in dense masses toward the city. Here they encountered the Corinthian exiles, and discovering that they had fallen upon foes, swerved aside in the reverse direction. In this predicament some mounted by the ladders of the city wall, and, leaping down from its summit, were destroyed;[1] others yielded up their lives, thrust through, as they jostled at the foot of the steps; others again were literally trampled under one another's feet and suffocated.

The Lacedaemonians had no difficulty in the choice of victims; for at that instant a work was assigned to them to do,[2] such as they could hardly have hoped or prayed for. To find delivered into their hands a mob of helpless enemies, in an ecstasy of terror, presenting their unarmed sides in such sort that none turned to defend himself, but each victim rather seemed to contribute what he could toward his own destruction—if that was not divine interposition, I know now what to call it. Miracle or not, in that little space so many fell, and the corpses lay piled so thick, that eyes familiar with the stacking of corn or wood or piles of stones were called upon to gaze at layers of human bodies. Nor did the guard of the Boeotians in the port itself[3] escape death; some were slain upon the ramparts, others on the roofs of the dock-houses, which they had scaled for refuge. Nothing remained but for the Corinthians and Argives to carry away their dead under cover of a truce; whilst the allies of Lacedaemon poured in their reinforcements. When these were collected, Praxitas decided in the first place to raze enough of the walls to allow a free broadway for an army on march. This done, he put himself at the head of his troops and advanced on the road to Megara, taking by assault, first Sidus and next Crommyon. Leaving garrisons in these two fortresses, he retraced his steps, and finally fortifying Epieiceia as a garrison outpost to protect the territory of the allies, he at once disbanded his troops and himself withdrew to Lacedaemon.

392–391 BC.[4] After this the great armaments of both belligerents had ceased to exist. The states merely furnished garrisons—the one set at

---

1 Or, "plunged from its summit into perdition." See Thuc. ii. 4.
2 Or, "Heaven assigned to them a work..." Lit. "The God..."
3 I.e. "of Lechaeum."
4 So Grote and Curtius; al. 393 BC.

Corinth, the other set at Sicyon—and were content to guard the walls. Though even so, a vigorous war was carried on by dint of the mercenary troops with which both sides were furnished.

A signal incident in the period was the invasion of Phlius by Iphicrates. He laid an ambuscade, and with a small body of troops adopting a system of guerilla war, took occasion of an unguarded sally of the citizens of Phlius to inflict such losses on them, that though they had never previously received the Lacedaemonians within their walls, they received them now. They had hitherto feared to do so lest it might lead to the restoration of the banished members of their community, who gave out that they owed their exile to their Lacedaemonian sympathies;[1] but they were now in such abject fear of the Corinthian party that they sent to fetch the Lacedaemonians, and delivered the city and citadel to their safe keeping. These latter, however, well disposed to the exiles of Phlius, did not, at the time they held the city, so much as breathe the thought of bringing back the exiles; on the contrary, as soon as the city seemed to have recovered its confidence, they took their departure, leaving city and laws precisely as they had found them on their entry.

To return to Iphicrates and his men: they frequently extended their incursions even into Arcadia in many directions,[2] following their usual guerilla tactics, but also making assaults on fortified posts. The heavy infantry of the Arcadians positively refused to face them in the field, so profound was the terror in which they held these light troops. In compensation, the light troops themselves entertained a wholesome dread of the Lacedaemonians, and did not venture to approach even within javelin-range of their heavy infantry. They had been taught a lesson when, within that distance, some of the younger hoplites had made a dash at them, catching and putting some of them to the sword. But however profound the contempt of the Lacedaemonians for these light troops, their contempt for their own allies was deeper. (On one occasion[3] a reinforcement of Mantineans had sallied from the walls between Corinth and Lechaeum to engage the peltasts, and had no sooner come under attack than they swerved, losing some of their men as they made good their retreat. The Lacedaemonians were unkind enough to poke fun at these unfortunates.

---

1 Lit. *"laconism."*
2 See Thuc. ii. 4.
3 See Grote, ix. 472 note. Lechaeum was not taken by the Lacedaemonians until the Corinthian long walls had been rebuilt by the Athenians. Possibly the incidents in this section (S. 17) occurred after the capture of Lechaeum. The historian introduces them parenthetically, as it were, in illustration of his main topic—the success of the peltasts.

"Our allies," they said, "stand in as much awe of these peltasts as children of the bogies and hobgoblins of their nurses." For themselves, starting from Lechaeum, they found no difficulty in marching right round the city of Corinth with a single Lacedaemonian division and the Corinthian exiles.)[1]

The Athenians, on their side, who felt the power of the Lacedaemonians to be dangerously close, now that the walls of Corinth had been laid open, and even apprehended a direct attack upon themselves, determined to rebuild the portion of the wall severed by Praxitas. Accordingly they set out with their whole force, including a suite of stonelayers, masons, and carpenters, and within a few days erected a quite splendid wall on the side facing Sicyon toward the west,[2] and then proceeded with more leisure to the completion of the eastern portion.

To turn once more to the other side: the Lacedaemonians, indignant at the notion that the Argives should be gathering the produce of their lands in peace at home, as if war were a pastime, marched against them. Agesilaus commanded the expedition, and after ravaging their territory from one end to the other, crossed their frontier at Tenea[3] and swooped down upon Corinth, taking the walls which had been lately rebuilt by the Athenians. He was supported on the sea side by his brother Teleutias[4] with a naval force of about twelve triremes, and the mother of both was able to congratulate herself on the joint success of both her sons; one having captured the enemy's walls by land and the other his ships and naval arsenal by sea, on the same day. These achievements sufficed Agesilaus for the present; he disbanded the army of the allies and led the state troops home.

V

390 BC.[5] Subsequently the Lacedaemonians made a second expedition against Corinth. They heard from the exiles that the citizens contrived to preserve all their cattle in Peiraeum; indeed, large numbers derived their subsistence from the place. Agesilaus was again in command of the expedition. In the first instance he advanced upon the Isthmus. It was the month of the Isthmian games,[6] and here he found the Argives engaged in

---

1 Or, adopting Schneider's conjecture, {estratopedeuonto}, add "and encamping."

2 See Thuc. vi. 98.

3 Reading {Tenean}, Koppen's emendation for {tegean}. In the parallel passage ("Ages." ii. 17) the text has {kata ta stena}. See Grote, "H. G." ix. 471.

4 See below, IV. viii. 11.

5 Al. 392 BC. The historian omits the overtures for peace, 391 BC (or 391–390) referred to in Andoc. "De Pace." See Jebb, "Att. Or." i. 83, 108; Grote, "H. G." ix. 474; Curtius, "H. G." Eng. tr. iv. 261.

6 Grote and Curtius believe these to be the Isthmian games of 390 BC, not of 392 BC, as Sauppe and others suppose. See Peter, "Chron. Table," p. 89, note 183; Jowett, "Thuc." ii. 468, note on VIII. 9, 1.

conducting the sacrifice to Poseidon, as if Corinth were Argos. So when they perceived the approach of Agesilaus, the Argives and their friends left the offerings as they lay, including the preparations for the breakfast, and retired with undisguised alarm into the city by the Cenchrean road.[1] Agesilaus, though he observed the movement, refrained from giving chase, but taking up his quarters in the temple, there proceeded to offer victims to the god himself, and waited until the Corinthian exiles had celebrated the sacrifice to Poseidon, along with the games. But no sooner had Agesilaus turned his back and retired, than the Argives returned and celebrated the Isthmian games afresh; so that in this particular year there were cases in which the same competitors were twice defeated in this or that contest, or conversely, the same man was proclaimed victor twice over.

On the fourth day Agesilaus led his troops against Peiraeum, but finding it strongly defended, he made a sudden retrograde march after the morning meal in the direction of the capital, as though he calculated on the betrayal of the city. The Corinthians, in apprehension of some such possible catastrophe, sent to summon Iphicrates with the larger portion of his light infantry. These passed by duly in the night, not unobserved, however, by Agesilaus, who at once turned round at break of day and advanced on Piraeum. He himself kept to the low ground by the hot springs,[2] sending a division to scale the top of the pass. That night he encamped at the hot springs, while the division bivouacked in the open, in possession of the pass. Here Agesilaus distinguished himself by an invention as seasonable as it was simple. Among those who carried provisions for the division not one had thought of bringing fire. The altitude was considerable; there had been a fall of rain and hail toward evening and the temperature was low; besides which, the scaling party were clad in thin garments suited to the summer season. There they sat shivering in the dark, with scarcely heart to attack their suppers, when Agesilaus sent up to them as many as ten porters carrying fire in earthen pots. One found his way up one way, one another, and presently there were many bonfires blazing—magnificently enough, since there was plenty of wood to hand; so that all fell to oiling themselves and many supped over again. The same night the sky was lit up by the blaze of the temple of Poseidon—set on fire no one knows how.

When the men in Piraeum perceived that the pass was occupied, they at once abandoned all thought of self-defense and fled for refuge to the

---

1 Lit. *"road to Cenchreae."*
2 Near mod. *Lutraki.*

Heraion[1]—men and women, slaves and free-born, with the greater part of their flocks and herds. Agesilaus, with the main body, meanwhile pursued his march by the sea-shore, and the division, simultaneously descending from the heights, captured the fortified position of Oenoe, appropriating its contents. Indeed, all the troops on that day reaped a rich harvest in the supplies they brought in from various farmsteads. Presently those who had escaped into the Heraion came out, offering to leave it to Agesilaus to decide what he would do with them. He decided to deliver up to the exiles all those concerned with the late butchery, and that all else should be sold. And so from the Heraion streamed out a long line of prisoners, whilst from other sides embassies arrived in numbers; and among these a deputation from the Boeotians, anxious to learn what they should do to obtain peace. These latter Agesilaus, with a certain loftiness of manner, affected not even to see, although Pharax,[2] their proxenus, stood by their side to introduce them. Seated in a circular edifice on the margin of the lake,[3] he surveyed the host of captives and valuables as they were brought out. Beside the prisoners, to guard them, stepped the Lacedaemonian warriors from the camp, carrying their spears—and themselves plucked all gaze their way, so readily will success and the transient fortune of the moment rivet attention. But even while Agesilaus was still thus seated, wearing a look betokening satisfaction at some great achievement, a horseman came galloping up; the flanks of his charger streamed with sweat. To the many inquiries what news he brought, the rider responded never a word; but being now close beside Agesilaus, he leaped from his horse, and running up to him with lowering visage narrated the disaster of the Spartan division[4] at Lechaeum. At these tidings the king sprang instantly from his seat, clutching his spear, and bade his herald summon to a meeting the generals, captains of fifties, and commanders of foreign brigades.[5] When these had rapidly assembled he bade them, seeing that the morning meal had not yet been tasted, to swallow hastily what they could, and with all possible speed to overtake him. But for himself, he, with the officers of the royal staff,[6] set off at once without breakfast. His bodyguard, with their heavy arms, accompanied him with all speed—himself in advance, the officers following behind. In this fashion he had already passed beyond the warm springs, and was well

---

1 Or, "Heraeum," i.e. sanctuary of Hera, on a promontory so called. See Leake, "Morea," iii. 317.
2 See "Hell." III. ii. 12, if the same.
3 Or, "on the round pavilion by the lake" (mod. Vuliasmeni).
4 Technically "mora."
5 Lit. the polemarchs, pentecontors, and xenagoi.
6 See "Pol. Lac." xiii. 1.

within the plateau of Lechaeum, when three horsemen rode up with further news: the dead bodies had been picked up. On receipt of these tidings he commanded the troops to order arms, and having rested them a little space, led them back again to the Heraion. The next day he spent in disposing of the captured property.[1]

The ambassadors of the Boeotians were then summoned, and, being asked to explain the object of their coming, made no further mention of the word "peace," but replied that, if there was nothing to hinder it, they wished to have a pass to their own soldiers within the capital. The king answered with a smile: "I know your desire is not so much to see your soldiers as to feast your eyes on the good fortune of your friends, and to measure its magnitude. Wait then, I will conduct you myself; with me you will be better able to discover the true value of what has taken place." And he was as good as his word. Next day he sacrificed, and led his army up to the gates of Corinth. The trophy he respected, but not one tree did he leave standing—chopping and burning, as proof positive that no one dared to face him in the field. And having so done, he encamped about Lechaeum; and as to the Theban ambassadors, in lieu of letting them pass into the city, he sent them off by sea across to Creusis.

But in proportion to the unwontedness of such a calamity befalling Lacedaemonians, a widespread mourning fell upon the whole Laconian army, those alone excepted whose sons or fathers or brothers had died at their post. The bearing of these resembled that of conquerors,[2] as with bright faces they moved freely to and fro, glorying in their domestic sorrow. Now the tragic fate which befell the division was on this wise: It was the unvaried custom of the men of Amyclae to return home at the Hyacinthia,[3] to join in the sacred paean, a custom not to be interrupted by active service or absence from home or for any other reason. So, too, on this occasion, Agesilaus had left behind all the Amyclaeans serving in any part of his army at Lechaeum. At the right moment the general in command of the garrison at that place had posted the garrison troops of the allies to guard the walls during his absence, and put himself at the head of his division of heavy infantry with that of the cavalry,[4] and led the Amyclaeans past the walls of Corinth. Arrived at a point within three miles or so[5] of Sicyon,

---

[1] See Grote, "H. G." ix. 480, in reference to "Ages." vii. 6.
[2] See Grote, "H. G." ix. 488.
[3] Observed on three days of the month Hecatombaeus (=July). See Muller's "Dorians," ii. 360. For Amyclae, see Leake, "Morea," i. ch. iv. p. 145 foll.; Baedeker's "Greece," p. 279.
[4] See below, "Hell." VI. iv. 12; and "Pol. Lac." xi. 4, xiii. 4.
[5] Lit. "twenty or thirty stades."

the polemarch turned back himself in the direction of Lechaeum with his heavy infantry regiment, six hundred strong, giving orders to the cavalry commandant to escort the Amyclaeans with his division as far as they required, and then to turn and overtake him. It cannot be said that the Lacedaemonians were ignorant of the large number of light troops and heavy infantry inside Corinth, but owing to their former successes they arrogantly presumed that no one would attack them. Within the capital of the Corinthians, however, their scant numbers—a thin line of heavy infantry unsupported by light infantry or cavalry—had been noted; and Callias, the son of Hipponicus,[1] who was in command of the Athenian hoplites, and Iphicrates at the head of his peltasts, saw no risk in attacking with the light brigade. Since if the enemy continued his march by the high road, he would be cut up by showers of javelins on his exposed right flank; or if he were tempted to take the offensive, they with their peltasts, the nimblest of all light troops, would easily slip out of the grasp of his hoplites.

With this clearly-conceived idea they led out their troops; and while Callias drew up his heavy infantry in line at no great distance from the city, Iphicrates and his peltasts made a dash at the returning division.

The Lacedaemonians were presently within range of the javelins.[2] Here a man was wounded, and there another dropped, not to rise again. Each time orders were given to the attendant shield-bearers[3] to pick up the men and bear them into Lechaeum; and these indeed were the only members of the mora who were, strictly speaking, saved. Then the polemarch ordered the ten-years-service men[4] to charge and drive off their assailants. Charge, however, as they might, they took nothing by their pains—not a man could they come at within javelin range. Being heavy infantry opposed to light troops, before they could get to close quarters the enemy's word of command sounded "Retire!" whilst as soon as their own ranks fell back, scattered as they were in consequence of a charge where each man's individual speed had told, Iphicrates and his men turned right about and renewed the javelin attack, while others, running alongside, harassed their exposed flank. At the very first charge the assailants had shot down nine or ten, and, encouraged by this success, pressed on with increasing audacity. These attacks told so severely that the polemarch a second time gave the

---

1 See Cobet, *"Prosop. Xen." p. 67 foll.*
2 See Grote, *"H. G." ix. 467, note on the improvements of Iphicrates.*
3 Grote, *"H. G." ix. 484; cf. "Hell." IV. viii. 39; "Anab." IV. ii. 20; Herod. ix. 10-29.*
4 *Youngest rank and file, between eighteen and twenty-eight years of age, who formed the first line. The Spartan was liable to service at the age of eighteen. From twenty-eight to thirty-three he would belong to the fifteen-years-service division (the second line); and so on. See below, IV. vi. 10.*

order (and this time for the fifteen-years-service men) to charge. The order was promptly obeyed, but on retiring they lost more men than on the first occasion, and it was not until the pick and flower of the division had succumbed that they were joined by their returning cavalry, in whose company they once again attempted a charge. The light infantry gave way, but the attack of the cavalry was feebly enforced. Instead of pressing home the charge until at least they had sabred some of the enemy, they kept their horses abreast of their infantry skirmishers,[1] charging and wheeling side by side.

Again and again the monotonous tale of doing and suffering repeated itself, except that as their own ranks grew thinner and their courage ebbed, the courage of their assailants grew bolder and their numbers increased. In desperation they massed compactly upon the narrow slope of a hillock, distant a couple of furlongs[2] or so from the sea, and a couple of miles[3] perhaps from Lechaeum. Their friends in Lechaeum, perceiving them, embarked in boats and sailed round until they were immediately under the hillock. And now, in the very slough of despair, being so sorely troubled as man after man dropped dead, and unable to strike a blow, to crown their distress they saw the enemy's heavy infantry advancing. Then they took to flight; some of them threw themselves into the sea; others—a mere handful—escaped with the cavalry into Lechaeum. The death-roll, including those who fell in the second fight and the final flight, must have numbered two hundred and fifty slain, or thereabouts.[4] Such is the tale of the destruction of the Lacedaemonian mora.

Subsequently, with the mutilated fragment of the division, Agesilaus turned his back upon Lechaeum, leaving another division behind to garrison that port. On his passage homeward, as he wound his way through the various cities, he made a point of arriving at each as late in the day as possible, renewing his march as early as possible next morning. Leaving Orchomenus at the first streak of dawn, he passed Mantinea still under cover of darkness. The spectacle of the Mantineans rejoicing at their misfortune would have been too severe an ordeal for his soldiers.

But Iphicrates had not yet reached the summit of his good fortune. Success followed upon success. Lacedaemonian garrisons had been placed in Sidus and Crommyon by Praxitas when he took these fortresses, and

---

1 See Thuc. iv. 125.
2 Lit. "two stades."
3 Lit. "sixteen or seventeen stades."
4 See Grote, "H. G." ix. 486.

again in Oenoe, when Peiraeum was taken quite lately by Agesilaus. One and all of these now fell into the hands of Iphicrates. Lechaeum still held out, garrisoned as it was by the Lacedaemonians and their allies; while the Corinthian exiles, unable since[1] the disaster of the mora any longer to pass freely by land from Sicyon, had the sea passage still open to them, and using Lechaeum as their base,[2] kept up a game of mutual annoyance with the party in the capital.

VI

390–389 BC.[3] At a later date the Achaeans, being in possession of Calydon, a town from old times belonging to Aetolia, and having further incorporated the Calydonians as citizens,[4] were under the necessity of garrisoning their new possession. The reason was, that the Arcarnanians were threatening the place with an army, and were aided by contingents from Athens and Boeotia, who were anxious to help their allies.[5] Under the strain of this combined attack the Achaeans despatched ambassadors to Lacedaemon, who on arrival complained of the unfair conduct of Lacedaemon toward themselves. "We, sirs," they said, "are ever ready to serve in your armies, in obedience to whatever orders you choose to issue; we follow you whithersoever you think fit to lead; but when it comes to our being beleaguered by the Acarnanians, with their allies the Athenians and Boeotians, you show not the slightest concern. Understand, then, that if things go on thus we cannot hold out; but either we must give up all part in the war in Peloponnesus and cross over in full force to engage the Arcarnanians, or we must make peace with them on whatever terms we can." This language was a tacit threat that if they failed to obtain the assistance they felt entitled to from Lacedaemon they would quit the alliance.

The ephors and the assembly concluded that there was no alternative but to assist the Achaeans in their campaign against the Acarnanians. Accordingly they sent out Agesilaus with two divisions and the proper complement of allies. The Achaeans none the less marched out in full force themselves. No sooner had Agesilaus crossed the gulf than there was a general flight of the population from the country districts into the towns, whilst the flocks and herds were driven into remote districts that they might

---

1 Lit. "owing to."
2 The illustrative incidents narrated in chapter iv. 17 may belong to this period.
3 According to others (who suppose that the Isthmia and the events recorded in chapter v. 1–19 above belong to 392 BC), we have now reached 391 BC.
4 Or, "having conferred a city organization on the Calydonians."
5 See Thuc. ii. 68.

not be captured by the troops. Being now arrived on the frontier of the enemy's territory, Agesilaus sent to the general assembly of the Acarnanians at Stratus,[1] warning them that unless they chose to give up their alliance with the Boeotians and Athenians, and to take instead themselves and their allies, he would ravage their territory through its length and breadth, and not spare a single thing. When they turned a deaf ear to this summons, the other proceeded to do what he threatened, systematically laying the district waste, felling the timber and cutting down the fruit-trees, while slowly moving on at the rate of ten or twelve furlongs a day. The Acarnanians, owing to the snail-like progress of the enemy, were lulled into a sense of security. They even began bringing down their cattle from their alps, and devoted themselves to the tillage of far the greater portion of their fields. But Agesilaus only waited till their rash confidence reached its climax; then on the fifteenth or sixteenth day after he head first entered the country he sacrificed at early dawn, and before evening had traversed eighteen miles[2] or so of country to the lake[3] round which were collected nearly all the flocks and herds of the Acarnanians, and so captured a vast quantity of cattle, horses, and grazing stock of all kinds, besides numerous slaves.

Having secured this prize, he stayed on the spot the whole of the following day, and devoted himself to disposing of the captured property by public sale. While he was thus engaged, a large body of Arcarnanian light infantry appeared, and availing themselves of the position in which Agesilaus was encamped against the mountain side, assailed him with volleys of sling-stones and rocks from the razor-edge of the mountain, without suffering any scathe themselves. By this means they succeeded in dislodging and forcing his troops down into the level plain, and that too at an hour when the whole camp was engaged in preparations for the evening meal. As night drew on, the Acarnanians retired; sentinels were posted, and the troops slept in peace.

Next day Agesilaus led off his army. The exit from the plain and meadow-land round the lake was a narrow aperture through a close encircling range of hills. In occupation of this mountain barrier the Acarnanians, from the

---

1 "The Akarnanians had, in early times, occupied the hill of Olpai as a place for judicial proceedings common to the whole nation" (see Thuc. iii. 105). "But in Thucydides" own time Stratos had attained its position as the greatest city of Akarnania, and probably the Federal Assemblies were already held there" (Thuc. ii. 80). "In the days of Agesilaos we find Stratos still more distinctly marked as the place of Federal meeting."—Freeman, "Hist. Fed. Gov." ch. iv. p. 148 foll., "On the constitution of the League."
2 Lit. "one hundred and sixty stades."
3 See Thuc. ii. 80; vi. 106.

vantage-ground above, poured down a continuous pelt of stones and other missiles, or, creeping down to the fringes, dogged and annoyed them so much that the army was no longer able to proceed. If the heavy infantry or cavalry made sallies from the main line they did no harm to their assailants, for the Acarnanians had only to retire and they had quickly gained their strongholds. It was too severe a task, Agesilaus thought, to force his way through the narrow pass so sorely beset. He made up his mind, therefore, to charge that portion of the enemy who dogged his left, though these were pretty numerous. The range of hills on this side was more accessible to heavy infantry and horse alike. During the interval needed for the inspection of victims, the Acarnanians kept plying them with javelins and bullets, and, coming into close proximity, wounded man after man. But presently came the word of command, "Advance!" and the fifteen-years-service men of the heavy infantry[1] ran forward, accompanied by the cavalry, at a round pace, the general himself steadily following with the rest of the column. Those of the Acarnanians who had crept down the mountain side at that instant in the midst of their sharpshooting turned and fled, and as they climbed the steep, man after man was slain. When, however, the top of the pass was reached, there stood the hoplites of the Acarnanians drawn up in battle line, and supported by the mass of their light infantry. There they steadily waited, keeping up a continuous discharge of missiles the while, or launching their long spears; whereby they dealt wounds to the cavalry troopers and death in some cases to the horses. But when they were all but within the clutches of the advancing heavy infantry[2] of the Lacedaemonians their firmness forsook them; they swerved and fled, and there died of them on that day about three hundred. So ended the affair.

Agesilaus set up a trophy of victory, and afterward making a tour of the country, he visited it with fire and sword.[3] Occasionally, in obedience to pressure put upon him by the Achaeans, he would assault some city, but did not capture a single one. And now, as the season of autumn rapidly approached, he prepared to leave the country; whereupon the Achaeans, who looked upon his exploits as abortive, seeing that not a single city, willingly or unwillingly, had as yet been detached from their opponents, begged him, as the smallest service he could render them, at any rate to stay long enough in the country to prevent the Acarnanians from sowing their corn. He answered that the course they suggested ran

---

1 I.e. "the first two ranks." See above, IV. v. 14.
2 See "Ages." ii. 20, for an extraordinary discrepancy.
3 Or lit. "burning and felling."

counter to expediency. "You forget," he said, "that I mean to invade your enemies again next summer; and therefore the larger their sowing now, the stronger will be their appetite for peace hereafter." With this retort he withdrew overland through Aetolia, and by roads, moreover, which no army, small or great, could possibly have traversed without the consent of the inhabitants. The Aetolians, however, were only too glad to yield the Spartan king a free passage, cherishing hopes as they did that he would aid them to recover Naupactus. On reaching Rhium[1] he crossed the gulf at that point and returned homeward, the more direct passage from Calydon to Peloponnesus being effectually barred by an Athenian squadron stationed at Oeniadae.

VII

389–388 BC.[2] On the expiration of winter, and in fulfillment of his promise to the Achaeans, Agesilaus called out the ban once more with early spring to invade the Acarnanians. The latter were apprised of his intention, and, being persuaded that owing to the midland situation of their cities they would just as truly be blockaded by an enemy who chose to destroy their corn as they would be if besieged with entrenchments in regular form, they sent ambassadors to Lacedaemon, and made peace with the Achaeans and alliance with the Lacedaemonians. Thus closes this page of history concerning the affairs of Arcarnania.

To turn to the next. There was a feeling on the part of the Lacedaemonians[3] that no expedition against Athens or Boeotia would be safe so long as a state so important and so close to their own frontier as Argos remained in open hostility behind them. Accordingly they called out the ban against Argos. Now when Agesipolis learned that the duty of leadership devolved on him, and, moreover, that the sacrifices before crossing the frontier were favorable, he went to Olympia and consulted the will of the god. "Would it be lawful to him," he inquired, "not to accept the holy truce, on the ground that the Argives made the season for it[4] depend not on a fixed date, but on the prospect of a Lacedaemonian invasion?" The god indicated to the inquirer that he might lawfully repudiate any holy truce which was fraudulently antedated.[5] Not content with this, the young king, on leaving Olympia, went at once to

---

1 Or Antirrhium (as more commonly called).
2 According to others, 390 BC.
3 Or, "It was agreed by the Lacedaemonians."
4 I.e. "the season of the Carneia."
5 Or, "wrongfully put forward." See below, V. i. 29; iii. 28; Paus. III. v. 8; Jebb. "Att. Or." i. p. 131; Grote, "H. G." ix. 494 foll.; Jowett, "Thuc." ii. 315; note to Thuc. V. liv. 3.

Delphi, and at that shrine put the same question to Apollo: "Were his views in accordance with his Father's as touching the holy truce?"—to which the son of Zeus made answer: "Yea, altogether in accordance."[1]

Then without further hesitation, picking up his army at Phlius (where, during his absence to visit the temples, the troops had been collecting), he advanced by Nemea into the enemy's territory. The Argives, on their side, perceiving that they would be unable to hinder his advance, in accordance with their custom sent a couple of heralds, garlanded, and presented their usual plea of a holy truce. Agesipolis answered them curtly that the gods were not satisfied with the justice of their plea, and, refusing to accept the truce, pushed forward, causing thereby great perplexity and consternation throughout the rural districts and the capital itself.

But while he was getting his evening meal that first evening in the Argive territory—just at the moment when the after-dinner libation had been poured out—the god sent an earthquake; and with one consent the Lacedaemonians, beginning with the officers of the royal quarters, sang the sacred hymn of Poseidon. The soldiers, in general, expected to retreat, arguing that, on the occurrence of an earthquake once before, Agis had retired from Elis. But Agesipolis held another view: if the god had sent his earthquake at the moment when he was meditating invasion, he should have understood that the god forbade his entrance; but now, when the invasion was a thing effected, he must needs take it as a signal of his approval.[2] Accordingly next morning he sacrificed to Poseidon, and advanced a short distance further into the country.

The late expedition of Agesilaus into Argos[3] was still fresh in men's minds, and Agesipolis was eager to ascertain from the soldiers how close his predecessor had advanced to the fortification walls; or again, how far he had gone in ravaging the open country—not unlike a competitor in the pentathlon,[4] eager to cap the performance of his rival in each event. On

---

1 Grote; cf. Aristot. "Rhet." ii. 33.
2 Or, "interpret the signal as a summons to advance."
3 See above, "Hell." IV. iv. 19.
4 The pentathlon of Olympia and the other great games consisted of five contests, in the following order—(1) leaping, (2) discus-throwing, (3) javelin-throwing, (4) running, (5) wrestling. Cf. Simonides, {alma podokeien diskon akonta palen}, where, "metri gratia," the order is inverted. The competitors were drawn in pairs. The odd man who drew a bye in any particular round or heat was called the "ephedros." The successful athletes of the pairs, that is, those who had won any three events out of five, would then again be drawn against each other, and so on until only two were left, between whom the final heat took place. See, for an exhaustive discussion of the subject, Prof. Percy Gardner, "The Pentathlon of the Greeks" ("Journal of Hellenic Studies," vol. i. 9, p. 210 foll. pl. viii.), from whom this note is taken.

one occasion it was only the discharge of missiles from the towers which forced him to recross the trenches round the walls; on another, profiting by the absence of the majority of the Argives in Laconian territory, he came so close to the gates that their officers actually shut out their own Boeotian cavalry on the point of entering, in terror lest the Lacedaemonians might pour into the town in company, and these Boeotian troopers were forced to cling, like bats to a wall, under each coign of vantage beneath the battlements. Had it not been for the accidental absence of the Cretans,[1] who had gone off on a raid to Nauplia, without a doubt numbers of men and horses would have been shot down. At a later date, while encamping in the neighborhood of the Enclosures,[2] a thunder-bolt fell into his camp. One or two men were struck, while others died from the effect of the concussion on their brains. At a still later period he was anxious to fortify some sort of garrison outpost in the pass of Celusa,[3] but upon offering sacrifice the victims proved lobeless,[4] and he was constrained to lead back and disband his army—not without serious injury inflicted on the Argives, as the result of an invasion which had taken them wholly by surprise.

VIII

394 BC. Such were the land operations in the war. Meanwhile another series of events was being enacted on the sea and within the seaboard cities; and these I will now narrate in detail. But I shall confine my pen to the more memorable incidents, and others of less account I shall pass over.

In the first place, then, Pharnabazus and Conon, after defeating the Lacedaemonians in the naval engagement of Cnidus, commenced a tour of inspection round the islands and the maritime states, expelling from them, as they visited them, one after another the Spartan governors.[5] Everywhere they gave consolatory assurances to the citizens that they had no intention of establishing fortress citadels within their walls, or in any way interfering with their self-government.[6] Such words fell soothingly upon the ears of those to whom they were addressed; the proposals were courteously accepted; all were eager to present Pharnabazus with gifts of friendship and hospitality. The satrap, indeed, was only applying the instructions of his

---

1 See Thuc. vii. 57.
2 {peri tas eirktas}—what these were no one knows, possibly a stone quarry used as a prison. Cf. "Cyrop." III. i. 19; "Mem." II. i. 5; see Grote, "H. G." ix. 497; Paus. III. v. 8.
3 Or Celossa. See Strabo, viii. 382.
4 I.e. "hopeless." See above, III. iv. 15.
5 Lit. "the Laconian harmosts."
6 See Hicks, 70, "Honors to Konon," Inscript. found at Erythrae in Ionia. Cf. Diod. xiv. 84.

master Conon on these matters—who had taught him that if he acted thus all the states would be friendly to him, whereas, if he showed any intention to enslave them, the smallest of them would, as Conon insisted, be capable of causing a world of trouble, and the chances were, if apprehensions were once excited, he would find himself face to face with a coalition of united Hellas. To these admonitions Pharnabazus lent a willing ear.

Accordingly, when disembarking at Ephesus, he presented Conon with a fleet of forty sail,[1] and having further instructed him to meet him at Sestos,[2] set off himself by land along the coast to visit his own provinces. For here it should be mentioned that his old enemy Dercylidas happened to be in Abydos at the time of the sea-fight;[3] nor had he at a later date suffered eclipse with the other governors,[4] but on the contrary, had kept tight hold of Abydos and still preserved it in attachment to Lacedaemon. The course he had adopted was to summon a meeting of the Abydenians, when he made them a speech as follows: "Sirs, today it is possible for you, who have before been friends to my city, to appear as benefactors of the Lacedaemonians. For a man to prove faithful to his friends in the heyday of their good fortune is no great marvel; but to prove steadfast when his friends are in misfortune—that is a service monumental for all time. But do not mistake me. It does not follow that, because we have been defeated in a great sea-fight, we are therefore annihilated.[5] Certainly not. Even in old days, you will admit, when Athens was mistress of the sea, our state was not powerless to benefit friends or chastise enemies. Moreover, in proportion as the rest of the cities have joined hands with fortune to turn their backs upon us, so much the more certainly will the grandeur of your fidelity shine forth. Or, is anyone haunted by the fear that we may find ourselves blockaded by land and sea?—let him consider that at present there is no Hellenic navy whatever on the seas, and if the barbarian attempts to clutch the empire of the sea, Hellas will not sit by and suffer it; so that, if only in self-defense, she must inevitably take your side."

To this the Abydenians lent no deaf ears, but rather responded with willingness approaching enthusiasm—extending the hand of fellowship to the ex-governors, some of whom were already flocking to Abydos as a harbor of refuge, whilst others they sent to summon from a distance.

---

1 See Diod. xiv. 83.
2 See above, "Hell." II. i. 27 foll.
3 See above, "Hell." IV. iii. 3.
4 Lit. "harmosts."
5 Or, "we are beaten, ergo, it is all over with us."

So when a number of efficient and serviceable men had been collected, Dercylidas ventured to cross over to Sestos—lying, as it does, not more than a mile[1] distant, directly facing Abydos. There he not only set about collecting those who held lands in the Chersonese through Lacedaemonian influence, but extended his welcome also to the governors[2] who had been driven out of European states.[3] He insisted that, if they came to think of it, not even was their case desperate, reminding them that even in Asia, which originally belonged to the Persian monarch, places were to be found—such as the little state of Temnos, or Aegae, and others, capable of administering their affairs, unsubjected to the king of Persia. "But," he added, "if you want a strong impregnable position, I cannot conceive what better you can find than Sestos. Why, it would need a combined naval and military force to invest that port." By these and such like arguments he rescued them from the lethargy of despair.

Now when Pharnabazus found Abydos and Sestos so conditioned, he gave them to understand that unless they chose to eject the Lacedaemonians, he would bring war to bear upon them; and when they refused to obey, having first assigned to Conon as his business to keep the sea closed against them, he proceeded in person to ravage the territory of the men of Abydos. Presently, finding himself no nearer the fulfillment of his object—which was their reduction—he set off home himself and left it to Conon the while so to conciliate the Hellespontine states that as large a naval power as possible might be mustered against the coming spring. In his wrath against the Lacedaemonians, in return for the treatment he had received from them, his paramount object was to invade their territory and exact what vengeance he could.

393 BC. The winter was thus fully taken up with preparations; but with the approach of spring, Pharnabazus and Conon, with a large fleet fully manned, and a foreign mercenary brigade to boot, threaded their way through the islands to Melos.[4] This island was to serve as a base of operations against Lacedaemon. And in the first instance he sailed down to Pherae[5] and ravaged that district, after which he made successive descents at various other points on the seaboard, and did what injury he could. But in apprehension of the harborless character of the coast, coupled with

1 Lit. *"eight stades."*
2 Lit. *"harmosts."*
3 See Demos. *"de Cor."* 96.
4 See Lys. xix. *"de bon. Arist."* 19 foll.; and Hicks, 71, *"Honors to Dionysios I. and his court"*; Grote, *"H. G."* ix. 453.
5 Mod. Kalamata.

the enemy's facility of reinforcement and his own scarcity of supplies, he very soon turned back and sailed away, until finally he came to moorings in the harbor of Phoenicus in Cythera. The occupants of the city of the Cytherians, in terror of being taken by storm, evacuated the walls. To dismiss these under a flag of truce across to Laconia was his first step; his second was to repair the fortress in question and to leave a garrison in the island under an Athenian governor—Nicophemus. After this he set sail to the Isthmus of Corinth, where he delivered an exhortation to the allies begging them to prosecute the war vigorously, and to show themselves faithful to the Great King; and so, having left them all the moneys he had with him, set off on his voyage home.

But Conon had a proposal to make:—If Pharnabazus would allow him to keep the fleet, he would undertake, in the first place, to support it free of expense from the islands; besides which, he would sail to his own country and help his fellow citizens the Athenians to rebuild their long walls and the fortifications round Piraeus. No heavier blow, he insisted, could well be inflicted on Lacedaemon. "In this way, I can assure you," he added, "you will win the eternal gratitude of the Athenians and wreak consummate vengeance on the Lacedaemonians, since at one stroke you will render null and void that on which they have bestowed their utmost labor." These arguments so far weighed with Pharnabazus that he despatched Conon to Athens with alacrity, and further supplied him with funds for the restoration of the walls. Thus it was that Conon, on his arrival at Athens, was able to rebuild a large portion of the walls—partly by lending his own crews, and partly by giving pay to carpenters and stone-masons, and meeting all the necessary expenses. There were other portions of the walls which the Athenians and Boeotians and other states raised as a joint voluntary undertaking.

Nor must it be forgotten that the Corinthians, with the funds left them by Pharnabazus, manned a fleet—the command of which they entrusted to their admiral Agathinus—and so were undisputed masters of the sea within the gulf round Achaia and Lechaeum.

393–391 BC. The Lacedaemonians, in opposition, fitted out a fleet under the command of Podanemus. That officer, in an attack of no great moment, lost his life, and Pollis,[1] his second in command, was presently in his turn obliged to retire, being wounded, whereupon Herippidas took command of the vessels. On the other hand, Proaenus the Corinthian, who had relieved Agathinus, evacuated Rhium, and the Lacedaemonians recovered that post.

---

1 See "Hell." I. i. 23.

Subsequently Teleutias succeeded to Herippidas's fleet, and it was then the turn of that admiral to dominate the gulf.[1]

392 BC. The Lacedaemonians were well informed of the proceedings of Conon. They knew that he was not only restoring the fortifications of Athens by help of the king's gold, but maintaining a fleet at his expense besides, and conciliating the islands and seaboard cities toward Athens. If, therefore, they could indoctrinate Tiribazus—who was a general of the king—with their sentiments, they believed they could not fail either to draw him aside to their own interests, or, at any rate, to put a stop to his feeding Conon's navy. With this intention they sent Antalcidas to Tiribazus:[2] his orders were to carry out this policy and, if possible, to arrange a peace between Lacedaemon and the king. The Athenians, getting wind of this, sent a counter-embassy, consisting of Hermogenes, Dion, Callisthenes, and Callimedon, with Conon himself. They at the same time invited the attendance of ambassadors from the allies, and there were also present representatives of the Boeotians, of Corinth, and of Argos. When they had arrived at their destination, Antalcidas explained to Tiribazus the object of his visit: he wished, if possible, to cement a peace between the state he represented and the king—a peace, moreover, exactly suited to the aspirations of the king himself; in other words, the Lacedaemonians gave up all claim to the Hellenic cities in Asia as against the king, while for their own part they were content that all the islands and other cities should be independent. "Such being our unbiased wishes," he continued, "for what earthly reason should (the Hellenes or) the king go to war with us? or why should he expend his money? The king is guaranteed against attack on the part of Hellas, since the Athenians are powerless apart from our hegemony, and we are powerless so long as the separate states are independent." The proposals of Antalcidas sounded very pleasantly in the ears of Tiribazus, but to the opponents of Sparta they were the merest talk. The Athenians were apprehensive of an agreement which provided for the independence of the cities in the islands, whereby they might be deprived of Lemnos, Imbros, and Scyros. The Thebans, again, were afraid of being compelled to let the Boeotian states go free. The Argives did not see how such treaty contracts and covenants were compatible with the realisation of their own

---

1 *According to Grote ("H. G." ix. 471, note 2), this section summarises the Lacedaemonian maritime operations in the Corinthian Gulf from the late autumn of 393 BC till the appointment of Teleutias in the spring or early summer of 391 BC, the year of the expedition of Agesilaus recounted above, "Hell." IV. iv. 19.*

2 *See Plut. "Ages." xxiii. (Clough, iv. p. 27); and for the date 392 BC (al. 393 BC) see Grote, "H. G." ix. 498.*

great object—the absorption of Corinth by Argos. And so it came to pass that this peace[1] proved abortive, and the representatives departed each to his own home.

Tiribazus, on his side, thought it hardly consistent with his own safety to adopt the cause of the Lacedaemonians without the concurrence of the king—a scruple which did not prevent him from privately presenting Antalcidas with a sum of money, in hopes that when the Athenians and their allies discovered that the Lacedaemonians had the wherewithal to furnish a fleet, they might perhaps be more disposed to desire peace. Further, accepting the statements of the Lacedaemonians as true, he took on himself to secure the person of Conon, as guilty of wrongdoing toward the king, and shut him up.[2] That done, he set off up country to the king to recount the proposals of Lacedaemon, with his own subsequent capture of Conon as a mischievous man, and to ask for further guidance on all these matters.

On the arrival of Tiribazus at the palace, the king sent down Struthas to take charge of the seaboard district. The latter, however, was a strong partisan of Athens and her allies, since he found it impossible to forget the long list of evils which the king's country had suffered at the hands of Agesilaus; so that the Lacedaemonians, contrasting the hostile disposition of the new satrap toward themselves with his friendliness to the Athenians, sent Thibron to deal with him by force of arms.

391 BC.[3] That general crossed over and established his base of operations in Ephesus and the towns in the plain of the Maeander—Priene, Leucophrys, and Achilleum—and proceeded to harry the king's territory, sparing neither live nor dead chattels. But as time went on, Struthas, who could not but note the disorderly, and indeed recklessly scornful manner in which the Lacedaemonian brought up his supports on each occasion, despatched a body of cavalry into the plain. Their orders were to gallop down and scour the plain, making a clean sweep[4] of all they could lay their hands on. Thibron, as it befell, had just finished breakfast, and was returning to the mess with Thersander the flute player. The latter was not only a good flute player, but, as affecting Lacedaemonian manners, laid claim to personal prowess. Struthas, then, seeing the disorderly advance of the supports and

---

1 See Andoc. "de Pace"; Jebb, "Attic Or." i. 83, 128 foll. Prof. Jebb assigns this speech to 390 BC rather than 391 BC. See also Grote, "H. G." ix. 499; Diod. xiv. 110.
2 See Diod. xiv. 85; and Corn. Nep. 5.
3 Al. 392 BC, al. 390 BC.
4 See "Hell." VII. i. 40; "Cyrop." I. iv. 17; III. iii. 23; "Anab." VI. iii. 3.

the paucity of the vanguard, appeared suddenly at the head of a large body of cavalry, all in orderly array. Thibron and Thersander were the first to be cut down, and when these had fallen the rest of the troops were easily turned. A mere chase ensued, in which man after man was felled to Earth, though a remnant contrived to escape into the friendly cities; still larger numbers owed their safety to their late discovery of the business on hand. Nor, indeed, was this the first time the Spartan commander had rushed to the field, without even issuing a general order. So ends the history of these events.

390 BC.[1] We pass on to the arrival at Lacedaemon of a party of Rhodian exiles expelled by the popular party. They insisted that it was not equitable to allow the Athenians to subjugate Rhodes and thus build up so vast a power. The Lacedaemonians were alive to the fact that the fate of Rhodes depended on which party in the state prevailed: if the democracy were to dominate, the whole island must fall into the hands of Athens; if the wealthier classes,[2] into their own. Accordingly they fitted out for them a fleet of eight vessels, and put Ecdicus in command of it as admiral.

At the same time they despatched another officer on board these vessels named Diphridas, on a separate mission. His orders were to cross over into Asia and to secure the states which had received Thibron. He was also to pick up the survivors of Thibron's army, and with these troops, aided by a second army which he would collect from any other quarter open to him, he was to prosecute the war against Struthas. Diphridas followed out his instructions, and among other achievements was fortunate enough to capture Tigranes,[3] the son-in-law of Struthas, with his wife, on their road to Sardis. The sum paid for their ransom was so large that he at once had the wherewithal to pay his mercenaries. Diphridas was no less attractive than his predecessor Thibron; but he was of a more orderly temperament, steadier, and incomparably more enterprising as a general; the secret of this superiority being that he was a man over whom the pleasures of the body exercised no sway. He became readily absorbed in the business before him—whatever he had to do he did it with a will.

Ecdicus having reached Cnidus, there learned that the democracy in Rhones were entirely masters of the situation. They were dominant by

---

1 Grote, "H. G." ix. 504; al. 391 BC.
2 Or, "the Lacedaemonians were not slow to perceive that the whole island of Rhodes was destined to fall either into the hands of Athens or of themselves, according as the democracy or the wealthier classes respectively dominated."
3 See "Anab." VII. viii. 9 for a similar exploit.

land and sea; indeed they possessed a fleet twice the size of his own. He was therefore content to keep quiet in Cnidus until the Lacedaemonians, perceiving that his force was too small to allow him to benefit their friends, determined to relieve him. With this view they ordered Teleutias to take the twelve ships which formed his squadron (at present in the gulf adjoining Achaia and Lechaeum),[1] and to feel his way round to Ecdicus: that officer he was to send home. For himself, he was to undertake personally to protect the interests of all who cared to be their friends, whilst injuring the enemy by every possible means.

So then Teleutias, having reached Samos, where he added some vessels to his fleet, set sail to Cnidus. At this point Ecdicus returned home, and Teleutias, continuing his voyage, reached Rhodes, at the head now of seven-and-twenty vessels. It was during this portion of the voyage that he fell in with Philocrates, the son of Ephialtes, who was sailing from Athens to Cyprus with ten triremes, in aid of their ally Evagoras.[2] The whole flotilla fell into the Spartan's hands—a curious instance, it may be added, of cross purposes on the part of both belligerents. Here were the Athenians, supposed to be on friendly terms with the king, engaged in sending an allied force to support Evagoras, who was at open war with him; and here again was Teleutias, the representative of a people at war with Persia, engaged in crippling a fleet which had been despatched on a mission hostile to their adversary. Teleutias put back into Cnidus to dispose of his captives, and so eventually reached Rhodes, where his arrival brought timely aid to the party in favor of Lacedaemon.

389 BC.[3] And now the Athenians, fully impressed with the belief that their rivals were laying the basis of a new naval supremacy, despatched Thrasybulus the Steirian to check them, with a fleet of forty sail. That officer set sail, but abstained from bringing aid to Rhodes, and for good reasons. In Rhodes the Lacedaemonian party had hold of the fortress, and would be out of reach of his attack, especially as Teleutias was close at hand to aid them with his fleet. On the other hand, his own friends ran no danger of succumbing to the enemy, as they held the cities and were numerically much stronger, and they had established their superiority in the field. Consequently he made for the Hellespont, where, in the absence of any rival power, he hoped to achieve some stroke of good fortune

---

1 See above, IV. viii. 11.
2 See Diod. xiv. 98; Hicks, 72; Kohler, "C. I. A." ii. p. 397; Isoc. "Evag." 54–57; Paus. I. iii. 1; Lys. "de bon. Ar." 20; Dem. p. 161.
3 Grote, "H. G." ix. 507.

for his city. Thus, in the first place, having detected the rivalries existing between Medocus,[1] the king of the Odrysians, and Seuthes,[2] the rival ruler of the seaboard, he reconciled them to each other, and made them friends and allies of Athens; in the belief that if he secured their friendship the Hellenic cities on the Thracian coast would show greater proclivity to Athens. Such being the happy state of affairs not only in Europe but as regards the states in Asia also, thanks to the friendly attitude of the king to his fellow citizens, he sailed into Byzantium and sold the tithe-duty levied on vessels arriving from the Euxine. By another stroke he converted the oligarchy of Byzantium into a democracy. The result of this was that the Byzantine demos[3] were no longer sorry to see as vast a concourse of Athenians in their city as possible. Having so done, and having further won the friendship of the men of Calchedon, he set sail south of the Hellespont. Arrived at Lesbos, he found all the cities devoted to Lacedaemon with the exception of Mytilene. He was therefore loth to attack any of the former until he had organized a force within the latter. This force consisted of four hundred hoplites, furnished from his own vessels, and a corps of exiles from the different cities who had sought shelter in Mytilene; to which he added a stout contingent, the pick of the Mytileneian citizens themselves. He stirred the ardour of the several contingents by suitable appeals: representing to the men of Mytilene that by their capture of the cities they would at once become the chiefs and patrons of Lesbos; to the exiles he made it appear that if they would but unite to attack each several city in turn, they might all reckon on their particular restoration; while he needed only to remind his own warriors that the acquisition of Lesbos meant not only the attachment of a friendly city, but the discovery of a mine of wealth. The exhortations ended and the contingents organized, he advanced against Methymna.

Therimachus, who chanced to be the Lacedaemonian governor at the time, on hearing of the meditated attack of Thrasybulus, had taken a body of marines from his vessels, and, aided by the citizens of Methymna themselves, along with all the Mytileneian exiles to be found in that place, advanced to meet the enemy on their borders. A battle was fought and Therimachus was slain, a fate shared by several of the exiles of his party.

---

1 Al. Amedocus.
2 For Seuthes, see above, "Hell." III. ii. 2, if the same.
3 For the varying fortunes of the democrats at Byzantium in 408 BC and 405 BC, see above, ("Hell." I. iii. 18; II. ii. 2); for the present moment, 390–389 BC, see Demosth. "c. Lept." 475; for the admission of Byzantium into the new naval confederacy in 378 BC, see Hicks, 68; Kohler, "C. I. A." ii. 19; and for 363 BC, Isocr. "Phil." 53; Diod. xv. 79; and for its commercial prosperity, Polyb. iv. 38-47.

As a result[1] of his victory the Athenian general succeeded in winning the adhesion of some of the states; or, where adhesion was refused, he could at least raise supplies for his soldiers by freebooting expeditions, and so hastened to reach his goal, which was the island of Rhodes. His chief concern was to support as powerful an army as possible in those parts, and with this object he proceeded to levy money aids, visiting various cities, until he finally reached Aspendus, and came to moorings in the river Eurymedon. The money was safely collected from the Aspendians, and the work completed, when, taking occasion of some depredations[2] of the soldiers on the farmsteads, the people of the place in a fit of irritation burst into the general's quarters at night and butchered him in his tent.

So perished Thrasybulus,[3] a good and great man by all admission. In room of him the Athenians chose Agyrrhius,[4] who was despatched to take command of the fleet. And now the Lacedaemonians—alive to the fact that the sale of the Euxine tithe-dues had been negotiated in Byzantium by Athens; aware also that as long as the Athenians kept hold on Calchedon the loyalty of the other Hellespontine cities was secured to them (at any rate while Pharnabazus remained their friend)—felt that the state of affairs demanded their serious attention. They attached no blame indeed to Dercylidas. Anaxibius, however, through the friendship of the ephors, contrived to get himself appointed as governor, on a mission to Abydos. With the requisite funds and ships, he promised to exert such hostile pressure upon Athens that at least her prospects in the Hellespont would cease to be so sunny. His friends the ephors granted him in return for these promises three ships of war and funds to support a thousand mercenaries, and so they despatched him on his mission. Reaching Abydos, he set about improving his naval and military position. First he collected a foreign brigade, by help of which he drew off some of the Aeolid cities from Pharnabazus. Next he set on foot a series of retaliatory expeditions against the states which attacked Abydos, marching upon them and ravaging their territories; and lastly, manning three vessels besides those which he already held in the harbor of Abydos, he intercepted and brought into port all the merchant ships of Athens or of her allies which he could lay hands on.

---

1 *According to some critics, 389 BC is only now reached.*
2 *See Diod. xiv. 94.*
3 *"Thus perished the citizen to whom, more than anyone else, Athens owed not only her renovated democracy, but its wise, generous, and harmonious working, after renovation."—Grote, "H. G." ix. 509.*
4 *For this statesman, see Demosth. "c. Timocr." 742; Andoc. "de Myst." 133; Aristot. "Ath. Pol." 41, and Mr. Kenyon's notes ad loc.; Aristoph. "Eccles." 102, and the Schol. ad loc.; Diod. xiv. 99; Curtius, "H. G." Eng tr. iv. 280.*

Getting wind of these proceedings, the Athenians, fearing lest the fair foundation laid for them by Thrasybulus in the Hellespont should be ruined, sent out Iphicrates with eight vessels and twelve hundred peltasts. The majority of them[1] consisted of troops which he had commanded at Corinth. In explanation it may be stated that the Argives, when once they had appropriated Corinth and incorporated it with Argos, gave out they had no further need of Iphicrates and his troops; the real fact being that he had put to death some of the partisans of Argos.[2] And so it was he turned his back on Corinth and found himself at home in Athens at the present crisis.

389–388 BC. When Iphicrates first reached the Chersonese he and Anaxibius carried on war against each other by the despatch of guerilla or piratic bands across the straits. But as time wore on, information reached him of the departure of Anaxibius to Antandrus, accompanied by his mercenaries and his own bodyguard of Laconians and two hundred Abydenian hoplites. Hearing further that Anaxibius had won the friendly adhesion of Antandrus, Iphicrates conjectured that after establishing a garrison in that place he would make the best of his way back, if only to bring the Abydenians home again. He therefore crossed in the night, selecting a desert point on the Abydene coast, from which he scaled the hills above the town and planted himself in ambuscade within their folds. The triremes which brought him across had orders at break of day to coast up northwards along the Chersonese, which would suggest the notion that he was only out on one of his customary voyages to collect money. The sequel more than fulfilled his expectations. Anaxibius began his return march, and if report speaks truly, he did so notwithstanding that the victims were against his marching that day; contemptuously disregarding the warning, and satisfied that his march lay all along through a friendly country and was directed to a friendly city. Besides which, those whom he met assured him that Iphicrates was off on a voyage to Proconnesus: hence the unusual absence of precaution on the march. On his side Iphicrates saw the chance, but, so long as the troops of Anaxibius lingered on the level bottoms, refused to spring from his lair, waiting for the moment when the Abydenian division in the van was safely landed in the plain of Cremaste, at the point where the gold mines stand; the main column following on the downward slope, and Anaxibius with his Laconians just beginning the

---

1 Or, "The mass of them."
2 See Grote, "H. G." ix. p. 491 note. The "Argolising" or philo-Argeian party, as opposed to the philo-Laconian party. See above, "Hell." IV. iv. 6.

descent. At that instant Iphicrates set his ambuscade in motion, and dashed against the Spartan at full speed. The latter quickly discerned that there was no hope of escape as he scanned the long straggling line of his attenuated column. The troops in advance, he was persuaded, would never be able to come back to his aid up the face of that acclivity; besides which, he observed the utter bewilderment of the whole body at sight of the ambuscade. He therefore turned to those next him, and spoke as follows: "Sirs, it is good for me to die on this spot, where honor bids me; but for you, sirs, yonder your path lies, haste and save yourselves[1] before the enemy can close with us." As the words died on his lips he took from the hands of his attendant shield-bearer his heavy shield, and there, at his post, unflinchingly fought and fell; not quite alone, for by his side faithfully lingered a favorite youth, and of the Lacedaemonian governors who had rallied to Abydos from their several cities yet other twelve fought and fell beside the pair. The rest fled, dropping down one by one as the army pursued them to the walls of the city. The death-roll amounted to something like fifty hoplites of the Abydenians, and of the rest two hundred. After this exploit Iphicrates returned to the Chersonese.[2]

BOOK V

I

388 BC. Such was the state of affairs in the Hellespont, so far at least as Athens and Sparta are concerned. Eteonicus was once more in Aegina; and notwithstanding that the Aeginetans and Athenians had up to this time held commercial intercourse, yet now that the war was plainly to be fought out on the sea, that officer, with the concurrence of the ephorate, gave permission to anyone who liked to plunder Attica.[3] The Athenians retaliated by despatching a body of hoplites under their general Pamphilus, who constructed a fort against the Aeginetans,[4] and proceeded to blockade them by land and sea with ten warships. Teleutias, however, while threading his way among the islands in question of contributions, had chanced to reach a point where he received information of the turn in affairs with

---

1 Or, "sauve qui peut."
2 See Hicks, 76; and below, "Hell." V. i. 31.
3 Or, "determined to let slip the hounds of war"; or, more prosaically, "issued letters of marque." See Grote, "H. G." ix. 517.
4 I.e. in Aegina as an {epiteikhisma}.

regard to the construction of the fortress, whereupon he came to the rescue of the beleaguered Aeginetans, and so far succeeded that he drove off the enemy's blockading squadron. But Pamphilus kept a firm hold on the offensive fortress, and was not to be dislodged.

After this the new admiral Hierax arrived from Lacedaemon. The naval force was transferred into his successor's hands, and under the happiest auspices Teleutias set sail for home. As he descended to the seashore to start on his homeward voyage there was not one among his soldiers who had not a warm shake of the hand for their old admiral. Here one presented him with a crown, and there another with a victor's wreath; and those who arrived too late, still, as the ship weighed anchor, threw garlands into the sea and wafted him many a blessing with prayerful lips. I am well aware that in the above incident I have no memorable story of munificence, peril, or invention to narrate, but in all sincerity I protest that a man may find food for reflection in the inquiry what Teleutias had done to create such a disposition in his subordinates. Here we are brought face to face with a true man's work more worthy of account than multitudes of riches or adventure.[1]

The new admiral Hierax, taking with him the larger portion of the fleet, set sail once more for Rhodes. He left behind him twelve vessels in Aegina under his vice-admiral Gorgopas, who was now installed as governor of that island. In consequence of this chance the Athenian troops inside the fortres were more blockaded than the Aeginetans themselves, so much so that a vote was passed by the Athenian assembly, in obedience to which a large fleet was manned, and the garrison, after four months" sojourn in Aegina, were brought back. But this was no sooner done than they began to be harassed by Gorgopas and the privateers again. To operate aganst these they fitted out thirteen vessels, choosing Eunomus as admiral in command. Hierax was still in Rhodes when the Lacedaemonians sent out a new admiral, Antalcidas; they believed that they could not find a better mode of gratifying Tiribazus. Accordingly Antalcidas, after visiting Aegina in order to pick up the vessels under Gorgopas, set sail for Ephesus. At this point he sent back Gorgopas with his twelve ships to Aegina, and appointed his vice-admiral Nicolochus to command the remainder of the fleet.

Nicolochus was to relieve Abydos, and thither set sail; but in the course

---

1 See Grote, "H. G." ix. 518: "The ideal of government as it presented itself to Xenophon was the paternal despotism or something like it," {to ethelonton arkhein}. Cf. "Cyrop." passim, "Heiro," and his various other compositions.

of the voyage turned aside to Tenedos, where he ravaged the territory, and, with the money so secured, sailed on to Abydos. The Athenian generals[1] on their side, collecting from Samothrace, Thasos, and the fortresses in that quarter, hastened to the relief of Tenedos; but, finding that Nicolochus had continued his voyage to Abydos, they selected the Chersonese as their base, and proceeded to blockade him and his fleet of five-and-twenty vessels with the two-and-thirty vessels under their joint command.

Meanwhile Gorgopas, returning from Ephesus, fell in with the Athenian admiral Eunomus, and, shunning an encounter at the moment, sought shelter in Aegina, which he reached a little before sunset; and at once disembarking his men, set them down to their evening meal; whilst Eunomus on his side, after hanging back for a little while, sailed away. Night fell, and the Athenian, showing the customary signal light to prevent his squadron straggling, led the way in the darkness. Gorgopas instantly got his men on board again, and, taking the lantern for his guide, followed the Athenians, craftily lagging behind a little space, so as not to show himself or raise any suspicion of his presence. In place of the usual cry of the boatswains timed the rowers by a clink of stones, and silently the oars slid, feathering through the waves[2]; and just when the squadron of Eunomus was touching the coast, off Cape Zoster[3] in Attica, the Spartan sounded the bugle-note for the charge. Some of Eunomus's vessels were in the act of discharging their crews, others were still getting to their moorings, whilst others were as yet only bearing down to land. The engagement was fought by the light of the moon, and Gorgopas captured four triremes, which he tied astern, and so set sail with his prizes in tow toward Aegina. The rest of the Athenian squadron made their escape into the harbor of Piraeus.

It was after these events that Chabrias[4] commenced his voyage to Cyprus, bringing relief to Evagoras. His force consisted at first of eight hundred light troops and ten triremes, but was further increased by other vessels from Athens and a body of heavy infantry. Thus reinforced, the admiral chose a night and landed in Aegina; and secreted himself in ambuscade with his light troops in hollow ground some way beyond the temple of Heracles. At break of day, as prearranged, the Athenian hoplites made their appearance under command of Demaenetus, and began mounting up

---

1 And among the rest Iphicrates and Diotimus. See below, S. 25; above, IV. viii. 39.
2 Lit. "the boatswains employing a clink of stones and a sliding motion of the oars."
3 I.e. "Cape Girdle," mod. Cape Karvura. See Tozer, "Geog. of Greece," pp. 78, 372.
4 According to Diod. xiv. 92, Chabrias had been for some time in Corinth. See also above, IV. viii. 24.

between two and three miles[1] beyond the Kerakleion at Tripurgia, as it is called. The news soon reached Gorgopas, who sallied out to the rescue with the Aeginetans and the marines of his vessels, being further accompanied by eight Spartans who happened to be with him. Not content with these he issued orders inviting any of the ships' crews, who were free men, to join the relief party. A large number of these sailors responded. They armed themselves as best they could, and the advance commenced. When the vanguard were well past the ambuscade, Chabrias and his men sprang up from their hiding-place, and poured a volley of javelins and stones upon the enemy. At the same moment the hoplites, who had disembarked,[2] were advancing, so that the Spartan vanguard, in the absence of anything like collective action, were speedily cut down, and among them fell Gorgopas with the Lacedaemonians. At their fall the rest of course turned and fled. One hundred and fifty Aeginetans were numbered among the slain, while the loss incurred by the foreigners, metics, and sailors who had joined the relief party, reached a total of two hundred. After this the Athenians sailed the sea as freely as in the times of actual peace. Nor would anything induce the sailors to row a single stroke for Eteonicus—even under pressure—since he had no pay to give.

Subsequently the Lacedaemonians despatched Teleutias once again to take command of the squadron, and when the sailors saw it was he who had come, they were overjoyed. He summoned a meeting and addressed them thus: "Soldiers, I am back again, but I bring with me no money. Yet if God be willing, and your zeal flag not, I will endeavor to supply you with provisions without stint. Be well assured, as often as I find myself in command of you, I have but one prayer—that your lives may be spared no less than mine; and as for the necessaries of existence, perhaps it would astonish you if I said I would rather you should have them than I. Yet by the gods I swear I would welcome two days' starvation in order to spare you one. Was not my door open in old days to every comer? Open again it shall stand now; and so it shall be; where your own board overflows, you shall look in and mark the luxury of your general; but if at other times you see him bearing up against cold and heat and sleepless nights, you must apply the lesson to yourselves and study to endure those evils. I do not bid you do aught of this for self-mortification's sake, but that you may derive some after-blessing from it. Soldiers, let Lacedaemon, our own mother-city, be to you an example. Her good fortune is reputed to stand high. That you

---

1 Lit. *"about sixteen stades."*
2 Or, reading {oi anabebekotes}, *"who had scaled the height."* See Hartman, *"Anal. Xen."* p. 364.

know; and you know too, that she purchased her glory and her greatness not by faint-heartedness, but by choosing to suffer pain and incur dangers in the day of need. 'Like city,' I say, 'like citizens.' You, too, as I can bear you witness, have been in times past brave; but today must we strive to be better than ourselves. So shall we share our pains without repining, and when fortune smiles, mingle our joys; for indeed the sweetest thing of all surely is to flatter no man, Hellene or Barbarian, for the sake of hire; we will suffice to ourselves, and from a source to which honor pre-eminently invites us; since, I need not remind you, abundance won from the enemy in war furnishes forth not bodily nutrition only, but a feast of glory the wide world over."

So he spoke, and with one voice they all shouted to him to issue what orders he thought fit; they would not fail him in willing service. The general's sacrifice was just concluded, and he answered: "Good, then, my men; go now, as doubtless you were minded, and take your evening meal, and next provide yourselves, please, with one day's food. After that repair to your ships without delay, for we have a voyage on hand, whither God wills, and must arrive in time." So then, when the men returned, he embarked them on their ships, and sailed under cover of night for the great harbor of Piraeus: at one time he gave the rowers rest, passing the order to take a snatch of sleep; at another he pushed forward toward his goal with rise and fall of oars. If anyone supposes that there was a touch of madness in such an expedition—with but twelve triremes to attack an enemy possessed of a large fleet—he should consider the calculations of Teleutias. He was under the firm persuasion that the Athenians were more careless than ever about their navy in the harbor since the death of Gorgopas; and in case of finding warships riding at anchor—even so, there was less danger, he conjectured, in attacking twenty ships in the port of Athens than ten elsewhere; for, whereas, anywhere outside the harbor the sailors would certainly be quartered on board, at Athens it was easy to divine that the captains and officers would be sleeping at their homes, and the crews located here and there in different quarters.

This minded he set sail, and when he was five or six furlongs[1] distant from the harbor he lay on his oars and rested. But with the first streak of dawn he led the way, the rest following. The admiral's orders to the crews were explicit. They were on no account to sink any merchant vessel; they were equally to avoid damaging[2] their own vessels, but if at any point they

---

1 Lit. "five or six stades."
2 See Hartman, "Anal. Xen." pp. 365, 366.

espied a warship at her moorings they must try and cripple her. The trading vessels, provided they had got their cargoes on board, they must seize and tow out of the harbor; those of larger tonnage they were to board wherever they could and capture the crews. Some of his men actually jumped on to the Deigma quay,[1] where they seized hold of various traders and pilots and deposited them bodily on board ship. So the Spartan admiral carried out his program.

As to the Athenians, meanwhile, some of them who got wind of what was happening rushed from indoors outside to see what the commotion meant, others from the streets home to get their arms, and others again were off to the city with the news. The whole of Athens rallied to the rescue at that instant, heavy infantry and cavalry alike, the apprehension being that Piraeus was taken. But the Spartan sent off the captured vessels to Aegina, telling off three or four of his triremes to convoy them thither; with the rest he followed along the coast of Attica, and emerging in seemingly innocent fashion from the harbor, captured a number of fishing smacks, and passage boats laden with passengers crossing to Piraeus from the islands; and finally, on reaching Sunium he captured some merchantmen laden with corn or other merchandise. After these performances he sailed back to Aegina, where he sold his prizes, and with the proceeds was able to provide his troops with a month's pay, and for the future was free to cruise about and make what reprisals chance cast in his way. By such a procedure he was able to support a full quota of mariners on board his squadron, and procured to himself the prompt and enthusiastic service of his troops.

388–387 BC. Antalcidas had now returned from the Persian court with Tiribazus. The negotiations had been successful. He had secured the alliance of the Persian king and his military cooperation in case the Athenians and their allies refused to abide by the peace which the king dictated. But learning that his second in command, Nicolochus, was being blockaded with his fleet by Iphicrates and Diotimus[2] in Abydos, he set off at once by land for that city. Being come thither he took the fleet one night and put out to sea, having first spread a story that he had invitations from a party in Calchedon; but as a matter of fact he came to anchorage in Percote and there kept quiet. Meanwhile the Athenian forces under Demaenetus and Dionysius and Leontichus and Phanias had got wind of his movement, and were in hot pursuit toward Proconnesus. As soon as they were well past,

---

1 See Grote ("H. G." ix. 523): cf. Thuc. ii. 94, the attempt of Brasidas on the port of Megara. For the wealth of Piraeus, Grote "H. G." ix. 351. See below, "Pol. Ath." i. 17; "Rev." iii. 13.
2 See above; Lysias, "de bon. Arist." (Jebb, "Att. Or." i. p. 327).

the Spartan veered round and returned to Abydos, trusting to information brought him of the approach of Polyxenus with the Syracusan[1] and Italian squadron of twenty ships, which he wished to pick up and incorporate with his own.

A little later the Athenian Thrasybulus[2] (of Collytus) was making his way up with eight ships from Thrace, his object being to effect a junction with the main Athenian squadron. The scouts signalled the approach of eight triremes, whereupon Antalcidas, embarking his marines on board twelve of the fastest sailers of his fleet, ordered them to make up their full complements, where defective, from the remaining vessels; and so lay to, skulking in his lair with all possible secrecy. As soon as the enemy's vessels came sailing past he gave chase; and they catching sight of him took to flight. With his swiftest sailors he speedily overhauled their laggards, and ordering his vanguard to let these alone, he followed hard on those ahead. But when the foremost had fallen into his clutches, the enemy's hinder vessels, seeing their leaders taken one by one, out of sheer despondency fell an easy prey to the slower sailors of the foe, so that not one of the eight vessels escaped.

Presently the Syracusan squadron of twenty vessels joined him, and again another squadron from Ionia, or rather so much of that district as lay under the control of Tiribazus. The full quota of the contingent was further made up from the territory of Ariobarzanes (which whom Antalcidas kept up a friendship of long standing), in the absence of Pharnabazus, who by this date had already been summoned up country on the occasion of his marriage with the king's daughter. With this fleet, which, from whatever sources derived, amounted to more than eighty sail, Antalcidas ruled the seas, and was in a position not only to cut off the passage of vessels bound to Athens from the Euxine, but to convoy them into the harbors of Sparta's allies.

The Athenians could not but watch with alarm the growth of the enemy's fleet, and began to fear a repetition of their former discomfiture. To be trampled under foot by the hostile power seemed indeed no remote possibility, now that the Lacedaemonians had procured an ally in the person of the Persian monarch, and they were in little less than a state of siege themselves, pestered as they were by privateers from Aegina. On

---

1 *See below, VI. ii. 4 foll; Hicks, 71, 84, 88.*
2 *His name occurs on the famous stele of the new Athenian confederacy, 378 BC. See Hicks, 81; Kohler, "C. I. A." ii. 17; Demos. "de. Cor." p. 301; Arist. "Rhet." ii. 23; Demos. "c. Timocr." 742.*

all these grounds the Athenians became passionately desirous of peace.[1] The Lacedaemonians were equally out of humor with the war for various reasons—what with their garrison duties, one mora at Lechaeum and another at Orchomenus, and the necessity of keeping watch and ward on the states, if loyal not to lose them, if disaffected to prevent their revolt; not to mention that reciprocity of annoyance[2] of which Corinth was the center. So again the Argives had a strong appetite for peace; they knew that the ban had been called out against them, and, it was plain, that no fictitious alteration of the calendar would any longer stand them in good stead. Hence, when Tiribazus issued a summons calling on all who were willing to listen to the terms of peace sent down by the king[3] to present themselves, the invitation was promptly accepted. At the opening of the conclave[4] Tiribazus pointed to the king's seal attached to the document, and proceeded to read the contents, which ran as follows:

"The king, Artaxerxes, deems it just that the cities in Asia, with the islands of Clazomenae and Cyprus, should belong to himself; the rest of the Hellenic cities he thinks it just to leave independent, both small and great, with the exception of Lemnos, Imbros, and Scyros, which three are to belong to Athens as of yore. Should any of the parties concerned not accept this peace, I, Artaxerxes, will war against him or them with those who share my views. This will I do by land and by sea, with ships and with money."

After listening to the above declaration the ambassadors from the several states proceeded to report the same to their respective governments. One and all of these took the oaths[5] to ratify and confirm the terms unreservedly, with the exception of the Thebans, who claimed to take the oaths in behalf of all Boeotians. This claim Agesilaus repudiated: unless they chose to take the oaths in precise conformity with the words of the king's edict, which insisted on "the future autonomy of each state, small or great," he would not admit them. To this the Theban ambassadors made no other reply, except that the instructions they had received were different. "Pray go, then," Agesilaus retorted, "and ask the question; and you may inform your countrymen that if they will not comply, they will be excluded from the treaty." The Theban ambassadors departed, but Agesilaus, out

---

1 See, at this point, Grote on the financial condition of Athens and the "Theorikon," "H. G." ix. 525.
2 Or, "that give-and-take of hard knocks."
3 See Hicks, 76.
4 At Sardis, doubtless.
5 At Sparta, doubtless.

of hatred to the Thebans, took active measures at once. Having got the consent of the ephors he forthwith offered sacrifice. The offerings for crossing the frontier were propitious, and he pushed on to Tegea. From Tegea he despatched some of the knights right and left to visit the perioeci and hasten their mobilisation, and at the same time sent commanders of foreign brigades to the allied cities on a similar errand. But before he had started from Tegea the answer from Thebes arrived; the point was yielded, they would suffer the states to be independent. Under these circumstances the Lacedaemonians returned home, and the Thebans were forced to accept the truce unconditionally, and to recognize the autonomy of the Boeotian cities.[1] But now the Corinthians were by no means disposed to part with the garrison of the Argives. Accordingly Agesilaus had a word of warning for both. To the former he said, "if they did not forthwith dismiss the Argives," and to the latter, "if they did not instantly quit Corinth," he would march an army into their territories. The terror of both was so great that the Argives marched out of Corinth, and Corinth was once again left to herself;[2] whereupon the "butchers"[3] and their accomplices in the deed of blood determined to retire from Corinth, and the rest of the citizens welcomed back their late exiles voluntarily.

Now that the transactions were complete, and the states were bound by their oaths to abide by the peace sent down to them by the king, the immediate result was a general disarmament, military and naval forces being alike disbanded; and so it was that the Lacedaemonians and Athenians, with their allies, found themselves in the enjoyment of peace for the first time since the period of hostilities subsequent to the demolition of the walls of Athens. From a condition which, during the war, can only be described as a sort of even balance with their antagonists, the Lacedaemonians now emerged; and reached a pinnacle of glory consequent upon the Peace of Antalcidas,[4] so called. As guarantors of the peace presented by Hellas to the king, and as administrators personally of the autonomy of the states, they had added Corinth to their alliance; they had obtained the

---

1 See Freeman, op. cit. pp. 168, 169.
2 See "Ages." ii. 21; Grote, "H. G." ix. 537.
3 {oi sphageis}, a party catchword (in reference to the incidents narrated above, "Hell." IV. iv. 2). See below, {ton bareon demagogon}, "Hell." V. ii. 7; {oi kedomenoi tes Peloponnesou}, "Hell." VII. v. 1; above, {oi sphageis}, "Hell." III. ii. 27, of the philo-Laconian oligarchs in Elis. See Dem. "c. Lept." 473.
4 Or, more correctly, the peace "under," or "at the date of," {ep "Antalkidou"}. See Grote, "H. G." x. 1, note 1.

independence of the states of Boeotia at the expense of Thebes,[1] which meant the gratification of an old ambition; and lastly, by calling out the ban in case the Argives refused to evacuate Corinth, they had put a stop to the appropriation of that city by the Argives.

II

386 BC. Indeed the late events had so entirely shaped themselves in conformity with the wishes of the Lacedaemonians, that they determined to go a step farther and chastise those of their allies who either had borne hard on them during the war, or otherwise had shown themselves less favorable to Lacedaemon than to her enemies.[2] Chastisement was not all; they must lay down such secure foundations for the future as should render the like disloyalty impossible again.[3] As the first step toward this policy they sent a dictatorial message to the Mantinaeans, and bade them raze their fortifications, on the sole ground that they could not otherwise trust them not to side with their enemies. Many things in their conduct, they alleged, from time to time, had not escaped their notice: their frequent despatches of corn to the Argives while at war with Lacedaemon; at other times their refusal to furnish contingents during a campaign, on the pretext of some holy truce or other;[4] or if they did reluctantly take the field—the miserable inefficiency of their service. "But, more than that," they added, "we note the jealousy with which you eye any good fortune which may betide our state; the extravagant pleasure[5] you exhibit at the sudden descent of some disaster."

This very year, moreover, it was commonly said,[6] saw the expiration, as

---

1 Or, "they had made the states of Boeotia independent of Thebes." See Grote, "H. G." x. 44.
2 See Hartman, "An. Xen." p. 367 foll.; Busolt, "Die Lak." p. 129 foll.
3 Or, "they determined to chastise... and reduce to such order that disloyalty should be impossible."
4 See above, "Hell." IV. ii. 16.
5 Ib. IV. v. 18.

6 As to this point, see Curtius, "H. G." V. v. (iv. 305 note, Eng. trans.) There appears to be some confusion. According to Thuc. v. 81, "When the Argives deserted the alliance (with Mantinea, Athens, and Elis, making a new treaty of alliance with Lacedaemon for fifty years) the Mantineans held out for a time, but without the Argives they were helpless, and so they came to terms with the Lacedaemonians, and gave up their claims to supremacy over the cities in Arcadia, which had been subject to them.... These changes were effected at the close of winter (418 BC) toward the approach of spring (417 BC), and so ended the fourteenth year of the war." Jowett. According to Diod. xv. 5, the Lacedaemonians attacked Mantinea within two years after the Peace of Antalcidas, apparently in 386 BC According to Thuc. v. 82, and "C. I. A. 50, in 417 BC Argos had reverted to her alliance with Athens, and an attempt to connect the city with the sea by long walls was made, certain other states in Peloponnese being privy to the project" (Thuc. v. 83)—an attempt frustrated by Lacedaemon early in 416 BC. Is it possible that a treaty of alliance between Mantinea and Lacedaemon for thirty years was formally signed in 416 BC?

far as the Mantineans were concerned, of the thirty years' truce, consequent upon the battle of Mantinea. On their refusal, therefore, to raze their fortification walls the ban was called out against them. Agesilaus begged the state to absolve him from the conduct of this war on the plea that the city of Mantinea had done frequent service to his father[1] in his Messenian wars. Accordingly Agesipolis led the expedition—in spite of the cordial relations of his father Pausanias[2] with the leaders of the popular party in Mantinea.

385 BC. The first move of the invader was to subject the enemy's territory to devastation; but failing by such means to induce them to raze their walls, he proceeded to draw lines of circumvallation round the city, keeping half his troops under arms to screen the entrenching parties whilst the other half pushed on the work with the spade. As soon as the trench was completed, he experienced no further difficulty in building a wall round the city. Aware, however, of the existence of a huge supply of corn inside the town, the result of the bountiful harvest of the preceding year, and averse to the notion of wearing out the city of Lacedaemon and her allies by tedious campaigning, he hit upon the expedient of damming up the river which flowed through the town.

It was a stream of no inconsiderable size.[3] By erecting a barrier at its exit from the town he caused the water to rise above the basements of the private dwellings and the foundations of the fortification walls. Then, as the lower layers of bricks became saturated and refused their support to the rows above, the wall began to crack and soon to totter to its fall. The citizens for some time tried to prop it with pieces of timber, and used other devices to avert the imminent ruin of their tower; but finding themselves overmatched by the water, and in dread lest the fall at some point or other of the circular wall[4] might deliver them captive to the spear of the enemy, they signified their consent to raze their walls. But the Lacedaemonians now steadily refused any form of truce, except on the further condition that the Mantineans would suffer themselves to be broken up and distributed into villages. They, looking the necessity in the face, consented to do even that. The sympathisers with Argos among them, and the leaders of their democracy, thought their fate was sealed. Then the father treated with the

---

1 I.e. Archidamus.
2 See above, "Hell." III. v. 25.
3 I.e. the Ophis. See Leake, "Morea," III. xxiv. p. 71; Pausan. "Arcad." 8; Grote, "H. G." x. 48, note 2.
4 Or, "in the circuit of the wall."

son, Pausanias with Agesipolis, on their behalf, and obtained immunity for them—sixty in number—on condition that they should quit the city. The Lacedaemonian troops stood lining the road on both sides, beginning from the gates, and watched the outgoers; and with their spears in their hands, in spite of bitter hatred, kept aloof from them with less difficulty than the Mantineans of the better classes themselves—a weighty testimony to the power of Spartan discipline, be it said. In conclusion, the wall was razed, and Mantinea split up into four parts,[1] assuming once again its primitive condition as regards inhabitants. The first feeling was one of annoyance at the necessity of pulling down their present houses and erecting others, yet when the owners[2] found themselves located so much nearer their estates round about the villages, in the full enjoyment of aristocracy, and rid forever of "those troublesome demagogues," they were delighted with the turn which affairs had taken. It became the custom for Sparta to send them, not one commander of contingents,[3] but four, one for each village; and the zeal displayed, now that the quotas for military service were furnished from the several village centers, was far greater than it had been under the democratic system. So the transactions in connection with Mantinea were brought to a conclusion, and thereby one lesson of wisdom was taught mankind—not to conduct a river through a fortress town.

384–383 BC. To pass on. The party in exile from Phlius, seeing the severe scrutiny to which the behavior of the allies of Lacedaemon during the late war was being subjected, felt that their opportunity had come. They repaired to Lacedaemon, and laid great emphasis on the fact that, so long as they had been in power themselves at home, "their city used to welcome Lacedaemonians within her walls, and her citizens flocked to the campaign under their leadership; but no sooner had they been driven into exile than a change had come. The men of Phlius now flatly refused to follow Lacedaemon anywhere; the Lacedaemonians, alone of all men living, must not be admitted within their gates." After listening to their story, the ephors agreed that the matter demanded attention. Then they sent to the state of Phlius a message to this effect; the Phliasian exiles were friends of Lacedaemon; nor did it appear that they owed their exile to any misdoing. Under the circumstances, Lacedaemon claimed their recall from

---

1 See Diod. xv. 5; Strab. viii. 337; Ephor. fr. 138, ed. Did.; and Grote, "H. G." x. 51.
2 Or, "holders of properties." The historian is referring not to the population at large, I think, but to the rich landowners, i.e. the {Beltistoi}, and is not so partial as Grote supposes ("H. G." x. 51 foll.)
3 Technically {ʒenagoi}, Lacedaemonian officers who commanded the contingents of the several allies. See above, "Hell." III. v. 7; Thuc. ii. 76; and Arnold's note ad loc.; also C. R. Kennedy, "ap. Dict. of Greek and Roman Antiquities," s.v.; Muller, "Dorians," ii. 250, Eng. tr.; Busolt, "Die Lak." p. 125.

banishment, not by force, but as a concession voluntarily granted. When the matter was thus stated, the Phliasians were not without alarm that an army might much upon Phlius, and a party inside the town might admit the enemy within the walls; for within the walls of Phlius were to be found many who, either as blood relations or for other reasons, were partisans of the exiles, and as so often happens, at any rate in the majority of states, there was a revolutionary party who, in their ardour to reform, would welcome gladly their restoration. Owing to fears of this character, a formal decree was passed: to welcome home the exiles, and to restore to them all undisputed property, the purchasers of the same being indemnified from the treasury of the state; and in the event of any ambiguity or question arising between the parties, the same to be determined before a court of justice. Such was the position of affairs in connection with the Phliasian exiles at the date in question.

383 BC.[1] And now from yet another quarter ambassadors arrived at Lacedaemon: that is to say, from Acanthus and Apollonia, the two largest and most important states of the Olynthian confederacy. The ephorate, after learning from them the object of their visit, presented them to the assembly and the allies, in presence of whom Cleigenes of Acanthus made a speech to this effect:

"Men of Lacedaemon and of the allied states," he said, "are you aware of a silent but portentous growth within the bosom of Hellas?[2] Few here need to be told that for size and importance Olynthus now stands at the head of the Thracian cities. But are you aware that the citizens of Olynthus had already brought over several states by the bribe of joint citizenship and common laws; that they have forcibly annexed some of the larger states; and that, so encouraged, they have taken in hand further to free the cities of Macedonia from Amyntas the king of the Macedonians; that, as soon as their immediate neighbors had shown compliance, they at once proceeded to attack larger and more distant communities; so much so, that when we started to come hither, we left them masters not only of many other places, but of Pella itself, the capital of Macedonia. Amyntas,[3] we saw plainly, must ere long withdraw from his cities, and was in fact already all but in name an outcast from Macedonia.

"The Olynthians have actually sent to ourselves and to the men of Apollonia a joint embassy, warning us of their intention to attack us if we

---

1 Al. 382 BC.
2 Or, "are you aware of a new power growing up in Hellas?"
3 For Amyntas's reign, see Diod. xiv. 89, 92; xv. 19; Isocr. "Panegyr." 126, "Archid." 46.

refuse to present ourselves at Olynthus with a military contingent. Now, for our parts, men of Lacedaemon, we desire nothing better than to abide by our ancestral laws and institutions, to be free and independent citizens; but if aid from without is going to fail us, we too must follow the rest and coalesce with the Olynthians. Why, even now they muster no less than eight hundred[1] heavy infantry and a considerably larger body of light infantry, while their cavalry, when we have joined them, will exceed one thousand men. At the date of our departure we left embassies from Athens and Boeotia in Olynthus, and we were told that the Olynthians themselves had passed a formal resolution to return the compliment. They were to send an embassy on their side to the aforesaid states to treat of an alliance. And yet, if the power of the Athenians and the Thebans is to be further increased by such an accession of strength, look to it," the speaker added, "whether hereafter you will find things so easy to manage in that quarter.

"They hold Potidaea, the key to the isthmus of Pallene, and therefore, you can well believe, they can command the states within that peninsula. If you want any further proof of the abject terror of those states, you have it in the fact that notwithstanding the bitter hatred which they bear to Olynthus, not one of them has dared to send ambassadors along with us to apprise you of these matters.

"Reflect, how you can reconcile your anxiety to prevent the unification of Boeotia with your neglect to hinder the solidifying of a far larger power—a power destined, moreover, to become formidable not on land only, but by sea? For what is to stop it, when the soil itself supplies timber for shipbuilding,[2] and there are rich revenues derived from numerous harbors and commercial centers?—it cannot but be that abundance of food and abundance of population will go hand in hand. Nor have we yet reached the limits of Olynthian expansion; there are their neighbors to be thought of—the kingless or independent Thracians. These are already today the devoted servants of Olynthus, and when it comes to their being actually under her, that means at once another vast accession of strength to her. With the Thracians in her train, the gold mines of Pangaeus would stretch out to her the hand of welcome.

"In making these assertions, we are but uttering remarks ten thousand

---

1 See Grote, "H. G." x. 72; Thirlwall, "H. G." v. 12 (ch. xxxvii).

2 See Hicks, 74, for a treaty between Amyntas and the Chalcidians, 390–389 BC: "The article of the treaty between Amyntas III., father of Philip, and the Chalcidians, about timber, etc., reminds us that South Macedonia, the Chalcidic peninsula, and Amphipolis were the chief sources whence Athens derived timber for her dockyards." Thuc. iv. 108; Diod. xx. 46; Boeckh, "P. E. A." p. 250; and for a treaty between Athens and Amyntas, 382 BC, see Hicks, 77; Kohler, "C. I. A." ii. 397, 423.

times repeated in the democracy of Olynthus. And as to their confident spirit, who shall attempt to describe it? It is God, for aught I know, who, with the growth of a new capacity, gives increase also to the proud thoughts and vast designs of humanity. For ourselves, men of Lacedaemon and of the allied states, our task is completed. We have played our parts in announcing to you how things stand there. To you it is left to determine whether what we have described is worthy of your concern. One only thing further you ought to recognize: the power we have spoken of as great is not as yet invincible, for those states which are involuntary participants in the citizenship of Olynthus will, in prospect of any rival power appearing in the field, speedily fall away. On the contrary, let them be once closely knit and welded together by the privileges of intermarriage and reciprocal rights of holding property in land—which have already become enactments; let them discover that it is a gain to them to follow in the wake of conquerors (just as the Arcadians,[1] for instance, find it profitable to march in your ranks, whereby they save their own property and pillage their neighbors'); let these things come to pass, and perhaps you may find the knot no longer so easy to unloose."

At the conclusion of this address, the Lacedaemonians requested the allies to speak, bidding them give their joint advice as to the best course to be pursued in the interests of Peloponnese and the allies. Thereupon many members, and especially those who wished to gratify the Lacedaemonians, agreed in counseling active measures; and it was resolved that the states should severally send contingents to form a total of ten thousand men. Proposals were also made to allow any state, so wishing, to give money instead of men, at the rate of three Aeginetan obols[2] a day per man; or where the contingent consisted of cavalry, the pay given for one horseman was to be the equivalent to that of four hoplites; while, in the event of any defaulting in service, the Lacedaemonians should be allowed to mulct the said state of a stater per man per diem. These resolutions were passed, and the deputies from Acanthus rose again. They argued that, though excellent, these resolutions were not of a nature to be rapidly carried into effect. Would it not be better, they asked, pending the mobilisation of the troops, to despatch an officer at once in command of a force from Lacedaemon

---

1 *For the point of the comparison, see Freeman, "Hist. Fed. Gov." ch. iv. "Real nature of the Olynthian scheme," pp. 190 foll., and note 2, p. 197; also Grote, "H. G." x. 67 foll., 278 foll.*

2 *I.e. "rather more than sixpence a day for a hoplite, and two shillings for a horseman." "The Aeginetan stater weighed about 196 grains, rather more than two of our shillings, and was divided into two drachms of 98 grains, each of which contained six obols of about 16 grains each." See Percy Gardner, "Types of Greek Coins," "Hist. Int." p. 8; Jowett, note to Thuc. III. lxx. 4, vol. i. pp. 201, 202.*

and the other states, not too large to start immediately. The effect would be instantaneous, for the states which had not yet given in their adhesion to Olynthus would be brought to a standstill, and those already forcibly enrolled would be shaken in their alliance. These further resolutions being also passed, the Lacedaemonians despatched Eudamidas, accompanied by a body of neodamodes, with perioeci and Sciritae,[1] to the number of two thousand odd. Eudamidas lost no time in setting out, having obtained leave from the ephors for his brother Phoebidas to follow later with the remainder of the troops assigned to him. Pushing on himself to the Thracian territory, he set about despatching garrisons to various cities at their request. He also secured the voluntary adhesion of Potidaea, although already a member of the Olynthian alliance; and this town now served as his base of operations for carrying on war on a scale adapted to his somewhat limited armament.

Phoebidas, when the remaining portion of his brother's forces was duly mustered, put himself at their head and commenced his march. On reaching Thebes the troops encamped outside the city, round the gymnasium. Faction was rife within the city. The two polemarchs in office, Ismenias and Leontiades, were diametrically opposed,[2] being the respective heads of antagonistic political clubs. Hence it was that, while Ismenias, ever inspired by hatred to the Lacedaemonians, would not come anywhere near the Spartan general, Leontiades, on the other hand, was assiduous in courting him; and when a sufficient intimacy was established between them, he made a proposal as follows: "You have it in your power," he said, addressing Phoebidas, "this very day to confer supreme benefit on your country. Follow me with your hoplites, and I will introduce you into the citadel. That done, you may rest assured Thebes will be completely under the thumb of Lacedaemon and of us, your friends. At present, as you see, there is a proclamation forbidding any Theban to take service with you against Olynthus, but we will change all that. You have only to act with us as we suggest, and we shall at once be able to furnish you with large supplies of infantry and cavalry, so that you will join your brother with a magnificent reinforcement, and pending his proposed reduction of Olynthus, you will have accomplished the reduction of a far larger state than that—to wit, this city of Thebes."

The imagination of Phoebidas was kindled as he listened to the tempting

---

1 Or, "new citizens, provincials, and Sciritae."
2 See Grote, "H. G." vol. x. p. 80: "We have little or no information respecting the government of Thebes," etc. The "locus classicus" seems to be Plut. "de Genio Socratis." See Freeman, op. cit. ch. iv. S. 2, "Of the Boeotian League," pp. 154–184; and, in reference to the seizure of the Kadmeia, p. 170.

proposal. To do a brilliant deed was far dearer to him than life;[1] on the other hand, he had no reasoning capacity, and would seem to have been deficient altogether in sound sense. The consent of the Spartan secured, Leontiades bade him set his troops in motion, as if everything were ready for his departure. "And anon, when the hour is come," added the Theban, "I will be with you, and show you the way myself."

The senate was seated in the arcade or stoa in the marketplace, since the Cadmeia was in possession of the women who were celebrating the Thesmophoria.[2] It was noon of a hot summer's day; scarcely a soul was stirring in the streets. This was the moment for Leontiades. He mounted on horseback and galloped off to overtake Phoebidas. He turned him back, and led him without further delay into the acropolis. Having posted Phoebidas and his soldiers inside, he handed him the key of the gates, and warning him not to suffer anyone to enter into the citadel without a pass from himself, he straightway betook himself to the senate. Arrived there, he delivered himself thus: "Sirs, the Lacedaemonians are in possession of the citadel; but that is no cause for despondency, since, as they assure us, they have no hostile intention, except, indeed, toward anyone who has an appetite for war. For myself, and acting in obedience to the law, which empowers the polemarch to apprehend all persons suspected of capital crimes, I hereby seize the person of Ismenias as an arch-fomenter of war. I call upon you, sirs, who are captains of companies, and you who are ranked with them, to do your duty. Arise and secure the prisoner, and lead him away to the place appointed."

Those who were privy to the affair, it will be understood, presented themselves, and the orders were promptly carried out. Of those not in the secret, but opposed to the party of Leontiades, some sought refuge at once outside the city in terror for their lives; whilst the rest, albeit they retired to their houses at first, yet when they found that Ismenias was imprisoned in the Cadmeia, and further delay seemed dangerous, retreated to Athens. These were the men who shared the views of Androcleidas and Ismenias, and they must have numbered about three hundred.

Now that the transactions were concluded, another polemarch was chosen in place of Ismenias, and Leontiades at once set out to Lacedaemon. There he found the ephors and the mass of the community highly incensed against Phoebidas, "who had failed to execute the orders assigned to him by

---

1 Or, "Renown was his mistress." See Grote, "H. G." x. 84.
2 An ancient festival held by women in honor of Demeter and Persephone ({to Thesmophoro}), who gave the first impulse to civil society, lawful marriage, etc. See Herod. ii. 171; Diod. v. 5.

the state." Against this general indignation, however, Agesilaus protested.[1] If mischief had been wrought to Lacedaemon by this deed, it was just that the doer of it should be punished; but, if good, it was a time-honored custom to allow full scope for impromptu acts of this character. "The sole point you have to look to," he urged, "is whether what has been done is good or evil." After this, however, Leontiades presented himself to the assembly[2] and addressed the members as follows: "Sirs, Lacedaemonians, the hostile attitude of Thebes toward you, before the occurrence of late events, was a topic constantly on your lips, since time upon time your eyes were called upon to witness her friendly bearing to your foes in contrast with her hatred of your friends. Can it be denied that Thebes refused to take part with you in the campaign against your direst enemy, the democracy in Piraeus; and balanced that lukewarmness by on onslaught on the Phocians, whose sole crime was cordiality to yourselves?[3] Nor is that all. In full knowledge that you were likely to be engaged in war with Olynthus, she proceeded at once to make an alliance with that city. So that up to the last moment you were in constant expectation of hearing that the whole of Boeotia was laid at the feet of Thebes. With the late incidents all is changed. You need fear Thebes no longer. One brief despatch[4] in cipher will suffice to procure a dutiful subservience to your every wish in that quarter, provided only you will take as kindly an interest in us as we in you."

This appeal told upon the meeting, and the Lacedaemonians[5] resolved formally, now that the citadel had been taken, to keep it, and to put Ismenias on his trial. In consequence of this resolution a body of commissioners[6] was despatched, three Lacedaemonians and one for each of the allied states, great and small alike. The court of inquiry thus constituted, the sittings commenced, and an indictment was preferred against Ismenias. He was accused of playing into the hands of the barbarian; of seeking amity with the Persians to the detriment of Hellas; of accepting sums of money as bribes from the king; and, finally, of being, along with Androcleidas, the prime cause of the whole intestine trouble to which Hellas was a prey. Each of these charges was met by the defendant, but to no purpose, since he failed to disabuse the court of their conviction that the grandeur of his designs

---

1 See "Ages." vii.
2 "Select Committee." See "Hell." II. iv. 38; and below, VI. iii. 3.
3 See above, "Hell." III. v. 4.
4 Lit. "scytale."
5 See Grote, "H. G." vol. x. p. 85; Diod. xv. 20; Plut. "Pelop." vi.; ib. "de Genio Socratis," V. vii. 6 A; Cor. Nep. "Pelop." 1.
6 Lit. "Dicasts."

was only equalled by their wickedness.[1] The verdict was given against him, and he was put to death. The party of Leontiades thus possessed the city; and went beyond the injunctions given them in the eager performance of their services.

382 BC. As a result of these transactions the Lacedaemonians pressed on the combined campaign against Olynthus with still greater enthusiasm. They not only set out Teleutias as governor, but by their united efforts furnished him with an aggregate army of ten thousand men.[2] They also sent despatches to the allied states, calling upon them to support Teleutias in accordance with the resolution of the allies. All the states were ready to display devotion to Teleutias, and to do him service, since he was a man who never forgot a service rendered him. Nor was Thebes an exception; for was not the governor a brother of Agesilaus? Thebes, therefore, was enthusiastic in sending her contribution of heavy infantry and cavalry. The Spartan conducted his march slowly and surely, taking the utmost pains to avoid injuring his friends, and to collect as large a force as possible. He also sent a message in advance to Amyntas, begging him, if he were truly desirous of recovering his empire, to raise a body of mercenaries, and to distribute sums of money among the neighboring kings with a view to their alliance. Nor was that all. He sent also to Derdas, the ruler of Elimia, pointing out to him that the Olynthians, having laid at their feet the great power of Macedonia, would certainly not suffer his lesser power to escape unless they were stayed up by force in arms in their career of insolence. Proceeding thus, by the time he had reached the territory of the allied powers he was at the head of a very considerable army. At Potidaea he halted to make the necessary disposition of his troops, and thence advanced into the territory of the enemy. As he approached the hostile city, he abstained from felling and firing alike, being persuaded that to do so was only to create difficulties in his own path, whether advancing or retreating; it would be time enough, when he retired from Olynthus, to fell the trees and lay them as a barrier in the path of any assailant in the rear.

Being now within a mile or so[3] of the city he came to a halt. The left division was under his personal command, for it suited him to advance in a line opposite the gate from which the enemy sallied; the other division of

---

1 Or, "that he was a magnificent malefactor." See Grote, "H. G." vol. ix. p. 420, "the great wicked man" (Clarendon's epithets for Cromwell); Plato, "Meno." 90 B; "Republic," 336 A, "a rich and mighty man." See also Plut. "Ages." xxxii. 2, Agesilaus's exclamation at sight of Epaminondas, {o tou megalopragmonos anthropou}.
2 Lit. "sent out along with him the combined force of ten thousand men," in ref to S. 20 above.
3 Lit. "ten stades."

the allies stretched away to the right. The cavalry were thus distributed: the Laconians, Thebans, and all the Macedonians present were posted on the right. With his own division he kept Derdas and his troopers, four hundred strong. This he did partly out of genuine admiration for this body of horse, and partly as a mark of courtesy to Derdas, which should make him not regret his coming.

Presently the enemy issued forth and formed in line opposite, under cover of their walls. Then their cavalry formed in close order and commenced the attack. Dashing down upon the Laconians and Boeotians they dismounted Polycharmus, the Lacedaemonian cavalry general, inflicting a hundred wounds on him as he lay on the ground, and cut down others, and finally put to flight the cavalry on the right wing. The flight of these troopers infected the infantry in close proximity to them, who in turn swerved; and it looked as if the whole army was about to be worsted, when Derdas at the head of his cavalry dashed straight at the gates of Olynthus, Teleutias supporting him with the troops of his division. The Olynthian cavalry, seeing how matters were going, and in dread of finding the gates closed upon them, wheeled round and retired with alacrity. Thus it was that Derdas had his chance to cut down man after man as their cavalry ran the gauntlet past him. In the same way, too, the infantry of the Olynthians retreated within their city, though, owing to the closeness of the walls in their case, their loss was trifling. Teleutias claimed the victory, and a trophy was duly erected, after which he turned his back on Olynthus and devoted himself to felling the fruit-trees. This was the campaign of the summer. He now dismissed both the Macedonians and the cavalry force of Derdas. Incursions, however, on the part of the Olynthians themselves against the states allied to Lacedaemon were frequent; lands were pillaged, and people put to the sword.

III

381 BC. With the first symptoms of approaching spring the Olynthian cavalry, six hundred strong, had swooped into the territory of Apollonia— about the middle of the day—and dispersing over the district, were employed in pillaging; but as luck would have it, Derdas had arrived that day with his troopers, and was breakfasting in Apollonia. He noted the enemy's incursion, but kept quiet, biding his time; his horses were ready saddled, and his troopers armed cap-a-pied. As the Olynthians came galloping up contemptuously, not only into the suburbs, but to the very gates of the city, he seized his opportunity, and with his compact and well-ordered squadron

dashed out; whereupon the invaders took to flight. Having once turned them, Derdas gave them no respite, pursuing and slaughtering them for ten miles or more,[1] until he had driven them for shelter within the very ramparts of Olynthus. Report said that Derdas slew something like eighty men in this affair. After this the Olynthians were more disposed to keep to their walls, contenting themselves with tilling the merest corner of their territory.

Time advanced, and Teleutias was in conduct of another expedition against the city of Olynthus. His object was to destroy any timber[2] still left standing, or fields still cultivated in the hostile territory. This brought out the Olynthian cavalry, who, stealthily advancing, crossed the river which washes the walls of the town, and again continued their silent march right up to the adversary's camp. At sight of an audacity which nettled him, Teleutias at once ordered Tlemonidas, the officer commanding his light infantry division, to charge the assailants at the run. On their side the men of Olynthus, seeing the rapid approach of the light infantry, wheeled and quietly retired until they had recrossed the river, drawing the enemy on, who followed with conspicuous hardihood. Arrogating to themselves the position of pursuers toward fugitives, they did not hesitate to cross the river which stood between them and their prey. Then the Olynthian cavalry, choosing a favorable moment, when those who had crossed seemed easy to deal with, wheeled and attacked them, putting Tlemonidas himself to the sword with more than a hundred others of his company. Teleutias, when he saw what was happening, snatched up his arms in a fit of anger and began leading his hoplites swiftly forward, ordering at the same time his peltasts and cavalry to give chase and not to slacken. Their fate was the fate of many before and since, who, in the ardour of pursuit, have come too close to the enemy's walls and found it hard to get back again. Under a hail of missiles from the walls they were forced to retire in disorder and with the necessity of guarding themselves against the missiles. At this juncture the Olynthians sent out their cavalry at full gallop, backed by supports of light infantry; and finally their heavy infantry reserves poured out and fell upon the enemy's lines, now in thorough confusion. Here Teleutias fell fighting, and when that happened, without further pause the troops immediately about him swerved. Not one soul longer cared to make a stand, but the flight became general, some fleeing toward Spartolus, others in the direction of Acanthus, a third set seeking refuge within the walls

---

1 Lit. "ninety stades."
2 I.e. fruit-trees.

of Apollonia, and the majority within those of Potidaea. As the tide of fugitives broke into several streams, so also the pursuers divided the work between them; this way and that they poured, dealing death wholesale. So perished the pith and kernel of the armament.

Such calamities are not indeed without a moral. The lesson they are meant to teach mankind, I think, is plain. If in a general sense one ought not to punish anyone, even one's own slave, in anger—since the master in his wrath may easily incur worse evil himself than he inflicts—so, in the case of antagonists in war, to attack an enemy under the influence of passion rather than of judgment is an absolute error. For wrath is but a blind impulse devoid of foresight, whereas to the penetrating eye of reason a blow parried may be better than a wound inflicted.[1]

When the news of what had happened reached Lacedaemon it was agreed, after due deliberation, that a force should be sent, and of no trifling description, if only to quench the victors" pride, and to prevent their own achievements from becoming null and void. In this determination they sent out King Agesipolis, as general, attended, like Agesilaus[2] on his Asiatic campaign, by thirty Spartans.[3] Volunteers flocked to his standard. They were partly the pick and flower of the provincials,[4] partly foreigners of the class called Trophimoi,[5] or lastly, bastard sons of Spartans, comely and beautiful of limb, and well versed in the lore of Spartan chivalry. The ranks of this invading force were further swelled by volunteers from the allied states, the Thessalians notably contributing a corps of cavalry. All were animated by the desire of becoming known to Agesipolis, so that even Amyntas and Derdas in zeal of service outdid themselves. With this promise of success Agesipolis marched forward against Olynthus.

Meanwhile the state of Phlius, complimented by Agesipolis on the amount of the funds contributed by them to his expedition and the celerity with which the money had been raised, and in full belief that while one king was in the field they were secure against the hostile attack of the other (since it was hardly to be expected that both kings should be absent from Sparta at one moment), boldly desisted from doing justice by her lately reinstated citizens. On the one hand, these exiles claimed that points in dispute should be determined before an impartial court of justice; the citizens, on the other,

---

1 *See, for the same sentiment, "Horsemanship," vi. 13. See also Plut. "Pel." and "Marc." (Clough, ii. p. 278).*
2 *See above, "Hell." III. iv. 2.*
3 *Lit. "Spartiates." The new army was sent out 380 BC, according to Grote.*
4 *Lit. "beautiful and brave of the Perioeci."*
5 *Xenophon's own sons educated at Sparta would belong to this class. See Grote, "H. G." x. 91.*

insisted on the claimants submitting the cases for trial in the city itself. And when the latter demurred to that solution, asking "What sort of trial that would be where the offenders were also the judges?" they appealed to deaf ears. Consequently the restored party appealed at Sparta, to prefer a complaint against their city. They were accompanied by other members of the community, who stated that many of the Phliasians themselves besides the appellants recognized the injustice of their treatment. The state of Phlius was indignant at this manouvre, and retaliated by imposing a fine on all who had betaken themselves to Lacedaemon without a mandate from the state. Those who incurred the fine hesitated to return home; they preferred to stay where they were and enforce their views: "It is quite plain now who were the perpetrators of all the violence—the very people who originally drove us into exile, and shut their gates upon Lacedaemon; the confiscators of our property one day, the ruthless opponents of its restoration the next. Who else but they have now brought it about that we should be fined for appearing at Lacedaemon? and for what purpose but to deter anyone else for the future from venturing to expose the proceedings at Phlius?" Thus far the appellants. And in good sooth the conduct of the men of Phlius did seem to savour of insolence; so much so that the ephors called out the ban against them.

380 BC. Nor was Agesilaus otherwise than well satisfied with this decision, not only on the ground of old relations of friendly hospitality between his father Archidamus and the party of Podanemus, who were numbered among the restored exiles at this time, but because personally he was bound by similar ties himself toward the adherents of Procles, son of Hipponicus. The border sacrifices proving favorable, the march commenced at once. As he advanced, embassy after embassy met him, and would fain by presents of money avert invasion. But the king answered that the purpose of his march was not to commit wrongdoing, but to protect the victims of injustice. Then the petitioners offered to do anything, only they begged him to forgo invasion. Again he replied—How could he trust to their words when they had lied to him already? He must have the warrant of acts, not promises. And being asked, "What act (would satisfy him)?" he answered once more, saying, "The same which you performed aforetime, and suffered no wrong at our hands"—in other words, the surrender of the acropolis.[1] But to this they could not bring themselves. Whereupon he invaded the territory of Phlius, and promptly drawing lines of circumvallation, commenced the siege. Many of the Lacedaemonians

---

1 See above, IV. iv. 15.

objected, for the sake of a mere handful of wretched people, so to embroil themselves with a state of over five thousand men.[1] For, indeed, to leave no doubt on this score, the men of Phlius met regularly in assembly in full view of those outside. But Agesilaus was not to be beaten by this move. Whenever any of the townsmen came out, drawn by friendship or kinship with the exiles, in every case the king's instructions were to place the public messes[2] at the service of the visitors, and, if they were willing to go through the course of gymnastic training, to give them enough to procure necessaries. All members of these classes were, by the general's strict injunctions, further to be provided with arms, and loans were to be raised for the purpose without delay. Presently the superintendents of this branch of the service were able to turn out a detachment of over a thousand men, in the prime of bodily perfection, well disciplined and splendidly armed, so that in the end the Lacedaemonians affirmed: "Fellow soldiers of this stamp are too good to lose." Such were the concerns of Agesilaus.

Meanwhile Agesipolis on leaving Macedonia advanced straight upon Olynthus and took up a strategical position in front of the town. Finding that no one came out to oppose him, he occupied himself for the present with pillaging any remnant of the district till intact, and with marching into the territory allied with the enemy, where he destroyed the corn. The town of Torone he attacked and took by storm. But while he was so engaged, in the height of mid-summer he was attacked by a burning fever. In this condition his mind reverted to a scene once visited, the temple of Dionysus at Aphytis, and a longing for its cool and sparkling waters and embowered shades[3] seized him. To this spot accordingly he was carried, still living, but only to breathe his last outside the sacred shrine, within a week of the day on which he sickened. His body was laid in honey and conveyed home to Sparta, where he obtained royal sepulchre.

When the news reached Agesilaus he displayed none of the satisfaction which might possibly have been expected at the removal of an antagonist. On the contrary, he wept and pined for the companionship so severed, it being the fashion at Sparta for the kings when at home to mess together and to share the same quarters. Moreover, Agesipolis was admirably suited to Agesilaus, sharing with the merriment of youth in tales of the chase and horsemanship and boyish loves;[4] while, to crown all, the touch of reverence

---

1 See Grote, "H. G." x. 45, note 4; and below, V. iv. 13.
2 See "Pol. Lac." v.
3 Lit. "shady tabernacles."
4 See "Ages." viii. 2.

due from younger to elder was not wanting in their common life. In place of Agesipolis, the Lacedaemonians despatched Polybiades as governor to Olynthus.

379 BC. Agesilaus had already exceeded the time during which the supplies of food in Phlius were expected to last. The difference, in fact, between self-command and mere appetite is so great that the men of Phlius had only to pass a resolution to cut down the food expenditure by one half, and by doing so were able to prolong the siege for twice the calculated period. But if the contrast between self-restraint and appetite is so great, no less startling is that between boldness and faint-heartedness. A Phliasian named Delphion, a real hero, it would seem, took to himself three hundred Phliasians, and not only succeeded in preventing the peace-party from carrying out their wishes, but was equal to the task of incarcerating and keeping safely under lock and key those whom he mistrusted. Nor did his ability end there. He succeeded in forcing the mob of citizens to perform garrison duty, and by vigorous patrolling kept them constant to the work. Over and over again, accompanied by his personal attendants, he would dash out of the walls and drive in the enemy's outposts, first at one point and then at another of the beleaguering circle. But the time eventually came when, search as they might by every means, these picked defenders[1] could find no further store of food within the walls, and they were forced to send to Agesilaus, requesting a truce for an embassy to visit Sparta, adding that they were resolved to leave it to the discretion of the authorities at Lacedaemon to do with their city what they liked. Agesilaus granted a pass to the embassy, but, at the same time, he was so angry at their setting his personal authority aside, that he sent to his friends at home and arranged that the fate of Phlius should be left to his discretion. Meanwhile he proceeded to tighten the cordon of investment, so as to render it impossible that a single soul inside the city should escape. In spite of this, however, Delphion, with one comrade, a branded dare-devil, who had shown great dexterity in relieving the besieging parties of their arms, escaped by night. Presently the deputation returned with the answer from Lacedaemon that the state simply left it entirely to the discretion of Agesilaus to decide the fate of Phlius as seemed to him best. Then Agesilaus announced his verdict. A board of one hundred—fifty taken from the restored exiles, fifty from those within the city—were in the first place to make inquisition as to who deserved to live and who to die, after which they were to lay down laws as the basis of a new constitution. Pending the carrying out of these

---

1 See below, "Hell." VII. i. 19.

transactions, he left a detachment of troops to garrison the place for six months, with pay for that period. After this he dismissed the allied forces, and led the state[1] division home. Thus the transactions concerning Phlius were brought to a conclusion, having occupied altogether one year and eight months.

Meanwhile Polybiades had reduced the citizens of Olynthus to the last stage of misery through famine. Unable to supply themselves with corn from their own land, or to import it by sea, they were forced to send an embassy to Lacedaemon to sue for peace. The plenipotentiaries on their arrival accepted articles of agreement by which they bound themselves to have the same friends and the same foes as Lacedaemon, to follow her lead, and to be enrolled among her allies; and so, having taken an oath to abide by these terms, they returned home.

On every side the affairs of Lacedaemon had signally prospered: Thebes and the rest of the Boeotian states lay absolutely at her feet; Corinth had become her most faithful ally; Argos, unable longer to avail herself of the subterfuge of a movable calendar, was humbled to the dust; Athens was isolated; and, lastly, those of her own allies who displayed a hostile feeling toward her had been punished; so that, to all outward appearance, the foundations of her empire were at length absolutely well and firmly laid.

IV

Abundant examples might be found, alike in Hellenic and in foreign history, to prove that the Divine powers mark what is done amiss, winking neither at impiety nor at the commission of unhallowed acts; but at present I confine myself to the facts before me.[2] The Lacedaemonians, who had pledged themselves by oath to leave the states independent, had laid violent hands on the acropolis of Thebes, and were eventually punished by the victims of that iniquity single-handed—the Lacedaemonians, be it noted, who had never before been mastered by living man; and not they alone, but those citizens of Thebes who introduced them to their acropolis, and who wished to enslave their city to Lacedaemon, that they might play the tyrant themselves—how fared it with them? A bare score of the fugitives were sufficient to destroy their government. How this happened I will now narrate in detail.

---

1 {*to politokon*}, the citizen army. See above, IV. iv. 19; "Pol. Lac." xi.
2 Or, "it is of my own subject that I must now speak." For the "peripety," or sudden reversal of circumstances, on which the plot of the "Hellenica" hinges, see Grote, "H. G." x. 100–108. Cf. Soph. "Oed. Tyr." 450; "Antig." 1066; Thuc. v. 116; "Hellenica Essays," "Xenophon," p. 382 foll. This passage is perhaps the key to the historian's position.

There was a man named Phyllidas—he was secretary to Archias, that is, to the polemarchs.[1] Beyond his official duties, he had rendered his chief other services, and all apparently in an exemplary fashion. A visit to Athens in pursuance of some business brought this man into contact with a former acquaintance of his, Melon, one of the exiles who had fled for safety to Athens. Melon had various questions to ask touching the sort of tyranny practiced by Archias in the exercise of the polemarchy, and by Philip. He soon discovered that affairs at home were still more detestable to Phyllidas than to himself. It only remained to exchange pledges, and to arrange the details of what was to be done. After a certain interval Melon, accompanied by six of the trustiest comrades he could find among his fellow exiles, set off for Thebes. They were armed with nothing but daggers, and first of all crept into the neighborhood under cover of night. The whole of the next day they lay concealed in a desert place, and drew near to the city gates in the guise of laborers returning home with the latest comers from the fields. Having got safely within the city, they spent the whole of that night at the house of a man named Charon, and again the next day in the same fashion. Phyllidas meanwhile was busily taken up with the concerns of the polemarchs, who were to celebrate a feast of Aphrodite on going out of office. Among other things, the secretary was to take this opportunity of fulfillling an old undertaking, which was the introduction of certain women to the polemarchs. They were to be the most majestic and the most beautiful to be found in Thebes. The polemarchs, on their side (and the character of the men is sufficiently marked), were looking forward to the pleasures of the night with joyful anticipation. Supper was over, and thanks to the zeal with which the master of the ceremonies responded to their mood, they were speedily intoxicated. To their oft-repeated orders to introduce their mistresses, he went out and fetched Melon and the rest, three of them dressed up as ladies and the rest as their attendant maidens. Having brought them into the treasury of the polemarchs" residence,[2] he returned himself and announced to Archias and his friends that the women would not present themselves as long as any of the attendants remained in the room; whereupon they promptly bade all withdraw, and Phyllidas, furnishing the servants with a stoup of wine, sent them off to the house of one of them. And now at last he introduced the mistresses, and led them

---

1 Lit. "to Archias and his (polemarchs)"; but the Greek phrase does not, as the English would, imply that there were actually more than two polemarchs, viz. Archias and Philippus. Hypates and Leontiades belonged to the faction, but were neither of them polemarchs.
2 Lit. "Polemarcheion."

to their seats beside their respective lords. It was preconcerted that as soon as they were seated they were to throw aside their veils and strike home. That is one version of the death of the polemarchs.[1] According to another, Melon and his friends came in as revellers, and so despatched their victims.

That over, Phyllidas, with three of the band, set off to the house of Leontiades. Arrived there, he knocked on the door, and sent in word that he had a message from the polemarchs. Leontiades, as chance befell, was still reclining in privacy after dinner, and his wife was seated beside him working wools. The fidelity of Phyllidas was well known to him, and he gave orders to admit him at once. They entered, slew Leontiades, and with threats silenced his wife. As they went out they ordered the door to be shut, threatening that if they found it open they would kill everyone in the house. And now that this deed was done, Phyllidas, with two of the band, presented himself at the prison, telling the gaoler he had brought a man from the polemarchs to be locked up. The gaoler opened the door, and was at once despatched, and the prisoners were released. These they speedily supplied with arms taken from the armoury in the stoa, and then led them to the Ampheion,[2] and bade them take up a position there, after which they at once made a proclamation calling on all Thebans to come out, horse and foot, seeing that the tyrants were dead. The citizens, indeed, as long as it was night, not knowing whom or what to trust, kept quiet, but when day dawned and revealed what had occurred, the summons was responded to with alacrity, heavy infantry and cavalry under arms alike sallying forth. Horsemen were also despatched by the now restored exiles to the two Athenian generals on the frontier; and they, being aware of the object of the message (promptly responded).[3]

On the other hand, the Lacedaemonian governor in the citadel, as soon as that night's proclamation reached his ears, was not slow to send to Plataeae[4] and Thespiae for reinforcements. The approach of the Plataeans was perceived by the Theban cavalry, who met them and killed a score of them and more, and after that achievement returned to the city, to find the Athenians from the frontier already arrived. Then they assaulted the acropolis. The troops within recognized the paucity of their own numbers,

---

1 Or, "and so, according to the prevalent version of the matter, the polemarchs were slain. But some say that..."
2 See plan of Thebes, "Dict. Geog."; Arrian, "Anab." i. 8; Aesch. "Sept. c. Theb." 528.
3 Supply {epeboethoun}. There is a lacuna in the MSS. at this point.
4 This city had been refounded in 386 BC (Isocr. "Plat." 20, 21). See Freeman, op. cit. ch. iv. p. 170: "Its restoration implied not only a loss of Theban supremacy, but the actual loss of that portion of the existing Theban territory which had formerly formed the Plataian district."

whilst the zeal of their opponents (one and all advancing to the attack) was plainly visible, and loud were the proclamations, promising rewards to those who should be first to scale the walls. All this so worked upon their fears that they agreed to evacuate the place if the citizens would allow them a safe-conduct to retire with their arms. To this request the others gladly yielded, and they made a truce. Oaths were taken on the terms aforesaid, and the citizens dismissed their adversaries. For all that, as the garrison retired, those of them who were recognized as personal foes were seized and put to death. Some were rescued through the good offices of the Athenian reinforcements from the frontier, who smuggled them across and saved them. The Thebans were not content with putting the men to death; if any of them had children, these also were sacrificed to their vengeance.

378 BC. When the news of these proceedings reached Sparta the first thing the Lacedaemonians did was to put to death the governor, who had abandoned the Cadmeia instead of awaiting reinforcements, and the next was to call out the ban against Thebes. Agesilaus had little taste to head the expedition; he pointed out that he had seen more than forty years' service,[1] and that the exemption from foreign duty applicable to others at that age was applicable on the same principle to the king. Such were the ostensible grounds on which he excused himself from the present expedition, but his real objections lay deeper. He felt certain that if he led the expedition his fellow citizens would say: "Agesilaus caused all this trouble to the state in order to aid and abet tyrants." Therefore he preferred to leave his countrymen to settle the matter themselves as they liked. Accordingly the ephors, instructed by the Theban exiles who had escaped the late massacres, despatched Cleombrotus. He had not commanded before, and it was the depth of winter.

Now while Chabrias, with a body of Athenian peltasts, kept watch and ward over the road through Eleutherae, Cleombrotus made his way up by the direct route to Plataeae. His column of light infantry, pushing forward in advance, fell upon the men who had been released from the Theban prison, guarding the summit, to the number of about one hundred and fifty. These, with the exception of one or two who escaped, were cut down by the peltasts, and Cleombrotus descended in person upon Plataeae, which was still friendly to Sparta. Presently he reached Thespiae, and that was the base for an advance upon Cynoscephalae, where he encamped on Theban territory. Here he halted sixteen days, and then again fell back upon Thespiae. At this latter place he now left Sphodrias as governor, with

---

1 *And was therefore more than fifty-eight years old at this date. See "Ages." i. 6.*

a third portion of each of the contingents of the allies, handing over to him all the moneys he had brought with him from home, with directions to supplement his force with a contingent of mercenaries.

While Sphodrias was so employed, Cleombrotus himself commenced his homeward march, following the road through Creusis at the head of his own moiety of the troops, who indeed were in considerable perplexity to discover whether they were at war with the Thebans or at peace, seeing that the general had led his army into Theban territory, had inflicted the minimum of mischief, and again retired. No sooner, however, was his back turned than a violent wind storm assailed him in his rear, which some construed as an omen clearly significant of what was about to take place. Many a blow this assailant dealt them, and as the general and his army, crossing from Creusis, scaled that face of the mountain[1] which stretches seaward, the blast hurled headlong from the precipices a string of asses, baggage and all: countless arms were wrested from the bearers" grasp and whirled into the sea; finally, numbers of the men, unable to march with their arms, deposited them at different points of the pass, first filling the hollow of their shields with stones. For the moment, then, they halted at Aegosthena, on Megarian soil, and supped as best they could. Next day they returned and recovered their arms. After this adventure the contingents lost no time in returning to their several homes, as Cleombrotus disbanded them.

Meanwhile at Athens and Thebes alike fear reigned. To the Athenians the strength of the Lacedaemonians was unmistakable: the war was plainly no longer confined to Corinth; on the contrary, the Lacedaemonians had ventured to skirt Athenian territory and to invade Thebes. They were so worked upon by their alarm that the two generals who had been privy to the insurrection of Melon against Leontiades and his party had to suffer: the one was formally tried and put to death; the other, refusing to abide his trial, was banished.

The apprehensions of the Thebans were of a different sort: their fear was rather lest they should find themselves in single-handed war with Lacedaemon. To prevent this they hit upon the following expedient. They worked upon Sphodrias,[2] the Spartan governor left in Thespiae, by offering him, as at least was suspected, a substantial sum, in return for which he was to make an incursion into Attica; their great object being to involve Athens and Lacedaemon in hostilities. Sphodrias lent a willing ear, and,

---

1 I.e. "Cithaeron."
2 See Plut. "Pel." xiv. (Clough, ii. p. 214).

pretending that he could easily capture Piraeus in its present gateless condition, gave his troops an early evening meal and marched out of Thespiae, saying that he would reach Piraeus before daybreak. As a matter of fact day overtook him at Thria, nor did he take any pains even to draw a veil over his intentions; on the contrary, being forced to turn aside, he amused himself by recklessly lifting cattle and sacking houses. Meanwhile some who chanced upon him in the night had fled to the city and brought news to the men of Athens that a large body of troops was approaching. It needs no saying with what speed the cavalry and heavy infantry armed themselves and stood on guard to protect the city. As chance befell, there were some Lacedaemonian ambassadors in Athens at the moment, at the house of Callias their proxenos; their names were Etymocles, Aristolochus, and Ocyllus. Immediately on receipt of the news the Athenians seized these three and imprisoned them, as not improbably concerned in the plot. Utterly taken aback by the affair themselves, the ambassadors pleaded that, had they been aware of an attempt to seize Piraeus, they would hardly have been so foolish as to put themselves into the power of the Athenians, or have selected the house of their proxenos for protection, where they were so easily to be found. It would, they further urged, soon be plain to the Athenians themselves that the state of Lacedaemon was quite as little cognisant of these proceedings as they. "You will hear before long"—such was their confident prediction—"that Sphodrias has paid for his behavior by his life." On this wise the ambassadors were acquitted of all concern in the matter and dismissed. Sphodrias himself was recalled and indicted by the ephors on the capital charge, and, in spite of his refusal to face the trial, he was acquitted. This miscarriage of justice, as it seemed to many, who described it as unprecedented in Lacedaemon, has an explanation.

Sphodrias had a son named Cleonymus. He was just at the age when youth emerges from boyhood, very handsome and of high repute among his fellows. To this youth Archidamus, the son of Agesilaus, was passionately attached. Now the friends of Cleombrotus, as comrades of Sphodrias, were disposed to acquit him; but they feared Agesilaus and his friends, not to mention the intermediate party, for the enormity of his proceeding was clear. So when Sphodrias addressed his son Cleonymus: "You have it in your power, my son, to save your father, if you will, by begging Archidamus to dispose Agesilaus favorably to me at my trial." Thus instructed, the youth did not shrink from visiting Archidamus, and implored him for his sake to save his father. Now when Archidamus saw how Cleonymus wept, he too was melted to tears as he stood beside him, but to his petition he made answer thus: "Nay, Cleonymus, it is the bare truth I tell you, I cannot so much as look my father in the face;[1] if I wished anything transacted for me in the city I would beg assistance from the whole world sooner than from my father. Still, since it is you who bid me, rest assured I will do my best to bring this about for you as you desire." He then left the common hall[2] and retired home to rest, but with dawn he arose and kept watch that his father might not go out without his knowledge. Presently, when he saw him ready to go forth, first some citizen was present, and then another and another; and in each case he stepped aside, while they held his father in conversation. By and by a stranger would come, and then another; and so it went on until he even found himself making way for a string of petitioning attendants. At last, when his father had turned his back on the Eurotas, and was entering his house again, he was fain to turn his back also and be gone without so much as accosting him. The next day he fared no better: all happened as on the previous day. Now Agesilaus, although he had his suspicions why his son went to and fro in this way, asked no questions, but left him to take his own course. Archidamus, on his side, was longing, as was natural, to see his friend Cleonymus; but how he was to visit him, without having held the desired conversation with his father, he knew not. The friends of Sphodrias, observing that he who was once so frequent a visitor had ceased coming, were in agony; he must surely have been deterred by the reproaches of his father. At last, however, Archidamus dared to go to his father, and said, "Father, Cleonymus bids me ask you to save his father; grant me this boon, if possible, I beg you." He answered: "For yourself, my son, I can make excuse, but how shall my city make excuse for me if I fail to condemn that man who, for his own base purpose, traffics to the injury of the state?" For the moment the other made no reply, but retired crestfallen before the verdict of justice. Afterward, whether the thought was his own or that he was prompted by some other, he came and said, "Father, if Sphodrias had done no wrong you would have released him, that I know; but now, if he has done something wrong, may he not be excused by you for our sakes?" And the father answered: "If it can be done without loss of honor on our parts, so shall it be." At that word the young man, in deep despondency, turned and went. Now one of the friends of Sphodrias, conversing with Etymocles, remarked to him: "You are all bent on putting Sphodrias to death, I take it, you friends of Agesilaus?" And Etymocles replied: "If that be so, we all are bent on one thing, and Agesilaus on another, since in all

---

1 See *"Cyrop."* I. iv. 12.
2 Lit. *"the Philition."* See *"Pol. Lac."* iii. 6.

his conversations he still harps upon one string: that Sphodrias has done a wrong there is no denying, yet Sphodrias is a man who, from boyhood to ripe manhood,[1] was ever constant to the call of honor. To put such a man as that to death is hard; nay, Sparta needs such soldiers." The other accordingly went off and reported what he had just heard to Cleonymus; and he in the joy of his heart went straightway to Archidamus and said: "Now we know that you care for us; rest assured, Archidamus, that we in turn will take great pains that you shall never have cause to blush for our friendship." Nor did his acts belie his words; but so long as he lived he was ever faithful to the code of Spartan chivalry; and at Leuctra, fighting in front of the king side by side with Deinon the polemarch, thrice fell or ever he yielded up his breath—foremost of the citizens amidst the foe. And so, albeit he caused his friend the bitterest sorrow, yet to that which he had promised he was faithful, seeing he wrought Archidamus no shame, but contrariwise shed luster on him.[2] In this way Sphodrias obtained his acquittal.

At Athens the friends of Boeotia were not slow to instruct the people that his countrymen, so far from punishing Sphodrias, had even applauded him for his designs on Athens; and in consequence of this the Athenians not only furnished Piraeus with gates, but set to work to build a fleet, and displayed great zeal in sending aid to the Boeotians.[3] The Lacedaemonians, on their side, called out the ban against the Thebans; and being persuaded that in Agesilaus they would find a more prudent general than Cleombrotus had proved, they begged the former to undertake the expedition.[4] He, replying that the wish of the state was for him law, began making preparations to take the field.

Now he had come to the conclusion that without the occupation of Mount Cithaeron any attack on Thebes would be difficult. Learning then that the men of Cleitor were just now at war with the men of Orchomenus,[5] and were maintaining a foreign brigade, he came to an understanding with the Cleitorians that in the event of his needing it, this force would be at his service; and as soon as the sacrifices for crossing the frontier proved

---

1 Lit. "who, whether as child, boy, or young man"; and for the three stages of growth, see "Pol. Lac." ii. iii. iv.
2 I.e. both in life and in death.
3 For the new Athenian confederacy of Delos of this year, 378 BC, see "Pol. Lac." xiv. 6; "Rev." v. 6; Diod. xv. 28–30; Plut. "Pelop." xv.; Hicks, 78, 81; and for an alliance between Athens and Chalcis in Euboea, see Hicks, 79; and for a treaty with Chios, Hicks, 80.
4 See "Ages." ii. 22.
5 In Arcadia. See Busolt, "Die Lak." 120 foll.

favorable, he sent to the commander of the Cleitorian mercenaries, and handing him a month's pay, ordered him to occupy Cithaeron with his men. This was before he himself reached Tegea. Meanwhile he sent a message to the men of Orchomenus that so long as the campaign lasted they must cease from war. If any city during his campaign abroad took on itself to march against another city, his first duty, he declared, would be to march against such offending city in accordance with a decree of the allies.

Thus crossing Cithaeron he reached Thespiae,[1] and from that base made the territory of Thebes his objective. Finding the great plain fenced round with ditch and palisade, as also the most valuable portions of the country, he adopted the plan of shifting his encampment from one place to another. Regularly each day, after the morning meal, he marched out his troops and ravaged the territory, confining himself to his own side of the palisadings and trench. The appearance of Agesilaus at any point whatever was a signal to the enemy, who within the circuit of his entrenchment kept moving in parallel line to the invader, and was ever ready to defend the threatened point. On one occasion, the Spartan king having retired and being well on the road back to camp, the Theban cavalry, hitherto invisible, suddenly dashed out, following one of the regularly constructed roads out of the entrenchment. Taking advantage of the enemy's position—his light troops breaking off to supper or busily preparing the meal, and the cavalry, some of them on their legs just[2] dismounted, and others in the act of mounting—on they rode, pressing the charge home. Man after man of the light troops was cut down; and three cavalry troopers besides—two Spartans, Cleas and Epicydidas by name, and the third a provincial[3] named Eudicus, who had not had time to mount their horses, and whose fate was shared by some Theban[4] exiles. But presently Agesilaus wheeled about and advanced with his heavy infantry to the succour; his cavalry dashed at the enemy's cavalry, and the flower of the heavy infantry, the ten-years-service men, charged by their side. The Theban cavalry at that instant looked like men who had been imbibing too freely in the noontide heat—that is to say, they awaited the charge long enough to hurl their spears; but the volley sped without effect, and wheeling about within that distance they left twelve of their number dead upon the field.

---

1 By Cynoscephalae. See "Ages." ii. 22.
2 Read, after Courier, {arti} for the vulg. {eti}; or, better still, adopt Hartman's emendation (op. cit. p. 379), {ton men ede katabebekoton ton de katabainonton}, and translate "some—already dismounted, and others dismounting."
3 Lit. "one of the perioeci."
4 Reading {Thebaion} after Dind. for {'Athenaion}.

Agesilaus had not failed to note with what regularity the enemy presented himself after the morning meal. Turning the observation to account, he offered sacrifice with day's dawn, and marched with all possible speed, and so crossed within the palisadings, through what might have been a desert, as far as defense or sign of living being went. Once well inside, he proceeded to cut down and set on fire everything up to the city gates. After this exploit he beat a retreat, retiring into Thespiae, where he fortified their citadel for them. Here he left Phoebidas as governor, while he himself crossed the passes back into Megara. Arrived here he disbanded the allies, and led the city troops homeward.

After the departure of Agesilaus, Phoebidas devoted himself to harrying the Thebans by sending out robber bands, and laid waste their land by a system of regular incursions. The Thebans, on their side, desiring to retaliate, marched out with their whole force into the territory of Thespiae. But once well inside the district they found themselves closely beset by Phoebidas and his light troops, who would not give them the slightest chance to scatter from their main body, so that the Thebans, heartily vexed at the turn their foray had taken, beat a retreat quicker than they had come. The muleteers threw away with their own hands the fruits they had captured, in their anxiety to get home as quickly as possible; so dire a dread had fallen upon the invading army. This was the chance for the Spartan to press home his attack boldly, keeping his light division in close attendance on himself, and leaving the heavy infantry under orders to follow him in battle order. He was in hopes even that he might put the enemy to complete rout, so valiantly did he lead the advance, encouraging the light troops to "come to a close grip with the invadors," or summoning the heavy infantry of the Thespiaeans to "bring up their supports." Presently the Theban cavalry as they retired found themselves face to face with an impassable glen or ravine, where in the first instance they collected in a mob, and next wheeled right-about-face in sheer resourcelessness where to cross. The handful of light troops who formed the Spartan vanguard took fright at the Thebans and fled, and the Theban horsemen seeing this put in practice the lesson of attack which the fugitives taught them. As for Phoebidas himself, he and two or three with him fell sword in hand, whereupon his mercenary troops all took to their heels.

When the stream of fugitives reached the Thespiaean heavy infantry reserves, they too, in spite of much boasting beforehand that they would never yield to Thebans, took to flight, though there was now absolutely no pursuit whatever, for it was now late. The number slain was not large, but, for all that, the men of Thespiae did not come to a standstill until they found themselves safe inside their walls. As a sequel, the hopes and spirits of the Thebans were again kindled into new life, and they made campaigns against Thespiae and the other provincial cities of Boeotia.[1] It must be admitted that in each case the democratical party retired from these cities to Thebes; since absolute governments had been established in all of them on the pattern previously adopted at Thebes; and the result was that the friends of Lacedaemon in these cities also needed her assistance.[2] After the death of Phoebidas the Lacedaemonians despatched a polemarch with a division by sea to form the garrison of Thespiae.

377 BC. With the advent of spring[3] the ephors again called out the ban against Thebes, and requested Agesilaus to lead the expedition, as on the former campaign. He, holding to his former theory with regard to the invasion, even before sacrificing the customary frontier sacrifice, sent a despatch to the polemarch at Thespiae, with orders to seize the pass which commands the road over Cithaeron, and to guard it against his arrival. Then, having once more crossed the pass and reached Plataeae, he again made a feint of marching first into Thespiae, and so sent a despatch ordering supplies to be in readiness, and all embassies to be waiting his arrival there; so that the Thebans concentrated their attention on the approaches from Thespiae, which they strongly guarded. Next morning, however, Agesilaus sacrificed at daybreak and set out on the road to Erythrae,[4] and completing in one day what was a good two days' march for an army, gave the Thebans the slip, and crossed their palisade-work at Scolus before the enemy had arrived from the closely-guarded point at which he had effected his entrance formerly. This done he proceeded to ravage the eastward-facing districts of the city of Thebes as far as the territory of Tanagra, for at that date Tanagra was still in the hands of Hypatodorus and his party, who were friends of the Lacedaemonians. After that he turned to retire, keeping the walls of Thebes on his left. But the Thebans, who had stolen, as it were, upon the scene, drew up at the spot called "The Old Wife's Breast,"[5] keeping the trench and palisading in their

---

1 Lit. "their other perioecid cities." For the significance of this title as applied by the Thebans (and perhaps commonly) to the other cities of Boeotia, see Freeman, op. cit. ch. iv. pp. 157, 173 foll.
2 See Grote, "H. G." x. 174; Freeman, op. cit. iv. 171, 172.
3 See for affairs of Delos, never actually named by Xenophon, between 377 and 374 BC, the Sandwich Marble in Trinity College, Cambridge; Boeckh, "C. I. G" 158, and "P. E. A." ii. p. 78 foll.; Hicks, 82.
4 Erythrae (Redlands) stands between Hysiae and Scolus, east of Katzula.—Leake, "N. Gr." ii. 329. See Herod. ix. 15, 25; Thuc. iii. 24; Paus. IX. ii. 1; Strab. IX. ii.
5 Lit. "Graos Stethos."

rear: they were persuaded that here, if anywhere, lay their chance to risk a decisive engagement, the ground at this point being somewhat narrow and difficult to traverse. Agesilaus, however, in view of the situation, refused to accept the challenge. Instead of marching upon them he turned sharp off in the direction of the city; and the Thebans, in alarm for the city in its undefended state, abandoned the favorable ground on which they were drawn up in battle line, and retired at the double toward the city along the road to Potniae, which seemed the safer route. This last move of Agesilaus may be described as a stroke of genius:[1] while it allowed him to retire to a distance, it forced the enemy themselves to retreat at the double. In spite of this, however, one or two of the polemarchs, with their divisions, charged the foe as he raced past. But again the Thebans, from the vantage-ground of their heights, sent volleys of spears upon the assailants, which cost one of the polemarchs, Alypetus, his life. He fell pierced by a spear. But again from this particular crest the Thebans on their side were forced to turn in flight; so much so that the Sciritae, with some of the cavalry, scaled up and speedily cut down the rearmost ranks of the Thebans as they galloped past into the city. When, however, they were close under cover of their walls the Thebans turned, and the Sciritae seeing them retreated at more than a steady walking pace. No one, it is true, was slain; but the Thebans all the same set up a trophy in record of the incident at the point where the scaling party had been forced to retreat.

And now, since the hour was come, Agesilaus fell back and encamped on the very site on which he had seen the enemy drawn up in battle array. Next day he retired by the road to Thespiae. The light troops, who formed a free corps in the pay of the Thebans, hung audaciously at his heels. Their shouts could be heard calling out to Chabrias[2] for not bringing up his supports; when the cavalry of the Olynthians (who now contributed a contingent in accordance with their oaths)[3] wheeled round on them, caught the pursuers in the heat of their pursuit, and drove them uphill, putting large numbers of them to the sword—so quickly are infantry overhauled by cavalry on steep ground which can be ridden over. Being arrived within the walls of Thespiae, Agesilaus found the citizens in a state of party feud, the men of Lacedaemonian proclivities desiring to put their political opponents, one

---

1 Or, *"and this move of Agesilaus was regarded as a very pretty one."*
2 For the exploits of Chabrias, who commanded a division of mixed Athenians and mercenaries (see above, S. 14), see Dem. "c. Lept." 479; Polyaen. ii. 1, 2; Diod. xv. 32, 33, who gives interesting details; Grote, "H. G." x. 172 foll.
3 See above, "Hell." V. iii. 26.

of whom was Menon, to death[1]—a proceeding which Agesilaus would not sanction. After having healed their differences and bound them over by solemn oath to keep the peace with one another, he at once retired, taking his old route across Cithaeron to Megara. Here once more he disbanded the allies, and at the head of the city troops himself marched back to Sparta.

The Thebans had not gathered in the fruits of their soil for two years now, and began to be sorely pinched for want of corn; they therefore sent a body of men on board a couple of triremes to Pagasae, with ten talents[2] in hand for the purchase of corn. But while these commissioners were engaged in effecting their purchases, Alcetas, the Lacedaemonian who was garrisoning Oreus,[3] fitted out three triremes, taking precautions that no rumor of his proceedings should leak out. As soon as the corn was shipped and the vessels under weigh, he captured not only the corn but the triremes, escort and all, numbering no less than three hundred men. This done he locked up his prisoners in the citadel, where he himself was also quartered. Now there was a youth, the son of a native of Oreus, fair of mien and of gentle breeding,[4] who danced attendance on the commandant: and the latter must needs leave the citadel and go down to busy himself with this youth. This was a piece of carelessness which the prisoners did not fail to observe, and turned to good account by seizing the citadel, whereupon the town revolted, and the Thebans experienced no further difficulty in obtaining corn supplies.

376 BC. At the return of spring Agesilaus lay sick—a bedridden invalid. The history of the case is this: During the withdrawal of his army from Thebes the year before, when at Megara, while mounting from the Aphrodision[5] to the Government house he ruptured a vein or other vessel of the body. This was followed by a rush of blood to his sound leg. The knee was much swelled, and the pain intolerable, until a Syracusan surgeon made an incision in the vein near the ankle. The blood thus let flowed night and day; do what they could to stop the discharge, all failed, till the patient fainted away; then it ceased. In this plight Agesilaus was conveyed home

---

1 Or, "under the pretext of furthering Laconian interests there was a desire to put political opponents to death." For "Menon," Diod. conj. "Melon."
2 = 2,437 pounds: 10 shillings.
3 Oreus, formerly called Histiaea, in the north of Euboea. See Thuc. vii. 57, viii. 95; Diod. xv. 30; Grote, "H. G." ix. 263. For Pagasae at the north extremity of the Pagasaean Gulf, "the cradle of Greek navigation," see Tozer, "Geog. Gr." vi. p. 124; Strab. IX. v. 15.
4 Or, "beautiful and brave if ever youth was."
5 Pausanius (I. xi. 6) mentions a temple of Aphrodite {'Epistrophoa} (Verticordia), on the way up to the Carian Acropolis of Megara.

on a litter to Lacedaemon, and remained an invalid the rest of that summer and throughout the winter.

But to resume: at the first burst of spring the Lacedaemonians again called out the ban, and gave orders to Cleombrotus to lead the expedition. The king found himself presently with his troops at the foot of Cithaeron, and his light infantry advanced to occupy the pass which commands the road. But here they found a detachment of Thebans and Athenians already in occupation of the desired height, who for a while suffered them to approach; but when they were close upon them, sprang from their position and charged, putting about forty to the sword. This incident was sufficient to convince Cleombrotus that to invade Thebes by this mountain passage was out of the question, and in this faith he led back and disbanded his troops.

The allies met in Lacedaemon, and arguments were adduced on the part of the allies to show that faintheartedness would very soon lead to their being absolutely worn out by the war. They had got it in their power, it was urged, to fit out a fleet far outnumbering that of Athens, and to reduce that city by starvation; it was open to them, in the self-same ships, to carry an army across into Theban territory, and they had a choice of routes—the road into Phocis, or, if they preferred, by Creusis. After thus carefully considering the matter they manned a fleet of sixty triremes, and Pollis was appointed admiral in command. Nor indeed were their expectations altogether belied. The Athenians were soon so closely blockaded that their corn vessels could get no farther than Geraestus;[1] there was no inducing them to coast down father south, with a Lacedaemonian navy hovering about Aegina and Ceos and Andros. The Athenians, making a virtue of necessity, manned their ships in person, gave battle to Pollis under the leadership of Chabrias, and came out of the sea-fight[2] victorious.

375 BC. Then the corn supplies flowed freely into Athens. The Lacedaemonians, on their side, were preparing to transport an army across the water into Boeotia, when the Thebans sent a request to the Athenians urging them to despatch an armament round Peloponnesus, under the persuasion that if this were done the Lacedaemonians would find it impossible at once to guard their own or the allied territory in that part of the world, and at the same time to convery an army of any size to operate against Thebes. The proposals fell in with the present temper of the Athenians, irritated with Lacedaemon on account of the exploit

---

1 *The promontory at the southern extremity of Euboea.*
2 *Battle of Naxos, 376 BC. For interesting details, see Diod. xv. 35, 35.*

of Sphodrias. Accordingly they eagerly manned a fleet of sixty vessels, appointing Timotheus as admiral in command, and despatched it on a cruise round Peloponnesus.

The Thebans, seeing that there had been no hostile invasion of their territory for so long (neither during the campaign of Cleombrotus nor now,[1] whilst Timotheus prosecuted his coasting voyage), felt emboldened to carry out a campaign on their own account against the provincial cities;[2] and one by one they again recovered them.

Timotheus in his cruise reached Corcyra, and reduced it at a blow. That done, he neither enslaved the inhabitants nor drove them into exile, nor changed their laws. And of this conduct he reaped the benefit of the increased cordiality[3] of all the cities of those parts. The Lacedaemonians thereupon fitted out and despatched a counter fleet, with Nicolochus in command, an officer of consummate boldness. This admiral no sooner caught sight of Timotheus's fleet than without hesitation, and in spite of the absence of six Ambraciot vessels which formed part of his squadron, he gave battle, with fifty-five ships to the enemy's sixty. The result was a defeat at the moment, and Timotheus set up a trophy at Alyzia. But as soon as the six missing Ambraciot vessels had reinforced him—the ships of Timotheus meanwhile being docked and undergoing repairs—he bore down upon Alyzia in search of the Athenian, and as Timotheus refused to put out to meet him, the Lacedaemonian in turn set up a trophy on the nearest group of islands.

374 BC. Timotheus, after repairing his original squadron and manning more vessels from Corcyra, found himself at the head of more than seventy

---

1 Lit. "nor at the date of Timotherus's periplus." To the historian writing of the events of this period several years later, the coasting voyage of Timotheus is a single incident ({periepleuse}), and as Grote ("H. G." x. 185, note 3) observes, the words may "include not simply the time which Timotheus took in actually circumnavigating Peloponnesos, but the year which he spent afterward in the Ionian sea, and the time which he occupied in performing his exploits near Korkyra, Leukas, and the neighborhood generally." For the character and exploits of Timotheus, son of Conon, see Isocr. "Or." xv. "On the Antidosis," SS. 101–139; Jebb, "Att. Or." ii. p. 140 foll.; Rehdantz, "Vit. Iphicr. Chabr. Timoth. Atheniensium."
2 Or, "the cities round about their territory," lit. "the perioecid cities." For the import of the epithet, see V. iv. 46; Freeman, op. cit. iv. 173, note 1, in reference to Grote, "H. G." x. 183, note 4. For the battle of Tegyra see Grote, ib. 182; Plut. "Pelop." 17; Diod. xv. 57 ("evidently this battle," Grote); Callisthenes, fr. 3, ed. Did. Cf. Steph. Byz., {Tegura}.
3 The Corcyraeans, Acarnanians, and Cephallenians join the alliance 375 BC; see Hicks, 83. "This decree dates from the autumn of 375 BC, immediately after Timotheos's visit to Korkyra (Xen. "Hell." V. iv. 64). The result was that the names of Korkyra, Kephallenia, and Akarnania were inscribed upon the list (No. 81), and an alliance was made with them." (See "C. I. A." ii. p. 399 foll.; Hicks, loc. cit.; "Hell." VI. v. 23); "C. I. A." ii. 14. The tablet is in the Asclepeian collection at the entrance of the Acropolis at Athens. See Milchofer, "Die Museum Athens," 1881, p. 45.

ships. His naval superiority was undisputed, but he was forced to send to Athens for moneys, seeing his fleet was large and his wants not trifling.

BOOK VI

I

374 BC. The Athenians and Lacedaemonians were thus engaged. But to return to the Thebans. After the subjugation of the cities in Boeotia, they extended the area of aggression and marched into Phocis. The Phocians, on their side, sent an embassy to Lacedaemon, and pleaded that without assistance from that power they must inevitably yield to Thebes. The Lacedaemonians in response conveyed by sea into the territory of Phocis their king Cleombrotus, at the head of four regiments and the contingents of the allies.

About the same time Polydamus of Pharsalus arrived from Thessaly to address the general assembly[1] of Lacedaemon. He was a man of high repute throughout the whole of Thessaly, while in his native city he was regarded as so true a gentleman that the faction-ridden Pharsalians were content to entrust the citadel to his keeping, and to allow their revenues to pass through his hands. It was his privilege to disburse the money needed for sacred rites or other expenditure, within the limits of their written law and constitution. Out of these moneys this faithful steward of the state was able to garrison and guard in safety for the citizens their capital. Every year he rendered an account of his administration in general. If there was a deficit he made it up out of his own pocket, and when the revenues expanded he paid himself back. For the rest, his hospitality to foreigners and his magnificence were on a true Thessalian scale. Such was the style and character of the man who now arrived in Lacedaemon and spoke as follows:

"Men of Lacedaemon, it is in my capacity as "proxenos" and "benefactor" (titles borne by my ancestry from time immemorial) that I claim, or rather am bound, in case of any difficulty to come to you, and, in case of any complication dangerous to your interests in Thessaly, to give you warning. The name of Jason, I feel sure, is not unknown to Lacedaemonian ears. His power as a prince is sufficiently large, and his fame widespread. It is of Jason I have to speak. Under cover of a treaty of peace he has lately conferred

---

[1] {pros to koinon}, "h.e. vel ad ad senatum vel ad ephoros vel ad concionem."—Sturz, "Lex. Xen." s.v.

with me, and this is the substance of what he urged: "Polydamas," he said, "if I chose I could lay your city at my feet, even against its will, as the following considerations will prove to you. See," he went on, "the majority and the most important of the states of Thessaly are my allies. I subdued them in campaigns in which you took their side in opposition to myself. Again, you do not need to be told that I have six thousand mercenaries who are a match in themselves, I take it, for any single state. It is not the mere numbers on which I insist. No doubt as large an army could be raised in other quarters; but these citizen armies have this defect—they include men who are already advanced in years, with others whose beards are scarcely grown. Again, it is only a fraction of the citizens who attend to bodily training in a state, whereas with me no one takes mercenary service who is not as capable of endurance as myself."

"And here, Lacedaemonians, I must tell you what is the bare truth. This Jason is a man stout of limb and robust of body, with an insatiable appetite for toil. Equally true is it that he tests the mettle of those with him day by day. He is always at their head, whether on a field-day under arms, or in the gymnasium, or on some military expedition. The weak members of the corps he weeds out, but those whom he sees bear themselves stout-heartedly in the face of war, like true lovers of danger and of toil, he honors with double, treble, and quadruple pay, or with other gifts. On the bed of sickness they will not lack attendance, nor honor in their graves. Thus every foreigner in his service knows that his valour in war may obtain for him a livelihood—a life replete at once with honor and abundance.[1]

"Then with some parade he pointed out to me what I knew before, that the Maracians, and the Dolopians, and Alcetas the hyparch[2] in Epirus, were already subject to his sway; "so that I may fairly ask you, Polydamas," he proceeded, "what I have to apprehend that I should not look on your future subjugation as mere child's play. Perhaps someone who did not know me, and what manner of man I am, might put it to me: "Well! Jason, if all you say be true, why do you hesitate? why do you not march at once against Pharsalia?" For the good reason, I reply, that it suits me better to win you voluntarily than to annex you against your wills. Since, if you are forced, you will always be planning all the mischief you can against me, and I on my side shall be striving to diminish your power; whereas if you throw in your lot with mine trustfully and willingly, it is certain we shall do what

---

1 Or, "a life satisfying at once to soul and body."

2 Or, "his underlord in Epirus." By hyparch, I suppose, is implied that Alcetas regarded Jason as his suzerain. Diodorus (xv. 13, 36) speaks of him as "king" of the Molossians.

we can to help each other. I see and know, Polydamas, that your country fixes her eyes on one man only, and that is yourself: what I guarantee you, therefore, is that, if you will dispose her lovingly to myself, I on my side will raise you up to be the greatest man in Hellas next to me. Listen, while I tell you what it is in which I offer you the second prize. Listen, and accept nothing which does not approve itself as true to your own reasoning. First, is it not plain to us both, that with the adhesion of Pharsalus and the swarm of pettier states dependent on yourselves, I shall with infinite ease become Tagos[1] of all the Thessalians; and then the corollary—Thessaly so united—sixteen thousand cavalry and more than ten thousand heavy infantry leap into life. Indeed, when I contemplate the physique and proud carriage of these men, I cannot but persuade myself that, with proper handling, there is not a nation or tribe of men to which Thessalians would deign to yield submission. Look at the broad expanse of Thessaly and consider: when once a Tagos is established here, all the tribes in a circle round will lie stilled in subjection; and almost every member of each of these tribes is an archer born, so that in the light infantry division of the service our power must needs excel. Furthermore, the Boeotians and all the rest of the world in arms against Lacedaemon are my allies; they clamour to follow my banner, if only I will free them from Sparta's yoke. So again the Athenians, I make sure, will do all they can to gain our alliance; but with them I do not think we will make friends, for my persuasion is that empire by sea will be even easier to acquire than empire by land; and to show you the justice of this reasoning I would have you weigh the following considerations. With Macedonia, which is the timber-yard[2] of the Athenian navy, in our hands we shall be able to construct a far larger fleet than theirs. That stands to reason. And as to men, which will be the better able to man vessels, think you—Athens, or ourselves with our stalwart and numerous Penestae?[3] Which will better support mariners—a nation which, like our own, out of her abundance exports her corn to foreign parts, or Athens, which, but for foreign purchases, has not enough to support herself? And so as to wealth

---

1 Or, "Prince," and below, "Thessaly so converted into a Principality." "The Tagos of Thessaly was not a King, because his office was not hereditary or even permanent; neither was he exactly a Tyrant, because his office had some sort of legal sanction. But he came much nearer to the character either of a King or of a Tyrant than to that of a Federal President like the General of the Achaians.... Jason of Pherai acts throughout like a King, and his will seems at least as uncontrolled as that of his brother sovereign beyond the Kambunian hills. Even Jason seems to have been looked upon as a Tyrant (see below, "Hell." VI. iv. 32); possibly, like the Athenian Demos, he himself did not refuse the name" (cf. Arist. "Pol." iii. 4, 9).—Freeman, "Hist. Fed. Gov." "No True Federation in Thessaly," iv. pp. 152 foll.

2 See above, and Hicks, 74.

3 Or, "peasantry."

in general it is only natural, is it not, that we, who do not look to a string of little islands for supplies, but gather the fruits of continental peoples, should find our resources more copious? As soon as the scattered powers of Thessaly are gathered into a principality, all the tribes around, I repeat, will become our tributaries. I need not tell you that the king of Persia reaps the fruits, not of islands, but of a continent, and he is the wealthiest of men! But the reduction of Persia will be still more practicable, I imagine, than that of Hellas, for there the men, save one, are better versed in slavery than in prowess. Nor have I forgotten, during the advance of Cyrus, and afterward under Agesilaus, how scant the force was before which the Persian quailed."

"Such, Lacedaemonians, were the glowing arguments of Jason. In answer I told him that what he urged was well worth weighing, but that we, the friends of Lacedaemon, should so, without a quarrel, desert her and rush into the arms of her opponents, seemed to me sheer madness. Whereat he praised me, and said that now must he needs cling all the closer to me if that were my disposition, and so charged me to come to you and tell you the plain truth, which is, that he is minded to march against Pharsalus if we will not hearken to him. Accordingly he bade me demand assistance from you; 'and if they suffer you,'[1] he added, 'so to work upon them that they will send you a force sufficient to do battle with me, it is well: we will abide by war's arbitrament, nor quarrel with the consequence; but if in your eyes that aid is insufficient, look to yourself. How shall you longer be held blameless before that fatherland which honors you and in which you fare so well?' "[2]

"These are the matters," Polydamas continued, "which have brought me to Lacedaemon. I have told you the whole story; it is based partly on what I see to be the case, and partly on what I have heard from yonder man. My firm belief is, men of Lacedaemon, that if you are likely to despatch a force sufficient, not in my eyes only, but in the eyes of all the rest of Thessaly, to cope with Jason in war, the states will revolt from him, for they are all in alarm as to the future development of the man's power; but if you think a company of newly-enfranchised slaves and any amateur

---

1 Or, reading {theoi}, after Cobet; translate "if providentially they should send you."
2 Reading {kai e su pratteis}, after Cobet. The chief MSS. give {ouk ede anegkletos an dikaios eies en te patridi e se tima kai su prattois ta kratista}, which might be rendered either, "and how be doing best for yourself?" (lit. "and you would not be doing best for yourself," {ouk an} carried on from previous clause), or (taking {prattois} as pure optative), "may you be guided to adopt the course best for yourself!" "may the best fortune attend you! Farewell." See Otto Keller, op. cit. ad loc. for various emendations.

general will suffice, I advise you to rest in peace. You may take my word for it, you will have a great power to contend against, and a man who is so prudent a general that, in all he essays to do, be it an affair of secrecy, or speed, or force, he is wont to hit the mark of his endeavours: one who is skilled, should occasion serve, to make the night of equal service to him with the day;[1] or, if speed be needful, will labor on while breakfasting or taking an evening meal. And as for repose, he thinks that the time for it has come when the goal is reached or the business on hand accomplished. And to this same practice he has habituated those about him. Right well he knows how to reward the expectations of his soldiers, when by the extra toil which makes the difference they have achieved success; so that in his school all have laid to heart that maxim, "Pain first and pleasure after."[2] And in regard to pleasure of the senses, of all men I know, he is the most continent; so that these also are powerless to make him idle at the expense of duty. You must consider the matter then and tell me, as befits you, what you can and will do."

Such were the representations of Polydamas. The Lacedaemonians, for the time being, deferred their answer; but after calculating the next day and the day following how many divisions[3] they had on foreign service, and how many ships on the coast of Laconia to deal with the foreign squadron of the Athenians, and taking also into account the war with their neighbors, they gave their answer to Polydamas: "For the present they would not be able to send him sufficient aid: under the circumstances they advised him to go back and make the best settlement he could of his own affairs and those of his city." He, thanking the Lacedaemonians for their straightforwardness, withdrew.

The citadel of Pharsalus he begged Jason not to force him to give up: his desire was to preserve it for those who had entrusted it to his safe keeping; his own sons Jason was free to take as hostages, and he would do his best to procure for him the voluntary adhesion of his city by persuasion, and in every way to further his appointment as Tagos of Thessaly. Accordingly, after interchange of solemn assurances between the pair, the Pharsalians were let alone and in peace, and ere long Jason was, by general consent, appointed Tagos of all the Thessalians. Once fairly vested with that authority, he drew up a list of the cavalry and heavy infantry which the several states were capable of furnishing as their quota, with the result that

---

1 See *"Cyrop."* III. i. 19.
2 For this sentiment, see *"Mem."* II. i. 20 *et passim*.
3 Lit. *"morai."*

his cavalry, inclusive of allies, numbered more than eight thousand, while his infantry force was computed at not less than twenty thousand; and his light troops would have been a match for those of the whole world—the mere enumeration of their cities would be a labor in itself.[1] His next act was a summons to all the dwellers round[2] to pay tribute exactly the amount imposed in the days of Scopas.[3] And here in this state of accomplishment we may leave these matters. I return to the point reached when this digression into the affairs of Jason began.

II

374 BC. The Lacedaemonians and their allies were collecting in Phocia, and the Thebans, after retreating into their own territory, were guarding the approaches. At this juncture the Athenians, seeing the Thebans growing strong at their expense without contributing a single penny to the maintenance of the fleet, while they themselves, what with money contributions, and piratical attacks from Aegina, and the garrisoning of their territory, were being pared to the bone, conceived a desire to cease from war. In this mood they sent an embassy to Lacedaemon and concluded peace.[4]

374–373 BC. This done, two of the ambassadors, in obedience to a decree of the state, set sail at once from Laconian territory, bearing orders to Timotheus to sail home, since peace was established. That officer, while obeying his orders, availed himself of the homeward voyage to land certain Zacynthian exiles[5] on their native soil, whereupon the Zacynthian city party sent to Lacedaemon and complained of the treatment they had received from Timotheus; and the Lacedaemonians, without further consideration, decided that the Athenians were in the wrong, and proceeded

---

1 See "Cyrop." I. i. 5.
2 Lit. perioeci.
3 It is conjectured that the Scopadae ruled at Pherae and Cranusa in the earlier half of the fifth century BC; see, for the change of dynasty, what is said of Lycophron of Pherae in "Hell." II. iii. 4. There was a famous Scopas, son of Creon, to whom Simonides addressed his poem—

> {Andr' agathon men alatheos genesthai khalepon khersin te kai posi kai noo tetragonon, aneu psogou tetugmenon.}

a sentiment criticised by Plato, "Protag." 359 A. "Now Simonides says to Scopas, the son of Creon, the Thessalian:

> 'Hardly on the one hand can a man become truly good; built four-square in hands and feet and mind, a work without a flaw.'

Do you know the poem?"—Jowett, "Plat." i. 153. But whether this Scopas is the Scopas of our text and a hero of Jason's is not clear.
4 See Curtius, "H. G." vol. iv. p. 376 (Eng. trans.)
5 See Hicks, 81, p. 142.

to equip another navy, and at length collected from Laconia itself, from Corinth, Leucas,[1] Ambracia, Elis, Zacynthus, Achaia, Epidaurus, Troezen, Hermione, and Halieis, a force amounting to sixty sail. In command of this squadron they appointed Mnasippus admiral, with orders to attack Corcyra, and in general to look after their interests in those seas. They, moreover, sent an embassy to Dionysius, instructing him that his interests would be advanced by the withdrawal of Corcyra from Athenian hands.

373 BC. Accordingly Mnasippus set sail, as soon as his squadron was ready, direct to Corcyra; he took with him, besides his troops from Lacedaemon, a body of mercenaries, making a total in all of no less than fifteen hundred men. His disembarked, and soon became master of the island, the country district falling a prey to the spoiler. It was in a high state of cultivation, and rich with fruit-trees, not to speak of magnificent dwelling-houses and wine-cellars fitted up on the farms: so that, it was said, the soldiers reached such a pitch of luxury that they refused to drink wine which had not a fine bouquet. A crowd of slaves, too, and fat beasts were captured on the estates.

The general's next move was to encamp with his land forces about three-quarters of a mile[2] from the city district, so that any Corcyraean who attempted to leave the city to go into the country would certainly be cut off on that side. The fleet he stationed on the other side of the city, at a point where he calculated on detecting and preventing the approach of convoys. Besides which he established a blockade in front of the harbor when the weather permitted. In this way the city was completely invested.

The Corcyraeans, on their side, were in the sorest straits. They could get nothing from their soil owing to the vice in which they were gripped by land, whilst owing to the predominance of the enemy at sea nothing could be imported. Accordingly they sent to the Athenians and begged for their assistance. They urged upon them that it would be a great mistake if they suffered themselves to be robbed of Corcyra. If they did so, they would not only throw away a great advantage to themselves, but add a considerable strength to their enemy; since, with the exception of Athens, no state was capable of furnishing a larger fleet or revenue. Moreover, Corcyra lay favorably[3] for commanding the Corinthian gulf and the cities which line its shores; it was splendidly situated for injuring the rural districts of Laconia, and still more splendidly in relation to the opposite shores of the continent of Epirus, and the passage between Peloponnesus and Sicily.

---

1 *Ibid.* 81, 86.
2 Lit. *"five stades."*
3 See Thuc. i. 36.

This appeal did not fall on deaf ears. The Athenians were persuaded that the matter demanded their most serious attention, and they at once despatched Stesicles as general,[1] with about six hundred peltasts. They also requested Alcetas to help them in getting their troops across. Thus under cover of night the whole body were conveyed across to a point in the open country, and found their way into the city. Nor was that all. The Athenians passed a decree to man sixty ships of war, and elected[2] Timotheus admiral. The latter, being unable to man the fleet on the spot, set sail on a cruise to the islands and tried to make up the complements of his crews from those quarters. He evidently looked upon it as no light matter to sail round Peloponnesus as if on a voyage of pleasure, and to attack a fleet in the perfection of training.[3] To the Athenians, however, it seemed that he was wasting the precious time seasonable for the coastal voyage, and they were not disposed to condone such an error, but deposed him, appointing Iphicrates in his stead. The new general was no sooner appointed than he set about getting his vessels manned with the utmost activity, putting pressure on the trierarchs. He further procured from the Athenians for his use not only any vessels cruising on the coast of Attica, but the *Paralus* and *Salaminia*[4] also, remarking that, if things turned out well yonder, he would soon send them back plenty of ships. Thus his numbers grew to something like seventy sail.

Meanwhile the Corcyraeans were sore beset with famine: desertion became every day more frequent, so much so that Mnasippus caused proclamation to be made by herald that all deserters would be sold there and then;[5] and when that had no effect in lessening the stream of runaways, he ended by driving them back with the lash. Those within the walls, however, were not disposed to receive these miserable slaves within the lines, and numbers died outside. Mnasippus, not blind to what was happening, soon persuaded himself that he had as good as got the city into his possession: and he began to try experiments on his mercenaries. Some of them he had already paid off;[6] others still in his service had as much as two months' pay owing to them by the general, who, if report spoke true, had no lack of money, since the majority of the states, not caring for a

---

1 The name of the general was Ctesicles, according to Diod. xv. 47. Read {strategon} for {tagon}, with Breitenbach, Cobet, etc. For Alcetas, see above, "Hell." VI. i. 7.
2 I.e. by show of hands, {ekheirotonoun}.
3 See Jowett, note to Thuc. VIII. xcv. 2, ii. p. 525.
4 The two sacred galleys. See Thuc. iii. 33; Aristoph. "Birds," 147 foll.
5 Or, "he would knock them all down to the hammer."
6 Or, "cut off from their pay."

campaign across the seas, sent him hard cash instead of men. But now the beleaguered citizens, who could espy from their towers that the outposts were less carefully guarded than formerly, and the men scattered about the rural districts, made a sortie, capturing some and cutting down others. Mnasippus, perceiving the attack, donned his armor, and, with all the heavy troops he had, rushed to the rescue, giving orders to the captains and brigadiers[1] to lead out the mercenaries. Some of the captains answered that it was not so easy to command obedience when the necessaries of life were lacking; whereat the Spartan struck one man with his staff, and another with the butt of his spear. Without spirit and full of resentment against their general, the men mustered—a condition very unfavorable to success in battle. Having drawn up the troops, the general in person repulsed the division of the enemy which was opposite the gates, and pursued them closely; but these, rallying close under their walls, turned right about, and from under cover of the tombs kept up a continuous discharge of darts and other missiles; other detachments, dashing out at other gates, meanwhile fell heavily on the flanks of the enemy. The Lacedaemonians, being drawn up eight deep, and thinking that the wing of their phalanx was of inadequate strength, essayed to wheel around; but as soon as they began the movement the Corcyraeans attacked them as if they were fleeing, and they were then unable to recover themselves,[2] while the troops next in position abandoned themselves to flight. Mnasippus, unable to succour those who were being pressed owing to the attack of the enemy immediately in front, found himself left from moment to moment with decreasing numbers. At last the Corcyraeans collected, and with one united effort made a final rush upon Mnasippus and his men, whose numbers were now considerably reduced. At the same instant the townsmen,[3] eagerly noticing the posture of affairs, rushed out to play their part. First Mnasippus was slain, and then the pursuit became general; nor could the pursuers well have failed to capture the camp, barricade and all, had they not caught sight of the mob of traffickers with a long array of attendants and slaves, and thinking that here was a prize indeed, desisted from further chase.

 The Corcyraeans were well content for the moment to set up a trophy and to give back the enemy's dead under a flag of truce; but the after-consequences were even more important to them in the revival of strength

---

1 Lit. "lochagoi and taxiarchs."
2 Or, "to retaliate"; or, "to complete the movement."
3 Reading, after Dindorf, {oi politai}, or, if with the MSS., {oi oplitai}; translate "the heavy-armed among the assailants saw their advantage and pressed on."

and spirits which were sunk in despondency. The rumor spread that Iphicrates would soon be there—he was even at the doors; and in fact the Corcyraeans themselves were manning a fleet. So Hypermenes, who was second in command to Mnasippus and the bearer of his despatches, manned every vessel of the fleet as full as it would hold, and then sailing round to the entrenched camp, filled all the transports with prisoners and valuables and other stock, and sent them off. He himself, with his marines and the survivors of his troops, kept watch over the entrenchments; but at last even this remnant in the excess of panic and confusion got on board the men-of-war and sailed off, leaving behind them vast quantities of corn and wine, with numerous prisoners and invalided soldiers. The fact was, they were sorely afraid of being caught by the Athenians in the island, and so they made safely off to Leucas.

Meanwhile Iphicrates had commenced his voyage of circumnavigation, partly voyaging and partly making every preparation for an engagement. He at once left his large sails behind him, as the voyage was only to be the prelude of a battle; his flying jibs, even if there was a good breeze, were but little used, since by making his progress depend on sheer rowing, he hoped at once to improve the physique of his men and the speed of his attack. Often when the squadron was about to put into shore for the purpose of breakfast or supper, he would seize the moment, and draw back the leading wing of the column from the land off the point in question; and then facing round again with the triremes posted well in line, prow for prow, at a given signal let loose the whole fleet in a stoutly contested race for the shore. Great was the triumph in being the first to take in water or whatever else they might need, or the first to breakfast; just as it was a heavy penalty on the late-comers, not only to come short in all these objects of desire, but to have to put out to sea with the rest as soon as the signal was given; since the first-comers had altogether a quiet time of it, whilst the hindmost must get through the whole business in hot haste. So again, in the matter of outposts, if he chanced to be getting the morning meal on hostile territory, pickets would be posted, as was right and proper, on the land; but, apart from these, he would raise his masts and keep look-out men on the maintops. These commanded of course a far wider prospect from their lofty perches than the outposts on the level ground. So too, when he dined or slept he had no fires burning in the camp at night, but only a beacon kindled in front of the encampment to prevent any unseen approach; and frequently in fine weather he put out to sea immediately after the evening meal, when, if the breeze favored, they ran along and took their rest simultaneously, or if they depended on oars he gave his mariners repose by turns. During the voyage in daytime he would at one time signal to "sail in column," and at another signal "abreast in line." So that whilst they prosecuted the voyage they at the same time became (both as to theory and practice) well versed in all the details of an engagement before they reached the open sea—a sea, as they imagined, occupied by their foes. For the most part they breakfasted and dined on hostile territory; but as he confined himself to bare necessaries he was always too quick for the enemy. Before the hostile reinforcement would come up he had finished his business and was out to sea again.

At the date of Mnasippus's death he chanced to be off Sphagiae in Laconian territory. Reaching Elis, and coasting past the mouth of the Alpheus, he came to moorings under Cape Ichthus,[1] as it is called. The next day he put out from that port for Cephallenia, so drawing up his line and conducting the voyage that he might be prepared in every detail to engage if necessary. The tale about Mnasippus and his demise had reached him, but he had not heard it from an eye-witness, and suspected that it might have been invented to deceive him and throw him off his guard. He was therefore on the look-out. It was, in fact, only on arrival in Cephallenia that he learned the news in an explicit form, and gave his troops rest.

I am well aware that all these details of practice and manouvring are customary in anticipation of a sea-fight, but what I single out for praise in the case before us is the skill with which the Athenian admiral attained a twofold object. Bearing in mind that it was his duty to reach a certain point at which he expected to fight a naval battle without delay, it was a happy discovery on his part not to allow tactical skill, on the one hand, to be sacrificed to the pace of sailing,[2] nor, on the other, the need of training to interfere with the date of arrival.

After reducing the towns of Cephallenia, Iphicrates sailed to Corcyra. There the first news he heard was that the triremes sent by Dionysius were expected to relieve the Lacedaemonians. On receipt of this information he set off in person and surveyed the country, in order to find a spot from which it would be possible to see the vessels approaching and to signal to the city. Here he stationed his look-out men. A code of signals was agreed upon to signify "vessels in sight," "mooring," etc.; which done he gave his orders to twenty of his captains of men-of-war who were to follow him at a given word of command. Any one who failed to follow him must not grumble at the penalty; that he warned them. Presently the vessels were

---

1 *Cape Fish, mod. Cape Katakolon, protecting harbor of Pyrgos in Elis.*
2 *Lit. "the voyage."*

signalled approaching; the word of command was given, and then the enthusiasm was a sight to see—every man of the crews told off for the expedition racing to join his ship and embark. Sailing to the point where the enemy's vessels lay, he had no difficulty in capturing the crews, who had disembarked from all the ships with one exception. The exception was that of Melanippus the Rhodian, who had advised the other captains not to stop at this point, and had then manned his own vessel and sailed off. Thus he encountered the ships of Iphicrates, but contrived to slip through his fingers, while the whole of the Syracusan vessels were captured, crews and all.

Having cut the beaks off the prows, Iphicrates bore down into the harbor of Corcyra with the captured triremes in tow. With the captive crews themselves he came to an agreement that each should pay a fixed sum as ransom, with one exception, that of Crinippus, their commander. Him he kept under guard, with the intention apparently of exacting a handsome sum in his case or else of selling him. The prisoner, however, from vexation of spirit, put an end to his own life. The rest were sent about their business by Iphicrates, who accepted the Corcyraeans as sureties for the money. His own sailors he supported for the most part as laborers on the lands of the Corcyraeans, while at the head of his light infantry and the hoplites of the contingent he crossed over into Acarnania, and there lent his aid to any friendly state that needed his services; besides which he went to war with the Thyrians,[1] a sturdy race of warriors in possession of a strong fortress.

372 BC. Having attached to his squadron the navy also of Corcyra, with a fleet numbering now about ninety ships he set sail, in the first instance to Cephallenia, where he exacted money—which was in some cases voluntarily paid, in others forcibly extorted. In the next place he began making preparations partly to harass the territory of the Lacedaemonians, and partly to win over voluntarily the other states in that quarter which were hostile to Athens; or in case of refusal to go to war with them.

The whole conduct of the campaign reflects, I think, the highest credit on Iphicrates. If his strategy was admirable, so too was the instinct which led him to advise the association with himself of two such colleagues as Callistratus and Chabrias—the former a popular orator but no great friend

---

1 *Thyreum (or Thyrium), in Acarnania, a chief city at the time of the Roman wars in Greece; and according to Polybius (xxxviii. 5), a meeting-place of the League on one occasion. See "Dict. Anct. Geog." s.v.; Freeman, op. cit. iv. 148; cf. Paus. IV. xxvi. 3, in reference to the Messenians and Naupactus; Grote, "H. G." x. 212.*

of himself politically,[1] the other a man of high military reputation. Either he looked upon them as men of unusual sagacity, and wished to profit by their advice, in which case I commend the good sense of the arrangement, or they were, in his belief, antagonists, in which case the determination to approve himself a consummate general, neither indolent nor incautious, was bold, I admit, but indicative of a laudable self-confidence. Here, however, we must part with Iphicrates and his achievements to return to Athens.

III

The Athenians, forced to witness the expatriation from Boeotia of their friends the Plataeans (who had sought an asylum with themselves), forced also to listen to the supplications of the Thespiaeans (who begged them not to suffer them to be robbed of their city), could no longer regard the Thebans with favor;[2] though, when it came to a direct declaration of war, they were checked in part by a feeling of shame, and partly by considerations of expediency. Still, to go hand in hand with them, to be a party to their proceedings, this they absolutely refused, now that they saw them marching against time-honored friends of the city like the Phocians, and blotting out states whose loyalty in the great Persian war was conspicuous no less than their friendship to Athens. Accordingly the People passed a decree to make peace; but in the first instance they sent an embassy to Thebes, inviting that state to join them if it pleased them on an embassy which they proposed to send to Lacedaemon to treat of peace. In the next place they despatched such an embassy on their own account. Among the commissioners appointed were Callias the son of Hipponicus, Autocles the son of Strombichides, Demostratus the son of Aristophon, Aristocles, Cephisodotus,[3] Melanopus, and Lycaethus.

371 BC. (These were formally introduced to the Deputies of the Lacedaemonians and the allies.[4]) Nor ought the name of Callistratus to be omitted. That statesman and orator was present. He had obtained furlough from Iphicrates on an undertaking either to send money for the fleet or

---

1 Reading with the MSS. {ou mala epitedeion onta}. See Grote, "H. G." x. 206. Boeckh ("P. E. A.," trans. Cornewall Lewis, p. 419) wished to read {eu mala} for {ou mala k.t.l.}, in which case translate "the former a popular orator, and a man of singular capacity"; and for {epitedeion} in that sense, see "Hipparch." i. 8; for {eu mala}, see "Hipparch." i. 25. For details concerning Callistratus, see Dindorf, op. cit. note ad. loc.; Curtius, "H. G." iv. 367, 381 foll., v. 90. For Chabrias, Rehdantz, op. cit. In the next sentence I have again adhered to the reading of the MSS., but the passage is commonly regarded as corrupt; see Otto Keller, op. cit. p. 215 for various emendations.
2 Plataea destroyed in 373 BC. See Jowett, "Thuc." ii. 397.
3 See below, "Hell." VII. i. 12; Hicks, 87.
4 The bracketed words read like an annotator's comment, or possibly they are a note by the author.

to arrange a peace. Hence his arrival in Athens and transactions in behalf of peace. After being introduced to the assembly[1] of the Lacedaemonians and to the allies, Callias,[2] who was the dadouchos (or torch-holder) in the mysteries, made the first speech. He was a man just as well pleased to praise himself as to hear himself praised by others. He opened the proceedings as follows:

"Lacedaemonians, the duty of representing you as proxenos at Athens is a privilege which I am not the first member of my family to enjoy; my father's father held it as an heirloom of our family and handed it down as a heritage to his descendants. If you will permit me, I should like to show you the disposition of my fatherland toward yourselves. If in times of war she chooses us as her generals, so when her heart is set upon quiet she sends us out as her messengers of peace. I myself have twice already[3] stood here to treat for conclusion of war, and on both embassies succeeded in arranging a mutually agreeable peace. Now for the third time I am come, and I flatter myself that today again I shall obtain a reconciliation, and on grounds exceptionally just. My eyes bear witness that our hearts are in accord; you and we alike are pained at the effacement of Plataeae and Thespiae. Is it not then reasonable that out of agreement should spring concord rather than discord? It is never the part, I take it, of wise men to raise the standard of war for the sake of petty differences; but where there is nothing but unanimity they must be marvellous folk who refuse the bond of peace. But I go further. It were just and right on our parts even to refuse to bear arms against each other; since, as the story runs, the first strangers to whom our forefather Triptolemus showed the unspeakable mystic rites of Demeter and Core, the mother and the maiden, were your ancestors;—I speak of Heracles, the first founder of your state, and of your two citizens, the great twin sons of Zeus—and to Peloponnesus first he gave as a gift the seed of Demeter's corn-fruits. How, then, can it be just or right either that you should come and ravage the corn crops of those from whom you got the sacred seed of corn, or that we should not desire that they to whom the gift was given should share abundantly of this boon? But if, as it would seem, it is a fixed decree of heaven that war shall never cease among men, yet ought we—your people and our people—to be as slow as possible to begin it, and being in it, as swift as possible to bring it to an end."

---

1 See above, *"Hell."* II. iv. 38.
2 See above, *"Hell."* IV. v. 13; Cobet, *"Prosop. Xen."* p. 67 foll.; Xen. *"Symp."*; Plat. *"Protag."*; Andoc. *"de Myst."* If this is one and the same person he must have been an elderly man at this date, 371 BC
3 387 BC and 374; see Curtius, *"H. G."* vol. iv. p. 376 (Eng. ed.)

After him Autocles[1] spoke: he was of repute as a versatile lawyer and orator, and addressed the meeting as follows: "Lacedaemonians, I do not conceal from myself that what I am about to say is not calculated to please you, but it seems to me that, if you wish the friendship which we are cementing to last as long as possible, we are wise to show each other the underlying causes of our wars. Now, you are perpetually saying that the states ought to be independent; but it is you yourselves who most of all stand in the way of independence—your first and last stipulation with the allied states being that they should follow you whithersoever you choose to lead; and yet what has this principle of follow-my-leader got to do with independent action?[2] Again, you pick quarrels without consulting your allies, and lead them against those whom you account enemies; so that in many cases, with all their vaunted independence, they are forced to march against their greatest friends; and, what is still more opposed to independence than all else, you are forever setting up here your decarchies and there your thirty commissioners, and your chief aim in appointing these officers and governors seems to be, not that they should fulfill their office and govern legally, but that they should be able to keep the cities under their heels by sheer force. So that it looks as if you delighted in despotisms rather than free constitutions. Let us go back to the date[3] at which the Persian king enjoined the independence of the states. At that time you made no secret of your conviction that the Thebans, if they did not suffer each state to govern itself and to use the laws of its own choice, would be failing to act in the spirit of the king's rescript. But no sooner had you got hold of Cadmeia than you would not suffer the Thebans themselves to be independent. Now, if the maintenance of friendship be an object, it is no use for people to claim justice from others while they themselves are doing all they can to prove the selfishness of their aims."

These remarks were received in absolute silence, yet in the hearts of those who were annoyed with Lacedaemon they stirred pleasure. After Autocles spoke Callistratus: "Trespasses, men of Lacedaemon, have been committed on both sides, yours and ours, I am free to confess; but still it is not my view that because a man has done wrong we can never again have dealings with him. Experience tells me that no man can go very far without a slip, and it seems to me that sometimes the transgressor by

---

1 For the political views of Autocles, see Curtius, "H. G." iv. 387, v. 94 (Eng. tr.); see also Grote, "H. G." x. 225.
2 Or, "what consistency is there between these precepts of yours and political independence?"
3 Sixteen years before—387 BC. See "Pol. Lac." xiv. 5.

reason of his transgression becomes more tractable, especially if he be chastened through the error he has committed, as has been the case with us. And so on your own case I see that ungenerous acts have sometimes reaped their own proper reward: blow has been met by counter-blow; and as a specimen I take the seizure of the Cadmeia in Thebes. Today, at any rate, the very cities whose independence you strove for have, since your unrighteous treatment of Thebes, fallen one and all of them again into her power.[1] We are schooled now, both of us, to know that grasping brings not gain. We are prepared, I hope, to be once more moderate under the influence of a mutual friendship. Some, I know, in their desire to render our peace[2] abortive accuse us falsely, as though we were come hither, not seeking friendship, but because we dread the arrival of some[3] Antalcidas with moneys from the king. But consider, what arrant nonsense they talk! Was it not, pray, the great king who demanded that all the states in Hellas should be independent? and what have we Athenians, who are in full agreement with the king, both in word and deed, to fear from him? Or is it conceivable that he prefers spending money in making others great to finding his favorite projects realized without expense?

"Well! what is it really that has brought us here? No especial need or difficulty in our affairs. That you may discover by a glance at our maritime condition, or, if you prefer, at the present posture of our affairs on land. Well, then, how does the matter stand? It is obvious that some of our allies please us no better than they please you;[4] and, possibly, in return for your former preservation of us, we may be credited with a desire to point out to you the soundness of our policy.

"But, to revert once more to the topic of expediency and common interests. It is admitted, I presume, that, looking at the states collectively, half support your views, half ours; and in every single state one party is for Sparta and another for Athens. Suppose, then, we were to shake hands, from what quarter can we reasonably anticipate danger and trouble? To put the case in so many words, so long as you are our friends no one

---

1 Reading, with Breitenbach and Hartman, {as} instead of {os espoudasate k.t.l.}
2 Or, more lit. "to avert the peace" as an ill-omened thing.
3 Without inserting {tis}, as Hartman proposes ("An. Xen." p. 387), that, I think, is the sense. Antalcidas is the arch-diplomat—a name to conjure with, like that of Bismarck in modern European politics. But see Grote, "H. G." x. 213, note 2.
4 See, for this corrupt passage, Otto Keller, op. cit. p. 219; Hartman, op. cit. p. 387; and Breitenbach, n. ad loc. In the next sentence I should like to adopt Hartman's emendation (ib.) {on orthos egnote} for the MSS. {a orthos egnomen}, and translate "we may like to prove to you the soundness of your policy at the time." For the "preservation" referred to, see below, VI. v. 35, and above, II. ii. 20.

can vex us by land; no one, whilst we are your supports, can injure you by sea. Wars like tempests gather and grow to a head from time to time, and again they are dispelled. That we all know. Some future day, if not today, we shall crave, both of us, for peace. Why, then, need we wait for that moment, holding on until we expire under the multitude of our ills, rather than take time by the forelock and, before some irremediable mischief betide, make peace? I cannot admire the man who, because he has entered the lists and has scored many a victory and obtained to himself renown, is so eaten up with the spirit of rivalry that he must needs go on until he is beaten and all his training is made futile. Nor again do I praise the gambler who, if he makes one good stroke of luck, insists on doubling the stakes. Such conduct in the majority of cases must end in absolute collapse. Let us lay the lesson of these to heart, and forbear to enter into any such lists as theirs for life or death; but, while we are yet in the heyday of our strength and fortune, shake hands in mutual amity. So assuredly shall we through you and you through us attain to an unprecedented pinnacle of glory throughout Hellas."

The arguments of the speakers were approved, and the Lacedaemonians passed a resolution to accept peace on a threefold basis: the withdrawal of the governors from the cities,[1] the disbanding of armaments naval and military, and the guarantee of independence to the states. "If any state transgressed these stipulations, it lay at the option of any power whatsoever to aid the states so injured, while, conversely, to bring such aid was not compulsory on any power against its will." On these terms the oaths were administered and accepted by the Lacedaemonians on behalf of themselves and their allies, and by the Athenians and their allies separately state by state. The Thebans had entered their individual name among the states which accepted the oaths, but their ambassadors came the next day with instructions to alter the name of the signatories, substituting for Thebans Boeotians.[2] But Agesilaus answered to this demand that he would alter nothing of what they had in the first instance sworn to and subscribed. If they did not wish to be included in the treaty, he was willing to erase their name at their bidding. So it came to pass that the rest of the world made peace, the sole point of dispute being confined to the Thebans; and the Athenians came to the conclusion that there was a fair prospect of

---

1 Grote ("H. G." x. 236) thinks that Diod. xv. 38 ({exagogeis}) belongs to this time, not to the peace between Athens and Sparta in 374 BC

2 See, for a clear explanation of the matter, Freeman, "Hist. Red. Gov." iv. p. 175, note 3, in reference to Grote, ib. x. 231 note, and Paus. IX. xiii. 2; Plut. "Ages." 28; Thirlwall, "H. G." v. p 69 note.

the Thebans being now literally decimated.[1] As to the Thebans themselves, they retired from Sparta in utter despondency.

IV

In consequence of the peace the Athenians proceeded to withdraw their garrisons from the different sates, and sent to recall Iphicrates with his fleet; besides which they forced him to restore everything captured subsequently to the late solemn undertaking at Lacedaemon. The Lacedaemonians acted differently. Although they withdrew their governors and garrisons from the other states, in Phocis they did not do so. Here Cleombrotus was quartered with his army, and had sent to ask directions from the home authorities. A speaker, Prothous, maintained that their business was to disband the army in accordance with their oaths, and then to send round invitations to the states to contribute what each felt individually disposed, and lay such sum in the temple of Apollo; after which, if any attempt to hinder the independence of the states on any side were manifested, it would be time enough then again to invite all who cared to protect the principle of autonomy to march against its opponents. "In this way," he added, "I think the goodwill of heaven will be secured, and the states will suffer least annoyance." But the Assembly, on hearing these views, agreed that this man was talking nonsense. Puppets in the hands of fate![2] An unseen power, it would seem, was already driving them onward; so they sent instructions to Cleombrotus not to disband the army, but to march straight against the Thebans if they refused to recognize the autonomy of the states. (Cleombrotus, it is understood, had, on hearing the news of the establishment of peace, sent to the ephorate to ask for guidance; and then they sent him the above instructions, bidding him under the circumstances named to march upon Thebes.[3])

The Spartan king soon perceived that, so far from leaving the Boeotian states their autonomy, the Thebans were not even preparing to disband their army, clearly in view of a general engagement; he therefore felt justified in marching his troops into Boeotia. The point of ingress which he adopted was not that which the Thebans anticipated from Phocis, and where they were keeping guard at a defile; but, marching through Thisbae by a mountainous and unsuspected route, he arrived before Creusis, taking

---

1 Or, "*as the saying is, taken and tithed.*" See below, VI. v. 35, *and for the origin of the saying,* Herod. vii. 132.

2 See Grote, "H. G." x. 237: "*The miso-Theban impulse now drove them on with a fury which overcame all other thoughts... a misguiding inspiration sent by the gods—like that of the Homeric Ate.*"

3 *This passage reads like an earlier version for which the above was substituted by the author.*

that fortress and capturing twelve Theban war-vessels besides. After this achievement he advanced from the seaboard and encamped in Leuctra on Thespian territory. The Thebans encamped in a rising ground immediately opposite at no great distance, and were supported by no allies except the Boeotians.

At this juncture the friends of Cleombrotus came to him and urged upon him strong reasons for delivering battle. "If you let the Thebans escape without a battle," they said, "you will run great risks of suffering the extreme penalty at the hands of the state. People will call to mind against you the time when you reached Cynoscephelae and did not ravage a square foot of Theban territory; and again, a subsequent expedition when you were driven back foiled in your attempt to make an entry into the enemy's country—while Agesilaus on each occasion found his entry by Mount Cithaeron. If then you have any care for yourself, or any attachment to your fatherland, march you against the enemy." That was what his friends urged. As to his opponents, what they said was, "Now our fine friend will show whether he really is so concerned on behalf of the Thebans as he is said to be."

Cleombrotus, with these words ringing in his ears, felt driven[1] to join battle. On their side the leaders of Thebes calculated that, if they did not fight, their provincial cities[2] would hold aloof from them and Thebes itself would be besieged; while, if the commonalty of Thebes failed to get supplies, there was every prospect that the city itself would turn against them; and, seeing that many of them had already tasted the bitterness of exile, they came to the conclusion that it was better for them to die on the field of battle than to renew that experience. Besides this they were somewhat encouraged by the recital of an oracle which predicted that the Lacedaemonians would be defeated on the spot where the monument of the maidens stood, who, as the story goes, being violated by certain Lacedaemonians, had slain themselves.[3] This sepulchral monument the Thebans decked with ornaments before the battle. Furthermore, tidings were brought them from the city that all the temples had opened of their own accord; and the priestesses asserted that the gods revealed victory. Again, from the Heracleion men said that the arms had disappeared, as though Heracles himself had sallied forth to battle. It is true that another

---

1 Or, "was provoked."
2 Lit. "perioecid." See Thuc. iv. 76, Arnold's note, and "Hell." V. iv. 46, 63.
3 See Diod. xv. 54; Paus. IX. xiii. 3; Plut. "Pelop." xx.

interpretation[1] of these marvels made them out to be one and all the artifices of the leaders of Thebes. However this may be, everything in the battle turned out adverse to the Lacedaemonians; while fortune herself lent aid to the Thebans and crowned their efforts with success. Cleombrotus held his last council "whether to fight or not," after the morning meal. In the heat of noon a little goes a long way; and the people said that it took a somewhat provocative effect on their spirits.[2]

Both sides were now arming, and there was the unmistakeable signs of approaching battle, when, as the first incident, there issued from the Boeotian lines a long train bent on departure—these were the furnishers of the market, a detachment of baggage bearers, and in general such people as had no inclination to join in the fight. These were met on their retreat and attacked by the mercenary troops under Hiero, who got round them by a circular movement.[3] The mercenaries were supported by the Phocian light infantry and some squadrons of Heracleot and Phliasian cavalry, who fell upon the retiring train and turned them back, pursuing them and driving them into the camp of the Boeotians. The immediate effect was to make the Boeotian portion of the army more numerous and closer packed than before. The next feature of the combat was that in consequence of the flat space of plain[4] between the opposing armies, the Lacedaemonians posted their cavalry in front of their squares of infantry, and the Thebans followed suit. Only there was this difference—the Theban cavalry was in a high state of training and efficiency, owing to their war with the Orchomenians and again their war with Thespiae, whilst the cavalry of the Lacedaemonians was at its worst at this period.[5] The horses were reared and kept by the wealthiest members of the state; but whenever the ban was called out, an appointed trooper appeared who took the horse with any sort of arms which might be presented to him, and set off on the expedition at a moment's notice. Moreover, these troopers were the least able-bodied of the men: raw recruits set simply astride their horses, and devoid of soldierly ambition. Such was the cavalry of either antagonist.

The heavy infantry of the Lacedaemonians, it is said, advanced by sections three files abreast,[6] allowing a total depth to the whole line of not

---

1 Or, "it is true that some people made out these marvels."
2 Or, "they were somewhat excited by it."
3 Or, "surrounded them."
4 See Rustow and Kochly, op. cit. p. 173.
5 See "Hipparch." ix. 4; also "Cyrop." VIII. viii.
6 It would appear that the "enomoty" (section) numbered thirty-six files. See "Pol. Lac." xi. 4; xiii. 4. For further details as to the tactical order of the Thebans, see Diod. xv. 55; Plut. "Pelop." xxiii.

more than twelve. The Thebans were formed in close order of not less than fifty shields deep, calculating that victory gained over the king's division of the army implied the easy conquest of the rest.

Cleombrotus had hardly begun to lead his division against the foe when, before in fact the troops with him were aware of his advance, the cavalry had already come into collision, and that of the Lacedaemonians was speedily worsted. In their flight they became involved with their own heavy infantry; and to make matters worse, the Theban regiments were already attacking vigorously. Still strong evidence exists for supposing that Cleombrotus and his division were, in the first instance, victorious in the battle, if we consider the fact that they could never have picked him up and brought him back alive unless his vanguard had been masters of the situation for the moment.

When, however, Deinon the polemarch and Sphodrias, a member of the king's council, with his son Cleonymus,[1] had fallen, then it was that the cavalry and the polemarch's adjutants,[2] as they are called, with the rest, under pressure of the mass against them, began retreating; and the left wing of the Lacedaemonians, seeing the right borne down in this way, also swerved. Still, in spite of the numbers slain, and broken as they were, as soon as they had crossed the trench which protected their camp in front, they grounded arms on the spot[3] whence they had rushed to battle. This camp, it must be borne in mind, did not lie at all on the level, but was pitched on a somewhat steep incline. At this juncture there were some of the Lacedaemonians who, looking upon such a disaster as intolerable, maintained that they ought to prevent the enemy from erecting a trophy, and try to recover the dead not under a flag of truce but by another battle. The polemarchs, however, seeing that nearly a thousand men of the total Lacedaemonian troops were slain; seeing also that of the seven hundred Spartans themselves who were on the field something like four hundred lay dead;[4] aware, further, of the despondency which reigned among the allies, and the general disinclination on their parts to fight longer (a frame of mind not far removed in some instances from positive satisfaction at what had taken place)—under the circumstances, I say, the polemarchs called a council of the ablest representatives of the shattered army[5] and deliberated

---

1 See above, V. iv. 33.
2 {sumphoreis}. For the readings of this corrupt passage see Otto Keller.
3 Or, "in orderly way." See Curt. "H. G." iv. 400.
4 See "Ages." ii. 24.
5 {tous epikairiotatous}. See above, III. iii. 10; "Cyrop." VII. iv. 4; VIII. iv. 32, vi. 2.

as to what should be done. Finally the unanimous opinion was to pick up the dead under a flag of truce, and they sent a herald to treat for terms. The Thebans after that set up a trophy and gave back the bodies under a truce.

After these events, a messenger was despatched to Lacedaemon with news of the calamity. He reached his destination on the last day of the gymnopaediae,[1] just when the chorus of grown men had entered the theatre. The ephors heard the mournful tidings not without grief and pain, as needs they must, I take it; but for all that they did not dismiss the chorus, but allowed the contest to run out its natural course. What they did was to deliver the names of those who had fallen to their friends and families, with a word of warning to the women not to make any loud lamentations but to bear their sorrow in silence; and the next day it was a striking spectacle to see those who had relations among the slain moving to and fro in public with bright and radiant looks, whilst of those whose friends were reported to be living barely a man was to be seen, and these flitted by with lowered heads and scowling brows, as if in humiliation.

After this the ephors proceeded to call out the ban, including the forty-years-service men of the two remaining regiments;[2] and they proceeded further to despatch the reserves of the same age belonging to the six regiments already on foreign service. Hitherto the Phocian campaign had only drawn upon the thirty-five-years-service list. Besides these they now ordered out on active service the troops retained at the beginning of the campaign in attendance on the magistrates at the government offices. Agesilaus being still disabled by his infirmity, the city imposed the duty of command upon his son Archidamus. The new general found eager co-operators in the men of Tegea. The friends of Stasippus at this date were still living,[3] and they were stanch in their Lacedaemonian proclivities, and wielded considerable power in their state. Not less stoutly did the Mantineans from their villages under their aristocratic form of government flock to the Spartan standard. Besides Tegea and Mantinea, the Corinthians and Sicyonians, the Phliasians and Achaeans were equally enthusiastic to joining the campaign, whilst other states sent out soldiers. Then came the fitting out and manning of ships of war on the part of the Lacedaemonians themselves and of the Corinthians, whilst the Sicyonians were requested to furnish a supply of vessels on board of which it was proposed to transport

---

1 *The festival was celebrated annually about midsummer. See Herod. vi. 67; Thuc. v. 82, and Arnold's note; Pollux. iv. 105; Athen. xiv. 30, xv. 22; Muller, "Dorians," ii. 389.*
2 *I.e. everyone up to fifty-eight years of age.*
3 *See below, VI. v. 9.*

the army across the gulf. And so, finally, Archidamus was able to offer the sacrifices usual at the moment of crossing the frontier. But to return to Thebes.

Immediately after the battle the Thebans sent a messenger to Athens wearing a chaplet. Whilst insisting on the magnitude of the victory they at the same time called upon the Athenians to send them aid, for now the opportunity had come to wreak vengeance on the Lacedaemonians for all the evil they had done to Athens. As it chanced, the senate of the Athenians was holding a session on the Acropolis. As soon as the news was reported, the annoyance caused by its announcement was unmistakeable. They neither invited the herald to accept of hospitality nor sent back one word in reply to the request for assistance. And so the herald turned his back on Athens and departed.

But there was Jason still to look to, and he was their ally. To him then the Thebans sent, and earnestly besought his aid, their thoughts running on the possible turn which events might take. Jason on his side at once proceeded to man a fleet, with the apparent intention of sending assistance by sea, besides which he got together his foreign brigade and his own cavalry; and although the Phocians and he were implacable enemies,[1] he marched through their territory to Boeotia. Appearing like a vision to many of the states before his approach was even announced—at any rate before levies could be mustered from a dozen different points—he had stolen a march upon them and was a long way ahead, giving proof that expedition is sometimes a better tool to work with than sheer force.

When he arrived in Boeotia the Thebans urged upon him that now was the right moment to attack the Lacedaemonians: he with his foreign brigade from the upper ground, they face to face in front; but Jason dissuaded them from their intention. He reminded them that after a noble achievement won it was not worth their while to play for so high a stake, involving a still greater achievement or else the loss of victory already gained. "Do you not see," he urged, "that your success followed close on the heels of necessity? You ought then to reflect that the Lacedaemonians in their distress, with a choice between life and death, will fight it out with reckless desperation. Providence, as it seems, ofttimes delights to make the little ones great and the great ones small."[2]

By such arguments he diverted the Thebans from the desperate adventure. But for the Lacedaemonians also he had words of advice,

---

1 Or, "though the Phocians maintained a war 'a outrance' with him."
2 Cf. "Anab." III. ii. 10.

insisting on the difference between an army defeated and an army flushed with victory. "If you are minded," he said, "to forget this disaster, my advice to you is to take time to recover breath and recruit your energies. When you have grown stronger then give battle to these unconquered veterans.[1] At present," he continued, "you know without my telling you that among your own allies there are some who are already discussing terms of friendship with your foes. My advice is this: by all means endeavor to obtain a truce. This," he added, "is my own ambition: I want to save you, on the ground of my father's friendship with yourselves, and as being myself your representative."[2] Such was the tenor of his speech, but the secret of action was perhaps to be found in a desire to make these mutual antagonists put their dependence on himself alone. Whatever his motive, the Lacedaemonians took his advice, and commissioned him to procure a truce.

As soon as the news arrived that the terms were arranged, the polemarchs passed an order round: the troops were to take their evening meal, get their kit together, and be ready to set off that night, so as to scale the passes of Cithaeron by next morning. After supper, before the hour of sleep, the order to march was given, and with the generals at their head the troops advanced as the shades of evening fell, along the road to Creusis, trusting rather to the chance of their escaping notice, than to the truce itself. It was weary marching in the dead of night, making their retreat in fear, and along a difficult road, until they fell in with Archidamus's army of relief. At this point, then, Archidamus waited till all the allies had arrived, and so led the whole of the united armies back to Corinth, from which point he dismissed the allies and led his fellow citizens home.

Jason took his departure from Boeotia through Phocis, where he captured the suburbs of Hyampolis[3] and ravaged the country districts, putting many to the sword. Content with this, he traversed the rest of Phocis without meddling or making. Arrived at Heraclea,[4] he knocked down the fortress of the Heracleots, showing that he was not troubled by any apprehension lest

---

1 Or, "the invincibles."
2 Lit. "your proxenos."
3 *An ancient town in Phocis (see Hom. "Il." ii. 521) on the road leading from Orchomenus to Opus, and commanding a pass from Locris into Phocis and Boeotia. See Herod. viii. 28; Paus. ix. 35, S. 5; Strab. ix. 424; "Dict. of Geog." s.v.*
4 *Or, "Heracleia Trachinia," a fortress city founded (as a colony) by the Lacedaemonians in 426 BC, to command the approach to Thermopylae from Thessaly, and to protect the Trachinians and the neighboring Dorians from the Oetean mountaineers. See "Dict. of Geog." "Trachis"; Thuc. iii. 92, 93, v. 51, 52; Diod. xii. 59.*

when the pass was thrown open somebody or other might march against his own power at some future date. Rather was he haunted by the notion that some one or other might one day seize Heraclea, which commanded the pass, and bar his passage into Hellas—should Hellas ever be his goal.[1] At the moment of his return to Thessaly he had reached the zenith of his greatness. He was the lawfully constituted Prince[2] of Thessaly, and he had under him a large mercenary force of infantry and cavalry, and all in the highest perfection of training. For this twofold reason he might claim the title great. But he was still greater as the head of a vast alliance. Those who were prepared to fight his battles were numerous, and he might still count upon the help of many more eager to do so; but I call Jason greatest among his contemporaries, because not one among them could afford to look down upon him.[3]

370 BC. The Pythian games were now approaching, and an order went round the cities from Jason to make preparation for the solemn sacrifice of oxen, sheep and goats, and swine. It was reported that although the requisitions upon the several cities were moderate, the number of beeves did not fall short of a thousand, while the rest of the sacrificial beasts exceeded ten times that number. He issued a proclamation also to this effect: a golden wreath of victory should be given to whichever city could produce the best-bred bull to head the procession in honor of the god. And lastly there was an order issued to all the Thessalians to be ready for a campaign at the date of the Pythian games. His intention, as people said, was to act as manager of the solemn assembly and games in person. What the thought was that passed through his mind with reference to the sacred money, remains to this day uncertain; only, a tale is rife to the effect that in answer to the inquiry of the Delphians, "What ought we to do, if he takes any of the treasures of the god?" the god made answer, "He would see to that himself." This great man, his brain teeming with vast designs of this high sort, came now to his end. He had ordered a military inspection. The cavalry of the Pheraeans were to pass muster before him. He was already seated, delivering answers to all petitioners, when seven striplings approached, quarrelling, as it seemed, about some matter. Suddenly by these seven the Prince was despatched; his throat gashed, his body gored with wounds. Stoutly his guard rushed to the rescue with their long spears,

---

1 370 BC. *The following sections 28–37 form an episode concerning Thessalian affairs between 370 BC and 359 BC.*

2 Lit. *"Tagos."*

3 *For a similar verbal climax see below, VI. v. 47.*

and one of the seven, while still in the act of aiming a blow at Jason, was thrust through with a lance and died; a second, in the act of mounting his horse, was caught, and dropped dead, the recipient of many wounds. The rest leaped on the horses which they had ready waiting and escaped. To whatever city of Hellas they came honors were almost universally accorded them. The whole incident proves clearly that the Hellenes stood in much alarm of Jason. They looked upon him as a tyrant in embryo.

So Jason was dead; and his brothers Polydorus and Polyphron were appointed princes[1] in his place. But of these twain, as they journeyed together to Larissa, Polydorus was slain in the night, as he slept, by his brother Polyphron, it was thought; since a death so sudden, without obvious cause, could hardly be otherwise accounted for.

Polyphron governed for a year, and by the year's end he had refashioned his princedom into the likeness of a tyranny. In Pharsalus he put to death Polydamas[2] and eight other of the best citizens; and from Larissa he drove many into exile. But while he was thus employed, he, in his turn, was done to death by Alexander, who slew him to avenge Polydorus and to destroy the tyranny. This man now assumed the reins of office, and had no sooner done so than he showed himself a harsh prince to the Thessalians: harsh too and hostile to the Thebans and Athenians,[3] and an unprincipled freebooter everywhere by land and by sea. But if that was his character, he too was doomed to perish shortly. The perpetrators of the deed were his wife's brothers.[4] The counselor of it and the inspiring soul was the wife herself. She it was who reported to them that Alexander had designs against them; who hid them within the house a whole day; who welcomed home her husband deep in his cups and laid him to rest, and then while the lamp still burned brought out the prince's sword. It was she also who, perceiving her brothers shrank bank, fearing to go in and attack Alexander, said to them, "If you do not be quick and do the deed, I will wake him up!" After they had gone in, she, too, it was who caught and pulled to the door, clinging fast to the knocker till the breath was out of her husband's body.[5] Her fierce hatred against the man is variously explained. By some it was said to date from the day when Alexander, having imprisoned his own favorite—who was a fair young stripling—when his wife supplicated him

---

1 Lit. "*Tagoi.*"

2 See above, VI. i. 2 *foll.*

3 See Dem. "*c. Aristocr.*" 120; Diod. xv. 60 *foll.*

4 359 or 358 BC.

5 The woman's name was Thebe. See Diod. xvi. 14; Cicero, "*de Inven.*" II. xlix. 144; "*de Div.*" I. xxv. 52; "*de Off.*" II. vii. 25; Ovid, "*Ibis,*" iii. 21 *foll.*

to release the boy, brought him forth and stabbed him in the throat. Others say it originated through his sending to Thebes and seeking the hand of the wife of Jason in marriage, because his own wife bore him no children. These are the various causes assigned to explain the treason of his wife against him. Of the brothers who executed it, the eldest, Tisiphonus, in virtue of his seniority accepted, and up to the date of this history[1] succeeded in holding, the government.

V

The above is a sketch of Thessalian affairs, including the incidents connected with Jason, and those subsequent to his death, down to the government of Tisiphonus. I now return to the point at which we digressed.

371 BC. Archidamus, after the relief of the army defeated at Leuctra, had led back the united forces. When he was gone, the Athenians, impressed by the fact that the Peloponessians still felt under an obligation to follow the Lacedaemonians to the field, whilst Sparta herself was by no means as yet reduced to a condition resembling that to which she had reduced Athens, sent invitations to those states which cared to participate in the peace authorized by the great king.[2] A congress met, and they passed a resolution in conjunction with those who wished to make common cause with them to bind themselves by oath as follows: "I will abide by the treaty terms as conveyed in the king's rescript, as also by the decrees of the Athenians and the allies. If anyone marches against any city among those which have accepted this oath, I will render assistance to that city with all my strength." The oath gave general satisfaction, the Eleians alone gainsaying its terms and protesting that it was not right to make either the Marganians or the Scilluntians or the Triphylians independent, since these cities belonged to them, and were a part of Elis. [3]The Athenians, however, and the others passed the decree in the precise language of the king's rescript: that all states—great and small alike—were to be independent; and they sent out administrators of the oath, and enjoined upon them to administer it to the highest authorities in each state. This oath they all, with the exception of the Eleians, swore to.

371–370 BC. As an immediate consequence of this agreement, the Mantineans, on the assumption that they were now absolutely independent, met in a body and passed a decree to make Mantinea into a single state

---

1 Or, "portion of my work"; lit. "argument," {logos}. See {Kuprianos, Peri ton "Ell"}: p. 111.
2 I.e. in 387 BC, the peace "of" Antalcidas. See Grote, "H. G." x. 274.
3 See Busolt, op. cit. p. 186.

and to fortify the town.¹ The proceeding was not overlooked by the Lacedaemonians, who thought it would be hard if this were done without their consent. Accordingly they despatched Agesilaus as ambassador to the Mantineans, choosing him as the recognized ancestral friend of that people. When the ambassador arrived, however, the chief magistrates had no inclination to summon a meeting of the commons to listen to him, but urged him to make a statement of his wishes to themselves. He, on his side, was ready to undertake for himself and in their interests that, if they would at present desist from their fortification work, he would bring it about that the defensive walls should be built with the sanction of Lacedaemon and without cost. Their answer was, that it was impossible to hold back, since a decree had been passed by the whole state of Mantinea to build at once. Whereupon Agesilaus went off in high dudgeon; though as to sending troops to stop them,² the idea seemed impracticable, as the peace was based upon the principle of autonomy. Meanwhile the Mantineans received help from several of the Arcadian states in the building of their walls; and the Eleians contributed actually three talents³ of silver to cover the expense of their construction. And here leaving the Mantineans thus engaged, we will turn to the men of Tegea.

There were in Tegea two political parties. The one was the party of Callibius and Proxenus, who were for drawing together the whole Arcadian population in a confederacy,⁴ in which all measures carried in the common assembly should be held valid for the individual component states. The program of the other (Stasippus's) party was to leave Tegea undisturbed and in the enjoyment of the old national laws. Perpetually defeated in the Sacred College,⁵ the party of Callibius and Proxenus were persuaded that if only the commons met they would gain an easy victory by an appeal to the multitude; and in this faith they proceeded to march out the citizen

---

1 For the restoration of Mantinea, see Freeman, "Fed. Gov." iv. p. 198; Grote, "H. G." x. 283 foll.
2 See above, V. ii. 1, sub anno 386 BC.
3 = 731 pounds: 5 shillings. See Busolt, op. cit. p. 199.
4 Although the historian does not recount the foundation of Megalopolis (see Pausanias and Diodorus), the mention of the common assembly of the League {en to koino} in this passage and, still more, of the Ten Thousand (below, "Hell." VII. i. 38), implies it. See Freeman, op. cit. iv. 197 foll.; Grote, "H. G." x. 306 foll., ii. 599; "Dict. of Geog." "Megalopolis." As to the date of its foundation Pausanias (VIII. xxvii. 8) says "a few months after the battle of Leuctra," before midsummer 370 BC; Diodorus (xv. 72) says 368 BC. The great city was not built in a day. Messene, according to Paus. IV. xxvii. 5, was founded between the midsummers of 370 BC and 369 BC.
5 Lit. "in the Thearoi." For the Theari, see Thuc. v. 47, Arnold's note; and "C. I. G." 1756 foll.; and for the revolution at Tegea here recounted, see Grote, "H. G." x. 285 foll.

soldiers.[1] At sight of this Stasippus and his friends on their side armed in opposition, and proved not inferior in numbers. The result was a collision and battle, in which Proxenus and some few others with him were slain and the rest put to flight; though the conquerors did not pursue, for Stasippus was a man who did not care to stain his hands with the blood of his fellow citizens.[2]

Callibius and his friends had retired under the fortification walls and gates facing Mantinea; but, as their opponents made no further attempts against them, they here collected together and remained quiet. Some while ago they had sent messages to the Mantineans demanding assistance, but now they were ready to discuss terms of reconciliation with the party of Stasippus. Presently they saw the Mantineans advancing; whereupon some of them sprang to the walls, and began calling to them to bring succour with all speed. With shouts they urged upon them to make haste, whilst others threw open wide the gates to them. Stasippus and his party, perceiving what was happening, poured out by the gates leading to Pallantium,[3] and, outspeeding their pursuers, succeeded in reaching the temple of Artemis, where they found shelter, and, shutting to the doors, kept quiet. Following close upon their heels, however, their foes scaled the temple, tore off the roof, and began striking them down with the tiles. They, recognising that there was no choice, called upon their assailants to desist, and undertook to come forth. Then their opponents, capturing them like birds in a fowler's hand, bound them with chains, threw them on to the prisoner's van,[4] and led them off to Tegea. Here with the Mantineans they sentenced and put them to death.

The outcome of these proceedings was the banishment to Lacedaemon of the Tegeans who formed the party of Stasippus, numbering eight hundred; but as a sequel to what had taken place, the Lacedaemonians determined that they were bound by their oaths to aid the banished Tegeans and to avenge the slain. With this purpose they marched against the Mantineans, on the ground that they had violated their oaths in marching against Tegea with an armed force. The ephors called out the ban and the state commanded Agesilaus to head the expedition.

---

1 Or, "they mustered under arms."
2 Or, "opposed to a wholesale slaughter of the citizens."
3 Pallantium, one of the most ancient towns of Arcadia, in the Maenalia (Paus. VIII. xliv. 5; Livy, i. 5), situated somewhat south of the modern Tripolitza (see "Dict. of Anc. Geog."); like Asea and Eutaea it helped to found Megalopolis (Paus. VIII. xxvii. 3, where for {"Iasaia"} read {"Asea"}); below, VII. v. 5; Busolt, op. cit. p. 125.
4 For the sequel of the matter, see above, "Hell." VI. iv. 18; Busolt, op. cit. p. 134.

Meanwhile most of the Arcadian contingents were mustering at Asea.[1] The Orchomenians not only refused to take part in the Arcadian league, on account of their personal hatred to Mantinea, but had actually welcomed within their city a mercenary force under Polytropus, which had been collected at Corinth. The Mantineans themselves were forced to stay at home to keep an eye on these. The men of Heraea and Lepreum made common cause with the Lacedaemonians in a campaign against Mantinea.

Finding the frontier sacrifices favorable, Agesilaus began his march at once upon Arcadia. He began by occupying the border city of Eutaea, where he found the old men, women, and children dwelling in their houses, while the rest of the population of a military age were off to join the Arcadian league. In spite of this he did not stir a finger unjustly against the city, but suffered the inhabitants to continue in their homes undisturbed. The troops took all they needed, and paid for it in return; if any pillage had occurred on his first entrance into the town, the property was hunted up and restored by the Spartan king. Whilst awaiting the arrival of Polytropus's mercenaries, he amused himself by repairing such portions of their walls as necessity demanded.

Meanwhile the Mantineans had taken the field against Orchomenus; but from the walls of that city the invaders had some difficulty in retiring, and lost some of their men. On their retreat they found themselves in Elymia;[2] here the heavy infantry of the Orchomenians ceased to follow them; but Polytropus and his troops continued to assail their rear with much audacity. At this conjuncture, seeing at a glance that either they must beat back the foe or suffer their own men to be shot down, the Mantineans turned right about and met the assailant in a hand-to-hand encounter. Polytropus fell fighting on that battlefield; and of the rest who took to flight, many would have shared his fate, but for the opportune arrival of the Phliasian cavalry, who swooped round to the conqueror's rear and checked him in his pursuit.[3]

---

1 *Asea is placed by Leake ("Travels in Morea," i. 84; iii. 34) near Frangovrysi, a little south of Pallantium.*

Heraea, the most important town of Arcadia in the Cynuria, near Elis, on the high road to Olympia, and commanding other main roads. See Leake, "Peloponnesiaca," p. 1 foll.; "Morea," ii. 91.

Lepreum, chief town of the Triphylia (Herod. iv. 148, ix. 28; Thuc. v. 31; above, III. ii. 25; Paus. V. v. 3; Polyb. iv. 77 foll.; Strab. viii. 345), near modern Strovitzi; Leake, "Morea," i. 56; Dodwell, "Tour," ii. 347.

Eutaea is placed by Leake between Asea and Pallantium at Barbitza ("Morea," iii. 31); but see Grote, "H. G." x. 288.

2 *Elymia, mentioned only by Xenophon, must have been on the confines of the Mantinice and Orchomenus, probably at Levidhi.— Leake, "Morea," iii. 75; "Peloponn." p. 229.*

3 *See "Cyrop." VII. i. 36.*

Content with this achievement, the Mantineans retired homeward; while Agesilaus, to whom the news was brought, no longer expecting that the Orchomenian mercenaries could effect a junction with himself, determined to advance without further delay.[1] On the first day he encamped for the evening meal in the open country of Tegea, and the day following crossed into Mantinean territory. Here he encamped under the westward-facing[2] mountains of Mantinea, and employed himself in ravaging the country district and sacking the farmsteads; while the troops of the Arcadians who were mustered in Asea stole by night into Tegea. The next day Agesilaus shifted his position, encamping about two miles'[3] distance from Mantinea; and the Arcadians, issuing from Tegea and clinging to the mountains between Mantinea and that city, appeared with large bodies of heavy infantry, wishing to effect a junction with the Mantineans. The Argives, it is true, supported them, but they were not in full force. And here counsellors were to be found who urged on Agesilaus to attack these troops separately; but fearing lest, in proportion as he pressed on to engage them, the Mantineans might issue from the city behind and attack him on flank and rear, he decided it was best to let the two bodies coalesce, and then, if they would accept battle, to engage them on an open and fair field.

And so ere long the Arcadians had effected their object and were united with the Mantineans. The next incident was the sudden apparition at break of day, as Agesilaus was sacrificing in front of the camp, of a body of troops. These proved to be the light infantry from Orchomenus, who in company with the Phliasian cavalry had during the night made their way across past the town of Mantinea; and so caused the mass of the army to rush to their ranks, and Agesilaus himself to retire within the lines. Presently, however, the newcomers were recognized as friends; and as the sacrifices were favorable, Agesilaus led his army forward a stage farther after breakfast. As the shades of evening descended he encamped unobserved within the fold of the hills behind the Mantinean territory, with mountains in close proximity all round.[4]

On the next morning, as day broke, he sacrificed in front of the army;

---

1 See "Ages." ii. 23.
2 See Leake, "Morea," iii. 73.
3 Lit. "twenty stades."
4 Lit. "within the hindmost bosom of the Mantinice." In reference to the position, Leake ("Morea," iii. 75) says: "The northern bay (of the Mantinic plain between Mantinea and the Argon) corresponds better by its proximity to Mantinea; by Mount Alesium it was equally hidden from the city, while its small dimensions, and the nearness of the incumbent mountains, rendered it a more hazardous position to an army under the circumstances of that of Agesilaus" (than had he encamped in the Argon itself). For the Argon (or Inert Plain), see Leake, ib. 54 foll.

and observing a mustering of men from the city of Mantinea on the hills which overhung the rear of his army, he decided that he must lead his troops out of the hollow by the quickest route. But he feared lest, if he himself led off, the enemy might fall upon his rear. In this dilemma he kept quiet; presenting a hostile front to the enemy, he sent orders to his rear to face about to the right,[1] and so getting into line behind his main body, to move forward upon him; and in this way he at once extricated his troops from their cramped position and kept continually adding to the weight and solidity of his line. As soon as the phalanx was doubled in depth he emerged upon the level ground, with his heavy infantry battalions in this order, and then again extended his line until his troops were once more nine or ten shields deep. But the Mantineans were no longer so ready to come out. The arguments of the Eleians who had lent them their cooperation had prevailed: that it was better not to engage until the arrival of the Thebans. The Thebans, it was certain, would soon be with them; for had they not borrowed ten talents[2] from Elis in order to be able to send aid? The Arcadians with this information before them kept quiet inside Mantinea. On his side Agesilaus was anxious to lead off his troops, seeing it was midwinter; but, to avoid seeming to hurry his departure out of fear, he preferred to remain three days longer and no great distance from Mantinea. On the fourth day, after an early morning meal, the retreat commenced. His intention was to encamp on the same ground which he had made his starting-point on leaving Eutaea. But as none of the Arcadians appeared, he marched with all speed and reached Eutaea itself, although very late, that day; being anxious to lead off his troops without catching a glimpse of the enemy's watch-fires, so as to silence the tongues of anyone pretending that he withdrew in flight. His main object was in fact achieved. To some extent he had recovered the state from its late despondency, since he had invaded Arcadia and ravaged the country without anyone caring to offer him battle. But, once arrived on Laconian soil, he dismissed the Spartan troops to their homes and disbanded the provincials[3] to their several cities.

370–369 BC. The Arcadians, now that Agesilaus had retired, realizing that he had disbanded his troops, while they themselves were fully mustered, marched upon Heraea, the citizens of which town had not only refused to join the Arcadian league, but had joined the Lacedaemonians in their invasion of Arcadia. For this reason they entered the country, burning the homesteads and cutting down the fruit-trees.

---

1 See *"Anab." IV. iii. 29; "Pol. Lac." xi. 10.*
2 *2,437 pounds: 10 shillings. See Busult, op. cit. p. 199.*
3 *Lit. "perioeci"; and below, SS. 25, 32.*

Meanwhile news came of the arrival of the Theban reinforcements at Mantinea, on the strength of which they left Heraea and hastened to fraternize[1] with their Theban friends. When they were met together, the Thebans, on their side, were well content with the posture of affairs: they had duly brought their succour, and no enemy was any longer to be discovered in the country; so they made preparations to return home. But the Arcadians, Argives and Eleians were eager in urging them to lead the united forces forthwith into Laconia: they dwelt proudly on their own numbers, extolling above measure the armament of Thebes. And, indeed, the Boeotians one and all were resolute in their military manouvres and devotion to arms,[2] exulting in the victory of Leuctra. In the wake of Thebes followed the Phocians, who were now their subjects, Euboeans from all the townships of the island, both sections of the Locrians, the Acarnanians,[3] and the men of Heraclea and of Melis; while their force was further swelled by Thessalian cavalry and light infantry. With the full consciousness of facts like these, and further justifying their appeal by dwelling on the desolate condition of Lacedaemon, deserted by her troops, they entreated them not to turn back without invading the territory of Laconia. But the Thebans, albeit they listened to their prayers, urged arguments on the other side. In the first place, Laconia was by all accounts most difficult to invade; and their belief was that garrisons were posted at all the points most easily approached. (As a matter of fact, Ischolaus was posted at Oeum in the Sciritid, with a garrison of neodamodes and about four hundred of the youngest of the Tegean exiles; and there was a second outpost on Leuctrum above the Maleatid.[4]) Again it occurred to the Thebans

---

1 Or, "effect a junction with."
2 Or, "in practicing gymnastics about the place of arms." See "Pol. Lac." xii. 5.
3 See "Hell." IV. vii. 1; "Ages." ii. 20. For a sketch of the relations of Acarnania to Athens and Sparta, see Hicks, No. 83, p. 150; and above, "Hell." V. iv. 64.
4 Leuctrum, a fortress of the district Aegytis on the confines of Arcadia and Laconia ("in the direction of Mount Lycaeum," Thuc. v. 54). See Leake, "Morea," ii. 322; also "Peloponn." p. 248, in which place he corrects his former view as to the situation of Leuctrum and the Maleatid.

Oeum or Ium, the chief town of the Sciritis, probably stood in the Klisura or series of narrow passes through the watershed of the mountains forming the natural boundary between Laconia and Arcadia (in the direct line north from Sparta to Tegea), "Dict. of Anc. Geog." s.v. Leake says ("Morea," iii. 19, 30 foll.) near the modern village of Kolina; Baedeker ("Greece," p. 269) says perhaps at Palaeogoulas.

Caryae. This frontier town was apparently (near Arachova) on the road from Thyrea (in the direction of the Argolid) to Sparta (Thuc. v. 55; Paus. III. x. 7; Livy, xxxiv. 26, but see Leake, "Morea," iii. 30; "Peloponn." p. 342).

Sellasia, probably rightly placed "half an hour above Vourlia" (Baedeker, "Greece," p. 269). The famous battle of Sellasia, in the spring of 221 BC, in which the united Macedonians under Antigonus and the Achaeans finally broke the power of Sparta, was fought in the little valley where the stream Gorgylus joins the river Oenus and the Khan of Krevatas now stands. For a plan, see "Dict. of Anc. Geog." s.v.

that the Lacedaemonian forces, though disbanded, would not take long to muster, and once collected they would fight nowhere better than on their own native soil. Putting all these considerations together, they were not by any means impatient to march upon Lacedaemon. A strong counter-impulse, however, was presently given by the arrival of messengers from Caryae, giving positive information as to the defenseless condition of the country, and offering to act as guides themselves; they were ready to lose their lives if they were convicted of perfidy. A further impulse in the same direction was given by the presence of some of the provincials,[1] with invitations and promises of revolt, if only they would appear in the country. These people further stated that even at the present moment, on a summons of the Spartans proper, the provincials did not care to render them assistance. With all these arguments and persuasions echoing from all sides, the Thebans at last yielded, and invaded. They chose the Caryan route themselves, while the Arcadians entered by Oeum in the Sciritid.[2]

By all accounts Ischolaus made a mistake in not advancing to meet them on the difficult ground above Oeum. Had he done so, not a man, it is believed, would have scaled the passes there. But for the present, wishing to turn the help of the men of Oeum to good account, he waited down in the village; and so the invading Arcadians scaled the heights in a body. At this crisis Ischolaus and his men, as long as they fought face to face with their foes, held the superiority; but, presently, when the enemy, from rear and flank, and even from the dwelling-houses up which they scaled, rained blows and missiles upon them, then and there Ischolaus met his end, and every man besides, save only one or two who, failing to be recognized, effected their escape.

After these achievements the Arcadians marched to join the Thebans at Caryae, and the Thebans, hearing what wonders the Arcadians had performed, commenced their descent with far greater confidence. Their first exploit was to burn and ravage the district of Sellasia, but finding themselves ere long in the flat land within the sacred enclosure of Apollo, they encamped for the night, and the next day continued their march along the Eurotas. When they came to the bridge they made no attempt to cross it to attack the city, for they caught sight of the heavy infantry in the temple of Alea[3] ready to meet them. So, keeping the Eurotas on their right, they tramped along, burning and pillaging homesteads stocked with numerous

---

1 *"Perioeci."*

2 *Diodorus (xv. 64) gives more details; he makes the invaders converge upon Sellasia by four separate routes. See Leake, "Morea," iii. 29 foll.*

3 *See Pausanias, III. xix. 7.*

stores. The feelings of the citizens may well be imagined. The women who had never set eyes upon a foe[1] could scarcely contain themselves as they beheld the cloud of smoke. The Spartan warriors, inhabiting a city without fortifications, posted at intervals, here one and there another, were in truth what they appeared to be—the veriest handful. And these kept watch and ward. The authorities passed a resolution to announce to the helots that whosoever among them chose to take arms and join a regiment should have his freedom guaranteed to him by solemn pledges in return for assistance in the common war.[2] More than six thousand helots, it is said, enrolled themselves, so that a new terror was excited by the very incorporation of these men, whose numbers seemed to be excessive. But when it was found that the mercenaries from Orchomenus remained faithful, and reinforcements came to Lacedaemon from Phlius, Corinth, Epidaurus, and Pellene, and some other states, the dread of these new levies was speedily diminished.

The enemy in his advance came to Amyclae.[3] Here he crossed the Eurotas. The Thebans wherever they encamped at once formed a stockade of the fruit-trees they had felled, as thickly piled as possible, and so kept ever on their guard. The Arcadians did nothing of the sort. They left their camping-ground and took themselves off to attack the homesteads and loot. On the third or fourth day after their arrival the cavalry advanced, squadron by squadron, as far as the racecourse,[4] within the sacred enclosure of Gaiaochos. These consisted of the entire Theban cavalry and the Eleians, with as many of the Phocian or Thessalian or Locrian cavalry as were present. The cavalry of the Lacedaemonians, looking a mere handful, were drawn up to meet them. They had posted an ambuscade chosen from their heavy infantry, the younger men, about three hundred in number, in the house of the Tyndarids[5]; and while the cavalry charged, out rushed the three hundred at the same instant at full pace. The enemy did not wait to receive the double charge, but swerved, and at sight of that many also of the infantry took to headlong flight. But the pursuers presently paused; the Theban army remained motionless; and both parties returned to their camps. And now the hope, the confidence strengthened that an attack upon the city itself would never come; nor did it. The invading army broke up

---

1 See Plutarch, "Ages." xxxi. 3 (Clough, vol. iv. p. 38); Aristot. "Pol." ii. 9–10.
2 See below, VII. ii. 2.
3 For this ancient (Achaean) town, see Paus. III. ii. 6; Polyb. v. 19. It lay only twenty stades (a little more than two miles) from the city of Sparta.
4 Or, "hippodrome." See Paus. III. ii. 6.
5 Paus. III. xvi. 2.

from their ground, and marched off on the road to Helos and Gytheum.[1] The unwalled cities were consigned to the flames, but Gytheum, where the Lacedaemonians had their naval arsenal, was subjected to assault for three days. Certain of the provincials[2] also joined in this attack, and shared the campaign with the Thebans and their friends.

The news of these proceedings set the Athenians deeply pondering what they ought to do concerning the Lacedaemonians, and they held an assembly in accordance with a resolution of the senate. It chanced that the ambassadors of the Lacedaemonians and the allies still faithful to Lacedaemon were present. The Lacedaemonian ambassadors were Aracus, Ocyllus, Pharax, Etymocles, and Olontheus, and from the nature of the case they all used, roughly speaking, similar arguments. They reminded the Athenians how they had often in old days stood happily together, shoulder to shoulder, in more than one great crisis. They (the Lacedaemonians), on their side, had helped to expel the tyrant from Athens, and the Athenians, when Lacedaemon was besieged by the Messenians, had heartily leant her a helping hand.[3] Then they fell to enumerating all the blessings that marked the season when the two states shared a common policy, hinting how in common they had warred against the barbarians, and more boldly recalling how the Athenians with the full consent and advice of the Lacedaemonians were chosen by united Hellas leaders of the common navy[4] and guardians of all the common treasure, while they themselves were selected by all the Hellenes as confessedly the rightful leaders on land; and this also not without the full consent and concurrence of the Athenians.

One of the speakers ventured on a remark somewhat to this strain: "If you and we, sirs, can only agree, there is hope today that the old saying may be fulfillled, and Thebes be 'taken and tithed.'"[5] The Athenians, however, were not in the humor to listen to that style of argument. A sort of suppressed murmur ran through the assembly which seemed to say, "That language may be well enough now; but when they were well off they pressed hard enough on us." But of all the pleas put forward by

---

1 See Baedeker's "Greece," p. 279. Was Gytheum taken? See Grote, "H. G." x. 305; Curt. "H. G." Eng. trans. iv. 431.

2 "Perioeci." See above, III. iii. 6; VI. v. 25; below, VII. ii. 2; Grote, "H. G." x. 301. It is a pity that the historian should hurry us off to Athens just at this point. The style here is suggestive of notes ({upomnemata}) unexpanded.

3 In reference (1) to the expulsion of the Peisistratidae (Herod. v. 64); (2) the "third" Messenian war (Thuc. i. 102).

4 See "Revenues," v. 6.

5 Or, "the Thebans be decimated"; for the phrase see above, "Hell." VI. iii. 20.

the Lacedaemonians, the weightiest appeared to be this: that when they had reduced the Athenians by war, and the Thebans wished to wipe Athens off the face of the Earth, they (the Lacedaemonians) themselves had opposed the measure.[1] If that was the argument of most weight, the reasoning which was the most commonly urged was to the effect that "the solemn oaths necessitated the aid demanded. Sparta had done no wrong to justify this invasion on the part of the Arcadians and their allies. All she had done was to assist the men of Tegea when[2] the Mantineans had marched against that township contrary to their solemn oaths." Again, for the second time, at these expressions a confused din ran through the assembly, half the audience maintaining that the Mantineans were justified in supporting Proxenus and his friends, who were put to death by the party with Stasippus; the other half that they were wrong in bringing an armed force against the men of Tegea.

Whilst these distinctions were being drawn by the assembly itself, Cleiteles the Corinthian got up and spoke as follows: "I daresay, men of Athens, there is a double answer to the question, Who began the wrongdoing? But take the case of ourselves. Since peace began, no one can accuse us either of wantonly attacking any city, or of seizing the wealth of any, or of ravaging a foreign territory. In spite of which the Thebans have come into our country and cut down our fruit-trees, burnt to the ground our houses, filched and torn to pieces our cattle and our goods. How then, I put it to you, will you not be acting contrary to your solemn oaths if you refuse your aid to us, who are so manifestly the victims of wrongdoings? Yes; and when I say solemn oaths, I speak of oaths and undertakings which you yourselves took great pains to exact from all of us." At that point a murmur of applause greeted Cleiteles, the Athenians feeling the truth and justice of the speaker's language.

He sat down, and then Procles of Phlius got up and spoke as follows: "What would happen, men of Athens, if the Lacedaemonians were well out of the way? The answer to that question is obvious. You would be the first object of Theban invasion. Clearly; for they must feel that you and you alone stand in the path between them and empire over Hellas. If this be so, I do not consider that you are more supporting Lacedaemon by a campaign in her behalf than you are helping yourselves. For imagine the Thebans, your own sworn foes and next-door neighbors, masters of Hellas! You will find it a painful and onerous exchange indeed for the distant antagonism of

---

1 See "Hell." II. ii. 19; and "Hell." III. v. 8.
2 Lit. "because," {oti}.

Sparta. As a mere matter of self-interest, now is the time to help yourselves, while you may still reckon upon allies, instead of waiting until they are lost, and you are forced to fight a life-and-death battle with the Thebans single-handed. But the fear suggests itself, that should the Lacedaemonians escape now, they will live to cause you trouble at some future date. Lay this maxim to heart, then, that it is not the potential greatness of those we benefit, but of those we injure, which causes apprehension. And this other also, that it behoves individuals and states alike so to better their position[1] while yet in the zenith of their strength that, in the day of weakness, when it comes, they may find some succour and support in what their former labors have achieved.[2] To you now, at this time, a heaven-sent opportunity is presented. In return for assistance to the Lacedaemonians in their need, you may win their sincere, unhesitating friendship for all time. Yes, I say it deliberately, for the acceptance of these benefits at your hands will not be in the presence of one or two chance witnesses. The all-seeing gods, in whose sight tomorrow is even as today, will be cognisant of these things. The knowledge of them will be jointly attested by allies and enemies; nay, by Hellenes and barbarians alike, since to not one of them is what we are doing a matter of unconcern. If, then, in the presence of these witnesses, the Lacedaemonians should prove base toward you, no one will ever again be eager in their cause. But our hope, our expectation should rather be that they will prove themselves good men and not base; since they beyond all others would seem persistently to have cherished a high endeavor, reaching forth after true praise, and holding aloof from ugly deeds.

"But there are further considerations which it were well you should lay to heart. If danger were ever again to visit Hellas from the barbarian world outside, in whom would you place your confidence if not in the Lacedaemonians? Whom would you choose to stand at your right hand in battle if not these, whose soldiers at Thermopylae to a man preferred to fall at their posts rather than save their lives by giving the barbarian free passage into Hellas? Is it not right, then, considering for what thing's sake they displayed that bravery in your companionship, considering also the good hope there is that they will prove the like again—is it not just that you and we should lend them all countenance and goodwill? Nay, even for us their allies' sake, who are present, it would be worth your while to manifest this goodwill. Need you be assured that precisely those who continue faithful to them in their misfortunes would in like manner be ashamed not

---

1 Lit. "to acquire some good."
2 Or, "for what," etc.

to requite you with gratitude? And if we seem to be but small states, who are willing to share their dangers with them, lay to heart that there is a speedy cure for this defect: with the accession of your city the reproach that, in spite of all our assistance, we are but small cities, will cease to be.

"For my part, men of Athens, I have hitherto on hearsay admired and envied this great state, whither, I was told, everyone who was wronged or stood in terror of aught needed only to betake himself and he would obtain assistance. Today I no longer hear, I am present myself and see these famous citizens of Lacedaemon here, and by their side their trustiest friends, who have come to you, and ask you in their day of need to give them help. I see Thebans also, the same who in days bygone failed to persuade the Lacedaemonians to reduce you to absolute slavery,[1] today asking you to suffer those who saved you to be destroyed.

"That was a great deed and of fair renown, attributed in old story to your ancestors, that they did not suffer those Argives who died on the Cadmeia[2] to lie unburied; but a fairer wreath of glory would you weave for your own brows if you suffer not these still living Lacedaemonians to be trampled under the heel of insolence and destroyed. Fair, also, was that achievement when you stayed the insolence of Eurystheus and saved the sons of Heracles;[3] but fairer still than that will your deed be if you rescue from destruction, not the primal authors[4] merely, but the whole city which they founded; fairest of all, if because yesterday the Lacedaemonians won you your preservation by a vote which cost them nothing, you today shall bring them help with arms, and at the price of peril. It is a proud day for some of us to stand here and give what aid we can in pleading for assistance to brave men. What, then, must you feel, who in very deed are able to render that assistance! How generous on your parts, who have been so often the friends and foes of Lacedaemon, to forget the injury and remember only the good they have done! How noble of you to repay, not for yourselves only, but for the sake of Hellas, the debt due to those who proved themselves good men and true in her behalf!"

After these speeches the Athenians deliberated, and though there was

---

1 See "Hell." II. ii. 19; III. v. 8, in reference to 405 BC.
2 In reference to the Seven against Thebes, see Herod. IX. xxvii. 4; Isoc. "Paneg." 55.
3 Herod. IX. xxvii. 3; see Isoc. "Paneg." 56. "The greatness of Sparta was founded by the succour which Athens lent to the Heraklid invaders of the Peloponnese—a recollection which ought to restrain Sparta from injuring or claiming to rule Athens. Argos, Thebes, Sparta were in early times, as they are now, the foremost cities of Hellas; but Athens was the greatest of them all—the avenger of Argos, the chastiser of Thebes, the patron of those who founded Sparta."—Jebb, "Att. Or." ii. 154.
4 Plut. "Lyc." vi.

opposition, the arguments of gainsayers[1] fell upon deaf ears. The assembly finally passed a decree to send assistance to Lacedaemon in force, and they chose Iphicrates general. Then followed the preliminary sacrifices, and then the general's order to his troops to take the evening meal in the grove of the Academy.[2] But the general himself, it is said, was in no hurry to leave the city; many were found at their posts before him. Presently, however, he put himself at the head of his troops, and the men followed cheerily, in firm persuasion that he was about to lead them to some noble exploit. On arrival at Corinth he frittered away some days, and there was a momentary outburst of discontent at so much waste of precious time; but as soon as he led the troops out of Corinth there was an obvious rebound. The men responded to all orders with enthusiasm, heartily following their general's lead, and attacking whatever fortified place he might confront them with.

And now reverting to the hostile forces on Laconian territory, we find that the Arcadians, Argives, and Eleians had retired in large numbers. They had every inducement so to do since their homes bordered on Laconia; and off they went, driving or carrying whatever they had looted. The Thebans and the rest were no less anxious to get out of the country, though for other reasons, partly because the army was melting away under their eyes day by day, partly because the necessities of life were growing daily scantier, so much had been either fairly eaten up and pillaged or else recklessly squandered and reduced to ashes. Besides this, it was winter; so that on every ground there was a general desire by this time to get away home.

As son as the enemy began his retreat from Laconian soil, Iphicrates imitated his movement, and began leading back his troops out of Arcadia into Corinthia. Iphicrates exhibited much good generalship, no doubt, with which I have no sort of fault to find. But it is not so with that final feature of the campaign to which we are now come. Here I find his strategy either meaningless in intent or inadequate in execution. He made an attempt to keep guard at Oneion, in order to prevent the Boeotians making their way out homeward; but left meanwhile far the best passage through Cenchreae unguarded. Again, when he wished to discover whether or not the Thebans had passed Oneion, he sent out on a reconnaissance the whole of the Athenian and Corinthian cavalry; whereas, for the object in view, the eyes of a small detachment would have been as useful as a whole regiment;[3] and when it came to falling back, clearly the smaller number had a better chance

---

1 *As to the anti-Laconian or Boeotian party at Athens, see Curtius, "H. G." vol. v. ch. ii. (Eng. tr.)*
2 *See Baedeker, "Greece," p. 103.*
3 *See "Hipparch." viii. 10 foll.*

of hitting on a traversable road, and so effecting the desired movement quietly. But the height of folly seems to have been reached when he threw into the path of the enemy a large body of troops which were still too weak to cope with him. As a matter of fact, this body of cavalry, owing to their very numbers, could not help covering a large space of ground; and when it became necessary to retire, had to cling to a series of difficult positions in succession, so that they lost not fewer than twenty horsemen.[1] It was thus the Thebans effected their object and retired from Peloponnese.

BOOK VII

I

369 BC. In the following year[2] plenipotentiary ambassadors[3] from the Lacedaemonians and their allies arrived at Athens to consider and take counsel in what way the alliance between Athens and Lacedaemon might be best cemented. It was urged by many speakers, foreigners and Athenians also, that the alliance ought to be based on the principle of absolute equality,[4] "share and share alike," when Procles of Phlius put forward the following argument:

"Since you have already decided, men of Athens, that it is good to secure the friendship of Lacedaemon, the point, as it appears to me, which you ought now to consider is, by what means this friendship may be made to last as long as possible. The probability is, that we shall hold together best by making a treaty which shall suit the best interests of both parties. On most points we have, I believe, a tolerable unanimity, but there remains the question of leadership. The preliminary decree of your senate anticipates a division of the hegemony, crediting you with the chief maritime power, Lacedaemon with the chief power on land; and to me, personally, I confess, that seems a division not more established by human invention than preordained by some divine naturalness or happy fortune. For, in the first place, you have a geographical position pre-eminently adapted for naval supremacy; most of the states to whom the sea is important are massed round your own, and all of these are inferior to you in strength. Besides,

---

1 See Diod. xv. 63; Plut. "Pelop." 24.
2 I.e. the official year from spring to spring. See Peter, "Chron. Table" 95, note 215; see Grote, "H. G." x. 346, note 1.
3 See Hicks, 89.
4 For the phrase {epi toi isois kai omoiois}, implying "share and share alike," see Thuc. i. 145, etc.

you have harbors and roadsteads, without which it is not possible to turn a naval power to account. Again, you have many ships of war. To extend your naval empire is a traditional policy; all the arts and sciences connected with these matters you possess as home products, and, what is more, in skill and experience of nautical affairs you are far ahead of the rest of the world. The majority of you derive your livelihood from the sea, or things connected with it; so that in the very act of minding your own affairs you are training yourselves to enter the lists of naval combat.[1] Again, no other power in the world can send out a larger collective fleet, and that is no insignificant point in reference to the question of leadership. The nucleus of strength first gained becomes a rallying-point, round which the rest of the world will gladly congregate. Furthermore, your good fortune in this department must be looked upon as a definite gift of God: for, consider among the numberless great sea-fights which you have fought how few you have lost, how many you have won. It is only rational, then, that your allies should much prefer to share this particular risk with you. Indeed, to show you how natural and vital to you is this maritime study, the following reflection may serve. For several years the Lacedaemonians, when at war with you in old days, dominated your territory, but they made no progress toward destroying you. At last God granted them one day to push forward their dominion on the sea, and then in an instant you completely succumbed to them.[2] Is it not self-evident that your safety altogether depends upon the sea? The sea is your natural element—your birthright; it would be base indeed to entrust the hegemony of it to the Lacedaemonians, and the more so, since, as they themselves admit, they are far less acquainted with this business than yourselves; and, secondly, your risk in naval battles would not be for equal stakes—theirs involving only the loss of the men on board their ships, but yours, that of your children and your wives and the entire state.

"And if this is a fair statement of your position, turn, now, and consider that of the Lacedaemonians. The first point to notice is, that they are an inland power; as long as they are dominant on land it does not matter how much they are cut off from the sea—they can carry on existence happily enough. This they so fully recognize, that from boyhood they devote themselves to training for a soldier's life. The keystone of this training is obedience to command,[3] and in this they hold the same pre-eminence on

---

1 See "Pol. Ath." i. 19 foll.
2 See "Hell." II. i.
3 Or, "the spirit of discipline." See "Mem." III. v. 16; IV. iv. 15; Thuc. ii. 39; "Pol. Lac." viii.

land which you hold on the sea. Just as you with your fleets, so they on land can, at a moment's notice, put the largest army in the field; and with the like consequence, that their allies, as is only rational, attach themselves to them with undying courage.[1] Further, God has granted them to enjoy on land a like good fortune to that vouchsafed to you on sea. Among all the many contests they have entered into, it is surprising in how few they have failed, in how many they have been successful. The same unflagging attention which you pay to maritime affairs is required from them on land, and, as the facts of history reveal, it is no less indispensable to them. Thus, although you were at war with them for several years and gained many a naval victory over them, you never advanced a step nearer to reducing them. But once worsted on land, in an instant they were confronted with a danger affecting the very lives of child and wife, and vital to the interests of the entire state. We may very well understand, then, the strangeness, not to say monstrosity, in their eyes, of surrendering to others the military leadership on land, in matters which they have made their special study for so long and with such eminent success. I end where I began. I agree absolutely with the preliminary decrees of your own senate, which I consider the solution most advantageous to both parties. My prayer[2] is that you may be guided in your deliberations to that conclusion which is best for each and all of us."

Such were the words of the orator, and the sentiments of his speech were vehemently applauded by the Athenians no less than by the Lacedaemonians who were present. Then Cephisodotus[3] stepped forward and addressed the assembly. He said, "Men of Athens, do you not see how you are being deluded? Lend me your ears, and I will prove it to you in a moment. There is no doubt about your leadership by sea: it is already secured. But suppose the Lacedaemonians in alliance with you: it is plain they will send you admirals and captains, and possibly marines, of Laconian breed; but who will the sailors be? Helots obviously, or mercenaries of some sort. These are the folk over whom you will exercise your leadership. Reverse the case. The Lacedaemonians have issued a general order summoning you to join them in the field; it is plain again, you will be sending your heavy infantry and your cavalry. You see what follows. You have invented a pretty machine, by which they become leaders of your very selves, and you become the leaders either of their slaves or of the dregs of their state.

---

1 Or, "with unlimited confidence."
2 See above, "Hell." VI. i. 13, {kai su prattois ta kratista}, "and so may the best fortune attend you!"—if that reading and rendering be adopted.
3 See above, "Hell." VI. iii. 2; Hicks, 87.

I should like to put a question to the Lacedaemonian Timocrates seated yonder. Did you not say just now, Sir, that you came to make an alliance on terms of absolute equality, 'share and share alike'? Answer me." "I did say so." "Well, then, here is a plan by which you get the perfection of equality. I cannot conceive of anything more fair and impartial than that 'turn and turn about' each of us should command the navy, each the army; whereby whatever advantage there may be in maritime or military command we may each of us share."

These arguments were successful. The Athenians were converted, and passed a decree vesting the command in either state[1] for periods of five days alternately.

369 BC.[2] The campaign was commenced by both Athenians and Lacedaemonians with their allies, marching upon Corinth, where it was resolved to keep watch and ward over Oneion jointly. On the advance of the Thebans and their allies the troops were drawn out to defend the pass. They were posted in detachments at different points, the most assailable of which was assigned to the Lacedaemonians and the men of Pellene.[3]

The Thebans and their allies, finding themselves within three or four miles[4] of the troops guarding the pass, encamped in the flat ground below; but presently, after a careful calculation of the time it would take to start and reach the goal in the gloaming, they advanced against the Lacedaemonian outposts. In spite of the difficulty they timed their movements to a nicety, and fell upon the Lacedaemonians and Pellenians just at the interval when the night pickets were turning in and the men were leaving their shakedowns and retiring for necessary purposes.[5] This was the instant for the Thebans to fling themselves upon them; they plied their weapons with good effect, blow upon blow. Order was pitted against disorder, preparation against disarray. When, however, those who escaped from the thick of the business had retired to the nearest rising ground, the Lacedaemonian polemarch, who might have taken as many heavy, or light, infantry of the allies as he wanted, and thus have held the position (no bad one, since it enabled him to get his supplies safely enough from Cenchreae), failed to do so. On the contrary, and in spite of the great perplexity of the Thebans as to how they

---

1 See "Revenues," v. 7.
2 See Grote, "H. G." x. 349 foll.; al. 368 BC.
3 "During the wars of Epameinondas Pellene adhered firmly to her Spartan policy, at a time when other cities were, to say the least, less strenuous in the Spartan cause."—Freeman, "Hist. Fed. Gov." p. 241. Afterward Pellene is found temporarily on the Theban side ("Hell." VII. ii. 11).
4 Lit. "thirty stades."
5 Or, "intent on their personal concerns." See "Hell." II. iv. 6; "Hipparch." vii. 12.

were to get down from the high level facing Sicyon or else retire the way they came, the Spartan general made a truce, which in the opinion of the majority, seemed more in favor of the Thebans than himself, and so he withdrew his division and fell back.

The Thebans were now free to descend without hindrance, which they did; and, effecting a junction with their allies the Arcadians, Argives, and Eleians, at once attacked[1] Sicyon and Pellene, and, marching on Epidaurus, laid waste the whole territory of that people. Returning from that exploit with a consummate disdain for all their opponents, when they found themselves near the city of Corinth they advanced at the double against the gate facing toward Phlius; intending if they found it open to rush in. However, a body of light troops sallied out of the city to the rescue, and met the advance of the Theban picked corps[2] not one hundred and fifty yards[3] from the walls. Mounting on the monuments and commanding eminences, with volleys of sling stones and arrows they laid low a pretty large number in the van of the attack, and routing them, gave chase for three or four furlongs'[4] distance. After this incident the Corinthians dragged the corpses of the slain to the wall, and finally gave them up under a flag of truce, erecting a trophy to record the victory. As a result of this occurrence the allies of the Lacedaemonians took fresh heart.

At the date of the above transactions the Lacedeamonians were cheered by the arrival of a naval reinforcement from Dionysius, consisting of more than twenty warships, which conveyed a body of Celts and Iberians and about fifty cavalry. The day following, the Thebans and the rest of the allies, posted, at intervals, in battle order, and completely filling the flat land down to the sea on one side, and up to the knolls on the other which form the buttresses of the city, proceeded to destroy everything precious they could lay their hands on in the plain. The Athenian and Corinthian cavalry, eyeing the strength, physical and numerical, of their antagonists, kept at a safe distance from their armament. But the little body of cavalry lately arrived from Dionysius spread out in a long thin line, and one at one point and one at another galloped along the front, discharging their missiles as they dashed forward, and when the enemy rushed against them, retired, and again wheeling about, showered another volley. Even while so engaged they would dismount from their horses and take breath; and if

---

1 *And took (apparently); see below; Diod. xv. 69.*
2 *See "Anab." III. iv. 43; and above, "Hell." V. iii. 23.*
3 *Lit. "four plethra."*
4 *Lit. "three or four stades."*

their foemen galloped up while they were so dismounted, in an instant they had leapt on their horses' backs and were in full retreat. Or if, again, a party pursued them some distance from the main body, as soon as they turned to retire, they would press upon them, and discharging volleys of missiles, made terrible work, forcing the whole army to advance and retire, merely to keep pace with the movements of fifty horsemen.

369–368 BC. After this the Thebans remained only a few more days and then turned back homeward; and the rest likewise to their several homes. Thereupon the troops sent by Dionysius attacked Sicyon. Engaging the Sicyonians in the flat country, they defeated them, killing about seventy men and capturing by assault the fortres of Derae.[1] After these achievements this first reinforcement from Dionysius re-embarked and set sail for Syracuse.

Up to this time the Thebans and all the states which had revolted from Lacedaemon had acted together in perfect harmony, and were content to campaign under the leadership of Thebes; but now a certain Lycomedes,[2] a Mantinean, broke the spell. Inferior in birth and position to none, while in wealth superior, he was for the rest a man of high ambition. This man was able to inspire the Arcadians with high thoughts by reminding them that to Arcadians alone the Peloponnese was in a literal sense a fatherland; since they and they alone were the indigenous inhabitants of its sacred soil, and the Arcadian stock the largest among the Hellenic tribes—a good stock, moreover, and of incomparable physique. And then he set himself to panegyrise them as the bravest of the brave, adducing as evidence, if evidence were needed, the patent fact, that everyone in need of help invariably turned to the Arcadians.[3] Never in old days had the Lacedaemonians yet invaded Athens without the Arcadians. "If then," he added, "you are wise, you will be somewhat chary of following at the beck and call of anybody, or it will be the old story again. As when you marched in the train of Sparta you only enhanced her power, so today, if you follow Theban guidance without thought or purpose instead of claiming a division of the headship, you will speedily find, perhaps, in her only a second edition of Lacedaemon."[4]

---

1 *"East of Sicyon was Epieiceia (see above, "Hell." IV. ii. 14, iv. 13) on the river Nemea. In the same direction was the fortress Derae." ("Dict. Anct. Geog." "Topography of Sicyonia"), al. Gerae. So Leake ("Morea," iii. 376), who conjectures that this fortress was in the maritime plain.*
2 *For the plan of an Arcadian Federation and the part played by Lycomedes, its true author, "who certainly merits thereby a high place among the statesmen of Greece," see Freeman, "Hist. Fed. Gov." ch. iv. p. 199 foll.*
3 *For this claim on the part of the Arcadians, see "Anab." VI. ii. 10 foll.*
4 *Or, "Lacedaemonians under another name."*

These words uttered in the ears of the Arcadians were sufficient to puff them up with pride. They were lavish in their love of Lycomedes, and thought there was no one his equal. He became their hero; he had only to give his orders, and they appointed their magistrates[1] at his bidding. But, indeed, a series of brilliant exploits entitled the Arcadians to magnify themselves. The first of these arose out of an invasion of Epidaurus by the Argives, which seemed likely to end in their finding their escape barred by Chabrias and his foreign brigade with the Athenians and Corinthians. Only, at the critical moment the Arcadians came to the rescue and extricated the Argives, who were closely besieged, and this in spite not only of the enemy, but of the savage nature of the ground itself. Again they marched on Asine[2] in Laconian territory, and defeated the Lacedaemonian garrison, putting the polemarch Geranor, who was a Spartan, to the sword, and sacking the suburbs of the town. Indeed, whenever or wherever they had a mind to send an invading force, neither night nor wintry weather, nor length of road nor mountain barrier could stay their march. So that at this date they regarded their prowess as invincible.[3] The Thebans, it will be understood, could not but feel a touch of jealousy at these pretensions, and their former friendship to the Arcadians lost its ardour. With the Eleians, indeed, matters were worse. The revelation came to them when they demanded back from the Arcadians certain cities[4] of which the Lacedaemonians had deprived them. They discovered that their views were held of no account, but that the Triphylians and the rest who had revolted from them were to be made much of, because they claimed to be Arcadians.[5] Hence, as contrasted with the Thebans, the Eleians cherished feelings toward their late friends which were positively hostile.

368 BC. Self-esteem amounting to arrogance—such was the spirit which animated each section of the allies, when a new phase was introduced by the arrival of Philiscus[6] of Abydos on an embassy from Ariobarzanes[7] with large sums of money. This agent's first step was to assemble a congress of Thebans, allies, and Lacedaemonians at Delphi to treat of peace. On their

---

1 {arkhontas}, see below, "Hell." VII. iv. 33. *The formal title of these Federal magistrates may or may not have been {arkhontes}; Freeman, "H. F. G." 203, note 6.*
2 *See Grote, "H. G." x. 356.*
3 *Or, "regarded themselves as the very perfection of soldiery."*
4 *In reference to "Hell." III. ii. 25 foll., see Freeman, op. cit. p. 201, and below, "Hell." VII. iv. 12 (365 BC); Busolt, op. cit. p. 186 foll., in reference to Lasion.*
5 *Busolt, p. 150.*
6 *See Hicks, 84, p. 152; Kohler, "C. I. A." ii. 51; Grote, "H. G." x. 357; Curtius, "H. G." (Eng. tr.) iv. 458; Diod. xv. 90.*
7 *See above, V. i. 28; "Ages." ii. 26.*

arrival, without attempting to communicate or take counsel with the god as to how peace might be re-established, they fell to deliberating unassisted; and when the Thebans refused to acquiesce in the dependency of Messene[1] upon Lacedaemon, Philiscus set about collecting a large foreign brigade to side with Lacedaemon and to prosecute the war.

Whilst these matters were still pending, the second reinforcements from Dionysius[2] arrived. There was a difference of opinion as to where the troops should be employed, the Athenians insisting that they ought to march into Thessaly to oppose the Thebans, the Lacedaemonians being in favor of Laconia; and among the allies this latter opinion carried the day. The reinforcement from Dionysius accordingly sailed round to Laconia, where Archidamus incorporated them with the state troops and opened the campaign. Caryae he took by storm, and put everyone captured to the sword, and from this point marching straight upon the Parrhasians of Arcadia, he set about ravaging the country along with his Syracusan supporters.

Presently when the Arcadians and Argives arrived with succours, he retreated and encamped on the knolls above Medea.[3] While he was there, Cissidas, the officer in charge of the reinforcement from Dionysius, made the announcement that the period for his stay abroad had elapsed; and the words were no sooner out of his lips than off he set on the road to Sparta. The march itself, however, was not effected without delays, for he was met and cut off by a body of Messenians at a narrow pass, and was forced in these straits to send to Archidamus and beg for assistance, which the latter tendered. When they had got as far as the bend[4] on the road to Eutresia, there were the Arcadians and Argives advancing upon Laconia and apparently intending, like the Messenians, to shut the Spartan off from the homeward road.

Archidamus, debouching upon a flat space of ground where the roads to Eutresia and Medea converge, drew up his troops and offered battle. When happened then is thus told:—He passed in front of the regiments

---

1 See Hicks, 86.

2 See above, SS. 20, 22, p. 191 foll. The date is 368 BC according to Grote, "H. G." x. 362 foll.; al. 367 BC.

3 Or, "Melea," or "Malea." E. Curtius conjectures {Meleas} for {Medeas} of the MSS., and probably the place referred to is the township of Malea in the Aegytis (Pausan. VIII. xxvii. 4); see above, "Hell." VI. v. 24, "the Maleatid." See Dind. "Hist. Gr.," Ox. MDCCCLIII., note ad loc.; Curtius, "H. G." iv. 459; Grote, "H. G." x. 362.

4 Or, "the resting-place"; cf. mod. "Khan." L. and S. cf. Arist. "Frogs," 113. "Medea," below, is probably "Malea," (see last note).

and addressed them in terms of encouragement thus: "Fellow citizens, the day has come which calls upon us to prove ourselves brave men and look the world in the face with level eyes.[1] Now are we to deliver to those who come after us our fatherland intact as we received it from our fathers; now will we cease hanging our heads in shame before our children and wives, our old men and our foreign friends, in sight of whom in days of old we shone forth conspicuous beyond all other Hellenes."

The words were scarcely uttered (so runs the tale), when out of the clear sky came lightnings and thunderings,[2] with propitious manifestation to him; and it so happened that on his right wing there stood a sacred enclosure and a statue of Heracles, his great ancestor. As the result of all these things, so deep a strength and courage came into the hearts of his soldiers, as they tell, that the generals had hard work to restrain their men as they pushed forward to the front. Presently, when Archidamus led the advance, a few only of the enemy cared to await them at the spear's point, and were slain; the mass of them fled, and fleeing fell. Many were cut down by the cavalry, many by the Celts. When the battle ceased and a trophy had been erected, the Spartan at once despatched home Demoteles, the herald, with the news. He had to announce not only the greatness of the victory, but the startling fact that, while the enemy's dead were numerous, not one single Lacedaemonian had been slain.[3] Those in Sparta to whom the news was brought, as says the story, when they heard it, one and all, beginning with Agesilaus, and, after him, the elders and the ephors, wept for joy—so close akin are tears to joy and pain alike. There were others hardly less pleased than the Lacedaemonians themselves at the misfortune which had overtaken the Arcadians: these were the Thebans and Eleians—so offensive to them had the boastful behavior of these men become.

The problem perpetually working in the minds of the Thebans was how they were to compass the headship of Hellas; and they persuaded themselves that, if they sent an embassy to the King of Persia, they could not but gain some advantage by his help. Accordingly they did not delay, but called together the allies, on the plea that Euthycles the Lacedaemonian was already at the Persian court. The commissioners sent up were, on the part of the Thebans, Pelopidas;[4] on the part of the Arcadians, Antiochus,

---

1 See Plut. "Ages." 53 (Clough, vol. iv. p. 41).
2 See Xen. "Apolog." 12; Homer, "Il." ii. 353; "Od." xx. 113 foll.
3 According to Diod. xv. 72, ten thousand of the enemy fell.
4 See Plut. "Pelop." 30 (Clough, vol. ii. p. 230). For the date see Grote, "H. G." x. 365, 379; Curtius, "H. G." iv. 460.

the pancratiast; and on that of the Eleians, Archidamus. There was also an Argive in attendance. The Athenians on their side, getting wind of the matter, sent up two commissioners, Timagoras and Leon.

When they arrived at the Persian court the influence of Pelopidas was preponderant with the Persian. He could point out that, besides the fact that the Thebans alone among all the Hellenes had fought on the king's side at Plataeae,[1] they had never subsequently engaged in military service against the Persians; nay, the very ground of Lacedaemonian hostility to them was that they had refused to march against the Persian king with Agesilaus,[2] and would not even suffer him to sacrifice to Artemis at Aulis (where Agamemnon sacrificed before he set sail for Asia and captured Troy). In addition, there were two things which contributed to raise the prestige of Thebes, and redounded to the honor of Pelopidas. These were the victory of the Thebans at Leuctra, and the indisputable fact that they had invaded and laid waste the territory of Laconia. Pelopidas went on to point out that the Argives and Arcadians had lately been defeated in battle by the Lacedaemonians, when his own countrymen were not there to assist. The Athenian Timagoras supported all these statements of the Theban by independent testimony, and stood second in honor after Pelopidas.

At this point of the proceedings Pelopidas was asked by the king, what special clause he desired inserted in the royal rescript. He replied as follows: "Messene to be independent of Lacedaemon, and the Athenians to lay up their ships of war. Should either power refuse compliance in these respects, such refusal to be a casus belli; and any state refusing to take part in the military proceedings consequent, to be herself the first object of attack." These clauses were drawn up and read to the ambassadors, when Leon, in the hearing of the king, exclaimed: "Upon my word! Athenians, it strikes me it is high time you looked for some other friend than the great king." The secretary reported the comment of the Athenian envoy, and produced presently an altered copy of the document, with a clause inserted: "If the Athenians have any better and juster views to propound, let them come to the Persian court and explain them."[3]

Thus the ambassadors returned each to his own home and were variously received. Timagoras, on the indictment of Leon, who proved that his fellow commissioner not only refused to lodge with him at the king's court, but in every way played into the hands of Pelopidas, was put to death. Of the

---

1 See Thuc. iii. 58, 59, 60.
2 See above, "Hell." III. iv. 3; Lincke, "Zur. Xen. Krit." p. 315.
3 See Grote, "H. G." x. 402; and "Ages." viii. 3.

other joint commissioners, the Eleian, Archidamus, was loud in his praises of the king and his policy, because he had shown a preference to Elis over the Arcadians; while for a converse reason, because the Arcadian league was slighted, Antiochus not only refused to accept any gift, but brought back as his report to the general assembly of the Ten Thousand,[1] that the king appeared to have a large army of confectioners and pastry-cooks, butlers and doorkeepers; but as for men capable of doing battle with Hellenes, he had looked carefully, and could not discover any. Besides all which, even the report of his wealth seemed to him, he said, bombastic nonsense. "Why, the golden plane-tree that is so belauded is not big enough to furnish shade to a single grasshopper."[2]

At Thebes a conference of the states had been convened to listen to the great king's letter. The Persian who bore the missive merely pointed to the royal seal, and read the document; whereupon the Thebans invited all, who wished to be their friends, to take an oath to what they had just heard, as binding on the king and on themselves. To which the ambassadors from the states replied that they had been sent to listen to a report, not to take oaths; if oaths were wanted, they recommended the Thebans to send ambassadors to the several states. The Arcadian Lycomedes, moreover, added that the congress ought not to be held at Thebes at all, but at the seat of war, wherever that might be. This remark brought down the wrath of the Thebans on the speaker; they exclaimed that he was bent on breaking up the alliance. Whereupon the Arcadian refused to take a seat in the congress at all, and got up and betook himself off there and then, accompanied by all the Arcadian envoys. Since, therefore, the assembled representatives refused to take the oaths at Thebes, the Thebans sent to the different states, one by one in turn, urging each to undertake solemnly to act in accordance with the great king's rescript. They were persuaded that no individual state would venture to quarrel with themselves and the Persian monarch at once. As a matter of fact, however, when they arrived at Corinth—which was the first stated vist—the Corinthians stood out and gave as their answer, that they had no desire for any common oath or undertaking with the king. The rest of the states followed suit, giving answers of a similar tenor, so that this striving after empire on the part of Pelopidas and the Thebans melted like a cloud-castle into air.

367 BC.[3] But Epaminondas was bent on one more effort. With a view to

---

1 See above, VI. v. 6; Freeman, "Hist. Fed. Gov." 202; Demosth. "F. L." 220, etc.
2 Or, "the golden plane-tree they romance about would not suffice to," etc.
3 367 BC, according to Grote, "H. G." x. 365, note 1; al. 366 BC.

forcing the Arcadians and the rest of the allies to pay better heed to Thebes, he desired first to secure the adhesion of the Achaeans, and decided to march an army into Achaea. Accordingly, he persuaded the Argive Peisias, who was at the head of military affairs in Argos, to seize and occupy Oneion in advance. Persias, having ascertained that only a sorry guard was maintained over Oneion by Naucles, the general commanding the Lacedaemonian foreign brigade, and by Timomachus the Athenian, under cover of night seized and occupied with two thousand heavy infantry the rising ground above Cenchreae, taking with him provisions for seven days. Within the interval the Thebans arrived and surmounted the pass of Oneion; whereupon the allied troops with Epaminondas at their head, advanced into Achaea. The result of the campaign was that the better classes of Achaea gave in their adhesion to him; and on his personal authority Epaminondas insisted that there should be no driving of the aristocrats into exile, nor any modification of the constitution. He was content to take a pledge of fealty from the Achaeans to this effect: "Verily and indeed we will be your allies, and follow whithersoever the Thebans lead."[1]

So he departed home. The Arcadians, however, and the partisans of the opposite faction in Thebes were ready with an indictment against him: "Epaminondas," they said, "had merely swept and garnished Achaea for the Lacedaemonians, and then gone off." The Thebans accordingly resolved to send governors[2] into the states of Achaea; and those officers on arrival joined with the commonalty and drove out the better folk, and set up democracies throughout Achaea. On their side, these exiles coalesced, and, marching upon each separate state in turn, for they were pretty numerous, speedily won their restoration and dominated the states. As the party thus reinstated no longer steered a middle course, but went heart and soul into an alliance with Lacedaemon, the Arcadians found themselves between the upper and the nether millstone—that is to say, the Lacedaemonians and the Achaeans.

At Sicyon, hitherto,[3] the constitution was based on the ancient laws; but at this date Euphron (who during the Lacedaemonian days had been the greatest man in Sicyon, and whose ambition it was to hold a like pre-

---

1 See Freeman, "Hist. Fed. Gov." p. 241: "We read of local oligarchies (in the several cities of Achaia) which Epameinondas found and left in possession, but which the home government of Thebes thought good to expel, and to substitute democracies under the protection of Theban harmosts. This policy did not answer, as the large bodies of exiles thus formed contrived to recover the cities, and to bring them to a far more decided Spartan partisanship than before."
2 Lit. "harmosts."
3 See Grote, "H. G." x. 379.

eminence under their opponents) addressed himself to the Argives and Arcadians as follows: "If the wealthiest classes should ever come into power in Sicyon, without a doubt the city would take the first opportunity of readopting a Laconian policy; whereas, if a democracy be set up," he added, "you may rest assured Sicyon will hold fast by you. All I ask you is to stand by me; I will do the rest. It is I who will call a meeting of the people; and by that selfsame act I shall give you a pledge of my good faith and present you with a state firm in its alliance. All this, be assured," he added, "I do because, like yourselves, I have long ill brooked the pride of Lacedaemon, and shall be glad to escape the yoke of bondage."

These proposals found favor with the Arcadians and the Argives, who gladly gave the assistance demanded. Euphron straightway, in the marketplace, in the presence of the two powers concerned,[1] proceeded to convene the Demos, as if there were to be a new constitution, based on the principle of equality.[2] When the convention met, he bade them appoint generals: they might choose whom they liked. Whereupon they elected Euphron himself, Hippodamus, Cleander, Acrisius, and Lysander. When these matters were arranged he appointed Adeas, his own son, over the foreign brigade, in place of the former commander, Lysimenes, whom he removed. His next step was promptly to secure the fidelity of the foreign mercenaries by various acts of kindness, and to attach others; and he spared neither the public nor the sacred moneys for this object. He had, to aid him, further, the property of all the citizens whom he exiled on the ground of Laconism, and of this without scruple he in every case availed himself. As for his colleagues in office, some he treacherously put to death, others he exiled, by which means he got everything under his own power, and was now a tyrant without disguise. The method by which he got the allies to connive at his doings was twofold. Partly he worked on them by pecuniary aid, partly by the readiness with which he lent the support of his foreign troops on any campaign to which they might invite him.

II

366 BC. Matters had so far progressed that the Argives had already fortified the Trikaranon above the Heraion as an outpost to threaten Phlius, while the Sicyonians were engaged in fortifying Thyamia[3] on their frontier;

---

1 Lit. "the Argives and the Arcadians."
2 Lit. "on fair and equal terms." See Thuc. v. 79.
3 "Thyamia is placed by Ross on the lofty hill of Spiria, the northern prolongation of Tricaranum, between the villages Stimanga and Skrapani."—"Dict. Anct. Geog." "Phlius."

and between the two the Phliasians were severely pinched. They began to suffer from dearth of necessaries; but, in spite of all, remained unshaken in their alliance. It is the habit of historians, I know, to record with admiration each noble achievement of the larger powers, but to me it seems a still more worthy task to bring to light the great exploits of even a little state found faithful in the performance of fair deeds.

370–369 BC. Now these Phliasians were friends of Lacedaemon while at the zenith of her power. After her disaster on the field of Leuctra, when many of the Perioeci, and the helots to a man, revolted; when, more than that, the allies, save only quite a few, forsook her;[1] and when united Hellas, so to speak, was marching on her—these Phliasians remained stanch in their allegiance; and, in spite of the hostility of the most powerful states of the Peloponnese, to wit the Arcadians and the Argives, they insisted on coming to her aid. It fell to their lot to cross into Prasiae as the rearguard of the reinforcements, which consisted of the men of Corinth, of Epidaurus and of Troezen, of Hermione, Halieis, and Sicyon and Pellene, in the days before any of these had revolted.[2] Not even when the commander of the foreign brigade, picking up the divisions already across, left them behind and was gone—not even so did they flinch or turn back, but hired a guide from Prasiae, and though the enemy was massed round Amyclae, slipped through his ranks, as best they could, and so reached Sparta. It was then that the Lacedaemonians, besides other honors conferred upon them, sent them an ox as a gift of hospitality.

369 BC. Later on, when the enemy had retired from Laconia, the Argives, ill brooking so much zeal for Lacedaemon on the part of Phlius, marched in full force against the little state, and fell to ravaging their territory. Even then they remained undaunted; and when the enemy turned to retire, destroying all that he could lay hands upon, out dashed the cavalry of the Phliasians and dogged his retreat. And notwithstanding that the Argive's rear consisted of the whole of his cavalry, with some companies of infantry to support them, they attacked him, sixty in number, and routed his whole rearguard. They slew, indeed, but a few of them; but, having so slain that handful, they paused and erected a trophy in full sight of the Argive army with as little concern as if they had cut down their enemies to a man.

Once again the Lacedaemonians and their allies were guarding Oneion,[3] and the Thebans were threatening to scale the pass. The Arcadians and

---

1 See above, "VI." v. 29.
2 See "Hell." VII. i. 18.
3 369 BC? al. 368 BC. See above, "Hell." VII. i. 15; Grote, "H. G." x. 346.

Eleians[1] were moving forward through Nemea to effect a junction with the Thebans, when a hint was conveyed to them by some Phliasian exiles, "Only show yourselves before Phlius and the town is yours." An agreement was made, and in the dead of night a party consisting of the exiles themselves and others with them, about six hundred in number, planted themselves close under the walls with scaling-ladders. Presently the scouts from the Trikaranon signalled to the city that the enemy was advancing. The citizens were all attention; their eyes fixed upon their scouts. Meanwhile the traitors within were likewise signalling to those seated under lee of the walls "to scale"; and these, scaling up, seized the arms of the guards, which they found abandoned, and fell to pursuing the day sentinels, ten in number (one out of each squad of five being always left on day duty).[2] One of these was put to the sword as he lay asleep, and a second as he was escaping to the Heraion; but the other eight day-pickets leapt down the wall on the side toward the city, one after another. The scaling party now found themselves in undisputed possession of the citadel. But the shouting had reached the city below: the citizens rallied to the rescue; and the enemy began by sallying forth from the citadel, and did battle in the forefront of the gate leading down to the city. By and by, being strongly beleaguered by the ever-increasing reinforcements of the citizens, they retired, falling back upon the citadel; and the citizens along with the enemy forced their way in. The center of the citadel was speedily deserted; for the enemy scaled the walls and towers, and showered blows and missiles upon the citizens below. These defended themselves from the ground, or pressed the encounter home by climbing the ladders which led to the walls. Once masters of certain towers on this side and the other of the invaders, the citizens came to close quarters with them with reckless desperation. The invaders, pushed and pommelled by dint of such audacity and hard hitting, were cooped up like sheep into narrower and narrower space. But at that critical moment the Arcadians and the Argives were circling round the city, and had begun to dig through the walls of the citadel from its upper side.[3] Of the citizens inside some were beating down their assailants on the wall;[4] others, those of them who were climbing up from outside and were still on the scaling-ladders, whilst a third set were delivering battle against

---

1 See above, "Hell." VII. i. 18, and below, S. 8.
2 Or, "one member of both the squads of five was left behind"—i.e. two out of the ten could not keep up with the rest in their flight, and were taken and killed; one indeed had not started, but was killed in sleep.
3 Or, "downwards" (L. and S.); or, "in front," "von vorn" (Buchs).
4 Reading, {tous eti toi teikhous}. See Otto Keller for various emendations of the passage.

those who had mounted the towers. These last had found fire in the men's quarters, and were engaged in setting the towers and all ablaze, bringing up sheaves of corn and grass—an ample harvesting, as luck would have it, garnered off the citadel itself. Thereupon the occupants of the towers, in terror of the flames, leapt down one by one, while those on the walls, under the blows of the defenders, tumbled off with similar expedition; and as soon as they had once begun to yield, the whole citadel, in almost less time than it takes to tell, was cleared of the enemy. In an instant out dashed the cavalry, and the enemy, seeing them, beat a hasty retreat, leaving behind scaling-ladders and dead, besides some comrades hopelessly maimed. In fact, the enemy, what between those who were slain inside and those who leapt from the walls, lost not less than eighty men. And now it was a goodly sight to see the brave men grasp one another by the hand and pledge each other on their preservation, whilst the women brought them drink and cried for joy. Not one there present but in very sooth was overcome by laughter mixed with tears.[1]

Next year also[2] Phlius was invaded by the Argives and all the Arcadians. The reason of this perpetually-renewed attack on Phlius is not far to seek: partly it was the result of spleen, partly the little township stood midway between them, and they cherished the hope that through want of the necessaries of life they would bring it over. During this invasion the cavalry and the picked troop of the Phliasians, assisted by some Athenian knights, made another famous charge at the crossing of the river.[3] They made it so hot for the enemy that for the rest of that day he was forced to retire under the mountain ridges, and to hold aloof as if afraid to trample down the corn-crops of a friendly people on the flat below.

Again another time[4] the Theban commander in Sicyon marched out against Phlius, taking with him the garrison under his personal command, with the Sicyonians and Pellenians (for at the date of the incident these states followed in the wake of Thebes). Euphron was there also with his mercenaries, about two thousand in number, to share the fortunes of the field. The mass of the troops began their descent on the Heraion by the Trikaranon, intending to ravage the flat bottom below. At the gate leading to Corinth the Theban general left his Sicyonians and Pellenians on the

---

1 *In true Homeric fashion, as Pollux (ii. 64) observes. See Homer, "Il." vi. 484. See above, VII. i. 32; "Cyrop." VII. v. 32; "Hiero," iii. 5; "Sym." ii. 24; "Antony and Cleopatra," III. ii. 43.*
2 *368 BC (or 367 BC).*
3 *The Asopus.*
4 *367 BC (or 366 BC).*

height, to prevent the Phliasians getting behind him at this point and so over the heads of his troops as they lay at the Heraion beneath.[1] As soon as the citizens of Phlius found that hostile troops were advancing on their corn-land, out dashed the cavalry with the chosen band of the Phliasians and gave battle, not suffering the enemy to penetrate into the plain. The best part of the day was spent in taking long shots at one another on that field; Euphron pushing his attack down to the point where cavalry could operate, the citizens retaliating as far as the Heraion. Presently the time to withdraw had come, and the enemy began to retire, following the circle of the Trikaranon; the short cut to reach the Pellenians being barred by the ravine which runs in front of the walls. The Phliasians escorted their retreating foes a little way up the steep, and then turning off dashed along the road beside the walls, making for the Pellenians and those with them; whereupon the Theban, perceiving the haste of the Phliasians, began racing with his infantry to outspeed them and bring succour to the Pellenians. The cavalry, however, arrived first and fell to attacking the Pellenians, who received and withstood the shock, and the cavalry drew back. A second time they charged, and were supported by some infantry detachments, which had now come up. It ended in a hand-to-hand fight; and eventually the enemy gave way. On the field lay dead some Sicyonians, and of the Pellenians many a good man. In record of the feat the Phliasians began to raise a trophy, as well they might; and loud and clear the paean rang. As to the Theban and Euphron, they and all their men stood by and stared at the proceedings, like men who had raced to see a sight. After all was over the one party retired to Sicyon and the other withdrew into their city.

That too was another noble exploit of the Phliasians, when they took the Pellenian Proxenus prisoner and, although suffering from scarcity at the time, sent him back without a ransom. "As generous as brave," such is their well-earned title who were capable of such performance.

The heroic resolution with which these men maintained their loyalty to their friends is manifest. When excluded from the fruits of their own soil, they contrived to live, partly by helping themselves from the enemy's territory, partly by purchasing from Corinth, though to reach that market they must run the gauntlet of a thousand risks; and having reached it their troubles began afresh. There were difficulties in providing the requisite sum, difficulties in arranging with the purveyors, and it was barely possible to find sureties for the very beasts which should carry home their marketing. They had reached the depth of despair, and were absolutely at a loss what

---

1 Lit. *"above the Heraion"* (where his main body lay).

to do, when they arranged with Chares to escort their convoy. Once safe inside Phlius, they begged him to help them to convey their useless and sick folk to Pellene.[1] These they left at that place; and after making purchases and packing as many beasts of burthen as they could, they set off to return in the night, not in ignorance that they would be laid in wait for by the enemy, but persuaded that the want of provisions was a worse evil than mere fighting.

The men of Phlius pushed forward with Chares; presently they stumbled on the enemy and at once grappled to their work. Pressing hard on the foe, they called cheerily to one another, and shouted at the same time to Chares to bring up his aid. In short, the victory was theirs; and the enemy was driven off the road; and so they got themselves and their supplies safely home. The long night-watching superinduced sleep which lasted well into the next day. But Chares was no sooner out of bed then he was accosted by the cavalry and the pick of the heavy infantry with the following appeal: "Chares, today you have it in your power to perform the noblest deed of arms. The Sicyonians are fortifying an outpost on our borders, they have plenty of stone-masons but a mere handful of hoplites. We the knights of Phlius and we the flower of our infantry force will lead the way; and you shall follow after with your mercenaries. Perhaps when you appear on the scene you will find the whole thing finished, or perhaps your coming will send the enemy flying, as happened at Pellene. If you do not like the sound of these proposals, sacrifice and take counsel of the gods. Our belief is that the gods will bid you yet more emphatically than we to take this step. Only this, Chares, you must well consider, that if you do take it you will have established an outpost on the enemy's frontier; you will have saved from perdition a friendly city; you will win eternal glory in your own fatherland; and among friends and foes alike no name will be heralded with louder praise than that of Chares."

Chares was persuaded, and proceeded to offer sacrifice. Meanwhile the Phliasian cavalry were donning their breastplates and bridling their horses, and the heavy infantry made every preparation for the march. Then they took their arms, fell into line, and tramped off to the place of sacrifice. Chares with the soothsayer stepped forward to meet them, announcing that the victims were favorable. "Only wait for us," they exclaimed; "we will sally forth with you at once." The heralds' cry "To arms!" was sounded, and with a zeal which was almost miraculous the mercenaries themselves rushed out. As soon as Chares began the march, the Phliasian cavalry and

---

1 *What is the date of this incident? See above, "Hell." VII. ii. 3; below VII. iv. 17.*

infantry got in front of him. At first they led off at a smart pace; presently they began to bowl[1] along more quickly, and finally the cavalry were tearing over the ground might and main, whilst the infantry, at the greatest pace compatible with keeping their ranks, tore after them; and behind them, again, came Chares zealously following up in their rear. There only remained a brief interval of daylight before the sun went down, and they came upon the enemy in the fortress, some washing, some cooking a savoury meal, others kneading their bread, others making their beds. These, when they saw the vehemence of the attack, at once, in utter panic, took to flight, leaving behind all their provisions for the brave fellows who took their place. They, as their reward, made a fine supper off these stores and others which had come from home, pouring out libations for their good fortune and chanting the battle-hymn; after which they posted pickets for the night and slumbered well. The messenger with the news of their success at Thyamia arrived at Corinth in the night. The citizens of that state with hearty friendship at once ordered out by herald all the oxen and beasts of burthen, which they loaded with food and brought to Phlius; and all the while the fortress was building day by day these convoys of food were duly despatched.

III

But on this topic enough, perhaps, has been said to demonstrate the loyalty of the men of Phlius to their friends, their bravery in war, and, lastly, their steadfastness in maintaining their alliance in spite of famine.

367–366 BC. It seems to have been somewhere about this date that Aeneas the Stymphalian,[2] who had become general of the Arcadians, finding that the state of affairs in Sicyon was intolerable, marched up with his army into the acropolis. Here he summoned a meeting of the Sicyonian aristocrats already within the walls, and sent to fetch those others who had been banished without a decree of the people.[3] Euphron, taking fright at these proceedings, fled for safety to the harbor-town of Sicyon. Hither he summoned Pasimelus from Corinth, and by his instrumentality handed

---

1 See "Anab." VII. iii. 46.
2 Is this man the famous writer {o taktikos}, a portion of whose works, the "Treatise on Siege Operations," has been preserved (recently re-edited by Arnold Hug—"Commentarius Poliorceticus," Lips. Trubner, 1884)? So Casaubon supposed. Cf. "Com. Pol." 27, where the writer mentions {paneia} as the Arcadian term for "panics." Readers of the "Anabasis" will recollect the tragic end of another Aeneas, also of Stymphalus, an Arcadian officer. On the official title {strategos} (general), Freeman ("Hist. Fed. Gov." 204) notes that "at the head of the whole League there seems to have been, as in so many other cases, a single Federal general." Cf. Diod. xv. 62.
3 See above, VII. i. 46.

over the harbor to the Lacedaemonians. Once more reappearing in his old character, he began to pose as an ally of Sparta. He asserted that his fidelity to Lacedaemon had never been interrupted; for when the votes were given in the city whether Sicyon should give up her allegiance to Lacedaemon, "I, with one or two others," said he, "voted against the measure; but afterward these people betrayed me, and in my desire to avenge myself on them I set up a democracy. At present all traitors to yourselves are banished—I have seen to that. If only I could get the power into my own hands, I would go over to you, city and all, at once. All that I can do at present, I have done; I have surrendered to you this harbor." That was what Euphron said to his audience there, but of the many who heard his words, how many really believed his words is by no means evident. However, since I have begun the story of Euphron, I desire to bring it to its close.

Faction and party strife ran high in Sicyon between the better classes and the people, when Euphron, getting a body of foreign troops from Athens, once more obtained his restoration. The city, with the help of the commons, he was master of, but the Theban governor held the citadel. Euphron, perceiving that he would never be able to dominate the state whilst the Thebans held the acropolis, collected money and set off to Thebes, intending to persuade the Thebans to expel the aristocrats and once again to hand over the city to himself. But the former exiles, having got wind of this journey of his, and of the whole intrigue, set off themselves to Thebes in front of him.[1] When, however, they saw the terms of intimacy on which he associated with the Theban authorities, in terror of his succeeding in his mission some of them staked their lives on the attempt and stabbed Euphron in the Cadmeia, where the magistrates and senate were seated. The magistrates, indeed, could not but indict the perpetrators of the deed before the senate, and spoke as follows:

"Fellow citizens, it is our duty to arraign these murderers of Euphron, the men before you, on the capital charge. Mankind may be said to fall into two classes: there are the wise and temperate,[2] who are incapable of any wrong and unhallowed deed; and there are the base, the bad, who do indeed such things, but try to escape the notice of their fellows. The men before you are exceptional. They have so far exceeded all the rest of men in audacity and foul villainy that, in the very presence of the magistrates and of yourselves, who alone have the power of life and death, they have taken

---

1 Or, "on an opposition journey."
2 Lit. "the sound of soul."

the law into their own hands,[1] and have slain this man. But they stand now before the bar of justice, and they must needs pay the extreme penalty; for, if you spare them, what visitor will have courage to approach the city? Nay, what will become of the city itself, if license is to be given to anyone who chooses to murder those who come here, before they have even explained the object of their visit? It is our part, then, to prosecute these men as arch-villains and miscreants, whose contempt for law and justice is only matched by the supreme indifference with which they treat this city. It is your part, now that you have heard the charges, to impose upon them that penalty which seems to be the measure of their guilt."

Such were the words of the magistrates. Among the men thus accused, all save one denied immediate participation in the act. It was not their hands that had dealt the blow. This one not only confessed the deed, but made a defense in words somewhat as follows:

"As to treating you with indifference, men of Thebes, that is not possible for a man who knows that with you lies the power to deal with him as you list. Ask rather on what I based my confidence when I slew the man; and be well assured that, in the first place, I based it on the conviction that I was doing right; next, that your verdict will also be right and just. I knew assuredly how you dealt with Archias[2] and Hypates and that company whom you detected in conduct similar to that of Euphron: you did not stay for formal voting, but at the first opportunity within your reach you guided the sword of vengeance, believing that by the verdict of mankind a sentence of death had already been passed against the conspicuously profane person, the manifest traitor, and him who lays to his hand to become a tyrant. See, then, what follows. Euphron was liable on each of these several counts: he was a conspicuously profane person, who took into his keeping temples rich in votive offerings of gold and silver, and swept them bare of their sacred treasures; he was an arrant traitor—for what treason could be more manifest than Euphron's? First he was the bosom friend of Lacedaemon, but presently chose you in their stead; and, after exchange of solemn pledges between yourselves and him, once more turned round and played the traitor to you, and delivered up the harbor to your enemies. Lastly, he was most undisguisedly a tyrant, who made not free men only, but free fellow citizens his slaves; who put to death, or drove into exile, or robbed of their wealth and property, not malefactors, note you, but the mere victims of his whim and fancy; and these were

---

1 Or, "they have been judge and jury both, and executioners to boot."
2 See above, V. iv. 2.

ever the better folk. Once again restored by the help of your sworn foes and antagonists, the Athenians, to his native town of Sicyon, the first thing he did was to take up arms against the governor from Thebes; but, finding himself powerless to drive him from the acropolis, he collected money and betook himself hither. Now, if it were proved that he had mustered armed bands to attack you, I venture to say, you would have thanked me that I slew him. What then, when he came furnished with vile moneys, to corrupt you therewith, to bribe you to make him once more lord and master of the state? How shall I, who dealt justice upon him, justly suffer death at your hands? For to be worsted in arms implies injury certainly, but of the body only: the defeated man is not proved to be dishonest by his loss of victory. But he who is corrupted by filthy lucre, contrary to the standard of what is best,[1] is at once injured and involved in shame.

"Now if he had been your friend, however much he was my national foe, I do confess it had been scarce honorable of me to have stabbed him to death in your presence: but why, I should like to ask, should the man who betrayed you be less your enemy than mine? 'Ah, but,' I hear someone retort, 'he came of his own accord.' I presume, sir, you mean that had he chanced to be slain by somebody at a distance from your state, that somebody would have won your praise; but now, on the ground that he came back here to work mischief on the top of mischief, 'he had the right to live!'[2] In what part of Hellas, tell me, sir, do Hellenes keep a truce with traitors, double-dyed deserters, and tyrants? Moreover, I must remind you that you passed a resolution—if I mistake not, it stands recorded in your parliamentary minutes—that 'renegades are liable to be apprehended[3] in any of the allied cities.' Now, here is a renegade restoring himself without any common decree of the allied states: will anyone tell me on what ground this person did not deserve to die? What I maintain, sirs, is that if you put me to death, by so doing you will be aiding and abetting your bitterest foe; while, by a verdict sanctioning the justice of my conduct, you will prove your willingness to protect the interests not of yourselves only, but of the whole body of your allies."

The Thebans on hearing these pleadings decided that Euphron had only suffered the fate which he deserved. His own countrymen, however, conveyed away the body with the honors due to a brave and good man,

---

1 Or, as we should say, "in violation of conscience."
2 Or, "he was wrongfully slain."
3 For this right of extradition see Plut. "Lys." xxvii.

and buried him in the marketplace, where they still pay pious reverence to his memory as "a founder of the state." So strictly, it would seem, do the mass of mankind confine the term brave and good to those who are the benefactors of themselves.

IV

366 BC. And so ends the history of Euphron. I return to the point reached at the commencement of this digression.[1] The Phliasians were still fortifying Thyamia, and Chares was still with them, when Oropus[2] was seized by the banished citizens of that place. The Athenians in consequence despatched an expedition in full force to the point of danger, and recalled Chares from Thyamia; whereupon the Sicyonians and the Arcadians seized the opportunity to recapture the harbor of Sicyon. Meanwhile the Athenians, forced to act single-handed, with none of their allies to assist them, retired from Oropus, leaving that town in the hands of the Thebans as a deposit till the case at issue could be formally adjudicated.

Now Lycomedes[3] had discovered that the Athenians were harboring a grievance against her allies, as follows:—They felt it hard that, while Athens was put to vast trouble on their account, yet in her need not a man among them stepped forward to render help. Accordingly he persuaded the assembly of Ten Thousand to open negotiations with Athens for the purpose of forming an alliance.[4] At first some of the Athenians were vexed that they, being friends of Lacedaemon, should become allied to her opponents; but on further reflection they discovered it was no less desirable for the Lacedaemonians than for themselves that the Arcadians should become independent of Thebes. That being so, they were quite ready to accept an Arcadian alliance. Lycomedes himself was still engaged on this transaction when, taking his departure from Athens, he died, in a manner which looked like divine intervention.

Out of the many vessels at his service he had chosen the one he liked best, and by the terms of contract was entitled to land at any point he might desire; but for some reason, selected the exact spot where a body of

---

1 See above, *VII. ii. 23; iii. 3; Diod. xv. 76.*
2 See *Thuc. viii. 60.*
3 See above, *VII. i. 23.*
4 This proves that "the Ten Thousand made war and peace in the name of all Arkadia"; cf. "Hell." *VII. i. 38; Diod. xv. 59.* "They received and listened to the ambassadors of other Greek states"; Demosth. "F. L." 220. "They regulated and paid the standing army of the Federation"; "Hell." *VII. iv. 22, 23; Diod. xv. 62.* "They sat in judgment on political offenders against the collective majority of the Arkadian League"; "Hell." *VII. iv. 33;* Freeman, "Hist. Fed. Gov." 203, note 1.

Mantinean exiles lay. Thus he died; but the alliance on which he had set his heart was already consummated.

Now an argument was advanced by Demotion[1] in the Assembly of Athens, approving highly of the friendship with the Arcadians, which to his mind was an excellent thing, but arguing that the generals should be instructed to see that Corinth was kept safe for the Athenian people. The Corinthians, hearing this, lost no time in despatching garrisons of their own large enough to take the place of the Athenian garrisons at any point where they might have them, with orders to these latter to retire: "We have no further need of foreign garrisons," they said. The garrisons did as they were bid.

As soon as the Athenian garrison troops were met together in the city of Corinth, the Corinthian authorities caused proclamation to be made inviting all Athenians who felt themselves wronged to enter their names and cases upon a list, and they would recover their dues. While things were in this state, Chares arrived at Cenchreae with a fleet. Learning what had been done, he told them that he had heard there were designs against the state of Corinth, and had come to render assistance. The authorities, while thanking him politely for his zeal, were not any the more ready to admit the vessels into the harbor, but bade him sail away; and after rendering justice to the infantry troops, they sent them away likewise. Thus the Athenians were quit of Corinth. To the Arcadians, to be sure, they were forced by the terms of their alliance to send an auxiliary force of cavalry, "in case of any foreign attack upon Arcadia." At the same time they were careful not to set foot on Laconian soil for the purposes of war.

The Corinthians had begun to realizeon how slender a thread their political existence hung. They were overmastered by land still as ever, with the further difficulty of Athenian hostility, or quasi-hostility, now added. They resolved to collect bodies of mercenary troops, both infantry and horse. At the head of these they were able at once to guard their state and to inflict much injury on their neighboring foes. To Thebes, indeed, they sent ambassadors to ascertain whether they would have any prospect of peace if they came to seek it. The Thebans bade them come: "Peace they should have." Whereupon the Corinthians asked that they might be allowed to visit their allies; in making peace they would like to share it with

---

[1] *Of Demotion nothing more, I think, is known. Grote ("H. G." x. 397) says: "The public debates of the Athenian assembly were not favorable to the success of a scheme like that proposed by Demotion, to which secrecy was indispensable. Compare another scheme" (the attempted surprise of Mitylene, 428 BC), "divulged in like manner, in Thuc. iii. 3."*

those who cared for it, and would leave those who preferred war to war. This course also the Thebans sanctioned; and so the Corinthians came to Lacedaemon and said:

"Men of Lacedaemon, we, your friends, are here to present a petition, and on this wise. If you can discover any safety for us whilst we persist in warlike courses, we beg that you will show it us; but if you recognize the hopelessness of our affairs, we would, in that case, proffer this alternative: if peace is alike conducive to your interests, we beg that you would join us in making peace, since there is no one with whom we would more gladly share our safety than with you; if, on the other hand, you are persuaded that war is more to your interest, permit us at any rate to make peace for ourselves. So saved today, perhaps we may live to help you in days to come; whereas, if today we be destroyed, plainly we shall never at any time be serviceable again."

The Lacedaemonians, on hearing these proposals, counselled the Corinthians to arrange a peace on their own account; and as for the rest of their allies, they permitted any who did not care to continue the war along with them to take a respite and recruit themselves. "As for ourselves," they said, "we will go on fighting and accept whatever Heaven has in store for us,"—adding, "never will we submit to be deprived of our territory of Messene, which we received as an heirloom from our fathers."[1]

Satisfied with this answer, the Corinthians set off to Thebes in quest of peace. The Thebans, indeed, asked them to agree on oath, not to peace only but an alliance; to which they answered: "An alliance meant, not peace, but merely an exchange of war. If they liked, they were ready there and then," they repeated, "to establish a just and equitable peace." And the Thebans, admiring the manner in which, albeit in danger, they refused to undertake war against their benefactors, conceded to them and the Phliasians and the rest who came with them to Thebes, peace on the principle that each should hold their own territory. On these terms the oaths were taken.

Thereupon the Phliasians, in obedience to the compact, at once retired from Thyamia; but the Argives, who had taken the oath of peace on precisely the same terms, finding that they were unable to procure the continuance of the Phliasian exiles in the Trikaranon as a point held within the limits of Argos,[2] took over and garrisoned the place, asserting now that this land was theirs—land which only a little while before they were ravaging as hostile territory. Further, they refused to submit the case to arbitration in answer to the challenge of the Phliasians.

---

1 See Isocr. "Or." vi. "Archidamos," S. 70; Jebb, "Att. Or." ii. 193.
2 Or, "as a post held by them within the territory of the state." The passage is perhaps corrupt.

It was nearly at the same date that the son of Dionysius[1] (his father, Dionysius the first, being already dead) sent a reinforcement to Lacedaemon of twelve triremes under Timocrates, who on his arrival helped the Lacedaemonians to recover Sellasia, and after that exploit sailed away home.

366–365 BC. Not long after this the Eleians seized Lasion,[2] a place which in old days was theirs, but at present was attached to the Arcadian league. The Arcadians did not make light of the matter, but immediately summoned their troops and rallied to the rescue. Counter-reliefs came also on the side of Elis—their Three Hundred, and again their Four Hundred.[3] The Eleians lay encamped during the day face to face with the invader, but on a somewhat more level position. The Arcadians were thereby induced under cover of night to mount on to the summit of the hill overhanging the Eleians, and at day-dawn they began their descent upon the enemy. The Eleians soon caught sight of the enemy advancing from the vantage ground above them, many times their number; but a sense of shame forbade retreat at such a distance. Presently they came to close quarters; there was a hand-to-hand encounter; the Eleians turned and fled; and in retiring down the difficult ground lost many men and many arms.

Flushed with this achievement the Arcadians began marching on the cities of the Acroreia,[4] which, with the exception of Thraustus, they captured, and so reached Olympia. There they made an entrenched camp on the hill of Kronos, established a garrison, and held control over the Olympian hill-country. Margana also, by help of a party inside who gave it up, next fell into their hands.

These successive advantages gained by their opponents reacted on the Eleians, and threw them altogether into despair. Meanwhile the Arcadians were steadily advancing upon their capital.[5] At length they arrived, and penetrated into the marketplace. Here, however, the cavalry and the rest of the Eleians made a stand, drove the enemy out with some loss, and set up a trophy.

It should be mentioned that the city of Elis had previously been in a

---

1 Concerning Dionysius the first, see above, *VII. i. 20 foll. 28*.
2 See above, *VII. i. 26*; Freeman, "Hist. Fed. Gov." p. 201.
3 From the sequel it would appear that the former were a picked corps of infantry and the latter of cavalry. See Thuc. ii. 25; Busolt, op. cit. p. 175 foll.
4 The mountainous district of Elis on the borders of Arcadia, in which the rivers Peneius and Ladon take their rise; see "Dict. of Anct. Geog." s.v.; above, *III. ii. 30, IV. ii. 16*. Thraustus was one of the four chief townships of the district. For Margana, see above, *III. ii. 25, 30, IV. ii. 16, VI. v. 2*.
5 I.e. Elis.

state of disruption. The party of Charopus, Thrasonidas and Argeius were for converting the state into a democracy; the party of Eualcas, Hippias, and Stratolas[1] were for oligarchy. When the Arcadians, backed by a large force, appeared as allies of those who favored a democratic constitution, the party of Charopus were at once emboldened; and, having obtained the promise of assistance from the Arcadians, they seized the acropolis. The Knights and the Three Hundred did not hesitate, but at once marched up and dislodged them; with the result that about four hundred citizens, with Argeius and Charopus, were banished. Not long afterward these exiles, with the help of some Arcadians, seized and occupied Pylus;[2] where many of the commons withdrew from the capital to join them, attracted not only by the beauty of the position, but by the great power of the Arcadians, in alliance with them.

There was subsequently another invasion of the territory of the Eleians on the part of the Arcadians, who were influenced by the representations of the exiles that the city would come over to them. But the attempt proved abortive. The Achaeans, who had now become friends with the Eleians, kept firm guard on the capital, so that the Arcadians had to retire without further exploit than that of ravaging the country. Immediately, however, on marching out of Eleian territory they were informed that the men of Pellene were in Elis; whereupon they executed a marvellously long night march and seized the Pellenian township of Olurus[3] (the Pellenians at the date in question having already reverted to their old alliance with Lacedaemon). And now the men of Pellene, in their turn getting wind of what had happened at Olurus, made their way round as best they could, and got into their own city of Pellene; after which there was nothing for it but to carry on war with the Arcadians in Olurus and the whole body of their own commons; and in spite of their small numbers they did not cease till they had reduced Olurus by siege.

365 BC. [4]The Arcadians were presently engaged on another campaign against Elis. While they were encamped between Cyllene[5] and the capital

---

1 See below, *VII. iv. 31;* Busolt, *op. cit.* p. 175.

2 *Pylus, a town in "hollow" Elis, upon the mountain road from Elis to Olympia, at the place where the Ladon flows into the Peneius (Paus. VI. xxii. 5), near the modern village of Agrapidokhori.*— Baedeker, *"Greece,"* p. 320. See Busolt, p. 179.

3 *This fortress (placed by Leake at modern Xylokastro) lay at the entrance of the gorge of the Sys, leading from the Aigialos or coast-land into the territory of Pellene, which itself lay about sixty stades from the sea at modern Zougra. For the part played by Pellene as one of the twelve Achaean states at this period, see above.*

4 See Grote, *"H. G."* x. 429 foll.; al. 364 BC.

5 *The port town of Elis.*

the Eleians attacked them, but the Arcadians made a stand and won the battle. Andromachus, the Eleian cavalry general, who was regarded as responsible for the engagement, made an end of himself; and the rest withdrew into the city. This battle cost the life also of another there present—the Spartan Socleides; since, it will be understood, the Lacedaemonians had by this time become allies of the Eleians. Consequently the Eleians, being sore pressed on their own territory, sent an embassy and begged the Lacedaemonians to organise an expedition against the Arcadians. They were persuaded that in this way they would best arrest the progress of the Arcadians, who would thus be placed between the two foes. In accordance with this suggestion Archidamus marched out with a body of the city troops and seized Cromnus.[1] Here he left a garrison—three out of the twelve regiments[2]— and so withdrew homeward. The Arcadians had just ended their Eleian campaign, and, without disbanding their levies, hastened to the rescue, surrounded Cromnus with a double line of trenches, and having so secured their position, proceeded to lay siege to those inside the place. The city of Lacedaemon, annoyed at the siege of their citizens, sent out an army, again under Archidamus, who, when he had come, set about ravaging Arcadia to the best of his power, as also the Sciritid, and did all he could to draw off, if possible, the besieging army. The Arcadians, for all that, were not one whit the more to be stirred: they seemed callous to all his proceedings.

Presently espying a certain rising ground, across which the Arcadians had drawn their outer line of circumvallation, Archidamus proposed to himself to take it. If he were once in command of that knoll, the besiegers at its foot would be forced to retire. Accordingly he set about leading a body of troops round to the point in question, and during this movement the light infantry in advance of Archidamus, advancing at the double, caught sight of the Arcadian Eparitoi[3] outside the stockade and attacked them, while the cavalry made an attempt to enforce their attack simultaneously. The Arcadians did not swerve: in compact order they waited impassively. The Lacedaemonians charged a second time: a second time they swerved not, but on the contrary began advancing. Then, as the hoarse roar and shouting deepened, Archidamus himself advanced in support of his troops. To do so he turned aside along the carriage-road leading to Cromnus, and moved onward in column two

---

1 Cromnus, a township near Megalopolis. See Callisthenes, ap. Athen. 10, p. 452 A. See Schneider's note ad loc.
2 Lit. "lochi." See Arnold's note to Thuc. v. 68; below, VII. v. 10.
3 So the troops of the Arcadian Federation were named. Diodorus (xv. 62) calls them "the select troops," {tous kaloumenous epilektous}.

abreast,[1] which was his natural order. When they came into close proximity to one another—Archidamus's troops in column, seeing they were marching along a road; the Arcadians in compact order with shields interlinked—at this conjuncture the Lacedaemonians were not able to hold out for any length of time against the numbers of the Arcadians. Before long Archidamus had received a wound which pierced through his thigh, whilst death was busy with those who fought in front of him, Polyaenidas and Chilon, who was wedded to the sister of Archidamus, included. The whole of these, numbering no less than thirty, perished in this action. Presently, falling back along the road, they emerged into the open ground, and now with a sense of relief the Lacedaemonians got themselves into battle order, facing the foe. The Arcadians, without altering their position, stood in compact line, and though falling short in actual numbers, were in far better heart—the moral result of an attack on a retreating enemy and the severe loss inflicted on him. The Lacedaemonians, on the other hand, were sorely down-hearted: Archidamus lay wounded before their eyes; in their ears rang the names of those who had died, the fallen being not only brave men, but, one may say, the flower of Spartan chivalry. The two armies were now close together, when one of the older men lifted up his voice and cried: "Why need we fight, sirs? Why not rather make truce and part friends?" Joyously the words fell on the ears of either host, and they made a truce. The Lacedaemonians picked up their dead and retired; the Arcadians withdrew to the point where their advance originally began, and set up a trophy of victory.

Now, as the Arcadians lay at Cromnus, the Eleians from the capital, advancing in the first instance upon Pylus, fell in with the men of that place, who had been beaten back from Thalamae.[2] Galloping along the road, the cavalry of the Eleians, when they caught sight of them, did not hesitate, but dashed at them at once, and put some to the sword, while others of them fled for safety to a rising knoll. Ere long the Eleian infantry arrived, and succeeded in dislodging this remnant on the hillock also; some they slew, and others, nearly two hundred in number, they took alive, all of whom where either sold, if foreigners, or, if Eleian exiles, put to death. After this the Eleians captured the men of Pylus and the place itself, as no one came to their rescue, and recovered the Marganians.

The Lacedaemonians presently made a second attempt on Cromnus by a

---

1 See above, III. i. 22.
2 *A strong fortress in an unfrequented situation, defended by narrow passes (Leake, "Morea," ii. 204); it lay probably in the rocky recesses of Mount Scollis (modern Santameri), on the frontier of Achaea, near the modern village of Santameri. See Polyb. iv. 75. See Busolt, op. cit. p. 179.*

night attack, got possession of the part of the palisading facing the Argives, and at once began summoning their besieged fellow citizens to come out. Out accordingly came all who happened to be within easy distance, and who took time by the forelock. The rest were not quick enough; a strong Arcadian reinforcement cut them off, and they remained shut up inside, and were eventually taken prisoners and distributed. One portion of them fell to the lot of the Argives, one to the Thebans,[1] one to the Arcadians, and one to the Messenians. The whole number taken, whether true-born Spartans or Perioeci, amounted to more than one hundred.

364 BC. And now that the Arcadians had leisure on the side of Cromnus, they were again able to occupy themselves with the Eleians, and to keep Olympia still more strongly garrisoned. In anticipation of the approaching Olympic year,[2] they began preparations to celebrate the Olympian games in conjunction with the men of Pisa, who claim to be the original presidents of the Temple.[3] Now, when the month of the Olympic Festival—and not the month only, but the very days, during which the solemn assembly is wont to meet, were come, the Eleians, in pursuance of preparations and invitations to the Achaeans, of which they made no secret, at length proceeded to march along the road to Olympia. The Arcadians had never imagined that they would really attack them; and they were themselves just now engaged with the men of Pisa in carrying out the details of the solemn assembly. They had already completed the chariot-race, and the foot-race of the pentathlon.[4] The competitors entitled to enter for the wrestling match had left the racecourse, and were getting through their bouts in the space between the racecourse and the great altar.

It must be understood that the Eleians under arms were already close at hand within the sacred enclosure.[5] The Arcadians, without advancing

---

1 "The Thebans must have been soldiers in garrison at Tegea, Megalopolis, or Messene."—Grote, "H. G." x. 433.

2 I.e. "Ol. 104. 1" (July 364 BC).

3 For this claim on the part of the Pisatans (as the old inhabitants), see above, III. ii. 31; Paus. VI. xxii. 2; Diod. xv. 78; Busolt, op. cit. p. 154.

4 As to the pentathlon, see above, IV. vii. 5. Whether the preceding {ippodromia} was, at this date, a horse or chariot race, or both, I am unable to say.

5 "The {temenos} must here be distinguished from the Altis, as meaning the entire breadth of consecrated ground at Olympia, of which the Altis formed a smaller interior portion enclosed with a wall. The Eleians entered into a {temenos} before they crossed the river Kladeus, which flowed through the {temenos}, but alongside the Altis. The tomb of Oenomaus, which was doubtless included in the {temenos}, was on the right bank of the Kladeus (Paus. VI. xxi. 3); while the Altis was on the left bank of the river."— Grote, "H. G." x. 438, note 1. For the position of the Altis (Paus. V. x. 1) and several of the buildings here mentioned, and the topography of Olympia in general, see Baedeker's "Greece," p. 322 foll.; and Dorpfeld's Plan ("Olympia und Umgegend," Berlin, 1882), there reproduced.

farther to meet them, drew up their troops on the river Cladaus, which flows past the Altis and discharges itself into the Alpheus. Their allies, consisting of two hundred Argive hoplites and about four hundred Athenian cavalry, were there to support them. Presently the Eleians formed into line on the opposite side of the stream, and, having sacrificed, at once began advancing. Though heretofore in matters of war despised by Arcadians and Argives, by Achaeans and Athenians alike, still on this day they led the van of the allied force like the bravest of the brave. Coming into collision with the Arcadians first, they at once put them to flight, and next receiving the attack of the Argive supports, mastered these also. Then having pursued them into the space between the senate-house, the temple of Hestia, and the theatre thereto adjoining, they still kept up the fighting as fiercely as ever, pushing the retreating foe toward the great altar. But now being exposed to missiles from the porticoes and the senate-house and the great temple,[1] while battling with their opponents on the level, some of the Eleians were slain, and among others the commander of the Three Hundred himself, Stratolas. At this state of the proceedings they retired to their camp.

The Arcadians and those with them were so terrified at the thought of the coming day that they gave themselves neither respite nor repose that night, but fell to chopping up the carefully-compacted booths and constructing them into palisades; so that when the Eleians did again advance the next day and saw the strength of the barriers and the number mounted on the temples, they withdrew to their city. They had proved themselves to be warriors of such mettle as a god indeed by the breath of his spirit may raise up and bring to perfection in a single day, but into which it were impossible for mortal men to convert a coward even in a lifetime.

363 BC. The employment of the sacred treasures of the temple by the Arcadian magistrates[2] as a means of maintaining the Eparitoi[3] aroused protest. The Mantineans were the first to pass a resolution forbidding such use of the sacred property. They set the example themselves of providing the necessary quota for the Troop in question from their state exchequer, and this sum they sent to the federal government. The latter, affirming that the Mantineans were undermining the Arcadian league, retaliated by citing their leading statesmen to appear before the assembly of Ten Thousand; and on their refusal to obey the summons, passed sentence upon

---
1 Or, "from the porticoes of the senate-house and the great temple."
2 See above, VII. i. 24. "Were these magistrates, or merely popular leaders?"—Freeman, "Hist. Fed. Gov." p. 203, note 3.
3 Or, "Select Troop." See above.

them, and sent the Eparitoi to apprehend them as convicted persons. The Mantineans, however, closed their gates, and would not admit the Troop within their walls. Their example was speedily followed: others among the Ten Thousand began to protest against the enormity of so applying the sacred treasures; it was doubly wrong to leave as a perpetual heirloom to their children the imputation of a crime so heinous against the gods. But no sooner was a resolution passed in the general assembly[1] forbidding the use of the sacred moneys for profane purposes than those (members of the league) who could not have afforded to serve as Eparitoi without pay began speedily to melt away; while those of more independent means, with mutual encouragement, began to enrol themselves in the ranks of the Eparitoi— the feeling being that they ought not to be a mere tool in the hands of the corps, but rather that the corps itself should be their instrument. Those members of the government who had manipulated the sacred money soon saw that when they came to render an account of their stewardship, in all likelihood they would lose their heads. They therefore sent an embassy to Thebes, with instructions to the Theban authorities warning them that, if they did not open a campaign, the Arcadians would in all probability again veer round to Lacedaemon.

The Thebans, therefore, began making preparations for opening a campaign, but the party who consulted the best interests of Peloponnese[2] persuaded the general assembly of the Arcadians to send an embassy and tell the Thebans not to advance with an army into Arcadia, unless they sent for them; and whilst this was the language they addressed to Thebes, they reasoned among themselves that they could dispense with war altogether. The presidency over the temple of Zeus, they were persuaded, they might easily dispense with; indeed, it would at once be a more upright and a holier proceeding on their parts to give it back, and with such conduct the god, they thought, might be better pleased. As these were also the views and wishes of the Eleians, both parties agreed to make peace, and a truce was established.

362 BC. The oaths were ratified; and among those who swore to them were included not only the parties immediately concerned, but the men of Tegea, and the Theban general himself, who was inside Tegea with three hundred heavy infantry of the Boeotians. Under these

---

1 "The common formula for a Greek confederation, {to koinon ton "Arkadon}, is used as an equivalent of {oi mupioi}" (here and below, SS. 35, 38)—Freeman, op. cit. 202, note 4.
2 See below, VII. v. 1, {oi kedouenoi tes Peloponnesou}. I regard these phrases as self-laudatory political catchwords.

circumstances the Arcadians in Tegea remained behind feasting and keeping holy day, with outpouring of libations and songs of victory, to celebrate the establishment of peace. Here was an opportunity for the Theban and those of the government who regarded the forthcoming inquiry with apprehension. Aided by the Boeotians and those of the Eparitoi who shared their sentiments, they first closed the gates of the fortress of Tegea, and then set about sending to the various quarters to apprehend those of the better class. But, inasmuch as there were Arcadians present from all the cities, and there was a general desire for peace, those apprehended must needs be many. So much so, that the prison-house was eventually full to overflowing, and the town-hall was full also. Besides the number lodged in prison, a number had escaped by leaping down the walls, and there were others who were suffered to pass through the gates (a laxity easily explained, since no one, excepting those who were anticipating their own downfall, cherished any wrathful feeling against anybody). But what was a source of still graver perplexity to the Theban commander and those acting with him—of the Mantineans, the very people whom they had set their hearts on catching, they had got but very few. Nearly all of them, owing to the proximity of their city, had, in fact, betaken themselves home. Now, when day came and the Mantineans learned what had happened, they immediately sent and forewarned the other Arcadian states to be ready in arms, and to guard the passes; and they set the example themselves by so doing. They sent at the same time to Tegea and demanded the release of all Mantineans there detained. With regard to the rest of the Arcadians they further claimed that no one should be imprisoned or put to death without trial. If anyone had any accusation to bring against any, than by the mouth of their messengers there present they gave notice that the state of Mantinea was ready to offer bail, "Verily and indeed to produce before the general assembly of the Arcadians all who might be summoned into court." The Theban accordingly, on hearing this, was at a loss what to make of the affair, and released his prisoners. Next day, summoning a congress of all the Arcadians who chose to come, he explained, with some show of apology, that he had been altogether deceived; he had heard, he said, that "the Lacedaemonians were under arms on the frontier, and that some of the Arcadians were about to betray Tegea into their hands." His auditors acquitted him for the moment, albeit they knew that as touching themselves he was lying. They sent, however, an embassy to Thebes and there accused him as deserving of death. Epaminondas (who was at that time the general at the head of the war department) is reported to have maintained that the Theban commander had acted far more rightly when he seized than when he let go the prisoners. "Thanks to you," he argued, "we have been brought into a state of war, and then you, without our advice or opinion asked, make peace on your own account; would it not be reasonable to retort upon you the charge of treason in such conduct? Anyhow, be assured," he added, "we shall bring an army into Arcadia, and along with those who share our views carry on the war which we have undertaken."

V

362 BC. This answer was duly reported to the general assembly of the Arcadians, and throughout the several states of the league. Consequently the Mantineans, along with those of the Arcadians who had the interests of Peloponnesus at heart, as also the Eleians and the Achaeans, came to the conclusion that the policy of the Thebans was plain. They wished Peloponnesus to be reduced to such an extremity of weakness that it might fall an easy prey into their hands who were minded to enslave it. "Why else," they asked, "should they wish us to fight, except that we may tear each other to pieces, and both sides be driven to look to them for support? or why, when we tell them that we have no need of them at present, do they insist on preparing for a foreign campaign? Is it not plain that these preparations are for an expedition which will do us some mischief?"

In this mood they sent to Athens,[1] calling on the Athenians for military aid. Ambassadors also went to Lacedaemon on behalf of the Eparitoi, summoning the Lacedaemonians, if they wished to give a helping hand, to put a stop to the proceedings of any power approaching to enslave Peloponnesus. As regards the headship, they came to an arrangement at once, on the principle that each of the allied states should exercise the generalship within its own territory.

While these matters were in progress, Epaminondas was prosecuting his march at the head of all the Boeotians, with the Euboeans, and a large

---

1 For a treaty of alliance between Athens, the Arkadians, Achaeans, Eleians, and Phliasians, immediately before Mantinea, 362 BC, {epi Molonos arkhontos}, see Hicks, 94; Kohler, "C. I. A." ii. p. 405. It is preserved on a stele ("broken at bottom; but the top is surmounted by a relief representing Zeus enthroned, with a thunderbolt; a female figure (= the {Summakhia}?) approaches lifting her veil, while Athena stands by") now standing among the sculptures from the Asklepieion on the Acropolis at Athens. See Milchhofer, p. 47, no. 7, "Die Museum," Athens, 1881. For the date, see Demosth. "c. Polycl." 1207.

body of Thessalians, furnished both by Alexander[1] and by his opponents. The Phocians were not represented. Their special agreement only required them to render assistance in case of an attack on Thebes; to assist in a hostile expedition against others was not in the bond. Epaminondas, however, reflected that inside Peloponnesus itself they might count upon the Argives and the Messenians, with that section of the Arcadians which shared their views. These latter were the men of Tegea and Megalopolis, of Asea and Pallantium, with any townships which owing to their small size or their position in the midst of these larger cities were forced to follow their lead.

Epaminondas advanced with rapid strides; but on reaching Nemea he slackened speed, hoping to catch the Athenians as they passed, and reflecting on the magnitude of such an achievement, whether in stimulating the courage of his own allies, or in plunging his foes into despondency; since, to state the matter concisely, any blow to Athens would be a gain to Thebes. But during his pause at Nemea those who shared the opposite policy had time to converge on Mantinea. Presently the news reached Epaminondas that the Athenians had abandoned the idea of marching by land, and were preparing to bring their supports to Arcadia by sea through Lacedaemon. This being so, he abandoned his base of Nemea and pushed on to Tegea.

That the strategy of the Theban general was fortunate I will not pretend to assert, but in the particular combination of prudence and daring which stamps these exploits, I look upon him as consummate. In the first place, I cannot but admire the sagacity which led him to form his camp within the walls of Tegea, where he was in greater security that he would have been if entrenched outside, and where his future movements were more completely concealed from the enemy. Again, the means to collect material and furnish himself with other necessaries were readier to his hand inside the city; while, thirdly, he was able to keep an eye on the movements of his opponents marching outside, and to watch their successful dispositions as well as their mistakes. More than this: in spite of his sense of superiority to his antagonists, over and over again, when he saw them gaining some

---

1 *For Alexander of Pherae, see above, VI. iv. 34. In 363 BC the Thebans had sent an army under Pelopidas into Thessaly to assist their allies among the Thessalians with the Phthiot Achaeans and the Magnetes against Alexander. At Kynos Kephelae Alexander was defeated, but Pelopidas was slain (see Grote, "H. G." x. 420 foll.). "His death, as it brought grief, so likewise it produced advantage to the allies; for the Thebans, as soon as they heard of his fall, delayed not their revenge, but presently sent seven thousand foot and seven hundred horse, under the command of Malcitas and Diogiton. And they, finding Alexander weak and without forces, compelled him to restore the cities he had taken, to withdraw his garrisons from the Magnesians and Achaeans of Phthiotos and swear to assist the Thebans against whatsoever enemies they should require."—Plut. "Pelop." 35 (Clough, ii. 236).*

advantage in position, he refused to be drawn out to attack them. It was only when he saw plainly that no city was going to give him its adhesion, and that time was slipping by, that he made up his mind that a blow must be struck, failing which, he had nothing to expect save a vast ingloriousness, in place of his former fame.[1] He had ascertained that his antagonists held a strong position round Mantinea, and that they had sent to fetch Agesilaus and the whole Lacedaemonian army. He was further aware that Agesilaus had commenced his advance and was already at Pellene.[2] Accordingly he passed the word of command[3] to his troops to take their evening meal, put himself at their head and advanced straight upon Sparta. Had it not been for the arrival (by some providential chance) of a Cretan, who brought the news to Agesilaus of the enemy's advance, he would have captured the city of Sparta like a nest of young birds absolutely bereft of its natural defenders. As it was, Agesilaus, being forewarned, had time to return to the city before the Thebans came, and here the Spartans made distribution of their scanty force and maintained watch and ward, albeit few enough in numbers, since the whole of their cavalry were away in Arcadia, and so was their foreign brigade, and so were three out of their twelve regiments.[4]

Arrived within the city of Sparta,[5] Epaminondas abstained from gaining an entry at a point where his troops would have to fight on level ground and under attack from the houses above; where also their large numbers would give them no superiority over the small numbers of the foemen. But, singling out a position which he conceived would give him the advantage, he occupied it and began his advance against the city upon a downward instead of an upward incline.

With regard to what subsequently took place, two possible explanations suggest themselves: either it was miraculous, or it may be maintained that there is no resisting the fury of desperation. Archidamus, advancing at the head of but a hundred men, and crossing the one thing which might have been expected to form an obstacle to the enemy,[6] began marching uphill

---

1 Or, "dull obscurity in place of renown."
2 Pellene (or Pellana), a town of Laconia on the Eurotas, and on the road from Sparta to Arcadia; in fact the frontier fortress on the Eurotas, as Sellasia on the Oenus; "Dict. of Anct. Geog." s.v.; see Paus. iii. 20, S. 2; Strab. viii. 386; Polyb. iv. 81, xvi. 37; Plut. "Agis," 8; Leake, "Morea," iii. 14 foll.
3 Cf. "Hipparch." iv. 9.
4 Lit. "lochi." See above, VII. iv. 20; "Pol. Lac." xi. 4.
5 Grote ("H. G." x. 455) says: "Though he crossed the Eurotas and actually entered into the city of Sparta," as the words {epei de egeneto en te polei ton Spartiaton} certainly seem to me to imply. Others interpret "in the close neighborhood of."
6 Or, "to serve as his defense"; or, "the one obstacle to his progress," i.e. Archidamus's. It was a miraculous thing that the Thebans did not stop him.

against his antagonists. At this crisis these fire-breathing warriors, these victorious heroes of Leuctra,[1] with their superiority at every point, aided, moreover, by the advantage of their position, did not withstand the attack of Archidamus and those with him, but swerved in flight.

The vanguard of Epaminondas's troops were cut down; when, however, flushed with the glory of their victory, the citizens followed up their pursuit beyond the right point, they in turn were cut down—so plainly was the demarking line of victory drawn by the finger of God. So then Archidamus set up a trophy to note the limit of his success, and gave back those who had there fallen of the enemy under a truce. Epaminondas, on his side, reflecting that the Arcadians must already be hastening to the relief of Lacedaemon, and being unwilling to engage them in conjunction with the whole of the Lacedaemonian force, especially now that the star of Sparta's fortune shone, whilst theirs had suffered some eclipse, turned and marched back the way he came with all speed possible into Tegea. There he gave his heavy infantry pause and refreshment, but his cavalry he sent on to Mantinea; he begged them to "have courage and hold on," instructing them that in all likelihood they would find the flocks and herds of the Mantineans and the entire population itself outside their walls, especially as it was the moment for carrying the corn. So they set off.

The Athenian cavalry, started from Eleusis, had made their evening meal at the Isthmus, and passing through Cleonae, as chance befell, had arrived at Mantinea and had encamped within the walls in the houses. As soon as the enemy were seen galloping up with evidently hostile intent, the Mantineans fell to praying the Athenian knights to lend them all the succour they could, and they showed them all their cattle outside, and all their laborers, and among them were many children and graybeards who were free-born citizens. The Athenians were touched by this appeal, and, though they had not yet broken fast, neither the men themselves nor their horses, went out eagerly to the rescue. And here we must needs pause to admire the valour of these men also. The enemy whom they had to cope with far outnumbered them, as was plain to see, and the former misadventure of the cavalry in Corinth was not forgotten.[2] But none of these things entered into their calculations now—nor yet the fact that they were on the point of engaging Thebans and Thessalians, the finest cavalry in the world by all repute. The only thing they thought of was the shame and the dishonor, if,

---

1 See Mahaffy, "Hist. Gk. Lit." vol. ii. p. 268, 1st ed. See above, "Hell." VI. iv. 24; Diod. xv. 39, 56.
2 Or, "and in Corinth an untoward incident had been experienced by the cavalry." See Grote, "H. G." x. 458, note 2. Possibly in reference to "Hell." VI. v. 51, 52.

being there, they did not lend a helping hand to their allies. In this mood, so soon as they caught sight of the enemy, they fell with a crash upon him in passionate longing to recover the old ancestral glory. Nor did they fight in vain—the blows they struck enabled the Mantineans to recover all their property outside, but among those who dealt them died some brave heroes;[1] brave heroes also, it is evident, were those whom they slew, since on either side the weapons wielded were not so short but that they could lunge at one another with effect. The dead bodies of their own men they refused to abandon; and there were some of the enemy's slain whom they restored to him under a flag of truce.

The thoughts now working in the mind of Epaminondas were such as these: that within a few days he would be forced to retire, as the period of the campaign was drawing to a close; if it ended in his leaving in the lurch those allies whom he came out to assist, they would be besieged by their antagonists. What a blow would that be to his own fair fame, already somewhat tarnished! Had he not been defeated in Lacedaemon, with a large body of heavy infantry, by a handful of men? defeated again at Mantinea, in the cavalry engagement, and himself the main cause finally of a coalition between five great powers—that is to say, the Lacedaemonians, the Arcadians, the Achaeans, the Eleians, and the Athenians? On all grounds it seemed to him impossible to steal past without a battle. And the more so as he computed the alternatives of victory or death. If the former were his fortune, it would resolve all his perplexities; if death, his end would be noble. How glorious a thing to die in the endeavor to leave behind him, as his last legacy to his fatherland, the empire of Peloponnesus! That such thoughts should pass through his brain strikes me as by no means wonderful, as these are thoughts distinctive to all men of high ambition. Far more wonderful to my mind was the pitch of perfection to which he had brought his army. There was no labor which his troops would shrink from, either by night or by day; there was no danger they would flinch from; and, with the scantiest provisions, their discipline never failed them.

And so, when he gave his last orders to them to prepare for impending battle, they obeyed with alacrity. He gave the word; the cavalry fell to whitening their helmets, the heavy infantry of the Arcadians began inscribing their clubs as the crest on their shields,[2] as though they were Thebans, and all were engaged in sharpening their lances and swords and polishing their heavy shields. When the preparations were complete and he had led them

---

1 Probably Xenophon's own son Gryllus was among them.
2 Grote ("H. G." x. 463) has another interpretation.

out, his next movement is worthy of attention. First, as was natural, he paid heed to their formation, and in so doing seemed to give clear evidence that he intended battle; but no sooner was the army drawn up in the formation which he preferred, than he advanced, not by the shortest route to meet the enemy, but toward the westward-lying mountains which face Tegea, and by this movement created in the enemy an expectation that he would not do battle on that day. In keeping with this expectation, as soon as he arrived at the mountain-region, he extended his phalanx in long line and piled arms under the high cliffs; and to all appearance he was there encamping. The effect of this manouvre on the enemy in general was to relax the prepared bent of their souls for battle, and to weaken their tactical arrangements. Presently, however, wheeling his regiments (which were marching in column) to the front, with the effect of strengthening the beak-like[1] attack which he proposed to lead himself, at the same instant he gave the order, "Shoulder arms, forward," and led the way, the troops following.

When the enemy saw them so unexpectedly approaching, not one of them was able to maintain tranquility: some began running to their divisions, some fell into line, some might be seen bitting and bridling their horses, some donning their cuirasses, and one and all were like men about to receive rather than to inflict a blow. He, the while, with steady impetus pushed forward his armament, like a ship-of-war prow forward. Wherever he brought his solid wedge to bear, he meant to cleave through the opposing mass, and crumble his adversary's host to pieces. With this design he prepared to throw the brunt of the fighting on the strongest half of his army, while he kept the weaker portion of it in the background, knowing certainly that if worsted it would only cause discouragement to his own division and add force to the foe. The cavalry on the side of his opponents were disposed like an ordinary phalanx of heavy infantry, regular in depth and unsupported by foot-soldiers interspersed among the horses.[2] Epaminondas again differed in strengthening the attacking point of his cavalry, besides which he interspersed footmen between their lines in the belief that, when he had once cut through the cavalry, he would have wrested victory from the antagonist along his whole line; so hard is it to find troops who will care to keep their own ground when once they

---

1 Or, "the wedge-like attack of his own division"; see Grote, "H. G." x. 469 foll. I do not, however, think that the attacking column was actually wedge-shaped like the "acies cuneata" of the Romans. It was the unusual depth of the column which gave it the force of an ironclad's ram. Cf. "Cyrop." II. iv. for {eis metopon}.

2 See Rustow and Kochly, p. 176; and for the {amippoi} Harpocration, s.v.; Pollus, i. 131; "Hipparch." v. 13; Thuc. v. 58; Herod. vii. 158; Caes. "B. G." i. 48; "B. Civ." iii. 84.

see any of their own side flying. Lastly, to prevent any attempt on the part of the Athenians, who were on the enemy's left wing, to bring up their reliefs in support of the portion next them, he posted bodies of cavalry and heavy infantry on certain hillocks in front of them, intending to create in their minds an apprehension that, in case they offered such assistance, they would be attacked on their own rear by these detachments. Such was the plan of encounter which he formed and executed; nor was he cheated in his hopes. He had so much the mastery at his point of attack that he caused the whole of the enemy's troops to take flight.

But after he himself had fallen, the rest of the Thebans were not able any longer to turn their victory rightly to account. Though the main battle line of their opponents had given way, not a single man afterward did the victorious hoplites slay, not an inch forward did they advance from the ground on which the collision took place. Though the cavalry had fled before them, there was no pursuit; not a man, horseman or hoplite, did the conquering cavalry cut down; but, like men who have suffered a defeat, as if panic-stricken[1] they slipped back through the ranks of the fleeing foemen. Only the footmen fighting among the cavalry and the light infantry, who had together shared in the victory of the cavalry, found their way round to the left wing as masters of the field, but it cost them dear; here they encountered the Athenians, and most of them were cut down.

The effective result of these achievements was the very opposite of that which the world at large anticipated. Here, where well-nigh the whole of Hellas was met together in one field, and the combatants stood rank against rank confronted, there was no one doubted that, in the event of battle, the conquerors would this day rule; and that those who lost would be their subjects. But God so ordered it that both belligerents alike set up trophies as claiming victory, and neither interfered with the other in the act. Both parties alike gave back their enemy's dead under a truce, and in right of victory; both alike, in symbol of defeat, under a truce took back their dead. And though both claimed to have won the day, neither could show that he had thereby gained any accession of territory, or state, or empire, or was better situated than before the battle. Uncertainty and confusion, indeed, had gained ground, being tenfold greater throughout the length and breadth of Hellas after the battle than before.

At this point I lay aside my pen: the sequel of the story may haply commend itself[2] to another.

---

1 Or, "they timorously slipped back."
2 Or, "win the attention of some other writer."

EPICTETUS

THE ENCHIRIDION

BY EPICTETUS

Translated by Elizabeth Carter

1. Some things are in our control and others not. Things in our control are opinion, pursuit, desire, aversion, and, in a word, whatever are our own actions. Things not in our control are body, property, reputation, command, and, in one word, whatever are not our own actions.

The things in our control are by nature free, unrestrained, unhindered; but those not in our control are weak, slavish, restrained, belonging to others. Remember, then, that if you suppose that things which are slavish by nature are also free, and that what belongs to others is your own, then you will be hindered. You will lament, you will be disturbed, and you will find fault both with gods and men. But if you suppose that only to be your own which is your own, and what belongs to others such as it really is, then no one will ever compel you or restrain you. Further, you will find fault with no one or accuse no one. You will do nothing against your will. No one will hurt you, you will have no enemies, and you not be harmed.

Aiming therefore at such great things, remember that you must not allow yourself to be carried, even with a slight tendency, toward the attainment of lesser things. Instead, you must entirely quit some things and for the present postpone the rest. But if you would both have these great things, along with power and riches, then you will not gain even the latter, because you aim at the former too: but you will absolutely fail of the former, by which alone happiness and freedom are achieved.

Work, therefore to be able to say to every harsh appearance, "You are but an appearance, and not absolutely the thing you appear to be." And then examine it by those rules which you have, and first, and chiefly, by this: whether it concerns the things which are in our own control, or those which are not; and, if it concerns anything not in our control, be prepared to say that it is nothing to you.

2. Remember that following desire promises the attainment of that of which you are desirous; and aversion promises the avoiding that to which

you are averse. However, he who fails to obtain the object of his desire is disappointed, and he who incurs the object of his aversion wretched. If, then, you confine your aversion to those objects only which are contrary to the natural use of your faculties, which you have in your own control, you will never incur anything to which you are averse. But if you are averse to sickness, or death, or poverty, you will be wretched. Remove aversion, then, from all things that are not in our control, and transfer it to things contrary to the nature of what is in our control. But, for the present, totally suppress desire: for, if you desire any of the things which are not in your own control, you must necessarily be disappointed; and of those which are, and which it would be laudable to desire, nothing is yet in your possession. Use only the appropriate actions of pursuit and avoidance; and even these lightly, and with gentleness and reservation.

3. With regard to whatever objects give you delight, are useful, or are deeply loved, remember to tell yourself of what general nature they are, beginning from the most insignificant things. If, for example, you are fond of a specific ceramic cup, remind yourself that it is only ceramic cups in general of which you are fond. Then, if it breaks, you will not be disturbed. If you kiss your child, or your wife, say that you only kiss things which are human, and thus you will not be disturbed if either of them dies.

4. When you are going about any action, remind yourself what nature the action is. If you are going to bathe, picture to yourself the things which usually happen in the bath: some people splash the water, some push, some use abusive language, and others steal. Thus you will more safely go about this action if you say to yourself, "I will now go bathe, and keep my own mind in a state conformable to nature." And in the same manner with regard to every other action. For thus, if any hindrance arises in bathing, you will have it ready to say, "It was not only to bathe that I desired, but to keep my mind in a state conformable to nature; and I will not keep it if I am bothered at things that happen.

5. Men are disturbed, not by things, but by the principles and notions which they form concerning things. Death, for instance, is not terrible, else it would have appeared so to Socrates. But the terror consists in our notion of death that it is terrible. When therefore we are hindered, or disturbed, or grieved, let us never attribute it to others, but to ourselves; that is, to our own principles. An uninstructed person will lay the fault of his own bad condition upon others. Someone just starting instruction will lay the fault on himself. Some who is perfectly instructed will place blame neither on others nor on himself.

6. Don't be prideful with any excellence that is not your own. If a horse should be prideful and say, "I am handsome," it would be supportable. But when you are prideful, and say, "I have a handsome horse," know that you are proud of what is, in fact, only the good of the horse. What, then, is your own? Only your reaction to the appearances of things. Thus, when you behave conformably to nature in reaction to how things appear, you will be proud with reason; for you will take pride in some good of your own.

7. Consider when, on a voyage, your ship is anchored; if you go on shore to get water you may along the way amuse yourself with picking up a shellish, or an onion. However, your thoughts and continual attention ought to be bent toward the ship, waiting for the captain to call on board; you must then immediately leave all these things, otherwise you will be thrown into the ship, bound neck and feet like a sheep. So it is with life. If, instead of an onion or a shellfish, you are given a wife or child, that is fine. But if the captain calls, you must run to the ship, leaving them, and regarding none of them. But if you are old, never go far from the ship: lest, when you are called, you should be unable to come in time.

8. Don't demand that things happen as you wish, but wish that they happen as they do happen, and you will go on well.

9. Sickness is a hindrance to the body, but not to your ability to choose, unless that is your choice. Lameness is a hindrance to the leg, but not to your ability to choose. Say this to yourself with regard to everything that happens, then you will see such obstacles as hindrances to something else, but not to yourself.

10. With every accident, ask yourself what abilities you have for making a proper use of it. If you see an attractive person, you will find that self-restraint is the ability you have against your desire. If you are in pain, you will find fortitude. If you hear unpleasant language, you will find patience. And thus habituated, the appearances of things will not hurry you away along with them.

11. Never say of anything, "I have lost it"; but, "I have returned it." Is your child dead? It is returned. Is your wife dead? She is returned. Is your estate taken away? Well, and is not that likewise returned? "But he who took it away is a bad man." What difference is it to you who the giver assigns to take it back? While he gives it to you to possess, take care of it; but don't view it as your own, just as travelers view a hotel.

12. If you want to improve, reject such reasonings as these: "If I neglect my affairs, I'll have no income; if I don't correct my servant, he will be

bad." For it is better to die with hunger, exempt from grief and fear, than to live in affluence with perturbation; and it is better your servant should be bad, than you unhappy.

Begin therefore from little things. Is a little oil spilt? A little wine stolen? Say to yourself, "This is the price paid for apathy, for tranquillity, and nothing is to be had for nothing." When you call your servant, it is possible that he may not come; or, if he does, he may not do what you want. But he is by no means of such importance that it should be in his power to give you any disturbance.

13. If you want to improve, be content to be thought foolish and stupid with regard to external things. Don't wish to be thought to know anything; and even if you appear to be somebody important to others, distrust yourself. For, it is difficult to both keep your faculty of choice in a state conformable to nature, and at the same time acquire external things. But while you are careful about the one, you must of necessity neglect the other.

14. If you wish your children, and your wife, and your friends to live forever, you are stupid; for you wish to be in control of things which you cannot, you wish for things that belong to others to be your own. So likewise, if you wish your servant to be without fault, you are a fool; for you wish vice not to be vice," but something else. But, if you wish to have your desires undisappointed, this is in your own control. Exercise, therefore, what is in your control. He is the master of every other person who is able to confer or remove whatever that person wishes either to have or to avoid. Whoever, then, would be free, let him wish nothing, let him decline nothing, which depends on others else he must necessarily be a slave.

15. Remember that you must behave in life as at a dinner party. Is anything brought around to you? Put out your hand and take your share with moderation. Does it pass by you? Don't stop it. Is it not yet come? Don't stretch your desire toward it, but wait till it reaches you. Do this with regard to children, to a wife, to public posts, to riches, and you will eventually be a worthy partner of the feasts of the gods. And if you don't even take the things which are set before you, but are able even to reject them, then you will not only be a partner at the feasts of the gods, but also of their empire. For, by doing this, Diogenes, Heraclitus and others like them, deservedly became, and were called, divine.

16. When you see anyone weeping in grief because his son has gone abroad, or is dead, or because he has suffered in his affairs, be careful that the appearance may not misdirect you. Instead, distinguish within your own mind, and be prepared to say, "It's not the accident that distresses this

person., because it doesn't distress another person; it is the judgment which he makes about it." As far as words go, however, don't reduce yourself to his level, and certainly do not moan with him. Do not moan inwardly either.

17. Remember that you are an actor in a drama, of such a kind as the author pleases to make it. If short, of a short one; if long, of a long one. If it is his pleasure you should act a poor man, a cripple, a governor, or a private person, see that you act it naturally. For this is your business, to act well the character assigned you; to choose it is another's.

18. When a raven happens to croak unluckily, don't allow the appearance hurry you away with it, but immediately make the distinction to yourself, and say, "None of these things are foretold to me; but either to my paltry body, or property, or reputation, or children, or wife. But to me all omens are lucky, if I will. For whichever of these things happens, it is in my control to derive advantage from it."

19. You may be unconquerable, if you enter into no combat in which it is not in your own control to conquer. When, therefore, you see anyone eminent in honors, or power, or in high esteem on any other account, take heed not to be hurried away with the appearance, and to pronounce him happy; for, if the essence of good consists in things in our own control, there will be no room for envy or emulation. But, for your part, don't wish to be a general, or a senator, or a consul, but to be free; and the only way to this is a contempt of things not in our own control.

20. Remember, that not he who gives ill language or a blow insults, but the principle which represents these things as insulting. When, therefore, anyone provokes you, be assured that it is your own opinion which provokes you. Try, therefore, in the first place, not to be hurried away with the appearance. For if you once gain time and respite, you will more easily command yourself.

21. Let death and exile, and all other things which appear terrible be daily before your eyes, but chiefly death, and you win never entertain any abject thought, nor too eagerly covet anything.

22. If you have an earnest desire of attaining to philosophy, prepare yourself from the very first to be laughed at, to be sneered by the multitude, to hear them say, "He is returned to us a philosopher all at once," and "Whence this supercilious look?" Now, for your part, don't have a supercilious look indeed; but keep steadily to those things which appear best to you as one appointed by God to this station. For remember that, if you adhere to the same point, those very persons who at first ridiculed will

afterward admire you. But if you are conquered by them, you will incur a double ridicule.

23. If you ever happen to turn your attention to externals, so as to wish to please anyone, be assured that you have ruined your scheme of life. Be contented, then, in everything with being a philosopher; and, if you wish to be thought so likewise by anyone, appear so to yourself, and it will suffice you.

24. Don't allow such considerations as these distress you. "I will live in dishonor, and be nobody anywhere." For, if dishonor is an evil, you can no more be involved in any evil by the means of another, than be engaged in anything base. Is it any business of yours, then, to get power, or to be admitted to an entertainment? By no means. How, then, after all, is this a dishonor? And how is it true that you will be nobody anywhere, when you ought to be somebody in those things only which are in your own control, in which you may be of the greatest consequence? "But my friends will be unassisted."—What do you mean by unassisted? They will not have money from you, nor will you make them Roman citizens. Who told you, then, that these are among the things in our own control, and not the affair of others? And who can give to another the things which he has not himself? "Well, but get them, then, that we too may have a share." If I can get them with the preservation of my own honor and fidelity and greatness of mind, show me the way and I will get them; but if you require me to lose my own proper good that you may gain what is not good, consider how inequitable and foolish you are. Besides, which would you rather have, a sum of money, or a friend of fidelity and honor? Rather assist me, then, to gain this character than require me to do those things by which I may lose it. Well, but my country, say you, as far as depends on me, will be unassisted. Here again, what assistance is this you mean? "It will not have porticoes nor baths of your providing." And what signifies that? Why, neither does a smith provide it with shoes, or a shoemaker with arms. It is enough if everyone fully performs his own proper business. And were you to supply it with another citizen of honor and fidelity, would not he be of use to it? Yes. Therefore neither are you yourself useless to it. "What place, then, say you, will I hold in the state?" Whatever you can hold with the preservation of your fidelity and honor. But if, by desiring to be useful to that, you lose these, of what use can you be to your country when you are become faithless and void of shame.

25. Is anyone preferred before you at an entertainment, or in a compliment, or in being admitted to a consultation? If these things are

good, you ought to be glad that he has gotten them; and if they are evil, don't be grieved that you have not gotten them. And remember that you cannot, without using the same means [which others do] to acquire things not in our own control, expect to be thought worthy of an equal share of them. For how can he who does not frequent the door of any [great] man, does not attend him, does not praise him, have an equal share with him who does? You are unjust, then, and insatiable, if you are unwilling to pay the price for which these things are sold, and would have them for nothing. For how much is lettuce sold? Fifty cents, for instance. If another, then, paying fifty cents, takes the lettuce, and you, not paying it, go without them, don't imagine that he has gained any advantage over you. For as he has the lettuce, so you have the fifty cents which you did not give. So, in the present case, you have not been invited to such a person's entertainment, because you have not paid him the price for which a supper is sold. It is sold for praise; it is sold for attendance. Give him then the value, if it is for your advantage. But if you would, at the same time, not pay the one and yet receive the other, you are insatiable, and a blockhead. Have you nothing, then, instead of the supper? Yes, indeed, you have: the not praising him, whom you don't like to praise; the not bearing with his behavior at coming in.

26. The will of nature may be learned from those things in which we don't distinguish from each other. For example, when our neighbor's boy breaks a cup, or the like, we are presently ready to say, "These things will happen." Be assured, then, that when your own cup likewise is broken, you ought to be affected just as when another's cup was broken. Apply this in like manner to greater things. Is the child or wife of another dead? There is no one who would not say, "This is a human accident." but if anyone's own child happens to die, it is presently, "Alas I how wretched am I!" But it should be remembered how we are affected in hearing the same thing concerning others.

27. As a mark is not set up for the sake of missing the aim, so neither does the nature of evil exist in the world.

28. If a person gave your body to any stranger he met on his way, you would certainly be angry. And do you feel no shame in handing over your own mind to be confused and mystified by anyone who happens to verbally attack you?

29. In every affair consider what precedes and follows, and then undertake it. Otherwise you will begin with spirit; but not having thought of the consequences, when some of them appear you will shamefully desist.

"I would conquer at the Olympic games." But consider what precedes and follows, and then, if it is for your advantage, engage in the affair. You must conform to rules, submit to a diet, refrain from dainties; exercise your body, whether you choose it or not, at a stated hour, in heat and cold; you must drink no cold water, nor sometimes even wine. In a word, you must give yourself up to your master, as to a physician. Then, in the combat, you may be thrown into a ditch, dislocate your arm, turn your ankle, swallow dust, be whipped, and, after all, lose the victory. When you have evaluated all this, if your inclination still holds, then go to war. Otherwise, take notice, you will behave like children who sometimes play like wrestlers, sometimes gladiators, sometimes blow a trumpet, and sometimes act a tragedy when they have seen and admired these shows. Thus you too will be at one time a wrestler, at another a gladiator, now a philosopher, then an orator; but with your whole soul, nothing at all. Like an ape, you mimic all you see, and one thing after another is sure to please you, but is out of favor as soon as it becomes familiar. For you have never entered upon anything considerately, nor after having viewed the whole matter on all sides, or made any scrutiny into it, but rashly, and with a cold inclination. Thus some, when they have seen a philosopher and heard a man speaking like Euphrates (though, indeed, who can speak like him?), have a mind to be philosophers too. Consider first, man, what the matter is, and what your own nature is able to bear. If you would be a wrestler, consider your shoulders, your back, your thighs; for different persons are made for different things. Do you think that you can act as you do, and be a philosopher? That you can eat and drink, and be angry and discontented as you are now? You must watch, you must labor, you must get the better of certain appetites, must quit your acquaintance, be despised by your servant, be laughed at by those you meet; come off worse than others in everything, in magistracies, in honors, in courts of judicature. When you have considered all these things round, approach, if you please; if, by parting with them, you have a mind to purchase apathy, freedom, and tranquillity. If not, don't come here; don't, like children, be one while a philosopher, then a publican, then an orator, and then one of Caesar's officers. These things are not consistent. You must be one man, either good or bad. You must cultivate either your own ruling faculty or externals, and apply yourself either to things within or without you; that is, be either a philosopher, or one of the vulgar.

30. Duties are universally measured by relations. Is anyone a father? If so, it is implied that the children should take care of him, submit to him in everything, patiently listen to his reproaches, his correction. But he is

a bad father. Is you naturally entitled, then, to a good father? No, only to a father. Is a brother unjust? Well, keep your own situation toward him. Consider not what he does, but what you are to do to keep your own faculty of choice in a state conformable to nature. For another will not hurt you unless you please. You will then be hurt when you think you are hurt. In this manner, therefore, you will find, from the idea of a neighbor, a citizen, a general, the corresponding duties if you accustom yourself to contemplate the several relations.

31. Be assured that the essential property of piety toward the gods is to form right opinions concerning them, as existing and as governing the universe with goodness and justice. And fix yourself in this resolution, to obey them, and yield to them, and willingly follow them in all events, as produced by the most perfect understanding. For thus you will never find fault with the gods, nor accuse them as neglecting you. And it is not possible for this to be effected any other way than by withdrawing yourself from things not in our own control, and placing good or evil in those only which are. For if you suppose any of the things not in our own control to be either good or evil, when you are disappointed of what you wish, or incur what you would avoid, you must necessarily find fault with and blame the authors. For every animal is naturally formed to fly and abhor things that appear hurtful, and the causes of them; and to pursue and admire those which appear beneficial, and the causes of them. It is impractical, then, that one who supposes himself to be hurt should be happy about the person who, he thinks, hurts him, just as it is impossible to be happy about the hurt itself. Hence, also, a father is reviled by a son, when he does not impart to him the things which he takes to be good; and the supposing empire to be a good made Polynices and Eteocles mutually enemies. On this account the husbandman, the sailor, the merchant, on this account those who lose wives and children, revile the gods. For where interest is, there too is piety placed. So that, whoever is careful to regulate his desires and aversions as he ought, is, by the very same means, careful of piety likewise. But it is also incumbent on everyone to offer libations and sacrifices and first fruits, conformably to the customs of his country, with purity, and not in a slovenly manner, nor negligently, nor sparingly, nor beyond his ability.

32. When you have recourse to divination, remember that you know not what the event will be, and you come to learn it of the diviner; but of what nature it is you know before you come, at least if you are a philosopher. For if it is among the things not in our own control, it can by no means be either good or evil. Don't, therefore, bring either desire or aversion

with you to the diviner (else you will approach him trembling), but first acquire a distinct knowledge that every event is indifferent and nothing to you., of whatever sort it may be, for it will be in your power to make a right use of it, and this no one can hinder; then come with confidence to the gods, as your counselors, and afterward, when any counsel is given you, remember what counselors you have assumed, and whose advice you will neglect if you disobey. Come to divination, as Socrates prescribed, in cases of which the whole consideration relates to the event, and in which no opportunities are afforded by reason, or any other art, to discover the thing proposed to be learned. When, therefore, it is our duty to share the danger of a friend or of our country, we ought not to consult the oracle whether we will share it with them or not. For, though the diviner should forewarn you that the victims are unfavorable, this means no more than that either death or mutilation or exile is portended. But we have reason within us, and it directs, even with these hazards, to the greater diviner, the Pythian god, who cast out of the temple the person who gave no assistance to his friend while another was murdering him.

33. Immediately prescribe some character and form of conduce to yourself, which you may keep both alone and in company.

Be for the most part silent, or speak merely what is necessary, and in few words. We may, however, enter, though sparingly, into discourse sometimes when occasion calls for it, but not on any of the common subjects, of gladiators, or horse races, or athletic champions, or feasts, the vulgar topics of conversation; but principally not of men, so as either to blame, or praise, or make comparisons. If you are able, then, by your own conversation bring over that of your company to proper subjects; but, if you happen to be taken among strangers, be silent.

Don't allow your laughter be much, nor on many occasions, nor profuse.

Avoid swearing, if possible, altogether; if not, as far as you are able.

Avoid public and vulgar entertainments; but, if ever an occasion calls you to them, keep your attention upon the stretch, that you may not imperceptibly slide into vulgar manners. For be assured that if a person be ever so sound himself, yet, if his companion be infected, he who converses with him will be infected likewise.

Provide things relating to the body no further than mere use; as meat, drink, clothing, house, family. But strike off and reject everything relating to show and delicacy.

As far as possible, before marriage, keep yourself pure from familiarities with women, and, if you indulge them, let it be lawfully. But don't therefore be troublesome and full of reproofs to those who use these liberties, nor frequently boast that you yourself don't.

If anyone tells you that such a person speaks ill of you, don't make excuses about what is said of you, but answer: "He does not know my other faults, else he would not have mentioned only these."

It is not necessary for you to appear often at public spectacles; but if ever there is a proper occasion for you to be there, don't appear more solicitous for anyone than for yourself; that is, wish things to be only just as they are, and him only to conquer who is the conqueror, for thus you will meet with no hindrance. But abstain entirely from declamations and derision and violent emotions. And when you come away, don't discourse a great deal on what has passed, and what does not contribute to your own amendment. For it would appear by such discourse that you were immoderately struck with the show.

Go not [of your own accord] to the rehearsals of any (authors), nor appear [at them] readily. But, if you do appear, keep your gravity and sedateness, and at the same time avoid being morose.

When you are going to confer with anyone, and particularly of those in a superior station, represent to yourself how Socrates or Zeno would behave in such a case, and you will not be at a loss to make a proper use of whatever may occur.

When you are going to any of the people in power, represent to yourself that you will not find him at home; that you will not be admitted; that the doors will not be opened to you; that he will take no notice of you. If, with all this, it is your duty to go, bear what happens, and never say [to yourself], "It was not worth so much." For this is vulgar, and like a man dazed by external things.

In parties of conversation, avoid a frequent and excessive mention of your own actions and dangers. For, however agreeable it may be to yourself to mention the risks you have run, it is not equally agreeable to others to hear your adventures. Avoid, likewise, an endeavor to excite laughter. For this is a slippery point, which may throw you into vulgar manners, and, besides, may be apt to lessen you in the esteem of your acquaintance. Approaches to indecent discourse are likewise dangerous. Whenever, therefore, anything of this sort happens, if there be a proper opportunity, rebuke him who makes advances that way; or, at least, by silence and blushing and a forbidding look, show yourself to be displeased by such talk.

34. If you are struck by the appearance of any promised pleasure, guard

yourself against being hurried away by it; but let the affair wait your leisure, and procure yourself some delay. Then bring to your mind both points of time: that in which you will enjoy the pleasure, and that in which you will repent and reproach yourself after you have enjoyed it; and set before you, in opposition to these, how you will be glad and applaud yourself if you abstain. And even though it should appear to you a seasonable gratification, take heed that its enticing, and agreeable and attractive force may not subdue you; but set in opposition to this how much better it is to be conscious of having gained so great a victory.

35. When you do anything from a clear judgment that it ought to be done, never shun the being seen to do it, even though the world should make a wrong supposition about it; for, if you don't act right, shun the action itself; but, if you do, why are you afraid of those who censure you wrongly?

36. As the proposition, "Either it is day or it is night," is extremely proper for a disjunctive argument, but quite improper in a conjunctive one, so, at a feast, to choose the largest share is very suitable to the bodily appetite, but utterly inconsistent with the social spirit of an entertainment. When you eat with another, then, remember not only the value of those things which are set before you to the body, but the value of that behavior which ought to be observed toward the person who gives the entertainment.

37. If you have assumed any character above your strength, you have both made an ill figure in that and quitted one which you might have supported.

38. When walking, you are careful not to step on a nail or turn your foot; so likewise be careful not to hurt the ruling faculty of your mind. And, if we were to guard against this in every action, we should undertake the action with the greater safety.

39. The body is to everyone the measure of the possessions proper for it, just as the foot is of the shoe. If, therefore, you stop at this, you will keep the measure; but if you move beyond it, you must necessarily be carried forward, as down a cliff; as in the case of a shoe, if you go beyond its fitness to the foot, it comes first to be gilded, then purple, and then studded with jewels. For to that which once exceeds a due measure, there is no bound.

40. Women from fourteen years old are flattered with the title of "mistresses" by the men. Therefore, perceiving that they are regarded only as qualified to give the men pleasure, they begin to adorn themselves, and in that to place ill their hopes. We should, therefore, fix our attention on making them sensible that they are valued for the appearance of decent, modest and discreet behavior.

41. It is a mark of want of genius to spend much time in things relating to the body, as to be long in our exercises, in eating and drinking, and in the discharge of other animal functions. These should be done incidentally and slightly, and our whole attention be engaged in the care of the understanding.

42. When any person harms you, or speaks badly of you, remember that he acts or speaks from a supposition of its being his duty. Now, it is not possible that he should follow what appears right to you, but what appears so to himself. Therefore, if he judges from a wrong appearance, he is the person hurt, since he too is the person deceived. For if anyone should suppose a true proposition to be false, the proposition is not hurt, but he who is deceived about it. Setting out, then, from these principles, you will meekly bear a person who reviles you, for you will say upon every occasion, "It seemed so to him."

43. Everything has two handles, the one by which it may be carried, the other by which it cannot. If your brother acts unjustly, don't lay hold on the action by the handle of his injustice, for by that it cannot be carried; but by the opposite, that he is your brother, that he was brought up with you; and thus you will lay hold on it, as it is to be carried.

44. These reasonings are unconnected: "I am richer than you, therefore I am better"; "I am more eloquent than you, therefore I am better." The connection is rather this: "I am richer than you, therefore my property is greater than yours"; "I am more eloquent than you, therefore my style is better than yours." But you, after all, are neither property nor style.

45. Does anyone bathe in a mighty little time? Don't say that he does it ill, but in a mighty little time. Does anyone drink a great quantity of wine? Don't say that he does ill, but that he drinks a great quantity. For, unless you perfectly understand the principle from which anyone acts, how should you know if he acts ill? Thus you will not run the hazard of assenting to any appearances but such as you fully comprehend.

46. Never call yourself a philosopher, nor talk a great deal among the unlearned about theorems, but act conformably to them. Thus, at an entertainment, don't talk how persons ought to eat, but eat as you ought. For remember that in this manner Socrates also universally avoided all ostentation. And when persons came to him and desired to be recommended by him to philosophers, he took and recommended them, so well did he bear being overlooked. So that if ever any talk should happen among the unlearned concerning philosophic theorems, be you, for the most part, silent. For there is great danger in immediately throwing out what you have

not digested. And, if anyone tells you that you know nothing, and you are not nettled at it, then you may be sure that you have begun your business. For sheep don't throw up the grass to show the shepherds how much they have eaten; but, inwardly digesting their food, they outwardly produce wool and milk. Thus, therefore, do you likewise not show theorems to the unlearned, but the actions produced by them after they have been digested.

47. When you have brought yourself to supply the necessities of your body at a small price, don't pique yourself upon it; nor, if you drink water, be saying upon every occasion, "I drink water." But first consider how much more sparing and patient of hardship the poor are than we. But if at any time you would inure yourself by exercise to labor, and bearing hard trials, do it for your own sake, and not for the world; don't grasp statues, but, when you are violently thirsty, take a little cold water in your mouth, and spurt it out and tell nobody.

48. The condition and characteristic of a vulgar person, is, that he never expects either benefit or hurt from himself, but from externals. The condition and characteristic of a philosopher is, that he expects all hurt and benefit from himself. The marks of a proficient are, that he censures no one, praises no one, blames no one, accuses no one, says nothing concerning himself as being anybody, or knowing anything: when he is, in any instance, hindered or restrained, he accuses himself; and, if he is praised, he secretly laughs at the person who praises him; and, if he is censured, he makes no defense. But he goes about with the caution of sick or injured people, dreading to move anything that is set right, before it is perfectly fixed. He suppresses all desire in himself; he transfers his aversion to those things only which thwart the proper use of our own faculty of choice; the exertion of his active powers toward anything is very gentle; if he appears stupid or ignorant, he does not care, and, in a word, he watches himself as an enemy, and one in ambush.

49. When anyone shows himself overly confident in ability to understand and interpret the works of Chrysippus, say to yourself, " Unless Chrysippus had written obscurely, this person would have had no subject for his vanity. But what do I desire? To understand nature and follow her. I ask, then, who interprets her, and, finding Chrysippus does, I have recourse to him. I don't understand his writings. I seek, therefore, one to interpret them." So far there is nothing to value myself upon. And when I find an interpreter, what remains is to make use of his instructions. This alone is the valuable thing. But, if I admire nothing but merely the interpretation, what do I become more than a grammarian instead

of a philosopher? Except, indeed, that instead of Homer I interpret Chrysippus. When anyone, therefore, desires me to read Chrysippus to him, I rather blush when I cannot show my actions agreeable and consonant to his discourse.

50. Whatever moral rules you have deliberately proposed to yourself. abide by them as they were laws, and as if you would be guilty of impiety by violating any of them. Don't regard what anyone says of you, for this, after all, is no concern of yours. How long, then, will you put off thinking yourself worthy of the highest improvements and follow the distinctions of reason? You have received the philosophical theorems, with which you ought to be familiar, and you have been familiar with them. What other master, then, do you wait for, to throw upon that the delay of reforming yourself? You are no longer a boy, but a grown man. If, therefore, you will be negligent and slothful, and always add procrastination to procrastination, purpose to purpose, and fix day after day in which you will attend to yourself, you will insensibly continue without proficiency, and, living and dying, persevere in being one of the vulgar. This instant, then, think yourself worthy of living as a man grown up, and a proficient. Let whatever appears to be the best be to you an inviolable law. And if any instance of pain or pleasure, or glory or disgrace, is set before you, remember that now is the combat, now the Olympiad comes on, nor can it be put off. By once being defeated and giving way, proficiency is lost, or by the contrary preserved. Thus Socrates became perfect, improving himself by everything. attending to nothing but reason. And though you are not yet a Socrates, you ought, however, to live as one desirous of becoming a Socrates.

51. The first and most necessary topic in philosophy is that of the use of moral theorems, such as, "We ought not to lie"; the second is that of demonstrations, such as, "What is the origin of our obligation not to lie"; the third gives strength and articulation to the other two, such as, "What is the origin of this is a demonstration." For what is demonstration? What is consequence? What contradiction? What truth? What falsehood? The third topic, then, is necessary on the account of the second, and the second on the account of the first. But the most necessary, and that whereon we ought to rest, is the first. But we act just on the contrary. For we spend all our time on the third topic, and employ all our diligence about that, and entirely neglect the first. Therefore, at the same time that we lie, we are immediately prepared to show how it is demonstrated that lying is not right.

52. Upon all occasions we ought to have these maxims ready at hand:

> "Conduct me, Jove, and you, O Destiny,
> Wherever your decrees have fixed my station."
>> (Cleanthes)

> "I follow cheerfully; and, did I not,
> Wicked and wretched, I must follow still
> Whoever yields properly to Fate, is deemed
> Wise among men, and knows the laws of heaven."
>> (Euripides, Frag. 965)

And this third:

> "O Crito, if it thus pleases the gods, thus let it be. Anytus and Melitus may kill me indeed, but hurt me they cannot."
>> (Plato's Crito and Apology)

EPICURUS

LETTER TO MENOECEUS

BY Epicurus

Translated by Robert Drew Hicks

Greeting.
 Let no one be slow to seek wisdom when he is young nor weary in the search thereof when he is grown old. For no age is too early or too late for the health of the soul. And to say that the season for studying philosophy has not yet come, or that it is past and gone, is like saying that the season for happiness is not yet or that it is now no more. Therefore, both old and young ought to seek wisdom, the former in order that, as age comes over him, he may be young in good things because of the grace of what has been, and the latter in order that, while he is young, he may at the same time be old, because he has no fear of the things which are to come. So we must exercise ourselves in the things which bring happiness, since, if that be present, we have everything, and, if that be absent, all our actions are directed toward attaining it.

Those things which without ceasing I have declared to you, those do, and exercise yourself in those, holding them to be the elements of right life. First believe that God is a living being immortal and happy, according to the notion of a god indicated by the common sense of humankind; and so do not affirm of him anything that is foreign to upholding both his happiness and his immortality. For truly there are gods, and knowledge of them is evident; but they are not such as the multitude believe, seeing that people do not steadfastly maintain the notions they form respecting them. Not the person who denies the gods worshipped by the multitude, but he who affirms of the gods what the multitude believes about them is truly impious. For the utterances of the multitude about the gods are not true preconceptions but false assumptions; hence it is that the greatest evils happen to the wicked and the greatest blessings happen to the good from the hand of the gods, seeing that they are always favorable to their own good qualities and take pleasure in people like to themselves, but reject as alien whatever is not of their kind.

Accustom yourself to believe that death is nothing to us, for good and evil simply awareness, and death is the privation of all awareness; therefore a right understanding that death is nothing to us makes the mortality of life enjoyable, not by adding to life an unlimited time, but by taking away the yearning after immortality. For life has no terror; for those who thoroughly apprehend that there are no terrors for them in ceasing to live. Foolish, therefore, is the person who says that he fears death, not because it will pain when it comes, but because it pains in the prospect. Whatever causes no annoyance when it is present, causes only a groundless pain in the expectation. Death, therefore, the most awful of evils, is nothing to us, seeing that, when we are, death is not come, and, when death is come, we are not. It is nothing, then, either to the living or to the dead, for with the living it is not and the dead exist no longer. But in the world, at one time people shun death as the greatest of all evils, and at another time choose it as a respite from the evils in life. The wise person does not deprecate life nor does he fear the cessation of life. The thought of life is no offense to him, nor is the cessation of life regarded as an evil. And even as people choose of food not merely and simply the larger portion, but the more pleasant, so the wise seek to enjoy the time which is most pleasant and not merely that which is longest. And he who admonishes the young to live well and the old to make a good end speaks foolishly, not merely because of the desirability of life, but because the same exercise at once teaches to live well and to die well. Much worse is he who says that it were good not to be born, but when once one is born to pass with all speed through the gates of Hades. For if he truly believes this, why does he not depart from life? It were easy for him to do so, if once he were firmly convinced. If he speaks only in mockery, his words are foolishness, for those who hear believe him not.

We must remember that the future is neither wholly ours nor wholly not ours, so that neither must we count upon it as quite certain to come nor despair of it as quite certain not to come.

We must also reflect that of desires some are natural, others are groundless; and that of the natural some are necessary as well as natural, and some natural only. And of the necessary desires some are necessary if we are to be happy, some if the body is to be rid of uneasiness, some if we are even to live. He who has a clear and certain understanding of these things will direct every preference and aversion toward securing health of body and tranquility of mind, seeing that this is the sum and end of a happy life. For the end of all our actions is to be free from pain and fear, and, when once we have attained all this, the tempest of the soul is laid; seeing that the living creature has no need to go in search of something that is lacking, nor to look anything else by which the good of the soul and of the body will be fulfilled. When we are pained pleasure, then, and then only, do we feel the need of pleasure. For this reason we call pleasure the alpha and omega of a happy life. Pleasure is our first and kindred good. It is the starting point of every choice and of every aversion, and to it we always come back, inasmuch as we make feeling the rule by which to judge of every good thing. And since pleasure is our first and native good, for that reason we do not choose every pleasure whatever, but often pass over many pleasures when a greater annoyance ensues from them. And often we consider pains superior to pleasures when submission to the pains for a long time brings us as a consequence a greater pleasure. While therefore all pleasure because it is naturally akin to us is good, not all pleasure is worthy of choice, just as all pain is an evil and yet not all pain is to be shunned. It is, however, by measuring one against another, and by looking at the conveniences and inconveniences, that all these matters must be judged. Sometimes we treat the good as an evil, and the evil, on the contrary, as a good. Again, we regard independence of outward things as a great good, not so as in all cases to use little, but so as to be contented with little if we have not much, being honestly persuaded that they have the sweetest enjoyment of luxury who stand least in need of it, and that whatever is natural is easily procured and only the vain and worthless hard to win. Plain fare gives as much pleasure as a costly diet, when one the pain of want has been removed, while bread an water confer the highest possible pleasure when they are brought to hungry lips. To habituate one's self therefore, to simple and inexpensive diet supplies all that is needful for health, and enables a person to meet the necessary requirements of life without shrinking, and it places us in a better condition when we approach at intervals a costly fare and renders us fearless of fortune.

When we say, then, that pleasure is the end and aim, we do not mean the pleasures of the prodigal or the pleasures of sensuality, as we are understood to do by some through ignorance, prejudice, or willful misrepresentation. By pleasure we mean the absence of pain in the body and of trouble in the soul. It is not an unbroken succession of drinking-bouts and of merrymaking, not sexual love, not the enjoyment of the fish and other delicacies of a luxurious table, which produce a pleasant life; it is sober reasoning, searching out the grounds of every choice and avoidance, and banishing those beliefs through which the greatest disturbances take possession of the soul. Of all this the end is prudence. For this reason prudence is a more precious thing even than the other virtues, for lead a life of pleasure which is not also a life of prudence, honor, and justice; nor lead a life of prudence, honor, and justice, which is not also a life of pleasure. For the virtues have grown into one with a pleasant life, and a pleasant life is inseparable from them.

Who, then, is superior in your judgment to such a person? He holds a holy belief concerning the gods, and is altogether free from the fear of death. He has diligently considered the end fixed by nature, and understands how easily the limit of good things can be reached and attained, and how either the duration or the intensity of evils is but slight. Destiny which some introduce as sovereign over all things, he laughs to scorn, affirming rather that some things happen of necessity, others by chance, others through our own agency. For he sees that necessity destroys responsibility and that chance or fortune is inconstant; whereas our own actions are free, and it is to them that praise and blame naturally attach. It were better, indeed, to accept the legends of the gods than to bow beneath destiny which the natural philosophers have imposed. The one holds out some faint hope that we may escape if we honor the gods, while the necessity of the naturalists is deaf to all entreaties. Nor does he hold chance to be a god, as the world in general does, for in the acts of a god there is no disorder; nor to be a cause, though an uncertain one, for he believes that no good or evil is dispensed by chance to people so as to make life happy, though it supplies the starting point of great good and great evil. He believes that the misfortune of the wise is better than the prosperity of the fool. It is better, in short, that what is well judged in action should not owe its successful issue to the aid of chance.

Exercise yourself in these and kindred precepts day and night, both by yourself and with him who is like to you; then never, either in waking or in dream, will you be disturbed, but will live as a god among people. For people lose all appearance of mortality by living in the midst of immortal blessings.

PRINCIPAL DOCTRINES

BY EPICURUS

Translated by Robert Drew Hicks

1. A happy and eternal being has no trouble himself and brings no trouble upon any other being; hence he is exempt from movements of anger and partiality, for every such movement implies weakness
2. Death is nothing to us; for the body, when it has been resolved into its elements, has no feeling, and that which has no feeling is nothing to us.
3. The magnitude of pleasure reaches its limit in the removal of all pain. When pleasure is present, so long as it is uninterrupted, there is no pain either of body or of mind or of both together.
4. Continuous pain does not last long in the body; on the contrary, pain, if extreme, is present a short time, and even that degree of pain which barely outweighs pleasure in the body does not last for many days together. Illnesses of long duration even permit of an excess of pleasure over pain in the body.
5. It is impossible to live a pleasant life without living wisely and well and justly, and it is impossible to live wisely and well and justly without living pleasantly. Whenever any one of these is lacking, when, for instance, the person is not able to live wisely, though he lives well and justly, it is impossible for him to live a pleasant life.
6. In order to obtain security from other people any means whatever of procuring this was a natural good.
7. Some people have sought to become famous and renowned, thinking that thus they would make themselves secure against their fellow humans. If, then, the life of such persons really was secure, they attained natural good; if, however, it was insecure, they have not attained the end which by nature's own prompting they originally sought.
8. No pleasure is in itself evil, but the things which produce certain pleasures entail annoyances many times greater than the pleasures themselves.
9. If all pleasure had been capable of accumulation,—if this had gone

on not only be recurrences in time, but all over the frame or, at any rate, over the principal parts of human nature, there would never have been any difference between one pleasure and another, as in fact there is.

10. If the objects which are productive of pleasures to profligate persons really freed them from fears of the mind,—the fears, I mean, inspired by celestial and atmospheric phenomena, the fear of death, the fear of pain; if, further, they taught them to limit their desires, we should never have any fault to find with such persons, for they would then be filled with pleasures to overflowing on all sides and would be exempt from all pain, whether of body or mind, that is, from all evil.

11. If we had never been molested by alarms at celestial and atmospheric phenomena, nor by the misgiving that death somehow affects us, nor by neglect of the proper limits of pains and desires, we should have had no need to study natural science.

12. It would be impossible to banish fear on matters of the highest importance, if a person did not know the nature of the whole universe, but lived in dread of what the legends tell us. Hence without the study of nature there was no enjoyment of unmixed pleasures.

13. There would be no advantage in providing security against our fellow humans, so long as we were alarmed by occurrences over our heads or beneath the earth or in general by whatever happens in the boundless universe.

14. When tolerable security against our fellow humans is attained, then on a basis of power sufficient to afford supports and of material prosperity arises in most genuine form the security of a quiet private life withdrawn from the multitude.

15. Nature's wealth at once has its bounds and is easy to procure; but the wealth of vain fancies recedes to an infinite distance.

16. Fortune but seldom interferes with the wise person; his greatest and highest interests have been, are, and will be, directed by reason throughout the course of his life.

17. The just person enjoys. the greatest peace of mind, while the unjust is full of the utmost disquietude.

18. Pleasure in the body admits no increase when once the pain of want has been removed; after that it only admits of variation. The limit of pleasure in the mind, however, is reached when we reflect on the things themselves and their congeners which cause the mind the greatest alarms.

19. Unlimited time and limited time afford an equal amount of pleasure, if we measure the limits of that pleasure by reason.

20. The body receives as unlimited the limits of pleasure; and to provide it requires unlimited time. But the mind, grasping in thought what the end and limit of the body is, and banishing the terrors of futurity, procures a complete and perfect life, and has no longer any need of unlimited time. Nevertheless it does not shun pleasure, and even in the hour of death, when ushered out of existence by circumstances, the mind does not lack enjoyment of the best life.

21. He who understands the limits of life knows how easy it is to procure enough to remove the pain of want and make the whole of life complete and perfect. Hence he has no longer any need of things which are not to be won save by labor and conflict.

22. We must take into account as the end all that really exists and all clear evidence of sense to which we refer our opinions; for otherwise everything will be full of uncertainty and confusion.

23. If you fight against all your sensations, you will have no standard to which to refer, and thus no means of judging even those judgments which you pronounce false.

24. If you reject absolutely any single sensation without stopping to discriminate with respect to that which awaits confirmation between matter of opinion and that which is already present, whether in sensation or in feelings or in any immediate perception of the mind, you will throw into confusion even the rest of your sensations by your groundless belief and so you will be rejecting the standard of truth altogether. If in your ideas based upon opinion you hastily affirm as true all that awaits confirmation as well as that which does not, you will not escape error, as you will be maintaining complete ambiguity whenever it is a case of judging between right and wrong opinion.

25. If you do not on every separate occasion refer each of your actions to the end prescribed by nature, but instead of this in the act of choice or avoidance swerve aside to some other end, your acts will not be consistent with your theories.

26. All such desires as lead to no pain when they remain ungratified are unnecessary, and the longing is easily got rid of, when the thing desired is difficult to procure or when the desires seem likely to produce harm.

27. Of all the means which are procured by wisdom to ensure happiness throughout the whole of life, by far the most important is the acquisition of friends.

28. The same conviction which inspires confidence that nothing we have to fear is eternal or even of long duration, also enables us to see that even

in our limited conditions of life nothing enhances our security so much as friendship.

29. Of our desires some are natural and necessary others are natural, but not necessary; others, again, are neither natural nor necessary, but are due to illusory opinion.

30. Those natural desires which entail no pain when not gratified, though their objects are vehemently pursued, are also due to illusory opinion; and when they are not got rid of, it is not because of their own nature, but because of the person's illusory opinion.

31. Natural justice is a symbol or expression of usefullness, to prevent one person from harming or being harmed by another.

32. Those animals which are incapable of making covenants with one another, to the end that they may neither inflict nor suffer harm, are without either justice or injustice. And those tribes which either could not or would not form mutual covenants to the same end are in like case.

33. There never was an absolute justice, but only an agreement made in reciprocal association in whatever localities now and again from time to time, providing against the infliction or suffering of harm.

34. Injustice is not in itself an evil, but only in its consequence, viz. the terror which is excited by apprehension that those appointed to punish such offenses will discover the injustice.

35. It is impossible for the person who secretly violates any article of the social compact to feel confident that he will remain undiscovered, even if he has already escaped ten thousand times; for right on to the end of his life he is never sure he will not be detected.

36. Taken generally, justice is the same for all, to wit, something found useful in mutual association; but in its application to particular cases of locality or conditions of whatever kind, it varies under different circumstances.

37. Among the things accounted just by conventional law, whatever in the needs of mutual association is attested to be useful, is thereby stamped as just, whether or not it be the same for all; and in case any law is made and does not prove suitable to the usefulness of mutual association, then this is no longer just. And should the usefulness which is expressed by the law vary and only for a time correspond with the prior conception, nevertheless for the time being it was just, so long as we do not trouble ourselves about empty words, but look simply at the facts.

38. Where without any change in circumstances the conventional laws, when judged by their consequences, were seen not to correspond with the

notion of justice, such laws were not really just; but wherever the laws have ceased to be useful in consequence of a change in circumstances, in that case the laws were for the time being just when they were useful for the mutual association of the citizens, and subsequently ceased to be just when they ceased to be useful.

39. He who best knew how to meet fear of external foes made into one family all the creatures he could; and those he could not, he at any rate did not treat as aliens; and where he found even this impossible, he avoided all association, and, so far as was useful, kept them at a distance.

40. Those who were best able to provide themselves with the means of security against their neighbors, being thus in possession of the surest guarantee, passed the most agreeable life in each other's society; and their enjoyment of the fullest intimacy was such that, if one of them died before his time, the survivors did not mourn his death as if it called for sympathy.

EDITOR'S NOTE

COVER ART

The cover art for *Ancient Greek Philosophers* was inspired by a photograph of a calyx krater (a type of vase) currently owned by the British Museum. Calyx kraters—so called because their shape resembles the cup, or calyx, of a flower—were often found in the dining rooms of ancient Greece. They were used to dilute wine with water, and were usually placed in the center of the room for a symposium. Unlike paintings or other significant art sculptures, most calyx kraters don't have unique names, even though each scene painted on them is unique. In the ancient era from which they hail, they were likely just everyday objects in the household, much like nice serving dishes are today.

Characteristic of early fifth-century Attic (Athenian) red pottery, our calyx krater scene depicts the sun god Helios as a beardless youth, rising at dawn upward to the heavens from the sea, riding in his chariot drawn by four winged horses. The bright, shining crown of sunrays behind his head may have been meant to depict the godly enlightenment he brings to the world, just as the philosophers hoped to enlighten the public with knowledge and logic.

On the back cover, four gods of the stars, shown as boys, dive under the Sun to disappear into the water as a new day begins and darkness is once again vanquished by the light.

ENDPAPER ART

Kidnapping of Europa

Tile mosaics were unique to the elite residences in which they appeared in ancient Greece. Created—or at least directed in design—by the homeowner, they often relayed clues to guests about the personal beliefs and intellectual interests of the hosts. Images selected, and their placement in the home, were important. Some households meant for their mosaics to be viewed in a certain order. A guest may have been greeted by a salutary scene of the Three Muses in the entryway, indicating the host was a patron of science and the arts. Then they would move on to displays of Dionysus, the god of wine, or other merry, mythological tableaus in the dining room or salon where celebrations and other gatherings were held.

The endpapers of *Ancient Greek Philosophers* are devised from a photograph of the mosaic *Kidnapping of Europa*, which depicts a Greek myth about the goddess Europa. The legend is that Zeus, ruler of Olympus and known for his love of adventure, was enamored of Europa and decided the best way to seduce her was to transform into a bull and hide among her father's herds. When Europa saw Zeus as a bull, she climbed onto his back and he ran away with her, swimming across the sea to the island of Crete, where he then revealed his identity and made Europa the first queen of Crete. Zeus later re-created his image of the bull in the stars as the constellation Taurus.

The Greek philosopher Herodotus recounted this tale without embellishment in his work *Histories*, leaving historians to speculate that the story may have been an account of a Phoenician aristocrat being abducted by Greeks (likely Cretans). It later became the myth we know today.

Kidnapping of Europa was excavated from ruins of the ancient city Zeugma, which dates back to the second century AD. It's now displayed in the Zeugma Mosaic Museum in Gaziantep, Turkey.